BaseBall america®
2015 PROSPECT
HANDBOOK

BASEBALL AMERICA INC. DURHAM, N.C.

Baseball america®
2015 PROSPECT HANDBOOK

Editors
MATT EDDY, JOHN MANUEL

Assistant Editors
BEN BADLER, J.J. COOPER, MICHAEL LANANNA,
VINCENT LARA-CINISOMO, JOSH LEVENTHAL,
WILL LINGO, JOSH NORRIS, JIM SHONERD

Database and Application Development
BRENT LEWIS

Contributing Writers
BILL BALLEW, MIKE BERARDINO, JACK ETKIN,
AARON FITT, DERRICK GOOLD,
TOM HAUDRICOURT,
CLINT LONGENECKER, STEVE MELEWSKI,
BILL MITCHELL, JOHN PERROTTO,
JUAN C. RODRIGUEZ, ALEX SPEIER

Photo Editor
JIM SHONERD

Design & Production
SARA HIATT MCDANIEL, LINWOOD WEBB

Cover Photo
KRIS BRYANT BY JOHN WILLIAMSON

NO PORTION OF THIS BOOK MAY BE
REPRINTED OR REPRODUCED WITHOUT
THE WRITTEN CONSENT OF THE PUBLISHER.

FOR ADDITIONAL COPIES, VISIT OUR
WEBSITE AT BASEBALLAMERICA.COM OR
CALL 1-800-845-2726 TO ORDER.

US $32.95, PLUS SHIPPING AND HANDLING PER ORDER.
EXPEDITED SHIPPING AVAILABLE.

DISTRIBUTED BY SIMON & SCHUSTER
ISBN: 978-1-932391-55-8

STATISTICS PROVIDED BY MAJOR LEAGUE BASEBALL
ADVANCED MEDIA AND COMPILED BY
BASEBALL AMERICA.

© 2015 by TEN: The Enthusiast Network Magazines, LLC.
All Rights Reserved. Printed in the USA.

Baseball america®

GENERAL MANAGER Will Lingo @willingo

EDITORIAL
EDITOR IN CHIEF John Manuel @johnmanuelba
MANAGING EDITOR J.J. Cooper @jjcoop36
NEWS EDITOR Josh Leventhal @joshlev44
ASSOCIATE EDITOR Matt Eddy @matteddyba
WEB EDITOR Vincent Lara-Cinisomo @vincelara
NATIONAL WRITER Ben Badler @benbadler
ASSISTANT EDITORS Michael Lananna @mlananna
Josh Norris @jnorris427
Jim Shonerd @jimshonerdba

PRODUCTION
DESIGN & PRODUCTION DIRECTOR Sara Hiatt McDaniel
MULTIMEDIA MANAGER Linwood Webb

ADVERTISING
ADVERTISING DIRECTOR George Shelton
DIRECT MARKETING MANAGER Ximena Caceres
MARKETPLACE MANAGER Kristopher M. Lull
ADVERTISING ACCOUNT EXECUTIVE Abbey Langdon

BUSINESS
CUSTOMER SERVICE Ronnie McCabe, C.J. McPhatter
ACCOUNTING/OFFICE MANAGER Hailey Carpenter
TECHNOLOGY MANAGER Brent Lewis

STATISTICAL SERVICE
MAJOR LEAGUE BASEBALL ADVANCED MEDIA

ACTION / OUTDOOR GROUP
MANAGEMENT
PRODUCTION DIRECTOR Kasey Kelley
EDITORIAL DIRECTOR, DIGITAL Chris Mauro
FINANCE DIRECTOR Adam Miner
DIRECTOR OF SALES/OUTDOOR Chris Engelsman
DIRECTOR OF SALES/ACTION Adam Cozens

DIGITAL GROUP
DIGITAL DIRECTOR, ENGINEERING Jeff Kimmel
SENIOR PRODUCT MANAGER Rishi Kumar
SENIOR PRODUCT MANAGER Marc Bartell
CREATIVE DIRECTOR Peter Tracy
DIGITAL CONTENT STRATEGIES MANAGER Kristopher Heineman
SOCIAL MEDIA MANAGER Aaron Carrera

MANUFACTURING & PRODUCTION OPERATIONS
VP, MANUFACTURING & AD OPERATIONS Greg Parnell
SENIOR DIRECTOR, AD OPERATIONS Pauline Atwood
PRODUCTION MANAGER Jason Jopling
ARCHIVIST Thomas Voehringer

TEN: THE ENTHUSIAST NETWORK, LLC
CHAIRMAN Peter Englehart
CHIEF EXECUTIVE OFFICER Scott P. Dickey
EVP, CHIEF FINANCIAL OFFICER Bill Sutman
EVP, CHIEF CREATIVE OFFICER Alan Alpanian
EVP, SPORTS & ENTERTAINMENT Norb Garrett
EVP, CHIEF CONTENT OFFICER Angus MacKenzie
EVP, OPERATIONS Kevin Mullan
SVP, ENTERPRISES Tyler Schulze
EVP, SALES & MARKETING Eric Schwab
SVP, DIGITAL OPERATIONS Dan Bednar
VP, SALES OPERATIONS Matt Boice
SVP, FINANCIAL PLANNING Mike Cummings
SVP, AUTOMOTIVE DIGITAL Geoff DeFrance
VP, EDITORIAL OPERATIONS Amy Diamond
EVP, AFTERMARKET AUTOMOTIVE Doug Evans
SVP, CONTENT STRATEGY, AUTOMOTIVE David Freiburger
SVP, DIGITAL, SPORTS & ENTERTAINMENT Greg Morrow
VP, DIGITAL MONETIZATION Elisabeth Murray
SVP, MARKETING Ryan Payne
EVP, MIND OVER EYE Bill Wadsworth

CONSUMER MARKETING,
ENTHUSIAST MEDIA SUBSCRIPTION COMPANY, INC.
SVP, CIRCULATION Tom Slater
**VP, RETENTION &
OPERATIONS FULFILLMENT** Donald T. Robinson III

INTRODUCTION

The 15th edition of Baseball America's Prospect Handbook looks much like the first edition. It's bigger, and better—I'm confident it's better. The book keeps evolving over the years as our staff has evolved and as the game has evolved.

Power was almost taken for granted in those early writeups; many scouting reports said players needed to "get stronger," without thinking what consequences "getting stronger" might bring. Many reports praise pitchers for throwing 90-92 mph, which almost seems quaint in an era when we reported on more than 50 pitchers hitting 100 mph in the minors leagues in 2014.

So as the game has evolved, the Handbook has evolved with it. We report on unsigned international players in the Appendix, with players from Cuba and Korea. We have expanded our statistical analysis, this year introducing strikeout and power ratios for hitters and pitchers who are in organization Top 10s. And we delve deeper into explaining both baseball's 20-80 scouting scale and our own BA Grades, a key addition to the Handbook four years ago.

The book has changed, but its mission has not. You're holding 900 scouting reports to help you plan your fantasy team, follow your favorite organization more astutely, or just to bring you closer to the game we all love. I welcome your feedback on the book (johnmanuel@baseballamerica.com) and hope you enjoy it.

JOHN MANUEL
EDITOR IN CHIEF
BASEBALL AMERICA

EDITOR'S NOTE: Transactions for this book go through Dec. 11. As always, you can find players even if they have changed organizations by using the handy index in the back. >> For the purposes of this book, a prospect is any player who has no more than 50 innings pitched, 30 relief appearances or 130 at-bats in the major leagues, regardless of major league service time. Finally, the grades you'll find for each team's drafts are based solely on the quality of the players signed, with no consideration given to the players draft picks were traded for or how many picks a team might have lost.

TABLE OF CONTENTS

In the midst of their minor league home run chase, Las Vegas natives Joey Gallo (left) and Kris Bryant took grounders together prior to the Futures Game at Target Field in Minneapolis

For the fourth year in a row, Baseball America has assigned Grades and Risk Factors for each and every one of the 900 prospects in the Prospect Handbook. For the BA Grade, we used a 20-to-80 scale, similar to the scale scouts use, to keep it familiar. However, most major league clubs put an overall numerical grade on players, called the Overall Future Potential or OFP. Often the OFP is merely an average of the player's tools.

The BA Grade is not an OFP. It's a measure of a prospect's value, and it attempts to gauge the player's realistic ceiling. We've continued to adjust our grades to try to be more realistic, and less optimistic, and keep refining the grade vetting process. The vast majority of the players in this book rest in the

BA GRADE

50 Risk: High

50 High/45 Medium range, because the vast majority of worthwhile prospects in the minors are players who either have a chance to be everyday regulars but are far from that possibility, or players who are closer to the majors but who are likely to be role players and useful contributors. Few future franchise players or perennial all-stars graduate from the minors in any given year.

BA Grade Scale

GRADE	HITTER ROLE	PITCHER ROLE	EXAMPLES
75-80	Franchise Player	No. 1 starter	Clayton Kershaw, Buster Posey, Mike Trout
65-70	Perennial All-Star	No. 2 starter	Alex Gordon, Cole Hamels, Anthony Rendon
55-60	First-Division Regular	No. 3 starter, Elite closer	Aroldis Chapman, Ian Desmond, Chris Tillman
50	Solid-Average Regular	No. 4 starter, Elite set-up reliever	Mike Leake, Andrew Miller, Daniel Murphy
45	Second-Division Regular, Utilityman	No. 5 starter, Set-up reliever	Matt Dominguez, Scott Feldman, Craig Stammen
40	Reserve	Swingman, Relief specialist	Brandon Barnes, Randy Choate

RISK FACTORS

SAFE: Has shown realistic ceiling in big leagues; ready to contribute in 2015.

LOW: Likely to reach realistic ceiling, certain big league career barring injury.

MEDIUM: Still some work to do to turn tools into major league-caliber skills, but fairly polished player.

HIGH: Most draft picks in their first seasons, players with plenty of projection left or players whose injury history is worrisome. Players with concussion histories have at least a High risk factor.

EXTREME: Teenagers in Rookie ball, players with significant injury histories or players whose struggle with a key skill (control for pitchers or plate discipline for hitters) is a significant barrier to them ever reaching their potential.

Explaining The 20-80 Scouting Scale

None of the authors of this book is a scout, but we all have spoken to plenty of scouts to report on the prospects and scouting reports enclosed in the Prospect Handbook. So we have to use their lingo, and the 20-80 scouting scale is part of that.

Many of these grades are measurable data, such as fastball velocity and speed (usually timed from home to first or in workouts over 60 yards). A fastball grade doesn't stem solely from its velocity—command and life are crucial elements as well—but throwing 100 mph will earn a player an 80 grade. Secondary pitches are graded in a similar fashion. The more swings-and-misses a pitch induces from hitters and the sharper the bite of the movement, the better the grade.

Velocity steadily has increased over the past decade. Many scouts still think of a 88-91 mph fastball as average, but major league Pitch f/x data says it's below-average; in 2014, big league starting pitchers averaged 91.4 mph. Lefthanded starters averaged 1.3 mph less on their fastballs last year than righthanders, so reduce each velocity by 1 mph to scale it for lefthanders. Fastballs earn their grades based on the average range of the pitch over the course of a typical outing, not touching or bumping the peak velocity on occasion.

A move to the bullpen complicates in another direction. Pitchers airing it out for one inning should throw harder than someone trying to last six or seven innings, so add 1-2 mph for relievers. Yes, nowadays an 80 fastball for a reliever needs to sit at 98-99 mph. That may seem excessive, but we found more than 50 minor league relievers who touched 100 mph last season. Many of them aren't even significant prospects.

Hitting ability is as much a skill as it is a tool, but the physical elements—hand-eye coordination, swing mechanics, bat speed—are key factors in the hit tool grade. Raw power generally is measured by how far a player can hit the ball, but game power is graded by how many home runs the hitter projects to hit in the majors, preferably an average over the course of a career. Those numbers are in flux as big league offensive levels change. Some teams consider the player reaching that level of production as a validation of the power tool grade, while others do not.

Arm strength can be evaluated by observing the velocity and carry of throws, measured in workouts with radar guns or measured in games for catchers with pop times—the time it takes from the pop of the ball in the catcher's mitt to the pop of the ball in the fielder's glove at second base. Defense takes different factors into account by position but starts with proper footwork and technique, incorporates physical attributes such as hands, short-area quickness and fluid actions, then adds subtle skills such as instincts and anticipation as a last layer.

Not every team uses the wording below. Some use a 2-to-8 scale without half-grades, and others use above-average and plus synonymously. But for the Handbook, consider this BA's 20-80 scale.

20: As bad as it gets for a big leaguer. Think R.A. Dickey's fastball or Brendan Ryan's bat.

30: Poor, but not unplayable, such as Ben Revere's arm or Elvis Andrus' power.

40: Below-average, such as Derek Norris' arm, or Huston Street's fastball velocity.

45: Fringe-average. Kevin Correia's fastball and Daniel Murphy's defense qualify.

50: Major league average. Jason Hammel's fastball or Desmond Jennings' power.

55: Above-average. Michael Brantley's power, or Brandon McArthur's fastball.

60: Plus. Think Corey Kluber's slider, Doug Fister's command or Robinson Cano's defense.

70: Plus-Plus. Among the best tools in the game, such as Felix Hernandez's changeup, or Robinson Cano's hitting ability.

80: Top of the scale. Some scouts consider only one player's tool in all of the major leagues to be 80. Think Billy Hamilton's speed, or Aroldis Chapman's 103 mph fastball.

20-80 Measurables

SPEED 60-Yard Dash Times (In Seconds)	SPEED Home-First (In Secs.) RHH—LHH		POWER Grade Home Runs	FASTBALL Velocity (Starters) Grade Velocity	ARM STRENGTH Catcher: Pop Times To Second Base (In Seconds)
80 . . . . < 6.44	80 . . . . 4.00—3.90		80 . . . . .35+	80 . . . . . 97+ mph	80 . . . . < 1.74
70 . . . . . .6.45-6.64	70 . . . . 4.10—4.00		70 29-34	70 96	70 . . . . . .1.75-1.84
60 . . . . . .6.65-6.84	65 . . . . 4.15—4.05		65 25-30	65 95	60 . . . . . .1.85-1.94
50 . . . . . .6.85-6.99	60 . . . . 4.20—4.10		60 21-26	60 94	50 . . . . . .1.95-2.04
40 . . . . . .7.00-7.24	55 . . . . 4.25—4.15		55 17-22	55 93	40 . . . . . .2.05-2.14
30 . . . . . .7.25-7.44	50 . . . . 4.30—4.20		50 14-18	50 91-92	30 . . . . . .2.15-2.24
20 . . . . > 7.45	45 . . . . 4.35—4.25		45 11-15	45 90	20 . . . . > 2.25
	40 . . . . 4.40—4.30		40 7-12	40 88-89	
	30 . . . . 4.50—4.40		30 4-8	30 86-87	
	20 . . . . 4.60—4.50		20 0-5	20 . . . . .85 or less	

How To Place Minor League Performance In Context

In addition to the detailed scouting reports and tools information available for the 900 players in this Prospect Handbook, we have introduced a new wrinkle for one-third of players in the 2015 edition. Now readers will find a performance-overview box for the Top 10 Prospects in each organization.

Performance is displayed level by level, to note how a player fared after a promotion to a higher level in 2014 and also to keep distinct league run-scoring environments separate.

To avoid clutter and reduce the number of potentially misleading small samples, we print a maximum of two performance lines for players who spent time in more than two leagues in 2014, and we always display the leagues at which he spent the most time, as measured by plate appearances (for batters) or batters faced (for pitchers).

Here are the various league averages in 2014 for the two major leagues plus all 16 domestic minor leagues:

LEAGUE	LGE	LVL	BAge	PAge	R/G	AVG	OBP	SLG	BB	SO	ISO	HR/9
American	AL	MLB	28.7	28.4	4.18	.253	.316	.390	7.7%	19.8%	.137	0.9
National	NL	MLB	28.2	28.5	3.95	.249	.312	.383	7.6%	20.9%	.133	0.8
International	IL	AAA	26.9	26.9	4.36	.261	.331	.393	8.8%	19.4%	.132	0.8
Pacific Coast	PCL	AAA	26.6	26.8	5.03	.276	.344	.427	8.7%	19.8%	.152	1.0
Eastern	EL	AA	24.7	24.6	4.35	.261	.327	.392	8.2%	19.0%	.131	0.8
Southern	SL	AA	24.5	24.4	4.31	.254	.328	.382	8.9%	18.7%	.128	0.7
Texas	TL	AA	24.1	24.4	4.18	.251	.322	.373	8.7%	20.1%	.121	0.7
California	CAL	Hi A	22.8	23.2	5.22	.270	.340	.426	8.6%	20.7%	.156	1.0
Carolina	CAR	Hi A	22.9	22.8	4.41	.255	.327	.379	8.6%	19.7%	.123	0.6
Florida State	FSL	Hi A	22.6	23.2	4.21	.257	.325	.371	8.2%	18.9%	.113	0.5
Midwest	MWL	Lo A	21.4	22.0	4.37	.252	.322	.370	8.3%	20.9%	.118	0.6
South Atlantic	SAL	Lo A	21.5	21.8	4.58	.261	.330	.381	8.3%	19.8%	.120	0.6
New York-Penn	NYP	SS	21.0	21.5	4.15	.251	.318	.357	7.6%	20.0%	.106	0.4
Northwest	NWL	SS	21.1	21.5	4.89	.256	.334	.370	9.0%	20.8%	.114	0.6
Appalachian	APP	R	20.2	20.5	4.55	.252	.327	.356	8.7%	21.6%	.104	0.5
Pioneer	PIO	R	20.5	21.2	5.64	.279	.348	.425	8.4%	20.1%	.145	0.8
Arizona	AZL	R	19.5	20.3	5.03	.248	.328	.352	9.3%	23.2%	.104	0.4
Gulf Coast	GCL	R	19.6	20.3	4.37	.249	.331	.346	9.3%	19.3%	.097	0.3

BAge: Average age of batters in league. **PAge:** Average age of pitchers in league. **R/G:** Runs per game.
ISO: Isolated slugging percentage, which expresses power production as extra bases per at-bat

With the major league strikeout rate soaring to new heights each season, pay particular attention to the SO% column, which is strikeouts divided by plate appearances. A good rule of thumb: The strikeout rate is approximately 20 percent at all full-season levels and the two short-season (SS) leagues. The Rookie-level rate is about 21 percent.

The overall walk rate (BB%) generally ranges from about 8-9 percent, depending on level, while ISO (isolated power) ranges from .113 (Florida State) to .137 (American) in the full-season leagues—with the notable exceptions of the California (.156) and Pacific Coast (.152) leagues, which are outliers for their highly favorable hitting conditions.

Using Kris Bryant and Daniel Norris as examples, we can cross-reference how their performance compares with the average rates for players in leagues in which they played.

Kris Bryant, 3b, Cubs	LGE	PA	BB%	SO%	ISO	
	SL	297	14.5	25.9	.347	
	PCL	297	14.5	28.6	.324	
Daniel Norris, lhp, Blue Jays	LGE	BF	SO%	BB%	HR/9	
	FSL	262	29.0	6.9	0.00	
	EL	155	31.6	11.0	1.26	

Throughout this edition of the Prospect Handbook, you'll notice that we print statistics only for each of the past three seasons. Omitting statistics prior to 2012 creates more space to run expanded scouting reports for each club's Top 10 Prospects and the new performance-overview boxes.

We hope the modifications and additions enhance your Prospect Handbook experience.

—MATT EDDY

MINOR LEAGUE DEPTH CHART

AN OVERVIEW

Another feature of the Prospect Handbook is a depth chart of every organization's minor league talent. This shows you at a glance what kind of talent a system has and provides even more prospects beyond the Top 30.

Players are usually listed on the depth charts where we think they'll ultimately end up. To help you better understand why players are slotted at particular positions, we show you here what scouts look for in the ideal candidate at each spot, with individual tools ranked in descending order.

LF
Power
Hitting
Fielding
Arm Strength
Speed

CF
Fielding
Hitting
Speed
Power
Arm Strength

RF
Power
Hitting
Arm Strength
Fielding
Speed

3B
Power
Hitting
Fielding
Arm Strength
Speed

SS
Fielding
Arm Strength
Hitting
Speed
Power

2B
Hitting
Fielding
Power
Speed
Arm Strength

1B
Power
Hitting
Fielding
Arm Strength
Speed

C
Fielding
Hitting
Arm Strength
Power
Speed

STARTING PITCHERS			
No. 1 starter	**No. 2 starter**	**No. 3 starter**	**No. 4-5 starters**
• Two plus pitches	• Two plus pitches	• One plus pitch	• Command of two major
• Average third pitch	• Average third pitch	• Two average pitches	league pitches
• Plus-plus command	• Average command	• Average command	• Average velocity
• Plus makeup	• Average makeup	• Average makeup	• Consistent breaking ball
			• Decent changeup

CLOSER
• One dominant pitch
• Second plus pitch
• Plus command
• Plus-plus makeup

When Baseball America ranks prospects, there's almost always a byline attributing the ranking to the person who finally put the players in order, who decided, "OK, this guy's No. 6 and this guy's No. 7." But in truth, all of our rankings are more than one person's opinion. They are most often a reflection of the consensus of sources on the subject—managers, coaches, scouts, front-office personnel, the whole spectrum—filtered through the expertise of our writers and editors.

Except here, really. In this section of the Handbook, we get personal. Sifting through all of the information we've gathered to this point, four of our editors give their own personal takes on the game's top 50 prospects. This helps form the basis of the arguments that shape Baseball America's official Top 100 Prospects list, which is released each February. We consider it the definitive guide to the best talent in the minor leagues, and you can find it in our print edition or online at BaseballAmerica.com.

The rules for these lists are the same for any prospect who appears in the Handbook: no more than 130 at-bats, 50 innings or 30 relief appearances in the major leagues. We do not consider service time in our eligibility requirements. These rankings represent how each person regarded the top minor league talent in the game at a moment in time. Ask us again in a few months how these prospects stack up, and you'll get a different answer.

Injuries plagued Byron Buxton throughout the 2014 season

BEN BADLER

1. Byron Buxton, of, Twins	26. Orlando Arcia, ss, Brewers
2. Kris Bryant, 3b, Cubs	27. Manuel Margot, of, Red Sox
3. Addison Russell, ss, Cubs	28. Tyler Glasnow, rhp, Pirates
4. Jorge Soler, of, Cubs	29. Luis Severino, rhp, Yankees
5. Carlos Correa, ss, Astros	30. Rusney Castillo, of, Red Sox
6. Corey Seager, ss, Dodgers	31. Tyrone Taylor, of, Brewers
7. Joey Gallo, 3b, Rangers	32. Marcos Molina, rhp, Mets
8. Joc Pederson, of, Dodgers	33. Braden Shipley, rhp, Diamondbacks
9. Francisco Lindor, ss, Indians	34. Jake Lamb, 3b, Diamondbacks
10. J.P. Crawford, ss, Phillies	35. Steven Souza, of, Nationals
11. Noah Syndergaard, rhp, Mets	36. Austin Meadows, of, Pirates
12. Julio Urias, lhp, Dodgers	37. Andrew Heaney, lhp, Angels
13. Miguel Sano, 3b, Twins	38. Aaron Sanchez, rhp, Blue Jays
14. Lucas Giolito, rhp, Nationals	39. Daniel Robertson, ss, Athletics
15. Kyle Schwarber, of/c, Cubs	40. Franklin Barreto, ss, Athletics
16. Carlos Rodon, lhp, White Sox	41. Alex Jackson, of, Mariners
17. Dilson Herrera, 2b, Mets	42. Jorge Polanco, ss, Twins
18. Blake Swihart, c, Red Sox	43. Brandon Nimmo, of, Mets
19. Daniel Norris, lhp, Blue Jays	44. Jameson Taillon, rhp, Pirates
20. Dalton Pompey, of, Blue Jays	45. Michael Taylor, of, Nationals
21. Robert Stephenson, rhp, Reds	46. Raul A. Mondesi, ss, Royals
22. Jesse Winker, of, Reds	47. Ryan McMahon, 3b, Rockies
23. David Dahl, of, Rockies	48. Matt Wisler, rhp, Padres
24. Alex Meyer, rhp, Twins	49. Aaron Nola, rhp, Phillies
25. Jake Thompson, rhp, Rangers	50. Alex Reyes, rhp, Cardinals

J.J. COOPER

1. Kris Bryant, 3b, Cubs
2. Byron Buxton, of, Twins
3. Carlos Correa, ss, Astros
4. Addison Russell, ss, Cubs
5. Joey Gallo, 3b, Rangers
6. Corey Seager, ss, Dodgers
7. Francisco Lindor, ss, Indians
8. Joc Pederson, of, Dodgers
9. Lucas Giolito, rhp, Nationals
10. Miguel Sano, 3b, Twins
11. Julio Urias, lhp, Dodgers
12. Noah Syndergaard, rhp, Mets
13. Jorge Soler, of, Cubs
14. Blake Swihart, c, Red Sox
15. Robert Stephenson, rhp, Reds
16. Tyler Glasnow, rhp, Pirates
17. Jon Gray, rhp, Rockies
18. Archie Bradley, rhp, Diamondbacks
19. Daniel Norris, lhp, Blue Jays
20. Carlos Rodon, lhp, White Sox
21. Luis Severino, rhp, Yankees
22. J.P. Crawford, ss, Phillies
23. Henry Owens, lhp, Red Sox
24. Dylan Bundy, rhp, Orioles
25. Jameson Taillon, rhp, Pirates
26. Aaron Sanchez, rhp, Blue Jays
27. Mark Appel, rhp, Astros
28. Kyle Schwarber, c, Cubs
29. Eddie Butler, rhp, Rockies
30. Dalton Pompey, of, Blue Jays
31. Alex Jackson, of, Mariners
32. Jose Berrios, rhp, Twins
33. David Dahl, of, Rockies
34. Jesse Winker, of, Reds
35. Reynaldo Lopez, rhp, Nationals
36. Hunter Harvey, rhp, Orioles
37. Aaron Nola, rhp, Phillies
38. Raul A. Mondesi, ss, Royals
39. Yasmany Tomas, of/3b, Diamondbacks
40. D.J. Peterson, 3b/1b, Mariners
41. Brandon Finnegan, lhp, Royals
42. Kohl Stewart, rhp, Twins
43. Alex Meyer, rhp, Twins
44. Raisel Iglesias, rhp, Reds
45. C.J. Edwards, rhp, Cubs
46. Maikel Franco, 3b, Phillies
47. Trea Turner, ss, Padres
48. Hunter Renfroe, of, Padres
49. Kevin Plawecki, c, Mets
50. Kyle Zimmer, rhp, Royals

MATT EDDY

1. Byron Buxton, of, Twins
2. Carlos Correa, ss, Astros
3. Kris Bryant, 3b, Cubs
4. Addison Russell, ss, Cubs
5. Corey Seager, ss, Dodgers
6. Joey Gallo, 3b, Rangers
7. Francisco Lindor, ss, Indians
8. Joc Pederson, of, Dodgers
9. Lucas Giolito, rhp, Nationals
10. Noah Syndergaard, rhp, Mets
11. Daniel Norris, lhp, Blue Jays
12. Miguel Sano, 3b, Twins
13. J.P. Crawford, ss, Phillies
14. Tyler Glasnow, rhp, Pirates
15. Jorge Soler, of, Cubs
16. Julio Urias, lhp, Dodgers
17. Carlos Rodon, lhp, White Sox
18. Blake Swihart, c, Red Sox
19. Braden Shipley, rhp, Diamondbacks
20. Robert Stephenson, rhp, Reds
21. Alex Jackson, of, Mariners
22. Jose Peraza, 2b, Braves
23. Kyle Schwarber, of/c, Cubs
24. David Dahl, of, Rockies
25. Jameson Taillon, rhp, Pirates
26. Jon Gray, rhp, Rockies
27. Matt Wisler, rhp, Padres
28. Brandon Finnegan, lhp, Royals
29. Yasmany Tomas, of/3b, Diamondbacks
30. Steve Matz, lhp, Mets
31. Raul A. Mondesi, ss, Royals
32. Dylan Bundy, rhp, Orioles
33. Kyle Freeland, lhp, Rockies
34. Michael Taylor, of, Nationals
35. Luis Severino, rhp, Yankees
36. Brandon Nimmo, of, Mets
37. Mark Appel, rhp, Astros
38. Dilson Herrera, 2b, Mets
39. Dalton Pompey, of, Blue Jays
40. C.J. Edwards, rhp, Cubs
41. Maikel Franco, 3b, Phillies
42. Archie Bradley, rhp, Diamondbacks
43. Aaron Sanchez, rhp, Blue Jays
44. Henry Owens, lhp, Red Sox
45. Aaron Blair, rhp, Diamondbacks
46. Alex Reyes, rhp, Cardinals
47. Steven Souza, of, Nationals
48. J.T. Realmuto, c, Marlins
49. Rusney Castillo, of, Red Sox
50. Andrew Susac, c, Giants

Older brother Kyle Seager is an all-star, but younger brother Corey may be even better

Carlos Correa's athleticism serves him well, making him the Astros' future cornerstone

JOHN MANUEL

1. Kris Bryant, 3b, Cubs
2. Byron Buxton, of, Twins
3. Addison Russell, ss, Cubs
4. Carlos Correa, ss, Astros
5. Corey Seager, ss, Dodgers
6. Joey Gallo, 3b, Rangers
7. J.P. Crawford, ss, Phillies
8. Lucas Giolito, rhp, Nationals
9. Joc Pederson, of, Dodgers
10. Jorge Soler, of, Cubs
11. Tyler Glasnow, rhp, Pirates
12. Julio Urias, lhp, Dodgers
13. Miguel Sano, 3b, Twins
14. Francisco Lindor, ss, Indians
15. Carlos Rodon, lhp, White Sox
16. Daniel Norris, lhp, Blue Jays
17. Robert Stephenson, rhp, Reds
18. Matt Wisler, rhp, Padres
19. Blake Swihart, c, Red Sox
20. Raul A. Mondesi, ss, Royals
21. Kyle Schwarber, of/c, Cubs
22. Alex Jackson, of, Mariners
23. Archie Bradley, rhp, Diamondbacks
24. Aaron Nola, rhp, Phillies
25. Mark Appel, rhp, Astros
26. Braden Shipley, rhp, Diamondbacks
27. Jon Gray, rhp, Rockies
28. Yasmany Tomas, of/3b, Diamondbacks
29. Dylan Bundy, rhp, Orioles
30. Jameson Taillon, rhp, Pirates
31. Tyler Kolek, rhp, Marlins
32. Dalton Pompey, of, Blue Jays
33. Jose Berrios, rhp, Twins
34. Daniel Robertson, ss, Athletics
35. C.J. Edwards, rhp, Cubs
36. Eduardo Rodriguez, lhp, Red Sox
37. Luis Severino, rhp, Yankees
38. Steve Matz, lhp, Mets
39. Andrew Heaney, lhp, Angels
40. Aaron Blair, rhp, Diamondbacks
41. Rusney Castillo, of, Red Sox
42. Reynaldo Lopez, rhp, Nationals
43. Henry Owens, lhp, Red Sox
44. J.T. Realmuto, c, Marlins
45. Aaron Sanchez, rhp, Blue Jays
46. Franklin Barretto, ss, Athletics
47. Michael Taylor, of, Nationals
48. Brandon Nimmo, of, Mets
49. David Dahl, of, Rockies
50. Austin Meadows, of, Pirates

Team	2014	2013	2012	2011	2010
1. Chicago Cubs	4	13	14	8	15

The Royals parlayed homegrown talent into a 2014 World Series appearance. The Cubs are following that same playbook, amassing an enviable collection of impact talent heavy on bats that should soon end their own World Series drought.

2. Minnesota Twins	3	10	19	13	7

Even though 2014 was a lost season for blue-chippers Byron Buxton and Miguel Sano, the Twins have a formidable farm system, mixing starting pitching that's close to the big leagues led by Jose Berrios and Alex Meyer with up-the-middle position prospects like Nick Gordon and Jorge Polanco.

3. Los Angeles Dodgers	14	19	23	12	24

Only the Cubs have a better trio of prospects than the Dodgers, who have wisely held on to Corey Seager, Joc Pederson and Julio Urias. Beyond the big three, several players took a big leap forward, improving the depth that was previously a weakness.

4. New York Mets	10	26	24	20	22

With sharp trades, quality drafts and a strong international program, the Mets have successfully tapped into all means of talent procurement to build a powerhouse farm system. Prospects Noah Syndergaard, Steven Matz and Rafael Montero are ready to help an already formidable major league rotation in 2015.

5. Boston Red Sox	2	6	10	17	6

Even with the prospect graduations of Xander Bogaerts and Mookie Betts, the Red Sox still have one of the game's deepest systems. Boston usually has hit on its biggest investments to find high-ceiling talent, whether it's in the draft for first-rounders like Blake Swihart or internationally with Rafael Devers and Manuel Margot.

6. Arizona Diamondbacks	13	7	4	22	27

Baseball's worst team has help on the way. Six of the team's top eight prospects have reached Double-A, while Yasmany Tomas should also go straight to the majors. With the No. 1 overall pick in 2015, the Diamondbacks could turn the ship around quickly with the right moves.

7. Pittsburgh Pirates	1	8	13	19	16

Productive drafts and Latin American signings have helped the Pirates cultivate one of the game's most balanced farm systems. The organization has a quality blend of pitching and position prospects at all levels, which should help them maintain another high ranking as they continue to graduate players to Pittsburgh.

8. Colorado Rockies	11	20	16	10	10

Jon Gray and Eddie Butler are two big arms on the cusp of a rotation spot in Colorado, while 2014 first-rounder Kyle Freeland has the polish to move quickly. A stacked low Class A Asheville club included David Dahl and Ryan McMahon, a pair of dynamic prospects who can impact the game at the plate and in the field.

9. Toronto Blue Jays	15	12	5	4	28

After Marcus Stroman showed tantalizing talent in his 2014 rookie season, the Blue Jays should have two more young arms helping next year in Daniel Norris and Aaron Sanchez. A breakthrough season for Dalton Pompey, the addition of two first-round picks in Max Pentecost and Jeff Hoffman, along with the emergence of promising young Latin American players in the lower levels have bolstered the Blue Jays' young pipeline.

10. Houston Astros	5	9	17	26	30

The Astros' plan to tear it all down and embark on a lengthy rebuild has produced a good but not elite farm system. Carlos Correa is a cornerstone player and the system is deep, though the possibility of contending for a playoff spot is likely still a few years away. The Astros should move up in these rankings next year, as they will have two of the top five picks in the 2015 draft after they didn't sign Brady Aiken, the No. 1 overall pick in 2014.

11. Texas Rangers	9	3	2	15	2

The system is full of high-risk, high-reward prospects, with breakout seasons from Joey Gallo and Nomar Mazara providing a taste of what could happen when everything clicks. While most of the position players are a year out from Texas, righthanders Jake Thompson and Alex Gonzalez could boost the rotation by midseason.

12. Washington Nationals	21	16	1	14	21

Betting on players who fell due to injury concerns has benefited the Nationals, who scored big on Anthony Rendon, have a potential ace in Lucas Giolito and could make another big strike if 2014 first-rounder Erick Fedde makes a full recovery from Tommy John.

13. Kansas City Royals	8	18	3	1	17

Now that they're winning, can the Royals continue to keep the pipeline filled with prospects without getting their annual pick near the top of the draft? The system is understandably starting to slip, though one of the game's premier international programs should help.

14. San Diego Padres	6	15	8	9	20

Pitching, with Matt Wisler on the cusp of San Diego and Joe Ross not far behind, is the sytem's strength. Top bats such as Trea Turner, Hunter Renfroe and Austin Hedges are divisive prospects. New GM A.J. Preller, who helped the Rangers build one of the game's top farm systems, should be fascinating to watch transform the Padres.

15. St. Louis Cardinals	7	1	12	24	29

The Cardinals' tremendous success through homegrown talent has been obvious at the big league level. The quality of the farm system has backed up since it ranked No. 1 two years ago due to graduations, but it's still a solid crop slanted toward pitching.

Team	2014	2013	2012	2011	2010
16. Cincinnati Reds	16	14	7	6	23

Pitching is the strength of the system, with Robert Stephenson, Raisel Iglesias and Anthony Desclafani all capable of helping in Cincinnati in 2015. But other than Jesse Winker, the Reds are thin on bats, especially in the infield.

Team	2014	2013	2012	2011	2010
17. Tampa Bay Rays	20	4	11	3	1

The Rays continue to rely on trading arbitration-eligible stars to get younger and cheaper, with the midseason David Price deal netting top prospect Willy Adames. There's already a thin margin for error when a team has to continually part with its best players, but that's become magnified due to a run of bad drafts and international talent that's mostly congregated at the lower levels.

Team	2014	2013	2012	2011	2010
18. New York Yankees	18	11	6	5	18

It's going to be a challenge yet again for the Yankees to tap the farm system for big league contributions in 2015. Latin American talent headlined by Luis Severino has helped make up for a lack of success in the draft in a middle-of-the-road farm system. That trend could continue after the Yankees signed 10 of the top 30 international prospects for July 2 last year.

Team	2014	2013	2012	2011	2010
19. Oakland Athletics	23	25	26	28	12

Giving up Addison Russell and Billy McKinney to the A's was a stunning trade at the time, a huge blow to the farm system that could come back to haunt the organization. Offseason trades of Josh Donaldson and Jeff Samardzija improved the farm system, but came at a high price. They must get more out of their Latin American program.

Team	2014	2013	2012	2011	2010
20. Chicago White Sox	24	29	30	27	19

Gambling on raw athletes with big tools in the draft has left the organization with several unproductive players who swing and miss liberally. Things are more promising on the pitching side, thanks largely to the influx of two potential front-end starters in Carlos Rodon and Spencer Adams from the 2014 draft.

Team	2014	2013	2012	2011	2010
21. Milwaukee Brewers	29	22	25	30	14

Tyrone Taylor and Orlando Arcia have the ability to impact the game at the plate and in the field at premium positions. But neither has reached Double-A, and the decline in the system after them is steep, with much riding on a daring 2014 draft.

Team	2014	2013	2012	2011	2010
22. Philadelphia Phillies	22	23	27	11	5

J.P. Crawford, Aaron Nola and Maikel Franco make a formidable trio at the top of the farm system. After that, you might want to avert your eyes. A rebuild should be in order to infuse the organization with much-needed young talent.

Team	2014	2013	2012	2011	2010
23. Cleveland Indians	17	24	29	7	3

Francisco Lindor is the crown jewel of the farm system and could be in Cleveland after the all-star break. It's a top-heavy system that falls off quickly though, with four of their top 10 prospects members of a promising 2014 draft haul.

Team	2014	2013	2012	2011	2010
24. Seattle Mariners	25	2	9	18	11

Seattle's best young talent is no longer prospect-eligible, with Taijuan Walker and James Paxton graduating and poised to play key roles in 2015. Aside from No. 1 prospect Alex Jackson, there aren't many potentially above-average big leaguers on the farm.

Team	2014	2013	2012	2011	2010
25. Miami Marlins	27	5	28	29	8

The Marlins can build around a talented young outfield of Giancarlo Stanton, Marcell Ozuna and Christian Yelich, though losing Jose Fernandez to Tommy John surgery was a brutal blow. Trades thinned the farm system, which benefits from a remarkably effective Dominican scouting group that already has Ozuna in the big leagues along with four of the team's top 10 prospects, despite limited resources.

Team	2014	2013	2012	2011	2010
26. San Francisco Giants	19	28	21	23	4

Homegrown players helped fuel the Giants to three World Series titles in five years. They no longer have high-end players like Buster Posey or Madison Bumgarner in the farm system, though, so the formula to sustain that success will have to be tweaked.

Team	2014	2013	2012	2011	2010
27. Los Angeles Angels	30	18	16	25	25

With Andrew Heaney, Sean Newcomb and Ricardo Sanchez, three promising lefthanders sit atop the farm system. Otherwise, it's mostly spare parts, with a pitching focus in the draft leaving the system bare of athletes and position-player prospects.

Team	2014	2013	2012	2011	2010
28. Baltimore Orioles	12	17	20	21	9

Dan Duquette engineered a masterful, remarkably quick turnaround at the major league level in Baltimore. He's going to have to keep making shrewd moves because the talent on the farm is light, as even top prospect Dylan Bundy was shaky in his return from Tommy John, while a forearm injury ended the season in July for No. 2 prospect Hunter Harvey.

Team	2014	2013	2012	2011	2010
29. Atlanta Braves	26	21	15	2	13

An organization once revered for its scouting and player development has seen its farm system go in the tank following a run of thin drafts and quick rises to the majors. It's no wonder the organization decided to clean house and bring back former scouting director Roy Clark as a special assistant to overhaul operations.

Team	2014	2013	2012	2011	2010
30. Detroit Tigers	28	27	22	25	26

With four consecutive AL Central titles, it's hard to argue with the Tigers' methods. GM Dave Dombrowski's penchant for shipping away prospects hasn't bitten the Tigers yet, but there's little impact talent or immediate help coming from the farm.

Arizona Diamondbacks

BY BILL MITCHELL

For a team on its way to the majors' worst record at 64-98, following two straight .500 seasons, it came as no surprise that the Diamondbacks contemplated significant changes as the 2014 season wore on.

The biggest splash came in May, with the announcement that Hall of Fame manager Tony La Russa was joining the organization in a new role of chief baseball officer. He had been working in the commissioner's office since retiring as the manager of the Cardinals after the 2011 season. After taking most of the summer to evaluate the organization, La Russa's first major move was the removal of Kevin Towers as general manager, a post he'd held since 2010.

La Russa hired his former ace with the Athletics, Dave Stewart, as the new GM on Sept. 25. Stewart had worked as assistant GM with the Blue Jays but had been an agent since 2001.

Manager Kirk Gibson and bench coach Alan Trammell were fired just before the end of the regular season, and A's bench coach Chip Hale will take over as manager.

A University of Arizona product and former big leaguer, Hale had been the D-backs' third base coach from 2007-09 as well as previously managing in their minor league system. Former D-backs infielder Andy Green, who managed at Double-A Mobile in 2013-14, was named bench coach.

The makeover continued throughout the front office. La Russa hired De Jon Watson, previously the Dodgers' farm director, as senior vice president of baseball operations. Scouting director Ray Montgomery, who had been one of the internal candidates for the GM job, later left the organization to accept the same position with the Brewers.

Arizona hired Nationals special assistant Deric Ladnier to replace him. The former Royals scouting director will direct the organization's efforts as they pick No. 1 overall in 2015 for the first time since taking Justin Upton to start the 2005 draft.

The No. 1 pick is about the only good thing produced in 2014. The organization increased payroll heading into 2014, but nearly all of its moves backfired. Free agent pickup Bronson Arroyo and 2013 all-star Pat Corbin both needed Tommy John surgery, decimating the rotation. Slugger Mark Trumbo, acquired from the Angels, missed nearly three months with a broken foot, and key pieces such as reliever David Hernandez (Tommy John surgery) and A.J. Pollock (broken hand) also missed time.

The lack of starting-pitcher depth, once an organizational strength, hurt the team more than anything. Projected future rotation members Ian

GM Kevin Towers and manager Kirk Gibson did not survive a 98-loss season in Arizona

TOP PROSPECTS OF THE DECADE

Year	Player, Pos.	2014 Org
2005	Carlos Quentin, of	Padres
2006	Stephen Drew, ss	Yankees
2007	Justin Upton, of	Braves
2008	Carlos Gonzalez, of	Rockies
2009	Jarrod Parker, rhp	Athletics
2010	Jarrod Parker, rhp	Athletics
2011	Jarrod Parker, rhp	Athletics
2012	Trevor Bauer, rhp	Indians
2013	Tyler Skaggs, lhp	Angels
2014	Archie Bradley, rhp	Diamondbacks

Kennedy, Trevor Bauer and Tyler Skaggs had all been traded, and No. 1 prospect Archie Bradley was not yet ready to contribute due to a flexor strain in his right elbow early in the season and command troubles when he returned.

The offseason renovations continued with the major league roster. The new front office traded catcher Miguel Montero to the Cubs, shortstop Didi Gregorius to the Yankees (in a three-team deal) and lefthander Wade Miley to the Red Sox, adding mostly young pitchers in return, as well as second baseman Domingo Leyba from the Tigers in the Gregorius deal.

Arizona also added major league-ready talent by signing Cuban outfielder Yasmany Tomas to a six-year, $68.5 million contract and getting right-hander Jeremy Hellickson in a trade with the Rays.

General manager: Dave Stewart. **Farm director:** Mike Bell. **Scouting director:** Deric Ladnier.

Class	Team	League	W	L	PCT	Finish	Manager
Majors	Arizona Diamondbacks	National	64	98	.395	30th (30)	Kirk Gibson
Triple-A	Reno Aces	Pacific Coast	81	63	.563	t-1st (16)	Phil Nevin
Double-A	Mobile Bay Bears	Southern	79	58	.577	3rd (10)	Andy Green
High A	Visalia Rawhide	California	75	65	.536	4th (10)	Robby Hammock
Low A	*South Bend Silver Hawks	Midwest	83	56	.597	2nd (16)	Mark Haley
Short season	Hillsboro Hops	Northwest	48	28	.632	1st (8)	J.R. House
Rookie	Missoula Osprey	Pioneer	36	40	.474	7th (8)	Audo Vicente
Rookie	Diamondbacks	Arizona	29	27	.518	5th (8)	Luis Urueta
Overall Minor League Record			**431**	**337**	**.561**	**2nd (30)**	

*Affiliate will be Kane County (Midwest) in 2015.

THIS YEAR'S TOP 30

Player, Pos.	Status
1. Archie Bradley, rhp	65/High
2. Braden Shipley, rhp	60/Medium
3. Aaron Blair, rhp	60/Medium
4. Yasmany Tomas, of/3b	60/High
5. Touki Toussaint, rhp	65/Extreme
6. Jake Lamb, 3b	50/Low
7. Brandon Drury, 3b/2b	50/Medium
8. Peter O'Brien, c/1b	50/High
9. Domingo Leyba, 2b/ss	55/Extreme
10. Nick Ahmed, ss	45/Low
11. Robbie Ray, lhp	50/High
12. Jake Barrett, rhp	45/Medium
13. Jose Martinez, rhp	55/Extreme
14. Cody Reed, lhp	55/Extreme
15. Jose Herrera, c	55/Extreme
16. Jimmie Sherfy, rhp	50/High
17. Anthony Banda, lhp	50/High
18. Andrew Chafin, lhp	45/Medium
19. Socrates Brito, of	50/High
20. Sergio Alcantara, ss	50/Extreme
21. Stryker Trahan, c/of	50/Extreme
22. Mitch Haniger, of	45/Medium
23. Jeferson Mejia, rhp	50/Extreme
24. Marcus Wilson, of	50/Extreme
25. Brent Jones, rhp	45/High
26. Zach Borenstein, of	45/High
27. Isan Diaz, 2b/ss	50/Extreme
28. Matt Railey, of	50/Extreme
29. Enrique Burgos, rhp	45/High
30. Daniel Palka, 1b/of	45/High

LAST YEAR'S TOP 30

Player, Pos.	Status
1. Archie Bradley, rhp	No. 1
2. Braden Shipley, rhp	No. 2
3. Chris Owings, ss	Majors
4. Matt Davidson, 3b	(White Sox)
5. Aaron Blair, rhp	No. 3
6. Jose Martinez, rhp	No. 13
7. David Holmberg, lhp	(Reds)
8. Stryker Trahan, c	No. 21
9. Matt Stites, rhp	Majors
10. Brandon Drury, 3b	No. 7
11. Jake Barrett, rhp	No. 12
12. Jake Lamb, 3b	No. 6
13. Sergio Alcantara, ss	No. 20
14. Justin Williams, of	(Rays)
15. Jimmie Sherfy, rhp	No. 16
16. Zeke Spruill, rhp	Dropped out
17. Daniel Palka, 1b	No. 30
18. Nick Ahmed, ss	No. 10
19. Evan Marshall, rhp	Majors
20. Michael Perez, c	Dropped out
21. Daniel Gibson, lhp	Dropped out
22. Geordy Parra, rhp	Dropped out
23. Chase Anderson, rhp	Majors
24. Andrew Chafin, lhp	No. 18
25. Alfredo Marte, of	(Angels)
26. Joe Munoz, ss	Dropped out
27. Jamie Westbrook, 2b	Dropped out
28. Andrew Velazquez, ss/2b	(Rays)
29. Bo Schultz, rhp	(Blue Jays)
30. Jose Herrera, c	No. 15

BEST TOOLS

Best Hitter for Average	Jake Lamb
Best Power Hitter	Yasmany Tomas
Best Strike-Zone Discipline	Sergio Alcantara
Fastest Baserunner	Matt McPhearson
Best Athlete	Socrates Brito
Best Fastball	Enrique Burgos
Best Curveball	Braden Shipley
Best Slider	Will Locante
Best Changeup	Braden Shipley
Best Control	Aaron Blair
Best Defensive Catcher	Michael Perez
Best Defensive Infielder	Nick Ahmed
Best Infield Arm	Sergio Alcantara
Best Defensive Outfielder	Evan Marzilli
Best Outfield Arm	Socrates Brito

PROJECTED 2018 LINEUP

Catcher	Peter O'Brien
First Base	Paul Goldschmidt
Second Base	Brandon Drury
Third Base	Jake Lamb
Shortstop	Chris Owings
Left Field	Mark Trumbo
Center Field	A.J. Pollock
Right Field	Yasmany Tomas
No. 1 Starter	Pat Corbin
No. 2 Starter	Archie Bradley
No. 3 Starter	Braden Shipley
No. 4 Starter	Aaron Blair
No. 5 Starter	Touki Toussaint
Closer	Addison Reed

ARIZONA DIAMONDBACKS

TOP 2015 ROOKIE: Yasmany Tomas, of. The slugging Cuban will provide much-needed power from the middle of the order.
BREAKOUT PROSPECT: Anthony Banda, lhp. Acquired in the Gerardo Parra trade, he thrived after joining the D-backs with increased control.
SLEEPER: Fernery Ozuna. 2b/3b. Gamer with tools does everything well and could break out in first full-season assignment.

SOURCE OF TOP 30 TALENT			
Homegrown	21	Acquired	9
College	8	Trades	9
Junior college	0	Rule 5 draft	0
High school	7	Independent leagues	0
Draft-and-follow	0	Free agents/waivers	0
Nondrafted free agents	0		
International	6		

LF
Zach Borenstein (26)
Matt Railey (28)
Francis Martinez
Grant Heyman
Alex Glenn

CF
Marcus Wilson (24)
Evan Marzilli
Chuck Taylor
Colin Bray
Matt McPhearson
Jose Ordaz

RF
Yasmany Tomas (4)
Socrates Brito (19)
Mitch Haniger (22)
Gerard Hernandez
Remy Cordero

3B
Jake Lamb (6)
Brandon Drury (7)
Tyler Humphreys
Marlon Arroyo

SS
Nick Ahmed (10)
Sergio Alcantara (20)
Raul Navarro
Sean Jamieson
Justin Gonzalez

2B
Domingo Leyba (9)
Isan Diaz (27)
Fernery Ozuna
Jamie Westbrook
Henry Castillo
Kevin Medrano

1B
Daniel Palka (30)
Kevin Cron
Rudy Flores

C
Peter O'Brien (8)
Jose Herrera (15)
Stryker Trahan (21)
Michael Perez
Ronnie Freeman
Elvin Soto

LHP

LHSP	LHRP
Robbie Ray (11)	Will Locante
Cody Reed (14)	Daniel Gibson
Anthony Banda (17)	Zac Curtis
Andrew Chafin (18)	Patrick Schuster
Hector Hernandez	Jared Miller
Anfernee Benitez	Cody Wheeler

RHP

RHSP	RHRP
Archie Bradley (1)	Jake Barrett (12)
Braden Shipley (2)	Jimmie Sherfy (16)
Aaron Blair (3)	Enrique Burgos (29)
Touki Toussaint (5)	Kaleb Fleck
Jose Martinez (13)	Mason McCullough
Jeferson Mejia (23)	J.R. Bradley
Brent Jones (25)	Kevin Munson
A.J. Schugel	Seth Simmons
Yefrey Ramirez	Zach Hedges
Blake Perry	Joey Krehbiel
Brad Keller	
Wei-Chieh Huang	
Felipe Perez	

2014

BEST PURE HITTER: The Diamondbacks got two high school bats they believe in, both under 6 feet tall. OF Matt Railey (3) performed as a prep against strong competition, and had a hamstring injury interrupt a hot streak at Rookie-level Missoula. SS Isan Diaz (2s) earns Jose Vidro comparisons for his strong frame and Puerto Rican heritage.

BEST POWER: 1B Kevin Cron (14) has size (6-foot-5, 245 pounds) and strength that gives him plus raw power, which played better with wood than it did with metal. He hit 12 homers in his debut after hitting just 14 in three seasons at Texas Christian.

FASTEST RUNNER: OF Marcus Wilson (2s) has posted blazing 6.5-second times over 60 yards, plus speed that plays better presently in center field than on the bases.

BEST DEFENSIVE PLAYER: Wilson is a long strider with a lean, long-limbed 6-foot-3, 175-pound frame. He reminds the Diamondbacks of former Astros outfielder Brian Hunter, a teammate of Arizona scouting director Ray Montgomery.

BEST FASTBALL: In a velocity-heavy draft, Arizona loaded up on power arms. RHP Mason McCullough (5) hit 98 mph regularly in the spring and 101 mph this summer. LHP Cody Reed (2) pitches anywhere from 88-94 mph, touching 96 in the spring, and gets lots of ugly swings with his fastball thanks to natural deception.

BEST SECONDARY PITCH: RHP Touki Toussaint (1) has dastardly secondary stuff to go with a plus fastball that has touched 97. His curveball has tremendous spin and flashes 80 on the 20-80 scouting scale. His changeup also flashes plus.

BEST PRO DEBUT: Cron hit .291/.356/.498 overall and helped Hillsboro win the short-season Northwest League. LHP Zac Curtis (6) saved every Hops playoff victory after going 2-1, 1.00 with 14 saves and 42 strikeouts in 27 innings. 1B Trevor Mitsui (30) swatted 12 homers with Rookie-level Missoula while hitting .331/.386/.546 overall.

BEST ATHLETE: Wilson may be a two-year Rookie-ball player but has the raw athleticism the Diamondbacks coveted.

MOST INTRIGUING BACKGROUND: Cron's father Chris, an ex-big leaguer, is the Diamondbacks' minor league hitting coordinator. His older brother C.J. is the Angels' DH. LHP Lawrence Pardo (38) is the son of Astros scout Larry, who pitched parts of seven minor league seasons.

CLOSEST TO THE MAJORS: Curtis, McCullough and RHP Brent Jones (4) all could move quickly in relief roles, with Curtis' fast start and lefthandedness giving him the edge.

BEST LATE-ROUND PICK: While he often struggled at TCU, Cron was a third-rounder out of high school and played like one in his pro debut.

THE ONE WHO GOT AWAY: The Diamondbacks wanted to make runs at several players, particularly RHP Jacob Bukauskas (20), the highest-ranked player on the BA 500 who went to college. He's at North Carolina.

ASSESSMENT: Arizona's class is as high-risk, high-reward as any class save the Marlins. A breakthrough by Cron would be a nice boost to the power arms the Diamondbacks amassed.

2013

RHPs Braden Shipley (1) and Aaron Blair (1s) have traveled together, reaching Double-A in their first full season. OF Justin Williams (2) was traded to the Rays in the Jeremy Hellickson trade.

GRADE: B+

2012

3B Jake Lamb (6) sped to the majors and looks like the jewel of the class, as C/OF Stryker Trahan (1) struggles. SS Andrew Velazquez (7) broke out in 2014 and was traded to Tampa for Jeremy Hellickson.

GRADE: C

2011

Arizona used two top-10 overall picks on RHPs, giving up quickly on Trevor Bauer while Archie Bradley stalled a bit in 2014. LHP Andrew Chafin (1s) and RHP Evan Marshall (4) have reached the majors.

GRADE: B

TOP DRAFT PICKS OF THE DECADE

Year	Player, Pos.	2014 Org
2005	Justin Upton, of	Braves
2006	Max Scherzer, rhp	Tigers
2007	Jarrod Parker, rhp	Athletics
2008	Daniel Schlereth, lhp	Tigers
2009	Bobby Borchering, 3b	Astros
2010	*Barret Loux, rhp	Cubs
2011	Trevor Bauer, rhp	Indians
2012	Stryker Trahan, c	Diamondbacks
2013	Braden Shipley, rhp	Diamondbacks
2014	Touki Toussaint, rhp	Diamondbacks

*Did not sign

LARGEST BONUSES IN CLUB HISTORY

Travis Lee, 1996	$10,000,000
Justin Upton, 2005	$6,100,000
John Patterson, 1996	$6,075,000
Archie Bradley, 2011	$5,000,000
Stephen Drew, 2004	$4,000,000

1 ARCHIE BRADLEY, RHP

Born: Aug. 10, 1992. **B-T:** R-R. **Ht.:** 6-4. **Wt.:** 235.
Drafted: HS—Broken Arrow, Okla., 2011 (1st round).
Signed by: Kyle Denny.

The Diamondbacks drafted Bradley No. 7 overall in 2011, compensation for not signing Barret Loux the previous year. Arizona paid a $5 million bonus to keep the multi-sport athlete from heading to Oklahoma to play football for the Sooners. After just two Rookie-league appearances in 2011, Bradley went right to low Class A South Bend in 2012 and shot through the system, ranking as one of the game's top pitching prospects. His 2014 was a disappointment for all involved, however. Bradley came to big league camp in 2014 with a shot at making the big league rotation and pitched well in his first few spring-training outings. He accompanied the team in its season-opening trip to Australia, pitching in one of the exhibition games prior to the official series against the Dodgers. After struggling in his last two spring starts, Bradley was assigned to Triple-A Reno to begin the regular season, a point of contention with his agent, who accused Arizona of holding Bradley back for service-time considerations. After five starts with Reno, Bradley was diagnosed with a mild flexor strain in his right elbow and the organization shut him down until June. After rehabbing at the team's training facility and pitching in one Rookie-level Arizona League game, Bradley was assigned to Double-A Mobile to get him into a better pitcher's park for the remainder of the season. His fastball velocity was down and curveball not as sharp, which some observers attributed to the early start to his season and the push to make the rotation. Bradley then got in extra work with a post-season assignment to the Arizona Fall League.

Bradley's AFL performance was encouraging, with much of his fastball velocity returning. His heater, which during the regular season was 91-93 mph, sat 92-95 and touched 97. The low-80s curveball, previously a plus pitch, lacked depth in part because of a lower arm slot, but showed more break and flashed above-average in the AFL. He used his changeup more frequently while he was learning to pitch without his best fastball and curve, and it's an average pitch in the upper 80s with armside sink. Most importantly, Bradley added an 88-91 mph slider that plays off his fastball, changing the look for hitters facing him. It projects to be an above-average pitch and one that he can use to get swings and misses. Bradley's high three-quarters arm slot gets the ball over his front side and allows him to pound the fastball down in the zone. His command suffers when he's inconsistent with his delivery and his front side flies open, but he projects to be able to repeat the delivery due to his athleticism.

Some evaluators now see Bradley as a future No. 3 starter, with the proviso that improved command will get him back to the original projection of a frontline starter. The Diamondbacks will be cautious with Bradley in spring training and, despite the organization's need for starting pitchers, may start him back at Double-A. If all goes well, he'll make his major league debut at some point in 2015.

BA GRADE

65 Risk: High

SCOUTING GRADES

Fastball: 65
Slider: 55
Changeup 50
Control: 45

Based on 20-80 scouting scale and future projection rather than present tools.

LGE	BF	SO%	BB%	HR/9
SL	240	19.2	15.0	0.33
PCL	113	20.4	10.6	0.00

BILL MITCHELL

Year	Club (League)	Class	W	L	ERA	G	GS	CG	SV	IP	H	HR	BB	SO	K/9	WHIP	AVG
2012	South Bend (MWL)	LoA	12	6	3.84	27	27	0	0	136	87	6	84	152	10.1	1.26	.181
2013	Visalia (CAL)	HiA	2	0	1.26	5	5	0	0	29	22	1	10	43	13.5	1.12	.218
	Mobile (SL)	AA	12	5	1.97	21	21	2	0	123	93	5	59	119	8.7	1.23	.214
2014	Reno (PCL)	AAA	1	4	5.18	5	5	0	0	24	26	0	12	23	8.5	1.56	.277
	Diamondbacks (AZL)	R	0	0	4.50	1	1	0	0	4	5	0	1	6	13.5	1.50	.278
	Mobile (SL)	AA	2	3	4.12	12	12	1	0	55	45	2	36	46	7.6	1.48	.231
Minor League Totals			29	18	3.14	73	72	3	0	373	279	14	202	393	9.5	1.29	.210

2 BRADEN SHIPLEY, RHP

Born: Feb. 22, 1992. **B-T:** R-R. **Ht.:** 6-3. **Wt.:** 190. **Drafted:** Nevada, 2013 (1st round). **Signed by:** John Bartsch.

The Diamondbacks eagerly called Shipley's name when it was time to make the 15th overall pick in 2013, as he'd been rumored to go in the top 10. Primarily a shortstop as a freshman at Nevada, Shipley's arm was too good to keep him off the mound in his next two seasons. After finishing his debut season at low Class A South Bend in 2013, Shipley returned there to start 2014 and pitched at three levels and finished at Double-A Mobile. He ranked as the No. 3 prospect in the Midwest League and No. 4 in the California League. Shipley functions as a fifth infielder on the mound thanks to his plus athleticism and shortstop background. His fastball is a plus pitch in the mid-90s with late life and armside sink. His equalizer pitch is a high-80s changeup that he can throw in any count, coming out of the same release point as his fastball and getting early-contact outs for him. His 12-to-6 curveball is a power pitch with bite that dives hard to the bottom of the zone. It improved in 2014, with a cleaner release. Shipley's clean delivery projects to give him plus command. He's a fierce competitor with a strong desire to improve. Shipley projects as at least a No. 3 starter. After getting a brief taste of Double-A at the end of 2014, he'll return there with a promotion to Triple-A Reno at some point in 2015.

BA GRADE	
60	Risk: Medium

LGE	BF	SO%	BB%	HR/9
MWL	189	21.7	5.8	0.20
CAL	252	27.0	8.3	1.04

Year	Club (League)	Class	W	L	ERA	G	GS	CG	SV	IP	H	HR	BB	SO	K/9	WHIP	AVG
2013	Hillsboro (NWL)	SS	0	2	7.58	8	8	0	0	19	30	1	6	24	11.4	1.89	.357
	South Bend (MWL)	LoA	0	1	2.61	4	4	0	0	21	14	2	8	16	7.0	1.06	.194
2014	South Bend (MWL)	LoA	4	2	3.74	8	8	0	0	46	46	1	11	41	8.1	1.25	.263
	Visalia (CAL)	HiA	2	4	4.03	10	10	0	0	60	57	7	21	68	10.1	1.29	.258
	Mobile (SL)	AA	1	2	3.60	4	4	0	0	20	14	3	10	18	8.1	1.20	.203
Minor League Totals			7	11	4.13	34	34	0	0	166	161	14	56	167	9.1	1.31	.259

3 AARON BLAIR, RHP

Born: May 26, 1992. **B-T:** R-R. **Ht.:** 6-5. **Wt.:** 230. **Drafted:** Marshall, 2013 (first round supplemental). **Signed by:** Rick Matsko.

Blair was Marshall's highest-drafted player ever after the Diamondbacks popped him 36th overall in 2013. He joined Braden Shipley in low Class A South Bend's playoff rotation at the end of his 2013 pro debut, and they were on the same three-city odyssey in 2014, starting at South Bend and finishing at Double-A Mobile. Blair tied for second in the minors with 171 strikeouts in 2014, ranking as the No. 5 prospect in the California League and No. 11 in the Southern League. Increased arm speed and an improved curveball caused Blair's stock to jump in 2014 with most evaluators now projecting him as more than just a durable, back-of-the rotation innings burner. The heavy life on his 91-95 mph fastball generates weak contact from opposing hitters, and he's touched 97. He ditched his slider and instead improved the power and shape on the high-70s curveball to give him a potential plus pitch that gets swings and misses. He gets on the side of it at times, but it has better power and 11-to-5 shape. Blair has a good feel for an above-average changeup. He has good control, and some scouts project solid-average command thanks to his clean, repeatable delivery and big hands. Blair could begin 2015 at Triple-A Reno and has a good shot at getting a call to the big leagues. He has a No. 3 starter ceiling, though his flyball tendencies may not be best-suited for Chase Field.

BA GRADE	
60	Risk: Medium

LGE	BF	SO%	BB%	HR/9
CAL	313	25.9	6.7	0.75
SL	182	25.3	8.8	0.78

Year	Club (League)	Class	W	L	ERA	G	GS	CG	SV	IP	H	HR	BB	SO	K/9	WHIP	AVG
2013	Hillsboro (NWL)	SS	1	1	2.90	8	8	0	0	31	25	2	13	28	8.1	1.23	.225
	South Bend (MWL)	LoA	0	2	3.57	3	3	0	0	18	19	0	4	13	6.6	1.30	.279
2014	South Bend (MWL)	LoA	1	2	4.04	6	6	1	0	36	25	2	14	44	11.1	1.09	.188
	Visalia (CAL)	HiA	4	2	4.35	13	13	0	0	72	70	6	21	81	10.1	1.26	.251
	Mobile (SL)	AA	4	1	1.94	8	8	0	0	46	30	4	16	46	8.9	0.99	.185
Minor League Totals			10	8	3.46	38	38	1	0	203	169	14	68	212	9.4	1.17	.224

4 YASMANY TOMAS, OF/3B

Born: Nov. 14, 1990. **B-T:** R-R. **Ht.:** 6-1. **Wt.:** 252. **Signed:** Cuba, 2014. **Signed by:** Junior Naboa.

Arizona hopes to have solved a power shortage in its everyday lineup by signing Tomas to a six-year, $68.5 million contract on Dec. 9. The slugger starred for Industriales in Cuba's *Serie Nacional*, busting out in the 2011-12 season when he batted .301/.340/.580 with 16 home runs in 226 plate appearances. He also played in the 2013 World Baseball Classic. Plus-plus raw power is the calling card for Tomas, a strong man with big lift in his swing. Tomas does a good job of staying inside the ball and can drive pitches to the opposite field. At times he sells out for power, resulting in a swing with holes and a tendency to chase pitches out of the zone, and he'll swing through offspeed pitches. The combination could result in high strikeout totals. He projects to be an average defender and could handle either outfield corner position, but his plus arm will likely target him for right field. He also has some experience at third base, which the Diamondbacks intend to explore. Tomas is athletic and runs well considering his thick build, recording speeds to first as fast as 4.4 seconds. He will be just 24 on Opening Day and won't have played a competitive game in more than a year, so an initial assignment to Triple-A Reno would probably be beneficial. Tomas more likely will break camp in Arizona's everyday lineup, either in an outfield corner or perhaps at third base.

BA GRADE	
60	Risk: High

LGE	PA	BB%	SO%	ISO
Did not play				

Year	Club (League)	Class	AVG	G	AB	R	H	2B	3B	HR	RBI	BB	SO	SB	CS	OBP	SLG
Did not play—Signed 2015 contract																	

5 TOUKI TOUSSAINT, RHP

Born: June 20, 1996. **B-T:** R-R. **Ht.:** 6-3. **Wt.:** 185. **Drafted:** HS—Coral Springs, Fla., 2014 (1st round). **Signed by:** Frankie Thon Jr.

The Diamondbacks were thrilled to find Toussaint's name on the draft board when their turn came for the 16th overall pick in 2014. They convinced him to forego his commitment to Vanderbilt with a $2.7 million bonus. Toussaint was born in Haiti and lived there until he was 6, and he didn't begin playing baseball until he was 11. While he's less experienced than most high school pitchers in his draft class, he's a showcase veteran who can match the ceiling of any prep arm in the 2014 draft. Toussaint made his pro debut in the Rookie-level Arizona League before moving up to Rookie-level Missoula in 2014. With big hands and a long wingspan, he uses explosive arm speed to deliver a fastball in the 90-95 mph range with plus life. He's athletic and the ball comes out of his hand easy. He has a natural ability to spin the ball, thus the jewel of Toussaint's arsenal is a 74-77 mph curveball that projects as a double-plus pitch. He has a good feel for a slightly above-average changeup with tumble that ranges from 79-84 mph with enough potential that it could develop into a third plus pitch. Toussaint struggled with command as a pro in 2014, but he looked more comfortable on the mound in instructional league with more consistency in repeating his high three-quarters delivery. Toussaint may be ready for an assignment to low Class A Kane County in 2015, though he may stay in extended spring training for a while to limit his innings and keep him out of the Midwest League's coldest weather. Touissant has ace potential if he tames his control.

BA GRADE	
65	Risk: Extreme

LGE	BF	SO%	BB%	HR/9
AZL	74	23.0	16.2	0.00
PIO	73	20.5	8.2	3.29

Year	Club (League)	Class	W	L	ERA	G	GS	CG	SV	IP	H	HR	BB	SO	K/9	WHIP	AVG
2014	Diamondbacks (AZL)	R	1	1	4.80	7	5	0	0	15	14	0	12	17	10.2	1.73	.237
	Missoula (PIO)	R	1	3	12.51	5	5	0	0	14	24	5	6	15	9.9	2.20	.381
Minor League Totals			2	4	8.48	12	10	0	0	29	38	5	18	32	10.0	1.95	.311

6 JAKE LAMB, 3B

Born: Oct. 9, 1990. **B-T:** L-R. **Ht.:** 6-3. **Wt.:** 220. **Drafted:** Washington, 2012 (6th round). **Signed by:** Donnie Reynolds.

Lamb's breakout season in 2014 shows that the Diamondbacks guessed right when they believed they could iron out his swing coming out of college. They jumped the 2012 sixth-rounder to high Class A Visalia in 2013, a season interrupted by a broken left hamate bone in his wrist, but he made up for lost time in the Arizona Fall League. He opened 2014 at Double-A Mobile and finished in the majors, winning the Southern League MVP award along the way after leading the SL in batting (.318) and ranking second in on-base percentage (.399), slugging (.551) and RBIs (79). The improvement in Lamb's bat came when he adjusted his swing to better handle inside pitches, with an approach more suited for hitting for a high average. He has above-average power to all fields, driving the ball even in Mobile's pitcher-friendly park. His long swing can lead to high strikeout totals, but he has a good approach at the plate and draws his share of walks. Lamb is a solid defender at the hot corner with good hands and an above-average arm. He's athletic but is a below-average runner, especially out of the box. His work ethic is strong. Slotted as the top third baseman on the Diamondbacks' depth chart, Lamb will head to spring training as the odds-on favorite to earn a starting job in 2015.

BA GRADE

50 Risk: Low

LGE	PA	BB%	SO%	ISO
SL	439	11.4	22.6	.233
NL	133	4.5	27.8	.143

Year	Club (League)	Class	AVG	G	AB	R	H	2B	3B	HR	RBI	BB	SO	SB	CS	OBP	SLG
2012	Missoula (PIO)	R	.329	67	280	47	92	22	5	9	57	24	51	8	2	.390	.539
2013	Diamondbacks (AZL)	R	.294	5	17	4	5	2	0	0	5	2	5	0	0	.381	.412
	Visalia (CAL)	HiA	.303	64	231	44	70	20	0	13	47	48	70	0	0	.424	.558
2014	Mobile (SL)	AA	.318	103	374	60	119	35	5	14	79	50	99	0	0	.399	.551
	Reno (PCL)	AAA	.500	5	18	3	9	4	0	1	5	3	4	2	0	.571	.889
	Arizona (NL)	MAJ	.230	37	126	15	29	4	1	4	11	6	37	1	1	.263	.373
Major League Totals			.230	37	126	15	29	4	1	4	11	6	37	1	1	.263	.373
Minor League Totals			.321	244	920	158	295	83	10	37	193	127	229	10	2	.406	.553

7 BRANDON DRURY, 3B/2B

Born: Aug. 21, 1992. **B-T:** R-R. **Ht.:** 6-2. **Wt.:** 190. **Drafted:** HS—Grants Pass, Ore., 2010 (13th round). **Signed by:** Brett Evert (Braves).

Drury was the youngest among the five players acquired in the January 2013 blockbuster trade that sent outfielder Justin Upton to the Braves, but he may wind up providing Arizona's best return from the deal. The Oregon native was coming off a down 2012 season with the Braves' low Class A affiliate but has boosted his stock with two strong seasons in the Diamondbacks organization. Drury ranked third in the high Class A California League in doubles (35) in 2014 despite being promoted to Double-A Mobile in late July. He generates above-average power with his strength and good bat speed, and supporters believe he has the ingredients to be great hitter. He has a short, compact swing but struggles with good offspeed pitches. Drury is a well below-average runner, but his first-step quickness, good hands and strong, accurate arm project to make him at least an average defender at third base. He got some reps at second base during the Arizona Fall League and may have the tools and work ethic to become an average defender at the keystone. Added to the Diamondbacks' 40-man roster in November, Drury will return to Mobile for more seasoning in 2015, with a move to Triple-A Reno not far off. With Jake Lamb ahead of him on the third-base depth chart, Drury might meet the least resistance at second base.

BA GRADE

50 Risk: Medium

LGE	PA	BB%	SO%	ISO
CAL	478	8.6	15.9	.219
SL	116	6.0	16.4	.181

Year	Club (League)	Class	AVG	G	AB	R	H	2B	3B	HR	RBI	BB	SO	SB	CS	OBP	SLG
2012	Rome (SAL)	LoA	.229	123	445	47	102	22	3	6	51	20	73	3	4	.270	.333
2013	South Bend (MWL)	LoA	.302	134	526	78	159	51	4	15	85	47	92	1	1	.362	.500
2014	Visalia (CAL)	HiA	.300	107	430	73	129	35	1	19	81	41	76	4	3	.366	.519
	Mobile (SL)	AA	.295	29	105	12	31	7	0	4	14	7	19	0	0	.345	.476
Minor League Totals			.281	508	1963	270	551	145	9	55	302	130	345	13	10	.331	.448

8 PETE O'BRIEN, C/1B

DAVID SCHOFIELD

Born: July 15, 1990. **B-T:** R-R. **Ht.:** 6-3. **Wt.:** 215. **Drafted:** Miami, 2012 (2nd round). **Signed by:** Carlos Marti (Yankees).

O'Brien has hit home runs throughout both his amateur and professional careers. He had slugged 33 when the Diamondbacks acquired him from the Yankees in a July 2014 deadline deal for big leaguer Martin Prado. O'Brien fouled a ball off his shin in his fourth game with his new organization and missed the rest of the regular season. He made up for lost time with a return trip to the Arizona Fall League. O'Brien is Arizona's most enigmatic prospect. While he has top-of-the-scale raw power and excellent makeup, scouts aren't sold on his ability to handle quality pitchers, either at the plate or behind it. His strength and good bat speed allow him to hit the ball out to any part of the park, but evaluators point to his long swing and suscep- ibility to big velocity and good breaking balls. Behind the plate, he has a strong arm, receives well within his body and has hands that work well, but he needs to improve his blocking ability, lateral mobility and transfer on his throws. While the Yankees tried him at the infield and outfield corners, O'Brien is determined to develop into a good catcher with Arizona. He has put in the work there, report- ing early for the AFL to work with catching coordinator Bill Plummer and later with big league bench coach Glenn Sherlock. O'Brien's high baseball IQ gives him a shot to stick behind the plate, but he has a lot of work to do. He'll likely return to Double-A Mobile as the everyday catcher in 2015, and if he can handle the position, he could be a star. If not, he may also top out as a bench bat or future DH.

BA GRADE

50 Risk: High

LGE	PA	BB%	SO%	ISO
FSL	119	3.4	24.4	.366
EL	294	5.4	26.2	.310

Year	Club (League)	Class	AVG	G	AB	R	H	2B	3B	HR	RBI	BB	SO	SB	CS	OBP	SLG
2012	Yankees (GCL)	R	.357	4	14	2	5	2	0	0	2	0	1	0	0	.357	.500
	Staten Island (NYP)	SS	.202	48	198	27	40	8	0	10	32	10	61	0	1	.249	.394
2013	Charleston, SC (SAL)	LoA	.325	53	194	47	63	22	1	11	41	22	58	0	0	.394	.619
	Tampa (FSL)	HiA	.265	66	253	31	67	17	3	11	55	19	76	0	1	.314	.486
2014	Tampa (FSL)	HiA	.321	30	112	19	36	9	1	10	19	4	29	0	0	.353	.688
	Trenton (EL)	AA	.245	72	274	47	67	14	1	23	51	16	77	0	0	.296	.555
	Mobile (SL)	AA	.385	4	13	1	5	0	0	1	4	1	5	0	0	.429	.615
Minor League Totals			.267	277	1058	174	283	72	6	66	204	72	307	0	2	.319	.534

9 DOMINGO LEYBA, 2B/SS

Born: Sept. 11, 1995. **B-T:** B-R. **Ht.:** 5-11. **Wt.:** 160. **Signed:** Dominican Republic, 2012. **Signed by:** Miguel Rodriguez/Carlos Santana/Ramon Perez/Miguel Garcia (Tigers).

Arizona acquired Leyba from the Tigers in December as part of the three-team trade that shipped Didi Gregorius to the Yankees. Leyba, who signed with Detroit in 2012 for $400,000, had opened 2014 at short-season Connecticut. He hit even better once he was moved up to low Class A West Michigan for the final month of the 2014 season and Midwest League playoffs, then went to the Arizona Fall League. Leyba doesn't have any dynamic tools, but he's a fundamentally-sound player who grows on scouts the more they see him. He has a quick bat, squares up good velocity and has good barrel control, lacing line drives to all fields. He's not big, but he's strong for his size, though he's mostly a gap hitter. Leyba has solid strike- zone management, though he will have to learn to lay off high fastballs. A fringe-average runner who spent most of his time at second base, where he may be best suited, he played shortstop during the final two weeks of the season. His hands and footwork are solid, and his average arm plays up due to a quick release. The Tigers had pushed Leyba aggressively, and he responded to the challenge. Arizona hopes to benefit and could continue pushing him to high Class A Visalia in 2015.

BA GRADE

55 Risk: Extreme

LGE	PA	BB%	SO%	ISO
NYP	154	5.2	11.0	.111
MWL	124	4.8	10.5	.086

Year	Club (League)	Class	AVG	G	AB	R	H	2B	3B	HR	RBI	BB	SO	SB	CS	OBP	SLG
2013	Tigers (DSL)	R	.348	57	201	51	70	15	8	5	36	34	26	16	8	.446	.577
2014	Connecticut (NYP)	SS	.264	37	144	20	38	11	1	1	17	8	17	1	2	.303	.375
	West Michigan (MWL)	LoA	.397	30	116	20	46	7	0	1	7	6	13	1	2	.431	.483
Minor League Totals			.334	124	461	91	154	33	9	7	60	48	56	18	12	.400	.490

10 NICK AHMED, SS

Born: March 15, 1990. **B-T:** R-R. **Ht.:** 6-3. **Wt.:** 205. **Drafted:** Connecticut, 2011 (2nd round). **Signed by:** Kevin Barry (Braves).

A college teammate of the Astros' George Springer and Red Sox farmhand Matt Barnes, Ahmed was one of five players the Diamondbacks got from the Braves in the 2013 Justin Upton trade. Regarded as one of the top defensive shortstops in the minors, the Connecticut product struggled at the plate in his first season with the Diamondbacks organization in 2013, but took advantage of hitter-happy conditions at Triple-A Reno in 2014. Ahmed made his big league debut as an emergency callup in July and returned in September after Reno's playoff run ended. No one doubts Ahmed's ability to play shortstop at a plus level. He can be a game-changer with the glove, with soft hands, a strong, accurate arm and a quick release. He has a quick first step and makes virtually all the routine plays. He's an above-average runner who can steal a base. His approach at the plate improved in 2014 when he lowered his hands and created a better path to the zone, allowing his swing to make better contact and generate more line-drive pop. He doesn't have

BA GRADE	
45	**Risk:** Low

LGE	PA	BB%	SO%	ISO
PCL	452	8.2	12.2	.113
NL	75	4.0	13.3	.071

much power but can drive balls into the gap. Ahmed profiles best as a light-hitting regular shortstop with Gold Glove-caliber defense. He increased his versatility by showing that he could also handle second base. He'll challenge Chris Owings and Cliff Pennington for the everyday job in Arizona, likely heading back to Reno at least to start the 2015 season.

Year	Club (League)	Class	AVG	G	AB	R	H	2B	3B	HR	RBI	BB	SO	SB	CS	OBP	SLG
2012	Lynchburg (CAR)	HiA	.269	130	506	84	136	36	4	6	49	49	102	40	10	.337	.391
2013	Mobile (SL)	AA	.236	136	487	58	115	21	5	4	46	33	72	26	7	.288	.324
2014	Reno (PCL)	AAA	.312	104	407	57	127	26	4	4	47	37	55	14	6	.373	.425
	Arizona (NL)	MAJ	.200	25	70	9	14	2	0	1	4	3	10	0	1	.233	.271
Major League Totals			.200	25	70	9	14	2	0	1	4	3	10	0	1	.233	.271
Minor League Totals			.269	429	1648	245	443	96	15	18	166	149	275	98	29	.333	.378

11 ROBBIE RAY, LHP

BA GRADE	
50	**Risk:** High

Born: Oct. 1, 1991. **B-T:** L-L. **Ht.:** 6-2. **Wt.:** 195. **Drafted:** HS— Brentwood, Tenn., 2010 (12th round). **Signed by:** Paul Faulk (Nationals).

Only one year after being the centerpiece prospect in the trade that sent Doug Fister from the Tigers to the Nationals, Ray was on the move again, with the Diamondbacks acquiring him from Detroit in a three-team deal centered on Didi Gregorius in December 2014. Ray's stock did not improve in 2014 with an uninspiring season. He got rocked during his major league debut in May, then spent most of the season at Triple-A Toledo before coming back up in August and September. Ray's fastball ranges from the low- to mid-90s, and he touched 97 mph in the AFL. His strikeout rate dropped precipitously in 2014 because he doesn't have an out pitch among his secondary offerings. His changeup is an average pitch that he throws with good arm speed, along with solid sink and tail, but the lack of a reliable breaking ball continues to hamper him. He's thrown a slider and a curveball, though he scrapped the curve toward the end of the season to focus on the slider, which is below-average. Ray is athletic but scouts have questioned his pitching savvy. Without a second plus pitch or better command, Ray profiles as a No. 4 starter, but the Diamondbacks believe he has the potential to be at least a mid-rotation arm. He'll go to spring training with a shot at earning a rotation job but could also spend time on the Triple-A Reno shuttle.

Year	Club (League)	Class	W	L	ERA	G	GS	CG	SV	IP	H	HR	BB	SO	K/9	WHIP	AVG
2012	Potomac (CAR)	HiA	4	12	6.56	22	21	0	0	106	122	14	49	86	7.3	1.62	.292
2013	Potomac (CAR)	HiA	6	3	3.11	16	16	3	0	84	60	9	41	100	10.7	1.20	.205
	Harrisburg (EL)	AA	5	2	3.72	11	11	1	0	58	56	4	21	60	9.3	1.33	.247
2014	Toledo (IL)	AAA	7	6	4.22	20	19	0	0	100	106	6	44	75	6.7	1.50	.277
	Detroit (AL)	MAJ	1	4	8.16	9	6	0	0	29	43	5	11	19	6.0	1.88	.350
Major League Totals			1	4	8.16	9	6	0	0	29	43	5	11	19	6.0	1.88	.350
Minor League Totals			24	26	4.27	90	87	4	0	438	415	36	193	418	8.6	1.39	.253

12 JAKE BARRETT, RHP

BA GRADE	
45	**Risk:** Medium

Born: July 22, 1991. **B-T:** R-R. **Ht.:** 6-3. **Wt.:** 230. **Drafted:** Arizona State, 2012 (3rd round). **Signed by:** Matt Smith.

Barrett played both high school and college ball in the Phoenix area, and it's likely he'll complete the trifecta by making it to Chase Field for his big league debut sometime in 2015. An unsigned third-round pick out of high school by the Blue Jays, Barrett instead attended nearby Arizona State, working first as a starter before becoming the Sun Devils closer. The Diamondbacks took him in the third round in 2012, signing him for $392,900. Barrett is a durable, big-bodied strike thrower with a plus fastball that sits 93-96 mph and gets up as high as 98. He works down in the zone, using both sides of the plate, and gets plenty of armside tail on the heater. His slider, which flashes plus, has sharp down tilt with bite. He doesn't often use his changeup, but it gives him a pitch to keep lefthanders from sitting on his fastball. After closing for Triple-A Reno in the second half of 2014, Barrett should get a shot at the big leagues. With an aggressive demeanor and ability to take the ball every day, he's got closer potential.

Year	Club (League)	Class	W	L	ERA	G	GS	CG	SV	IP	H	HR	BB	SO	K/9	WHIP	AVG
2012	South Bend (MWL)	LoA	0	3	5.84	25	0	0	6	25	28	2	13	25	9.1	1.66	.283
2013	Visalia (CAL)	HiA	2	1	1.98	28	0	0	15	27	21	2	9	37	12.2	1.10	.198
	Mobile (SL)	AA	1	1	0.36	24	0	0	14	25	18	2	3	22	8.0	0.85	.196
2014	Mobile (SL)	AA	1	2	2.39	25	0	0	12	26	25	0	12	24	8.2	1.41	.260
	Reno (PCL)	AAA	1	0	3.72	30	0	0	16	29	22	3	15	23	7.1	1.28	.220
Minor League Totals			5	7	2.86	132	0	0	63	132	114	9	52	131	8.9	1.26	.231

13 JOSE MARTINEZ, RHP

BA GRADE
55 Risk: Extreme

Born: April 14, 1994. **B-T:** R-R. **Ht.:** 6-1. **Wt.:** 160. **Signed:** Dominican Republic, 2011. **Signed by:** Junior Noboa.

Originally signed from the Dominican Republic for $55,000 in 2011, Martinez was on the fast track through the Arizona system thanks to an electric arm and plus curveball. After making his full-season debut at low Class A South Bend in 2014, Martinez's progress was derailed after two starts when he was diagnosed with a stress fracture in his right elbow. Prior to the injury, he possessed a quick arm that delivered his fastball up to 99 mph from a smaller frame. Even with the elbow soreness, he was still working at 94-96 mph. He also has a plus curveball, a hard pitch with late bite and tilt. A healthy Martinez should head to low Class A Kane County, the organization's new Midwest League affiliate, though he may start 2015 in extended spring training to keep his innings count down.

Year	Club (League)	Class	W	L	ERA	G	GS	CG	SV	IP	H	HR	BB	SO	K/9	WHIP	AVG
2012	Diamondbacks (DSL)	R	5	2	1.72	14	14	0	0	73	57	0	22	71	8.7	1.08	.218
	Yakima (NWL)	SS	0	1	4.22	2	2	0	0	11	8	1	6	8	6.8	1.31	.205
2013	Hillsboro (NWL)	SS	2	3	4.03	10	10	0	0	38	20	3	25	30	7.1	1.18	.159
2014	South Bend (MWL)	LoA	1	1	6.00	2	2	0	0	6	8	1	4	3	4.5	2.00	.348
Minor League Totals			8	7	2.81	28	28	0	0	128	93	5	57	112	7.9	1.17	.207

14 CODY REED, LHP

BA GRADE
55 Risk: Extreme

Born: June 7, 1996. **B-T:** R-L. **Ht.:** 6-3. **Wt.:** 245. **Drafted:** HS— Ardmore, Ala., 2014 (2nd round). **Signed by:** Joe Mason.

The Royals drafted their own Cody Reed—a second-rounder from Northwest Mississippi CC—in 2013. The Diamondbacks' version also hails from the South (Ardmore, Ala.), also is lefthanded and also went in the second round (2014). Reed made a strong debut in 2014, pitching his way to Rookie-level Missoula. He's a big-bodied southpaw who will constantly needs to work on his conditioning. While his high school velocity topped out at 96 mph in the spring before the draft, he worked in the 90-91 range, topping off at 93, at Missoula. Reed projects to have a plus fastball with good angle that he keeps down in the zone. His slider with sharp break also is a quality pitch. His changeup still is a work in progress, but he shows a good feel for it. With advanced pitchability and confidence in his repertoire, Reed could make the jump to low Class A Kane County in 2015. Since he won't turn 19 until June, his more likely assignment will be at short-season Hillsboro. He has the durability to be a mid-rotation starter.

Year	Club (League)	Class	W	L	ERA	G	GS	CG	SV	IP	H	HR	BB	SO	K/9	WHIP	AVG
2014	Diamondbacks (AZL)	R	0	1	2.18	10	7	0	0	21	17	0	5	26	11.3	1.06	.218
	Missoula (PIO)	R	0	1	2.25	4	4	0	0	12	3	1	7	14	10.5	0.83	.081
Minor League Totals			0	2	2.20	14	11	0	0	33	20	1	12	40	11.0	0.98	.174

15 JOSE HERRERA, C

BA GRADE
55 Risk: Extreme

Born: Feb. 24, 1997. **B-T:** B-R. **Ht.:** 5-10. **Wt.:** 185. **Signed:** Venezuela, 2013. **Signed by:** Marlon Urdaneta.

The Diamondbacks' top international signee in 2013, Herrera signed for $1.06 million on July 2. Rather than starting the switch-hitting catcher in the Dominican Summer League, Arizona challenged the 17-year-old in 2014 with an initial assignment to the Rookie-level Arizona League, where he started 75 percent of the team's games. He already has advanced catching skills and polish uncommon for his age. Herrera has good hands, frames well and knows how to call a game, and his above-average to plus arm helped him throw out 34 percent of basestealers. With a good approach at the plate and some feel to hit, he projects to have enough bat to complement his skills behind the plate. He needs to smooth out his swing, but he's a patient hitter with life in the bat and present gap power that should translate to over-the-fence pop as he matures physically. He'll spend his second pro season in 2015 with one of the organization's three short-season affiliates.

Year	Club (League)	Class	AVG	G	AB	R	H	2B	3B	HR	RBI	BB	SO	SB	CS	OBP	SLG
2014	Diamondbacks (AZL)	R	.227	43	154	24	35	4	1	0	14	23	37	1	0	.337	.266
	Missoula (PIO)	R	.286	2	7	2	2	1	0	0	1	2	2	0	0	.444	.429
Minor League Totals			.230	45	161	26	37	5	1	0	15	25	39	1	0	.342	.273

16 JIMMIE SHERFY, RHP

BA GRADE

50 Risk: High

Born: Dec. 27, 1991. **B-T:** R-R. **Ht.:** 6-0. **Wt.:** 175. **Drafted:** Oregon, 2013 (10th round). **Signed by:** Donnie Reynolds.

One of the most dominant closers in college as an Oregon sophomore and junior, Sherfy's small stature, max-effort delivery and injury history caused him to drop in the 2013 draft, and the Diamondbacks scooped him up for a $100,000 bonus in the 10th round. He dominated hitters in his 11 games at high Class A Visalia to start 2014, striking out 23 of the 44 batters he faced. While he still has a high-maintenance delivery, Sherfy cleaned it up to better stay online. He generates plus velocity from his small frame because of his athleticism and arm speed. His fastball is electric, a 96-97 mph heater that touches 99 with late sink and life. His slider at 82-85 mph is short and tight with a little bit of tilt. While he doesn't use it much, his changeup gives Sherfy an effective third pitch. He'll challenge for a Triple-A Reno roster spot to open 2015 and could pitch his way to Chase Field sooner than later.

Year	Club (League)	Class	W	L	ERA	G	GS	CG	SV	IP	H	HR	BB	SO	K/9	WHIP	AVG
2013	Hillsboro (NWL)	SS	0	0	0.00	9	0	0	5	9	3	0	1	17	17.0	0.44	.100
	South Bend (MWL)	LoA	1	1	2.16	9	0	0	2	8	10	0	3	12	13.0	1.56	.286
2014	Visalia (CAL)	HiA	2	0	3.27	11	0	0	6	11	6	2	5	23	18.8	1.00	.158
	Mobile (SL)	AA	3	1	4.97	37	0	0	1	38	34	4	18	45	10.7	1.37	.241
Minor League Totals			6	2	3.66	66	0	0	14	66	53	6	27	97	13.2	1.21	.217

17 ANTHONY BANDA, LHP

BA GRADE

50 Risk: High

Born: Aug. 18, 1993. **B-T:** L-L. **Ht.:** 6-2. **Wt.:** 190. **Drafted:** San Jacinto (Texas) JC, 2012 (10th round). **Signed by:** Brian Sankey (Brewers).

The Diamondbacks drafted Banda in the 33rd round out of a Texas high school, but he didn't sign, attending San Jacinto (Texas) JC instead. The Brewers signed him for $125,000 in 2012 as a 10th-rounder, and the Diamondbacks finally got their man in the July 2014 trade of outfielder Gerardo Parra. Banda profiles as a back-end starter, with intriguing potential and improved control. The loose-armed lefty took a big step forward after the Diamondbacks acquired him, sharpening his strike-throwing considerably after the move. Banda has started to fulfill projections, jumping his fastball up to 94 mph with good movement. He's got an easy delivery and does a good job in keeping his front side closed, so there may be more velocity coming down the line. He's got an at-least-average 79-80 mph curveball with good shape and an average 84-87 mph changeup that flashes better. A 2015 trip to high Class A Visalia in the hitter-friendly California League will be a good test.

Year	Club (League)	Class	W	L	ERA	G	GS	CG	SV	IP	H	HR	BB	SO	K/9	WHIP	AVG
2012	Brewers (AZL)	R	2	3	5.83	14	4	0	0	42	54	3	24	43	9.3	1.87	.309
2013	Helena (PIO)	R	3	4	4.45	14	14	0	0	61	64	7	25	45	6.7	1.47	.274
2014	Wisconsin (MWL)	LoA	6	6	3.66	20	14	0	2	84	84	4	38	83	8.9	1.46	.263
	South Bend (MWL)	LoA	3	0	1.54	6	6	0	0	35	32	2	7	34	8.7	1.11	.237
Minor League Totals			14	13	3.95	54	38	0	2	221	234	16	94	205	8.3	1.48	.271

18 ANDREW CHAFIN, LHP

BA GRADE

45 Risk: Medium

Born: June 17, 1990. **B-T:** R-L. **Ht.:** 6-2. **Wt.:** 205. **Drafted:** Kent State, 2011 (1st round supplemental). **Signed by:** Nate Birtwell.

Chafin has bounced around the upper levels of the system since signing for $875,000 as the 43rd overall pick in 2011. Projected to move to the bullpen at several points in his career, the Kent State lefty began the 2014 season back in the rotation at Double-A Mobile after pitching there for most of 2013. He proved to be effective in his second go-round with the Bay Bears, earning a promotion to Triple-A Reno and his first big league time in mid-August, when he tossed five scoreless innings at Cleveland, close to his hometown of Wakeman, Ohio. He returned to the majors in September for two more starts. Chafin's velocity has bounced around in pro ball, often settling in the upper 80s with his fastball, but he sat 91-93 in the majors. His strikeout rate has diminished as he's climbed the ladder, though he throws with a funky delivery that provides deception and helps the ball get on hitters quickly. His slider, once a plus pitch, remains effective in the low 80s, and his changeup gives him a third average pitch, if not a tick above. Chafin will go to spring training with the big league team hoping to win a spot in the rotation but will more likely return to Reno.

Year	Club (League)	Class	W	L	ERA	G	GS	CG	SV	IP	H	HR	BB	SO	K/9	WHIP	AVG
2012	Visalia (CAL)	HiA	6	6	4.93	30	22	0	0	122	112	12	69	150	11.0	1.48	.241
2013	Visalia (CAL)	HiA	3	1	4.65	6	6	0	0	31	32	1	14	32	9.3	1.48	.262
	Mobile (SL)	AA	10	7	2.85	21	21	2	0	126	118	5	41	87	6.2	1.26	.252
2014	Mobile (SL)	AA	4	1	1.96	9	9	0	0	55	49	4	19	41	6.7	1.24	.243
	Reno (PCL)	AAA	5	6	5.34	17	16	0	0	93	111	11	39	73	7.1	1.62	.298
	Arizona (NL)	MAJ	0	1	3.86	3	3	0	0	14	13	0	8	10	6.4	1.50	.265
Major League Totals			0	1	3.86	3	3	0	0	14	13	0	8	10	6.4	1.50	.265
Minor League Totals			28	21	3.99	84	75	2	0	428	423	33	182	385	8.1	1.41	.259

19 SOCRATES BRITO, OF

BA GRADE
50 Risk: High

Born: Sept. 6, 1992. **B-T:** L-L. **Ht.:** 6-2. **Wt.:** 200. **Signed:** Dominican Republic, 2010. **Signed by:** Junior Noboa.

Ever since signing in 2010, Brito has been more about tools and future projection, but his promising season at high Class A Visalia in 2014 hinted at future production. His plus raw power started to emerge in games, more with doubles to the gap, but the loft he generates in his swing indicates that more balls will leave the park as he gets stronger. He's now a borderline plus runner who has the basestealing instincts to swipe 38 bats in 2014. Brito split time in both right and center field, with scouts remarking that his defense exceeded expectations. His plus arm ranks as the best among outfielders in the system, and he also rates as the organization's most athletic player. The Diamondbacks saw enough to add Brito to the 40-man roster in November. He'll experience his first big league spring training camp in 2015.

Year	Club (League)	Class	AVG	G	AB	R	H	2B	3B	HR	RBI	BB	SO	SB	CS	OBP	SLG
2012	Missoula (PIO)	R	.312	69	279	47	87	15	5	4	39	21	73	15	9	.357	.444
2013	South Bend (MWL)	LoA	.264	129	523	61	138	24	9	2	49	37	124	27	9	.313	.356
2014	Visalia (CAL)	HiA	.293	128	518	82	152	30	5	10	62	36	109	38	10	.339	.429
Minor League Totals			.284	403	1638	230	466	76	27	17	187	116	371	98	42	.332	.395

20 SERGIO ALCANTARA, SS

BA GRADE
50 Risk: Extreme

Born: July 10, 1996. **B-T:** B-R. **Ht.:** 5-10. **Wt.:** 150. **Signed:** Dominican Republic, 2012. **Signed by:** Junior Noboa.

Alcantara, the nephew of former big league infielder Anderson Hernandez, signed with Arizona for $700,000 in 2012 just after turning 16, and he has played above his age level in both of his pro seasons. He's already a plus defender at shortstop with a double-plus arm, and he drew raves from opposing managers at Rookie-level Missoula for his defensive play in 2014. Despite his youth and relative inexperience, Alcantara displays advanced plate discipline, for he led his league in walks in both of 2013 and 2014. He's still not fully developed physically, especially his upper half, which is reflected in his modest batting average (career .244) and high strikeout rate. A switch-hitter, Alcantara has a decent feel for the barrel, good bat speed and instincts. He projects as a gap-to-gap hitter with occasional power once his body fills out, and is an average runner who could improve with age. Alcantara will still be just 18 in spring training, so he'll probably head to short-season Hillsboro.

Year	Club (League)	Class	AVG	G	AB	R	H	2B	3B	HR	RBI	BB	SO	SB	CS	OBP	SLG
2013	Diamondbacks (AZL)	R	.243	48	169	31	41	5	4	0	16	44	36	3	2	.398	.320
2014	Missoula (PIO)	R	.244	70	266	48	65	11	0	1	18	48	62	8	4	.361	.297
Minor League Totals			.244	118	435	79	106	16	4	1	34	92	98	11	6	.376	.306

21 STRYKER TRAHAN, OF/C

BA GRADE
50 Risk: Extreme

Born: April 25, 1994. **B-T:** L-R. **Ht.:** 5-11. **Wt.:** 215. **Drafted:** HS— Lafayette, La., 2012 (1st round). **Signed by:** Rusty Pendergrass.

To say that 2014 was a challenging year for Trahan is an understatement. The 2012 first-round pick moved from catcher to right field for his first full-season assignment at low Class A South Bend to help his bat develop more quickly. The change had the opposite effect with the Louisiana native hitting just .198 in 95 games. The Diamondbacks put Trahan back behind the plate in late July and sent him to short-season Hillsboro, where he rebounded a hit, and he helped the Hops win the Northwest League title. Working with hitting coach Mark Grace, Trahan made adjustments to hit from a slightly more closed stance in order to keep his stride length down, as well as moving his hands up slightly. He has plus raw power to all fields, but he can't always get to it in games as he struggles with quality offspeed stuff. Trahan also showed improvement in his catching skills and, most importantly, got his body in better shape. His release and footwork need improvement to take advantage of his strong arm, and he calls a good game, but he needs to stay focused for all nine innings. Trahan needs many more reps behind the plate but should get them now that he's in condition to handle the rigors of everyday catching. He'll get a fresh start in 2015, returning to low Class A with Kane County.

Year	Club (League)	Class	AVG	G	AB	R	H	2B	3B	HR	RBI	BB	SO	SB	CS	OBP	SLG
2012	Diamondbacks (AZL)	R	.281	49	167	29	47	11	3	5	25	40	48	8	1	.422	.473
2013	Missoula (PIO)	R	.254	59	236	44	60	15	2	10	33	24	57	1	0	.328	.462
2014	South Bend (MWL)	LoA	.198	95	368	47	73	21	1	13	52	30	146	3	0	.264	.367
	Hillsboro (NWL)	SS	.257	30	113	15	29	7	1	6	22	15	23	2	2	.344	.496
Minor League Totals			.236	233	884	135	209	54	7	34	132	109	274	14	3	.324	.429

22 MITCH HANIGER, OF

BA GRADE

45 Risk: Medium

Born: Dec. 23, 1990. **B-T:** R-R. **Ht.:** 6-2. **Wt.:** 215. **Drafted:** Cal Poly, 2012 (first round supplemental). **Signed by:** Dan Huston (Brewers).

Haniger was one of two players acquired by Arizona in the July 2014 trade that sent Gerardo Parra to the Brewers. Haniger has struggled with injuries since turning pro. A knee injury limiting him to 14 games in 2012, while both hamstring and elbow problems kept him on the sidelines for much of the second half of 2014. After a good 2013 season which included a stint in the Arizona Fall League, Haniger looked like he wasn't far from contributing in the big leagues. Instead, he got off to a slow start at Double-A Huntsville in 2014 before hitting the disabled list. He's a streaky hitter with plus pull-side power who handles lefthanders much better than righties. Haniger's best tool is his plus arm, allowing him to handle either corner-outfield position as an average defender with fringy speed. A half-season of Double-A should get Haniger a promotion to Triple-A Reno in 2015.

Year	Club (League)	Class	AVG	G	AB	R	H	2B	3B	HR	RBI	BB	SO	SB	CS	OBP	SLG
2012	Wisconsin (MWL)	LoA	.286	14	49	9	14	4	0	1	8	7	13	1	0	.379	.429
2013	Wisconsin (MWL)	LoA	.297	41	145	24	43	12	2	5	25	25	24	7	0	.399	.510
	Brevard County (FSL)	HiA	.250	88	328	52	82	24	3	6	43	32	68	2	2	.323	.396
2014	Huntsville (SL)	AA	.255	67	243	41	62	7	1	10	34	19	41	4	0	.316	.416
	Diamondbacks (AZL)	R	.200	4	15	4	3	1	0	1	4	1	6	0	0	.250	.467
	Mobile (SL)	AA	.333	8	24	5	8	3	0	0	5	3	4	0	0	.433	.458
Minor League Totals			.264	222	804	135	212	51	6	23	119	87	156	14	2	.342	.428

23 JEFFERSON MEJIA, RHP

BA GRADE

50 Risk: Extreme

Born: Aug. 2, 1994. **B-T:** R-R. **Ht.:** 6-7. **Wt.:** 220. **Signed:** Dominican Republic, 2013. **Signed by:** Jose Serra (Cubs).

Arizona's deal to send catcher Miguel Montero to the Cubs was largely viewed as a salary dump, but the trade netted them an intriguing raw prospect in Mejia. Presumably old enough to sign in 2012 but ruled ineligible for one year due to issues with his age, Mejia finally inked a contract with the Cubs one year later for $850,000. He made his U.S. debut in the Rookie-level Arizona League in 2014, where he was emerging as one of the Cubs' more intriguing arms, with club officials calling him a lottery ticket. Arizona got a pitcher who is all about arm strength and projection, improving his velocity and pitch location during the season. He's a big-bodied kid who delivers a mid- to high-90s fastball using an over-the-top delivery with downward plane and hard sink. His delivery is fairly clean, but he struggles with command, and his secondary pitches—a slurvy breaking ball and nascent changeup—are not yet ready for prime time. While he has an upside as a starter, Mejia has a long way to go and most likely will open 2015 in extended spring training.

Year	Club (League)	Class	W	L	ERA	G	GS	CG	SV	IP	H	HR	BB	SO	K/9	WHIP	AVG
2013	Cubs 1 (DSL)	R	0	0	3.00	3	3	0	0	9	6	0	3	6	6.0	1.00	.222
2014	Cubs (AZL)	R	2	4	2.48	12	2	0	0	40	30	1	17	45	10.1	1.18	.204
Minor League Totals			2	4	2.57	15	5	0	0	49	36	1	20	51	9.4	1.14	.207

24 MARCUS WILSON, OF

BA GRADE

50 Risk: Extreme

Born: Aug. 15, 1996. **B-T:** R-R. **Ht.:** 6-3. **Wt.:** 175. **Drafted:** HS— Gardena, Calif., 2014 (2nd round supplemental). **Signed by:** Hal Kurtzman.

Arizona was rewarded with a pair of competitive balance picks after the second round of the 2014 draft, using both choices on high-potential high school players in Isan Diaz and Wilson. The Diamondbacks signed Wilson for $1 million to keep him from heading to Arizona State. He has a tall, lanky frame with room to add weight and muscle. He's got decent bat speed and has strong wrists that can help the ball jump off his bat, but his swing gets long when he tries to compensate for his weakness. He's at least an average runner with first-step quickness now, and he should get faster with strength and better running techniques. The Diamondbacks see Wilson as a natural center fielder with an average arm and good instincts that help him get good jumps and reads. He'll head to one of Arizona's Rookie-level affiliates in 2015.

Year	Club (League)	Class	AVG	G	AB	R	H	2B	3B	HR	RBI	BB	SO	SB	CS	OBP	SLG
2014	Diamondbacks (AZL)	R	.206	39	131	15	27	2	2	1	22	16	40	4	2	.297	.275
Minor League Totals			.206	39	131	15	27	2	2	1	22	16	40	4	2	.297	.275

25 BRENT JONES, RHP

Born: Jan. 10, 1993. **B-T:** R-R. **Ht.:** 6-3. **Wt.:** 215. **Drafted:** Cornell, 2014 (4th round). **Signed by:** Mike Serbalik.

Jones was a high school star in New Mexico before heading across country for an Ivy League education at Cornell. It's not surprising that he's a cerebral pitcher with advanced pitchability, with more premium velocity than normally seen from the Ivy League. Arizona grabbed Jones in the fourth round in 2014, signing him for $350,000. After beginning his pro career with eight solid starts at short-season Hillsboro, Jones moved up to low Class A South Bend for the rest of his first season. Sporting a competitive demeanor on the mound, he deals a fastball that sits 88-93 mph and was up as high as 97 in college. He induces lots of groundballs with the sink on his heater. His 79-82 mph curveball that he throws with a spike grip flashes plus at times but lacks consistency. He lacks a feel for his rarely-used 81-84 mph changeup and will need to develop it if he wants to stay in the rotation. It has average potential. Jones could move quickly as a high-floor reliever and may get to high Class A Visalia in 2015.

Year	Club (League)	Class	W	L	ERA	G	GS	CG	SV	IP	H	HR	BB	SO	K/9	WHIP	AVG
2014	Hillsboro (NWL)	SS	2	1	3.90	6	6	0	0	28	22	2	10	18	5.9	1.16	.218
	South Bend (MWL)	LoA	5	2	2.80	8	8	1	0	35	41	1	12	27	6.9	1.50	.285
Minor League Totals			7	3	3.29	14	14	1	0	63	63	3	22	45	6.4	1.35	.257

26 ZACH BORENSTEIN, OF

Born: July 23, 1990. **B-T:** L-R. **Ht.:** 6-0. **Wt.:** 225. **Drafted:** Eastern Illinois, 2011 (23rd round). **Signed by:** Joel Murrie (Angels).

Borenstein's big breakout year came in 2013 when he led the high Class A California League in batting (.337), home runs (28) and slugging (.631) to win the league's MVP award. This despite missing a month with a hip flexor injury. The Diamondbacks acquired Borenstein in a four-player deal with the Angels in July 2014, and he batted a cumulative .258/.320/.432 with 15 homers for four total clubs. His plus power potential comes from solid bat speed and a good swing. His power is counterbalanced by a low contact rate (24 percent strikeouts in 2014), which will keep his batting average down. He's an average, max-effort runner who will lose some speed as he matures. As an average defender with a below-average arm, Borenstein fits best in left field, but he could also handle right field in a backup role. Left off the 40-man roster, Borenstein will go as far as his bat takes him, which will be Triple-A Reno in 2015.

Year	Club (League)	Class	AVG	G	AB	R	H	2B	3B	HR	RBI	BB	SO	SB	CS	OBP	SLG
2012	Cedar Rapids (MWL)	LoA	.266	79	293	42	78	25	3	11	50	27	60	13	5	.339	.485
2013	Inland Empire (CAL)	HiA	.337	112	407	76	137	22	7	28	95	43	88	5	5	.403	.631
2014	Salt Lake (PCL)	AAA	.256	30	117	11	30	4	0	2	22	3	33	0	2	.279	.342
	Arkansas (TL)	AA	.266	48	184	23	49	13	2	5	28	21	53	6	4	.338	.440
	Mobile (SL)	AA	.241	23	87	13	21	4	2	3	14	12	17	3	0	.333	.437
	Reno (PCL)	AAA	.260	20	73	12	19	4	1	5	15	7	22	0	1	.321	.548
Minor League Totals			.286	343	1274	198	365	78	19	56	245	130	294	39	18	.359	.509

27 ISAN DIAZ, 2B/SS

Born: May 27, 1996. **B-T:** L-R. **Ht.:** 5-10. **Wt.:** 185. **Drafted:** HS— Springfield, Mass., 2014 (2nd round supplemental). **Signed by:** Mike Serbalik.

The Diamondbacks signed Diaz, who was born in Puerto Rico but grew up in Massachusetts, for a $750,000 bonus as a 2014 supplemental second-rounder. Regarded as a bat-first middle infielder during his high school days, he showed the opposite traits in his debut in the Rookie-level Arizona League. Diaz played a better-than-expected shortstop but struggled with the bat. He looked better in instructional league, and scouts believe the bat will come around because he has good hands, a good feel for the barrel, and a natural, easy swing. He struggles with offspeed stuff but has a strong lower half and projects to have average power if it all clicks. He's a fringe-average runner who won't steal a lot of bases, especially as he grows bigger. While he spent more time at shortstop in Rookie ball, Diaz's future is at second base. He could be an above-average defender there as well as being able to handle shortstop in a utility role. He'll likely move to Rookie-level Missoula in 2015.

Year	Club (League)	Class	AVG	G	AB	R	H	2B	3B	HR	RBI	BB	SO	SB	CS	OBP	SLG
2014	Diamondbacks (AZL)	R	.187	49	182	22	34	7	5	3	21	25	56	6	5	.289	.330
Minor League Totals			.187	49	182	22	34	7	5	3	21	25	56	6	5	.289	.330

28 MATT RAILEY OF

BA GRADE

50 Risk: Extreme

Born: March 16, 1995. **B-T:** L-L. **Ht.:** 5-11. **Wt.:** 190. **Drafted:** HS— Tallahassee, Fla., 2014 (3rd round). **Signed by:** Luke Wrenn.

Railey teamed with Cubs draft pick Carson Sands at North Florida Christian High in Tallahassee, Fla., with both players choosing pro ball in 2014 over their Florida State commitments. The Diamondbacks picked Railey in the third round, signing him for $600,000. A torn hamstring ended his first pro season after just 13 games at Rookie-level Missoula. He returned in time to get action in instructional league but was primarily limited to a DH role and scouts didn't really get a good look at him. Railey is more of a line-drive hitter with a quick, short-to-the-ball swing, but with above-average raw power he projects to be able to drive balls over the fence. Railey doesn't have the instincts for center field and his below-average arm may keep him out of right field, so his bat will have to play for him to be a regular. He's expected to be back to full speed by spring training before reporting to one of Arizona's three short-season affiliates.

Year	Club (League)	Class	AVG	G	AB	R	H	2B	3B	HR	RBI	BB	SO	SB	CS	OBP	SLG
2014	Missoula (PIO)	R	.267	13	45	7	12	5	1	2	7	4	7	1	1	.327	.556
Minor League Totals			.267	13	45	7	12	5	1	2	7	4	7	1	1	.327	.556

29 ENRIQUE BURGOS, RHP

BA GRADE

45 Risk: High

Born: Nov. 23, 1990. **B-T:** R-R. **Ht.:** 6-4. **Wt.:** 250. **Signed:** Panama, 2007. **Signed by:** Junior Noboa/Jose Diaz Perez.

Burgos has often teased as an intriguing arm with little command and limited pitchability. He figured it out in 2014 with a strong season in the high Class A Visalia bullpen, earning a spot on the 40-man roster. The key for Burgos' improvement was a bump in velocity, with a fastball now up to a lively 99 mph, and enough control to get by. He struck out a career-best 13.7 per nine innings and matched his best walk rate (4.3 per nine) in 2014. The big-bodied Burgos delivers his pitches with a live, loose arm, with a max-effort delivery that he doesn't always repeat. He also throws a plus slider in the mid-80s that gives him a pitch to complement the heater. Burgos profiles as a seventh-inning reliever and is still a bit of a wild card, but he just turned 24 and will move up to Double-A Mobile in 2015.

Year	Club (League)	Class	W	L	ERA	G	GS	CG	SV	IP	H	HR	BB	SO	K/9	WHIP	AVG
2012	Yakima (NWL)	SS	2	3	2.35	25	0	0	4	38	28	1	19	40	9.4	1.23	.201
2013	South Bend (MWL)	LoA	2	2	3.88	49	0	0	17	46	29	1	49	50	9.7	1.68	.179
2014	Visalia (CAL)	HiA	3	3	2.47	55	0	0	29	55	37	5	26	83	13.7	1.15	.188
Minor League Totals			20	18	4.55	182	52	0	50	364	333	25	246	376	9.3	1.59	.245

30 DANIEL PALKA, 1B/OF

BA GRADE

45 Risk: High

Born: Oct. 28, 1991. **B-T:** L-L. **Ht.:** 6-2. **Wt.:** 220. **Drafted:** Georgia Tech, 2013 (3rd round). **Signed by:** T.R. Lewis.

Palka led the Atlantic Coast Conference in home runs at Georgia Tech in 2013, prompting the Diamondbacks to pop him in the third round and sign him for $550,000. He made his full-season debut in 2014 and tied for the low Class A Midwest League home run lead despite a broken hamate bone ending his season in mid-August. He's got legit raw power generated by strong hands, but holes in the inner half and lack of ideal bat speed concern many scouts. Palka handles southpaws just as well as righthanders, posting an identical .798 OPS against both sides in 2014. He swings and misses frequently, which he'll need to address as he moves higher in the system, but he draws his fair share of walks. Palka will be ready to move to the friendly hitting environs of the high Class A California League in 2015.

Year	Club (League)	Class	AVG	G	AB	R	H	2B	3B	HR	RBI	BB	SO	SB	CS	OBP	SLG
2013	Missoula (PIO)	R	.302	56	205	36	62	20	0	7	38	29	45	2	2	.386	.502
	Hillsboro (NWL)	SS	.340	12	47	10	16	1	2	2	10	7	16	1	0	.418	.574
2014	South Bend (MWL)	LoA	.248	118	455	63	113	23	5	22	82	56	129	9	3	.332	.466
Minor League Totals			.270	186	707	109	191	44	7	31	130	92	190	12	5	.354	.484

Atlanta Braves

BY BILL BALLEW

Team president John Schuerholz envisioned big things for the Braves in 2014 as he successfully planned for the team to build a new, taxpayer-funded stadium in suburban Cobb County for the 2017 season while three men identified with the Braves—former manager Bobby Cox and aces Tom Glavine and Greg Maddux—were inducted into the Hall of Fame.

It turned into a nightmare, however, and Schuerholz is determined not to repeat it. One year after winning the National League East by 10 games with a 96-66 record in 2013, the Braves fell to 79-83 and 17 games behind the first-place Nationals.

Schuerholz responded by taking a wrecking ball to the front office in late September and October, reiterating all the while that the farm system must be the lifeblood of the organization. And while it is unlikely that the minor league system will generate the same type of productivity it did in the late 1980s and '90s, Schuerholz is determined to put forth the effort to make that scenario a reality.

Every new hire brings with him a deep commitment to building from within, beginning with president of baseball operations John Hart, who as general manager of the Indians guided them to two World Series appearances in the mid-'90s. Hart's new special assistants to the GM include former Yankees scouting guru Gordon Blakeley and prodigal son Roy Clark, who guided the Braves' scouting efforts for nearly a decade in the 2000s before stints with the Nationals and Dodgers.

Dave Trembley returns as the farm director after a two-year stint with the Astros, while Brian Bridges was promoted from the Southeast crosschecker to scouting director, replacing the fired Tony DeMacio.

Though the challenge to return to the days when Atlanta won 14 consecutive division titles is substantial, the cupboard is not bare. Prior to the 2014 season, the Braves locked up many of their young, homegrown major leaguers, including righthander Julio Teheran, closer Craig Kimbrel, first baseman Freddie Freeman and shortstop Andrelton Simmons. Lefthander Alex Wood blossomed into a No. 2 starter in 2014, and lefty Mike Minor provides another foundation piece.

But outfielder Jason Heyward, one of Clark's signature picks as Atlanta's 2007 first-rounder, never signed an extension, prompting the Braves to trade him to the Cardinals in a November deal that netted power righthanders in big leaguer Shelby Miller and prospect Tyrell Jenkins. They add pitching depth to a system heavier at the top with position players, such as catcher Christian Bethancourt

Braves president John Schuerholz turned over the team's front office, starting with new general manager John Hart

TOP PROSPECTS OF THE DECADE

Year	Player, Pos.	2014 Org
2005	Jeff Francoeur, of	Padres
2006	Jarrod Saltalamacchia, c	Marlins
2007	Jarrod Saltalamacchia, c	Marlins
2008	Jordan Schafer, of	Braves
2009	Tommy Hanson, rhp	White Sox
2010	Jason Heyward, of	Braves
2011	Julio Teheran, rhp	Braves
2012	Julio Teheran, rhp	Braves
2013	Julio Teheran, rhp	Braves
2014	Lucas Sims, rhp	Braves

and second baseman Jose Peraza, who are both on the verge of becoming starters in the big leagues.

While the Braves have some arms, the system appears thinner than it has in years, particularly with lefthanded pitchers as well as impact position players at the corners, an exception being 2014 first-round pick Braxton Davidson.

General manager: John Hart. **Farm director:** Dave Trembley. **Scouting director:** Brian Bridges.

Class	Team	League	W	L	PCT	Finish	Manager
Majors	Atlanta Braves	National	79	83	.488	t-16th (30)	Fredi Gonzalez
Triple-A	Gwinnett Braves	International	65	77	.458	11th (14)	Brian Snitker
Double-A	Mississippi Braves	Southern	83	56	.597	1st (10)	Aaron Holbert
High A	*Lynchburg Hillcats	Carolina	68	71	.489	4th (8)	Luis Salazar
Low A	Rome Braves	South Atlantic	56	84	.400	t-12th (14)	Jonathan Schuerholz
Rookie	Danville Braves	Appalachian	38	30	.559	2nd (10)	Randy Ingle
Rookie	Braves	Gulf Coast	29	30	.492	9th (16)	Rocket Wheeler
Overall Minor League Record			**339**	**348**	**.493**	**19th (30)**	

*Affiliate will be Carolina (Carolina) in 2015.

THIS YEAR'S TOP 30

No.	Player, Pos.	Grade
1.	Jose Peraza, 2b	55/Medium
2.	Lucas Sims, rhp	55/High
3.	Christian Bethancourt, c	55/High
4.	Jason Hursh, rhp	50/Medium
5.	Ozhaino Albies, ss	55/Extreme
6.	Braxton Davidson, of	50/High
7.	Tyrell Jenkins, rhp	50/High
8.	Johan Camargo, ss	50/High
9.	Garrett Fulenchek, rhp	55/Extreme
10.	Kyle Kubitza, 3b	45/Medium
11.	Arodys Vizcaino, rhp	50/High
12.	Chasen Shreve, lhp	45/Low
13.	Shae Simmons, rhp	45/Medium
14.	Mauricio Cabrera, rhp	50/High
15.	Wes Parsons, rhp	45/High
16.	Alec Grosser, rhp	50/Extreme
17.	Tanner Murphy, c	50/Extreme
18.	Cody Martin, rhp	40/Low
19.	Williams Perez, rhp	45/Medium
20.	Juan Jaime, rhp	45/High
21.	Max Povse, rhp	45/High
22.	Victor Reyes, of	50/Extreme
23.	Todd Cunningham, of	40/Medium
24.	Chad Sobotka, rhp	50/Extreme
25.	Daniel Castro, ss/2b	40/Medium
26.	Dan Winkler, rhp	50/Extreme
27.	Carlos Salazar, rhp	45/High
28.	Aaron Northcraft, rhp	40/Medium
29.	Elmer Reyes, ss/2b	40/Medium
30.	Luis Merejo, lhp	50/Extreme

LAST YEAR'S TOP 30

No.	Player, Pos.	Status
1.	Lucas Sims, rhp	No. 2
2.	Christian Bethancourt, c	No. 3
3.	J.R. Graham, rhp	(Twins)
4.	Jason Hursh, rhp	No. 4
5.	Mauricio Cabrera, rhp	No. 14
6.	Jose Peraza, ss	No. 1
7.	David Hale, rhp	Majors
8.	Victor Caratini, 3b/c	(Cubs)
9.	Tommy La Stella, 2b	(Cubs)
10.	Sean Gilmartin, lhp	(Twins)
11.	Cody Martin, rhp	No. 18
12.	Edward Salcedo, 3b	Dropped out
13.	Josh Elander, rhp	Dropped out
14.	Victor Reyes, of	No. 22
15.	Joey Terdoslavich, of/1b	Dropped out
16.	Shae Simmons, rhp	No. 13
17.	Carlos Salazar, rhp	No. 27
18.	Kyle Wren, of	(Brewers)
19.	Johan Camargo, ss	No. 8
20.	Wes Parsons, rhp	No. 15
21.	Tanner Murphy, c	No. 17
22.	Kyle Kubitza, 3b	No. 10
23.	Todd Cunningham, of	No. 23
24.	Matt Lipka, of	Dropped out
25.	Aaron Northcraft, rhp	No. 28
26.	Luis Merejo, lhp	No. 30
27.	Juan Jaime, rhp	No. 20
28.	Tyler Brosius, rhp	Dropped out
29.	Robby Hefflinger, of	Dropped out
30.	James Hoyt, rhp	Dropped out

BEST TOOLS

Best Hitter for Average	Jose Peraza
Best Power Hitter	Joey Terdoslavich
Best Strike-Zone Discipline	Braxton Davidson
Fastest Baserunner	Jose Peraza
Best Athlete	Matt Lipka
Best Fastball	Shae Simmons
Best Curveball	Lucas Sims
Best Slider	Cody Martin
Best Changeup	Chasen Shreve
Best Control	Chasen Shreve
Best Defensive Catcher	Christian Bethancourt
Best Defensive Infielder	Johan Camargo
Best Infield Arm	Kyle Kubitza
Best Defensive Outfielder	Todd Cunningham
Best Outfield Arm	Edward Salcedo

PROJECTED 2018 STARTING LINEUP

Catcher	Christian Bethancourt
First Base	Freddie Freeman
Second Base	Jose Peraza
Third Base	Kyle Kubitza
Shortstop	Andrelton Simmons
Left Field	Justin Upton
Center Field	Todd Cunningham
Right Field	Nick Markakis
No. 1 Starter	Julio Teheran
No. 2 Starter	Mike Minor
No. 3 Starter	Alex Wood
No. 4 Starter	Lucas Sims
No. 5 Starter	Jason Hursh
Closer	Craig Kimbrel

ATLANTA BRAVES

TOP 2015 ROOKIE: Christian Bethancourt, c. His consistency at the plate and focus behind it will determine whether he platoons or takes the job on a full-time basis.
BREAKOUT PROSPECT: Alec Grosser, rhp. The former high school quarterback has a low-mileage arm, a low-90s fastball and improving curveball that could allow him to blossom.
SLEEPER: Kyle Kinman, lhp. The 23-year-old reliever from tiny Bellevue (Neb.) showed a sharp curveball and a fastball that touches the mid-90s.

SOURCE OF TOP 30 TALENT			
Homegrown	29	Acquired	1
College	9	Trades	0
Junior college	1	Rule 5 draft	0
High school	7	Independent leagues	0
Draft-and-follow	0	Free agents/waivers	1
Nondrafted free agents	1		
International	11		

LF
Josh Elander
Justin Black

CF
Todd Cunningham (23)
Matt Lipka
Connor Oliver
Joseph Darius

RF
Braxton Davidson (6)
Victor Reyes (22)
Edward Salcedo
Fernelys Sanchez

3B
Kyle Kubitza (10)
Jordan Edgerton
Dylan Manwaring

SS
Ozhaino Albies (5)
Johan Camargo (8)
Daniel Castro (25)
Elmer Reyes (29)

2B
Jose Peraza (1)
Phil Gosselin
Luke Dykstra

1B
Joey Terdoslavich

C
Christian Bethancourt (3)
Tanner Murphy (17)

LHP

LHSP	LHRP
Luis Merejo (30)	Chasen Shreve (12)
Yean Carlos Gil	Ian Thomas
Matt Marksberry	Brady Feigl
	Kyle Kinman
	Michael Flores

RHP

RHSP	RHRP
Lucas Sims (2)	Arodys Vizcaino (11)
Jason Hursh (4)	Shae Simmons (13)
Tyrell Jenkins (7)	Mauricio Cabrera (14)
Garrett Fulenchek (9)	Juan Jaime (20)
Wes Parsons (15)	Chad Sobotka (24)
Alec Grosser (16)	Carlos Salazar (27)
Cody Martin (18)	Brandon Cunniff
Williams Perez (19)	James Hoyt
Max Povse (21)	John Cornely
Dan Winkler (26)	Ryne Harper
Aaron Northcraft (28)	Tyler Brosiius
Gus Schlosser	Alex Wilson
Andry Ubiera	Nate Hyatt

2014

BEST PURE HITTER: The Braves weren't the only ones convicted on the bat of OF/1B Braxton Davidson (1), who has a chance to be a middle-of-the-order presence. He's shown the ability to make adjustments and has fine strike-zone awareness.

BEST POWER HITTER: Davidson showed plus power with wood on the showcase circuit, though he focused more on contact this spring and didn't homer after signing. 3B Jordan Edgerton (9) has hand-eye coordination and strength that allow him to hit for solid power as well.

FASTEST RUNNER: OF Joseph Daris (14) gives the Braves a true burner with 80 speed and an explosive first step.

BEST DEFENSIVE PLAYER: OF Sean Godfrey (22) was a college senior with tools. He has an average arm if not a tick above and has 70 speed that allows him to play center.

BEST FASTBALL: A two-way player at Southern Mississippi, RHP Brad Roney (8) will focus on pitching as a pro and has run his fastball up as high as 98 mph since signing. RHP Garrett Fulenchek (2) has athleticism and repeats his delivery more consistently than Roney, pounding the bottom of the zone with a lively 89-93 mph fastball.

BEST SECONDARY PITCH: Omaha product LHP Kyle Kinman (25) led NAIA with 141 strikeouts and can show two plus pitches: a fastball that has touched 95 and a plus, hard curveball with power and late action. RHP Chad Sobotka (4) has also shown a plus slider when healthy and was throwing it in instructional league. LHP Chris Diaz (5) has the group's best changeup, at times a plus pitch as well.

BEST PRO DEBUT: Godfrey finished the season at high Class A Lynchburg and hit .321/.358/.464 overall, stealing 18 bases in 20 tries. Sinkerballing RHP Max Povse (3) went 4-2, 3.42 at Rookie-level Danville, allowing only one home run.

BEST ATHLETE: Daris was a high school running back and linebacker and has strength and explosiveness in his 5-foot-10, 170-pound body.

MOST INTRIGUING BACKGROUND: 2B Luke Dykstra (7) is the son of ex-big leaguer Len. C Sal Giardina's (31) father Sal Sr. coached at Lynn (Fla.), and his brother Carmine has reached Double-A with the Angels. Unsigned SS Grayson Byrd (39) is the son of Paul Byrd, who won 109 games in the majors and spent parts of two seasons in Atlanta. Unsigned LHP Tucker Baca (32) is the son of Mark, a national crosschecker for the Nationals.

CLOSEST TO THE MAJORS: Kinman and Diaz have very different repertoires, but both could move quickly as lefthanded relievers. Diaz still may start, giving Kinman the edge.

BEST LATE-ROUND PICK: Godfrey, Daris and Kinman all have carrying tools to become big league role players.

THE ONE WHO GOT AWAY: The Braves made a run at OF/RHP Ashton Perritt (17), whose fastball has touched 95 mph in the past. He returned to Liberty. RHP Jake Godfrey (21) had a rough spring and wound up as part of Louisiana State's boffo recruiting class.

ASSESSMENT: Tony DeMacio's final draft class with the Braves may provide good value, but a thinned farm system and Frank Wren's firing as GM led to an overhaul of the scouting department.

2013

RHPs Jason Hursh (1) and Alec Grosser (11) and C Tanner Murphy (4) have stood out so far. The Braves already traded C Victor Caratini (2) and OF Kyle Wren (8).

GRADE: D

2012

LHP Alex Wood (2) already has 14 big league wins. RHP Lucas Sims (1) is the Braves' top pitching prospect. RHP Shae Simmons (22) has reached Atlanta's bullpen.

GRADE: B

2011

The best player left in the system is 3B Kyle Kubitza (3). Atlanta has traded big leaguers SS Nick Ahmed (2) and 2B Tommy La Stella (8).

GRADE: C

TOP DRAFT PICKS OF THE DECADE

Year	Player, Pos.	2014 Org
2005	Joey Devine, rhp	Out of baseball
2006	Cody Johnson, of	Out of baseball
2007	Jason Heyward, of	Braves
2008	Brett DeVall (1s)	Out of baseball
2009	Mike Minor, lhp	Braves
2010	Matt Lipka, ss (1s)	Braves
2011	Sean Gilmartin, lhp	Twins
2012	Lucas Sims, rhp	Braves
2013	Jason Hursh, rhp	Braves
2014	Braxton Davidson, of	Braves

LARGEST BONUSES IN CLUB HISTORY

Mike Minor, 2009	$2,420,000
Jeff Francoeur, 2002	$2,200,000
Matt Belisle, 1998	$1,750,000
Braxton Davidson, 2014	$1,705,000
Jason Hursh, 2013	$1,704,200

1 JOSE PERAZA, 2B

Born: April 30, 1994. **B-T:** R-R. **Ht.:** 6-0. **Wt.:** 165.
Signed: Venezuela, 2010. **Signed by:** Rolando Petit.

BA GRADE

55 Risk: Medium

SCOUTING GRADES

Batting: 60.
Power: 30.
Speed: 80.
Defense: 55.
Arm: 55.

Based on 20-80 scouting scale and future projection rather than present grades.

LGE	PA	BB%	SO%	ISO
CAR	304	3.3	10.5	.113
SL	195	3.6	7.7	.086

MIKE JANES

Signed out of Venezuela for $350,000 in 2010, Peraza has emerged as a top prospect over the past three seasons by displaying an incredible feel for the game. He made his U.S. debut in 2012 and ranked as the No. 10 prospect in the Rookie-level Gulf Coast League prior to spending the last five-plus weeks in the Appalachian League. He then stole 64 bases at low Class A Rome in 2013 before busting out as a prospect in 2014, when he stole 60 bases (to rank third in the minors) as he raced to Double-A Mississippi in the second half. Along the way, Peraza started for the World team in the Futures Game in Minneapolis, collecting a single in two at-bats. He helped guide Mississippi to a second-half record of 44-26.

Peraza employs speed, quickness and intellect with tremendous instincts for the game, which led to a combined .339 average in 2014, ninth-best in the minors. A spray hitter with a good understanding of the strike zone, Peraza has the hand-eye coordination to hit all types of pitches but is patient enough to wait for those he can handle and winds up barreling the ball more often than not. He has quick wrists and strong hands that generate a compact swing. He's tinkered with moving his hands in his stance to give him more of a trigger, because he has below-average power. Peraza keeps the ball on the ground by rarely getting under pitches and uses his plus speed to get on base. He has been timed as fast as 3.9 seconds from home to first base, which is top-of-the-scale speed that makes him one of the fastest players in the minors. Once on base, he creates an instant distraction for pitchers and the defense. He reads pitchers well and has a great first step in stealing bases. He made a seamless move from shortstop to second base in 2014 while displaying steady, soft hands with above-average range and solid arm strength. He is not flashy in the field but makes all of the routine plays and was voted best defensive second baseman by high Class A Carolina League managers. Peraza's other weakness other than his modest pop is his unwillingness to walk, which may set him back as a future leadoff man.

Some scouts questioned Atlanta's decision to shift Peraza off shortstop to the less-demanding job at second base. With Andrelton Simmons entrenched at shortstop, the Braves gave Peraza a chance to accelerate his timetable by moving him to second, and he seized the opportunity. The organization considered calling up Peraza in August when Simmons was sidelined with an injury, but Peraza was battling a mild groin strain at the time. The Braves traded second baseman Tommy La Stella to the Cubs in November, meaning the musical chairs at that position will end soon in Atlanta. In anticipation of filling the Braves' longstanding need at second, Peraza will compete with Phil Gosselin in big league camp this spring for the starting job and could wind up bypassing Triple-A Gwinnett with an impressive showing.

Year	Club (League)	Class	AVG	G	AB	R	H	2B	3B	HR	RBI	BB	SO	SB	CS	OBP	SLG
2012	Braves (GCL)	R	.318	21	85	17	27	3	3	0	10	4	6	10	3	.348	.424
	Danville (APP)	R	.281	32	121	21	34	4	0	1	18	9	18	15	2	.351	.339
2013	Rome (SAL)	LoA	.288	114	448	72	129	18	8	1	47	34	64	64	15	.341	.371
2014	Lynchburg (CAR)	HiA	.342	66	284	44	97	13	8	1	27	10	32	35	7	.365	.454
	Mississippi (SL)	AA	.335	44	185	35	62	7	3	1	17	7	15	25	8	.363	.422
Minor League Totals			.306	343	1358	218	415	50	25	5	141	79	162	177	42	.351	.390

2 LUCAS SIMS, RHP

BA GRADE

55 Risk: High

LGE	BF	SO%	BB%	HR/9
CAR	676	15.8	8.4	0.69

Born: May 10, 1994. **B-T:** R-R. **Ht.:** 6-2. **Wt.:** 195. **Drafted:** HS—Snellville, Ga., 2012 (1st round). **Signed by:** Brian Bridges.

Selected 21st overall in 2012, Sims had his workload restricted by Atlanta during his first two tastes of pro ball. He was the youngest player in the high Class A Carolina League on Opening Day 2014 and it showed with just 4.9 strikeouts per nine innings in the first three months, but he finished strong with a rate of 7.6 in July and August. The competitive Sims made impressive strides in his feel for pitching in the second half of 2014. An athletic pitcher who has fine-tuned his delivery, his best offering is a plus fastball that sits in the low to mid-90s and reaches 96 mph regularly. The pitch has good run, which creates lots of swings and misses. Sims uses the pitch on both sides of the plate and can overpower some hitters with his heater's explosiveness. His slider and curve often blend into a slurvy breaking ball in the upper 70s, and his improved command of the pitch contributed to his late-season success at Lynchburg. He has worked hard on his changeup since signing but shows an inconsistent feel for the pitch. While his overall control is solid, Sims needs to continue to improve his sequencing to get more strikeouts. Sims learned from his mistakes and became a better all-around pitcher. A potential No. 3 starter in the big leagues, he should make the jump to Double-A Mississippi in 2015.

Year	Club (League)	Class	W	L	ERA	G	GS	CG	SV	IP	H	HR	BB	SO	K/9	WHIP	AVG
2012	Braves (GCL)	R	0	0	1.29	3	3	0	0	7	2	1	1	10	12.9	0.43	.091
	Danville (APP)	R	2	4	4.33	8	8	0	0	27	26	2	12	29	9.7	1.41	.243
2013	Rome (SAL)	LoA	12	4	2.62	28	18	1	0	117	83	3	46	134	10.3	1.11	.203
2014	Lynchburg (CAR)	HiA	8	11	4.19	28	28	0	0	157	146	12	57	107	6.1	1.30	.247
Minor League Totals			22	19	3.54	67	57	1	0	307	257	18	116	280	8.2	1.21	.228

3 CHRISTIAN BETHANCOURT, C

BA GRADE

55 Risk: High

LGE	PA	BB%	SO%	ISO
IL	365	3.6	16.7	.125
NL	117	2.6	22.2	.027

Born: Sept. 2, 1991. **B-T:** R-R. **Ht.:** 6-2. **Wt.:** 215. **Signed:** Panama, 2008. **Signed by:** Luis Ortiz.

Bethancourt saw his first extended activity in the big leagues in 2014 after being hailed as the organization's catcher of the future for the past six seasons. The Panama native initially gained attention as a 12-year-old in the 2004 Little League World Series and signed with the Braves four years later for $600,000. He was called up in June and again in September, when he served as everyday catcher. Scouts have long raved about Bethancourt's tools behind the plate. He has plus arm strength with a quick release and outstanding carry and accuracy on his throws. He threw out 36 percent of basestealers at Triple-A Gwinnett. A good athlete with quick feet, he moves well but has a tendency to lose his focus by backhanding balls in the dirt, and he had 16 passed balls in 2014, including six in his short big league stint. Bethancourt's swing is quick and generates good bat speed with the ability to drive the ball. He is aggressive at the plate, struggles with strike-zone discipline and tends to swing early in the count instead of waiting for a pitch he can drive. He does make consistent contact, however, and he runs well on the basepaths. The Braves saw enough of Bethancourt in Atlanta last year to feel comfortable with him handling the catching responsibilities in 2015. His lack of plate discipline may hinder him at the plate, so he will need to excel defensively to win a majority share at the position.

Year	Club (League)	Class	AVG	G	AB	R	H	2B	3B	HR	RBI	BB	SO	SB	CS	OBP	SLG
2012	Mississippi (SL)	AA	.243	71	268	30	65	5	1	2	26	11	45	8	6	.275	.291
2013	Mississippi (SL)	AA	.277	90	358	42	99	21	0	12	45	16	57	11	7	.305	.436
	Atlanta (NL)	MAJ	.000	1	1	0	0	0	0	0	0	0	1	0	0	.000	.000
2014	Gwinnett (IL)	AAA	.283	91	343	33	97	17	1	8	48	13	61	7	1	.308	.408
	Atlanta (NL)	MAJ	.248	31	113	7	28	3	0	0	9	3	26	1	1	.274	.274
Major League Totals			.246	32	114	7	28	3	0	0	9	3	27	1	1	.271	.272
Minor League Totals			.270	539	2037	216	550	98	11	34	250	93	350	55	23	.300	.379

4 JASON HURSH, RHP

Born: Oct. 2, 1991. **B-T:** R-R. **Ht.:** 6-3. **Wt.:** 190. **Drafted:** Oklahoma State, 2013 (1st round). **Signed by:** Gerald Turner.

An unsigned 2010 sixth-round pick out of high school just north of Dallas, Hursh spurned the Pirates and went to Oklahoma State, where he had to have Tommy John surgery in 2012. The Braves had interest in him out of high school but correctly considered him unsignable. They took Hursh 31st overall in 2013 and pushed him to Double-A Mississippi a year later, when he earned the organization's pitcher of the year award. Hursh is a big, strong and durable pitcher who works quickly and throws on a downhill plane, producing quality low strikes. His fastball sits in the 91-93 mph range and touches 95 with armside run and occasional cutting action. His overhand curveball was inconsistent in 2014, but he showed the ability to change speeds with the pitch while throwing it for strikes. His changeup has a chance to develop into a plus offering with his above-average feel for the pitch. By pounding the lower part of the strike zone with his heavy artillery, Hursh forces batters to hit the ball on the ground and was among the minors' stingiest pitchers for home runs allowed. The Braves love Hursh's confident demeanor and his overall feel for pitching. With the Atlanta rotation projected to be stocked in 2015, Hursh should spend the year at Triple-A Gwinnett. Some scouts believe his future could be in the bullpen, which could get him to the big leagues earlier. If not he looks like a quality No. 4 starter.

BA GRADE

50 Risk: Medium

LGE	BF	SO%	BB%	HR/9
SL	615	13.5	7.0	0.30

Year	Club (League)	Class	W	L	ERA	G	GS	CG	SV	IP	H	HR	BB	SO	K/9	WHIP	AVG
2013	Rome (SAL)	LoA	1	1	0.67	9	9	0	0	27	20	1	10	15	5.0	1.11	.206
2014	Mississippi (SL)	AA	11	7	3.58	27	26	1	0	148	151	5	43	83	5.0	1.31	.272
Minor League Totals			12	8	3.13	36	35	1	0	175	171	6	53	98	5.0	1.28	.262

5 OZHAINO ALBIES, SS

Born: Jan. 7, 1997. **B-T:** B-R. **Ht.:** 5-9. **Wt.:** 150. **Signed:** Curacao, 2013. **Signed by:** Dargello Lodowica.

Unlike several other suitors, the Braves ignored Albies' small stature and signed him for $350,000 out of Curacao. In addition to making his professional debut in the U.S. in 2014 as a 17-year-old, he excelled while being named the top prospect in the Rookie-level Appalachian League, which he led in batting (.356) and on-base percentage (.429). Scouts and opponents alike rave about Albies' energy and ability. One of the youngest players in pro ball in 2014, he demonstrated an uncannily advanced feel for the game despite playing it at top speed. A natural top-of-the-lineup batter who should hit for a high average, Albies has a quick swing with plus bat speed from both sides of the plate. He stays inside the ball and makes consistent contact with his superior hand-eye coordination, yet he's strong enough to drive the ball from gap to gap. His strike-zone judgment is far beyond his years, and he keeps the ball out of the air in order to take advantage of his plus speed. Defensively, Albies has soft hands with above-average range at shortstop, which he pairs with a strong, accurate arm with a quick release that led to a league-average .950 fielding percentage in 2014. Albies has already progressed quickly and could continue to move at a rapid rate as he enters the full-season ranks. He will open 2015 at low Class A Rome.

BA GRADE

55 Risk: Extreme

LGE	PA	BB%	SO%	ISO
GCL	78	14.1	7.7	.048
APP	161	10.6	10.6	.096

Year	Club (League)	Class	AVG	G	AB	R	H	2B	3B	HR	RBI	BB	SO	SB	CS	OBP	SLG
2014	Braves (GCL)	R	.381	19	63	16	24	3	0	0	5	11	6	7	2	.481	.429
	Danville (APP)	R	.356	38	135	25	48	4	3	1	14	17	17	15	3	.429	.452
Minor League Totals			.364	57	198	41	72	7	3	1	19	28	23	22	5	.446	.444

6 BRAXTON DAVIDSON, OF

Born: June 18, 1996. **B-T:** L-L. **Ht.:** 6-2. **Wt.:** 210. **Drafted:** HS—Asheville, N.C., 2014 (1st round). **Signed by:** Billy Best.

After several strong performances on the showcase circuit in 2013, including a three-homer performance in the Tournament of Stars, Davidson was the 32nd overall pick in the 2014 draft. He started to drive the ball with consistency midway through his stint in the Rookie-level Gulf Coast League, where he ranked as the No. 12 prospect. Davidson's strength is his plus hit tool. He's a patient hitter with an advanced feel for the strike zone and has made noticeable improvements with his contact rate over the past year. Despite failing to hit a home run in his first taste of pro ball, Davidson has plus raw power to all fields. He's quick to the ball and uses his natural strength to drive pitches with authority from the left side of the plate. His on-base percentage projects to be high due to his ability to draw walks. His below-average speed plays higher due to his intelligence on the basepaths. Davidson made the shift from left to right field in instructional league and has enough arm strength to stay there. If not, he could return to his high school position of first base. The Braves will be patient with Davidson, who turned 18 two weeks after the draft. A potential 20-home run hitter, he will challenge for a spot at low Class A Rome in spring training.

BA GRADE

50 Risk: High

LGE	PA	BB%	SO%	ISO
GCL	140	15.7	22.9	.081
APP	46	19.6	21.7	.056

Year	Club (League)	Class	AVG	G	AB	R	H	2B	3B	HR	RBI	BB	SO	SB	CS	OBP	SLG
2014	Braves (GCL)	R	.243	37	111	23	27	7	1	0	8	22	32	0	0	.400	.324
	Danville (APP)	R	.167	13	36	1	6	2	0	0	3	9	10	0	0	.348	.222
Minor League Totals			.224	50	147	24	33	9	1	0	11	31	42	0	0	.387	.299

7 TYRELL JENKINS, RHP

Born: July 20, 1992. **B-T:** R-R. **Ht.:** 6-4. **Wt.:** 204. **Drafted:** HS—Henderson, Texas, 2010 (1st round supplemental). **Signed By:** Ralph Garr Jr. (Cardinals).

Jenkins signed for $1.3 million in 2010 when the Cardinals lured him away from a Baylor football scholarship, but injuries and slow development chipped away at his prospect stock ever since. He threw six no-hit innings in his 2014 debut in mid-June after he returned from shoulder surgery, then pitched well in the Arizona Fall League. The Braves acquired him from the Cardinals in the four-player deal headlined by Jason Heyward and Shelby Miller. Jenkins has athleticism and a fine pitcher's frame, as well as quality arm strength. His fastball remains a plus pitch, and though he hasn't shown consistent 96 mph velocity as he did pre-injury, he still sits at 92-93 with sinking and cutting life and hits 95 regularly. Shoulder problems have precluded Jenkins from ever pitching 100 innings in a season, and he had surgery in 2013 to repair lat-muscle damage. The lost development time has hampered Jenkins' command, and he still struggles with his release point

BA GRADE

50 Risk: High

LGE	BF	SO%	BB%	HR/9
FSL	309	13.3	7.4	0.73

and the consistency of his secondary stuff. His upper-70s curveball has power and above-average potential, while his average changeup has its moments when he trusts it, but his over-reliance on his fastball leads to high contact rates and below-average strikeout totals. Added to the 40-man roster in November, Jenkins gives the Braves an athletic starter with upside to go with significant durability questions. He'll get his first Double-A exposure in 2015 at Mississippi and still has a mid-rotation ceiling.

Year	Club (League)	Class	W	L	ERA	G	GS	CG	SV	IP	H	HR	BB	SO	K/9	WHIP	AVG
2012	Quad Cities (MWL)	LoA	4	4	5.14	19	19	0	0	82	84	5	36	80	8.7	1.46	.267
2013	Peoria (MWL)	LoA	4	4	4.74	10	10	2	0	49	51	4	24	34	6.2	1.52	.267
	Palm Beach (FSL)	HiA	0	0	4.50	3	3	0	0	10	13	0	1	6	5.4	1.40	.310
2014	Palm Beach (FSL)	HiA	6	5	3.28	13	13	0	0	74	74	6	23	41	5.0	1.31	.264
Minor League Totals			18	15	4.23	58	58	2	0	275	287	18	99	218	7.1	1.41	.273

8 JOHAN CAMARGO, SS

Born: Dec. 13, 1993. **B-T:** B-R. **Ht.:** 6-0. **Wt.:** 160. **Signed:** Panama, 2010.
Signed by: Luis Ortiz.

The Braves scout Panama as heavily as any team, and Camargo could follow in the footsteps of Christian Bethancourt and Randall Delgado to the big leagues. Camargo struggled early at low Class A Rome in 2014 before rebounding and earning a late-season promotion to high Class A Lynchburg. Camargo is a steady, fluid player with outstanding hand-eye coordination. He handles the bat well while using a disciplined line-drive approach to spray the ball to all fields from both sides of the plate. He has an advanced knowledge and feel for the strike zone, makes consistent contact and rarely strikes out. His power is lacking, but he has worked hard to add strength to drive the ball more often as his game develops. He has soft, steady hands and easy, smooth actions on defense, which allow him to make plays in the hole and up the middle consistently. His speed and quickness both rate as fringe-average, but his anticipation, body control and knowledge of the game should enable him to remain at shortstop at higher levels.

BA GRADE	
50	Risk: High

LGE	PA	BB%	SO%	ISO
SAL	478	7.1	10.5	.057
CAR	62	1.6	21.0	.086

He has above-average arm strength and makes accurate throws with good carry. The Braves neglected to add Camargo to the 40-man roster becaue they believed he's far enough away offensively to be unworthy of Rule 5 draft attention. He will most likely open the 2015 season back in the Carolina League at Atlanta's new affiliate in Carolina, with a mid-summer promotion to Double-A Mississippi a possibility.

Year	Club (League)	Class	AVG	G	AB	R	H	2B	3B	HR	RBI	BB	SO	SB	CS	OBP	SLG
2012	Braves (DSL)	R	.343	59	198	38	68	14	1	2	26	25	27	6	3	.433	.455
2013	Danville (APP)	R	.294	57	228	28	67	7	4	0	14	18	31	3	3	.359	.360
2014	Rome (SAL)	LoA	.267	115	420	53	112	16	4	0	40	34	50	7	6	.320	.324
	Lynchburg (CAR)	HiA	.259	17	58	7	15	2	0	1	6	1	13	0	0	.262	.345
Minor League Totals			.290	248	904	126	262	39	9	3	86	78	121	16	12	.352	.363

9 GARRETT FULENCHEK, RHP

Born: June 7, 1996. **B-T:** R-R. **Ht.:** 6-4. **Wt.:** 205. **Drafted:** HS—Howe, Texas, 2014 (2nd round). **Signed by:** Gerald Turner.

A Dallas Baptist recruit, Fulenchek kept getting better in his final prep season. He first emerged as a potential top pick during the latter part of 2013 with a solid showing in the Perfect Game World Wood Bat Championship, then had a strong senior spring. The Braves signed him for $1 million as a second-round selection in 2014. A former basketball player with long arms, strong legs and above-average athleticism, Fulenchek has low mileage on his arm and is considered raw by some scouts. The righthander is a power pitcher with a quick arm and impressive mound presence who works off his heavy fastball that sits in the low 90s and touches 95 mph. His heater features above-average life with armside run and natural sinking action from his high three-quarters arm slot. He also throws a mid-80s slider that should develop into at least an average offering and a below-average changeup that needs work in order for him to remain in the rotation. Fulenchek's delivery

BA GRADE	
55	Risk: Extreme

LGE	BF	SO%	BB%	HR/9
GCL	169	17.2	13.0	0.48

requires some effort, and he spent time in the Rookie-level Gulf Coast League trying to iron out his mechanics, which should improve his control. The Braves like to challenge young players and will give Fulenchek the opportunity to jump to low Class A Rome to open the 2015 campaign. A potential mid-rotation starter in the big leagues, he likely will need plenty of development time.

Year	Club (League)	Class	W	L	ERA	G	GS	CG	SV	IP	H	HR	BB	SO	K/9	WHIP	AVG
2014	Braves (GCL)	R	0	7	4.78	12	10	0	0	38	34	2	22	29	6.9	1.49	.238
Minor League Totals			0	7	4.78	12	10	0	0	38	34	2	22	29	6.9	1.49	.238

10 KYLE KUBITZA, 3B

Born: July 15, 1990. **B-T:** L-R. **Ht.:** 6-3. **Wt.:** 215. **Drafted:** Texas State, 2011 (3rd round). **Signed by:** John Barron.

Few players have developed more impressively over the last few years in the organization than Kubitza, whose brother Aaron pitches in the Tigers system. The highest-drafted position player in Texas State history blossomed in his third full pro season in 2014 at Double-A Mississippi. In addition to hitting 35 points above his career average, he led the Southern League in on-base percentage (.405) and walks (55), placed second in triples (11) and ranked fourth in runs (76). A fiery player, Kubitza combines a smooth line-drive swing from the left side with one of the best eyes at the plate in the organization. His power has increased with experience and he uses his quick wrists to drive the ball in the gaps. He can be exploited with a minor hitch in his swing, and he can be too patient with inconsistent umpires, leading to high strikeout totals. Though not a quick-twitch athlete, Kubitza runs well with excellent instincts on the basepaths. He has one of the strongest infield arms in the game, with soft hands that suit him at third base. He moves well to his left but tends to boot the occasional routine ball. Kubitza should open the 2015 season at Triple-A Gwinnett. Scouts are mixed on whether he will be an everyday third baseman or more of a bench bat, but he could get his first shot in Atlanta by the end of the year.

BA GRADE		
45	**Risk:**	**Medium**

LGE	PA	BB%	SO%	ISO
SL	529	14.6	25.1	.175

Year	Club (League)	Class	AVG	G	AB	R	H	2B	3B	HR	RBI	BB	SO	SB	CS	OBP	SLG
2012	Rome (SAL)	LoA	.239	128	448	68	107	24	9	9	59	73	127	18	11	.349	.393
2013	Lynchburg (CAR)	HiA	.260	132	435	75	113	28	6	12	57	80	132	8	16	.380	.434
2014	Mississippi (SL)	AA	.295	132	440	76	130	31	11	8	55	77	133	21	6	.405	.470
Minwor League Totals			.271	436	1485	255	402	99	29	30	205	254	430	56	36	.381	.437

11 ARODYS VIZCAINO, RHP

BA GRADE		
50	**Risk:**	**High**

Born: Nov. 13, 1990. **B-T:** R-R. **Ht.:** 6-0. **Wt.:** 190. **Signed:** Dominican Republic, 2007. **Signed By:** Alfredo Dominguez (Yankees).

Originally signed for $800,000 by the Yankees, Vizcaino made his major league debut for the Braves in 2011, but he missed the next two seasons recovering from Tommy John surgery, with a May 2013 setback following a second surgery to remove debris from his elbow. He's been traded three times, the latest bringing him back to the Braves from the Cubs in a deal that included Tommy La Stella and four international bonus slots also changing hands. When healthy, Vizcaino still has premium stuff that plays at the back of a bullpen in high-leverage situations. He retains two swing-and-miss offerings, with a plus-plus fastball that reached 99 mph in his September big league work and sits in the 95-98 mph range. His fastball has above-average life as well, with run and sink, and he uses it aggressively. Vizcaino's hard, mid-80s curveball also still can be a plus pitch. He's still regaining his feel for the strike zone, though, and he has had worse control out of the bullpen than he had as a starter. He occasionally uses a firm, almost vestigial changeup from his starter days. Vizcaino's durability remains his biggest issue. If he can stay off the disabled list, he should give the Braves another set-up option in front of Craig Kimbrel in 2015.

Year	Club (League)	Class	W	L	ERA	G	GS	CG	SV	IP	H	HR	BB	SO	K/9	WHIP	AVG
2012	Did not play—Injured																
2013	Did not play—Injured																
2014	Daytona (FSL)	HiA	0	0	1.00	9	0	0	1	9	6	0	4	10	10.0	1.11	.194
	Tennessee (SL)	AA	1	1	2.63	14	0	0	1	14	7	1	3	16	10.5	0.73	.149
	Iowa (PCL)	AAA	0	0	5.40	17	0	0	0	18	25	1	11	16	7.9	1.96	.325
	Chicago (NL)	MAJ	0	0	5.40	5	0	0	0	5	5	1	3	4	7.2	1.60	.263
Major League Totals			1	1	4.84	22	0	0	0	22	21	2	12	21	8.5	1.48	.244
Minor League Totals			20	16	2.99	105	50	0	2	310	271	18	86	321	9.3	1.15	.229

12 CHASEN SHREVE, LHP

BA GRADE		
45	**Risk:**	**Low**

Born: July 12 1990. **B-T:** L-L. **Ht.:** 6-3. **Wt.:** 190. **Drafted:** JC of Southern Nevada, 2011 (11th round). **Signed by:** Bump Merriweather.

Shreve's older brother Colby was an eighth-round pick of the Braves in 2007 who didn't sign. The Phillies signed him for $400,000 a year later and he reached Double-A before being released in 2014. Chasen, who attended JC of Southern Nevada with Bryce Harper, had a breakthrough 2014. His control has improved steadily since signing with Atlanta, and his overall stuff has continued to get better as he has added strength to his tall, solid frame. Shreve threw harder than ever in 2014, reaching 92-94 mph as he stopped cruising and began to throw his hardest with every pitch. As a result, his strikeout rate jumped, and he earned a callup from Double-A Mississippi to the majors in July. He made a stopover at Triple-A Gwinnett before returning to the majors in September. Shreve's funky lower arm angle creates deception and generates solid movement on all of his offerings. His best pitch is a plus changeup that features outstanding fade and depth and has proven effective against righthanders at higher levels. He mixes it with a low-80s slider and maintained quality stuff in back-to-back outings. Shreve pounds the zone and has a good chance to earn a full-time spot in Atlanta's 2015 bullpen.

Year	Club (League)	Class	W	L	ERA	G	GS	CG	SV	IP	H	HR	BB	SO	K/9	WHIP	AVG
2012	Mississippi (SL)	AA	2	1	3.93	11	0	0	0	18	17	1	16	16	7.9	1.80	.243
	Lynchburg (CAR)	HiA	4	4	2.15	32	0	0	1	46	44	2	17	41	8.0	1.33	.262
2013	Mississippi (SL)	AA	3	1	4.43	36	0	0	0	43	43	1	22	28	5.9	1.52	.272
	Lynchburg (CAR)	HiA	0	1	2.75	14	0	0	2	20	15	1	8	15	6.9	1.17	.197
2014	Mississippi (SL)	AA	3	2	2.48	36	0	0	7	54	42	2	9	76	12.6	0.94	.213
	Gwinnett (IL)	AAA	2	1	3.72	10	0	0	2	10	9	2	3	11	10.2	1.24	.273
	Atlanta (NL)	MAJ	0	0	0.73	15	0	0	0	12	10	0	3	15	10.9	1.05	.217
Major League Totals			0	0	0.73	15	0	0	0	12	10	0	3	15	10.9	1.05	.217
Minor League Totals			21	16	3.22	181	0	0	17	277	263	13	104	275	8.9	1.33	.254

13 SHAE SIMMONS, RHP

BA GRADE

45 Risk: Medium

Born: Sept. 3, 1990. **B-T:** R-R. **Ht.:** 5-9. **Wt.:** 180. **Drafted:** Southeast Missouri State, 2012 (22nd round). **Signed by:** Terry Tripp.

Former scouting director Paul Snyder used to encourage his scouts to "find a big leaguer" regardless of the round a player was taken. The Braves did just that with Simmons, an undersized reliever who sped from the 22nd round in 2012 to the majors in two years. Simmons went 14-for-14 in save opportunities and did not allow a run in 19 of his 20 Double-A Mississippi outings prior to being promoted to Atlanta at the end of May. He continued to have success in the big leagues before shoulder discomfort sidelined him in late July. Simmons is a classic power pitcher with a heavy fastball that sits at 95-97 mph and touches 100. He also has an above-average, yet inconsistent, slider that is unhittable when he generates the proper tilt. He mixes in an overhand curveball to keep hitters off-balance. Simmons' delivery requires some effort, and his 5-foot-9 frame already had raised questions about his durability. The Braves proceeded cautiously with his shoulder ailment last year. If healthy, Simmons will return to the Atlanta bullpen in 2015 as a set-up man.

Year	Club (League)	Class	W	L	ERA	G	GS	CG	SV	IP	H	HR	BB	SO	K/9	WHIP	AVG
2012	Braves (GCL)	R	2	0	0.00	7	1	0	0	14	5	0	8	15	9.4	0.91	.109
	Danville (APP)	R	0	2	3.48	9	0	0	2	10	11	0	8	21	18.3	1.84	.256
2013	Rome (SAL)	LoA	1	1	1.49	39	0	0	24	42	26	0	15	66	14.0	0.97	.169
	Mississippi (SL)	AA	0	0	2.45	11	0	0	0	11	5	0	7	16	13.1	1.09	.139
2014	Mississippi (SL)	AA	0	0	0.78	20	0	0	14	23	15	0	6	30	11.7	0.91	.183
	Atlanta (NL)	MAJ	1	2	2.91	26	0	0	1	22	15	1	11	23	9.6	1.20	.197
	Gwinnett (IL)	AAA	0	1	36.00	2	2	0	0	1	3	0	2	1	9.0	5.00	.600
Major League Totals			1	2	2.91	26	0	0	1	22	15	1	11	23	9.6	1.20	.197
Minor League Totals			3	4	1.76	88	3	0	40	102	65	0	46	149	13.1	1.09	.178

14 MAURICIO CABRERA, RHP

BA GRADE

50 Risk: High

Born: Sept. 22, 1993. **B-T:** R-R. **Ht.:** 6-2. **Wt.:** 180. **Signed:** Dominican Republic, 2010. **Signed by:** Roberto Aquino.

Cabrera signed for $400,000 in 2010, led the Rookie-level Appalachian League with an opponent average of .213 in 2012, then ranked as the No. 10 prospect in the South Atlantic League in 2013. He often struggled at high Class A Lynchburg in 2014 when he missed two months with forearm discomfort before returning in July and putting together a productive stint in instructional league. Cabrera continued to have difficulty with his control, walking 5.9 batters per nine innings in 19 appearances. He has a live arm that generates a mid-90s fastball and has reached triple digits. His slurvy curveball shows promise but lacks consistency, and his changeup has been little more than a show-me offering. Cabrera moved to the bullpen upon his midseason return. He has a chance to dominate if he improves his strike-throwing ability. A return to high Class A seems likely for 2015.

Year	Club (League)	Class	W	L	ERA	G	GS	CG	SV	IP	H	HR	BB	SO	K/9	WHIP	AVG
2012	Danville (APP)	R	2	2	2.97	12	12	0	0	58	45	2	23	48	7.5	1.18	.213
2013	Rome (SAL)	LoA	3	8	4.18	24	24	1	0	131	118	3	71	107	7.3	1.44	.243
2014	Braves (GCL)	R	0	0	6.75	3	2	0	0	4	3	0	2	3	6.8	1.25	.214
	Lynchburg (CAR)	HiA	1	1	5.59	19	3	0	0	29	24	1	19	26	8.1	1.48	.226
Minor League Totals			7	16	4.13	77	50	1	0	274	241	9	139	220	7.2	1.39	.236

15 WES PARSONS, RHP

BA GRADE
45 Risk: High

Born: Sept. 9, 1992. **B-T:** R-R. **Ht.:** 6-5. **Wt.:** 190. **Signed:** Jackson State (Tenn.) CC, 2012 (NDFA). **Signed by:** Terry Tripp.

The Braves are one of the more successful teams when it comes to signing nondrafted pitchers. The tradition dates to Kerry Ligtenberg in the mid-1990s and was solidified with recent big leaguer Brandon Beachy. Parsons could join that club after being bypassed by every major league organization coming out of high school as well as after his one year at Jackson State (Tenn.) CC, before Atlanta signed him from the Northwoods League in 2012 for $200,000. Displaying a free-and-easy delivery that he repeats well, Parsons uses his 6-foot-5 height to his advantage by pitching downhill. He has above-average movement on his low-90s fastball that touches 95 mph. His slider has mid-80s power but is more of a groundball pitch than a swing-and-miss offering. He's made strides with his inconsistent changeup. Parsons missed two weeks in July with biceps tendinitis and pitched poorly when affected by the injury (7.98 ERA in July and August). His arm has low mileage after he focused on golf during much of his high school career, and he may still offer some projection. He should remain in the rotation in 2015, moving up to Double-A Mississippi, but could move to the bullpen if his changeup doesn't improve.

Year	Club (League)	Class	W	L	ERA	G	GS	CG	SV	IP	H	HR	BB	SO	K/9	WHIP	AVG
2013	Rome (SAL)	LoA	7	7	2.63	19	19	1	0	110	91	5	21	101	8.3	1.02	.224
2014	Lynchburg (CAR)	HiA	4	7	5.00	23	23	0	0	113	119	10	34	96	7.6	1.35	.271
Minor League Totals			11	14	3.83	42	42	1	0	223	210	15	55	197	8.0	1.19	.248

16 ALEC GROSSER, RHP

BA GRADE
50 Risk: Extreme

Born: Jan. 12, 1995. **B-T:** R-R. **Ht.:** 6-3. **Wt.:** 1990. **Drafted:** HS— Alexandria, Va., 2013 (11th round). **Signed by:** Lyle Kerns.

A high school quarterback at T.C. Williams who emerged late in the draft process due to his limited experience on the mound, Grosser was a George Mason commit who signed for $400,000 after slipping through the first 10 rounds of the draft in 2013. The raw righthander made the most of his initial professional instruction and was named the No. 8 prospect in the Rookie-level Appalachian League in 2014. Grosser is an excellent athlete with a strong body who competes well with great composure on the mound. His fastball sits in the low 90s and touches 93 mph with above-average sinking action that generated the highest groundout/airout ratio (2.71) among starters in the Appy League. His slider is a heavy offering in the low- to mid-80s and gives him two potential plus pitches as he gains experience. His changeup improved as the season progressed but still has a ways to go. Grosser has ironed out some mechanical issues, which led to better control after his first few outings in 2014. The development of his changeup will play a major role in whether he sticks in the rotation. Grosser should make the jump to low Class A Rome in 2015.

Year	Club (League)	Class	W	L	ERA	G	GS	CG	SV	IP	H	HR	BB	SO	K/9	WHIP	AVG
2013	Braves (GCL)	R	1	3	2.15	13	5	0	0	29	12	0	15	23	7.1	0.92	.125
2014	Danville (APP)	R	4	3	3.68	13	12	0	0	64	60	0	22	63	8.9	1.29	.244
Minor League Totals			5	6	3.19	26	17	0	0	93	72	0	37	86	8.3	1.17	.211

17 TANNER MURPHY, C

BA GRADE
50 Risk: Extreme

Born: Feb. 27, 1995. **B-T:** R-R. **Ht.:** 6-2. **Wt.:** 215. **Drafted:** HS—Malden, Mo., 2013 (4th round). **Signed by:** Terry Tripp.

The Braves wanted to improve their catching depth in the 2013 draft and achieved that feat in part by signing fourth-rounder Murphy for $250,000. Atlanta liked his solid yet projectable frame and raw strength that started to show itself last season at Rookie-level Danville. Murphy split his time in high school between pitching and catching and was clocked in the low 90s off the mound. His footwork has improved behind the plate but remains a work in progress in order to take full advantage of his above-average arm. Murphy moves well as far as blocking balls is concerned and shows a take-charge approach as a leader of the defense. His plus raw power should generate 15-20 home runs annually at higher levels. He has strong hands and forearms and shows a good feel for the strike zone. He has worked to shorten his swing, cutting his strikeout rate from his 2013 pro debut, and has developed more of a line-drive swing path. Murphy has a long road ahead but has the tools to develop into a major league catcher. He should move up to low Class A Rome in 2015.

Year	Club (League)	Class	AVG	G	AB	R	H	2B	3B	HR	RBI	BB	SO	SB	CS	OBP	SLG
2013	Braves (GCL)	R	.227	32	97	7	22	3	0	0	8	12	34	5	0	.313	.258
2014	Danville (APP)	R	.242	50	157	21	38	8	0	5	19	30	38	2	1	.361	.389
Minor League Totals			.236	82	254	28	60	11	0	5	27	42	72	7	1	.343	.339

18 CODY MARTIN, RHP

BA GRADE

40 Risk: Low

Born: Sept. 4, 1989. **B-T:** R-R. **Ht.:** 6-2. **Wt.:** 225. **Drafted:** Gonzaga, 2011 (7th round). **Signed by:** Brett Evert.

Martin has spent most of the past three minor league campaigns as a starter after a career closing at Gonzaga. Martin has an excellent feel for pitching while mixing his four fringy-to-average offerings with aplomb to keep hitters off-balance. His below-average fastball has good late movement while sitting in the 86-90 mph range, reaching 92. He pairs the heater with a hard slider in the mid-80s that serves as his strikeout pitch. Martin throws a curveball and changeup with late action for strikes. His mechanics can get a little off-kilter on occasion, but he tends to correct the problem quickly. He's an extreme flyball pitcher. The Braves didn't protect Martin on the 40-man roster, and he wasn't selected in the Rule 5 draft. If he doesn't earn a spot with Atlanta, he'll head to Triple-A Gwinnett for a third straight season in 2015.

Year	Club (League)	Class	W	L	ERA	G	GS	CG	SV	IP	H	HR	BB	SO	K/9	WHIP	AVG
2012	Lynchburg (CAR)	HiA	12	7	2.93	22	19	1	0	107	93	7	34	123	10.3	1.18	.235
2013	Mississippi (SL)	AA	3	3	2.82	16	11	0	0	67	63	3	27	71	9.5	1.34	.250
	Gwinnett (IL)	AAA	3	4	3.49	13	11	1	1	70	59	6	31	66	8.5	1.29	.232
2014	Gwinnett (IL)	AAA	7	8	3.52	27	26	1	1	156	151	17	56	142	8.2	1.33	.254
Minor League Totals			26	22	3.07	100	67	3	11	433	386	35	153	451	9.4	1.24	.240

19 WILLIAMS PEREZ, RHP

BA GRADE

45 Risk: Medium

Born: May 21, 1991. **B-T:** R-R. **Ht.:** 6-1. **Wt.:** 230. **Signed:** Venezuela, 2009. **Signed by:** Rolando Petit/Carlos Torres.

Perez has put together consecutive strong seasons. With Double-A Mississippi in 2014 he allowed two earned runs or fewer in 19 of his 25 starts, ranking second in the Southern League with a 2.91 ERA. Perez's success is centered on his ability to work off his low-90s, two-seam fastball with good late action. He has made major strides in getting ahead in the count and using the inner half. He also throws an above-average changeup with sink as well, and he spots his below-average slider. Perez keeps hitters off-balance with his willingness to throw any of his three offerings at any time in the count while using both sides of the plate. He pitches to contact and relies on the plus movement of his pitches that prevents hard contact. The potential back-end starter should spend most of 2015 at Triple-A Gwinnett.

Year	Club (League)	Class	W	L	ERA	G	GS	CG	SV	IP	H	HR	BB	SO	K/9	WHIP	AVG
2012	Danville (APP)	R	4	3	4.15	13	9	0	1	56	54	5	9	54	8.6	1.12	.245
2013	Rome (SAL)	LoA	5	4	4.24	14	13	1	0	70	73	5	18	59	7.6	1.30	.274
	Lynchburg (CAR)	HiA	6	2	2.62	9	9	0	0	55	50	4	18	47	7.7	1.24	.239
2014	Mississippi (SL)	AA	7	6	2.91	26	25	0	0	133	119	4	39	94	6.4	1.19	.241
Minor League Totals			28	23	3.43	104	84	1	1	477	452	26	124	392	7.4	1.21	.251

20 JUAN JAIME, RHP

BA GRADE

45 Risk: High

Born: Aug. 2, 1987. **B-T:** R-R. **Ht.:** 6-2. **Wt.:** 235. **Signed:** Dominican Republic, 2004. **Signed by:** Ismael Cruz (Expos).

Jaime originally signed with the Expos but didn't make his major league debut until 10 years later. He required Tommy John surgery in 2010 and missed two full seasons. The Braves signed him in August 2011 following his release from the Diamondbacks, then moved him to the bullpen full time. He has struck out 13.8 batters per nine innings since then. Jaime can dominate with an upper-90s fastball. He just doesn't throw enough strikes with it, having walked 6.5 per nine as a Brave. His effortful delivery features recoil and his fastball lacks life. He mixes in an average changeup that can be effective, and he offers a slurvy curveball. Jaime is yet another middle relief option for Atlanta's 2015 bullpen.

Year	Club (League)	Class	W	L	ERA	G	GS	CG	SV	IP	H	HR	BB	SO	K/9	WHIP	AVG
2012	Lynchburg (CAR)	HiA	1	3	3.16	42	0	0	18	51	31	4	33	73	12.8	1.25	.173
2013	Mississippi (SL)	AA	2	5	4.07	35	0	0	0	42	30	1	28	70	15.0	1.38	.201
2014	Gwinnett (IL)	AAA	1	0	3.51	43	0	0	18	41	27	1	36	63	13.8	1.54	.181
	Atlanta (NL)	MAJ	0	0	5.84	16	0	0	0	12	14	1	9	18	13.1	1.86	.280
Major League Totals			0	0	5.84	16	0	0	0	12	14	1	9	18	13.1	1.86	.280
Minor League Totals			15	11	3.01	171	14	1	37	260	166	10	179	366	12.7	1.33	.180

21 MAX POVSE, RHP

BA GRADE

45 Risk: High

Born: Aug. 23, 1993. **B-T:** R-R. **Ht.:** 6-7. **Wt.:** 220. **Drafted:** UNC Greensboro, 2014 (3rd round). **Signed by:** Billy Best.

Povse spent three seasons at UNC Greensboro. He added nearly 40 pounds to his frame in college and saw his fastball velocity increase from 86-89 mph to 90-93. He had a durable but inconsistent career, posting a 5.38 ERA during an era of declining offense, but was a third-round pick in 2014 who signed for $425,000 nonetheless. Povse has good athleticism and repeats his delivery well. His fastball has plus sinking action and touches 95 mph. His low- to mid-80s slider has the potential to be a solid-average offering and he does a good job of generating groundballs with the pitch. Povse's fringy changeup needs added depth in order to prevent him from being vulnerable against lefthanders. After a solid pro debut at Rookie-level Danville in 2014, Povse should move up to low Class A Rome in 2015.

Year	Club (League)	Class	W	L	ERA	G	GS	CG	SV	IP	H	HR	BB	SO	K/9	WHIP	AVG
2014	Danville (APP)	R	4	2	3.42	12	11	0	0	47	42	1	11	37	7.0	1.12	.235
Minor League Totals			4	2	3.42	12	11	0	0	47	42	1	11	37	7.0	1.12	.235

22 VICTOR REYES, OF

BA GRADE
50 Risk: Extreme

Born: Oct. 5, 1994. **B-T:** B-R. **Ht.:** 6-3. **Wt.:** 190. **Signed:** Venezuela, 2011. **Signed by:** Rolando Petit.

Reyes was the Braves' top international acquisition in 2011 when he signed for $365,000. In his first full-season assignment in 2014, he hit well against righthanders on a weak low Class A Rome club before a lower-leg infection cut his campaign short in mid-July. Reyes has a disciplined and patient approach and covers the plate well without expanding the zone. He generates above-average bat speed and drives the ball into the gaps when he keeps his weight back. With his long arms, he needs to stay inside the ball to keep from getting beat on pitches on the inner half. A lean and lanky player, Reyes is still maturing and growing into his body. The Braves expected him to hit for power upon signing him but that tool has yet to materialize. Reyes moved to right field in 2104 and performed well, displaying good athleticism and an above-average arm with solid carry on his throws. He likely will begin 2015 at high Class A Carolina.

Year	Club (League)	Class	AVG	G	AB	R	H	2B	3B	HR	RBI	BB	SO	SB	CS	OBP	SLG
2012	Braves (DSL)	R	.296	52	162	40	48	3	0	0	33	31	39	12	6	.418	.315
2013	Braves (GCL)	R	.357	31	112	22	40	8	1	0	21	12	20	5	1	.414	.446
	Danville (APP)	R	.321	18	81	12	26	3	0	0	4	3	9	0	0	.345	.358
2014	Rome (SAL)	LoA	.259	89	332	32	86	13	0	0	34	24	58	12	7	.309	.298
Minor League Totals			.291	190	687	106	200	27	1	0	92	70	126	29	14	.359	.333

23 TODD CUNNINGHAM, OF

BA GRADE
40 Risk: Medium

Born: March 20, 1989. **B-T:** B-R. **Ht.:** 6-0. **Wt.:** 200. **Drafted:** Jacksonville State, 2010 (2nd round). **Signed by:** Brian Bridges.

The Braves know what they have in Cunningham, who made his major league debut in 2013 and has spent most of the last two seasons at Triple-A Gwinnett. He performed better in repeating the assignment. Cunningham makes consistent contact with a smooth, compact swing from both sides of the plate. He has below-average power but will take a walk and knows his role whether he leads off or bats second. An excellent bunter, he had 13 sacrifice bunts in 2014 and is proficient at executing the hit-and-run. He's an above-average runner who can steal a base, and a solid-average defender in center field—and he grades as plus in left field—but with below-average arm strength that precludes him from right field. His arm accuracy, though, helped him rack up 11 assists in 2014. Cunningham fits best as an extra outfielder.

Year	Club (League)	Class	AVG	G	AB	R	H	2B	3B	HR	RBI	BB	SO	SB	CS	OBP	SLG
2012	Mississippi (SL)	AA	.309	120	466	77	144	23	6	3	51	38	51	24	8	.364	.403
2013	Atlanta (NL)	MAJ	.250	8	8	2	2	0	0	0	0	0	3	0	0	.250	.250
	Gwinnett (IL)	AAA	.265	116	427	60	113	13	5	2	38	41	62	20	7	.342	.333
2014	Gwinnett (IL)	AAA	.287	120	470	59	135	28	2	8	58	35	79	19	8	.347	.406
Major League Totals			.250	8	8	2	2	0	0	0	0	0	3	0	0	.250	.250
Minor League Totals			.278	512	1939	289	540	85	21	18	191	162	274	85	33	.349	.372

24 CHAD SOBOTKA, RHP

BA GRADE
50 Risk: Extreme

Born: July 10, 1993. **B-T:** R-R. **Ht.:** 6-6. **Wt.:** 195. **Drafted:** South Carolina-Upstate, 2014 (4th round). **Signed by:** Billy Best.

Sobotka did not pitch in 2014 after suffering a back injury in February, but the Braves thought enough of the tall righthander's potential to draft him in the fourth round and sign him for $400,000. At his best, Sobotka repeats his delivery well despite his tall, lanky body. His frame projects to add needed size and strength. He throws both a two-seam and four-seam fastball and employs different arm slots. His two-seam heater has plus movement, which leads to command issues. He has shown the potential for a plus slider and will need to develop that pitch as well as a changeup in order to remain a starter at higher levels.

Sobotka will enter 2015 having not pitched competitively in more than a year, though he looked good during instructional league while touching 95 mph. Provided he is healthy in spring training, Sobotka should begin his pro career at low Class A Rome.

Year	Club (League)	Class	W	L	ERA	G	GS	CG	SV	IP	H	HR	BB	SO	K/9	WHIP	AVG
2014	Did not play—Injured																

25 DANIEL CASTRO, SS/2B

BA GRADE 40 Risk: Medium

Born: Nov. 14, 1992. **B-T:** R-R. **Ht.:** 5-11. **Wt.:** 175. **Signed:** Mexico, 2009. **Signed by:** Manuel Samaniego.

Castro spent two seasons playing in the Dominican Summer League after signing with the Braves, but then he returned to his native Mexico to play a year and a half with Saltillo. He batted higher than .300 in Mexico and earned all-star honors in 2013 prior to making his U.S. debut at high Class A Lynchburg that season. Castro took over as Lynchburg's shortstop in 2014, while Jose Peraza moved to second base. Castro does a good job of barreling pitches with his compact, line-drive stroke from the right side, and while he lacks home run power, he has some doubles pop. He is a smart baserunner but has fringy speed. He shows soft, steady hands on defense with good footwork. He moves well and positions himself correctly to make plays. His accuracy and the carry on his throws help his average arm play up. Castro profiles as a utility infielder. After passing unselected through the Rule 5 draft, Castro should return to Mississippi.

Year	Club (League)	Class	AVG	G	AB	R	H	2B	3B	HR	RBI	BB	SO	SB	CS	OBP	SLG
2012	Saltillo (MEX)	AAA	.291	60	117	22	34	3	3	3	18	3	19	0	1	.308	.444
2013	Saltillo (MEX)	AAA	.312	80	282	49	88	15	3	8	38	13	36	6	0	.339	.472
	Lynchburg (CAR)	HiA	.284	26	88	10	25	1	1	0	7	7	6	3	1	.337	.318
2014	Lynchburg (CAR)	HiA	.292	70	257	33	75	16	3	1	34	10	20	7	4	.320	.389
	Mississippi (SL)	AA	.277	51	173	23	48	9	1	4	20	5	18	2	1	.300	.410
Minor League Totals			.273	361	1163	173	317	53	12	16	136	68	129	30	17	.315	.380

26 DAN WINKLER, RHP

BA GRADE 50 Risk: Extreme

Born: Feb. 2, 1990. **B-T:** R-R. **Ht.:** 6-2. **Wt.:** 210. **Drafted:** Central Florida, 2011 (20th round). **Signed by:** John Cedarburg (Rockies).

Winkler was selected by the Braves in the major league phase of the Rule 5 draft, so Atlanta needs to keep him in the majors leagues all year or offer him back to the Rockies. That's a likely outcome because of an injury wrinkle. After leading the minors with 175 strikeouts in 2013, Winkler dominated the Texas League until he had Tommy John surgery on July 1. His unusual delivery creates deception and makes his ordinary stuff play much better. He has a low three-quarters arm slot with an inverted elbow in the back of his arm swing, which helps conceal the ball. He pitches at 88-90 mph and touches 92 with a fastball he commands well. Winkler began throwing a cutter, and he commands it better than his slider, enabling him to bore the pitch in on lefties. Winkler's changeup is effective. He's an extreme flyball pitcher, which could fit better at Turner Field than at Coors Field.

Year	Club (League)	Class	W	L	ERA	G	GS	CG	SV	IP	H	HR	BB	SO	K/9	WHIP	AVG
2012	Asheville (SAL)	LoA	11	10	4.46	25	25	0	0	145	152	16	47	136	8.4	1.37	.269
2013	Modesto (CAL)	HiA	12	5	2.97	22	22	0	0	130	84	15	37	152	10.5	0.93	.184
	Tulsa (TL)	AA	1	2	3.04	5	5	0	0	27	23	3	10	23	7.8	1.24	.240
2014	Tulsa (TL)	AA	5	2	1.41	12	12	1	0	70	33	5	17	71	9.1	0.71	.139
Minor League Totals			33	22	3.35	76	76	1	0	430	356	45	130	447	9.4	1.13	.224

27 CARLOS SALAZAR, RHP

BA GRADE 45 Risk: High

Born: Nov. 23, 1994. **B-T:** R-R. **Ht.:** 6-0. **Wt.:** 200. **Drafted:** HS— Kerman, Calif., 2013 (3rd round). **Signed by:** Brett Evert.

Salazar was one of the hardest-throwing high school pitchers available in the 2013 draft, and the Braves coaxed him from his Fresno State commitment with a $625,000 bonus. After limiting Salazar to 13 innings in his pro debut, Atlanta pushed him to low Class A Rome to open 2014 and watched him struggle. He walked more than he struck out and was demoted to Rookie-level Danville, shifting to the bullpen. Salazar regained his confidence and held Appalachian League hitters to a .147 average. While his control is lacking, Salazar has the raw ability to succeed. His fastball sits at 92-94 mph, has touched 97 and shows excellent late life. Through long hours with the Braves coaches, his curveball and changeup have shown flashes of potential. Salazar lacks physical projection, though he has present strength and velocity. The development of his secondary offerings will determine whether he starts or relieves. Salazar will try Rome again in 2015.

Year	Club (League)	Class	W	L	ERA	G	GS	CG	SV	IP	H	HR	BB	SO	K/9	WHIP	AVG
2013	Braves (GCL)	R	0	3	6.92	8	4	0	0	13	18	0	5	14	9.7	1.77	.321
2014	Rome (SAL)	LoA	1	6	10.60	10	10	0	0	36	47	2	38	27	6.8	2.38	.320
	Danville (APP)	R	2	1	2.51	17	0	0	0	29	15	0	18	34	10.7	1.15	.147
Minor League Totals			3	10	6.98	35	14	0	0	77	80	2	61	75	8.7	1.82	.262

28 AARON NORTHCRAFT, RHP

BA GRADE
40 Risk: Medium

Born: May 28, 1990. **B-T:** R-R. **Ht.:** 6-4. **Wt.:** 225. **Drafted:** HS— Newport Beach, Calif., 2009 (10th round). **Signed by:** Tom Battista.

Northcraft continued his career trend of having to make adjustments when he reaches a new level. That was the case in 2013, when he made the move to Double-A Mississippi, where he returned to start 2014 and limited opposing hitters to a .228 average. However, Triple-A Gwinnett hitters battered him at a .317 clip following a midseason bump in 2014. Northcraft works quickly on the mound and creates some deception with his low three-quarters arm slot. He has above-average sinking action on his 89-91 mph fastball that generates groundballs. He also has solid movement on his changeup and knows how to mix in his fringe-average curveball and slider. Northcraft has a solid mound presence, throws strikes and mixes his pitches well, which generates high strikeout totals. Northcraft's durability gives him a chance to be a No. 5 starter, and the Braves elected to protect him on the 40-man roster instead of Cody Martin. He will take another swing at Gwinnett in 2105.

Year	Club (League)	Class	W	L	ERA	G	GS	CG	SV	IP	H	HR	BB	SO	K/9	WHIP	AVG
2012	Lynchburg (CAR)	HiA	10	11	3.98	27	27	2	0	152	143	4	53	160	9.5	1.29	.247
2013	Mississippi (SL)	AA	8	8	3.42	26	26	0	0	137	124	7	51	121	7.9	1.28	.241
2014	Mississippi (SL)	AA	7	3	2.88	13	12	0	0	66	57	2	24	62	8.5	1.23	.228
	Gwinnett (IL)	AAA	0	7	6.54	13	12	0	0	65	86	6	31	51	7.1	1.81	.317
Minor League Totals			40	43	3.91	127	118	2	0	639	616	31	245	559	7.9	1.35	.252

29 ELMER REYES, SS/2B

BA GRADE
40 Risk: Medium

Born: Nov. 26, 1990. **B-T:** R-R. **Ht.:** 5-11. **Wt.:** 170. **Signed:** Nicaragua, 2009. **Signed by:** Marvin Throneberry.

Reyes signed as an 18-year-old out of Nicaragua and has made a methodical climb through the organization, reaching Triple-A Gwinnett in 2014. His steady performance has pushed him past more talented, higher-dollar players at every level. Reyes is a smooth defender at shortstop with a quick first step, above-average lateral range and soft hands. He has above-average arm strength and a quick release that allows him to make throws from the hole or going up the middle. Aggressive at the plate with a good approach, Reyes stands upright and sprays line drives from gap to gap. The ball does not jump off his bat, but he has doubles power. He has a decent feel for the strike zone but doesn't draw many walks, and his average speed doesn't lead to stolen bases. Reyes' glove helps profile him as a utility infielder. He's on the 40-man roster but likely will start 2015 back at Gwinnett.

Year	Club (League)	Class	AVG	G	AB	R	H	2B	3B	HR	RBI	BB	SO	SB	CS	OBP	SLG
2012	Rome (SAL)	LoA	.251	112	379	49	95	26	6	5	36	15	64	5	5	.296	.391
2013	Lynchburg (CAR)	HiA	.285	123	438	57	125	30	4	5	60	20	73	7	1	.321	.406
2014	Mississippi (SL)	AA	.303	58	211	25	64	16	1	2	28	7	48	3	2	.339	.417
	Gwinnett (IL)	AAA	.286	55	206	27	59	16	2	3	24	5	45	2	0	.318	.427
Minor League Totals			.267	560	1983	264	529	136	19	23	225	85	351	33	15	.314	.389

30 LUIS MEREJO, LHP

BA GRADE
50 Risk: Extreme

Born: Oct. 8, 1994. **B-T:** L-L. **Ht.:** 6-0. **Wt.:** 170. **Signed:** Dominican Republic, 2011. **Signed by:** Matias Laureano Fortunato.

Merejo moved quickly after signing with the Braves out of the Dominican for $65,000 in 2011. He reached Rookie-level Danville in 2013 before requiring Tommy John surgery in late August of that year. When healthy, he demonstrates an impressive feel for pitching for such a young player. He works quickly and repeats his delivery, which gives him above-average control and allows him to work ahead in the count with consistency. His fastball sits in the low 90s and touches 94 mph. His tight curveball and promising changeup showed noticeable improvement prior to his injury. Merejo will pitch 2015 as a 20-year-old and could still open the season at low Class A Rome. The Braves will be cautious with his workload.

Year	Club (League)	Class	W	L	ERA	G	GS	CG	SV	IP	H	HR	BB	SO	K/9	WHIP	AVG
2012	Braves (GCL)	R	0	5	4.61	10	8	0	0	41	38	1	9	53	11.6	1.15	.245
2013	Braves (GCL)	R	0	0	0.00	2	0	0	0	6	4	0	4	1	1.5	1.33	.182
	Danville (APP)	R	1	0	0.00	3	1	0	0	10	8	0	5	11	9.9	1.30	.222
2014	Did not play—Injured																
Minor League Totals			1	5	3.32	15	9	0	0	57	50	1	18	65	10.3	1.19	.235

Baltimore Orioles

BY STEVE MELEWSKI

After winning 93 and 85 games the previous two seasons, the 2014 Orioles proved that their success was not a fluke by claiming the American League East with 96 victories. They reached the AL Championship Series for the first time since 1997 but came up short against the Royals.

After posting a losing record for 14 consecutive seasons, Baltimore now has recorded three straight winning seasons for the first time since 1992-94. They did it with a season that went anything but according to plan. The Orioles finished third in the AL in ERA, even though their big free agent pickup, righthander Ubaldo Jimenez, bombed and was pulled from the rotation in August, returning only after the division title was in hand. Manager Buck Showalter handled the pitching staff deftly and had the benefit of six healthy starters. Chris Tillman, Wei-Yin Chen, Bud Norris, Miguel Gonzalez, rookie Kevin Gausman and Jimenez made 161 of the team's 162 starts. And when Tommy Hunter stumbled in an early audition as closer, Showalter resuscitated the career of lefty Zach Britton, reinventing him as a groundballing reliever.

The lineup did not have the same good fortune. Catcher Matt Wieters was reduced to advanced scouting come playoff time, missing all but 26 games due to elbow surgery. And a knee injury felled inconsistent young star Manny Machado for the second straight season, this time to his right knee (it was his left in 2013). Chris Davis, hitting just .196 with less than half of last year's 53 home runs, missed much of September and the playoffs due to a 25-game amphetamines suspension.

The Orioles kept their bullpen fresh by making good use of their minor league affiliates and finding players with options remaining. They used 46 players this season and pitchers Gonzalez, Norris, Ryan Webb and T.J. McFarland all made at least one minor league appearance. Relievers such as Preston Guilmet and Evan Meek were on the shuttle between Baltimore and Triple-A Norfolk.

Executive vice president Dan Duquette continued to push the right buttons, whether by acquiring depth, like catcher Nick Hundley when Wieters needed surgery, or adding a key trade deadline piece such as reliever Andrew Miller from the Red Sox for top pitching prospect Eduardo Rodriguez. Duquette was still making moves in late August and acquired infielder Kelly Johnson and outfielder Alejandro De Aza, who both made the playoff roster.

Showalter coaxed monster seasons from Steve

Nelson Cruz delivered on his free agent promise with a big league-best 40 homers

TOP PROSPECTS OF THE DECADE

Year	Player, Pos.	2014 Org
2005	Nick Markakis, of	Orioles
2006	Nick Markakis, of	Orioles
2007	Billy Rowell, 3b	Out of baseball
2008	Matt Wieters, c	Orioles
2009	Matt Wieters, c	Orioles
2010	Brian Matusz, lhp	Orioles
2011	Manny Machado, ss	Orioles
2012	Dylan Bundy, rhp	Orioles
2013	Dylan Bundy, rhp	Orioles
2014	Dylan Bundy, rhp	Orioles

Pearce (.293/.373/.556, 21 HR) and major league home run champ Nelson Cruz, who signed for one year and $8 million coming off last year's 50-game suspension stemming from the Biogenesis scandal. They helped the O's lead the majors with 211 home runs, but Cruz left as a free agent for Seattle.

The Orioles feel good about their player development operation led by Brian Graham and having players like Jonathan Schoop, Gausman and Caleb Joseph contribute to the winning was a positive. Dylan Bundy (2011) returned from Tommy John surgery and remains the organization's top prospect, while Hunter Harvey (2013) had a strong full-season debut halted in late July by a forearm injury.

The entire rotation and most of the bullpen should return, giving the Orioles confidence in their chances to return to the playoffs in 2015.

General Manager: Dan Duquette. **Farm Director:** Brian Graham. **Scouting Director:** Gary Rajsich.

Class	Team	League	W	L	PCT	Finish	Manager
Majors	Baltimore Orioles	American	96	66	.593	t-2nd (30)	Buck Showalter
Triple-A	Norfolk Tides	International	65	79	.451	13th (14)	Ron Johnson
Double-A	Bowie Baysox	Eastern	72	70	.507	6th (12)	Gary Kendall
High A	Frederick Keys	Carolina	65	72	.474	t-7th (10)	Luis Pujols
Low A	Delmarva Shorebirds	South Atlantic	66	73	.475	7th (14)	Ryan Minor
Short-season	Aberdeen IronBirds	New York-Penn	27	48	.360	14th (14)	Matt Murrullo
Rookie	Orioles	Gulf Coast	29	31	.483	10th (16)	Orlando Gomez
Overall 2014 Minor League Record			324	373	.465	25th (30)	

THIS YEAR'S TOP 30

No.	Player, Pos.	Grade/Risk
1.	Dylan Bundy, rhp	65/High
2.	Hunter Harvey, rhp	60/High
3.	Christian Walker, 1b	50/Medium
4.	Chance Sisco, c	55/High
5.	Dariel Alvarez, of	50/Medium
6.	Zach Davies, rhp	45/Medium
7.	Tim Berry, lhp	45/Medium
8.	Mike Wright, rhp	45/Medium
9.	Mike Yastrzemski, of	45/Medium
10.	Jomar Reyes, 3b	55/Extreme
11.	Pat Connaughton, rhp	50/High
12.	Tyler Wilson, rhp	45/Medium
13.	Jon Keller, rhp	45/Medium
14.	Henry Urrutia, of	50/High
15.	Drew Dosch, 3b	50/High
16.	Stephen Tarpley, lhp	50/High
17.	Jason Garcia, rhp	50/Extreme
18.	Steven Brault, lhp	45/High
19.	Mike Ohlman, c	45/High
20.	David Hess, rhp	45/High
21.	Adrian Marin, ss	45/High
22.	Parker Bridwell, rhp	45/High
23.	Brian Gonzalez, lhp	45/High
24.	Logan Verrett, rhp	40/Low
25.	Josh Hart, of	45/High
26.	Branden Kline, rhp	45/High
27.	Mychal Givens, rhp	45/High
28.	Jonah Heim, c	50/Extreme
29.	Ofelky Peralta, rhp	50/Extreme
30.	Trey Mancini, 1b	45/High

LAST YEAR'S TOP 30

No.	Player, Pos.	Status
1.	Dylan Bundy, rhp	No. 1
2.	Kevin Gausman, rhp	Majors
3.	Eduardo Rodriguez, lhp	(Red Sox)
4.	Hunter Harvey, rhp	No. 2
5.	Jonathan Schoop, 2b/ss	Majors
6.	Tim Berry, lhp	No. 7
7.	Henry Urrutia, of	No. 14
8.	Mike Wright, rhp	No. 8
9.	Michael Ohlman, c	No. 19
10.	Chance Sisco, c	No. 4
11.	Zach Davies, rhp	No. 6
12.	Adrian Marin, ss	No. 21
13.	Josh Hart, of	No. 25
14.	Steven Brault, lhp	No. 18
15.	Dariel Alvarez, of	No. 5
16.	Travis Seabrooke, lhp	Dropped out
17.	Jon Keller, rhp	No. 13
18.	Christian Walker, 1b	No. 3
19.	Parker Bridwell, rhp	No. 22
20.	Branden Kline, rhp	No. 26
21.	Stephen Tarpley, lhp	No. 16
22.	Ofelky Peralta, rhp	No. 29
23.	Mychal Givens, rhp	No. 27
24.	Oliver Drake, rhp	Dropped out
25.	Trey Mancini, 1b	No. 30
26.	Jonah Heim, c	No. 28
27.	Chris Jones, lhp	Dropped out
28.	Josh Stinson, rhp	(Pirates)
29.	Glynn Davis, of	Dropped out
30.	Jason Gurka, lhp	(Free Agent)

BEST TOOLS

Best Hitter for Average	Chance Sisco
Best Power Hitter	Christian Walker
Best Strike-Zone Discipline	Drew Dosch
Fastest Baserunner	Daniel Franco
Best Athlete	Pat Connaughton
Best Fastball	Tanner Scott
Best Curveball	Dylan Bundy
Best Slider	Tyler Wilson
Best Changeup	Zach Davies
Best Control	Zach Davies
Best Defensive Catcher	Brian Ward
Best Defensive Infielder	Jason Esposito
Best Infield Arm	Jason Esposito
Best Defensive Outfielder	Mike Yastrzemski
Best Outfield Arm	Dariel Alvarez

PROJECTED 2018 LINEUP

Catcher	Matt Wieters
First Base	Christian Walker
Second Base	Jonathan Schoop
Third Base	Ryan Flaherty
Shortstop	Manny Machado
Left Field	Mike Yastrzemski
Center Field	Adam Jones
Right Field	Dariel Alvarez
Designated Hitter	Chris Davis
No. 1 Starter	Kevin Gausman
No. 2 Starter	Dylan Bundy
No. 3 Starter	Chris Tillman
No. 4 Starter	Hunter Harvey
No. 5 Starter	Wei-Yin Chen
Closer	Zach Britton

BALTIMORE ORIOLES

TOP 2015 ROOKIE: Dylan Bundy, rhp. The 2011 first-rounder should return to 2012 form and help the Orioles in the second half.
BREAKOUT PROSPECT: Stephen Tarpley, lhp. Stuff generates swings and misses, and he logged a 2.56 ERA and 3.5 SO/BB ratio in August.
SLEEPER: Alex Murphy, c. The 2013 sixth-rounder's bat is ahead of the glove, but he should make a full recovery from labrum surgery on his non-throwing shoulder.

SOURCE OF TOP 30 TALENT			
Homegrown	28	Acquired	2
College	10	Trades	0
Junior college	1	Rule 5 draft	2
High school	13	Independent leagues	0
Draft-and-follow	0	Free agents/waivers	0
Nondrafted free agents	0		
International	4		

LF
Henry Urrutia (14)
Jamill Moquette
Conor Bierfeldt

CF
Josh Hart (25)
Glynn Davis
Greg Lorenzo
Jay Gonzalez

RF
Dariel Alvarez (5)
Mike Yastrzemski (9)
John Ruettiger

3B
Jomar Reyes (10)
Drew Dosch (15)
Jason Esposito

SS
Adrian Marin (21)
Ozzie Martinez
Jared Breen
Jeff Kemp

2B
Garabez Rosa
Anthony Caronia

1B
Christian Walker (3)
Trey Mancini (30)
Riley Palmer
Carlos Diaz

C
Chance Sisco (4)
Mike Ohlman (19)
Jonah Heim (28)
Brian Ward
Alex Murphy
Austin Wynns

LHP

LHSP	LHRP
Tim Berry (7)	Chris Jones
Stephen Tarpley (16)	Matt Trowbridge
Steven Brault (18)	
Brian Gonzalez (23)	
Travis Seabrooke	
Mitch Horacek	
Luis Gonzalez	
John Means	

RHP

RHSP	RHRP
Dylan Bundy (1)	Jon Keller (13)
Hunter Harvey (2)	Jason Garcia (17)
Zach Davies (6)	Mychal Givens (27)
Mike Wright (8)	Derrick Bleeker
Pat Connaughton (11)	Jimmy Yacabonis
Tyler Wilson (12)	Brady Wager
David Hess (20)	David Richardson
Parker Bridwell (22)	Dylan Rheault
Logan Verrett (24)	Matt Hobgood
Branden Kline (26)	
Ofelky Peralta (29)	
Lazaro Leyva	
Jean Cosme	

2014

BEST PURE HITTER: 3B Austin Anderson (9) was a consistent producer in the SEC the last two years who walked more than he struck out. Anderson has a simple, direct swing from the left side that produces power to the gaps.

BEST POWER HITTER: OF Jamill Moquete (32) has a great-looking body at 6-foot-3, 215 pounds that has drawn physical comparisons to Matt Kemp. He started playing baseball later but has physical ability, including plus raw power.

FASTEST RUNNER: OF Jay Gonzalez (10) is a 70-grade runner. The lefthanded hitter has wiry strength and some pop, but is at his best offensively when he employs a slash-and-dash approach.

BEST DEFENSIVE PLAYER: Gonzalez, who began his college career at Auburn before attending Mount Olive, has the potential to remain in center field.

BEST FASTBALL: LHP Tanner Scott (6), who got a third-round bonus, was up to 98 before the draft and touched 100 this summer. He is working on improving his delivery, but no other lefthander in the 2014 draft has been up to triple digits. RHP Pat Connaughton (4) was up to 97, as was RHP David Hess (5). Projectable RHP Jean Cosme took a big step forward this summer and touched 96 after touching 93 in the spring with a loose, fast arm.

BEST SECONDARY PITCH: LHP Brian Gonzalez (3) was the first player the Orioles selected. He has a strong build and easy delivery with advanced feel for a plus changeup. Hess' curveball flashes plus, as does LHP John Means' (11) curve. RHP Patrick Baker (29) is a reliever with a heater up to 95 and curveball that shows above-average potential.

BEST PRO DEBUT: Gonzalez did not allow an earned run in 25 innings in the Gulf Coast League while striking out a batter an inning and registering just eight walks.

BEST ATHLETE: Connaughton has been a two-year starter at small forward for the Notre Dame basketball team. The athletic, versatile Connaughton scored 13.8 points per game and ranked in the top three for the Fighting Irish in nearly every significant statistic. Infielder Steve Wilkerson (8) was recruited by colleges as a quarterback before focusing on baseball at Clemson.

MOST INTRIGUING BACKGROUND: Connaughton.

CLOSEST TO THE MAJORS: Hess had three straight outings this summer where he touched 97 mph and sat in the mid-90s while showing feel for a changeup and a plus breaking ball. His ability to throw his fastball to both sides of the plate and his strong, sturdy frame have drawn comparisons to Nationals righthander Jordan Zimmerman.

BEST LATE-ROUND PICK: Means is a strike-throwing lefthander with feel for secondary stuff.

THE ONE WHO GOT AWAY: Prep RHP Connor Seabold (19) has a chance to develop at Cal State Fullerton.

ASSESSMENT: The Orioles were the last team to pick in the 2014 draft and did not make their first selection until the third round. They took pitchers with their first five picks, a number of whom have taken significant steps forward since signing.

2013

A high school-heavy draft by O's standards landed RHP Hunter Harvey (1) and C Chance Sisco (2) and college sleepers 3B Drew Dosch (7), OF Mike Yastrzemski (14) and RHP Jon Keller (22).

GRADE: B

2012

Kevin Gausman (1) may be primed to emerge as Baltimore's ace. 1B Christian Walker (4) hit his way to the majors, while LHP Josh Hader (19) was traded to Houston for Bud Norris.

GRADE: B

2011

RHP Dylan Bundy (1) reached the majors quickly but has to prove he's fully back from Tommy John surgery. The rest of the class has disappointed, though there's hope for RHPs Mike Wright (3) and Tyler Wilson (10).

GRADE: C

TOP DRAFT PICKS OF THE DECADE

Year	Player, Pos.	2014 Org
2005	Brandon Snyder, 1b	Red Sox
2006	Billy Rowell, 3b	Out of baseball
2007	Matt Wieters, c	Orioles
2008	Brian Matusz, lhp	Orioles
2009	Matt Hobgood, rhp	Orioles
2010	Manny Machado, ss	Orioles
2011	Dylan Bundy, rhp	Orioles
2012	Kevin Gausman, rhp	Orioles
2013	Hunter Harvey, rhp	Orioles
2014	Brian Gonzalez, lhp (3rd round)	Orioles

LARGEST BONUSES IN CLUB HISTORY

Matt Wieters, 2007	$6,000,000
Manny Machado, 2010	$5,250,000
Kevin Gausman, 2012	$4,320,000
Dylan Bundy, 2011	$4,000,000
Adam Loewen, 2002	$3,200,000

1 DYLAN BUNDY, RHP

Born: Nov. 15, 1992. **B-T:** B-R Ht.: **6-1. Wt.:** 195.
Drafted: HS—Owasso, Okla., 2011 (1st round).
Signed by: Ernie Jacobs.

Considered among the most advanced high school pitchers in years, Bundy went fourth overall in a deep 2011 draft and signed a $6.225 million major league contract that included a $4 million bonus. He had a very strong 2012 that included a sensational debut in the South Atlantic League, where over 30 dominant innings he gave up five hits while not allowing a single earned run with two walks to 40 strikeouts. Bundy went 9-3, 2.08 over three levels of the minors that year and made two September relief appearances for Baltimore, making him the fourth 19-year-old to pitch in the majors in the last decade. Bundy's velocity was down during a 2013 spring training start and he was shut down. It eventually led to ligament-reconstructive surgery performed by Dr. James Andrews on June 27. Bundy's goal was to return by that date in 2014 and he did, pitching for short-season Aberdeen on June 15 last summer.

The pre-surgery Bundy pitched in the mid-90s, sometimes touching 97 and 98. He showed a plus curveball with sharp break and a changeup that made dramatic improvement through the 2012 season and was often a plus pitch by the end of the year. In 2014, Bundy pitched in extended-spring training games before moving to Aberdeen and high Class A Frederick, where he threw a total of 41 innings. He didn't pitch after Aug. 5 due to a lat strain that is now fully healed. The Orioles limited Bundy to 75-pitch outings, and he was never quite as electric as he was pre-surgery. Bundy's fastball sat mostly in the 91-94 mph range but one pitch touched 96 in his last Frederick start. He was more 90-92 mph at extended spring, but the velocity ticked up a bit deeper in the season. His secondary pitches were solid but inconsistent at times in both quality and command, understandable coming off surgery. The Orioles were pleased with his healthy arm and he didn't have a single setback. His last start was his best—he got seven of his 13 outs via strikeout and allowed no walks. He should have a normal offseason and will enter the 2015 season with a strong chance to pitch at the same high level

he did in 2012.

The Orioles are confident in Bundy's stuff and future at the front of their rotation. One question for next season is how many innings Bundy will be allowed to work. He'll be back in full force in 2015 if he follows the same Dave Walker-designed rehab program as lefty Tsuyoshi Wada, who had surgery while with the Orioles and tossed 180 total innings in the Cubs organization in 2014. He's expected to start the season back at Double-A Bowie.

BA GRADE

65 Risk: High

SCOUTING GRADES

Fastball: 70.
Curveball: 65.
Changeup: 60.
Control: 65.

Based on 20-80 scouting scale and future projection rather than present tools.

LGE	BF	SO%	BB%	HR/9
NYP	56	39.3	5.4	0.00
CAR	117	12.8	11.1	0.00

BRIAN WESTERHOLT

Year	Club (League)	Class	W	L	ERA	G	GS	CG	SV	IP	H	HR	BB	SO	K/9	WHIP	AVG
2012	Delmarva (SAL)	LoA	1	0	0.00	8	8	0	0	30	5	0	2	40	12.0	0.23	.053
	Frederick (CAR)	HiA	6	3	2.84	12	12	0	0	57	48	5	18	66	10.4	1.16	.233
	Bowie (EL)	AA	2	0	3.24	3	3	0	0	17	14	1	8	13	7.0	1.32	.230
	Baltimore (AL)	MAJ	0	0	0.00	2	0	0	0	2	1	0	1	0	0.0	1.20	.200
2013	Did not play—Injured																
2014	Aberdeen (NYP)	SS	0	1	0.60	3	3	0	0	15	10	0	3	22	13.2	0.87	.189
	Frederick (CAR)	HiA	1	2	4.78	6	6	0	0	26	28	0	13	15	5.1	1.56	.283
Major League Totals			0	0	0.00	2	0	0	0	2	1	0	1	0	0.0	1.20	.200
Minor League Totals			10	6	2.42	32	32	0	0	145	105	6	44	156	9.7	1.03	.205

2 HUNTER HARVEY, RHP

Born: Dec. 9, 1994. **B-T:** R-R. **Ht.:** 6-4. **Wt.:** 178. **Drafted:** HS—Catawba, N.C., 2013 (1st round). **Signed by:** Chris Gale.

The son of former big league closer Bryan Harvey, Hunter Harvey was the 22nd overall pick in 2013 and the Orioles signed him to a slot bonus of $1,947,600. Harvey earned a spot in the Futures Game with a strong first half in 2014, but was shut down in late July with a flexor mass muscle strain in his right forearm. Harvey showed excellent command of a fastball that sat in the 92-94 mph range, touching 95 and 96. He showed a sharp, plus curveball from 72-77 mph with tight spin that can overmatch hitters at times. His changeup made big gains during the season but remains his third-best pitch. He has the potential for three plus pitches. His pedigree was displayed in his mound presence, composure and pitching smarts. One scout said he's everything you want in a top of the rotation starter. As Harvey advances he will need to improve at holding runners on base. He sometimes throws across his body, which may have led to his injured forearm. Harvey said that doctors told him he would not need surgery, and Orioles officials said the same. Health and experience stand between him and the front of the Orioles' future rotation. He should pitch at high Class A Frederick in 2015. His big league ETA could be 2017.

BA GRADE

60 Risk: High

LGE	BF	SO%	BB%	HR/9
SAL	365	29.0	9.0	0.51

Year	Club (League)	Class	W	L	ERA	G	GS	CG	SV	IP	H	HR	BB	SO	K/9	WHIP	AVG
2013	Orioles (GCL)	R	0	0	1.35	5	5	0	0	13	10	0	2	18	12.2	0.90	.208
	Aberdeen (NYP)	SS	0	1	2.25	3	3	0	0	12	11	0	4	15	11.3	1.25	.239
2014	Delmarva (SAL)	LoA	7	5	3.18	17	17	0	0	88	66	5	33	106	10.9	1.13	.209
Minor League Totals			7	6	2.87	25	25	0	0	113	87	5	39	139	11.1	1.12	.212

3 CHRISTIAN WALKER, 1B

Born: March 28, 1991. **B-T:** R-R. **Ht.:** 6-2. **Wt.:** 180. **Drafted:** South Carolina, 2012 (4th round). **Signed by:** Chris Gale.

Walker was a rock in South Carolina's lineup for three seasons that included back-to-back College World Series championships and a runner-up finish in 2012. A fourth-round pick that season, he needed just more than two seasons to reach the major leagues, homering off the Red Sox's Rubby de la Rosa to right-center field on Sept. 20. Known as a solid hitter with gap-to-gap power, Walker's game took a big step forward in 2014 with an organization-best 27 home runs. Working with new minor league hitting coordinator Jeff Manto to increase his power, he produced all-fields power by using his legs more in his short swing. Walker keeps his bat in the zone a long time, recognizes pitches and has good bat speed. A modest athlete, Walker has improved his footwork but is more competent than an asset defensively, and is a below-average runner. Walker's makeup will be the separator if he becomes a regular. He should start 2015 as Triple-A Norfolk's first baseman. If the Orioles don't retain Chris Davis (a free agent after 2015), Walker could be his replacement.

BA GRADE

50 Risk: Medium

LGE	PA	BB%	SO%	ISO
EL	411	9.2	20.2	.216
IL	188	9.6	26.1	.169

Year	Club (League)	Class	AVG	G	AB	R	H	2B	3B	HR	RBI	BB	SO	SB	CS	OBP	SLG
2012	Aberdeen (NYP)	SS	.284	22	81	12	23	5	0	2	9	10	14	2	1	.376	.420
2013	Delmarva (SAL)	LoA	.353	31	116	19	41	5	0	3	20	11	16	0	3	.420	.474
	Frederick (CAR)	HiA	.288	55	215	25	62	17	0	8	35	17	41	2	0	.343	.479
	Bowie (EL)	AA	.242	17	62	7	15	5	0	0	1	6	10	0	0	.319	.323
2014	Bowie (EL)	AA	.301	95	366	58	110	15	2	20	77	38	83	2	1	.367	.516
	Norfolk (IL)	AAA	.259	44	166	15	43	10	0	6	19	18	49	0	0	.335	.428
	Baltimore (AL)	MAJ	.167	6	18	1	3	1	0	1	1	1	9	0	0	.211	.389
Major League Totals			.167	6	18	1	3	1	0	1	1	1	9	0	0	.211	.389
Minor League Totals			.292	264	1006	136	294	57	2	39	161	100	213	6	5	.361	.469

4 CHANCE SISCO, C

Born: Feb. 24, 1995. **B-T:** L-R. **Ht.:** 6-2. **Wt.:** 190. **Drafted:** HS—Lake Elsinore, Calif., 2013 (2nd round). **Signed by:** Mark Ralston.

The 61st overall selection in the 2013 draft, Sisco signed for a $785,000 bonus, which was under slot for that draft position. The Orioles drafted Sisco for his bat, with his catching skills a real bonus. He didn't begin catching full-time until his senior season of high school, after primarily playing shortstop previously. Sisco can hit. He batted .371/.475/.465 in the Rookie-level Gulf Coast League and won the low Class A South Atlantic League batting title in his first full season in 2014. Scouts like Sisco's controlled, line-drive swing, and he uses the whole field and seldom overswings. He lets the ball travel and uses left-center often. Some scouts want to see him pull the ball more with authority, which the Orioles expect to develop with time. Defensively, Sisco is raw with enough arm strength but plenty of work to do to improve his receiving and footwork. His 16 passed balls led the Sally League, and he threw out just 20 percent of opposing basestealers. Sisco got stronger last year, which should help him handle the rigors of catching. The Orioles will keep Sisco behind the plate for the foreseeable future, as he's much more valuable as a potential offensive catcher. He'll get his third year at the position at high Class A Frederick in 2015.

BA GRADE	
55	Risk: High

LGE	PA	BB%	SO%	ISO
SAL	478	8.8	16.5	.108

Year	Club (League)	Class	AVG	G	AB	R	H	2B	3B	HR	RBI	BB	SO	SB	CS	OBP	SLG
2013	Orioles (GCL)	R	.371	31	97	15	36	4	1	1	11	17	21	1	1	.475	.464
	Aberdeen (NYP)	SS	.200	2	5	1	1	0	0	0	0	1	2	0	0	.333	.200
2014	Delmarva (SAL)	LoA	.340	114	426	56	145	27	2	5	63	42	79	1	2	.406	.448
Minor League Totals			.345	147	528	72	182	31	3	6	74	60	102	2	3	.419	.449

5 DARIEL ALVAREZ, OF

Born: Nov. 7, 1988. **B-T:** R-R. **Ht.:** 6-2. **Wt.:** 180. **Signed:** Cuba, 2013. **Signed by:** Fred Ferreira/Joel Bradley/Gustavo Bencid.

Alvarez spent four seasons playing in Cuba's Serie Nacional before he left the island, making his way to Mexico in 2012. After nearly a year, he was cleared to sign with a U.S. team and signed with the Orioles for an $800,000 bonus in July 2013. He hit his way to a spot in the 2014 Futures Game. Alvarez showed an ability to make adjustments all year, hitting .306/.330/.472 between Double-A and Triple-A in his first full U.S. season. He's aggressive, so he'll likely never walk much, but covers the plate and makes consistent hard contact, showing solid power to all fields. He'll need to continue to improve laying off breaking stuff for his power to play. While he projects as a corner outfielder, the Orioles played him in center this year and he handled it well, with average or better range thanks to good jumps and average speed. Alvarez threw 93-95 mph during workouts when some clubs looked at him as pitcher, and his arm is a weapon in right field. Alvarez is an option for right field now that the Orioles did not re-sign Nick Markakis, whose team option (at $17.5 million) was declined. The Orioles preferred to bring back Markakis and give Alvarez more time at Triple-A to temper his aggressiveness, but he should reach Baltimore in 2015 at some point.

BA GRADE	
50	Risk: Medium

LGE	PA	BB%	SO%	ISO
EL	381	3.4	9.2	.178
IL	183	4.4	14.8	.139

Year	Club (League)	Class	AVG	G	AB	R	H	2B	3B	HR	RBI	BB	SO	SB	CS	OBP	SLG
2013	Orioles (GCL)	R	.444	3	9	2	4	2	1	1	2	1	1	0	0	.500	1.222
	Frederick (CAR)	HiA	.436	10	39	5	17	2	0	2	7	2	1	1	2	.463	.641
	Bowie (EL)	AA	.194	9	31	2	6	0	0	1	1	1	9	0	0	.219	.290
2014	Bowie (EL)	AA	.309	91	359	52	111	20	1	14	68	13	35	7	4	.332	.487
	Norfolk (IL)	AAA	.301	44	173	23	52	17	2	1	19	8	27	1	1	.328	.439
Minor League Totals			.311	157	611	84	190	41	4	19	97	25	73	9	7	.336	.484

6 ZACH DAVIES, RHP

Born: Feb. 7, 1993. **B-T:** R-R. **Ht.:** 6-0. **Wt.:** 150. **Drafted:** HS—Gilbert, Ariz., 2011 (26th round). **Signed by:** John Gillette.

Davies got a $575,000 bonus despite his low draft round in the last year under the old draft rules when the Orioles signed him away from his Arizona State commitment. Buck Showalter picked him to make an exhibition start against the big league club in March, and Davies struck out J.J. Hardy and Chris Davis with changeups in the first inning. Davies is a strike-thrower with a plus pitch, his changeup. He throws it with such good arm action that one scout said he had to look at his radar gun to be sure it was his changeup. One club official cited his delivery as the best in the system—smooth, free and easy, repeatable—leading to good command of his sinking 86-91 mph fastball. Davies' curveball is his third pitch, and it's solid-average as well. He's slightly built, leading to consistent durability concerns, and he missed most of May with shoulder tendinitis. He pitched well after returning, but at his size, he has little physical projection left and

BA GRADE

45 Risk: Medium

LGE	BF	SO%	BB%	HR/9
EL	465	23.4	6.9	0.65

likely has maxed out his fastball velocity. Davies got to go home to Arizona to pitch in the Fall League, seeking to make up for lost innings and get more upper-level experience. He should re-join Tim Berry in the rotation, this time at Triple-A Norfolk, in 2015 and likewise projects as a back-of-the-rotation starter

Year	Club (League)	Class	W	L	ERA	G	GS	CG	SV	IP	H	HR	BB	SO	K/9	WHIP	AVG
2012	Delmarva (SAL)	LoA	5	7	3.86	25	17	0	1	114	109	11	46	91	7.2	1.36	.255
2013	Frederick (CAR)	HiA	7	9	3.69	26	26	0	0	149	145	10	38	132	8.0	1.23	.256
2014	Bowie (EL)	AA	10	7	3.35	21	20	0	0	110	106	8	32	109	8.9	1.25	.249
Minor League Totals			22	23	3.64	72	63	0	1	373	360	29	116	332	8.0	1.28	.254

7 TIM BERRY, LHP

Born: March 18, 1991. **B-T:** L-L. **Ht.:** 6-3. **Wt.:** 180. **Drafted:** HS—San Marcos, Calif., 2009 (50th round). **Signed by:** Mark Ralston.

The Orioles drafted Berry after he had Tommy John surgery as a high school senior and signed him away from an Oregon commitment for $125,000. A 50th-round pick, Berry already has made it to the majors—at least for a single day. Added to the 40-man roster in November 2013, Berry was on the major league roster for one day in June before the Orioles sent him back down. Berry is a three-pitch lefthander who pitches off his 88-92 mph fastball that can reach 94 with some sink. His changeup has developed into his best secondary pitch, with some scouts giving it plus grades and others not quite as bullish. Berry's slurvy 75-77 mph slider has more sweeping action than depth, grades as fringe-average at its best and is more often a below-average pitch. Because of his changeup, he's generally been equally effective against righthanded hitters as he is against lefties. He has a loose arm and good delivery but still didn't pitch after Aug. 10 due to mild shoul-

BA GRADE

45 Risk: Medium

LGE	BF	SO%	BB%	HR/9
EL	555	19.5	8.1	0.81

der tendinitis. Berry was in the process of having a strong finish when he was shut down. Although he had Tommy John surgery in high school, he's had a pretty solid record of durability until this recent shoulder issue. He should progress to Triple-A for 2015 and projects as a back-end starter if he's not pushed to the bullpen by a big league need.

Year	Club (League)	Class	W	L	ERA	G	GS	CG	SV	IP	H	HR	BB	SO	K/9	WHIP	AVG
2012	Delmarva (SAL)	LoA	2	7	5.02	10	10	0	0	52	60	3	17	44	7.6	1.48	.282
	Frederick (CAR)	HiA	5	5	4.32	15	13	0	0	75	83	6	20	61	7.3	1.37	.285
	Bowie (EL)	AA	0	1	37.80	1	1	0	0	2	7	0	2	4	21.6	5.40	.583
2013	Frederick (CAR)	HiA	11	7	3.85	27	27	0	0	152	156	13	40	119	7.0	1.29	.265
2014	Bowie (EL)	AA	6	7	3.51	23	23	0	0	133	122	12	45	108	7.3	1.25	.249
Minor League Totals			27	35	4.23	116	100	0	0	551	548	45	199	455	7.4	1.36	.262

8 MIKE WRIGHT, RHP

Born: Jan. 3, 1990. **B-T:** R-R. **Ht.:** 6-6. **Wt.:** 215. **Drafted:** East Carolina, 2011 (3rd round). **Signed by:** Chris Gale.

The organization's Jim Palmer award winner in 2013 as its top minor league pitcher, Wright got off to a slow start in 2014 but had a very strong finish at Triple-A. He pitched to an 0.76 ERA with a .176 opponents average in five August starts, including falling one out short of a no-hitter against Durham in his next-to-last start. Scouts look at Wright and see a tall, strong, hard-throwing durable starter—albeit one without a picture-perfect delivery. Wright throws across his body from the first-base side of the rubber and lands on a stiff front leg. His fastball works between 89-93 mph, touching 95, with good sink. He throws both a slider and curveball as well as a changeup, which some scouts leaned to as his best secondary pitch, a solid-average offering. His low-80s slider also can be solid-average, and his fringy curve gives hitters another look. He doesn't have a put-away pitch or the stuff to elevate as a starter. The Orioles believe his fastball would play

BA GRADE

45 Risk: Medium

LGE	BF	SO%	BB%	HR/9
IL	622	16.6	6.6	0.63

up in the 96-98 mph range if he was airing it out on every pitch out of the bullpen. Wright is likely to return to the Triple-A rotation in 2015, and the Orioles added him to the 40-man this winter since he was Rule 5 eligible for the first time. He needs to avoid another slow start if he hopes to make a run at a major league spot in 2015.

Year	Club (League)	Class	W	L	ERA	G	GS	CG	SV	IP	H	HR	BB	SO	K/9	WHIP	AVG
2012	Frederick (CAR)	HiA	5	2	2.91	8	8	0	0	46	47	3	5	35	6.8	1.12	.266
	Bowie (EL)	AA	5	3	4.91	12	12	0	0	62	71	7	17	45	6.5	1.41	.289
2013	Bowie (EL)	AA	11	3	3.26	26	26	0	0	144	152	9	39	136	8.5	1.33	.267
	Norfolk (IL)	AAA	0	0	0.00	1	1	0	0	7	6	0	0	2	2.7	0.90	.231
2014	Norfolk (IL)	AAA	5	11	4.61	26	26	0	0	143	159	10	41	103	6.5	1.40	.281
Minor League Totals			29	21	4.08	85	81	0	0	447	485	35	112	363	7.3	1.33	.275

9 MIKE YASTRZEMSKI, OF

Born: Aug. 23, 1990. **B-T:** L-L. **Ht.:** 6-0. **Wt.:** 185. **Drafted:** Vanderbilt, 2013 (14th round). **Signed by:** Adrian Dorsey.

The grandson of Hall of Famer Carl Yastrzemski, the younger Yaz was drafted twice before the Orioles signed him—by Carl's Red Sox out of high school in 2009 and by the Mariners in 2012. The Orioles signed him after a four-year career as a starter at Vanderbilt and he finished his first full season at Double-A, blazing through three levels. With no offensive tool that rates plus, Yaz just keeps hitting, making the South Atlantic League all-star game and hitting for the cycle with high Class A Frederick. He hit to all fields with some power with solid pitch recognition. Yastrzemski credits a strong mental approach as a key to his success. Scouts say he's baseball's equivalent of a gym rat who plays hard and never takes a pitch off. His smarts and savvy play at the plate, where he was able to often work himself into fastball counts; on the bases, as his average speed plays up; and defensively, as he takes good routes and closes on the ball well. His arm rates solid-average but is very accurate, helping him rack up 15 assists. Yaz will return to Double-A, where he ended last year. He profiles as a championship-caliber fourth outfielder, but could be more if he keeps hitting like he did in 2014.

BA GRADE

45 Risk: Medium

LGE	PA	BB%	SO%	ISO
SAL	288	6.6	22.2	.248
EL	201	7.0	16.9	.163

Year	Club (League)	Class	AVG	G	AB	R	H	2B	3B	HR	RBI	BB	SO	SB	CS	OBP	SLG
2013	Aberdeen (NYP)	SS	.273	57	205	28	56	13	4	3	25	24	44	8	8	.362	.420
2014	Delmarva (SAL)	LoA	.306	63	258	52	79	14	10	10	44	19	64	12	4	.365	.554
	Frederick (CAR)	HiA	.312	23	93	21	29	7	2	1	19	8	16	5	0	.364	.462
	Bowie (EL)	AA	.250	43	184	23	46	13	4	3	12	14	34	1	2	.310	.413
Minor League Totals			.284	186	740	124	210	47	20	17	100	65	158	26	14	.351	.470

10 JOMAR REYES, 3B

Born: Feb. 20, 1997. **B-T:** R-R. **Ht.:** 6-3. **Wt.:** 220. **Signed:** Dominican Republic, 2014. **Signed by:** Fred Ferreira/Calvin Maduro/Enrique Constante.

The Orioles signed the then 16-year-old Reyes out of the Dominican Republic in January 2014 to a $350,000 bonus, the largest in franchise history for a Dominican amateur. Reyes ranked as the No. 18 prospect in the Rookie-level Gulf Coast League in his debut. Reyes skipped the Dominican Summer League and went straight to the U.S. for his pro debut because he was clearly ready physically. One scout said he got pitched to like Hank Aaron late in the summer and he led the GCL in intentional walks. Reyes has two plus tools: his arm and his power. Imposing physically, Reyes looks even bigger and taller than his listed 6-foot-3, 220 pounds. He has plenty of strength and plus power to his pull side and to the middle of the field and good bat speed. Reyes' power potential excited Orioles brass. His ability to drive the ball fits with his corner infield defensive profile. He has below-average speed but plenty of arm strength for third base and he made progress during the season. His hands are decent, but he needs to improve his footwork and could wind up at first base. The Orioles were delighted with Reyes' pro debut in the GCL. They thought he could handle that league at 17 and he did. Reyes has a chance to break camp in 2015 as the starting third baseman at low Class A Delmarva.

BA GRADE	
55	Risk: Extreme

LGE	PA	BB%	SO%	ISO
GCL	207	7.2	18.4	.140

Year	Club (League)	Class	AVG	G	AB	R	H	2B	3B	HR	RBI	BB	SO	SB	CS	OBP	SLG
2014	Orioles (GCL)	R	.285	53	186	23	53	10	2	4	29	15	38	1	0	.333	.425
Minor League Totals			.285	53	186	23	53	10	2	4	29	15	38	1	0	.333	.425

11 PAT CONNAUGHTON, RHP

BA GRADE	
50	Risk: High

Born: Jan. 6, 1993. **B-T:** R-R. **Ht.:** 6-5. **Wt.:** 210. **Drafted:** Notre Dame, 2014 (4th round). **Signed by:** Dan Durst.

Connaughton has drawn comparisons with fellow Notre Dame two-sport athlete Jeff Samardzija, both for his amateur background and live arm. Instead of football, though, Connaughton starred in basketball, and he will spend his senior year on the court for the Irish before focusing on baseball in summer 2015. The Orioles signed him for $428,100 out of the fourth round, and one member of the front office believes Connaughton could become "a different animal" once he drops basketball. He pitched effectivley at short-season Aberdeen in a 15-inning look before he headed back to campus for a summer tour of Italy with the basketball team. Connaughton's fastball ranged from 91-96 mph with late movement, while his slider and changeup still need a lot of development. For now, the Orioles will keep him in the rotation. Connaughton is a high-energy guy with strong makeup, and his tremendous athleticism will be a plus on the mound. Baltimore expects him to begin 2015 in the low Class A Delmarva rotation.

Year	Club (League)	Class	W	L	ERA	G	GS	CG	SV	IP	H	HR	BB	SO	K/9	WHIP	AVG
2014	Aberdeen (NYP)	SS	0	1	2.45	6	4	0	0	15	13	0	3	10	6.1	1.09	.228
Minor League Totals			0	1	2.45	6	4	0	0	15	13	0	3	10	6.1	1.09	.228

12 TYLER WILSON, RHP

BA GRADE	
45	Risk: Medium

Born: Sept. 25, 1989. **B-T:** R-R. **Ht.:** 6-1. **Wt.:** 195. **Drafted:** Virginia, 2011 (10th round). **Signed by:** Chris Gale.

No longer is Wilson overlooked after the Orioles added him to the 40-man roster in November. Drafted out of Virginia after his senior year in 2011, he's made slow, steady progress through the system, culminating in his being named Baltimore's minor league pitcher of the year in 2014. He went 14-8, 3.67 in 28 starts at Double-A Bowie and Triple-A Norfolk and tied for ninth in the minors with 157 innings. Wilson's strong season was the result of a solid-average fastball, improved secondary pitches and a work ethic that one Baltimore staff member ranked as good as any in the organization. Wilson pitched at 90-94 mph, showing an uptick in velocity after a winter of workouts. His slider and changeup now also rate solid-average. His slider showed tight spin and good depth. A strike-thrower, Wilson has averaged 2.3 walks per nine in his career. Wilson's ceiling is a back-end starter, and he should return to Norfolk in 2015.

Year	Club (League)	Class	W	L	ERA	G	GS	CG	SV	IP	H	HR	BB	SO	K/9	WHIP	AVG
2012	Delmarva (SAL)	LoA	3	3	5.06	6	6	0	0	32	30	4	11	29	8.2	1.28	.252
	Frederick (CAR)	HiA	7	7	3.49	19	19	0	0	111	95	12	19	114	9.2	1.03	.228
2013	Frederick (CAR)	HiA	1	1	4.48	11	11	0	0	62	57	4	25	48	6.9	1.32	.242
	Bowie (EL)	AA	7	5	3.83	16	16	1	0	89	85	13	22	70	7.1	1.20	.246
2014	Bowie (EL)	AA	10	5	3.72	16	16	0	0	97	101	10	22	91	8.5	1.27	.266
	Norfolk (IL)	AAA	4	3	3.60	12	12	0	0	70	61	8	21	66	8.5	1.17	.239
Minor League Totals			32	24	3.73	88	88	1	0	494	448	55	125	445	8.1	1.16	.240

13 JON KELLER, RHP

BA GRADE

45 Risk: Medium

Born: Aug. 8, 1992. **B-T:** R-R. **Ht.:** 6-5. **Wt.:** 206. **Drafted:** Tampa, 2013 (22nd round). **Signed by:** Jim Thrift.

The Kellers are a power pitching family. Keller's younger brother Mitch was the Pirates' second-round pick in 2014 out of high school. Jon was drafted by the Mariners in the 11th round in 2010. He did not sign and went to Nebraska. After two years in the Cornhuskers rotation, he transferred to Tampa and led the NCAA Division II team to the College World Series. A power pitcher, Keller fell to the Orioles in the 22nd round in 2013 due to medical concerns. He had thoracic outlet syndrome surgery in spring 2012 and also has dealt with an elbow strain in his past. He ended 2014 with a torn oblique muscle that did not require surgery. He is expected to be at full health for spring training. Keller pounds the zone with a fastball that works often in the low 90s but touched 96 mph. He features a solid delivery and throws with good downhill angle. He throws a hard slider that could be a plus pitch. His changeup is a distant third pitch at this point. Keller moved from low Class A Delmarva to high Class A Frederick in July and might have even made Double-A Bowie if he had not gotten injured. Keller appears destined to stay in the bullpen, where he could move fast. Look for him to begin 2015 in Frederick and then possibly move up.

Year	Club (League)	Class	W	L	ERA	G	GS	CG	SV	IP	H	HR	BB	SO	K/9	WHIP	AVG
2013	Orioles (GCL)	R	1	2	4.11	6	5	0	0	15	17	0	2	18	10.6	1.24	.274
	Aberdeen (NYP)	SS	1	0	3.00	1	0	0	0	3	1	0	1	2	6.0	0.67	.100
2014	Delmarva (SAL)	LoA	3	0	1.59	24	0	0	5	57	39	1	14	66	10.5	0.94	.192
	Frederick (CAR)	HiA	0	0	8.31	2	0	0	0	4	8	0	7	5	10.4	3.46	.400
Minor League Totals			5	2	2.50	33	5	0	5	79	65	1	24	91	10.3	1.12	.220

14 HENRY URRUTIA, OF

BA GRADE

50 Risk: High

Born: Feb. 13, 1987. **B-T:** L-R. **Ht.:** 6-3. **Wt.:** 180. **Signed:** Cuba, 2012. **Signed by:** Fred Ferreira.

A Cuban defector who signed with the Orioles for $778,500 in July 2012, Urrutia's visa issues kept him out of games until April 19, 2013, but by July he had reached Baltimore. The promise of that season faded somewhat when he needed sports-hernia surgery early in May 2014 and missed more than two months. Urrutia never regained the offensive form he showed when he was the Orioles' minor league player of the year in 2013. Limited to 51 games at Triple-A Norfolk, he failed to homer and posted a .623 OPS, though he hit .303 in 122 at-bats after his return. Despite Urrutia taking a step backward, the Orioles remain high on his lefthanded bat. He has a level, line-drive swing with solid contact and plate discipline skills. A gap-to-gap hitter, he may never hit for much home-run power, but his hit tool alone could get him back to the majors. He's a below-average defender in left field but has shown improvement in reading the ball off the bat, and his first step is now quicker, but he will probably never be an average defender. Urrutia's bat will need to get him past Triple-A, where likely will begin 2015.

Year	Club (League)	Class	AVG	G	AB	R	H	2B	3B	HR	RBI	BB	SO	SB	CS	OBP	SLG
2013	Bowie (EL)	AA	.365	52	200	33	73	16	0	7	37	24	36	1	1	.433	.550
	Norfolk (IL)	AAA	.316	29	114	16	36	5	1	2	13	8	15	0	0	.358	.430
	Baltimore (AL)	MAJ	.276	24	58	5	16	0	1	0	2	0	11	0	0	.276	.310
2014	Orioles (GCL)	R	.184	14	49	4	9	1	0	0	2	3	11	0	0	.231	.204
	Norfolk (IL)	AAA	.270	51	204	14	55	12	1	0	17	5	50	2	1	.284	.338
Major League Totals			.276	24	58	5	16	0	1	0	2	0	11	0	0	.276	.310
Minor League Totals			.305	146	567	67	173	34	2	9	69	40	112	3	2	.349	.420

15 DREW DOSCH, 3B

BA GRADE

50 Risk: High

Born: June 24, 1992. **B-T:** L-R. **Ht.:** 6-2. **Wt.:** 200. **Drafted:** Youngstown State, 2013 (7th round). **Signed by:** Adrian Dorsey.

The Orioles drafted Dosch in 2013 just weeks after he had surgery for a torn anterior cruciate ligament in his knee, convinced he would make a full recovery. Baltimore general manager Dan Duquette saw Dosch play as an all-star in the Cape Cod League in the summer of 2012, so the organization was pleased to draft him in the seventh round the following year. Dosch finished seventh in the South Atlantic League in batting (.314) in 2014, headlined by a July in which he hit .364 in 107 at-bats. The Orioles feel that his mature approach is as good as any in their system. He uses the whole field, lets the ball travel deep in the hitting zone, and has above-average plate-discipline skills. The lefthanded hitter has shown the ability to make adjustments well. One scout compared his smooth, compact swing to Wade Boggs. Dosch has below-average speed, and scouts debate whether he will develop more than below-average power. His defense at third also is a question. He has arm strength, and his hands are decent, but his agility and consistency need to improve. Dosch will begin 2015 as the third baseman at high Class A Frederick.

Year	Club (League)	Class	AVG	G	AB	R	H	2B	3B	HR	RBI	BB	SO	SB	CS	OBP	SLG
2013	Did not play—Injured																
2014	Delmarva (SAL)	LoA	.314	128	500	76	157	22	4	5	50	47	97	5	3	.379	.404
Minor League Totals			.314	128	500	76	157	22	4	5	50	47	97	5	3	.379	.404

16 STEPHEN TARPLEY, LHP

BA GRADE
50 Risk: High

Born: Feb. 17, 1993. **B-T:** R-L. **Ht.:** 6-2. **Wt.:** 180. **Drafted:** Scottsdale (Ariz.) CC, 2013 (3rd round). **Signed by:** Jim Gillette.

An Indians eighth-round pick out of high school in 2011, Tarpley chose to attend Southern California, where he made 13 starts as a freshman. He transferred to Scottsdale (Ariz.) CC, and the Orioles drafted him in round three in 2013 and signed him to a slot $525,000 bonus. The strong-armed Tarpley made big improvement during a 2014 season that began with him struggling during extended spring training starts and ended with him dominating at short-season Aberdeen. In his last two starts with the IronBirds, he allowed one run in 15 innings with 18 strikeouts. Tarpley pitches in the low 90s, touching 94 mph, with a hard curveball, a changeup he commands well and a slider. During the season, Tarpley made big strides in repeating his delivery, which led to more consistent command. If that continues, he may have No. 3 starter potential. He likely will begin 2015 in the low Class A Delmarva rotation.

Year	Club (League)	Class	W	L	ERA	G	GS	CG	SV	IP	H	HR	BB	SO	K/9	WHIP	AVG
2013	Orioles (GCL)	R	0	1	2.14	7	7	0	0	21	20	0	3	25	10.7	1.10	.256
2014	Aberdeen (NYP)	SS	3	5	3.66	13	12	0	0	66	69	4	24	60	8.1	1.40	.279
Minor League Totals			3	6	3.30	20	19	0	0	87	89	4	27	85	8.8	1.33	.274

17 JASON GARCIA, RHP

BA GRADE
50 Risk: Extreme

Born: Nov. 21, 1992. **B-T:** R-R. **Ht.:** 6-0. **Wt.:** 185. **Drafted:** HS—Land O' Lakes, Fla., 2010 (17th round). **Signed by:** Anthony Turco (Red Sox).

After he missed most of 2013 as he recovered from Tommy John surgery, Garcia came back with explosive stuff, sitting at 94-98 mph and touching triple digits in 2014 while also featuring a slider that garnered some swings and misses. The Orioles selected him from the Red Sox in the major league phase of the Rule 5 draft in December. Orioles scout Danny Haas worked as a crosschecker with Boston when they selected Garcia in the 17th round of the 2010 draft. Baltimore got a good chance to scout him when he struck out 14 of 18 Orioles hitters in a fall instructional league game, including Chance Sisco, Christian Walker and Chris Davis. Garcia's mid-80s slider is a present average pitch, and if it becomes more consistent he has potential closer stuff. His fastball features a late burst up in the zone that makes it seem unhittable at times. Garcia must improve his control (career walk rate of 4.6 per nine innings), but his delivery is easy enough that evaluators believe he can do just that. He finished the 2014 season in the low Class A bullpen, so he faces a four-level leap to the majors if he's going to stick as a Rule 5 pick.

Year	Club (League)	Class	W	L	ERA	G	GS	CG	SV	IP	H	HR	BB	SO	K/9	WHIP	AVG
2012	Greenville (SAL)	LoA	6	6	6.16	28	22	0	2	115	135	8	67	95	7.4	1.75	.297
2013	Greenville (SAL)	LoA	2	2	4.21	9	1	0	1	36	33	3	16	36	8.9	1.35	.239
2014	Lowell (NYP)	SS	1	1	3.48	5	4	0	0	21	19	0	7	22	9.6	1.26	.238
	Greenville (SAL)	LoA	2	1	3.79	9	3	0	3	36	31	0	17	37	9.3	1.35	.242
Minor League Totals			15	16	4.69	73	51	0	6	293	301	12	149	247	7.6	1.53	.266

18 STEVEN BRAULT, LHP

BA GRADE
45 Risk: High

Born: April 29, 1992. **B-T:** L-L. **Ht.:** 6-1. **Wt.:** 185. **Drafted:** Regis (Colo.), 2013 (11th round). **Signed by:** John Gillette.

A former two-way college player, Brault has produced on the mound since being drafted in 2013 out of D-II Regis in Denver. He was the first player to be Rocky Mountain Conference first-team as a pitcher and outfielder. Brault played center field and hit .397, and his athleticism has helped him on the mound. In two pro seasons, he has logged a 2.61 ERA and 1.01 WHIP, yielding just five homers over 189 innings. Brault profiles as a command-and-control lefty with a fastball that ranges from 88-92 mph. His changeup is his best secondary pitch, and he also throws a slider. Brault has a solid delivery, fields his position well and changes speeds. After throwing 130 innings at low Class A Delmarva, Brault should get a shot at the high Class A Frederick rotation in 2015. His ceiling is a back-end starter.

Year	Club (League)	Class	W	L	ERA	G	GS	CG	SV	IP	H	HR	BB	SO	K/9	WHIP	AVG
2013	Aberdeen (NYP)	SS	1	2	2.09	12	12	0	0	43	35	1	12	38	8.0	1.09	.227
2014	Delmarva (SAL)	LoA	9	8	3.05	22	21	1	0	130	107	4	28	115	8.0	1.04	.227
	Frederick (CAR)	HiA	2	0	0.55	3	3	1	0	16	7	0	2	9	5.0	0.55	.127
Minor League Totals			12	10	2.61	37	36	2	0	189	149	5	42	162	7.7	1.01	.219

19 MIKE OHLMAN, C

BA GRADE

45 Risk: High

Born: Dec. 14, 1990. **B-T:** R-R. **Ht.:** 6-5. **Wt.:** 215. **Drafted:** HS— Bradenton, Fla., 2009 (11th round). **Signed by:** John Martin.

After back-to-back seasons of hitting over .300, including a .313 mark in 2013 when he won the high Class A Carolina League batting title, Ohlman's numbers took a big hit in his first year at Double-A Bowie. He hit .236/.310/.318 with two homers and his OPS fell from .934 in 2013 to .628. While he had the same up-the-middle approach, he just could not find consistency. Selected in the 11th round in 2009, Ohlman received an overslot bonus of $995,000, then joined the 40-man roster in November 2013. On defense, Ohlman needs to improve his receiving. He's gotten better blocking, and he has the arm strength, but his throwing is inconsistent. Some scouts wonder if Ohlman's offense would benefit from a position change. He should return to Double-A in 2015.

Year	Club (League)	Class	AVG	G	AB	R	H	2B	3B	HR	RBI	BB	SO	SB	CS	OBP	SLG
2012	Orioles (GCL)	R	.276	8	29	5	8	3	0	1	3	2	10	1	0	.323	.483
	Delmarva (SAL)	LoA	.304	51	171	27	52	16	2	2	28	33	27	0	1	.411	.456
2013	Frederick (CAR)	HiA	.313	100	361	61	113	29	4	13	53	56	93	5	0	.410	.524
2014	Bowie (EL)	AA	.236	113	403	40	95	25	1	2	33	43	86	0	0	.310	.318
Minor League Totals			.254	465	1609	197	408	103	10	24	206	216	401	11	3	.345	.375

20 DAVID HESS, RHP

BA GRADE

45 Risk: High

Born: July 10, 1993. **B-T:** R-R. **Ht.:** 6-2. **Wt.:** 210. **Drafted:** Tennessee Tech, 2014 (5th round). **Signed by:** Adrian Dorsey.

Hess impressed the Orioles with a 33-inning pro debut at short-season Aberdeen and low Class A Delmarva in 2014. He walked eight, fanned 36 and had a 1.11 WHIP. Hess signed for a slightly underslot $280,000. At Tennessee Tech, he pitched out of the bullpen in his first two seasons but worked as a starter as a junior, sitting 89-93 mph with his fastball and touching 96. The Orioles saw a similar velocity in 2014. He also throws a slider and changeup which rate right now as solid-average. Hess showed some polish on the mound, and while he could eventually wind up in a bullpen role, the Orioles will develop him as a starter. One front office executive said Hess reminds him of righthander Bud Norris, with a similar body and delivery. He's a strike-thrower with solid makeup. Hess, who pitched a scoreless inning with one strikeout in the New York-Penn League all-star game, could begin 2015 in the Delmarva rotation.

Year	Club (League)	Class	W	L	ERA	G	GS	CG	SV	IP	H	HR	BB	SO	K/9	WHIP	AVG
2014	Aberdeen (NYP)	SS	2	1	3.20	8	5	0	0	25	22	1	8	24	8.5	1.18	.242
	Delmarva (SAL)	LoA	0	0	3.38	2	2	0	0	8	7	0	0	12	13.5	0.88	.233
Minor League Totals			2	1	3.24	10	7	0	0	33	29	1	8	36	9.7	1.11	.240

21 ADRIAN MARIN, SS

BA GRADE

45 Risk: High

Born: March 8, 1994. **B-T:** R-R. **Ht.:** 6-0. **Wt.:** 180. **Drafted:** HS—Miami, 2012 (3rd round). **Signed by:** Juan Alvarez.

The Orioles selected Marin out of Gulliver Prep in Miami with the 99th overall pick in 2012 and signed him to a slot bonus of $481,100. He has since posted modest stats but held his own at high Class A Frederick in 2014 at age 20. Then he had an impressive instructional league performance where one scout said he looked re-energized. Marin shows average or below tools across the board, with slightly above-average speed, but he adds a high baseball IQ and the ability to make adjustments. He needs to make more consistent contact, use the whole field, and improve his bunting. The Orioles feel he can stay at shortstop, and he's described as a fundamentally sound defender in the mold of J.J. Hardy. Marin has an accurate arm, strong instincts and good anticipation in playing the position. He has a solid-average glove and arm. Even after his modest performance at Frederick, he has a shot to begin next season at Double-A Bowie.

Year	Club (League)	Class	AVG	G	AB	R	H	2B	3B	HR	RBI	BB	SO	SB	CS	OBP	SLG
2012	Orioles (GCL)	R	.287	47	178	24	51	7	3	0	13	11	34	6	1	.339	.360
	Delmarva (SAL)	LoA	.286	6	21	5	6	0	0	0	2	1	2	2	0	.348	.286
2013	Delmarva (SAL)	LoA	.265	108	388	30	103	19	2	4	48	23	90	11	4	.311	.356
2014	Frederick (CAR)	HiA	.232	115	431	40	100	30	1	5	42	21	103	12	4	.271	.341
Minor League Totals			.255	276	1018	99	260	56	6	9	105	56	229	31	9	.300	.349

22 PARKER BRIDWELL, RHP

BA GRADE

45 Risk: High

Born: Aug. 2, 1991. **B-T:** R-R. **Ht.:** 6-4. **Wt.:** 190. **Drafted:** HS—Hereford, Texas, 2010 (9th round). **Signed by:** Ernie Jacobs.

Bridwell's above-average stuff makes him a prospect, but his inconsistency keeps him from being a better one. He can wow observers with performances like his late-season, eight-inning one-hitter with no walks and 13 strikeouts for high Class A Frederick. A three-sport star at Hereford (Texas) High, Bridwell drew some interest from college football programs as a quarterback before the Orioles drafted him in 2010. He led the organization in strikeouts in 2013 and was third with 142 in 2014. Bridwell's fastball sits in the 90-93 mph range, touching 95. He often struggles with command and repeating his delivery. His changeup is his best secondary pitch, ahead of his slider, with swing-and-miss potential. Bridwell is athletic with a good feel for pitching, if not pitch execution. He did well in a bullpen role in the Arizona Fall League, a possible glimpse into his future, but will remain in the rotation at Double-A Bowie.

Year	Club (League)	Class	W	L	ERA	G	GS	CG	SV	IP	H	HR	BB	SO	K/9	WHIP	AVG
2012	Delmarva (SAL)	LoA	5	9	5.98	23	22	1	0	114	122	15	63	71	5.6	1.62	.281
2013	Delmarva (SAL)	LoA	8	9	4.73	26	26	0	0	143	141	9	59	144	9.1	1.40	.255
2014	Frederick (CAR)	HiA	7	10	4.45	26	26	1	0	142	123	11	70	142	9.0	1.36	.234
Minor League Totals			22	36	4.99	96	92	2	0	480	469	37	231	433	8.1	1.46	.257

23 BRIAN GONZALEZ, LHP

BA GRADE

45 Risk: High

Born: Oct. 25, 1995. **B-T:** R-L. **Ht.:** 6-1. **Wt.:** 230. **Drafted:** HS—Southwest Ranches, Fla., 2014 (3rd round). **Signed by:** Kelvin Colon.

After signing free agents Nelson Cruz and Ubaldo Jimenez following the 2013 season, the Orioles didn't make their first selection in the 2014 draft until day two and round three. They selected Gonzalez with the 90th pick out of Archbishop McCarthy High, where he played for a powerhouse that won three consecutive state titles. Gonzalez signed for $700,000, which was $105,800 over slot. He impressed the Orioles with his maturity and advanced pitchability, flashing a little more velocity than he had in high school with a fastball that ranged from 88-92 mph and topped out at 94. He also throws a changeup and a solid curveball that could get tighter. All three pitches right now rate as solid average. Gonzalez felt his changeup was ahead of his curveball in high school because his dad would not allow him to throw a curve until he was 16. Former major league pitcher Alex Fernandez worked with Gonzalez's prep team, teaching him how to pitch inside and change speeds. Gonzalez could become a durable innings-eater because he has a clean, athletic delivery. He will likely open 2015 with low Class A Delmarva.

Year	Club (League)	Class	W	L	ERA	G	GS	CG	SV	IP	H	HR	BB	SO	K/9	WHIP	AVG
2014	Orioles (GCL)	R	0	0	0.00	8	8	0	0	25	11	0	8	25	9.1	0.77	.134
	Aberdeen (NYP)	SS	0	1	5.00	2	2	0	0	9	10	0	2	11	11.0	1.33	.286
Minor League Totals			0	1	1.34	10	10	0	0	34	21	0	10	36	9.6	0.92	.179

24 LOGAN VERRETT, RHP

BA GRADE

40 Risk: Low

Born: June 19, 1990. **B-T:** R-R. **Ht.:** 6-2. **Wt.:** 190. **Drafted:** Baylor, 2011 (3rd round). **Signed by:** Max Semler (Mets).

After three seasons in the Mets system and with 308 innings the last two seasons between Double-A and Triple-A under his belt, Verrett joined the Orioles when they selected him in the major league phase of the Rule 5 draft in December. A strike-thrower who has walked just 1.7 batters per nine over his career, Verrett succeeds with intelligence more than stuff. He mixes four usable pitches, none of which is plus. His fastball ranges from 88-92 mph and his slider is solid-average. He throws the slider in any count and uses it to neutralize righthanded hitters, though lefties hit .311 and slugged .463 against him in 2014. Verrett adds and subtracts from a changeup and curveball to keep hitters off-balance. The Orioles feel he is ready to compete for a big league job and will give him a chance to do so in spring training.

Year	Club (League)	Class	W	L	ERA	G	GS	CG	SV	IP	H	HR	BB	SO	K/9	WHIP	AVG
2012	Savannah (SAL)	LoA	3	2	3.06	11	11	1	0	65	57	7	9	67	9.3	1.02	.228
	St. Lucie (FSL)	HiA	2	0	2.09	6	6	1	0	39	30	4	4	26	6.1	0.88	.205
2013	Binghamton (EL)	AA	12	6	4.25	24	24	0	0	146	136	21	31	132	8.1	1.14	.249
2014	Las Vegas (PCL)	AAA	11	5	4.33	28	28	1	0	162	188	17	34	119	6.6	1.37	.291
Minor League Totals			28	13	3.89	69	69	3	0	411	411	49	78	344	7.5	1.19	.259

25 JOSH HART, OF

BA GRADE

45 Risk: High

Born: Oct. 2, 1994. **B-T:** L-L. **Ht.:** 6-2. **Wt.:** 180. **Drafted:** HS—Lilburn, Ga., 2013 (1st round supplemental). **Signed by:** Arthur McConnehead.

The Orioles drafted Hart 37th overall in 2013 and signed the Georgia high schooler for $1.45 million. So far his performance has not quite matched his promise. A hamstring injury limited him in 2013, and he missed five weeks in 2014 after having arthroscopic surgery on his right knee to repair a torn meniscus. Hart has been projected as a speedy, top-of-the-order hitter with little power. Some scouts feel he'll eventually show gap-to-gap pop, but he'll need improved plate discipline to increase his on-base ability and take advantage of his speed. Hart is a solid-average defender who can stay in center field. His arm rates below-average but has improved and could become average. Despite Hart's poor output at low Class A Delmarva in 2014, the Orioles feel he has a shot to start at high Class A Frederick in 2015.

Year	Club (League)	Class	AVG	G	AB	R	H	2B	3B	HR	RBI	BB	SO	SB	CS	OBP	SLG
2013	Orioles (GCL)	R	.228	33	123	14	28	5	2	0	9	13	23	11	3	.312	.301
	Aberdeen (NYP)	SS	.100	3	10	0	1	0	0	0	0	1	4	0	0	.182	.100
2014	Orioles (GCL)	R	.167	6	24	2	4	0	1	0	0	1	2	2	0	.200	.250
	Delmarva (SAL)	LoA	.255	85	326	22	83	5	1	1	28	21	86	11	5	.301	.285
Minor League Totals			.240	127	483	38	116	10	4	1	37	36	115	24	8	.297	.284

26 BRANDEN KLINE, RHP

BA GRADE

45 Risk: High

Born: Sept. 29, 1991. **B-T:** R-R. **Ht.:** 6-3. **Wt.:** 205. **Drafted:** Virginia, 2012 (2nd round). **Signed by:** Chris Gale.

The Orioles made Kline the 65th overall selection in 2012 after his three-year career at Virginia, where he was an all-Atlantic Coast Conference closer in 2011 and a top starter in 2012. Limited to 35 innings in 2013 after he had surgery in late May to repair a right ankle/fibula fracture, Kline logged 143 innings in 2014, mostly at high Class A Frederick. Kline throws a fastball, slider and changeup. He pitches between 90-95 mph with velocity that can fluctuate. He is athletic and pitches with solid mechanics and good downhill plane. His secondary pitches still need more development to consistently grade as solid-average, but it's more an issue of command than pure stuff. He projects to have a ceiling as a back-end starter, but his future could be in a bullpen role. He should begin 2015 in the Double-A Bowie rotation.

Year	Club (League)	Class	W	L	ERA	G	GS	CG	SV	IP	H	HR	BB	SO	K/9	WHIP	AVG
2012	Aberdeen (NYP)	SS	0	0	4.50	4	4	0	0	12	12	1	4	12	9.0	1.33	.273
2013	Delmarva (SAL)	LoA	1	2	5.86	7	7	0	0	35	41	4	14	32	8.2	1.56	.289
2014	Frederick (CAR)	HiA	8	6	3.84	23	23	0	0	127	143	9	32	95	6.8	1.38	.288
	Bowie (EL)	AA	0	2	5.94	3	3	0	0	17	18	1	11	9	4.9	1.74	.290
Minor League Totals			9	10	4.44	37	37	0	0	191	214	15	61	148	7.0	1.44	.287

27 MYCHAL GIVENS, RHP

BA GRADE

45 Risk: High

Born: May 13, 1990. **B-T:** R-R. **Ht.:** 6-1. **Wt.:** 210. **Drafted:** HS—Tampa, 2009 (2nd round). **Signed by:** John Martin.

When the Orioles drafted Givens with the 54th pick in 2009 and signed him for $800,000, they saw the potential to develop a strong, athletic shortstop who could grow into power. But after three seasons and an empty .247 average, the Orioles moved him to the mound in 2013. Givens had pitched a bit in high school, and the early results have been positive. Using a unique low-three-quarters arm slot, he has shown a plus arm with a fastball touching 96 mph. Givens' fastball shows good life and heavy sink, and he could be a future groundball machine. He recorded a 2.27 groundout-to-airout ratio at high Class Frederick and Double-A Bowie in 2014. His slider and changeup rate average, and the latter has made gains. He struggled with control in 2014 before making an adjustment in the Arizona Fall League, pitching out of a crouch to more easily get to his arm slot. Givens will begin 2015 in Triple-A Norfolk.

Year	Club (League)	Class	W	L	ERA	G	GS	CG	SV	IP	H	HR	BB	SO	K/9	WHIP	AVG
2013	Delmarva (SAL)	LoA	2	3	4.22	28	0	0	3	43	34	1	19	36	7.6	1.24	.219
2014	Frederick (CAR)	HiA	1	2	3.24	18	0	0	3	33	21	2	16	27	7.3	1.11	.174
	Bowie (EL)	AA	0	0	3.91	18	0	0	0	25	19	0	23	28	9.9	1.66	.209
Minor League Totals			3	5	3.82	64	0	0	6	101	74	3	58	91	8.1	1.30	.202

Year	Club (League)	Class	AVG	G	AB	R	H	2B	3B	HR	RBI	BB	SO	SB	CS	OBP	SLG
2012	Delmarva (SAL)	LoA	.243	100	337	43	82	15	0	2	27	39	49	13	8	.330	.306
Minor League Totals			.247	254	907	108	224	36	2	6	84	91	134	36	22	.331	.311

28 JONAH HEIM, C

BA GRADE

50 Risk: Extreme

Born: June 27, 1995. **B-T:** B-R. **Ht.:** 6-3. **Wt.:** 195. **Drafted:** HS— Amherst, N.Y., 2013 (4th round). **Signed by:** Kirk Fredriksson.

The Orioles see Heim as a solid switch-hitting catching prospect with a lot of potential, but also with a lot of development to come due to his youth. They gave the lean, 6-foot-3 backstop $389,700 to bypass his Michigan State commitment. He needs to add strength, but Baltimore is encouraged by his offense and defense already. Heim has a great body and strong makeup. He has a fundamentally-sound swing where he gets his hands to the ball with a direct bat path and above-average bat speed, and has potential to hit for average with gap power. Right now he is not stronger from one side of the plate or the other. Like most young players, Heim needs to improve his plate discipline. On defense, he shows potential with solid skills across the board, including above-average arm strength and consistent pop times of under two seconds on throws to second base. The Orioles feel he is mature on defense, a smart kid and a real student of the game. He likely will start 2015 at low Class A Delmarva.

Year	Club (League)	Class	AVG	G	AB	R	H	2B	3B	HR	RBI	BB	SO	SB	CS	OBP	SLG
2013	Orioles (GCL)	R	.185	27	81	8	15	5	0	0	4	10	13	1	1	.275	.247
2014	Orioles (GCL)	R	.244	26	78	8	19	9	0	0	5	6	9	3	0	.306	.359
	Aberdeen (NYP)	SS	.143	20	70	2	10	2	0	1	2	2	15	0	0	.164	.214
Minor League Totals			.192	73	229	18	44	16	0	1	11	18	37	4	1	.253	.275

29 OFELKY PERALTA, RHP

BA GRADE

50 Risk: Extreme

Born: April 20, 1997. **B-T:** R-R. **Ht.:** 6-5. **Wt.:** 195. **Signed:** Dominican Republic, 2013. **Signed by:** Fred Ferreira.

Peralta displayed mid-90s velocity during his pro debut in the Dominican Summer League in 2014, but he is very much a raw prospect who needs to improve his mechanics and control. Orioles international guru Fred Ferreira signed Peralta to a $325,000 bonus in September 2013 the same day he saw him throw for the first time during a showcase in San Pedro de Macoris. The Orioles found Peralta to be a likable, hard-working pitcher in 2014, but one who struggled to throw consistent strikes, with a walk rate of 6.9 per nine innings. He improved during the season, allowing only one earned run in his last 14 innings. A tall, lean 17-year-old, Peralta's fastball worked from 91-95 mph. He also throws a slider and changeup. He had problems repeating his delivery and getting his long arms and legs working together. The Orioles probably will move Peralta to the U.S. in 2015 and start him in extended spring, with a move to the Rookie-level Gulf Coast League in June.

Year	Club (League)	Class	W	L	ERA	G	GS	CG	SV	IP	H	HR	BB	SO	K/9	WHIP	AVG
2014	Orioles2 (DSL)	R	0	4	3.12	11	11	0	0	43	28	0	37	33	6.9	1.50	.187
Minor League Totals			0	4	3.12	11	11	0	0	43	28	0	37	33	6.9	1.50	.187

30 TREY MANCINI, 1B

BA GRADE

45 Risk: High

Born: March 18, 1992. **B-T:** R-R. **Ht.:** 6-4. **Wt.:** 215. **Drafted:** Notre Dame, 2013 (8th round). **Signed by:** Kirk Fredriksson.

A senior sign out of Notre Dame, Mancini made a strong first impression by setting a short-season Aberdeen record with 84 hits in 2013. The hit parade continued in 2014, when he hit .317 at low Class A Delmarva prior to a midseason promotion to high Class A Frederick. Mancini has a feel for hitting with an excellent approach. He is focused at the plate and shows raw power, but not consistently. For now, he is a righthanded gap-to-gap hitter who can drive the ball well to right-center field. His hit tool is above his power tool, but Mancini sometimes gets too aggressive at the plate. His defense grades as solid-average, with speed that is a step below-average. Mancini isn't the smoothest defender, committing nine errors in 2014, but Orioles officials say he picks the ball out of the dirt well, and he has a solid-average arm. Mancini probably will return to Frederick to begin the 2015 season.

Year	Club (League)	Class	AVG	G	AB	R	H	2B	3B	HR	RBI	BB	SO	SB	CS	OBP	SLG
2013	Aberdeen (NYP)	SS	.328	68	256	43	84	18	2	3	35	20	43	3	1	.382	.449
2014	Delmarva (SAL)	LoA	.317	68	268	30	85	13	3	3	42	14	52	1	1	.357	.422
	Frederick (CAR)	HiA	.251	69	275	37	69	19	0	7	41	14	43	0	1	.295	.396
Minor League Totals			.298	205	799	110	238	50	5	13	118	48	138	4	3	.344	.422

Boston Red Sox

BY ALEX SPEIER

The Red Sox entered 2014 as defending champions and concluded the year humbled by their second last-place finish in three years, their precipitous decline reflecting in no small part on the unrealized hopes for what had appeared to be an emerging young core.

The organization viewed the championship as the potential point of departure for what GM Ben Cherington had described as "the next great Red Sox team," a term meant to signify sustainable championship hopes fueled by an impressive prospect pipeline. With a significant amount of a championship core returning, the team felt it could begin to assimilate position players into everyday roles in 2014, in advance of a wave of homegrown pitchers who would join the roster as soon as late 2014 or early 2015.

The logic seemed sound. Xander Bogaerts was a postseason star in 2013; there was no hesitation at the idea of committing to him at shortstop for 2014. Will Middlebrooks had endured an up-and-down 2013, but had shown enough over two big league seasons that the Sox felt he was ready for a primary role. Jackie Bradley hadn't been ready for the big leagues in 2013, but his track record suggested that he should be able to get on base enough to be a potential starter (the team hedged its bet slightly by signing Grady Sizemore) given his jaw-dropping defense.

Instead, those three players endured lengthy periods in which they appeared overmatched. Middlebrooks struggled with both health and performance and never hit for power. Bradley was overpowered, striking out with enough frequency to cast doubt on his future as an everyday big leaguer. Bogaerts, after a breathtaking start, endured a two and a half month slump that, coincidentally or not, coincided with a temporary move from short to third.

Those struggles—in place of reliable veteran production in 2013—contributed to the team's spiral from contention by late-July and a trade deadline selloff of veterans. More broadly, the challenges faced by those young players left team owners questioning the pace of the team's commitment to prospects.

"What we won't do is make the same mistake we made this year, which is assume that so many of our young players were ready for prime time," Red Sox CEO Larry Lucchino said at the end of the year. "I guess we miscalculated the preparation level."

Of course, the team also witnessed immensely promising developments among its young players.

Boston looks for more from Xander Bogaerts after an up-and-down rookie season

TOP PROSPECTS OF THE DECADE

Year	Player, Pos.	2014 Org
2005	Hanley Ramirez, ss	Dodgers
2006	Andy Marte, 3b	Diamondbacks
2007	Daisuke Matsuzaka, rhp	Mets
2008	Clay Buchholz, rhp	Red Sox
2009	Lars Anderson, 1b	Cubs
2010	Ryan Westmoreland, of	Out of baseball
2011	Jose Iglesias, ss	Tigers
2012	Will Middlebrooks, 3b	Red Sox
2013	Xander Bogaerts, ss	Red Sox
2014	Xander Bogaerts, ss	Red Sox

Bogaerts recovered from his struggles with a strong September, and the team thinks he'll use the lessons of his age 21 season as a springboard to success.

Mookie Betts blitzed from Double-A to the big leagues by midseason and showed star potential as a 21-year-old who moved from second to the outfield.

After signing with the Sox in August, Cuban outfielder Rusney Castillo showed impact across-the-board tools in his big league debut.

And catcher Christian Vazquez showed Gold Glove defensive potential and passable offense in a half-season in the big leagues.

The Sox have endured a three-year period of unprecedented volatility, going worst-to-first-to-worst. Yet as devastating as the 2014 season was, the glimpses of those potential core players along with the steady advance of future impact players like catcher Blake Swihart and third baseman Rafael Devers has created a belief that the ultimate goal of sustainable success may be closer at hand than the last-place finish of 2014 would suggest.

General manager: Ben Cherington. **Farm director:** Ben Crockett. **Scouting director:** Amiel Sawdaye.

Class	Team	League	W	L	PCT	Finish	Manager
Majors	Boston Red Sox	American	71	91	.438	25th (30)	John Farrell
Triple-A	Pawtucket Red Sox	International	79	65	.549	t-2nd (14	Kevin Boles
Double-A	Portland Sea Dogs	Eastern	88	54	.620	1st (12)	Billy McMillon
High A	Salem Red Sox	Carolina	68	68	.500	3rd (8)	Carlos Febles
Low A	Greenville Drive	South Atlantic	60	79	.432	10th (14)	Darren Fenster
Short season	Lowell Spinners	New York-Penn	37	38	.493	t-6th (14)	Joe Oliver
Rookie	Red Sox	Gulf Coast	36	24	.600	4th (16)	Tom Kotchman
Overall Minor League Record			368	328	.529	5th (30)	

THIS YEAR'S TOP 30

No.	Player, Pos.	Grade
1.	Blake Swihart, c	60/Medium
2.	Henry Owens, lhp	55/Medium
3.	Rusney Castillo, of	55/Medium
4.	Eduardo Rodriguez, lhp	55/Medium
5.	Brian Johnson, lhp	50/Low
6.	Rafael Devers, 3b	60/Extreme
7.	Manuel Margot, of	55/High
8.	Matt Barnes, rhp	50/Medium
9.	Deven Marrero, ss	50/Medium
10.	Garin Cecchini, 3b/of	50/Medium
11.	Michael Chavis, ss/3b	55/High
12.	Sam Travis, 1b	50/High
13.	Javier Guerra, ss	55/Extreme
14.	Michael Kopech, rhp	55/Extreme
15.	Trey Ball, lhp	55/Extreme
16.	Anthony Ranaudo, rhp	45/Low
17.	Sean Coyle, 2b/3b	50/High
18.	Edwin Escobar, lhp	45/Low
19.	Travis Shaw, 1b	45/Medium
20.	Teddy Stankiewicz, rhp	50/High
21.	Bryce Brentz, of	45/Medium
22.	Steven Wright, rhp	45/Medium
23.	Mauricio Dubon, ss	50/High
24.	Wendell Rijo, 2b	50/High
25.	Carlos Asuaje, 2b/3b/of	45/Medium
26.	Joe Gunkel, rhp	50/High
27.	Nick Longhi, 1b/of	50/Extreme
28.	Justin Haley, rhp	45/High
29.	Henry Ramos, of	50/Extreme
30.	Pat Light, rhp	45/High

LAST YEAR'S TOP 30

No.	Player, Pos.	Status
1.	Xander Bogaerts, ss/3b	Majors
2.	Henry Owens, lhp	No. 2
3.	Jackie Bradley, of	Majors
4.	Allen Webster, rhp	Majors
5.	Blake Swihart, c	No. 1
6.	Garin Cecchini, 3b	No. 10
7.	Mookie Betts, 2b	Majors
8.	Brandon Workman, rhp	Majors
9.	Matt Barnes, rhp	No. 8
10.	Trey Ball, lhp	No. 15
11.	Anthony Ranaudo, rhp	No. 16
12.	Christian Vazquez, c	Majors
13.	Manuel Margot, of	No. 7
14.	Brian Johnson, lhp	No. 5
15.	Deven Marrero, ss	No. 9
16.	Bryce Brentz, of	No. 21
17.	Drake Britton, lhp	Majors
18.	Wendell Rijo, 2b	No. 24
19.	Teddy Stankiewicz, 2b	No. 20
20.	Rafael Devers, 3b	No. 6
21.	Cody Kukuk, lhp	Dropped out
22.	Jamie Callahan, rhp	Dropped out
23.	Daniel McGrath, lhp	Dropped out
24.	Simon Mercedes, rhp	Dropped out
25.	Dan Butler, c	Dropped out
26.	Travis Shaw, 1b	No. 19
27.	Javier Guerra, ss	No. 13
28.	Tzu-Wei Lin, ss	Dropped out
29.	Alex Wilson, rhp	Majors
30.	Sean Coyle, 2b	No. 17

BEST TOOLS

Best Hitter for Average	Garin Cecchini
Best Power Hitter	Rafael Devers
Best Strike-Zone Discipline	Garin Cecchini
Fastest Baserunner	Manuel Margot
Best Athlete	Blake Swihart
Best Fastball	Eduardo Rodriguez
Best Curveball	Brian Johnson
Best Slider	Michael Kopech
Best Changeup	Henry Owens
Best Control	Brian Johnson
Best Defensive Catcher	Blake Swihart
Best Defensive Infielder	Deven Marrero
Best Infield Arm	Deven Marrero
Best Defensive Outfielder	Manuel Margot
Best Outfield Arm	Henry Ramos

PROJECTED 2018 LINEUP

Catcher	Blake Swihart
First Base	Rafael Devers
Second Base	Dustin Pedroia
Third Base	Hanley Ramirez
Shortstop	Xander Bogaerts
Left Field	Mookie Betts
Center Field	Manuel Margot
Right Field	Rusney Castillo
Designated Hitter	Pablo Sandoval
No. 1 Starter	Rick Porcello
No. 2 Starter	Clay Buchholz
No. 3 Starter	Henry Owens
No. 4 Starter	Eduardo Rodriguez
No. 5 Starter	Joe Kelly
Closer	Matt Barnes

BOSTON RED SOX

TOP 2015 ROOKIE: Rusney Castillo, of. For $72.5 million, the Red Sox are betting on the Cuban defector's ability to make an immediate impact.

BREAKOUT PROSPECT: Javier Guerra, ss. The 18-year-old played Gold Glove-caliber defense in the Gulf Coast League; if he matures as a hitter, he has star potential.

SLEEPER: Jake Cosart, rhp. The converted outfielder has a lightning-quick arm and shows the potential to work at 93-97 mph as a starter with a hammer breaking ball.

SOURCE OF TOP 30 TALENT			
Homegrown	27	Acquired	3
College	10	Trades	3
Junior college	1	Rule 5 draft	0
High school	11	Independent leagues	0
Draft-and-follow	0	Free agents/waivers	0
Nondrafted free agents	0		
International	5		

LF
Bryce Brentz (21)
Keury De La Cruz
Trenton Kemp

CF
Rusney Castillo (3)
Manuel Margot (7)
Yoan Aybar
Luis Alexander Basabe

RF
Henry Ramos (29)
Danny Mars

3B
Rafael Devers (6)
Garin Cecchini (10)
Jordan Betts

SS
Deven Marrero (9)
Javier Guerra (13)
Mauricio Dubon (23)
Tzu-Wei Lin

2B
Michael Chavis (11)
Sean Coyle (17)
Wendell Rijo (24)
Carlos Asuaje (25)
Victor Acosta
Reed Gragnani

1B
Sam Travis (12)
Travis Shaw (19)
Nick Longhi (27)
Jantzen Witte
Josh Ockimey

C
Blake Swihart (1)
Dan Butler

LHP

LHSP	LHRP
Henry Owens (2)	Edwin Escobar (18)
Eduardo Rodriguez (4)	Drake Britton
Brian Johnson (5)	Cody Kukuk
Trey Ball (15)	
Javier Gonzalez	
Daniel McGrath	

RHP

RHSP	RHRP
Matt Barnes (8)	Joe Gunkel (26)
Michael Kopech (14)	Pat Light (30)
Anthony Ranaudo (16)	Heath Hembree
Teddy Stankiewicz (20)	Dalier Hinojosa
Steven Wright (22)	Jonathan Aro
Justin Haley (28)	Simon Mercedes
Jake Cosart	Kyle Martin
Pat McAvoy	Noe Ramirez
Anderson Espinoza	Jamie Callahan
Christopher Acosta	
Keith Couch	
Luis Diaz	

2014

BEST PURE HITTER: 1B Sam Travis (2) was one of the top righthanded college bats in the draft. His natural strength produces bat speed and a direct swing, leading to high contact rates in college and in his pro debut.

BEST POWER HITTER: 3B Michael Chavis (1) unleashes plus bat speed from a compact stroke, producing plus raw power and a different sound off his bat. Both Chavis and Travis have a chance to hit for both average and power. 1B Josh Ockimey (5) has 70-grade raw power.

FASTEST RUNNER: Switch-hitting OF Danny Mars (6) is a plus runner who gets out of the box quickly with a line drive stroke. Overslot OF Trenton Kemp (15) is an explosive athlete with plus speed.

BEST DEFENSIVE PLAYER: C Devon Fisher (20) had one of the strongest catching arms in the draft, drawing at least plus grades, though it needs to be more accurate. He signed for $300,000.

BEST FASTBALL: RHP Michael Kopech (1) has a loose, quick arm and the ball explodes out of his hand with plus life, touching 98 in the spring and 96 this summer. RHP Jake Cosart (3) has elite arm speed and sat 92-95, touching 97 after signing. RHP Kevin McAvoy (4) can pitch off his low-90s fastball with heavy, sinking life.

BEST SECONDARY PITCH: The breaking balls for both Kopech (slider) and Cosart (curveball) have at least plus potential. RHP Karsten Whitson (11) used to have a wipeout slider; it has shown flashes of returning during instructs. RHP Chandler Shepherd (13) and Jalen Beeks (12) have above-average to plus changeups.

BEST PRO DEBUT: McAvoy produced a 1.91 ERA and 7.7 strikeout-walk ratio in 28 innings. Travis hit .316/.351/.467 with seven home runs and 44 RBIs across two levels, reaching low Class A Greenville. 3B Jordan Betts (18) finished fourth in the New York-Penn League in home runs (10) while hitting .269/.333/.479.

BEST ATHLETE: RHP Kevin Steen (9) led his team deep into the state playoffs in basketball, limiting his mound time this spring. The 6-foot-1 Steen has impressive leaping ability capable of producing highlight-reel dunks. He has a quick arm and could take a jump once he gains strength to his lean, long-limbed body.

MOST INTRIGUING BACKGROUND: Cosart is the younger brother of Marlins righthander Jarred Cosart. Whitson turned down $2.1 million as the ninth pick in the 2010 draft and signed for $100,000 this year. OF Derek Miller (23) is the son of Blake Miller, vice president of security and parking for the Texas Rangers.

CLOSEST TO THE MAJORS: Travis and Beeks.

BEST LATE-ROUND PICK: Whitson provides value and upside. Josh Pennington (29) had Tommy John surgery but is athletic with a fastball that sits in the low-90s.

THE ONE WHO GOT AWAY: Projectable LHP David Peterson (28) could go in the top few rounds after three years at Oregon.

ASSESSMENT: Boston began its high-upside draft class with two high schoolers and tied for the most prep signees of any American League team with eight.

2013

Early returns on the class have been iffy; RHP Teddy Stankiewicz (2) and 2B Carlos Asuaje (11) have performed, but LHP Trey Ball (1) is among those who had a tough welcome to pro ball.

GRADE: D

2012

SS Deven Marrero (1) has played as advertised, while LHP Brian Johnson (1s) dominated Double-A in 2014. Boston's unsigned included RHP Carson Fulmer (15), SS Alex Bregman (29).

GRADE: C

2011

2B/OF Mookie Betts (5) emerged as a potential star in 2014, while OF Jackie Bradley (1s) struggled as a rookie. C Blake Swihart (1) and LHP Henry Owens (1s) rank among Boston's top prospects.

GRADE: A

TOP DRAFT PICKS OF THE DECADE

Year	Player, Pos.	2014 Org
2005	Jacoby Ellsbury, of	Yankees
2006	Jason Place, of	Out of baseball
2007	Nick Hagadone, lhp (1st round supp.)	Indians
2008	Casey Kelly, rhp	Padres
2009	Reymond Fuentes, of	Padres
2010	Kolbrin Vitek, 3b	Out of baseball
2011	Matt Barnes, rhp	Red Sox
2012	Deven Marrero, ss	Red Sox
2013	Trey Ball, lhp	Red Sox
2014	Michael Chavis, ss	Red Sox

LARGEST BONUSES IN CLUB HISTORY

Jose Iglesias, 2009	$6,250,000
Rusney Castillo, 2014	$5,400,000
Dalier Hinojosa, 2013	$4,000,000
Casey Kelly, 2008	$3,000,000
Trey Ball, 2013	$2,750,000

1 BLAKE SWIHART, C

Born: April 3, 1992. **B-T:** B-R. **Ht.:** 6-1. **Wt.:** 185.
Drafted: HS—Rio Rancho, N.M., 2011 (1st round).
Signed by: Matt Mahoney.

As a sophomore in high school, Swihart identified an opportunity to improve his prospect status by broadening his baseball horizons. A righthanded-hitting and righthanded-throwing player who moved all over the field, Swihart commenced an education in both switch-hitting and catching. Good move. Though he remained a work in progress in both areas, by the time Swihart was draft-eligible in 2011, the Sox saw him as one of the best high school bats in the draft with a chance to bring rarely seen athleticism to catching. Given the limited exposure to both catching and switch-hitting as an amateur, the Sox anticipated that it might take Swihart time to excel. But after a modest pro debut in low Class A in 2012, he's emerged as perhaps the top catching prospect in the game.

How many catchers are there like Swihart in the minors? "There are none," said one evaluator, a testament to his offensive and defensive potential as well as his head-turning athleticism. He has made huge strides behind the plate, where he now profiles as an above-average defender who led the Eastern League by a wide margin while gunning down 47 percent of attempted base thieves, with pop times averaging about 1.9 seconds and getting below 1.8 on occasion. Evaluators marvel that he has the athleticism and speed to play virtually anywhere on the field—some even suggested he could play center or second—though behind the plate, he has a chance to be a two-way force. Offensively, though he shows an aggressive approach that limits his walks, he displays good pitch recognition, typically swings at strikes and sends line drives screaming to the gaps. Though still stronger from the right side, he shows above-average bat speed and bat control from both sides of the plate, and he won't be beaten by velocity, while switch-hitting will limit his vulnerability to breaking balls. His swing is geared for line drives, but after hitting nine combined homers in his first two full pro seasons, Swihart cleared that total with 13 homers in 2014.

There's a chance that his aggressive tendencies will be exploited by advanced pitching, which could result in a challenging transition to the big leagues after a lengthy apprenticeship in Pawtucket in 2015. Yet even evaluators who recognize the potential that his floor could be that of a backup concede the likelihood that he has the skill set to be at least a solid defense-first primary catcher. And even with limited power totals, Swihart's ability to hit for average and amass extra-base hits while leading a pitching staff could allow him to emerge as a perennial all-star.

BA GRADE

60 Risk: Medium

SCOUTING GRADES

Batting: 60.
Power: 50.
Speed: 50.
Defense: 65.
Arm: 65.

Based on 20-80 scouting scale and future projection rather than present tools.

LGE	PA	BB%	SO%	ISO
EL	380	7.6	17.1	.187
IL	71	2.8	21.1	.116

KEN BABBITT

Year	Club (League)	Class	AVG	G	AB	R	H	2B	3B	HR	RBI	BB	SO	SB	CS	OBP	SLG
2012	Greenville (SAL)	LoA	.262	92	344	44	90	17	4	7	53	26	68	6	2	.307	.395
2013	Salem (CAR)	HiA	.298	103	376	45	112	29	7	2	42	41	63	7	8	.366	.428
2014	Portland (EL)	AA	.300	92	347	47	104	23	3	12	55	29	65	7	1	.353	.487
	Pawtucket (IL)	AAA	.261	18	69	6	18	3	1	1	9	2	15	1	0	.282	.377
Minor League Totals			.284	307	1142	142	324	72	15	22	159	98	213	21	11	.338	.431

2 HENRY OWENS, LHP

Born: July 21, 1992. **B-T:** L-L. **Ht.:** 6-7. **Wt.:** 210. **Drafted:** HS—Huntington Beach, Calif., 2011 (1st round supplemental). **Signed by:** Tom Battista.

Owens built on a dominant 2013 season by opening 2014 with a rain-shortened, six-inning, nine-strikeout no-hitter for Portland. He earned the nod as the starter for the U.S. team in the Futures Game. Owens is comfortable working at 89-92 mph (though he'll touch 94) thanks to an excellent changeup that he sells to great effect. He emphasized his curveball this year, a point he hammered home by opening the Futures Game with a hook. He also shows an advanced feel for pitching that exceeds his age, including the ability to read swings and adapt. With ongoing strength gains, Owens continues to make strides in locking in his delivery, contributing to a decrease in his walk rate that was accompanied by working more consistently down in the zone for quick outs. He'll need to develop the curveball further and may ultimately incorporate a slider or cutter. Owens' combination of stuff, makeup and feel for pitching makes him a safe bet for the big league rotation. Most believe he has a mid-rotation ceiling (some see a chance for a No. 2 starter), with a reasonable probability of getting there or close to that point, despite less-than-eye-popping velocity.

BA GRADE

55 Risk: Medium

LGE	BF	SO%	BB%	HR/9
EL	493	25.6	9.5	0.45
IL	156	28.2	7.7	0.95

Year	Club (League)	Class	W	L	ERA	G	GS	CG	SV	IP	H	HR	BB	SO	K/9	WHIP	AVG
2012	Greenville (SAL)	LoA	12	5	4.87	23	22	0	0	102	100	10	47	130	11.5	1.45	.256
2013	Salem (CAR)	HiA	8	5	2.92	20	20	0	0	105	66	6	53	123	10.6	1.14	.180
	Portland (EL)	AA	3	1	1.78	6	6	0	0	30	18	3	15	46	13.6	1.09	.167
2014	Portland (EL)	AA	14	4	2.60	20	20	3	0	121	89	6	47	126	9.4	1.12	.201
	Pawtucket (IL)	AAA	3	1	4.03	6	6	0	0	38	32	4	12	44	10.4	1.16	.230
Minor League Totals			40	16	3.34	75	74	3	0	396	305	29	174	469	10.7	1.21	.211

3 RUSNEY CASTILLO, OF

Born: Sept. 7, 1987. **B-T:** R-R. **Ht.:** 5-8. **Wt.:** 186. **Signed:** Cuba, 2014. **Signed by:** Allard Baird.

The Red Sox won the bidding war for Castillo's services with the largest guarantee ever conferred upon a player from Cuba, signing him in August to a contract through 2020 for $72.5 million. His first game action in roughly a year and a half was singularly impressive given the layoff, as Castillo was able to show the diverse skill set that convinced the Sox to project him as an everyday outfielder. Castillo checks a lot of boxes. He has a big swing that permits him to generate above-average raw power (with perhaps 20-home run potential) yet he has the hand-eye coordination to limit his swings and misses, even with an aggressive approach. He also showed the ability to learn and adjust, implementing a leg kick as a timing mechanism in September that paid immediate dividends with a pair of homers. Defensively, he runs strong routes and shows the speed to have above-average range. His arm is average, perhaps a tick below, but his fundamentals, quick release and accuracy permit it to play well. His speed doesn't play out of the box due to his swing, but he has 20/20 potential. The Sox signed Castillo to be an everyday outfielder, most likely in center, starting in 2015. At the least, his complement of skills creates the likelihood of an average center fielder, with upside well beyond that.

BA GRADE

55 Risk: Medium

LGE	PA	BB%	SO%	ISO
AL	40	7.5	15.0	.194

Year	Club (League)	Class	AVG	G	AB	R	H	2B	3B	HR	RBI	BB	SO	SB	CS	OBP	SLG
2014	Boston (AL)	MAJ	.333	10	36	6	12	1	0	2	6	3	6	3	0	.400	.528
Major League Totals			.333	10	36	6	12	1	0	2	6	3	6	3	0	.400	.528

4 EDUARDO RODRIGUEZ, LHP

Born: April 7, 1993. **B-T:** L-L. **Ht.:** 6-2. **Wt.:** 200. **Signed:** Venezuela, 2010. **Signed by:** Calvin Maduro (Orioles).

If Rodriguez were judged based solely on his first six weeks in the Sox organization after being traded by the Orioles in exchange for Andrew Miller, he likely would have ranked as the top prospect in the system. Among the Sox's cluster of upper levels starting prospects, Rodriguez is the one with clear top-of-the-rotation stuff. Rodriguez sits at 92-94 mph but regularly touched 96 and 97 in his outings with the Red Sox. He complements that with a killer changeup that he sells well—some evaluators thought it was superior to Owens'—and a slider that sometimes grades as slightly below-average but shows the potential to be average or slightly above. Once with the Sox, he started using his changeup to lefties and attacking the inside of the plate to excellent effect. He shows impressive athleticism and a repeatable delivery. Rodriguez's explosive fastball and changeup after joining the Sox both graded as plus offerings. If his slider develops to at least average, his potential is immense. "That kid can be Johan Santana Part 2," one evaluator said. "If his breaking ball improves one tick, he's going to be outstanding." He should start 2015 in Triple-A, but if he pitches as he did in Portland, a mid-year move to the big leagues wouldn't be surprising.

BA GRADE

55 Risk: Medium

LGE	BF	SO%	BB%	HR/9
EL	509	21.2	7.3	0.45

Year	Club (League)	Class	W	L	ERA	G	GS	CG	SV	IP	H	HR	BB	SO	K/9	WHIP	AVG
2012	Delmarva (SAL)	LoA	5	7	3.70	22	22	1	0	107	103	4	30	73	6.1	1.24	.251
2013	Frederick (CAR)	HiA	6	4	2.85	14	14	0	0	85	78	4	25	66	7.0	1.21	.245
	Bowie (EL)	AA	4	3	4.22	11	11	1	0	60	53	5	24	59	8.9	1.29	.237
2014	Bowie (EL)	AA	3	7	4.79	16	16	1	0	83	90	5	29	69	7.5	1.44	.274
	Portland (EL)	AA	3	1	0.96	6	6	0	0	37	30	1	8	39	9.4	1.02	.222
Minor League Totals			25	27	3.26	93	92	4	1	486	437	20	162	418	7.7	1.23	.240

5 BRIAN JOHNSON, LHP

Born: Dec. 7, 1990. **B-T:** L-L. **Ht.:** 6-3. **Wt.:** 240. **Drafted:** Florida, 2012 (1st round). **Signed by:** Anthony Turco.

A two-way standout in college, Johnson's transition to pro ball was hindered by a liner off the face in his 2012 pro debut that resulted in a disjointed offseason and an equally disjointed 2013 season that was stunted by shoulder tendinitis. With a healthy offseason, however, Johnson looked like a big leaguer virtually every time he took the mound, running off an impressive string of two or fewer earned runs in 23 of his last 24 starts between three levels (he finished the year with a Triple-A playoff start). Johnson has a diverse arsenal of four average or better pitches and knows how to use it to considerable effect, working at a blistering pace while changing speeds and locations in a fashion sometimes evocative of Mark Buehrle. Johnson sits at 88-92 mph but will add (he can reach back for 94) and subtract to keep hitters off-balance. He doesn't have a single overpowering swing-and-miss pitch, but his execution is superb and his control has improved to a tick above-average. Though Johnson started 2014 in high Class A, his sprint across three levels could continue into 2015. He's expected to open in Pawtucket, but if the need arises, his polish suggests he could be a consideration for the big leagues in early 2015.

BA GRADE

50 Risk: Low

LGE	BF	SO%	BB%	HR/9
CAR	109	30.3	6.4	0.00
EL	452	21.9	7.1	0.46

Year	Club (League)	Class	W	L	ERA	G	GS	CG	SV	IP	H	HR	BB	SO	K/9	WHIP	AVG
2012	Lowell (NYP)	SS	0	0	0.00	4	4	0	0	6	2	0	1	4	6.4	0.53	.111
2013	Red Sox (GCL)	R	0	0	0.00	2	2	0	0	5	1	0	2	7	12.6	0.60	.067
	Greenville (SAL)	LoA	1	6	2.87	15	15	0	0	69	50	4	28	69	9.0	1.13	.197
	Salem (CAR)	HiA	1	0	1.64	2	2	0	0	11	9	0	5	8	6.5	1.27	.225
2014	Salem (CAR)	HiA	3	1	3.86	5	5	0	0	26	23	0	7	33	11.6	1.17	.230
	Portland (EL)	AA	10	2	1.75	20	20	2	0	118	78	6	32	99	7.6	0.93	.189
Minor League Totals			15	9	2.23	48	48	2	0	234	163	10	75	220	8.4	1.02	.194

6 RAFAEL DEVERS, 3B

Born: Oct. 24, 1996. **B-T:** L-R. **Ht.:** 6-0. **Wt.:** 200. **Signed:** Dominican Republic, 2013. **Signed by:** Eddie Romero/Manny Nanita.

Regarded as the best pure bat on the international amateur market in 2013, Devers delivered on that status in his 2014 pro debut. He announced his presence by clubbing an opposite-field homer in the DSL opener and didn't stop mashing. At 17, he led two Sox affiliates in home runs, becoming the first Sox 17-year-old to make the in-season jump from the DSL to the States in years. Devers' ability to drive the ball out of the park to all fields at such a young age suggests a player with an enormous ceiling as a potential middle-of-the-order fixture, depending on how he develops against lefthanders. There are questions about whether he'll outgrow third, where he committed 18 errors in 51 games. For now he shows the hands and feet to complement a plus arm which suggests he could stay at the position. Multiple evaluators cited the potential for a Pablo Sandoval-style defender. Devers will compete in spring training for a spot as a third baseman in low Class A Greenville as an 18-year-old in 2015. Regardless of whether his future is at first or third, his progression will be monitored closely for a potential game-changing bat that could anchor a lineup in his prime.

BA GRADE

60 Risk: Extreme

LGE	PA	BB%	SO%	ISO
DSL	128	16.4	15.6	.202
GCL	174	8.0	17.2	.172

Year	Club (League)	Class	AVG	G	AB	R	H	2B	3B	HR	RBI	BB	SO	SB	CS	OBP	SLG
2014	Red Sox (DSL)	R	.337	28	104	26	35	6	3	3	21	21	20	4	1	.445	.538
	Red Sox (GCL)	R	.312	42	157	21	49	11	2	4	36	14	30	1	0	.374	.484
Minor League Totals			.322	70	261	47	84	17	5	7	57	35	50	5	1	.404	.506

7 MANUEL MARGOT, OF ~to S.D.- Padres

Born: Sept. 28, 1994. **B-T:** R-R. **Ht.:** 5-11. **Wt.:** 175. **Signed:** Dominican Republic, 2011. **Signed by:** Craig Shipley/Manny Nanita.

When the Red Sox signed Margot out of the Dominican Republic, they saw a player with five-tool potential and the defense to stick in center. After showing an ability to hit for average, get on base and steal bases while playing solid outfield defense in Lowell in 2013, Margot was one of five minor leaguers with at least 10 homers and 40 or more steals. There's electricity in virtually everything Margot does. His strong wrists create plus bat speed, and while aggressive, he has the barrel control to limit his strikeouts. His speed plays both out of the box and as a basestealer. It remains an open question whether he'll have the plate discipline to be a true top-of-the-order hitter, but he has a chance to deliver across-the-board impact with the floor of at least a very good fourth outfielder based on his defense. He's likely close to maxed out physically, so there's not a great deal of power projection, but it wouldn't be a shock if improved knowledge of his swing yielded home run totals in the high teens. Margot will open 2015 at the same level where he offered a tantalizing first glimpse at the end of 2014 in Salem. He has a chance to move up to Double-A by the end of the year if he can show an ability to remain under control and manage his at-bats.

BA GRADE

55 Risk: High

LGE	PA	BB%	SO%	ISO
SAL	413	9.0	11.9	.162
CAR	56	3.6	8.9	.220

Year	Club (League)	Class	AVG	G	AB	R	H	2B	3B	HR	RBI	BB	SO	SB	CS	OBP	SLG
2012	Red Sox (DSL)	R	.285	68	260	49	74	10	7	4	45	36	25	33	9	.382	.423
2013	Lowell (NYP)	SS	.270	49	185	29	50	8	2	1	21	22	40	18	8	.346	.351
2014	Greenville (SAL)	LoA	.286	99	370	61	106	20	5	10	45	37	49	39	13	.355	.449
	Salem (CAR)	HiA	.340	16	50	4	17	5	0	2	14	2	5	3	2	.364	.560
Minor League Totals			.286	232	865	143	247	43	14	17	125	97	119	93	32	.362	.427

8 MATT BARNES, RHP

Born: June 17, 1990. **B-T:** R-R. **Ht.:** 6-4. **Wt.:** 205. **Drafted:** Connecticut, 2011 (1st round). **Signed by:** Ray Fagnant.

Barnes exploded onto the scene in his debut in Greenville in 2012, but since then his progress has been more deliberate. He sought to develop a consistent breaking ball. His 2014 season opened ingloriously with shoulder tenderness, but after a bad first half, he had a second-half breakthrough and a September callup. Despite his spring training health hiccup, Barnes has a big, durable frame that suggests the ability to handle a starter's workload. Whether that proves his big league destiny remains to be seen. Some scouts believe that his fastball and change are good enough to succeed as a back-end starter if he can incorporate the occasional show-me breaking ball, but he does demonstrate an ability to spin a curve even if his command and control of the pitch are inconsistent. If it comes—or if he develops a slider or cutter—he has a No. 3 starter's ceiling. However, the fact that the Sox gave him a September look in the bullpen suggests a potential near-term big league path for him. The Sox are keeping the door open for Barnes to be a starter, at least for now. It remains to be seen whether he spends 2015 working toward such a role in the Pawtucket rotation or if the team decides to use him out of the bullpen in the big leagues.

BA GRADE

50 Risk: Medium

LGE	BF	SO%	BB%	HR/9
IL	538	19.1	8.6	0.56
AL	39	20.5	5.1	1.00

Year	Club (League)	Class	W	L	ERA	G	GS	CG	SV	IP	H	HR	BB	SO	K/9	WHIP	AVG
2012	Greenville (SAL)	LoA	2	0	0.34	5	5	0	0	27	12	0	4	42	14.2	0.60	.130
	Salem (CAR)	HiA	5	5	3.58	20	20	1	0	93	85	6	25	91	8.8	1.18	.250
2013	Portland (EL)	AA	5	10	4.33	24	24	0	0	108	112	11	46	135	11.3	1.46	.265
	Pawtucket (IL)	AAA	1	0	0.00	1	1	0	0	5	3	0	2	7	11.8	0.94	.167
2014	Pawtucket (IL)	AAA	8	9	3.95	23	22	0	0	128	119	8	46	103	7.3	1.29	.247
	Boston (AL)	MAJ	0	0	4.00	5	0	0	0	9	11	1	2	8	8.0	1.44	.306
Major League Totals			0	0	4.00	5	0	0	0	9	11	1	2	8	8.0	1.44	.306
Minor League Totals			21	24	3.64	73	72	1	0	361	331	25	123	378	9.4	1.26	.244

9 DEVEN MARRERO, SS

Born: Aug. 25, 1990. **B-T:** R-R. **Ht.:** 6-1. **Wt.:** 185. **Drafted:** Arizona State, 2012 (1st round). **Signed by:** Vaughn Williams.

A down offensive year as a junior caused Marrero to fall to the Sox with the No. 24 pick of the 2012 draft, and in an injury-filled 2013 season, it appeared that his struggles at Arizona State might have been a harbinger. But after spending the final month of 2013 in Double-A without a single extra-base hit, a healthy Marrero showed far greater offensive impact—including some pop—in repeating in Portland. Marrero's calling card is his defense, where he combines standout range to both sides (the result of positioning and instincts as opposed to speed) with tremendously consistent hands and a strong throwing arm to create a potential Gold Glove defensive package. Offensively, most view him as a future bottom-of-the-order hitter but with a respectable floor given his ability to keep the barrel in the zone and line the ball from gap to gap with the occasional ability to turn on a pitch and drive it. He has required adjustment time in his transitions between levels, but he's also shown the aptitude to adjust. Marrero stands a good chance of being an everyday big league shortstop for a number of years. Marrero will likely get most of 2015 to establish himself in Pawtucket before starting a very interesting conversation about the Sox' shortstop position for 2016.

BA GRADE

50 Risk: Medium

LGE	PA	BB%	SO%	ISO
EL	307	11.1	18.6	.142
IL	202	5.9	18.3	.075

Year	Club (League)	Class	AVG	G	AB	R	H	2B	3B	HR	RBI	BB	SO	SB	CS	OBP	SLG
2012	Lowell (NYP)	SS	.268	64	246	45	66	14	3	2	24	34	48	24	6	.358	.374
2013	Salem (CAR)	HiA	.256	85	332	50	85	20	0	2	21	42	60	21	2	.341	.334
	Portland (EL)	AA	.236	19	72	7	17	0	0	0	5	10	16	6	0	.321	.236
2014	Portland (EL)	AA	.291	68	268	42	78	19	2	5	39	34	57	12	5	.371	.433
	Pawtucket (IL)	AAA	.210	50	186	23	39	11	0	1	20	12	37	4	1	.260	.285
Minor League Totals			.258	286	1104	167	285	64	5	10	109	132	218	67	16	.338	.352

10 GARIN CECCHINI, 3B/OF

Born: April 20, 1991. **B-T:** L-R. **Ht.:** 6-2. **Wt.:** 210. **Drafted:** HS—Lake Charles, La., 2010 (4th round). **Signed by:** Matt Dorey.

Cecchini appeared like a potential mid-2014 big league option at third base after leading the minors in on-base percentage (.443) with Salem and Portland in 2013. Instead, he lost the approach that had been a staple of his first three pro seasons. He finished strong and then hit well when afforded a season-ending big league opportunity. Cecchini struggled while focusing on not getting beaten on the inner half of the plate, and in the process, he slipped from an up-the-middle/opposite-field approach with high contact and walk rates to a pull-conscious hitter with high strikeout rates. He ironed that out by the end of the year, and impressed by driving balls from gap to gap in the big leagues. Defensively, Cecchini remains a below-average to fringy defender at third with an erratic throwing arm, but he shows a tremendous work ethic. He also started playing left field. Cecchini still has a considerable offensive ceiling as a player capable of hitting over .300 with high OBPs, and everyone seems to agree he'll hit. But given his typically modest extra-base totals, his value would take a hit if he ends up in left field or first base. He's expected to open 2015 back in Pawtucket but will be an immediate depth option.

BA GRADE

50 Risk: Medium

	LGE	PA	BB%	SO%	ISO
	IL	458	9.6	21.6	.108
	AL	36	8.3	30.6	.194

Year	Club (League)	Class	AVG	G	AB	R	H	2B	3B	HR	RBI	BB	SO	SB	CS	OBP	SLG
2012	Greenville (SAL)	LoA	.305	118	455	84	139	38	4	4	62	61	90	51	6	.394	.433
2013	Salem (CAR)	HiA	.350	63	214	44	75	19	4	5	33	43	34	15	7	.469	.547
	Portland (EL)	AA	.296	66	240	36	71	14	3	2	28	51	52	8	2	.420	.404
2014	Pawtucket (IL)	AAA	.263	114	407	52	107	21	1	7	57	44	99	11	1	.341	.371
	Boston (AL)	MAJ	.258	11	31	6	8	3	0	1	4	3	11	0	0	.361	.452
Major League Totals			.258	11	31	6	8	3	0	1	4	3	11	0	0	.361	.452
Minor League Totals			.298	393	1430	237	426	104	13	21	203	216	294	97	18	.396	.433

11 MICHAEL CHAVIS, SS/3B

BA GRADE

55 Risk: High

Born: Aug. 11, 1995. **B-T:** R-R. **Ht.:** 5-10. **Wt.:** 190. **Drafted:** HS—Marietta, Ga., 2014 (1st round). **Signed by:** Brian Moehler.

Selected 26th overall in 2014 and signed for $1,870,500, Chavis adjusted to pro ball after a slow initial start. With a thick, compact frame that is likely close to maxed out, Chavis generates tremendous bat speed. While he will swing and miss, he has a chance to hit 20 or more homers. A high school shortstop, Chavis embraced his first prolonged exposure to third base enthusiastically, and that's where he's expected to spend 2015 as he competes for a spot at low Class A Greenville. He has an above-average arm and the short-area quickness for third. Several Red Sox officials consider second base is his best fit, though first base or left field also are possibilities given his plus raw power. If his bat develops, Chavis will profile at any position, particularly if he remains under control instead of swinging for oncoming traffic.

Year	Club (League)	Class	AVG	G	AB	R	H	2B	3B	HR	RBI	BB	SO	SB	CS	OBP	SLG
2014	Red Sox (GCL)	R	.269	39	134	21	36	12	3	1	16	15	38	5	3	.347	.425
Minor League Totals			.269	39	134	21	36	12	3	1	16	15	38	5	3	.347	.425

12 SAM TRAVIS, 1B

BA GRADE

50 Risk: High

Born: Aug. 27, 1993. **B-T:** R-R. **Ht.:** 6-0. **Wt.:** 195. **Drafted:** Indiana, 2014 (2nd round). **Signed by:** Blair Henry.

Perhaps the most commonly heard refrain about Travis is that he "hits the (bleep) out of the ball." His hitting is very advanced, for he barrels the ball with striking consistency, something that was evident both in his pro debut and in the instructional league, where he hit over .500. It remains to be seen how often he generates the loft to produce home runs, but he hits the ball hard enough to grow into plus power and 20 or more home runs. One evaluator described Travis as having a "Captain Caveman" approach, but with the barrel control to limit strikeouts and a flat, righthanded swing plane that generates screaming line drives to the pull side and right-center field. His ceiling is capped by his position, for Travis is most likely a first baseman, though with some demonstrated ability to play left field in college. He has a chance to open 2015 at high Class A Salem and reach Double-A Portland by the end of the year.

Year	Club (League)	Class	AVG	G	AB	R	H	2B	3B	HR	RBI	BB	SO	SB	CS	OBP	SLG
2014	Lowell (NYP)	SS	.333	40	165	28	55	5	1	4	30	4	18	5	1	.364	.448
	Greenville (SAL)	LoA	.290	27	107	12	31	11	1	3	14	7	14	0	1	.330	.495
Minor League Totals			.316	67	272	40	86	16	2	7	44	11	32	5	2	.351	.467

13 JAVIER GUERRA, SS — to SD Padres

BA GRADE
55 Risk: Extreme

Born: Sept. 29, 1995. **B-T:** L-R. **Ht.:** 5-11. **Wt.:** 155. **Signed:** Panama, 2012. **Signed by:** Eddie Romero/Cris Garibaldo.

Rookie-level Gulf Coast League manager Tom Kotchman called Guerra the best defensive shortstop he's had in 35 years, and evaluators for other organizations back the view of Guerra as a potential Gold Glover at shortstop. He exudes confidence and control in all his actions, with an easy lefthanded swing that allows Red Sox evaluators to dream about his upside as a shortstop with above-average offensive potential and elite defense. He combines plus arm strength with pinpoint accuracy and the ability to make throws from all angles. Though he walked just five times against 42 strikeouts in the GCL, he showed the ability to drive fastballs with pull power at age 18. His weakest tool is his below-average speed. Guerra's makeup and game instincts have team officials convinced he could experience developmental leaps in the future. His bat lags behind his glove, so it's possible he could be ticketed for short-season Lowell in 2015, but long term, Guerra has the best package of tools of any shortstop in the organization.

Year	Club (League)	Class	AVG	G	AB	R	H	2B	3B	HR	RBI	BB	SO	SB	CS	OBP	SLG
2013	Red Sox (DSL)	R	.248	60	210	27	52	9	0	0	23	33	40	7	4	.356	.290
2014	Red Sox (GCL)	R	.269	51	201	21	54	14	4	2	26	5	42	1	5	.286	.408
Minor League Totals			.258	111	411	48	106	23	4	2	49	38	82	8	9	.325	.348

14 MICHAEL KOPECH, RHP

BA GRADE
55 Risk: Extreme

Born: April 30, 1996. **B-T:** R-R. **Ht.:** 6-3. **Wt.:** 195. **Drafted:** HS—Mount Pleasant, Texas, 2014 (1st round). **Signed by:** Tim Collinsworth.

Signed for $1.5 million as the 33rd overall pick in 2014, Kopech lights up the radar gun like few Red Sox draftees in recent years. He touched 99 mph as a high school senior, regularly touched 97 in his outings in the Rookie-level Gulf Coast League and sat in the mid-90s. He does so with a max-effort delivery that creates questions about his future control and ability to remain healthy, but he has a starting pitcher's frame and elite arm speed, with a chance for unusual power out of the rotation. In addition to his fastball, Kopech also features a slider that appears to have wipeout potential, and while he didn't incorporate a changeup as an amateur, he shows the potential to take something off the ball. If Kopech manages to control his power stuff and develop a three-pitch mix, then he has a chance to be a front-of-the-rotation starter down the road. At the least, the Red Sox can envision his fastball/slider combination playing late in games.

Year	Club (League)	Class	W	L	ERA	G	GS	CG	SV	IP	H	HR	BB	SO	K/9	WHIP	AVG
2014	Red Sox (GCL)	R	0	1	4.61	8	8	0	0	14	11	0	9	16	10.5	1.46	.216
Minor League Totals			0	1	4.61	8	8	0	0	14	11	0	9	16	10.5	1.46	.216

15 TREY BALL, LHP

BA GRADE
55 Risk: Extreme

Born: June 27, 1994. **B-T:** L-L. **Ht.:** 6-6. **Wt.:** 175. **Drafted:** HS—New Castle, Ind., 2013 (1st round). **Signed by:** John Pyle.

The Red Sox used their highest pick (No. 7 overall) in 20 years on Ball, who signed for $2.75 million, the second-largest draft bonus in club history. As a two-way high school player from a cold-weather climate, he had limited amateur pitching experience. Still, no one anticipated that, 11 starts into his pro career, Ball would be 1-7, 7.27. To his credit, Ball rebounded in his final 11 starts, working to a 2.70 ERA. He showed good downward angle on his fastball, which sat by the end of the year at 91-92 mph while topping out at 95. His changeup progressed into a solid offering with the potential to be above-average, and he showed improvement in his curveball after switching from a knuckle-curve to a conventional grip. His athleticism permits a clean, repeatable delivery and he showed an excellent work ethic even through his struggles. Ball still offers plenty of projection, but plenty of uncertainty, and evaluators differ on his ceiling, suggesting the potential for anything from a No. 2 to a No. 4 starter. Now that he's acclimated to pro ball, Ball's future should come into sharper view in 2015, when he could open at high Class A Salem.

Year	Club (League)	Class	W	L	ERA	G	GS	CG	SV	IP	H	HR	BB	SO	K/9	WHIP	AVG
2013	Red Sox (GCL)	R	0	1	6.43	5	5	0	0	7	10	1	6	5	6.4	2.29	.357
2014	Greenville (SAL)	LoA	5	10	4.68	22	22	0	0	100	111	9	39	68	6.1	1.50	.280
Minor League Totals			5	11	4.79	27	27	0	0	107	121	10	45	73	6.1	1.55	.285

16 ANTHONY RANAUDO, RHP

BA GRADE

45 Risk: Low

Born: Sept. 9, 1989. **B-T:** R-R. **Ht.:** 6-7. **Wt.:** 245. **Drafted:** Louisiana State, 2010 (1st round supplemental). **Signed by:** Matt Dorey.

Ranaudo reached the majors in September for the first time, with poor results. However he also threw a career-high 177 innings, as well as leading the Triple-A International League in wins, ERA and opponents' average. He won his league's pitcher of the year award for a second consecutive season. Ranaudo's failed big league cameo resulted from reduced stuff—he sat mostly at a straight 92-94 mph with below-average secondary offerings. He retains the potential to be a steady back-end starter if the life on his fastball and curveball improve following a productive offseason. Ranaudo made mechanical adjustments in 2014, removing excess movement from the back swing of his delivery, which resulted in improved command. He also added a slider to pair with his at-times-plus curveball to allow him to change planes. Ranaudo's aptitude and self-awareness suggest a pitcher capable of making the adjustments to be a valuable big leaguer whether as a back-end starter or a middle reliever.

Year	Club (League)	Class	W	L	ERA	G	GS	CG	SV	IP	H	HR	BB	SO	K/9	WHIP	AVG
2012	Portland (EL)	AA	1	3	6.69	9	9	0	0	38	41	4	27	27	6.5	1.81	.283
2013	Portland (EL)	AA	8	4	2.95	19	19	0	0	110	80	9	40	106	8.7	1.09	.204
	Pawtucket (IL)	AAA	3	1	2.97	6	5	0	0	30	32	1	7	21	6.2	1.29	.271
2014	Pawtucket (IL)	AAA	14	4	2.61	24	24	1	0	138	112	9	54	111	7.2	1.20	.223
	Boston (AL)	MAJ	4	3	4.81	7	7	0	0	39	39	10	16	15	3.4	1.40	.260
Major League Totals			4	3	4.81	7	7	0	0	39	39	10	16	15	3.4	1.40	.260
Minor League Totals			35	18	3.46	84	83	1	0	443	380	33	174	382	7.8	1.25	.233

17 SEAN COYLE, 2B/3B

BA GRADE

50 Risk: High

Born: Jan. 17, 1992. **B-T:** R-R. **Ht.:** 5-8. **Wt.:** 180. **Drafted:** HS—Fort Washington, Pa., 2010 (3rd round). **Signed by:** Chris Calciano.

Coyle rekindled his prospect status by pulverizing the ball at Double-A Portland in 2014, particularly in a first half. He still showed a considerable amount of swing and miss (25 percent strikeout rate), but his increased willingness to drive the ball to all fields (with impressive power to right-center) contributed to a jump in his hard-hit rate. An average runner, Coyle also showed solid defensive actions both at second base and in his first trial at third, where he has an average arm. However, in the continuation of a career pattern, injuries restricted him to 97 games in 2014 and contributed to significant durability questions from a 5-foot-8 player who has never played more than 116 games in a season. The uncertainty about Coyle's ability to stay on the field inhibits his prospect status, even as he joined the 40-man roster in the offseason and prepared for an assignment to Triple-A Pawtucket in 2015.

Year	Club (League)	Class	AVG	G	AB	R	H	2B	3B	HR	RBI	BB	SO	SB	CS	OBP	SLG
2012	Salem (CAR)	HiA	.249	116	437	60	109	31	2	9	63	29	116	16	0	.316	.391
2013	Red Sox (GCL)	R	.150	6	20	3	3	0	0	1	3	3	6	1	1	.292	.300
	Greenville (SAL)	LoA	.320	6	25	4	8	3	0	1	4	3	9	0	1	.393	.560
	Salem (CAR)	HiA	.241	48	195	41	47	9	1	14	28	24	65	11	0	.321	.513
2014	Portland (EL)	AA	.295	96	336	60	99	23	1	16	61	38	95	13	1	.371	.512
Minor League Totals			.258	381	1407	250	363	94	11	55	223	158	402	61	9	.344	.458

18 EDWIN ESCOBAR, LHP

BA GRADE

45 Risk: Low

Born: April 22, 1992. **B-T:** L-L. **Ht.:** 6-1. **Wt.:** 185. **Signed:** Venezuela, 2008. **Signed by:** Wilmer Becerra/Rafic Saab (Rangers).

Originally signed by the Rangers, Escobar was traded to San Francisco so Texas could keep Rule 5 draft pick Ben Snyder back in 2010. Four-plus years later, the Giants traded Escobar shortly before the trade deadline as the primary piece for Jake Peavy. Escobar rebounded from a tough start at Triple-A Fresno to produce a number of solid starts at Triple-A Pawtucket, throwing particularly well in the postseason. He sits in the low 90s but runs his fastball up to 95 mph with the potential to get swings and misses on his slider—his best secondary pitch—and changeup. Escobar sometimes favors secondary offerings over his fastball, so he has a mix that suggests either a future as back-end starter or reliever, potentially a matchup arm, given his dominance against Triple-A lefties (.200/.244/.230 with 25 percent strikeouts) and struggles against righties. His crossfire delivery also affords deception versus lefthanders. Escobar could provide a lefthanded bullpen option early in 2015 or he could offer pitching depth (or trade value) at Pawtucket.

Year	Club (League)	Class	W	L	ERA	G	GS	CG	SV	IP	H	HR	BB	SO	K/9	WHIP	AVG
2012	Augusta (SAL)	LoA	7	8	2.96	22	22	0	0	131	121	7	32	122	8.4	1.17	.241
2013	San Jose (CAL)	HiA	3	4	2.89	16	14	0	0	75	68	3	17	92	11.1	1.14	.234
	Richmond (EL)	AA	5	4	2.67	10	10	0	0	54	44	2	13	54	9.0	1.06	.219
2014	Fresno (PCL)	AAA	3	8	5.11	20	20	0	0	111	128	16	37	96	7.8	1.49	.287
	Pawtucket (IL)	AAA	0	2	4.28	5	5	0	0	27	33	3	8	20	6.6	1.50	.297
	Boston (AL)	MAJ	0	0	4.50	2	0	0	0	2	1	0	0	2	9.0	0.50	.143
Major League Totals			0	0	4.50	2	0	0	0	2	1	0	0	2	9.0	0.50	.143
Minor League Totals			25	42	4.13	119	111	0	0	558	577	40	185	548	8.8	1.37	.264

19 TRAVIS SHAW, 1B

BA GRADE
45 Risk: Medium

Born: April 16, 1990. **B-T:** L-R. **Ht.:** 6-4. **Wt.:** 235. **Drafted:** Kent State, 2011 (9th round). **Signed by:** Jon Adkins.

After a 2013 struggle at Double-A Portland, Shaw implemented a leg kick that paid immediate dividends with a monster Arizona Fall League performance that carried over to a repeat assignment in 2014. He hit his way out of Portland after 47 games before hitting a wall at Triple-A Pawtucket, with a spike in strikeout rate and drop in walk rate. Still, Shaw showed at least average power, with the ability to drive the ball out from left-center to right field, and he led the system with 21 homers. Shaw's willingness to drive the ball to the opposite produces both solid plate discipline and a potentially average hit tool and excellent fit for Fenway Park. That, in combination with above-average first base defense and good instincts that draw from a lifetime around the game (his father Jeff was an all-star closer), suggests a player who could be a second-division first baseman or a primary platoon option on a playoff team.

Year	Club (League)	Class	AVG	G	AB	R	H	2B	3B	HR	RBI	BB	SO	SB	CS	OBP	SLG
2012	Salem (CAR)	HiA	.305	99	354	69	108	31	3	16	73	59	81	11	2	.411	.545
	Portland (EL)	AA	.227	31	110	13	25	13	0	3	12	21	34	1	1	.353	.427
2013	Portland (EL)	AA	.221	127	444	57	98	21	4	16	50	78	117	7	3	.342	.394
2014	Portland (EL)	AA	.305	47	177	35	54	8	1	11	37	29	23	5	5	.406	.548
	Pawtucket (IL)	AAA	.262	81	313	43	82	21	1	10	41	28	76	2	0	.321	.431
Minor League Totals			.263	444	1609	251	423	108	9	64	250	250	378	29	9	.365	.461

20 TEDDY STANKIEWICZ, RHP

BA GRADE
50 Risk: High

Born: Nov. 25, 1993. **B-T:** R-R. **Ht.:** 6-4. **Wt.:** 190. **Drafted:** Seminole State (Okla.) JC, 2013 (2nd round). **Signed by:** Chris Mears.

The highest unsigned high school player from the 2012 draft, Stankiewicz spurned the Mets and spent a year at Seminole State (Okla.) JC before signing with the Red Sox for $915,000 after being picked 30 spots higher than in 2012. The steadiest performer in the low Class A Greenville rotation in 2014, Stankiewicz pounded the strike zone with a four-pitch mix and, more often than not, pitched deep into games and led the Drive in wins, innings and strikeouts. He mostly pitched to contact with a fastball that sat at 92 mph and topped out around 95, with his slider having been a more consistent secondary offering than his curveball or changeup. Stankiewicz, the long-limbed righty, has the athleticism to repeat his delivery and command the ball, traits that pair with his pitch mix and average velocity to make him a potential back-end starter. He could ultimately exceed that projection if any of his pitches plays up and develops into a legitimate out pitch. Stankiewicz will move up to high Class A Salem in 2015.

Year	Club (League)	Class	W	L	ERA	G	GS	CG	SV	IP	H	HR	BB	SO	K/9	WHIP	AVG
2013	Lowell (NYP)	SS	0	0	2.29	9	9	0	0	20	17	1	2	15	6.9	0.97	.227
2014	Greenville (SAL)	LoA	11	8	3.72	25	25	0	0	140	141	9	29	102	6.5	1.21	.260
Minor League Totals			11	8	3.54	34	34	0	0	160	158	10	31	117	6.6	1.18	.256

21 BRYCE BRENTZ, OF

BA GRADE
45 Risk: Medium

Born: Dec. 30, 1988. **B-T:** R-R. **Ht.:** 6-0. **Wt.:** 200. **Drafted:** Middle Tennessee State, 2010 (1st round supplemental). **Signed by:** Danny Watkins.

Few players in the upper levels of the Red Sox system divide opinion as much as Brentz. He'll show power that some view as plus to double-plus, with the potential to send rockets into orbit. Yet his all-or-nothing approach tends to lead to high strikeout rates and inconsistency. Brentz missed two and a half months with a hamstring injury, and he showed a huge platoon split in which he slugged .685 against lefties and struggled against righties, hitting just .223/.335/.363. He repeated the pattern in a season-ending taste of the big leagues. As such, Brentz probably fits best as the righthanded hitter on an outfield corner, though some scouts believe he could eventually make an impact as a late-developing everyday outfielder. His fringy range and strong arm suggest a future in right field. Brentz made a concerted effort to improve his plate discipline in 2014, on which he'll continue to focus in 2015 as he embarks on a third season at

Pawtucket at age 26.

Year	Club (League)	Class	AVG	G	AB	R	H	2B	3B	HR	RBI	BB	SO	SB	CS	OBP	SLG
2012	Portland (EL)	AA	.296	122	456	62	135	30	1	17	76	40	130	7	5	.355	.478
	Pawtucket (IL)	AAA	.118	5	17	0	2	0	0	0	0	1	6	0	0	.167	.118
2013	Red Sox (GCL)	R	.235	6	17	3	4	2	0	2	8	1	4	0	0	.316	.706
	Pawtucket (IL)	AAA	.264	82	326	36	86	16	1	17	56	20	86	1	0	.312	.475
2014	Red Sox (GCL)	R	.056	7	18	1	1	1	0	0	0	3	5	0	0	.190	.111
	Lowell (NYP)	SS	.125	2	8	2	1	0	0	0	1	1	2	0	0	.200	.125
	Pawtucket (IL)	AAA	.243	63	230	42	56	11	2	12	53	32	58	0	1	.341	.465
	Boston (AL)	MAJ	.308	9	26	5	8	2	0	2	0	0	9	0	0	.308	.385
Major League Totals			.308	9	26	5	8	2	0	0	2	0	9	0	0	.308	.385
Minor League Totals			.266	471	1792	265	477	99	12	83	327	159	482	16	13	.330	.474

22 STEVEN WRIGHT, RHP

BA GRADE
45 Risk: Medium

Born: Aug. 30, 1984. **B-T:** R-R. **Ht.:** 6-1. **Wt.:** 220. **Drafted:** Hawaii, 2006 (2nd round). **Signed by:** Don Lyle (Indians).

Though surgery just before spring training 2014 to repair a sports hernia delayed the start of his fourth year as a full-time knuckleballer, Wright experienced a breakthrough in the execution of his signature pitch. At the encouragement of Triple-A Pawtucket pitching coach Rich Sauveur, he decided to slow down his pitch from a low- to mid-80s offering to the mid-70s, with the slower speed making the pitch easier to control, and also more tantalizing to hitters. The improvement to Wright's walk rate was palpable. Wright walked 2.1 batters per nine innings at Pawtucket in 2014, compared with a rate of 4.4 per nine from 2011-13. He even threw more strikes in the big leagues, finishing his stint with five capable innings against the Yankees. Indeed, of all the pitchers offered an open audition for the 2015 rotation, Wright showed the most consistent ability to throw strikes and generate swings and misses. What that means going forward is a mystery, as few pretend to know whether Wright is more likely to become the next Tim Wakefield or the next Charlie Zink. Regardless, Wright showed enough in 2014 that the team views him as a meaningful contributor in 2015. He could compete for the No. 5 starter spot in spring training.

Year	Club (League)	Class	W	L	ERA	G	GS	CG	SV	IP	H	HR	BB	SO	K/9	WHIP	AVG
2012	Akron (EL)	AA	9	6	2.49	20	20	1	0	116	86	8	62	101	7.9	1.28	.207
	Portland (EL)	AA	1	0	1.50	1	1	0	0	6	5	0	2	2	3.0	1.17	.238
	Pawtucket (IL)	AAA	0	1	3.15	4	4	0	0	20	19	1	5	16	7.2	1.20	.238
2013	Boston (AL)	MAJ	2	0	5.40	4	1	0	0	13	12	0	9	10	6.8	1.58	.245
	Pawtucket (IL)	AAA	8	7	3.46	24	24	3	0	135	130	10	65	99	6.6	1.44	.254
2014	Portland (EL)	AA	1	0	3.60	1	1	0	0	5	5	1	1	4	7.2	1.20	.278
	Pawtucket (IL)	AAA	5	5	3.41	15	15	1	0	95	86	9	22	68	6.4	1.14	.240
	Boston (AL)	MAJ	0	1	2.57	6	1	0	0	21	21	2	4	22	9.4	1.19	.256
Major League Totals			2	1	3.67	10	2	0	0	34	33	2	13	32	8.4	1.34	.252
Minor League Totals			53	46	3.79	231	148	6	7	935	905	86	342	746	7.2	1.33	.254

23 MAURICIO DUBON, SS

BA GRADE
50 Risk: High

Born: July 19, 1994. **B-T:** R-R. **Ht.:** 6-0. **Wt.:** 165. **Drafted:** HS— Sacramento, 2013 (26th round). **Signed by:** Demond Smith.

Dubon moved from Honduras to the U.S. in high school to pursue baseball, a decision that paid off when he was drafted out of high school in California in 2013. He has shown outstanding hand-eye coordination and a clean swing to hit line drives to all fields, with occasional pull power. He also showed skill as a bunter at short-season Lowell to help boost his average to .320, second in the New York-Penn League. He rarely walked but also rarely struck out. Despite limited experience as an amateur, Dubon showed smooth actions and average range at shortstop thanks to good body control and footwork, perhaps owing to his soccer-playing background. Future strength gains likely will help determine whether he has the offensive profile of a starter or a utility player. Next up is an assignment to low Class A Greenville.

Year	Club (League)	Class	AVG	G	AB	R	H	2B	3B	HR	RBI	BB	SO	SB	CS	OBP	SLG
2013	Red Sox (GCL)	R	.245	20	53	8	13	3	0	0	4	1	12	6	2	.298	.302
2014	Lowell (NYP)	SS	.320	66	256	40	82	8	1	3	34	9	26	7	8	.337	.395
Minor League Totals			.307	86	309	48	95	11	1	3	38	10	38	13	10	.330	.379

24 WENDELL RIJO, 2B

BA GRADE
50 Risk: High

Born: Sept. 4, 1995. **B-T:** R-R. **Ht.:** 5-11. **Wt.:** 170. **Signed:** Dominican Republic, 2012. **Signed by:** Eddie Romero/Victor Rodriguez Jr.

The son of Dodgers Dominican scout Rafael Rijo, Wendell signed for $575,000 in July 2012 and then showed considerable polish as one of the youngest players in the South Atlantic League in 2014. He posted above-average numbers across the board at low Class A Greenville. Rijo has clear potential to deliver above-average offensive impact at second base, with a high average and modest power. Though he has strong hand-eye coordination, he seems focused at times on generating power, an approach that could be exposed as he moves up. Some have expressed concern about his commitment to defense, for Rijo shows concentration lapses in the field, and there isn't a clear fallback defensive position for him if he doesn't stick at second. Still, given that he will be just 19 for most of the 2015 season suggests he has room to improve his concentration and refine his tools. He could be headed for high Class A Salem in 2015.

Year	Club (League)	Class	AVG	G	AB	R	H	2B	3B	HR	RBI	BB	SO	SB	CS	OBP	SLG
2013	Red Sox (GCL)	R	.271	49	170	28	46	15	0	0	20	22	29	15	5	.368	.359
	Lowell (NYP)	SS	.357	3	14	1	5	1	1	0	1	0	3	0	1	.357	.571
2014	Greenville (SAL)	LoA	.254	111	409	56	104	27	6	9	46	56	103	16	6	.348	.416
Minor League Totals			.261	163	593	85	155	43	7	9	67	78	135	31	12	.354	.403

25 CARLOS ASUAJE, 2B/3B/OF — *to SD Padres*

BA GRADE

45 Risk: Medium

Born: Nov. 2, 1991. **B-T:** L-R. **Ht.:** 5-9. **Wt.:** 160. **Drafted:** Nova Southeastern (Fla.), 2013 (11th round). **Signed by:** Willie Romay.

After a nondescript pro debut at short-season Lowell in 2013, Asuaje defied expectations by consistently barreling pitches with a swing that seemed much too big for his unassuming, 5-foot-9 frame. Asuaje led the organization in slugging percentage (.533), extra-base hits (65) and RBIs (101) in 129 games at two Class A levels. While Asuaje holds little back at the plate, he typically swings at strikes. He dominated Class A competition at age 22, so his performance in the high minors will be more telling than his 2014 output. Asuaje is a serviceable if below-average defender at third base, but he looked playable at both second base and in left field. He's an average runner with a chance to hit for average and contribute gap power. Despite an unusual profile, he has a chance to play his way into contention for a larger role, perhaps as a multi-position extra. He will reach Double-A Portland at some point in 2015.

Year	Club (League)	Class	AVG	G	AB	R	H	2B	3B	HR	RBI	BB	SO	SB	CS	OBP	SLG
2013	Lowell (NYP)	SS	.269	52	171	19	46	12	1	1	20	27	33	4	3	.366	.368
2014	Greenville (SAL)	LoA	.305	90	325	59	99	24	10	11	73	41	56	7	4	.391	.542
	Salem (CAR)	HiA	.323	39	155	27	50	14	2	4	28	18	34	1	3	.398	.516
Minor League Totals			.300	181	651	105	195	50	13	16	121	86	123	12	10	.386	.490

26 JOE GUNKEL, RHP

BA GRADE

50 Risk: High

Born: Dec. 30, 1991. **B-T:** R-R. **Ht.:** 6-5. **Wt.:** 225. **Drafted:** West Chester (Pa.), 2013 (18th round). **Signed by:** Chris Calciano.

The 6-foot-5 Gunkel was the talk of instructional league in 2013 after signing out of NCAA Division II West Chester (Pa.), for he showed a 90-94 mph fastball with life and command from a low arm slot. He comes at hitters with a long wingspan and a low-three-quarters release point that evaluators have compared with Justin Masterson, Kevin Brown and Jered Weaver. At low Class A Greenville, Gunkel overmatched opponents with a three-pitch mix including a slider and a changeup. His performance regressed following a promotion to high Class A Salem, and given his low arm slot, retiring lefthanders, as he did in 2014 with a .172 opponent average, always will be key to his continued advancement. While Gunkel probably will shift to the bullpen at some point, he hasn't shown any indication that a move is imminent.

Year	Club (League)	Class	W	L	ERA	G	GS	CG	SV	IP	H	HR	BB	SO	K/9	WHIP	AVG
2013	Red Sox (GCL)	R	0	0	0.00	1	0	0	0	1	0	0	0	1	9.0	0.00	.000
	Lowell (NYP)	SS	3	0	1.35	14	0	0	5	20	8	0	3	32	14.4	0.55	.114
2014	Greenville (SAL)	LoA	3	0	2.28	17	5	0	2	51	26	3	11	62	10.9	0.72	.149
	Salem (CAR)	HiA	3	5	4.64	10	10	1	0	52	62	3	13	39	6.7	1.43	.294
Minor League Totals			9	5	3.10	42	15	1	7	125	96	6	27	134	9.7	0.99	.209

27 NICK LONGHI, 1B/OF

BA GRADE

50 Risk: Extreme

Born: Aug. 16, 1995. **B-T:** R-L. **Ht.:** 6-2. **Wt.:** 205. **Drafted:** HS—Venice, Fla., 2013 (30th round). **Signed by:** Willie Romay.

Longhi's disappointment about slipping to the 30th round of the 2013 draft amid signability concerns was mitigated by the fact that the Springfield, Mass., native was taken by the team he grew up following. Longhi enjoyed a standout performance with short-season Lowell through mid-July, when he suffered a torn ligament in his thumb while running the bases. He has a sweet, righthanded swing with the ability to stay inside the ball and drive it to all fields, suggesting an above-average to plus hit tool. Though he didn't hit any homers in 2014, Longhi's strong wrists and forearms suggest the potential to deliver average to above-average power. As a lefthanded thrower, he's limited to first base or left field, but his offensive approach should carry him. Longhi will be a candidate to break with low Class A Greenville in 2015.

Year	Club (League)	Class	AVG	G	AB	R	H	2B	3B	HR	RBI	BB	SO	SB	CS	OBP	SLG
2013	Red Sox (GCL)	R	.178	16	45	4	8	5	0	1	4	3	12	1	0	.245	.356
2014	Lowell (NYP)	SS	.330	30	109	19	36	10	1	0	10	11	22	0	3	.388	.440
Minor League Totals			.286	46	154	23	44	15	1	1	14	14	34	1	3	.347	.416

28 JUSTIN HALEY, RHP

BA GRADE

45 Risk: High

Born: June 16, 1991. **B-T:** R-R. **Ht.:** 6-5. **Wt.:** 230. **Drafted:** Fresno State, 2012 (6th round). **Signed by:** Demond Smith.

Haley underwhelmed in his first full pro season in 2013, and he spent the early stages of 2014 piggybacking with other starters in the high Class A Salem rotation, but he performed his way into a starting role and excelled. After he walked 5.3 batters per nine innings in 2013, Haley dropped that figure nearly in half (2.7 per nine) while at Salem before six solid season-ending starts at Double-A Portland. Haley angles the ball down at the bottom of the zone with a fastball that typically sits 90-93 mph and touches 94, and he features has some deception in his delivery that allows somewhat pedestrian stuff to play up. Haley's breaking ball and changeup played as average offerings in 2014, and while his stuff is hardly eye-popping, his performance could make him a potential No. 5 starter in time.

Year	Club (League)	Class	W	L	ERA	G	GS	CG	SV	IP	H	HR	BB	SO	K/9	WHIP	AVG
2012	Lowell (NYP)	SS	0	1	1.89	13	12	0	0	33	23	1	16	33	8.9	1.17	.200
2013	Greenville (SAL)	LoA	7	11	3.68	26	24	0	0	125	97	10	74	124	9.0	1.37	.219
2014	Salem (CAR)	HiA	7	4	2.82	19	11	1	1	93	77	4	23	74	7.2	1.08	.229
	Portland (EL)	AA	3	2	1.19	6	6	0	0	38	30	2	16	33	7.9	1.22	.222
Minor League Totals			17	18	2.87	64	53	1	1	288	227	17	129	264	8.2	1.23	.221

29 HENRY RAMOS, OF

BA GRADE

50 Risk: Extreme

Born: April 15, 1992. **B-T:** B-R. **Ht.:** 6-2. **Wt.:** 190. **Drafted:** HS—Maunabo, P.R., 2010 (5th round). **Signed by:** Edgar Perez.

A tremendous athlete who had limited playing experience as an amateur, Ramos seemed as if he might be in the midst of a career breakthrough at Double-A Portland in 2014. The switch-hitter was one of the team's top performers through 48 games before fouling a ball off the side of his left knee, creating a stress fracture on the opposite side of the knee that ended his season. Ramos returned to the field by the end of instructional league and appeared to be unhindered as a runner. His plus range, plus arm and average speed in right field suggest a player who could fill an extra outfielder role in the big leagues. Ramos has shown improved pitch recognition as he's moved up the ladder, and he has the strength to drive the ball out of the park. "If he hits at all," said one National League evaluator, "he's a starter."

Year	Club (League)	Class	AVG	G	AB	R	H	2B	3B	HR	RBI	BB	SO	SB	CS	OBP	SLG
2012	Greenville (SAL)	LoA	.254	122	441	61	112	24	4	8	63	44	101	12	10	.327	.381
2013	Salem (CAR)	HiA	.252	129	469	69	118	27	7	12	55	55	100	11	12	.330	.416
2014	Portland (EL)	AA	.326	48	181	26	59	9	2	2	23	11	38	2	4	.368	.431
Minor League Totals			.266	434	1583	215	421	85	18	30	212	140	351	52	38	.328	.399

30 PAT LIGHT, RHP

BA GRADE

45 Risk: High

Born: March 29, 1991. **B-T:** R-R. **Ht.:** 6-6. **Wt.:** 225. **Drafted:** Monmouth, 2012 (1st round supplemental). **Signed by:** Ray Fagnant.

Hamstring injuries wrecked Light's first full pro season in 2013 and, though healthy enough to make 25 starts and shoulder 132 innings in 2014, he proved less-than-overpowering. However, he displayed tremendous arm strength at times, his fastball reaching the triple digits on occasion at the end of the year. In the past, Light topped out near 94 mph as a starter, but his lack of a consistent slider or changeup allowed hitters to sit on his heater. While the Red Sox had yet to make a decision about Light's role in 2015, he could turn into a very different animal if moved to the bullpen at Double-A Portland. He could jump onto a more aggressive development path if he makes the role switch, and his raw arm strength could place him in a high-leverage bullpen role.

Year	Club (League)	Class	W	L	ERA	G	GS	CG	SV	IP	H	HR	BB	SO	K/9	WHIP	AVG
2012	Lowell (NYP)	SS	0	2	2.37	12	12	0	0	30	27	1	5	30	8.9	1.05	.243
2013	Red Sox (GCL)	R	0	0	0.00	3	3	0	0	6	4	0	2	3	4.5	1.00	.190
	Greenville (SAL)	LoA	1	4	8.89	10	9	0	0	28	44	4	14	28	8.9	2.05	.346
2014	Greenville (SAL)	LoA	2	0	4.15	3	3	0	0	17	15	1	4	19	9.9	1.10	.231
	Salem (CAR)	HiA	6	6	4.93	22	22	1	0	115	135	10	33	57	4.5	1.46	.295
Minor League Totals			9	12	4.89	50	49	1	0	197	225	16	58	137	6.3	1.44	.288

Chicago Cubs

BY JOHN MANUEL

MIKE JANES

The Cubs' top prospect heading into 2014, Javier Baez hit just .169 in the majors but learned that his power will play

Did the Cubs play a 2014 season? Did that happen?

With all that has gone on since the season ended, forgive Cubs fans if they have flushed away thoughts of the team's 73-89 season, their fifth straight fifth-place finish in the National League Central. It was a bridge year to the future, and in the offseason, the Cubs built a brand new bridge (and started rebuilding Wrigley Field).

Entering 2014, the Cubs believed they had building blocks for the lineup, starting with 24-year-old regulars Anthony Rizzo at first base and shortstop Starlin Castro. Both had struggled in 2013 but bounced back with strong seasons, as Rizzo hit 32 homers while Castro posted the highest OPS of his career (.777) and made his third all-star team.

The Cubs also found out who won't be part of the future—such as Mike Olt and Junior Lake— and saw the debuts of three key rookies. Last year's No. 1, Javier Baez, swatted nine home runs as a second baseman but found out his all-or-nothing approach won't work against big league pitchers, striking out 95 times in 213 at-bats while batting .169. Versatile Arismendy Alcantara had his moments but also struggled while settling in as the team's new center fielder. Cuban right fielder Jorge Soler had the best debut, in just 89 at-bats, showing off profile right-field tools. Meanwhile righthander Kyle Hendricks had the best rookie debut on the mound and looks like a back-of-the-rotation option for when the team becomes competitive.

Now that looks like it could be in 2015, with two huge moves that accelerated the organization's timetable. Chicago swooped in when Rays manager Joe Maddon had a two-week window to opt out of his contract, firing Rick Renteria after one season as Cubs manager to strike while Maddon was available. Second, team president Theo Epstein, general manager Jed Hoyer and assistant GM Jason McLeod tapped into their Red Sox roots to sign Jon Lester to the largest contract in franchise history, a six-year, $155 million deal that gave the Cubs a new ace.

Lester ended 2014 playing for the Athletics with Jeff Samardzija, the Cubs' ace the last two seasons who will be contributing indirectly on the North Side for years. Chicago traded him to the Athletics and got consecutive first-round picks in return, with hard-hitting shortstop Addison Russell (2012) and smooth-swinging outfielder Billy McKinney (2013), who both made an immediate impact.

Russell joins 2014 Minor League Player of

TOP PROSPECTS OF THE DECADE

Year	Player, Pos.	2014 Org
2005	Brian Dopirak, 1b	Out of baseball
2006	Felix Pie, of	Hanwha (Korea)
2007	Felix Pie, of	Hanwha (Korea)
2008	Josh Vitters, 3b	Cubs
2009	Josh Vitters, 3b	Cubs
2010	Starlin Castro, ss	Cubs
2011	Chris Archer, rhp	Rays
2012	Brett Jackson, of	Diamondbacks
2013	Javier Baez, ss	Cubs
2014	Javier Baez, ss	Cubs

the Year Kris Bryant, who hit 43 homers while reaching Triple-A, plus Baez in giving the Cubs an enviable group of athletic infielders with pop. The organization then added more impact talent through the draft, executing its plan perfectly. Chicago got perhaps the draft's best hitter, catcher/outfielder Kyle Schwarber, at No. 4 overall for a below-slot bonus, then used the savings to sign three million-dollar high school pitchers, adding much-needed organizational pitching depth.

Adding Lester (plus re-signing Jason Hammel) doesn't mean the Cubs are contenders yet. But it does mean they don't have to wait for a home-grown ace. When the team's young hitters are ready, Chicago will be ready, and don't be surprised if that happens in 2015.

General manager: Jed Hoyer. **Farm director:** Jaron Madison. **Scouting director:** Matt Dorey.

Class	Team	League	W	L	PCT	Finish	Manager:
Majors	Chicago Cubs	National	73	89	.451	t-22nd (30)	Rick Renteria
Triple-A	Iowa Cubs	Pacific Coast	74	70	.514	t-7th (16)	Marty Pevey
Double-A	Tennessee Smokies	Southern	66	73	.475	5th (10)	Buddy Bailey
High A	*Daytona Cubs	Florida State	67	69	.493	8th (12)	Dave Keller
Low A	†Kane County Cougars	Midwest	91	49	.650	1st (18)	Mark Johnson
Short season	#Boise Hawks	Northwest	41	35	.539	3rd (8)	Gary Van Tol
Rookie	Cubs	Arizona	22	34	.393	12th (13)	Jimmy Gonzalez
Overall Minor League Record			**361**	**330**	**.522**	**7th (30)**	

*Affiliate will be Myrtle Beach (Carolina) in 2015. †Affiliate will be South Bend (Midwest) in 2015.
#Affiliate will be Eugene (Northwest) in 2015.

THIS YEAR'S TOP 30

No.	Player, Pos.	Grade
1.	Kris Bryant, 3b	75/Medium
2.	Addison Russell, ss	70/Medium
3.	Jorge Soler, of	65/Medium
4.	Kyle Schwarber, c/of	65/High
5.	C.J. Edwards, rhp	60/High
6.	Billy McKinney, of	55/Medium
7.	Albert Almora, of	50/Medium
8.	Gleyber Torres, ss	55/High
9.	Pierce Johnson, rhp	55/High
10.	Duane Underwood, rhp	60/Extreme
11.	Jen-Ho Tseng, rhp	50/Medium
12.	Jake Stinnett, rhp	55/High
13.	Victor Caratini, c	50/High
14.	Rob Zastryzny, lhp	50/High
15.	Mark Zagunis, c/of	50/High
16.	Corey Black, rhp	50/High
17.	Jacob Hannemann, of	50/High
18.	Paul Blackburn, rhp	50/High
19.	Justin Steele, lhp	50/Extreme
20.	Eloy Jimenez, of	50/Extreme
21.	Bijan Rademacher, of	45/High
22.	Eric Jokisch, lhp	40/Low
23.	Trevor Clifton, rhp	50/Extreme
24.	Jeimer Candelario, 3b	45/High
25.	Dan Vogelbach, 1b	45/High
26.	Carson Sands, lhp	50/Extreme
27.	Kevonte Mitchell, of	50/Extreme
28.	Dylan Cease, rhp	50/Extreme
29.	James Norwood, rhp	45/High
30.	Daury Torrez, rhp	45/High

LAST YEAR'S TOP 30

No.	Player, Pos.	Status
1.	Javier Baez, ss	Majors
2.	Kris Bryant, 3b	No. 1
3.	C.J. Edwards, rhp	No. 5
4.	Albert Almora, of	No. 7
5.	Jorge Soler, of	No. 3
6.	Pierce Johnson, rhp	No. 9
7.	Arismendy Alcantara, 2b/ss	Majors
8.	Jeimer Candelario, 3b	No. 24
9.	Dan Vogelbach, 1b	No. 25
10.	Arodys Vizcaino, rhp	(Braves)
11.	Kyle Handricks, rhp	Majors
12.	Paul Blackburn, rhp	No. 18
13.	Christian Villanueva, 3b	Dropped out
14.	Mike Olt, 3b	Majors
15.	Corey Black, rhp	No. 16
16.	Eloy Jimenez, of	No. 20
17.	Jacob Hannemann, of	No. 17
18.	Dillon Maples, rhp	Dropped out
19.	Tyler Skulina, rhp	Dropped out
20.	Rob Zastryzny, lhp	No. 14
21.	Ivan Pineyro, rhp	Dropped out
22.	Kyuji Fujikawa	Free Agent
23.	Gleyber Torres, ss	No. 8
24.	Dallas Beeler, rhp	Dropped out
25.	Armando Rivero, rhp	Dropped out
26.	Matt Szczur, of	Dropped out
27.	Zach Cates, rhp	Dropped out
28.	Ben Wells, rhp	Dropped out
29.	Rubi Silva, of	Dropped out
30.	Danny Lockhart, 2b	Dropped out

BEST TOOLS

Best Hitter for Average	Kyle Schwarber
Best Power Hitter	Kris Bryant
Best Strike-Zone Discipline	Mark Zagunis
Fastest Baserunner	Jacob Hannemann
Best Athlete	Matt Szczur
Best Fastball	Duane Underwood
Best Curveball	C.J. Edwards
Best Slider	Jake Stinnett
Best Changeup	Jen-Ho Tseng
Best Control	Jen-Ho Tseng
Best Defensive Catcher	Victor Caratini
Best Defensive Infielder	Carlos Penalver
Best Infield Arm	Kris Bryant
Best Defensive Outfielder	Albert Almora
Best Outfield Arm	Jorge Soler

PROJECTED 2018 LINEUP

Catcher	Kyle Schwarber
First Base	Anthony Rizzo
Second Base	Starlin Castro
Third Base	Javier Baez
Shortstop	Addison Russell
Left Field	Kris Bryant
Center Field	Billy McKinney
Right Field	Jorge Soler
No. 1 Starter	Jon Lester
No. 2 Starter	Jake Arrieta
No. 3 Starter	C.J. Edwards
No. 4 Starter	Kyle Hendricks
No. 5 Starter	Duane Underwood
Closer	Corey Black

CHICAGO CUBS

TOP 2015 ROOKIE: Kris Bryant, 3b. He may not be there Opening Day, but he'll hit when he gets to Chicago.

BREAKOUT PROSPECT: Jake Stinnett, rhp. The ex-Maryland ace has all the pieces to be a starter if his arm is fresh.

SLEEPER: Juan Paniagua, rhp. He gained experience as starter in 2014 and could take off with shift to bullpen in 2015.

SOURCE OF TOP 30 TALENT

Homegrown	25	Acquired	5
College	9	Trades	5
Junior college	1	Rule 5 draft	0
High school	9	Independent leagues	0
Draft-and-follow	0	Free agents/waivers	0
Nondrafted free agents	0		
International	6		

LF
Billy McKinney (6)
Bijan Rademacher (21)
Shawon Dunston Jr.
Rubi Silva

CF
Albert Almora (7)
Jacob Hannemann (17)
Kevonte Mitchell (27)
Matt Szczur
Trey Martin

RF
Jorge Soler (3)
Eloy Jimenez (20)
Charcer Burks

3B
Kris Bryant (1)
Jeimer Candelario (24)
Christian Villanueva

SS
Addison Russell (2)
Gleyber Torres (8)
Carlos Penalver

2B
Danny Lockhart
Logan Watkins
Stephen Bruno
Chesny Young

1B
Dan Vogelbach (25)

C
Kyle Schwarber (4)
Victor Caratini (13)
Mark Zagunis (15)
Gioskar Amaya

LHP

LHSP	LHRP
Rob Zastryzny (14)	Zac Rosscup
Justin Steele (19)	Tommy Thorpe
Eric Jokisch (22)	Ariel Ovando
Carson Sands (26)	

RHP

RHSP	RHRP
C.J. Edwards (5)	Corey Black (16)
Pierce Johnson (9)	James Norwood (29)
Duane Underwood (10)	Juan Paniagua
Jen-Ho Tseng (11)	Armando Rivero
Jake Stinnett (12)	Blake Parker
Paul Blackburn (18)	Donn Roach
Trevor Clifton (23)	Tony Zych
Dylan Cease (28)	Zach Cates
Daury Torrez (30)	Scott Frazier
Dallas Beeler	Jordan Brink
Jonathan Martinez	
Tyler Skulina	
Ivan Pineyro	
Erick Leal	
Dillon Maples	
Adin Diaz	
Jeremy Null	
Ben Wells	

2014

BEST PURE HITTER: Several scouting directors contacted for this feature called C/OF Kyle Schwarber (1) the best hitter in the draft, wowed by his combination of strength, short swing and confident presence in the box.

BEST POWER HITTER: Schwarber has plus power from pole to pole and made hitting home runs look easy in his debut, mashing 18 over three regular season levels (and one more in the high Class A Florida State League playoffs) after hitting 14 in the spring for Indiana.

FASTEST RUNNER: Five-foot-9, 170-pound OF Calvin Graves (27) has no power to speak of but is an aggressive 60 runner who stole 92 bases in four seasons at Division II Franklin Pierce (N.H.).

BEST DEFENSIVE PLAYER: 2B Andrew Ely (32) was an all-league defender in the Pacific-12 Conference with sure hands, good range and instincts to spare.

BEST FASTBALL: RHP James Norwood (7) and RHP Jake Stinnett (2) have the best present fastballs, with the Cubs giving Norwood a slight edge. Both reach 97 mph regularly as starters, and pitch in the 92-95 mph range as starters. RHP Dylan Cease (6) came out of the gate hitting 98 mph this spring but got hurt and needed Tommy John surgery after signing in July.

BEST SECONDARY PITCH: Stinnett has improved his feel for a hard, late slider that has power in the 78-83 mph range.

BEST PRO DEBUT: Schwarber made pro ball look too easy, hitting .344/.428/.634 with 18 homers and a 39-57 walk-strikeout ratio in 262 at-bats. He struggled more with the defensive part of the game. OF Kevonte Mitchell (13) hit .294/.374/.371 in the Rookie-level Arizona League, showing a more advanced swing than expected and stealing 19 bases in 20 tries.

BEST ATHLETE: At 6-foot-4, 185 pounds, Mitchell was a first-team all-Missouri basketball player as a junior, but he was committed to play baseball at Southeast Missouri State.

MOST INTRIGUING BACKGROUND: OF Joey Martarano (22) was one of Idaho's top prep players in 2013 but didn't sign and attended Boise State to play football. The Cubs drafted him in 2014 and signed him while allowing him to continue playing linebacker for the Broncos. LHP Carson Sands (4) has a younger brother Cole who is a priority follow for the 2015 draft.

CLOSEST TO MAJORS: Schwarber's arrival will depend mostly on his ability to catch. If the Cubs decide to stick him in left field, he'll be in Wrigley Field in 2015.

BEST LATE-ROUND PICK: RHP Jeremy Null (15) had back problems in the spring and saw his velocity drop into the mid-to-upper 80s. The 6-foot-8, 230-pounder threw the ball better this summer after signing and was back up to reaching 93 mph with good downhill plane.

THE ONE WHO GOT AWAY: Athletic OF Isiah Gilliam (23) was ruled ineligible this spring at Parkview High in Lilburn, Ga., limiting looks at the athletic switch-hitter. He'll make up for lost time at Chipola (Fla.) JC.

ASSESSMENT: The Cubs executed a plan deftly, getting the consensus top bat in Schwarber and saving enough to add needed million-dollar arms in Stinnett, Sands, Steele and Cease.

2013

3B Kris Bryant (1) won Minor League Player of the Year in 2014. LHP Rob Zastryzny (2) and OF Jacob Hannemann (3) reached high Class A in their first seasons. RHP Trevor Clifton (12) is a hard-throwing sleeper.

GRADE: A

2012

OF Albert Almora (1), RHPs Pierce Johnson (1s) and Duane Underwood (2) are Top 10 prospects, while RHP Paul Blackburn (1s) and OF Bijan Rademacher (13) made the Top 30.

GRADE: B

2011

SS Javier Baez (1) has terrifying power and swing-and-miss tendencies. The rest of this class has fallen short of hopes thus far.

GRADE: C

TOP DRAFT PICKS OF THE DECADE

Year	Player, Pos.	2014 Org
2005	Mark Pawelek, lhp	Out of baseball
2006	Tyler Colvin, of	Giants
2007	Josh Vitters, 3b	Cubs
2008	Andrew Cashner, rhp	Padres
2009	Brett Jackson, of	Diamondbacks
2010	Hayden Simpson, rhp	Out of baseball
2011	Javier Baez, ss	Cubs
2012	Albert Almora, of	Cubs
2013	Kris Bryant, 3b	Cubs
2014	Kyle Schwarber, c/of	Cubs

LARGEST BONUSES IN CLUB HISTORY

Kris Bryant, 2013	$6,708,400
Jorge Soler, 2012	$6,000,000
Mark Prior, 2001	$4,000,000
Kosuke Fukudome, 2007	$4,000,000
Albert Almora, 2012	$3,900,000

1 KRIS BRYANT, 3B

Born: Jan. 4, 1992. **B-T:** R-R. **Ht.:** 6-5. **Wt.:** 215.
Drafted: San Diego, 2013 (1st round).
Signed by: Alex Lantayo.

The Cubs did plenty of due diligence on drafting Bryant out of high school in 2010, under their previous administration, scouting him heavily out of Las Vegas' Bonanza High. The price wasn't right, as it turned out, for any team, and Bryant bypassed the Blue Jays (who drafted him in the 18th round) to go to San Diego. A three-year starter who also played for USA Baseball's Collegiate National Team, Bryant turned a corner in 2013, leading the nation in home runs (31) as well as walks, total bases and slugging percentage while playing third base, right field and center field for the Toreros. The No. 2 overall pick in 2013 signed for a Cubs club-record $6,708,400, then hit nine homers in his pro debut and was MVP of the Arizona Fall League. All he did for an encore was become the second player to win the Baseball America College and Minor League Player of the Year awards in consecutive years—the other being Alex Gordon in 2005-06—leading the minors with 43 home runs, 78 extra-base hits, a .661 slugging percentage and 1.098 OPS while ranking second with a .438 on-base percentage.

Bryant's biggest adjustment as an amateur was spreading out and simplifying his swing, and while he has some holes, as most tall sluggers do, his approach and pitch recognition make him an above-average hitter with lethal all-fields power. No one in the minor leagues gets to their raw power as much as Bryant, a baseball grinder whose father Mike played in the minors in the early 1980s and who works as a hitting coach in Las Vegas, having mentored Rangers No. 1 prospect Joey Gallo, among others. While Gallo, like last year's Cubs' top prospect Javier Baez, always seems to be seeing how far he can hit it, Bryant has an all-fields approach that belies his experience level. He works at his craft, soaking up coaches' information and applying it in ways that earns respect from coaches and teammates. Bryant's athleticism makes him an average defender at third base, where he's improved on balls in front of him, features an easy plus arm and ranges well to his left. He's not as good going to his right, and few tall, lanky players his size have stayed at the hot corner in the majors. His average speed—he's easy to grade because he runs virtually every ball out—would suit him well if he moves to the outfield, and he'd profile in right. Bryant's makeup earns nearly as many plaudits as his power, both for his work ethic and love of the game, which go hand in hand.

The Cubs have a surplus of athletic infielders who can hit, and it's conceivable either big league shortstops Baez and Starlin Castro or Double-A shortstop Addison Russell could wind up at third base, with Bryant shifting to the outfield. Bryant also could stay at third, where Luis Valbuena is keeping the hot corner warm in Chicago. Barring a poor start back at Triple-A Iowa, Bryant should arrive on the North Side as soon as the Cubs deem it financially feasible. Bryant has the talent, confidence and makeup to be one of the game's biggest stars. All he's waiting for is the playing time.

BA GRADE

75 Risk: Medium

SCOUTING GRADES

Batting: 60.
Power: 80.
Speed: 50.
Defense: 50.
Arm: 60.

Based on 20-80 scouting scale and future projection rather than present grades.

LGE	PA	BB%	SO%	ISO
SL	297	14.5	25.9	.347
PCL	297	14.5	28.6	.324

JOHN WILLIAMSON

Year	Club (League)	Class	AVG	G	AB	R	H	2B	3B	HR	RBI	BB	SO	SB	CS	OBP	SLG
2013	Cubs (AZL)	R	.167	2	6	0	1	1	0	0	2	0	1	0	0	.143	.333
	Boise (NWL)	SS	.354	18	65	13	23	8	1	4	16	8	17	0	0	.416	.692
	Daytona (FSL)	HiA	.333	16	57	9	19	5	1	5	14	3	17	1	0	.387	.719
2014	Tennessee (SL)	AA	.355	68	248	61	88	20	0	22	58	43	77	8	2	.458	.702
	Iowa (PCL)	AAA	.295	70	244	57	72	14	1	21	52	43	85	7	2	.418	.619
Minor League Totals			.327	174	620	140	203	48	3	52	142	97	197	16	4	.428	.666

2 ADDISON RUSSELL, SS

Born: Jan. 23, 1994. **B-T:** R-R. **Ht.:** 6-0. **Wt.:** 195. **Drafted:** HS—Pensacola, Fla., 2012 (1st round). **Signed by:** Kelcey Mucker (Athletics).

The 12th overall pick in 2012, Russell signed for $2.625 million and became the Athletics' top prospect. He was teammates in the Arizona Fall League in 2013 with Cubs prospects Albert Almora, Kris Bryant and Jorge Soler. His 2014 season got off to a slow start; he injured his hamstring on Opening Day and missed two months. When he returned, Russell was the key return for the Cubs when they traded Jeff Samardzija to the Athletics. He combines above-average athleticism with extremely quick hands and impressive strength to produce both plus hitting ability and power. He's nearly impossible to beat with a fastball when he's looking for it and stays back on offspeed stuff, trusting his fast hands and making plenty of high-impact contact. Defensively, Russell has the range and improved footwork to stay at shortstop. He has an average arm with a slight hitch in his throwing motion, but it's accurate and he has a good internal clock, so most scouts believe he can be an average defender. He's played some second base as well.

BA GRADE

70 Risk: Medium

LGE	PA	BB%	SO%	ISO
TL	57	14.0	14.0	.167
SL	205	4.4	17.1	.242

He's an above-average runner but not a burner. Russell's bat will play anywhere. Chicago shortstop Starlin Castro will play as a 25-year-old in 2015, so Russell should open the season at Triple-A Iowa.

Year	Club (League)	Class	AVG	G	AB	R	H	2B	3B	HR	RBI	BB	SO	SB	CS	OBP	SLG
2012	Athletics (AZL)	R	.415	26	106	29	44	4	5	6	29	14	23	9	1	.488	.717
	Vermont (NYP)	SS	.340	13	53	9	18	2	2	1	7	4	13	2	0	.386	.509
	Burlington (MWL)	LoA	.310	16	58	8	18	4	2	0	9	5	12	5	1	.369	.448
2013	Stockton (CAL)	HiA	.275	107	429	85	118	29	10	17	60	61	116	21	3	.377	.508
	Sacramento (PCL)	AAA	.077	3	13	1	1	0	0	0	0	0	9	0	0	.077	.077
2014	Stockton (CAL)	HiA	.188	5	16	0	3	0	0	0	1	2	6	1	0	.278	.188
	Midland (TL)	AA	.333	13	48	7	16	3	1	1	8	8	8	3	2	.439	.500
	Tennessee (SL)	AA	.294	50	194	32	57	11	0	12	36	9	35	2	2	.332	.536
Minor League Totals			.300	233	917	171	275	53	20	37	150	103	222	43	9	.379	.522

3 JORGE SOLER, OF

Born: Feb. 25, 1992. **B-T:** R-R. **Ht.:** 6-4. **Wt.:** 215. **Signed:** Cuba, 2012. **Signed by:** Louie Eljaua/Jose Serra/Alex Suarez.

Soler defected from Cuba in 2011, officially signing for a $6 million bonus as part of a nine-year, $30 million contract months after he and the Cubs were first linked. He had trouble understanding why he was in the minor leagues with that contract and also had trouble staying on the field in 2013 and 2014, getting too bulky and straining both hamstrings early in the latter season. A looser Soler took off in the second half, including a tantalizing big league callup that included three home runs in his first four games. Kris Bryant hits more homers, but Soler's create more buzz. His vicious bat speed, top-of-the-scale raw power and impressive feel for hitting make him a terror to pitchers. When locked in, he generates scorching line drives to all fields; some just don't stop going until they're over the fence. He's coachable, takes quality at-bats and isn't fazed by hitting with two strikes. Soler runs average at this point in his career and has an easy plus arm, fitting the right-field profile well. His biggest issues are concentration,

BA GRADE

65 Risk: Medium

LGE	PA	BB%	SO%	ISO
PCL	127	13.4	20.5	.336
NL	97	6.2	24.7	.281

competing consistently and staying healthy, none of which he has done yet over a full pro season. Soler is the best outfielder and righthanded power hitter on the Cubs' big league roster. If he stays healthy, he has the ability to be an all-star right fielder soon.

Year	Club (League)	Class	AVG	G	AB	R	H	2B	3B	HR	RBI	BB	SO	SB	CS	OBP	SLG
2012	Cubs (AZL)	R	.241	14	54	14	13	2	0	2	10	6	13	8	0	.328	.389
	Peoria (MWL)	LoA	.338	20	80	14	27	5	0	3	15	6	6	4	1	.398	.513
2013	Daytona (FSL)	HiA	.281	55	210	38	59	13	1	8	35	21	38	5	1	.343	.467
2014	Cubs (AZL)	R	.400	8	25	7	10	3	0	1	6	4	7	0	0	.500	.640
	Tennessee (SL)	AA	.415	22	65	13	27	9	1	6	22	12	15	0	1	.494	.862
	Iowa (PCL)	AAA	.282	32	110	22	31	11	1	8	29	17	26	0	1	.378	.618
	Chicago (NL)	MAJ	.292	24	89	11	26	8	1	5	20	6	24	1	0	.330	.573
Major League Totals			.292	24	89	11	26	8	1	5	20	6	24	1	0	.330	.573
Minor League Totals			.307	151	544	108	167	43	3	28	117	66	105	17	3	.383	.551

4 KYLE SCHWARBER, OF/C

Born: March 5, 1993. **B-T:** L-R. **Ht.:** 6-0. **Wt.:** 235. **Drafted:** Indiana, 2014 (1st round). **Signed by:** Stan Zielinski.

As a sophomore, Schwarber led Indiana to the 2013 College World Series, leading the first Big Ten Conference team to Omaha since Barry Larkin's 1984 Michigan club. The Cubs drafted him fourth overall in 2014, signing him for a $3.125 million bonus that was nearly $1.5 million below slot, savings the Cubs passed on to pitchers. Then Schwarber destroyed pro pitching in his debut, hitting 19 home runs (counting the playoffs) over three levels. He has thick, strong legs and swings from the ground up, incorporating his powerful lower half to deliver plus power with a short, furious, lefthanded stroke. He keeps his hands back and has the strength to hit the ball out to any part of the park. He has some movement in his load, a timing mechanism that may cause him issues going forward, but he has the savvy to adjust and has a .300-hitting, 30-homer ceiling. A college catcher, Schwarber has leadership skills and solid-average arm strength, but his receiving was rudimentary as an amateur, and he frequently dropped to one knee to handle breaking balls. The Cubs worked him exclusively behind the plate in instructional league, where his competitiveness and energy—even at the end of a very long season—made him a club-house leader. He has the tools to be a capable left fielder, having shown instincts for the position. With his bat, Schwarber—an average runner underway—could move quickly as an outfielder. The Cubs intend to catch him, with some club officials giving him a 50/50 shot to stay there, while sources outside the system aren't as sanguine. The offseason plan is for Schwarber to open as the Double-A Tennessee catcher, but the plan could change in spring training.

BA GRADE	
65	Risk: High

LGE	PA	BB%	SO%	ISO
MWL	96	11.5	17.7	.241
FSL	191	13.6	19.9	.258

Year	Club (League)	Class	AVG	G	AB	R	H	2B	3B	HR	RBI	BB	SO	SB	CS	OBP	SLG
2014	Boise (NWL)	SS	.600	5	20	7	12	1	1	4	10	2	2	0	1	.625	1.350
	Kane County (MWL)	LoA	.361	23	83	17	30	8	0	4	15	11	17	1	1	.448	.602
	Daytona (FSL)	HiA	.302	44	159	31	48	9	1	10	28	26	38	4	0	.393	.560
Minor League Totals			.344	72	262	55	90	18	2	18	53	39	57	5	2	.428	.634

5 C.J. EDWARDS, RHP

Born: Sept. 3, 1991. **B-T:** R-R. **Ht.:** 6-2. **Wt.:** 155. **Drafted:** HS—Prosperity, S.C., 2011 (48th round). **Signed by:** Chris Kemp (Rangers).

Signed for $50,000 in the 48th round (which no longer exists) by the Rangers, Edwards broke out in 2013 in low Class A and was a key piece the Cubs received in trade that sent Matt Garza to Texas. Edwards missed most of 2014 with a right shoulder strain, making four April starts at Double-A Tennessee and six more after returning in August. He didn't need surgery. At his best, Edwards delivers three above-average to plus pitches, with excellent body control leading to an easy, rhythmic delivery and strike-throwing ability. He's very tough for hitters to square up due to late cutting action on his fastball, which generally sat 90-93 mph in August and in his Arizona Fall League stint. The late life on the pitch has helped him miss barrels, saw off bats and yield just two homers in 237 career pro innings. His curveball improved over his 2013 model, with more snap now in the upper 70s. The changeup flashes plus, playing off his fastball. His feel for pitching returned, though his command showed rust. Durability remains Edwards' biggest concern, and he raised more questions this year than he answered, but Cubs officials believe he learned a lesson in how to prepare for a full season. Chicago's best pitching prospect likely will start 2015 back at Double-A, with front-of-the-rotation stuff and doubts over how often he can go to the post.

BA GRADE	
60	Risk: High

LGE	BF	SO%	BB%	HR/9
SL	193	23.8	10.9	0.19

Year	Club (League)	Class	W	L	ERA	G	GS	CG	SV	IP	H	HR	BB	SO	K/9	WHIP	AVG
2012	Rangers (AZL)	R	3	0	0.00	4	3	0	0	20	6	0	6	25	11.3	0.60	.094
	Spokane (NWL)	SS	2	3	2.11	10	10	0	0	47	26	0	19	60	11.5	0.96	.160
2013	Hickory (SAL)	LoA	8	2	1.83	18	18	1	0	93	62	0	34	122	11.8	1.03	.186
	Daytona (FSL)	HiA	0	0	1.96	6	6	0	0	23	14	1	7	33	12.9	0.91	.169
2014	Cubs (AZL)	R	0	0	1.59	2	2	0	0	6	2	0	4	8	12.7	1.06	.111
	Tennessee (SL)	AA	1	2	2.44	10	10	0	0	48	30	1	21	46	8.6	1.06	.180
Minor League Totals			14	7	1.86	50	49	1	0	237	140	2	91	294	11.2	0.97	.169

6 BILLY McKINNEY, OF

Born: Aug. 23, 1994. **B-T:** L-L. **Ht.:** 6-1. **Wt.:** 195. **Drafted:** HS—Plano, Texas, 2013 (1st round). **Signed by:** Armann Brown (Athletics).

The Cubs were stunned they were able to pry both Addison Russell and McKinney, the Athletics' top two prospects, away in the Jeff Samardzija/Jason Hammel trade. Signed in 2013 for $1.8 million, McKinney jumped to high Class A Stockton for his first full season but hit better at Daytona in the pitcher-friendly Florida State League after the trade. It's all about the approach with McKinney, a polished hitter who is quiet in the box, with a balanced setup and good hands. He'll bar his swing at times but generally has as smooth path to the ball and isn't afraid to hit with two strikes, or to use the whole field. McKinney's pitch recognition and situational-hitting skills are other plusses, leading some evaluators to believe he may wind up with average or a tick above home run production. A sore shoulder limited McKinney to DH duty down the stretch in 2014, and his fringy arm strength limits him to left or center field anyway. He's an average runner. McKinney isn't a profile left fielder, but his Todd Hollandsworth/Rusty Greer skillset blends well with the rest of the Cubs' aggressive, powerful bats. He's headed to Double-A Tennessee as a 20-year-old in 2015.

BA GRADE

55 Risk: Medium

LGE	PA	BB%	SO%	ISO
FSL	210	11.9	20.0	.131
CAL	333	10.8	17.4	.159

Year	Club (League)	Class	AVG	G	AB	R	H	2B	3B	HR	RBI	BB	SO	SB	CS	OBP	SLG
2013	Athletics (AZL)	R	.320	46	181	31	58	7	2	2	20	17	29	7	0	.383	.414
	Vermont (NYP)	SS	.353	9	34	5	12	2	1	1	6	3	4	1	1	.405	.559
2014	Stockton (CAL)	HiA	.241	75	290	42	70	12	2	10	33	36	58	5	3	.330	.400
	Daytona (FSL)	HiA	.301	51	176	30	53	12	4	1	36	25	42	1	0	.390	.432
Minor League Totals			.283	181	681	108	193	33	9	14	95	81	133	14	4	.364	.420

7 ALBERT ALMORA, OF

Born: April 16, 1994. **B-T:** R-R. **Ht.:** 6-2. **Wt.:** 180. **Drafted:** HS—Hialeah, Fla., 2012 (1st round). **Signed by:** John Koronka/Laz Llanos.

Almora signed for $3.9 million as the sixth overall pick in 2012. Injuries interrupted his first pro season, and he reached Double-A Tennessee in 2014 but has yet to thrive He has yet to thrive, however, hitting into 21 double plays and searching for consistency. Almora has first-round tools, starting with a line-drive bat with present strength, fine hand-eye coordination, bat speed to catch up to good fastballs and average raw power. He makes contact so easily, he gets himself out often swinging at pitcher's pitches. He was pitched backwards much of the season and struggled to adjust. He still employs a big leg kick and can get streaky, as evidenced by a .377/.395/.649 finishing kick with high Class A Daytona before his promotion. A bit more patience would go a long way to making Almora a big league regular considering his defense, which remains advanced. He reads hitters' swings, has excellent range despite fringe-average speed and owns an accurate, strong arm. His bilingual skills come in handy in the clubhouse, and his makeup and work ethic remain strong positives. The Cubs don't need Almora to be a star—just a grinder who can hit and play plus defense at a premium position. Those goals are attainable if he becomes more flexible in his hitting approach. He's headed back to Double-A to begin 2015 but now has Arismendy Alcantara ahead of him as Chicago's incumbent center fielder.

BA GRADE

50 Risk: Medium

LGE	PA	BB%	SO%	ISO
FSL	385	3.1	11.9	.123
SL	144	1.4	16.0	.121

Year	Club (League)	Class	AVG	G	AB	R	H	2B	3B	HR	RBI	BB	SO	SB	CS	OBP	SLG
2012	Cubs (AZL)	R	.347	18	75	18	26	5	1	1	13	2	8	5	1	.363	.480
	Boise (NWL)	SS	.292	15	65	9	19	7	0	1	6	0	5	0	1	.292	.446
2013	Kane County (MWL)	LoA	.329	61	249	39	82	17	4	3	23	17	30	4	4	.376	.466
2014	Daytona (FSL)	HiA	.283	89	367	55	104	20	2	7	50	12	46	6	3	.306	.406
	Tennessee (SL)	AA	.234	36	141	20	33	7	2	2	10	2	23	0	1	.250	.355
Minor League Totals			.294	219	897	141	264	56	9	14	102	33	112	15	10	.322	.424

8 GLEYBER TORRES, SS

Born: Dec. 13, 1996. **B-T:** R-R. **Ht.:** 6-1. **Wt.:** 175. **Signed:** Venezuela, 2013.
Signed by: Louie Eljaua/Hector Ortega.

The Cubs signed the two top-ranked players in the 2013 international signing class, Torres and outfielder Eloy Jimenez, who got more money but is much less polished. A $1.7 million signee, Torres finished his U.S. pro debut in 2014 by earning a promotion to short-season Boise before his 18th birthday. His maturity showed as he maintained his focus despite turmoil in his native Venezuela that prompted his family to move to the U.S. Torres is not the typical teen and draws comparisons with Cubs prospect Albert Almora for his baseball savvy and instincts. His hands, actions and above-average arm fit him for shortstop, and his internal clock helps him make routine plays look routine. His range may fit better at second base, where his bat should carry him. He has an advanced approach for any age, with strength that allows him to drive mistakes to the gaps and fight off pitchers' pitches. He's willing to draw walks and has a chance to be an above-average hitter with fringe-average power down the line. He's an average runner and won't be a big basestealer. Torres is expected to advance to full-season ball with Chicago's new low Class A South Bend affiliate. He's a couple of years away from the system's upper-levels, middle-infield glut and could be trade bait sooner than later.

BA GRADE

55 Risk: High

LGE	PA	BB%	SO%	ISO
AZL	183	13.7	18.0	.097
NWL	32	12.5	21.9	.393

Year	Club (League)	Class	AVG	G	AB	R	H	2B	3B	HR	RBI	BB	SO	SB	CS	OBP	SLG
2014	Cubs (AZL)	R	.279	43	154	33	43	6	3	1	29	25	33	8	7	.372	.377
	Boise (NWL)	SS	.393	7	28	4	11	2	3	1	4	4	7	2	0	.469	.786
Minor League Totals			.297	50	182	37	54	8	6	2	33	29	40	10	7	.386	.440

9 PIERCE JOHNSON, RHP

Born: May 10, 1991. **B-T:** R-R. **Ht.:** 6-3. **Wt.:** 170. **Drafted:** Missouri State, 2012 (1st round supplemental). **Signed by:** Stan Zielinksi.

Arvada, Colo., was the high school home for Johnson as well as Roy Halladay and Mark Melancon. Johnson signed in 2012 for $1.196 million. He has a long history of forearm trouble from his amateur days, when he also had knee and hand injuries, but has never had arm surgery. When he was disabled in 2014, it was due to hamstring issues and not his arm. Johnson walked eight in his second Double-A Tennessee start in 2014 and took a while to find his confidence thereafter. When he throws strikes, his stuff has proved hard to square up; opponents have hit .227 against him as a pro. Johnson's 90-94 mph fastball can reach 96 and has late life up in the zone. His upright finish can make it difficult for him to locate down in the zone, a developmental focus going forward. He throws both a hard late-breaking curveball with depth and sluvy shape in the low 80s and a short, cutter-like slider. He's learned to use his fringy changeup more effectively with pro experience. If Johnson puts it all together, he profiles as a No. 2 or 3 starter with two plus pitches and potentially above-average control. Chicago's 2014 ace, Jake Arrieta, had a similar (albeit more durable) career path, and Johnson's stuff is worth the wait. He could pitch his way to Triple-A Iowa with a strong, healthy spring training.

BA GRADE

55 Risk: High

LGE	BF	SO%	BB%	HR/9
MWL	39	20.5	7.7	0.82
SL	373	24.4	14.5	0.79

Year	Club (League)	Class	W	L	ERA	G	GS	CG	SV	IP	H	HR	BB	SO	K/9	WHIP	AVG
2012	Cubs (AZL)	R	0	0	0.00	2	2	0	0	3	4	0	0	2	6.0	1.33	.364
	Boise (NWL)	SS	0	0	4.50	4	4	0	0	8	10	0	3	12	13.5	1.63	.323
2013	Kane County (MWL)	LoA	5	5	3.10	13	13	0	0	70	68	4	22	74	9.6	1.29	.255
	Daytona (FSL)	HiA	6	1	2.22	10	8	0	0	49	41	1	21	50	9.2	1.27	.240
2014	Kane County (MWL)	LoA	0	1	2.45	2	2	0	0	11	4	1	3	8	6.5	0.64	.118
	Tennessee (SL)	AA	5	4	2.55	18	17	0	0	92	60	8	54	91	8.9	1.24	.194
Minor League Totals			16	11	2.68	49	46	0	0	232	187	14	103	237	9.2	1.25	.227

10 DUANE UNDERWOOD, RHP

Born: July 20, 1994. **B-T:** R-R. **Ht.:** 6-2. **Wt.:** 205. **Drafted:** HS—Marietta, Ga., 2012 (2nd round). **Signed by:** Keith Lockhart.

Underwood was a potential first-round pick as a prep senior before an erratic spring in which he didn't hold his top-end velocity. The Cubs signed him for a $1.05 million bonus and he struggled in his first two seasons. But having dropped 25-30 pounds, Underwood broke out at low Class A Kane County in 2014. He took off when his preparation started to match his ability. He not only had a better body but a better, more professional mindset. His weight loss unlocked his athleticism, allowing him to better repeat his delivery and locate his plus fastball. He had the highest average velocity of any Cubs minor league starter, and his heater can sit in the 94-96 mph range. He's learning to finish off hitters with a hard curve that flashes plus as well, thanks to its depth and late action. He needs to locate both pitches better against more advanced hitters. His changeup continues to improve and also flashes plus because he throws it with good arm speed. Consistency with location and preparation continue to be his biggest weaknesses. No one took as big of a step forward for the organization in 2014 as Underwood, who has the system's most electric stuff. If he combines better control with more consistent displays of the best of his repertoire, he could move quickly. He'll start 2015 at Chicago's new high Class A Myrtle Beach affiliate.

BA GRADE

60 **Risk:** Extreme

LGE	BF	SO%	BB%	HR/9
MWL	413	20.3	8.7	0.89

Year	Club (League)	Class	W	L	ERA	G	GS	CG	SV	IP	H	HR	BB	SO	K/9	WHIP	AVG
2012	Cubs (AZL)	R	0	1	5.19	5	5	0	0	9	7	1	6	7	7.3	1.50	.206
2013	Boise (NWL)	SS	3	4	4.97	14	11	0	0	54	62	4	27	36	6.0	1.64	.277
2014	Kane County (MWL)	LoA	6	4	2.50	22	21	0	0	101	85	10	36	84	7.5	1.20	.231
Minor League Totals			9	9	3.46	41	37	0	0	164	154	15	69	127	7.0	1.36	.246

11 JEN-HO TSENG, RHP

BA GRADE

50 **Risk:** Medium

Born: Oct. 3, 1994. **B-T:** L-R. **Ht.:** 6-1. **Wt.:** 210. **Signed:** Taiwan, 2013. **Signed by:** Steve Wilson/Paul Weaver.

With their hitters far ahead of their pitching depth, the Cubs signed Tseng out of Taiwan in 2013 for a $1.625 million bonus. He sent scouts mixed signals as an amateur, flashing 95 mph fastballs at times while pitching backwards with average velocity at other times, and he pitched poorly in the 2013 World Baseball Classic as a 17-year-old. That's in his past now after a strong debut season at low Class A Kane County in 2014. A consistent strike-thrower with the best control in the system, Tseng pitches at 87-92 mph with his fastball, reaching 94, and locates it all over the strike zone. He's the rare pitcher scouts project with potential plus command thanks to a compact, repeatable delivery. His changeup is his best pitch, a plus offering with tumble and good arm speed, and he has the confidence to double-up with it. His tight, mid-70s curveball plays solid-average, and he locates it well. Tseng gets more swings and misses with his secondary pitches than his fastball, profiling him toward the back of the rotation, but he's primed to move quickly with his durable frame and command. He'll start 2015 at high Class A Myrtle Beach.

Year	Club (League)	Class	W	L	ERA	G	GS	CG	SV	IP	H	HR	BB	SO	K/9	WHIP	AVG
2014	Kane County (MWL)	LoA	6	1	2.40	19	17	1	0	105	76	7	15	85	7.3	0.87	.204
Minor League Totals			6	1	2.40	19	17	1	0	105	76	7	15	85	7.3	0.87	.204

12 JAKE STINNETT, RHP

BA GRADE

55 **Risk:** High

Born: April 25, 1995. **B-T:** R-R. **Ht.:** 6-4. **Wt.:** 202. **Drafted:** Maryland, 2014 (2nd round). **Signed by:** Billy Swope.

The Cubs were stunned to get Stinnett with the 45th overall pick in 2014, considering how college seniors—especially those with actual tools and upside—speed up draft boards now. A California prep product, he went to Maryland as a third baseman but made 13 relief appearances as well in his first two seasons. He moved into the rotation as a junior, didn't sign as the Pirates' 29th-round pick in 2013 and blossomed in 2014, tossing 118 innings and ranking fifth in Division I with 132 strikeouts. He no-hit Massachusetts and struck out 14 in front of a bevy of scouts in a showdown with North Carolina State's Carlos Rodon in March, then led the Terrapins to their first regional (and first super regional) since 1971. Stinnett signed for $1 million and had his debut interrupted by a mishap during pitcher's fielding practice, having surgery to repair a damaged testicle. He's expected to be healthy for spring training, having regained most of the 15 pounds he lost convalescing from the injury, and could jump on the fast track thanks to his fine pitcher's frame, fairly fresh arm and big stuff. His heavy fastball peaks at 97 mph and can sit 92-95 mph, with bat-breaking armside run. His slider also earns plus grades, which features late three-quarters tilt in the 79-84 mph range. Stinnett's changeup is a clear third pitch and requires the most development. He has a pin in his elbow from a childhood injury, but so does Corey Kluber, and it hasn't hampered him as a pro. Stinnett likely will jump to high Class A Myrtle Beach in 2015.

Year	Club (League)	Class	W	L	ERA	G	GS	CG	SV	IP	H	HR	BB	SO	K/9	WHIP	AVG
2014	Cubs (AZL)	R	0	1	7.71	3	2	0	0	5	9	0	0	3	5.8	1.93	.409
	Boise (NWL)	SS	0	0	2.84	2	2	0	0	6	3	1	2	7	9.9	0.79	.130
Minor League Totals			0	1	4.91	5	4	0	0	11	12	1	2	10	8.2	1.27	.267

13 VICTOR CARATINI, C

BA GRADE
50 Risk: High

Born: Aug. 17, 1993. **B-T:** B-R. **Ht.:** 6-0. **Wt.:** 195. **Drafted:** Miami Dade JC, 2013 (2nd round). **Signed by:** Buddy Hernandez (Braves).

A Puerto Rico Baseball Academy alumnus, Caratini attended Southern for a year with Dodgers farmhand Jose De Leon but was academically ineligible and transferred to Miami Dade JC. He played third base and catcher there and hit his way into the second round of the 2013 draft, signing for $800,000. The Braves drafted him as a catcher and put him there full-time in his first full pro season, then traded him to the Cubs for two big leaguers—Emilio Bonifacio and James Russell. Caratini is a surer bet to catch than 2014 Cubs draftees Kyle Schwarber and Mark Zagunis, though he's still learning the position, too, and wore down at the end of his first full season at the position. He's learning nuances of blocking and receiving, using his solid-average arm to throw out 32 percent of basestealers at low Class A in 2014. He's a switch-hitter whose lefthanded swing is far ahead of his right-side stroke, with a chance for average power from that side. He's balanced at the plate, uses the whole field and is learning which pitches he can drive without selling out for power—and when to sell out. The Cubs like Caratini's plate discipline, ability to spot and lay off breaking balls and physicality, which should lend durability. For now, he's slotted for high Class A Myrtle Beach in 2015, a level behind Schwarber and ahead of Zagunis.

Year	Club (League)	Class	AVG	G	AB	R	H	2B	3B	HR	RBI	BB	SO	SB	CS	OBP	SLG
2013	Danville (APP)	R	.290	58	200	29	58	23	1	1	25	39	49	0	2	.415	.430
2014	Rome (SAL)	LoA	.279	87	323	42	90	18	4	5	42	34	59	1	1	.352	.406
	Kane County (MWL)	LoA	.264	14	53	7	14	4	1	0	13	4	10	0	0	.310	.377
Minor League Totals			.281	159	576	78	162	45	6	6	80	77	118	1	3	.371	.411

14 ROB ZASTRYZNY, LHP

BA GRADE
50 Risk: High

Born: March 26, 1992. **B-T:** R-L. **Ht.:** 6-3. **Wt.:** 205. **Drafted:** Missouri, 2013 (3rd round). **Signed by:** Ty Nichols.

Zastryzny was born in Edmonton, Alberta, but moved to Texas with his parents when he was 1 year old. Still, he was excited to be Trevor Gretzky's teammate in his pro debut in short-season Boise. Zastryzny jumped to high Class A for his first full season and struggled with the jump, with an 8.46 ERA at the end of April. He got better in at least one aspect every month, though, and was Daytona's Game One starter in the Florida State League playoffs, beating Dunedin. Zastryzny is neither a power pitcher nor a finesse lefty. He pitches off his 89-92 mph fastball that has heavy, late life and locates it up and down, in and out. He has to because he doesn't have a plus secondary pitch. He throws both a hard slider and loopier curveball, with the slider grading as fringe-average. Zastryzny nevertheless gets swings and misses with both the fastball and both breaking balls, for he hides the ball well in his cross-body delivery. His command is spottier than it needs to be at the major league level, and the Cubs believe improving his direction a bit will help him locate better, but they don't want to eliminate his deception, either. Zastryzny's improvement augurs well for his future as a potential back-end starter, with Double-A Tennessee his next stop.

Year	Club (League)	Class	W	L	ERA	G	GS	CG	SV	IP	H	HR	BB	SO	K/9	WHIP	AVG
2013	Boise (NWL)	SS	0	0	3.14	8	7	0	0	14	15	0	4	16	10.0	1.33	.268
	Kane County (MWL)	LoA	1	0	0.93	3	0	0	0	10	9	0	4	6	5.6	1.34	.257
2014	Daytona (FSL)	HiA	4	6	4.66	23	23	0	0	110	121	10	33	108	8.8	1.40	.279
Minor League Totals			5	6	4.23	34	30	0	0	134	145	10	41	130	8.7	1.39	.276

15 MARK ZAGUNIS, C/OF

BA GRADE
50 Risk: High

Born: Feb. 5, 1993. **B-T:** R-R. **Ht.:** 6-0. **Wt.:** 205. **Drafted:** Virginia Tech, 2014 (3rd round). **Signed by:** Billy Swope.

The son of a high school assistant coach, Zagunis nevertheless is a college draftee more notable for his athletic ability than his polish. He's an above-average runner, not just for a catcher, though his baserunning instincts could use improvement. In his first two seasons at Virginia Tech, he played as much outfield as catcher, and while his arm strength rates above-average, he remains a raw receiver and overall defender who also has to be more assertive as an on-field leader as a pro. At the plate, though, Zagunis' advanced approach translated to pro ball, as he walked (42) as often as he struck out and hit for average, including a 12-for-28 run with two home runs in the low Class A Midwest League playoffs. That helped Kane County run the table for the league title, with Zagunis as the DH. He puts together quality at-bats as often as anyone in the organization, recognizes pitches early and knows what pitches he can drive. Zagunis gears his swing for line drives to the gaps. His bat profiles better behind the plate, and the Cubs are loaded with outfielders. He's slated to return to the Midwest League, with new affiliate South Bend, for 2015, when his defense will be tested regularly.

Year	Club (League)	Class	AVG	G	AB	R	H	2B	3B	HR	RBI	BB	SO	SB	CS	OBP	SLG
2014	Cubs (AZL)	R	.125	2	8	1	1	1	0	0	1	1	2	0	0	.222	.250
	Boise (NWL)	SS	.299	41	154	32	46	9	2	2	27	31	31	11	2	.429	.422
	Kane County (MWL)	LoA	.280	14	50	11	14	6	1	0	4	10	9	5	0	.419	.440
Minor League Totals			.288	57	212	44	61	16	3	2	32	42	42	16	2	.420	.420

16 COREY BLACK, RHP

BA GRADE
50 Risk: High

Born: Aug. 4, 1991. **B-T:** R-R. **Ht.:** 5-11. **Wt.:** 175. **Drafted:** Faulkner (Ala.), 2012 (4th round). **Signed by:** D.J. Svihlik (Yankees).

The Cubs acquired Black from the Yankees for Alfonso Soriano, whom New York released in 2014, ending his career. Club officials are ecstatic because while they acknowledge that Black may be a reliever, his arm is special and he could be a weapon as a setup man. Black's athleticism and four-pitch mix make starting still possible, though. He reached a career high in starts and innings at Double-A Tennessee in 2014, still pumping 92-96 mph fastballs with plus late life, earning some comparisons to a young Tim Hudson for his smallish body and life. Commanding his fastball is one of Black's biggest bugaboos and may push him to the bullpen. So could his high-adrenaline style of pitching. At times, he's his own worst enemy, mentally and in terms of throwing harder when he's in trouble. Black's straight changeup improved significantly and was one of the system's best in 2014, and he stymied lefthanders to a .157/.264/.268 clip. He throws both a curve and slider, hard of course. He has more feel for the slider and throws the curve with more depth. Black, who had Tommy John surgery in high school, saw his walk rate jump, so he could move to the bullpen as soon as 2015. He profiles as a fine setup man and perhaps a closer.

Year	Club (League)	Class	W	L	ERA	G	GS	CG	SV	IP	H	HR	BB	SO	K/9	WHIP	AVG
2012	Yankees (GCL)	R	0	0	6.75	1	1	0	0	1	2	0	2	0	0.0	3.00	.333
	Staten Island (NYP)	SS	0	0	2.28	6	6	0	0	28	22	1	8	21	6.8	1.08	.222
	Charleston, SC (SAL)	LoA	2	2	3.80	5	5	0	0	24	18	0	5	29	11.0	0.97	.214
2013	Tampa (FSL)	HiA	3	8	4.25	19	19	0	0	83	79	2	45	88	9.6	1.50	.243
	Daytona (FSL)	HiA	4	0	2.88	5	5	0	0	25	22	3	10	28	10.1	1.28	.237
2014	Tennessee (SL)	AA	6	7	3.47	26	25	0	0	124	100	13	71	119	8.6	1.38	.224
Minor League Totals			15	17	3.57	62	61	0	0	285	243	19	141	285	9.0	1.35	.231

17 JACOB HANNEMANN, OF

BA GRADE
50 Risk: High

Born: April 29, 1991. **B-T:** L-L. **Ht.:** 6-1. **Wt.:** 195. **Drafted:** Brigham Young, 2013 (3rd round). **Signed by:** Steve McFarland.

Hannemann's football background—he was a two-sport athlete at Brigham Young—and two missed years due to his Mormon mission have left him old for his experience level. The Cubs focus on his athleticism, a combination of strength and explosiveness that makes him unique in the system and earns Jacoby Ellsbury comparisons. Hannemann has plus speed that helps him outrun mistakes in the outfield and helped him steal 37 bases, most in the organization. He could steal more as he learns the nuances of reading pitchers and how and when to take aggressive leads. His offense evolved as the season progressed, by far the most baseball he's played in a year. He still has rigidity to his swing and actions befitting a football player, which also shows up in his below-average arm, but he displayed more looseness as the season progressed. He'll have to improve his pitch recognition and draw more walks to fit the Ellsbury comparison. He picked up a confidence boost by holding his own in the Arizona Fall League in 2014, more experience he needed to gain. Hannemann likely begins 2015 back at high Class A, where he finished 2014, but could jump to Double-A Tennessee if his bat shows signs of real progress.

Year	Club (League)	Class	AVG	G	AB	R	H	2B	3B	HR	RBI	BB	SO	SB	CS	OBP	SLG
2013	Cubs (AZL)	R	.111	3	9	1	1	1	0	0	2	0	1	1	0	.111	.222
	Boise (NWL)	SS	.290	14	62	8	18	4	2	1	5	2	11	3	1	.313	.468
2014	Kane County (MWL)	LoA	.254	88	342	57	87	14	5	6	39	31	77	32	4	.321	.377
	Daytona (FSL)	HiA	.241	36	145	17	35	9	0	2	12	11	34	5	3	.299	.345
Minor League Totals			.253	141	558	83	141	28	7	9	58	44	123	41	8	.311	.376

18 PAUL BLACKBURN, RHP

BA GRADE
50 Risk: High

Born: Dec. 4, 1993. **B-T:** R-R. **Ht.:** 6-2. **Wt.:** 185. **Drafted:** HS— Brentwood, Calif., 2012 (1st round supplemental). **Signed by:** Scott Fairbanks.

Which is the real Blackburn? The command-and-control, pitchability righthander whose fastball generally sat in the 87-91 mph range during the 2014 regular season? Or the ace who dealt in the low Class A Midwest League playoffs, sitting 92-94 mph in a five-inning, one-hit, seven-strikeout shutout appearance? If that Blackburn shows up more regularly, the Cubs believe they'll have a No. 3 or 4 starter on their hands. He pitches off his sinking fastball, which he locates well. His best pitch at this point is his curveball, which has a chance to be plus because it has good shape and spin. Blackburn's changeup has potential to be average as well. He is a cerebral pitcher who keeps journals on opposing hitters and his own workout regimen, trying to learn what works and what doesn't. What he did in the playoffs worked, so the Cubs hope to see more of it at high Class A Myrtle Beach in 2015.

Year	Club (League)	Class	W	L	ERA	G	GS	CG	SV	IP	H	HR	BB	SO	K/9	WHIP	AVG
2012	Cubs (AZL)	R	2	0	3.48	9	6	0	0	21	23	2	7	13	5.7	1.45	.284
2013	Boise (NWL)	SS	2	3	3.33	13	12	0	0	46	41	3	29	38	7.4	1.52	.241
2014	Kane County (MWL)	LoA	9	4	3.23	24	24	0	0	117	108	6	31	75	5.8	1.19	.247
Minor League Totals			13	7	3.28	46	42	0	0	184	172	11	67	126	6.2	1.30	.250

19 JUSTIN STEELE, LHP

BA GRADE
50 Risk: Extreme

Born: July 11, 1995. **B-T:** L-L. **Ht.:** 6-1. **Wt.:** 180. **Drafted:** HS— Lucedale, Miss., 2014 (5th round). **Signed by:** Jonathan Davis.

The Cubs popped three straight prep pitchers in rounds four, five and six of the 2014 draft, then signed all three for seven-figure bonuses. Steele starts off with the best profile. Pried away from Southern Mississippi with a $1 million bonus, he is a lean athlete who impressed the Cubs after signing with his competitiveness, love of practice and athleticism. His arm works well and he's shown some present control with his fastball, throwing plenty of strikes with it. Steele's stuff isn't consistent from start to start, so sometimes he tops out at 90 mph and at other times he throws as hard as 95. He throws downhill but must improve his ability to hold his velocity over longer outings. The Cubs have seen him spin a breaking ball and he's thrown a changeup, but neither secondary pitch stands out on a consistent basis. Steele may start 2015 in extended spring training and report to the Cubs' new short-season Eugene affiliate.

Year	Club (League)	Class	W	L	ERA	G	GS	CG	SV	IP	H	HR	BB	SO	K/9	WHIP	AVG
2014	Cubs (AZL)	R	0	0	2.89	9	4	0	0	19	15	0	8	25	12.1	1.23	.217
Minor League Totals			0	0	2.89	9	4	0	0	19	15	0	8	25	12.1	1.23	.217

20 ELOY JIMENEZ, OF

BA GRADE
50 Risk: Extreme

Born: Nov. 27, 1996. **B-T:** R-R. **Ht.:** 6-4. **Wt.:** 205. **Signed:** Dominican Republic, 2013. **Signed by:** Louie Eljaua/Jose Serra/Carlos Reyes.

Jimenez was the top-rated player in the international signing class of 2013, thanks to profile right-field tools, and received the largest bonus at $2.8 million. He is still growing into his body, with his coordination catching up. Foot and shoulder injuries have slowed his progression as well, twice interrupting his 2014 debut in the Rookie-level Arizona League. He has impressed club officials with his intelligence, learning English quickly and returning to the Dominican to complete his high school diploma. He has basic fundamentals to improve, such as his throwing mechanics, which have gotten better but remain inconsistent. He has tremendous raw power with leverage in his swing and good natural balance. He must learn to use his legs more in his swing and incorporate his lower half better to make more contact and fly open with his hips less frequently. Jimenez likely will start 2015 in extended spring training and play at short-season Eugene.

Year	Club (League)	Class	AVG	G	AB	R	H	2B	3B	HR	RBI	BB	SO	SB	CS	OBP	SLG
2014	Cubs (AZL)	R	.227	42	150	13	34	8	2	3	27	10	32	3	1	.268	.367
Minor League Totals			.227	42	150	13	34	8	2	3	27	10	32	3	1	.268	.367

21 BIJAN RADEMACHER, OF

BA GRADE
45 Risk: High

Born: June 15, 1991. **B-T:** L-L. **Ht.:** 6-0. **Wt.:** 200. **Drafted:** Orange Coast (Calif.) JC, 2012 (13th round). **Signed by:** Denny Henderson.

Rademacher was a Cal State Fullerton recruit out of Anaheim's Canyon High, transferred to Orange Coast (Calif.) JC after a year and emerged as a draft prospect as both a hitter and pitcher. He signed for $100,000 as a hitter, and now has a chance to be an everyday corner outfielder. He has bat-to-ball skills

and has started to tap into his raw power. He put on a longball display during the Florida State League home run derby in 2014, though he uses a different swing during games, focusing on bat control. Better pitch recognition and a more aggressive cut, sacrificing some contact for power, would help Rademacher tap into his plus raw power. He's a solid runner and athlete who can play either outfield corner well, though his arm has backed up to fringe-average. Double-A Tennessee offers Rademacher his next test in 2015.

Year	Club (League)	Class	AVG	G	AB	R	H	2B	3B	HR	RBI	BB	SO	SB	CS	OBP	SLG
2012	Cubs (AZL)	R	.333	3	12	3	4	1	0	1	1	0	2	2	0	.333	.667
	Boise (NWL)	SS	.396	14	53	9	21	6	0	1	8	2	7	0	1	.411	.566
	Peoria (MWL)	LoA	.221	35	122	16	27	7	1	0	11	10	26	2	1	.280	.295
2013	Kane County (MWL)	LoA	.303	55	185	24	56	8	0	2	18	21	25	5	3	.374	.378
	Daytona (FSL)	HiA	.276	42	145	22	40	7	3	2	20	14	24	3	0	.338	.407
2014	Daytona (FSL)	HiA	.281	111	384	58	108	22	6	10	56	42	87	4	8	.363	.448
Minor League Totals			.284	260	901	132	256	51	10	16	114	89	171	16	13	.353	.416

22 ERIC JOKISCH, LHP

BA GRADE

40 Risk: Low

Born: July 29, 1989. **B-T:** R-L. **Ht.:** 6-2. **Wt.:** 185. **Drafted:** Northwestern, 2010 (11th round). **Signed by:** Stan Zielinski.

Jokisch is one of five Northwestern alumni who pitched in the majors in 2014 and will compete for the No. 5 starter's job in Chicago after reaching the big leagues for the first time. He ranked second in the Pacific Coast League in strikeouts (143) and fourth in WHIP in 2014. Jokisch pitches in the 86-90 mph range with his two- and four-seam fastballs, reaching 93 on occasion. He has to be fine with both, adding and subtracting to try to set up his changeup. It's his money pitch, earning above-average grades in the 76-80 mph range. He locates his short, firm slider and drops in a slow curve from time to time. He's been tremendously durable, averaging 159 innings the last three seasons. Jokisch is the classic crafty lefty, with the savvy to get through lineups multiple times in the minors. He'll have to turn his above-average control into true command to do it in the majors, and likely will start 2015 back at Triple-A Iowa.

Year	Club (League)	Class	W	L	ERA	G	GS	CG	SV	IP	H	HR	BB	SO	K/9	WHIP	AVG
2012	Daytona (FSL)	HiA	3	4	3.48	9	9	0	0	54	55	4	16	52	8.6	1.31	.267
	Tennessee (SL)	AA	7	2	2.91	18	17	1	0	105	86	7	33	63	5.4	1.13	.226
2013	Tennessee (SL)	AA	11	3	3.42	27	26	2	0	161	144	14	54	137	7.7	1.23	.240
2014	Iowa (PCL)	AAA	9	10	3.58	26	26	1	0	158	155	12	31	143	8.1	1.17	.255
	Chicago (NL)	MAJ	0	0	1.88	4	1	0	0	14	18	3	4	10	6.3	1.53	.290
Major League Totals			0	0	1.88	4	1	0	0	14	18	3	4	10	6.3	1.53	.290
Minor League Totals			42	35	3.50	123	99	4	1	648	608	56	198	544	7.6	1.24	.249

23 TREVOR CLIFTON, RHP

BA GRADE

50 Risk: Extreme

Born: May 11, 1995. **B-T:** R-R. **Ht.:** 6-4. **Wt.:** 170. **Drafted:** HS— Maryville, Tenn., 2013 (12th round). **Signed by:** Keith Rymon.

Clifton was the only prep pitcher from Tennessee who signed out of the 2013 draft. He got a $375,000 bonus, even though he's the rawest arm among the state's top arms. The slender Clifton remains green, with obvious signs of progress. He has a quick arm, pumping his fastball in the 92-94 mph range and hitting 96 at his best. His inconsistency manifests itself in many ways, such as erratic fastball velocity. He's polished his mechanics but still has work to do, especially in honing his hard curveball and slider. He's flashed a changeup but all his secondary stuff has a ways to go. Clifton hasn't grown into his body yet, lacking coordination and "man strength." His mid-rotation starter ceiling ranks among the highest among the system's pitchers, though, with a big test coming in 2015 at low Class A South Bend.

Year	Club (League)	Class	W	L	ERA	G	GS	CG	SV	IP	H	HR	BB	SO	K/9	WHIP	AVG
2013	Cubs (AZL)	R	0	0	6.97	8	1	0	0	10	13	0	8	15	13.1	2.03	.310
2014	Boise (NWL)	SS	4	2	3.69	13	13	0	0	61	59	3	30	54	8.0	1.46	.257
Minor League Totals			4	2	4.16	21	14	0	0	71	72	3	38	69	8.7	1.54	.265

24 JEIMER CANDELARIO, 3B

BA GRADE

45 Risk: High

Born: Nov. 24, 1993. **B-T:** B-R. **Ht.:** 6-1. **Wt.:** 180. **Signed:** Dominican Republic, 2010. **Signed by:** Jose Serra/Marino Encarnacion.

Candelario ended 2014 repeating low Class A, though he did help Kane County win the Midwest League title with nine hits and nine walks in a 7-0 playoff run. His offensive approach regressed from patient to passive, as he took too many early-count fastballs and was constantly behind. He hit for more power after being sent down from high Class A, and scouts like his swing (particularly from the left side) and power potential from both sides of the plate. Club officials respected that he took accountability for his problems; he simply has to find a way to be more aggressive. He has average arm strength and range at third base with solid actions. A below-average runner, Candelario returns to high Class A at Myrtle Beach.

Year	Club (League)	Class	AVG	G	AB	R	H	2B	3B	HR	RBI	BB	SO	SB	CS	OBP	SLG
2012	Boise (NWL)	SS	.281	71	278	34	78	14	0	6	47	26	55	2	1	.345	.396
2013	Kane County (MWL)	LoA	.256	130	500	71	128	35	1	11	57	68	88	1	0	.346	.396
2014	Daytona (FSL)	HiA	.193	62	218	24	42	10	2	5	26	23	44	0	3	.275	.326
	Kane County (MWL)	LoA	.250	63	244	32	61	19	3	6	37	18	45	0	1	.300	.426
Minor League Totals			.264	398	1489	211	393	94	8	33	220	185	274	7	9	.346	.404

25 DAN VOGELBACH, 1B

BA GRADE

45 Risk: High

Born: Dec. 17, 1992. **B-T:** L-R. **Ht.:** 6-0. **Wt.:** 250. **Drafted:** HS—Fort Myers, Fla., 2011 (2nd round). **Signed by:** Lukas McKnight.

Vogelbach, who signed for $1.6 million out of the 2011 draft, grinded through a full season in the high Class A Florida State League in 2014 and led Daytona in home runs, doubles, RBIs and walks. He offers plus power, and he makes good contact for a slugger, has good bat control and identifies pitches well. He improved defensively, making seven errors (two in the playoffs) after racking up 11 in 2013, but remains a poor defender at first base. His lack of athleticism means his bat has to carry him, and so far it has been merely good, not great. He struggles against lefthanders (.212/.298/.340 last season) and his poor speed leaves him prone to hitting into double plays. Vogelbach moves up to Double-A Tennessee in 2015, but he fits better long-term for an American League club as a DH.

Year	Club (League)	Class	AVG	G	AB	R	H	2B	3B	HR	RBI	BB	SO	SB	CS	OBP	SLG
2012	Cubs (AZL)	R	.324	24	102	16	33	12	2	7	31	12	14	1	0	.391	.686
	Boise (NWL)	SS	.322	37	143	23	46	9	1	10	31	23	34	0	1	.423	.608
2013	Kane County (MWL)	LoA	.284	114	433	55	123	21	0	17	71	57	76	4	4	.364	.450
	Daytona (FSL)	HiA	.280	17	50	13	14	2	0	2	5	16	13	1	0	.455	.440
2014	Daytona (FSL)	HiA	.268	132	482	71	129	28	1	16	76	66	91	4	4	.357	.429
Minor League Totals			.285	330	1234	182	352	75	4	53	220	176	230	11	9	.375	.481

26 CARSON SANDS, LHP

BA GRADE

50 Risk: Extreme

Born: March 28, 1995. **B-T:** L-L. **Ht.:** 6-3. **Wt.:** 195. **Drafted:** HS— Tallahassee, Fla., 2014 (4th round). **Signed by:** Tom Clark.

Sands signed for $1.1 million as part of the Cubs' prep pitching haul in 2014. Part of USA Baseball's 16U and 18U teams, he has continued to get better since, smoothing out his delivery and bumping up his velocity. Sands is a big-bodied lefthander who has touched 95 mph at times with downward plane to his fastball. He gets good armside action to his heater and throws strikes with it. His curveball and changeup have average potential, and the curve has improved its shape and consistency over the last two years. Sands' stuff was inconsistent after signing, and club officials were impressed with how he kept his composure when he struggled. His body has room to fill out, and he could wind up being a mid-rotation workhorse if it all comes together. He'll challenge for a full-season role in 2015.

Year	Club (League)	Class	W	L	ERA	G	GS	CG	SV	IP	H	HR	BB	SO	K/9	WHIP	AVG
2014	Cubs (AZL)	R	3	1	1.89	9	4	0	0	19	15	0	7	20	9.5	1.16	.221
Minor League Totals			3	1	1.89	9	4	0	0	19	15	0	7	20	9.5	1.16	.221

27 KEVONTE MITCHELL, OF

BA GRADE

50 Risk: Extreme

Born: Aug. 12, 1995. **B-T:** R-R. **Ht.:** 6-4. **Wt.:** 185. **Drafted:** HS— Kennett, Mo., 2014 (13th round). **Signed by:** Ty Nichols.

Mitchell's frame, Midwest roots and basketball background earn him comparisons with Matt Kemp. He averaged 24.4 points per game as a senior and had to start the baseball season as a DH due to a broken hand. The Cubs signed him for an above-slot $200,000 bonus. Lean and athletic, Mitchell not only impresses with his raw ability but with his surprising hitting aptitude. He's shown no fear of hitting with two strikes, identifies spin and has the ability to use the whole field. Mitchell is an above-average runner who should be able to handle center field in the minors if not longer as a long-strider. He has average arm strength as well, and projecting his power and his future impact is where it gets tricky, as his flat swing path currently precludes loft power. Mitchell likely will be tested at low Class A South Bend in 2015.

Year	Club (League)	Class	AVG	G	AB	R	H	2B	3B	HR	RBI	BB	SO	SB	CS	OBP	SLG
2014	Cubs (AZL)	R	.294	39	143	30	42	3	4	0	12	14	32	19	1	.374	.371

Minor League Totals		.294	39	143	30	42	3	4	0	12	14	32	19	1	.374	.371

28 DYLAN CEASE, RHP

BA GRADE

50 Risk: Extreme

Born: Dec. 28, 1995. **B-T:** R-R. **Ht.:** 6-1. **Wt.:** 175. **Drafted:** HS—Milton, Ga., 2014 (6th round). **Signed by:** Keith Lockhart.

Cease ranked just two spots ahead of fellow Cubs draftee James Norwood on Baseball America's Top 500 prospects list for the 2014 draft. To pry Cease away from a Vanderbilt commitment, however, the Cubs paid him $1.5 million, even though they knew he would need Tommy John surgery, which he had after the draft. Scouting directors voted him a Preseason High School All-American based off a strong junior high school season and showcase summer, as he ran his fastball up to 97 mph with easy velocity from a fluid delivery. Cease adds an inconsistent but at times above-average curveball that he used more in high school play than when he was on the showcase circuit. When healthy, he has a quick arm, good hand speed and even flashes an average changeup. He's a solid athlete who led Milton (Ga.) High to a state title in 2013. If Cease pitches in 2015, it will be in Rookie ball or instructional league, and the Cubs really won't know what their lottery ticket will be worth until 2016.

Year	Club (League)	Class	W	L	ERA	G	GS	CG	SV	IP	H	HR	BB	SO	K/9	WHIP	AVG
2014	Did not play—Injured																

29 JAMES NORWOOD, RHP

BA GRADE

45 Risk: High

Born: Dec. 24, 1993. **B-T:** R-R. **Ht.:** 6-2. **Wt.:** 205. **Drafted:** Saint Louis, 2014 (7th round). **Signed by:** Ty Nichols.

Norwood, who attended high school in the Bronx, wound up at the up-and-coming college program at Saint Louis, where last June he became the first Billiken drafted in the first 10 rounds since 1982. He lost crispness and velocity at the end of his first full year as a starter, and the Cubs took advantage, getting him in the seventh round and signing him for $175,000, when earlier in the spring he had appeared likely to go in the first three rounds. The Cubs took it easy with Norwood after signing him but expect to see him at full strength again in spring training. Norwood at times threw six pitches in college, and the Cubs will pare that repertoire significantly. His four-seam fastball has reached 98 mph, and the Cubs may ditch his two-seamer. They'd also like him to focus on one breaking ball, preferring his curveball to his cutter-type slider. He also throws a changeup. Norwood may wind up in the bullpen, but he will get a chance to start at low Class A South Bend in his first full season.

Year	Club (League)	Class	W	L	ERA	G	GS	CG	SV	IP	H	HR	BB	SO	K/9	WHIP	AVG
2014	Cubs (AZL)	R	0	0	13.50	2	0	0	0	2	4	0	1	2	9.0	2.50	.500
	Boise (NWL)	SS	0	2	7.00	8	4	0	0	18	16	3	7	18	9.0	1.28	.239
Minor League Totals			0	2	7.65	10	4	0	0	20	20	3	8	20	9.0	1.40	.267

30 DAURY TORREZ, RHP

BA GRADE

45 Risk: High

Born: June 11, 1993. **B-T:** R-R. **Ht.:** 6-3. **Wt.:** 170. **Signed:** Dominican Republic, 2010. **Signed by:** Juan Moncion/Jose Serra.

Signed for $25,000 as a 17-year-old in December 2010, Torrez finally reached full-season ball in 2014 and led low Class A Kane County in wins (11) and innings (131). He has not added much muscle to his skinny frame and may not have much projection left, but his fastball and pitchability may be enough. He works off a 91-92 mph fastball that reaches 95 with sink and average life, with above-average control and potential solid-average command. He pitches inside with it to neutralize lefthanders (.536 OPS). He's athletic and repeats his delivery, maintaining the quality of his stuff over six- and seven-inning outings. Torrez's consistency with his fastball contrasts with his inconsistent secondary stuff. His fringy slider helps him get groundballs, and he lacks conviction in his below-average changeup. Torrez does little things well such as holding runners and fielding his position. It adds up to a back-end starter profile and a step-at-a-time progression through the minors. Next stop: high Class A Myrtle Beach.

Year	Club (League)	Class	W	L	ERA	G	GS	CG	SV	IP	H	HR	BB	SO	K/9	WHIP	AVG
2012	Cubs 2 (DSL)	R	6	3	1.21	14	13	0	0	75	57	6	4	50	6.0	0.82	.213
2013	Cubs (AZL)	R	4	2	3.31	12	2	0	1	49	49	2	5	49	9.0	1.10	.255
	Kane County (MWL)	LoA	0	1	5.40	1	1	0	0	5	5	1	1	2	3.6	1.20	.313
2014	Kane County (MWL)	LoA	11	7	2.74	23	23	1	0	131	110	8	21	81	5.6	1.00	.226
Minor League Totals			22	15	2.60	66	40	1	2	301	263	17	36	207	6.2	0.99	.235

Chicago White Sox

BY JOHN MANUEL

The last time the White Sox had an Opening Day payroll below the $90 million (and change) level they had in 2014, they won the World Series.

But 2014 was not a repeat of 2005. Instead, Paul Konerko's farewell season in Chicago was, the Sox hope, a first step back into contention as the club improved by 10 wins over the previous year. Moreover, the roster churn necessary for the franchise, which has failed to post consecutive winning seasons since 2005-2006, has begun. Konerko, as expected, gave way to Cuban rookie Jose Abreu, who led the team in virtually every offensive category at .317/.383/.581 with 36 home runs and 107 RBIs.

He's one franchise cornerstone; the other remains lefthander Chris Sale, whose dazzling 12-4, 2.17 season, which included 10.8 strikeouts per nine innings, only lacked full health, as he missed a month early with a flexor muscle strain in his forearm.

The young foundation around those stars includes lefty Jose Quintana, who turned in another steady, 200-inning season and is just 25; outfielder Adam Eaton, who proved a sparkplug atop the lineup when healthy; and outfielder Avisail Garcia, just 23 and limited to 172 at-bats in 2014 by a torn labrum in his left shoulder.

The rest of the roster for the future, though, showed a need for significant change. Chicago had just $45 million committed for 2015 as October closed, with $14.25 million of that going to disappointing lefty John Danks and another $10 million to shortstop Alexei Ramirez. The club has an option on Ramirez for 2016 and hopes 2013 first-rounder Tim Anderson is ready to step in at the position after he reached Double-A at the end of 2014.

The Sox pitching staff needs plenty of help, especially with a lack of righthanded starters after the flops of rookie Erik Johnson (6.46 ERA in five starts) and second-year Brazilian pitcher Andre Rienzo (6.82). The White Sox were able to be aggressive thanks to their payroll, though, and traded four players, led by shortstop Marcus Semien, to the Athletics for Jeff Samardzija, who will be a free agent after the 2015 season.

They looked externally for bullpen help as well. Homegrown products Jake Petricka and Daniel Webb had their moments, but in general Robin Ventura's bullpen failed, with a 4.38 ERA that ranked 28th in the majors, ahead of just the Rockies and Astros. That helped explain the free-agent signings of David Robertson (four years, $46 million) and lefty Zach Duke (three years, $15 million).

Cuban Jose Abreu exceeded expectations as a rookie by slugging an AL-best .581

MIKE JANES

TOP PROSPECTS OF THE DECADE

Year	Player, Pos.	2014 Org
2005	Brian Anderson, of	Out of baseball
2006	Bobby Jenks, rhp	Out of baseball
2007	Ryan Sweeney, of	Cubs
2008	Aaron Poreda, lhp	Rangers
2009	Gordon Beckham, ss	Angels
2010	Jared Mitchell, of	White Sox
2011	Chris Sale, lhp	White Sox
2012	Addison Reed, rhp	Diamondbacks
2013	Courtney Hawkins, of	White Sox
2014	Jose Abreu, 1b	White Sox

Lefthander Carlos Rodon could be part of a bullpen turnaround or could become the fourth southpaw in the rotation; either way, the 2014 first-rounder, who received the largest signing bonus in White Sox history, will be deemed a disappointment if he is not part of the revival. He headlined a draft class that fell just short of $10 million in bonuses that also included righthander Spencer Adams and lefty Jace Fry, both of whom have future rotation potential.

The White Sox tell their farmhands every spring that the organization's goal is for them to help the big league team, either in Chicago or in trades. That played out this offseason under third-year general manager Rick Hahn, and the deals should expedite the White Sox's return to contention.

General manager: Rick Hahn. **Farm director:** Nick Capra. **Scouting director:** Doug Laumann.

Class	Team	League	W	L	PCT	Finish	Manager
Majors	Chicago White Sox	American	73	89	.451	t-22nd (30)	Robin Ventura
Triple-A	Charlotte Knights	International	63	81	.438	14th (14)	Joel Skinner
Double-A	Birmingham Barons	Southern	60	80	.429	t-9th (10)	Julio Vinas
High A	Winston-Salem Dash	Carolina	61	78	.439	8th (8)	Tommy Thompson
Low A	Kannapolis Intimidators	South Atlantic	62	75	.453	8th (14)	Pete Rose Jr.
Rookie	Great Falls Voyagers	Pioneer	39	37	.513	4th (8)	Charles Poe
Rookie	White Sox	Arizona	30	25	.545	t-4th (13)	Mike Gellinger
Overall Minor League Record			315	376	.456	27th (30)	

THIS YEAR'S TOP 30

No.	Player, Pos.	Grade
1.	Carlos Rodon, lhp	65/High
2.	Tim Anderson, ss	60/High
3.	Spencer Adams, rhp	60/High
4.	Micah Johnson, 2b	55/Medium
5.	Francellis Montas, rhp	55/High
6.	Micker Adolfo, of	55/Extreme
7.	Tyler Danish, rhp	50/Medium
8.	Trey Michalczewski, 3b	50/High
9.	Courtney Hawkins, of	50/High
10.	Jacob May, of	50/High
11.	Chris Beck, rhp	45/Medium
12.	Carlos Sanchez, 2b/ss	45/Medium
13.	Jace Fry, lhp	50/High
14.	Matt Davidson, 3b	50/High
15.	Kevan Smith, c	45/High
16.	Cleuluis Rondon, ss	45/High
17.	Thaddius Lowry, rhp	50/Extreme
18.	Trayce Thompson, of	45/High
19.	Tyler Saladino, 2b/ss	40/Low
20.	Luis Martinez, rhp	50/Extreme
21.	Brandon Brennan, rhp	45/High
22.	David Trexler, rhp	45/High
23.	Adam Engel, of	50/Extreme
24.	Jake Peter, 2b	45/High
25.	James Dykstra, rhp	45/High
26.	Keon Barnum, 1b	50/Extreme
27.	Onelki Garcia, lhp	45/High
28.	Michael Ynoa, rhp	45/High
29.	Jared Mitchell, of	45/High
30.	Andy Wilkins, 1b	40/Medium

LAST YEAR'S TOP 30

No.	Player, Pos.	Status
1.	Jose Abreu, 1b	Majors
2.	Erik Johnson, rhp	Majors
3.	Tim Anderson, ss	No. 2
4.	Marcus Semien, ss/2b/3b	(Athletics)
5.	Micah Johnson, 2b	No. 4
6.	Courtney Hawkins, of	No. 9
7.	Trayce Thompson, of	No. 18
8.	Chris Beck, rhp	No. 11
9.	Jacob May, of	No. 10
10.	Tyler Danish, rhp	No. 7
11.	Daniel Webb, rhp	Majors
12.	Carlos Sanchez, ss/2b	No. 12
13.	Jared Mitchell, of	No. 29
14.	Keon Barnum, 1b	No. 26
15.	Chris Bassitt, rhp	(Athletics)
16.	Scott Snodgress, lhp	(Angels)
17.	Leury Garcia, ss/of	Majors
18.	Micker Adolfo, of	No. 6
19.	Trey Michalczewski, 3b	No. 7
20.	Braulio Ortiz, rhp	Dropped out
21.	Jake Petricka, rhp	Majors
22.	Adam Engel, of	No. 25
23.	Keenyn Walker, of	Dropped out
24.	Myles Jaye, rhp	Dropped out
25.	Brandon Jacobs, of	(Diamondbacks)
26.	Cleuluis Rondon, ss	No. 16
27.	Andrew Mitchell, rhp	Dropped out
28.	Brad Goldberg, rhp	Dropped out
29.	Francellis Montas, rhp	No. 5
30.	Rangel Ravelo, 1b	(Athletics)

BEST TOOLS

Best Hitter for Average	Tim Anderson
Best Power Hitter	Courtney Hawkins
Best Strike-Zone Discipline	Kevan Smith
Fastest Baserunner	Micah Johnson
Best Athlete	Tim Anderson
Best Fastball	Francellis Montas
Best Curveball	David Trexler
Best Slider	Carlos Rodon
Best Changeup	Chris Beck
Best Control	James Dykstra
Best Defensive Catcher	Kevan Smith
Best Defensive Infielder	Cleuluis Rondon
Best Infield Arm	Cleuluis Rondon
Best Defensive Outfielder	Keenyn Walker
Best Outfield Arm	Adam Engel

PROJECTED 2018 LINEUP

Catcher	Kevan Smith
First Base	Trey Michalczewski
Second Base	Micah Johnson
Third Base	Conor Gillaspie
Shortstop	Tim Anderson
Left Field	Jacob May
Center Field	Adam Eaton
Right Field	Avisail Garcia
Designated Hitter	Jose Abreu
No. 1 Starter	Chris Sale
No. 2 Starter	Carlos Rodon
No. 3 Starter	Spencer Adams
No. 4 Starter	Jose Quintana
No. 5 Starter	Tyler Danish
Closer	Francellis Montas

CHICAGO WHITE SOX

TOP 2015 ROOKIE: Carlos Rodon, lhp. He may break in as a reliever, but he should make an impact.
BREAKOUT PROSPECT: Luis Martinez, rhp. One of Marco Paddy's first international signees is ready for his full-season closeup.
SLEEPER: Nick Basto, of. Former prep infielder has moved to the outfield; White Sox are banking on the bat, which has shown flashes of real power.

SOURCE OF TOP 30 TALENT			
Homegrown	25	Acquired	5
College	13	Trades	4
Junior college	2	Rule 5 draft	0
High school	7	Independent leagues	0
Draft-and-follow	0	Free agents/waivers	1
Nondrafted free agents	0		
International	3		

LF
Courtney Hawkins (9)
Jared Mitchell (29)
Nick Basto
Mason Robbins

CF
Jacob May (10)
Trayce Thompson (18)
Adam Engel (23)
Keenyn Walker
Louie Lechich

RF
Micker Adolfo (Zapata) (6)
Jason Coates
Zach Fish

3B
Trey Michalczewski (8)
Matt Davidson (14)

SS
Tim Anderson (2)
Cleuluis Rondon (16)

2B
Micah Johnson (4)
Carlos Sanchez (12)
Tyler Saladino (19)
Jake Peter (24)
Joey DeMichele
Jake Jarvis

1B
Keon Barnum (26)
Andy Wilkins (30)
Danny Hayes

C
Kevan Smith (15)
Brett Austin
Jose Barraza

LHP	
LHSP	**LHRP**
Carlos Rodon (1)	Onelki Garcia (27)
Jace Fry (13)	Jefferson Olacio
Andre Wheeler	Aaron Bummer
Chris Freudenberg	
Brian Clark	

RHP	
RHSP	**RHRP**
Spencer Adams (3)	Brandon Brennan (21)
Francellis Montas (5)	Michael Ynoa (28)
Tyler Danish (7)	Robinson Leyer
Chris Beck (11)	Kyle Hansen
Thaddius Lowry (17)	Braulio Ortiz
Luis Martinez (20)	Jose Brito
David Trexler (22)	Andrew Mitchell
James Dykstra (25)	Brad Goldberg
Mike Recchia	Matt Cooper
Zach Thompson	
Myles Jaye	
J.B. Wendelken	

2014

BEST PURE HITTER: 2B Jake Peter (7) earns the "pro hitter" cliche because it's true. He works counts, spoils pitchers' pitches and makes hard contact consistently because he has a plan at the plate.

BEST POWER HITTER: OF/C Zach Fish (11) has bat speed and strength to go with short arms. His above-average power will play more if he can move back to catcher, which he played earlier in his amateur career before moving to an outfield corner as a junior. He got off to a good start defensively in instructional league.

FASTEST RUNNER: The White Sox didn't get any burners, with OF Michael Suiter (24) tops in the group as an above-average runner.

BEST DEFENSIVE PLAYER: OF Louie Lechich (6) was a senior cost-saver with tools, particularly defensively. He covers a lot of ground in center field and has a strong arm that helped him work in the high 80s as a college pitcher.

BEST FASTBALL: LHP Carlos Rodon (1) has hit 97-98 mph when he's loose and pitched at 94-96 in short stints after signing. He needs to locate it better, particularly to his arm side. RHP David Trexler (17) bumped up his velocity after signing, sitting 92-96 mph while throwing consistent strikes.

BEST SECONDARY PITCH: Multiple scouts from multiple organizations have seen Rodon pitch with a consistent 70 slider, if not an 80, with mid-80s power and tilt. It's a devastating pitch that played in his debut as Rodon racked up 13.86 strikeouts per nine innings.

BEST PRO DEBUT: Peter so dominated Rookie-level Great Falls (1.023 OPS) that he jumped to high Class A Winston-Salem; he hit .332/.385/.477 overall with just 26 strikeouts in 241 at-bats. RHP Matt Cooper (16) went 4-2, 3.18 with 47 strikeouts in 34 innings for Great Falls.

BEST ATHLETE: Pitchers often don't win this category, but RHP Spencer Adams (2), a fine prep basketball player, does for the White Sox. Lechich also has long strides and athleticism in his tool set.

MOST INTRIGUING BACKGROUND: The Sox also drafted Rodon's college roommate and N.C. State teammate, C Brett Austin (4), but they didn't play together in their debuts. Unsigned 1B Jed Sprague (37) is the son of Ed Sprague Jr., who was an Olympic gold medalist for baseball in 1988, and Kristen Babb-Sprague, a gold medal-winning swimmer in 1992.

CLOSEST TO THE MAJORS: Had Rodon signed earlier, he would have reached the majors in September. He'll get there in 2015 if healthy, likely breaking into the bullpen first, and may not need any more minor league time.

BEST LATE-ROUND PICK: Trexler's development

is exciting; he showed above-average changeups and curveballs before and after the draft to go with an average-to-plus fastball, making him a possible future rotation-mate of Rodon's.

THE ONE WHO GOT AWAY: The Sox drafted mammoth RHP Bryce Montes de Oca (14) as a hedge, as insurance in case Rodon didn't sign. The 6-foot-7, 265-pounder headlines Missouri's strong recruiting class.

ASSESSMENT: Starting with Rodon, the White Sox loaded up on quality pitching, with Adams a very pleasant surprise in the second round. They give the Sox a pair of first-round talents.

2013

The White Sox are excited about the athleticism of SS Tim Anderson (1) and OF Jacob May (3) and the bat of 3B Trey Michalczewski (7). RHP Tyler Danish (2) heads a solid pitching haul.

GRADE: B

2012

Power-hitting top picks OF Courtney Hawkins (1) and 1B Keon Barnum (1s) have gone bust more than boom thus far. 2B Micah Johnson (9) has shown the most ability in the class so far.

GRADE: C

2011

Four picks have reached the majors already—three already out of the organization. SS Marcus Semien (6) and RHP Chris Bassitt (16) were traded together for Jeff Samardzija.

GRADE: C

TOP DRAFT PICKS OF THE DECADE

Year	Player, Pos.	2014 Org
2005	Lance Broadway, rhp	Out of baseball
2006	Kyle McCulloch, rhp	Out of baseball
2007	Aaron Poreda, lhp	Rangers
2008	Gordon Beckham, ss	Angels
2009	Jared Mitchell, of	White Sox
2010	Chris Sale, lhp	White Sox
2011	Keenyn Walker, of (1st round supp.)	White Sox
2012	Courtney Hawkins, of	White Sox
2013	Tim Anderson, ss	White Sox
2014	Carlos Rodon, lhp	White Sox

LARGEST BONUSES IN CLUB HISTORY

Jose Abreu, 2013	$10,000,000
Carlos Rodon, 2014	$6,582,000
Joe Borchard, 2000	$5,300,000
Dayan Viciedo, 2008	$4,000,000
Gordon Beckham, 2008	$2,600,000

1 CARLOS RODON, LHP

Born: Dec. 10, 1992. **B-T:** L-L. **Ht.:** 6-3. **Wt.:** 234.
Drafted: North Carolina State, 2014 (1st round).
Signed by: Abraham Fernandez.

Back spasms and diminished velocity helped drop Rodon to the 16th round of the 2011 draft out of Holly Springs (N.C.) High, and he went to North Carolina State after turning down the Brewers' offer of more than $500,000. His velocity jumped in college thanks to an improved strength and conditioning program and better mechanics, and he hit 97 mph regularly en route to Freshman of the Year honors. He topped himself in 2013, leading the nation in strikeouts and powering the Wolfpack back to the College World Series. A dominating stint with USA Baseball's Collegiate National Team, made him the No. 1 prospect for the 2014 draft. But an inconsistent junior season and a high price tag dropped him to No. 3 overall, where the White Sox signed him for a club-record $6.582 million bonus.

Rodon has one of the best sliders college baseball has seen in years, a 70-grade pitch (on the 20-80 scouting scale) he throws with power anywhere from 82-87 mph. He has feel for the pitch and can throw a harder, cut-fastball version of the pitch at up to 89 mph to get in on righthanders, or an 82-85 mph variety with serious depth and late tilt that gets swings and misses. Rodon lifted less and loosened up after signing, throwing more fastballs and changeups and fewer sliders in his 24-inning debut. The results included more 97s than he showed in the spring, when he often pitched in the 89-93 mph range. He lacks the fastball command to start at present, especially throwing strikes to his arm side. The White Sox are confident that increased flexibility will help Rodon finish out front in his delivery better, allowing him to throw the pitch for strikes. His changeup has flashed average if not a tick above, and he needs to throw it more than he did in college. Rodon's thick body and past back problems prompt scouts to question his overall athleticism, as do his spotty command, below-average defense and struggles to limit opposing basestealers.

The White Sox trust their pitching development to help Rodon become a true three-pitch starter. He has an ace's swagger and mentality and needs the fastball command and reps with his changeup to make it a reality. He could begin 2015 in the Double-A Birmingham or Triple-A Charlotte rotation, then join the big league bullpen in the second half to get his feet wet and control his workload, all as a prelude for a 2016 rotation spot. Rodon has better stuff than Chris Sale at a similar stage, and if he throws more quality fastball strikes, he'll join Sale atop the Chicago rotation in short order.

BA GRADE

65 Risk: High

SCOUTING GRADES

Fastball: 65.
Slider: 70.
Changeup: 50.
Control: 45.

Based on 20-80 scouting scale and future projection rather than present grades.

LGE	BF	SO%	BB%	HR/9
AZL	13	38.5	0.0	0.00
CAR	42	35.7	11.9	0.00
IL	53	34.0	15.1	0.00

BRIAN WESTERHOLT

Year	Club (League)	Class	W	L	ERA	G	GS	CG	SV	IP	H	HR	BB	SO	K/9	WHIP	AVG
2014	White Sox (AZL)	R	0	0	6.00	2	1	0	0	3	4	0	0	5	15.0	1.33	.308
	Winston-Salem (CAR)	HiA	0	0	1.86	4	2	0	0	10	7	0	4	15	14.0	1.24	.189
	Charlotte (IL)	AAA	0	0	3.00	3	3	0	0	12	9	0	8	18	13.5	1.42	.209
Minor League Totals			0	0	2.92	9	6	0	0	25	20	0	13	38	13.9	1.34	.215

2 TIM ANDERSON, SS

Born: June 23, 1993. **B-T:** R-R. **Ht.:** 6-1. **Wt.:** 180. **Drafted:** East Central (Miss.) JC, 2013 (1st round). **Signed by:** Warren Hughes.

Any team could have signed Anderson in the summer of 2012, when the junior-college freshman went undrafted and ranked as the No. 2 prospect in the Jayhawk League. Instead, he played his way into the 2013 first round with a fine sophomore season. Anderson's athleticism has allowed him to adjust to the speed of the pro game quickly. He's explosively quick and twitchy, with the burst and plus speed to steal bases and the strength to provide power to the gaps. He accepts instruction well and has the actions, above-average arm and range for shortstop, though his inexperience and rough footwork can lead to throwing errors. (His .897 fielding percentage was by far the worst in the Carolina League.) Some scouts see him as a better fit at second base or center field. Anderson has solid-average raw power and makes contact almost too readily, He'll tap into his power more with a more patient approach. He also tends to lose his timing at the plate, leaving his upper and lower halves out of sync and sapping his power. The White Sox rave about Anderson's aptitude and believe he can have a Brandon Phillips-type career, only at shortstop. With Alexei Ramirez signed for another year, Anderson will get another full minor league season, starting back at Double-A Birmingham.

BA GRADE

60 Risk: High

LGE	PA	BB%	SO%	ISO
CAR	300	2.3	22.7	.175
SL	45	0.0	20.0	.136

Year	Club (League)	Class	AVG	G	AB	R	H	2B	3B	HR	RBI	BB	SO	SB	CS	OBP	SLG
2013	Kannapolis (SAL)	LoA	.277	68	267	45	74	10	5	1	21	23	78	24	4	.348	.363
2014	Winston-Salem (CAR)	HiA	.297	68	286	48	85	18	7	6	31	7	68	10	3	.323	.472
	White Sox (AZL)	R	.200	5	15	2	3	0	0	2	2	2	5	0	1	.294	.600
	Birmingham (SL)	AA	.364	10	44	7	16	3	0	1	7	0	9	0	1	.364	.500
Minor League Totals			.291	151	612	102	178	31	12	10	61	32	160	34	9	.336	.430

3 SPENCER ADAMS, RHP

Born: April 13, 1996. **B-T:** R-R. **Ht.:** 6-3. **Wt.:** 171. **Drafted:** HS—Cleveland, Ga., 2014 (2nd round). **Signed by:** Kevin Burrell.

A three-sport athlete who excelled in basketball as a high schooler, Adams was committed to Georgia but started to move up draft boards in the summer of 2013, when he shined at the Metropolitan Baseball Classic. Opposing clubs were as surprised as the White Sox when Adams fell to them with the third pick of the second round, and he signed for $1,282,700. Adams is the best athlete among the organization's pitchers, showing plus control and the aptitude to apply adjustments quickly. He doesn't need to change much, for he has premium, front-of-the-rotation stuff. His fastball has touched 96 mph and can sit 93-95 at times, and he has excellent control of the pitch even though it features excellent life, both with sink and bat-sawing action. His arm path is short and consistent, and his projectable frame makes it probable he'll maintain his present velocity. Adams' slider was one of the better breaking balls in the draft, a low-80s out pitch that also could be a consistent future plus pitch. He needs more experience changing speeds and using his changeup without slowing his arm when he throws it. The White Sox hadn't drafted a prep pitcher this high since Gio Gonzalez in 2004, and they believe Adams has similar upside. He'll start at low Class A Kannapolis and projects to have a No. 2 starter ceiling.

BA GRADE

60 Risk: High

LGE	BF	SO%	BB%	HR/9
AZL	179	33.0	2.2	0.86

BILL MITCHELL

Year	Club (League)	Class	W	L	ERA	G	GS	CG	SV	IP	H	HR	BB	SO	K/9	WHIP	AVG
2014	White Sox (AZL)	R	3	3	3.67	10	9	0	0	42	49	4	4	59	12.7	1.27	.282
Minor League Totals			3	3	3.67	10	9	0	0	42	49	4	4	59	12.7	1.27	.282

4 MICAH JOHNSON, 2B

Born: Dec. 18, 1990. **B-T:** L-R. **Ht.:** 6-0. **Wt.:** 190. **Drafted:** Indiana, 2012 (9th round). **Signed by:** Mike Shirley.

If he's not careful, Johnson will pick up the injury-prone tag. He missed much of his junior season at Indiana with arm surgery, then lit up pro ball in 2013, leading the minors with 84 stolen bases and earning MVP honors in the Double-A Southern League playoffs. Johnson then missed two stretches with left hamstring problems in 2014. In an organization long on athletes, Johnson still stands out for his explosiveness and burst. He's physical and strong, with surprising pull power that allows him to punish mistakes. He focuses more on being a top-of-the-order igniter, with double-plus speed and reasonable contact skills, as well as a discerning-enough eye for a leadoff man. Johnson doesn't always adjust on pitches away, and he has to keep improving his footwork around the bag to turn the double play effectively. With hard hands, he struggles to consistently field the ball cleanly. With his plus range, he must learn which plays he can make and which ones he can't. The White Sox traded Gordon Beckham in 2014, leaving second base an open competition between Johnson, Carlos Sanchez and Marcus Semien. Johnson might be the best bet, but if he needs more polish, he will head back to Triple-A Charlotte.

BA GRADE

55 Risk: **Medium**

LGE	PA	BB%	SO%	ISO
SL	170	12.4	15.9	.137
IL	302	5.3	13.9	.095

Year	Club (League)	Class	AVG	G	AB	R	H	2B	3B	HR	RBI	BB	SO	SB	CS	OBP	SLG
2012	Great Falls (PIO)	R	.273	69	271	49	74	10	5	4	25	43	74	19	6	.375	.391
2013	Kannapolis (SAL)	LoA	.342	77	304	76	104	17	11	6	42	40	67	61	19	.422	.530
	Winston-Salem (CAR)HiA		.275	49	211	28	58	7	4	1	15	10	27	22	7	.309	.360
	Birmingham (SL)	AA	.238	5	21	2	5	0	0	0	1	0	4	1	0	.227	.238
2014	Birmingham (SL)	AA	.329	37	146	18	48	9	1	3	16	21	27	10	7	.414	.466
	Charlotte (IL)	AAA	.275	65	273	30	75	10	5	2	28	16	42	12	6	.314	.370
Minor League Totals			.297	302	1226	203	364	53	26	16	127	130	241	125	45	.366	.422

5 FRANCELLIS MONTAS, RHP

Born: March 21, 1993. **B-T:** R-R. **Ht.:** 6-2. **Wt.:** 185. **Signed:** Dominican Republic, 2009. **Signed by:** Manny Nanita (Red Sox).

The White Sox believe in their ability to develop pitchers, and Montas may be the latest example. He spent two years in the Dominican Summer League and had a 5.70 ERA in his first full season in the Red Sox system when the White Sox acquired him in the three-team Jake Peavy deal. Even with two knee injuries interrupting his 2014 season, Montas reached Double-A Birmingham and hit 100 mph in the Arizona Fall League. Montas shares physical similarities with Bartolo Colon and Livan Hernandez as a big-bodied Latin American righthander. He has a long arm stroke but easy velocity, regularly pitching at 96-100 mph. He tends to lose velocity over five or six innings, but he's got plenty to spare. He has the hand speed to spin a slider that at times flashes 70 potential on the 20-80 scouting scale. His changeup has its moments as well and can be an average pitch. The White Sox have simplified Montas' delivery, but his direction to the plate still wanders, as does his release point, leading to below-average control and poor command. Montas has closer written all over him, and his delivery and velocity remind some scouts of Rafael Soriano. The White Sox want to see if he can start, though, so he should return to Birmingham to begin 2015.

BA GRADE

55 Risk: **High**

LGE	BF	SO%	BB%	HR/9
CAR	242	23.1	5.8	0.29
SL	17	5.9	5.9	0.00

Year	Club (League)	Class	W	L	ERA	G	GS	CG	SV	IP	H	HR	BB	SO	K/9	WHIP	AVG
2012	Red Sox (GCL)	R	1	5	3.98	12	9	0	0	41	34	0	12	41	9.1	1.13	.228
	Lowell (NYP)	SS	0	0	0.00	1	1	0	0	4	5	0	1	4	9.8	1.64	.357
2013	Greenville (SAL)	LoA	2	9	5.70	19	18	1	0	85	94	10	32	96	10.1	1.48	.276
	Kannapolis (SAL)	LoA	3	2	4.56	5	5	0	0	26	20	1	18	31	10.9	1.48	.215
2014	Winston-Salem (CAR)	HiA	4	0	1.60	10	10	1	0	62	45	2	14	56	8.1	0.95	.202
	White Sox (AZL)	R	1	0	1.29	4	4	0	0	14	6	1	7	23	14.8	0.93	.128
	Birmingham (SL)	AA	0	0	0.00	1	1	0	0	5	1	0	1	1	1.8	0.40	.063
Minor League Totals			11	20	4.22	69	57	2	0	271	240	16	115	282	9.4	1.31	.237

6 MICKER ADOLFO, OF

Born: Sept. 11, 1996. **B-T:** R-R. **Ht.:** 6-3. **Wt.:** 200. **Signed:** Dominican Republic, 2013. **Signed by:** Marco Paddy.

Every "homegrown" Latin American player on the 2014 White Sox hailed either from Cuba or Brazil (Andre Rienzo), and Chicago hasn't featured true homegrown Latin American regulars since the days of Carlos Lee (Panama) and Magglio Ordonez (Venezuela). Adolfo, who was born in the Virgin Islands but trained in the Dominican Republic, is a $1.6 million investment in turning around an international program that was once criminally corrupt and unproductive under Dave Wilder. Adolfo has the long, lean look of an athlete and still draws physical comparisons with Michael Jordan. He has the right-field profile if he hits, with a plus arm that earns some double-plus grades, as well as plus raw power that helped him hit nine home runs in 16 games in instructional league. A long-strider, Adolfo is an above-average runner underway. He struggled to make contact in his first pro season due to long arms and a lack of an approach at the plate. The White Sox believe

BA GRADE:

55 Risk: Extreme

LGE	PA	BB%	SO%	ISO
AZL	198	7.1	42.9	.162

Adolfo grew from the difficulty and has learned what it takes to be a professional. While a long way from reaching his potential, Adolfo will be asked about in trades sooner than later thanks to his body, upside and power. The White Sox love to push prospects, but Adolfo would have to have a big spring to earn a full-season assignment and likely will head to Rookie-level Great Falls in 2015.

Year	Club (League)	Class	AVG	G	AB	R	H	2B	3B	HR	RBI	BB	SO	SB	CS	OBP	SLG
2014	White Sox (AZL)	R	.218	46	179	27	39	10	2	5	21	14	85	0	0	.279	.380
Minor League Totals			.218	46	179	27	39	10	2	5	21	14	85	0	0	.279	.380

7 TYLER DANISH, RHP

Born: Sept. 12, 1994. **B-T:** R-R. **Ht.:** 6-0. **Wt.:** 205. **Drafted:** HS—Plant City, Fla., 2013 (2nd round). **Signed by:** Joe Siers.

A year after signing for just over $1 million, Danish led the White Sox system with a 2.08 ERA, nearly a run better than any other qualifier, while reaching high Class A Winston-Salem in his first full season. It's a continuation of the success he had in high school, where he didn't give up a run as a prep senior. The White Sox love Danish's toughness and competitiveness on the mound, and his stuff ain't bad either. He's physically maxed out and pitches with a low arm slot that his present strength allows him to repeat while staying on top of the ball, driving it down in the strike zone. He gets extension out front that helps his 88-93 mph sinker and upper-70s slider have late life. He locates both pitches well, allowing him to rack up impressive groundball rates. His changeup, a below-average pitch as an amateur, now ranks as the best in the organization, flashing above-average. Danish is still learning to use it. He keeps the ball in the ballpark and attacks hitters aggressively, with no fear. Danish's ceiling is that of a back-of-the-

BA GRADE:

50 Risk: Medium

LGE	BF	SO%	BB%	HR/9
SAL	146	17.1	6.8	0.00
CAR	378	20.6	6.1	0.69

rotation starter if not aggressive reliever. The White Sox believe he'll be a big leaguer, though, and his makeup ranks among the best in the organization. Danish is on the fast track and will jump to Double-A Birmingham as a 20-year-old in 2015.

Year	Club (League)	Class	W	L	ERA	G	GS	CG	SV	IP	H	HR	BB	SO	K/9	WHIP	AVG
2013	Bristol (APP)	R	1	0	1.38	13	1	0	0	26	15	1	5	22	7.6	0.77	.165
	Kannapolis (SAL)	LoA	0	0	0.00	2	0	0	0	4	2	0	0	6	13.5	0.50	.143
2014	Kannapolis (SAL)	LoA	3	0	0.71	7	7	0	0	38	28	0	10	25	5.9	1.00	.206
	Winston-Salem (CAR)	HiA	5	3	2.65	18	18	0	0	92	87	7	23	78	7.7	1.20	.249
Minor League Totals			9	3	1.92	40	26	0	0	160	132	8	38	131	7.4	1.06	.224

8 TREY MICHALCZEWSKI, 3B

Born: Feb. 27, 1995. **B-T:** B-R. **Ht.:** 6-3. **Wt.:** 210. **Drafted:** HS—Jenks, Okla., 2013 (7th round). **Signed by:** Clay Overcash.

A tight end on Jenks High's state championship team in 2013, Michalczewski was deemed the top prep prospect in Oklahoma and signed for $500,000 as a seventh-rounder. He finished 2014 at high Class A Winston-Salem, though he ran out of gas and hit just .225 in the last two months. Michalczewski in some ways is a typical White Sox draftee, for he's strong, athletic and somewhat raw. He stands out with his grinder mentality and offensive aptitude. His swing is sound from both sides of the plate, though he has more feel from the left side and more length from the right. He's confident enough to go deep in counts, and he has the average-to-plus power to profile for an infield corner. The White Sox believe in his ability at third base, and he has a solid-average arm that should be enough for the hot corner. He can get flat-footed at times, leading to some botched routine plays, but moves well for his size, and the White Sox believe he has the agility and hands to be an average defender. Other organizations aren't as confident in Michalczewski as a third baseman as farm director Buddy Bell, a former Gold Glover at the position. The White Sox believe Michalczewski can develop into a player similar to current third baseman Conor Gillaspie.

BA GRADE:

50 Risk: High

LGE	PA	BB%	SO%	ISO
SAL	495	9.1	28.3	.160
CAR	84	10.7	25.0	.028

Year	Club (League)	Class	AVG	G	AB	R	H	2B	3B	HR	RBI	BB	SO	SB	CS	OBP	SLG
2013	Bristol (APP)	R	.236	56	195	25	46	5	2	3	21	23	56	2	0	.324	.328
2014	Kannapolis (SAL)	LoA	.273	116	432	57	118	25	7	10	70	45	140	6	3	.348	.433
	Winston-Salem (CAR)HiA		.194	19	72	5	14	2	0	0	5	9	21	1	0	.293	.222
Minor League Totals			.255	191	699	87	178	32	9	13	96	77	217	9	3	.336	.382

9 COURTNEY HAWKINS, OF

Born: Nov. 12, 1993. **B-T:** R-R. **Ht.:** 6-3. **Wt.:** 220. **Drafted:** HS—Corpus Christi, Texas, 2013 (1st round). **Signed by:** Keith Staab.

Hawkins became a draft star when he back-flipped on live TV after the White Sox drafted him in 2012. He signed for $2.475 million and immediately raked as a pro, finishing his debut season at high Class A Winston-Salem—but the game isn't that easy. Hawkins hit just .178 in a return engagement in 2013 and had a third stint with Winston-Salem in 2014. Hawkins showed a stubborn streak in his brutal 2013 campaign, but he lowered his hands in his setup and opened up a bit in his stance in 2014, helping him see the ball better and cover the outside corner more than he had previously. He always will strike out a lot and still must improve at identifying and laying off breaking balls, particularly against lefthanders (.174/.271/.273). He makes more contact now and has natural plus-plus power that plays when he does. He remains a fine athlete and an average runner with a solid-average arm. He played left field rather than center and right in 2014, and that may be his long-term home. Hawkins played the entire season as a 20-year-old, so it's way too early to write him off, and his adjustments and growing aptitude encouraged the White Sox. He has the power for a corner profile if he continues to mature at the plate. He's finally headed for Double-A Birmingham in 2015.

BA GRADE

50 Risk: High

LGE	PA	BB%	SO%	ISO
CAR	515	10.3	27.8	.200

Year	Club (League)	Class	AVG	G	AB	R	H	2B	3B	HR	RBI	BB	SO	SB	CS	OBP	SLG
2012	Bristol (APP)	R	.272	38	147	25	40	8	1	3	16	7	37	8	2	.314	.401
	Kannapolis (SAL)	LoA	.308	16	65	11	20	5	2	4	15	4	17	3	2	.352	.631
	Winston-Salem (CAR)HiA		.294	5	17	3	5	2	0	1	2	0	2	0	1	.294	.588
2013	Winston-Salem (CAR)HiA		.178	103	383	48	68	16	3	19	62	29	160	10	5	.249	.384
2014	Winston-Salem (CAR)HiA		.249	122	449	65	112	25	4	19	84	53	143	11	3	.331	.450
Minor League Totals			.231	284	1061	152	245	56	10	46	179	93	359	32	13	.300	.433

10 JACOB MAY, OF

Born: Jan. 23, 1992. **B-T:** B-R. **Ht.:** 5-10. **Wt.:** 180. **Drafted:** Coastal Carolina, 2013 (3rd round). **Signed by:** Kevin Burrell.

May has lofty bloodlines to live up to. His father Lee Jr. was a first-round pick in 1986 and reached Triple-A with the Mets, while his grandfather Lee Sr. hit 354 home runs in an 18-year major league career. His uncle Carlos, a first-round pick in 1966, also had a 10-year big league career. Jacob signed for $525,000 in 2013, played 66 games in his pro debut, then went straight to instructional league and the Australian Baseball League, where he played until January. Taking only one month off before 2014 spring training, he didn't have time to recharge. May's tremendous speed ticked down a grade in 2014 to double-plus, but he gets to top speed quickly, and he has the savvy for his speed to play on the bases and in center field. His below-average arm is playable but can be exploited. May's bat also backed up early at high Class A Winston-Salem in 2014, but he adjusted as the season went on. His swing had more length from the left side initially, but he closed up holes and made better contact. Scouts still prefer his righthanded swing. May has sneaky power and could hit 10-12 homers annually, although at times it suckers him into a more power-oriented approach, leading to the longer swing. If May hits, he profiles as a regular, earning Coco Crisp comparisons. He's headed to Double-A Birmingham to start 2015.

		BA GRADE	
	50	**Risk:** High	

LGE	PA	BB%	SO%	ISO
CAR	472	8.9	15.0	.137

Year	Club (League)	Class	AVG	G	AB	R	H	2B	3B	HR	RBI	BB	SO	SB	CS	OBP	SLG
2013	Great Falls (PIO)	R	.378	12	45	5	17	1	1	0	7	7	6	5	1	.481	.444
	Kannapolis (SAL)	LoA	.286	54	206	36	59	6	3	8	28	16	43	19	5	.346	.461
2014	Winston-Salem (CAR)	HiA	.258	109	415	66	107	31	10	2	27	42	71	37	8	.326	.395
Minor League Totals			.275	175	666	107	183	38	14	10	62	65	120	61	14	.344	.419

11 CHRIS BECK, RHP

BA GRADE	
45	**Risk:** Medium

Born: Sept. 4, 1990. **B-T:** R-R. **Ht.:** 6-3. **Wt.:** 225. **Drafted:** Georgia Southern, 2012 (2nd round). **Signed by:** Kevin Burrell.

The offseason trades of righthanders Chris Bassitt and Andre Rienzo and non-tendering of lefty Scott Snodgress left Beck as the most experienced starter in the system. Strong and durable, he has taken every turn the last two years and finished strong at Triple-A Charlotte in 2014. He profiles at the back of a rotation, and because he's a creature of habit who struggles when he's out of his routine, the bullpen may not be an option. Beck's breaking ball has backed up since college, when he flashed a plus-plus slider with power and depth. He has lost the feel for the slider as well as the proper shape on the pitch, which lacks depth and now resembles a cutter. As a result, he lacks a strikeout pitch and has had to focus on getting weak contact. His fastball can sit 92-95 mph, more frequently sitting 90-93, but he doesn't command it or consistently sink it. His changeup has evolved into an average pitch with some sink, and he throws a loopy, early-count curveball. If his plus slider ever returns, he could be a mid-rotation factor. In the meantime, he's rotation insurance at Triple-A Charlotte.

Year	Club (League)	Class	W	L	ERA	G	GS	CG	SV	IP	H	HR	BB	SO	K/9	WHIP	AVG
2012	Great Falls (PIO)	R	4	3	4.69	15	6	0	0	40	51	3	12	36	8.0	1.56	.319
2013	Winston-Salem (CAR)	HiA	11	8	3.11	21	21	1	0	119	117	11	42	57	4.3	1.34	.262
	Birmingham (SL)	AA	2	2	2.89	5	5	0	0	28	26	0	3	22	7.1	1.04	.250
2014	Birmingham (SL)	AA	5	8	3.39	20	20	1	0	117	116	7	31	57	4.4	1.26	.258
	Charlotte (IL)	AAA	1	3	4.05	7	7	0	0	33	36	1	13	28	7.6	1.47	.265
Minor League Totals			23	24	3.47	68	59	2	0	337	346	22	101	200	5.3	1.33	.267

12 CARLOS SANCHEZ, 2B/SS

BA GRADE	
45	**Risk:** Medium

Born: June 29, 1992. **B-T:** B-R. **Ht.:** 5-11. **Wt.:** 195. **Signed:** Venezuela, 2009. **Signed by:** Amador Arias.

A rare White Sox success story from Latin America, Sanchez finished 2012 at Triple-A Charlotte but stalled in 2013 after some offseason weight gain and a part-time move to shortstop. The trades of Gordon Beckham and Marcus Semien cleared two obstacles from Sanchez's path, and he got 100 at-bats as a September callup. Sanchez played shortstop again in 2014 but fits better at second base, where his range and above-average arm strength make him a plus defender. He's just fringe-average at short. He regained some quickness and burst in 2014 and has the above-average speed managers like to have on their bench. Sanchez's bat is sound from both sides of the plate but lacks explosiveness. His below-average power means he's unlikely to be more than a bottom-of-the-order option. Sanchez has the opportunity to earn the everyday second-base job in 2015 because he's more polished than Micah Johnson, but long-term Johnson has more tools and impact potential. Sanchez likely will compete with Tyler Saladino for a utility job.

Year	Club (League)	Class	AVG	G	AB	R	H	2B	3B	HR	RBI	BB	SO	SB	CS	OBP	SLG
2012	Winston-Salem (CAR)	HiA	.315	92	365	58	115	14	6	1	42	31	64	19	10	.374	.395
	Birmingham (SL)	AA	.370	30	119	17	44	9	1	0	13	10	22	7	5	.424	.462
	Charlotte (IL)	AAA	.256	11	39	4	10	2	0	0	1	0	6	0	0	.256	.308
2013	Charlotte (IL)	AAA	.241	112	432	50	104	20	2	0	28	29	76	16	7	.293	.296
2014	Charlotte (IL)	AAA	.293	110	437	60	128	19	6	7	57	36	84	16	4	.349	.412
	Chicago (AL)	MAJ	.250	28	100	6	25	5	0	0	5	3	25	1	1	.269	.300
Major League Totals			.250	28	100	6	25	5	0	0	5	3	25	1	1	.269	.300
Minor League Totals			.284	497	1860	270	528	80	18	10	192	175	339	74	39	.353	.362

13 JACE FRY, LHP

BA GRADE
50 Risk: High

Born: July 9, 1993. **B-T:** L-L. **Ht.:** 6-1. **Wt.:** 190. **Drafted:** Oregon State, 2013 (3rd round). **Signed by:** Adam Virchis.

A ninth-round pick in 2011 by the Athletics, Fry instead went to Oregon State, where he thrived as a freshman before requiring Tommy John surgery in June 2012. He returned in 2013 and was a key weekend pitcher for the Beavers, pitching 120 innings with a 1.80 ERA. That prompted the White Sox to draft him in the third round and sign him for $760,000. Fry wasn't completely healthy after signing and was used cautiously last year. When he did throw, though, he impressed, sitting at 90-92 mph with his fastball. Fry gets good sink on his fastball and locates it well. His average slider gives him a second pitch that helps him induce groundballs, and that's his game plan. His fringy curveball and changeup remain early-count offerings for strikes rather than putaway pitches. Fry has a chance to be a four-pitch, back-of-the-rotation lefty if he can stay healthy, and his ability to repeat his delivery bodes well for that long-term. He will be pushed to high Class A Winston-Salem for his full-season debut in 2015.

Year	Club (League)	Class	W	L	ERA	G	GS	CG	SV	IP	H	HR	BB	SO	K/9	WHIP	AVG
2014	Great Falls (PIO)	R	1	0	2.79	7	0	0	0	10	7	0	3	10	9.3	1.03	.206
Minor League Totals			1	0	2.79	7	0	0	0	10	7	0	3	10	9.3	1.03	.206

14 MATT DAVIDSON, 3B

BA GRADE
50 Risk: High

Born: March 26, 1991. **B-T:** R-R. **Ht.:** 6-2. **Wt.:** 225. **Drafted:** HS—Yucaipa, Calif., 2009 (1st round supp.). **Signed by:** Jeff Mousser (Diamondbacks).

Davidson had one of the worst years in the White Sox organization in 2014, mixing bad timing with an inability to get out of a slump. Acquired after the 2013 season from the Diamondbacks for Addison Reed, Davidson entered the season with hopes of competing for the third-base job in Chicago. When Conor Gillaspie beat him out, Davidson went to Triple-A Charlotte, pressed and expanded his strike zone, piling up strikeouts and bad at-bats. Davidson never really got out of his funk, with family issues complicating his struggles. When he's right, Davidson remains strong and quick to the ball, with plus power particularly to his pull side but with authority to the opposite field as well. He defended better than the White Sox expected, with average range and arm strength and enough first-step quickness for the job. The organization intends to give Davidson a mulligan, and his power gives him a better profile than Gillaspie, who is a better hitter. They'll compete again in spring training, but now Gillaspie is the incumbent.

Year	Club (League)	Class	AVG	G	AB	R	H	2B	3B	HR	RBI	BB	SO	SB	CS	OBP	SLG
2012	Mobile (SL)	AA	.261	135	486	81	127	28	2	23	76	69	126	3	4	.367	.469
2013	Reno (PCL)	AAA	.280	115	443	55	124	32	3	17	74	46	134	1	0	.350	.481
	Arizona (NL)	MAJ	.237	31	76	8	18	6	0	3	12	10	24	0	1	.333	.434
2014	Charlotte (IL)	AAA	.199	130	478	59	95	18	0	20	55	49	164	0	0	.283	.362
Major League Totals			.237	31	76	8	18	6	0	3	12	10	24	0	1	.333	.434
Minor League Totals			.256	721	2698	381	691	168	9	100	429	292	780	4	9	.339	.436

15 KEVAN SMITH, C

BA GRADE
45 Risk: High

Born: Sept. 24, 1991. **B-T:** R-R. **Ht.:** 6-4. **Wt.:** 230. **Drafted:** Pittsburgh, 2011 (7th round). **Signed by:** Phil Gulley.

The White Sox haven't drafted and developed a big league catcher since they spent high draft picks in the early 1990s on Mark Johnson (1994, first round) and Josh Paul (1996, second), neither of whom hit enough to be true regulars. Smith has a similar ceiling, but his makeup might allow him to coax a bit more out of his tools. The former University of Pittsburgh quarterback started as a freshman but wound up focusing on baseball thanks in part to injuries. Smith has proved durable at baseball's most demanding position, with a big, physical frame and enough athleticism to turn himself into a solid-average defender. He threw out 33 percent of basestealers at Double-A Birmingham in 2014, with his quick transfer helping his average arm play up. His leadership skills translate well. He relies on strength and savvy over bat speed at the plate. He'll compete with Rob Brantly, Adrian Nieto and Tyler Flowers for playing time in Chicago but likely will start the year at Triple-A Charlotte.

Year	Club (League)	Class	AVG	G	AB	R	H	2B	3B	HR	RBI	BB	SO	SB	CS	OBP	SLG
2012	Kannapolis (SAL)	LoA	.282	86	340	48	96	26	0	7	60	25	62	0	1	.344	.421
	Winston-Salem (CAR)HiA		.273	22	77	8	21	4	2	3	23	5	17	0	0	.314	.494
2013	Winston-Salem (CAR)HiA		.286	101	384	66	110	26	3	12	73	38	66	4	1	.370	.464
2014	Birmingham (SL)	AA	.290	106	389	45	113	21	3	10	48	46	68	1	1	.376	.437
Minor League Totals			.296	371	1393	213	412	99	11	41	252	142	243	7	5	.374	.471

16 CLEULUIS RONDON, SS

BA GRADE

45 Risk: High

Born: April 13, 1994. **B-T:** R-R. **Ht.:** 6-0. **Wt.:** 155. **Signed:** Venezuela, 2010. **Signed by:** Angel Escobar (Red Sox).

The Red Sox originally signed Rondon and traded him, along with Francellis Montas, to the White Sox in the three-team Jake Peavy trade in 2013. Rondon's first full year in his new organization revealed him as its best infield defender, with a magician's sleight of hand with the glove and easy plus arm strength. Rondon has a youthful penchant for botching routine plays, seeming to needlessly increase his degree of difficulty. Improved focus should make him a plus defender, and he led the minors in 2014 in double-plays (103) and total chances (648) while tying for the lead in assists (404). His offensive upside is less impressive. He has average speed and his hands do work at the plate. He has the bat control to make contact and no major swing issues, but he lacks power so his offensive impact will be low. A year at Double-A Birmingham will help reveal whether he hits enough to be a regular or is destined for a utility role.

Year	Club (League)	Class	AVG	G	AB	R	H	2B	3B	HR	RBI	BB	SO	SB	CS	OBP	SLG
2012	Red Sox (GCL)	R	.231	47	182	19	42	10	6	0	16	9	42	2	2	.270	.352
	Lowell (NYP)	SS	.000	2	4	0	0	0	0	0	0	0	1	0	0	.000	.000
2013	Lowell (NYP)	SS	.276	37	123	13	34	4	1	1	10	7	26	6	1	.326	.350
	Kannapolis (SAL)	LoA	.202	29	94	11	19	0	0	1	6	7	24	1	0	.279	.234
2014	Kannapolis (SAL)	LoA	.233	77	301	35	70	9	0	0	16	26	65	13	8	.295	.262
	Winston-Salem (CAR)HiA		.247	53	198	24	49	10	4	1	24	19	33	3	4	.315	.354
Minor League Totals			.225	307	1107	141	249	39	12	5	99	111	241	39	16	.307	.295

17 THADDIUS LOWRY, RHP

BA GRADE

50 Risk: Extreme

Born: Oct. 4, 1994. **B-T:** R-R. **Ht.:** 6-4. **Wt.:** 215. **Drafted:** HS—Spring, Texas, 2013 (5th round). **Signed by:** Keith Staab.

Signed away from a Texas Tech scholarship offer for $400,000 in 2013, Lowry has the classic size and arm strength of a power pitcher. He was a high school catcher until his senior season, so he's raw. The White Sox were careful with Lowry's workload in his first full season, starting him in extended spring training before he reported to low Class A Kannapolis in May. He showed flashes of a three-pitch mix and threw a five-inning, rain-shortened no-hitter against West Virginia on June 3. His fastball sits around 90-94 mph with sink. His inconsistent but above-average slider comes from a similar release point with deception and bite. He has shown an average changeup with life. Lowry still needs work on his delivery to stay tall and create better angle on his pitches. His inexperience shows most in his lack of feel for his craft. He could start 2015 back at Kannapolis, though the White Sox generally prefer to push their players.

Year	Club (League)	Class	W	L	ERA	G	GS	CG	SV	IP	H	HR	BB	SO	K/9	WHIP	AVG
2013	Bristol (APP)	R	3	5	5.48	15	7	0	0	44	55	2	22	30	6.1	1.74	.313
2014	Kannapolis (SAL)	LoA	4	6	4.76	17	17	1	0	87	103	5	29	43	4.4	1.52	.308
Minor League Totals			7	11	5.00	32	24	1	0	131	158	7	51	73	5.0	1.59	.310

18 TRAYCE THOMPSON, OF

BA GRADE

45 Risk: High

Born: March 15, 1991. **B-T:** R-R. **Ht.:** 6-3. **Wt.:** 215. **Drafted:** HS— Rancho Santa Margarita, Calif., 2009 (2nd round). **Signed by:** George Kachigian.

Thompson's basketball lineage includes his dad Mychal, the No. 1 pick in the 1978 NBA draft, and brother Klay, the star Golden State Warriors shooting guard. Trayce has similar upside in baseball, but his bat stands in his way. He's a graceful athlete and above-average defender in center field, a long-strider who gobbles up territory with plus range. His body and tools draw comparisons to Alex Rios, but Rios came to pro ball with a feel for hitting that Thompson never has exhibited. He has plus pull power that he doesn't get to consistently, instead flying open against soft stuff away. He lacks a consistent approach or offensive plan at the plate. He's an above-average runner who can steal a base and could fill a fourth outfielder role. Added to the 40-man roster in November, Thompson likely will move up to Triple-A Charlotte.

Year	Club (League)	Class	AVG	G	AB	R	H	2B	3B	HR	RBI	BB	SO	SB	CS	OBP	SLG
2012	Winston-Salem (CAR)	HiA	.254	116	449	77	114	28	5	22	90	45	144	18	3	.325	.486
	Birmingham (SL)	AA	.280	14	50	10	14	1	1	3	6	8	16	2	0	.379	.520
	Charlotte (IL)	AAA	.167	6	18	1	3	2	0	0	0	2	6	1	0	.250	.278
2013	Birmingham (SL)	AA	.229	135	507	78	116	23	5	15	73	60	139	25	8	.321	.383
2014	Birmingham (SL)	AA	.237	133	518	86	123	34	6	16	59	65	151	20	5	.324	.419
Minor League Totals			.237	630	2377	385	564	140	23	88	356	268	738	83	24	.321	.427

19 TYLER SALADINO, SS/2B

BA GRADE

40 Risk: Low

Born: July 20, 1989. **B-T:** R-R. **Ht.:** 6-0. **Wt.:** 200. **Drafted:** Oral Roberts, 2010 (7th round). **Signed by:** Clay Overcash.

A San Diego prep product, Saladino was having a key bounceback season in 2014 at Triple-A Charlotte when he tore his ulnar collateral ligament on a throw home from left field and required season-ending surgery. Saladino remains athletic enough to play shortstop, with an above-average arm pre-injury, and good enough footwork and soft hands stay in the dirt at any spot. He played left field and first base to stay in the Charlotte lineup in 2014 and is an average runner. Saladino has a sound approach at the plate, regularly ranking among the top players in the system in walk rate, and has the power to punish mistakes, but he lacks the hitting ability to be a first-division regular. However, he could be a first-division utility-man and is on the 40-man roster, so he could earn that chance in Chicago in 2015.

Year	Club (League)	Class	AVG	G	AB	R	H	2B	3B	HR	RBI	BB	SO	SB	CS	OBP	SLG
2012	Charlotte (IL)	AAA	.224	15	49	9	11	2	0	0	6	4	16	1	0	.296	.265
	Birmingham (SL)	AA	.237	112	418	71	99	15	4	4	39	75	91	38	8	.359	.321
2013	Birmingham (SL)	AA	.229	118	424	49	97	17	2	5	55	51	86	28	8	.316	.314
2014	Charlotte (IL)	AAA	.310	82	294	41	91	16	4	9	43	27	50	7	1	.367	.483
Minor League Totals			.262	489	1795	292	470	93	20	37	222	235	389	86	28	.353	.398

20 LUIS MARTINEZ, RHP

BA GRADE

50 Risk: Extreme

Born: Jan. 29, 1995. **B-T:** R-R. **Ht.:** 6-4. **Wt.:** 190. **Signed:** Venezuela, 2011. **Signed by:** Marco Paddy.

The White Sox hired Marco Paddy to revamp their international scouting efforts in November 2011, and one of his first deals was signing was Martinez for $250,000. He hit 92 mph with his fastball but soon had elbow issues that led to Tommy John surgery in 2012. He finally made his pro debut in 2014, and he got better as he went along, never giving up more than a run while pitching at least five innings in each of his Pioneer League starts. Martinez has a good pitcher's body with long arms, and he has retained some looseness in his arm and delivery despite the surgery. He's raw in terms of repeating his delivery and in his consistency of preparation, but at his best he has a fastball up to 95 mph that sits in the 89-93 range. He's shown the ability to spin a breaking ball, alternately described as a curveball and slider, and has started to tinker with a changeup. Martinez looks ready to jump to low Class A Kannapolis for 2015.

Year	Club (League)	Class	W	L	ERA	G	GS	CG	SV	IP	H	HR	BB	SO	K/9	WHIP	AVG
2012	Did not play--Injured																
2013	Did not play--Injured																
2014	White Sox (AZL)	R	3	2	4.09	7	6	0	0	33	31	3	16	40	10.9	1.42	.244
	Great Falls (PIO)	R	2	1	1.42	5	5	0	0	25	24	2	10	22	7.8	1.34	.261
Minor League Totals			5	3	2.93	12	11	0	0	58	55	5	26	62	9.6	1.39	.251

21 BRANDON BRENNAN, RHP

BA GRADE

45 Risk: High

Born: July 26, 1991. **B-T:** R-R. **Ht.:** 6-4. **Wt.:** 220. **Drafted:** Orange Coast (Calif.) JC, 2012 (4th round). **Signed by:** Mike Baker.

Brennan was also a starting quarterback at Capistrano Valley High in Southern California, but he was better at baseball. He pitched in the 2009 Under Armour All-America Game and was a 40th-round pick of the Rockies in 2010. Brennan headed to Oregon instead, then transferred to Orange Coast (Calif.) JC. After the White Sox drafted him, he struggled to get going thanks to Tommy John surgery that ended his 2013 season in June. He returned to game action less than a year later and finished his breakout season at high Class A Winston-Salem in 2014. He combines size and athletic ability with easy velocity, sitting in the 92-94 mph range and touching 97. His slider is his best secondary pitch, though a wandering release point causes it to flatten out too often. It has late bite when he's on top of it and features solid low-80s power. Brennan's changeup is just a show-me pitch at this stage. He has the body and the plus fastball to develop as a starter but may lack the feel for pitching. If he winds up in the bullpen, he could move quickly. He's expected to start 2015 in the Double-A Birmingham rotation.

Year	Club (League)	Class	W	L	ERA	G	GS	CG	SV	IP	H	HR	BB	SO	K/9	WHIP	AVG
2012	Great Falls (PIO)	R	3	2	4.34	14	7	0	0	37	44	2	16	31	7.5	1.61	.297
2013	Kannapolis (SAL)	LoA	4	9	5.53	15	15	0	0	81	99	7	27	54	6.0	1.55	.298
2014	Great Falls (PIO)	R	1	1	3.20	5	5	0	0	20	17	2	7	12	5.5	1.22	.243
	Kannapolis (SAL)	LoA	2	0	2.55	3	3	0	0	18	11	0	6	15	7.6	0.96	.172
	Winston-Salem (CAR)	HiA	2	0	2.93	6	6	0	0	31	32	1	12	22	6.5	1.43	.286
Minor League Totals			12	12	4.34	43	36	0	0	187	203	12	68	134	6.5	1.45	.280

22 DAVID TREXLER, RHP

BA GRADE

45 Risk: High

Born: Sept. 4, 1990. **B-T:** R-R. **Ht.:** 6-3. **Wt.:** 185. **Drafted:** North Florida, 2014 (17th round). **Signed by:** Joel Grampietro.

Trexler, already 24, will have to move quickly, and he has the arm to do it. He attended Florida State for two seasons and transferred to Gulf Coast (Fla.) CC for his redshirt sophomore season. He then spent two years at North Florida. The White Sox were excited to get him in the 17th round (for a $1,000 bonus), but they didn't expect him to come out throwing 92-96 mph in his pro debut. He gave up five home runs in 14 appearances but pitched aggressively off his power fastball, then kept throwing hard in instructional league. Trexler played off his four-seamer with a hard 12-to-6 curveball that also was better than it had been as an amateur. He throws a fringy changeup as well and has three pitches needed to start. It wouldn't be surprising if Trexler started 2015 at high Class A Winston-Salem or even Double-A Birmingham.

Year	Club (League)	Class	W	L	ERA	G	GS	CG	SV	IP	H	HR	BB	SO	K/9	WHIP	AVG
2014	White Sox (AZL)	R	0	0	0.00	4	0	0	0	7	5	0	0	6	7.7	0.71	.179
	Great Falls (PIO)	R	1	2	3.42	14	0	0	0	24	24	5	9	27	10.3	1.39	.258
Minor League Totals			1	2	2.64	18	0	0	0	31	29	5	9	33	9.7	1.24	.240

23 ADAM ENGEL, OF

BA GRADE

50 Risk: Extreme

Born: Dec. 9, 1991. **B-T:** R-R. **Ht.:** 6-1. **Wt.:** 215. **Drafted:** Louisville, 2013 (19th round). **Signed by:** Phil Gulley.

The White Sox have drafted a lot of toolsy outfielders of late, and most of them haven't hit enough to break through to the big leagues, including Engel. He has explosive athleticism and speed when he's at his best, though he missed time last year after he injured his right lat muscle. Engel combines size and strength along with an average arm and fly-catching skills in center field. His bat is his weakest tool. He has the strength to hit for power, but he has never shown the ability to tap into it. He has stiffness in his swing despite his athleticism, and it gets choppy. He struggled in the Australian Baseball League, hitting .185 while striking out 23 times in his first 92 at-bats, but was leading the league in stolen bases. Engel will head back to Winston-Salem in 2015, and if the bat ever clicks he has the tools to be a regular.

Year	Club (League)	Class	AVG	G	AB	R	H	2B	3B	HR	RBI	BB	SO	SB	CS	OBP	SLG
2013	Great Falls (PIO)	R	.301	56	239	44	72	12	3	3	30	21	34	31	8	.379	.414
2014	White Sox (AZL)	R	.364	8	33	6	12	3	3	1	3	3	6	2	0	.447	.727
	Kannapolis (SAL)	LoA	.261	74	307	54	80	14	7	6	30	29	86	28	11	.334	.410
	Winston-Salem (CAR)	HiA	.239	21	88	11	21	0	0	0	5	6	21	9	1	.296	.239
Minor League Totals			.277	159	667	115	185	29	13	10	68	59	147	70	20	.351	.405

24 JAKE PETER, 2B

BA GRADE

45 Risk: High

Born: April 5, 1993. **B-T:** L-R. **Ht.:** 6-1. **Wt.:** 195. **Drafted:** Creighton, 2014 (7th round). **Signed by:** J.J. Lally.

Peter was a surehanded second baseman at Creighton who also flashed mid-90s heat in limited pitching outings. Some scouts preferred him as a pitcher, but a tender elbow prompted him to stick to hitting as a junior. The White Sox signed him for a slot $203,800 bonus as a seventh-round pick in 2014 and pushed him to high Class A Winston-Salem to finish the year. Peter likely will prove to be the best hitter the White Sox drafted in a pitcher-heavy 2014 draft class. He is an average runner with a short, line-drive swing, with a polished approach that covers the plate well. He can pepper the gaps but has below-average home run power. He's a surehanded second baseman with a plus arm who excels turning the double play. He'll be the everyday second baseman at a Class A stop in 2015.

Year	Club (League)	Class	AVG	G	AB	R	H	2B	3B	HR	RBI	BB	SO	SB	CS	OBP	SLG
2014	Great Falls (PIO)	R	.388	37	152	26	59	11	6	2	21	13	13	1	1	.444	.579
	Winston-Salem (CAR)	HiA	.236	23	89	8	21	4	1	0	5	4	13	1	0	.277	.303
Minor League Totals			.332	60	241	34	80	15	7	2	26	17	26	2	1	.385	.477

25 JAMES DYKSTRA, RHP

BA GRADE	
45	Risk: High

Born: Nov. 22, 1990. **B-T:** R-R. **Ht.:** 6-4. **Wt.:** 190. **Drafted:** Cal State San Marcos, 2013 (6th round). **Signed by:** George Kachigian.

Dykstra's older brother Allan was a 2008 first-rounder by the Padres who has reached Triple-A. James played at Yavapai (Ariz.) JC and Louisiana State before finishing his career at NAIA Cal State San Marcos. An outfielder who converted to pitching while at Yavapai and pitched out of LSU's bullpen, Dykstra ranked second among all qualified minor league starters for lowest walk rate last year. He throws a ton of strikes and keeps the ball down and in the ballpark. He has to be fine because he has little life on a solid-average 88-92 mph fastball and no true plus pitch. He works fast, throws a changeup with confidence that qualifies as his best pitch, and throws his curveball for strikes. He'll need to add a cutter or get more life on his fastball to be more than a fringe starter. He'll move up to Double-A Birmingham for 2015.

Year	Club (League)	Class	W	L	ERA	G	GS	CG	SV	IP	H	HR	BB	SO	K/9	WHIP	AVG
2013	Great Falls (PIO)	R	0	0	5.06	6	0	0	0	5	10	0	5	2	3.4	2.81	.417
2014	Kannapolis (SAL)	LoA	6	8	2.64	16	16	1	0	99	101	3	10	82	7.5	1.12	.262
	Winston-Salem (CAR)	HiA	3	3	4.89	9	9	0	0	53	73	3	6	46	7.8	1.48	.322
Minor League Totals			9	11	3.48	31	25	1	0	158	184	6	21	130	7.4	1.30	.289

26 KEON BARNUM, 1B

BA GRADE	
50	Risk: Extreme

Born: Jan. 16, 1993. **B-T:** L-L. **Ht.:** 6-5. **Wt.:** 225. **Drafted:** HS—Tampa, 2012 (1st round supplemental). **Signed by:** Joe Siers.

The White Sox loved Barnum's raw power and swing in the 2012 draft, signing him for $950,000 as the 48th overall pick. He stayed healthy enough to play every day in 2014 for high Class A Winston-Salem, but the White Sox believe they have yet to see the real Barnum. They drafted him thinking they had another Ryan Howard on their hands, and in some ways they do. Like Howard, Barnum has soft hands and solid footwork around the bag at first. He doesn't sniff lefthanded pitchers, and he strikes out in bunches (leading the Carolina League with 163 in 2014). But while Howard hits plenty of home runs, Barnum puts on a batting-practice show but has just 16 career homers, as he gets beat hard in and soft away. He's a baseclogger. Barnum needs to start figuring out how to get to his power more consistently.

Year	Club (League)	Class	AVG	G	AB	R	H	2B	3B	HR	RBI	BB	SO	SB	CS	OBP	SLG
2012	Bristol (APP)	R	.279	13	43	6	12	1	0	3	8	5	13	0	0	.347	.512
2013	Kannapolis (SAL)	LoA	.254	56	201	22	51	13	1	5	26	19	65	0	0	.315	.403
2014	Winston-Salem (CAR)	HiA	.253	132	491	49	124	29	1	8	60	37	163	3	0	.306	.365
Minor League Totals			.254	201	735	77	187	43	2	16	94	61	241	3	0	.311	.384

27 ONELKI GARCIA, LHP

BA GRADE	
45	Risk: High

Born: Aug. 2, 1989. **B-T:** L-L. **Ht.:** 6-3. **Wt.:** 225. **Drafted:** Los Angeles (no school), 2012 (3rd round). **Signed by:** Dennis Moeller (Dodgers).

Garcia shook up the 2011 draft, as the Cuban defector was made eligible for two days before Major League Baseball declared him ineligible again. He was back in the 2012 draft, and the Dodgers took him and signed him for $382,000. The physical lefthander finished his first full pro season in the majors with a September callup. It was a lost year in 2014, though, as he had setbacks from offseason left elbow surgery and then had left knee surgery in January 2014 to repair torn cartilage. The Dodgers tried to sneak him off their 40-man roster in November, and the White Sox claimed Garcia on waivers. At his best, Garcia shows a 93-95 mph fastball, touching 97, with below-average control. He has a power low-80s slider. Throwing strikes and staying healthy would make Garcia a useful lefty option in the White Sox's 2015 bullpen.

Year	Club (League)	Class	W	L	ERA	G	GS	CG	SV	IP	H	HR	BB	SO	K/9	WHIP	AVG
2012	R. Cucamonga (CAL)	HiA	0	0	0.00	1	1	0	0	2	0	0	0	4	18.0	0.00	.000
2013	Chattanooga (SL)	AA	2	3	2.75	25	6	0	1	52	41	3	32	53	9.1	1.39	.215
	Albuquerque (PCL)	AAA	0	1	3.72	10	0	0	0	10	6	0	3	14	13.0	0.93	.176
	Los Angeles (NL)	MAJ	0	0	13.50	3	0	0	0	1	1	1	4	1	6.8	3.75	.200
2014	R. Cucamonga (CAL)	HiA	0	1	27.00	1	1	0	0	1	2	0	1	0	4.50	.500
Major League Totals			0	0	13.50	3	0	0	0	1	1	1	4	1	6.8	3.75	.200
Minor League Totals			2	5	3.06	37	8	0	1	65	49	3	36	71	9.9	1.31	.209

28 MICHAEL YNOA, RHP

BA GRADE	
45	Risk: High

Born: Sept. 24, 1991. **B-T:** R-R. **Ht.:** 6-7. **Wt.:** 210. **Signed:** Dominican Republic, 2008. **Signed by:** Trevor Schaffer (Athletics).

Ynoa was the most sought-after prospect on the 2008 international market and landed a $4.25 million bonus from the Athletics. Tommy John surgery and other ailments cost him the better part of three full years. The A's shifted him to the bullpen in 2014, then sent him to the White Sox as part of the deal headlined by Jeff Samardzija. Ynoa cuts loose his plus fastball in shorter stints, showing mid- to upper-90s velocity from an easy delivery. He shifted his breaking ball from a curve to a slider and found some success with it. His changeup is useful as well, showing depth to go with good arm speed. Ynoa remains unrefined. He tends to become predictable with his fastball, allowing hitters to sit on it, and his command is below-average, thanks to a delivery he struggles to repeat. The White Sox hope their pitching-development program can unlock Ynoa's talent as he embarks on his third minor league option year in 2015.

Year	Club (League)	Class	W	L	ERA	G	GS	CG	SV	IP	H	HR	BB	SO	K/9	WHIP	AVG
2012	Athletics (AZL)	R	0	1	5.40	6	6	0	0	10	11	1	9	6	5.4	2.00	.282
	Vermont (NYP)	SS	1	3	6.97	8	6	0	0	21	20	2	16	19	8.3	1.74	.247
2013	Beloit (MWL)	LoA	2	1	2.14	15	15	0	0	55	45	3	18	48	7.9	1.15	.221
	Stockton (CAL)	HiA	1	2	7.71	7	6	0	1	21	23	2	17	20	8.6	1.90	.274
2014	Stockton (CAL)	HiA	4	2	5.52	31	0	0	0	46	42	5	21	64	12.6	1.38	.247
Minor League Totals			8	10	4.81	70	36	0	1	161	147	14	85	168	9.4	1.44	.241

29 JARED MITCHELL, OF

BA GRADE

45 Risk: High

Born: Oct. 13, 1988. **B-T:** L-L. **Ht.:** 6-0. **Wt.:** 205. **Drafted:** Louisiana State, 2009 (1st round). **Signed by:** Warren Hughes.

The White Sox aren't waiting on Mitchell anymore. They've sent the former Louisiana State football player down to Double-A Birmingham in both 2013 and 2014 and removed him from the 40-man roster, and no one claimed him. Mitchell still has tools, with athleticism, strength and plus speed. He's a fair defender with an average arm and plays a passable center field, though he fits better in left. He'll always strike out a lot due to poor pitch recognition and a propensity to chase breaking balls. He showed more ability to adjust from at-bat to at-bat in 2014, with a career-best 19 home runs. He doesn't hit lefthanders well enough to be a regular, so his ceiling is that of a part-time player and reserve. He made enough progress to get called back up to Triple-A Charlotte in 2014, and he's likely headed there again for 2015.

Year	Club (League)	Class	AVG	G	AB	R	H	2B	3B	HR	RBI	BB	SO	SB	CS	OBP	SLG
2012	Birmingham (SL)	AA	.240	94	334	51	80	13	12	10	54	62	126	20	5	.368	.440
	Charlotte (IL)	AAA	.231	36	121	18	28	11	1	1	13	16	53	1	1	.329	.364
2013	Charlotte (IL)	AAA	.132	14	53	7	7	2	0	0	3	10	27	4	1	.277	.170
	Birmingham (SL)	AA	.174	76	247	23	43	6	2	5	20	41	96	13	5	.297	.275
2014	Birmingham (SL)	AA	.299	39	157	32	47	5	3	10	20	16	40	4	5	.367	.561
	Charlotte (IL)	AAA	.230	81	269	41	62	8	2	9	30	49	111	11	7	.360	.375
Minor League Totals			.230	503	1773	259	407	88	30	44	208	269	676	72	33	.338	.387

30 ANDY WILKINS, 1B

BA GRADE

40 Risk: Medium

Born: Sept. 13, 1988. **B-T:** L-R. **Ht.:** 6-1. **Wt.:** 220. **Drafted:** Arkansas, 2010 (5th round). **Signed by:** Clay Overcash.

Wilkins slammed 30 homers to lead the Triple-A International League last year and earned his first big league promotion, striking out in nearly half of his plate appearances with the White Sox. He has strength and a swing geared for loft power. He's short to the ball but lacks the bat speed to consistently keep up with premium velocity. Playing winter ball in Venezuela in 2013 helped him identify breaking stuff better, and he can punish mistakes to all parts of the park. He has some feel for hitting, but his defense and arm strength are below-average, and his speed is near the bottom of the scale. Wilkins should return to Triple-A Charlotte for 2015 as insurance, but he may need a new organization to get a big league opportunity.

Year	Club (League)	Class	AVG	G	AB	R	H	2B	3B	HR	RBI	BB	SO	SB	CS	OBP	SLG
2012	Birmingham (SL)	AA	.239	116	435	68	104	28	1	17	69	63	94	6	4	.335	.425
2013	Birmingham (SL)	AA	.288	67	243	37	70	16	0	10	49	38	58	3	0	.386	.477
	Charlotte (IL)	AAA	.265	58	215	25	57	13	0	7	30	14	52	2	1	.312	.423
2014	Charlotte (IL)	AAA	.293	127	491	79	144	38	1	30	85	34	91	0	1	.338	.558
	Chicago (AL)	MAJ	.140	17	43	2	6	2	0	0	2	2	22	0	0	.178	.186
Major League Totals			.140	17	43	2	6	2	0	0	2	2	22	0	0	.178	.186
Minor League Totals			.276	555	2095	318	579	142	3	93	362	238	417	20	10	.349	.480

Cincinnati Reds

BY J.J. COOPER

The Reds head into 2015 with a lot of opportunity, and a whole lot of uncertainty on the horizon.

After topping 90 wins and reaching the playoffs in 2012 and 2013, the 2014 season was a disaster in Cincinnati. First baseman Joey Votto spent months on the disabled list, and when he went down the Reds quickly demonstrated they didn't have a viable option to replace him in the lineup. Breakout seasons by third baseman Todd Frazier and catcher Devin Mesoraco weren't enough to make up for an unproductive outfield.

At the all-star break, the Reds had gone 51-44 and trailed the National League Central leaders by just one and a half games. They went 25-42 from that point forward, resorting to playing Brayan Pena at first base, pitching Dylan Axelrod and David Holmberg in the rotation and rotating a cast of underperformers in left field.

Cincinnati has gone through this before. After winning 91 games in 2010 and being swept in the NL Division Series, they fell back to 79 wins in 2011. The Reds made additions at that point, most notably trading first-rounders Yonder Alonso and Yasmani Grandal to the Padres for Mat Latos, and the club returned to its winning ways.

With an owner, Bob Castellini, who wants to win now, especially with the All-Star Game coming to Cincinnati in 2015, the Reds will try to prove that 2014 was another brief detour.

Cincinnati has retooled for 2015. By trading away arbitration-eligible righthanders Latos (to the Marlins) and Alfredo Simon (to the Tigers), the Reds have ensured that four of the club's five starters won't hit free agency at the same time after the season. Now they must worry only about ace Johnny Cueto and Mike Leake.

In the Latos and Simon trades, the Reds found a viable rotation option in righty Anthony DeSclafani, while shortstop Eugenio Suarez fills a dire need at shortstop. Last year, the Reds had no other option other than Zack Cozart even when Cozart was struggling at the plate. Suarez gives the team another viable shortstop as either competition or depth in case of injury.

The same issues that undermined the 2014 club's success still rest just under the surface. The Reds need a full, productive season from Votto because they do not have a viable replacement for him. They also need an everyday solution in left field, probably via a bargain free agent, because the best internal options—Jesse Winker, Yorman Rodriguez and Kyle Waldrop—aren't considered big league ready.

All-star seasons from catcher Devin Mesoraco (pictured) and Todd Frazier could not cover for the loss of Joey Votto

TOP PROSPECTS OF THE DECADE

Year	Player, Pos.	2014 Org
2005	Homer Bailey, rhp	Reds
2006	Homer Bailey, rhp	Reds
2007	Homer Bailey, rhp	Reds
2008	Jay Bruce, of	Reds
2009	Yonder Alonso, 1b	Padres
2010	Todd Frazier, 3b/of	Reds
2011	Aroldis Chapman, lhp	Reds
2012	Devin Mesoraco, c	Reds
2013	Billy Hamilton, of	Reds
2014	Robert Stephenson, rhp	Reds

Cincinnati could contend again in 2015 while retooling on the fly. They have an impressive amount of pitching depth at Double-A and Triple-A that could begin to help the club soon, and the everyday lineup and rotation is strong.

But over the long term, it's going to be hard for the Reds to keep up with the Pirates, Cardinals and Cubs, given their payroll obligations to Votto and second baseman Brandon Phillips.

In 2017, the Reds will devote roughly $70 million to four players. For a team that saw its payroll max out at $114 million in 2014, and was under $100 million just two years ago, it's going to be tough to figure out a way to make those numbers work.

General manager: Walt Jocketty. **Farm director:** Jeff Graupe. **Scouting director:** Chris Buckley.

Class	Team	League	W	L	PCT	Finish	Manager
Majors	Cincinnati Reds	National	76	86	.469	21st (30)	Bryan Price
Triple-A	Louisville Bats	International	68	75	.476	9th (14)	Jim Riggleman
Double-A	Pensacola Blue Wahoos	Southern	60	80	.429	t-9th (10	Delino DeShields
High A	*Bakersfield Blaze	California	78	62	.557	t-2nd (10)	Pat Kelly
Low A	Dayton Dragons	Midwest	68	70	.493	8th (16)	Jose Nieves
Rookie	Billings Mustangs	Pioneer	41	35	.539	3rd (8)	Dick Schofield
Rookie	Reds	Arizona	24	32	.429	11th (13)	Eli Marrero
Overall Minor League Record			339	354	.489	20th (30)	

*Affiliate will be Daytona (Florida State) in 2015.

THIS YEAR'S TOP 30

No.	Player, Pos.	Grade
1.	Robert Stephenson, rhp	65/High
2.	Raisel Iglesias, rhp	60/High
3.	Jesse Winker, of	55/Medium
4.	Michael Lorenzen, rhp	50/Medium
5.	Nick Howard, rhp	55/High
6.	Anthony DeSclafani, rhp	45/Medium
7.	Amir Garrett, lhp	50/High
8.	Nick Travieso, rhp	50/High
9.	Aristides Aquino, of	55/Extreme
10.	Yorman Rodriguez, of	50/High
11.	Alex Blandino, ss	50/High
12.	Ben Lively, rhp	45/Medium
13.	Kyle Waldrop, of	50/High
14.	Philip Ervin, of	50/High
15.	Sal Romano, rhp	50/High
16.	Jonathon Crawford, rhp	50/High
17.	Gavin LaValley, 3b/1b	50/High
18.	Taylor Sparks, 3b	50/Extreme
19.	Tucker Barnhart, c	40/Safe
20.	Jon Moscot, rhp	45/Low
21.	David Holmberg, lhp	40/Low
22.	Seth Mejias-Brean, 3b	45/High
23.	Wyatt Strahan, rhp	45/High
24.	Junior Arias, of	50/Extreme
25.	Sebastian Elizalde, of	45/High
26.	Tyler Mahle, rhp	45/High
27.	Chad Wallach, c	45/High
28.	Donald Lutz, 1b/of	40/Medium
29.	Jeremy Kivel, rhp	45/High
30.	Carlos Contreras, rhp	45/High

LAST YEAR'S TOP 30

No.	Player, Pos.	Status
1.	Robert Stephenson, rhp	No. 1
2.	Billy Hamilton, of	Majors
3.	Phil Ervin, of	No. 14
4.	Jesse Winker, of	No. 3
5.	Yorman Rodriguez, of	No. 11
6.	Michael Lorenzen, rhp	No. 4
7.	Carlos Contreras, rhp	No. 29
8.	Nick Travieso, rhp	No. 8
9.	Ben Lively, rhp	No. 12
10.	Tucker Barnhart, c	No. 19
11.	Jeremy Kivel, rhp	No. 29
12.	Ismael Guillon, lhp	Dropped out
13.	Daniel Corcino, rhp	Dropped out
14.	Junior Arias, of	No. 24
15.	Chad Rogers, rhp	Dropped out
16.	Donald Lutz, of	No. 28
17.	Jacob Constante, lhp	Dropped out
18.	Amir Garrett, lhp	No. 7
19.	Jackson Stephens, rhp	Dropped out
20.	Jonathan Reynoso, of	Dropped out
21.	Seth Mejias-Brean, 3b	No. 21
22.	K.J. Franklin, 3b	Dropped out
23.	Jon Moscot, rhp	No. 20
24.	Aristides Aquino, of	No. 9
25.	Sal Romano, rhp	No. 15
26.	Sebastian Elizalde, of	No. 25
27.	Tanner Rahier, 3b	Dropped out
28.	Curtis Partch, rhp	Free agent
29.	Reydel Medina, of	Dropped out
30.	Dan Langfield, rhp	Dropped out

BEST TOOLS

Best Hitter for Average	Jesse Winker
Best Power Hitter	Aristides Aquino
Best Strike-Zone Discipline	Jesse Winker
Fastest Baserunner	Junior Arias
Best Athlete	Amir Garrett
Best Fastball	Robert Stephenson
Best Curveball	Robert Stephenson
Best Slider	Nick Howard
Best Changeup	Ismael Guillon
Best Control	Ben Lively
Best Defensive Catcher	Tucker Barnhart
Best Defensive Infielder	Tanner Rahier
Best Infield Arm	Cory Thompson
Best Defensive Outfielder	Nick Benedetto
Best Outfield Arm	Yorman Rodriguez

PROJECTED 2018 LINEUP

Catcher	Devin Mesoraco
First Base	Joey Votto
Second Base	Alex Blandino
Third Base	Todd Frazier
Shortstop	Eugenio Suarez
Left Field	Jesse Winker
Center Field	Billy Hamilton
Right Field	Jay Bruce
No. 1 Starter	Johnny Cueto
No. 2 Starter	Homer Bailey
No. 3 Starter	Robert Stephenson
No. 4 Starter	Raisel Iglesias
No. 5 Starter	Michael Lorenzen
Closer	Aroldis Chapman

CINCINNATI REDS

TOP 2015 ROOKIE: Raisel Iglesias, rhp. After an excellent AFL stint, he is poised to take a prominent role in the big league bullpen.
BREAKOUT PROSPECT: Junior Arias, of. After injuries wiped out his 2014 season, he is ready to bounce back to show his power and speed.
SLEEPER: Jose Ortiz, c. He's a talented catcher who has work to both behind the plate and in the batter's box.

SOURCE OF TOP 30 TALENT			
Homegrown	26	Acquired	4
College	10	Trades	4
Junior college	0	Rule 5 draft	0
High school	10	Independent leagues	0
Draft-and-follow	0	Free agents/waivers	0
Nondrafted free agents	0		
International	6		

LF
Jesse Winker (3)
Kyle Waldrop (13)
Sebastian Elizalde (25)
Felix Perez

CF
Junior Arias (24)
Jonathan Reynoso
Beau Amaral
Gabriel Rosa

RF
Aristides Aquino (9)
Yorman Rodriguez (10)
Phillip Ervin (14)
Juan Duran

3B
Taylor Sparks (18)
Seth Mejias-Brean (22)
Montrell Marshall
Tanner Rahier

SS
Alex Blandino (11)
Carlton Daal
Cory Thompson

2B
Juan Perez
Shane Mardirosian
Ty Washington
Francis Azcona

1B
Gavin LaValley (17)
Donald Lutz (28)
Neftali Soto
K.J. Franklin
Sean Buckley

C
Tucker Barnhart (19)
Chad Wallach (27)
Joe Hudson
Jose Ortiz

LHP

LHSP	LHRP
Amir Garrett (7)	Ismael Guillon
David Holmberg (21)	Wandy Peralta
Jacob Constante	

RHP

RHSP	RHRP
Robert Stephenson (1)	Carlos Contreras (30)
Raisel Iglesias (2)	Jeremy Kivel (29)
Michael Lorenzen (4)	Drew Hayes
Nick Howard (5)	Daniel Corcino
Anthony DeSclafani (6)	Alejandro Chacin
Nick Travieso (8)	El'Hajj Muhammed
Ben Lively (12)	Jake Johnson
Sal Romano (15)	Dan Langfield
Jonathon Crawford (16)	Zach Weiss
Jon Moscot (20)	Carlos Gonzalez
Wyatt Strahan (23)	Chad Rogers
Tyler Mahle (26)	
Daniel Wright	
Jackson Stephens	
Mark Armstrong	

2014

BEST PURE HITTER: SS Alex Blandino (1), the second of the Reds' two first-round picks, hit .310 over two summers in the Cape Cod League, then used his loose, quick-wristed swing to hit .283/.367/.480 in his pro debut, spending more than half of it with low Class A Dayton. 1B/3B Gavin LaValley (4) has an advanced approach, particularly for a high school hitter who faced modest competition, and present strength.

BEST POWER HITTER: 3B Taylor Sparks (2) remains raw offensively and swings and misses a lot. But when he connects, the ball travels, and he has well-above-average raw power.

FASTEST RUNNER: 2B Shane Mardirosian (7) is a plus runner, if not a bit more. Sparks also earns 60 grades, getting to first base in 4.2 seconds from the right side at his best.

BEST DEFENSIVE PLAYER: Sparks has a chance to be a plus third baseman, with a plus arm, agility and first-step quickness. C Mitch Trees (11) has catch-and-throw tools but missed part of the summer with a bout of mononucleosis.

BEST FASTBALL: RHP Nick Howard (1) can sit in the 94-97 mph range even over multiple innings and touched 98 this spring. The Reds intend to develop the former Virginia closer as a starter next season.

BEST SECONDARY PITCH: Howard started as a sophomore and has retained his ability to keep his curveball and slider distinct. He throws both with power, a 79-82 mph curve and slider up to 85. The Reds have confidence in both pitches.

BEST PRO DEBUT: Blandino hit eight homers in his debut. RHP Wyatt Strahan (3) was one of the top pitchers in the Rookie-level Pioneer League, with 40 strikeouts, a 2.76 ERA and no home runs allowed in 42 innings.

BEST ATHLETE: Sparks is a potential power-speed corner bat if he can improve his contact rate. Reds officials compare his overall profile to that of Drew Stubbs.

MOST INTRIGUING BACKGROUND: 3B Montrell Marshall (12), who missed the season with a stress fracture in his lower back, is the first cousin of Reds second baseman Brandon Phillips. Trees is the first cousin of Nationals outfielder Jayson Werth. Unsigned LHP Logan Browning (36) is the son of ex-Reds lefty Tom Browning, now a minor league pitching coach in the system. C Seth Roadcap (39) is the son of Reds scout Steve.

CLOSEST TO THE MAJORS: Howard could have finished the year in the majors if the Reds move him as a reliever. He and Blandino both could move to Cincinnati quickly.

BEST LATE-ROUND PICK: Marshall has power, athleticism, and profiles for third base if he gets healthy.

THE ONE WHO GOT AWAY: The Reds tried to sign Alaskan OF Roderick Bynum (18) but ran up against their budget limit. The speedy basketball player wound up at Arizona Western CC.

ASSESSMENT: The Reds have had success drafting college infielders like Blandino and college pitchers like Howard. If Sparks comes into his own, he could be the top talent in the entire class.

2013

RHP Michael Lorenzen (1) has taken a leap forward after giving up hitting, and RHP Ben Lively (4) also has moved quickly. OF Phillip Ervin (1) stalled a bit in his first full season.

GRADE: C

2012

OF Jesse Winker (1s) is the system's top hitter and will move quicker than RHP Nick Travieso (1). RHP Jon Moscot (4) already has reached Triple-A, but the rest of the class has struggled.

GRADE: D

2011

RHP Robert Stephenson (1) is the system's top prospect. LHP Tony Cingrani (3) rocketed to the majors, though he back-slid in 2014. LHP Amir Garrett (22) and RHP Sal Romano (23) both have rotation upside.

GRADE: B

TOP DRAFT PICKS OF THE DECADE

Year	Player, Pos.	2014 Org
2005	Jay Bruce, of	Reds
2006	Drew Stubbs, of	Rockies
2007	Devin Mesoraco, c	Reds
2008	Yonder Alonso, 1b	Padres
2009	Mike Leake, rhp	Reds
2010	Yasmani Grandal, c	Padres
2011	Robert Stephenson, rhp	Reds
2012	Nick Travieso, rhp	Reds
2013	Phillip Ervin, of	Reds
2014	Nick Howard, rhp	Reds

LARGEST BONUSES IN CLUB HISTORY

Aroldis Chapman, 2010	$16,250,000
Raisel Iglesias, 2014	$5,000,000
Chris Gruler, 2002	$2,500,000
Yorman Rodriguez, 2008	$2,500,000
Homer Bailey, 2004	$2,300,000

1 ROBERT STEPHENSON, RHP

Born: Feb. 24, 1993. **B-T:** R-R. **Ht.:** 6-2. **Wt.:** 190.
Drafted: HS—Martinez, Calif., 2011 (1st round).
Signed by: Rich Bordi.

A member of an excellent 2011 high school pitching class that included Jose Fernandez, Dylan Bundy, Archie Bradley, Daniel Norris and Henry Owens, Stephenson has arguably the best pure arm strength of that group, though he has moved more slowly up the ladder than some of his peers (Fernandez, Bundy and Norris have reached the big leagues). After a dominating 2013 season that concluded with a poor stint at Double-A Pensacola, Stephenson threw five dominant innings for the Blue Wahoos in his 2014 debut, striking out 11, walking one and allowing only one hit in five scoreless innings. That proved to be his season highlight, for he never reached double-digits in strikeouts again, and he pitched through seven innings just three times all season. Stephenson was durable, but he also wasn't very effective. He led the Southern League in strikeouts (140) and finished second in opponent average (.224), but he also led in home runs (18) and walks allowed (74) and finished second worst in the league in ERA among qualifiers.

Stephenson's stuff didn't back up even while his ERA ballooned to 4.74. He still could run his double-plus fastball up to 99 mph at times and still sat 93-96. His 80-82 mph curveball still is a hard-breaking yo-yo that some scouts also project to end up as a double-plus pitch. And while his changeup is clearly his third pitch, it shows flashes of potential when he's not throwing it too firmly. Stephenson's feel for the game has not caught up to his stuff. He is prone to overthrowing when he gets in trouble. Much too often, Stephenson will try to throw an absolutely perfect curveball when he gets in trouble, which usually means he misses with it. The same problem happens with his fastball. Instead of taking a bit off to gain improved command of his heater, he humps up, which leads to him missing his target. Stephenson is slow to the plate and doesn't control the running game—12 of 13 basestealers were successful against him in 2014. There's nothing wrong with Stephenson that experience shouldn't fix. His delivery is relatively clean, and he has shown in the past that he can throw strikes, even if his 2014 walk rate indicates fringe-average control. Much like Homer

Bailey before him, Stephenson has to learn that a plus-plus fastball isn't always enough to succeed against more advanced hitters. Scouts and managers who saw him in the Southern League generally still project Stephenson as a front-end starter and thought of him as one of the more promising arms in baseball.

Because he hasn't mastered Double-A yet, Stephenson could end up heading back to Pensacola for a tuneup in 2015. Even if he doesn't begin the season in a crowded Triple-A Louisville rotation, he should get there before long. He should be part of the Reds' rotation in 2016 if he shows the expected improvements. He has all the makings of a future No. 2 starter, even if his 2014 season didn't offer a whole lot of statistical evidence.

BA GRADE

65 Risk: High

SCOUTING GRADES

Fastball: 70.
Curveball: 70.
Changeup: 50.
Control: 50.

Based on 20-80 scouting scale and future projection rather than present grades.

LGE	BF	SO%	BB%	HR/9
SL	601	23.3	12.3	1.19

BILL MITCHELL

Year	Club (League)	Class	W	L	ERA	G	GS	CG	SV	IP	H	HR	BB	SO	K/9	WHIP	AVG
2012	Billings (PIO)	R	1	0	2.05	7	7	0	0	31	22	2	8	37	10.9	0.98	.195
	Dayton (MWL)	LoA	2	4	4.19	8	8	0	0	34	32	4	15	35	9.2	1.37	.246
2013	Dayton (MWL)	LoA	5	3	2.57	14	14	0	0	77	56	5	20	96	11.2	0.99	.200
	Bakersfield (CAL)	HiA	2	2	3.05	4	4	0	0	21	19	3	2	22	9.6	1.02	.235
	Pensacola (SL)	AA	0	2	4.86	4	4	0	0	17	17	2	13	18	9.7	1.80	.274
2014	Pensacola (SL)	AA	7	10	4.74	27	26	0	0	137	114	18	74	140	9.2	1.38	.224
Minor League Totals			17	21	3.79	64	63	0	0	316	260	34	132	348	9.9	1.24	.221

2 RAISEL IGLESIAS, RHP

Born: Jan. 4, 1990. **B-T:** R-R. **Ht.:** 6-2. **Wt.:** 165. **Signed:** Cuba, 2014. **Signed by:** Tony Arias/Miguel Machado.

The Reds hit the jackpot by signing Cuban flame-thrower Aroldis Chapman to $30 million deal in 2010 and hope to get a similar payoff from a seven-year, $27 million deal with Iglesias. He worked primarily as a reliever in Cuba's Serie Nacional in 2013, with 50 strikeouts and 20 walks in 54 innings, working primarily as a reliever. He when he also pitched for the national team. He didn't return to the mound until the 2014 Arizona Fall League, where he led all relievers in opponent average (.045). The Reds view Iglesias as a starter candidate with four pitches. He sat at 92-95 mph in the AFL, right in line with what he showed with the national team, but he impressed even more with his feel for staying a step ahead of hitters. Iglesias' plus slider is his best secondary pitch, and he varies the shape of it to turn it into a potentially plus hard curveball earlier in the count for get-ahead strikes. His changeup is more advanced than expected for a pitcher with so little starting experience, but it's too firm at times. Iglesias' arm is loose and his delivery is athletic. Like many Cuban pitchers, he'll vary his arm slot a little at times, and some scouts worry that he won't repeat his delivery enough to throw consistent strikes. While Iglesias projects as a loose-armed starter, his long layoff means the Reds likely will send him to the big league bullpen for at least a year while he builds innings. He has the stuff to be a solid setup man now, but if he can improve his command, he has the assortment to be a mid-rotation starter.

BA GRADE

60 Risk: High

LGE	BF	SO%	BB%	HR/9
Did not play				

Year	Club (League)	Class	W	L	ERA	G	GS	CG	SV	IP	H	HR	BB	SO	K/9	WHIP	AVG
2014	Did not play—Signed 2015 contract																

3 JESSE WINKER, OF

Born: Aug. 17, 1993. **B-T:** L-L. **Ht.:** 6-3. **Wt.:** 210. **Drafted:** HS—Orlando, 2012 (1st round supplemental). **Signed by:** Greg Zunino.

The Reds' best pure hitter to come through the system since Jay Bruce, Winker produced at high Class A Bakersfield, and seemed set to build on that after a midseason promotion to Double-A Pensacola. But he injured his wrist diving for a flyball just 21 games into his time in the Southern League. He returned in time to play in the Arizona Fall League. Winker's advanced approach at the plate is the foundation of his success. He understands the strike zone very well, knows how to draw a walk and understands how to look for a certain pitch in a certain zone when he gets into a hitter's count. His swing is simple and geared for hitting for average. Winker has plus raw power, something that's apparent whenever he enters a home run derby, but when the games count, his swing is geared for line-drive doubles to the alleys. He projects as an above-average hitter with average power, but if he wanted to change his approach, he could boost his home run numbers at the expense of his average and on-base percentage. Winker is a below-average runner, but he's shown steady improvement on defense to become a steady, if less-than-rangy, left fielder. Winker will get to catch up for lost time in Pensacola in 2015. He is the team's long-term answer to its troublesome left-field position, but he's not ready to take over just yet.

BA GRADE

55 Risk: Medium

LGE	PA	BB%	SO%	ISO
CAL	249	16.1	18.5	.263
SL	92	15.2	23.9	.143

Year	Club (League)	Class	AVG	G	AB	R	H	2B	3B	HR	RBI	BB	SO	SB	CS	OBP	SLG
2012	Billings (PIO)	R	.338	62	228	42	77	16	3	5	35	40	50	1	3	.443	.500
2013	Dayton (MWL)	LoA	.281	112	417	73	117	18	5	16	76	63	75	6	1	.379	.463
2014	Bakersfield (CAL)	HiA	.317	53	205	42	65	15	0	13	49	40	46	5	1	.426	.580
	Pensacola (SL)	AA	.208	21	77	15	16	5	0	2	8	14	22	0	0	.326	.351
Minor League Totals			.297	248	927	172	275	54	8	36	168	157	193	12	5	.401	.489

4 MICHAEL LORENZEN, RHP

Born: Jan. 4, 1992. **B-T:** R-R. **Ht.:** 6-3. **Wt.:** 195. **Drafted:** Cal State Fullerton, 2013 (1st round supplemental). **Signed by:** Mike Misuraca.

The Reds work creatively to acquire pitchers in the draft. They've had success drafting lower-profile college pitchers with funky arm actions, and they've shown interest in those who serve as two-way players in college. Lorenzen served primarily as Cal State Fullerton's center fielder, but he also closed, recording 35 saves in 45 college innings. After Lorenzen's rough stint in the 2013 Arizona Fall League, the Reds still promoted him aggressively to Double-A Pensacola in 2014. He handled the aggressive assignment with no problems. He finished third in the Southern League with a 3.13 ERA. He has turned into a vastly different pitcher than he was in college, when he threw mostly 95-98 mph four-seamers up in the zone. As a starter, Lorenzen relied on a 92-95 mph two-seamer with sink and bore. It was a pitch-efficient, bat-breaking means of achieving results. He still showed the ability to run his four-seamer up to 97 mph when he wanted. Lorenzen impressed scouts with his competitive demeanor to go with his athleticism. His slurvy 82-84 mph slider works more vertically than a traditional slider, and some scouts describe it as a curveball, but it's an average pitch. His changeup is below-average, but he locates it and has shown aptitude for throwing it. Lorenzen's lack of strikeouts are a concern, but he has plenty of stuff and will head to Triple-A Louisville in 2015. He projects as a mid-rotation starter who could arrive in Cincinnati by the end of 2015.

BA GRADE

50 Risk: Medium

LGE	BF	SO%	BB%	HR/9
SL	504	16.7	8.7	0.67

Year	Club (League)	Class	W	L	ERA	G	GS	CG	SV	IP	H	HR	BB	SO	K/9	WHIP	AVG
2013	Reds (AZL)	R	0	0	0.00	1	1	0	0	1	1	0	0	1	9.0	1.00	.200
	Dayton (MWL)	LoA	1	0	0.00	9	0	0	2	8	7	0	2	7	7.6	1.08	.233
	Bakersfield (CAL)	HiA	0	1	6.35	5	0	0	2	6	6	1	5	6	9.5	1.94	.273
	Pensacola (SL)	AA	0	0	4.50	7	0	0	0	6	6	1	6	5	7.5	2.00	.286
2014	Pensacola (SL)	AA	4	6	3.13	24	24	0	0	121	112	9	44	84	6.3	1.29	.253
Minor League Totals			5	7	3.11	46	25	0	4	142	132	11	57	103	6.5	1.33	.253

5 NICK HOWARD, RHP

Born: April 6, 1993. **B-T:** R-R. **Ht.:** 6-3. **Wt.:** 215. **Drafted:** Virginia, 2014 (1st round). **Signed by:** Jeff Brookens

Howard flourished as a two-way star at Virginia. As a sophomore, he was the Cavaliers' third baseman and played some shortstop in addition to pitching in the weekend rotation. He moved to the bullpen as a junior, setting an Atlantic Coast Conference single-season record with 20 saves, while also serving as DH on a Virginia club that lost in the College World Series final when he gave up a game-winning homer to Vanderbilt's John Norwood. He signed for $1,990,500 as the 19th overall pick. Much like they had done with Michael Lorenzen, the Reds drafted Howard with the intention of moving him to the rotation. Howard sits at 92-95 mph as a starter and pairs his plus fastball with a pair of breaking balls. His high-70s curveball is the more developed of the two, with its 12-to-6 break, while his slider is harder at 82-84 mph with some tilt and depth. Both project as at least average pitches. Howard's changeup is the least advanced, but it has some deception and he shows some feel. It could be at least a fringe-average pitch. His simple, low-effort delivery combined with his athleticism should help him to develop big league average control, but he did struggled to hit his spots at low Class A Dayton. Howard is more advanced than Lorenzen at a similar stage. He'll head to Double-A Pensacola in 2015, and if he handles that assignment, a late-2016 arrival in Cincinnati isn't unreasonable.

BA GRADE

55 Risk: High

LGE	BF	SO%	BB%	HR/9
MWL	136	16.9	8.1	1.07

Year	Club (League)	Class	W	L	ERA	G	GS	CG	SV	IP	H	HR	BB	SO	K/9	WHIP	AVG
2014	Dayton (MWL)	LoA	2	1	3.74	11	5	0	0	34	28	4	11	23	6.1	1.16	.233
Minor League Totals			2	1	3.74	11	5	0	0	34	28	4	11	23	6.1	1.16	.233

6 ANTHONY DESCLAFANI, RHP

Born: April 18, 1990. **B-T:** R-R. **Ht.:** 6-1. **Wt.:** 190. **Drafted:** Florida, 2011 (6th round). **Signed by:** Joel Grampietro (Blue Jays).

Traded by the Blue Jays to the Marlins with Justin Nicolino and Henderson Alvarez, DeSclafani received the first shot to replace injured ace Jose Fernandez but could not lock down the spot and worked in relief exclusively during his September callup. He now heads to the Reds along with Chad Wallach for Mat Latos. DeSclafani pitches off a hard four-seam fastball that parks at 92-94 mph when he's at his best. He can get ground-balls with a two-seamer in the low 90s, and his hard 81-85 mph slider earns average grades for its velocity and late three-quarters tilt. DeSclafani does it all from an easy delivery and pounds the bottom of the zone. He doesn't miss many bats with his slider, though it has improved, and he needs to use and develop his fringe-average changeup, which is too firm and lacks separation. After sticking with the slider for a while, he reintroduced the curve and began throwing it regularly in the Arizona Fall League. If he can throw four pitches for strikes, he would give the Reds a potential No. 4 starter, and he'll compete for a rotation spot this spring.

BA GRADE

45 Risk: Medium

LGE	BF	SO%	BB%	HR/9
SL	175	21.7	5.7	0.84
PCL	249	23.7	8.4	0.30

Year	Club (League)	Class	W	L	ERA	G	GS	CG	SV	IP	H	HR	BB	SO	K/9	WHIP	AVG
2012	Lansing (MWL)	LoA	11	3	3.37	28	21	0	0	123	145	3	25	92	6.7	1.38	.307
2013	Jupiter (FSL)	HiA	4	2	1.67	12	12	0	0	54	48	3	9	53	8.8	1.06	.236
	Jacksonville (SL)	AA	5	4	3.36	13	13	0	0	75	74	7	14	62	7.4	1.17	.263
2014	Jacksonville (SL)	AA	3	4	4.19	8	8	0	0	43	45	4	10	38	8.0	1.28	.278
	New Orleans (PCL)	AAA	3	3	3.49	12	11	0	0	59	48	2	21	59	8.9	1.16	.218
	Miami (NL)	MAJ	2	2	6.27	13	5	0	0	33	40	4	5	26	7.1	1.36	.303
Major League Totals			2	2	6.27	13	5	0	0	33	40	4	5	26	7.1	1.36	.303
Minor League Totals			26	16	3.23	73	65	0	0	354	360	19	79	304	7.7	1.24	.269

7 AMIR GARRETT, LHP

Born: May 3, 1992. **B-T:** L-L. **Ht.:** 6-5. **Wt.:** 210. **Drafted:** HS—Henderson, Nev., 2011 (22nd round). **Signed by:** Clark Crist.

When the Reds signed Garrett for $1 million as a 22nd-round pick in 2011 they hoped that one day he would give up his basketball career to focus on baseball. After playing hoops for two seasons at St. John's and spending one year sitting out as a transfer at Cal State Northridge, Garrett attended spring training for the first time in 2014, decided to focus on baseball and went 5-4, 2.86 at low Class A Dayton during the second half. No Reds pitcher improved more in 2014. Garrett showed erratic control early, but in the second half he consistently showed a plus fastball (92-95 mph) that he can throw to both sides of the plate but is pretty straight. He throws a slurvy slider that is a bigger breaker than ideal but does have some power. Some scouts think it's too much of a chase pitch, but most see it as an average offering with a chance to end up as plus. Garrett's changeup is erratic, but at its best it's a fringe-average offering that is a little firm. His control has improved dramatically, but his command still has a way to go. With extremely long legs and arms, the 6-foot-5 lefty has to work to repeat his delivery, and he's slow to the plate. Given that he'll be 23 in 2015, Garrett could end up as a power reliever with a plus fastball and potentially plus slider. But he could grow to be a mid-rotation starter if he continues making strides.

BA GRADE

50 Risk: High

LGE	BF	SO%	BB%	HR/9
MWL	561	22.6	9.1	0.74

Year	Club (League)	Class	W	L	ERA	G	GS	CG	SV	IP	H	HR	BB	SO	K/9	WHIP	AVG
2012	Reds (AZL)	R	0	2	5.79	7	5	0	0	14	14	1	12	13	8.4	1.86	.255
	Billings (PIO)	R	0	0	0.00	2	2	0	0	6	4	0	1	5	7.5	0.83	.211
2013	Billings (PIO)	R	1	1	2.66	5	5	0	0	24	22	0	10	17	6.5	1.35	.250
	Dayton (MWL)	LoA	1	3	6.88	8	8	0	0	34	40	4	16	15	4.0	1.65	.294
2014	Dayton (MWL)	LoA	7	8	3.65	27	27	2	0	133	115	11	51	127	8.6	1.25	.231
Minor League Totals			9	14	4.09	49	47	2	0	211	195	16	90	177	7.5	1.35	.245

8 NICK TRAVIESO, RHP

Born: Jan. 31, 1994. **B-T:** R-R. **Ht.:** 6-2. **Wt.:** 215. **Drafted:** HS—Southwest Ranches, Fla., 2012 (1st round). **Signed by:** Tony Arias/Miguel Machado.

In the case of Travieso, the Reds had an inside advantage because international scouting director Tony Arias' son Nicholas played on the same Archbishop McCarthy High club that finished No. 1 in the country their junior year in 2011 and No. 5 their senior year. Travieso's stuff picked back up at low Class A Dayton after dipping in 2013. He went back to bringing his hands over his head to begin his windup later in the season, which coincided with his best run of 2014. He sat 92-95 mph and touched 97 in a 4-0, 1.56 August. Travieso generally sat at 90-93 mph, showing a tick above-average fastball and an 84-86 mph slider. His slider flashes above-average, but like many young pitchers, he throws as many loopy breaking balls as sliders with good tilt. His below-average changeup needs refinement. Travieso likes to pitch inside, and he impressed evaluators with his competitiveness. His delivery has some effort, but it hasn't kept him from throwing strikes, and he shows the potential for average control. After spending most of the past two seasons at Dayton, Travieso likely will head to high Class A Daytona in 2015, but he's shown enough feel that if the Reds have a need at Double-A Pensacola, he could skip a level. He projects as a No. 4 starter with a chance to be a little better than that if he can improve his secondary stuff.

BA GRADE

50 Risk: High

LGE	BF	SO%	BB%	HR/9
MWL	594	19.2	7.4	0.63

Year	Club (League)	Class	W	L	ERA	G	GS	CG	SV	IP	H	HR	BB	SO	K/9	WHIP	AVG
2012	Reds (AZL)	R	0	2	4.71	8	8	0	0	21	20	3	5	14	6.0	1.19	.250
2013	Dayton (MWL)	LoA	7	4	4.63	17	17	0	0	82	83	7	27	61	6.7	1.35	.263
2014	Dayton (MWL)	LoA	14	5	3.03	26	26	1	0	143	123	10	44	114	7.2	1.17	.229
Minor League Totals			21	11	3.71	51	51	1	0	245	226	20	76	189	6.9	1.23	.242

9 ARISTIDES AQUINO, OF

Born: April 22, 1994. **B-T:** R-R. **Ht.:** 6-4. **Wt.:** 190. **Signed:** Dominican Republic, 2011. **Signed by:** Richard Jimenez.

A tall, live-bodied right fielder with a big arm who wears No. 27, Aquino models his game after Vladimir Guerrero, right down to a batting stance that begins with a bat waggle above his head. Signed for $115,000 in 2011, Aquino struggled with contact issues in his first years in the organization, but he also showed flashes of immense potential. He broke out in 2014 at Rookie-level Billings, leading the Pioneer League with 23 doubles and 64 RBIs. A student of the game, Aquino has steadily improved, learning to speak English quickly. In 2013, he could drive a fastball but was an easy mark for offspeed offerings. In his return to Billings, he showed a better ability to stay back and drive the ball to the opposite field. With long arms, Aquino shows plus power when he can extend. He uses a big leg kick that may have to be toned down as he moves up the ladder, and he doesn't like to take ball four if he sees a pitch he likes. Aquino had an average arm when he signed, but it's now a plus weapon in right field—he led PL outfielders with 13 assists— and he has grown to be an average defender. His tick above-average speed has allowed him to be a threat on the bases. Aquino is one of the Reds' most well-rounded position prospects, and if he continues to improve, he'll make noise at low Class A Dayton in 2015.

BA GRADE

55 Risk: Extreme

LGE	PA	BB%	SO%	ISO
PL	307	4.9	21.5	.285

Year	Club (League)	Class	AVG	G	AB	R	H	2B	3B	HR	RBI	BB	SO	SB	CS	OBP	SLG
2012	Reds (DSL)	R	.197	65	239	28	47	11	0	3	26	24	65	5	8	.277	.280
2013	Reds (AZL)	R	.278	46	194	37	54	15	6	4	38	10	40	4	3	.325	.479
	Billings (PIO)	R	.212	15	66	13	14	1	1	3	10	2	22	1	1	.229	.394
2014	Billings (PIO)	R	.292	71	284	48	83	23	5	16	64	15	66	21	5	.342	.577
Minor League Totals			.240	257	985	153	236	54	16	29	159	72	256	35	27	.303	.415

10 YORMAN RODRIGUEZ, OF

Born: Aug. 15, 1992. **B-T:** R-R. **Ht:** 6-3. **Wt.:** 195. **Signed:** Venezuela, 2008. **Signed by:** Tony Arias.

At an age when he could be just entering pro ball had he been born in the U.S., Rodriguez is making his seventh Prospect Handbook appearance. Signed for a then-Venezuelan amateur bonus record of $2.5 million in 2008, he missed time in 2014 with an oblique injury that muted his production when he returned, but he finished strong and made his big league debut in September. Rodriguez has long been one of the toolsiest players in the system, but his plate discipline and his maturity had to catch up to his talent. He still frustrates scouts because he'll show a tick above-average run time followed by well below-average times in his next few at-bats, but when he's locked in, he shows everything a scout wants to see. Rodriguez has started to show an improved hitting approach by learning how to take a pitch the other way and knowing when to shrink or expand his strike zone. He can play all three outfield spots, but he fits best in right field where his plus arm is an asset. In center field, his average range makes him best as a fill-in. For a player who has reached the majors, Rodriguez's future potential is highly volatile. Scouts see him as a potential fourth outfielder, but one who could turn into more than that if the light switch clicks on. He's headed to Triple-A Louisville in 2015.

	BA GRADE	
50	**Risk:** High	

LGE	PA	BB%	SO%	ISO
SL	502	9.4	23.3	.127
NL	29	3.4	41.4	.000

Year	Club (League)	Class	AVG	G	AB	R	H	2B	3B	HR	RBI	BB	SO	SB	CS	OBP	SLG
2012	Bakersfield (CAL)	HiA	.156	23	90	7	14	4	0	0	7	3	39	4	0	.181	.200
	Dayton (MWL)	LoA	.271	65	258	35	70	17	3	6	44	12	61	7	5	.307	.430
2013	Bakersfield (CAL)	HiA	.251	63	251	41	63	20	4	9	35	22	77	6	3	.319	.470
	Pensacola (SL)	AA	.267	66	262	30	70	15	2	4	31	25	76	4	0	.329	.385
2014	Pensacola (SL)	AA	.262	119	450	69	118	20	5	9	40	47	117	12	5	.331	.389
	Cincinnati (NL)	MAJ	.222	11	27	3	6	0	0	0	2	1	12	0	1	.276	.222
Major League Totals			.222	11	27	3	6	0	0	0	2	1	12	0	1	.276	.222
Minor League Totals			.260	526	2029	275	527	106	24	40	255	161	568	75	25	.315	.395

11 ALEX BLANDINO, SS

	BA GRADE	
50	**Risk:** High	

Born: Nov. 6, 1992. **B-T:** R-R. **Ht.:** 6-0. **Wt.:** 190. **Drafted:** Stanford, 2014 (1st round). **Signed by:** Rich Bordi.

Blandino is the rare case of a college third baseman who moved to shortstop in pro ball. The 2014 first-rounder, who signed for $1.788 million, spent the vast majority of his time at third base for Stanford, though he played shortstop in the Cape Cod League. As one would expect, Blandino's move to shortstop had some hiccups. He has excellent instincts, but his lack of first-step quickness limits his range. His tick above-average arm allows him to play a little deeper to mitigate some of his range issues. He projects as a fringe-average to average shortstop who many scouts think will eventually move to second or third base,. At the plate, Blandino made strides during his junior year at unlocking his power, in part by becoming more pull-happy. He uses a toe tap that sometimes turns into a leg kick to start his swing, and he swings from a wide-open stance. Blandino's power is largely pull-oriented and can lead to him selling out and over-swinging, but he has shown the ability to drive the ball the other way. Blessed with plenty of bat speed, he has the ability to be an average hitter with fringe-average power. He's a below-average runner. He'll head to high Class A Daytona for his first full season in 2015.

Year	Club (League)	Class	AVG	G	AB	R	H	2B	3B	HR	RBI	BB	SO	SB	CS	OBP	SLG
2014	Billings (PIO)	R	.309	29	110	20	34	10	1	4	16	16	18	6	3	.412	.527
	Dayton (MWL)	LoA	.261	34	134	20	35	10	1	4	16	13	42	1	2	.329	.440
Minor League Totals			.283	63	244	40	69	20	2	8	32	29	60	7	5	.367	.480

12 BEN LIVELY, RHP

	BA GRADE	
45	**Risk:** Medium	

Born: March 5, 1992. **B-T:** R-R. **Ht.:** 6-4. **Wt.:** 190. **Drafted:** Central Florida, 2013 (4th round). **Signed by:** Greg Zunino.

When the Reds sent Lively to high Class A Bakersfield to begin 2014, they considered it an aggressive assignment. Lively went 5-0, 0.31 in April with a 40-to-1 strikeout-to-walk ratio and forced a promotion to Double-A Pensacola by June. Lively's success is based on a delivery that emphasizes deception over velocity. He gets excellent extension, but even more importantly, he keeps the ball behind his body during his takeaway and continues to keep it hidden behind his head from the batter's perspective until very late. His 88-92 mph fastball generates swings and misses up in the zone thanks in part to riding life. He shows a fringe-average curve that he uses as a get-me-over strike early in counts, then follows it up with a chase slider that is an average pitch. His changeup became more important in Double-A. He showed some feel for it, and it projects as an average pitch as well. Lively's deception and ability to pitch to all four corners of the zone give him more possible outcomes than most pitchers with no above-average pitch. He profiles at best as a No. 4 starter. He'll head to Triple-A Louisville in 2015.

Year	Club (League)	Class	W	L	ERA	G	GS	CG	SV	IP	H	HR	BB	SO	K/9	WHIP	AVG
2013	Billings (PIO)	R	0	3	0.73	12	12	0	0	37	21	0	12	49	11.9	0.89	.163
	Dayton (MWL)	LoA	0	1	2.25	1	1	0	0	4	2	0	1	7	15.8	0.75	.143
2014	Bakersfield (CAL)	HiA	10	1	2.28	13	13	0	0	79	57	6	16	95	10.8	0.92	.201
	Pensacola (SL)	AA	3	6	3.88	13	13	0	0	72	60	7	36	76	9.5	1.33	.232
Minor League Totals			13	11	2.58	39	39	0	0	192	140	13	65	227	10.6	1.07	.204

13 KYLE WALDROP, OF

BA GRADE
50 Risk: High

Born: Nov. 26, 1991. **B-T:** L-L. **Ht.:** 6-2. **Wt.:** 216. **Drafted:** HS—Fort Myers, Fla., 2010 (12th round). **Signed by:** Greg Zunino.

The Reds' most pleasant surprise in 2014 was the development of Waldrop at Double-A Pensacola. A former high school football player who had flashed potential in the past, sandwiched around a number of injuries, Waldrop dominated the high Class A California League and, more importantly, did the same thing after a midseason promotion to the Southern League and then in the Arizona Fall League. Waldrop has to hit because he's a fringe-average defensive left fielder without the speed (he's an average runner) or arm strength (a 40 on the 20-to-80 scouting scale) to handle another outfield spot. In the past, Waldrop had been a pull hitter who would succumb to good pitching but destroyed mistakes, but in 2014 he started using the whole field much better and stopped chasing as much. A bit of Waldrop's power melted away in the process, but it was a solid trade-off, for he now shows the potential to become an above-average hitter with still solid-average power. He and Jesse Winker are competing for the same spot in the Reds' future lineup because neither fits in right field. Added to the 40-man roster in November, Waldrop could make himself a candidate for Triple-A Louisville in 2015 with a strong spring.

Year	Club (League)	Class	AVG	G	AB	R	H	2B	3B	HR	RBI	BB	SO	SB	CS	OBP	SLG
2012	Dayton (MWL)	LoA	.284	117	416	59	118	21	6	8	50	38	77	10	6	.346	.421
2013	Bakersfield (CAL)	HiA	.258	129	504	66	130	32	4	21	54	32	121	20	8	.304	.462
2014	Bakersfield (CAL)	HiA	.359	65	256	54	92	20	1	6	32	22	56	11	2	.409	.516
	Pensacola (SL)	AA	.315	66	232	27	73	17	3	8	35	17	44	3	4	.359	.517
Minor League Totals			.289	452	1714	245	495	113	23	48	201	120	372	48	24	.337	.466

14 PHILLIP ERVIN, OF

BA GRADE
50 Risk: High

Born: July 17, 1992. **B-T:** R-R. **Ht.:** 5-11. **Wt.:** 190. **Drafted:** Samford, 2013 (1st round). **Signed by:** Ben Jones.

Ervin entered pro ball with a track record for hitting, but perceptions can change quickly when a 21-year-old, first-round college outfielder hits .237/.305/.376. While Ervin's full-season debut in 2014 was a disaster, scouts still saw flashes. His approach, contact skills and power were all less than advertised, however. Instead of dominating younger competition, Ervin looked overmatched. He had a wrist problem early in the year which helped lead to his slow start, but even when he was fully healthy, he got into a yank-and-pray approach that left him vulnerable to almost anything other than a fastball on the inner half. Injuries have been a recurring problem for Ervin, who hasn't been healthy for a full year in any of the past five seasons. The Reds have to hope a fresh start will allow him to return to the all-field approach he showed in college and at Rookie-level Billings in 2013. Among the encouraging signs for Ervin in 2014 were above-average speed and improved range and reads in center field, where he projects as at least a fringe-average defender. He'll head to high Class A Daytona in 2015.

Year	Club (League)	Class	AVG	G	AB	R	H	2B	3B	HR	RBI	BB	SO	SB	CS	OBP	SLG
2013	Billings (PIO)	R	.326	34	129	27	42	9	1	8	29	17	24	12	0	.416	.597
	Dayton (MWL)	LoA	.349	12	43	7	15	2	0	1	6	8	10	2	1	.451	.465
2014	Dayton (MWL)	LoA	.237	132	498	68	118	34	7	7	68	46	110	30	5	.305	.376
Minor League Totals			.261	178	670	102	175	45	8	16	103	71	144	44	6	.336	.424

15 SAL ROMANO, RHP

BA GRADE
50 Risk: High

Born: Oct. 12, 1993. **B-T:** L-R. **Ht.:** 6-4. **Wt.:** 220. **Drafted:** HS—Southington, Conn., 2011 (23rd round). **Signed by:** Lee Seras.

Romano had to catch up to the speed of pro competition, but in 2014 the righthander showed signs that he's doing just that. He made big strides with his control by keeping his lower half in sync in his delivery more consistently. While his massive frame doesn't leave room for projection, Romano can run his four-seamer up to 97 mph, but he pitches best when he's pounding the bottom of the zone with 91-94 sinking two-seamers. His power curveball flashes plus and would be even more effective if he landed it for a strike more often. To remain a starter, Romano must improve his well below-average changeup and continue to hone his control. Romano's two-pitch mix may eventually relegate him to the pen, but he could end up a No. 4 or 5 starter. Up next: high Class A Daytona in 2015.

Year	Club (League)	Class	W	L	ERA	G	GS	CG	SV	IP	H	HR	BB	SO	K/9	WHIP	AVG
2012	Billings (PIO)	R	5	6	5.32	15	15	0	0	64	74	1	23	52	7.3	1.51	.288
2013	Dayton (MWL)	LoA	7	11	4.86	25	25	0	0	120	134	10	57	89	6.7	1.59	.291
2014	Dayton (MWL)	LoA	8	11	4.12	28	28	0	0	149	169	9	42	128	7.7	1.42	.288
Minor League Totals			20	28	4.62	68	68	0	0	333	377	20	122	269	7.3	1.50	.289

16 JONATHON CRAWFORD, RHP

BA GRADE **50** Risk: High

Born: Nov. 1, 1991. **B-T:** R-R. **Ht.:** 6-2. **Wt.:** 205. **Drafted:** Florida, 2013 (1st round). **Signed by:** Jimmy Rough (Tigers).

Crawford stood out in a 2013 draft thin on college starters, pushing the Tigers to draft him at No. 20 overall and sign him for $2,001,700. The Reds landed him and shortstop Eugenio Suarez in the December Alfredo Simon trade. Crawford has a strong, athletic build and a plus fastball that sits at 90-94 mph with good sinking movement and touches 96. When he's at his best, he also shows a plus slider at 83-86 mph, but the breaking ball is the biggest wild card. When his slider is biting, he's tough to hit and has an out pitch to put hitters away. When the slider is off, it allows hitters to sit on his fastball. He flashes a changeup, but it's below-average. Crawford's short-arm delivery features effort. With his two-pitch mix, Crawford fits best as a reliever for some scouts, though if he can bring along his changeup, he has a chance to be a mid-rotation starter. He has a shot to jump to Double-A Pensacola with new club.

Year	Club (League)	Class	W	L	ERA	G	GS	CG	SV	IP	H	HR	BB	SO	K/9	WHIP	AVG
2013	Connecticut (NYP)	SS	0	2	1.89	8	8	0	0	19	15	0	9	21	9.9	1.26	.205
2014	West Michigan (MWL)	LoA	8	3	2.85	23	23	0	0	123	93	3	50	85	6.2	1.16	.220
Minor League Totals			8	5	2.73	31	31	0	0	142	108	3	59	106	6.7	1.18	.218

17 GAVIN LAVALLEY, 3B/1B

BA GRADE **50** Risk: High

Born: Dec. 28, 1994. **B-T:** R-R. **Ht.:** 6-3. **Wt.:** 235. **Drafted:** HS— Midwest City, Okla., 2014 (4th round). **Signed by:** Mike Keenan.

Getting a good feel on Oklahoma prep hitters isn't easy because they get to beat up on poor pitching. A two-sport star in high school, LaValley was an all-state offensive guard who dominated on the baseball diamond. He slimmed down for baseball season and should melt away more weight. LaValley has excellent bat speed and an advanced, all-field hitting approach that gives him a chance to both hit for average and produce at least average productive power. For his size, he showed nimble feet and a tick above-average arm. The Reds will let him continue to play third base for now, but scouts see him moving to first before long, as he lacks range. He's a well below-average runner. LaValley is one of the more advanced high school hitters the Reds have drafted in recent years. He could make the jump to low Class A Dayton in 2015.

Year	Club (League)	Class	AVG	G	AB	R	H	2B	3B	HR	RBI	BB	SO	SB	CS	OBP	SLG
2014	Reds (AZL)	R	.286	54	189	29	54	10	2	5	30	26	44	3	0	.374	.439
	Billings (PIO)	R	.190	5	21	2	4	0	0	1	2	0	10	0	0	.227	.333
Minor League Totals			.276	59	210	31	58	10	2	6	32	26	54	3	0	.361	.429

18 TAYLOR SPARKS, 3B

BA GRADE **50** Risk: Extreme

Born: April 3, 1993. **B-T:** R-R. **Ht.:** 6-4. **Wt.:** 200. **Drafted:** UC Irvine, 2014 (2nd round). **Signed by:** Mike Misuraca.

A 2014 second-rounder who helped UC Irvine reach the College World Series, Sparks is an outstanding athlete who plays a well above-average third base, with excellent range, outstanding body control, a quick first step and a strong arm. He's an above-average runner has plus raw power. If he could develop even an average hit tool, he could end up as an above-average big league regular. Sparks, whose father Don played nine seasons in pro ball, falls short of profiling as even an average hitter because his swing is not conducive to making consistent contact. He struck out 154 times in 2014 between college and pro ball. His other tools will earn him playing time, starting at low Class A Dayton in 2015, to correct his flaw.

Year	Club (League)	Class	AVG	G	AB	R	H	2B	3B	HR	RBI	BB	SO	SB	CS	OBP	SLG
2014	Billings (PIO)	R	.232	55	198	41	46	7	7	10	30	31	84	14	1	.350	.490
Minor League Totals			.232	55	198	41	46	7	7	10	30	31	84	14	1	.350	.490

19 TUCKER BARNHART, C

BA GRADE

40 Risk: Safe

Born: Jan. 7, 1991. **B-T:** R-R. **Ht.:** 5-10. **Wt.:** 185. **Drafted:** HS— Brownsburg, Ind., 2009 (10th round). **Signed by:** Rick Sellers.

Barnhart made his big league debut in 2014, filling in when Devin Mesoraco missed time with hamstring and oblique injuries. He performed as advertised. Barnhart won't ever hit enough to be a regular, especially because of the switch-hitter's long-running trouble with lefthanders. Hitting righthanded, Barnhart has a slow swing with no power, which explains why he's hit .153/.221/.186 against southpaws over the past four years. From the left side, he's much better. He still has no power, but he makes contact, sprays singles and draws walks. Defensively, Barnhart's plus, accurate arm helped him throw out 8 of 12 basestealers (66 percent) at the big league level. He calls a good game, and pitchers like throwing to him, but he needs to work on his pitch-framing skills. He'll compete with Brayan Pena for the backup job.

Year	Club (League)	Class	AVG	G	AB	R	H	2B	3B	HR	RBI	BB	SO	SB	CS	OBP	SLG
2012	Bakersfield (CAL)	HiA	.278	59	198	26	55	12	1	4	22	29	45	0	2	.371	.409
	Pensacola (SL)	AA	.200	41	130	10	26	4	1	2	12	11	22	1	1	.262	.292
2013	Pensacola (SL)	AA	.260	98	339	31	88	19	1	3	44	45	57	1	0	.348	.348
2014	Louisville (IL)	AAA	.246	78	256	18	63	9	3	1	29	28	34	0	1	.319	.316
	Cincinnati (NL)	MAJ	.185	21	54	3	10	0	0	1	1	4	10	0	0	.241	.241
Major League Totals			.185	21	54	3	10	0	0	1	1	4	10	0	0	.241	.241
Minor League Totals			.259	422	1408	154	365	79	8	13	168	174	251	8	6	.341	.354

20 JON MOSCOT, RHP

BA GRADE

45 Risk: Low

Born: Aug. 15, 1991. **B-T:** R-R. **Ht.:** 6-4. **Wt.:** 205. **Drafted:** Pepperdine, 2012 (4th round). **Signed by:** Rex de la Nuez.

Based on pure stuff, Moscot has more potential than Ben Lively, his Double-A Pensacola rotation-mate in 2014. Both righthanders lack a true plus pitch, but they succeed because they can throw three pitches for strikes at any point in the count. Moscot, a fourth-rounder from Pepperdine in 2012, has a touch more velocity on his fastball than Lively. He sits 89-92 mph with some cut and tail to his fastball, but he doesn't generate nearly as many swings and misses as Lively because he lacks the same deception. Moscot has above-average control that allows him to locate his potentially average slider and changeup. He has a big, durable frame. He heads to Triple-A Louisville, with a long-term future as a potential No. 5 starter.

Year	Club (League)	Class	W	L	ERA	G	GS	CG	SV	IP	H	HR	BB	SO	K/9	WHIP	AVG
2012	Reds (AZL)	R	0	1	0.00	2	1	0	0	2	3	0	5	1	3.9	3.43	.273
	Billings (PIO)	R	0	1	2.88	10	10	0	0	25	19	2	6	26	9.4	1.00	.213
2013	Bakersfield (CAL)	HiA	2	14	4.59	22	22	0	0	116	109	17	36	112	8.7	1.25	.247
	Pensacola (SL)	AA	2	1	3.19	6	6	0	0	31	34	3	12	28	8.1	1.48	.281
2014	Pensacola (SL)	AA	7	10	3.13	25	25	2	0	149	145	11	43	111	6.7	1.26	.255
	Louisville (IL)	AAA	1	1	5.71	3	3	0	0	17	15	5	7	9	4.7	1.27	.224
Minor League Totals			12	28	3.73	68	67	2	0	341	325	38	109	287	7.6	1.27	.251

21 DAVID HOLMBERG, LHP

BA GRADE

40 Risk: Low

Born: July 19, 1991. **B-T:** R-L. **Ht.:** 6-3. **Wt.:** 225. **Drafted:** HS—Port Charlotte, Fla., 2009 (2nd round). **Signed by:** Joe Siers (White Sox).

Holmberg didn't exactly make a great first impression following his trade to the Reds (for Ryan Hanigan) in December 2013. He showed up to spring training in poor shape and had to work his way into better condition during the season. Shelled in a pair of emergency starts, Holmberg did a much better job during a September callup. He intrigued evaluators when he was dominating hitters in low Class A thanks to a plus changeup, but scouts even then were wary of his lack of fastball velocity. It's a below-average 87-89 mph offering. Holmberg's fringy curveball forces him to rely on his changeup heavily. He walked very few batters in the low minors, but he has seen his walk rate soar as he neared the majors. That's not because he's lost his feel for throwing strikes; his lack of stuff forces him to nibble. Holmberg profiles as a useful depth option for the Reds to stash at Triple-A for spot-starter work.

Year	Club (League)	Class	W	L	ERA	G	GS	CG	SV	IP	H	HR	BB	SO	K/9	WHIP	AVG
2012	Visalia (CAL)	HiA	6	3	2.99	12	12	0	0	78	62	6	14	86	9.9	0.97	.214
	Mobile (SL)	AA	5	5	3.60	15	15	0	0	95	104	8	23	67	6.3	1.34	.281
2013	Arizona (NL)	MAJ	0	0	7.36	1	1	0	0	4	6	0	3	0	0.0	2.45	.375
	Mobile (SL)	AA	5	8	2.75	26	26	1	0	157	138	12	50	116	6.6	1.19	.239
2014	Louisville (IL)	AAA	2	6	4.66	18	18	0	0	93	119	4	33	56	5.4	1.64	.316
	Cincinnati (NL)	MAJ	2	2	4.80	7	5	0	0	30	27	8	16	18	5.4	1.43	.243
Major League Totals			2	2	5.08	8	6	0	0	34	33	8	19	18	4.8	1.54	.260
Minor League Totals			34	38	3.57	127	120	2	0	695	700	47	202	595	7.7	1.30	.261

22 SETH MEJIAS-BREAN, 3B

BA GRADE

45 Risk: High

Born: April 5, 1991. **B-T:** R-R. **Ht.:** 6-2. **Wt.:** 210. **Drafted:** Arizona, 2012 (8th round). **Signed by:** Clark Crist.

Mejias-Brean is the kind of unassuming player who may end up with a lengthy big league career. The most optimistic scouts see him as a potential everyday third baseman, but most see him as a backup corner bat. Mejias-Brean's swing does not generate much loft, so it's hard to project him as hitting more than 10 or so home runs a year, but he understands the strike zone and at his best draws a lot of walks to go with a hit tool that is at least average. Mejias-Brean's plus arm is his best asset defensively, but he also has quick reactions and athleticism. He will return to Double-A Pensacola in 2015 to prove he's better than his late Southern League slump.

Year	Club (League)	Class	AVG	G	AB	R	H	2B	3B	HR	RBI	BB	SO	SB	CS	OBP	SLG
2012	Billings (PIO)	R	.313	46	179	35	56	12	2	8	40	21	29	6	0	.389	.536
2013	Dayton (MWL)	LoA	.305	127	479	70	146	35	3	10	79	55	83	3	2	.381	.453
	Bakersfield (CAL)	HiA	.308	3	13	3	4	1	0	1	3	0	0	1	0	.308	.615
2014	Bakersfield (CAL)	HiA	.300	69	267	56	80	8	3	11	45	44	49	7	1	.396	.476
	Pensacola (SL)	AA	.235	65	226	23	53	7	2	3	22	32	50	1	4	.333	.323
Minor League Totals			.291	310	1164	187	339	63	10	33	189	152	211	18	7	.376	.448

23 WYATT STRAHAN, RHP

BA GRADE

45 Risk: High

Born: April 18, 1993. **B-T:** R-R. **Ht.:** 6-3. **Wt.:** 190. **Drafted:** Southern California, 2014 (3rd round). **Signed by:** Rex De La Nuez.

Coming into his junior year, Strahan looked nearly undraftable because he had walked more batters than he had struck out. But he managed to improve both his stuff and control in 2014. Strahan can generate swings and misses with his four-seam fastball at 94-96 mph up in the zone, but he's at his best when he's throwing his two-seamer at 92-93 with above-average sink. He mixes a slow, early-count curveball for a strike and a harder curve that is a two-strike chase pitch that flashes plus. His changeup is a below-average but useable pitch. Strahan's upright delivery isn't free and easy, and he finishes with pronounced recoil. Some scouts see a future power reliever, but the Reds will let Strahan start at low Class A Dayton.

Year	Club (League)	Class	W	L	ERA	G	GS	CG	SV	IP	H	HR	BB	SO	K/9	WHIP	AVG
2014	Billings (PIO)	R	0	3	2.76	14	14	0	0	42	48	0	12	40	8.5	1.42	.277
Minor League Totals			0	3	2.76	14	14	0	0	42	48	0	12	40	8.5	1.42	.277

24 JUNIOR ARIAS, OF

50 Risk: Extreme

Born: Jan. 9, 1992. **B-T:** R-R. **Ht.:** 6-1. **Wt.:** 200. **Signed:** Dominican Republic, 2008. **Signed by:** Richard Jimenez.

Arias has as much talent as any position player in the system, but his career has moved at a very slow pace. After trying and failing to handle shortstop and third base, he adapted much better to center field. Arias missed almost the entire 2014 season after breaking his leg sliding into third base on April 11. He made it back to Bakersfield midway through August, played with the Reds' advanced instructional league team and then headed to the Dominican Republic for winter ball. He has above-average raw power, but he expands the zone too much. He's an above-average runner and has an above-average arm that plays in right field, but he has the speed and range to be a fringe-average center fielder as well. After six pro seasons, he needs to make it to Double-A Pensacola and prove he can handle more advanced pitchers.

Year	Club (League)	Class	AVG	G	AB	R	H	2B	3B	HR	RBI	BB	SO	SB	CS	OBP	SLG
2012	Dayton (MWL)	LoA	.208	97	361	52	75	11	3	7	35	20	96	28	7	.255	.313
2013	Dayton (MWL)	LoA	.284	72	271	45	77	12	4	10	33	13	72	40	10	.323	.469
	Bakersfield (CAL)	HiA	.257	53	222	30	57	12	2	5	20	5	60	20	10	.283	.396
2014	Reds (AZL)	R	.167	12	36	4	6	1	0	0	0	9	14	6	0	.333	.194
	Bakersfield (CAL)	HiA	.271	17	70	15	19	2	0	3	10	5	18	9	3	.338	.429
Minor League Totals			.248	414	1582	270	393	73	19	45	180	102	458	124	44	.302	.404

25 SEBASTIAN ELIZALDE, OF

BA GRADE

45 Risk: High

Born: Nov. 20, 1991. **B-T:** L-R. **Ht.:** 6-0. **Wt.:** 175. **Signed:** Mexico, 2013. **Signed by:** Tony Arias.

Signed out of Mexico during the 2013 season, Elizalde had Tommy John surgery after signing, forcing him to wait until 2014 to make his U.S. debut. He showed an excellent understanding of the game both between the lines and in the clubhouse, where his experience playing with veterans in the Mexican League was apparent. A plus runner when he signed, Elizalde dealt with hamstring problems and generally graded as a fringe-average runner in 2014. His best-case scenario is as a top-of-the-order hitter with on-base skills, but more realistically he'll be a fourth outfielder who can play above-average defense in either outfield corner—he has an average, accurate arm—or can play center field in a pinch.

Year	Club (League)	Class	AVG	G	AB	R	H	2B	3B	HR	RBI	BB	SO	SB	CS	OBP	SLG
2012	Monterrey (MEX)	AAA	.276	74	134	25	37	9	4	2	14	15	37	7	3	.351	.448
2013	Monterrey (MEX)	AAA	.328	36	116	24	38	5	0	3	10	5	22	5	3	.361	.448
2014	Dayton (MWL)	LoA	.311	55	183	29	57	12	1	7	34	41	48	9	10	.439	.503
	Bakersfield (CAL)	HiA	.272	66	243	35	66	17	1	9	37	19	44	10	7	.330	.461
Minor League Totals			.294	268	715	122	210	46	6	22	100	82	157	31	23	.369	.467

26 TYLER MAHLE, RHP

BA GRADE

45 Risk: High

Born: Sept. 29, 1994. **B-T:** R-R. **Ht.:** 6-2. **Wt.:** 175. **Drafted:** HS— Westminster, Calif., 2013 (7th round). **Signed by:** Mike Misuraca.

Mahle is the kind of pitcher who often makes it to college as scouts wait to see if he matures as they project. The Reds decided to take a chance on his potential and paid him $250,000 as a seventh-rounder in 2013 to bypass UC Santa Barbara, where his brother Greg (drafted by the Angels in 2014) played. Mahle has skinny legs and a lanky frame, and his future depends a lot on whether he can add a tick to his fastball as he matures and gain strength. He had immediate success at Rookie-level Billings in 2014 because of his excellent control, finishing second in the Pioneer League with a 3.87 ERA. Mahle currently pitches at 88-92 mph, so he does have an average fastball on his better nights, but there's not any plus pitch in his assortment. His 11-to-5, slow curveball and slider both vary between below-average and average, and he has an average changeup. If he gains velocity, then his clean delivery and above-average control give him a chance to be a back-end starter as he embarks on an assignment to low Class A Dayton in 2015.

Year	Club (League)	Class	W	L	ERA	G	GS	CG	SV	IP	H	HR	BB	SO	K/9	WHIP	AVG
2013	Reds (AZL)	R	1	3	2.36	12	4	0	0	34	32	0	8	30	7.9	1.17	.237
2014	Billings (PIO)	R	5	4	3.87	15	15	2	0	77	80	5	15	71	8.3	1.24	.263
Minor League Totals			6	7	3.41	27	19	2	0	111	112	5	23	101	8.2	1.22	.255

27 CHAD WALLACH, C

BA GRADE

45 Risk: High

Born: Nov. 4, 1991. **B-T:** R-R. **Ht:** 6-3. **Wt.:** 215. **Drafted:** Cal State Fullerton, 2013 (5th round). **Signed by:** Tim McDonnell (Marlins).

The son of big leaguer Tim Wallach, Chad has been around the game all his life and it shows. The Cal State Fullerton product brings all the intangibles and physical tools teams want in a catcher. Selected by the Marlins in the fifth round of the 2013 draft, Wallach turned in a disappointing pro debut offensively at short-season Batavia in 2013, but he reworked his swing for 2014 and hit .321/.430/.476 at low Class A Greensboro. He joined the Reds organization in December as part of the Mat Latos trade. Wallach doesn't figure to hit for much power, instead relying on a more controlled swing to drive balls into the gaps, particularly right-center field. One of the seven homers Wallach did hit came off of Nationals top prospect Lucas Giolito. Defensively, he has improved and now clocks average pop times on throws to second base. He showed good game-calling skills and worked well with the staff at Greensboro. The big-framed Wallach will have to stay on top of his condition to maximize his durability and remain agile behind the plate. He moves well for his size and does a good job knocking down balls in the dirt, but he has had some trouble handling plus stuff. He'll head to high Class A Daytona for his Reds debut in 2015.

Year	Club (League)	Class	AVG	G	AB	R	H	2B	3B	HR	RBI	BB	SO	SB	CS	OBP	SLG
2013	Batavia (NYP)	SS	.226	43	146	19	33	6	0	0	13	11	27	0	0	.294	.267
2014	Jupiter (FSL)	HiA	.328	19	64	4	21	3	0	0	8	12	7	0	0	.436	.375
	Greensboro (SAL)	LoA	.321	78	271	50	87	19	1	7	49	50	39	3	0	.430	.476
Minor League Totals			.293	140	481	73	141	28	1	7	70	73	73	3	0	.392	.399

28 DONALD LUTZ, 1B/OF

BA GRADE

40 Risk: Medium

Born: Feb. 6, 1989. **B-T:** L-R. **Ht.:** 6-3. **Wt.:** 235. **Signed:** Germany, 2007. **Signed by:** Jim Stoeckel.

When Joey Votto missed much of 2014 with a series of injuries, Lutz stood as the logical replacement. The Reds looked past him, though, and chose backup catcher Brayan Pena. Even with the Reds out of the playoff race, Lutz served only as a pinch-hitter. He's a power hitter with a long, high-maintenance swing who struggles without regular at-bats, so his big league role was the worst use of his talents. He has been granted a fourth minor league option year, which gives the Reds one more year to evaluate him. The massive Lutz is an fringe-average runner, but he's below-average defensively in left field or at first base, which played a part in him not getting regular big league time. He has the power to produce 20-plus home runs, but his defense and his below-average hit tool will likely preclude him from an everyday big league job.

Year	Club (League)	Class	AVG	G	AB	R	H	2B	3B	HR	RBI	BB	SO	SB	CS	OBP	SLG
2012	Reds (AZL)	R	.643	4	14	3	9	2	2	0	5	3	4	0	0	.706	1.071
	Bakersfield (CAL)	HiA	.265	63	253	42	67	18	3	17	51	19	71	7	2	.325	.561
	Pensacola (SL)	AA	.242	40	149	17	36	5	1	5	15	13	32	1	3	.315	.389
2013	Cincinnati (NL)	MAJ	.241	34	58	5	14	1	0	1	8	1	14	2	0	.254	.310
	Pensacola (SL)	AA	.245	65	229	35	56	12	4	7	30	19	56	4	1	.318	.424
2014	Pensacola (SL)	AA	.360	23	89	16	32	7	2	6	16	7	17	1	0	.412	.685
	Louisville (IL)	AAA	.236	52	195	26	46	9	2	6	33	17	68	4	0	.307	.395
	Cincinnati (NL)	MAJ	.176	28	51	2	9	4	0	0	1	3	19	0	0	.222	.255
Major League Totals			.211	62	109	7	23	5	0	1	9	4	33	2	0	.239	.284
Minor League Totals			.273	475	1764	291	481	96	23	70	282	147	453	34	14	.338	.472

29 JEREMY KIVEL, RHP

BA GRADE

45 Risk: High

Born: Oct. 16, 1993. **B-T:** R-R. **Ht.:** 6-1. **Wt.:** 200. **Drafted:** HS—Spring, Texas, 2012 (10th round). **Signed by:** Bryan Ewing.

When the Reds selected Kivel in the 10th round of the 2012 draft, they knew they were getting a big arm they could dream on. But that dream always carried a lot of risk, and so far Kivel's control issues have kept him from tapping into his potential. The Reds decided to shift him to the bullpen, giving up the idea of developing him as a starter. Out of the pen, Kivel's fastball jumped back up to the 94-96 mph he showed early in his pro debut. His delivery and mentality never seemed to fit as a starter. He's an aggressive power pitcher with below-average control. The Reds hope that the move to the bullpen will help him throw more strikes as he simplifies to a power approach with his plus fastball and fringe-average slider.

Year	Club (League)	Class	W	L	ERA	G	GS	CG	SV	IP	H	HR	BB	SO	K/9	WHIP	AVG
2012	Did not play—Injured																
2013	Reds (AZL)	R	0	2	3.91	13	12	0	0	51	50	4	23	56	9.9	1.44	.249
2014	Billings (PIO)	R	1	4	5.31	13	9	0	0	41	54	4	21	44	9.7	1.84	.312
Minor League Totals			1	6	4.53	26	21	0	0	91	104	8	44	100	9.9	1.62	.278

30 CARLOS CONTRERAS, RHP

BA GRADE

45 Risk: High

Born: Jan. 8, 1991. **B-T:** R-R. **Ht.:** 5-11. **Wt.:** 205. **Signed:** Dominican Republic, 2008. **Signed by:** Richard Jimenez.

Contreras has long possessed one of the better arms in the Reds system. Used as a power reliever early in his career, he moved to the rotation in 2013, but after he went on the Double-A Pensacola disabled list last season with back spasms, he moved back to the bullpen when he returned. By late June, he was working out of the big league bullpen. His big league debut was a struggle because his always-shaky control fell apart with a tighter big league strike zone. Contreras has a long arm path that hinders his control. He has a 92-94 mph fastball, a fringe-average changeup he uses against lefties and a below-average slider he spots against righthanders. Contreras' stuff is good enough to retire big league hitters if he throws strikes, but he has yet to prove he can do that. If he doesn't improve his control, he'll be stuck at Triple-A Louisville, where he could begin 2015.

Year	Club (League)	Class	W	L	ERA	G	GS	CG	SV	IP	H	HR	BB	SO	K/9	WHIP	AVG
2012	Dayton (MWL)	LoA	0	1	3.20	40	0	0	16	51	29	6	19	51	9.1	0.95	.158
	Bakersfield (CAL)	HiA	1	0	2.70	9	0	0	4	10	9	1	5	12	10.8	1.40	.225
2013	Bakersfield (CAL)	HiA	5	7	3.80	18	18	0	0	90	70	9	41	96	9.6	1.23	.215
	Pensacola (SL)	AA	3	2	2.76	8	8	0	0	42	36	2	21	26	5.5	1.35	.238
2014	Pensacola (SL)	AA	2	1	2.70	9	3	0	0	20	15	0	11	27	12.2	1.30	.195
	Cincinnati (NL)	MAJ	0	1	6.52	17	0	0	0	19	19	2	17	19	8.8	1.86	.250
Major League Totals			0	1	6.52	17	0	0	0	19	19	2	17	19	8.8	1.86	.250
Minor League Totals			19	21	4.46	143	47	0	22	376	317	37	196	355	8.5	1.37	.228

Cleveland Indians

BY JIM SHONERD

Though the Indians missed out on an encore playoff appearance, they showed in 2014 that they shouldn't be fading from the conversation either.

A poor April ultimately doomed Cleveland's postseason aspirations, but they did play well enough the rest of the way to finish 85-77, marking the first time the franchise has had back-to-back winning seasons since its 1995-2001 heyday. Righthander Corey Kluber and outfielder Michael Brantley enjoyed breakout years, the former winning the Cy Young Award by going 18-9, 2.44 with 269 strikeouts while Brantley hit .327 with 20 homers and 23 steals.

Brantley and Kluber were both trade acquisitions, as were several of the Indians' other significant contributors. Still, the farm system had its fingerprints on the team's success as well.

Third baseman Lonnie Chisenhall, Cleveland's first-round pick in 2008, enjoyed his best offensive season, hitting .280 with 13 homers. Rookie Jose Ramirez took over the everyday shortstop role down the stretch after the Indians traded Asdrubal Cabrera to the Nationals.

Homegrown arms Cody Allen and Kyle Crockett, the first 2013 draftee to reach the majors, played key roles in the bullpen, while lefty T.J. House, a big-money high school signee back in 2008, finally broke through to the big leagues and gave the rotation a boost by going 5-3, 3.35 in 102 innings.

Whether Kluber and Brantley's big 2014 seasons end up being anomalies is a question that will have to be answered, but the Indians do appear set to remain competitive.

Most of the team's core is on the right side of 30—Nick Swisher, at age 33, was Cleveland's oldest regular in 2014—led by Brantley (27), Chisenhall (26), Gomes (27), Santana (28) and second baseman Jason Kipnis (27), who had a disappointing season but is still just a year removed from being an all-star in 2013.

Top prospect Francisco Lindor, a shortstop, should make the leap to the majors at some point in 2015, and the Indians have a strong crop of position players in the pipeline they can continue to build around. Along with Lindor, they have other quality hitters in the upper minors like shortstop Erik Gonzalez and outfielders Tyler Naquin and James Ramsey, the latter a trade acquisition from the Cardinals for Justin Masterson.

Taking advantage of owning three of the first 40 picks in the 2014 draft, the Indians added a pair of impact college bats, San Francisco's Bradley Zimmer (21st overall) and Virginia's Mike Papi

Corey Kluber was one of four imported prospects that starred for the Indians in 2014

TOP PROSPECTS OF THE DECADE

Year	Player, Pos.	2014 Org
2005	Adam Miller, rhp	Indians
2006	Adam Miller, rhp	Indians
2007	Adam Miller, rhp	Indians
2008	Adam Miller, rhp	Indians
2009	Carlos Santana, c	Indians
2010	Carlos Santana, c	Indians
2011	Lonnie Chisenhall, 3b	Indians
2012	Francisco Lindor, ss	Indians
2013	Francisco Lindor, ss	Indians
2014	Francisco Lindor, ss	Indians

(38th), both of whom could move through the system quickly.

Though the Indians turned to the college ranks for Zimmer with their top 2014 pick, they have largely gotten away from their tendency to lean on collegians at the top of the draft, starting with when they took Lindor in the first round in 2011. Looking at their track record, it's easy to see why.

The Indians took college or junior college players with their top pick every year from 2002-10, and only one of those players, Chisenhall, has made any meaningful impact in Cleveland, though at least righthander Jeremy Guthrie (2002) has found success elsewhere. In 2014, the Indians signed more high school players (nine) than any American League team, highlighted by No. 31 overall pick Justus Sheffield.

General manager: Chris Antonetti. **Farm director:** Ross Atkins. **Scouting director:** Brad Grant.

Class	Team	League	W	L	PCT	Finish	Manager
Majors	Cleveland Indians	American	85	77	.525	12th (30)	Terry Francona
Triple-A	Columbus Clippers	International	79	65	.549	t-2nd (14)	Chris Tremie
Double-A	Akron RubberDucks	Eastern	73	69	.514	t-4th (12)	David Wallace
High Class A	Carolina Mudcats*	Carolina	62	74	.456	7th (8)	Scooter Tucker
Low Class A	Lake County Captains	Midwest	65	74	.469	11th (16)	Mark Budzinski
Short-season	Mahoning Valley Scrappers	New York-Penn	33	42	.440	11th (14)	Ted Kubiak
Rookie	AZL Indians	Arizona	37	16	.698	1st (13)	Anthony Medrano
Overall 2014 Minor League Record			349	340	.507	15th (30)	

*Affiliate will be Lynchburg (Carolina) in 2015.

THIS YEAR'S TOP 30

No.	Player, Pos.	Grade
1.	Francisco Lindor, ss	65/Low
2.	Bradley Zimmer, of	60/Medium
3.	Clint Frazier, of	60/High
4.	Justus Sheffield, lhp	60/High
5.	Mike Papi, of/1b	55/Medium
6.	Tyler Naquin, of	50/Medium
7.	Francisco Mejia, c	55/Extreme
8.	Erik Gonzalez, ss	45/Low
9.	Bobby Bradley, 1b	50/High
10.	Cody Anderson, rhp	45/Medium
11.	Giovanny Urshela, 3b	45/Medium
12.	James Ramsey, of	45/Medium
13.	Yu-Cheng Chang, ss/3b	55/Extreme
14.	Mitch Brown, rhp	50/High
15.	Roberto Perez, c	45/Medium
16.	Carlos Moncrief, of	45/Medium
17.	Austin Adams, rhp	45/Medium
18.	Jesus Aguilar, 1b	45/Medium
19.	Nellie Rodriguez, 1b	50/High
20.	Dace Kime, rhp	50/High
21.	Luis Lugo, lhp	50/High
22.	Mike Clevinger, rhp	50/High
23.	Shawn Armstrong, rhp	45/Medium
24.	Adam Plutko, rhp	45/Medium
25.	Casey Shane, rhp	50/High
26.	Dorssys Paulino, of/ss	45/High
27.	Ryan Merritt, lhp	40/Medium
28.	Tony Wolters, c/2b	45/High
29.	Grant Hockin, rhp	45/High
30.	Ronny Rodriguez, inf	45/High

LAST YEAR'S TOP 30

No.	Player, Pos.	Status
1.	Francisco Lindor, ss	No. 1
2.	Clint Frazier, of	No. 3
3.	Trevor Bauer, rhp	Majors
4.	Tyler Naquin, of	No. 6
5.	Cody Anderson, rhp	No. 10
6.	Dorssys Paulino, ss	No. 26
7.	Ronny Rodriguez, ss/2b	No. 30
8.	C.C. Lee, rhp	Majors
9.	Jose Ramirez, 2b/ss	Majors
10.	Austin Adams, rhp	No. 17
11.	Kyle Crockett, lhp	Majors
12.	Francisco Mejia, c	No. 7
13.	Luigi Rodriguez, of	Dropped out
14.	Carlos Moncrief, of	No. 16
15.	Jesus Aguilar, 1b	No. 18
16.	Dace Kime, rhp	No. 20
17.	Joe Wendle, 2b	(Athletics)
18.	Adam Plutko, rhp	No. 24
19.	Erik Gonzalez, ss	No. 8
20.	Anthony Santander, of	Dropped out
21.	Luis Lugo, lhp	No. 21
22.	Shawn Morimando, lhp	Dropped out
23.	Casey Shane, rhp	No. 25
24.	Mitch Brown, rhp	No. 14
25.	Tony Wolters, c	No. 28
26.	Scott Barnes, rhp	(Rangers)
27.	Nellie Rodriguez, 1b	No. 19
28.	Trey Haley, rhp	Dropped out
29.	Shawn Armstrong, rhp	No. 23
30.	Sean Brady, lhp	Dropped out

BEST TOOLS

Best Hitter for Average	Francisco Lindor
Best Power Hitter	Clint Frazier
Best Strike-Zone Discipline	Mike Papi
Fastest Baserunner	Greg Allen
Best Athlete	Bradley Zimmer
Best Fastball	Austin Adams
Best Curveball	Mitch Brown
Best Slider	Justus Sheffield
Best Changeup	Adam Plutko
Best Control	Ryan Merritt
Best Defensive Catcher	Roberto Perez
Best Defensive Infielder	Francisco Lindor
Best Infield Arm	Erik Gonzalez
Best Defensive Outfielder	Greg Allen
Best Outfield Arm	Tyler Naquin

PROJECTED 2018 LINEUP

Catcher	Yan Gomes
First Base	Mike Papi
Second Base	Jason Kipnis
Third Base	Lonnie Chisenhall
Shortstop	Francisco Lindor
Left Field	Michael Brantley
Center Field	Bradley Zimmer
Right Field	Clint Frazier
Designated Hitter	Carlos Santana
No. 1 Starter	Corey Kluber
No. 2 Starter	Carlos Carrasco
No. 3 Starter	Trevor Bauer
No. 4 Starter	Danny Salazar
No. 5 Starter	Justus Sheffield
Closer	Cody Allen

CLEVELAND INDIANS

TOP 2015 ROOKIE: Francisco Lindor, ss. It's only a matter of time before he takes over the starting shortstop job.
BREAKOUT PROSPECT: Nellie Rodriguez, 1b. Carolina League pitchers will get to know his power in 2015.
SLEEPER: Sam Hentges, rhp. The 2014 fourth-round pick has solid mechanics and projects to add velocity to his fringe-average fastball.

SOURCE OF TOP 30 TALENT			
Homegrown	28	Acquired	2
College	8	Trades	2
Junior college	4	Rule 5 draft	0
High school	9	Independent leagues	0
Draft-and-follow	0	Free agents/waivers	0
Nondrafted free agents	0		
International	7		

LF
Mike Papi (5)
Dorssys Paulino (26)
Bryson Myles
LeVon Washington

CF
Clint Frazier (3)
Tyler Naquin (6)
James Ramsey (12)
Greg Allen
Silento Sayles

RF
Bradley Zimmer (2)
Carlos Moncrief (16)
Luigi Rodriguez
Anthony Santander

3B
Giovanny Urshela (11)
Yu-Cheng Chang (13)
Paul Hendrix

SS
Francisco Lindor (1)
Erik Gonzalez (8)
Alexis Pantoja

2B
Ronny Rodriguez (30)
Claudio Bautista

1B
Bobby Bradley (9)
Jesus Aguilar (18)
Nellie Rodriguez (19)
Leo Castillo
Emmanuel Tapia

C
Francisco Mejia (7)
Roberto Perez (15)
Tony Wolters (28)
Simeon Lucas
Li-Jen Chu
Eric Haase

LHP

LHSP	LHRP
Justus Sheffield (4)	Kenny Mathews
Luis Lugo (21)	Thomas Pannone
Ryan Merritt (27)	
Shawn Morimando	
Sean Brady	
Sam Hentges	

RHP

RHSP	RHRP
Cody Anderson (10)	Austin Adams (17)
Mitch Brown (14)	Shawn Armstrong (23)
Dace Kime (20)	Ben Heller
Mike Clevinger (22)	Justin Brantley
Adam Plutko (24)	Jeff Johnson
Casey Shane (25)	Bryan Price
Grant Hockin (29)	
Dylan Baker	
Jared Robinson	
Micah Miniard	
Julian Merryweather	
Leandro Linares	
Joseph Colon	
Kieran Lovegrove	
Cameron Hill	

2014

BEST PURE HITTER: All three of the Indians' position players drafted in the top three rounds—Bradley Zimmer (1), Mike Papi (1) and Bobby Bradley (3)—have strong cases for this category, but Zimmer gets the nod. Zimmer has a quick, direct and level stroke with the ability to drive the ball to all fields from a solid approach and strike zone awareness.

BEST POWER HITTER: Bradley has at least plus raw power and that power impacted games this summer, leading the Rookie level Arizona League in home runs and isolated slugging (.290).

FASTEST RUNNER: OF Greg Allen has at least plus speed, drawing some 70 grades from scouts. OF Jodd Carter (24) has at least 60 speed and ran the 60 in 6.5 seconds.

BEST DEFENSIVE PLAYER: Allen was one of the best defensive center fielders in the draft with speed, instincts and an average arm, while Alexis Pantojas (9) was one of the top prep defenders at shortstop with loose, athletic actions and at least an average arm.

BEST FASTBALL: RHP Julian Merryweather (5) threw strikes with his fastball earlier in his career, then saw his velocity jump after going to the Texas Baseball Ranch, touching 96. Justus Sheffield (1) and Grant Hockin (2) have both touched 95.

BEST SECONDARY PITCH: Sheffield has feel for secondary stuff with a curveball that has plus potential and a changeup with at least above-average potential. Hockin's slider is above-average with a chance to be plus.

BEST PRO DEBUT: Bradley was the MVP of the Arizona League after winning the triple crown by hitting .361 with eight home runs and 50 RBIs.

BEST ATHLETE: Zimmer has plus speed, arm strength and raw power with a long, rangy 6-foot-5 build. RHP Dominic DeMasi (31) averaged 39 yards per punt as the punter at Valdosta State.

MOST INTRIGUING BACKGROUND: Zimmer became a first-rounder two years after his brother, Kyle, was drafted fifth overall by the Royals. Sheffield's older brother Jordan is a righthander at Vanderbilt who could have went in the first round out of high school but had Tommy John surgery.

CLOSEST TO THE MAJORS: Zimmer and Papi could both move quickly as advanced lefthanded college bats who control the strike zone and saw time in the Midwest League.

MOST INTERESTING BACKGROUND: Contact-oriented OF Bobby Ison (21) was temporarily paralyzed from the waist down in eighth grade because of Guillain-Barre syndrome.

BEST LATE-ROUND PICK: Robinson has a low-90s fastball, strike-throwing ability and a four-pitch mix, with his curveball presently ahead of his slider.

THE ONE WHO GOT AWAY: Shelton State (Ala.) JC RHP Grayson Jones (14) touched the mid-90s with heavy sink and was in play for the Indians' remaining bonus pool money.

ASSESSMENT: Armed with three of the first 38 picks, the Indians got an impressive haul of talent, offering upside and probability in position players and pitchers.

2013

LHP Kyle Crockett (4), as expected, zoomed to the major league bullpen. OF Clint Frazier (1), the fifth overall pick, had a modest first full season; fellow prep picks LHP Sean Brady (5) and RHP Casey Shane (6) have upside.

GRADE: C

2012

The Tribe took OF Tyler Naquin (1) ahead of Texas A&M teammate Michael Wacha; RHP Mitch Brown (2) may have to suffice for pitching. 2B Joe Wendle (6) was flipped for Brandon Moss.

GRADE: D

2011

SS Francisco Lindor (1) may be good enough to be a star, and RHP Cody Allen (23) zoomed to the majors, and now is the club's closer. RHP Cody Anderson (14) backed up in '14.

GRADE: B

TOP DRAFT PICKS OF THE DECADE

Year	Player, Pos.	2014 Org
2005	Trevor Crowe, of	Tigers
2006	David Huff, lhp (1st round supp.)	Yankees
2007	Beau Mills, 3b/1b	Out of baseball
2008	Lonnie Chisenhall, 3b	Indians
2009	Alex White, rhp	Astros
2010	Drew Pomeranz, lhp	Athletics
2011	Francisco Lindor, ss	Indians
2012	Tyler Naquin, of	Indians
2013	Clint Frazier, of	Indians
2014	Bradley Zimmer, of	Indians

LARGEST BONUSES IN CLUB HISTORY

Danys Baez, 1999	$4,500,000
Clint Frazier, 2013	$3,500,000
Jeremy Guthrie, 2002	$3,000,000
Francisco Lindor, 2011	$2,650,000
Drew Pomeranz, 2010	$2,650,000

1 FRANCISCO LINDOR, SS

Born: Nov. 14, 1993. **B-T:** B-R. **Ht.:** 5-11. **Wt.:** 175.
Drafted: HS—Montverde, Fla., 2011 (1st round).
Signed by: Mike Soper.

Lindor's star was first born when his youth teams won 8- and 9-year old Puerto Rican championships. However, he and his father Miguel had designs on Francisco having a pro career from early on, which motivated the family to relocate to Florida when Lindor was 12, seeking to find him better competition. He settled at Montverde (Fla.) Academy, an international boarding school, and went on to a standout prep career, starring with USA Baseball's 16U national team. Lindor served as team captain for the American squad that won gold at the 2009 World Youth Championships in Taiwan. The Indians hadn't taken a high school player in the first round since 2001 but broke from tradition to select Lindor eighth overall in 2011, signing him for $2.9 million. Just 17 years old at the time he was drafted, he has consistently performed despite being young for his league throughout his time in the minors. He was the youngest position player to play in the Triple-A International League in 2014, yet held his own following his promotion from Double-A Akron in late July.

There are plusses almost everywhere with Lindor, both in terms of his tools and his intangibles. At the plate, he takes line-drive swings and makes consistent hard contact to all fields. He has outstanding hand-eye coordination and feel for the strike zone, which along with his speed allows his hit tool to play up. A switch-hitter since age 13, he's a little more comfortable from the right side—his natural side—but the club is confident he'll be a factor from both sides of the plate. Power is the one tool that won't be Lindor's forte, though he did show more of it last season than ever before. He got noticeably stronger in the weight room and worked to get in better hitting positions to tap more into his strength. He would at times get caught up in trying to pull the ball, but for the most part he shows an understanding of how pitchers want to attack him and what pitches he can drive. He has all the tools to be an above-average shortstop, with smooth hands and a strong arm. He has a knack for anticipation and the first-step quickness to always be in the right place at the right time. The team has long been enamored of his work ethic and leadership qualities.

Jose Ramirez played well enough at shortstop down the stretch for Cleveland in 2014 that the team doesn't feel it necessarily has to hand the job to Lindor for Opening Day. So even though he may open the year back at Columbus, he'll certainly make his big league debut at some point in 2015, barring injury. Whenever he does take over at shortstop for the Indians, he should stay there for years to come.

Year	Club (League)	Class	AVG	G	AB	R	H	2B	3B	HR	RBI	BB	SO	SB	CS	OBP	SLG
2012	Lake County (MWL)	LoA	.257	122	490	83	126	24	3	6	42	61	78	27	12	.352	.355
2013	Carolina (CAR)	HiA	.306	83	327	51	100	19	6	1	27	35	39	20	5	.373	.410
	Akron (EL)	AA	.289	21	76	14	22	3	1	1	7	14	7	5	2	.407	.395
2014	Akron (EL)	AA	.278	88	342	51	95	12	4	6	48	40	61	25	9	.352	.389
	Columbus (IL)	AAA	.273	38	165	24	45	4	0	5	14	9	36	3	7	.307	.388
Minor League Totals			.278	357	1419	227	394	62	14	19	140	160	226	81	35	.355	.381

2 BRADLEY ZIMMER, OF

Born: Nov. 27, 1992. **B-T:** L-R. **Ht.:** 6-4. **Wt.:** 185. **Drafted:** San Francisco, 2014 (1st round). **Signed by:** Don Lyle.

Zimmer and older brother Kyle got to play together at San Francisco in 2012, the year Kyle became the fifth overall pick in the draft by the Royals. Bradley carried with him that experience of seeing how his brother dealt with the pressure and became a first-round pick himself two years later. Bradley broke out as a sophomore, then earned first-team All-America honors as a junior, when he hit .368/.461/.573 for the Dons en route to being the 21st overall pick and signing for $1.9 million. Zimmer has the makings of a five-tool player. He has a calm approach at the plate and outstanding bat-to-ball skills. His power shows up more in the form of doubles for now, but he has the leverage in his swing to drive balls a long way when he gets his arms extended. He has a lanky, superbly athletic frame and catches eyes with his long strides on the bases and in center field. Scouts who watched Zimmer in college were mixed about whether he could stay in center, but the Indians like what they've seen. He's able to cover plenty of ground and has good instincts, and his plus arm strength would fit in right field. Zimmer reached low Class A Lake County at the tail end of his pro debut and should be advanced enough to handle high Class A in his first full season. He has all the ingredients to move though the system quickly and be an impact player on both sides of the ball.

BA GRADE

60 Risk: Medium

LGE	PA	BB%	SO%	ISO
NYP	197	9.6	15.2	.161
MWL	13	15.4	23.1	.636

Year	Club (League)	Class	AVG	G	AB	R	H	2B	3B	HR	RBI	BB	SO	SB	CS	OBP	SLG
2014	Mahoning Valley (NYP)	SS	.304	45	168	32	51	11	2	4	30	19	30	11	4	.401	.464
	Lake County (MWL)	LoA	.273	3	11	4	3	1	0	2	2	2	3	1	0	.385	.909
Minor League Totals			.302	48	179	36	54	12	2	6	32	21	33	12	4	.400	.492

3 CLINT FRAZIER, OF

Born: Sept. 6, 1994. **B-T:** R-R. **Ht.:** 6-1. **Wt.:** 190. **Drafted:** HS—Loganville, Ga., 2013 (1st round). **Signed by:** Brad Tyler.

Frazier weathered a difficult first full season. The fifth overall pick in 2013 after being the Baseball America High School Player of the Year—and the recipient of the largest draft bonus in franchise history at $3.5 million— had a challenging year at low Class A Lake County. A pulled hamstring held him back in spring training and he took some time to get his bat on track, though he did recover to hit .282/.367/.448 with nine homers in the second half. Frazier's pure tools stand out, especially at the plate. His hands are extremely fast and he whips his bat through the zone, which, combined with strong forearms, allows him generate plenty of raw power. His approach is another matter, for his 161 strikeouts were the third most in the Midwest League. He does show some ability to recognize pitches but needs to manage his at-bats better. By the end of the season, though, Frazier had made progress at staying back on balls and not getting to his front side too early.

BA GRADE

60 Risk: High

LGE	PA	BB%	SO%	ISO
MWL	542	10.3	29.7	.146

He's an above-average runner and the Indians would like to keep him in center field, though his play there needs more polish as well. His arm strength would play in right. One of Frazier or Bradley Zimmer will have to move off center field if the two are teammates next season at high Class A Lynchburg. The Indians remain high on Frazier's loud tools, but his rough edges need refinement.

Year	Club (League)	Class	AVG	G	AB	R	H	2B	3B	HR	RBI	BB	SO	SB	CS	OBP	SLG
2013	Indians (AZL)	R	.297	44	172	32	51	11	5	5	28	17	61	3	2	.362	.506
2014	Lake County (MWL)	LoA	.266	120	474	70	126	18	6	13	50	56	161	12	6	.349	.411
Minor League Totals			.274	164	646	102	177	29	11	18	78	73	222	15	8	.353	.437

4 JUSTUS SHEFFIELD, LHP

Born: May 13, 1996. **B-T:** L-L. **Ht.:** 5-10. **Wt.:** 196. **Drafted:** HS—Tullahoma, Tenn., 2014 (1st round). **Signed by:** Chuck Bartlett.

The Indians gained an extra 2014 first-round pick, No. 31 overall, as compensation for losing free agent Ubaldo Jimenez. They spent it on Sheffield, marking the third time in four years they've taken a high schooler in the first round. He passed on a chance to go to Vanderbilt and pitch alongside older brother Jordan, himself a highly regarded prospect, and signed with Cleveland for $1.6 million. Sheffield offers an exciting combination of power stuff from the left side and athleticism on the mound. His fastball typically sits in the low 90s with late life, but he was able to run it up to 95-96 mph in the Rookie-level Arizona League. He throws a hard, late-breaking slider that he can locate for a strike or use as a chase pitch. He shows good feel for a curveball as well, and the Indians believe it could also be an out-pitch in the future. His changeup is behind his other pitches but on par with most prep pitchers. Despite standing in at 5-foot-10, he nonetheless does a good job of getting down the hill with power to leverage balls down in the zone. From an ability standpoint, Sheffield is ready to tackle low Class A Lake County in his first full season, though the Indians might hold him back to control his workload. He has the upside to be a No. 2 starter if everything comes together.

BA GRADE

60 Risk: High

LGE	BF	SO%	BB%	HR/9
AZL	94	30.9	9.6	0.00

Year	Club (League)	Class	W	L	ERA	G	GS	CG	SV	IP	H	HR	BB	SO	K/9	WHIP	AVG
2014	Indians (AZL)	R	3	1	4.79	8	4	0	0	21	24	0	9	29	12.6	1.60	.286
Minor League Totals			3	1	4.79	8	4	0	0	21	24	0	9	29	12.6	1.60	.286

5 MIKE PAPI, OF/1B

Born: Sept. 19, 1992. **B-T:** L-R. **Ht.:** 6-2. **Wt.:** 190. **Drafted:** Virginia, 2014 (1st round supplemental). **Signed by:** Bob Mayer.

Papi turned down the Angels as a 30th-round pick out of high school and went on to star at Virginia. He won the Atlantic Coast Conference batting title at .381 his sophomore year and tied for the league's home run lead with 11 as a junior, when his Virginia team spent most of the season ranked No. 1 in the country and advanced to the College World Series finals before losing to Vanderbilt. The 38th overall pick in the 2014 draft, Papi signed with Cleveland in early July for $1.25 million. Papi already had a professional approach while he was in college, proving to be an intelligent, selective hitter. When he does swing, he makes consistent hard contact and looks to spray the ball all over the field. Virginia's cavernous home ballpark suppressed his power production, but he has strength and has earned plus power grades from scouts in the past. Papi began his college career in the outfield but mainly played first base for Virginia in 2014. The Indians at least want to give him a shot in the outfield again, because he's a fair athlete who posts occasional average run times to first base. He threw 90 mph off the mound in high school, so his arm plays in the outfield also. First base will always be a fallback option for Papi, but his bat is advanced enough that he could move through the system quickly. He, Bradley Zimmer and Clint Frazier should form an exciting heart of the order at high Class A Lynchburg in 2015.

BA GRADE

55 Risk: Medium

LGE	PA	BB%	SO%	ISO
NYP	9	0.0	0.0	.000
MWL	166	15.7	19.3	.096

Year	Club (League)	Class	AVG	G	AB	R	H	2B	3B	HR	RBI	BB	SO	SB	CS	OBP	SLG
2014	Mahoning Valley (NYP)	SS	.222	2	9	2	2	0	0	0	3	0	0	0	0	.222	.222
	Lake County (MWL)	LoA	.178	39	135	21	24	4	0	3	15	26	32	2	0	.305	.274
Minor League Totals			.181	41	144	23	26	4	0	3	18	26	32	2	0	.301	.271

6 TYLER NAQUIN, OF

Born: April 24, 1991. **B-T:** L-R. **Ht.:** 6-3. **Wt.:** 190. **Drafted:** Texas A&M, 2012 (1st round). **Signed by:** Kyle Van Hook.

Naquin finished his college career with back-to-back Big 12 Conference batting titles at Texas A&M and netted himself a $1.75 million bonus as the 15th overall pick in 2012. He has kept hitting as a pro and was coming on strong at Double-A Akron in 2014, hitting .333 in June, until a stray pitch broke his right hand on June 27, ending his season. Naquin always has been a handsy hitter, but he made an adjustment to broaden his stance in the middle of 2013. Things really started clicking when he hit .339 in the Arizona Fall League, and he continued to improve in 2014. He created more leverage in his swing and consistently stayed up the middle. He takes a quiet approach in the box and hits to all fields with a line-drive swing. Naquin shows pop at times, too, though he'll likely max out near 12 homers. He played right field in college but has moved to center as a pro. He runs well and his routes and jumps are solid. He has a plus arm that would play well in right field, and opponents already think twice about running on him, though he lacks ideal power for a corner. Some scouts are less enamored of Naquin's ability to stick in center and see him as a fourth outfielder. Naquin can be a top-of-the-order hitter and everyday center fielder if everything comes together, and he probably will begin 2015 at Triple-A Columbus, where he'll share center field with James Ramsey.

BA GRADE

50 Risk: Medium

LGE	PA	BB%	SO%	ISO
EL	341	8.5	20.8	.112

Year	Club (League)	Class	AVG	G	AB	R	H	2B	3B	HR	RBI	BB	SO	SB	CS	OBP	SLG
2012	Mahoning Valley (NYP)	SS	.270	36	137	22	37	11	2	0	13	17	26	4	3	.379	.380
2013	Carolina (CAR)	HiA	.277	108	448	69	124	27	6	9	42	41	112	14	7	.345	.424
	Akron (EL)	AA	.225	18	80	9	18	3	0	1	6	5	22	1	3	.271	.300
2014	Akron (EL)	AA	.313	76	304	54	95	12	5	4	30	29	71	14	3	.371	.424
Minor League Totals			.283	238	969	154	274	53	13	14	91	92	231	33	16	.352	.408

7 FRANCISCO MEJIA, C

Born: Oct. 27, 1995. **B-T:** B-R. **Ht.:** 5-10. **Wt.:** 175. **Signed:** Dominican Republic, 2012. **Signed by:** Ramon Pena.

The Indians have been aggressive with Mejia since signing him for $350,000 in 2012, skipping him over the Dominican Summer League in 2013 and sending him to short-season Mahoning Valley in 2014, where he was one of the New York-Penn League's youngest players. He's been up for the challenge, however, handling the demands of being the Scrappers' everyday catcher and cleanup hitter. Mejia idolizes Carlos Santana and frequently draws comparisons with him as a switch-hitting catching prospect in the Indians system. He has a natural feel for hitting and innate bat control, allowing him to drive almost anything. The Indians hope to see him dial back his aggressive approach, for the ease with which he makes contact sometimes works against him. Mejia generates plenty of bat speed and should develop average or better power from both sides. His rocket throwing arm might be his loudest tool, garnering some 70 grades on the 20-80 scouting scale. Other aspects of his catching are unrefined, with the Indians placing particular emphasis on getting his game-calling and his English up to par. Though he has a compact frame, Mejia runs well for a catcher. Mejia has all kinds of upside, perhaps as much as any player in the organization, but he's also several years away. He should get his first chance to tackle full-season ball in 2015 at low Class A Lake County.

BA GRADE

55 Risk: Extreme

LGE	PA	BB%	SO%	ISO
NYP	274	6.6	17.2	.125

Year	Club (League)	Class	AVG	G	AB	R	H	2B	3B	HR	RBI	BB	SO	SB	CS	OBP	SLG
2013	Indians (AZL)	R	.305	30	105	16	32	9	1	4	24	5	18	3	1	.348	.524
2014	Mahoning Valley (NYP)	SS	.282	66	248	32	70	17	4	2	36	18	47	2	4	.339	.407
Minor League Totals			.289	96	353	48	102	26	5	6	60	23	65	5	5	.342	.442

8 ERIK GONZALEZ, SS

Born: Aug. 31, 1991. **B-T:** R-R. **Ht.:** 6-0. **Wt.:** 175. **Signed:** Dominican Republic, 2008. **Signed by:** Andres Garcia.

Francisco Lindor isn't the only shortstop prospect for whom the Indians harbor high hopes. Gonzalez enjoyed a huge winter in the Dominican League and used it as a springboard into 2014. Just a .264 career hitter entering the year, Gonzalez hit a combined .309/.353/.428 at high Class A Carolina and Double-A Akron, where he moved when Lindor moved up to Triple-A. Gonzalez has been noted more for his defensive prowess in the past, but his bat has begun to catch up. He began incorporating a high leg kick two years ago and has gotten more comfortable with it and improved his timing. He generates good bat speed and has wiry strength, though his approach isn't geared for power. His plate discipline made progress in 2014 but remains his biggest area for improvement. His defense remains his calling card. He has an athletic frame—tall with long, lanky levers—and a strong arm. He makes plays look easy, ranging well to both sides. He also began putting his above-average speed to better use on the bases, reaching the 20-steal mark for the first time in his career. The Indians want to keep Gonzalez at shortstop as long as possible, which will require staying a level behind Lindor. If Gonzalez eventually does have to move, his strong arm would allow him to handle either second or third base.

BA GRADE	
45	Risk: Low

LGE	PA	BB%	SO%	ISO
CAR	336	6.8	19.3	.120
EL	136	5.1	16.9	.116

Year	Club (League)	Class	AVG	G	AB	R	H	2B	3B	HR	RBI	BB	SO	SB	CS	OBP	SLG
2012	Mahoning Valley (NYP)	SS	.220	60	214	30	47	9	1	2	18	11	50	9	1	.264	.299
2013	Lake County (MWL)	LoA	.259	93	355	59	92	23	7	9	49	24	71	10	4	.307	.439
	Carolina (CAR)	HiA	.242	39	153	16	37	9	5	0	27	5	38	1	2	.259	.366
2014	Carolina (CAR)	HiA	.289	74	308	44	89	14	7	3	46	23	65	15	6	.336	.409
	Akron (EL)	AA	.357	31	129	21	46	6	3	1	16	7	23	6	1	.390	.473
Minor League Totals			.275	463	1792	269	493	90	30	18	224	111	333	69	21	.320	.389

9 BOBBY BRADLEY, 1B

Born: May 29, 1996. **B-T:** L-R. **Ht.:** 6-1. **Wt.:** 225. **Drafted:** HS—Gulfport, Miss., 2014 (3rd round). **Signed by:** Mike Bradford.

The Indians paid Bradley an over-slot $912,500 bonus as a third-round pick in 2014 to entice him to turn pro rather than go to Louisiana State, and it paid immediate dividends. Despite turning 18 a week before the draft, Bradley became the Rookie-level Arizona League's first triple crown winner since 1989 by batting .361 with eight homers and 50 RBIs. He won league MVP honors and also led the league in slugging percentage (.652). Scouts typically view high school first basemen with heavy skepticism, but Bradley has the tools to overcome the bias. He has plenty of bat speed and impressive raw power from the left side. He knows the strike zone and hits with controlled aggression. His swing is balanced, and he keeps the bat in the hitting zone a long time, while showing a feel for taking balls the other way. Bradley improved his physique between his junior and senior years of high school, and the Indians believe he still can add more strength. He tried his hand at catching as a senior, but the Indians will develop him at first base, though he needs work there as well. He runs well for a first baseman, at least for now. Bradley could be an impact bat down the road, though he'll need time, like all high school players. Provided he keeps up with his conditioning and hits well enough in spring training, he should open his first full season at low Class A Lake County.

BILL MITCHELL

BA GRADE	
50	Risk: High

LGE	PA	BB%	SO%	ISO
AZL	176	9.1	20.5	.290

Year	Club (League)	Class	AVG	G	AB	R	H	2B	3B	HR	RBI	BB	SO	SB	CS	OBP	SLG
2014	Indians (AZL)	R	.361	39	155	39	56	13	4	8	50	16	36	3	0	.426	.652
Minor League Totals			.361	39	155	39	56	13	4	8	50	16	36	3	0	.426	.652

10 CODY ANDERSON, RHP

Born: Sept. 14, 1990. **B-T:** R-R. **Ht.:** 6-4. **Wt.:** 220. **Drafted:** Feather River (Calif.) JC, 2011 (14th round). **Signed by:** Don Lyle.

Anderson didn't begin to bear down on pitching until arriving at Feather River (Calif.) JC and finding he might not be able to make the team as an outfielder, his main position in high school. His pitching career picked up steam in 2013 when he earned high Class A Carolina League pitcher of the year honors, but his encore with Double-A Akron was disappointing. His velocity didn't degrade, for he still sat in the low 90s and topped out at 95 mph with life. His slider and curveball are both currently below-average, though the slider is a little further along. The slider is a hard, cutter-like offering, while the curve is softer with more downer action. He also throws a sinking changeup but doesn't use it often—it's too firm at about 86-88 mph. Anderson needs to work down in the zone more consistently and just pitch more assertively. There were times last year when he tried to be too fine and failed to attack hitters. Anderson appears destined for a repeat trip to Akron, though he should certainly get a crack at Triple-A Columbus if he pitches well. He has the potential to be a back-end starter, but he has many items to check off his to-do list.

BA GRADE
45 Risk: Medium

LGE	BF	SO%	BB%	HR/9
EL	544	14.9	8.3	1.22

Year	Club (League)	Class	W	L	ERA	G	GS	CG	SV	IP	H	HR	BB	SO	K/9	WHIP	AVG
2012	Lake County (MWL)	LoA	4	7	3.20	24	23	0	0	98	92	8	29	72	6.6	1.23	.249
2013	Carolina (CAR)	HiA	9	4	2.34	23	23	0	0	123	105	6	31	112	8.2	1.10	.236
	Akron (EL)	AA	0	0	5.68	3	3	0	0	13	16	2	9	10	7.1	1.97	.320
2014	Akron (EL)	AA	4	11	5.44	25	25	0	0	126	141	17	45	81	5.8	1.48	.285
Minor League Totals			17	22	3.75	78	75	0	0	365	358	33	118	278	6.9	1.30	.260

11 GIOVANNY URSHELA, 3B

BA GRADE
45 Risk: Medium

Born: Oct. 11, 1991. **B-T:** R-R. **Ht.:** 6-0. **Wt.:** 197. **Signed:** Colombia, 2008. **Signed by:** Jose Quintero.

Urshela long has been hailed within the system as a standout defensive player who needed his bat to come forward, which it did in 2014. He hit his way out of Double-A Akron in early May and then held his own as a 22-year-old at Triple-A Columbus. The Indians rewarded Urshela by adding him to the 40-man roster after the season. Introducing a slight leg kick last season allowed him to see the ball longer and in turn be more selective as far as picking out pitches to drive. Urshela has a muscular frame and can put on shows in batting practice, though his in-game power rates closer to average. He's never struggled to make contact, but by putting the ball in play so often, he rarely walks. Defense still is where Urshela shines most brightly, for he shows clean actions at third base and a plus throwing arm. He ranges well but is a below-average runner overall. Urshela figures to spend the bulk of 2015 at Columbus.

Year	Club (League)	Class	AVG	G	AB	R	H	2B	3B	HR	RBI	BB	SO	SB	CS	OBP	SLG
2012	Carolina (CAR)	HiA	.278	114	439	50	122	30	1	14	59	16	60	1	1	.309	.446
2013	Akron (EL)	AA	.270	116	445	42	120	23	2	8	43	14	48	1	1	.292	.384
2014	Akron (EL)	AA	.300	24	90	15	27	9	0	5	19	6	16	1	1	.347	.567
	Columbus (IL)	AAA	.276	104	395	63	109	27	6	13	65	30	51	0	2	.331	.473
Minor League Totals			.268	601	2308	269	618	131	12	53	302	109	302	16	10	.304	.404

12 JAMES RAMSEY, OF

BA GRADE
45 Risk: Medium

Born: Dec. 19, 1989. **B-T:** L-R. **Ht.:** 6-0. **Wt.:** 190. **Drafted:** Florida State, 2012 (1st round). **Signed by:** Rob Fidler (Cardinals).

Ramsey spurned the Twins as a 22nd-round pick in 2011 to return for his senior season at Florida State. Scouts have been divided on Ramsey's potential going back to his college days. He may lack a true carrying tool but should be well-rounded. He has an intelligent approach and doesn't try to do too much at the plate. Neither his hit nor power tools grade out as better than average. He's an above-average runner, though that speed hasn't translated into stolen bases, and the Indians can see him being an outstanding defender in center field. Ramsey has an average throwing arm and can handle any of the three outfield positions if need be. After being the odd-man out in a deep St. Louis outfield picture, Ramsey gets a fresh look with Cleveland, though he has no obvious avenue to the Indians' lefty-heavy lineup. He'll split time in center field with Naquin at Triple-A Columbus in 2015.

Year	Club (League)	Class	AVG	G	AB	R	H	2B	3B	HR	RBI	BB	SO	SB	CS	OBP	SLG
2012	Palm Beach (FSL)	HiA	.229	56	210	36	48	9	3	1	14	33	59	10	2	.333	.314
2013	Palm Beach (FSL)	HiA	.361	18	61	17	22	5	2	1	7	12	12	1	0	.481	.557
	Springfield (TL)	AA	.251	93	347	61	87	11	2	15	44	53	108	8	4	.356	.424
	Memphis (PCL)	AAA	.000	1	3	0	0	0	0	0	0	0	1	0	0	.000	.000
2014	Springfield (TL)	AA	.300	67	243	47	73	14	1	13	36	31	66	4	2	.389	.527
	Columbus (IL)	AAA	.284	28	109	17	31	9	1	3	16	13	34	1	0	.365	.468
Minor League Totals			.268	263	973	178	261	48	9	33	117	142	280	24	8	.368	.438

13 YU-CHENG CHANG, SS/3B

BA GRADE

55 Risk: Extreme

Born: Aug. 18, 1995. **B-T:** R-R. **Ht.:** 6-1. **Wt.:** 175. **Signed:** Taiwan, 2013.
Signed by: Allen Lin/Jason Lynn.

The Indians have been one of the most active teams scouting players in Taiwan, with reliever C.C. Lee being their most notable success so far, and they ponied up $500,000 to sign Chang in June 2013. Few who watch Chang would guess he's just 19 years old. He generates plenty of bat speed, while his swing draws comparisons with David Wright's. He has a feel for the barrel and should continue to add strength, giving him potentially above-average power. Scouts can see him moving to third base down the road after he spent the bulk of his time at shortstop in the Rookie-level Arizona League. His strong throwing arm should keep him on the left side of the infield. Chang's speed is average to a tick above and his range is solid for now, while at the same time he earns raves for his ability to slow the game down and not look rushed. That maturity gives him a chance to open 2015 at low Class A Lake County as a teenager.

Year	Club (League)	Class	AVG	G	AB	R	H	2B	3B	HR	RBI	BB	SO	SB	CS	OBP	SLG
2014	Indians (AZL)	R	.346	42	159	39	55	9	4	6	25	18	28	6	1	.420	.566
Minor League Totals			.346	42	159	39	55	9	4	6	25	18	28	6	1	.420	.566

14 MITCH BROWN, RHP

BA GRADE

50 Risk: High

Born: April 13, 1994. **B-T:** R-R. **Ht.:** 6-1. **Wt.:** 195. **Drafted:** HS— Rochester, Minn., 2012 (2nd round). **Signed by:** Les Pajari.

Brown became one of just two Minnesota high school pitchers taken inside the top two rounds of the draft in the last 30 years when the Indians snagged him at No. 79 overall in 2012 and signed him $800,000. After struggling to find a comfortable delivery in 2013, Brown was able to harness his effort level and incorporate his lower half much better as he made a second run at Lake County. His command was much improved, allowing him to get the most out of his four-pitch mix. His fastball and curveball have the makings of being plus pitches, the heater sitting in the low 90s and getting up to 96 mph with slight cutting action, while his hammer curve is the best in the system. He shows some feel for a changeup that has some armside life, and he also throws an early-count slider. The Indians like Brown's chances to stay in the rotation with his durable, athletic frame. He'll move up to high Class A Lynchburg in 2015.

Year	Club (League)	Class	W	L	ERA	G	GS	CG	SV	IP	H	HR	BB	SO	K/9	WHIP	AVG
2012	Indians (AZL)	R	2	0	3.58	8	8	0	0	28	20	3	10	26	8.5	1.08	.204
2013	Lake County (MWL)	LoA	1	1	11.49	5	5	0	0	16	21	4	11	18	10.3	2.04	.328
	Indians (AZL)	R	2	4	5.37	12	10	0	0	52	57	2	29	48	8.3	1.65	.284
2014	Lake County (MWL)	LoA	8	8	3.31	27	27	0	0	139	113	6	55	127	8.2	1.21	.226
Minor League Totals			13	13	4.35	52	50	0	0	234	211	15	105	219	8.4	1.35	.245

15 ROBERTO PEREZ, C

BA GRADE

45 Risk: Medium

Born: Dec. 23, 1988. **B-T:** R-R. **Ht.:** 5-11. **Wt.:** 225. **Drafted:** Lake City (Fla.) CC, 2008 (33rd round). **Signed by:** Mike Soper.

Perez played the 2013 season while afflicted with Bell's Palsy, a nerve condition that caused temporary paralysis on one side of his face. Healthy in 2014, Perez enjoyed a breakout year and served as Yan Gomes' understudy in Cleveland after being called up in July. Perez has long been known for his defense, but his offense took a major step forward in 2014 and gives him a chance to be more than just a defense-first backup. He shows outstanding bat-to-ball skills and takes short swings, allowing him to let the ball travel deep in the zone. Aside from being healthy and actually able to see the ball out of both eyes, the other big difference for Perez in 2014 was a more aggressive swing rather than a contact-oriented one, indicating he could have close to average power. Perez remains a standout defender. He calls a good game, receives the ball well and has an above-average throwing arm. He'll reprise his role as Gomes' backup in 2015.

Year	Club (League)	Class	AVG	G	AB	R	H	2B	3B	HR	RBI	BB	SO	SB	CS	OBP	SLG
2012	Akron (EL)	AA	.212	95	283	31	60	16	2	1	31	49	67	0	1	.336	.293
2013	Akron (EL)	AA	.247	32	93	10	23	6	0	2	10	32	25	1	1	.453	.376
	Columbus (IL)	AAA	.176	67	187	16	33	12	0	0	24	22	59	0	1	.269	.241
2014	Columbus (IL)	AAA	.305	53	174	29	53	11	1	8	43	29	51	1	0	.405	.517
	Cleveland (AL)	MAJ	.271	29	85	10	23	5	0	1	4	5	26	0	0	.311	.365
Major League Totals			.271	29	85	10	23	5	0	1	4	5	26	0	0	.311	.365
Minor League Totals			.236	514	1594	207	376	97	7	22	213	299	420	8	7	.363	.347

16 CARLOS MONCRIEF, OF

BA GRADE

45 Risk: Medium

Born: Nov. 3, 1988. **B-T:** L-R. **Ht.:** 6-0. **Wt.:** 220. **Drafted:** Chipola (Fla.) JC, 2008 (14th round). **Signed by:** Chuck Bartlett.

The Indians drafted Moncrief, a two-way player in high school and junior college, as a power-armed pitcher in 2008, but his mound career came to an end a year later after he compiled a 7.75 ERA over two stints in Rookie ball. He has fared much better since converting to the outfield in 2010. The Indians laud Moncrief's ability to make adjustments over the course of a season, and his second-half turnaround in 2014 boiled down to simplifying his approach and showing the plate discipline he had the year before. He has good hands and a short swing that should enable him to hit for solid averages. He'll show above-average raw power, primarily to his pull side. How much of that power he'll be able to tap into in games is more of a question. He's a serviceable defender in right field, for he runs well for his size and still has a plus throwing arm. Moncrief remains on the 40-man roster, but with no openings in the big league outfield, he'll have to bide his time at Columbus.

Year	Club (League)	Class	AVG	G	AB	R	H	2B	3B	HR	RBI	BB	SO	SB	CS	OBP	SLG
2012	Carolina (CAR)	HiA	.249	101	353	57	88	23	4	15	53	46	126	17	2	.339	.465
2013	Akron (EL)	AA	.284	129	489	77	139	26	7	17	75	55	98	15	7	.354	.470
2014	Columbus (IL)	AAA	.271	132	480	64	130	33	4	12	63	38	130	8	3	.328	.431
Minor League Totals			.257	555	2040	302	525	120	26	65	265	243	572	67	24	.339	.437

17 AUSTIN ADAMS, RHP

BA GRADE

45 Risk: Medium

Born: Aug. 19, 1986. **B-T:** R-R. **Ht.:** 5-11. **Wt.:** 190. **Drafted:** Faulkner (Ala.), 2009 (5th round). **Signed by:** Chuck Bartlett.

Shoulder surgery cost Adams the entire 2012 season and derailed his career as a starter, but he's taken well to the bullpen and made his big league debut in 2014. Adams attacks hitters with tailing fastballs in the upper 90s. He was clocked at 96-98 mph last season, touched 99 and has hit 100 in the past. He threw a curve and a slider as a starter but has gone to one breaking ball now—more of a slurvy slider. It's a quality pitch, with depth and sharp break in the upper 80s. Adams still throws his changeup and has feel for it, though it's clearly his third option. He did a better job of throwing strikes in 2014 than ever before, posting the lowest walk rate (2.7 per nine innings) of his career at Triple-A Columbus. He does need to do a better job of staying down in the zone, because his stuff flattens out when he elevates. Adams should be in the mix for the big league bullpen again in 2015.

Year	Club (League)	Class	W	L	ERA	G	GS	CG	SV	IP	H	HR	BB	SO	K/9	WHIP	AVG
2012	Did not play—Injured																
2013	Akron (EL)	AA	3	2	2.62	45	0	0	4	55	44	3	29	76	12.4	1.33	.215
2014	Columbus (IL)	AAA	3	2	2.50	42	0	0	5	54	44	4	16	52	8.7	1.11	.224
	Cleveland (AL)	MAJ	0	0	9.00	6	0	0	0	7	9	1	1	4	5.1	1.43	.310
Major League Totals			0	0	9.00	6	0	0	0	7	9	1	1	4	5.1	1.43	.310
Minor League Totals			28	20	3.18	156	46	0	11	394	364	29	159	400	9.1	1.33	.245

18 JESUS AGUILAR, 1B

BA GRADE

45 Risk: Medium

Born: June 30, 1990. **B-T:** R-R. **Ht.:** 6-3. **Wt.:** 250. **Signed:** Venezuela, 2007. **Signed by:** Jesus Mendoza.

Aguilar got to be winter-ball teammates with Bobby Abreu and Alex Gonzalez in the Venezuelan League following the 2013 season. The two long-time big leaguers helped him to mature his approach, and Aguilar took those lessons into the 2014 season. Aguilar remains the same hulking presence in the batter's box and has big-time righthanded power. He's at his best when he stays within himself and uses the whole field, which frees up his hands and allows him to show his power to all parts of the park. His swing does get long at times and he'll start pulling off balls, though he shows good bat speed. A below-average runner and thrower, Aguilar handles himself well enough at first base to not be a defensive liability. With no clear path to everyday playing time in Cleveland, Aguilar may find himself back in Columbus in 2015. The Indians value having his righthanded power around, given how many of their best hitters are lefties.

Year	Club (League)	Class	AVG	G	AB	R	H	2B	3B	HR	RBI	BB	SO	SB	CS	OBP	SLG
2012	Carolina (CAR)	HiA	.277	107	368	63	102	25	2	12	58	45	91	0	1	.365	.454
	Akron (EL)	AA	.292	20	72	12	21	6	0	3	13	13	24	0	0	.402	.500
2013	Akron (EL)	AA	.275	130	499	66	137	28	0	16	105	56	107	0	1	.349	.427
2014	Columbus (IL)	AAA	.304	118	427	69	130	31	0	19	77	64	96	0	0	.395	.511
	Cleveland (AL)	MAJ	.121	19	33	2	4	0	0	0	3	4	13	0	0	.211	.121
Major League Totals			.121	19	33	2	4	0	0	0	3	4	13	0	0	.211	.121
Minor League Totals			.276	685	2498	359	690	159	5	91	465	294	558	14	7	.357	.453

19 NELLIE RODRIGUEZ, 1B

BA GRADE

50 Risk: High

Born: June 12, 1994. **B-T:** R-R. **Ht.:** 6-2. **Wt.:** 225. **Drafted:** HS—New York, 2012 (15th round). **Signed by:** Brent Urcheck.

The Indians may have pushed Rodriguez too much when they sent him to Lake County in 2013 for his first full season, but he punished Midwest League pitchers in his encore, tying for the league home run title (22) and leading it in extra-base hits (57). Rodriguez is cut from the same cloth as Jesus Aguilar as a hulking righthanded-hitting first baseman. His swing doesn't always look picturesque, but he has a fine bat path and he can cover all parts of the plate. He has plenty of bat speed and raw power. Rodriguez piled up his share of strikeouts but was willing to take his walks as well. The onus will be on his bat to carry him. He has worked hard on his conditioning and could be an average defender, but that will never be his calling card. Rodriguez will move up to high Class A Lynchburg in 2015.

Year	Club (League)	Class	AVG	G	AB	R	H	2B	3B	HR	RBI	BB	SO	SB	CS	OBP	SLG
2012	Indians (AZL)	R	.229	32	109	19	25	7	3	4	17	24	41	0	0	.375	.459
2013	Lake County (MWL)	LoA	.194	47	160	18	31	7	0	1	13	26	53	0	0	.305	.256
	Mahoning Valley (NYP)	SS	.287	73	261	32	75	16	0	9	37	29	61	0	2	.366	.452
2014	Lake County (MWL)	LoA	.268	130	485	67	130	32	3	22	88	60	142	0	0	.349	.482
Minor League Totals			.257	282	1015	136	261	62	6	36	155	139	297	0	2	.349	.436

20 DACE KIME, RHP

BA GRADE

50 Risk: High

Born: March 6, 1992. **B-T:** R-R. **Ht.:** 6-4. **Wt.:** 200. **Drafted:** Louisville, 2013 (3rd round). **Signed by:** Junie Melendez.

Primarily a reliever in college, Kime's repertoire was deep enough that the Indians moved him to the rotation. He sits in the low 90s and tops out at 95 mph with a physical, durable body. Kime's curveball is his best pitch, featuring bite and top-to-bottom depth. He showed improved confidence and feel for his fading changeup as well. The Indians deemphasized his fourth pitch, a slider, early in 2014, but it's useable and did help him once he started throwing it more. Kime tended to get too high with his lead arm in his delivery, and the Indians worked with him to get in better position to be able to repeat his mechanics and thus his control, which will be crucial given that his fastball is fairly straight. Kime has the ingredients to be a starter, but he'll be looking for better results at high Class A Lynchburg in 2015.

Year	Club (League)	Class	W	L	ERA	G	GS	CG	SV	IP	H	HR	BB	SO	K/9	WHIP	AVG
2013	Mahoning Valley (NYP)	SS	0	2	2.92	9	9	0	0	25	19	0	16	26	9.5	1.42	.224
2014	Lake County (MWL)	LoA	7	14	5.22	28	28	0	0	136	148	12	56	108	7.1	1.50	.276
Minor League Totals			7	16	4.86	37	37	0	0	161	167	12	72	134	7.5	1.48	.269

21 LUIS LUGO, LHP

BA GRADE

50 Risk: High

Born: March 5, 1994. **B-T:** L-L. **Ht.:** 6-5. **Wt.:** 200. **Signed:** Venezuela, 2011. **Signed by:** Ramon Pena/Antonio Caballero.

The Indians had a busy 2011 on the international market, spending an estimated $3.58 million in bonuses. Lugo accounted for $415,000 of that total and looks like the pick of the litter. It's easy to project on Lugo's athletic 6-foot-5 frame, so he should add velocity to his 90-92 mph fastball. He already gets a lot of out of the velocity he has and improved the consistency of his mechanics. He hides the ball well in his delivery and pumps strikes to the bottom half of the zone. His changeup gets plus grades and he has feel for all of his pitches, including an 11-to-5 curveball and a harder slider. His curve is ahead of his slider now, but both have the potential to be average. Lugo will move up to high Class A Lynchburg for 2015, and his ultimate upside is tied largely to how much velocity he adds.

Year	Club (League)	Class	W	L	ERA	G	GS	CG	SV	IP	H	HR	BB	SO	K/9	WHIP	AVG
2012	Indians (AZL)	R	2	4	4.50	11	10	0	0	42	38	4	21	51	10.9	1.40	.242
2013	Mahoning Valley (NYP)	SS	1	4	1.97	11	11	0	0	50	39	1	11	30	5.4	0.99	.222
	Lake County (MWL)	LoA	0	1	3.77	3	3	0	0	14	14	1	5	14	8.8	1.33	.250
2014	Lake County (MWL)	LoA	10	9	4.92	27	22	0	0	126	124	16	40	146	10.4	1.30	.255
Minor League Totals			13	23	4.11	64	55	0	0	270	246	26	101	285	9.5	1.29	.242

22 MIKE CLEVINGER, RHP

Born: Dec. 21, 1990. **B-T:** R-R. **Ht.:** 6-4. **Wt.:** 220. **Drafted:** Seminole State (Fla.) JC, 2011 (4th round). **Signed by:** Tom Kotchman (Angels).

The Angels paid Clevinger $250,000 a few days before the August signing deadline in 2011 after he had a big summer in the Cape Cod League. His career stalled after having Tommy John surgery in 2012. The Indians remained intrigued and asked for Clevinger when the Angels came looking for bullpen help, and Cleveland got him straight up for righthander Vinnie Pestano in August 2014. The Indians felt like Clevinger had gotten away from the mechanics he'd shown on the Cape, in particular lowering his arm slot. After getting his delivery more over the top, he started showing velocity up to 97 mph at high Class A Carolina. He's a good athlete on the mound and has a feel for spinning the ball, showing three secondary pitches with solid-average upside in his curveball, slider and changeup. the Indians like his potential to remain in the rotation and will continue to develop him there. He'll move up to Double-A Akron in 2015.

Year	Club (League)	Class	W	L	ERA	G	GS	CG	SV	IP	H	HR	BB	SO	K/9	WHIP	AVG
2012	Cedar Rapids (MWL)	LoA	1	1	3.73	8	8	0	0	41	37	3	13	34	7.5	1.22	.243
2013	Angels (AZL)	R	0	0	3.00	2	2	0	0	3	2	0	2	3	9.0	1.33	.200
	Orem (PIO)	R	0	1	16.88	1	1	0	0	3	6	0	2	2	6.8	3.00	.429
2014	Burlington (MWL)	LoA	3	0	1.88	5	5	0	0	24	16	2	5	27	10.1	0.88	.186
	Inland Empire (CAL)	HiA	1	3	5.37	13	13	0	0	55	58	8	27	58	9.4	1.54	.272
	Carolina (CAR)	HiA	0	1	4.79	5	4	0	0	21	20	1	11	15	6.5	1.50	.270
Minor League Totals			5	6	4.36	37	33	0	0	151	142	14	62	144	8.6	1.35	.252

23 SHAWN ARMSTRONG, RHP

Born: Sept. 11, 1990. **B-T:** R-R. **Ht.:** 6-2. **Wt.:** 210. **Drafted:** East Carolina, 2011 (18th round). **Signed by:** Bob Mayer.

Armstrong has battled injuries on and off for years but looks to be finally closing in on the majors. Back to full strength in 2014, Armstrong excelled as closer at Double-A Akron and earned a spot on the 40-man roster. Armstrong doesn't lack for arm strength, running his fastball up to 96 mph and pitching in the low 90s. Getting his delivery more online to the plate helped him improve his fastball command and slash his walk rate from 5.7 per nine innings in 2013 to 3.5 a year later. He complements his heater with a cutter and a slider, which are essentially shorter and bigger versions of the same pitch, and both can get swings and misses. He still has a changeup as part of his arsenal but seldom throws it. Armstrong figures to start 2015 at Triple-A Columbus and should be an option for the big league pen if things go well.

Year	Club (League)	Class	W	L	ERA	G	GS	CG	SV	IP	H	HR	BB	SO	K/9	WHIP	AVG
2012	Lake County (MWL)	LoA	0	0	0.00	2	0	0	0	4	1	0	2	4	9.8	0.82	.091
	Carolina (CAR)	HiA	1	3	2.06	26	0	0	1	44	31	0	23	52	10.7	1.24	.205
	Akron (EL)	AA	1	0	0.89	17	0	0	3	20	12	0	12	22	9.7	1.18	.176
2013	Indians (AZL)	R	0	0	4.50	3	0	0	0	4	3	1	0	5	11.3	0.75	.200
	Akron (EL)	AA	2	3	4.09	30	0	0	0	33	32	2	21	43	11.7	1.61	.252
2014	Akron (EL)	AA	6	2	2.12	44	0	0	15	51	39	3	19	68	12.0	1.14	.211
	Columbus (IL)	AAA	0	0	5.40	5	0	0	0	5	4	1	3	4	7.2	1.40	.235
Minor League Totals			10	8	2.43	128	0	0	19	163	123	7	80	200	11.1	1.25	.212

24 ADAM PLUTKO, RHP

Born: Oct. 3, 1991. **B-T:** R-R. **Ht.:** 6-3. **Wt.:** 195. **Drafted:** UCLA, 2013 (11th round). **Signed by:** Carlos Muniz.

Plutko will live forever in UCLA lore as the ace of the Bruins' national championship team in 2013. He had gone to college after turning down the Astros as a sixth-round pick out of high school and parlayed his success into an 11th-round selection and well-over-slot $300,000 bonus from the Indians in 2013. Plutko's biggest assets remain his pitchability and ability to command the ball, which shows flashes of being elite. As was the case in college, he remains very fly ball-oriented, although his fastball has picked up some velocity, sitting in the 88-92 mph range and touching 93-94. His changeup has the best chance of any of his offerings to be a true plus pitch, while he can mix in a short slider and a bigger curveball well. The Indians liked that Plutko pitched more assertively last season, while his mechanics were already clean and easy and required no real alterations. Plutko could start 2015 back in high Class A although Double-A should come calling if things go well.

Year	Club (League)	Class	W	L	ERA	G	GS	CG	SV	IP	H	HR	BB	SO	K/9	WHIP	AVG
2014	Lake County (MWL)	LoA	3	1	3.93	10	10	0	0	53	49	1	12	66	11.3	1.16	.241
	Carolina (CAR)	HiA	4	9	4.08	18	18	0	0	97	99	11	18	78	7.2	1.21	.265
Minor League Totals			7	10	4.03	28	28	0	0	150	148	12	30	144	8.7	1.19	.257

25 CASEY SHANE, RHP

BA GRADE
50 Risk: High

Born: Aug. 23, 1995. **B-T:** R-R. **Ht.:** 6-4. **Wt.:** 200. **Drafted:** HS— Burleson, Texas, 2013 (6th round). **Signed by:** Mark Allen.

Once a standout on the high school showcase circuit, Shane fell in the 2013 draft after he got out of shape over the winter leading up to his senior season. The Indians signed him for $150,000 in the sixth round. Shane has put in the work both in the weight room and with his nutrition to change his body since turning pro, and his efforts began to bear fruit in the Rookie-level Arizona League in 2014. The crispness and consistency of his stuff stepped forward as he began to look more like his old self. His fastball, which had dipped into the 87-91 mph range in spring 2013, was back operating in the low 90s, touching 94. He didn't throw his changeup a ton as an amateur, but the pitch has improved to become his best secondary pitch. He also throws a hard three-quarters slider that's usable in the low 80s, and he toys around with a curveball. Shane shows feel for manipulating his secondary stuff and the ability to command the ball to both sides of the plate. Shane should get a shot to go to low Class A Lake County in 2015.

Year	Club (League)	Class	W	L	ERA	G	GS	CG	SV	IP	H	HR	BB	SO	K/9	WHIP	AVG
2013	Indians (AZL)	R	1	1	6.52	11	3	0	1	29	33	1	16	22	6.8	1.69	.282
2014	Indians (AZL)	R	5	0	2.72	10	9	0	0	46	38	1	15	40	7.8	1.14	.226
	Mahoning Valley (NYP)	SS	1	0	0.82	2	2	0	0	11	8	0	1	5	4.1	0.82	.205
Minor League Totals			7	1	3.75	23	14	0	1	86	79	2	32	67	7.0	1.29	.244

26 DORSSYS PAULINO, OF/SS

BA GRADE
45 Risk: High

Born: Nov. 21, 1994. **B-T:** R-R. **Ht.:** 6-0. **Wt.:** 175. **Signed:** Dominican Republic, 2011. **Signed by:** Ramon Pena/Claudio Brito/Felix Nivar.

The Indians expected Paulino to be the centerpiece of their 2011 international class after he signed for $1.1 million. Scouts had forecasted that Paulino would have to move off shortstop since his amateur days, and the Indians pulled the plug on him in May 2014, shifting him to left field with Lake County after he'd made 13 errors in 24 games. His defensive struggles had started bleeding over to his offense, and the position switch did seem to free up his approach. The Indians still like his bat. Paulino has a compact swing and a natural feel for timing, allowing him to handle plus stuff. He could grow into average power but he hits more to the gaps now, which hurts his profile if he stays in the outfield. The club envisions him handling any of the three outfield positions, though the fact Paulino's speed is just average will likely keep him on a corner. Paulino has age on his side as he heads to high Class A Lynchburg in 2015.

Year	Club (League)	Class	AVG	G	AB	R	H	2B	3B	HR	RBI	BB	SO	SB	CS	OBP	SLG
2012	Indians (AZL)	R	.355	41	172	42	61	14	6	6	30	15	31	9	1	.404	.610
	Mahoning Valley (NYP)	SS	.271	15	59	5	16	5	0	1	8	3	14	2	1	.306	.407
2013	Lake County (MWL)	LoA	.246	120	476	56	117	28	3	5	46	30	91	12	7	.297	.349
2014	Lake County (MWL)	LoA	.251	113	427	51	107	25	5	3	35	33	101	5	6	.311	.354
Minor League Totals			.265	289	1134	154	301	72	14	15	119	81	237	28	15	.319	.393

27 RYAN MERRITT, LHP

BA GRADE
40 Risk: Medium

Born: Feb. 21, 1992. **B-T:** L-L. **Ht.:** 6-0. **Wt.:** 165. **Drafted:** McLennan (Texas) CC, 2011 (16th round). **Signed by:** Kevin Cullen.

Merritt finished strong with a 2.35 ERA in the second half of the 2013 season at low Class A Lake County and carried that momentum into high Class A Carolina in 2014, leading the system in ERA (2.58). The Indians added him to the 40-man roster after the season. He stands out most for his command and feel for the zone, and he has issued just 1.5 walks per nine innings for his career. His clean delivery helps him locate any of his pitches anywhere he wants, and he shows a feel for adding and subtracting velocity. What Merritt lacks is a true plus pitch, which limits his upside. He has gotten stronger each year he's been in the system, and his fastball works at 88-92 mph now. He has an athletic frame and the Indians hope he can add a tick or two on his fastball. A curveball and changeup are his main secondary offerings, both projecting to be average. He can also a mix in a slider but didn't need it much last year. Merritt profiles as a back-of-the-rotation starter and will move up to Double-A Akron in 2015.

Year	Club (League)	Class	W	L	ERA	G	GS	CG	SV	IP	H	HR	BB	SO	K/9	WHIP	AVG
2011	Indians (AZL)	R	0	0	1.08	4	0	0	1	8	10	0	2	10	10.8	1.44	.278
2012	Mahoning Valley (NYP)	SS	3	4	4.09	14	14	0	0	66	82	3	17	40	5.5	1.50	.304
2013	Lake County (MWL)	LoA	6	9	3.42	24	23	0	0	126	142	10	18	91	6.5	1.27	.287
	Carolina (CAR)	HiA	0	0	5.00	2	2	0	0	9	7	1	1	6	6.0	0.89	.206
2014	Carolina (CAR)	HiA	13	3	2.58	25	25	2	0	160	128	12	25	127	7.1	0.95	.216
Minor League Totals			22	16	3.16	69	64	2	1	370	369	26	63	274	6.7	1.17	.258

28 TONY WOLTERS, C/2B

Born: June 9, 1992. **B-T:** L-R. **Ht.:** 5-10. **Wt.:** 1992. **Drafted:** HS—Vista, Calif., 2010 (3rd round). **Signed by:** Jason Smith.

Wolters has become one of the more unique prospects in the minors as a player who can catch one day and play middle infield the next. Drafted as a shortstop in the third round in 2010, he signed for $1.35 million, but his career outlook changed drastically in 2013 when he shifted behind the plate. A good athlete with a compact frame, he has soft hands and a quick transfer on throws that helps his average arm play up, and he caught 47 percent of basestealers in 2014. The Indians have told Wolters he can always go back to the infield, and he continues to see intermittent action at shortstop and second base, but he has embraced catching. Putting in so much time on defense has understandably taken away from Wolters' offense. His simple lefthanded swing can get long at times, but he has a feel for the barrel and good strength for his size. He joined the 40-man roster in November to keep him out of the Rule 5 draft. A return to Double-A Akron or move to Triple-A Columbus should be in play for 2015.

Year	Club (League)	Class	AVG	G	AB	R	H	2B	3B	HR	RBI	BB	SO	SB	CS	OBP	SLG
2012	Carolina (CAR)	HiA	.260	125	485	66	126	30	8	8	58	36	104	5	9	.320	.404
2013	Carolina (CAR)	HiA	.277	80	289	36	80	13	0	3	33	41	58	3	6	.369	.353
2014	Akron (EL)	AA	.249	94	341	36	85	15	2	1	34	35	74	3	2	.319	.314
Minor League Totals			.266	373	1401	190	373	68	13	13	148	144	290	32	21	.342	.361

29 GRANT HOCKIN, RHP

Born: March 5, 1996. **B-T:** R-R. **Ht.:** 6-4. **Wt.:** 200. **Drafted:** HS—La Verne, Calif., 2014 (2nd round). **Signed by:** Ryan Thompson.

Hockin grew up learning about the game from his grandfather, the late Hall of Famer Harmon Killebrew. His baseball bloodlines also extend to his uncle Cam Killebrew, who played three years in the minors, and older brother Chad Hockin, who pitches for Cal State Fullerton. Grant was set to go to UCLA before the Indians lured him away with a $1.1 million bonus as their 2014 second-round pick. The UCLA connection is fitting since Hockin is often compared with former Bruins ace Adam Plutko, whom he now joins in the Indians system, as a righthander who lacks a wipeout pitch but shows advanced command and feel for pitching. Hockin is a good athlete and has a clean delivery and three-quarters arm slot. He does a good job of leveraging his 89-91 mph fastball down in the zone, and he can touch 94 occasionally. His slider gets the highest marks from among his secondary pitches, showing sharp, two-plane break in the low 80s, but he can also spin a curveball and shows feel for a changeup, both of which can be average pitches. Hockin should get a shot to go to low Class A Lake County in 2015.

Year	Club (League)	Class	W	L	ERA	G	GS	CG	SV	IP	H	HR	BB	SO	K/9	WHIP	AVG
2014	Indians (AZL)	R	0	0	3.86	9	7	0	0	21	21	1	4	19	8.1	1.19	.266
Minor League Totals			0	0	3.86	9	7	0	0	21	21	1	4	19	8.1	1.19	.266

30 RONNY RODRIGUEZ, INF

Born: April 17, 1992. **B-T:** R-R. **Ht.:** 6-0. **Wt.:** 170. **Signed:** Dominican Republic, 2010. **Signed by:** Ramon Pena/Miguel Valdez.

Rodriguez's career has had its share of odd twists and turns. Born in the Dominican Republic, he came to the U.S. at age 12 and attended high school in the States before returning to the island. After Major League Baseball decided he wouldn't have to go through the draft, he signed with the Indians for $375,000 in 2010. He looked like one of the organization's top middle-infield prospects for a time, but other players have surpassed him while he had to repeat Double-A Akron in 2014. He saw action at all four infield positions at Akron, though he played primarily second and third base. His pure athleticism is his best asset. He ranges well along with having sure hands and a strong-enough arm to play on the left side of the infield. Whether he'll be able to hit enough to be more than a utility player is the big question. He has some wiry strength, but he can fall in love trying to drive balls and take too many big swings. He's at his best as a contact hitter, and the Indians want to see him improve his pitch selection. He could yet make a run at a big league bench job, but first he must conquer Double-A.

Year	Club (League)	Class	AVG	G	AB	R	H	2B	3B	HR	RBI	BB	SO	SB	CS	OBP	SLG
2012	Carolina (CAR)	HiA	.264	126	454	67	120	20	4	19	66	19	88	7	7	.300	.452
2013	Akron (EL)	AA	.265	116	468	62	124	25	6	5	52	16	76	12	3	.291	.376
2014	Akron (EL)	AA	.228	118	413	52	94	25	0	5	34	25	92	4	5	.270	.324
Minor League Totals			.252	458	1705	222	429	98	17	40	194	73	339	33	22	.284	.399

Colorado Rockies

BY JACK ETKIN

The Rockies entered the 2014 season hoping to build on their improvement the year before and finish with a winning record for the first time since 2010.

What resulted instead was a regime change following a 96-loss season, two shy of the club record set in 2012. The Rockies typically struggle away from Coors Field but reached new depths in 2014, losing 39 of their final 45 road games to finish 21-60 away from home.

Shortly after the season ended, general manager Dan O'Dowd turned down a five-year extension and resigned. So did his chief assistant Bill Geivett, when he learned he wouldn't be O'Dowd's replacement.

In O'Dowd's 15 seasons as GM, the Rockies made the playoffs twice (as a wild card) and had four winning records. In August 2012, a front-office restructuring resulted in O'Dowd getting more involved in overseeing the minor league system and Geivett having day-to-day responsibility for the major league team. The unusual arrangement ultimately didn't work.

Jeff Bridich, 37, who had spent 10 seasons in the Rockies' front office and the last three as farm director, was promoted to GM. Skeptics thought it was a more-of-the-same hire, but Bridich has brought new energy and a different perspective to an organization in need of a reboot. He also has the advantage of knowing the system well.

Bridich takes over a team that ranked last in the National League in ERA for both starters (4.89) and relievers (4.79) in 2014. The Rockies used 15 different starting pitchers in 2014, tying the club record. Injuries wracked the rotation and exposed a lack of pitching depth. The team fired both pitching coach Jim Wright and bullpen coach Bo McLaughlin, replacing them with outsiders Steve Foster and Darren Holmes—a former teammate of manager Walt Weiss in the Rockies' early years. The organization also replaced four members of the minor league field staff, another sign that Bridich will do things differently.

Compounding matters, core players such as shortstop Troy Tulowitzki, left fielder Carlos Gonzalez, right fielder Michael Cuddyer and third baseman Nolan Arenado missed significant time with injuries.

"Our general goal is just to get us back to playing meaningful games in September," Bridich said. "That's the challenge before us. I think it's both an aggressive and realistic goal for us."

In the past two seasons, homegrown players such as Arenado, corner outfielders Charlie Blackmon and Corey Dickerson and lefthander

Nolan Arenado looks like a cornerstone, but like many Rockies he missed time in 2014

TOP PROSPECTS OF THE DECADE

Year	Player, Pos.	2014 Org
2005	Ian Stewart, 3b	Angels
2006	Ian Stewart, 3b	Angels
2007	Troy Tulowitzki, ss	Rockies
2008	Franklin Morales, lhp	Rockies
2009	Dexter Fowler, of	Astros
2010	Tyler Matzek, lhp	Rockies
2011	Tyler Matzek, lhp	Rockies
2012	Drew Pomeranz, lhp	Athletics
2013	Nolan Arenado, 3b	Rockies
2014	Jon Gray, rhp	Rockies

Tyler Matzek have contributed in Colorado, with more help on the way from a farm system that has improved in recent years.

Top pitching prospects Jon Gray and Eddie Butler are close to the majors—Butler was there briefly last year—and so is lefthander Tyler Anderson, if he can stay healthy. Catcher Tom Murphy should contribute soon too, but the real strength of the system is at the lower levels.

Eleven of the organization's Top 30 Prospects spent 2014 at low Class A Asheville, the South Atlantic League champion, including lefthander Kyle Freeland. The organization's first-round pick in 2014, Freeland signed for nearly $900,000 below slot, freeing up money to sign players such as second baseman Forrest Wall, third baseman Kevin Padlo and shortstop Max George.

General manager: Jeff Bridich. **Farm director:** Zach Wilson. **Scouting director:** Bill Schmidt.

Class	Team	League	W	L	PCT	Finish	Manager
Majors	Colorado Rockies	National	66	96	.407	29th (30)	Walt Weiss
Triple-A	*Colo. Springs Sky Sox	Pacific Coast	53	91	.368	16th (16)	Glenallen Hill
Double-A	†Tulsa Drillers	Texas	71	68	.511	4th (8)	Kevin Riggs
High A	Modesto Nuts	California	43	97	.307	10th (10)	Don Sneddon
Low A	Asheville Tourists	South Atlantic	89	49	.645	1st (14)	Fred Ocasio
Short season	#Tri-City Dust Devils	Northwest	33	43	.434	6th (8)	Drew Saylor
Rookie	Grand Junction Rockies	Pioneer	43	33	.566	1st (8)	Anthony Sanders
Overall Minor League Record			332	381	.466	24th (30)	

*Affiliate will be Albuquerque (Pacific Coast) in 2015. †Affiliate will be New Britain (Eastern) in 2015. #Affiliate will be Boise (Northwest) in 2015.

THIS YEAR'S TOP 30

No.	Player, Pos.	Grade/Risk
1.	David Dahl, of	65/High
2.	Jon Gray, rhp	65/High
3.	Kyle Freeland, lhp	60/High
4.	Eddie Butler, rhp	55/High
5.	Ryan McMahon, 3b	55/High
6.	Tom Murphy, c	50/Medium
7.	Forrest Wall, 2b	55/Extreme
8.	Antonio Senzatela, rhp	50/High
9.	Rosell Herrera, 3b	50/High
10.	Raimel Tapia, of	50/High
11.	Ryan Castellani, rhp	55/Extreme
12.	Trevor Story, ss/3b	50/High
13.	Emerson Jimenez, ss	50/High
14.	Kevin Padlo, 3b	50/High
15.	Jairo Diaz, rhp	50/High
16.	Tyler Anderson, lhp	50/High
17.	Dom Nunez, c	50/High
18.	Jose Briceno, c	50/High
19.	Rayan Gonzalez, rhp	45/Medium
20.	Kyle Parker, of/1b	45/Medium
21.	Sam Moll, lhp	45/High
22.	Correlle Prime, 1b	45/High
23.	Scott Oberg, rhp	45/High
24.	Sam Howard, lhp	45/High
25.	Jayson Aquino, lhp	45/High
26.	Carlos Estevez, rhp	45/High
27.	Jordan Patterson, of	45/High
28.	Helmis Rodriguez, lhp	45/High
29.	Johendi Jiminian, rhp	45/High
30.	Wes Rogers, of	50/Extreme

LAST YEAR'S TOP 30

No.	Player, Pos.	Status
1.	Jon Gray, rhp	No. 2
2.	Eddie Butler, rhp	No. 4
3.	Rosell Herrera, ss	No. 9
4.	Kyle Parker, 1b/of	No. 20
5.	Chad Bettis, rhp	Majors
6.	David Dahl, of	No. 1
7.	Tom Murphy, c	No. 6
8.	Ryan McMahon, 3b	No. 5
9.	Trevor Story, ss	No. 12
10.	Raimel Tapia, of	No. 10
11.	Tyler Anderson, lhp	No. 16
12.	Tyler Matzek, lhp	Majors
13.	Scott Oberg, rhp	No. 23
14.	Rayan Gonzalez, rhp	No. 19
15.	Sam Moll, lhp	No. 21
16.	Charlie Culberson, 2b/ss/of	Majors
17.	Rob Scahill, rhp	(Pirates)
18.	Taylor Featherston, 2b	(Angels)
19.	Chris Jenson, rhp	(Athletics)
20.	Emerson Jimenez, ss	No. 13
21.	Cristhian Adames, ss	Dropped out
22.	Raul Fernandez, rhp	(White Sox)
23.	Francisco Sosa, of	Free agent
24.	Antonio Senzatela, rhp	No. 8
25.	Dan Houston, rhp	Dropped out
26.	Max White, of	Dropped out
27.	Johendi Jiminian, rhp	No. 29
28.	Jayson Aquino, lhp	No. 25
29.	Jose Briceno, c	No. 18
30.	Ryan Warner, rhp	(Angels)

BEST TOOLS

Best Hitter for Average	David Dahl
Best Power Hitter	Ryan McMahon
Best Strike-Zone Discipline	Michael Tauchman
Fastest Baserunner	Omar Carrizales
Best Athlete	David Dahl
Best Fastball	Kyle Freeland
Best Curveball	Scott Oberg
Best Slider	Kyle Freeland
Best Changeup	Nelson Gonzalez
Best Control	Tyler Anderson
Best Defensive Catcher	Dustin Garneau
Best Defensive Infielder	Emerson Jimenez
Best Infield Arm	Emerson Jimenez
Best Defensive Outfielder	David Dahl
Best Outfield Arm	Jared Simon

PROJECTED 2018 LINEUP

Catcher	Tom Murphy
First Base	Ryan McMahon
Second Base	D.J. LeMahieu
Third Base	Nolan Arenado
Shortstop	Troy Tulowitzki
Left Field	Corey Dickerson
Center Field	David Dahl
Right Field	Charlie Blackmon
No. 1 Starter	Jon Gray
No. 2 Starter	Kyle Freeland
No. 3 Starter	Eddie Butler
No. 4 Starter	Tyler Matzek
No. 5 Starter	Antonio Senzatela
Closer	Rex Brothers

COLORADO ROCKIES

TOP 2015 ROOKIE: Eddie Butler, rhp. He's stronger after offseason work and should avoid the 2014 delivery issues that affected his sinker, slider and changeup, all plus pitches with great movement.

BREAKOUT PROSPECT: Dom Nunez, c. He's a well above-average receiver with a line-drive stroke and a high baseball IQ ready for the challenge of a full-season league.

SLEEPER: Ken Roberts, lhp. After vastly improving his changeup in the Arizona Fall League, he has a third pitch and is an intriguing bullpen option.

SOURCE OF TOP 30 TALENT			
Homegrown	30	Acquired	0
College	13	Trades	0
Junior college	0	Rule 5 draft	0
High school	8	Independent leagues	0
Draft-and-follow	0	Free agents/waivers	0
Nondrafted free agents	0		
International	9		

LF
Michael Tauchman
Drew Weeks
Brian Humphries
Terry McClure

CF
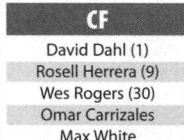
David Dahl (1)
Rosell Herrera (9)
Wes Rogers (30)
Omar Carrizales
Max White

RF

Raimel Tapia (10)
Kyle Parker (20)
Jordan Patterson (27)
Yonathan Daza

3B
Ryan McMahon (5)
Kevin Padlo (14)
Rafael Ynoa
Jayson Langfels
Shane Hoelscher

SS
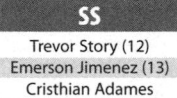
Trevor Story (12)
Emerson Jimenez (13)
Cristhian Adames

2B
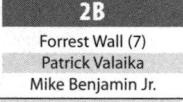
Forrest Wall (7)
Patrick Valaika
Mike Benjamin Jr.

1B
Correlle Prime (22)
Ben Paulsen
Ryan Casteel
Will Swanner
Henry Garcia
Sean Dwyer

C
Tom Murphy (6)
Dom Nunez (17)
Jose Briceno (18)
Dustin Garneau
Hamlet Marte
Chris O'Dowd
Rob Perkins

LHP

LHSP	LHRP
Kyle Freeland (3)	Sam Moll (21)
Tyler Anderson (16)	Ken Roberts
Sam Howard (24)	Trent Daniel
Jayson Aquino (25)	Yoely Bello
Helmis Rodriguez (28)	
Hunter Musgrave	
Dylan Craig	

RHP

RHSP	RHRP
Jon Gray (2)	Jairo Diaz (15)
Eddie Butler (4)	Rayan Gonzalez (19)
Antonio Senzatela (8)	Scott Oberg (23)
Ryan Castellani (11)	Carlos Estevez (26)
Johendi Jiminian (29)	Austin House
Konner Wade	Kyle Simon
Carlos Polanco	Nelson Gonzalez
Alex Balog	Shane Broyles
Javier Palacios	Matt Carasiti

2014

BEST PURE HITTER: 2B Forrest Wall (1s) has natural feel for hitting, surprising power and the speed to leg out extra hits. His contact ability translated in his pro debut, as he walked (27) almost as often as he struck out (32). He's as good a pure hitter as any player drafted in 2014. OF Drew Weeks (7) led Division I in hitting in the spring, hitting .430.

BEST POWER HITTER: 3B Kevin Padlo (5) has a strength-oriented swing and athleticism that helped him star in high school basketball at 6-foot-2, 200 pounds.

FASTEST RUNNER: Wall posts 70 run times to first base from the left side, which would play if he were to move to center field and which plays on the bases. OF Wes Rogers (4) has above-average speed that covers a lot of ground in the outfield.

BEST DEFENSIVE PLAYER: Rogers is raw but could be an above-average center fielder. SS/2B Chris Rabago (13) has sure hands and arm strength, so the Rockies tried him at catcher in instructional league.

BEST FASTBALL: LHP Kyle Freeland (1) pitched with similar stuff to what he showed in the spring, with a lively fastball touching 96 mph and consistently in the 91-94 range. He has excellent control and delivers his fastball with plane and angle, making it tough for hitters to square up. LHP Sam Howard (3) has touched 96 from the left side, while RHP Ryan Castellani (2) has hit 95 with a hard sinker.

BEST SECONDARY PITCH: Freeland's slider was so good in college, at 85-87 mph, he had a tendency to throw it too much.

BEST PRO DEBUT: Freeland went 3-0, 1.15 in 39 innings and helped low Class A Asheville win the South Atlantic League title. 3B Shane Hoelscher (17) led the short-season Northwest League in OBP during a .332/.427/.466 debut. Padlo, Wall and SS Max George (6) were three-quarters of the Rookie-level Grand Junction infield, with Padlo posting a 1.015 OPS, Wall .907 and George (.896).

BEST ATHLETE: Rogers lacks arm strength and needs to add strength but has fast-twitch traits.

MOST INTRIGUING BACKGROUND: Rabago's brother Hector converted from infielder to catcher in the Yankees system. RHP Hunter Brothers (30) is the younger brother of Rockies reliever Rex. RHP Gavin Glanz (23) is the son of Gary Glanz, a second-round pick in 1978.

CLOSEST TO THE MAJORS: Freeland has the fastball command to move quickly if healthy.

BEST LATE-ROUND PICK: Hoelscher and Rebago could be useful role players, as could RHP Grahamm Wiest (14), a command-oriented starter with an above-average changeup.

THE ONE WHO GOT AWAY: The Rockies signed every pick in the first 27 rounds but couldn't land sophomore-eligible 2B Landon Lassiter (28), who went back to North Carolina, or 1B Pavin Smith (32), now a freshman at Virginia.

ASSESSMENT: Kyle Freeland had an elbow issue before the draft and signed for a discount that helped the Rockies land Forrest Wall ($2 million) and three other above-slot preps.

2013

RHP Jon Gray (1) backed up in 2014, but his stuff had room to regress and he remains a formidable prospect. 3B Ryan McMahon (2) heads a group of intriguing bats including OF Jordan Patterson (4) and C Dom Nunez (6).

GRADE: B

2012

RHP Eddie Butler (1s) wasn't as good as he was in 2013 but still made his big league debut. OF David Dahl (1) recovered from a lost '13 season and has star-level tools. Colorado is counting on C Tom Murphy (3) to bounce back himself.

GRADE: B

2011

LHP Tyler Anderson (1) and SS Trevor Story (1s) still have a chance in a class defined by players that got away, such as unsigned C Peter O'Brien (3), RHP Ross Stripling (9) and OF Preston Tucker (16), plus Rule 5 draft losses 2B Taylor Featherston (5) and RHP Danny Winkler (20).

GRADE: D

TOP DRAFT PICKS OF THE DECADE

Year	Player, Pos.	2014 Org
2005	Troy Tulowitzki, ss	Rockies
2006	Greg Reynolds, rhp	Seibu (Japan)
2007	Casey Weathers, rhp	Rays
2008	Christian Friedrich, lhp	Rockies
2009	Tyler Matzek, lhp	Rockies
2010	Kyle Parker, of/1b	Rockies
2011	Tyler Anderson, lhp	Rockies
2012	David Dahl, of	Rockies
2013	Jon Gray, rhp	Rockies
2014	Kyle Freeland, lhp	Rockies

LARGEST BONUSES IN CLUB HISTORY

Jon Gray, 2013	$4,800,000
Tyler Matzek, 2009	$3,900,000
Greg Reynolds, 2006	$3,200,000
Jason Young, 2000	$2,750,000
David Dahl, 2012	$2,600,000

1 DAVID DAHL, OF

Born: April 1, 1994. **B-T:** L-R. **Ht.:** 6-2. **Wt.:** 195.
Drafted: HS—Birmingham, 2012 (1st round).
Signed by: Damon Iannelli.

The Rockies never had taken a high school outfielder with their first pick before drafting Dahl 10th overall in 2012 and signing him for $2.6 million, He won MVP honors in the Rookie-level Pioneer League in his 2012 debut, hitting a league-leading .379 with a 27-game hitting streak and 1.048 OPS. But 2013 was a lost season. After Dahl played Opening Day for low Class A Asheville, the Rockies sent him to extended spring training, a disciplinary measure for making his own airline reservation out of spring training. He returned to Asheville in late April but a week later suffered a season-ending torn right hamstring while running to first base. During his rehab, he developed lower back soreness that prevented him from participating in instructional league. Dahl returned to Asheville in 2014 seeking to be a team leader and he fulfilled that goal. After his long layoff, he was understandably rusty early in the season, but after hitting .368/.395/.513 in 117 at-bats to begin the second half, he earned a promotion to high Class A Modesto where he hit safely in his final 12 games. The Rockies wanted to give Dahl playoff experience and boost Asheville's chances in the postseason, so he returned there for the final two games of the regular season and then helped the Tourists win the South Atlantic League championship by hitting .367/.424/.700 in seven playoff games.

Dahl is a potential five-tool player. He is a pure hitter with very good hand-eye coordination who doesn't strike out too often. He can drive balls to all fields with an easy, loose, lefthanded swing. Dahl is a line-drive hitter, who occasionally will get away from that approach and try to hit home runs and attack pitches not in his hitting zone. He has extremely fast hands and has shown the ability to turn on inside fastballs in the low to mid-90s, an indication he will hit for power. He has the potential to hit 20-25 home runs if he reaches his ceiling. Dahl is a good bunter and being an above-average runner helps him maximize that part of his game. He's a gifted center fielder. He runs down balls without fear, running into walls twice in the same week while making catches at Modesto and charging and diving for balls without hesitation. Dahl's instincts, first-step quickness and routes are all above-average. He has an above-average arm that is very accurate.

Dahl's misspent 2013 season was a good teaching tool as far as dealing with and overcoming adversity and helping him mature. He could begin 2015 at Modesto but at some point during the season should reach Double-A New Britain. Toward the end of the 2016 season, Dahl could reach the big leagues where he has the potential to hit first, second or third in the lineup.

BA GRADE

65 Risk: High

SCOUTING GRADES

Batting: 60.
Power: 55.
Speed: 60.
Defense: 60.
Arm: 55.

Based on 20-80 scouting scale, where 50 represents major average, and future projection rather than present tools.

LGE	PA	BB%	SO%	ISO
SAL	422	5.5	15.4	.191
CAL	125	4.0	21.6	.200

Year	Club (League)	Class	AVG	G	AB	R	H	2B	3B	HR	RBI	BB	SO	SB	CS	OBP	SLG
2012	Grand Junction (PIO)	R	.379	67	280	62	106	22	10	9	57	21	42	12	7	.423	.625
2013	Asheville (SAL)	LoA	.275	10	40	9	11	4	1	0	7	2	8	2	0	.310	.425
2014	Modesto (CAL)	HiA	.267	29	120	14	32	8	2	4	14	5	27	3	0	.296	.467
	Asheville (SAL)	LoA	.309	90	392	69	121	33	6	10	41	23	65	18	5	.347	.500
Minor League Totals			.325	196	832	154	270	67	19	23	119	51	142	35	12	.364	.534

2 JON GRAY, RHP

Born: Nov. 5, 1991. **B-T:** R-R. **Ht.:** 6-4. **Wt.:** 235. **Drafted:** Oklahoma, 2013 (1st round). **Signed by:** Jesse Retzlaff.

Gray signed for a franchise-record $4.8 million after being taken third overall in the 2013 draft, topping the $3.9 million lefthander Tyler Matzek received in 2009. Gray began his pro career at Rookie-level Grand Junction, where he was told to throw only one slider per batter because he had thrown the pitch excessively at Oklahoma. He moved up to high Class A Modesto and went 4-0, 0.75 in five starts after the restriction was lifted. At Double-A Tulsa in 2014, Gray dealt with the rigors of his first full season and was shut down with shoulder fatigue after an Aug. 20 start and didn't return. After reaching 102 mph on multiple occasions in 2013 and sitting at 95-96 with his four-seam fastball in 2013, Gray topped out at 96 and pitched around 94 in 2014. He has above-average command of his fastball for someone who throws that hard. Gray tired as the 2014 season progressed, causing his front side to slightly drift open, and he wasn't able to maintain the on-line delivery he had earlier. He had enough feel that he could make the adjustment with his changeup, but he got around his slider a little bit. His changeup is above-average at 87-88 mph with a little run and sink, and Gray has plus command of the pitch. His slider is average but has the potential to be above-average and an out pitch. Expect Gray to begin 2015 at Triple-A Albuquerque, and he could easily reach the majors. He has a durable frame and projects to be as good as a No. 2 starter. His biggest advancements will come once he learns to read hitters and situations and develop pitchability with his quality stuff.

BA GRADE	
65	Risk: High

LGE	BF	SO%	BB%	HR/9
TL	508	22.2	8.1	0.72

Year	Club (League)	Class	W	L	ERA	G	GS	CG	SV	IP	H	HR	BB	SO	K/9	WHIP	AVG
2013	Grand Junction (PIO)	R	0	0	4.05	4	4	0	0	13	15	0	2	15	10.1	1.28	.278
	Modesto (CAL)	HiA	4	0	0.75	5	5	0	0	24	10	0	6	36	13.5	0.67	.128
2014	Tulsa (TL)	AA	10	5	3.91	24	24	0	0	124	107	10	41	113	8.2	1.19	.237
Minor League Totals			14	5	3.45	33	33	0	0	162	132	10	49	164	9.1	1.12	.226

3 KYLE FREELAND, LHP

Born: May 14, 1993. **B-T:** L-L. **Ht.:** 6-4. **Wt.:** 190. **Drafted:** Evansville, 2014 (1st round). **Signed by:** Scott Corman.

Freeland was born and raised in Denver and drafted out of high school by the Phillies in the 35th round in 2011. He opted to attend Evansville and was taken eighth overall by the Rockies in 2014 and signed for $2.3 million. Some clubs had medical concerns about Freeland, but not the Rockies since their doctor performed arthroscopic surgery on his left elbow when he was in high school. Freeland is a strike-thrower with double-plus control and two well above-average pitches. His fastball ranges from 90-97 mph and sits in the 92-93 range. He commands it to both sides of the plate and comes inside fearlessly, not just for intent but to get outs. Freeland has a wipeout 84-86 mph slider. He can throw it with a very tight, late break with tilt and boring action or with more of a horizontal, late sweeping action—or anywhere in between. Freeland's main focus in instructional league was developing his changeup, which he didn't throw often in college. It's firm at 84-88 mph, but thanks to an altered grip has some fade. He throws across his body but has a loose arm action and is just where he needs to be when releasing the ball. If Freeland doesn't begin 2015 at Double-A New Britain, he should get there at some point during the season and might even reach the majors where he profiles as high as No. 2 in a rotation.

BA GRADE	
60	Risk: High

LGE	BF	SO%	BB%	HR/9
PIO	66	22.7	3.0	0.00
SAL	82	22.0	4.9	0.42

Year	Club (League)	Class	W	L	ERA	G	GS	CG	SV	IP	H	HR	BB	SO	K/9	WHIP	AVG
2014	Grand Junction (PIO)	R	1	0	1.56	5	5	0	0	17	16	0	2	15	7.8	1.04	.254
	Asheville (SAL)	LoA	2	0	0.83	5	5	0	0	22	14	1	4	18	7.5	0.83	.179
Minor League Totals			3	0	1.15	10	10	0	0	39	30	1	6	33	7.6	0.92	.213

4 EDDIE BUTLER, RHP

Born: March 13, 1991. **B-T:** R-R. **Ht.:** 6-2. **Wt.:** 180. **Drafted:** Radford, 2012 (1st round supplemental). **Signed by:** Jay Matthews.

After being taken 46th overall in the 2012 draft and signing for $1 million, Butler finished the 2013 season at Double-A Tulsa. He returned there in 2014, and while trying to utilize his four-seamer more, he began overthrowing, causing his arm slot to rise slightly. His sinker didn't have the depth it had a year earlier, and his slider and curveball weren't as sharp. Hence, Butler wasn't ready when he made his major league debut on June 6. The following day, he showed up with soreness behind his right shoulder and ended up on the disabled list. Butler's sinker, changeup and slider are plus pitches with terrific movement. He also has a developing four-seamer that will get up to 97 mph and an average curveball that is more of a show-me pitch. Butler's sinker, his most dominant pitch, sits at 93-94 mph and has late action. So does his 87 mph changeup, which is his best secondary pitch. His 86 mph slider is sharp and tight but needs a bit more downward tilt. Butler eventually returned to Tulsa and made two late-September starts for the Rockies, but after the second he developed upper-back soreness that caused him to miss the Arizona Fall League. He has gotten stronger, which should help him maintain his delivery in 2015 at Triple-A Albuquerque. His raw stuff gives him a ceiling as a No. 2 starter.

BA GRADE

55 Risk: High

LGE	BF	SO%	BB%	HR/9
TL	450	14.0	7.1	0.83
NL	76	3.9	9.2	1.12

Year	Club (League)	Class	W	L	ERA	G	GS	CG	SV	IP	H	HR	BB	SO	K/9	WHIP	AVG
2012	Grand Junction (PIO)	R	7	1	2.13	13	12	0	0	68	59	1	13	55	7.3	1.06	.230
2013	Asheville (SAL)	LoA	5	1	1.66	9	9	0	0	54	25	2	25	51	8.4	0.92	.137
	Modesto (CAL)	HiA	3	4	2.39	13	13	0	0	68	58	7	21	67	8.9	1.17	.227
	Tulsa (TL)	AA	1	0	0.65	6	6	0	0	28	13	0	6	25	8.1	0.69	.138
2014	Modesto (CAL)	HiA	0	0	6.75	1	1	0	0	4	2	0	2	2	4.5	1.00	.125
	Colorado Springs (PCL)	AAA	0	1	10.13	1	1	0	0	5	8	0	3	4	6.8	2.06	.348
	Tulsa (TL)	AA	6	9	3.58	18	18	0	0	108	104	10	32	63	5.3	1.26	.254
	Colorado (NL)	MAJ	1	1	6.75	3	3	0	0	16	23	2	7	3	1.7	1.88	.343
Major League Totals			1	1	6.75	3	3	0	0	16	23	2	7	3	1.7	1.88	.343
Minor League Totals			22	16	2.64	61	60	0	0	335	269	20	102	267	7.2	1.11	.217

5 RYAN McMAHON, 3B

Born: Dec. 14, 1994. **B-T:** L-R. **Ht.:** 6-2. **Wt.:** 185. **Drafted:** HS—Santa Ana, Calif., 2013 (2nd round). **Signed by:** Jon Lukens.

McMahon was a quarterback at perennial California power Mater Dei High but signed with the Rockies for $1,327,600 instead of following through on his commitment to play baseball at Southern California. After ranking second in the Rookie-level Pioneer League in slugging (.583) in 2013, he moved up to low Class A Asheville and tied teammate Correlle Prime for the South Atlantic League lead in RBIs (102) and finished second in OPS (.860) and doubles (46) and tied for second in runs (93). McMahon has a loose, easy lefthanded swing and impressive power to all fields, particularly his pull side, for such a young hitter. He also has a chance to hit for average once his pitch recognition and plate discipline improve and he becomes a more mature, patient hitter. McMahon has a plus arm, soft hands and should develop plus range because he's an instinctual player. He makes the difficult reaction plays at third base and will make the more routine plays that have given him trouble once he gets his feet in synch with his arm. McMahon has a good feel for the game and, drawing on his days as a quarterback, has proven to be a leader on the field despite playing with older players. He will play at high Class A Modesto in 2015 and profiles as an impact middle-of-the-order run producer in the majors.

BA GRADE

55 Risk: High

LGE	PA	BB%	SO%	ISO
SAL	552	9.8	25.9	.220

Year	Club (League)	Class	AVG	G	AB	R	H	2B	3B	HR	RBI	BB	SO	SB	CS	OBP	SLG
2013	Grand Junction (PIO)	R	.321	59	218	42	70	18	3	11	52	28	59	4	6	.402	.583
2014	Asheville (SAL)	LoA	.282	126	482	93	136	46	3	18	102	54	143	8	5	.358	.502
Minor League Totals			.294	185	700	135	206	64	6	29	154	82	202	12	11	.372	.527

TONY FARLOW

6 TOM MURPHY, C

Born: April 3, 1991. **B-T:** R-R. **Ht.:** 6-1. **Wt.:** 220. **Drafted:** Buffalo, 2012 (3rd round). **Signed by:** Ed Santa.

Murphy is the fifth catcher the Rockies have taken as high as the third round since they began drafting in 1992. After beginning his first full season in 2013 at low Class A Asheville, he played his final 20 games of that season at Double-A Tulsa. He returned there in 2014, only to have his season end May 15 due to a right rotator cuff strain. Murphy avoided surgery and was at full strength toward the end of the season, but the Rockies decided not to risk playing him and having him enter the offseason in a rehab mode. Murphy is exceptionally strong and can impact a game on both sides of the ball. He has well above-average arm strength, an aggressive transfer and possesses above-average accuracy and receiving and blocking skills. Murphy is a leader who commands both the clubhouse and the pitching staff. He has a short, simple swing that generates plus power to all fields but needs to improve his strike-zone awareness and plate discipline. With his bat speed and strength, Murphy was looking to pull the ball too often early in the season, which made him vulnerable to pitches on the outer portion of the plate. Murphy likely will return to Tulsa to begin 2015, but with a few good months could move to Triple-A Albuquerque. The Rockies project him to be an everyday catcher, giving them an upgrade over Wilin Rosario.

BA GRADE

50 Risk: Medium

LGE	PA	BB%	SO%	ISO
TL	109	12.8	24.8	.202

Year	Club (League)	Class	AVG	G	AB	R	H	2B	3B	HR	RBI	BB	SO	SB	CS	OBP	SLG
2012	Tri-City (NWL)	SS	.288	55	212	26	61	13	3	6	38	14	52	1	1	.349	.462
2013	Asheville (SAL)	LoA	.288	80	288	55	83	26	2	19	74	37	87	4	5	.385	.590
	Tulsa (TL)	AA	.290	20	69	9	20	5	0	3	9	4	16	0	0	.338	.493
2014	Tulsa (TL)	AA	.213	27	94	16	20	4	0	5	15	14	27	0	0	.321	.415
Minor League Totals			.278	182	663	106	184	48	5	33	136	69	182	5	6	.360	.514

7 FORREST WALL, 2B

Born: Nov. 20, 1995. **B-T:** L-R. **Ht.:** 6-0. **Wt.:** 175. **Drafted:** HS—Maitland, Fla., 2014 (1st round supplemental). **Signed by:** John Cedarburg.

Wall is the highest drafted high school second baseman—35th overall—since the draft moved to a single phase in 1987. He committed to North Carolina but signed for an above-slot $2 million. He had labrum surgery on his right shoulder in November 2011 followed by a rushed rehab program that severely limited his arm strength. Wall is a pure hitter with loose hands who still finds a way to barrel up the ball because of his extraordinary hand-eye coordination, even when he opens his front hip prematurely and is off balance. He makes steady contact and drives the ball, especially to his pull side. His offspeed recognition is quite good for a young hitter, but he can chase fastballs up. Wall has above-average raw power that should become more a part of his game as he gains strength. Defensively, he needs work on his footwork and exchanges around second base turning double plays. His arm strength, while well below-average, improved during the 2014 season and could one day play as fringe-average as he continues in the Rockies' strength and rehab program. Wall should play at low Class A Asheville in 2015. If turning the double play proves too challenging, he could end up in center field, but he projects to be an impact bat at the top of the order.

BA GRADE

55 Risk: Extreme

LGE	PA	BB%	SO%	ISO
PIO	188	14.4	17.0	.172

Year	Club (League)	Class	AVG	G	AB	R	H	2B	3B	HR	RBI	BB	SO	SB	CS	OBP	SLG
2014	Grand Junction (PIO)	R	.318	41	157	48	50	6	6	3	24	27	32	18	5	.416	.490
Minor League Totals			.318	41	157	48	50	6	6	3	24	27	32	18	5	.416	.490

8 ANTONIO SENZATELA, RHP

TONY FARLOW

Born: Jan. 21, 1995. **B-T:** R-R. **Ht.:** 6-1. **Wt.:** 180. **Signed:** Venezuela, 2011.
Signed by: Rolando Fernandez/Orlando Medina/Carlos Gomez.

Senzatela signed for $250,000 in 2011 and dominated in the Dominican Summer League in 2012 and half of 2013 before being promoted in the middle of that year to short-season Tri-City. He served as the youngest and best starter in a strong low Class A Asheville rotation in 2014, going 8-1, 1.84 in 13 second-half starts and allowing one homer in 73 innings. Senzatela has a plus fastball that will reach 96 mph and sit around 93 with late life and a good downhill angle. Despite his youth, he has a mature body with little projection, so future velocity gains are unlikely. His fastball is fairly straight but is somewhat sneaky and gets on hitters quickly. Senzatela is able to command the pitch to both sides of the plate. The same with his straight changeup, which is an above-average pitch that works well off his fastball. After showing little feel for a curveball, he began working on a slider in instructional league and threw some good ones in sessions and live batting practice. He has the makings of a good slider, but it's a work in progress and lacks consistency. Senzatela will pitch at high Class A Modesto in 2015. He could be a No. 4 starter in the big leagues.

BA GRADE

50 Risk: High

LGE	BF	SO%	BB%	HR/9
SAL	602	14.8	6.0	0.68

Year	Club (League)	Class	W	L	ERA	G	GS	CG	SV	IP	H	HR	BB	SO	K/9	WHIP	AVG
2012	Rockies (DSL)	R	5	2	0.72	13	12	0	0	63	40	0	14	35	5.0	0.86	.179
2013	Rockies (DSL)	R	6	1	1.76	8	8	1	0	51	32	1	3	46	8.1	0.69	.179
	Tri-City (NWL)	SS	2	4	3.83	8	8	0	0	42	48	1	13	20	4.3	1.44	.282
2014	Asheville (SAL)	LoA	15	2	3.11	26	26	0	0	145	134	11	36	89	5.5	1.18	.243
Minor League Totals			28	9	2.48	55	54	1	0	301	254	13	66	190	5.7	1.06	.226

9 ROSELL HERRERA, SS/3B

Born: Oct. 16, 1992. **B-T:** B-R. **Ht.:** 6-3. **Wt.:** 190. **Signed:** Dominican Republic, 2009. **Signed by:** Rolando Fernandez/Jhonathan Leyba.

Herrera signed for $550,000 in 2009, played well in the Rookie-level Pioneer League in 2011 but saved his big breakthrough for low Class A Asheville in 2013, when he won both the South Atlantic League batting title (.343) and MVP honors. Inflammation in both wrists sabotaged his encore at high Class A Modesto in 2014, forcing him out for five weeks early in the season and bothering him for the balance of the year. Herrera has a long, loose body and loose actions. The switch-hitter is much better from the left side, while his long limbs give him extension and enable him to make adjustments to hit different pitches in and out of the zone. Herrera still has breaking-ball and count-management issues, but he has good bat speed and has developed a balanced approach. His long actions are a hindrance at shortstop and third base, where he's a below-average defender, so the Rockies tried him in center field during 2014 instructional league. Herrera is instinctively natural when it comes to reads and first-step quickness in the outfield and has a solid-average to plus arm. His accuracy will improve as he gets experience with outfield hops. The Rockies say the outfield is an addition for Herrera, not a conversion from the infield, and now that he has been fitted for special wrist braces, he should be at full health in 2015, when he faces a likely return to Modesto.

BA GRADE

50 Risk: High

LGE	PA	BB%	SO%	ISO
CAL	302	7.9	17.2	0.091

Year	Club (League)	Class	AVG	G	AB	R	H	2B	3B	HR	RBI	BB	SO	SB	CS	OBP	SLG
2012	Asheville (SAL)	LoA	.202	63	213	22	43	8	2	1	26	21	49	6	3	.271	.272
	Tri-City (NWL)	SS	.284	47	194	30	55	6	2	1	30	14	34	7	3	.332	.351
2013	Asheville (SAL)	LoA	.343	126	472	83	162	33	0	16	76	61	96	21	8	.419	.515
2014	Modesto (CAL)	HiA	.244	72	275	31	67	11	1	4	23	24	52	9	7	.302	.335
Minor League Totals			.277	438	1629	231	451	70	14	29	215	171	317	65	33	.348	.390

10 RAIMEL TAPIA, OF

TONY FARLOW

Born: Feb. 4, 1994. **B-T:** L-L. **Ht.:** 6-2. **Wt.:** 160. **Signed:** Dominican Republic, 2010. **Signed by:** Rolando Fernandez/Jhonathan Leyba/Hector Roa.

Tapia signed for $175,000 in 2010 and after two seasons in the Dominican Summer League, he led the Rookie-level Pioneer League in batting (.357) and hits (92) in 2013 and had a 29-game hitting streak. At low Class A Asheville in 2014, he finished third in the South Atlantic League in batting (.326), tied for second in runs (93) and tied for third in hits (157). Tapia has exceptional hand-eye coordination, uses his hands well and has plus bat speed and the ability to manipulate the barrel. He has an upright stance until he gets to two strikes, when he spreads out and squats way down, and consistently generates hard two-strike contact. He can be overly emotional when things aren't going his way on the field, and he can lose focus on defense. In batting practice, Tapia has easy pull-side power, and given his great swing it should start to play as he as he gains strength. He mostly played left field at Asheville until David Dahl moved up to high Class A Modesto and then took over in center field, which he is equipped to play. He is at least an average runner, whose reads and jumps are decent. He has plus arm strength, but his accuracy needs work. Tapia has at least average tools across the board aside from his power, and should play at high Class A Modesto in 2015.

BA GRADE	
50	Risk: High

LGE	PA	BB%	SO%	ISO
SAL	539	6.5	16.7	0.127

Year	Club (League)	Class	AVG	G	AB	R	H	2B	3B	HR	RBI	BB	SO	SB	CS	OBP	SLG
2012	Rockies (DSL)	R	.316	63	237	31	75	9	1	0	35	20	35	13	11	.383	.363
2013	Grand Junction (PIO)	R	.357	66	258	53	92	20	6	7	47	15	31	10	9	.399	.562
2014	Asheville (SAL)	LoA	.326	122	481	93	157	32	1	9	72	35	90	33	16	.382	.453
Minor League Totals			.318	318	1224	206	389	67	11	17	189	96	197	71	44	.376	.432

11 RYAN CASTELLANI, RHP

BA GRADE	
55	Risk: Extreme

Born: April 1, 1996. **B-T:** R-R. **Ht.:** 6-4. **Wt.:** 190. **Drafted:** HS—Phoenix, 2014 (2nd round). **Signed by:** Chris Forbes.

Castellani signed for $1.1 million as the 48th overall pick in the 2014 draft, then held his own against older players at short-season Tri-City. He has a strong, lanky pitcher's body, a loose arm action and a balanced, clean delivery. Castellani displayed a calmness and maturity beyond his years, a fearlessness about pitching inside and good downhill angle on his fastball. His sinker is an above-average pitch at 91-93 mph with late depth. He controls but doesn't command his changeup but can keep the pitch down and throws it comfortably and willingly. He worked on his glove-side fastball command and his slider in instructional league. He's working to make that pitch tighter with a late break. Castellani could have three plus pitches and projects to be a solid No. 3 starter if he reaches his ceiling. He could start 2015 in extended spring training but should end up at low Class A Asheville, if he doesn't begin the year there.

Year	Club (League)	Class	W	L	ERA	G	GS	CG	SV	IP	H	HR	BB	SO	K/9	WHIP	AVG
2014	Tri-City (NWL)	SS	1	2	3.65	10	10	0	0	37	35	2	9	25	6.1	1.19	.248
Minor League Totals			1	2	3.65	10	10	0	0	37	35	2	9	25	6.1	1.19	.248

12 TREVOR STORY, SS/3B

BA GRADE	
50	Risk: High

Born: Nov. 15, 1992. **B-T:** R-R. **Ht.:** 6-1. **Wt.:** 175. **Drafted:** HS—Irving, Texas, 2011 (1st round supplemental). **Signed by:** Dar Cox.

Story signed for $915,000 after the Rockies took him 45th overall in 2011, but his struggles to make consistent contact have kept him from fulfilling his potential. He has trouble with sliders down and away, and fastballs both in and up, and he needs to eliminate at least one of those holes in his swing. He carries his hands with him at times while striding, keeping him from reading and recognizing pitches. Story has good hand-eye coordination and plus bat speed but will pull off his lower half, causing balance issues that make it hard for him to get to anything spinning on the outer half of the plate. He has enough bat speed and bat strength to let the ball travel, and he did a better job last year of not sitting on his back side, though in Double-A he had trouble keeping his lower half closed. In the field, Story doesn't always react to balls as a shortstop must and seemed a step slow. He even played five games last year at second base, where he may end up. After struggling in Double-A last year, Story will probably return to that level to begin 2015 at the Rockies' new New Britain affiliate.

Year	Club (League)	Class	AVG	G	AB	R	H	2B	3B	HR	RBI	BB	SO	SB	CS	OBP	SLG
2012	Asheville (SAL)	LoA	.277	122	477	96	132	43	6	18	63	60	121	15	3	.367	.505
2013	Modesto (CAL)	HiA	.233	130	497	71	116	34	5	12	65	45	183	23	1	.305	.394
2014	Tri-City (NWL)	SS	.286	2	7	2	2	1	0	0	0	1	3	0	0	.375	.429
	Modesto (CAL)	HiA	.332	50	184	38	61	17	7	5	28	31	59	20	4	.436	.582
	Tulsa (TL)	AA	.200	56	205	29	41	8	1	9	20	28	82	3	1	.302	.380
Minor League Totals			.258	407	1549	273	400	111	21	50	204	191	489	74	10	.347	.454

13 EMERSON JIMENEZ, SS

BA GRADE

50 Risk: High

Born: Dec. 16, 1994. **B-T:** B-R. **Ht.:** 6-1. **Wt.:** 160. **Signed:** Dominican Republic, 2011. **Signed by:** Rolando Fernandez/Jhonathan Leyba/Martin Cabrera.

Jimenez started the 2014 season in extended spring training before heading to low Class A Asheville on May 20. The delay had nothing to do with his skills or injury. Instead, the Rockies wanted him to work on improving his English before heading off to a full-season league. Jimenez signed as a switch-hitter, but because he was undersized and lacked strength, the Rockies had him bat from his natural lefthanded side only. Now that he has filled out, Jimenez reinstituted his righthanded swing during instructional league in the Dominican Republic. He is an aggressive defensive player who can throw accurately from all angles with plus arm strength, and he makes all the agile reaction plays required of a premium shortstop. Jimenez projects to be a top-of-the-order hitter with the ability to hit line drives from gap to gap. He could open the 2015 season back at Asheville but should move to high Class A Modesto.

Year	Club (League)	Class	AVG	G	AB	R	H	2B	3B	HR	RBI	BB	SO	SB	CS	OBP	SLG
2012	Rockies (DSL)	R	.261	65	238	23	62	9	1	0	16	9	42	13	4	.289	.307
2013	Rockies (DSL)	R	.222	8	36	3	8	1	0	0	4	1	4	1	2	.243	.250
	Grand Junction (PIO)	R	.309	46	181	32	56	8	1	3	20	9	42	6	3	.344	.414
2014	Asheville (SAL)	LoA	.259	73	266	36	69	11	4	1	28	5	58	16	7	.276	.342
Minor League Totals			.270	192	721	94	195	29	6	4	68	24	146	36	16	.296	.344

14 KEVIN PADLO, 3B

BA GRADE

50 Risk: High

Born: July 15, 1996. **B-T:** R-R. **Ht.:** 6-2. **Wt.:** 200. **Drafted:** HS—Murrieta, Calif., 2014 (5th round). **Signed by:** Jon Lukens.

Padlo signed for an above-slot $650,000 bonus as the Rockies swayed him from a University of San Diego commitment. He is strong, with impressive power for a high school player. His strike-zone awareness is not bad for a young hitter, and he had nearly as many walks (31) as strikeouts (38) in his debut and thrived in pressure situations. He has no problem turning on a fastball, though he sometimes gets in trouble chasing fastballs up. Padlo can get pull-happy but drove the ball to the opposite field toward the end of the season. He has a solid, accurate arm with hands that are good enough for third base. He gets a little flat-footed at times and will emphasize skill work over strength work to gain agility and improve his footwork and first-step quickness. Padlo has a thick body for an 18-year-old and will have to watch his weight so his lower half get doesn't get too thick. He likely will play at low Class A Asheville in 2015.

Year	Club (League)	Class	AVG	G	AB	R	H	2B	3B	HR	RBI	BB	SO	SB	CS	OBP	SLG
2014	Grand Junction (PIO)	R	.300	48	160	32	48	15	4	8	44	31	38	6	1	.421	.594
Minor League Totals			.300	48	160	32	48	15	4	8	44	31	38	6	1	.421	.594

15 JAIRO DIAZ, RHP

BA GRADE

50 Risk: High

Born: May 27, 1991. **B-T:** R-R. **Ht:** 6-0. **Wt:** 195. **Signed:** Venezuela, 2007. **Signed by:** Leo Perez (Angels).

If the flame-throwing Diaz looks like a pitcher in a catcher's body, that's because he spent the first two years of his career behind the plate. An anemic bat coupled with a strong arm prompted a move to the mound in 2010. His triple-digit fastball and nasty slider carried him all the way to Anaheim in 2014, and the Rockies grabbed him in a December trade for Josh Rutledge. Diaz shortened his arm action significantly last year, adding deception, helping him repeat his delivery and producing better velocity. His powerful delivery has effort as he turns his hip toward third base and then explodes toward the hitter. His plus-plus fastball sits 97-98 mph and hits 100 at times, though it has below-average life and Diaz will need to command it better. His hard slider sits at 87-90 mph and is a true out pitch when it's on. He has a changeup with split action, but he uses it infrequently. Diaz made incredible strides in 2014, and the Rockies will look for him to earn a spot in the big league bullpen out of spring training.

Year	Club (League)	Class	W	L	ERA	G	GS	CG	SV	IP	H	HR	BB	SO	K/9	WHIP	AVG
2012	Cedar Rapids (MWL)	LoA	2	7	7.70	13	13	0	0	69	99	8	29	45	5.9	1.86	.343
	Orem (PIO)	R	5	6	5.30	14	14	0	0	75	93	5	23	61	7.4	1.55	.304
2013	Burlington (MWL)	LoA	0	3	3.97	32	0	0	8	34	27	3	11	28	7.4	1.12	.220
	Inland Empire (CAL)	HiA	0	2	8.87	13	0	0	0	22	38	3	14	21	8.5	2.33	.373
2014	Inland Empire (CAL)	HiA	2	3	4.78	29	0	0	4	32	31	2	10	37	10.4	1.28	.244
	Arkansas (TL)	AA	2	1	2.20	27	0	0	11	33	30	2	10	48	13.2	1.22	.252
	Los Angeles (AL)	MAJ	0	0	3.18	5	0	0	0	6	4	0	3	8	12.7	1.24	.200
Major League Totals			0	0	3.18	5	0	0	0	6	4	0	3	8	12.7	1.24	.200
Minor League Totals			18	27	5.36	159	41	0	26	368	423	27	137	322	7.9	1.52	.290

16 TYLER ANDERSON, LHP

Born: Dec. 30, 1989. **B-T:** L-L. **Ht.:** 6-4. **Wt.:** 215. **Drafted:** Oregon, 2011 (1st round). **Signed by:** Jesse Retzlaff.

Health has become a major concern with Anderson, who won Texas League pitcher of the year honors at Double-A Tulsa in 2014 after leading the circuit in ERA (1.98), opponent average (.216) and WHIP (1.11). He left a Sept. 10 playoff start after three innings, however, and doctors found a stress fracture in his left elbow, the same injury that caused him to be scratched from the Arizona Fall League in 2013. Anderson dealt with a sports hernia in 2012 and also missed nine weeks in 2013 with shoulder soreness. He missed two May starts last year with elbow soreness but otherwise was healthy until September. Anderson is analytical, extremely competitive and has a good feel for pitching as well as a deceptive delivery. He challenges hitters on the inner half and pitches to both sides of the plate with an 89-90 mph fastball that will reach 93. He has added an 86-89 mph cutter that has become his best secondary pitch, followed by a changeup that has average depth. He also has a curveball that he uses sparingly. If healthy, he should begin 2015 at Triple-A Albuquerque and projects as a back-end starter.

Year	Club (League)	Class	W	L	ERA	G	GS	CG	SV	IP	H	HR	BB	SO	K/9	WHIP	AVG
2012	Asheville (SAL)	LoA	12	3	2.47	20	20	2	0	120	102	5	28	81	6.1	1.08	.232
2013	Tri-City (NWL)	SS	1	1	0.60	3	3	0	0	15	9	0	3	13	7.8	0.80	.164
	Modesto (CAL)	HiA	3	2	3.25	13	13	0	0	75	62	10	24	63	7.6	1.15	.224
2014	Tulsa (TL)	AA	7	4	1.98	23	23	0	0	118	91	3	40	103	7.8	1.11	.216
Minor League Totals			23	10	2.38	59	59	2	0	328	264	18	95	260	7.1	1.09	.221

17 DOM NUNEZ, C

Born: Jan. 17, 1995. **B-T:** L-R. **Ht.:** 6-0. **Wt.:** 180. **Drafted:** HS—Elk Grove, Calif., 2013 (6th round). **Signed by:** Gary Wilson.

It took an above-slot bonus of $800,000 to keep Nunez from going to UCLA out of the 2013 draft. He played second base and shortstop in his pro debut but was considered a step slow, and the Rockies moved him behind the plate in instructional league that fall. Nunez returned to Rookie-level Grand Junction in 2014 and served as a team leader. He is an exceptional receiver whose footwork and exchange are quick, leading to pop times on throws to second base of about 1.9 seconds. He has more than enough arm strength but needs to improve his accuracy. His baseball IQ may be his greatest strength. Nunez is a line-drive, gap-to-gap hitter with pull power. His stroke can get a little long, resulting in a lot of balls in the air, though he did a much better job last season of staying in the middle of the field and swinging at strikes he could hit. He will make his full-season debut at low Class A Asheville in 2015.

Year	Club (League)	Class	AVG	G	AB	R	H	2B	3B	HR	RBI	BB	SO	SB	CS	OBP	SLG
2013	Grand Junction (PIO)	R	.200	55	195	24	39	13	1	3	23	18	34	11	8	.269	.323
2014	Grand Junction (PIO)	R	.313	46	176	30	55	12	0	8	40	21	28	5	7	.384	.517
Minor League Totals			.253	101	371	54	94	25	1	11	63	39	62	16	15	.324	.415

18 JOSE BRICENO, C

Born: Sept. 19, 1992. **B-T:** R-R. **Ht.:** 6-1. **Wt.:** 210. **Signed:** Venezuela, 2009. **Signed by:** Rolando Fernandez/Francisco Cartaya.

Briceno spent an entire year with a full-season club for the first time in 2014 and his catching improved dramatically. He has the tools to be a standout catcher, with a well above-average arm with above-average accuracy, and he recorded pop times of about 1.8 seconds on throws to second base thanks to an efficient exchange. He is working to block balls better, and if he gets that down he could move quickly. Briceno is a potential impact bat with impressive raw power to all fields. He tried too hard to hit home runs in the first half of the 2014 season, so he was pull-happy and guessing, which led to one in 141 at-bats. He settled down in the second half and hit 11 homers in 174 at-bats. Better posture at the plate helped him.

Briceno used to be hunched over and was vulnerable to fastballs inside, so he had to cheat, but now he is more upright and can handle all pitch types. He is introverted, so he'll have to work on his leadership, which the Rockies stressed in instructional league. He'll move up to high Class A Modesto in 2015.

Year	Club (League)	Class	AVG	G	AB	R	H	2B	3B	HR	RBI	BB	SO	SB	CS	OBP	SLG
2012	Grand Junction (PIO)	R	.391	7	23	5	9	0	0	2	5	2	2	0	0	.462	.652
2013	Asheville (SAL)	LoA	.264	26	91	12	24	6	0	1	8	5	20	1	0	.302	.363
	Grand Junction (PIO)	R	.333	36	153	32	51	16	0	9	30	5	30	8	2	.356	.614
2014	Asheville (SAL)	LoA	.283	84	315	38	89	23	1	12	50	16	57	8	4	.336	.476
Minor League Totals			.280	252	893	125	250	61	2	24	128	68	159	38	14	.342	.433

19 RAYAN GONZALEZ, RHP

BA GRADE

45 Risk: Medium

Born: Oct. 18, 1990. **B-T:** R-R. **Ht.:** 6-3. **Wt.:** 175. **Drafted:** Bethune-Cookman, 2012 (21st round). **Signed by:** John Cedarburg.

After not signing with the Athletics as an 18th-rounder out of high school in Puerto Rico, Gonzalez attended Bethune-Cookman, a historically black college in Daytona Beach, Fla., whose baseball coach Jason Beverlin recruits P.R. Gonzalez began the 2014 season at high Class A Modesto in a setup role but began closing in late May when Raul Fernandez faltered. Gonzalez did not allow a home run in 56 innings, making it two straight seasons totaling 110 innings in which he has not yielded a homer. He is an extreme groundball pitcher, whose groundout/airout ratio was 3.3 in 2014. Gonzalez has tremendous stuff and doesn't throw anything straight but has below-average command of three pitches. His heavy sinker ranges from 90-95 mph and sits around 93. He throws a changeup around 80 mph with good depth and a devastating 85-86 mph cutter with sharp bite and downward tilt. Gonzalez continually pitches himself into trouble, which shouldn't happen with stuff suited for the back end of the bullpen. But to be reliable in the eighth or ninth, Gonzalez will have to improve his control. He should begin the 2015 season at Double-A New Britain.

Year	Club (League)	Class	W	L	ERA	G	GS	CG	SV	IP	H	HR	BB	SO	K/9	WHIP	AVG
2012	Grand Junction (PIO)	R	0	3	6.75	22	0	0	0	24	33	3	15	27	10.1	2.00	.308
2013	Asheville (SAL)	LoA	2	3	2.68	49	0	0	12	54	51	0	21	70	11.7	1.34	.243
2014	Modesto (CAL)	HiA	4	5	3.99	50	0	0	11	56	65	0	22	64	10.2	1.54	.290
Minor League Totals			6	11	3.96	121	0	0	23	134	149	3	58	161	10.8	1.54	.275

20 KYLE PARKER, OF/1B

BA GRADE

45 Risk: Medium

Born: Sept. 30, 1989. **B-T:** R-R. **Ht.:** 6-0. **Wt.:** 205. **Drafted:** Clemson, 2010 (1st round). **Signed by:** Jay Matthews.

Parker made his major league debut in 2014, earning three stints with the Rockies that amounted to 18 games and three starts. He possesses righthanded power, which teams covet and which will be his make-or-break tool. A former quarterback at Clemson, he signed for $1.4 million after the Rockies took him 26th overall in 2010. Parker has decent bat speed but has had contact issues. He has the power to profile in right field, and he actually hits with more authority versus same-side pitchers, slugging .507 against righties since 2012, compared to .436 versus lefties. He started playing at first base in 2013, but right field is his best position. He is a below-average defensive player there but has a strong, accurate arm. At first base, he needs work reading groundballs and short hops. His plate discipline and ability to stay on the ball and go to right field have improved. Parker might not have the power output or show the on-base ability to start for a first-division team, but his power would play in a complementary role. He probably will head to Triple-A to open 2015.

Year	Club (League)	Class	AVG	G	AB	R	H	2B	3B	HR	RBI	BB	SO	SB	CS	OBP	SLG
2012	Modesto (CAL)	HiA	.308	102	390	86	120	18	6	23	73	66	88	1	2	.415	.562
2013	Tulsa (TL)	AA	.288	123	480	70	138	23	3	23	74	40	99	6	6	.345	.492
2014	Colo Springs (PCL)	AAA	.289	128	502	73	145	30	3	15	72	33	102	4	3	.336	.450
	Colorado (NL)	MAJ	.192	18	26	1	5	1	0	0	1	0	14	0	0	.192	.231
Major League Totals			.192	18	26	1	5	1	0	0	1	0	14	0	0	.192	.231
Minor League Totals			.292	470	1817	304	530	94	13	82	314	187	422	13	11	.364	.493

21 SAM MOLL, LHP

BA GRADE

45 Risk: High

Born: Jan. 3, 1992. **B-T:** L-L. **Ht.:** 5-10. **Wt.:** 185. **Drafted:** Memphis, 2013 (3rd round). **Signed by:** Scott Corman.

Elbow soreness delayed Moll's 2014 debut until Aug. 2, after he missed a month with a broken toe at the end of 2013. A starter in college, he seems destined to end up in the bullpen, where he could work in a high-leverage role facing tough lefthanded batters. For now he might continue starting for developmental reasons. He has flashed three plus pitches at times, with a feel for how to use them. Moll sits at 93-94 mph and touches 96 with a fastball that has a lot of run. He commands the pitch well but can miss up at times while reaching for more stuff. He has a putaway, mid-80s slider that can overmatch both righties and lefties and comes right out of his fastball slot with no change in his delivery. His changeup has depth and sink and is at times a plus pitch. Moll had minor surgery on his elbow on Sept. 19 and is expected to be ready to open the season at high Class A Modesto.

Year	Club (League)	Class	W	L	ERA	G	GS	CG	SV	IP	H	HR	BB	SO	K/9	WHIP	AVG
2013	Tri-City (NWL)	SS	3	1	1.80	10	6	0	0	30	20	0	10	29	8.7	1.00	.182
2014	Tri-City (NWL)	SS	0	1	4.15	9	0	0	0	13	17	1	4	7	4.8	1.62	.327
Minor League Totals			3	2	2.51	19	6	0	0	43	37	1	14	36	7.5	1.19	.228

22 CORRELLE PRIME, 1B

BA GRADE

45 Risk: High

Born: Feb. 18, 1994. **B-T:** R-R. **Ht.:** 6-5. **Wt.:** 220. **Drafted:** HS—Bradenton, Fla., 2012 (12th round). **Signed by:** John Cedarburg.

Prime spent his first two seasons at Rookie-level Grand Junction before moving up to low Class A Asheville in 2014 and blossoming into a prospect. He led the South Atlantic League in doubles (47), tied teammate Ryan McMahon for the lead in RBIs (102) and finished second in slugging (.520). An exceptionally hard worker with good makeup, Prime always had power to all fields but shortened his swing and learned to use his lower half. He began his pro career as an inside-out hitter who primarily hit with his hands and filled up right-center field. New swing mechanics have given him better balance and control of the barrel, enabling him to get on top of the ball and pull pitches on the inner half. Prime can hit balls that are down and middle-in a long way. His ability to adjust the bat head within the zone will be key for him moving up. He is decent defensively with soft hands and a good arm at first base, and he is working to improve his lateral movement. He should play at high Class A Modesto in 2015.

Year	Club (League)	Class	AVG	G	AB	R	H	2B	3B	HR	RBI	BB	SO	SB	CS	OBP	SLG
2012	Grand Junction (PIO)	R	.283	36	127	17	36	7	0	1	11	18	34	0	0	.377	.362
2013	Grand Junction (PIO)	R	.281	59	224	30	63	12	2	7	39	11	55	11	2	.318	.446
2014	Asheville (SAL)	LoA	.291	127	508	84	148	47	3	21	102	36	131	8	2	.336	.520
Minor League Totals			.288	222	859	131	247	66	5	29	152	65	220	19	4	.338	.477

23 SCOTT OBERG, RHP

BA GRADE

45 Risk: High

Born: March 13, 1990. **B-T:** R-R. **Ht.:** 6-2. **Wt.:** 205. **Drafted:** Connecticut, 2012 (15th round). **Signed by:** Mike Garlatti.

Tommy John surgery caused Oberg to miss his junior year at Connecticut, but he returned as a redshirt junior in 2012, recorded nine saves and was drafted by the Rockies in the 15th round. With a competitive edge and high level of aggressiveness, he has a closer's mentality and has converted 61 of 68 professional save opportunities. The Rockies would have called him up last season to help their leaky bullpen, but right shoulder soreness ended his season in August. Oberg throws a 93-96 mph fastball for strikes, but he needs to refine his command. He also owns a power curveball and an improved changeup. He has worked on a slider, throwing it well in warmups—but not in games. His slider would give him a pitch to open up both sides of the zone, while also providing more of a command breaking pitch, which would allay concerns that his sharp curveball might not be called for strikes in the big leagues. Oberg had what was termed minor shoulder surgery on Aug. 28 but is expected to be ready for spring training. If healthy, he would probably open the season at Triple-A but could contribute in the big leagues in 2015.

Year	Club (League)	Class	W	L	ERA	G	GS	CG	SV	IP	H	HR	BB	SO	K/9	WHIP	AVG
2012	Grand Junction (PIO)	R	0	2	2.33	25	0	0	13	27	20	2	6	29	9.7	0.96	.196
2013	Modesto (CAL)	HiA	1	6	1.86	56	0	0	33	53	34	4	27	61	10.3	1.14	.178
2014	Tulsa (TL)	AA	0	1	2.63	27	0	0	15	27	22	1	6	21	6.9	1.02	.218
Minor League Totals			1	9	2.17	108	0	0	61	108	76	7	39	111	9.3	1.07	.193

24 SAM HOWARD, LHP

BA GRADE

45 Risk: High

Born: March 5, 1993. **B-T:** L-L. **Ht.:** 6-3. **Wt.:** 180. **Drafted:** Georgia Southern, 2014 (3rd round). **Signed by:** Alan Matthews.

The Cubs drafted Howard in the 48th round in 2011, but he went to Georgia Southern and signed for $672,100 after the Rockies took him in the third round in 2014. He has a lanky body and a clean and easy delivery, and his fastball sits at 91-92 mph, touching 94 consistently. He throws an explosive fastball and improved his command of it as the 2014 season went on. During instructional league he worked on throwing with a good downhill angle, and hitters have a hard time elevating it when he does.

Howard came to pro ball with a poor curveball and cutter that was big and flat. In instructional league, he developed a better hybrid breaking ball with depth. He needs to tweak his grip on the pitch and stop trying to throw it so hard. His changeup is inconsistent but flashes plus and should be effective against righthanders. Howard does not handle failure well and needs to gain maturity in that area. He could start 2015 in extended spring training but should get a look at low Class A Asheville.

Year	Club (League)	Class	W	L	ERA	G	GS	CG	SV	IP	H	HR	BB	SO	K/9	WHIP	AVG
2014	Grand Junction (PIO)	R	1	3	5.40	14	13	0	0	53	73	6	10	42	7.1	1.56	.333
Minor League Totals			1	3	5.40	14	13	0	0	53	73	6	10	42	7.1	1.56	.333

25 JAYSON AQUINO, LHP

BA GRADE

45 Risk: High

Born: Nov. 22, 1992. **B-T:** L-L. **Ht.:** 6-1. **Wt.:** 180. **Signed:** Dominican Republic, 2009. **Signed by:** Rolando Fernandez, Jhonathan Leyba, Frank Roa.

Aquino spent the bulk of 2014 at high Class A Modesto before making his final two starts at Double-A Tulsa. A major challenge has been to throw his fastball more and not be overly reliant on his well above-average changeup. He improved in 2014, but more because of an organization mandate rather than making the adjustment himself. He touches 92 mph and pitches at 88-89 with his fastball that has run but not much sink. Aquino still needs to be able to command his fastball in to righthanders. His changeup is typically 10 mph slower than his fastball, has a little run and is his best pitch. But with runners on base, he falls into a pattern of throwing changeup after changeup. His 11-to-5 curveball is a tick above-average, but the pitch suffers because he tends to drift in his delivery. Aquino should return to Double-A to open 2015.

Year	Club (League)	Class	W	L	ERA	G	GS	CG	SV	IP	H	HR	BB	SO	K/9	WHIP	AVG
2012	Rockies (DSL)	R	6	1	1.52	9	9	2	0	65	45	1	9	74	10.2	0.83	.191
	Grand Junction (PIO)	R	4	0	1.87	7	7	0	0	43	32	2	11	36	7.5	0.99	.203
2013	Tri-City (NWL)	SS	0	1	3.13	4	4	0	0	23	21	1	5	16	6.3	1.13	.244
	Asheville (SAL)	LoA	9	4.78		11	10	0	0	64	66	4	21	57	8.0	1.36	.275
2014	Modesto (CAL)	HiA	5	10	5.40	16	16	1	0	95	113	7	30	74	7.0	1.51	.305
	Tulsa (TL)	AA	0	0	3.00	2	2	0	0	12	9	0	8	9	6.8	1.42	.205
Minor League Totals			27	26	2.84	75	74	8	0	454	376	16	115	405	8.0	1.08	.226

26 CARLOS ESTEVEZ, RHP

BA GRADE

45 Risk: High

Born: Dec. 28, 1992. **B-T:** R-R. **Ht.:** 6-4. **Wt.:** 210. **Signed:** Dominican Republic, 2011. **Signed by:** Rolando Fernandez/Jhonathan Leyba.

Estevez is broad-shouldered, with a big body and has a tremendous arm with a double-plus fastball and below-average secondary stuff. He creates a tremendous angle when he pitches down but doesn't do it enough. He topped out at 98 mph and often pitched at 95-96 with his fastball last season, but tends to pitch up in the zone. He has trouble spinning a curveball, which is why he began throwing a low-80s slider in 2014. His straight changeup is firm and sits around 87 mph. It's not a huge action pitch, but he throws it with enough speed variance from his fastball to be effective. Estevez's command is below-average on all his pitches, but he has an easy arm action and the potential to become a high-leverage reliever. He should pitch at high Class A Modesto in 2015.

Year	Club (League)	Class	W	L	ERA	G	GS	CG	SV	IP	H	HR	BB	SO	K/9	WHIP	AVG
2012	Rockies (DSL)	R	3	3	4.14	12	9	1	0	54	53	3	13	38	6.3	1.21	.259
2013	Tri-City (NWL)	SS	1	0	2.45	2	0	0	0	4	3	1	1	5	12.3	1.09	.214
	Grand Junction (PIO)	R	5	1	3.79	22	0	0	0	36	31	3	14	31	7.8	1.26	.240
2014	Asheville (SAL)	LoA	1	3	4.73	33	0	0	0	53	62	4	11	50	8.4	1.37	.294
Minor League Totals			13	9	4.08	77	15	2	0	181	182	13	53	151	7.5	1.30	.265

27 JORDAN PATTERSON, OF

BA GRADE

45 Risk: High

Born: Feb. 12, 1992. **B-T:** L-L. **Ht.:** 6-4. **Wt.:** 215. **Drafted:** South Alabama, 2013 (4th round). **Signed by:** Alan Matthews.

Patterson was a two-way player at South Alabama, where he also threw 90-93 mph as a lefthanded reliever. After a solid debut in 2013, he got off to a slow start in 2014 at low Class A Asheville, hitting .220 in April and .222 in May before making an adjustment that got him on track. He toned down excessive pre-pitch movement in his hands and wrists, while simplifying a leg kick that improved his timing, especially on offspeed pitches. Patterson has plus raw power, which should enable him to approach 20 homers in the big leagues. His swing can get a little long, but when his approach is right, he keeps his hands inside the ball and incorporates his back side to make consistent hard contact. Patterson is an average to tick above-average runner. He has a well above-average, accurate arm to go with above-average first-step quickness and range in right field. He should play at high Class A Modesto in 2015, and the Rockies love his makeup and deceptive athleticism.

Year	Club (League)	Class	AVG	G	AB	R	H	2B	3B	HR	RBI	BB	SO	SB	CS	OBP	SLG
2013	Grand Junction (PIO)	R	.291	60	206	44	60	12	0	10	37	19	37	10	6	.389	.495
2014	Asheville (SAL)	LoA	.278	125	453	69	126	27	0	14	66	46	118	25	8	.359	.430
Minor League Totals			.282	185	659	113	186	39	0	24	103	65	155	35	14	.369	.451

28 HELMIS RODRIGUEZ, LHP

BA GRADE

45 Risk: High

Born: June 10, 1994. **B-T:** L-L. **Ht.:** 6-1. **Wt.:** 185. **Signed:** Venezuela, 2010. **Signed by:** Rolando Fernandez/Francisco Cartaya.

Rodriguez led the short-season Northwest League in innings (91) and WHIP (1.09) last season while ranking second in ERA (1.97). Rodriguez, whose twin brother Herlis is an outfielder in the Phillies system, is not afraid to come inside to batters on either side of the plate. He pitches at 90 mph with his fastball, touching 93, and commands the pitch to both sides of the plate. Toward the end of the season he tinkered with a two-seam fastball. He has a well above-average changeup that he'll throw in any count. It has late action when thrown at 78-82 mph but can be too firm. In instructional league, Rodriguez put his curveball aside to work on a harder breaking pitch with sharp, late break. A groundball pitcher, he generated 2.3 groundouts for every airout in 2014 because of the angle and depth on his fastball and changeup. His ceiling is that of a No. 4 starter, and he will pitch at low Class A Asheville in 2015.

Year	Club (League)	Class	W	L	ERA	G	GS	CG	SV	IP	H	HR	BB	SO	K/9	WHIP	AVG
2012	Rockies (DSL)	R	4	1	1.82	12	12	0	0	74	60	3	12	53	6.4	0.97	.221
2013	Grand Junction (PIO)	R	2	4	5.10	15	7	0	0	55	60	5	16	36	5.9	1.39	.269
2014	Tri-City (NWL)	SS	4	7	1.97	15	15	0	0	91	82	2	18	41	4.0	1.09	.236
Minor League Totals			15	14	2.52	53	44	0	1	272	238	10	63	175	5.8	1.11	.232

29 JOHENDI JIMINIAN, RHP

BA GRADE

45 Risk: High

Born: Oct. 14, 1992. **B-T:** R-R. **Ht.:** 6-3. **Wt.:** 170. **Signed:** Dominican Republic, 2010. **Signed by:** Rolando Fernandez/Jhonathan Leyba/Frank Roa.

Jiminian spent two years in the Dominican Summer League and two in short-season leagues before moving up to low Class A Asheville in 2014. He pitches at 91 mph and tops out at 94 with a fastball that is pretty straight, but he has an active front side that provides deception. He struggles to stay on line and in sync in his delivery. His curveball is below-average, and his changeup is average. Jiminian has stuff but needs to command all his pitches better, which should happen if he can develop a repeatable delivery and mound rhythm. Otherwise, he could end up in the bullpen. He sometimes lacks fire on the mound and needs to be tougher and pitch inside more. Jiminian should pitch at high Class A Modesto in 2015.

Year	Club (League)	Class	W	L	ERA	G	GS	CG	SV	IP	H	HR	BB	SO	K/9	WHIP	AVG
2012	Grand Junction (PIO)	R	2	4	7.71	14	13	0	0	47	60	5	33	28	5.4	1.99	.311
2013	Tri-City (NWL)	SS	3	5	3.38	15	14	0	0	83	79	3	24	57	6.2	1.25	.256
2014	Asheville (SAL)	LoA	14	6	3.99	28	27	0	0	151	158	7	45	120	7.2	1.34	.269
Minor League Totals			28	23	4.21	83	79	0	0	395	400	20	142	283	6.4	1.37	.264

30 WES ROGERS, OF

BA GRADE

50 Risk: Extreme

Born: March 7, 1994. **B-T:** R-R. **Ht.:** 6-3. **Wt.:** 180. **Drafted:** Spartanburg Methodist (S.C.) JC, 2014 (4th round). **Signed by:** Jordan Czarniecki.

Rogers was drafted in the 28th round in 2012 by the Red Sox but didn't sign. He wasn't drafted after his first season at Spartanburg Methodist but hit .351/.479/.476 last season, and the Rockies signed him for $360,000 as their fourth-round pick. Rogers is a pure center fielder, and his lanky build and long strides have drawn comparisons to former Rockies center fielder Dexter Fowler. His first-step quickness and speed enable him to cover a lot of ground. He has a fringy arm. Rogers has bat speed and the strength to turn on fastballs but needs to improve his breaking ball recognition and put the ball in play more. He has the speed to steal bases but needs refinement. Rogers could play at low Class A Asheville in 2015.

Year	Club (League)	Class	AVG	G	AB	R	H	2B	3B	HR	RBI	BB	SO	SB	CS	OBP	SLG
2014	Grand Junction (PIO)	R	.283	30	113	25	32	3	2	3	16	13	25	15	1	.362	.425
Minor League Totals			.283	30	113	25	32	3	2	3	16	13	25	15	1	.362	.425

Detroit Tigers

BY BEN BADLER

No team has matched the consistent regular-season success of the Tigers over the last four seasons. Detroit has won more games than any team in baseball in that stretch. And while the Dodgers and Cardinals repeated as division champions in 2014, the Tigers rattled off their fourth straight American League Central title.

Yet the season still ended on a bitter note, with the Orioles sweeping the Tigers in the AL Division Series, the first time in four years the Tigers were unable to reach the AL Championship Series.

Several of the team's moves helped the Tigers' offense. Unloading Prince Fielder to the Rangers netted the Tigers second baseman Ian Kinsler, who was more valuable than Fielder in 2014. The move also enabled Miguel Cabrera to move back to first base and let rookie Nick Castellanos take over at third.

Picking up J.D. Martinez, whom the Astros released in spring training, ended up being one of the steals of the year. He hit .315/.358/.553 with 23 home runs in 441 at-bats, then batted fifth in the Tigers' lineup during the playoffs. With Victor Martinez leading the majors in OPS, the Tigers ranked second in baseball in runs scored.

Yet the bullpen continued to be a weakness for the Tigers, one that proved costly in the postseason. While the Tigers tried to upgrade with the offseason free agent signings of Joe Nathan and Joba Chamberlain, the former was completely ineffective and the latter caused plenty of headaches.

The Tigers paid a high prospect cost—righthanders Jake Thompson and Corey Knebel—to trade for Joakim Soria from the Rangers in July, but he didn't perform well immediately and quickly lost the trust of manager Brad Ausmus.

Giving Doug Fister to the Nationals for an underwhelming trade return of lefthanders Robbie Ray and Ian Krol and utility infielder Steve Lombardozzi also proved costly, and proved to be a rare misstep for general manager Dave Dombrowski, whose trading track record is among the best in the game.

The farm system remains light, but that's always been the case for the Tigers throughout their run of division titles. The system thinned out further with the Soria trade and the July acquisition of David Price, who gives the Tigers an ace for next season as they prepare for possibility departure of Max Scherzer, but also cost them low Class A shortstop Willy Adames, along with center fielder Austin Jackson and lefty Drew Smyly from the big league team. After the season, second base-

Rookie Nick Castellanos took over at third base after Miguel Cabrera shifted back across the diamond

TOP PROSPECTS OF THE DECADE

Year	Player, Pos.	2014 Org
2005	Curtis Granderson, of	Mets
2006	Justin Verlander, rhp	Tigers
2007	Cameron Maybin, of	Padres
2008	Rick Porcello, rhp	Tigers
2009	Rick Porcello, rhp	Tigers
2010	Jacob Turner, rhp	Cubs
2011	Jacob Turner, rhp	Cubs
2012	Jacob Turner, rhp	Cubs
2013	Nick Castellanos, 3b/of	Tigers
2014	Nick Castellanos, 3b	Tigers

man Devon Travis, who would have been the No. 1 prospect, went to Toronto in exchange for Anthony Gose. Middle infielder Domingo Leyba and Ray went to the Diamondbacks in a three-team deal that netted the Tigers righthander Shane Greene.

Few prospects in the organization have star potential. Steven Moya is an exception, with his electric power combined with a reckless offensive approach making for a high-risk, high-reward player. Derek Hill has exciting tools, but he's a 2014 high school draft pick who struggled in his pro debut.

The competition in the division has become stiffer with the emergence of the Royals. The talent level is still high in Detroit, but it's no longer an easy call to forecast them as AL Central favorites.

General manager: Dave Dombrowski. **Farm director:** Dave Owen. **Scouting director:** Scott Pleis.

Class	Team	League	W	L		Finish	Manager
Majors	Detroit Tigers	American	90	72	.556	t-5th (30)	Brad Ausmus
Triple-A	Toledo Mud Hens	International	69	74	.483	8th (14)	Larry Parrish
Double-A	Erie SeaWolves	Eastern	71	71	.500	7th (12)	Lance Parrish
High A	Lakeland Flying Tigers	Florida State	62	75	.453	10th (12)	Dave Huppert/Bill Dancy
Low A	West Michigan Whitecaps	Midwest	82	58	.586	3rd (16)	Andrew Graham
Short season	Connecticut Tigers	New York-Penn	42	34	.553	t-4th (14)	Mike Rabelo
Rookie	Tigers	Gulf Coast	34	25	.576	6th (16)	Basilio Cabrera
Overall Minor League Record			360	337	.516	9th (30)	

THIS YEAR'S TOP 30

No.	Player, Pos.	Grade
1.	Steven Moya, of	60/Extreme
2.	Buck Farmer, rhp	50/Medium
3.	Derek Hill, of	60/Extreme
4.	Kevin Ziomek, lhp	50/High
5.	Hernan Perez, ss/2b	45/Low
6.	James McCann, c	45/Low
7.	Tyler Collins, of	45/Low
8.	Austin Kubitza, rhp	50/High
9.	Bruce Rondon, rhp	45/High
10.	Dixon Machado, ss	45/High
11.	Zach Shepherd, 3b	50/Extreme
12.	Arvicent Perez, c	50/Extreme
13.	Kyle Lobstein, lhp	40/Low
14.	Joe Jimenez, rhp	45/High
15.	Steven Fuentes, 3b	45/High
16.	Drew VerHagen, rhp	40/Medium
17.	Jose Valdez, rhp	45/High
18.	Spencer Turnbull, rhp	45/High
19.	Mike Gerber, of	45/High
20.	Javier Betancourt, 2b/ss	45/High
21.	Angel Nesbitt, rhp	40/Medium
22.	Edgar de la Rosa, rhp	45/High
23.	Sandy Baez, rhp	50/Extreme
24.	Grayson Greiner, c	45/High
25.	Joe Mantiply, lhp	40/Medium
26.	Daniel Fields, of	40/Medium
27.	Melvin Mercedes, rhp	40/Medium
28.	Harold Castro, 2b	40/High
29.	Chad Green, rhp	40/High
30.	Joey Pankake, 3b/ss	40/High

LAST YEAR'S TOP 30

No.	Player, Pos.	Status
1.	Nick Castellanos, 3b/of	Majors
2.	Devon Travis, 2b	(Blue Jays)
3.	Bruce Rondon, rhp	No. 9
4.	Jake Thompson, rhp	(Rangers)
5.	Jonathon Crawford, rhp	(Reds)
6.	Corey Knebel, rhp	(Rangers)
7.	Eugenio Suarez, ss/2b	(Reds)
8.	Domingo Leyba, ss/2b	(Diamondbacks)
9.	Hernan Perez, 2b/ss	No. 5
10.	Kevin Ziomek, lhp	No. 4
11.	James McCann, c	No. 6
12.	Drew VerHagen, rhp	No. 17
13.	Jose Ortega, rhp	(Rockies)
14.	Javier Betancourt, ss	No. 21
15.	Steven Moya, of	No. 1
16.	Melvin Mercedes, rhp	No. 28
17.	Casey Crosby, lhp	Free agent
18.	Jose Valdez, rhp	No. 18
19.	Jordan Lennerton, 1b	Free agent
20.	Tyler Collins, of	No. 7
21.	Jose Alvarez, lhp	(Angels)
22.	Daniel Fields, of	No. 27
23.	Kyle Lobstein, lhp	No. 14
24.	Jeff Thompson, rhp	Dropped out
25.	Zac Reininger, rhp	Dropped out
26.	Bryan Holaday, c	Majors
27.	Ramon Cabrera, c	Free agent
28.	Steven Fuentes, 3b	No. 16
29.	Calvin Drummond, rhp	Dropped out
30.	Willy Adames, ss	(Rays)

BEST TOOLS

Best Hitter for Average	Hernan Perez
Best Power Hitter	Steven Moya
Best Strike-Zone Discipline	Jason Krizan
Fastest Baserunner	Derek Hill
Best Athlete	Derek Hill
Best Fastball	Bruce Rondon
Best Curveball	Kevin Ziomek
Best Slider	Buck Farmer
Best Changeup	Buck Farmer
Best Control	Drew VerHagen
Best Defensive Catcher	James McCann
Best Defensive Infielder	Dixon Machado
Best Infield Arm	Dixon Machado
Best Defensive Outfielder	Derek Hill
Best Outfield Arm	Steven Moya

2018 LINEUP

Catcher	Alex Avila
First Base	Miguel Cabrera
Second Base	Ian Kinsler
Third Base	Nick Castellanos
Shortstop	Jose Iglesias
Left Field	J.D. Martinez
Center Field	Derek Hill
Right Field	Steven Moya
Designated Hitter	Victor Martinez
No. 1 Starter	David Price
No. 2 Starter	Justin Verlander
No. 3 Starter	Anibal Sanchez
No. 4 Starter	Shane Greene
No. 5 Starter	Buck Farmer
Closer	Bruce Rondon

DETROIT TIGERS

TOP 2015 ROOKIE: Buck Farmer, rhp. After rapidly ascending to Detroit in 2014, he should log more innings for the big club in 2015, whether in the rotation or bullpen.

BREAKOUT PROSPECT: Zach Shepherd, 3b. The Australian teenager has a good combination of size, hitting ability and strength, and he took to third base quickly after playing shortstop as an amateur.

SOURCE OF TOP 30 TALENT			
Homegrown	29	Acquired	1
College	11	Trades	1
Junior college	1	Rule 5 draft	0
High school	2	Independent leagues	0
Draft-and-follow	0	Free agents/waivers	0
Nondrafted free agents	1		
International	14		

SLEEPER: Endrys Briceno, rhp. Tommy John surgery killed his 2014 season, but he hit 97 mph from a steep downhill plane when healthy.

LF
Tyler Collins (7)
Daniel Fields (26)
Jason Krizan
Julio Martinez

CF
Derek Hill (3)
Connor Harrell
Austin Schotts

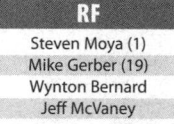

RF
Steven Moya (1)
Mike Gerber (19)
Wynton Bernard
Jeff McVaney

3B
Zach Shepherd (11)
Steven Fuentes (15)
Joey Pankake (30)
Luis Torrealba
Randel Alcantara

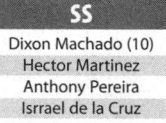

SS
Dixon Machado (10)
Hector Martinez
Anthony Pereira
Isrrael de la Cruz

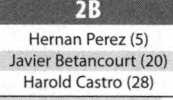

2B
Hernan Perez (5)
Javier Betancourt (20)
Harold Castro (28)

1B
Dean Green

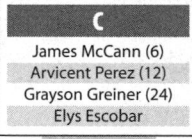

C
James McCann (6)
Arvicent Perez (12)
Grayson Greiner (24)
Elys Escobar

LHP

LHSP	**LHRP**
Kevin Ziomek (4)	Joe Mantiply (25)
Kyle Lobstein (13)	

RHP

RHSP	**RHRP**
Buck Farmer (2)	Bruce Rondon (9)
Austin Kubitza (8)	Joe Jimenez (14)
Drew VerHagen (16)	Jose Valdez (17)
Spencer Turnbull (18)	Angel Nesbitt (21)
Edgar de la Rosa (22)	Melvin Mercedes (27)
Sandy Baez (23)	Adam Ravenelle
Chad Green (29)	Kyle Ryan
Endrys Briceno	Zac Reininger
Francisco German	Montreal Robertson

2014

BEST PURE HITTER: OF Mike Gerber has plus raw power from the left side of the plate and hit 11 home runs this spring for Creighton. He continued to hit in pro ball across two levels (.298/.367/.492). OF Derek Hill (1) has the raw tools to become an above-average hitter with a quick, line-drive oriented swing.

BEST POWER HITTER: C Grayson Greiner (3) has a huge frame at 6-foot-6, 215 pounds with plus raw power from the right side and a swing path conducive to lifting the ball. A broken hamate bone in his left hand cut his first pro season short by roughly a month.

FASTEST RUNNER: Hill is at least a 70-grade runner who impacts the game in many ways with his speed, out of the box, on the bases and in center field.

BEST DEFENSIVE PLAYER: Hill was arguably the top prep center fielder in the class, capable of closing gaps quickly with his speed and tremendous defensive instincts. He is capable of highlight-reel catches and his arm improved significantly over the last year, showing above-average potential.

BEST FASTBALL: RHP Spencer Turnbull (2) is capable of running his fastball up to 98 with heavy, bat-breaking arm-side run and sink from a large, powerful body. RHP Adam Ravenelle (3) has a great pitcher's body and sat 93-95, touching 97.

BEST SECONDARY PITCH: Ravenelle's slider is an out pitch with at least plus potential.

BEST PRO DEBUT: Greiner hit .322/.394/.444 in the Midwest League before his late-season injury.

BEST ATHLETE: Hill was one of the top prep athletes in the class.

MOST INTRIGUING BACKGROUND: C Shane Zeile (5) is the nephew of 16-year major league veteran Todd Zeile (5), who also attended UCLA. Hill is the son of Dodgers scout Orsino Hill, who played in the minors for 12 years and served as a hitting coach before becoming a scout. 1B Magglio Ordonez (38) is the son of the former major leaguer by the same name who played for the Tigers for seven years.

CLOSEST TO THE MAJORS: Although Ravenelle threw just four innings in his debut after signing late following Vanderbilt's College World Series victory, he is likely the fastest-moving pitcher. With more consistent innings as a junior, Ravenelle's strike-throwing ability sharpened significantly.

BEST LATE-ROUND PICK: Gerber, who could have come out as a junior performing at a high level (.328.385/.567), lost more than a month of the season to an appendectomy. He finished this summer at low Class A.

THE ONE WHO GOT AWAY: RHP Alex Faedo (40) is the son of former big leaguer Landy Faedo. He suffered a turf toe injury early in the season that caused him to gain weight. But he was up to 94 last fall with a loose, easy arm. He will head to Florida.

ASSESSMENT: The Tigers picked a prep position player in the first round for the first time since Cameron Maybin in 2005, before turning their attention to SEC power arms.

2013

While Detroit traded RHP Jonathon Crawford (1) to the Reds for Alfredo Simon, this class has pitching depth, from since-traded Corey Knebel (1) to LHP Kevin Ziomek (2) to RHPs Buck Farmer (5), who zoomed to the majors, and Austin Kubitza (4).

GRADE: B

2012

Top prospects RHP Jake Thompson (2) and 2B Devon Travis (13) were traded in 2014 for Joakim Soria and Anthony Gose, respectively. RHP Drew VerHagen (4), who reached Detroit in 2014, is the best remaining hope.

GRADE: C

2011

Five Tigers draft picks have reached the majors; the most significant appear to be Cs James McCann (2), coming off a strong year in Triple-A, and Curt Casali (10), now with the Rays.

GRADE: C

TOP DRAFT PICKS OF THE DECADE

Year	Player, Pos.	2014 Org
2005	Cameron Maybin, of	Padres
2006	Andrew Miller, lhp	Orioles
2007	Rick Porcello, rhp	Tigers
2008	Ryan Perry, rhp	Nationals
2009	Jacob Turner, rhp	Cubs
2010	Nick Castellanos, 3b (1st round supp.)	Tigers
2011	James McCann, c (2nd round)	Tigers
2012	Jake Thompson, rhp (2nd round)	Rangers
2013	Jonathon Crawford, rhp	Tigers
2014	Derek Hill, of	Tigers

LARGEST BONUSES IN CLUB HISTORY

Jacob Turner, 2009	$4,700,000
Rick Porcello, 2007	$3,580,000
Andrew Miller, 2006	$3,550,000
Eric Munson, 1999	$3,500,000
Nick Castellanos, 2010	$3,450,000

1 STEVEN MOYA, OF

Born: Aug. 9, 1991. **B-T:** L-R. **Ht.:** 6-6. **Wt.:** 230.
Signed: Dominican Republic, 2008.
Signed by: Miguel Rodriguez/Ramon Perez/
Miguel Garcia.

Moya was born in Puerto Rico, but he grew up in the Dominican Republic and signed as an international free agent in 2008. Through his first three years in the system, he was a tall, lanky teenager with intriguing tools who was still learning to gain better body control and coordination of his long-levered frame, which showed in his underwhelming early performance. He struggled in the Rookie-level Gulf Coast League in 2010 and at low Class A West Michigan in 2011, but things started to click for him when he repeated the Midwest League in 2012—that is until Tommy John surgery cut his season short. A separated left shoulder in 2013 cut into his playing time again, but in 2014 Moya remained healthy, played more than 100 games for the first time in his career and had a breakthrough season at Double-A Erie. He led the Eastern League with 35 homers, which ranked fourth in the minors overall, and a .555 slugging average, then made his major league debut as a September callup, though he played sparingly in the big leagues.

Moya can make any ballpark feel small with his well above-average raw power. He has plenty of lift in his swing, hitting balls over the fence to all fields in games and tying for third in the minors with 71 extra-base hits in 2014. He has good bat speed, generates tremendous leverage and has developed a better feel for his swing. Strike-zone discipline is Moya's biggest obstacle. His long arms lead to a long swing and too much swinging and missing. He led the EL with 161 strikeouts, whiffing in 29 percent of his plate appearances. With a large strike zone to cover, he doesn't do himself any favors by frequently chasing pitches off the plate, which contributes to his high strikeout rate and hampers his on-base percentage because he walked in just 4 percent of his trips to the plate. With all the time he's missed with injuries, Moya doesn't have as much game experience as most players his age, so his believers think he can make the necessary adjustments. He is surprisingly athletic for his size, with average speed and a plus arm. He earned praise from scouts for his routes in right field, something that wasn't the case entering 2014. The attributes are all there for Moya to be an average

defensive right fielder.

Moya is a divisive prospect. Some scouts project him as a middle-of-the-order force, while others question whether he will make enough contact. With Torii Hunter gone, the Tigers have a hole in right field, but Moya should open 2015 at Triple-A Toledo. If he dominates the International League, he might be a candidate to bring up by midseason, but his hitting approach is still raw enough that a full season of Triple-A at-bats could help him make a smoother transition to the big leagues.

BA GRADE

60 Risk: Extreme

SCOUTING GRADES

Hit: 40
Power: 70
Run: 50
Field: 50
Arm: 60

Based on 20-80 scouting scale and future projection rather than present grades.

LGE	PA	BB%	SO%	ISO
EL	549	4.2	29.3	.280
AL	8	0.0	25.0	.000

TOMASSO DeROSA

Year	Club (League)	Class	AVG	G	AB	R	H	2B	3B	HR	RBI	BB	SO	SB	CS	OBP	SLG
2012	West Michigan (MWL)	LoA	.288	59	243	28	70	14	3	9	47	11	59	5	3	.319	.481
2013	Lakeland (FSL)	HiA	.255	93	365	52	93	19	5	12	55	18	106	6	0	.296	.433
2014	Erie (EL)	AA	.276	133	515	81	142	33	3	35	105	23	161	16	4	.306	.555
	Detroit (AL)	MAJ	.375	11	8	2	3	0	0	0	0	0	2	0	0	.375	.375
Major League Totals			.375	11	8	2	3	0	0	0	0	0	2	0	0	.375	.375
Minor League Totals			.251	471	1801	247	452	89	14	77	290	103	575	32	10	.295	.444

2 BUCK FARMER, RHP

Born: Feb. 20, 1991. **B-T:** L-R. **Ht.:** 6-4. **Wt.:** 225. **Drafted:** Georgia Tech, 2013 (5th round). **Signed by:** James Rough.

Farmer spent four seasons at Georgia Tech, then signed for $225,000 as a fifth-round pick in 2013. At 23, he started the year relatively old for the low Class A Midwest League, but after carving through the circuit he jumped to Double-A Erie for a pair of starts in August, made his major league debut on Aug. 13, then split the rest of the season between Detroit and Triple-A Toledo. Farmer is a solid strike-thrower who works downhill with a lively 90-95 mph fastball that generates sink and run and has peaked at 97. His slider was his best secondary pitch in college, but his changeup improved tremendously over the course of the season. His changeup was below-average early in the year, but it now flashes above-average with late drop. His average slider can be a swing-and-miss pitch. That may stem from his arm action, which along with his funky delivery provides deception but leads some scouts to project him as a reliever. Farmer has the stuff to be a back-end starter. Given the Tigers' bullpen woes, though, it may be tempting to move him there.

BA GRADE	
50	Risk: **Medium**

LGE	BF	SO%	BB%	HR/9
MWL	420	27.6	5.7	0.52
EL	49	22.4	8.2	0.75

Year	Club (League)	Class	W	L	ERA	G	GS	CG	SV	IP	H	HR	BB	SO	K/9	WHIP	AVG
2013	Connecticut (NYP)	SS	0	3	3.09	12	11	0	0	32	32	1	7	33	9.3	1.22	.258
2014	West Michigan (MWL)	LoA	10	5	2.60	18	18	0	0	104	91	6	24	116	10.1	1.11	.233
	Erie (EL)	AA	1	0	3.00	2	2	0	0	12	10	1	4	11	8.3	1.17	.222
	Toledo (IL)	AAA	1	1	9.82	2	2	0	0	7	11	1	4	2	2.5	2.05	.355
	Detroit (AL)	MAJ	0	1	11.57	4	2	0	0	9	12	2	5	11	10.6	1.82	.308
Major League Totals			0	1	11.57	4	2	0	0	9	12	2	5	11	10.6	1.82	.308
Minor League Totals			12	9	3.08	34	33	0	0	155	144	9	39	162	9.4	1.18	.244

3 DEREK HILL, OF

Born: Dec. 30, 1995. **B-T:** R-R. **Ht.:** 6-2. **Wt.:** 195. **Drafted:** HS—Elk Grove, Calif., 2014 (1st round). **Signed by:** Scott Cerny.

The Tigers used their first-round pick in 2014 on Hill, who signed for $2 million then got off to a hot start in the Rookie-level Gulf Coast League. After sitting out three weeks with lower back pain, he didn't play well when he returned and his numbers dipped further when he moved up to short-season Connecticut in August, though his tool set remains exciting. Hill is an explosive, quick-twitch athlete with double-plus speed. He's already a terrific defensive center fielder—the best among 2014 draft picks—who covers ample ground with good reads off the bat, direct routes and an average, accurate arm. Hill, the son of a minor league hitting coach, has a quick stroke, good balance and a contact-oriented swing. He is a line-drive hitter who doesn't loft the ball much, so with his below-average power, he may be more of a doubles and triples hitter than a home run threat. Hill showed a sound hitting approach in high school and early in the GCL season. Despite Hill's struggles in his pro debut, he still excited evaluators with his potential as a two-way threat who could hit near the top of a lineup. The next stop for him should be low Class A West Michigan.

BA GRADE	
60	Risk: **Extreme**

LGE	PA	BB%	SO%	ISO
GCL	119	13.4	16.0	.121
NYP	78	2.6	33.3	.041

Year	Club (League)	Class	AVG	G	AB	R	H	2B	3B	HR	RBI	BB	SO	SB	CS	OBP	SLG
2014	Tigers (GCL)	R	.212	28	99	12	21	2	2	2	11	16	19	9	1	.331	.333
	Connecticut (NYP)	SS	.203	19	74	8	15	1	1	0	3	2	26	2	1	.244	.243
Minor League Totals			.208	47	173	20	36	3	3	2	14	18	45	11	2	.296	.295

4 KEVIN ZIOMEK, LHP

Born: March 21, 1992. **B-T:** R-L. **Ht.:** 6-3. **Wt.:** 190. **Drafted:** Vanderbilt, 2013 (2nd round). **Signed by:** Harold Zonder.

Ziomek passed on signing with the Diamondbacks as a 13th-round pick out of high school in 2010. Instead he went to Vanderbilt, followed in the footsteps of Commodores lefties David Price and Mike Minor, then signed with the Tigers for $956,600 as a second-rounder in 2013. In his first full season, Ziomek led the low Class A Midwest League in ERA (2.27) and strikeouts per nine innings (11.1), though it's unusual that an organization that normally promotes its prospects aggressively left the fairly polished 22-year-old at West Michigan all season. Ziomek doesn't overpower with his arsenal, relying instead on mixing his pitches and hitting his spots. He throws strikes, works quickly and moves his 87-92 mph fastball around the strike zone with average life and good downhill angle. His low-80s slider is an average pitch, though it can get sweepy on him. His changeup is another average pitch. He adds and subtracts from his fringy curveball, throwing it with more velocity later in the count. His delivery isn't smooth, but his funkiness creates deception. Ziomek earns comparisons with former Tiger Drew Smyly, himself a second-round college lefty, though Smyly had made it to Double-A at the same age. Ziomek figures to advance to high Class A Lakeland in 2015 and could develop into a back-end starter.

BA GRADE

50 Risk: High

LGE	BF	SO%	BB%	HR/9
MWL	510	29.8	10.4	0.37

Year	Club (League)	Class	W	L	ERA	G	GS	CG	SV	IP	H	HR	BB	SO	K/9	WHIP	AVG
2013	Connecticut (NYP)	SS	0	1	4.50	4	4	0	0	8	5	0	5	3	3.4	1.25	.200
2014	West Michigan (MWL)	LoA	10	6	2.27	23	23	0	0	123	89	5	53	152	11.1	1.15	.201
Minor League Totals			10	7	2.40	27	27	0	0	131	94	5	58	155	10.6	1.16	.201

5 HERNAN PEREZ, SS/2B

Born: March 26, 1991. **B-T:** R-R. **Ht.:** 6-1. **Wt.:** 185. **Signed:** Venezuela, 2007. **Signed by:** Jesus Garces/Pedro Chavez.

After signing out of Venezuela at age 16 for $237,000, Perez didn't do anything to distinguish himself in his first four years with the organization. He built upon a 2013 breakout season at Double-A Erie with a solid 2014 at Triple-A Toledo. Perez's tools are nondescript, but he stands out for his smart, heady play in all areas of the game. He drags the bat at times, but he's a line-drive hitter who uses the whole field and makes consistent contact, albeit without much power. Perez would benefit from a more patient hitting approach, for he's susceptible to chasing off the plate. He's an average runner who's a 20-steal threat because of his acumen on the basepaths. Perez played a lot of second base coming up because he was teammates with the more defensively gifted Eugenio Suarez and Dixon Machado, but he showed that he's playable at shortstop, even if his range is a better fit at second base. He's a smooth defender with clean footwork and hands, along with an average, accurate arm. Perez is is blocked by Ian Kinsler, who is signed through 2017, at second base, and by Jose Iglesias (if healthy) at shortstop. Perez's best role is likely as a utility infielder.

BA GRADE

45 Risk: Low

LGE	PA	BB%	SO%	ISO
IL	596	6.0	10.9	.117
AL	6	16.7	16.7	.000

Year	Club (League)	Class	AVG	G	AB	R	H	2B	3B	HR	RBI	BB	SO	SB	CS	OBP	SLG
2012	Detroit (AL)	MAJ	.500	2	2	1	1	0	0	0	0	0	0	0	0	.500	.500
	Lakeland (FSL)	HiA	.261	124	441	50	115	11	4	5	44	24	70	27	4	.298	.338
2013	Erie (EL)	AA	.301	87	362	45	109	28	2	4	35	12	48	24	7	.325	.423
	Toledo (IL)	AAA	.299	16	67	3	20	3	0	0	4	5	7	4	0	.356	.343
	Detroit (AL)	MAJ	.197	34	66	13	13	0	1	0	5	2	15	1	0	.217	.227
2014	Toledo (IL)	AAA	.287	133	547	69	157	32	7	6	53	36	65	21	6	.331	.404
	Detroit (AL)	MAJ	.200	8	5	1	1	0	0	0	0	1	1	0	0	.333	.200
Major League Totals			.205	44	73	15	15	0	1	0	5	3	16	1	0	.234	.233
Minor League Totals			.262	735	2855	335	749	133	23	30	274	162	453	112	29	.304	.357

6 JAMES McCANN, C

Born: June 13, 1990. **B-T:** R-R. **Ht.:** 6-2. **Wt.:** 210. **Drafted:** Arkansas, 2011 (2nd round). **Signed by:** Chris Wimmer.

McCann always has earned praise for his defensive chops, but 2014 was the best offensive season of his career. He posted career highs in batting average (.295), on-base percentage (.343) and slugging (.427) while in Triple-A Toledo before his big league debut as a September callup. McCann is a quality receiver and a quiet defender. He has minimal foot speed but moves well behind the plate, rarely allowing a ball to get by him. He does the little things well, framing pitches and earning praise for his game-calling. His plus arm helped him throw out 42 percent of Triple-A basestealers, which ranked second in the International League. As McCann learned to leverage the ball better and tweaked his setup, his offense improved. He's a good fastball hitter with quick hands, though his barrel angle leaves length to his swing without ideal bat path. He's an aggressive hitter who has trouble with the soft stuff, though he doesn't swing and miss excessively. He should max out at around 8-12 home runs per year. McCann fits what teams look for in a backup catcher, which could help him carve out a long career. Given the offensive improvement he showed in 2014 and the struggles of Alex Avila, McCann could play a larger role with the Tigers in 2015.

BA GRADE
45 Risk: Low

LGE	PA	BB%	SO%	ISO
IL	460	5.4	19.6	.132
AL	12	0.0	16.7	.083

Year	Club (League)	Class	AVG	G	AB	R	H	2B	3B	HR	RBI	BB	SO	SB	CS	OBP	SLG
2012	Lakeland (FSL)	HiA	.288	45	160	24	46	10	0	0	20	10	29	3	0	.345	.350
	Erie (EL)	AA	.200	64	220	15	44	12	0	2	19	8	44	2	2	.227	.282
2013	Erie (EL)	AA	.277	119	441	50	122	30	1	8	54	30	85	3	3	.328	.404
2014	Toledo (IL)	AAA	.295	109	417	49	123	34	0	7	54	25	90	9	2	.343	.427
	Detroit (AL)	MAJ	.250	9	12	2	3	1	0	0	0	0	2	1	0	.250	.333
Major League Totals			.250	9	12	2	3	1	0	0	0	0	2	1	0	.250	.333
Minor League Totals			.266	351	1286	139	342	88	1	18	154	76	261	17	7	.314	.378

7 TYLER COLLINS, OF

Born: June 6, 1990. **B-T:** L-L. **Ht.:** 5-11. **Wt.:** 215. **Drafted:** Howard (Texas) JC, 2011 (6th round). **Signed by:** Tim Grieve.

Collins raked in his first full season in the high Class A Florida State League in 2012, but his strikeout rate soared upon reaching Double-A Erie. His performance rebounded in 2014, as he spent the first two weeks in Detroit for his big league debut before spending the rest of the minor league season at Triple-A Toledo. Strong and stocky, Collins can put a charge into the ball with average power, making him a potential 20-homer threat. Praised for his pure hitting ability earlier in his career, he got big with his swing and had trouble recognizing pitches last year when he got to Double-A. There's still some swing-and-miss to his game, but he has solid patience and in 2014 he did a better job of understanding his swing and anticipating how pitchers were attacking him, which helped boost his batting average and on-base percentage. Collins is a fringy runner with an average arm who split time between left and right field, even getting spot time in center, though he's much better suited for the corners. Collins gets the fourth-outfielder label thrown on him, though he could have value as a platoon outfielder. With Torii Hunter hitting the free agent market, the Tigers have an opening, though the club is much more likely to use Collins as a backup in 2015.

BA GRADE
45 Risk: Low

LGE	PA	BB%	SO%	ISO
IL	526	9.3	22.1	.160
AL	25	4.0	16.0	.125

Year	Club (League)	Class	AVG	G	AB	R	H	2B	3B	HR	RBI	BB	SO	SB	CS	OBP	SLG
2012	Lakeland (FSL)	HiA	.290	126	473	68	137	35	5	7	66	58	64	20	3	.371	.429
2013	Erie (EL)	AA	.240	129	466	67	112	29	0	21	79	51	122	4	5	.323	.438
2014	Toledo (IL)	AAA	.263	121	468	63	123	17	2	18	62	49	116	12	4	.335	.423
	Detroit (AL)	MAJ	.250	18	24	3	6	0	0	1	4	1	4	0	0	.280	.375
Major League Totals			.250	18	24	3	6	0	0	1	4	1	4	0	0	.280	.375
Minor League Totals			.270	419	1573	228	424	92	8	54	239	170	319	42	13	.345	.441

8 AUSTIN KUBITZA, RHP

Born: Nov. 16, 1991. **B-T:** R-R. **Ht.:** 6-5. **Wt.:** 225. **Drafted:** Rice, 2013 (4th round). **Signed by:** Tim Grieve.

A three-year starter at Rice, Kubitza ranked seventh in NCAA Division I with 11.0 strikeouts per nine innings his junior year in 2013, when the Tigers drafted him in the fourth round and signed him for $401,200. In his first full season, he ranked second in the low Class A Midwest League in ERA (2.34) and strikeouts (140) at West Michigan. Kubitza's fastball sits 87-90 mph and touches 92 but the ridiculous movement on the pitch stands out far more than its velocity. It dances all over the place with wicked sink and cutting action that makes it a nightmare for hitters to square up. The pitch makes him the most prolific groundball machine in the minors, with a 3.7 groundout/airout ratio that placed well ahead of Brewers lefthander Jed Bradley, who ranked No. 2 at 2.72. Kubitza also racks up plenty of strikeouts, though he doesn't have a true out pitch among his secondary weapons. He throws a slider that lower-level hitters will bite on,

BA GRADE

50 Risk: High

LGE	BF	SO%	BB%	HR/9
MWL	539	26.0	8.0	0.34

but scouts consider it a fringe-average offering. He has tried to work a changeup into the mix, but it's not a factor at this point. He has a crossfire delivery but is a solid strike thrower. Kubitza's unique skill set makes him tricky for scouts to project, with some believing he would fit best in the bullpen, though others believe his approach will continue to work as a starter at the higher levels because he gives hitters such an uncomfortable look. He should move on to high Class A Lakeland in 2015.

Year	Club (League)	Class	W	L	ERA	G	GS	CG	SV	IP	H	HR	BB	SO	K/9	WHIP	AVG
2013	Tigers (GCL)	R	0	0	2.16	6	0	0	0	8	5	0	1	5	5.4	0.72	.185
	Lakeland (FSL)	HiA	0	1	5.82	8	1	0	0	17	16	0	10	14	7.4	1.53	.254
2014	West Michigan (MWL)	LoA	10	2	2.34	23	23	0	0	131	98	5	43	140	9.6	1.08	.202
Minor League Totals			10	3	2.71	37	24	0	0	156	119	5	54	159	9.2	1.11	.207

9 BRUCE RONDON, RHP

Born: Dec. 9, 1990. **B-T:** R-R. **Ht.:** 6-3. **Wt.:** 275. **Signed:** Venezuela, 2007. **Signed by:** German Robles/Pedro Chavez/Miguel Garcia.

The Tigers have a stacked lineup, a rotation filled with frontline starters and won the American League Central four straight years. Yet the bullpen continues to be an annual source of frustration for the team. Rondon was expected to help solve the Tigers' relief woes in 2014, but instead he missed the entire season after having Tommy John surgery in March. With 30 major league relief appearances and 29 innings, Rondon barely meets our threshold to still qualify as a prospect. When healthy, he showed the stuff to pitch high-leverage innings. He has a monster frame to match his fastball, which sits at 97-100 mph and touched as high as 103. Beyond the top-of-the-scale velocity, his fastball also had good life, running in on righties to help him blow it by hitters and get grounders at an above-average clip. Rondon throws his hard slider up in the high 80s and it can be an average pitch, but it's not consistent yet. He improved his changeup in 2013, but

BA GRADE

45 Risk: High

LGE	BF	SO%	BB%	HR/9
Did not play				

it's not a pitch he throws much. He got away with below-average command prior to his surgery because his fastball was so tough for hitters to square up. The Tigers expect Rondon to be ready for spring training after his rehab process, though it remains to be seen whether he will still have the high-octane stuff he once possessed. If he does, he should be pitching late in games for the Tigers with a chance to be a closer eventually.

Year	Club (League)	Class	W	L	ERA	G	GS	CG	SV	IP	H	HR	BB	SO	K/9	WHIP	AVG
2012	Lakeland (FSL)	HiA	1	0	1.93	22	0	0	15	23	12	1	10	34	13.1	0.94	.152
	Erie (EL)	AA	0	1	0.83	21	0	0	12	22	15	1	9	23	9.6	1.11	.195
	Toledo (IL)	AAA	1	0	2.25	9	0	0	2	8	5	1	7	9	10.1	1.50	.167
2013	Toledo (IL)	AAA	1	1	1.52	30	0	0	14	30	14	1	13	40	12.1	0.91	.139
	Detroit (AL)	MAJ	1	2	3.45	30	0	0	1	29	28	2	11	30	9.4	1.36	.259
2014	Did not play—Injured																
Major League Totals			1	2	3.45	30	0	0	1	29	28	2	11	30	9.4	1.36	.259
Minor League Totals			7	11	2.39	170	16	1	79	226	146	6	124	253	10.1	1.20	.183

10 DIXON MACHADO, SS

Born: Feb. 22, 1992. **B-T:** R-R. **Ht.:** 6-1. **Wt.:** 170. **Signed:** Venezuela, 2008. **Signed by:** German Robles.

Machado had just three extra-base hits in 124 games at low Class A West Michigan in 2012, but he got stronger for the 2013 season. Regardless, he struggled on the field and was often sidelined with leg injuries, prompting the Tigers to remove him from the 40-man roster after adding him the year before. Machado switched up his offseason routine, focusing more on flexibility and agility, and his ability to stay on the field helped fuel a breakout season in 2014. Machado worked with high Class A Lakeland hitting coach Larry Herndon to tweak his setup and his load, both with his hands and his lower half. Machado has always used his hands well in his swing and has a steady, disciplined hitting approach to make frequent contact and draw walks. His power is mostly to the gaps with a focus on hitting line drives and getting on base. Defense is where Machado has always shined. He's smooth and sure-handed, with slightly above-average speed but plus range thanks to his quickness and instincts, making flashy plays with a plus arm. Machado could be a defensive-oriented backup, but the offensive outburst got him back on the 40-man after the 2014 season and gives him an outside shot to be an everyday player.

BA GRADE		
45	**Risk:**	**High**

LGE	PA	BB%	SO%	ISO
FSL	187	12.3	18.2	.082
EL	342	11.7	10.5	.137

Year	Club (League)	Class	AVG	G	AB	R	H	2B	3B	HR	RBI	BB	SO	SB	CS	OBP	SLG
2012	Lakeland (FSL)	HiA	.195	119	421	59	82	16	1	2	37	51	61	23	5	.283	.252
2013	Tigers (GCL)	R	.321	7	28	3	9	2	0	0	2	1	5	0	0	.345	.393
	Lakeland (FSL)	HiA	.215	37	149	19	32	5	2	1	12	10	19	1	0	.264	.295
2014	Lakeland (FSL)	HiA	.252	41	159	30	40	8	1	1	8	23	34	2	1	.348	.333
	Erie (EL)	AA	.305	90	292	45	89	23	1	5	32	40	36	8	5	.391	.442
Minor League Totals			.237	531	1901	270	451	66	11	12	157	220	296	99	27	.319	.302

11 ZACH SHEPHERD, 3B

BA GRADE		
50	**Risk:**	**Extreme**

Born: Sept. 14, 1995. **B-T:** R-R. **Ht.:** 6-3. **Wt.:** 185. **Signed:** Australia, 2012. **Signed by:** Glenn Williams/Kevin Hooker.

Detroit's top two international signings in 2012 were a pair of Dominican shortstops, Willy Adames and Domingo Leyba, and their third-largest bonus went to Shepherd, who signed for $325,000 as a shortstop out of Australia. He is a balanced hitter with a mature plan at the plate and a good blend of hitting, on-base ability and power. As he moves up the ladder, some scouts expect his profile to lean more heavily toward power, which is average now with the ability to leave the yard from his pull side over to the middle of the field, and should increase as he gets stronger. He didn't face much premium velocity in Australia, so he's still adjusting to quality fastballs. After he signed, Shepherd immediately moved to third base, where he has the tools to be a quality defender. He's a below-average runner but he's athletic and moves around well, with good hands and a strong, accurate arm. With third baseman Steven Fuentes one level ahead of him, Shepherd could spend 2015 at short-season Connecticut.

Year	Club (League)	Class	AVG	G	AB	R	H	2B	3B	HR	RBI	BB	SO	SB	CS	OBP	SLG
2014	Tigers (GCL)	R	.301	51	173	34	52	12	5	4	29	21	44	5	1	.373	.497
Minor League Totals			.301	51	173	34	52	12	5	4	29	21	44	5	1	.373	.497

12 ARVICENT PEREZ, C

BA GRADE		
50	**Risk:**	**Extreme**

Born: Jan. 14, 1994. **B-T:** R-R. **Ht.:** 5-10. **Wt.:** 178. **Signed:** Venezuela, 2011. **Signed by:** Alejandro Rodriguez.

Shortly after the 2011 season ended, the Tigers scooped up Perez for just $16,000 out of Venezuela. After a couple of seasons in the Venezuelan Summer League, he impressed scouts in the Rookie-level Gulf Coast League in 2014 and continued to play well upon an aggressive push to low Class A West Michigan for the final month of the season. Perez has skills on both sides of the ball, but he stands out immediately on defense. Perez has a plus arm and makes accurate throws, which enabled him to throw out 43 percent of basestealers in 2014. His blocking and receiving skills are advanced for his age, and he has a chance to be a plus defender once he learns more about the nuances of catching, such as game-calling and how to handle a pitching staff. Perez is an extremely aggressive hitter who goes up swinging at the first pitch, which is why he walked just twice in 135 plate appearances in 2014. His bat control is so good that he's a career .304 hitter despite being a bad-ball hitter, though he will have to show more plate discipline against better pitchers. While he does chase, he doesn't overswing to try to hit the ball out of the park, instead staying within his line-drive approach and gap power. He's ready for his first full-season test at West Michigan in 2015.

Year	Club (League)	Class	AVG	G	AB	R	H	2B	3B	HR	RBI	BB	SO	SB	CS	OBP	SLG
2012	Tigers (VSL)	R	.289	34	97	8	28	5	1	1	15	5	11	3	0	.336	.392
2013	Tigers (VSL)	R	.297	48	148	14	44	5	2	1	26	8	14	3	2	.338	.378
2014	Tigers (GCL)	R	.309	27	81	14	25	6	1	3	20	1	7	3	0	.310	.519
	West Michigan (MWL)LoA		.348	14	46	7	16	2	0	0	6	1	5	1	1	.375	.391
Minor League Totals			.304	123	372	43	113	18	4	5	67	15	37	10	3	.336	.414

13 KYLE LOBSTEIN, LHP

BA GRADE
40 Risk: Low

Born: Aug. 12, 1989. **B-T:** L-L. **Ht.:** 6-3. **Wt.:** 200. **Drafted:** HS— Flagstaff, Ariz., **2008 (2nd round)**. **Signed by:** Jayson Durocher (Rays).

When the Rays left Lobstein off their 40-man roster following the 2012 season, the Mets picked him in the Rule 5 draft. They turned around and sold him to the Tigers, who traded Curt Casali to Tampa Bay before the 2013 season to be keep Lobstein without Rule 5 restriction. The Tigers brought him up from Triple-A Toledo in to be their fifth starter in September 2014, and he held his own in that role for the rest of the season. Lobstein doesn't have a plus pitch, so he relies on keeping hitters off balance by mixing his stuff and moving the ball around the strike zone. His fastball sits 86-90 mph, and he usually tries to keep the pitch down and on the outer third of the plate. He throws a tight cutter at 83-86 mph that was effective against major league hitters and a good weapon against both righties and lefties. His 78-82 mph changeup is an average pitch he mainly uses when he's facing righthanded hitters. Lobstein also flips an occasional 74-78 mph curveball in when he's facing a lefty to give them another look. Lobstein has a chance to be a No. 5 starter, though he could end up shuttling between Detroit and Toledo.

Year	Club (League)	Class	W	L	ERA	G	GS	CG	SV	IP	H	HR	BB	SO	K/9	WHIP	AVG
2012	Montgomery (SL)	AA	8	7	4.06	27	27	0	0	144	140	12	69	129	8.1	1.45	.260
2013	Erie (EL)	AA	7	4	3.12	15	15	2	0	95	92	6	27	83	7.8	1.25	.262
	Toledo (IL)	AAA	6	3	3.48	13	13	0	0	72	73	2	25	65	8.1	1.35	.267
2014	Toledo (IL)	AAA	9	11	4.07	26	25	1	0	146	174	10	42	127	7.8	1.48	.299
	Detroit (AL)	MAJ	1	2	4.35	7	6	0	0	39	35	3	14	27	6.2	1.25	.236
Major League Totals			1	2	4.35	7	6	0	0	39	35	3	14	27	6.2	1.25	.236
Minor League Totals			52	48	3.77	146	144	5	0	811	808	63	276	702	7.8	1.34	.262

14 JOE JIMENEZ, RHP

BA GRADE
45 Risk: High

Born: Jan. 17, 1995. **B-T:** R-R. **Ht.:** 6-3. **Wt.:** 220. **Signed:** HS—Gurabo, P.R., **2013 (NDFA)**. **Signed by:** Rolando Casanova/German Geigel.

Jimenez signed with the Tigers as a nondrafted free agent out of the Puerto Rico Baseball Academy in 2013 and has quickly looked like a steal. After throwing in the low 90s in high school, Jimenez spiked his velocity up to 95-98 mph. Even though Jimenez has a long arm action and effort in his delivery, he's able to repeat his mechanics surprisingly well and throw plenty of strikes. His fastball is a swing-and-miss pitch, but he also made strides tightening up the break on his slider over the course of the season. He can manipulate the shape and speed of the pitch, throwing it softer for an early-count strike then ramping it up for a harder-breaking chase pitch when he's ahead in the count. With one plus pitch in his fastball and a second in his slider, Jimenez has the weapons to profile in a big league bullpen and the control to move quickly through the system if the Tigers want to push him, with low Class A West Michigan his next stop.

Year	Club (League)	Class	W	L	ERA	G	GS	CG	SV	IP	H	HR	BB	SO	K/9	WHIP	AVG
2013	Tigers (GCL)	R	3	0	0.50	8	0	0	1	18	9	0	6	24	12.0	0.83	.155
2014	Connecticut (NYP)	SS	3	2	2.70	23	0	0	4	27	22	1	6	41	13.8	1.05	.218
Minor League Totals			6	2	1.81	31	0	0	5	45	31	1	12	65	13.1	0.96	.195

15 STEVEN FUENTES, 3B

BA GRADE
45 Risk: High

Born: Oct. 21, 1994. **B-T:** B-R. **Ht.:** 5-11. **Wt.:** 180. **Signed:** Venezuela, 2011. **Signed by:** Oscar Garcia/Pedro Chavez.

One of the Tigers' top international signings in 2011, Fuentes signed for $210,000 as a 16-year-old out of Venezuela. He has good bat speed and had a solid season at the plate in 2014. He's still ironing some things out with his swing, working at his pitch recognition and trying to maintain a consistent hitting approach, though he doesn't swing and miss excessively. Most of the switch-hitter's struggles at short-season Connecticut came batting righthanded, where he struck out 20 times in 44 plate appearances. Fuentes uses the whole field and shows occasional pull power that should improve as he gets stronger. Signed as a shortstop, he's become big enough that he fits better at third base, slowing down from a plus runner to an average one. He's athletic and moves around well at the hot corner, where he has a quick first step, good range and a plus arm, though like many young infielders he's still learning to slow the game down. He's ready to move on to low Class A West Michigan in 2015.

Year	Club (League)	Class	AVG	G	AB	R	H	2B	3B	HR	RBI	BB	SO	SB	CS	OBP	SLG
2012	Tigers (VSL)	R	.257	59	226	23	58	8	4	2	25	18	47	8	8	.317	.354
2013	Tigers (GCL)	R	.272	46	151	26	41	10	2	2	24	12	41	5	0	.353	.404
2014	Connecticut (NYP)	SS	.295	55	200	30	59	13	7	3	19	16	51	6	2	.356	.475
Minor League Totals			.274	160	577	79	158	31	13	7	68	46	139	19	10	.340	.409

16 DREW VERHAGEN, RHP

BA GRADE

40 Risk: Medium

Born: Oct. 22, 1990. **B-T:** R-R. **Ht.:** 6-6. **Wt.:** 230. **Drafted:** Vanderbilt, 2012 (4th round). **Signed by:** Harold Zonder.

VerHagen, who had Tommy John surgery as a high school senior, made his major league debut with a spot start on July 19, 2014, but he went on the disabled list with a back strain afterward and didn't pitch the rest of the season. A massive 6-foot-6, VerHagen drops his pitches downhill and with good extension. His fastball is tough for hitters to barrel because of the angle, 90-94 mph velocity (with a peak of 96) and hard, heavy sink and run that results in plenty of groundballs. He throws slightly across his body, which also adds deception. The trouble with VerHagen is his low strikeout rate, which stems from a lack of a reliable secondary pitch. His best offspeed offering is a changeup, a fringy pitch that flashes average with solid sink. VerHagen's curveball is a slurvy pitch that will likely always be below-average. He's improved his strike-throwing ability each year, though he's still more control than command. VerHagen should go back to Triple-A Toledo to begin 2015, but he has a chance to be back up as a No. 5 starter.

Year	Club (League)	Class	W	L	ERA	G	GS	CG	SV	IP	H	HR	BB	SO	K/9	WHIP	AVG
2012	Tigers (GCL)	R	0	0	2.25	2	0	0	0	4	5	0	0	2	4.5	1.25	.313
	Lakeland (FSL)	HiA	0	3	3.67	8	6	0	0	27	20	0	14	17	5.7	1.26	.206
2013	Lakeland (FSL)	HiA	5	3	2.81	12	11	0	0	67	49	1	27	35	4.7	1.13	.207
	Erie (EL)	AA	2	5	3.00	12	12	1	0	60	53	3	17	40	6.0	1.17	.240
2014	Toledo (IL)	AAA	6	7	3.67	19	19	0	0	110	117	5	25	63	5.1	1.29	.275
	Detroit (AL)	MAJ	0	1	5.40	1	1	0	0	5	5	0	3	4	7.2	1.60	.294
Major League Totals			0	1	5.40	1	1	0	0	5	5	0	3	4	7.2	1.60	.294
Minor League Totals			13	18	3.28	53	48	1	0	269	244	9	83	157	5.3	1.22	.245

17 JOSE VALDEZ, RHP

BA GRADE

45 Risk: High

Born: March 1, 1990. **B-T:** R-R. **Ht.:** 6-1. **Wt.:** 200. **Signed:** Dominican Republic, 2009. **Signed by:** Carlos Santana/Ramon Perez/Miguel Garcia.

Valdez used steroids early in his career, which cost him a 50-game suspension when he was in the Dominican Summer League in 2010 after he tested positive for Boldenone, and he didn't make it to full-season ball until he was 23 in 2012. Since then, Valdez has garnered attention for his high-octane stuff, though everything about his game is erratic. A pure reliever, Valdez throws 93-98 mph with good angle. He has two plus pitches when he has his slider working, for it's a hard, three-quarters breaking ball that can miss bats in the high 80s and even reach into the low 90s at times. He has a changeup as well, though it's below-average. Valdez is a high-energy pitcher with a long arm action, effort to his delivery and a tendency to overthrow, which causes bouts of wildness, though his control has improved the last two seasons. Even if Valdez develops fringe-average control, his stuff is good enough to beat major league hitters. He will advance to Triple-A Toledo with a chance to make his major league debut in 2015.

Year	Club (League)	Class	W	L	ERA	G	GS	CG	SV	IP	H	HR	BB	SO	K/9	WHIP	AVG
2012	Tigers (GCL)	R	0	1	0.82	23	0	0	15	22	15	0	10	28	11.5	1.14	.188
2013	West Michigan (MWL)	LoA	1	1	2.73	27	0	0	16	26	16	0	20	35	12.0	1.37	.178
	Lakeland (FSL)	HiA	1	1	2.74	23	0	0	17	23	16	1	14	32	12.5	1.30	.195
2014	Erie (EL)	AA	2	3	4.11	47	0	0	18	57	56	6	26	66	10.4	1.44	.257
Minor League Totals			10	13	3.20	181	0	0	90	200	152	9	116	239	10.8	1.34	.213

18 SPENCER TURNBULL, RHP

BA GRADE

45 Risk: High

Born: Sept. 18, 1992. **B-T:** R-R. **Ht.:** 6-3. **Wt.:** 215. **Drafted:** Alabama, 2014 (2nd round). **Signed by:** Bryson Barber.

The Tigers used their second-round pick in 2014 on Turnbull, a right-hander out of Alabama who signed for $900,000. Turnbull throws two quality fastballs, including a four-seamer that sits 90-95 mph and hits 97. He also throws a two-seamer with hard, heavy sink that helps him rack up a lot of ground balls. His slider was his most improved pitch at Alabama. Turnbull used to get caught in between with his breaking ball, giving it three-quarters action and inconsistent snap, but he's turned it into more of a true power slider that's average. He doesn't miss many bats, though, and his cutter and changeup are both below-average. Turnbull has smoothed out parts of his delivery over the years, but his delivery features plenty of effort and some scouts aren't a fan of his arm action. Turnbull has a strong, physical frame that suggests he should be durable, though his mechanics, arsenal and shaky command could land him in the bullpen. He will be ticketed for low Class A West Michigan rotation in 2015.

Year	Club (League)	Class	W	L	ERA	G	GS	CG	SV	IP	H	HR	BB	SO	K/9	WHIP	AVG
2014	Tigers (GCL)	R	0	0	3.00	1	1	0	0	3	2	1	1	4	12.0	1.00	.200
	Connecticut (NYP)	SS	0	2	4.45	11	11	0	0	28	31	1	14	19	6.0	1.59	.270
Minor League Totals			0	2	4.31	12	12	0	0	31	33	2	15	23	6.6	1.53	.264

19 MIKE GERBER, OF

Born: July 8, 1992. **B-T:** L-R. **Ht.:** 6-2. **Wt.:** 175. **Drafted:** Creighton, 2014 (15th round). **Signed by:** Marty Miller.

The Tigers may have found a late-round bargain in Gerber, a promising hitter who went in the 15th round as a senior sign out of Creighton in 2014. His strong wrists and forearms help him generate plus raw power. He's an aggressive hitter who gave some scouts concerns in college because they worried about his contact rate, but he squared up plenty of pitches in pro ball. Pro scouts liked his balance, pitch recognition and that his bat stayed in the zone a long time, though he can get long at times and his offensive profile will likely always be power over hitting. Gerber was a quality defensive center fielder in college but he's not a burner and fits better in right field, where he played after signing and showed a plus arm. He should go to low Class A West Michigan in 2015 with a chance to boost his stock significantly.

Year	Club (League)	Class	AVG	G	AB	R	H	2B	3B	HR	RBI	BB	SO	SB	CS	OBP	SLG
2014	Connecticut (NYP)	SS	.286	57	217	40	62	16	4	7	37	17	48	8	4	.354	.493
	West Michigan (MWL)	LoA	.387	8	31	4	12	3	0	0	5	4	3	1	0	.457	.484
Minor League Totals			.298	65	248	44	74	19	4	7	42	21	51	9	4	.367	.492

20 JAVIER BETANCOURT, 2B/SS

Born: May 8, 1995. **B-T:** R-R. **Ht.:** 6-0. **Wt.:** 180. **Signed:** Venezuela, 2012. **Signed by:** Oscar Garcia/Pedro Chavez.

Betancourt is the nephew of former Mets third baseman Edgardo Alfonzo. Signed for $200,000 in 2011, Betancourt has good hand-eye coordination and makes frequent contact with a level, line-drive swing. He started to generate more loft in his swing in 2014 and can occasionally pull a ball over the fence, but he has gap power and his game will have to be about getting on base. He uses the whole field and has good pitch recognition, but his strong bat-to-ball skills get him in trouble because he's too aggressive, swinging at borderline pitches that result in weak contact. Betancourt mostly played second base, where he excelled and has a chance to be an above-average defender. He positions himself well, has good hands and feet and slows the game down. Despite fringy speed, he has good range to both sides, along with a fringe-average arm. Betancourt has a chance to develop into a player along the lines of Hernan Perez, though Betancourt is more advanced at the same age.

Year	Club (League)	Class	AVG	G	AB	R	H	2B	3B	HR	RBI	BB	SO	SB	CS	OBP	SLG
2012	Tigers (VSL)	R	.333	32	123	24	41	6	0	3	15	10	16	4	5	.391	.455
2013	Tigers (GCL)	R	.333	50	177	28	59	9	2	2	22	12	14	5	3	.379	.441
2014	West Michigan (MWL)	LoA	.269	134	558	67	150	18	3	6	54	26	81	9	6	.307	.344
Minor League Totals			.291	216	858	119	250	33	5	11	91	48	111	18	14	.334	.380

21 ANGEL NESBITT, RHP

Born: Dec. 4, 1990. **B-T:** R-R. **Ht.:** 6-1. **Wt.:** 237. **Signed:** Venezuela, 2009. **Signed by:** German Robles.

Nesbitt has slowly evolved into an intriguing relief prospect with a power arm whom the Tigers protected on the 40-man roster after the 2014 season. Nesbitt throws his fastball 93-97 mph with solid sink and armside run. His breaking ball, an 83-86 mph slider has made promising strides after being a nonfactor early in his career. It's not a knockout pitch, but it flashes average with solid bite, though it still gets slurvy on him when he gets caught in between. He throws a firm changeup with solid sink but right now is below-average, as he tends to slow his arm speed. Nesbitt's walk rate jumped upon reaching Double-A Erie, and while he's been a steady strike-thrower previously, his control and command both need improvement. Nesbitt will move to Triple-A Toledo in 2015, with a chance to help the Tigers as a middle reliever.

Year	Club (League)	Class	W	L	ERA	G	GS	CG	SV	IP	H	HR	BB	SO	K/9	WHIP	AVG
2012	Connecticut (NYP)	SS	4	3	4.71	20	0	0	0	36	49	1	11	23	5.7	1.65	.336
2013	West Michigan (MWL)	LoA	3	4	3.22	52	0	0	3	67	60	5	21	54	7.3	1.21	.235
2014	Lakeland (FSL)	HiA	2	0	0.79	24	0	0	14	34	23	0	8	36	9.4	0.90	.189
	Erie (EL)	AA	1	0	2.23	24	0	0	6	32	20	3	15	36	10.0	1.08	.177
Minor League Totals			13	12	3.71	178	8	0	35	279	281	15	104	213	6.9	1.38	.264

22 EDGAR DE LA ROSA, RHP

BA GRADE

45 Risk: High

Born: Nov. 12, 1990. **B-T:** R-R. **Ht.:** 6-8. **Wt.:** 235. **Signed:** Dominican Republic, 2009. **Signed by:** Miguel Rodriguez/Ramon Perez/Miguel Garcia.

De la Rosa is a gigantic human being who looks like he should be posting up down in the paint as a power forward at 6-foot-8, 235 pounds. Instead he throws heat off the mound anywhere from 92-98 mph with steep downhill plane and good extension, though he doesn't generate much movement on his fastball. De la Rosa's fastball is a plus pitch but his strikeout rate is low because he's still searching for a reliable secondary weapon. The pitch with the most potential is his fringy, high-80s changeup, on which he maintains his arm speed and drops late in the zone at times but flattens out at times. He throws a curveball and a slider, but both are below-average. De la Rosa is a solid strike thrower given all the long levers he has to keep in sync in his delivery. De la Rosa has shown durability to handle a starter's workload, though he needs to improve his soft stuff to avoid the bullpen. Extremely tall pitchers can take longer to develop, so the Tigers will be patient with him in case he can have a breakthrough. Double-A Erie is up next.

Year	Club (League)	Class	W	L	ERA	G	GS	CG	SV	IP	H	HR	BB	SO	K/9	WHIP	AVG
2012	Connecticut (NYP)	SS	4	4	3.10	15	15	0	0	73	66	3	35	54	6.7	1.39	.242
2013	West Michigan (MWL)	LoA	8	6	5.61	25	22	1	0	120	140	6	41	78	5.8	1.50	.297
2014	Lakeland (FSL)	HiA	7	9	3.30	26	26	1	0	139	116	13	53	91	5.9	1.22	.230
Minor League Totals			26	35	4.18	115	97	2	3	518	532	30	200	377	6.5	1.41	.269

23 SANDY BAEZ, RHP

BA GRADE

50 Risk: Extreme

Born: Nov. 25, 1993. **B-T:** R-R. **Ht.:** 6-2. **Wt.:** 180. **Drafted:** Dominican Republic, 2011. **Signed by:** Carlos Santana/Ramon Perez/Miguel Garcia.

When the Tigers scouted Baez as an amateur in the Dominican Republic, he had a good frame and a high-80s fastball, so they signed him after the 2011 season for $49,000. Since then his fastball has exploded into the mid-90s, making him one of the organization's most promising arms at the lower levels. Baez has an excellent build for a pitcher and the added strength has taken his fastball up to 92-94 mph and even 96 at times with good movement. He has developed feel to spin a power curveball, which is inconsistent but flashes average and should be a steadier pitch once he gains more experience. He pitches mostly with the fastball and curveball, which are ahead of his changeup. He hasn't had much need to throw his changeup yet, and some think it might develop into an average offering. Baez never has had trouble throwing strikes, so he should remain in the rotation as long as he can bring along his secondary stuff.

Year	Club (League)	Class	W	L	ERA	G	GS	CG	SV	IP	H	HR	BB	SO	K/9	WHIP	AVG
2012	Tigers (DSL)	R	0	3	5.21	10	9	0	0	38	43	1	12	42	9.9	1.45	.293
2013	Tigers (DSL)	R	8	1	2.05	14	10	1	1	61	41	0	16	50	7.3	0.93	.188
2014	Tigers (GCL)	R	1	2	3.06	12	12	0	0	62	62	3	16	48	7.0	1.26	.258
Minor League Totals			9	6	3.19	36	31	1	1	161	146	4	44	140	7.8	1.18	.241

24 GRAYSON GREINER, C

BA GRADE

45 Risk: High

Born: Oct. 11, 1992. **B-T:** R-R. **Ht.:** 6-6. **Wt.:** 215. **Drafted:** South Carolina, 2014 (3rd round). **Signed by:** Grant Brittain.

After the Tigers drafted him in the third round and signed him for $529,400, Greiner hit well at low Class A West Michigan for a month until a hit-by-pitch broke the hamate bone in his left wrist, necessitating season-ending surgery. There aren't many 6-foot-6 catchers, but Greiner's defense grades out surprisingly well. He's a quiet receiver who handles velocity well and doesn't let many balls get past him. He has a plus arm, but because of his slow release, he's not great at controlling the running game. He has solid-average raw power, though his long levers lead to a long swing. He didn't have any trouble making contact against lower-level pitchers in pro ball, but that will be tested once he faces more advanced pitchers at upper levels. Scouts mostly project Greiner as a backup catcher, but he has upside if he keeps hitting.

Year	Club (League)	Class	AVG	G	AB	R	H	2B	3B	HR	RBI	BB	SO	SB	CS	OBP	SLG
2014	West Michigan (MWL)	LoA	.322	26	90	11	29	5	0	2	16	11	18	0	0	.394	.444
Minor League Totals			.322	26	90	11	29	5	0	2	16	11	18	0	0	.394	.444

25 JOE MANTIPLY, LHP

BA GRADE

40 Risk: Medium

Born: March 1, 1991. **B-T:** R-L. **Ht.:** 6-4. **Wt.:** 215. **Drafted:** Virginia, 2013 (27th round). **Signed by:** Bill Buck.

A starter at Virginia Tech, Mantiply moved to the bullpen in 2014, which helped his strikeout rate jump to 9.4 per nine innings. Mantiply spent most of the season as a 23-year-old at low Class A West Michigan, but the Tigers skipped him to Double-A Erie in August, where he didn't miss a beat. He followed that up with a strong showing in the Arizona Fall League. Mantiply doesn't overpower, throwing 88-91 mph, but he's not afraid to pitch inside and can manipulate the movement on the pitch to generate sink and tail or cut the ball. He has an average changeup that managers voted the best in the Midwest League, and he has a fringy slider that flashes average. Mantiply has an unorthodox delivery and throws across his body, but that gives him needed deception, and he repeats his mechanics to throw consistent strikes, which gives him a chance to be a middle reliever in the majors.

Year	Club (League)	Class	W	L	ERA	G	GS	CG	SV	IP	H	HR	BB	SO	K/9	WHIP	AVG
2013	Connecticut (NYP)	SS	0	1	2.04	13	12	0	0	35	31	2	10	30	7.6	1.16	.235
2014	West Michigan (MWL)	LoA	6	3	2.40	38	0	0	8	71	57	2	19	76	9.6	1.07	.221
	Erie (EL)	AA	0	0	3.38	8	0	0	1	11	12	1	3	10	8.4	1.41	.293
Minor League Totals			6	4	2.38	59	12	0	9	117	100	5	32	116	8.9	1.13	.232

26 DANIEL FIELDS, OF

BA GRADE

40 Risk: Medium

Born: Jan. 23, 1991. **B-T:** L-R. **Ht.:** 6-2. **Wt.:** 215. **Drafted:** HS—Detroit, 2009 (6th round). **Signed by:** Tom Osowski.

A key draft pick for the Tigers in 2009, Fields signed in the sixth round for $1.625 million out of high school. His father is Tigers hitting coordinator Bruce Fields, but Daniel was regarded more for his athleticism than his hitting polish at the time, so it was stunning when the Tigers started him as a 19-year-old at high Class A Lakeland in 2010. Fields spent three years in Lakeland before showing signs of life at the plate at Double-A Erie in 2013, but he struggled again upon a promotion to Triple-A Toledo in 2014, including two months on the sidelines after he broke his right hand getting hit by a pitch in May. He is prone to swinging and missing, though he eliminated a leg kick during the 2014 season to try to simplify his approach and improve his timing, and he has average raw power. Fields is athletic but he's a fringe-average runner and isn't a true center fielder, profiling better in left field with a fringy arm. The Tigers already have lefthanded-hitting Tyler Collins on the cusp, and in the offseason they traded for center fielder Anthony Gose, another lefthanded hitter and a superior defender, so Fields doesn't have a clear path to Detroit, even as a reserve. Thus, he's slated to return to Toledo.

Year	Club (League)	Class	AVG	G	AB	R	H	2B	3B	HR	RBI	BB	SO	SB	CS	OBP	SLG
2012	Lakeland (FSL)	HiA	.266	62	244	31	65	11	4	1	26	19	55	14	7	.318	.357
	Erie (EL)	AA	.264	29	106	13	28	4	0	2	7	13	21	9	1	.352	.358
2013	Erie (EL)	AA	.284	118	457	71	130	27	6	10	58	45	130	24	7	.356	.435
2014	Tigers (GCL)	R	.167	2	6	2	1	1	0	0	0	0	2	0	0	.286	.333
	Erie (EL)	AA	.286	8	28	4	8	3	1	0	9	6	7	2	0	.429	.464
	Toledo (IL)	AAA	.219	75	274	29	60	10	3	6	26	15	76	8	2	.273	.343
Minor League Totals			.248	527	1922	240	477	83	24	35	219	202	543	69	30	.327	.371

27 MELVIN MERCEDES, RHP

BA GRADE

40 Risk: Medium

Born: Nov. 2, 1990. **B-T:** R-R. **Ht.:** 6-3. **Wt.:** 250. **Signed:** Dominican Republic, 2008. **Signed by:** Miguel Rodriguez/Ramon Perez.

The heavily-built Mercedes had a mediocre season pitching at Triple-A Toledo in 2014, but on Aug. 15 he went six up, six down in two scoreless innings in his major league debut against the Mariners, then returned to Toledo to finish the season. Mercedes is a sinker/slider pitcher who relies heavily on the former, a plus pitch at 93-96 mph that helps him get groundballs. There are times when he will flash a solid-average slider, but it comes and goes because he doesn't stay on top of the ball consistently. His strikeout rate dipped to 4.6 batters per nine innings in 2014, which is in part a reflection of his lack of an out pitch. He got in trouble at times in Triple-A when he went nearly exclusively to the sinker at the expense of his secondary pitches, which made him too predictable. Mercedes has violence and recoil in his mechanics, but he throws strikes consistently and works down in the zone. If he can bring along his slider, he could stick around as a middle reliever, though he's probably heading back to Triple-A in 2015.

Year	Club (League)	Class	W	L	ERA	G	GS	CG	SV	IP	H	HR	BB	SO	K/9	WHIP	AVG
2012	West Michigan (MWL)	LoA	0	3	2.80	37	0	0	9	64	54	3	23	43	6.0	1.20	.230
	Lakeland (FSL)	HiA	0	0	0.00	1	0	0	0	1	1	0	1	0	0.0	2.00	.250
2013	Lakeland (FSL)	HiA	3	1	0.96	24	0	0	11	28	23	1	5	17	5.5	1.00	.221
	Erie (EL)	AA	2	1	1.44	26	0	0	12	25	23	3	9	19	6.8	1.28	.237
2014	Detroit (AL)	MAJ	0	0	0.00	1	0	0	0	2	0	0	0	2	9.0	0.00	.000
	Toledo (IL)	AAA	0	3	4.92	46	0	0	3	60	69	8	16	31	4.6	1.41	.284
Major League Totals			0	0	0.00	1	0	0	0	2	0	0	0	2	9.0	0.00	.000
Minor League Totals			12	15	3.15	225	0	0	63	297	269	16	131	198	6.0	1.35	.240

28 HAROLD CASTRO, 2B

BA GRADE

40 Risk: High

Born: Nov. 30, 1993. **B-T:** L-R. **Ht.:** 6-0. **Wt.:** 165. **Signed:** Venezuela, 2011. **Signed by:** Pedro Chavez.

Castro looked like the next under-the-radar Venezuelan find for the Tigers, who signed him for $29,000 in March 2011. Once he got to low Class A West Michigan in 2013, he looked overmatched at the plate. He returned to the Midwest League to start 2014 and wasn't hitting well there, but by the end of May the Tigers bumped him up to high Class A Lakeland, where he performed better. Castro has a short, quick swing and good bat-to-ball skills. He hits to all fields and uses his hands well at the plate, flicking the ball to the opposite field on pitches on the outer third. Castro hit .299 in Lakeland but without a trace of secondary skills. He has an aggressive approach and minimal power. He needs to get stronger to deliver more impact and take a more selective approach to improve his on-base ability. Castro is athletic and runs above-average, but he has a fringy arm and below-average defense at second base.

Year	Club (League)	Class	AVG	G	AB	R	H	2B	3B	HR	RBI	BB	SO	SB	CS	OBP	SLG
2012	Tigers (GCL)	R	.311	51	193	24	60	14	2	1	21	10	25	15	3	.343	.420
2013	Lakeland (FSL)	HiA	.274	21	73	8	20	2	1	0	11	5	22	3	2	.316	.329
	West Michigan (MWL)	LoA	.231	41	147	17	34	7	1	1	11	2	40	5	1	.240	.313
2014	West Michigan (MWL)	LoA	.250	20	72	8	18	5	0	0	3	5	7	3	2	.304	.319
	Lakeland (FSL)	HiA	.299	57	211	17	63	5	0	0	10	9	40	8	8	.335	.322
Minor League Totals			.289	253	948	118	274	43	4	3	88	42	155	58	23	.323	.352

29 CHAD GREEN, RHP

BA GRADE

40 Risk: High

Born: May 24, 1991. **B-T:** L-R. **Ht.:** 6-3. **Wt.:** 210. **Drafted:** Louisville, 2013 (11th round). **Signed by:** Harold Zonder.

Green pitched well in 2014, but he was also a 23-year-old at low Class A West Michigan getting by more on polish than stuff. He pitches off a solid fastball, sitting in the low 90s and touching 94 mph with good movement. He's a prolific strike-thrower who hits his spots and gets ground balls at an above-average rate. Green's strikeout percentage was good in the Midwest League, but that probably will drop once he faces better hitters unless he can come up with a reliable secondary pitch. He throws a slider and a changeup, but both are below-average pitches. Green should move up to high Class A Lakeland in 2015, where his pitchability should still be good enough to work, but he will be tested at upper levels.

Year	Club (League)	Class	W	L	ERA	G	GS	CG	SV	IP	H	HR	BB	SO	K/9	WHIP	AVG
2013	Tigers (GCL)	R	1	0	3.00	2	0	0	0	3	3	1	0	6	18.0	1.00	.250
	Lakeland (FSL)	HiA	3	0	3.63	10	2	0	1	17	16	0	6	10	5.2	1.27	.242
2014	West Michigan (MWL)	LoA	6	4	3.11	23	23	0	0	130	121	8	28	125	8.6	1.14	.251
Minor League Totals			10	4	3.17	35	25	0	1	151	140	9	34	141	8.4	1.15	.250

30 JOEY PANKAKE, 3B/SS

BA GRADE

40 Risk: High

Born: Nov. 23, 1992. **B-T:** R-R. **Ht.:** 6-2. **Wt.:** 185. **Drafted:** South Carolina, 2014 (7th round). **Signed by:** Grant Brittain.

Pankake, who signed for $165,000 as a seventh-round pick in 2014, has close to average tools across the board. He is a smart hitter with a good approach, working counts and understanding how pitchers attack him. His barrel stays in the hitting zone, which helps him make consistent contact to all fields and stay on good breaking pitches. He's strong and has average raw power, though his offensive game will be more about hitting line drives and getting on base. The Tigers flipped Pankake between shortstop and third base in his debut at short-season Connecticut, but he's expected to see more time at third base going forward, since he doesn't project as a shortstop. He's still adjusting to the hot corner, where he has an average arm.

Year	Club (League)	Class	AVG	G	AB	R	H	2B	3B	HR	RBI	BB	SO	SB	CS	OBP	SLG
2014	Connecticut (NYP)	SS	.292	64	240	37	70	16	2	2	36	22	44	2	0	.345	.400
Minor League Totals			.292	64	240	37	70	16	2	2	36	22	44	2	0	.345	.400

Houston Astros

BY VINCENT LARA-CINISOMO

E ven in a 2014 season when the major league team made clear steps forward on the field and top prospects started to blossom, the Astros' season cannot be categorized as unqualified progress.

The full-scale rebuilding process, which gave Houston the top overall pick in three consecutive drafts, hit a pothole when the Astros failed to sign 2014 No. 1 pick Brady Aiken, the San Diego high school lefthander.

It was just the third time in the history of the draft (which began in 1965) that the No. 1 overall pick did not sign. Previous unsigned picks Danny Goodwin (1971) and Tim Belcher (1983) went on to become first-round picks again and, eventually, major leaguers.

In June, Aiken and the Astros agreed to the parameters of a contract including a $6.5 million bonus. Aiken even traveled to Houston, but he never signed. The Astros reportedly found an issue with Aiken's elbow during a physical, though they said privacy laws prevented disclosure of the southpaw's condition. Regardless, rumors of a small tear in the ulnar collateral ligament in Aiken's left elbow ran rampant.

The Astros' inability to sign Aiken jeopardized their reported signing of fifth-rounder Jacob Nix, a high school righthander, and a potential run at lefthander Mac Marshall, a 21st-round pick. The signings of both players hinged on Houston having access to the unused portion of Aiken's $7.9 million slot in its signing budget.

The taint of the failure to sign Aiken affected the Astros in many ways. First, they lost access to three talented amateur arms. But more important for the future, the organization is the subject of a grievance filed by Nix's representatives, Excel Sports Management, which also represents Aiken. Excel has alleged the Astros agreed to terms on a $1.5 million bonus, and if MLB forces Houston to honor that offer, then the Astros would by rule forfeit two 2015 draft picks for going over their 2014 bonus pool by a significant amount.

If the Astros retain those picks, they'll control the 2015 draft, when holding the second and fifth overall picks would give them by far the largest bonus pool in the industry.

Previous No. 1 overall picks Carlos Correa (2012) and Mark Appel (2013) had setbacks. Correa broke his right fibula in June, ending his season after 62 games, while Appel struggled at high Class A Lancaster before gaining his bearings in a late-season stint at Double-A Corpus Christi and in the Arizona Fall League.

The Astros' failure to sign Brady Aiken cast a long shadow over their 2014 efforts

TOP PROSPECTS OF THE DECADE

Year	Player, Pos.	2014 Org
2005	Chris Burke, 2b	Out of baseball
2006	Jason Hirsh, rhp	Out of baseball
2007	Hunter Pence, of	Giants
2008	J.R. Towles, c	Rangers
2009	Jason Castro, c	Astros
2010	Jason Castro, c	Astros
2011	Jordan Lyles, rhp	Rockies
2012	Jon Singleton, 1b	Astros
2013	Carlos Correa, ss	Astros
2014	Carlos Correa, ss	Astros

Still, the 2014 season delivered promise. The major league club won 19 more games than 2013, with Jose Altuve leading the majors in hits while young pitchers Dallas Keuchel and Collin McHugh thrived. For the first time since 2011, the Astros avoided the majors' worst record.

It wasn't enough to save manager Bo Porter, who was fired in September for reported philosophical differences with general manager Jeff Luhnow. New manager A.J. Hinch has experience playing and managing in the big leagues as well as working as a farm director, and better fits the organizational approach.

Despite all the drama, the Astros still gave fans a reason for optimism, though they'll have to stay tuned to see if Houston can advance to the 2017 World Series, as forecast by a now-famous Sports Illustrated cover.

General manager: Jeff Luhnow. **Farm director:** Quinton McCracken. **Scouting director:** Mike Elias.

Class	Team	League	W	L	PCT	Finish	Manager
Majors	Houston Astros	American	70	92	.432	t-26th (30)	Bo Porter/Tom Lawless
Triple-A	Oklahoma City RedHawks	Pacific Coast	74	70	.514	t-7th (16)	Tom Lawless/ Tony DeFrancesco
Double-A	Corpus Christi Hooks	Texas	33	37	.471	t-5th (8)	Keith Bodie
High A	Lancaster JetHawks	California	78	62	.557	t-2nd (10)	Rodney Linares
Low A	Quad Cities River Bandits	Midwest	70	69	.504	7th (16)	Omar Lopez
Short season	Tri-City ValleyCats	New York-Penn	48	28	.632	t-1st (14)	Ed Romero
Rookie	Greeneville Astros	Appalachian	32	34	.485	8th (10)	Josh Bonifay
Rookie	Astros	Gulf Coast	28	32	.467	11th (16)	Marty Malloy
Overall Minor League Record			363	332	.522	8th (30)	

THIS YEAR'S TOP 30

No.	Player, Pos.	Grade/Risk
1.	Carlos Correa, ss	70/Medium
2.	Mark Appel, rhp	60/Medium
3.	Mike Foltynewicz, rhp	55/High
4.	Vince Velasquez, rhp	55/High
5.	Michael Feliz, rhp	55/High
6.	Brett Phillips, of	55/High
7.	Colin Moran, 3b	50/Medium
8.	Rio Ruiz, 3b	50/High
9.	Teoscar Hernandez, of	50/High
10.	Josh Hader, lhp	50/High
11.	Lance McCullers Jr., rhp	50/High
12.	Domingo Santana, of	50/High
13.	Derek Fisher, of	50/High
14.	Preston Tucker, of	45/Medium
15.	J.D. Davis, 3b	50/High
16.	A.J. Reed, 1b	50/High
17.	Francis Martes, rhp	55/Extreme
18.	Tony Kemp, 2b/of	45/Medium
19.	Joe Musgrove, rhp	50/High
20.	Max Stassi, c	40/Low
21.	Adrian Houser, rhp	50/High
22.	Brady Rodgers, rhp	45/Medium
23.	Roberto Pena, c	45/High
24.	Ronald Torreyes, 2b/util	40/Low
25.	Andrew Aplin, of	40/Low
26.	Kent Emanuel, lhp	45/Medium
27.	Jake Buchanan, rhp	40/Low
28.	Asher Wojciechowski, rhp	45/High
29.	Andrew Thurman, rhp	45/High
30.	Danry Vasquez, of	45/High

LAST YEAR'S TOP 30

No.	Player, Pos.	Status
1.	Carlos Correa, ss	No. 1
2.	George Springer, of	Majors
3.	Mark Appel, rhp	No. 2
4.	Mike Foltynewicz, rhp	No. 3
5.	Lance McCullers Jr., rhp	No. 11
6.	Vince Velasquez, rhp	No. 4
7.	Jon Singleton, 1b	Majors
8.	Domingo Santana, of	No. 12
9.	Michael Feliz, rhp	No. 5
10.	Asher Wojciechowski, rhp	No. 28
11.	Rio Ruiz, 3b	No. 8
12.	Max Stassi, c	No. 20
13.	Delino DeShields Jr., of	(Rangers)
14.	Josh Hader, lhp	No. 10
15.	Andrew Thurman, rhp	No. 29
16.	Teoscar Hernandez, of	No. 9
17.	Kevin Chapman, lhp	Majors
18.	Nick Tropeano, rhp	(Angels)
19.	Andrew Aplin, of	No. 25
20.	Nolan Fontana, ss	Dropped out
21.	Jake Buchanan, rhp	No. 27
22.	Kyle Smith, rhp	Dropped out
23.	Kent Emanuel, lhp	No. 26
24.	Chris Lee, lhp	Dropped out
25.	Leo Heras, of	Dropped out
26.	Gonzalo Sanudo, rhp	Dropped out
27.	Jandel Gustave, rhp	(Royals)
28.	Reymin Guduan, lhp	Dropped out
29.	Danry Vasquez, of	No. 30
30.	Brett Phillips, of	No. 6

BEST TOOLS

Best Hitter For Average	Carlos Correa
Best Power Hitter	Telvin Nash
Best Strike-Zone Discipline	Rio Ruiz
Fastest Baserunner	Teoscar Hernandez
Best Athlete	Brett Phillips
Best Fastball	Mike Foltynewicz
Best Curveball	Lance McCullers Jr.
Best Slider	Mark Appel
Best Changeup	Vince Velasquez
Best Command	Brady Rodgers
Best Defensive Catcher	Roberto Pena
Best Defensive Infielder	Carlos Correa
Best Infield Arm	Carlos Correa
Best Defensive Outfielder	Brett Phillips
Best Outfield Arm	Brett Phillips

2018 LINEUP

Catcher	Jason Castro
First Base	Jon Singleton
Second Base	Jose Altuve
Shortstop	Carlos Correa
Third Base	Colin Moran
Left Field	George Springer
Center Field	Brett Phillips
Right Field	Teoscar Hernandez
Designated Hitter	A.J. Reed
No. 1 starter	Mark Appel
No. 2 Starter	Vince Velasquez
No. 3 Starter	Michael Feliz
No. 4 Starter	Dallas Keuchel
No. 5 Starter	Josh Hader
Closer	Mike Foltynewicz

HOUSTON ASTROS

TOP 2015 ROOKIE: Mark Appel, rhp. The No. 1 overall pick in 2013 struggled early in 2014, but he righted the ship and has an opportunity to make the rotation.
TOP 2015 BREAKOUT PROSPECT: Joe Musgrove, rhp. It's taken a while, but the physical righty is ready for his full-season closeup.
TOP 2015 SLEEPER: Osvaldo Duarte, ss/of. Stocky 5-foot-9 bundle of energy has double-plus speed and hit his way to U.S. in 2014.

SOURCE OF TOP 30 TALENT			
Homegrown	22	**Acquired**	**8**
College	10	Trades	8
Junior college	0	Rule 5 draft	0
High school	9	Independent leagues	0
Draft-and-follow	0	Free agents/waivers	0
Nondrafted free agents	0		
International	3		

LF
Teoscar Hernandez (9)
Derek Fisher (13)
Preston Tucker (14)
Danry Vasquez (30)
Leonardo Heras

CF
Brett Phillips (6)
Andrew Aplin (25)
James Ramsay
Jason Martin
Nestor Tejada
Ronny Rafael

RF
Domingo Santana (12)
Felix Lucas

3B
Colin Moran (7)
Rio Ruiz (8)
J.D. Davis (15)
Matt Duffy
Nick Tanielu

SS
Carlos Correa (1)
Wilson Amador
Miguel Angel Sierra
Joan Mauricio

2B
Tony Kemp (18)
Ronald Torreyes (24)
Nolan Fontana
Joe Sclafani

1B
A.J. Reed (16)
Conrad Gregor
Telvin Nash

C
Max Stassi (20)
Roberto Pena (23)
Tyler Heineman
Jacob Nottingham

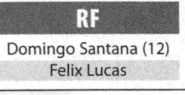

LHP

LHSP	LHRP
Josh Hader (10)	Reymin Guduan
Kent Emanuel (26)	Thomas Shirley
Chris Lee	
Luis Cruz	
Austin Nicely	
Bryan Radziewski	

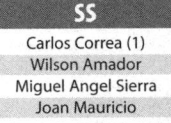

RHP

RHSP	RHRP
Mark Appel (2)	Mike Foltynewicz (3)
Vince Velasquez (4)	Lance McCullers Jr. (11)
Michael Feliz (5)	Andrew Thurman (29)
Francis Martes (17)	Gonzalo Sanudo
Joe Musgrove (19)	Kyle Westwood
Adrian Houser (21)	Francis Ramirez
Brady Rodgers (22)	Juan Minaya
Jake Buchanan (27)	Derick Velazquez
Asher Wojciehowski (28)	Dean Deetz
Franklin Perez	
Daniel Mengden	
Kyle Smith	
Brock Dykxhoorn	
Devonte German	

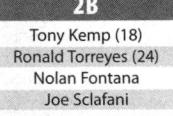

2014

BEST PURE HITTER: While all three of the college bats the Astros drafted in the top three rounds—OF Derek Fisher (1), 1B A.J. Reed (2) and 3B/1B J.D. Davis (3)—have a case, Davis gets the nod. He has bat speed and strength from the right side to go with plus power potential.

BEST POWER HITTER: Reed led all of college baseball with 23 home runs and a .399 isolated power. He has plus power potential from the left side. Fisher has plus raw power.

FASTEST RUNNER: OF Bobby Boyd (8) is at least a 70-grade runner with a short stroke from the left side. Fisher is also at least a plus runner.

BEST DEFENSIVE PLAYER: Boyd has the potential to be a plus defender in center with his speed, first-step quickness and instincts.

BEST FASTBALL: RHP Derick Velazquez (7) has an explosive fastball that sat 92-93 mph this summer, touching 96 with plus life to his arm side. RHP Dean Deetz (11) walked 6.8 per nine this summer, but his fastball was 92-94, touching 97.

BEST SECONDARY PITCH: RHP Daniel Mengden (4) is a tough, competitive strike-thrower who shows the makings of a plus changeup. Velazquez's changeup has plus potential and his slider flashes plus. Deetz's curveball shows at least above-average potential.

BEST PRO DEBUT: Davis impressed with his offensive production and his improved defense. Fisher likely would have been taken higher if not for a broken hamate in the spring. His beautiful lefthanded swing is short and compact, producing a .303/.378/.408 line this summer.

BEST ATHLETE: Fisher for his strong, angular 6-foot-1, 207-pound build and plus raw power-speed combo.

MOST INTRIGUING BACKGROUND: RHP Josh James (34) grew up in the Virgin Islands and didn't begin playing baseball until he was 17. He is the next product out of a loaded Western Oklahoma State JC program that has produced Andrelton Simmons and Sicnarf Loopstok. James is arguably the top pitching athlete of the Astros draft class with a fastball that ranges from 90-94 and slider that shows at least average potential, flashing above-average.

CLOSEST TO THE MAJORS: Reed combines lefthanded power with the potential to draw walks at an above-average clip.

BEST LATE-ROUND PICK: LHP Ben Smith (17) looked like a candidate to go in the top half-dozen rounds before needing Tommy John surgery after six starts. Nick Tanielu (14) is transitioning to second from third base. He is a natural, fluid and instinctual hitter with some pop from the right side.

THE ONE WHO GOT AWAY: LHP Brady Aiken (1) became the first No. 1 pick to go unsigned since Tim Belcher in 1983. Aiken's camp and the Astros had been tight-lipped on whether or not the two sides were involved in a grievance, and Aiken had yet to enroll either at UCLA, where he'd been committed, or in a junior college.

ASSESSMENT: After not signing Aiken with the first pick, Houston grabbed three college bats with hitting ability and power potential. The Astros have the second and fifth picks in the 2015 draft.

2013

RHP Mark Appel (1) had a rough year, but pitching guru Brent Strom seems to have repaired the damage. Is 5-foot-6 2B Tony Kemp (5) going to be the best of the rest? Unless he's another Altuve, that could be a light haul.

GRADE: C

2012

SS Carlos Correa (1), even after a broken leg, has looked like a No. 1 overall pick almost since Day One. A deep class also includes OF Brett Phillips (6), RHPs Lance McCullers Jr. (1s) and Brady Rodgers (3), 3B Rio Ruiz (4) and OFs Andrew Aplin (5) and Preston Tucker (7).

GRADE: A

2011

OF George Springer (1) swings and misses a lot but has star-level tools otherwise. RHPs Nick Tropeano (5), since traded, and slow-moving Adrian Houser (2), are the next-best products.

GRADE: B+

TOP DRAFT PICKS OF THE DECADE

Year	Player, Pos.	2014 Org
2005	Brian Bogusevic, lhp	Marlins
2006	Max Sapp, c	Out of baseball
2007	*Derek Dietrich, 3b (3rd round)	Marlins
2008	Jason Castro, c	Astros
2009	Jio Mier, ss	Astros
2010	Delino DeShields Jr., 2b	Astros
2011	George Springer, of	Astros
2012	Carlos Correa, ss	Astros
2013	Mark Appel, rhp	Astros
2014	*Brady Aiken, lhp	N/A

*Did not sign.

LARGEST BONUSES IN CLUB HISTORY

Mark Appel, 2013	$6,350,000
Carlos Correa, 2012	$4,800,000
Ariel Ovando, 2010	$2,600,000
George Springer, 2011	$2,525,000
Lance McCullers Jr., 2012	$2,500,000

1 CARLOS CORREA, SS

Born: Sept. 22, 1994. **B-T:** R-R. **Ht:** 6-4. **Wt:** 190.
Drafted: HS—Gurabo, P.R., 2012 (1st round).
Signed by: Larry Pardo/Joey Sola.

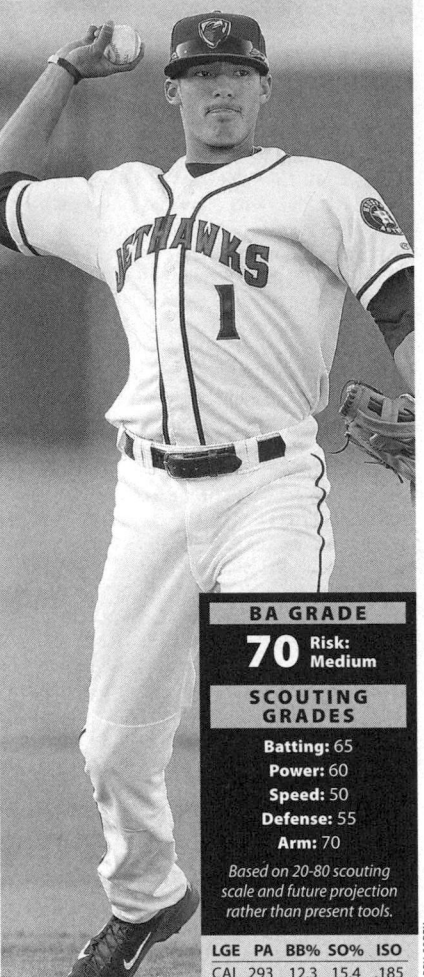

Two years after they drafted Correa No. 1 overall out of the Puerto Rico Baseball Academy, the Astros remain convinced they made the right choice in selecting him ahead of outfielder Byron Buxton—the No. 1 prospect in the game two years running—or college righthanders Mark Appel, Kyle Zimmer or Kevin Gausman. As a shortstop, Correa filled a void that Buxton, a center fielder, did not for Houston. He also signed for $4.8 million, which was $2.4 million less than the No. 1 overall bonus slot (and $1.3 million less than Buxton received from the Twins at No. 2 overall), savings the Astros passed on to sign draft picks such as Lance McCullers Jr. and Rio Ruiz. For an organization that was attempting a massive turnaround, Correa seemed a safer bet than Buxton. When healthy, Correa has delivered, ranking as the No. 2 prospect, behind Buxton, in the low Class A Midwest League in 2013, when he hit .320/.405/.467 in 117 games. He was off to a similarly strong start in 2014 when he broke his right fibula in late June and missed the remainder of the season at high Class A Lancaster.

At 6-foot-4, Correa is one of the bigger shortstops in the game, but his lean, athletic frame is a plus, as are most of his tools. He's an average runner underway who turns in some below-average run times out of the box. He's average when it comes to turning double plays, but he has excellent instincts, a quick first step, good hands and a double-plus arm, which helps him make the play in the hole and should allow him to thrive at shortstop in the near term. He's a plus hitter with plus raw power, though his homer totals haven't shown it yet because his swing lacks loft. He's capable of hitting 30 homers in a season once he has more experience, though scouts don't believe it will happen consistently. He hits the ball hard with regularity now, and one rival evaluator likened Correa to Albert Pujols (albeit with less power) for his ability to hammer the ball to the opposite field. His makeup is off the charts, with a natural ability to lead and a goal-oriented mindset unseen in a player who just turned 20. His size and arm strength allow for speculation that he'd easily slide to third base or right field when he reaches his late 20s.

Correa should be ready for spring training and was taking grounders during instructional league, though he did not play in the Arizona Fall League and will not play winter ball. The loss of half a season tempers hopes of Correa's quick rise, and he'll likely begin 2015 back at Lancaster for at least the start of the season. He might move off shortstop as he gets larger, but that won't be for four to five years at minimum. He'll play all of 2015 as a 20-year-old, eventually moving to Double-A Corpus Christi. Correa's strong character and work ethic paired with his on-field tools will make him one of the top shortstops in the majors once he arrives for good in 2016.

BA GRADE

70 Risk: Medium

SCOUTING GRADES

Batting: 65
Power: 60
Speed: 50
Defense: 55
Arm: 70

Based on 20-80 scouting scale and future projection rather than present tools.

LGE	PA	BB%	SO%	ISO
CAL	293	12.3	15.4	.185

LARRY GOREN

Year	Club (League)	Class	AVG	G	AB	R	H	2B	3B	HR	RBI	BB	SO	SB	CS	OBP	SLG
2012	Astros (GCL)	R	.232	39	155	23	36	11	1	2	9	7	36	5	1	.270	.355
	Greeneville (APP)	R	.371	11	35	5	13	3	1	1	3	5	8	1	0	.450	.600
2013	Quad Cities (MWL)	LoA	.320	117	450	73	144	33	3	9	86	58	83	10	10	.405	.467
2014	Lancaster (CAL)	HiA	.325	62	249	50	81	16	6	6	57	36	45	20	4	.416	.510
Minor League Totals			.308	229	889	151	274	63	11	18	155	106	172	36	15	.389	.465

2 MARK APPEL, RHP

Born: July 15, 1991. **B-T:** R-R. **Ht:** 6-5. **Wt:** 190. **Drafted:** Stanford, 2013 (1st round). **Signed by:** Brian Byrne.

The Astros considered taking Appel at No. 1 overall in 2012 but took Carlos Correa instead. They got Appel a year later anyway after he failed to sign with the Pirates in 2012. It worked out for both sides. Appel completed his management science and engineering degree at Stanford and ended up with a $6.35 million bonus as the top pick in 2013. High Class A California League hitters lit up Appel, but a midseason tutoring session with big league pitching coach Brent Strom helped synchronize the righthander's delivery and led to better results from his front-line stuff. He has three pitches that show plus. The question is whether they'll show plus on the same night. Appel needs to command his tight, mid-80s slider more, but he pitches at 92-98 mph consistently with his fastball, sitting 94-95. At his best, he has great command of his changeup and a wipeout slider, but he lacks deception and consistent command, and hitters get better swings at his fastball and slider as a result. His strong body and sound delivery should give him durability. After a solid Arizona Fall League performance, Appel will go to big league camp with a chance to compete for a job. The Astros don't have great urgency to fast-track him, so he probably will begin 2015 back at Double-A Corpus Christi.

BA GRADE

60 Risk: Medium

LGE	BF	SO%	BB%	HR/9
CAL	217	18.4	5.1	1.83
TL	165	23.0	7.9	0.46

Year	Club (League)	Class	W	L	ERA	G	GS	CG	SV	IP	H	HR	BB	SO	K/9	WHIP	AVG
2013	Tri-City (NYP)	SS	0	0	3.60	2	2	0	0	5	6	0	0	6	10.8	1.20	.300
	Quad Cities (MWL)	LoA	3	1	3.82	8	8	0	0	33	30	2	9	27	7.4	1.18	.236
2014	Lancaster (CAL)	HiA	2	5	9.74	12	12	0	0	44	74	9	11	40	8.1	1.92	.372
	Corpus Christi (TL)	AA	1	2	3.69	7	6	1	0	39	35	2	13	38	8.8	1.23	.236
Minor League Totals			6	8	5.93	29	28	1	0	121	145	13	33	111	8.2	1.47	.294

3 MIKE FOLTYNEWICZ, RHP

Born: Oct. 7, 1991. **B-T:** R-R. **Ht.:** 6-4. **Wt.:** 200. **Drafted:** HS—Minooka, Ill., 2010 (1st round). **Signed by:** Troy Hoerner.

Foltynewicz wasn't a consensus first-round pick when the Astros picked him 19th overall in 2010, but since signing for $1.3 million, he's developed into one of the top power arms in the minors, consistently throwing 96-100 mph. He made his major league debut in August, spending the last two months in the big league bullpen. Foltynewicz has an electric arm and crazy arm strength. He hits 100 mph in virtually every appearance and holds his top-of-the-scale velocity. His breaking ball—which some call a slider, some a curveball—is an above-average offering that misses bats. His aggressive, inefficient delivery costs him control, not to mention command, and he lacks feel for the strike zone. Trusting his premium stuff more would help. His changeup is below-average because he slows his arm noticeably when throwing it. Scouts who believe Foltynewicz can start liken him to Angels righty Garrett Richards, for he has top-of-the-rotation stuff with present below-average control. If he can't harness his delivery, he's a hard-throwing reliever. He likely will begin 2015 at Triple-A Fresno, though he could push his way on to the big league roster with a strong spring.

BA GRADE

55 Risk: High

LGE	BF	SO%	BB%	HR/9
PCL	448	22.8	11.6	0.88
AL	84	16.7	8.3	1.45

Year	Club (League)	Class	W	L	ERA	G	GS	CG	SV	IP	H	HR	BB	SO	K/9	WHIP	AVG
2012	Lexington (SAL)	LoA	14	4	3.14	27	27	0	0	152	145	11	62	125	7.4	1.36	.250
2013	Lancaster (CAL)	HiA	1	0	3.81	7	5	0	0	26	31	4	14	29	10.0	1.73	.290
	Corpus Christi (TL)	AA	5	3	2.87	23	16	0	3	103	75	8	52	95	8.3	1.23	.207
2014	Oklahoma City (PCL)	AAA	7	7	5.08	21	18	0	0	103	98	10	52	102	8.9	1.46	.260
	Houston (AL)	MAJ	0	1	5.30	16	0	0	0	19	23	3	7	14	6.8	1.61	.299
Major League Totals			0	1	5.30	16	0	0	0	19	23	3	7	14	6.8	1.61	.299
Minor League Totals			32	28	3.98	116	104	0	3	563	544	46	246	478	7.6	1.40	.258

4 VINCE VELASQUEZ, RHP

Born: June 7, 1992. **B-T:** B-R. **Ht.:** 6-3. **Wt.:** 185. **Drafted:** HS—Pomona, Calif.,
2010 (2nd round). **Signed by:** Tim Costic/Bobby Heck.

Health has been the bugaboo for Velasquez going back to high school.
He had a stress fracture and ligament strain in his right elbow in 2009 and
didn't pitch his junior season. After he was drafted in 2010 and lured away
from Cal State Fullerton for $655,830, he injured the ligament again and
missed the 2011 season after having Tommy John surgery. He missed two
months in 2014 with a groin injury. Velasquez's inability to stay on the
mound has been frustrating. He might have the highest ceiling of Houston's
pitching prospects thanks to an explosive fastball that plays beyond its 92-95
mph velocity (he tops out at 96 with late tailing life) and a plus changeup.
His curveball is a below-average pitch that needs tightening, but the Astros
believe he could get it to solid-average, and he throws it with requisite
power. Velasquez has a loose arm and athletic body to go with an aggressive
approach. His delivery features some crossfire action. Velasquez got needed

BA GRADE

55 Risk:
High

LGE	BF	SO%	BB%	HR/9
CAL	229	31.4	10.0	0.98

extra work in the Arizona Fall League. He will spend 2015 building endurance with an aim of exceeding
his career-best 125 innings. Expect Velasquez to return to high Class A Lancaster in 2015, at least to start
the season.

Year	Club (League)	Class	W	L	ERA	G	GS	CG	SV	IP	H	HR	BB	SO	K/9	WHIP	AVG
2012	Tri-City (NYP)	SS	4	1	3.35	9	9	0	0	46	37	2	17	51	10.1	1.18	.223
2013	Quad Cities (MWL)	LoA	9	4	3.19	25	16	0	3	110	90	7	33	123	10.1	1.12	.221
	Lancaster (CAL)	HiA	0	2	6.14	3	3	0	0	15	14	2	8	19	11.7	1.50	.259
2014	Astros (GCL)	R	0	1	2.08	3	3	0	0	9	5	0	2	19	19.7	0.81	.167
	Lancaster (CAL)	HiA	7	4	3.74	15	10	0	0	55	45	6	23	72	11.7	1.23	.223
Minor League Totals			22	14	3.45	63	47	0	3	264	215	21	88	309	10.5	1.15	.221

5 MICHAEL FELIZ, RHP

Born: June 28, 1993. **B-T:** R-R. **Ht:** 6-4. **Wt.:** 211. **Signed:** Dominican
Republic, 2010. **Signed by:** Felix Francisco/Rafael Belen/Jose Lima.

Feliz originally signed with the Athletics in 2010 for $800,000, but that
deal was voided when he tested positive for an anabolic steroid. He then
signed with the Astros for half of his initial bonus. Suspended for 50 games
in 2010, Feliz made it to the U.S. in 2011 and reached full-season ball for
the first time in 2014. The big-bodied Feliz throws a 90-96 mph fastball
that sits at 93 with movement. He's got an at-least-average breaking ball
(some call it a curve and some call it a slider) that flashes plus with sharp,
late break at times, and a still-developing changeup with some bottom to it.
Both secondary pitches are inconsistent at this point. Feliz has a fluid delivery that has minimal effort but good deception. He hides the ball and uses
a funky leg kick. Feliz showed steady improvement throughout the season.
He was sitting 90-93 early in the season but was touching 94-96 regularly
later while showing improved feel as well. Evaluators are excited about Feliz,

BA GRADE

55 Risk:
High

LGE	BF	SO%	BB%	HR/9
MWL	441	25.2	8.4	0.53

even though he lacks the control and consistency right now to project as more than a mid-rotation arm,
but if he commands his fastball and learns to pitch with runners on base, he has a lofty ceiling. He'll move
to high Class A Lancaster in 2015.

Year	Club (League)	Class	W	L	ERA	G	GS	CG	SV	IP	H	HR	BB	SO	K/9	WHIP	AVG
2012	Astros (GCL)	R	5	0	1.64	7	3	0	0	38	25	2	9	35	8.2	0.89	.185
	Greeneville (APP)	R	1	1	5.13	6	6	0	0	26	28	1	14	28	9.6	1.59	.269
2013	Tri-City (NYP)	SS	4	2	1.96	14	10	0	1	69	53	2	13	78	10.2	0.96	.209
2014	Quad Cities (MWL)	LoA	8	6	4.03	25	19	0	0	103	104	6	37	111	9.7	1.37	.263
Minor League Totals			18	13	3.40	67	51	0	1	299	272	14	97	309	9.3	1.23	.241

6 BRETT PHILLIPS, OF

Born: May 30, 1994. **B-T:** L-R. **Ht.:** 6-0. **Wt.:** 175. **Drafted:** HS—Seminole, Fla., 2012 (6th round). **Signed by:** John Martin.

Phillips decided against attending North Carolina State when the Astros ponied up $300,000 to sign him in 2012. His fast-twitch athleticism helped him become an all-county football player as a senior—the only year he played varsity. He led the low Class A Midwest League in slugging (.521) and outfield assists (14) in 2014 despite spending the last 27 games at high Class A Lancaster. The Astros already knew Phillips could be an above-average defender in center field, thanks to his above-average speed and double-plus arm—the best in the system, with accuracy and strength. He has range and instincts for the position. Phillips rates as a solid-average hitter with a chance to be above-average, and he has good bat control and strike-zone judgment. The big question is his power, but he's gotten stronger and has plenty of bat speed. Phillips still is learning to pull the ball consistently and handle pitches on the inner half. His speed doesn't play as well on the bases, where his lack of experience shows. Scouts who doubt Phillips' power potential see him as a fourth outfielder, while others believe he should hit enough to be an everyday outfielder. The Astros see him as a future regular in center field and will send him back to Lancaster to start 2015.

BA GRADE

55 Risk: High

LGE	PA	BB%	SO%	ISO
MWL	443	8.1	17.2	.219
CAL	128	10.9	15.6	.220

Year	Club (League)	Class	AVG	G	AB	R	H	2B	3B	HR	RBI	BB	SO	SB	CS	OBP	SLG
2012	Astros (GCL)	R	.251	54	175	26	44	7	6	0	13	28	48	7	5	.360	.360
2013	Quad Cities (MWL)	LoA	.231	12	39	4	9	2	0	0	3	3	10	1	3	.286	.282
	Greeneville (APP)	R	.247	29	85	9	21	7	1	0	9	17	21	4	3	.371	.353
2014	Quad Cities (MWL)	LoA	.302	103	384	68	116	21	12	13	58	36	76	18	10	.362	.521
	Lancaster (CAL)	HiA	.339	27	109	19	37	8	2	4	10	14	20	5	4	.421	.560
Minor League Totals			.287	225	792	126	227	45	21	17	93	98	175	35	23	.367	.461

7 COLIN MORAN, 3B

Born: Oct. 1, 1992. **B-T:** L-R. **Ht:** 6-4. **Wt:** 190. **Drafted:** North Carolina, 2013 (1st round). **Signed by:** Joel Matthews (Marlins).

The sixth overall pick by the Marlins in the 2013 draft, Moran had an excellent career at North Carolina, where he was the BA Freshman of the Year in 2011 and a Golden Spikes finalist as a junior. Moran came to Houston (along with Jake Marisnick) as part of trade package for right-hander Jarred Cosart. It's clear the Astros have long been fans of Moran, whose professional, even-keel demeanor often strikes scouts as low-energy, especially when he turns in bottom-of-the-scale run times. Houston believes in his profile, starting with average defense at third base with below-average range but good hands and a strong, accurate arm. The organization believes he has plus raw power, especially after seeing him blast a 425-foot homer off Royals first-rounder Brandon Finnegan. However, Moran's swing is geared to hit for average, manipulating the bat to produce liners to the gaps. He knows the strike zone, so he projects as at least an average hitter with modest on-base ability. Moran has earned comparisons with Bill Mueller and Dave Magadan as a third baseman lacking profile power. He likely will begin the 2015 season at Corpus Christi, but with big league incumbent Matt Dominguez coming off a .215 season, he could hit his way to Houston.

BA GRADE

50 Risk: Medium

LGE	PA	BB%	SO%	ISO
FSL	392	7.1	13.5	.100
TL	123	7.3	18.7	.107

Year	Club (League)	Class	AVG	G	AB	R	H	2B	3B	HR	RBI	BB	SO	SB	CS	OBP	SLG
2013	Greensboro (SAL)	LoA	.299	42	154	19	46	8	1	4	23	15	25	1	0	.354	.442
2014	Jupiter (FSL)	HiA	.294	89	361	34	106	21	0	5	33	28	53	1	2	.342	.393
	Corpus Christi (TL)	AA	.304	28	112	12	34	6	0	2	22	9	23	0	1	.350	.411
Minor League Totals			.297	159	627	65	186	35	1	11	78	52	101	2	3	.346	.408

8 RIO RUIZ, 3B

Born: May 22, 1994. **B-T:** L-R. **Ht.:** 6-1. **Wt.:** 180. **Drafted:** HS—La Puente, Calif., 2012 (4th round). **Signed by:** Tim Costic.

A fine high school quarterback at SoCal powerhouse Bishop Amat, Ruiz largely lost his senior season because of a knee injury and blood clot in his arm. The Astros drafted him anyway and paid him $1.85 million out of the fourth round in 2012 to bail on his Southern California commitment. He tied for the high Class A California League lead in doubles (37) in 2014. Ruiz's approach attracted the Astros in his amateur days, and he takes professional at-bats while maintaining a smooth stroke and balanced swing. He has made specific improvements to his hitting mechanics in the past year, cleaning up his collapsing front side. Ruiz's power hasn't translated to home runs yet, and scouts project average power thanks to good bat speed and his strike-zone judgment, which should allow him to become more aggressive in the future. Still somewhat raw, Ruiz lacks polished actions at third base and needs reps defensively, especially working on his backhand and being more consistent with his average arm. Ruiz doesn't have wow tools but he hits, and he fits the profile at third base. If he continues to improve the conditioning of his stocky frame, he will push Colin Moran to be the Astros' third baseman of the future. He likely will begin 2015 a level below Moran, probably at Double-A Corpus Christi.

BA GRADE

50 Risk: High

LGE	PA	BB%	SO%	ISO
CAL	602	13.6	15.1	.143

Year	Club (League)	Class	AVG	G	AB	R	H	2B	3B	HR	RBI	BB	SO	SB	CS	OBP	SLG
2012	Astros (GCL)	R	.271	23	85	13	23	8	2	0	11	12	22	2	0	.361	.412
	Greeneville (APP)	R	.220	15	50	8	11	3	1	1	7	4	10	0	0	.291	.380
2013	Quad Cities (MWL)	LoA	.260	114	416	46	108	33	1	12	63	50	92	12	3	.335	.430
2014	Lancaster (CAL)	HiA	.293	131	516	76	151	37	2	11	77	82	91	4	4	.387	.436
Minor League Totals			.275	283	1067	143	293	81	6	24	158	148	215	18	7	.361	.429

9 TEOSCAR HERNANDEZ, OF

Born: Oct. 15, 1992. **B-T:** R-R. **Ht.:** 6-2. **Wt.:** 180. **Signed:** Dominican Republic, 2011. **Signed by:** Felix Francisco/Rafael Belen/Francis Mojica.

Hernandez signed in 2011 for $20,000—or about $2.5 million less than fellow Dominican outfielder Ariel Ovando, whom he's far surpassed as a prospect. The Astros scouted Hernandez as a favor to Felix Francisco, then the team's Latin American director, whose brother-in-law was a friend of Hernandez's family. What comes up first from those who've seen Hernandez is excellent athleticism and power potential. He makes an impression with at least average raw power and serious snap in his bat thanks to strong hands. His stroke can get long, which makes swing and miss a part of his game going forward, and he likely will be an average to fringe-average hitter. He has a tendency to chase pitches off the plate. Hernandez has plus-plus speed (4.1 seconds to first base from the right side) but may slow down as he physically matures. He's an average to tick above defender with an above-average arm. The Astros laud his makeup. Hernandez is a boom-or-bust prospect whose free-swinging ways could keep him from reaching his potential. He profiles in right field and likely will return to Double-A Corpus Christi in 2015 after finishing the 2014 season there.

BA GRADE

50 Risk: High

LGE	PA	BB%	SO%	ISO
CAL	455	10.8	25.7	.256
TL	98	2.0	36.7	.189

Year	Club (League)	Class	AVG	G	AB	R	H	2B	3B	HR	RBI	BB	SO	SB	CS	OBP	SLG
2012	Astros (GCL)	R	.243	51	177	25	43	11	2	4	18	19	54	10	1	.325	.395
	Lexington (SAL)	LoA	.240	8	25	2	6	2	0	1	5	3	12	1	0	.310	.440
2013	Quad Cities (MWL)	LoA	.271	123	499	97	135	25	9	13	55	41	135	24	11	.328	.435
2014	Lancaster (CAL)	HiA	.294	96	391	72	115	33	8	17	75	49	117	31	6	.376	.550
	Corpus Christi (TL)	AA	.284	23	95	12	27	4	1	4	10	2	36	2	3	.299	.474
Minor League Totals			.275	366	1413	249	388	88	27	46	198	142	396	84	25	.344	.473

10 JOSH HADER, LHP

Born: April 7, 1994. **B-T:** L-L. **Ht.:** 6-3. **Wt.:** 160. **Drafted:** HS—Millersville, Md., 2012 (19th round). **Signed by:** Dean Albany (Orioles).

The Orioles drafted Hader as a local follow and signed him for $40,000 in 2012. He was developing into one of Baltimore's better prospects when the Astros acquired him for Bud Norris in July 2013. Hader's breakthrough 2014 season included being the high Class A California League pitcher of the year and reaching Double-A Corpus Christi by age 20. Hader is a young, thin, nasty lefthander with a Chris Sale body and arm slot, albeit from a shorter frame. He pitches with an above-average fastball at 88-93 mph that touches 96 and plays up. His low slot gives his heater running life and deception, and he pitches aggressively with it, busting hitters inside. Hader generally throws fastball strikes, but Double-A hitters didn't chase and he'll have to improve his control to remain a starter. His inconsistent slider and changeup flash average but generally are below-average pitches. Durability will always be a question because of Hader's size and how he slings the ball across his body. He's young enough that the Astros will give him plenty of time in the rotation, but his reliance on his fastball profiles him better as a reliever. He likely returns to Corpus Christi in 2015.

BA GRADE

50 Risk: High

LGE	BF	SO%	BB%	HR/9
CAL	421	26.6	9.0	0.78
TL	94	25.5	17.0	0.90

Year	Club (League)	Class	W	L	ERA	G	GS	CG	SV	IP	H	HR	BB	SO	K/9	WHIP	AVG
2012	Orioles (GCL)	R	2	0	2.66	12	0	0	2	20	12	2	7	35	15.5	0.93	.174
	Aberdeen (NYP)	SS	0	0	0.00	5	0	0	0	8	2	0	2	13	14.0	0.48	.074
2013	Delmarva (SAL)	LoA	3	6	2.65	17	17	0	0	85	67	4	42	79	8.4	1.28	.215
	Quad Cities (MWL)	LoA	2	0	3.22	5	5	0	0	22	14	0	12	16	6.4	1.16	.182
2014	Lancaster (CAL)	HiA	9	2	2.70	22	15	0	2	103	76	9	38	112	9.8	1.10	.206
	Corpus Christi (TL)	AA	1	1	6.30	5	4	0	0	20	16	2	16	24	10.8	1.60	.216
Minor League Totals			17	9	2.92	66	41	0	4	259	187	17	117	279	9.7	1.17	.202

11 LANCE McCULLERS JR., RHP

BA GRADE

50 Risk: High

Born: Oct. 2, 1993. **B-T:** L-R. **Ht.:** 6-1. **Wt.:** 190. **Drafted:** HS—Tampa, 2012 (1st round supplemental). **Signed by:** John Martin.

McCullers signed for $2.5 million as part of the Astros' 2012 draft class, the first under the current regime led by general manager Jeff Luhnow. The son of the former major league reliever of the same name, McCullers is not as tall as the other top-shelf pitchers in the organization, but he has a power fastball that touches 98 mph with a double-plus breaking ball that has been described within the organization as a curveball and outside of it as a slider. One thing is for certain: It is a strikeout pitch—but only when he knows where it's going. Well below-average control remains one of McCullers' bigger issues, which is in part due to a crossfire delivery. He doesn't always finish upright and doesn't get great extension, though back soreness—considered minor but enough to send him to the disabled list in June—may have contributed. He walked a career-worst 5.2 batters per nine innings in 2014, and his career rate of 4.6 is untenable for a righthanded starter. His changeup has improved to flash average in pro ball. With his delivery, poor control and competitive nature, McCullers probably faces a future in the bullpen. Just 21, he might begin 2015 back at high Class A Lancaster, if only to start the season.

Year	Club (League)	Class	W	L	ERA	G	GS	CG	SV	IP	H	HR	BB	SO	K/9	WHIP	AVG
2012	Astros (GCL)	R	0	1	1.64	4	4	0	0	11	10	0	2	12	9.8	1.09	.227
	Greeneville (APP)	R	0	3	4.80	4	4	0	0	15	10	2	10	17	10.2	1.33	.182
2013	Quad Cities (MWL)	LoA	6	5	3.18	25	19	0	0	105	92	3	49	117	10.1	1.35	.239
2014	Lancaster (CAL)	HiA	3	6	5.47	25	18	0	4	97	95	18	56	115	10.7	1.56	.255
Minor League Totals			9	15	4.19	58	45	0	4	228	207	23	117	261	10.3	1.42	.242

12 DOMINGO SANTANA, OF

BA GRADE

50 Risk: High

Born: Aug. 5, 1992. **B-T:** R-R. **Ht.** 6-5. **Wt.:** 228. **Signed:** Dominican Republic, 2009. **Signed by:** Sal Agnostinelli (Phillies).

Part of the haul from the July 2011 trade of Hunter Pence to the Phillies, Santana certainly looks the part but is the subject of the widest gulf in opinion in the Astros system. He reached the majors in 2014 but had a disastrous debut, striking out in 14 of his 18 plate appearances. The big, righthanded slugger has above-average raw power and an above-average throwing arm, as well as the athleticism and average speed to make him a profile right fielder. Santana has a feast-or-famine approach and might push 200 strikeouts as an everyday regular, but he also could hit 25-30 homers. Scouts don't believe he'll be able to tap into that power because of poor bat control, poor strike-zone discipline and a long swing with a low bat path. Santana can look awful against secondary offerings and get beat by velocity, a deadly combination. Scouts have begun to question his aptitude and inconsistent energy level. Still, Santana is just 22 and has had success at upper levels. He will get a chance to win a corner-outfield spot in Houston in 2015, but he's young enough to go to Houston's new Triple-A Fresno affiliate without it being a huge setback.

Year	Club (League)	Class	AVG	G	AB	R	H	2B	3B	HR	RBI	BB	SO	SB	CS	OBP	SLG
2012	Lancaster (CAL)	HiA	.302	119	457	87	138	26	6	23	97	55	148	7	1	.385	.536
2013	Corpus Christi (TL)	AA	.252	112	416	72	105	23	2	25	64	46	139	12	5	.345	.498
2014	Houston (AL)	MAJ	.000	6	17	1	0	0	0	0	0	1	14	0	0	.056	.000
	Oklahoma City (PCL)	AAA	.296	120	443	63	131	27	2	16	81	64	149	6	4	.384	.474
Major League Totals			.000	6	17	1	0	0	0	0	0	1	14	0	0	.056	.000
Minor League Totals			.273	604	2203	352	602	134	15	90	359	264	764	42	22	.364	.470

13 DEREK FISHER, OF

BA GRADE
50 Risk: High

Born: Aug. 21, 1993. **B-T:** L-R. **Ht:** 6-1. **Wt.:** 207. **Drafted:** Virginia, 2014 (1st round supplemental). **Signed by:** Tim Bittner.

Fisher was a sixth-round pick out of a Pennsylvania high school but turned down the Rangers for a three-year career at Virginia, which he helped lead to the College World Series finals in 2014. He had a down junior season due in part to a broken right hamate but still went 37th overall in the draft, signing for $1,534,100. Fisher had a strong pro debut at short-season Tri-City and has first-round offensive tools. He's an above-average runner who matched his three-year college stolen-base total (17) in his pro debut. Fisher's swing has changed from high school to college and he is able to barrel the ball more often now. He has strength and exceptional bat speed that give him plus-plus raw power, and he made more contact as his college career evolved. Still, he's never tapped into that power consistently, and the Astros will be satisfied if he hits 15-20 homers annually. Defensively, he remains below-average as a route runner and fielder with a below-average arm, but he's athletic enough to be an average defender in left field. If he ever taps into his power, Fisher will profile as a big league regular.

Year	Club (League)	Class	AVG	G	AB	R	H	2B	3B	HR	RBI	BB	SO	SB	CS	OBP	SLG
2014	Astros (GCL)	R	.667	1	3	0	2	1	0	0	1	0	0	0	0	.750	1.000
	Tri-City (NYP)	SS	.303	41	152	31	46	4	3	2	18	16	35	17	4	.378	.408
Minor League Totals			.310	42	155	31	48	5	3	2	18	17	35	17	4	.386	.419

14 PRESTON TUCKER, OF

BA GRADE
45 Risk: Medium

Born: July 6, 1990. **B-T:** L-L. **Ht.:** 6-0. **Wt.:** 215. **Drafted:** Florida, 2012 (7th round). **Signed by:** John Martin.

Tucker's younger brother Kyle, a 2015 draft prospect, will likely get drafted higher than Preston was, but Tucker has made himself into a legitimate prospect since signing as a senior (for $100,000) in 2012. After hitting 57 homers in four years at Florida, Tucker has done nothing but hit since turning pro, with 57 homers in two and a half seasons. As a thick-bodied lefthanded hitter with strong hands and enormous forearms, Tucker will go as far as his bat takes him. He has above-average power with a fringe-average hit tool to go with an aggressive approach. Tucker has solid strike-zone discipline and impacts the ball with a quick, simple swing that he fires through the zone. He has handled lefthanders in his career and hit .319 with seven homers against them in 2014, when he spent the second half at Triple-A. Tucker's below-average speed and fair athleticism, as well as his fringy arm, keep him tethered to left field if not first base. Tucker isn't yet on the 40-man roster, so he probably will begin 2015 at Triple-A Fresno.

Year	Club (League)	Class	AVG	G	AB	R	H	2B	3B	HR	RBI	BB	SO	SB	CS	OBP	SLG
2012	Tri-City (NYP)	SS	.321	42	165	32	53	7	0	8	38	18	16	1	2	.390	.509
2013	Lancaster (CAL)	HiA	.326	75	298	61	97	18	1	15	74	29	45	3	0	.384	.544
	Corpus Christi (TL)	AA	.262	60	237	36	62	14	1	10	29	27	46	0	1	.347	.456
2014	Corpus Christi (TL)	AA	.276	65	261	41	72	17	0	17	43	26	46	3	3	.348	.536
	Oklahoma City (PCL)	AAA	.287	73	275	38	79	18	0	7	51	31	74	2	0	.356	.429
Minor League Totals			.294	315	1236	208	363	74	2	57	235	131	227	9	6	.364	.495

15 J.D. DAVIS, 3B

BA GRADE
50 Risk: High

Born: April 27, 1993. **B-T:** R-R. **Ht.:** 6-3. **Wt.:** 215. **Drafted:** Cal State Fullerton, 2014 (3rd round). **Signed by:** Brad Budzinski.

An unsigned fifth-round pick out of high school, Davis played both infield corners and right field at Cal State Fullerton and also pitched for three seasons, starting earlier in his career but closing as a junior. The Astros saw Davis play third base while Matt Chapman, the Athletics' first-rounder in 2014, was injured, so they plugged him in at the hot corner after signing him for $748,600 and were pleased. At best, he'll be an average defender with a plus arm, but club officials were impressed at how nimble and agile he was for his size. It's at the plate where Davis shines. He had the best debut of Houston's 2014 draftees, reaching low Class A Quad Cities for 43 games and carrying his above-average raw power into games while showing opposite-field power. He projects as an average hitter, though scouts were concerned in his Titans career that he was susceptible to breaking balls. He's a below-average runner. He could return to Quad Cities to begin 2015 and will remain at third base for now.

Year	Club (League)	Class	AVG	G	AB	R	H	2B	3B	HR	RBI	BB	SO	SB	CS	OBP	SLG
2014	Tri-City (NYP)	SS	.279	30	111	18	31	7	1	5	20	15	25	1	0	.382	.495
	Quad Cities (MWL)	LoA	.303	43	155	20	47	9	0	8	32	13	41	4	0	.363	.516
Minor League Totals			.293	73	266	38	78	16	1	13	52	28	66	5	0	.371	.508

16 A.J. REED, 1B

Born: May 10, 1993. **B-T:** L-L. **Ht.:** 6-4. **Wt.:** 240. **Drafted:** Kentucky, 2014 (2nd round). **Signed by:** Nick Venuto.

Reed pitched and hit in high school and at Kentucky, and scouts long were divided over which was his ultimate destination as a pro. He did both exceptionally well in 2014, tying for the Southeastern Conference lead with 12 wins while leading the nation in home runs (23) and slugging (.735). The combination made him the College Player of the Year and Golden Spikes Award winner, and the offensive explosion convinced scouts he fits better as a hitter. After signing for $1.35 million as the 42nd overall pick in 2014, Reed had a solid pro debut, showing plus power to all fields and joining fellow draftee J.D. Davis at low Class A Quad Cities in August. Reed was not selective when his pro career began but made adjustments as the season went on and now understands that pitchers can locate better than in college. Power is Reed's lone plus tool, and he's a raw defender at first base, where he did not take groundballs often, even in practice, at Kentucky to conserve energy. He's fairly light on his feet, but he doesn't run well enough to give the outfield a try. Reed should start at high Class A Lancaster in 2015.

Year	Club (League)	Class	AVG	G	AB	R	H	2B	3B	HR	RBI	BB	SO	SB	CS	OBP	SLG
2014	Tri-City (NYP)	SS	.306	34	124	22	38	11	0	5	30	22	22	2	0	.420	.516
	Quad Cities (MWL)	LoA	.272	34	125	21	34	9	1	7	24	8	32	0	0	.326	.528
Minor League Totals			.289	68	249	43	72	20	1	12	54	30	54	2	0	.375	.522

17 FRANCIS MARTES, RHP

Born: Nov. 24, 1995. **B-T:** R-R. **Ht.:** 6-0. **Wt.:** 170. **Signed:** Dominican Republic 2012. **Signed by:** Albert Gonzalez/Sandy Nin/Domingo Ortega (Marlins).

The Marlins signed Martes for just $87,000 in 2012, then saw his fastball velocity jump into the low 90s in his first pro season in the Dominican Summer League. He jumped to the U.S. in 2014 and attracted the Astros' attention, and Houston added him as a piece in the July trade that shipped Jarred Cosart to Miami while bringing Colin Moran and Jake Marisnick to the Astros. One source said the Astros insisted on Martes to seal the deal. He pitched better after the trade, though his Rookie-level Gulf Coast League season ended early with tightness in his biceps. He can pitch off his fastball that sits in the low 90s and has touched 97 mph with excellent life, which can make it hard to command. His changeup flashes above-average at times and should be a consistent plus pitch for him in the future. While his slider and curveball tend to blend together, at least he has shown the ability to spin the ball. He has a nice, repeatable delivery, which should make him a more consistent strike-thrower in the future. He'll have a chance to earn a spot in the low Class A Quad Cities piggyback rotation in 2015.

Year	Club (League)	Class	W	L	ERA	G	GS	CG	SV	IP	H	HR	BB	SO	K/9	WHIP	AVG
2013	Marlins (DSL)	R	3	3	3.04	12	6	0	0	50	51	1	14	33	5.9	1.29	.267
2014	Marlins (GCL)	R	2	2	5.18	8	6	0	0	33	29	0	20	33	9.0	1.48	.232
	Astros (GCL)	R	1	1	0.82	4	3	0	0	11	5	0	3	12	9.8	0.73	.132
Minor League Totals			6	6	3.53	24	15	0	0	94	85	1	37	78	7.4	1.29	.240

18 TONY KEMP, 2B/OF

Born: Oct. 31, 1991. **B-T:** L-R. **Ht.:** 5-6. **Wt.:** 165. **Drafted:** Vanderbilt, 2013 (5th round). **Signed by:** Nick Venuto.

The strong, athletic Kemp will always face questions because of his size—he's listed at the same 5-foot-6 height as Jose Altuve, but he appears slighter—and like the Astros' all-star second baseman, he's driven by his doubters. The Southeastern Conference player of the year in 2013, Kemp walked more than he struck out in college, then led the Astros system in batting (.316) in 2014 while walking (73) more than he struck out (67). Kemp controls the bat head and makes consistent line-drive contact, though he has below-average power. His play at second base is fringe-average thanks to a below-average arm, but his hands and feet are adequate. He's a plus runner, and the Astros will give him time in center field—he played some left field as a freshman at Vanderbilt—to increase his versatility. Kemp's makeup is off the charts, but he'll have to maximize his tools to be an everyday regular. He could jump to Triple-A Fresno in 2015.

Year	Club (League)	Class	AVG	G	AB	R	H	2B	3B	HR	RBI	BB	SO	SB	CS	OBP	SLG
2013	Tri-City (NYP)	SS	.282	48	177	25	50	7	2	1	13	21	29	17	9	.355	.362
	Quad Cities (MWL)	LoA	.255	27	98	21	25	1	1	1	9	19	18	4	2	.387	.316
2014	Lancaster (CAL)	HiA	.336	72	295	79	99	19	4	4	37	45	35	28	7	.433	.468
	Corpus Christi (TL)	AA	.292	59	233	42	68	11	4	4	21	28	32	13	6	.381	.425
Minor League Totals			.301	206	803	167	242	38	11	10	80	113	114	62	24	.396	.413

19 JOE MUSGROVE, RHP

BA GRADE
50 Risk: High

Born: Dec. 4, 1992. **B-T:** R-R. **Ht:** 6-5. **Wt:** 230. **Drafted:** HS—El Cajon, Calif., 2011 (1st round supplemental). **Signed by:** Andrew Tinnish (Blue Jays).

Drafted by the Blue Jays in 2011 and signed for $500,000, Musgrove stalled in short-season ball after getting traded to the Astros in a 10-player deal in July 2012, hampered by injuries that had kept him grounded in the Rookie-level Gulf Coast League. While he hasn't reached full-season ball yet, Musgrove regained his shine in 2014 at short-season Tri-City, where he ranked as one of the better pitching prospects in the New York-Penn League. Musgrove works downhill with a low- to mid-90s fastball that peaked at 97 mph, and the plus velocity is magnified by armside movement, for his heater bores in on righthanders. He has a three-pitch mix that includes an inconsistent but at times plus curveball and a promising changeup. He profiles as a mid-rotation workhorse. He'll jump to low Class A Quad Cities in 2015.

Year	Club (League)	Class	W	L	ERA	G	GS	CG	SV	IP	H	HR	BB	SO	K/9	WHIP	AVG
2012	Bluefield (APP)	R	0	0	1.13	2	1	0	0	8	5	0	0	9	10.1	0.63	.179
	Greeneville (APP)	R	0	1	7.00	4	0	0	0	9	14	0	4	10	10.0	2.00	.359
2013	Astros (GCL)	R	1	3	4.41	11	3	0	0	33	43	1	4	30	8.3	1.44	.303
2014	Tri-City (NYP)	SS	7	1	2.81	15	13	0	0	77	64	4	10	67	7.8	0.96	.224
Minor League Totals			9	6	3.51	41	24	0	0	151	145	6	23	134	8.0	1.11	.250

20 MAX STASSI, C

BA GRADE
40 Risk: Low

Born: March 15, 1991. **B-T:** R-R. **Ht.:** 5-10. **Wt.:** 205. **Drafted:** HS—Yuba City, Calif., 2009 (4th round). **Signed by:** Jermaine Clark (Athletics).

Stassi comes from a rich baseball family that includes his father Jim, a catcher who reached Triple-A with the Giants, and brother Brock, who played for the Phillies' Double-A Reading club in 2014. He's the first family member since his great uncle Myril Hoag (1931-45) to reach the majors, though. Acquired from the Athletics in the deal that sent Jed Lowrie away in February 2013, Stassi largely stayed healthy in 2014 in what was otherwise a down year at Triple-A Oklahoma City. He posted a .674 OPS, his lowest in a full minor league season. As an average defender with plus raw power, Stassi has intriguing tools for a backstop. He handles pitchers well and is a good receiver, but he has a fringe-average arm. Evaluators believe he'll hit enough to be a major league catcher, but his long swing makes him overmatched against top velocity. He's ticketed for Triple-A again in 2015.

Year	Club (League)	Class	AVG	G	AB	R	H	2B	3B	HR	RBI	BB	SO	SB	CS	OBP	SLG
2012	Stockton (CAL)	HiA	.268	84	314	48	84	18	0	15	45	27	83	3	1	.331	.468
2013	Corpus Christi (TL)	AA	.277	76	289	40	80	20	1	17	60	19	68	1	1	.333	.529
	Houston (AL)	MAJ	.286	3	7	0	2	0	0	1	0	2	0	0	.375	.286
2014	Oklahoma City (PCL)	AAA	.247	101	392	49	97	20	2	9	45	22	103	1	0	.296	.378
	Houston (AL)	MAJ	.350	7	20	2	7	2	0	0	4	0	6	0	0	.350	.450
Major League Totals			.333	10	27	2	9	2	0	0	5	0	8	0	0	.357	.407
Minor League Totals			.252	416	1577	216	397	89	4	56	228	132	429	9	6	.318	.420

21 ADRIAN HOUSER, RHP

BA GRADE
50 Risk: High

Born: Feb. 2, 1993. **B-T:** R-R. **Ht.:** 6-4. **Wt.:** 228. **Drafted:** HS—Locust Grove, Okla., 2011 (2nd round). **Signed by:** Jim Stevenson.

Houston kicked off its 2011 draft—the last of the pre-Jeff Luhnow era—with outfielder George Springer and then Houser, an Oklahoma prep who signed for $535,000. Houser comes from a baseball family, as his father coached him in high school and his cousin Bob Davis was a big league backstop for eight seasons. Houser has moved slowly as a pro, finally reaching full-season ball in 2014. He gets scouts' attention with a fastball that often sits 93-95 mph with cut and tail away from righthanders, and he can maintain his velocity deep into games. He made real progress with an above-average cutter and flashes above-average with his 11-to-5 curve. He's shown feel for his curve that he lacks with his nascent slider and changeup, which flashes average. Houser has a solid, repeatable delivery and the durable body and good-not-great stuff to profile as a back-end starter. He should move up to high Class A Lancaster in 2015.

Year	Club (League)	Class	W	L	ERA	G	GS	CG	SV	IP	H	HR	BB	SO	K/9	WHIP	AVG
2012	Greeneville (APP)	R	3	4	4.19	11	11	0	0	58	53	1	23	54	8.4	1.31	.245
2013	Tri-City (NYP)	SS	0	4	3.42	14	9	0	0	50	57	1	10	39	7.0	1.34	.291
2014	Quad Cities (MWL)	LoA	5	6	4.14	25	17	0	0	109	99	5	37	93	7.7	1.25	.242
Minor League Totals			10	18	4.05	62	48	0	0	265	258	8	95	230	7.8	1.33	.256

22 BRADY RODGERS, RHP

Born: Sept. 17, 1990. **B-T:** R-R. **Ht.:** 6-2. **Wt.:** 187. **Drafted:** Arizona State, 2012 (3rd round). **Signed by:** Jim Stevenson.

BA GRADE
45 Risk: Medium

The former Arizona State control specialist—he walked just 36 batters in 286 college innings—has retained plus pitchability and strong command as a pro. He ranked ninth in 2014 among qualified minor league starters in lowest walk percentage (3.4 percent), spending virtually all year at Double-A Corpus Christi. Rodgers' knack for pitching goes with a solid four-pitch mix. He has average 89-93 mph velocity on his sinking fastball, with a slider that flashes plus when he gets on top of it. He throws it with some power in the low 80s, about 10 mph harder than his average curveball, and adds a deceptive changeup with sink. He's wiry and competitive, with the athleticism to field his position and stifle opposing running games. Rodgers profiles as a back-end starter and will report to Triple-A Fresno for 2015.

Year	Club (League)	Class	W	L	ERA	G	GS	CG	SV	IP	H	HR	BB	SO	K/9	WHIP	AVG
2012	Tri-City (NYP)	SS	7	2	2.89	12	12	0	0	62	62	5	11	49	7.1	1.14	.251
2013	Oklahoma City (PCL)	AAA	0	0	1.80	1	1	0	0	5	5	0	0	4	7.2	1.00	.263
	Corpus Christi (TL)	AA	1	0	0.00	1	1	0	0	5	5	0	0	6	10.8	1.00	.238
	Lancaster (CAL)	HiA	10	8	5.38	27	18	0	1	112	135	14	23	104	8.4	1.41	.300
2014	Oklahoma City (PCL)	AAA	1	0	0.00	1	1	0	0	6	2	0	1	4	6.0	0.50	.111
	Corpus Christi (TL)	AA	5	12	4.77	26	17	0	2	121	135	15	19	87	6.5	1.28	.287
Minor League Totals			24	22	4.40	68	50	0	3	311	342	34	54	254	7.4	1.27	.281

23 ROBERTO PENA, C

Born: June 8, 1992. **B-T:** B-R. **Ht.:** 6-0. **Wt.:** 217. **Drafted:** HS—Caguas, P.R., 2010 (7th round). **Signed by:** Joey Sola.

BA GRADE
45 Risk: High

A converted shortstop and son of former major league catcher Bert Pena, Pena is the best defensive catcher in the system, with an above-average to plus throwing arm that plays up due to exceptional accuracy. Pena has thrown out about 55 percent of basestealers in his career. Pena also gets high marks for his framing and receiving and his leadership on the field. His .996 fielding percentage led the high Class A California League, as did throwing out 57 percent of basestealers. Because of catching depth, the Astros did not add him to the 40-man roster, exposing him to the Rule 5 draft. Pena is a below-average runner and hitter with improving power, though nine of his 13 homers were struck at favorable hitting conditions at high Class A Lancaster. Pena's premium defense could make him a big leaguer if his bat continues to improve. He'll head to Double-A iafter being passed over in the Rule 5 draft.

Year	Club (League)	Class	AVG	G	AB	R	H	2B	3B	HR	RBI	BB	SO	SB	CS	OBP	SLG
2012	Lexington (SAL)	LoA	.245	61	220	21	54	12	0	2	22	10	43	1	2	.278	.327
	Lancaster (CAL)	HiA	.213	21	75	10	16	4	0	1	11	5	15	0	0	.259	.307
2013	Quad Cities (MWL)	LoA	.249	86	325	43	81	19	0	5	32	22	52	2	0	.297	.354
2014	Lancaster (CAL)	HiA	.249	93	350	48	87	19	0	13	54	25	63	1	2	.306	.414
Minor League Totals			.238	382	1392	163	331	71	1	26	169	86	255	4	5	.284	.346

24 RONALD TORREYES, 2B/UTIL

Born: Sept. 2, 1992. **B-T:** R-R. **Ht.:** 5-10. **Wt.:** 150. **Signed:** Venezuela, 2010. **Signed by:** Jose Fuentes (Reds).

BA GRADE
40 Risk: Low

The slightly built Torreyes has already been traded twice. Originally signed by the Reds, he joined the Cubs in the Sean Marshall deal prior to the 2012 season. The Astros acquired him from Chicago in July 2013, sending the Cubs two international bonus slots worth nearly $785,000. Torreyes is a high-energy player who can play second base, shortstop and third base, though he lacks the arm strength to play the left side on a consistent basis. He projects to be an above-average defender at the keystone, however, because of his soft hands. While he projects as an above-average hitter, he has well below-average power.

He doesn't draw many walks. He's just an average runner. The Astros added Torreyes to the 40-man roster in November and he profiles as a utilityman.

Year	Club (League)	Class	AVG	G	AB	R	H	2B	3B	HR	RBI	BB	SO	SB	CS	OBP	SLG
2012	Daytona (FSL)	HiA	.264	115	421	62	111	23	5	6	47	32	29	13	4	.326	.385
2013	Tennessee (SL)	AA	.263	65	224	32	59	13	4	2	25	22	15	4	0	.340	.384
	Corpus Christi (TL)	AA	.278	38	151	19	42	6	2	0	12	6	14	1	1	.310	.344
2014	Oklahoma City (PCL)	AAA	.298	126	460	65	137	20	5	2	46	25	26	12	9	.345	.376
Minor League Totals			.306	502	1883	303	577	100	33	18	217	123	122	67	38	.362	.423

25 ANDREW APLIN, OF

Born: March 21, 1991. **B-T:** L-L. **Ht.:** 6-0. **Wt.:** 200. **Drafted:** Arizona State, 2012 (5th round). **Signed by:** Mike Brown.

BA GRADE
40 Risk: Low

Aplin has moved quickly since signing for $220,000 in the Astros' deep 2012 draft class. He reached Triple-A Oklahoma City at the end of 2014 and added reps in the Arizona Fall League, playing all three outfield spots for Surprise. Aplin profiles as an extra outfielder, given his defensive prowess, high-energy playing style and flawed offensive game. He has a high-maintenance, lefthanded swing that starts with a pronounced leg kick. He consistently has produced below-average power and derives most of his offensive value from his excellent strike-zone discipline. He's an average defender whose route-running and instincts serve him well in center field. Aplin likely won't hit enough to be a regular, but he could be a contributor. He should start the year back at Triple-A.

Year	Club (League)	Class	AVG	G	AB	R	H	2B	3B	HR	RBI	BB	SO	SB	CS	OBP	SLG
2012	Tri-City (NYP)	SS	.348	44	164	38	57	9	5	4	25	24	22	20	7	.441	.537
	Lancaster (CAL)	HiA	.260	24	104	19	27	4	2	3	13	4	16	4	3	.287	.423
2013	Lancaster (CAL)	HiA	.278	128	500	102	139	32	7	9	107	83	63	24	6	.376	.424
2014	Corpus Christi (TL)	AA	.267	98	356	49	95	11	1	6	50	65	56	21	8	.379	.354
	Oklahoma City (PCL)	AAA	.260	28	96	14	25	3	1	0	15	15	15	5	3	.348	.313
Minor League Totals			.281	322	1220	222	343	59	16	22	210	191	172	74	27	.377	.410

26 KENT EMANUEL, LHP

Born: June 4, 1992. **B-T:** L-L. **Ht.:** 6-3. **Wt.:** 190. **Drafted:** North Carolina, 2013 (3rd round). **Signed by:** Tim Bittner.

BA GRADE
45 Risk: Medium

After a strong career at North Carolina that included two College World Series trips, Emanuel helped high Class A Lancaster win the California League title in 2014. While he has a terrific pitcher's body, he offers little to no projection. Emanuel has a solid-average, four-offering mix with pitchability. His fringy fastball ranges from 86-90 mph from a crossfire delivery that adds deception. He can vary the break on his slow curveball, which can get loopy at times. His slider is sweepy, while he has feel for his changeup. Emanuel profiles as a No. 5 starter, but the Astros coaxed better results out of Dallas Keuchel, and he has a similar profile as Emanuel. He'll have to work to earn a spot at Double-A Corpus Christi in 2015.

Year	Club (League)	Class	W	L	ERA	G	GS	CG	SV	IP	H	HR	BB	SO	K/9	WHIP	AVG
2013	Astros (GCL)	R	0	0	0.00	4	4	0	0	9	6	0	2	8	8.0	0.89	.188
2014	Quad Cities (MWL)	LoA	0	2	2.45	6	4	0	0	22	20	3	4	17	7.0	1.09	.241
	Lancaster (CAL)	HiA	9	5	4.59	21	14	0	2	102	111	12	19	76	6.7	1.27	.278
Minor League Totals			9	7	3.92	31	22	0	2	133	137	15	25	101	6.8	1.22	.267

27 JAKE BUCHANAN, RHP

Born: Sept. 24, 1989. **B-T:** R-R. **Ht.:** 6-0 **Wt.:** 235. **Drafted:** North Carolina State, 2010 (8th round). **Signed by:** J.D. Alleva.

BA GRADE
40 Risk: Low

The Astros have a deep inventory of pitchers at the upper levels, with Buchanan counting himself among those fortunate to work with big league pitching coach Brent Strom. Buchanan has thrived as a pro by relying on his two-seam fastball with sink in the 87-91 mph range and cutter-type slider in the low 80s. He mixes in a 77-79 mph curveball and changeup, even throwing a rare four-seamer. Buchanan works more in and out than up and down in the zone and has to sequence well to overcome his fringy stuff. His knack for pitching makes him a potential back-end starter, but his lack of swing-and-miss stuff limits his upside.

Year	Club (League)	Class	W	L	ERA	G	GS	CG	SV	IP	H	HR	BB	SO	K/9	WHIP	AVG
2012	Oklahoma City (PCL)	AAA	0	1	10.13	3	1	0	0	8	17	1	5	5	5.6	2.75	.459
	Corpus Christi (TL)	AA	5	9	4.96	27	19	0	0	134	171	11	33	83	5.6	1.52	.310
2013	Corpus Christi (TL)	AA	7	2	2.09	18	13	0	1	82	67	4	9	44	4.8	0.93	.226
	Oklahoma City (PCL)	AAA	5	5	3.89	12	12	0	0	76	85	6	13	55	6.5	1.28	.285

2014	Oklahoma City (PCL)	AAA	7	5	3.87	16	15	1	0	88	95	7	16	46	4.7	1.26	.275
	Houston (AL)	MAJ	1	3	4.58	17	2	0	0	35	41	4	12	20	5.1	1.50	.297
Major League Totals			1	3	4.58	17	2	0	0	35	41	4	12	20	5.1	1.50	.297
Minor League Totals			33	37	3.98	116	100	2	1	616	667	42	123	379	5.5	1.28	.277

28 ASHER WOJCIECHOWSKI, RHP

Born: Dec. 21, 1988. **B-T:** R-R. **Ht.:** 6-4. **Wt.:** 240. **Drafted:** The Citadel, 2010 (1st round supplemental). **Signed by:** John Hendricks (Blue Jays).

BA GRADE

45 Risk: High

Wojciechowski had two plus pitches while in college, reaching 96 mph with his fastball and flashing a plus slider. His stuff has backed up as a pro, and the Blue Jays traded their 2010 sandwich pick to Houston in the July 2012 deal that sent J.A. Happ to Toronto. The 2014 season was a lost one for Wojciechowski, who appeared on the precipice of his big league debut after a fine 2013. He pitched just 76 innings because of a lat-muscle injury, then pitched for Licey in the Dominican League in winter ball to make up for lost time. At his best, Wojciechowski has average 90-93 mph velocity with an average slider and changeup. He can show his fastball to both sides of the plate and keep it down. He's competitive and polished and on the 40-man roster, so he'll compete for a major league job—bullpen or rotation—in the spring, given good health. Because of limited relief experience, he could wind up at Triple-A Fresno in 2015.

Year	Club (League)	Class	W	L	ERA	G	GS	CG	SV	IP	H	HR	BB	SO	K/9	WHIP	AVG
2012	Dunedin (FSL)	HiA	7	3	3.57	18	18	0	0	93	91	3	22	76	7.3	1.21	.261
	Corpus Christi (TL)	AA	2	2	2.06	8	8	0	0	44	30	0	14	34	7.0	1.01	.190
2013	Corpus Christi (TL)	AA	2	1	2.08	6	3	0	1	26	17	1	7	27	9.3	0.92	.189
	Oklahoma City (PCL)	AAA	9	7	3.56	22	21	2	0	134	116	10	44	104	7.0	1.19	.229
2014	Oklahoma City (PCL)	AAA	4	4	4.74	15	14	0	0	76	89	10	21	59	7.0	1.45	.293
Minor League Totals			35	26	3.75	97	89	2	1	515	505	39	143	407	7.1	1.26	.255

29 ANDREW THURMAN, RHP

Born: Dec. 10, 1991. **B-T:** R-R. **Ht.:** 6-3. **Wt.:** 200. **Drafted:** UC Irvine, 2013 (2nd round). **Signed by:** Brad Budzinski.

BA GRADE

45 Risk: High

A second-rounder in 2013 drafted as a potential back-end starter candidate, Thurman saw his prospect status take a hit in 2014 when his stuff backed up at low Class A. He showed average velocity on his fastball but it tended to be flatter the harder he threw, though he locates the pitch well. Thurman's changeup, which flashes a tick above-average, is now his second-best offering, with his slider and curveball grading consistently below-average and ineffective. His delivery is below-average, with one evaluator calling him stiff with a hard landing on his front foot. Large-framed and not particularly athletic, Thurman is aggressive with his two chief pitches. He now projects as a reliever in the majors, and he'll head to high Class A Lancaster in 2015.

Year	Club (League)	Class	W	L	ERA	G	GS	CG	SV	IP	H	HR	BB	SO	K/9	WHIP	AVG
2013	Tri-City (NYP)	SS	4	2	3.86	12	5	0	1	40	43	5	11	43	9.8	1.36	.277
2014	Quad Cities (MWL)	LoA	7	9	5.38	26	20	0	1	115	122	9	40	107	8.3	1.40	.275
Minor League Totals			11	11	4.99	38	25	0	2	155	165	14	51	150	8.7	1.39	.275

30 DANRY VASQUEZ, OF

Born: Jan. 8, 1994. **B-T:** L-R. **Ht.:** 6-3. **Wt.:** 177. **Signed:** Venezuela, 2010. **Signed by:** Oscar Garcia/Pedro Chavez (Tigers).

BA GRADE

45 Risk: High

The Tigers signed Vasquez in July 2010 for $1.4 million, and the Astros acquired the lefty swinger at the 2013 deadline for reliever Jose Veras. The 6-foot-3 Vasquez has an innate ability to hit and control the bat, but evaluators question how much power he will develop. Vasquez has been pegged as a below-average runner and defender. He has more feel to hit than raw power, though one scout said he projects to have average power because he will fill out. He would need to add significant power to profile as a starting left fielder, though he has feel for the barrel and controls the strike zone well enough to perhaps fill a part-time role. The Astros did not protect Vasquez from the Rule 5 draft, though no team selected him.

Year	Club (League)	Class	AVG	G	AB	R	H	2B	3B	HR	RBI	BB	SO	SB	CS	OBP	SLG
2012	West Michigan (MWL)	LoA	.162	29	99	5	16	3	0	1	7	7	20	0	0	.218	.222
	Connecticut (NYP)	SS	.311	72	289	36	90	16	2	2	35	13	45	6	4	.341	.401
2013	West Michigan (MWL)	LoA	.283	97	375	47	106	16	5	6	40	31	56	9	8	.334	.400
	Quad Cities (MWL)	LoA	.288	32	118	12	34	2	1	3	20	6	15	2	0	.323	.398
2014	Lancaster (CAL)	HiA	.291	114	423	67	123	30	2	5	47	40	68	1	2	.353	.407
Minor League Totals			.281	398	1510	192	425	75	11	19	179	104	238	21	16	.328	.383

Kansas City Royals

BY J.J. COOPER

Congratulations, Dayton Moore. As general manager, you've led the Royals out of the wilderness.

Kansas City won 89 games in 2014, its most in the last quarter-century. The Royals made their first playoff appearance in 29 years. They became the first team to ever win their first eight playoff games in a single season, and they returned to the World Series for the first time since 1985.

In the process, they may have developed a new generation of Royals fans, who found out that the home team doesn't always have to be hapless.

GM Dayton Moore made the Royals winners by building a foundation of prospects

It was the season Royals fans have dreamed of for decades, but in many cases never thought was possible.

So now what will the Royals do for an encore?

Long before the Royals made the playoffs, Moore and his front office have talked about the need to follow up success with more success. Even before they had ever had any big league success, they were planning for the follow-up.

Kansas City has worked to ensure that the nucleus of the first wave can stay together for a while. Because so many young players arrived in a two-year span, the Royals can keep the majority of the American League pennant winners together for the short term, though rising arbitration salaries will likely force some cost-saving trades at some point.

Kansas City has all three members of its rally-killing relief combo—righthanders Kelvin Herrera, Wade Davis and Greg Holland—under contract through at least 2016. The same is true for four-fifths of the rotation, where only No. 1 starter James Shields, a free agent, is not likely to return for 2015.

Besides DH Billy Butler, whose $12.5 million team option the Royals declined, and right fielder Nori Aoki, the other seven members of the everyday lineup are under contract for at least the next year, with left fielder Alex Gordon the only one not under contract through 2017.

The Royals wouldn't have made it to the World Series without help from a second wave of prospects. Kansas City used righthander Jake Odorizzi as part of its deal to acquire Shields and Davis, while righty Yordano Ventura's speedy development provided the Royals with a much-needed starter behind Shields in 2014. Christian Colon, the 2010 first-round pick, filled in as a utility infielder.

Other members of the second wave have either sputtered (outfielders Bubba Starling and Brett Eibner) or been traded for bench help (righthander Jason Adam).

TOP PROSPECTS OF THE DECADE

Year	Player, Pos.	2014 Org
2005	Billy Butler, 1b	Royals
2006	Alex Gordon, 3b	Royals
2007	Alex Gordon, 3b	Royals
2008	Mike Moustakas, 3b	Royals
2009	Mike Moustakas, 3b	Royals
2010	Mike Montgomery, lhp	Rays
2011	Eric Hosmer, 1b	Royals
2012	Mike Montgomery, lhp	Rays
2013	Kyle Zimmer, rhp	Royals
2014	Kyle Zimmer, rhp	Royals

But as the young major leaguers' salaries begin to rise, the Royals will need a new group of prospects to arrive to provide inexpensive help over the next couple of years. They seem well equipped on the pitching side.

Between lefthanders Brandon Finnegan and Sean Manaea and righthanders Kyle Zimmer and Miguel Almonte, the Royals have four quality pitching prospects who all will spend time at Double-A (or higher) in 2015. Kansas City will need at least one of them to provide quality innings in 2015, and contributions by two or more in 2016 would provide much-needed rotation flexibility.

The Royals are not as deep in position prospects, and few of the club's best minor league hitters produced in 2014.

The Royals will have to adjust to a new world where they are no longer a group of inept underdogs. It's an adjustment that Kansas City has long dreamed of, and one the organization is looking to prove is not just a one-season fluke.

General manager: Dayton Moore. **Farm director:** Scott Sharp. **Scouting director:** Lonnie Goldberg.

Class	Team	League	W	L	PCT	Finish	Manager
Majors	Kansas City Royals	American	89	73	.549	7th (30)	Ned Yost
Triple-A	Omaha Storm Chasers	Pacific Coast	76	67	.531	6th (16)	Brian Poldberg
Double-A	Northwest Arkansas Naturals	Texas	53	87	.379	8th (8)	Vance Wilson
High A	Wilmington Blue Rocks	Carolina	65	72	.474	t-5th (8)	Darryl Kennedy
Low A	Lexington Legends	South Atlantic	57	83	.407	11th (14)	Brian Buchanan
Rookie	Burlington Royals	Appalachian	28	40	.412	9th (10	Tommy Shields
Rookie	Idaho Falls Chukars	Pioneer	38	38	.500	5th (8)	Omar Ramirez
Overall Minor League Record			317	387	.450	28th (30)	

THIS YEAR'S TOP 30

No.	Player, Pos.	Grade
1.	Raul A. Mondesi, ss	65/High
2.	Brandon Finnegan, lhp	60/High
3.	Sean Manaea, lhp	55/Medium
4.	Kyle Zimmer, rhp	65/Extreme
5.	Hunter Dozier, 3b	55/Medium
6.	Miguel Almonte, rhp	55/High
7.	Foster Griffin, lhp	50/High
8.	Scott Blewett, rhp	50/High
9.	Jorge Bonifacio, of	50/High
10.	Christian Colon, ss/2b	45/Low
11.	Brian Flynn, lhp	45/Medium
12.	Chase Vallot, c	50/High
13.	Orlando Calixte, ss	50/High
14.	Erik Skoglund, lhp	50/High
15.	Lane Adams, of	45/Medium
16.	Christian Binford, rhp	45/Medium
17.	Glenn Sparkman, rhp	50/High
18.	Bubba Starling, of	55/Extreme
19.	Pedro Fernandez, rhp	50/High
20.	Cheslor Cuthbert, 3b/1b	45/Medium
21.	Marten Gasparini, ss	55/Extreme
22.	Elier Hernandez, of	50/High
23.	Niklas Stephenson, rhp	50/High
24.	Brandon Downes, of	50/High
25.	Ryan O'Hearn, 1b	50/High
26.	Wander Franco, 3b	50/High
27.	Francisco Pena, c	45/Medium
28.	Cam Gallagher, c	45/High
29.	Paulo Orlando, of	40/Low
30.	Jandel Gustave, rhp	50/Extreme

LAST YEAR'S TOP 30

No.	Player, Pos.	Status
1.	Kyle Zimmer, rhp	No. 4
2.	Yordano Ventura, rhp	Majors
3.	Raul A. Mondesi, ss	No. 1
4.	Jorge Bonifacio, of	No. 9
5.	Miguel Almonte, rhp	No. 6
6.	Sean Manea, lhp	No. 3
7.	Hunter Dozier, 3b	No. 5
8.	Bubba Starling, of	No. 18
9.	Jason Adam, rhp	(Twins)
10.	Christian Binford, rhp	No. 16
11.	Elier Hernandez, of	No. 22
12.	Sam Selman, lhp	Dropped out
13.	Orlando Calixte, ss	No. 13
14.	Cheslor Cuthbert, 3b	No. 20
15.	Michael Mariot, rhp	Dropped out
16.	Pedro Fernandez, rhp	No. 19
17.	Brett Eibner, of	Dropped out
18.	Lane Adams, of	No. 15
19.	Samir Duenez, 1b/of	Dropped out
20.	Marten Gasparini, ss	No. 21
21.	Chris Dwyer, lhp	Dropped out
22.	Donnie Joseph, lhp	Dropped out
23.	Cam Gallagher, c	No. 28
24.	Zane Evans, c	Dropped out
25.	Christian Colon, 2b/ss	No. 10
26.	Bryan Brickhouse, rhp	Dropped out
27.	Angel Baez, rhp	Dropped out
28.	Cody Reed, lhp	Dropped out
29.	Christhian Vasquez, of	Dropped out
30.	Terrance Gore, of	Dropped out

BEST TOOLS

Best Hitter for Average	Hunter Dozier
Best Power Hitter	Chase Vallot
Best Strike-Zone Discipline	Hunter Dozier
Fastest Baserunner	Terrance Gore
Best Athlete	Bubba Starling
Best Fastball	Kyle Zimmer
Best Curveball	Kyle Zimmer
Best Slider	Brandon Finnegan
Best Changeup	Miguel Almonte
Best Control	Christian Binford
Best Defensive Catcher	Cam Gallagher
Best Defensive Infielder	Raul A. Mondesi
Best Infield Arm	Raul A. Mondesi
Best Defensive Outfielder	Bubba Starling
Best Outfield Arm	Brett Eibner

PROJECTED 2018 LINEUP

Catcher	Salvador Perez
First Base	Eric Hosmer
Second Base	Raul A. Mondesi
Third Base	Hunter Dozier
Shortstop	Alcides Escobar
Left Field	Alex Gordon
Center Field	Lorenzo Cain
Right Field	Jorge Bonifacio
Designated Hitter	Mike Moustakas
No. 1 Starter	Yordano Ventura
No. 2 Starter	Danny Duffy
No. 3 Starter	Brandon Finnegan
No. 4 Starter	Sean Manaea
No. 5 Starter	Kyle Zimmer
Closer	Wade Davis

KANSAS CITY ROYALS

TOP 2015 ROOKIE: Brandon Finnegan, lhp. After contributing in the playoffs, he will either start or relieve in Kansas City in 2015.
BREAKOUT PROSPECT: Brandon Downes, of. Injuries ruined his junior year at Virginia, but he has all-around tools to impress.
SLEEPER: Gerson Garabito, rhp. After dominating the Dominican Summer League in 2014, the hard-thrower should jump to Rookie ball.

SOURCE OF TOP 30 TALENT

Homegrown	28	Acquired	2
College	8	Trades	1
Junior college	1	Rule 5 draft	0
High school	8	Independent leagues	0
Nondrafted free agents	1	Free agents/waivers	1
International	10		

LF
Elier Hernandez (22)
Terrance Gore
Whit Merrifield
Cristhian Vasquez
Robert Pehl

CF
Lane Adams (15)
Bubba Starling (18)
Paulo Orlando (29)
Reymond Fuentes
Alfredo Escalera
Amalani Fukofuka

RF
Jorge Bonifacio (9)
Brandon Downes (24)
Brawlun Gomez

3B
Hunter Dozier (5)
Wander Franco (26)

SS
Raul A. Mondesi (1)
Orlando Calixte (13)
Marten Gasparini (21)
Ryan Jackson
Humberto Arteaga
Jack Lopez
Corey Toupes

2B
Christian Colon (10)
Ramon Torres
Justin Trapp

1B
Cheslor Cuthbert (20)
Ryan O'Hearn (25)
Samir Duenez
Matt Fields
Cody Stubbs
Josh Banuelos

C
Chase Vallot (12)
Francisco Pena (27)
Cam Gallagher (28)
Santiago Nessy
Meibrys Viloria
Zane Evans
Chad Johnson

LHP

LHSP	LHRP
Brandon Finnegan (2)	Sam Selman
Sean Manaea (3)	Cody Reed
Foster Griffin (7)	Luis Rico
Brian Flynn (11)	Scott Alexander
Eric Skoglund (14)	Tim Hill
Chris Dwyer	
Jonathan Dziedzic	

RHP

RHSP	RHRP
Kyle Zimmer (4)	Pedro Fernandez (19)
Miguel Almonte (6)	Jandel Gustave (30)
Scott Blewett (8)	Reid Redman
Christian Binford (16)	Malcolm Culver
Glenn Sparkman (17)	Robinson Yambati
Niklas Stephenson (23)	Matt Alvarez
Gerson Garabito	Andrew Edwards
Bryan Brickhouse	Angel Baez
Jake Junis	Mark Peterson
Yimauri Pena	Aroni Nina
	Jose Rodriguez
	Alec Mills
	Ali Williams

2014

BEST PURE HITTER: 1B Ryan O'Hearn (8) has a quick, loose stroke from the left side with natural loft. He was young for the college class, 20 on draft day, and won MVP honors in the Pioneer League after hitting .361/.448/.590 with 13 home runs.

BEST POWER HITTER: C Chase Vallot (1) had some of the best power in the prep class, at least 70-grade raw. He finished tied for third in home runs (seven) and had the third-highest ISO (.188) in the Appalachian League.

FASTEST RUNNER: Athletic switch-hitting OF DonAndre Clark (33) is a top-of-the-scale runner who has posted runs times as low as 3.84 to first. OF Rudy Martin (20) is a small-framed 70-grade runner from the left side of the plate.

BEST DEFENSIVE PLAYER: OF Brandon Downes (7) is an above-average defensive center fielder who is a plus runner underway with great instincts and a plus arm.

BEST FASTBALL: Although his 2014 season began in February, LHP Brandon Finnegan (1) was still able to reach back for 95 and 96 mph in the playoffs (after touching 97 in the spring). His fastball has been a swing-and-miss offering at the major league level with plus to plus-plus life as the ball jumps out of his hand. RHP Scott Blewett (2), who signed for a late first-round bonus, has a great frame at 6-foot-6 and heater up to 96 mph while sitting 91-94 at his best. RHP Evan Beal (21) touched 97.

BEST SECONDARY PITCH: Blewett's 12-6 downer curveball has plus potential. Finnegan's changeup has improved, giving him a second plus secondary pitch to go with his slider. Both the curve and change of LHP Foster Griffin (1) flash plus.

BEST PRO DEBUT: Finnegan raced through three levels while posting a 1.33 ERA and 26 strikeouts in 27 innings to emerge as a key reliever on the Royals' playoff roster.

BEST ATHLETE: Downes is an above-average athlete who can run and throw while providing at least average power from the right side. OF Logan Moon (6) is an average to above-average runner with a plus arm and simple swing.

MOST INTRIGUING BACKGROUND: Griffin, the son of a former professional golfer, is a scratch golfer both left and righthanded. Cole Way (38) is a 6-foot-11, 235-pound lefthander who was the starting punter on Tulsa's football team.

CLOSEST TO THE MAJORS: Finnegan was the first member of the 2014 draft class to make the majors.

BEST LATE-ROUND PICK: 3B Manny Olloque (16) is a competitive, projectable position player who was young for the class and made contact at a well above-average clip in his pro debut.

THE ONE WHO GOT AWAY: OF Scott Heineman (19) will return for his senior season at Oregon

ASSESSMENT: The Royals signed four players for at least $1 million each and brought in three high-upside high school players in Foster Griffin, Scott Blewett and Chase Vallot.

2013

The Royals gambled and won when they took 3B Hunter Dozier (1) eighth overall and got their man, LHP Sean Manaea (1s), with the 34th pick. RHP Glenn Sparkman (20) put himself on the map in 2014, leading the minors in ERA.

GRADE: B

2012

Injuries stalled RHP Kyle Zimmer (1), who has shown tantalizing pitches when healthy. He's the only member of the draft class in the system's Top 30, though RHP Alec Mills (22) is a hard-throwing sleeper.

GRADE: C

2011

OF Bubba Starling (1) is unlikely to live up to expectations created by his $7.5 million bonus. RHPs Aaron Brooks (9) and Spencer Patton (24) reached the majors but appear to be role players; the same goes for speedy OF Terrance Gore (20).

GRADE: D

TOP DRAFT PICKS OF THE DECADE

Year	Player, Pos.	2014 Org
2005	Alex Gordon, 3b	Royals
2006	Luke Hochevar, rhp	Royals
2007	Mike Moustakas, 3b	Royals
2008	Eric Hosmer, 1b	Royals
2009	Aaron Crow, rhp	Royals
2010	Christian Colon, ss	Royals
2011	Bubba Starling, of	Royals
2012	Kyle Zimmer, rhp	Royals
2013	Hunter Dozier, 3b	Royals
2014	Brandon Finnegan, lhp	Royals

LARGEST BONUSES IN CLUB HISTORY

Bubba Starling, 2011	$7,500,000
Eric Hosmer, 2008	$6,000,000
Alex Gordon, 2005	$4,000,000
Mike Moustakas, 2007	$4,000,000
Sean Manaea, 2013	$3,550,000

1 RAUL A. MONDESI, SS

Born: July 27, 1995. **B-T:** B-R. **Ht.:** 6-1. **Wt.:** 165.
Signed: Dominican Republic, 2011.
Signed by: Edis Perez/Alvin Cuevas.

The son of former Dodgers right fielder Raul Mondesi, Raul Adalberto was the second-most prominent international signing the Royals landed in 2011 He signed for $2 million, while Dominican outfielder Elier Hernandez signed for $3 million. But ever since Hernandez and Mondesi came to the States in 2012, the latter has established himself as the Royals' best position prospect. Mondesi was the youngest player in the high Class A Carolina League when the 2014 season began. The Royals were so taken by his spring training performance that they half-expected him to reach Double-A Northwest Arkansas by midseason, but after a strong April, he failed to hit better than .215 in any of the final four months of the season. He did hit six home runs and four triples in August.

Mondesi's tools are outstanding. In the words of one scout: "Every now and then you see flashes. You could put a lot of 70s and 80s (on the 20-80 scouting scale) on him." But Mondesi has to improve his approach and his ability to work counts to get a chance to take advantage of his excellent bat speed. He is a 70 runner who will turn in top-of-the-scale 80 times occasionally. He has a strong arm, soft hands and excellent short-stop actions, and he's sure-handed for his age (.963 fielding percentage). He projects as an above-average defender at shortstop. The wiry-strong Mondesi has a chance to one day hit 12-15 home runs as he matures. His combination of speed and pop helped him lead the Carolina League with 12 triples. He also has improved as a bunter, and roughly 15 percent of his singles in 2014 were bunt hits. He also has the tools to be at least an average hitter, and possibly better than that, but he's yet to show that in long stretches. Too often, Mondesi over-aggressively swings at everything, leaving himself in bad counts. His two-strike approach is even worse, as he'll expand the zone to chase unhittable breaking balls and fastballs. His swing has no obvious mechanical flaws from either side, but too often he gets caught lunging because of poor pitch recognition that disconnects his legs from his swing.

Mondesi presented one of the toughest player evaluations scouts faced in 2014. His tools are exceptional, but his contact issues meant that those tools were only seen sporadically. Scouts around baseball generally wrote off Mondesi's awful season as a byproduct of being 18 in the Carolina League. He's still the most talented player in the Royals' system and one of the top shortstop prospects in the game. The Royals have moved Mondesi aggressively, but it's time to let him catch up to his competition. He's the Royals' long-term answer at shortstop, but for now a return to Wilmington is likely.

BA GRADE

65 Risk: High

SCOUTING GRADES

Batting: 60.
Power: 45.
Speed: 70.
Defense: 60.
Arm: 60.

Based on 20-80 scouting scale and future projection rather than present grades.

LGE	PA	BB%	SO%	ISO
CAR	472	5.1	25.8	.143

Year	Club (League)	Class	AVG	G	AB	R	H	2B	3B	HR	RBI	BB	SO	SB	CS	OBP	SLG
2012	Idaho Falls (PIO)	R	.290	50	207	35	60	7	2	3	30	19	65	11	2	.346	.386
2013	Lexington (SAL)	LoA	.261	125	482	61	126	13	7	7	47	34	118	24	10	.311	.361
2014	Wilmington (CAR)	HiA	.211	110	435	54	92	14	12	8	33	24	122	17	4	.256	.354
Minor League Totals			.247	285	1124	150	278	34	21	18	110	77	305	52	16	.297	.363

2 BRANDON FINNEGAN, LHP

Born: April 14, 1993. **Ht.:** 5-11. **Wt.:** 185. **B-T:** L-L. **Drafted:** Texas Christian, 2014 (1st round). **Signed by:** Chad Lee/Gregg Miller.

The first pitcher to ever pitch in the College World Series and the World Series in the same season, Finnegan fell into the Royals' lap at 17th overall only because of an ill-timed shoulder issue. Considered in the mix to go in the top five picks, he left a late-April start early with shoulder tightness. After a week off, he returned to action and showed no ill effects. Finnegan made just 13 minor league appearances before joining the big league club, becoming the primary lefty reliever almost immediately and making seven playoff appearances. Finnegan isn't your typical first-round starter prospect. He's 5-foot-11 and his delivery is not without effort. The Royals, and some other teams' scouts, believe he's strong enough and athletic enough to repeat his mechanics, but others see him as a power reliever. Finnegan has run his fastball up to 98 mph at his best, but he sat at 92-94 as a pro reliever, and the Royals wouldn't be shocked to see him sit at 90-92 as a starter. His slider is at least average pretty much every time he takes the mound and is above-average regularly. His changeup, which he rarely used in short relief outings, is less consistent, but was an above-average pitch in college. Finnegan will get a chance to earn a spot in the Royals' rotation in spring training, but considering his lack of pro starting experience, he likely won't be ready for that role yet. He's ready to help a big league club as a reliever, however, so the Royals might opt to deploy him in that role, perhaps at the risk of affecting his long-term development as a starter.

BA GRADE

60 Risk: High

LGE	BF	SO%	BB%	HR/9
CAR	49	26.5	4.1	0.60
TL	56	23.2	3.6	1.50

Year	Club (League)	Class	W	L	ERA	G	GS	CG	SV	IP	H	HR	BB	SO	K/9	WHIP	AVG
2014	Wilmington (CAR)	HiA	0	1	0.60	5	5	0	0	15	5	1	2	13	7.8	0.47	.106
	NW Arkansas (TL)	AA	0	3	2.25	8	0	0	0	12	15	2	2	13	9.8	1.42	.283
	Kansas City (AL)	MAJ	0	1	1.29	7	0	0	0	7	6	0	1	10	12.9	1.00	.222
Major League Totals			0	1	1.29	7	0	0	0	7	6	0	1	10	12.9	1.00	.222
Minor League Totals			0	4	1.33	13	5	0	0	27	20	3	4	26	8.7	0.89	.200

3 SEAN MANAEA, LHP

Born: Feb. 1, 1992. **B-T:** R-L. **Ht.:** 6-5. **Wt.:** 235. **Drafted:** Indiana State, 2013 (1st round supplemental). **Signed by:** Jason Bryans.

The Royals signed 2013 first-round pick Hunter Dozier to a below-slot deal in order to free up money to sign Manaea for $3.55 million in the sandwich round. The potential top-five pick suffered a torn labrum in his hip, but after turning pro and having surgery, Manaea showed no ill effects in 2014. Early in the season, Manaea would lean back early in his delivery, which caused him to open up too soon and spin off the mound. That left his fastball up in the zone and made his slider too sweepy. After getting more upright and direct in his finish, Manaea posted a 1.45 ERA in his final 10 starts at high Class A Wilmington. He gets excellent extension and downhill plane on his plus 90-95 mph fastball that has a touch of late life. Manaea's slider became an above-average pitch late in 2014 as it became tighter with more tilt. His changeup is a potentially average pitch with late fade. The long-limbed Manaea never has had pinpoint control and may struggle to achieve more than average grades on that front. He's too easy to run on (24 steals in 29 attempts), but he lowered his leg kick from the stretch to speed up from a glacial 1.7 to a still-slow 1.4 seconds to the plate. Manaea made big strides in his first pro season, but he still has to demonstrate he can be more precise with his pitches. He heads to Double-A Northwest Arkansas with the raw ingredients to be a future No. 3 starter.

BA GRADE

55 Risk: Medium

LGE	BF	SO%	BB%	HR/9
CAR	514	28.4	10.5	0.37

Year	Club (League)	Class	W	L	ERA	G	GS	CG	SV	IP	H	HR	BB	SO	K/9	WHIP	AVG
2014	Wilmington (CAR)	HiA	7	8	3.11	25	25	1	0	122	102	5	54	146	10.8	1.28	.228
Minor League Totals			7	8	3.11	25	25	1	0	122	102	5	54	146	10.8	1.28	.228

4 KYLE ZIMMER, RHP

Born: Sept. 13, 1991. **B-T:** R-R .**Ht.:** **6-3. Wt.:** 215. **Drafted:** San Francisco, 2012 (1st round). **Signed by:** Max Valencia.

The Royals must be tempted to send Zimmer to the mound covered in bubble wrap. In 2014 he missed time with a biceps injury and followed that with a lat injury that postponed his season debut until Aug. 17. He pitched well in the Triple-A playoffs, made two excellent starts in the Arizona Fall League, then was shut down again with a tight shoulder and a bone bruise. In October, he had exploratory arthroscopic surgery in which doctors performed labrum and rotator-cuff cleanup. Zimmer could be back by May 1, but his timetable has frequently been pushed back in the past. When healthy, Zimmer has shown front-line starter stuff. He has three potentially plus pitches, led by a double-plus 93-97 mph fastball and equally-potent, sharp-breaking curveball. His changeup is at least average as well, and his slider flashes average. Injuries have been the only thing preventing Zimmer from joining the big league team. Doctors haven't been able to find any one underlying issue that ties Zimmer's lengthy list of injuries together, but one of the key attributes of a front-line starter is durability, something he has not achieved. If he can stay healthy, Zimmer is the Royals' most talented pitching prospect.

BA GRADE

65 Risk: Extreme

LGE	BF	SO%	BB%	HR/9
PIO	23	21.7	17.4	0.00

Year	Club (League)	Class	W	L	ERA	G	GS	CG	SV	IP	H	HR	BB	SO	K/9	WHIP	AVG
2012	Royals (AZL)	R	1	0	0.90	3	3	1	0	10	5	0	0	13	11.7	0.50	.152
	Kane County (MWL)	LoA	2	3	2.43	6	6	0	0	30	34	1	8	29	8.8	1.42	.301
2013	Wilmington (CAR)	HiA	4	8	4.82	18	18	1	0	90	80	9	31	113	11.3	1.24	.237
	NW Arkansas (TL)	AA	2	1	1.93	4	4	0	0	19	11	2	5	27	13.0	0.86	.162
2014	Idaho Falls (PIO)	R	0	0	1.93	6	5	0	0	5	5	0	4	5	9.6	1.93	.263
Minor League Totals			9	12	3.66	37	36	2	0	153	135	12	48	187	11.0	1.20	.236

5 HUNTER DOZIER, 3B

Born: Aug. 22, 1991. **B-T:** R-R. **Ht.:** 6-4. **Wt.:** 220. **Drafted:** Stephen F. Austin State, 2013 (1st round). **Signed by:** Mitch Thompson.

Dozier will be linked with lefthander Sean Manaea for as long as the two players remain Royals. The organization reached to take the former with the eighth overall pick in the 2013 draft, believing he wouldn't last until the Royals' second pick at No. 34, which they used to select Manaea and bestow him with an above-slot bonus. Dozier showed an extremely advanced approach at high Class A Wilmington. He employs a simple swing, making use of a slight toe tap as a timing mechanism before taking a balanced, short stroke best geared for line drives up the middle. Dozier always has demonstrated a good idea of the strike zone and an ability to draw walks. All of that fell apart after his promotion. He became pull-happy, overaggressive and began chasing poor pitches. Defensively, Dozier has adapted quickly to third base after moving off shortstop. He's becoming more confident at positioning himself and deciding when to play up or back on hitters. His arm strength and accuracy improved after he fixed a tendency early in the season to throw with a lowered front arm. Dozier's second-half performance at Double-A was an uncharacteristic hiccup, and he'll return to Northwest Arkansas in 2015.

BA GRADE

55 Risk: Medium

LGE	PA	BB%	SO%	ISO
CAR	267	13.1	21.0	.134
TL	267	11.6	26.2	.103

Year	Club (League)	Class	AVG	G	AB	R	H	2B	3B	HR	RBI	BB	SO	SB	CS	OBP	SLG
2013	Lexington (SAL)	LoA	.327	15	55	6	18	6	0	0	9	3	5	0	0	.373	.436
	Idaho Falls (PIO)	R	.303	54	218	43	66	24	0	7	43	35	32	3	1	.403	.509
2014	Wilmington (CAR)	HiA	.295	66	224	36	66	18	0	4	39	35	56	7	3	.397	.429
	NW Arkansas (TL)	AA	.209	64	234	33	49	12	0	4	21	31	70	3	3	.303	.312
Minor League Totals			.272	199	731	118	199	60	0	15	112	104	163	13	6	.368	.416

6 MIGUEL ALMONTE, RHP

BRAD GLAZIER

Born: April 4, 1993. **B-T:** R-R. **Ht:** 6-2. **Wt.:** 180. **Signed:** Dominican Republic, 2010. **Signed by:** Fausto Morel/Alvin Cuevas.

The Royals have had plenty of success developing Dominican pitchers whom they originally signed for inexpensive bonuses. Almonte signed for just $25,000, but he quickly established himself as one of the organization's best pitching prospects with a breakthrough performance at low Class A Lexington in 2013. Almonte's flaws became much more apparent at high Class A Wilmington in 2014. He was able to rely on his changeup to hand-cuff hitters at low Class A Lexington, but against more advanced Carolina League hitters, his lack of present feel for mixing his pitches was apparent. Almonte's fastball generally sits 91-95 mph and touches 97, but he struggles to locate it to the glove side and too often leaves it up in the zone. When his delivery gets out of whack, his fastball leaks back over the heart of the plate. He commands his plus changeup better than his fastball, which contributes to him becoming too reliant on the pitch. His slurvy curveball always has

BA GRADE	
55	Risk: High.

LGE	BF	SO%	BB%	HR/9
CAR	463	21.8	6.9	0.73

been a below-average pitch, partly because he throws from a low arm slot. Eventually he may need to switch to a harder slider or cutter, which would better fit his release point. Some scouts believe Almonte's future lies in the bullpen, where he could try to blow hitters away with a plus fastball and changeup. The Royals have every incentive to see if he can sequence his pitches better and improve his command to stick as a starter. He'll head to Double-A Northwest Arkansas for further refinement.

Year	Club (League)	Class	W	L	ERA	G	GS	CG	SV	IP	H	HR	BB	SO	K/9	WHIP	AVG
2012	Royals (DSL)	R	6	1	1.44	10	10	0	0	50	34	2	8	46	8.3	0.84	.194
	Royals (AZL)	R	2	1	2.33	6	2	0	0	27	22	0	5	28	9.3	1.00	.212
2013	Lexington (SAL)	LoA	6	9	3.10	25	25	1	0	131	115	6	36	132	9.1	1.16	.237
2014	Wilmington (CAR)	HiA	6	8	4.49	23	22	0	0	110	107	9	32	101	8.2	1.26	.259
Minor League Totals			20	19	3.33	69	60	1	0	330	289	17	88	316	8.6	1.14	.237

7 FOSTER GRIFFIN, LHP

Born: July 27, 1995. **Ht.:** 6-3. **Wt.:** 200. **B-T:** L-L. **Drafted:** HS—Orlando, 2014 (1st round). **Signed by:** Jim Buckley/Gregg Kilby.

Of the 31 players drafted and signed by the Royals in 2014, 11 of them were lefthanded pitchers, including first-round picks Brandon Finnegan and Griffin. A lanky lefty with an excellent body, Griffin led Orlando's The First Academy to a National High School Invitational title. Limited to three innings per start in his pro debut at Rookie-level Burlington, he allowed just four extra-base hits in 28 innings. Griffin could end up with three above-average pitches. A plus athlete, he might gain a tick or two on his fastball, but at 88-92 mph he already is effective at getting good angle. He can run his fastball in on righthanders and shows an ability to locate the pitch to both sides of the plate. Griffin is a strike-thrower with a clean delivery. His 79-91 mph changeup has solid deception and some late fade to generate swings and misses. His curveball is a tight downward breaker at its best,

BA GRADE	
50	Risk: High

LGE	BF	SO%	BB%	HR/9
APP	115	16.5	10.4	0.64

but too often is a slower, loopier pitch he can't always control. Griffin is the most prominent high school lefty the Royals have had in the system since the days of Mike Montgomery, Danny Duffy and John Lamb. He'll head to low Class A Lexington in 2015 and his polish gives him a chance to excel once he gets accustomed to the heavier workload of pro ball.

Year	Club (League)	Class	W	L	ERA	G	GS	CG	SV	IP	H	HR	BB	SO	K/9	WHIP	AVG
2014	Burlington (APP)	R	0	2	3.21	11	11	0	0	28	19	2	12	19	6.1	1.11	.186
Minor League Totals			0	2	3.21	11	11	0	0	28	19	2	12	19	6.1	1.11	.186

8 SCOTT BLEWETT, RHP

BRIAN WESTERHOLT

Born: April 10, 1996. **B-T:** R-R. **Ht.:** 6-6. **Wt.:** 210. **Drafted:** HS—Baldwinsville, N.Y., 2014 (2nd round). **Signed by:** Bobby Gandalfo/Keith Connolly.

Blewett is the first high school righthander from the state of New York to be selected in the top two rounds since Steve Karsay back in 1990. He attended the same Baker High in Baldwinsville as Jason Grilli. Blewett went 23-0 in his prep career, though a muscle strain in his shoulder gave him a scare just before the draft. He returned in time to prove his health, go in the second round to the Royals and sign for $1.8 million. Blewett is a big-bodied, wide-shouldered righthander with present physicality. His nearly over-the-top delivery increases the plane he gets from his 6-foot-6 frame. At his best, he pitches at 90-92 mph, touching 94 with good sink as he works down in the zone. When he struggles, he rushes his delivery and leaves the ball up too often. Blewett's curveball has gone from fringy to potentially plus in the past year. It's a 12-to-6 hammer with swing-and-miss potential. Working limited innings in his pro debut, he didn't use his fringy changeup much. Blewett's control is below-average at this point, but as a Northeastern arm, he has plenty of development ahead of him. Blewett is a high-risk, high-reward prospect. His control and command will have to improve for him to reach his potential ceiling as a mid-rotation starter.

BA GRADE

50 Risk: High

LGE	BF	SO%	BB%	HR/9
APP	126	23.0	11.9	0.96

Year	Club (League)	Class	W	L	ERA	G	GS	CG	SV	IP	H	HR	BB	SO	K/9	WHIP	AVG
2014	Burlington (APP)	R	1	2	4.82	8	7	0	0	28	27	3	15	29	9.3	1.50	.262
Minor League Totals			1	2	4.82	8	7	0	0	28	27	3	15	29	9.3	1.50	.262

9 JORGE BONIFACIO, OF

Born: June 4, 1993. **B-T:** R-R. **Ht.:** 6-1. **Wt.:** 215. **Signed:** Dominican Republic, 2009. **Signed by:** Edis Perez.

The younger brother of long-time big league speedster Emilio Bonifacio, Jorge has been one of the more productive hitters in the Royals system. After hitting .280 or better in each of his first three pro seasons, however, Bonifacio's average and power both cratered in 2014. Bonifacio, like Hunter Dozier, has an up-the-middle approach that is better suited to hitting for average than cranking home runs. His wide stance makes it difficult for him to use his legs fully in his swing, but when he has tried to narrow his base, he doesn't look as comfortable at the plate. Bonifacio has the bat speed to catch up to most any fastball with a simple stroke, but he's proven vulnerable to sliders and changeups off the outer half at Double-A Northwest Arkansas. He has above-average raw power, but it's never translated to productive in-game power, and he probably won't develop that power without hurting his average. A strong-bodied right fielder with a strong arm, Bonifacio has average range and below-average speed. Bonifacio still is the Royals' best hope for an in-house option to become an everyday corner outfielder, but he's no closer to filling that role than he was a year ago. At his best, he's a useful complementary regular whose solid average and on-base skills help compensate for a lack of profile power.

BA GRADE

50 Risk: High

LGE	PA	BB%	SO%	ISO
TL	566	8.8	22.4	.079

Year	Club (League)	Class	AVG	G	AB	R	H	2B	3B	HR	RBI	BB	SO	SB	CS	OBP	SLG
2012	Kane County (MWL)	LoA	.282	105	412	54	116	20	6	10	61	30	84	6	3	.336	.432
2013	Royals (AZL)	R	.300	9	30	4	9	3	2	0	6	4	6	1	0	.400	.533
	Wilmington (CAR)	HiA	.296	54	206	32	61	11	3	2	29	23	40	0	2	.368	.408
	NW Arkansas (TL)	AA	.301	25	93	15	28	7	0	2	19	11	23	2	1	.371	.441
2014	NW Arkansas (TL)	AA	.230	132	505	49	116	20	4	4	51	50	127	8	3	.302	.309
Minor League Totals			.272	456	1722	211	468	97	26	26	230	166	396	36	22	.339	.404

10 CHRISTIAN COLON, SS/2B

Born: May 14, 1989. **B-T:** R-R. **Ht.:** 6-1. **Wt.:** 180. **Drafted:** Cal State Fullerton, 2010 (1st round). **Signed by:** Scott Groot.

Colon was the first player ever named team captain of the USA Baseball collegiate national team and was a key member of Cal State Fullerton's 2009 College World Series team. He might be better known as the player the Royals drafted fourth overall in 2010 instead of Chris Sale. Colon made his big league debut in 2014 and earned a spot on the postseason roster. Colon doesn't have any one exceptional tool, but he is productive because he does everything well enough. He's a below-average runner, but he's heady enough to steal a bag against a slow pitcher. He's an average defender at second, a tick above that at third and a below-average defender at shortstop who can fill in as a backup. He doesn't make many flashy plays, but he is reliable and sure-handed. At the plate, Colon's whole-field approach is geared to hit for average with below-average power. Colon is ready to be the Royals' utility infielder, and he could grow into a slightly larger role. As a regular, his only fit would be at second base.

BA GRADE

45 Risk: Low

LGE	PA	BB%	SO%	ISO
PCL	388	7.7	7.5	.122
AL	49	6.1	8.2	.156

Year	Club (League)	Class	AVG	G	AB	R	H	2B	3B	HR	RBI	BB	SO	SB	CS	OBP	SLG
2012	Royals (AZL)	R	.364	7	22	6	8	3	0	0	4	4	0	1	1	.481	.500
	NW Arkansas (TL)	AA	.289	73	273	33	79	9	2	5	27	31	27	12	6	.364	.392
	Omaha (PCL)	AAA	.412	5	17	4	7	1	0	1	5	2	1	0	0	.429	.647
2013	Omaha (PCL)	AAA	.273	131	512	72	140	12	3	12	58	41	57	15	4	.335	.379
2014	Omaha (PCL)	AAA	.311	86	344	55	107	18	0	8	47	30	29	15	4	.366	.433
	NW Arkansas (TL)	AA	.250	2	8	1	2	1	0	0	0	1	2	1	0	.333	.375
	Kansas City (AL)	MAJ	.333	21	45	8	15	5	1	0	6	3	4	2	0	.375	.489
Major League Totals			.333	21	45	8	15	5	1	0	6	3	4	2	0	.375	.489
Minor League Totals			.281	491	1912	278	537	70	9	37	232	168	200	63	26	.344	.385

11 BRIAN FLYNN, LHP

BA GRADE

45 Risk: Medium

Born: April 19, 1990. **B-T:** L-L. **Ht:** 6-7. **Wt.:** 240. **Drafted:** Wichita State, 2011 (7th round). **Signed by:** Chris Wimmer (Tigers).

A 6-foot-7 lefty with low-90s velocity, Flynn is difficult for other teams to miss, which explains how he's been traded twice in the past two years. First the Tigers traded him to the Marlins as part of the haul for Anibal Sanchez, then Detroit shipped him to the Royals for Aaron Crow last November. Flynn arrived at Marlins camp in 2014 as one of the favorites to earn a big league rotation spot. That bid never got on track because he couldn't command the bottom of the strike zone and his delivery was a mess. Flynn shows average to solid-average velocity and sink on his fastball, and his low-80s changeup plays as average when his delivery is in sync and he's commanding his fastball. Neither his curveball nor slider plays consistently as a reliable third pitch, but his fastball, changeup and average control give him back-end starter potential.

Year	Club (League)	Class	W	L	ERA	G	GS	CG	SV	IP	H	HR	BB	SO	K/9	WHIP	AVG
2012	Lakeland (FSL)	HiA	8	4	3.71	18	18	0	0	102	113	5	32	84	7.4	1.42	.280
	Erie (EL)	AA	0	1	9.00	1	1	0	0	5	8	1	2	5	5.4	2.00	.381
	Jacksonville (SL)	AA	3	0	3.80	8	8	0	0	45	48	3	13	32	6.4	1.36	.273
2013	Jacksonville (SL)	AA	1	1	1.57	4	4	0	0	23	18	2	3	25	9.8	0.91	.222
	New Orleans (PCL)	AAA	6	11	2.80	23	23	0	0	138	127	7	40	122	8.0	1.21	.246
	Miami (NL)	MAJ	0	2	8.50	4	4	0	0	18	27	4	13	15	7.5	2.22	.370
2014	Miami (NL)	MAJ	0	1	9.00	2	1	0	0	7	12	0	3	6	7.7	2.14	.375
	New Orleans (PCL)	AAA	8	10	4.06	25	25	1	0	140	169	13	50	104	6.7	1.57	.302
Major League Totals			0	3	8.64	6	5	0	0	25	39	4	16	21	7.6	2.20	.371
Minor League Totals			33	29	3.49	92	92	1	0	520	541	34	163	427	7.4	1.35	.270

12 CHASE VALLOT, C

BA GRADE

50 Risk: High

Born: Aug. 21, 1996. **B-T:** R-R. **Ht. 5-11. Wt.:** 205. **Drafted:** HS—Lafayette, La., 2014 (1st round supplemental). **Signed by:** Travis Ezi/Gregg Kilby.

One of the better power bats on the 2013 summer showcase circuit, albeit with a big swing and lots of swing and miss, Vallot improved his stock with a strong senior season. He hit .545 with 13 home runs and led St. Thomas More High to its first Louisiana state title in more than 20 years. The Royals knew that Vallot's defense needed a lot of work, and it showed at Rookie-level Burlington. Early in the Appalachian League season, he could not cleanly catch pitchers with plus stuff—but by the time instructional league rolled around, he was able to catch Aaron Crow with no issues. Vallot needs to improve his hands and stop stabbing at pitches. His footwork and technique are also very raw, which keeps his plus arm from generating even average pop times consistently. At the plate, Vallot has the best raw power in the system with a chance to hit 25 or more home runs if he makes consistent contact. He has good bat speed, but his simple swing is geared for power with leverage, length and an uppercut finish that generates flyballs and strikeouts. How Vallot looks in the spring will determine whether he goes to low Class A Lexington or Rookie-level Idaho Falls.

Year	Club (League)	Class	AVG	G	AB	R	H	2B	3B	HR	RBI	BB	SO	SB	CS	OBP	SLG
2014	Burlington (APP)	R	.215	53	186	29	40	14	0	7	27	26	81	0	1	.329	.403
Minor League Totals			.215	53	186	29	40	14	0	7	27	26	81	0	1	.329	.403

13 ORLANDO CALIXTE, SS

BA GRADE

50 Risk: High

Born: Feb. 3, 1992. **B-T:** R-R. **Ht.:** 6-0. **Wt.:** 175. **Signed:** Dominican Republic 2010. **Signed by:** Alvin Cuevas/Hector Pineda.

Calixte can be a frustrating prospect for scouts to watch and evaluate. His tools are always better than the results, but that's now been the case for five seasons. Calixte has his virtues. For example, he has excellent bat speed that produces fringe-average power. At shortstop he should be a tick above-average defender with quick hands and smooth actions and average range. His above-average arm allows him to make plays in the hole, but he struggles going to his left. Calixte needs to improve his accuracy after he committed 16 throwing errors at Double-A Northwest Arkansas on his way to leading the Texas League with 26 miscues. He focused on shortstop in 2014, but he's played second and third base adequately in the past. At the plate, the righty-hitting Calixte's swing is too big and he is too pull-happy, largely because he doesn't appear to recognize spin quickly enough. With Raul A. Mondesi coming up behind him in the system and Christian Colon ahead of him as the Royals' presumptive utility infielder, Calixte will head to Triple-A Omaha knowing he's got plenty of competition. He has the tools to be an everyday regular with more refinement, but without a better approach, even a utility job is out of reach.

Year	Club (League)	Class	AVG	G	AB	R	H	2B	3B	HR	RBI	BB	SO	SB	CS	OBP	SLG
2012	Kane County (MWL)	LoA	.241	62	228	31	55	13	4	10	34	21	44	2	5	.303	.465
	Wilmington (CAR)	HiA	.281	63	256	38	72	17	4	4	28	15	65	8	3	.326	.426
2013	NW Arkansas (TL)	AA	.250	123	484	59	121	25	4	8	36	42	131	14	11	.312	.368
2014	NW Arkansas (TL)	AA	.241	96	374	43	90	15	1	11	37	27	92	9	5	.288	.374
Minor League Totals			.243	445	1697	200	413	81	14	36	178	138	415	47	29	.300	.371

14 ERIC SKOGLUND, LHP

BA GRADE

50 Risk: High

Born: Oct. 26, 1992. **B-T:** L-L. **Ht.:** 6-7. **Wt.:** 200. **Drafted:** Central Florida, 2014 (3rd round). **Signed by:** Jim Buckley/Gregg Kilby.

A 16th-round pick of the Pirates out of high school, Skoglund put his time at Central Florida to good use. He gained 10 pounds per year to go from a 6-foot-7, 170-pound pencil in high school to a still lanky but much more solid 200 pounds. Skoglund earned American Athletic Conference pitcher of the year honors as a junior. Skoglund struggled through his pro debut when he threw plenty of strikes but gave up too much solid contact at Rookie-level Idaho Falls. He throws an average 90-91 mph fastball with some life and an average 80-83 mph slider that he pairs with a below-average changeup that he doesn't really trust. His pitches play up because he locates well with average control, a rare trait for a young, long-levered pitcher. As he presently stands, Skoglund projects as a back-end starter, but one who could end up being more than that if he gains some more strength and velocity.

Year	Club (League)	Class	W	L	ERA	G	GS	CG	SV	IP	H	HR	BB	SO	K/9	WHIP	AVG
2014	Idaho Falls (PIO)	R	0	2	5.09	9	8	0	0	23	30	2	9	25	9.8	1.70	.316
Minor League Totals			0	2	5.09	9	8	0	0	23	30	2	9	25	9.8	1.70	.316

15 LANE ADAMS, OF

BA GRADE

45 Risk: Medium

Born: Nov. 13, 1989. **B-T:** R-R. **Ht.:** 6-2. **Wt.:** 204. **Drafted:** HS—Red Oak, Okla., 2009 (13th round). **Signed by:** Steve Gossett.

Royals area scout Steve Gossett convinced the club to take a flier on Adams even though he was much more accomplished as a basketball player. His athleticism allowed him to compete against more experienced competitors. Added to the 40-man roster after the 2013 season to protect him from the Rule 5 draft, he got off to a brutal start at Double-A Northwest Arkansas and he missed much of July with a wrist injury. Adams recovered to post a .924 OPS over the second half and reached the majors in September as a pinch-runner/defensive replacement. He is a plus-plus runner who is a plus defender in center field. He's not a good fit in right field because of his fringe-average arm. Offensively, Adams has some strength and shows pull power, but he projects as an average hitter with the ability to hit 8-10 home runs and plenty of doubles. He most likely winds up as a fourth outfielder. He heads to Triple-A Omaha in 2015.

Year	Club (League)	Class	AVG	G	AB	R	H	2B	3B	HR	RBI	BB	SO	SB	CS	OBP	SLG
2012	Kane County (MWL)	LoA	.298	67	262	40	78	13	4	5	44	21	48	11	1	.349	.435
	Wilmington (CAR)	HiA	.240	68	262	37	63	10	1	6	25	21	64	8	4	.302	.355
2013	Wilmington (CAR)	HiA	.276	87	323	56	89	23	2	7	39	43	66	23	6	.362	.424
	NW Arkansas (TL)	AA	.244	44	156	30	38	7	1	5	26	18	45	15	0	.333	.397
2014	Burlington (APP)	R	.500	3	10	3	5	2	2	0	4	4	1	0	0	.643	1.100
	NW Arkansas (TL)	AA	.269	105	405	65	109	25	3	11	36	45	86	38	9	.352	.427
	Kansas City (AL)	MAJ	.000	6	3	1	0	0	0	0	0	0	2	0	0	.000	.000
Major League Totals			.000	6	3	1	0	0	0	0	0	0	2	0	0	.000	.000
Minor League Totals			.267	534	2024	338	541	109	23	42	234	220	473	133	25	.344	.406

16 CHRISTIAN BINFORD, RHP

BA GRADE

45 Risk: Medium

Born: Dec. 20, 1992. **B-T:** R-R. **Ht.:** 6-7. **Wt.:** 215. **Drafted:** HS– Mercersburg, Pa., 2011 (30th round). **Signed by:** Jim Farr.

As was the case with Brandon Finnegan and Sean Manaea, the Royals were able to land Binford late because he came with an injury history. He had Tommy John surgery in high school, so most scouts expected to see him go to Virginia as a projectable starter. The Royals, however, convinced him to sign for $575,000 as a 30th-round pick in 2011. After an excellent start at high Class A Wilmington in 2014, Binford moved up to Double-A Arkansas in July, then moved to the Triple-A Omaha bullpen. The move did not suit him and he did not get called up. Binford is one of the few minor league pitchers with above-average present command. He doesn't just throw strikes—he locates to the corners. He carved hitters up with well-placed two-seamers down and in to righthanders. His fastball is average at best (89-91 mph), but it's been effective because he gets excellent extension and locates it. His slurve has morphed into two pitches. His slider is his second-best pitch, for he can throw it consistently for strikes, but he mixes in a slurvy curveball that is more of a chase pitch and a straight 80 mph change with little fade but good arm speed. Binford has no true plus pitch, but he succeeds with pitch movement and command. He will return to Northwest Arkansas with a chance to become a No. 5 starter, but one who has little margin for error.

Year	Club (League)	Class	W	L	ERA	G	GS	CG	SV	IP	H	HR	BB	SO	K/9	WHIP	AVG
2012	Burlington (APP)	R	2	3	2.03	8	8	0	0	40	40	1	4	31	7.0	1.10	.252
2013	Lexington (SAL)	LoA	8	7	2.67	23	23	0	0	135	129	7	25	130	8.7	1.14	.253
2014	Wilmington (CAR)	HiA	5	4	2.40	14	14	0	0	83	72	2	11	92	10.0	1.00	.231
	NW Arkansas (TL)	AA	3	2	3.19	8	8	0	0	48	45	7	6	38	7.1	1.06	.247
	Omaha (PCL)	AAA	0	1	5.40	4	0	0	0	10	16	1	5	9	8.1	2.10	.348
Minor League Totals			18	17	2.68	57	53	0	0	316	302	18	51	300	8.6	1.12	.250

17 GLENN SPARKMAN, RHP

BA GRADE

50 Risk: High

Born: May 11, 1992. **B-T:** R-R. **Ht.:** 6-2. **Wt.:** 210. **Drafted:** Wharton (Texas) JC, 2013 (20th round). **Signed by:** Mitch Thompson.

The surprise star of the Royals' 2014 farm system was Sparkman, a previously little-noticed 20th-round pick. After starting the year in the high Class A Wilmington bullpen, he pitched his way into the rotation and finished the year with the second best ERA in the minors at 1.56. A friendly home ballpark helped, but he performed slightly better on the road. Sparkman's success was based on a combination of his deceptive delivery and his ability to throw to all four quadrants of the strike zone. He leads with his elbow, then brings his hand and the ball forward with a quick over-the-top release. Sparkman gets more swings and misses than one would expect from a 90-93 mph fastball. He mixes in a potentially average changeup with a little late fade and a potentially average hard slider at 83-84 mph. The pitch doesn't have much depth but cuts enough to swerve away from the sweet spot of opponents' bats. His curveball is generally below-average and loopy. Sparkman's four pitches all play up because he has present above-average control and average command. He'll head to Double-A Northwest Arkansas as a starter.

Year	Club (League)	Class	W	L	ERA	G	GS	CG	SV	IP	H	HR	BB	SO	K/9	WHIP	AVG
2013	Idaho Falls (PIO)	R	1	0	1.72	20	0	0	2	37	25	1	10	47	11.5	0.95	.194
2014	Wilmington (CAR)	HiA	8	3	1.56	29	18	0	1	121	94	2	25	117	8.7	0.98	.213
Minor League Totals			9	3	1.60	49	18	0	3	158	119	3	35	164	9.4	0.98	.209

18 BUBBA STARLING, OF

BA GRADE
55 Risk: Extreme

Born: Aug. 3, 1992. **B-T:** R-R. **Ht.:** 6-4. **Wt.:** 205. **Drafted:** HS—Gardner, Kan., 2011 (1st round). **Signed by:** Blake Davis.

If hitting for average weren't required to reach the majors, then Starling would already be an all-star. He turned down a chance to be Nebraska's quarterback to sign with the Royals for $7.5 million as the fifth overall pick in 2011. He's an excellent center fielder with plus range and an above-average arm. He turns in average to tick above-average times coming out of the box, but he's an above-average runner underway. But as a hitter, Starling is still a long way from where he needs to be. He simply struggles to square up the ball. Part of it is a pitch-recognition issue, but part of it appears to be a hand-eye coordination issue. The Royals see signs of an improved approach. He no longer is a consistent victim of sliders off the plate. Starling's tools (and his signing bonus) give the organization every reason to be patient, but it's harder to find scouts for other teams who still view him as a future regular. Starling can hope the better hitting environment at Double-A Northwest Arkansas gives him a shot of confidence in 2015.

Year	Club (League)	Class	AVG	G	AB	R	H	2B	3B	HR	RBI	BB	SO	SB	CS	OBP	SLG
2012	Burlington (APP)	R	.275	53	200	35	55	8	2	10	33	28	70	10	1	.371	.485
2013	Lexington (SAL)	LoA	.241	125	435	51	105	21	4	13	63	53	128	22	3	.329	.398
2014	Wilmington (CAR)	HiA	.218	132	482	67	105	23	4	9	54	49	150	17	2	.304	.338
Minor League Totals			.237	310	1117	153	265	52	10	32	150	130	348	49	6	.326	.388

19 PEDRO FERNANDEZ, RHP

BA GRADE
50 Risk: High

Born: May 25, 1994. **B-T:** R-R. **Ht.:** 6-0. **Wt.:** 175. **Signed:** Dominican Republic, 2011. **Signed by:** Edis Perez/Alvin Cuevas.

Figuring out when to promote a player to a higher level is not always an easy call. After Fernandez dominated the Dominican Summer League and the Rookie-level Arizona League in 2013, the Royals watched him look equally impressive in extended spring training in 2014. Emboldened, they assigned him to low Class A Lexington in June and watched him struggle to handle a tougher level of competition. Fernandez is a short righthander. His arm swing is long in the back as he takes the ball away from his glove to begin his motion, but prior to 2014, he had shown an ability to repeat this complex delivery. Fernandez gets good extension out front, which helps his plus fastball play up further. He sits at 90-93 mph, but he'll touch 97 when he humps up. His fringe-average slurvy breaking ball shows some tilt, but it's slower than the typical slider and doesn't feature as much break as the typical curveball. His changeup has shown flashes, but it wasn't as consistent in 2014. Most likely he heads back to Lexington in 2015 to try to reassert himself as a starter prospect.

Year	Club (League)	Class	W	L	ERA	G	GS	CG	SV	IP	H	HR	BB	SO	K/9	WHIP	AVG
2012	Royals (DSL)	R	3	2	1.93	12	10	0	0	51	44	0	14	49	8.6	1.13	.237
2013	Royals (DSL)	R	0	0	0.75	4	2	0	0	12	5	0	3	15	11.3	0.67	.128
	Royals (AZL)	R	0	1	1.82	8	7	0	0	35	28	3	8	38	9.9	1.04	.215
2014	Lexington (SAL)	LoA	1	8	4.99	16	8	0	3	61	50	6	33	60	8.8	1.35	.225
Minor League Totals			4	11	2.99	40	27	0	3	159	127	9	58	162	9.2	1.16	.220

20 CHESLOR CUTHBERT, 3B/1B

BA GRADE
45 Risk: Medium

Born: Nov. 16, 1992. **B-T:** R-R. **Ht.:** 6-0. **Wt.:** 193. **Signed:** Nicaragua, 2009. **Signed by:** Orlando Esteves/Juan Lopez.

After making rapid progress early in his career, Cuthbert has settled into a bit of a holding pattern. Cuthbert showed improvement in his return to Double-A Northwest Arkansas in 2014, and he earned a 25-game trial at Triple-A Omaha. He always has demonstrated an ability to draw walks, but despite a relatively simple, compact swing, his hit tool hasn't matched expectations. He needs to be at least an average hitter, for his tick below-average power hasn't turned into an asset. Cuthbert slid over to first base when Hunter Dozier joined the Double-A club, and he's played second base sporadically as well. At third base, Cuthbert is sure-handed, but his range is limited. He's a well below-average runner whose thick lower half hints that he'll continue to slow down. He has the hands and arm to be a range-limited second baseman, but he doesn't profile at first base. Cuthbert now looks like a bench bat.

Year	Club (League)	Class	AVG	G	AB	R	H	2B	3B	HR	RBI	BB	SO	SB	CS	OBP	SLG
2012	Wilmington (CAR)	HiA	.240	124	475	47	114	18	0	7	59	37	80	6	3	.296	.322
2013	Wilmington (CAR)	HiA	.280	60	225	32	63	21	2	2	31	27	37	1	2	.354	.418
	NW Arkansas (TL)	AA	.215	64	237	25	51	16	0	6	28	20	51	5	2	.279	.359
2014	NW Arkansas (TL)	AA	.276	96	355	35	98	19	1	10	48	36	67	9	3	.342	.420
	Omaha (PCL)	AAA	.264	25	91	12	24	5	0	2	16	9	12	1	1	.330	.385
Minor League Totals			.255	482	1811	208	462	99	7	38	248	174	347	26	12	.321	.380

21 MARTEN GASPARINI, SS

BA GRADE

55 Risk: Extreme

Born: May 24, 1997. **B-T:** B-R. **Ht.:** 6-0. **Wt.:** 165. **Signed:** Italy, 2013.
Signed by: Nick Leto.

Gasparini received the highest bonus ever for a European amateur at $1.3 million. Gasparini's pro debut was nearly wiped out by a hamstring injury that cost him a month and limited him even before that. In limited action at Rookie-level Burlington, he showed a plus arm and the actions and range to stay at shortstop, though his reliability is lacking, for he made 15 errors in 22 games, 11 of them fielding miscues. Before the hamstring problem, Gasparini showed above-average speed. At the plate, he is understandably raw. The switch-hitter's lefthanded swing is more powerful and more consistent than his righthanded stroke, which gets too long. Gasparini will return to Burlington in 2015. He has the highest ceiling of any Royals' shortstop other than Raul A. Mondesi, but he's likely five or six years away.

Year	Club (League)	Class	AVG	G	AB	R	H	2B	3B	HR	RBI	BB	SO	SB	CS	OBP	SLG
2014	Burlington (APP)	R	.191	19	68	11	13	2	1	0	1	3	32	4	1	.225	.250
	Idaho Falls (PIO)	R	.455	4	11	4	5	0	0	1	3	1	2	2	0	.500	.727
Minor League Totals			.228	23	79	15	18	2	1	1	4	4	34	6	1	.265	.316

22 ELIER HERNANDEZ, OF

BA GRADE

50 Risk: High

Born: Nov. 21, 1994. **B-T:** R-R. **Ht.:** 6-3. **Wt.:** 200. **Signed:** Dominican Republic 2011. **Signed by:** Rene Francisco.

Hernandez had the good fortune to sign for $3 million as a 16-year-old. He had the misfortune to sign that deal the same year as Raul A. Mondesi agreed to terms for $2 million. When the two players made their debuts together at Rookie-level Idaho Falls in 2012, Mondesi quickly outclassed Hernandez, whose swing is fairly straightforward, but he hasn't shown the consistent pop that was expected. Hernandez's overaggressiveness has been an issue and he has struggled to recognize and lay off sliders off the plate. He improved his reads and comfort level in right field in 2014, showing signs he can become an average defender, but his average arm may force an eventual move to left. Hernandez still is young enough to take big strides forward, but so far he hasn't shown the requisite hitting or power potential to fit as a corner outfielder. He will still be one of the younger players in the high Class A Carolina League.

Year	Club (League)	Class	AVG	G	AB	R	H	2B	3B	HR	RBI	BB	SO	SB	CS	OBP	SLG
2012	Idaho Falls (PIO)	R	.208	60	250	30	52	10	4	0	34	14	66	2	0	.256	.280
2013	Idaho Falls (PIO)	R	.301	66	289	44	87	15	8	3	44	18	62	9	2	.350	.439
2014	Lexington (SAL)	LoA	.264	111	420	54	111	19	4	9	34	16	99	5	5	.296	.393
Minor League Totals			.261	237	959	128	250	44	16	12	112	48	227	16	7	.302	.377

23 NIKLAS STEPHENSON, RHP

BA GRADE

50 Risk: High

Born: Nov. 16, 1993. **B-T:** R-R. **Ht.:** 6-3. **Wt.:** 197. **Signed:** HS— Encinitas, Calif., 2012 (NDFA). **Signed by:** Dan Drake.

The Royals decided after the 2013 season to have five minor league pitchers experiment with a weighted ball as part of an offseason training program. They didn't see much difference for four of the pitchers, but for Stephenson it transformed him from a likely release candidate to one who now is a legitimate prospect. He gained nearly 10 mph on his fastball to regularly sit at a plus 92-95 mph and touch 97. Stephenson has cleaned up his arm action as well. He's shorter in back and more consistent in terms of repeating his delivery. He was an above-average strike-thrower at Rookie-level Burlington in 2014, with a chance to have at least average control. His breaking ball and changeup flash average, but Stephenson's curveball is a pitch he uses consistently, while his changeup is one he's just starting to feel comfortable throwing. His delivery has some effort and a little bit of recoil after he releases the ball, but the Royals will develop him as a starter so long as he throws strikes. Next up: a rotation spot at low Class A Lexington.

Year	Club (League)	Class	W	L	ERA	G	GS	CG	SV	IP	H	HR	BB	SO	K/9	WHIP	AVG
2012	Royals (AZL)	R	0	0	5.63	7	0	0	0	8	11	1	3	3	3.4	1.75	.333
2013	Burlington (APP)	R	0	0	8.10	12	0	0	0	23	37	2	12	15	5.8	2.10	.378
2014	Burlington (APP)	R	3	3	2.14	11	6	0	0	59	45	2	9	47	7.2	0.92	.205
	Lexington (SAL)	LoA	1	0	4.00	2	2	0	0	9	11	0	3	4	4.0	1.56	.306
Minor League Totals			4	3	3.99	32	8	0	0	99	104	5	27	69	6.3	1.32	.269

24 BRANDON DOWNES, OF

BA GRADE
50 Risk: High

Born: Sept. 29, 1992. **B-T:** R-R. **Ht.:** 6-2. **Wt.:** 175. **Drafted:** Virginia, 2014 (7th round). **Signed by:** Jim Farr/Keith Connolly.

As a sophomore in 2013, Downes led a 50-win Virginia team in multiple offensive categories. A two-home-run game against future first-round pick Jeff Hoffman early in his junior season seemed to hint at a big year, but Downes soon after suffered a right wrist injury he tried to play through. That left him dragging a slow bat through the zone, but after signing as a seventh-rounder in 2014, his bat speed returned, and he once again showed the tools to be a center fielder with plenty of power. Downes is among the best athletes in the Royals system. He is a solid-average runner who runs faster than that once underway. He's shown a tick above-average power potential to go with an average hit tool. Downes may not fit in spacious Kauffman Stadium as a center fielder—his range is simply average—but he can also play right field with an above-average arm. He could prove to be the steal of the Royals' 2014 draft class.

Year	Club (League)	Class	AVG	G	AB	R	H	2B	3B	HR	RBI	BB	SO	SB	CS	OBP	SLG
2014	Idaho Falls (PIO)	R	.308	41	169	31	52	13	4	3	23	10	41	6	4	.358	.485
Minor League Totals			.308	41	169	31	52	13	4	3	23	10	41	6	4	.358	.485

25 RYAN O'HEARN, 1B

BA GRADE
50 Risk: High

Born: July 26, 1993. **B-T:** L-L. **Ht:** 6-3. **Wt.:** 200. **Drafted:** Sam Houston State, 2014 (8th round). **Signed by:** Justin Lehr/Gregg Miller.

After O'Hearn hit .262 with little power as a junior, the Royals sensed they might be among the few who still believed in his bat. They told O'Hearn, their 2014 eighth-round pick, to trust his power as a pro, and he responded by hitting 13 home runs at Rookie-level Idaho Falls to win Pioneer League MVP honors. (He hit just four bombs in three college seasons.) O'Hearn's compact swing and all-fields approach actually is more geared to spraying the ball around, but his power allows some of those line drives to clear the fence. O'Hearn is an average defender at first base who also is a playable, if below-average, right fielder.

Year	Club (League)	Class	AVG	G	AB	R	H	2B	3B	HR	RBI	BB	SO	SB	CS	OBP	SLG
2014	Idaho Falls (PIO)	R	.361	64	249	61	90	16	1	13	54	39	59	3	2	.444	.590
Minor League Totals			.361	64	249	61	90	16	1	13	54	39	59	3	2	.444	.590

26 WANDER FRANCO, 3B

BA GRADE
50 Risk: High

Born: Dec. 13, 1994. **B-T:** B-R. **Ht.:** 6-2. **Wt.:** 170. **Signed:** Dominican Republic, 2011. **Signed by:** Edis Perez.

Franco has a brother, also named Wander, who is a shortstop in the Astros system. The Royals' Wander is a lanky switch-hitting third baseman with natural bat-to-ball skills and a smooth swing from both sides of the plate. A shoulder injury hindered him in 2014, forcing him to hit righthanded only. Franco has a loose, handsy swing and projects as an above-average hitter, but will he fill out and gain much-needed core strength? He presently has well below-average power. Pre-injury, Franco showed a tick above-average arm that fit at third base. He has the athleticism to stick at third as an average defender.

Year	Club (League)	Class	AVG	G	AB	R	H	2B	3B	HR	RBI	BB	SO	SB	CS	OBP	SLG
2012	Royals (DSL)	R	.311	66	235	45	73	13	5	2	38	44	30	13	7	.431	.434
2013	Royals (AZL)	R	.277	43	159	27	44	11	4	0	23	13	30	2	4	.331	.396
2014	Idaho Falls (PIO)	R	.323	42	158	19	51	13	3	3	19	8	36	3	1	.374	.500
Minor League Totals			.304	151	552	91	168	37	12	5	80	65	96	18	12	.388	.442

27 FRANCISCO PENA, C

BA GRADE
45 Risk: Medium

Born: Oct. 12, 1989. **B-T:** R-R. **Ht.:** 6-2. **Wt.:** 230. **Signed:** Dominican Republic, 2006. **Signed by:** Ismael Cruz (Mets).

The son of long-time big league catcher Tony Pena, Francisco Pena faded from the prospect radar as he struggled with his weight and inconsistency. The Royals made him their top priority on the minor league free agent market after the 2013 season, signing him to a major league contract and adding him to the 40-man roster. Pena responded with the best season of his pro career. His pull-happy hitting approach leaves him vulnerable to pitches away. Defensively, he has good hands and a strong enough arm to fire off sub-2.0-second pop times on throws to second base despite inconsistent mechanics. He threw out nearly 40 percent of basestealers in 2014. Pena does have defensive hiccups, namely on balls in the dirt, when he too often stabs at the ball. He profiles as a well below-average hitter with average power potential.

Year	Club (League)	Class	AVG	G	AB	R	H	2B	3B	HR	RBI	BB	SO	SB	CS	OBP	SLG
2012	St. Lucie (FSL)	HiA	.254	41	142	19	36	10	1	4	22	11	29	0	0	.305	.423
	Binghamton (EL)	AA	.198	40	126	14	25	7	0	3	17	16	25	1	0	.299	.325
2013	Binghamton (EL)	AA	.246	21	69	4	17	6	0	0	4	7	4	0	1	.321	.333
	Las Vegas (PCL)	AAA	.257	68	218	22	56	15	1	9	39	10	40	1	0	.294	.459
2014	Kansas City (AL)	MAJ	—	1	0	0	0	0	0	0	0	0	0	0	0	—	—
	Omaha (PCL)	AAA	.240	96	342	53	82	13	0	27	61	16	65	0	3	.280	.515
Major League Totals			—	1	0	0	0	0	0	0	0	0	0	0	0	—	—
Minor League Totals			.236	689	2441	250	577	116	6	67	304	152	480	6	7	.285	.371

28 CAM GALLAGHER, C

Born: Dec. 6, 1992. **B-T:** R-R. **Ht.:** 6-3. **Wt.:** 210. **Drafted:** HS—Lancaster, Pa., 2011 (2nd round). **Signed by:** Jim Farr.

BA GRADE

45 Risk: High

Gallagher was thought to be a power-first catcher with average-at-best defensive tools. Nowadays, he's an excellent receiver who has shown no productive power. Gallagher's soft hands are his best asset, and he's an excellent receiver with an extremely accurate arm. He will show plenty of pop times of 1.9 seconds, but it's his ability to put throws on the bag consistently that explains why he led the high Class A Carolina League by catching 40 percent of basestealers. Gallagher shows bat speed in batting practice, but when the pitches start to count, that bat speed seems to disappear for a contact-oriented approach. The Royals remain patient as Gallagher heads to Double-A Northwest Arkansas in 2015.

Year	Club (League)	Class	AVG	G	AB	R	H	2B	3B	HR	RBI	BB	SO	SB	CS	OBP	SLG
2012	Burlington (APP)	R	.276	36	127	13	35	10	0	3	15	10	16	1	3	.331	.425
2013	Lexington (SAL)	LoA	.212	66	222	19	47	15	0	2	18	24	28	0	0	.302	.306
2014	Wilmington (CAR)	HiA	.228	96	312	24	71	18	0	5	34	37	38	1	0	.306	.333
Minor League Totals			.221	226	769	64	170	43	0	12	76	81	101	2	3	.298	.324

29 PAULO ORLANDO, OF

Born: Nov. 1, 1985. **B-T:** R-R. **Ht.:** 6-3. **Wt.:** 180. **Signed:** Brazil, 2005. **Signed by:** Orlando Santana (White Sox).

BA GRADE

40 Risk: Low

The Royals were willing to add Orlando, an 11-year pro with no big league experience, to the 40-man roster this offseason after re-signing him to minor league contracts each of the past three seasons to keep him in the organization. A native of Brazil, Orlando's limited exposure to the game helps explain why he's still making strides at age 29. He's an above-average center fielder with a plus arm The long-legged Orlando is a plus runner. He has learned to use the whole field and cut down his swing, aiming for contact and line drives. He's an average hitter with below-average power. Orlando's best fit is as an extra outfielder.

Year	Club (League)	Class	AVG	G	AB	R	H	2B	3B	HR	RBI	BB	SO	SB	CS	OBP	SLG
2012	NW Arkansas (TL)	AA	.279	116	420	54	117	18	2	6	40	30	57	21	6	.329	.374
2013	Omaha (PCL)	AAA	.276	92	293	41	81	9	3	5	46	22	56	8	3	.326	.379
2014	Omaha (PCL)	AAA	.301	136	501	61	151	21	9	6	63	39	86	34	9	.355	.415
Minor League Totals			.275	1017	3726	544	1023	164	63	63	414	221	749	200	69	.324	.403

30 JANDEL GUSTAVE, RHP

Born: Oct. 12, 1992. **B-T:** R-R. **Ht.:** 6-2 **Wt.:** 160. **Signed:** Dominican Republic, 2010. **Signed by:** Felix Francisco/Rafael Belen (Astros).

BA GRADE

50 Risk: Extreme

The long-limbed, lean Gustave finally reached full-season ball with the Astros in 2014, his fifth pro season, before the Royals snagged him in the Rule 5 draft in December. He possesses a fastball that clips triple-digits. Gustave went back to the bullpen when he returned from an oblique injury in late August. It was in relief that he touched 100 mph and sat 95-98. Gustave's control improved this season as he trimmed his walk rate to 3.3 per nine innings, an immense improvement from his career ratio of 6.7. He is limited to a reliever ceiling because he lacks dependable secondary offerings. Scouts say he needs more tilt on the slider to make it an effective swing-and-miss pitch. His delivery is clean, but he lacks a feel for repeating his release point and arm slot. Gustave faces long odds of sticking in a stacked Royals bullpen.

Year	Club (League)	Class	W	L	ERA	G	GS	CG	SV	IP	H	HR	BB	SO	K/9	WHIP	AVG
2012	Astros (GCL)	R	2	1	5.79	10	4	0	0	28	24	0	27	22	7.1	1.82	.224
2013	Greeneville (APP)	R	2	3	2.68	10	10	0	0	44	38	2	23	49	10.1	1.40	.235
2014	Quad Cities (MWL)	LoA	5	5	5.01	23	14	0	2	79	94	3	29	82	9.3	1.56	.289
Minor League Totals			9	18	5.73	71	34	0	2	196	204	7	146	199	9.1	1.78	.266

Los Angeles Angels

BY BILL MITCHELL

The Angels went all-in for 2014, seeking to return to the postseason for the first time since 2009, and in that way the strategy paid off.

Major League Baseball's best record, at 98-64, was based in Anaheim. But the Angels couldn't get past the American League Division Series, getting swept by the Royals in three games, although two of the losses came in 11 innings.

The Angels' success guarantees another year of stability for third-year general manager Jerry Dipoto and Mike Scioscia, who finished his 15th season as manager.

Los Angeles' roster and $128 million payroll features expensive free agents surrounding MVP Mike Trout, and bringing in Albert Pujols, Josh Hamilton and C.J. Wilson all cost the Angels high draft picks. So the club went the trade route in 2014 in order to build a contender.

A November 2013 trade brought in third baseman David Freese and veteran reliever Fernando Salas from the Cardinals in exchange for outfielders Peter Bourjos and Randal Grichuk.

Then the Angels sent homegrown slugger Mark Trumbo to the Diamondbacks in a three-team deal that netted pitching depth in lefthanders Tyler Skaggs from the Arizona and Hector Santiago from the White Sox. Skaggs, who was originally drafted by the Angels, got back on track with 18 solid starts before having Tommy John surgery in August, while Santiago filled the role of swingman for the Halos. The Angels rebuilt their bullpen on the fly, and the last big deal came in July, when four of the organization's top prospects were bundled to the Padres for experienced closer Huston Street and minor league reliever Trevor Gott.

The Angels farm system already ranked last out of 30 organizations prior to the flurry of trades, but several homegrown rookies still made a major league impact. Rookie DH/first baseman C.J. Cron provided a power bat in the lineup, and righthander Mike Morin provided a consistent relief arm. The biggest boost came from 27-year-old righty Matt Shoemaker, who spent parts of four seasons at Triple-A Salt Lake. He filled the void when ace Garrett Richards went down for the season in August with a serious knee injury and went 16-4, 3.04 overall.

The talent left on the farm remains thin, though three of the organization's six affiliates qualified for postseason play in 2014. More importantly, the Angels had a first-round pick for the first time since 2011, taking college lefthander Sean Newcomb. He quickly jumped to the top of the

Rookie Matt Shoemaker went 16-4, 3.04 and filled in for No. 1 starter Garrett Richards

TOP PROSPECTS OF THE DECADE

Year	Player, Pos.	2014 Org
2005	Casey Kotchman, 1b	Out of baseball
2006	Brandon Wood, ss	Sugar Land (Atlantic)
2007	Brandon Wood, ss	Sugar Land (Atlantic)
2008	Brandon Wood, ss	Sugar Land (Atlantic)
2009	Nick Adenhart, rhp	Deceased
2010	Hank Conger, c	Angels
2011	Mike Trout, of	Angels
2012	Mike Trout, of	Angels
2013	Kaleb Cowart, 3b	Angels
2014	Taylor Lindsey, 2b	Padres

prospect list with an impressive pro debut, and he should move quickly through the system. Scouting director Ric Wilson has moved the organization to a more college-focused plan, looking for players who control the strike zone on both sides of the ball.

The Angels' last two drafts have been pitcher-heavy, with their first five picks in 2014 and first seven in 2013 being pitchers. The organization's renewed emphasis on signing Latin American prospects, which began with the opening of a new complex in the Dominican Republic, and the work of international scouting director Carlos Gomez also show signs of boosting the farm system.

But the emphasis on developing pitching depth has left the system devoid of projectable position players, with only one hitter among the Top 10 Prospects.

General manager: Jerry Dipoto. **Farm director:** Bobby Scales. **Scouting director:** Ric Wilson.

Class	Team	League	W	L	PCT	Finish	Manager
Majors	Los Angeles Angels	American	98	64	.605	1st (30)	Mike Scioscia
Triple-A	Salt Lake Bees	Pacific Coast	60	84	.417	15th (16)	Keith Johnson
Double-A	Arkansas Travelers	Texas	75	65	.536	3rd (8)	Phillip Wellman
High A	Inland Empire 66ers	California	62	78	.443	9th (10)	Denny Hocking
Low A	Burlington Bees	Midwest	68	71	.489	9th (16)	Bill Richardson
Rookie	Orem Owlz	Pioneer	42	33	.560	2nd (8)	Dave Stapleton
Rookie	AZL Angels	Arizona	30	25	.545	t-4th (13)	Elio Sarmiento
Overall Minor League Record			337	356	.486	21st (30)	

THIS YEAR'S TOP 30

No.	Player, Pos.	Grade
1.	Andrew Heaney, lhp	55/Low
2.	Sean Newcomb, lhp	60/High
3.	Ricardo Sanchez, lhp	55/Extreme
4.	Cam Bedrosian, rhp	50/Medium
5.	Chris Ellis, rhp	50/High
6.	Joe Gatto, rhp	50/High
7.	Victor Alcantara, rhp	50/High
8.	Alex Yarbrough, 2b	45/Medium
9.	Nick Tropeano, rhp	45/Medium
10.	Kyle McGowin, rhp	50/High
11.	Taylor Featherston, 2b/ss	45/Medium
12.	Julio Garcia, ss	55/Extreme
13.	Trevor Gott, rhp	50/High
14.	Nate Smith, lhp	45/High
15.	Kody Eaves, 2b	50/Extreme
16.	Danny Reynolds, rhp	45/High
17.	Hunter Green, lhp	50/High
18.	Drew Rucinski, rhp	45/High
19.	Jake Jewell, rhp	50/Extreme
20.	Jose Suarez, lhp	50/Extreme
21.	Jett Bandy, c	40/Medium
22.	Eduar Lopez, rhp	50/Extreme
23.	Eric Stamets, ss	40/Medium
24.	Kaleb Cowart, 3b	45/High
25.	Carlos Perez, c	40/Medium
26.	Greg Mahle, lhp	40/Medium
27.	Natanael Delgado, of	50/Extreme
28.	Chad Hinshaw, of	45/High
29.	Cal Towey, 3b/of	45/High
30.	Keynan Middleton, rhp	50/Extreme

LAST YEAR'S TOP 30

Player, Pos.	Status
1. Taylor Lindsey, 2b	(Padres)
2. C.J. Cron, 1b	Majors
3. Kaleb Cowart, 3b	No. 24
4. R.J. Alvarez, rhp	(Padres)
5. Mark Sappington, rhp	(Rays)
6. Hunter Green, lhp	No. 17
7. Ricardo Sanchez, lhp	No. 3
8. Alex Yarbrough, 2b	No. 8
9. Zach Borenstein, of	(Diamondbacks)
10. Cam Bedrosian, rhp	No. 4
11. Ryan Brasier, rhp	Dropped out
12. Jose Rondon, ss	(Padres)
13. Eric Stamets, ss	No. 23
14. Mike Morin, rhp	Majors
15. Victor Alcantara, rhp	No. 7
16. Natanael Delgado, of	No. 27
17. Mike Clevinger, rhp	(Indians)
18. Mike Fish, of	Dropped out
19. Cal Towey, 3b	No. 29
20. A.J. Schugel, rhp	(Diamondbacks)
21. Buddy Boshers, lhp	Free agent
22. Nick Maronde, lhp	(Indians)
23. Joe Krehbiel, rhp	(Diamondbacks)
24. Eduar Lopez, rhp	No. 22
25. Jett Bandy, c	No. 21
26. Keynan Middleton, rhp	No. 30
27. Erick Salcedo, ss	Dropped out
28. Andrew Ray, of	Retired
29. Kyle McGowin, rhp	No. 10
30. Reid Scoggins, rhp	Released

BEST TOOLS

Best Hitter for Average	Alex Yarbrough
Best Power Hitter	Fran Whitten
Best Strike-Zone Discipline	Cal Towey
Fastest Baserunner	Ayendy Perez
Best Athlete	Eric Stamets
Best Fastball	Victor Alcantara
Best Curveball	Sean Newcomb
Best Slider	Andrew Heaney
Best Changeup	Nate Smith
Best Control	Andrew Heaney
Best Defensive Catcher	Jett Bandy
Best Defensive Infielder	Eric Stamets
Best Infield Arm	Kaleb Cowart
Best Defensive Outfielder	Chad Hinshaw
Best Outfield Arm	Ranyelmy Mendoza

PROJECTED 2018 LINEUP

Catcher	Chris Iannetta
First Base	C.J. Cron
Second Base	Alex Yarbrough
Third Base	David Freese
Shortstop	Erick Aybar
Left Field	Josh Hamilton
Center Field	Mike Trout
Right Field	Kole Calhoun
Designated Hitter	Albert Pujols
No. 1 Starter	Garrett Richards
No. 2 Starter	Jered Weaver
No. 3 Starter	Andrew Heaney
No. 4 Starter	Sean Newcomb
No. 5 Starter	Tyler Skaggs
Closer	Cam Bedrosian

LOS ANGELES ANGELS

TOP 2015 ROOKIE: Cam Bedrosian, rhp. After getting a taste of the majors in 2014, he should get more time as a middle reliever and potential closer-in-waiting.

BREAKOUT PROSPECT: Danny Reynolds, rhp. He generates a lot of velocity out of a small frame and will head to Triple-A to position himself as another power arm that the Angels can call upon.

SOURCE OF TOP 30 TALENT			
Homegrown	24	Acquired	6
College	10	Trades	4
Junior college	2	Rule 5 draft	1
High school	6	Independent leagues	1
Draft-and-follow	0	Free agents/waivers	0
Nondrafted free agents	0		
International	6		

SLEEPER: Alan Busenitz, rhp. A 25th-round pick in 2013, he has been a favorite under-the-radar player of the Angels and will get the opportunity to take his 96 mph fastball and power curve to the rotation in 2015.

LF
Natanael Delgado (27)
Caleb Adams
Mike Fish
Mike Hermosillo

CF
Chad Hinshaw (28)
Bo Way
Mark Shannon
Johan Sala

RF
Alex Abbott
Ricky Martinez
Kentrail Davis
Junior Pedie

3B
Kaleb Cowart (24)
Cal Towey (29)
Chris Curley
Zach Houchins
Angel Rosa
Brian Hernandez

SS
Julio Garcia (12)
Eric Stamets (23)
Shawn O'Malley
Erick Salcedo
Franklin Torres
Jake Yacinich
Pedro Ruiz

2B
Alex Yarbrough (8)
Taylor Featherston (11)
Kody Eaves (15)
Sherman Johnson
Andrew Daniel

1B
Eric Aguilera
Mike Snyder
Wade Hinkle
Ryan Seiz
Fran Whitten

C
Jett Bandy (21)
Carlos Perez (25)
Zach Wright
Keinner Pina

LHP

LHSP	LHRP
Andrew Heaney (1)	Greg Mahle (26)
Sean Newcomb (2)	Chris O'Grady
Ricardo Sanchez (3)	Tyler DeLoach
Nate Smith (14)	Jonah Wesely
Hunter Green (17)	
Jose Suarez (20)	
Kramer Sneed	

RHP

RHSP	RHRP
Chris Ellis (5)	Cam Bedrosian (4)
Joe Gatto (6)	Victor Alcantara (7)
Nick Tropeano (9)	Trevor Gott (13)
Kyle McGowin (10)	Danny Reynolds (16)
Jake Jewell (19)	Drew Rucinski (18)
Eduar Lopez (22)	Austin Adams
Keynan Middleton (30)	Alan Busenitz
Jordan Kipper	Kevin Johnson
Harrison Cooney	Eduard Santos
Austin Robichaux	Eduardo Paredes
Jared Ruxer	Kurt Spomer
Jeremy Rhoades	
Garrett Nuss	
Yency Almonte	
Andres Heredia	
Crucito Mieses	

2014

BEST PURE HITTER: Lefthanded-hitting OF Bo Way (7) had a track record of hitting in college and continued to hit this summer while using all fields with a line-drive oriented stroke, gap-to-gap approach and knowledge of the strike zone.

BEST POWER HITTER: 1B Fran Whitten (37) has 70-grade raw power from the left side of the plate.

FASTEST RUNNER: OF Caleb Adams is an above-average to plus runner underway with at least average tools across the board. Way is also at least an above-average runner underway.

BEST DEFENSIVE PLAYER: Zach Houchins (13) has the potential to be at least an average defender at third base with an above-average arm, good hands and ability to come in well on plays in front of him.

BEST FASTBALL: LHP Sean Newcomb (1) had some of the easiest velocity in the entire draft and some of easiest lefthanded velocity of the last decade. His fastball sits 91-94 mph and he has touched 98. RHP Joe Gatto (2) had some of the easiest righthanded velocity in the draft and the ball jumps out of his hand, sitting 90-93 while touching 95.

BEST SECONDARY PITCH: Newcomb shows the makings of a plus changeup. RHP Chris Ellis (3) has a power slider at 83-86 mph with at least above-average potential to go with an above-average changeup. While Gatto is learning to make his curveball more consistent, it flashes plus potential with tight shape, power and swing-and-miss potential.

BEST PRO DEBUT: Way hit .347/.412/.510 this summer with a 21-to-29 strikeout-to-walk ratio. He has the ability to play all three outfield positions and gets good jumps with his advanced defensive instincts in center field. 3B Andrew Daniel's (11) best tool is his righthanded bat and he hit .340/.408/.510 this summer for Rookie-level Ogden.

BEST ATHLETE: Gatto played quarterback for his high school football team as a freshman and sophomore and starred on the school's basketball team as a junior.

MOST INTRIGUING BACKGROUND: SS Jose Rodriguez (34) is the first player the Angels have drafted out of Puerto Rico since the 2004 draft.

CLOSEST TO THE MAJORS: Newcomb and LHP Greg Mahle (15) offers advanced pitchability to go with tenacity and poise. Mahle varies his arm slot to give lefthanded hitters a different look, ranging from low three-quarters to high three-quarters and varying his velocity from 85 to 94.

BEST LATE-ROUND PICK: Mahle (15) and RHP Jared Ruxer (12) both stand out. Ruxer had the stuff to go in the top half-dozen rounds but he had Tommy John surgery just before the draft.

Robichaux has a track record of throwing strikes with three pitches that show at least average potential, though his other tools will need to develop.

THE ONE WHO GOT AWAY: Junior college 2B Blaine Prescott (16) is at least a 70 runner who got some 80 grades from scouts after running times of 4.0 from the right side.

ASSESSMENT: After picking seven straight pitchers at the top of the 2013 draft, the Angels again stockpiled hard-throwing arms by picking five straight to begin the 2014 draft.

2013

Raw LHP Hunter Green (2) and RHP Keynan Middleton (3) are off to very slow starts. RHP Elliot Morris (4), traded to the Padres, may be the class' top prospect along with RHP Kyle McGowin (5) and intriguing OF Chad Hinshaw (15).

GRADE: D

2012

A productive pitching draft landed fast-moving relievers LHP Michael Roth (9) and RHP Mike Morin (13) and since-traded RHP R.J. Alvarez (3). 2B Alex Yarbrough (4) could hit his way to being Howie Kendrick's replacement in 2015.

GRADE: C

2011

1B/DH C.J. Cron (1) will bring value at the plate. LHP Nick Marone (3) has reached the majors but has been designated for assignment twice. OF Zach Borenstein (23), now a Diamondback, keeps hitting.

GRADE: C

TOP DRAFT PICKS OF THE DECADE

Year	Player, Pos.	2014 Org
2005	Trevor Bell, rhp (1st round supp)	Reds
2006	Hank Conger, c	Angels
2007	Jon Bachanov, rhp (1st rd supp)	Out of baseball
2008	Tyler Chatwood, rhp (2nd round)	Rockies
2009	Randal Grichuk, of	Cardinals
2010	Kaleb Cowart, 3b	Angels
2011	C.J. Cron, 1b	Angels
2012	R.J. Alvarez, rhp (3rd round)	Padres
2013	Hunter Green, lhp (2nd round)	Angels
2014	Sean Newcomb, lhp	Angels

LARGEST BONUSES IN CLUB HISTORY

Jered Weaver, 2004	$4,000,000
Kendrys Morales, 2004	$3,000,000
Sean Newcomb, 2014	$2,518,400
Kaleb Cowart, 2010	$2,300,000
Troy Glaus, 1997	$2,250,000

1 ANDREW HEANEY, LHP

Born: June 5, 1991. **B-T:** L-L. **Ht.:** 6-3. **Wt.:** 180.
Drafted: Oklahoma State, 2012 (1st round).
Signed by: Steve Taylor (Marlins).

Marlins scouting director Stan Meek, a former player and assistant coach at Oklahoma, has strong ties to the Sooner State and has tapped into those ties in the draft. He hit early with 2002 fourth-rounder Josh Johnson and has gone to the well more frequently of late, missing with 2009 first-rounder Chad James but hitting on catcher J.T. Realmuto (third round, 2010) and Heaney, the ninth overall pick in 2012. Ranked among the best lefthanded college starters entering the 2012 draft, Heaney earned the same distinction in the minors heading into the 2014 season. A last-hour sign for $2.6 million, Heaney opened his third pro season in 2014 at Double-A Jacksonville. He made an 83-inning layover at Triple-A New Orleans, where he continued performing well, before the Marlins summoned him. He made his major league debut on June 19 with enormous expectations, but Marlins fans looking for a lefthanded complement to ace Jose Fernandez didn't get him in Heaney, who lost each of his first three big league starts. Miami optioned him back to Triple-A, and he didn't start again in the big leagues until Miami's 160th game. Traded twice during the Winter Meetings, Heaney first went from the Marlins to Dodgers as part of the package for Dan Haren and Dee Gordon, then moved from the Dodgers to Angels in a straight-up swap for Howie Kendrick.

At his best, Heaney's fastball sits in the low 90s and he complements it with a plus slider in the low 80s and a plus changeup with armside sink. He tired in the second half of what was actually his first full season, as a lat strain in 2013 limited him to 95 innings that season. When he tired, he lost some arm speed and didn't maintain his release point, causing his stuff to flatten out, so strength gains are an obvious area for improvement. Heaney's fastball generally misses down when it misses, and while he was homer-prone in the majors, he hasn't been in the minors, allowing just 0.5 per nine innings. He's still developing a feel for his changeup, which he throws too hard at times. Heaney has a clean delivery and easy arm

action, but he can be susceptible to the running game, often timed at 1.3 seconds or more to the plate, when 1.2 is considered average. He needs to focus on maintaining a quicker delivery and shortened stride length. When he's going well, Heaney also pitches with an excellent, aggressive tempo. He has above-average control and threw nearly two-thirds of his pitches in the minors for strikes. That figure dipped slightly to 63.7 percent while in the majors, but he threw first-pitch strikes at a better than 60 percent rate.

About the only thing Heaney lacks right now is experience. He benefitted from working with Marlins big league coaches Reid Cornelius and Chuck Hernandez in September, getting his feet wet in preparation for an expanded role. An offseason spent getting stronger would position him well to compete for a rotation spot with the Angels.

BA GRADE

55 Risk: Low

SCOUTING GRADES

Fastball: 55
Slider: 60
Changeup: 60
Control: 60

Based on 20-80 scouting scale and future projection rather than present tools.

LGE	BF	SO%	BB%	HR/9
SL	218	23.9	6.0	0.34
PCL	350	26.0	6.6	0.97

BILL MITCHELL

Year	Club (League)	Class	W	L	ERA	G	GS	CG	SV	IP	H	HR	BB	SO	K/9	WHIP	AVG
2012	Marlins (GCL)	R	0	0	2.57	2	2	0	0	7	7	0	2	9	11.6	1.29	.259
	Greensboro (SAL)	LoA	1	2	4.95	4	4	0	0	20	25	0	4	21	9.5	1.45	.287
2013	Jupiter (FSL)	HiA	5	2	0.88	13	12	0	0	62	45	2	17	66	9.6	1.01	.193
	Jacksonville (SL)	AA	4	1	2.94	6	6	1	0	34	31	2	9	23	6.1	1.19	.242
2014	Jacksonville (SL)	AA	4	2	2.35	9	8	0	0	54	45	2	13	52	8.7	1.08	.223
	New Orleans (PCL)	AAA	5	4	3.87	15	15	1	0	84	75	9	23	91	9.8	1.17	.234
	Miami (NL)	MAJ	0	3	5.83	7	5	0	0	29	32	6	7	20	6.1	1.33	.281
Major League Totals			0	3	5.83	7	5	0	0	29	32	6	7	20	6.1	1.33	.281
Minor League Totals			19	11	2.77	49	47	2	0	260	228	15	68	262	9.1	1.14	.228

2 SEAN NEWCOMB, LHP

Born: June 12, 1993. **B-T:** L-L. **Ht.:** 6-5. **Wt.:** 240. **Drafted:** Hartford, 2014 (1st round). **Signed by:** Nick Gorneault.

Ric Wilson had made only one first-round pick as the Angels' scouting director, even though he'd been on the job since October 2010. Happy to be back in the early part of the draft, he continued a recent emphasis on adding pitching depth to the organization with the selection of Newcomb. The 15th overall pick, Newcomb signed at the deadline for $2,158,400. A tight end in football during high school who was recruited by several major colleges, Newcomb filled out only one questionnaire from professional teams as a prep senior and preferred baseball to football even though Hartford was his only recruiting visit. After a shaky freshman season in which he walked 38 batters in 45 innings, his stock took off the next year when he ranked second in NCAA Division I in strikeouts per nine innings (11.5). His pro debut included four starts at low Class A Burlington, and one Midwest League playoff start that included six strikeouts in five, one-run innings. Newcomb is a big-bodied lefthander who draws comparisons with former Red Sox ace Jon Lester for his size, physical appearance and delivery. He projects to have three plus pitches, with a riding, 91-95 mph fastball that has life above the barrel. Scouts believe he throws his heater with some of the easiest velocity of any pitcher in the draft in recent memory, and it has touched as high as 98 mph. Newcomb's fastball gets on the batter quickly, and his overall command keeps the hitter in swing mode in pitchers' counts. His best secondary pitch is a curveball he delivers at 74-80 mph, with a spin rate already well above major league average. He's shown aptitude with his breaking ball, considering it was a below-average pitch when he was a sophomore. His third pitch is a changeup at 78-82 mph that he throws with armside action and good arm speed. While his changeup sometimes flattens out when left up in the zone, it projects to be at least average. Newcomb uses a high-three-quarters delivery, which he repeats well. He has very good makeup and is mature and composed on the mound. Newcomb's body is built to burn innings, making him a potential mid-rotation starter capable of logging 200-plus innings per year. He will jump on the fast track and should be ready for high Class A Inland Empire out of spring training, with a move to Double-A Arkansas before the end of the 2015 season.

BA GRADE 60 Risk: High

LGE	BF	SO%	BB%	HR/9
AZL	12	25.0	8.3	3.00
MWL	52	28.8	9.6	0.77

Year	Club (League)	Class	W	L	ERA	G	GS	CG	SV	IP	H	HR	BB	SO	K/9	WHIP	AVG
2014	Angels (AZL)	R	0	0	3.00	2	2	0	0	3	3	1	1	3	9.0	1.33	.273
	Burlington (MWL)	LoA	0	1	6.94	4	4	0	0	12	13	1	5	15	11.6	1.54	.289
Minor League Totals			0	1	6.14	6	6	0	0	15	16	2	6	18	11.0	1.50	.286

3 RICARDO SANCHEZ, LHP

Born: April 11, 1997. **B-T:** L-L. **Ht:** 5-11. **Wt:** 195. **Signed:** Venezuela, 2013. **Signed by:** Lebi Ochoa/Carlos Ramirez.

The Angels showed their renewed commitment to the Latin America market when they signed Sanchez, one of the top pitchers in the 2013 international class, on July 2 for $580,000. He previously had international experience when he was the winning pitcher for his native Venezuela against Cuba in the 2012 15U World Championship. The Angels brought Sanchez to instructional league when he was still just 16, and he made his pro debut in 2014 in the Rookie-level Arizona League just two months after his 17th birthday. Sanchez has a smooth, natural delivery that belies his age and experience level, but he needs more consistency in repeating it. The ball comes out of his hand effortlessly and he can spin a 70-75 mph curveball that projects to be a plus pitch. His fastball was in the 94-95 mph range at times after he arrived in the U.S., though the AZL coaching staff had him dial it back a bit in order to better command it. Sanchez needs to improve his 82-85 mph changeup so as not to rely on the breaking ball as much, and he's slowly been developing more of a feel for the pitch. Sanchez needs experience and health, but he has tantalizing upside. He most likely will remain behind in extended spring training in 2015 before reporting to Rookie-level Orem in June.

BA GRADE 55 Risk: Extreme

LGE	BF	SO%	BB%	HR/9
AZL	182	23.6	12.1	0.00

Year	Club (League)	Class	W	L	ERA	G	GS	CG	SV	IP	H	HR	BB	SO	K/9	WHIP	AVG
2014	Angels (AZL)	R	2	2	3.49	12	9	0	0	39	40	0	22	43	10.0	1.60	.258
Minor League Totals			2	2	3.49	12	9	0	0	39	40	0	22	43	10.0	1.60	.258

4 CAM BEDROSIAN, RHP

Born: Oct. 2, 1991. **B-T:** R-R. **Ht:** 6-0. **Wt:** 205. **Drafted:** HS—Sharpsburg, Ga.,
2010 (1st round). **Signed by:** Chris McAlpin.

The Angels took three Georgia high school players in the first round
of the 2010 draft, and the son of 1987 Cy Young Award winner Steve
Bedrosian has been the best so far. Cam missed most of his first two pro
seasons to Tommy John surgery before converting to the bullpen in 2013.
Healthy in 2014, he moved through three levels of the minors en route to
making his big league debut in June. Like his father before him, Bedrosian
is a bulldog on the mound, best suited for a late-inning relief role with his
stuff playing up in short stints. His fastball, which he keeps down in the
zone, touches 97 mph and sits in the 93-94 range. He also throws a power
slider that flashes plus, and he continues developing a curveball that shows
potential. For a reliever, Bedrosian has some feel for pitching. His results
in 17 big league games were mixed because he pitched up in the zone too
much, but he still struck out more than a batter per inning. Bedrosian will
head to spring training with a chance to make the Opening Day roster,
though a crowded bullpen may push him back to Triple-A Salt Lake for more seasoning.

BA GRADE

50 Risk: Medium

LGE	BF	SO%	BB%	HR/9
TL	114	50.0	8.8	0.28
AL	93	21.5	12.9	0.93

Year	Club (League)	Class	W	L	ERA	G	GS	CG	SV	IP	H	HR	BB	SO	K/9	WHIP	AVG
2012	Cedar Rapids (MWL)	LoA	3	11	6.31	21	21	0	0	83	91	5	52	48	5.2	1.73	.286
2013	Burlington (MWL)	LoA	1	5	5.30	37	2	0	7	54	55	4	22	69	11.4	1.42	.258
	Inland Empire (CAL)	HiA	0	0	0.00	7	0	0	0	9	4	0	7	9	9.3	1.27	.143
2014	Inland Empire (CAL)	HiA	0	0	0.00	5	0	0	1	6	1	0	2	15	23.8	0.53	.056
	Arkansas (TL)	AA	1	0	1.11	30	0	0	15	32	10	1	10	57	15.9	0.62	.097
	Salt Lake (PCL)	AAA	1	1	7.71	8	0	0	2	7	5	0	6	10	12.9	1.57	.192
	Los Angeles (AL)	MAJ	0	1	6.52	17	0	0	0	19	23	2	12	20	9.3	1.81	.288
Major League Totals			0	1	6.52	17	0	0	0	19	23	2	12	20	9.3	1.81	.288
Minor League Totals			6	19	4.71	113	27	0	25	203	179	10	106	218	9.7	1.41	.238

5 CHRIS ELLIS, RHP

Born: Sept. 22, 1992. **B-T:** R-R. **Ht:** 6-5. **Wt:** 205. **Drafted:** Mississippi, 2014
(3rd round). **Signed by:** J.T. Zink.

Originally drafted by the Dodgers in the 50th round out of high school,
Ellis instead headed to Mississippi, pitching out of the bullpen and battling
an abdominal strain that interrupted his sophomore season. After a successful summer in the Cape Cod League, he became the Rebels' Friday-night
starter in 2014, helping them reach the College World Series while becoming a third-round pick. He signed for $575,000. Ellis has a good pitcher's
body that gives his pitches downward angle. His live, sinking fastball, which
gets up to 95 mph and sits at 90-92 when working as a starter, runs in on
batters. He throws a sharp-breaking, hard slider at 83-85 mph, which gets
power from his high-three-quarters arm slot, and he's toyed with a slider in
the past that he may add again as a pro. Ellis' 79-81 mph changeup also is
an above-average pitch with good fade. He has enough feel and confidence
to throw his changeup to both lefthanders and righthanders. He showed
durability as a junior in his first full season as a starter. The Angels hope to keep Ellis in the rotation, and
he profiles as a No. 3 or 4 starter. After being handled carefully in his pro debut at Rookie-level Orem,
where he worked no more than three innings per appearance, he'll debut in full-season ball in 2015,
probably at low Class A Burlington.

BA GRADE

50 Risk: High

LGE	BF	SO%	BB%	HR/9
PIO	65	24.6	12.3	1.15

Year	Club (League)	Class	W	L	ERA	G	GS	CG	SV	IP	H	HR	BB	SO	K/9	WHIP	AVG
2014	Orem (PIO)	R	0	1	6.89	9	2	0	0	16	17	2	8	16	9.2	1.60	.309
Minor League Totals			0	1	6.89	9	2	0	0	16	17	2	8	16	9.2	1.60	.309

6 JOE GATTO, RHP

Born: June 14, 1995. **B-T:** R-R. **Ht:** 6-3. **Wt:** 204. **Drafted:** HS—Richland, N.J., 2014 (2nd round). **Signed by:** Nick Gorneault.

The Angels successfully drafted a New Jersey high school product in 2009 with their selection of Mike Trout at No. 25 overall. They will be satisfied if 2014 Jersey prep product Gatto turns into a useful starting pitcher in a few years. He netted $1.2 million to pass up his North Carolina commitment after being taken in the second round. Gatto has an ideal pitcher's body with big hands, long arms and present strength. The ball comes out of his hand easily and with good extension. The Angels saw Gatto's fastball up to 97 mph this spring, though he usually sits in the 90-93 range. A former three-sport prep, he's athletic and has a smooth delivery with easy velocity. He also showed an upper-70s slurvy curveball with power in the spring, but the velocity on both pitches backed up after he signed as he focused on throwing strikes. His curveball has good depth when he's right and projects as an above-average pitch if not a bit better. His changeup can be firm at 82-87 mph but flashed above-average in the past. Gatto finished instructional league in fine form, and since he's old for his high school class—he turned 19 just three days prior to signing—he's headed for low Class A Burlington in 2015.

BA GRADE	
50	**Risk:** High

LGE	BF	SO%	BB%	HR/9
AZL	115	13.0	7.8	0.36
PIO	8	12.5	0.0	4.50

Year	Club (League)	Class	W	L	ERA	G	GS	CG	SV	IP	H	HR	BB	SO	K/9	WHIP	AVG
2014	Angels (AZL)	R	2	1	5.40	10	6	0	0	25	33	1	9	15	5.4	1.68	.320
	Orem (PIO)	R	0	0	4.50	1	1	0	0	2	3	1	0	1	4.5	1.50	.375
Minor League Totals			2	1	5.33	11	7	0	0	27	36	2	9	16	5.3	1.67	.324

7 VICTOR ALCANTARA, RHP

Born: April 3, 1993. **B-T:** R-R. **Ht:** 6-2. **Wt:** 190. **Signed:** Dominican Republic, 2011. **Signed by:** Roman Ocumarez.

Regarded as more of a wild card in his first two pro seasons, with a strong arm but unpredictable control, Alcantara improved significantly in 2014 and made an appearance at the Futures Game at Target Field in Minneapolis. He moved into the low Class A Burlington rotation for good in late May and won a Midwest League playoff start with six scoreless innings. Alcantara possesses a powerful right arm, delivering a plus fastball up to 98 mph, but he pitches more effectively in the 93-94 range. His heater became a better pitch in 2014 as he added more sink to go with its natural movement. His slider also is an above-average pitch that he throws 88-89 mph with enough depth to miss barrels. His firm changeup that averages 89 mph can be at least an average pitch. Alcantara throws with a lot of effort from a high-three-quarters delivery and needs to be more consistent with his release point and delivery. As a result, he lacks control, not to mention command, having walked 4.3 batters per nine innings in 2014. Opponents hit just .219 against him, though, so his stuff clearly plays. Alcantara will move up to high Class A Inland Empire in 2015. He's got the pitches to remain in the rotation if he continues to improve his control and game-management skills, but he could also get to the big leagues as a hard-throwing reliever.

BA GRADE	
50	**Risk:** High

LGE	BF	SO%	BB%	HR/9
MWL	519	22.5	11.6	0.43

Year	Club (League)	Class	W	L	ERA	G	GS	CG	SV	IP	H	HR	BB	SO	K/9	WHIP	AVG
2012	Angels (DSL)	R	5	4	2.13	14	14	0	0	72	51	0	40	77	9.6	1.26	.199
2013	Orem (PIO)	R	2	5	7.47	17	12	0	0	59	73	10	35	48	7.3	1.83	.304
2014	Burlington (MWL)	LoA	7	6	3.81	27	20	0	1	125	98	6	60	117	8.4	1.26	.219
Minor League Totals			14	15	4.18	58	46	0	1	256	222	16	135	242	8.5	1.39	.235

8 ALEX YARBROUGH, 2B

Born: Aug. 3, 1991. **B-T:** B-R. **Ht:** 6-0. **Wt:** 195. **Drafted:** Mississippi, 2012 (4th round). **Signed by:** J.T. Zink.

The Mississippi product and first-team All-American in 2012 has risen steadily through the organization on the strength of his natural hitting ability and hard-nosed style of play since being taken in the fourth round in 2012. Yarbrough earned the Texas League MVP award in 2014 after leading the league in hits (154) and doubles (38) and ranking second in RBIs (77). Yarbrough is a pure hitter from both sides of the plate, though he has a better stroke from the left side. He's got more doubles power to the gaps than over-the-fence pop. His bat would have even more value if he was more selective at the plate and cut down on strikeouts, for he fanned 21 percent of the time in 2014. Yarbourgh's value comes mostly from his hitting ability, though his gamer mentality helps his team in many ways. He's just fair defensively at second base, with slow actions around the bag and below-average range and arm strength. He has become more efficient at turning the double play but projects as a fringy defender. He's a below-average runner. Yarbrough and double-play partner Eric Stamets will again move up together, this time to Triple-A Salt Lake. The Angels' 2014 trade of Taylor Lindsey removes one potential roadblock for Yarbrough, who projects as a starting second baseman in the big leagues and could allow the club to use Howie Kendrick as trade bait.

BA GRADE

45 Risk: Medium

LGE	PA	BB%	SO%	ISO
TL	592	5.6	20.9	.112

Year	Club (League)	Class	AVG	G	AB	R	H	2B	3B	HR	RBI	BB	SO	SB	CS	OBP	SLG
2012	Cedar Rapids (MWL)	LoA	.287	58	244	35	70	12	9	0	27	10	20	9	2	.320	.410
	Arkansas (TL)	AA	.111	5	18	1	2	1	0	0	0	0	3	0	0	.111	.167
2013	Inland Empire (CAL)	HiA	.313	136	582	77	182	32	10	11	80	27	106	14	4	.341	.459
2014	Arkansas (TL)	AA	.285	136	544	66	155	38	4	5	77	33	124	6	6	.321	.397
Minor League Totals			.295	335	1388	179	409	83	23	16	184	70	253	29	12	.327	.422

9 NICK TROPEANO, RHP

Born: Aug. 27, 1990. **B-T:** R-R. **Ht:** 6-4. **Wt:** 205. **Drafted:** Stony Brook, 2011 (5th round). **Signed by:** John Kosciak (Astros).

It cost the Angels backup catcher Hank Conger to acquire a low-risk, back-of-the-rotation starter candidate in Tropeano in a November 2014 trade with the Astros. An ace at Stony Brook, Tropeano capped a solid minor league career by beating the Mariners with five innings of work in his big league debut on Sept. 10. Tropeano lowered his walk rate at Triple-A Oklahoma City while keeping his strikeout rate in line with his career numbers. His fringy fastball plays up because of his innate deception, ranging from 90-92 mph and touching 93 on occasion. His changeup is the separator for Tropeano and is his bread and butter offering. It's a plus pitch that he throws at any time in the count and to both lefties and righties. His 78-81 mph slider is fringe-average, and he needs to get on top of the ball to improve the depth on the pitch. Tropeano's delivery is "not the prettiest," one evaluator said, as the righthander jerks his body toward first base after making a pitch. That might end up pushing him to the bullpen. Tropeano will head to spring training with a chance to earn a spot in the big league rotation, but he has two minor league options remaining and could spend ample time at Triple-A Salt Lake.

BA GRADE

45 Risk: Medium

LGE	BF	SO%	BB%	HR/9
PCL	486	24.7	6.8	0.79
AL	91	14.3	9.9	0.00

Year	Club (League)	Class	W	L	ERA	G	GS	CG	SV	IP	H	HR	BB	SO	K/9	WHIP	AVG
2012	Lexington (SAL)	LoA	6	4	2.78	15	14	0	0	87	77	3	26	97	10.0	1.18	.238
	Lancaster (CAL)	HiA	6	3	3.31	12	12	0	0	71	72	8	21	69	8.8	1.32	.265
2013	Corpus Christi (TL)	AA	7	10	4.11	28	20	1	5	134	140	15	39	130	8.8	1.34	.275
2014	Oklahoma City (PCL)	AAA	9	5	3.03	23	20	0	0	125	90	11	33	120	8.7	0.99	.202
	Houston (AL)	MAJ	1	3	4.57	4	4	0	0	22	19	0	9	13	5.4	1.29	.241
Major League Totals			1	3	4.57	4	4	0	0	22	19	0	9	13	5.4	1.29	.241
Minor League Totals			31	24	3.26	90	78	1	5	470	421	38	140	479	9.2	1.19	.241

10 KYLE McGOWIN, RHP

Born: Nov. 27, 1991. **B-T:** R-R. **Ht:** 6-3. **Wt:** 180. **Drafted:** Savanah
State, 2013 (5th round). **Signed by:** Todd Hogan.

The Angels have emphasized pitching in the last two drafts, making
McGowin a fifth-rounder in 2013 from Savannah State. During his last
year in school he led the Tigers to a Mid-Eastern Athletic Conference title
while finishing second among NCAA Division I pitchers in strikeouts
(128). McGowin pitched sparingly in his first pro season, then missed part
of 2014 with an elbow injury. He celebrated on Twitter when he learned he
did not need Tommy John surgery. McGowin throws from a regular three-
quarters arm slot with a repeatable delivery and a clean arm action, but with
a wider slot that gives his pitches good sink. His fastball sits usually in the
90-93 mph range with plus life, and he gets really good action on the two-
seamer. McGowin's best pitch is a plus slider that averages 82 mph, which he
complements with an average changeup at 79-80 mph. His stuff stays down
in the zone, making him a good groundball pitcher. McGowin reached
Double-A Arkansas for one start in 2014 and likely will return there in
2015. He projects as a back-end starter but has to prove he's durable enough to hold up over a full season.

BA GRADE

50 Risk: High

LGE	BF	SO%	BB%	HR/9
CAL	239	20.1	6.7	0.62
TL	21	14.3	0.0	1.80

Year	Club (League)	Class	W	L	ERA	G	GS	CG	SV	IP	H	HR	BB	SO	K/9	WHIP	AVG
2013	Orem (PIO)	R	1	1	6.28	9	1	0	0	14	12	2	5	12	7.5	1.19	.218
2014	Inland Empire (CAL)	HiA	1	5	2.93	10	10	0	0	58	51	4	16	48	7.4	1.15	.236
	Arkansas (TL)	AA	0	1	5.40	1	1	0	0	5	6	1	0	3	5.4	1.20	.286
	Angels (AZL)	R	0	0	0.00	1	1	0	0	2	2	0	1	2	9.0	1.50	.250
Minor League Totals			2	7	3.62	21	13	0	0	80	71	7	22	65	7.3	1.17	.237

11 TAYLOR FEATHERSTON, 2B/SS

BA GRADE:

45 Risk: Medium

Born: Oct. 8, 1989. **B-T:** R-R. **Ht.:** 6-1. **Wt.:** 185. **Drafted:** Texas
Christian, 2011 (5th round). **Signed by:** Dar Cox (Rockies).

Featherston has moved up one level a year since the Rockies drafted him in the fifth round in 2011.
He joined the Angels as a major league Rule 5 pick in December. Featherston has big power for a middle
infielder. He likes to ambush fastballs and attack early, but that approach leads to too big a swing as
Featherston seeks more power. He has a line-drive swing and now hits the ball to the right side more
frequently. He profiles as a utility player in the majors but needs to increase his versatility with more time
at third base. Featherston has enough range and good arm strength at shortstop. He makes instinctive
plays but needs to keep working on staying aggressive and coming through the ball on the routine plays.
Featherston will compete with Grant Green and Josh Rutledge for time around the infield in 2015.

Year	Club (League)	Class	AVG	G	AB	R	H	2B	3B	HR	RBI	BB	SO	SB	CS	OBP	SLG
2012	Asheville (SAL)	LoA	.299	105	378	75	113	30	4	12	53	53	87	15	4	.393	.495
2013	Modesto (CAL)	HiA	.292	116	469	87	137	31	10	13	81	30	110	17	4	.342	.484
2014	Tulsa (TL)	AA	.260	127	497	69	129	33	4	16	57	38	114	14	6	.322	.439
Minor League Totals			.276	397	1513	250	418	102	21	43	211	138	349	49	15	.346	.457

12 JULIO GARCIA, SS

BA GRADE

55 Risk: Extreme

Born: July 31, 1997. **B-T:** R-R. **Ht.:** 6-0. **Wt.:** 175. **Signed:** Dominican
Republic, 2014. **Signed by:** Alfredo Ulloa.

The switch-hitting Garcia garnered little attention during the 2013 international signing period, primarily because he was too small and too slow. The Angels signed the late-blooming Garcia in July 2014
for $565,000. Since signing, he has grown to 6 feet tall and should grow bigger and stronger with age.
Garcia projects to be a plus or better defender with excellent hands, quick-twitch actions at shortstop and
a plus arm. He's flashy and can get careless, and like many young shortstops will likely make a lot of errors
early in his career. Garcia projects as a gap hitter from both sides of the plate when he matures physically.
While still a below-average runner, he could have average speed in time. The difference between Garcia's
current abilities and his future projection is immense, but the Angels believe he may develop into a potential all-star. He will make his domestic debut in the Rookie-level Arizona League in 2015.

Year	Club (League)	Class	AVG	G	AB	R	H	2B	3B	HR	RBI	BB	SO	SB	CS	OBP	SLG
2014	Angels (DSL)	R	.162	18	68	6	11	1	0	0	5	7	19	2	2	.234	.176
Minor League Totals			.162	18	68	6	11	1	0	0	5	7	19	2	2	.234	.176

13 TREVOR GOTT, RHP

BA GRADE	
50	Risk: High

Born: Aug. 26, 1992. **B-T:** R-R. **Ht.:** 6-0. **Wt.:** 190. **Drafted:** Kentucky, 2013 (6th round). **Signed by:** Mark Conner (Padres).

The Angels surrendered four prospects in their July trade with the Padres to acquire closer Huston Street, but they got back one piece for the farm system in Gott. The former Kentucky closer set career and single-season saves records for the Wildcats before being a sixth-round pick in 2013. Gott brings plenty of arm speed from a smaller frame, with a fastball that sits in the 93 mph range, and reportedly has scraped 99, with late armside sink and plus life. His 79-81 mph slider shows life and flashes plus, but it's more of a slurve with just modest vertical break. Primarily a two-pitch reliever, Gott uses his 85 mph changeup infrequently. His delivery features a head jerk at the end, which could affect his command. Gott spent the second half of 2014 at Double-A Arkansas and finished the year with a successful Arizona Fall League stint. He should be ready for Triple-A Salt Lake in 2015 and has the ceiling of a high-leverage reliever

Year	Club (League)	Class	W	L	ERA	G	GS	CG	SV	IP	H	HR	BB	SO	K/9	WHIP	AVG
2013	Eugene (NWL)	SS	0	0	2.08	4	0	0	0	4	4	0	3	8	16.6	1.62	.250
	Fort Wayne (MWL)	LoA	2	2	2.56	27	0	0	4	32	23	1	12	33	9.4	1.11	.205
2014	Lake Elsinore (CAL)	HiA	2	4	3.16	29	0	0	16	31	28	3	9	31	8.9	1.18	.239
	San Antonio (TL)	AA	0	0	4.63	10	0	0	0	12	11	0	9	11	8.5	1.71	.256
	Arkansas (TL)	AA	2	1	1.53	13	0	0	2	18	11	0	7	18	9.2	1.02	.186
Minor League Totals			6	7	2.79	83	0	0	22	97	77	4	40	101	9.4	1.21	.222

14 NATE SMITH, LHP

BA GRADE	
45	Risk: High

Born: Aug. 28, 1991. **B-T:** L-L. **Ht.:** 6-3. **Wt.:** 200. **Drafted:** Furman, 2013 (8th round). **Signed by:** Todd Hogan.

Smith was an economical $12,000 senior sign after the end of his four-year career at Furman, with the Angels taking him in the eighth round in 2013. He jumped to high Class A Inland Empire as the club's No. 1 starter in 2014 before a midseason promotion to Double-A Arkansas. It's all about pitchability and deception for Smith. His fringe-average fastball ranges from 87-91 mph and more often sits in the high 80s, but he pounds the zone with strikes using an high-three-quarters to over-the-top delivery. His best pitch is a plus changeup that he commands well at 76 mph. Smith also has two breaking balls—an average slider in the 80-81 mph range and a slightly below-average curveball in the mid-70s. He's got a solid work ethic, projecting as a back-end starter with a low ceiling but high floor. Smith pitched just as effectively at Double-A as he did in the first half of the season, with a 2.89 ERA and 9.7 strikeouts per nine innings. He could break camp at Triple-A Salt Lake with a good spring training.

Year	Club (League)	Class	W	L	ERA	G	GS	CG	SV	IP	H	HR	BB	SO	K/9	WHIP	AVG
2013	Orem (PIO)	R	2	2	3.86	15	9	0	0	35	34	4	7	31	8.0	1.17	.264
2014	Inland Empire (CAL)	HiA	6	3	3.07	10	10	0	0	56	41	3	14	51	8.2	0.99	.201
	Arkansas (TL)	AA	5	3	2.89	11	11	0	0	62	48	3	30	67	9.7	1.25	.218
Minor League Totals			13	8	3.18	36	30	0	0	153	123	10	51	149	8.8	1.14	.222

15 KODY EAVES, 2B

BA GRADE	
50	Risk: Extreme

Born: July 8, 1993. **B-T:** L-R. **Ht.:** 6-0. **Wt.:** 175. **Drafted:** HS— Pasadena, Texas, 2012 (16th round). **Signed by:** Rudy Vasquez.

A 16th-round pick in 2012 from Pasadena (Texas) Memorial High, Eaves was ready to head to Texas Christian before the Angels signed him for an over-slot $100,000 bonus. The second baseman put himself on the prospect radar in 2014 at low Class A Burlington when he made the Midwest League all-star team. Eaves is an instinctual player who plays with lots of energy. He needs to learn to pace himself to handle the grind of a full season, for he started strongly in 2014 only to tire down the stretch. Eaves has a line-drive, pull approach that results in more doubles than home runs. His instincts on the bases and slightly above-average speed allowed him to steal 25 bases, but he also was caught 10 times. Eaves needs to decide which kind of hitter he wants to be in order to cut down on strikeouts (24 percent). Despite his 30 errors in 2014, Eaves' double-play pivot is at least average, and he's got the potential to be a better defender. The Angels are optimistic about Eaves as he advances to high Class A Inland Empire in 2015.

Year	Club (League)	Class	AVG	G	AB	R	H	2B	3B	HR	RBI	BB	SO	SB	CS	OBP	SLG
2012	Angels (AZL)	R	.261	42	165	25	43	7	5	2	19	16	34	6	0	.328	.400
2013	Orem (PIO)	R	.277	67	264	45	73	14	6	1	24	20	40	22	6	.326	.386
2014	Burlington (MWL)	LoA	.268	130	549	74	147	37	7	10	45	29	142	25	10	.308	.415
Minor League Totals			.269	239	978	144	263	58	18	13	88	65	216	53	16	.317	.405

16 DANNY REYNOLDS, RHP

BA GRADE

45 Risk: High

Born: May 2, 1991. **B-T:** R-R. **Ht.:** 6-0. **Wt.:** 170. **Drafted:** HS—Las Vegas, 2009 (6th round). **Signed by:** Jeff Scholzen.

Drafted by the Angels in the sixth round in 2009, Reynolds pitched just 34 total innings in his first three pro seasons. Finally healthy in 2012, he missed even more time with a 50-game suspension for a drug of abuse. The righthander's first complete season came in 2013, when he logged 26 starts at high Class A Inland Empire but went 11-10, 5.39. Reynolds' career finally took off in 2014 with a move to the bullpen, which suited his aggressive manner on the mound, and he posted a combined 2.90 ERA at three levels. A strong athlete, Reynolds' quick arm allows him to achieve big-time velocity out of a smaller frame. His fastball typically reaches 96-97 mph and has touched triple digits. His slider, called a power slurve by scouts, is at least an average offering. While inconsistent, the pitch is nearly unhittable when Reynolds stays on top of the ball. His high-three-quarters delivery got better when he shortened his stride, allowing him to drive the ball downhill better. Added to the 40-man roster in November, Reynolds faces a probable assignment to Triple-A Salt Lake, with a big league promotion possible in 2015.

Year	Club (League)	Class	W	L	ERA	G	GS	CG	SV	IP	H	HR	BB	SO	K/9	WHIP	AVG
2012	Cedar Rapids (MWL)	LoA	1	3	2.91	11	10	1	0	53	45	4	20	35	6.0	1.23	.237
	Inland Empire (CAL)	HiA	1	3	5.45	6	6	0	0	33	39	3	8	25	6.8	1.42	.298
2013	Inland Empire (CAL)	HiA	11	10	5.39	26	26	0	0	145	144	19	64	114	7.1	1.43	.262
2014	Salt Lake (PCL)	AAA	1	0	0.00	1	0	0	0	2	1	0	1	3	13.5	1.00	.143
	Inland Empire (CAL)	HiA	0	0	1.80	11	0	0	0	20	11	0	7	19	8.6	0.90	.159
	Arkansas (TL)	AA	3	2	3.60	30	0	0	2	40	42	1	15	41	9.2	1.43	.273
Minor League Totals			20	20	4.37	109	42	1	11	327	317	28	121	265	7.3	1.34	.258

17 HUNTER GREEN, LHP

BA GRADE

50 Risk: Extreme

Born: July 12, 1995. **B-T:** L-L. **Ht.:** 6-4. **Wt.:** 175. **Drafted:** HS—Bowling Green, Ky., 2013 (2nd round). **Signed by:** John Burden.

The Angels made Green their top draft selection in 2013, signing him for $942,000 as a second-round pick out of high school. Issues with his back, which affected him as an amateur, flared up again and kept him on the sideline for all of 2014. While he missed a year of development, Green still is younger than many players drafted a year after him, so the Angels don't see his lost year as a major setback. He worked on strengthening his core this year and needs to continue to add weight to his slender frame. Green threw simulated games before the end of the 2014 season, and he intended to pitch in instructional league before he had a setback. When healthy, he pitches with an easy delivery from a low-three-quarters arm slot, which affords him good armside run on his low-90s fastball. He flirted with a quality curveball and changeup in high school, but with just 17 pro innings, he hasn't had time to develop feel for them. He could break camp at low Class A Burlington in 2015 with a productive and healthy spring training, though he most likely faces a spring in extended spring training.

Year	Club (League)	Class	W	L	ERA	G	GS	CG	SV	IP	H	HR	BB	SO	K/9	WHIP	AVG
2013	Angels (AZL)	R	0	1	4.32	8	7	0	0	17	16	0	16	11	5.9	1.92	.254
2014	Did not play—Injured																
Minor League Totals			0	1	4.32	8	7	0	0	17	16	0	16	11	5.9	1.92	.254

18 DREW RUCINSKI, RHP

BA GRADE

45 Risk: High

Born: Dec. 30, 1988. **B-T:** R-R. **Ht.:** 6-2. **Wt.:** 190. **Signed:** Frontier League, 2011. **Signed by:** Junie Melendez (Indians).

Rucinski's pro career sounds like the storyline for a future Disney Studio sports movie, with a path that took the Ohio State alum from the independent Frontier League to the big leagues in less than a year. Undrafted in 2011, the righthander signed with Rockford, where he made one appearance before the Indians signed him. Rucinski advanced to low Class A Lake County in 2011, but Cleveland released him following spring training in 2012, so he headed back to the Frontier League. The Angels signed him in August 2013 to plug a hole at high Class A Inland Empire. Rucinski made the Double-A Arkansas team out of spring training in 2014 and quickly became the Travelers' top starter. Los Angeles summoned him to the majors on two occasions, once in July and then again as a September callup. Rucinski pitches with a herky-jerky delivery that adds deception and allows him to pitch up in the zone. His 91-94 mph fastball has riding life, and he throws an 84 mph splitter as his out pitch. He rounds out his arsenal with a fringy slider and changeup, both which are delivered around 80 mph. He's got strong work habits and shows maturity on the mound. Rucinski will report to spring training hoping to continue his unlikely adventure.

Year	Club (League)	Class	W	L	ERA	G	GS	CG	SV	IP	H	HR	BB	SO	K/9	WHIP	AVG
2012	Rockford (FRN)	IND	7	4	3.13	22	15	1	1	104	96	9	26	91	7.9	1.18	--
2013	Rockford (FRN)	IND	4	6	2.88	15	15	2	0	100	86	4	27	101	9.1	1.13	--
	Inland Empire (CAL)	HiA	2	2	1.86	5	5	0	0	29	29	0	4	21	6.5	1.14	.266
2014	Arkansas (TL)	AA	10	6	3.15	26	26	2	0	149	142	7	41	140	8.5	1.23	.257
	Los Angeles (AL)	MAJ	0	0	4.91	3	0	0	0	7	9	0	2	8	9.8	1.50	.290
Major League Totals			0	0	4.91	3	0	0	0	7	9	0	2	8	9.8	1.50	.290
Minor League Totals			16	8	2.93	53	31	2	0	215	207	10	55	208	8.7	1.22	.259

19 JAKE JEWELL, RHP

BA GRADE

50 Risk: Extreme

Born: May 16, 1993. **B-T:** R-R. **Ht.:** 6-3. **Wt.:** 200. **Drafted:** Northeastern Oklahoma A&M JC, 2014 (5th round). **Signed by:** Drew Chadd.

After struggling in the rotation as a freshman at Northeastern Oklahoma A&M JC, Jewell worked as a closer in his second year, saving eight games for the Golden Norsemen in 2014. The Angels signed their 2014 fifth-round pick for $250,000. He moved back into a starting role in his first pro season, and he pitched effectively in the Rookie-level Arizona League. Jewell throws four pitches for strikes and all project to play as a tick above-average. His fastball gets up to 96 mph and sits 92-94 with late tail. Jewell's curveball is a hard 11-to-5 downer, with his other breaking ball a power slider at 84-86 mph. He also works in a 78 mph changeup that features some fade. He delivers his four-pitch mix with a repeatable high-three-quarters delivery, and he has a loose arm and strong build. While some scouts think Jewell will wind up in the bullpen, the Angels believe he has the pitches and strength to start.

Year	Club (League)	Class	W	L	ERA	G	GS	CG	SV	IP	H	HR	BB	SO	K/9	WHIP	AVG
2014	Angels (AZL)	R	1	0	1.48	9	6	0	0	30	23	0	12	26	7.7	1.15	.213
	Orem (PIO)	R	0	2	8.76	3	3	0	0	12	22	1	4	9	6.6	2.11	.386
Minor League Totals			1	2	3.59	12	9	0	0	43	45	1	16	35	7.4	1.43	.273

20 JOSE SUAREZ, LHP

BA GRADE

50 Risk: Extreme

Born: Jan. 3, 1998. **B-T:** L-L. **Ht.:** 5-10. **Wt.:** 170. **Signed:** Venezuela, 2014. **Signed by:** Lebi Ochoa/Carlos Ramirez.

The buzz on Suarez began early in 2014 instructional league. Suarez was an unheralded signing earlier in the year for $300,000, and he impressed observers with his smooth delivery, competitive nature and advanced pitchability for a teenager. His general feel for his craft is impressive. He probably won't develop better than average velocity, and he pitches at 88 mph now. Already physically mature with a solid core, Suarez might add a tick to his heater as he grows taller. He gets decent plane from his high-three-quarters delivery with all of his pitches coming from the same slot. His average changeup is his best pitch, and a 74-77 mph curveball with snap has improved since signing. He already shows above-average control of the running game. Suarez's ordinary stuff and feel for the strike zone has earned him comparisons with Royals lefthander Jason Vargas. He will make his pro debut in the Rookie-level Arizona League in 2015.

Year	Club (League)	Class	W	L	ERA	G	GS	CG	SV	IP	H	HR	BB	SO	K/9	WHIP	AVG
2014	Did not play—Signed 2015 contract																

21 JETT BANDY, C

BA GRADE

40 Risk: Medium

Born: March 26, 1990. **B-T:** R-R. **Ht.:** 6-4. **Wt.:** 235. **Drafted:** Arizona, 2011 (31st round). **Signed by:** John Gracio.

Bandy became the primary catcher at Double-A Arkansas in 2014 when his bat began to show more life. The 31st-round pick from Arizona in 2011 previously had been viewed strictly as a good catch-and-throw receiver. While he lacks bat speed, Bandy is a big-bodied athlete with pull power who took a more relaxed approach at the plate and became a more selective hitter. Pitchers love throwing to Bandy because of his size and agility coupled with the fact that he calls a good game and blocks well. He's got a plus arm, throwing out 40 percent of basestealers in 2014, up from 32 percent the previous year. Like most catchers, he's a below-average runner. Bandy will move up to Triple-A Salt Lake in 2015 following his offseason addition to the 40-man roster, and he has a shot to have a career as a valuable big league backup.

Year	Club (League)	Class	AVG	G	AB	R	H	2B	3B	HR	RBI	BB	SO	SB	CS	OBP	SLG
2012	Inland Empire (CAL)	HiA	.247	94	324	42	80	22	1	7	46	20	51	1	1	.318	.386
2013	Arkansas (TL)	AA	.241	78	245	26	59	17	2	4	28	14	39	0	1	.303	.376
2014	Arkansas (TL)	AA	.250	93	312	38	78	12	0	13	40	33	63	2	4	.348	.413
Minor League Totals			.257	315	1066	141	274	70	3	29	146	77	176	5	6	.337	.410

22 EDUAR LOPEZ, RHP

Born: Feb. 21, 1995. **B-T:** R-R. **Ht.:** 6-0. **Wt.:** 180. **Signed:** Dominican
Republic, 2012. **Signed by:** Roman Ocumarez.

BA GRADE

50 Risk: Extreme

Lopez is another example of the effectiveness of the Angels international scouting department when it comes to finding Latin players who don't get scooped up immediately at the July 2 international signing period. Eligible in 2011, Lopez instead signed in February 2012 for $45,000. Unrefined when he signed, he spent two years in the Dominican Summer League before making his U.S. debut in the Rookie-level Arizona League in 2014. Lopez has a strong, stocky body built for durability, and he delivers an over-powering four-seam fastball up to 96 mph. His putaway pitch is an overhand curveball that he throws 78-83 mph. One of the goals for Lopez in 2014 was to develop a changeup, and he now throws it as a hard pitch from 88-90 mph that looks like a sinking two-seamer. His control isn't bad for a young power pitcher, but needs to be more fine. The biggest question regarding Lopez's future is whether he develops more of a feel for pitching. He'll remain in the rotation for now but may profile better out of the bullpen.

Year	Club (League)	Class	W	L	ERA	G	GS	CG	SV	IP	H	HR	BB	SO	K/9	WHIP	AVG
2012	Angels (DSL)	R	2	1	3.54	12	11	0	0	53	42	5	23	83	14.0	1.22	.212
2013	Angels (DSL)	R	6	3	1.88	14	13	0	0	62	27	0	42	83	12.0	1.11	.132
2014	Angels (AZL)	R	0	3	4.68	11	8	0	0	42	41	1	25	53	11.3	1.56	.258
Minor League Totals			8	7	3.19	37	32	0	0	158	110	6	90	219	12.5	1.27	.196

23 ERIC STAMETS, SS

Born: Sept. 25, 1991. **B-T:** R-R. **Ht.:** 6-0. **Wt.:** 185. **Drafted:** Evansville,
2012 (6th round). **Signed by:** John Burden.

BA GRADE

40 Risk: Medium

Stamets was the highest-drafted player from Evansville in 24 years when the Angels took the shortstop in the sixth round in 2012, though that honor now goes to Rockies lefthander Kyle Freeland, a 2014 first-round pick. Stamets would be one of the top prospects in baseball if he could hit as well as he plays defense. He's a plus defender with sure hands, quick feet, excellent range and a strong, accurate arm, and he's the best athlete in the organization. He also is an average runner and opportunistic basestealer. At the plate, Stamets is a slap hitter with a short stroke who makes weak contact. He's got a little power when he makes good contact, but he lacks consistency at the plate. He could have a major league career as a utility infielder based strictly on his defense. Stamets will advance to Triple-A Salt Lake in 2015 and could get a call to the big leagues if the Angels need a slick-fielding reserve infielder.

Year	Club (League)	Class	AVG	G	AB	R	H	2B	3B	HR	RBI	BB	SO	SB	CS	OBP	SLG
2012	Cedar Rapids (MWL)	LoA	.274	62	248	34	68	13	1	1	20	15	35	7	2	.323	.347
2013	Inland Empire (CAL)	HiA	.281	126	506	80	142	28	4	4	53	34	66	16	4	.335	.375
2014	Arkansas (TL)	AA	.235	106	344	46	81	13	1	4	23	24	62	11	1	.293	.314
Minor League Totals			.265	294	1098	160	291	54	6	9	96	73	163	34	7	.319	.350

24 KALEB COWART, 3B

Born: June 2, 1992. **B-T:** B-R. **Ht.:** 6-3. **Wt.:** 225. **Drafted:** HS—Adel,
Ga., 2010 (1st round). **Signed by:** Chris McAlpin.

BA GRADE

45 Risk: High

Cowart embarked on a good career path during his first couple of years after the Angels selected the High School Player of the Year with the first of three first-round picks in 2010. The switch-hitting third baseman ranked as the Angels' top prospect in 2013 after a breakthrough year at two Class A levels, but Cowart hit a wall at Double-A Arkansas, batting a cumulative .222/.286/.312 in more than a 1,000 Texas League plate appearances. He's got plenty of raw power but doesn't get to it in games. At times he looks comfortable in the batter's box, and other times he's leaking forward and doesn't keep his weight balanced. Cowart still grades as a plus defender at the hot corner with an elite arm that grades as a double-plus tool, and he has excellent makeup. The Angels instructed Cowart to bat strictly lefthanded during his time in the Arizona Fall League to allow him to focus on improving one side, so that he could then mirror the improvements with his natural right side. He also was highly regarded as a pitcher during his high school days, so if he doesn't make strides at the plate, a switch to the mound is a strong possibility in the future.

Year	Club (League)	Class	AVG	G	AB	R	H	2B	3B	HR	RBI	BB	SO	SB	CS	OBP	SLG
2012	Cedar Rapids (MWL)	LoA	.293	66	263	42	77	16	3	9	54	22	44	9	4	.348	.479
	Inland Empire (CAL)	HiA	.259	69	263	48	68	15	4	7	49	45	67	5	3	.366	.426
2013	Arkansas (TL)	AA	.221	132	498	48	110	20	1	6	42	38	124	14	5	.279	.301
2014	Arkansas (TL)	AA	.223	126	435	48	97	18	4	6	54	43	99	26	7	.295	.324
Minor League Totals			.247	472	1768	236	437	81	15	36	246	174	423	65	23	.316	.371

25 CARLOS PEREZ, C

BA GRADE

40 Risk: Medium

Born: Oct. 27, 1990. **B-T:** R-R. **Ht.:** 6-0. **Wt.:** 210. **Signed:** Venezuela, 2008. **Signed by:** Rafael Moncado (Blue Jays).

Lost in a logjam of catchers with the Blue Jays, Perez joined the Astros in July 2012 as part of the 10-player deal that sent lefthander J.A. Happ to Toronto. Something similar happened in Houston, where catchers such as Roberto Pena, Max Stassi, Tyler Heineman, Rene Garcia and Jacob Nottingham put Perez behind the eight ball. As such, the Astros traded Pena, along with righthander Nick Tropeano, to the Angels in November 2014 for big league catcher Hank Conger. The Astros liked Perez's defensive tools, grading him an above-average defender with good pop times on throws to second base and a solid arm. However, he still ranked behind Pena in those areas, and the players were too similar offensively to justify keeping both. The bat is the question with Perez, for he makes good contact but doesn't drive the ball due to below-average bat speed. Pitchers like throwing to him, giving him a ceiling as a solid backup catcher. He'll head to spring training with a good shot at replacing Conger as the Angels' backup to starter Chris Iannetta.

Year	Club (League)	Class	AVG	G	AB	R	H	2B	3B	HR	RBI	BB	SO	SB	CS	OBP	SLG
2012	Lansing (MWL)	LoA	.275	71	273	48	75	22	5	5	40	35	38	3	2	.358	.447
	Lancaster (CAL)	HiA	.318	26	88	11	28	6	1	0	10	6	17	0	1	.368	.409
2013	Corpus Christi (TL)	AA	.283	16	53	6	15	4	0	1	5	4	11	0	0	.356	.415
	Oklahoma City (PCL)	AAA	.269	75	264	29	71	14	0	2	32	25	39	1	1	.328	.345
2014	Oklahoma City (PCL)	AAA	.259	88	301	33	78	16	2	6	34	29	54	3	0	.323	.385
Minor League Totals			.277	538	1934	273	536	111	27	20	253	238	325	29	19	.359	.393

26 GREG MAHLE, LHP

BA GRADE

40 Risk: Medium

Born: April 17, 1993. **B-T:** L-L. **Ht.:** 6-2. **Wt.:** 230. **Drafted:** UC Santa Barbara, 2014 (15th round). **Signed by:** Dan Cox.

One of the more intriguing players in the system, Mahle is a kind of a Swiss army knife who throws a wide variety of pitches from a variety of arm angles. His fastball usually ranges from 90-93 mph from a high-three-quarters delivery and 86-90 mph when he's throwing sidearm or lower. His slider velocity ranges from 75-82 mph, depending on arm slot. His above-average curveball has screwball action and is thrown at 78-80 mph with hard fade, which makes Mahle effective against righthanders and could make him more than a matchup reliever. His changeup with good action earns a plus grade. His delivery, complete with a head snap, isn't pretty, but he stays online to the plate. When Mahle uses his submarine delivery, the ball comes to the batter at an unusual angle, making it hard to pick up. Mahle could move quickly, perhaps even making it to the big leagues in 2015.

Year	Club (League)	Class	W	L	ERA	G	GS	CG	SV	IP	H	HR	BB	SO	K/9	WHIP	AVG
2014	Orem (PIO)	R	1	1	0.00	5	0	0	1	8	5	0	3	11	12.4	1.00	.172
	Burlington (MWL)	LoA	0	1	3.38	18	0	0	1	29	20	1	12	38	11.7	1.09	.190
Minor League Totals			1	2	2.65	23	0	0	2	37	25	1	15	49	11.8	1.07	.187

27 NATANAEL DELGADO, OF

BA GRADE

50 Risk: Extreme

Born: Oct. 23, 1995. **B-T:** L-L. **Ht.:** 6-1. **Wt.:** 185. **Signed:** Dominican Republic, 2012 **Signed by:** Roman Ocumarez.

One of the more projectable power bats on the international market in 2012, Delgado signed with the Angels for $280,000. He debuted at age 17 in the Arizona League in 2013 and followed with a stop in the Pioneer League in 2014, making the Top 20 Prospect lists for both Rookie-level leagues. Delgado has gotten stronger and thicker since signing, giving him plus raw power but also reducing his speed and arm strength. He's now projected as a bat-only left fielder who will have to continue to hit to have value. He has struggled to stay healthy in his two pro seasons, being hit in the face with a pitch before his debut season and suffering a concussion late in 2014. Delgado has extremely strong hands and above-average bat speed, giving him power to all fields. He is very comfortable in the batter's box with a solid approach, and he handles lefthanders well. Delgado hasn't made much progress on defense and is a below-average runner, but he should be serviceable in left field. He's ready to move to full-season ball with an assignment to low Class A Burlington in 2015.

Year	Club (League)	Class	AVG	G	AB	R	H	2B	3B	HR	RBI	BB	SO	SB	CS	OBP	SLG
2013	Angels (AZL)	R	.271	51	192	23	52	16	2	3	33	11	43	4	0	.311	.422
2014	Orem (PIO)	R	.301	38	153	23	46	8	4	3	21	5	34	4	0	.333	.464
Minor League Totals			.284	89	345	46	98	24	6	6	54	16	77	8	0	.321	.441

28 CHAD HINSHAW, OF

BA GRADE

45 Risk: High

Born: Sept. 10, 1990. **B-T:** R-R. **Ht.:** 6-1. **Wt.:** 205. **Drafted:** Illinois State, 2013 (15th round). **Signed by:** Joel Murrie.

Merely a name on the organization's center-field depth chart after being selected in the 15th round in 2013, Hinshaw boosted his stock with a strong 2014 season split between low Class A Burlington and high Class A Inland Empire. The four-year starter at Illinois State batted a cumulative .270/.365/.477 with 16 home runs and 41 stolen bases. Hinshaw has a high baseball IQ and is an average defender in center field with a good arm and good first step. He's an above-average defender in the corners, with an average arm that will allow him to handle all three positions. A plus runner, Hinshaw uses his speed effectively on defense and on the bases. His improvement as a hitter came when he learned to drive the ball with a shorter swing in the zone, though he still swings and misses frequently. Already 24, Hinshaw may be ready for an assignment to Double-A Arkansas in 2015, and his combination of solid tools could spell a future as an extra outfielder in the majors.

Year	Club (League)	Class	AVG	G	AB	R	H	2B	3B	HR	RBI	BB	SO	SB	CS	OBP	SLG
2013	Orem (PIO)	R	.258	26	89	24	23	2	0	0	8	13	21	9	1	.412	.281
2014	Burlington (MWL)	LoA	.282	59	206	51	58	13	3	6	24	28	63	25	8	.403	.461
	Inland Empire (CAL)	HiA	.261	65	264	49	69	14	8	10	46	15	65	16	7	.333	.489
Minor League Totals			.268	150	559	124	150	29	11	16	78	56	149	50	16	.373	.445

29 CAL TOWEY, 3B/OF

BA GRADE

45 Risk: High

Born: Feb. 6, 1990. **B-T:** L-R. **Ht.:** 6-1. **Wt.:** 215. **Drafted:** Baylor, 2013 (17th round). **Signed by:** Rudy Vasquez.

As a four-year starter at Baylor, Towey was playing below his experience level in his debut at Rookie-level Orem in 2013, when he led the Pioneer League with a phenomenal .492 on-base percentage. The Angels jumped the lefthanded hitter two levels to high Class A Inland Empire in 2014 and Towey followed with a solid season there. He possesses an excellent batting eye, but that selectivity contributed to his high strikeout total (137) because he needs to not take so many called third strikes. He's more of a gap-top-gap hitter, though he maximizes his average raw power in games. A tick below-average runner who is aggressive on the bases, Towey saw time behind the plate during spring training in 2014, but the Angels didn't see the development necessary for the experiment to continue. He's an average defender at third base and is working hard to quicken his feet. He also can handle a corner outfield position with his above-average arm strength. Scouts see a fringy bat with some position versatility, which may allow Towey to get big league time in a multi-positional role. He moves to Double-A Arkansas in 2015.

Year	Club (League)	Class	AVG	G	AB	R	H	2B	3B	HR	RBI	BB	SO	SB	CS	OBP	SLG
2013	Orem (PIO)	R	.317	70	230	69	73	16	6	8	53	67	59	13	3	.492	.543
2014	Inland Empire (CAL)	HiA	.279	128	477	72	133	24	6	10	63	51	137	21	15	.364	.417
Minor League Totals			.291	198	707	141	206	40	12	18	116	118	196	34	18	.411	.458

30 KEYNAN MIDDLETON, RHP

BA GRADE

50 Risk: Extreme

Born: Sept. 12, 1993. **B-T:** R-R. **Ht.:** 6-2. **Wt.:** 185. **Drafted:** Lane (Ore.) CC, 2013 (3rd round). **Signed by:** Jason Ellison.

The Angels knew when they drafted Middleton in the third round in 2013 that he would be a long-term project. He was more of a basketball player in junior college, but instead he decided to pursue a career on the mound. He's very athletic but never really focused on baseball until turning pro. Middleton is still very inconsistent with his delivery but showed improvement in 2014 in a return trip to Rookie-level Orem. He struggles to repeat his high-three-quarter delivery, and he doesn't always have the same delivery from the windup and stretch positions. His fastball ranges from 92-95 mph, and he's starting to show more consistency with the 82-83 hard curveball. His changeup, which he'll need to develop to remain in the rotation, is still a work in progress. Middleton was at his best in two outings during the Pioneer League playoffs, when he didn't give up an earned run in a combined seven innings, striking out 11 batters. The Angels will hope that he can ride that momentum into his first full-season assignment in 2015.

Year	Club (League)	Class	W	L	ERA	G	GS	CG	SV	IP	H	HR	BB	SO	K/9	WHIP	AVG
2013	Orem (PIO)	R	1	3	8.10	6	6	0	0	23	29	4	15	15	5.8	1.89	.319
	Angels (AZL)	R	0	0	6.35	4	1	0	0	6	3	0	3	5	7.9	1.06	.143
2014	Orem (PIO)	R	5	4	6.45	14	14	0	0	67	69	9	30	53	7.1	1.48	.260
Minor League Totals			6	7	6.84	24	21	0	0	96	101	13	48	73	6.8	1.55	.268

Los Angeles Dodgers

BY BEN BADLER

After winning 94 games behind Major League Player of the Year Clayton Kershaw and capturing the National League West title for the second straight season, the Dodgers weren't exactly in desperate need of a major overhaul. Yet after the 2014 season ended with the Dodgers eliminated in the first round of the playoffs, widespread change began quickly, starting at the top.

General manager Ned Colletti, who reached the playoffs five times in his nine seasons running the team, was pushed aside and retained as a senior advisor when the Dodgers hired Rays general manager Andrew Friedman to run the show as the president of baseball operations, signing him to a five-year, $35 million contract.

Friedman brought aboard Athletics assistant GM Farhan Zaidi as his GM; former Padres GM Josh Byrnes as vice president of baseball operations; Billy Gasparino as scouting director, after he served in the same role for the Padres; and Gabe Kapler as farm director.

Friedman also hired two top Red Sox scouts, adding David Finley as VP of international and amateur scouting and Galen Carr as the director of player personnel.

Meanwhile, the organization lost three of its top people, with scouting director Logan White going to the Padres, national crosschecker Roy Clark going back to the Braves and farm director De Jon Watson becoming the Diamondbacks' VP of baseball operations. White was one of the Dodgers' longest-tenured employees, having run the scouting department with various titles for most of the last dozen years.

The shuffling of all the cooks in the kitchen is only the beginning. Second baseman Dee Gordon is out, replaced by Howie Kendrick from the Angels, with more changes on the way.

Baseball's fattest payroll commands the most attention when it comes to the Dodgers, but the organization has built one of the game's better farm systems, especially at the top. Aside from the Cubs, the Dodgers' top three prospects are as strong as any other organization's in baseball. Corey Seager, a shortstop for now who likely moves to third base, is one of the most talented hitters in the minors. Center fielder Joc Pederson is a 2015 Rookie of the Year frontrunner, while teenage lefthander Julio Urias has the makings of a future ace, combining plus stuff with the feel for pitching beyond his years.

After the vaunted trio, the Dodgers farm system is in a better place than it was a year ago because of the emergence of depth beyond them. Their top 2014 draft picks—first-round righthander

Homegrown ace Clayton Kershaw was the BA Major League Player of the Year

TOP PROSPECTS OF THE DECADE

Year	Player, Pos.	2014 Org
2005	Joel Guzman, ss/of	Out of baseball
2006	Chad Billingsley, rhp	Dodgers
2007	Andy LaRoche, 3b	Blue Jays
2008	Clayton Kershaw, lhp	Dodgers
2009	Andrew Lambo, of	Pirates
2010	Dee Gordon, ss	Dodgers
2011	Dee Gordon, ss	Dodgers
2012	Zach Lee, rhp	Dodgers
2013	Hyun-Jin Ryu, lhp	Dodgers
2014	Joc Pederson, of	Dodgers

Grant Holmes and outfielder Alex Verdugo—both had strong debuts and look like potential impact talents.

Aside from Ross Stripling missing 2014 after having Tommy John surgery, Zach Lee was the only major disappointment among the team's top prospects. The rest of the system is filled with players who took steps forward in 2014, such as righthander Jose De Leon who went from a 23rd-rounder in 2013 to looking like a potential mid-rotation starter or better, and outfielder Scott Schebler, who led the Double-A Southern League in homers, triples and slugging percentage.

Ownership has given Friedman money, big league talent and a strong farm system to work with, with the understanding that making the playoffs is no longer good enough.

TOM DiPACE

General manager: Farhan Zaidi. **Farm director:** Gabe Kapler. **Scouting director:** Billy Gasparino.

Class	Team	League	W	L	PCT	Finish	Manager
Majors	Los Angeles Dodgers	National	94	68	.580	4th (30)	Don Mattingly
Triple-A	*Albuquerque Isotopes	Pacific Coast	62	80	.437	14th (16)	Damon Berryhill
Double-A	†Chattanooga Lookouts	Southern	61	77	.442	8th (10)	Razor Shines
High A	Rancho Cucamonga Quakes	California	65	75	.464	8th (10)	P.J. Forbes
Low A	Great Lakes Loons	Midwest	66	73	.475	10th (16)	Bill Haselman
Rookie	Ogden Raptors	Pioneer	37	38	.493	6th (8)	Jack McDowell
Rookie	AZL Dodgers	Arizona	25	31	.446	9th (13)	John Shoemaker
Overall Minor League Record			316	374	.458	26th (30)	

* Affiliate will be Oklahoma City (Pacific Coast) in 2015. † Affiliate will be Tulsa (Texas) in 2015.

THIS YEAR'S TOP 30

No.	Player, Pos.	Grade
1.	Corey Seager, ss	70/Medium
2.	Joc Pederson, of	65/Low
3.	Julio Urias, lhp	70/High
4.	Grant Holmes, rhp	60/High
5.	Alex Verdugo, of	55/High
6.	Jose De Leon, rhp	55/High
7.	Chris Anderson, rhp	55/High
8.	Scott Schebler, of	50/Medium
9.	Tom Windle, lhp	50/High
10.	Chris Reed, lhp	45/Medium
11.	Julian Leon, c	50/High
12.	Yimi Garcia, rhp	45/Medium
13.	Zach Lee, rhp	45/Medium
14.	Pedro Baez, rhp	45/Medium
15.	Austin Barnes, c/2b/3b	45/Medium
16.	Darnell Sweeney, 2b	45/Medium
17.	Ross Stripling, rhp	50/Extreme
18.	Erisbel Arruebarrena, ss	40/Low
19.	Zach Bird, rhp	50/Extreme
20.	Cody Bellinger, 1b	50/Extreme
21.	Alexander Guerrero, 2b	45/High
22.	Jharel Cotton, rhp	45/High
23.	Jacob Rhame, rhp	45/High
24.	John Richy, rhp	45/High
25.	Carlos Frias, rhp	40/Low
26.	Chris O'Brien, c	45/High
27.	Jeff Brigham, rhp	50/Extreme
28.	Brock Stewart, rhp	45/High
29.	A.J. Vanegas, rhp	45/High
30.	Kyle Farmer, rhp	40/High

LAST YEAR'S TOP 30

No.	Player, Pos.	Status
1.	Joc Pederson, of	No. 2
2.	Corey Seager, ss	No. 1
3.	Julio Urias, lhp	No. 3
4.	Zach Lee, rhp	No. 13
5.	Chris Anderson, rhp	No. 7
6.	Chris Withrow, rhp	Majors
7.	Alexander Guerrero, 2b	No. 21
8.	Chris Reed, lhp	No. 10
9.	Onelki Garcia, lhp	(White Sox)
10.	Ross Stripling, rhp	No. 17
11.	Jose Dominguez, rhp	(Rays)
12.	Tom Windle, lhp	No. 9
13.	Yimi Garcia, rhp	No. 12
14.	Cody Bellinger, 1b	No. 20
15.	Jacob Scavuzzo, of	Dropped out
16.	Matt Magill, rhp	(Reds)
17.	Scott Schebler, of	No. 8
18.	Justin Chigbogu, 1b	Dropped out
19.	Pedro Baez, rhp	No. 14
20.	Victor Gonzalez, lhp	Dropped out
21.	Zach Bird, rhp	No. 19
22.	Jesmuel Valentin, 2b/ss	(Phillies)
23.	Ibandel Isabel, of	Dropped out
24.	Hector Nelo, rhp	(Reds)
25.	Darnell Sweeney, ss/2b	No. 16
26.	Tyler Ogle, 1b/c	Dropped out
27.	Jon Garcia, of	Dropped out
28.	Ariel Sandoval, of	Dropped out
29.	Victor Arano, rhp	(Phillies)
30.	Brandon Dixon, 3b	Dropped out

BEST TOOLS

Best Hitter for Average	Corey Seager
Best Power Hitter	Joc Pederson
Best Strike-Zone Discipline	Austin Barnes
Fastest Baserunner	James Baldwin III
Best Athlete	James Baldwin III
Best Fastball	Jacob Rhame
Best Curveball	Julio Urias
Best Slider	Tom Windle
Best Changeup	Julio Urias
Best Control	Yimi Garcia
Best Defensive Catcher	Spencer Navin
Best Defensive Infielder	Erisbel Arruebarrena
Best Infield Arm	Erisbel Arruebarrena
Best Defensive Outfielder	Joc Pederson
Best Outfield Arm	Johan Mieses

PROJECTED 2018 LINEUP

Catcher	Julian Leon
First Base	Adrian Gonzalez
Second Base	Howie Kendrick
Third Base	Corey Seager
Shortstop	Erisbel Arruebarrena
Left Field	Alex Verdugo
Center Field	Joc Pederson
Right Field	Yasiel Puig
No. 1 Starter	Clayton Kershaw
No. 2 Starter	Zack Greinke
No. 3 Starter	Julio Urias
No. 4 Starter	Hyun-Jin Ryu
No. 5 Starter	Grant Holmes
Closer	Kenley Jansen

LOS ANGELES DODGERS

TOP 2015 ROOKIE: Joc Pederson, of. On most clubs, he would have already been up in 2014, but now he's a strong Rookie of the Year candidate.

BREAKOUT PROSPECT: Julian Leon, c. The offensive-minded backstop could become one of the game's best catching prospects if he continues his hot hitting.

SLEEPER: Johan Mieses, of. He's ready to bring his slightly above-average raw power and plus arm to the U.S. after two years in the DSL.

SOURCE OF TOP 30 TALENT			
Homegrown	29	Acquired	1
College	13	Trades	1
Junior college	2	Rule 5 draft	0
High school	7	Independent leagues	0
Draft-and-follow	0	Free agents/waivers	0
Nondrafted free agents	0		
International	7		

LF	CF	RF
Scott Schebler (8)	Joc Pederson (2)	Alex Verdugo (5)
Jared Walker	Noel Cuevas	Johan Mieses
Ibandel Isabel	James Baldwin III	Michael Medina
Jacob Scavuzzo	Devan Ahart	Romer Cuadrado
		Joey Curletta
		Jeremy Rathjen

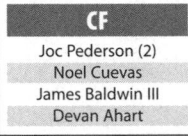

3B	SS	2B	1B
Corey Seager (1)	Erisbel Arruebarrena (18)	Darnell Sweeney (16)	Cody Bellinger (20)
	Moises Perez	Alex Guerrero (21)	Justin Chigbogu
		Enrique Hernandez	O'Koyea Dickson
		Brandon Dixon	

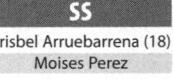
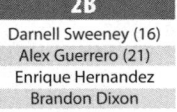

C
Julian Leon (11)
Austin Barnes (15)
Chris O'Brien (26)
Kyle Farmer (30)
Spencer Navin
Tyler Ogle

LHP		RHP	
LHSP	**LHRP**	**RHSP**	**RHRP**
Julio Urias (3)	Adam Liberatore	Grant Holmes (4)	Yimi Garcia (12)
Tom Windle (9)	Daniel Coulombe	Jose De Leon (6)	Pedro Baez (14)
Chris Reed (10)	Victor Gonzalez	Chris Anderson (7)	Jacob Rhame (23)
Jairo Pacheco	Michael Johnson	Zach Lee (13)	Carlos Frias (25)
		Ross Stripling (17)	Jeff Brigham (27)
		Zach Bird (19)	Brock Stewart (28)
		Jharel Cotton (22)	A.J. Vanegas (29)
		John Richy (24)	Kyle Farmer (30)
		Mike Bolsinger	Victor Araujo
		Scott Barlow	Ralston Cash
		William Soto	

2014

BEST PURE HITTER: Most teams seemed to prefer OF Alex Verdugo (2) on the mound as a lefthander. He wanted to hit, though, and the Dodgers like his overall offensive profile. He repeats his swing and has bat speed to go with impressive strike-zone judgment (20 walks, 18 strikeouts in his debut).

BEST POWER HITTER: In some ways, Verdugo's profile resembles that of Joc Pederson. Pederson has bigger power, but Verdugo should have average or better home run pop eventually, while making more contact than Pederson. The Dodgers project 3B Jared Walker (5) with future above-average power as well.

FASTEST RUNNER: Verdugo and OF Devin Ahart (16) have above-average speed, and the savvy Verdugo stole 11 bases in his debut without getting caught.

BEST DEFENSIVE PLAYER: Verdugo has the tools and arm strength (he regularly hit 92 mph last summer) to be a profile right fielder, and he's athletic enough to handle center field for now.

BEST FASTBALL: Dodgers scouts put consistent 70s on RHP Grant Holmes' (1) heater, reaching up to 97 mph and sitting 94-96 every time out. He uses his fastball aggressively as well. RHP Jeff Brigham (4) hit 97 mph early in the spring and has plus sink that helps him get ground balls by the bushel. RHP A.J. Vanegas (11) also can hit 97.

BEST SECONDARY PITCH: Holmes calls his breaking ball a power curve while the Dodgers consider it a plus slider. It's late and sharp at 83 mph when he's going well, and he throws it for strikes.

BEST PRO DEBUT: Verdugo hit .353/.421/.511 between two Rookie-ball levels. Ahart hit .344/.376/.463 overall, mostly at Rookie-level Ogden and also at low Class A Great Lakes. Vanegas struck out 33 and gave up just four runs in 27 innings.

BEST ATHLETE: RHP Kam Uter (12), signed for $200,000, was once committed to Vanderbilt to play football as a wide receiver before deciding to focus on baseball.

MOST INTRIGUING BACKGROUND: Holmes' older brother Colby pitches in the Braves system. RHP Brock Stewart (6), a two-way player at Illinois State, is the son of Jeff Stewart, former Illinois State coach and current area scout for the Padres. Unsigned RHP Sam Moore (40) led Division I with 23 saves, one shy of the single-season record.

CLOSEST TO THE MAJORS: Vanegas has had trouble staying healthy as an amateur, but if does, he won't need much matriculation in the minors.

BEST LATE-ROUND PICK: Uter flashed a good curveball, his fastball has reached 92 and he has a fairly clean arm action. At 6-foot-3, 200 pounds, his body has projection left, particularly as he focuses solely on baseball.

THE ONE WHO GOT AWAY: The Dodgers intended to sign LHP Christian Trent (29), an eligible sophomore who helped Ole Miss reach the College World Series last spring, but couldn't reach an agreement.

ASSESSMENT: Holmes and Verdugo will carry the load in a top-heavy group, though the development of Uter and college picks like Richy, Brigham and Vanegas would help deepen the class.

2013

Top picks RHP Chris Anderson (1) and LHP Tom Windle (2) had ups and downs in the high Class A California League. 1B Cody Bellinger (4) gives the Dodgers a unique, non-profile prospect.

GRADE: C

2012

SS Corey Seager (1) led the minors in batting in 2014 and has star potential. Three relievers—LHPs Paco Rodriguez (2), Onelki Garcia (3) and Danny Coulombe (25)—have reached the majors. RHPs Ross Stripling (5) and Zach Bird (9) and 2B Darnell Sweeney (13) have upside to be regulars.

GRADE: A

2011

LHP Chris Reed (1) has stalled at Double-A. At least he's in the system's Top 30; no other 2011 draft pick is. Unsigned RHPs Max Povse (42) and Chris Ellis (50) became third-rounders in 2014.

GRADE: D

TOP DRAFT PICKS OF THE DECADE

Year	Player, Pos.	2014 Org
2005	*Luke Hochevar, rhp (1st round supp.)	Royals
2006	Clayton Kershaw, lhp	Dodgers
2007	Chris Withrow, rhp	Dodgers
2008	Ethan Martin, rhp	Phillies
2009	Aaron Miller, lhp (1st round supp.)	Dodgers
2010	Zach Lee, rhp	Dodgers
2011	Chris Reed, lhp	Dodgers
2012	Corey Seager, ss	Dodgers
2013	Chris Anderson, rhp	Dodgers
2014	Grant Holmes, rhp	Dodgers

*Did not sign.

LARGEST BONUSES IN CLUB HISTORY

Yasiel Puig, 2012	$12,000,000
Alex Guerrero, 2013	$10,000,000
Erisbel Arruebarrena, 2014	$7,500,000
Hiroki Kuroda, 2007	$7,300,000
Zach Lee, 2010	$5,250,000

1 COREY SEAGER, SS

Born: April 27, 1994. **B-T:** L-R. **Ht.:** 6-4. **Wt.:** 215.
Drafted: HS—Concord, N.C., 2012 (1st round).
Signed by: Lon Joyce.

The Seagers look poised to become the next great baseball family. Corey's older brother Kyle, a Mariners third baseman, signed a seven-year, $100 million contract extension after a 2014 season in which he made the all-star team and won a Gold Glove. Similar accolades should soon be in store for Corey, who has an even higher ceiling. The No. 18 overall pick in the 2012 draft, he signed with the Dodgers for $2.35 million, immediately started raking and hasn't stopped since. After reaching high Class A Rancho Cucamonga as a 19-year-old at the end of the 2013 season, Seager returned there to open 2014 and quickly showed he was too advanced for that level, despite missing time with a right hamstring strain. A promotion to Double-A Chattanooga after the Futures Game in July did little to slow down Seager, who still won the Cal League MVP despite his abbreviated time there. He led the entire minors in hitting (.349) and doubles (50) in 2014, then continued to hit in the Arizona Fall League, batting .281 with a league-leading 10 doubles.

Seager is one of the most dominant offensive forces in the minors. He's an aggressive lefthanded hitter with an advanced hitting approach well beyond his years. He has a loose, easy swing with good balance that unleashes terrific bat speed with a compact path that helps him stay inside the ball. He hits the ball with high exit speed to all fields, controlling the barrel through the hitting zone and rarely mis-hitting a ball. He's a potential .300 hitter, though he does swing-and-miss some when he chases sliders down and out of the strike zone, but his pitch recognition and plate discipline are both solid. He doesn't overswing, maintaining his line-drive approach and allowing the power to come naturally. It's average raw power now, with a chance to grow into plus power and produce 25 or more home runs in his prime. Seager has come through the system as a shortstop, but few expect he will stay there much longer. He's still filling out his 6-foot-4 frame and is already a below-average runner who lacks the range or quick-twitch actions to stay in the middle of the diamond long term. That's fine, because Seager has all the attributes to be an above-average defender at third base, where his range would be above-average. He got better breaks off the bat last year because he improved his ability to read swings, with a good sense of timing, sound hands and a plus arm that he leaned on heavily at short, where he played deep to mask his limited range. Scouts complained about Seager's low-energy play in 2013, particularly in the AFL, but did so less as he matured and learned how to grind through a season in 2014.

With third baseman Juan Uribe signed through 2015, the Dodgers have the perfect bridge to allow Seager another year to develop in the minors, most likely at Triple-A Oklahoma City, before bringing him up to Los Angeles full time. He's a star in the making who should hit in the middle of the lineup and become one of the best players in baseball in the near future.

BA GRADE

70 Risk: Medium

SCOUTING GRADES

Batting: 70
Power: 60.
Speed: 40.
Defense: 60.
Arm: 60.

Based on 20-80 scouting scale and future projection rather than present grades.

LGE	PA	BB%	SO%	ISO
CAL	365	8.2	20.8	.281
SL	161	6.2	24.2	.189

MIKE JANES

Year	Club (League)	Class	AVG	G	AB	R	H	2B	3B	HR	RBI	BB	SO	SB	CS	OBP	SLG
2012	Ogden (PIO)	R	.309	46	175	34	54	9	2	8	33	21	33	8	2	.383	.520
2013	Great Lakes (MWL)	LoA	.309	74	272	45	84	18	3	12	57	34	58	9	4	.389	.529
	R. Cucamonga (CAL)	HiA	.160	27	100	10	16	2	1	4	15	12	31	1	0	.246	.320
2014	R. Cucamonga (CAL)	HiA	.352	80	327	61	115	34	2	18	70	30	76	5	1	.411	.633
	Chattanooga (SL)	AA	.345	38	148	28	51	16	3	2	27	10	39	1	1	.381	.534
Minor League Totals			.313	265	1022	178	320	79	11	44	202	107	237	24	8	.380	.541

2 JOC PEDERSON, OF

Born: April 21, 1992. **B-T:** L-L. **Ht.:** 6-1. **Wt.:** 185. **Drafted:** HS—Palo Alto, Calif., 2010 (11th round). **Signed by:** Orsino Hill.

In most organizations, Pederson would have been up by the 2014 all-star break, but a congested outfield in Los Angeles kept Pederson in the Triple-A Pacific Coast League, where he won the MVP award, until he made his major league debut as a September callup. Pederson took advantage of Albuquerque's extremely hitter-friendly conditions, blasting 33 homers, stealing 30 bases and leading the PCL in walks (100) and on-base percentage (.435). He also hit .274/.385/.523 in 63 road games and showed all the attributes that should allow his success to translate to the majors. Pederson is about as well-rounded as prospects come, showing five average to plus tools. He has good balance, keeps his weight back and explodes through the zone with good bat speed, a sound stroke and plus raw power. He's an aggressive hitter with some movement in the box, and while his strikeout rate jumped from 22 percent at Double-A Chattanooga in 2013 to 27 percent in 2014, he's also a patient hitter who understands the strike zone and should draw plenty of walks. He's a slightly above-average runner with an aggressive mindset on the basepaths, making him a threat to steal 20 bases. His reads and routes off the bat in center field improved, making him an average defender for the position with an above-average arm, albeit with inconsistent accuracy. Once the Dodgers sort through their outfield logjam, Pederson should emerge as the center fielder in Los Angeles. He has a chance to become an above-average player immediately, with future star potential.

BA GRADE

65 Risk: Low

LGE	PA	BB%	SO%	ISO
PCL	553	18.1	26.9	.279
NL	38	23.7	28.9	.000

Year	Club (League)	Class	AVG	G	AB	R	H	2B	3B	HR	RBI	BB	SO	SB	CS	OBP	SLG
2012	R. Cucamonga (CAL)	HiA	.313	110	434	96	136	26	4	18	70	51	81	26	14	.396	.516
2013	Chattanooga (SL)	AA	.278	123	439	81	122	24	3	22	58	70	114	31	8	.381	.497
2014	Albuquerque (PCL)	AAA	.303	121	445	106	135	17	4	33	78	100	149	30	13	.435	.582
	Los Angeles (NL)	MAJ	.143	18	28	1	4	0	0	0	0	9	11	0	0	.351	.143
Major League Totals			.143	18	28	1	4	0	0	0	0	9	11	0	0	.351	.143
Minor League Totals			.302	441	1641	342	495	87	13	84	271	268	412	113	40	.405	.524

3 JULIO URIAS, LHP

Born: Aug. 12, 1996. **B-T:** L-L. **Ht.:** 5-11. **Wt.:** 185. **Signed:** Mexico, 2012. **Signed by:** Mike Brito.

Urias signed as part of a a package deal from Mexico City of the Mexican League shortly after his 16th birthday and has been better than the Dodgers ever dreamed. After dominating at low Class A Great Lakes as a 16-year-old in 2013, Urias got off to a slow start in 2014 but quickly became one of the best pitchers in the high Class A California League at age 17. Urias was younger than many 2014 high school draft picks, so the Dodgers limited him to mostly three to five innings per start. His fastball sits at 89-94 mph and can reach 97. Scouts are split on whether they prefer his curveball or changeup, but that's only because both are plus pitches. His low-80s changeup can devastate hitters with its sink and fade, while his hard, sharp curveball misses plenty of bats when he stays on top of the ball. Both pitches earn future double-plus grades from some scouts, and Urias isn't afraid to throw either pitch in any count. He fills up the strike zone using pitchability beyond his years, with an easy arm action and clean mechanics. Urias has a noticeable medical condition on his left eye that scared some teams off when he was an amateur, but it doesn't hold him back on the mound. The Dodgers try to tap the brakes to take pressure off Urias, but it's hard to control the excitement around a pitcher with a chance to be a true No. 1 starter. He's ready to handle Double-A Chattanooga and on pace to reach Los Angeles in 2016 as a 19-year-old.

BA GRADE

70 Risk: High

LGE	BF	SO%	BB%	HR/9
CAL	356	30.6	10.4	0.41

Year	Club (League)	Class	W	L	ERA	G	GS	CG	SV	IP	H	HR	BB	SO	K/9	WHIP	AVG
2013	Great Lakes (MWL)	LoA	2	0	2.48	18	18	0	0	54	44	5	16	67	11.1	1.10	.227
2014	R. Cucamonga (CAL)	HiA	2	2	2.36	25	20	0	0	88	60	4	37	109	11.2	1.11	.194
Minor League Totals			4	2	2.41	43	38	0	0	142	104	9	53	176	11.2	1.11	.206

4 GRANT HOLMES, RHP

BILL MITCHELL

Born: March 22, 1996. **B-T:** L-R. **Ht.:** 6-1. **Wt.:** 215. **Drafted:** HS—Conway, S.C. 2014 (1st round). **Signed by:** Lon Joyce.

The Dodgers spent their 2014 first-round pick on Holmes, popping him at No. 18 overall to make him the highest drafted South Carolina high school righthander in modern history. After signing for $2.5 million, Holmes threw plenty of strikes and struck out more than a batter per inning in his pro debut in Rookie ball. He has a strong, filled-out frame with broad shoulders and two power pitches. His fastball parks anywhere from 91-96 mph and peaks at 98. Holmes calls his breaking ball a power curveball, while the Dodgers refer to it as a slider. Either way, it's a plus pitch in the low-80s with three-quarters break. Those two pitches help him strike out a lot of hitters, though he's still learning to take something off his breaking ball for an early-count strike instead of trying to induce a swing and a miss with every pitch. Holmes has mostly focused on two pitches, but he worked on his changeup during instructional league and it's flashed above-average. There's some recoil at the end of his delivery, and his long arm stroke wouldn't typically suggest above-average control, but he's athletic, repeats his delivery and threw plenty of strikes in his pro debut. He does get in trouble when he leaves his fastball up in the strike zone. Holmes is reminiscent of righthander Chad Billingsley, the Dodgers' 2003 first-round pick out of high school. He will open his first full season in low Class A Great Lakes, with a chance to develop into a No. 2 or 3 starter.

BA GRADE

60 Risk: High

LGE	BF	SO%	BB%	HR/9
AZL	118	28.0	5.9	0.60
PIO	78	32.1	7.7	0.49

Year	Club (League)	Class	W	L	ERA	G	GS	CG	SV	IP	H	HR	BB	SO	K/9	WHIP	AVG
2014	Dodgers (AZL)	R	1	2	3.00	7	6	0	0	30	20	2	7	33	9.9	0.90	.187
	Ogden (PIO)	R	1	1	4.91	4	4	0	0	18	19	1	6	25	12.3	1.36	.271
Minor League Totals			2	3	3.72	11	10	0	0	48	39	3	13	58	10.8	1.08	.220

5 ALEX VERDUGO, OF

MIKE JANES

Born: May 15, 1996. **B-T:** L-L. **Ht.:** 6-0. **Wt.:** 200. **Drafted:** HS—Tucson, 2014 (2nd round). **Signed by:** Dustin Yount.

Verdugo was a two-way standout in high school, but other teams focused on his pro future on the mound. He had a fastball he could run into the low 90s with a potentially above-average slider, a nice delivery and the ability to throw strikes consistently. Verdugo preferred hitting, though, and the Dodgers also liked him in that role, signing him for $914,600 as a second-rounder in 2014. The early returns have been superb, with Verdugo raking in the Rookie-level Arizona League. He has a simple, repeatable swing with good bat speed and a mature hitting approach. He makes consistent contact, recognizes breaking pitches and doesn't chase much out of the zone, which makes him a threat to hit for a high batting average and draw plenty of walks. He has good balance and occasional power, working the gaps and hitting line drives to all fields. His above-average speed is surprising for his thick build, and his savvy on the basepaths helped him go 11-for-11 on steals in his pro debut. That speed and athleticism is enough to start in center field, though he projects to slow down and could end up in right field, where he has a plus arm. If hitting doesn't work out, Verdugo always has pitching as a fallback option, but that won't happen any time soon. He heads to low Class A Great Lakes in 2015.

BA GRADE

55 Risk: High

LGE	PA	BB%	SO%	ISO
AZL	196	10.2	7.1	.171
PIO	20	0.0	20.0	.050

Year	Club (League)	Class	AVG	G	AB	R	H	2B	3B	HR	RBI	BB	SO	SB	CS	OBP	SLG
2014	Dodgers (AZL)	R	.347	49	170	28	59	14	3	3	33	20	14	8	0	.423	.518
	Ogden (PIO)	R	.400	5	20	3	8	1	0	0	8	0	4	3	0	.400	.450
Minor League Totals			.353	54	190	31	67	15	3	3	41	20	18	11	0	.421	.511

6 JOSE DE LEON, RHP

Born: Aug. 7, 1992. **B-T:** R-R. **Ht.:** 6-2. **Wt.:** 185. **Drafted:** Southern, 2013 (24th round). **Signed by:** Matthew Paul.

Born in Puerto Rico, De Leon went undrafted out of high school before spending three seasons at Southern, including a sophomore season when he led the Southwestern Athletic Conference in strikeouts. When the Dodgers drafted him in the 24th round in 2013, he threw 90-93 mph but was pudgy and didn't have an out pitch. The Dodgers were stunned to see his stock soar in 2014, as he lost weight, cranked up his stuff and made mechanical adjustments en route to a breakthrough season, followed by strong winter ball showing in the Puerto Rican League. De Leon started 2014 in extended spring training, which shows how lightly he was regarded as a college draft pick coming into the year. He steadily lost weight and improved his conditioning, which helped him make mechanical adjustments, moving from the third base side of the rubber to the first base side to help him stay more online to the plate. His fastball also jumped up to 93-96 mph and his breaking ball improved, going from a sweepy pitch to a hard, power pitch at 80-82 mph with hybrid action between a true curveball and a slider. By any name, the pitch gets swings and misses. De Leon didn't need to throw his fringe-average changeup much during the season, but he focused on it during instructional league and it has a chance to be an average pitch. His remarkable transformation has taken him from long shot to a potential mid-rotation starter, perhaps more if his changeup improves. If he continues his dominance, he could zip through the system quickly.

BA GRADE	
55	Risk: High

LGE	BF	SO%	BB%	HR/9
PIO	228	33.8	8.3	0.33
MWL	86	48.8	2.3	0.40

Year	Club (League)	Class	W	L	ERA	G	GS	CG	SV	IP	H	HR	BB	SO	K/9	WHIP	AVG
2013	Dodgers (AZL)	R	2	3	4.01	9	8	0	0	34	32	1	18	35	9.4	1.49	.256
	Ogden (PIO)	R	1	2	12.10	5	5	0	0	19	35	5	3	18	8.4	1.97	.380
2014	Ogden (PIO)	R	5	0	2.65	10	8	0	0	54	44	2	19	77	12.8	1.16	.217
	Great Lakes (MWL)	LoA	2	0	1.19	4	4	0	0	23	14	1	2	42	16.7	0.71	.171
Minor League Totals			10	5	4.15	28	25	0	0	130	125	9	42	172	11.9	1.28	.249

7 CHRIS ANDERSON, RHP

Born: July 29, 1992. **B-T:** R-R. **Ht.:** 6-4. **Wt.:** 215. **Drafted:** Jacksonville, 2013 (1st round). **Signed by:** Scott Hennessy.

Anderson was the Dodgers' first-round pick (No. 18 overall) in 2013 and made his full-season debut at high Class A Rancho Cucamonga in 2014. While the California League inflated his ERA, Anderson improved in the second half and punctuated his season with a 44-7 K-BB mark in August and double-digit strikeouts in his final three starts. Early in the season, Anderson's stuff was flat and he ran up high pitch counts early in games. In the second half, he made adjustments that helped him keep the ball down in the zone. His fastball ticked up, his slider started to work again and he made big strides with his changeup. At his best, Anderson sat 90-94 mph and touched 97 with downhill angle and boring life down in the zone. He had trouble throttling his slider early in the year, but by the second half it was better and flashing above-average again. The Dodgers pushed him to use his changeup more often, which paid off, with Anderson taking the pitch from a firm, below-average offering into a slightly above-average weapon against lefties and righties with improved separation from his fastball. He also mixes in an early-count curveball to change eye levels and give hitters a slower offering as a get-me-over strike. He became more pitch-efficient later in the season but still needs to improve his command and control. With a strong, durable build and the stuff to miss bats, Anderson has the makings of a mid-rotation starter, with command his biggest developmental need. The new Double-A Tulsa affiliate is his next test.

BA GRADE	
55	Risk: High

LGE	BF	SO%	BB%	HR/9
CAL	602	24.3	10.5	0.74

Year	Club (League)	Class	W	L	ERA	G	GS	CG	SV	IP	H	HR	BB	SO	K/9	WHIP	AVG
2013	Great Lakes (MWL)	LoA	3	0	1.96	12	12	0	0	46	32	0	24	50	9.8	1.22	.201
2014	R. Cucamonga (CAL)	HiA	7	7	4.62	27	25	0	0	134	147	11	63	146	9.8	1.56	.282
Minor League Totals			10	7	3.94	39	37	0	0	180	179	11	87	196	9.8	1.48	.263

8 SCOTT SCHEBLER, OF

Born: Oct. 6, 1990. **B-T:** L-R. **Ht.:** 6-1. **Wt.:** 208. **Drafted:** Des Moines Area CC, 2010 (26th round). **Signed by:** Scott Little.

When Scott Van Slyke came through the Dodgers' system as a 14th-round pick, he dealt with detractors at every level. Schebler, who signed for $300,000 as a 26th-rounder in 2010, has faced similar skepticism from scouts but has now strung together two stellar offensive seasons, with improvement across the board upon making the jump to Double-A Chattanooga in 2014. He led the Southern League in home runs (28), triples (14) and slugging (.556). Schebler sliced his strikeout rate from 26 percent in 2013 to 20 percent in 2014 while facing better pitchers. Early in the season, teams had success against Schebler by pitching him away and getting him to chase sliders off the plate. In the second half, he improved his pitch recognition, tightened up his plate discipline and forced pitchers to come into the zone, where he made them pay. Scouts who once questioned his bat speed and ability to cover the inner third of the plate saw a quicker stroke in 2014. Schebler has above-average raw power that plays in games. He's an average runner who played center field in a pinch, but he mostly split time between left and right field, with left a better fit due to his below-average arm. While he's on the 40-man roster, Schebler has no big league opportunity in the foreseeable future. He's headed to Triple-A Oklahoma City for 2015 and could develop into a solid everyday left fielder.

BA GRADE

50 Risk: Medium

LGE	PA	BB%	SO%	ISO
SL	560	8.0	19.6	.276

Year	Club (League)	Class	AVG	G	AB	R	H	2B	3B	HR	RBI	BB	SO	SB	CS	OBP	SLG
2012	Great Lakes (MWL)	LoA	.260	137	515	67	134	32	8	6	67	30	99	17	11	.312	.388
2013	R. Cucamonga (CAL)	HiA	.296	125	477	95	141	29	13	27	91	35	140	16	5	.360	.581
2014	Chattanooga (SL)	AA	.280	135	489	82	137	23	14	28	73	45	110	10	4	.365	.556
Minor League Totals			.279	472	1793	291	501	101	45	74	290	124	451	45	21	.342	.510

9 TOM WINDLE, LHP

Born: March 10, 1992. **B-T:** L-L. **Ht.:** 6-4. **Wt.:** 215. **Drafted:** Minnesota, 2013 (2nd round). **Signed by:** Chet Sergo.

Like fellow Dodgers lefty Chris Reed, Windle was a reliever in college. But after two seasons in Minnesota's bullpen, he impressed scouts as a starter the next summer in the Cape Cod League and started for the Gophers as a junior before the Dodgers made him a second-round pick in 2013. He had a solid first full season in 2014 in the hitter-friendly high Class A California League. Windle entered pro ball with two effective pitches in his fastball and slider. He throws 88-93 mph with downhill plane and the ability to sink, run and cut his fastball. His 82-86 mph slider is above-average when he keeps it down, with sharp tilt and two-plane depth. Windle can also backdoor his slider to righthanders, but the Dodgers pounded on him to improve his changeup, which went from below-average and very hittable early in 2014 to flashing average once he started to use it more in games. Windle throws slightly across his body and his delivery has effort, but it lends him some extra deception without preventing him from throwing consistent strikes. The continued development of Windle's changeup will dictate whether he can remain in the rotation, with a chance to be a No. 4 starter, perhaps a tick better. If not, he has plenty of stuff to be effective in a return to the bullpen. He will go to Double-A Tulsa to start 2015.

BA GRADE

50 Risk: High

LGE	BF	SO%	BB%	HR/9
CAL	606	18.3	7.3	0.90

Year	Club (League)	Class	W	L	ERA	G	GS	CG	SV	IP	H	HR	BB	SO	K/9	WHIP	AVG
2013	Great Lakes (MWL)	LoA	5	1	2.68	13	12	0	0	54	50	2	20	51	8.6	1.30	.242
2014	R. Cucamonga (CAL)	HiA	12	8	4.26	26	25	0	0	139	147	14	44	111	7.2	1.37	.271
Minor League Totals			17	9	3.82	39	37	0	0	193	197	16	64	162	7.6	1.35	.263

10 CHRIS REED, LHP

Born: May 20, 1990. **B-T:** L-L. **Ht.:** 6-4. **Wt.:** 195. **Drafted:** Stanford, 2011 (1st round). **Signed by:** Orsino Hill.

Reed was a closer at Stanford, but the Dodgers immediately made him a starter after making him a first-round pick in 2011. The Dodgers were split on whether to keep him in the rotation or move him to the bullpen in 2014, but the decision to keep him as a starter helped his secondary pitches develop. Reed is a good athlete who attacks hitters from a three-quarters arm slot with a sinking 90-94 mph two-seamer that makes him a groundball pitcher. He found a more consistent arm slot with his low-80s slider in 2014 to give him a weapon against lefties, earning average to solid-average grades on the pitch. He threw his changeup more frequently to righthanded hitters in 2014, giving him a chance for a third average pitch. He's not wild, but his command and control both need to improve. The Dodgers would like to keep Reed as a starter, but with a stacked rotation, the easiest path to the big leagues could be through the bullpen. He will return to Triple-A, with a chance to be a back-end starter or late-inning reliever.

BA GRADE

45 Risk: Medium

LGE	BF	SO%	BB%	HR/9
SL	554	20.0	9.9	0.66
PCL	113	15.9	9.7	2.11

Year	Club (League)	Class	W	L	ERA	G	GS	CG	SV	IP	H	HR	BB	SO	K/9	WHIP	AVG
2012	R. Cucamonga (CAL)	HiA	1	4	3.09	7	6	0	0	35	25	1	14	38	9.8	1.11	.203
	Chattanooga (SL)	AA	0	4	4.84	12	11	0	0	35	31	2	20	29	7.4	1.44	.242
2013	Chattanooga (SL)	AA	4	11	3.86	29	25	1	0	138	128	9	63	106	6.9	1.39	.250
2014	Chattanooga (SL)	AA	4	8	3.22	23	23	0	0	137	114	10	55	111	7.3	1.23	.226
	Albuquerque (PCL)	AAA	0	3	10.97	5	5	0	0	21	37	5	11	18	7.6	2.25	.378
Minor League Totals			9	31	4.12	79	73	1	0	373	344	28	167	311	7.5	1.37	.247

11 JULIAN LEON, C

BA GRADE

50 Risk: High

Born: Jan. 24, 1996. **B-T:** R-R. **Ht.:** 5-11. **Wt.:** 215. **Signed:** Mexico, 2012. **Signed by:** Mike Brito.

Julio Urias was the organization's top signing out of Mexico after the 2012 international signing period opened. Now Leon, who like Urias signed that summer as a 16-year-old from Mexico City of the Mexican League, has emerged as a legitimate prospect himself. He has a thick, squatty build and is an offensive-oriented catcher. He swing stays short, with strong hands and wrists that help him generate average raw power. There's some swing-and-miss to his game, but it's not excessive, and he's not a free-swinger, showing patience to draw walks. While scouts liked Leon's offensive game, he has work to do behind the plate. He has a plus arm and led the Rookie-level Pioneer League by throwing out 30 percent of basestealers, but he needs to speed up his transfer. Leon should stick behind the plate, but his receiving, blocking and footwork need to improve. He's ready for his first full-season trial at low Class A Great Lakes in 2015.

Year	Club (League)	Class	AVG	G	AB	R	H	2B	3B	HR	RBI	BB	SO	SB	CS	OBP	SLG
2013	Dodgers (AZL)	R	.247	26	81	12	20	3	1	3	19	7	21	0	1	.319	.420
2014	Ogden (PIO)	R	.332	63	223	39	74	14	1	12	57	31	53	1	1	.420	.565
Minor League Totals			.309	89	304	51	94	17	2	15	76	38	74	1	2	.394	.526

12 YIMI GARCIA, RHP

BA GRADE

45 Risk: Medium

Born: Aug. 18, 1990. **B-T:** R-R. **Ht.:** 6-1. **Wt.:** 175. **Signed:** Dominican Republic, 2009. **Signed by:** Bienvenido Tavarez.

Garcia hasn't started a game since Rookie ball, but he plowed through the minors to reach the majors in 2014 despite the lack of an attention-grabbing pitch. He has averaged 11 strikeouts per nine innings in the minors while keeping his walk rate low, and he performed at a similar level with Los Angeles. Garcia throws 89-95 mph with good movement. He gets great extension, which makes his fastball sneak up on hitters. He made a mechanical adjustment to separate his hands away from his head to try to stay on top of his fringe-average 79-83 mph slider. It has tight spin but occasionally comes in flat like a cutter. Garcia has also messed around with a splitter, but he doesn't use it much. He pounds the strike zone and locates his stuff especially well down in the zone. That control and deception explain why he's been so effective, and that should allow him to continue to have success in short relief outings and potentially throw high-leverage innings. He could play a key role in Dodgers' 2015 bullpen.

Year	Club (League)	Class	W	L	ERA	G	GS	CG	SV	IP	H	HR	BB	SO	K/9	WHIP	AVG
2012	Great Lakes (MWL)	LoA	4	4	3.02	40	0	0	14	42	42	0	17	60	13.0	1.42	.253
	R. Cucamonga (CAL)	HiA	2	1	2.53	9	0	0	2	11	7	0	5	22	18.6	1.13	.175
2013	Chattanooga (SL)	AA	4	6	2.54	49	0	0	19	60	35	9	14	85	12.7	0.81	.164

2014	Albuquerque (PCL)	AAA	4	2	3.10	47	0	0	5	61	58	5	18	69	10.2	1.25	.249
	Los Angeles (NL)	MAJ	0	0	1.80	8	0	0	0	10	6	2	1	9	8.1	0.70	.171
Major League Totals			0	0	1.80	8	0	0	0	10	6	2	1	9	8.1	0.70	.171
Minor League Totals			22	19	3.10	194	10	0	45	311	272	19	96	380	11.0	1.18	.234

13 ZACH LEE, RHP

BA GRADE
45 Risk: Medium

Born: Sept. 13, 1991. **B-T:** R-R. **Ht.:** 6-3. **Wt.:** 190. **Drafted:** HS—McKinney, Texas, 2010 (1st round). **Signed by:** Calvin Jones.

It was a big deal when the Dodgers convinced Lee to give up the chance to play quarterback and pitch for Louisiana State. He had lost some luster before reaching Triple-A, but he fell flat in his first exposure to the level. Albuquerque is unforgiving for pitchers, but Lee's strikeout rate also dissolved, and scouts backed up the stats with reports that his stuff wasn't sharp. His fastball sits 88-92 mph at hits 94, and the sink helps him gets groundballs. Lee had trouble missing barrels though because his secondary stuff regressed. Lee has never had a true wipeout pitch, but his slider and changeup both were fringy in 2014, occasionally flashing a tick better, with an early-count curveball mixed in. He throws strikes but his pitch-ability approach will only work against major league hitters if his stuff returns to average or better. If it does, he has a chance to rebound as a back-end starter, but he's headed back for another season in Triple-A.

Year	Club (League)	Class	W	L	ERA	G	GS	CG	SV	IP	H	HR	BB	SO	K/9	WHIP	AVG
2012	R. Cucamonga (CAL)	HiA	2	3	4.55	12	12	0	0	55	60	9	10	52	8.5	1.27	.270
	Chattanooga (SL)	AA	4	3	4.25	13	13	0	0	66	69	6	22	51	7.0	1.39	.272
2013	Chattanooga (SL)	AA	10	10	3.22	28	25	1	0	143	132	13	35	131	8.3	1.17	.247
2014	Albuquerque (PCL)	AAA	7	13	5.38	28	27	0	0	151	177	18	54	97	5.8	1.53	.297
Minor League Totals			32	35	4.16	105	101	1	0	523	539	55	153	422	7.3	1.32	.266

14 PEDRO BAEZ, RHP

BA GRADE
45 Risk: Medium

Born: March 11, 1988. **B-T:** R-R. **Ht.:** 6-2. **Wt.:** 230. **Signed:** Dominican Republic, 2007. **Signed by:** Elvio Jimenez.

Baez signed with the Dodgers in 2007 for $200,000, which was one of the most significant bonuses the organization handed out to a Latin American amateur during a time when penny-pinching was the norm in that arena. After six seasons as a third baseman, he shifted to the mound in 2013 and took to it surprisingly quickly. Baez reached the majors in August 2014 and became one of the club's most reliable relievers down the stretch. His velocity improved from 2013, as he threw 93-97 mph and touched 100 in 2014. He pitches heavily off his fastball, throwing consistent strikes at a remarkable rate for someone with his inexperience, and he moves the ball all around to all quadrants of the strike zone. Baez throws a fringy 86-88 mph slider with short break, and an occasional changeup when he faces a lefty, but he lacks a true swing-and-miss secondary pitch. Coming up with one would help his strikeout rate, but if not he still has the stuff to be a steady middle reliever, one who should open 2015 in the big league bullpen.

Year	Club (League)	Class	W	L	ERA	G	GS	CG	SV	IP	H	HR	BB	SO	K/9	WHIP	AVG
2013	R. Cucamonga (CAL)	HiA	2	2	3.63	32	0	0	2	35	41	3	15	32	8.3	1.62	.295
	Chattanooga (SL)	AA	1	1	4.24	16	0	0	0	23	26	3	8	23	8.9	1.46	.283
2014	Chattanooga (SL)	AA	2	1	2.79	17	0	0	6	19	15	0	9	18	8.4	1.24	.208
	Albuquerque (PCL)	AAA	0	0	4.76	23	0	0	6	23	27	4	4	20	7.9	1.37	.303
	Los Angeles (NL)	MAJ	0	0	2.63	20	0	0	0	24	16	3	5	18	6.8	0.88	.188
Major League Totals			0	0	2.63	20	0	0	0	24	16	3	5	18	6.8	0.88	.188
Minor League Totals			5	4	3.87	88	0	0	14	100	109	10	36	93	8.4	1.45	.278

Year	Club (League)	Class	AVG	G	AB	R	H	2B	3B	HR	RBI	BB	SO	SB	CS	OBP	SLG
2012	Chattanooga (SL)	AA	.216	78	273	41	59	13	4	4	36	33	64	5	3	.319	.337
	R. Cucamonga (CAL)	HiA	.228	50	184	19	42	14	1	7	23	14	44	2	1	.287	.429
Minor League Totals			.248	530	1850	258	458	112	10	45	286	145	452	26	12	.309	.392

15 AUSTIN BARNES, C/2B

BA GRADE
45 Risk: Medium

Born: Dec. 28, 1989. **B-T:** R-R. **Ht.:** 5-10. **Wt.:** 190. **Drafted:** Arizona State, 2011 (9th round). **Signed by:** Scott Stanley (Marlins).

Primarily a second baseman in 2012, Barnes caught almost exclusively in 2013, and the Marlins sent him back to high Class A Jupiter to start 2014 to let him catch every day. He hit his way to Double-A anyway and played second and third base as well as catching. In December, the Marlins shipped him to the Dodgers with lefthander Andrew Heaney (who was flipped to the Angels for Howie Kendrick) in a package for second baseman Dee Gordon. Barnes makes a lot of hard contact thanks to a gap-to-gap approach, barrel awareness and excellent hand-eye coordination. He has below-average power and speed. Defensively, Barnes fits better as a catcher, where he's an average receiver and thrower. Some scouts question his durability as a catcher due to his modest size. His hands are a bit hard in the infield, but he's an improved second baseman with the tools to be an average defender. At the very least, Barnes should enjoy a nice major league career as a utility man like his uncle, Mike Gallego.

Year	Club (League)	Class	AVG	G	AB	R	H	2B	3B	HR	RBI	BB	SO	SB	CS	OBP	SLG
2012	Greensboro (SAL)	LoA	.318	123	478	76	152	36	3	12	65	59	61	9	2	.401	.481
2013	Jupiter (FSL)	HiA	.260	98	350	42	91	15	1	4	38	52	59	5	2	.367	.343
	Jacksonville (SL)	AA	.339	19	62	10	21	2	2	1	7	12	10	0	0	.446	.484
2014	Jupiter (FSL)	HiA	.317	44	180	24	57	11	2	1	14	19	25	3	3	.385	.417
	Jacksonville (SL)	AA	.296	78	284	56	84	20	2	12	43	50	36	8	0	.406	.507
Minor League Totals			.298	419	1573	241	468	97	10	31	186	217	213	31	8	.390	.431

16 DARNELL SWEENEY, 2B/SS

BA GRADE

45 Risk: Medium

Born: Feb. 1, 1991. **B-T:** B-R. **Ht.:** 6-1. **Wt.:** 180. **Drafted:** Central Florida, 2012 (13th round). **Signed by:** Scott Hennessey.

Sweeney's plus speed and athleticism have always drawn scouts to him, but it's his evolution as a hitter that has taken him from a raw tools player and turned him into a prospect on the cusp of the big leagues. Prone to swing and miss, he cut down his strikeout rate from 25 percent at high Class A Rancho Cucamonga in 2013 to 20 percent after moving up to Double-A Chattanooga in 2014. Sweeney has a quick bat, a line-drive approach and good strike-zone discipline. He has fringe-average power, with a chance for 12-15 home runs. Sweeney is a poor basestealer who's still learning how to read pitchers' moves to home after succeeding in just 48 percent of his attempts in 2014. He spent most of 2014 at second base with time mixed in at shortstop and center field. He's below-average at each position, lacking the natural footwork and actions for the infield, with an average arm. Scouts highest on Sweeney see an everyday second baseman, though others see a potential utility man. He heads to Triple-A for 2015.

Year	Club (League)	Class	AVG	G	AB	R	H	2B	3B	HR	RBI	BB	SO	SB	CS	OBP	SLG
2012	Ogden (PIO)	R	.303	16	66	12	20	1	2	0	9	8	10	2	.380	.379
	Great Lakes (MWL)	LoA	.291	51	199	34	58	8	4	5	23	24	41	17	4	.372	.447
2013	R. Cucamonga (CAL)	HiA	.275	134	552	79	152	34	16	11	77	43	151	48	20	.329	.455
2014	Chattanooga (SL)	AA	.288	132	490	88	141	34	5	14	57	77	117	15	16	.387	.463
Minor League Totals			.284	333	1307	213	371	77	27	30	167	153	317	90	42	.361	.453

17 ROSS STRIPLING, RHP

BA GRADE

50 Risk: Extreme

Born: Nov. 23, 1989. **B-T:** R-R. **Ht.:** 6-3. **Wt.:** 190. **Drafted:** Texas A&M (5th round). **Signed by:** Clint Bowers.

Stripling was a fast mover who pitched well at Double-A Chattanooga in 2013, but he missed 2014 after having Tommy John surgery. The Dodgers hope he can return by midseason 2015. When healthy, Stripling filled up the strike zone with a sinking 88-94 mph fastball with good armside run, generating downhill plane and getting a lot of grounders. His stuff grades out around average across the board, with scouts split on whether they prefer his curveball or his short, mid-80s slider. He maintains his arm speed when he throws the changeup, which flashes average but lacks much movement. Stripling's polish had put him on the fast track, but the goal now is just for his stuff to return to where it was before surgery, pitch in 2015, then perhaps emerge as a back-end starter candidate in 2016.

Year	Club (League)	Class	W	L	ERA	G	GS	CG	SV	IP	H	HR	BB	SO	K/9	WHIP	AVG
2012	Ogden (PIO)	R	1	0	1.24	14	12	0	0	36	26	0	6	37	9.2	0.88	.197
2013	R. Cucamonga (CAL)	HiA	2	0	2.94	6	6	0	0	34	24	1	11	34	9.1	1.04	.198
	Chattanooga (SL)	AA	6	4	2.78	21	16	0	1	94	91	4	19	83	7.9	1.17	.251
2014	Did not play—Injured																
Minor League Totals			9	4	2.47	41	34	0	1	164	141	5	36	154	8.5	1.08	.229

18 ERISBEL ARRUEBARRENA, SS

BA GRADE

40 Risk: Low

Born: March 25, 1990. **B-T:** R-R. **Ht.:** 6-0. **Wt.:** 200. **Signed:** Cuba, 2014. **Signed by:** Mike Tosar/Patrick Guerrero/Bob Engle.

Arruebarrena was the shortstop for the Cuban national team at several international tournaments, capturing the attention of scouts for his defense. After he signed with the Dodgers for five years and $25 million, Arruebarrena played briefly in the big leagues in 2014 but looked overmatched even in the minors at the plate. He was also suspended five games by the Triple-A Pacific Coast League for his role in a benches-clearing brawl. Scouts rave about Arruebarrena's defense. He's a below-average runner but he has good range because of his quick first step and reads off the bat. He can make the acrobatic play with quick actions, sound hands and a plus-plus arm. Arruebarrena's hitting will never be good, but the hope is he can at least be adequate to play every day. His swing is long, his pitch recognition is poor and he chases balls out of the strike zone, with below-average power. He's going to give Triple-A another crack in 2015.

Year	Club (League)	Class	AVG	G	AB	R	H	2B	3B	HR	RBI	BB	SO	SB	CS	OBP	SLG
2014	Chattanooga (SL)	AA	.208	25	96	10	20	4	1	1	6	4	31	0	0	.252	.302
	Albuquerque (PCL)	AAA	.333	26	84	7	28	3	2	1	11	10	26	1	1	.400	.452
	Dodgers (AZL)	R	.222	5	18	3	4	2	0	2	4	0	10	0	0	.222	.667
	R. Cucamonga (CAL)	HiA	.245	12	49	8	12	4	1	2	11	2	24	1	0	.259	.490
	Los Angeles (NL)	MAJ	.195	22	41	4	8	1	0	0	4	3	17	0	0	.244	.220
Major League Totals			.195	22	41	4	8	1	0	0	4	3	17	0	0	.244	.220
Minor League Totals			.259	68	247	28	64	13	4	6	32	16	91	2	1	.304	.417

19 ZACH BIRD, RHP

BA GRADE

50 Risk: Extreme

Born: July 14, 1994. **B-T:** R-R. **Ht.:** 6-4. **Wt.:** 205. **Drafted:** HS—Jackson, Miss., 2012 (9th round). **Signed by:** Matthew Paul.

Bird struggled while repeating low Class A Great Lakes in 2014, but his stuff and performance looked completely different that August. He sat 89-94 mph early in the season, but by the end he was sitting 93-96 mph and cracked 99. In August, Bird ditched the windup and started to pitch exclusively from the stretch. That simplified his delivery, allowing him to focus on attacking hitters more aggressively, and he posted a 38-to-8 SO/BB ratio in 26 innings in the season's final month. Bird has an electric fastball, but his secondary stuff needs work. His breaking stuff, though still fringy, improved. His changeup is below-average and is a big reason why lefties teed off on him for a .291/.381/.445 line in 207 plate appearances in 2014. Bird's stiff-shouldered arm action concerns some scouts, and his crossfire delivery causes him to finish closed off. That doesn't help his control, which is trending in the right direction but needs to improve. Bird is still raw but has the chance to develop into a back-end starter. If not, his power arm would play well in the bullpen, with high Class A Rancho Cucamonga his next destination.

Year	Club (League)	Class	W	L	ERA	G	GS	CG	SV	IP	H	HR	BB	SO	K/9	WHIP	AVG
2012	Dodgers (AZL)	R	1	2	4.54	10	10	0	0	40	36	2	17	46	10.4	1.34	.237
2013	Ogden (PIO)	R	2	4	5.77	9	9	0	0	44	43	3	19	44	9.1	1.42	.247
	Great Lakes (MWL)	LoA	2	5	5.10	19	11	0	0	60	56	5	45	50	7.5	1.68	.249
2014	Great Lakes (MWL)	LoA	6	17	4.25	26	24	1	0	119	118	9	55	110	8.3	1.46	.259
Minor League Totals			11	28	4.74	64	54	1	0	262	253	19	136	250	8.6	1.48	.251

20 CODY BELLINGER, 1B

BA GRADE

50 Risk: Extreme

Born: July 13, 1995. **B-T:** L-L. **Ht.:** 6-4. **Wt.:** 180. **Drafted:** HS— Chandler, Ariz., 2013 (4th round). **Signed by:** Dustin Yount.

The polish Bellinger shows in all facets is no surprise, given that his father Clay spent four seasons in the big leagues. His swing works well and he makes frequent contact with a sound hitting approach. Bellinger's swing is geared more for line drives than loft, and power is the biggest question mark. He's mostly a gap-to-gap guy right now, with some scouts projecting 10-15 home runs, which would be light for a first baseman. Others point to his quick-twitch hands and the room in his frame to add muscle and think average or better power will come. No one doubts his defense at first base. He's light on his feet with slick actions, smooth hands and a strong arm. He's even a solid-average runner, plenty speedy to play the corner outfield, but his defense is so good at first there's no point in moving him. Bellinger has a chance to break out if the power comes, with a season at low Class A Great Lakes on deck.

Year	Club (League)	Class	AVG	G	AB	R	H	2B	3B	HR	RBI	BB	SO	SB	CS	OBP	SLG
2013	Dodgers (AZL)	R	.210	47	162	25	34	9	6	1	30	31	46	3	3	.340	.358
2014	Dodgers (AZL)	R	.150	5	20	2	3	1	0	0	0	1	5	0	0	.190	.200
	Ogden (PIO)	R	.328	46	195	49	64	13	6	3	34	14	35	8	0	.368	.503
Minor League Totals			.268	98	377	76	101	23	12	4	64	46	86	11	3	.347	.424

21 ALEX GUERRERO, 2B

BA GRADE

45 Risk: High

Born: Dec. 20, 1986. **B-T:** R-R. **Ht.:** 5-10. **Wt.:** 200. **Signed:** Cuba, 2013. **Signed by:** Mike Tosar/Patrick Guerrero/Bob Engle.

Guerrero was one of the top offensive shortstops in Cuba's *Serie Nacional*, but the Cubans used him sparingly on the national team. Many scouts were skeptical after watching him in the Dominican Republic, but that didn't dissuade the international scouts for the Dodgers, who signed him after the 2013 season to a four-year, $28 million deal that included a $10 million signing bonus. The Dodgers' major league staff shared that skepticism, so Guerrero spent 2014 at Triple-A Albuquerque. He missed nearly two months, though, when he was involved in a fight with teammate Miguel Olivo, who bit off part of Guerrero's ear, requiring surgery. Guerrero has the power to hit 20 home runs, but he's a pull-oriented hitter with holes in his swing, though he didn't strike out excessively. He expands the zone and has trouble hanging in against breaking pitches. Guerrero lacks the first-step quickness for shortstop and has trouble at second base, where he has an average arm but lacks natural infield actions. The offseason trade for Howie Kendrick shows the Dodgers' lack of faith in Guerrero, who will repeat Triple-A as a 28-year-old.

Year	Club (League)	Class	AVG	G	AB	R	H	2B	3B	HR	RBI	BB	SO	SB	CS	OBP	SLG
2014	Dodgers (AZL)	R	.348	7	23	6	8	1	0	2	6	3	5	0	0	.414	.652
	R. Cucamonga (CAL)	HiA	.368	5	19	3	7	4	1	0	2	2	2	0	0	.429	.684
	Albuquerque (PCL)	AAA	.329	65	243	38	80	14	5	15	49	10	44	4	0	.364	.613
	Los Angeles (NL)	MAJ	.077	11	13	0	1	0	0	0	0	0	6	0	0	.077	.077
Major League Totals			.077	11	13	0	1	0	0	0	0	0	6	0	0	.077	.077
Minor League Totals			.333	77	285	47	95	19	6	17	57	15	51	4	0	.373	.621

22 JHAREL COTTON, RHP

BA GRADE 45 Risk: High

Born: Jan. 19, 1992. **B-T:** R-R. **Ht.:** 5-11. **Wt.:** 195. **Drafted:** East Carolina, 2012 (20th round). **Signed by:** Clair Rierson.

After getting tagged for a 7.07 ERA in the first half of 2014 at high Class A Rancho Cucamonga, Cotton posted a 2.55 ERA with 93 strikeouts and 18 walks in 85 innings after the all-star break. His fastball ticked up slightly, bumping up to 88-94 mph and touching 95, although it can flatten out. At midseason, Dodgers officials in the stands noticed he was tipping his pitches and pointed it out to Cotton. Once he started to disguise his pitches, the results followed. Cotton backs up his fastball with a plus changeup featuring late fade. He maintains his arm speed when he throws it, making him equally effective against lefties as he is against righthanders. Cotton needs to improve his below-average curveball, which has decent depth but gets slurvy. He'll sneak in a cutter as well. He has good pitchability and throws strikes to both sides of the plate, with the total package making him an intriguing sleeper with a chance to slot into the back of the rotation. Double-A Tulsa will be a key test for Cotton in 2015.

Year	Club (League)	Class	W	L	ERA	G	GS	CG	SV	IP	H	HR	BB	SO	K/9	WHIP	AVG
2012	Ogden (PIO)	R	1	0	1.20	5	1	0	0	15	9	0	3	20	12.0	0.80	.180
2013	Great Lakes (MWL)	LoA	2	5	3.55	11	9	1	0	58	42	4	17	58	8.9	1.01	.200
	Chattanooga (SL)	AA	0	2	8.10	8	0	0	0	10	15	0	3	11	9.9	1.80	.341
	R. Cucamonga (CAL)	HiA	0	0	1.59	2	2	0	0	6	4	0	3	8	4.8	1.24	.190
2014	R. Cucamonga (CAL)	HiA	6	10	4.05	25	20	1	0	127	113	18	34	138	9.8	1.16	.239
Minor League Totals			9	17	3.84	51	32	2	0	216	183	22	60	230	9.6	1.13	.229

23 JACOB RHAME, RHP

BA GRADE 45 Risk: High

Born: March 16, 1993. **B-T:** R-R. **Ht.:** 6-1. **Wt.:** 190. **Drafted:** Grayson County (Texas) CC, 2013 (6th round). **Signed by:** Calvin Jones.

Rhame signed with the Dodgers for $300,000 as a 2013 sixth-rounder, when he sat 88-93 mph and touched 95. That's the range he started throwing in 2014, but as the year progressed he began bumping mid- to upper-90s heat, topping out at 100 mph. Rhame has a low-90s two-seamer he tends to rely on too much, but he's at his best when he's pumping his four-seamer in the 95-100 mph range. He introduced a hard, upper-80s slider into his mix and it flashes average, with an occasional changeup as well. He tweaked his arm action in 2014, going from a long, wrappy path with a wiggle and transitioning to a cleaner arm circle before exploding out front, and he's now one of the best strike-throwers in the organization. Rhame could move quickly, with a chance to pitch high-leverage relief innings within a few years.

Year	Club (League)	Class	W	L	ERA	G	GS	CG	SV	IP	H	HR	BB	SO	K/9	WHIP	AVG
2013	Ogden (PIO)	R	1	2	4.58	20	0	0	8	20	19	2	9	21	9.6	1.42	.257
2014	Great Lakes (MWL)	LoA	5	4	2.00	51	0	0	9	67	48	3	14	90	12.0	0.92	.198
Minor League Totals			6	6	2.59	71	0	0	17	87	67	5	23	111	11.5	1.03	.211

24 JOHN RICHY, RHP

BA GRADE 45 Risk: High

Born: July 28, 1992. **B-T:** R-R. **Ht.:** 6-4. **Wt.:** 215. **Drafted:** Nevada-Las Vegas, 2014 (3rd round). **Signed by:** Bobby Darwin.

The Dodgers have shown an affinity for tall, strong pitchers in the draft, like Richy, who signed for $534,400 as a third-round pick from Nevada-Las Vegas in 2014. He sits at 89-92 mph and touches 94 with sink. There's no wipeout pitch in his arsenal, but Richy throws strikes with a balanced four-pitch mix. Some scouts prefer his mid-70s curveball to his low-80s slider, though they both earn average grades at their best, along with a solid changeup he throws for strikes. Richy throws with effort, but he repeats his delivery and is a consistent strike-thrower. That ability to fill up the zone with solid stuff profiles him as a potential back-end starter. He finished 2014 at low Class A Great Lakes and could return there in 2015.

Year	Club (League)	Class	W	L	ERA	G	GS	CG	SV	IP	H	HR	BB	SO	K/9	WHIP	AVG
2014	Ogden (PIO)	R	0	0	5.71	8	5	0	0	17	20	1	4	17	8.8	1.38	.278
	Great Lakes (MWL)	LoA	0	0	1.65	4	4	0	0	16	14	0	7	14	7.7	1.29	.230
Minor League Totals			0	0	3.74	12	9	0	0	34	34	1	11	31	8.3	1.34	.256

25 CARLOS FRIAS, RHP

BA GRADE

40 Risk: Low

Born: Nov. 13, 1989. **B-T:** R-R. **Ht.:** 6-4. **Wt.:** 170. **Signed:** Dominican Republic, 2007. **Signed by:** Ezequiel Sepulveda.

Frias became a minor league free agent after the 2013 season, but he quickly re-signed with the Dodgers. He made his major league debut in August 2014, then he stuck with the big league club the final two months of the season, though he got hit hard. Frias was a starter in the minors, but most of his action in the majors came in long relief, and he projects best in that role. He pitches off a mixture of four- and two-seam fastballs that range from 91-97 mph. He can manipulate the movement on his fastball, imparting cutting, sinking or riding action on the pitch. Frias is a solid strike-thrower, but he doesn't miss many bats. His best secondary pitch is his solid-average, upper-80s slider, which has short break like a cutter. He will drop an occasional 76-81 mph curveball and an even more infrequent changeup in the mid-80s, but both are below-average. The Dodgers have room in their bullpen for Frias to carve out a role, though he could shuttle back and forth between Los Angeles and Triple-A Oklahoma City.

Year	Club (League)	Class	W	L	ERA	G	GS	CG	SV	IP	H	HR	BB	SO	K/9	WHIP	AVG
2012	R. Cucamonga (CAL)	HiA	0	1	12.71	3	1	0	0	6	9	0	8	5	7.9	3.00	.375
	Ogden (PIO)	R	7	4	4.15	15	15	0	0	78	83	5	21	67	7.7	1.33	.269
2013	Great Lakes (MWL)	LoA	5	3	2.63	12	12	0	0	68	66	3	23	49	6.5	1.30	.258
	R. Cucamonga (CAL)	HiA	2	3	4.11	8	8	0	0	46	52	4	11	48	9.4	1.37	.280
	Chattanooga (SL)	AA	1	1	3.94	8	2	0	0	16	15	2	7	8	4.5	1.38	.254
2014	Chattanooga (SL)	AA	2	1	3.38	5	5	0	0	32	34	2	9	14	3.9	1.34	.274
	Albuquerque (PCL)	AAA	8	4	5.01	16	15	2	0	92	114	4	21	65	6.4	1.47	.307
	Los Angeles (NL)	MAJ	1	1	6.12	15	2	0	0	32	33	4	7	29	8.1	1.24	.254
Major League Totals			1	1	6.12	15	2	0	0	32	33	4	7	29	8.1	1.24	.254
Minor League Totals			40	34	4.23	132	89	2	0	542	564	31	204	441	7.3	1.42	.270

26 CHRIS O'BRIEN, C

BA GRADE

45 Risk: High

Born: July 24, 1989. **B-T:** B-R. **Ht.:** 6-0. **Wt.:** 219. **Drafted:** Wichita State, 2011 (18th round). **Signed by:** Scott Little.

O'Brien's father Charlie spent 15 seasons catching in the big leagues for eight different teams. Chris, who followed in his father's footsteps by catching at Wichita State, had struggled at the plate as a pro until 2014, having the best year of his career upon jumping to Double-A Chattanooga. O'Brien stays within the strike zone and puts the ball in play frequently. He's more of a doubles threat than a masher, but he has solid on-base potential. He earns praise for his game-calling and the way he handles a pitching staff. He has a thick, heavy frame, so his lateral agility isn't great, but his receiving skills are adequate. He has a fringy arm that he used to throw out 29 percent of basestealers in 2014. As a switch-hitting catcher who's better from the left side, O'Brien has a chance to get to the big leagues as a backup or platoon catcher.

Year	Club (League)	Class	AVG	G	AB	R	H	2B	3B	HR	RBI	BB	SO	SB	CS	OBP	SLG
2012	R. Cucamonga (CAL)	HiA	.252	80	302	33	76	11	3	7	44	23	54	1	0	.305	.377
2013	Dodgers (AZL)	R	.226	9	31	4	7	0	0	2	5	4	7	0	0	.306	.419
	R. Cucamonga (CAL)	HiA	.195	64	210	28	41	12	1	3	21	18	51	0	0	.257	.305
2014	Chattanooga (SL)	AA	.266	116	354	33	94	32	4	7	53	41	66	3	0	.341	.438
Minor League Totals			.251	315	1065	123	267	71	11	23	158	104	210	7	0	.316	.403

27 JEFF BRIGHAM, RHP

BA GRADE

50 Risk: Extreme

Born: Feb. 16, 1992. **B-T:** R-R. **Ht.:** 6-0. **Wt.:** 200. **Drafted:** Washington, 2014 (4th round). **Signed by:** Henry Jones.

Tommy John surgery kept Brigham off the mound in 2013, but he looked sharp upon his return in 2014 as a redshirt junior for Washington. His power arm prompted the Dodgers to take him in the fourth round and sign him for $396,300. He looked good in his pro debut at Rookie-level Ogden, limited to no more than four innings per start, but his arm started barking again after the season, so the Dodgers didn't let him pitch during instructional league. Brigham's primary weapon is his fastball, which cruises at 90-94 mph but can ramp up to 98. His heater has good movement, with lively tail and sink that helps him generate groundballs. He showed an effective slider in pro ball that flashes average but also got sweepy and slurvy on him at times, along with a below-average changeup. Brigham has starting experience, but given his medical history and lack of any type of durable track record, it's safer to project him as a reliever. He will be 23 in 2015, so the Dodgers might be tempted to push him.

Year	Club (League)	Class	W	L	ERA	G	GS	CG	SV	IP	H	HR	BB	SO	K/9	WHIP	AVG
2014	Ogden (PIO)	R	0	3	3.58	11	10	0	0	33	32	2	16	33	9.1	1.47	.267
Minor League Totals			0	3	3.58	11	10	0	0	33	32	2	16	33	9.1	1.47	.267

28 BROCK STEWART, RHP

BA GRADE

45 Risk: High

Born: Oct. 3, 1991. **B-T:** L-R. **Ht.:** 6-3. **Wt.:** 170. **Drafted:** Illinois State, 2014 (6th round). **Signed by:** Chet Sergo.

Stewart was a two-way player at Illinois State who spent most of his time at third base, with occasional work out of the bullpen in 2014 as a redshirt junior. The Dodgers were intrigued by his arm strength and popped him in the sixth round and signed him for $190,000. Stewart already has a plus fastball from 92-96 mph, and there's reason to believe he could push the upper 90s once he's able to incorporate his lower half into his delivery. His 78-82 mph slider is still erratic, though it's ahead of his below-average changeup. Stewart has little mileage on his arm and his feel for pitching is understandably raw, but his baseball upbringing gives him a high general baseball IQ. The Dodgers are even tempted to develop him as a starter in 2015, with an assignment to low Class A Great Lakes most likely.

Year	Club (League)	Class	W	L	ERA	G	GS	CG	SV	IP	H	HR	BB	SO	K/9	WHIP	AVG
2014	Ogden (PIO)	R	3	2	3.41	17	1	0	3	34	36	1	17	45	11.8	1.54	.259
Minor League Totals			3	2	3.41	17	1	0	3	34	36	1	17	45	11.8	1.54	.259

29 A.J. VANEGAS, RHP

BA GRADE

45 Risk: High

Born: Aug. 16, 1992. **B-T:** R-R. **Ht.:** 6-3. **Wt.:** 205. **Drafted:** Stanford, 2014 (11th round). **Signed by:** Orsino Hill.

The Padres drafted Vanegas in the seventh round in 2011 and offered him a bonus that approached $2 million, but he turned them down to stay in state to play at Stanford. His stock fell after his junior season when mononucleosis and surgery to repair a herniated disc in his back limited him to nine innings. Back problems hampered Vanegas again as a senior in 2014, when he threw 41 innings and signed with the Dodgers for $100,000 in the 11th round. Exclusively a reliever his final two seasons at Stanford, Vanegas pitched in the bullpen in his pro debut and will stay there. He throws two plus pitches, with a 93-97 mph fastball and a power slider, though at times his slider shortens up and becomes flat like a cutter. He doesn't show much of a third pitch, but he only needs two as a reliever. His pitchability and control are understandably behind for his age given the time he's missed. Health will dictate Vanegas' 2015 assignment.

Year	Club (League)	Class	W	L	ERA	G	GS	CG	SV	IP	H	HR	BB	SO	K/9	WHIP	AVG
2014	Ogden (PIO)	R	1	0	1.89	16	0	0	4	19	14	0	14	26	12.3	1.47	.203
	Great Lakes (MWL)	LoA	1	0	0.00	5	0	0	1	8	3	0	0	7	7.6	0.36	.111
Minor League Totals			2	0	1.32	21	0	0	5	27	17	0	14	33	10.9	1.13	.177

30 KYLE FARMER, C

BA GRADE

40 Risk: High

Born: Aug. 17, 1990. **B-T:** R-R. **Ht.:** 6-0. **Wt.:** 200. **Drafted:** Georgia, 2013 (8th round). **Signed by:** Lon Joyce.

Farmer was a four-year starter at shortstop for Georgia when the Dodgers signed him for $40,000 as an eighth-round pick in 2013. They immediately put him behind the plate. Farmer showed good bat-to-ball skills in 2014 at low Class A Great Lakes, where he rarely struck out, though his whiff rate spiked and overall production dropped precipitously once he got to high Class A Rancho Cucamonga in June, a red flag for a player who turned 24 before the season ended. Farmer has good pitch recognition, but he doesn't walk a ton, and his well-below-average power makes him mostly a gap hitter. Farmer did a solid job for a first-year catcher of throwing out 30 percent of basestealers, with quick feet and an above-average arm, though his release is long. He has the hands to catch, but his receiving and blocking are raw. Farmer is likely headed back to the California League and projects as a backup catcher.

Year	Club (League)	Class	AVG	G	AB	R	H	2B	3B	HR	RBI	BB	SO	SB	CS	OBP	SLG
2013	Ogden (PIO)	R	.347	41	167	37	58	19	0	4	36	7	21	1	1	.386	.533
2014	Great Lakes (MWL)	LoA	.310	57	229	25	71	16	4	2	35	15	24	9	3	.357	.441
	R. Cucamonga (CAL)	HiA	.238	36	130	8	31	5	1	0	15	10	28	2	0	.306	.292
Minor League Totals			.304	134	526	70	160	40	5	6	86	32	73	12	4	.354	.433

Miami Marlins

BY JUAN RODRIGUEZ

resh off their respective promotions to president of baseball operations and general manager, Michael Hill and Dan Jennings were tasked in 2014 with re-tooling a 100-loss team that featured one of the worst offenses in baseball history. They delved into the free agent market for upgrades and landed catcher Jarrod Saltalamacchia, third baseman Casey McGehee, first baseman Garrett Jones and second baseman Rafael Furcal.

With the exception of McGehee, those acquisitions disappointed due to injury or non-performance.

Yet the Marlins still became just the third National League team since 1969 to lose 100 games and win at least 77 the following season thanks in part to a homegrown outfield.

Right fielder Giancarlo Stanton, 24, had an MVP-worthy season after hitting .288/.395/.555 and leading the majors with 37 home runs.

He would have finished with gaudier numbers had a Mike Fiers pitch to the face not ended his season on Sept. 11. Regardless, the Marlins made him the face of the franchise with a 13-year, $325 million extension in November, making him the highest-paid player in North American sports.

The foundation around Stanton is taking shape. Left fielder Christian Yelich, 22, and center fielder Marcell Ozuna, 23, both became offensive and defensive forces. Miami improved its offensive output from 3.1 runs per game in 2013 to 4.0 in 2014, keeping the team on the periphery of the NL wild-card race into August.

Making that feat all the more notable was that the Marlins got just eight starts from ace Jose Fernandez, the NL Rookie of the Year in 2013, before losing him for the season in May to Tommy John surgery.

The Marlins hope they found another future rotation anchor in righthander Tyler Kolek, the No. 2 overall pick in the 2014 draft. The Marlins signed the 6-foot-6, 260-pound Texan for $6 million. He lacks Fernandez's polish, but scouts consider him perhaps the hardest-throwing pitcher in draft history, as he consistently hit 100 mph this spring.

With Fernandez on the shelf, the Marlins got a breakout season from righthander Henderson Alvarez and found another key rotation piece in righthander Jarred Cosart, acquired from the Astros in July for a package that jettisoned 2013 first-round pick Colin Moran.

The Marlins' upper-level starting pitching depth looked like an organizational strength at the start

The Marlins gave Giancarlo Stanton $325 million, then began building around him

TOP PROSPECTS OF THE DECADE

Year	Player, Pos.	2014 Org
2005	Jeremy Hermida, of	Brewers
2006	Jeremy Hermida, of	Brewers
2007	Chris Volstad, rhp	Angels
2008	Cameron Maybin, of	Padres
2009	Cameron Maybin, of	Padres
2010	Giancarlo Stanton, of	Marlins
2011	Matt Dominguez, 3b	Astros
2012	Christian Yelich, of	Marlins
2013	Jose Fernandez, rhp	Marlins
2014	Andrew Heaney, lhp	Marlins

of 2014, but righthander Anthony DeSclafani and lefties Andrew Heaney and Brian Flynn failed to seize on their first big league opportunities, and Flynn and Heaney—set to be the Marlins' No. 1 prospect for a second season—were traded after the season.

DeSclafani and Heaney began the 2014 season at Double-A Jacksonville, but the Suns rode other prospects to the Southern League title. Lefthander Justin Nicolino, righthander Jose Urena and catcher J.T. Realmuto all played critical roles and could reach Miami in 2015.

ORGANIZATION OVERVIEW

General Manager: Dan Jennings. **Farm Director:** Brian Chattin. **Scouting Director:** Stan Meek.

Class	Team	League	W	L	PCT	Finish	Manager
Majors	Miami Marlins	National	77	85	.475	t-18th (30)	Mike Redmond
Triple-A	New Orleans Zephyrs	Pacific Coast	70	74	.486	t-11th (16)	Andy Haines
Double-A	Jacksonville Suns	Southern	81	59	.579	2nd (10)	Andy Barkett
High A	Jupiter Hammerheads	Florida State	50	87	.365	11th (12)	Brian Schneider
Low A	Greensboro Grasshoppers	South Atlantic	87	53	.621	t-3rd (14)	Dave Berg
Short season	Batavia Muckdogs	New York-Penn	34	42	.447	10th (14)	Angel Espada
Rookie	Marlins	Gulf Coast	25	35	.417	t-12th (16)	Julio Garcia
Overall Minor League Record			347	350	.498	17th (30)	

THIS YEAR'S TOP 30

No.	Player, Pos.	Grade
1.	Tyler Kolek, rhp	65/Extreme
2.	J.T. Realmuto, c	55/Medium
3.	Justin Nicolino, lhp	50/Medium
4.	Jose Urena, rhp	50/Medium
5.	Avery Romero, 2b	55/High
6.	Domingo German, rhp	50/High
7.	Isael Soto, of	55/Extreme
8.	Trevor Williams, rhp	50/High
9.	Brian Anderson, 3b/2b	50/High
10.	Jarlin Garcia, lhp	50/High
11.	Austin Dean, of	50/High
12.	Justin Bohn, ss	45/Medium
13.	Matt Ramsey, rhp	45/Medium
14.	Justin Twine, ss	55/Extreme
15.	Justin Bour, 1b	45/Medium
16.	Brian Schales, 3b	50/High
17.	J.T. Riddle, ss/3b	45/Medium
18.	Adam Conley, lhp	45/Medium
19.	Michael Mader, lhp	50/High
20.	Gabe Castellanos, lhp	50/Extreme
21.	Anfernee Seymour, of/ss	50/Extreme
22.	Brian Ellington, rhp	45/High
23.	Viosergy Rosa, 1b	45/High
24.	Jorgan Cavanerio, rhp	50/Extreme
25.	Javier Lopez, ss	50/Extreme
26.	Felix Munoz, 1b	45/High
27.	Miguel Del Pozo, lhp	45/High
28.	Andrew McKirahan, lhp	45/High
29.	Austin Brice, rhp	50/Extreme
30.	Colby Suggs, rhp	50/Extreme

LAST YEAR'S TOP 30

No.	Player, Pos.	Status
1.	Andrew Heaney, lhp	(Angels)
2.	Colin Moran, 3b	(Astros)
3.	Jake Marisnick, of	(Astros)
4.	Justin Nicolino, lhp	No. 3
5.	Anthony DeSclafani, rhp	(Reds)
6.	Brian Flynn, lhp	(Royals)
7.	Jose Urena, rhp	No. 4
8.	Adam Conley, lhp	No. 18
9.	Avery Romero, 2b	No. 5
10.	J.T. Realmuto, c	No. 2
11.	Trevor Williams, rhp	No. 8
12.	Arquimedes Caminero, rhp	Dropped out
13.	Jesus Solorzano, of	Dropped out
14.	Austin Dean, of	No. 11
15.	Sam Dyson, rhp	Majors
16.	Angel Sanchez, rhp	(Pirates)
17.	Colby Suggs, rhp	No. 30
18.	Nick Wittgren, rhp	Dropped out
19.	Brent Keys, of	Dropped out
20.	Austin Barnes, c	(Dodgers)
21.	Grant Dayton, lhp	Dropped out
22.	Kyle Jensen, of	(Dodgers)
23.	Edgar Olmos, lhp	Dropped out
24.	Mark Canha, 1b	(Athletics)
25.	Tyler Higgins, rhp	Dropped out
26.	Javier Lopez, ss	No. 25
27.	Austin Brice, rhp	No. 29
28.	Jarlin Garcia, lhp	Dropped out
29.	Josh Hodges, rhp	Dropped out
30.	Michael Brady, rhp	(Angels)

BEST TOOLS

Best Hitter for Average	Avery Romero
Best Power Hitter	Justin Bour
Best Strike-Zone Discipline	Chad Wallach
Fastest Baserunner	Anfernee Seymour
Best Athlete	Justin Twine
Best Fastball	Tyler Kolek
Best Curveball	Austin Brice
Best Slider	Matt Milroy
Best Changeup	Justin Nicolino
Best Control	Justin Nicolino
Best Defensive Catcher	J.T. Realmuto
Best Defensive Infielder	Austin Nola
Best Infield Arm	Brian Anderson
Best Defensive Outfielder	Ryan Aper
Best Outfield Arm	Isael Soto

2018 LINEUP

Catcher	J.T. Realmuto
First Base	Justin Bour
Second Base	Dee Gordon
Third Base	Avery Romero
Shortstop	Adeiny Hechavarria
Left Field	Christian Yelich
Center Field	Marcell Ozuna
Right Field	Giancarlo Stanton
No. 1 Starter	Jose Fernandez
No. 2 Starter	Henderson Alvarez
No. 3 Starter	Jarred Cosart
No. 4 Starter	Tyler Kolek
No. 5 Starter	Justin Nicolino
Closer	Jose Urena

MIAMI MARLINS

TOP 2015 ROOKIE: Matt Ramsey, rhp. A bulldog reliever with a power fastball/curveball combination will land in the big league bullpen at some point.

BREAKOUT PROSPECT: Javier Lopez, ss. Among the Marlins' most tooled up prospects, he has struggled with injuries and translating those plus tools into baseball skills.

SLEEPER: Mason Davis, 2b. The Citadel alum had a strong offensive debut and has athleticism to be a contributor down the line.

SOURCE OF TOP 30 TALENT			
Homegrown	26	Acquired	4
College	6	Trades	2
Junior college	3	Rule 5 draft	2
High school	8	Independent leagues	0
Draft-and-follow	0	Free agents/waivers	0
Nondrafted free agents	0		
International	9		

LF
Austin Dean (11)
Stone Garrett
Matt Jeungel
K.J. Woods
Zach Sullivan

CF
Ryan Aper
Yefri Perez
Casey Soltis
Austin Wates
John Norwood

RF
Isael Soto (7)
Jesus Solorzano
Carlos Lopez
Yordy Cabrera

3B
Brian Anderson (9)
Brian Schales (16)
Zack Cox

SS
Justin Bohn (12)
J.T. Riddle (17)
Anfernee Seymour (21)
Javier Lopez (25)
Austin Nola
Garvis Lara

2B
Avery Romero (5)
Justin Twine (14)
Mason Davis

1B
Justin Bour (15)
Viosergy Rosa (23)
Felix Munoz (26)

C
J.T. Realmuto (2)
Blake Anderson
Roy Morales

LHP

LHSP	LHRP
Justin Nicolino (3)	Miguel Del Pozo (27)
Jarlin Garcia (10)	Andrew McKirahan (28)
Adam Conley (18)	Grant Dayton
Michael Mader (19)	Sean Townsley
Gabe Castellanos (20)	Greg Nappo
Chipper Smith	
Chris Sadberry	
Dillon Peters	
Ben Holmes	

RHP

RHSP	RHRP
Tyler Kolek (1)	Matt Ramsey (13)
Jose Urena (4)	Brian Ellington (22)
Domingo German (6)	Colby Suggs (30)
Trevor Williams (8)	Arquimedes Caminero
Jorgan Cavanerio (24)	Nick Wittgren
Austin Brice (29)	Juancito Martinez
Matt Milroy	Tyler Higgins
Jake Esch	
Mike Mater	
Scott Lyman	
Nick White	
Jordan Holloway	

2014

BEST PURE HITTER: 2B/3B Brian Anderson (3) hit better with wood than he had in the spring with metal bats. OF Casey Soltis (5) has shown an advanced feel to hit, plate discipline and a short, repeatable swing.

BEST POWER HITTER: OF Stone Garrett (8) passes the eye test with a muscular 6-foot-2, 195-pound frame. There's some stiffness to his swing the Marlins will need to loosen up to tap into his plus raw power. He didn't homer in his debut.

FASTEST RUNNER: This class has several speedsters but none can touch SS/OF Anfernee Seymour (7). The Bahamas native ran a 6.14-second 60-yard dash in a team pre-draft workout, making him the fastest player director Stan Meek has ever scouted.

BEST DEFENSIVE PLAYER: The Marlins are convicted in C Blake Anderson (1s) behind the plate, where he shows athleticism and agility. The Mississippi prep product got off to a rough start with 13 passed balls in 26 games.

BEST FASTBALL: Meek was one of many scouts this spring who said that RHP Tyler Kolek (1) was the hardest-throwing pitcher, on a consistent basis, he had ever seen, consistently hitting 100 mph with his fastball.

BEST SECONDARY PITCH: RHP Nick White (11) has good shape and power on his upper-70s 12-to-6 curveball. LHP Michael Mader (3) also flashes plus with his curve.

BEST PRO DEBUT: Brian Anderson hit 13 homers in three seasons for Arkansas, then hit 11 during his .300/.363/.496 debut with short-season Batavia and low Class A Greensboro. 2B Mason Davis (19) hit a combined .313/.389/.453 at the same two stops, though with more time in Batavia.

BEST ATHLETE: SS Justin Twine (2) has power and speed in his 5-foot-11, 205-pound frame that helped him excel in track and as a running quarterback in football.

MOST INTRIGUING BACKGROUND: LHP Ben Holmes (9; formerly known as Ben Wetzler) was suspended by the NCAA in the spring for contact with an agent after failing to sign with the Phillies as a 2013 fifth-rounder. He went on to lead the nation with a 0.78 ERA for Oregon State. Davis' father Fred played briefly in the NFL in 1987. At 6-foot-5, 250 pounds, Kolek has the largest listed weight of any first-round pitcher in draft history.

CLOSEST TO THE MAJORS: Anderson, particularly if he can handle third.

BEST LATE-ROUND PICK: Colorado prep RHP Jordan Holloway (20) got $400,000 thanks to a fastball that touches 94 mph and a projectable 6-foot-4, 180-pound frame. The class also got a boost when the Marlins signed OF John Norwood, who hit the game-winning home run for Vanderbilt in the College World Series, as a non drafted free agent in August.

THE ONE WHO GOT AWAY: 3B Mitchell Robinson (22) headed to Florida International.

ASSESSMENT: Attention centers on Kolek's velocity and size, but the Marlins are also excited about their speedy group of athletes, which Meek calls the best in his 13-year tenure.

2013

The Marlins quickly soured on 3B Colin Moran (1), trading him to the Astros in the Jarred Cosart trade. They've also dealt C Chad Wallach (5) while liking the early returns from RHP Trevor Williams (2) and SS Justin Bohn (7).

GRADE: C

2012

The Marlins also soured on LHP Andrew Heaney (1) even after he reached the majors; he was traded for Dee Gordon. 2B Avery Romero (3) may be the system's top hitter. OF Austin Dean (4) and sleeper RHP Brian Ellington (16) are Top 30 prospects.

GRADE: C

2011

RHP Jose Fernandez (1) had a monster rookie season, but Tommy John surgery scuttled his sophomore year. Since-traded 2B/C Austin Barnes (9) was the best of the rest of a class that also includes LHP Adam Conley (2).

GRADE: A

TOP DRAFT PICKS OF THE DECADE

Year	Player, Pos.	2014 Org
2005	Chris Volstad, rhp	Angels
2006	Brett Sinkbeil, rhp	Out of baseball
2007	Matt Dominguez, 3b	Astros
2008	Kyle Skipworth, c	Marlins
2009	Chad James, lhp	Rangers
2010	Christian Yelich, of	Marlins
2011	Jose Fernandez, rhp	Marlins
2012	Andrew Heaney, lhp	Marlins
2013	Colin Moran, 3b	Astros
2014	Tyler Kolek, rhp	Marlins

LARGEST BONUSES IN CLUB HISTORY

Tyler Kolek, 2014	$6,000,000
Josh Beckett, 1999	$3,625,000
Colin Moran, 2013	$3,516,500
Adrian Gonzalez, 2000	$3,000,000
Andrew Heaney, 2012	$2,600,000

1 TYLER KOLEK, RHP

Born: Dec. 15, 1995. **B-T:** R-R. **Ht.:** 6-5. **Wt.:** 260.
Drafted: HS—Shepherd, Texas, 2014 (1st round).
Signed by: Ryan Wardinsky.

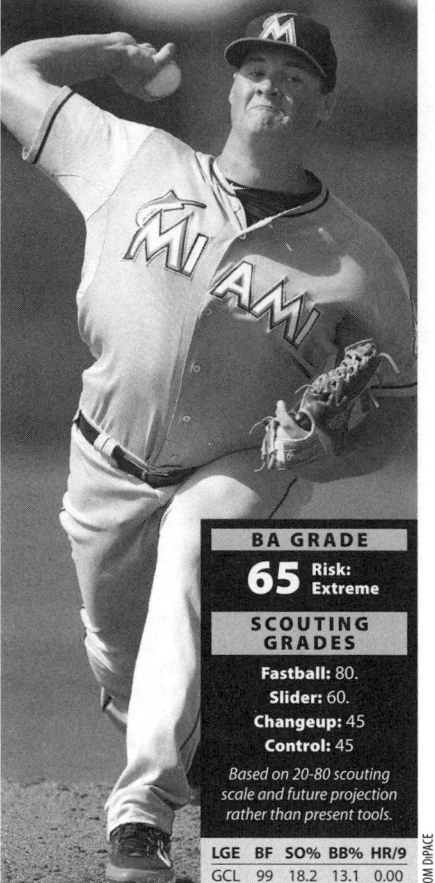

The last time the Marlins held the second overall pick in the draft, they went to the Texas prep pitcher ranks and got a future World Series MVP in Josh Beckett. Going to the same well last June, they nabbed Kolek, a country-strong fireballer whom they signed for $6 million. That broke Beckett's 15-year-old club record for the largest bonus in Marlins history. Baseball America research indicates that at 6-foot-5, 260 pounds, Kolek is the heaviest first-round high school righthander in draft history. Long-time scouts consider Kolek the hardest-throwing amateur in draft history, both for peak velocity (102 mph) and for consistently hitting 100. This after his junior year was cut short due to a broken arm he sustained during a baserunning collision. He came back hitting 99 mph in Texas' Area Code Games tryouts. His younger brother Stephen also is a big-bodied, hard-throwing righty who is draft-eligible in 2015.

Kolek has unprecedented size and arm strength, and he has coordination and arm speed to boot. The combination creates top-end velocity, even by today's radar-gun standards. Area scouts in Texas often had side bets with each other to see who could guess the velocity of his first warmup pitch, which often was as high as 97 mph, and he hit 100 virtually every time out in the spring. However, his fastball backed up a bit to 91-94 mph in the Rookie-level Gulf Coast League after signing due to a back issue and inconsistent direction in his delivery. The Marlins got him back on track in instructional league, with improved arm speed and more consistent stride, and they believe he'll pitch with a heavy, 95-97 mph heater consistently. Another key aspect of Kolek's fastball is its heavy sinking life, and scouts believe he'll break a lot of wood bats and induce a lot of groundballs. He gets tremendous extension in his delivery at his best, with a long stride to the plate and the ability to get over his front side and finish his pitches. Kolek's top-of-the-scale fastball helps his secondary stuff play up. He's shown an ability to spin the ball, with proper arm speed, though both his slider and power curveball need polish. He doesn't land either pitch consistently for strikes at this point, but both have flashed above-average, with an upper-70s curveball with depth and mid-80s slider with some tilt. At times they blend into one pitch, and he may wind up concentrating on one breaking ball as he develops. Kolek's changeup will be a focal point

for his 2015 development, because while he threw it in bullpens and showcases, he didn't throw it in games as a senior. Kolek is considered a solid athlete who's coordinated even at his massive size, but he'll be tested holding runners and fielding his position. He showed improvement in his debut but at times was a slow as 1.5 seconds to the plate.

Heading into the draft, the industry had no comparison point for Kolek, who is off the charts in so many ways. He encouraged Marlins officials by improving in instructional league after encountering a bit of adversity and losing something off his fastball in the GCL. Look for Kolek to open 2015 at low Class A Greensboro. The progression of his changeup and fastball command will be key early indicators to see if he hops on a Jose Fernandez-like fast track or if he'll need more time to develop. He could become the next great Texas-bred power pitcher.

BA GRADE

65 Risk: **Extreme**

SCOUTING GRADES

Fastball: 80.
Slider: 60.
Changeup: 45
Control: 45

Based on 20-80 scouting scale and future projection rather than present tools.

LGE	BF	SO%	BB%	HR/9
GCL	99	18.2	13.1	0.00

TOM DiPACE

Year	Club (League)	Class	W	L	ERA	G	GS	CG	SV	IP	H	HR	BB	SO	K/9	WHIP	AVG
2014	Marlins (GCL)	R	0	3	4.50	9	8	0	0	22	22	0	13	18	7.4	1.59	.275
Minor League Totals			0	3	4.50	9	8	0	0	22	22	0	13	18	7.4	1.59	.275

2 J.T. REALMUTO, C

Born: March 18, 1991. **B-T:** R-R. **Ht.:** 6-1. **Wt.:** 215. **Drafted:** HS—Midwest City, Okla, 2010 (3rd round). **Signed by:** Steve Taylor.

When he wasn't throwing touchdown passes in high school, Realmuto was manning shortstop on the baseball field. After signing him for $600,000 as a third-round pick in 2010, the Marlins transitioned him to catcher, and it proved a savvy move. When starter Jarrod Saltalamacchia missed time with a concussion in 2014, the Marlins called up Realmuto from Double-A Jacksonville to make his big league debut rather than summon Kyle Skipworth or Rob Brantly from Triple-A. Realmuto's athleticism and plus arm strength shine behind the plate. He runs well for a catcher and his game-calling and handling of pitchers have earned praise from Miami manager Mike Redmond. Realmuto threw out 39 percent of basestealers in 2014, posting pop times of 1.85 seconds on throws to second base, and he projects as an above-average defender overall. His offensive numbers in 2013 suffered as a result of his emphasis on defense, but he got back on track in 2014, focusing on a shorter swing and all-fields approach. His bat stays in the zone longer, and he has the strength for gap power, though consistent double-digit home run seasons aren't likely in his future. Realmuto profiles as an everyday catcher with two-way potential, but he may have to wait a bit at Triple-A New Orleans for his opportunity. Saltalamacchia is signed through 2016, and the Marlins exercised their 2015 club option on Jeff Mathis.

BA GRADE

55 Risk: Medium

LGE	PA	BB%	SO%	ISO
SL	423	9.7	13.9	.163
NL	30	3.3	26.7	.103

Year	Club (League)	Class	AVG	G	AB	R	H	2B	3B	HR	RBI	BB	SO	SB	CS	OBP	SLG
2012	Jupiter (FSL)	HiA	.256	123	446	63	114	16	0	8	46	37	64	13	5	.319	.345
2013	Jacksonville (SL)	AA	.239	106	368	41	88	21	3	5	39	36	68	9	1	.310	.353
2014	Jacksonville (SL)	AA	.299	97	375	66	112	25	6	8	62	41	59	18	5	.369	.461
	Miami (NL)	MAJ	.241	11	29	4	7	1	1	0	9	1	8	0	0	.267	.345
Major League Totals			.241	11	29	4	7	1	1	0	9	1	8	0	0	.267	.345
Minor League Totals			.267	434	1577	218	421	78	12	33	200	147	280	53	18	.334	.394

3 JUSTIN NICOLINO, LHP

Born: Nov. 22, 1991. **B-T:** L-L. **Ht.:** 6-3. **Wt.:** 190. **Drafted:** HS—Orlando, 2010 (2nd round). **Signed by:** Carlos Rodriguez (Blue Jays).

The Marlins acquired Nicolino from the Blue Jays as part of the November 2012 megadeal that sent Jose Reyes, Mark Buehrle and others to Toronto. Nicolino won over Miami manager Mike Redmond when he pitched for him at low Class A Lansing in the Blue Jays system. He pitched effectively at Double-A Jacksonville in 2014, winning Southern League pitcher of the year honors after leading the circuit in wins (14), ERA (2.85) and WHIP (1.07). Nicolino struck out just 4.3 batters per nine innings in 2014—fewer than all but six qualified minor league starters—but the Marlins aren't worried. He induces plenty of weak contact early in the count thanks to off-the-charts pitchability and a smooth, repeatable delivery. Nicolino has elite control, as evidenced by ranking third in the minors with 1.1 walks per nine. He incorporated a cutter in 2014 that he showed five or six times a game, but often he could log several innings using nothing but fastballs and changeups, precisely placed. He has to be fine, for only his changeup earns above-average grades. Nicolino's 88-91 mph fastball can reach 93 but lacks life. His mid- to upper-70s curveball bounced back to average late in 2014 after he'd struggled with it early. Nicolino likely will advance to Triple-A New Orleans in 2015. His overall profile is rare—most scouts project him as a No. 4 starter—but with his plus command he could reach a higher ceiling.

BA GRADE

50 Risk: Medium

LGE	BF	SO%	BB%	HR/9
SL	686	11.8	2.9	0.53

Year	Club (League)	Class	W	L	ERA	G	GS	CG	SV	IP	H	HR	BB	SO	K/9	WHIP	AVG
2012	Lansing (MWL)	LoA	10	4	2.46	28	22	0	0	124	112	6	21	119	8.6	1.07	.241
2013	Jupiter (FSL)	HiA	5	2	2.23	18	18	1	0	97	89	4	18	64	6.0	1.11	.247
	Jacksonville (SL)	AA	3	2	4.96	9	9	1	0	45	63	2	12	31	6.2	1.65	.341
2014	Jacksonville (SL)	AA	14	4	2.85	28	28	2	0	170	162	10	20	81	4.3	1.07	.249
Minor League Totals			38	14	2.64	98	89	5	0	498	465	22	84	368	6.7	1.10	.248

4 JOSE URENA, RHP

BA GRADE

50 Risk: Medium

LGE	BF	SO%	BB%	HR/9
SL	652	18.6	4.4	0.78

Born: Sept. 12, 1991. **B-T:** R-R. **Ht.:** 6-2. **Wt.:** 197. **Signed:** Dominican Republic, 2008 **Signed by:** Albert Gonzalez/Sandy Nin.

Originally signed for $52,000, Urena capped his 2013 season with a solid second half as a starter at high Class A Jupiter. He teamed with lefty Justin Nicolino in 2014 to give Double-A Jacksonville a pair of aces in the Suns' Southern League championship season, ranking second in the league to Nicolino in wins (13) and WHIP (1.14) while also ranking second in strikeouts (121). Urena's fastball/changeup combination is reminiscent of ex-Marlins reliever Juan Carlos Oviedo (formerly Leo Nunez). His plus fastball can sit at 94-95 mph, bumping 96, while his plus changeup is firm in the upper 80s with run and sink. Though his delivery is on the funky side, Urena repeats it and generally doesn't have issues controlling the strike zone, though below-average command makes him more hittable than his stuff suggests. Once Urena started trusting his stuff, he was able to get over a slow start in 2014 (6.66 ERA in April). His breaking ball, a hard slider, remains below-average but has its moments, and it remains the biggest obstacle to him missing more bats. The Marlins will have to decide whether Urena is a starter or a reliever. He has expressed a desire to keep starting, and the Marlins for the time appear willing to accommodate him, aware that patience now could yield a bigger payoff later. Don't be surprised to see Urena make his big league debut in relief sometime in 2015.

Year	Club (League)	Class	W	L	ERA	G	GS	CG	SV	IP	H	HR	BB	SO	K/9	WHIP	AVG
2012	Greensboro (SAL)	LoA	9	6	3.38	27	22	1	2	138	143	13	29	101	6.6	1.24	.266
2013	Jupiter (FSL)	HiA	10	7	3.73	27	26	0	0	150	148	8	29	107	6.4	1.18	.257
2014	Jacksonville (SL)	AA	13	8	3.33	26	25	0	0	162	155	14	29	121	6.7	1.14	.255
Minor League Totals			44	37	3.60	122	103	4	4	632	632	41	134	458	6.5	1.21	.260

5 AVERY ROMERO, 2B

BA GRADE

55 Risk: High

LGE	PA	BB%	SO%	ISO
SAL	399	6.3	11.8	.109
FSL	108	6.5	12.0	.080

Born: May 11, 1993. **B-T:** R-R. **Ht.:** 5-8. **Wt.:** 190. **Drafted:** HS—St. Augustine, Fla., 2012 (3rd round). **Signed by:** Brian Kraft.

Romero's older brother Jordan, who played at NAIA Embry-Riddle (Fla.), was the better-fielding shortstop in high school, pushing Avery off the position when they played on the same team. He shifted to second base full time upon turning pro. At low Class A Greensboro in 2014, he ranked fifth in the South Atlantic League in batting (.320), helping lead the Grasshoppers to the league's best record. The Marlins sent him back down for the playoffs after he also hit .320 during a month-long promotion to high Class A Jupiter. Romero might have the quickest bat in the organization, consistently showing the ability to turn on good fastballs. He showed improved balance and worked on plate-coverage issues in 2014 as well. A below-average runner, Romero is a gap-to-gap hitter who has the strength to drive balls out of the park as his pitch recognition improves. Defensively, he has improved significantly since his amateur days, showing that despite his stocky body he has quick enough feet and solid hands to handle second base, along with a solid-average arm. Romero already has shown he can hit in the Florida State League and should return to Jupiter to start 2015. He could hop on the fast track if he keeps hitting, though Dee Gordon now blocks his path at second base.

Year	Club (League)	Class	AVG	G	AB	R	H	2B	3B	HR	RBI	BB	SO	SB	CS	OBP	SLG
2012	Marlins (GCL)	R	.223	33	121	8	27	6	0	3	15	10	21	0	1	.309	.347
	Jamestown (NYP)	SS	.381	7	21	3	8	0	0	0	4	3	0	1	0	.458	.381
2013	Batavia (NYP)	SS	.297	56	209	27	62	18	0	2	30	15	34	3	4	.357	.411
	Greensboro (SAL)	LoA	.147	9	34	5	5	1	0	1	5	4	5	0	0	.237	.265
2014	Jupiter (FSL)	HiA	.320	26	100	12	32	8	0	0	10	7	13	4	1	.370	.400
	Greensboro (SAL)	LoA	.320	92	366	51	117	23	1	5	46	25	47	6	4	.366	.429
Minor League Totals			.295	223	851	106	251	56	1	11	110	64	120	14	10	.353	.402

6 DOMINGO GERMAN, RHP

Born: Aug. 4, 1992. **B-T:** R-R. **Ht.:** 6-2. **Wt.:** 175. **Signed:** Dominican Republic, 2009. **Signed by:** Albert Gonzalez/Sandy Nin/Alix Martinez.

German had never pitched in full-season ball until 2014, when he broke out in a big way at low Class A Greensboro. The Marlins' lone representative at the 2014 Futures Game, he impressed with a scoreless inning that featured strikeouts of top prospects Kris Bryant and Joey Gallo. Pitchability isn't German's strength right now, but throwing strikes is. He has an easy delivery he repeats well to go with a loose, live arm that produces above-average life on a heavy sinking fastball that sits in the 91-96 mph range and touches 97. He got his share of groundballs with his fastball and with his low-80s changeup, a pitch he's shown he knows how to use and that flashes average potential. German throws his slurvy curveball with low-80s power and 10-to-4 break. It's his third pitch at this point, which has some scouts projecting him as a future reliever. He's still in the early stages of learning pitch sequencing and how to set up hitters. German's control of a plus fastball makes him a prospect, but he'll need to develop his secondary stuff to be a future rotation option in Miami. Added to the 40-man roster in November, he is set to move up to high Class A Jupiter for 2015 and hopes to follow the career path of fellow live-armed Dominican Jose Urena.

BA GRADE

50 Risk: High

LGE	BF	SO%	BB%	HR/9
SAL	504	22.4	5.0	0.44

Year	Club (League)	Class	W	L	ERA	G	GS	CG	SV	IP	H	HR	BB	SO	K/9	WHIP	AVG
2012	Marlins (GCL)	R	2	0	1.61	13	0	0	0	22	17	0	16	29	11.7	1.48	.215
2013	Marlins (GCL)	R	3	0	1.38	5	5	0	0	26	15	1	5	27	9.3	0.77	.167
	Batavia (NYP)	SS	2	3	1.76	8	8	0	0	41	33	0	5	34	7.5	0.93	.213
2014	Greensboro (SAL)	LoA	9	3	2.48	25	25	0	0	123	116	6	25	113	8.2	1.14	.249
Minor League Totals			20	10	2.33	77	44	0	6	294	248	8	91	286	8.8	1.15	.229

7 ISAEL SOTO, OF

Born: Nov. 2, 1996. **B-T:** L-L. **Ht.:** 6-0. **Wt.:** 190. **Signed:** Dominican Republic, 2013. **Signed by:** Albert Gonzalez/Sandy Nin/Domingo Ortega.

Part of Miami's 2013 international signing class, Soto signed for $310,000, and the Marlins jumped him straight to the U.S. when he made his pro debut in the Rookie-level Gulf Coast League as a 17-year-old in 2014. His present strength was evident, as he slugged .426 and ranked second in the GCL with seven home runs. Soto is raw, but he opened eyes in the GCL, putting up better numbers at a younger age than Marcell Ozuna did at the same level. He earns some comparisons with Ozuna, and other comps to a lefthanded version of Raul Mondesi, thanks to his stocky body and plus, right-field arm. The ball sounds different coming off Soto's bat, and he's aggressive, at times to a fault, as are many young sluggers. He also has short, stocky arms that contribute to his short swing and direct path to the ball. He makes fair contact and consistently gets to his power in games, driving the ball to all fields. He's an average runner now, and the Marlins may give him some time in center field in 2015. The Marlins don't need young outfielders—they already have three in Miami—so Soto doesn't need to be fast-tracked. Nevertheless, he's headed to low Class A Greensboro for 2015. He fits the profile of a corner outfielder as long as he keeps hitting.

MIKE JANES

BA GRADE

55 Risk: Extreme

LGE	PA	BB%	SO%	ISO
GCL	199	5.0	23.6	.175

Year	Club (League)	Class	AVG	G	AB	R	H	2B	3B	HR	RBI	BB	SO	SB	CS	OBP	SLG
2014	Marlins (GCL)	R	.251	50	183	26	46	9	1	7	23	10	47	1	2	.302	.426
Minor League Totals			.251	50	183	26	46	9	1	7	23	10	47	1	2	.302	.426

8 TREVOR WILLIAMS, RHP

Born: April 25, 1992. **B-T:** R-R. **Ht.:** 6-3. **Wt.:** 228. **Drafted:** Arizona State, 2013 (2nd round). **Signed by:** Scott Stanley.

Williams previously pitched for two traditional powers. The San Diego native attended Rancho Bernardo High, where he played for coach Sam Blalock, and he attended Arizona State. A down junior season in 2013, in which his ERA doubled to 4.12, dropped him to the second round, where he signed for a $1,261,400 bonus. He made the high Class A Florida State League all-star team in 2014, then finished at Double-A Jacksonville. Marlins officials consider Williams among the system's most cerebral pitchers, and his advanced approach makes up for not having a plus pitch. He throws both a four- and two-seam fastball from a drop-and-drive delivery, pitching up and down in the zone with low-90s velocity and keeping the ball down. He has reached 96 mph in shorter stints when pitching as a reliever. Williams gave up just five home runs in 2014 and gets his share of groundball outs. He added an upper-80s cutter-type slider in 2014 and has more confidence in his changeup than his low-70s, early count curveball. Williams lacks a putaway pitch but has a chance to be an innings-eating No. 4 starter. He should start 2015 back at Double-A and could approach his career minor league innings total (178).

BA GRADE

50 Risk: High

LGE	BF	SO%	BB%	HR/9
FSL	537	16.8	5.4	0.35
SL	71	19.7	8.5	0.00

Year	Club (League)	Class	W	L	ERA	G	GS	CG	SV	IP	H	HR	BB	SO	K/9	WHIP	AVG
2013	Marlins (GCL)	R	0	0	4.50	1	1	0	0	2	3	0	0	1	4.5	1.50	.300
	Batavia (NYP)	SS	0	2	2.48	10	10	0	0	29	26	0	8	20	6.2	1.17	.228
	Greensboro (SAL)	LoA	0	0	0.00	1	1	0	0	3	2	0	0	3	9.0	0.67	.182
2014	Jupiter (FSL)	HiA	8	6	2.79	23	23	0	0	129	138	5	29	90	6.3	1.29	.277
	Jacksonville (SL)	AA	0	1	6.00	3	3	0	0	15	22	0	6	14	8.4	1.87	.344
Minor League Totals			8	9	2.98	38	38	0	0	178	191	5	43	128	6.5	1.31	.274

9 BRIAN ANDERSON, 3B/2B

Born: May 19, 1993. **B-T:** R-R **Ht:** 6-3. **Wt.:** 185. **Drafted:** Arkansas, 2014 (3rd round). **Signed by:** Brian Kraft.

Like many picks of scouting director Stan Meek, Anderson has Oklahoma ties, and he was a prep teammate of Mets farmhand Michael Fulmer. A 20th-round pick out of high school (Twins), Anderson didn't sign and helped lead Arkansas to the College World Series while playing the outfield as a freshman. He was a consistent hitter for the Razorbacks while playing several positions and signed for $600,000 as a 2014 third-rounder. In Anderson, the Marlins landed a hitter with a fluid, smooth, fundamentally sound swing and plus raw power. The ball jumps off his bat thanks in part to an advanced feel for hitting and strength that belies his slender but athletic frame. He played second base at short-season Batavia but moved to third base, in deference to Avery Romero, at low Class A Greensboro. He showed mid-90s velocity in fall workouts at Arkansas and has plenty of arm for third. He's an above-average runner whose defensive shuffling has kept him from developing proficiency at any position. At times the game speeds up on him defensively, and he'll need plenty of reps to prove he can handle third. If Anderson continues to tap into his power as a pro—he hit 11 homers in his debut after hitting 13 in three college seasons—he could give the Marlins a profile third baseman. He's ticketed for high Class A Jupiter to start 2015.

BA GRADE

50 Risk: High

LGE	PA	BB%	SO%	ISO
NYP	85	7.1	12.9	.182
SAL	172	7.6	16.3	.203

Year	Club (League)	Class	AVG	G	AB	R	H	2B	3B	HR	RBI	BB	SO	SB	CS	OBP	SLG
2014	Batavia (NYP)	SS	.273	20	77	11	21	3	1	3	12	6	11	1	1	.333	.455
	Greensboro (SAL)	LoA	.314	39	153	27	48	7	0	8	37	13	28	0	0	.378	.516
Minor League Totals			.300	59	230	38	69	10	1	11	49	19	39	1	1	.363	.496

10 JARLIN GARCIA, LHP

Born: Jan. 18, 1993. **B-T:** L-L. **Ht.:** 6-2. **Wt.:** 170. **Signed:** Dominican Republic, 2010. **Signed by:** Albert Gonzalez, Sandy Nin.

MIKE JANES

Garcia signed as a 17-year-old and it took him three seasons to reach full-season ball. In the interim, he grew physically and developed one of the organization's better curveballs. He led the low Class A South Atlantic League in lowest walk rate (1.35/9 IP) while leading Greensboro in victories, and he didn't give up an earned run in his final four starts, spanning 18 innings. Athletic and live-bodied, Garcia shows excellent control of a live, above-average fastball in the 90-95 mph range. His curveball still flashes above-average as well in the upper 70s, but somewhere between instructional league and the 2014 season, he lost the feel for it. His slinging delivery sometimes makes it tough for him to stay on top of the pitch. To avoid going through a full season without a breaking ball, Garcia started throwing a hard slider, and he has a changeup with some fade that is firm in the low 80s. Despite his athleticism, he needs polish defensively, both field-ing and holding runners. Garcia's strong finish restored optimism to what had been a season of struggles. He wasn't protected on the 40-man roster but he wasn't picked in the Rule 5 draft, so the Marlins can send him to high Class A Jupiter. A consistent breaking ball would give him a mid-rotation ceiling.

BA GRADE
50 Risk: High

LGE	BF	SO%	BB%	HR/9
SAL	569	19.5	3.7	0.88

Year	Club (League)	Class	W	L	ERA	G	GS	CG	SV	IP	H	HR	BB	SO	K/9	WHIP	AVG
2012	Marlins (GCL)	R	1	3	3.60	12	4	0	0	40	38	2	14	32	7.2	1.30	.242
2013	Batavia (NYP)	SS	2	3	3.10	15	15	0	0	70	58	7	18	74	9.6	1.09	.221
2014	Greensboro (SAL)	LoA	10	5	4.38	25	25	0	0	134	152	13	21	111	7.5	1.29	.286
Minor League Totals			18	16	3.78	66	52	0	1	295	295	25	65	263	8.0	1.22	.257

11 AUSTIN DEAN, OF

BA GRADE
50 Risk: High

Born: Oct. 14, 1993. **B-T:** R-R. **Ht.:** 6-1. **Wt.:** 190. **Drafted:** HS—Spring, Texas, 2012 (4th round). **Signed by:** Ryan Wardinsky.

An infielder in high school, Dean has logged no professional innings on the dirt. The Marlins immediately moved the 2012 fourth-rounder to left field, where he projects as an everyday player with power. Dean has totaled just 14 homers in 784 minor league at-bats, but the Marlins expect the power to continue developing. He hit a career-best .308 in 99 games at low Class A Greensboro in 2014, building on his solid debut at short-season Batavia in 2013. An aggressive, hard-nosed player, Dean does just about everything well offensively. His best attribute is outstanding bat speed. He lowered his strikeout rate from 20 percent in 2013 to 16 percent in 2014. What he lacks is a plus throwing arm, which may not be as much of an issue if Dean ultimately moves back to first base from left field. Dean probably doesn't have sufficient foot speed to man center field, but he has recorded average run times from home to first.

Year	Club (League)	Class	AVG	G	AB	R	H	2B	3B	HR	RBI	BB	SO	SB	CS	OBP	SLG
2012	Marlins (GCL)	R	.223	47	148	15	33	11	0	2	15	24	35	2	2	.337	.338
2013	Batavia (NYP)	SS	.268	56	213	28	57	12	7	2	19	17	47	0	2	.325	.418
	Greensboro (SAL)	LoA	.200	7	20	4	4	1	0	1	3	4	5	0	0	.346	.400
2014	Greensboro (SAL)	LoA	.308	99	403	67	124	20	4	9	58	38	72	4	4	.371	.444
Minor League Totals			.278	209	784	114	218	44	11	14	95	83	159	6	8	.351	.416

12 JUSTIN BOHN, SS

BA GRADE
45 Risk: Medium

Born: Nov. 2, 1992. **B-T:** R-R. **Ht.:** 6-0. **Wt.:** 180. **Drafted:** Feather River (Calif.) JC, 2013 (7th round). **Signed by:** John Hughes.

Signed away from Oregon State for $525,000 in 2013, Bohn will man shortstop at Double-A Jacksonville in 2015 after delivering a strong full-season debut between two Class A levels. While he doesn't have flashy tools, with average range and arm strength, scouts watching him over a five-game series see him make all the plays at shortstop and consistently drive balls to the gaps. Bohn hits for a solid average from a simple set-up and level swing, and the Marlins anticipate the hit tool to continue developing through the upper levels. Bohn ruptured a ligament in his finger toward the end of the 2014 season, and the Marlins thought he might not be able to fulfill his Arizona Fall League assignment. The injury did not require surgery, and he ranked among Salt River's top hitters (.328/.409/.431) in 58 at-bats. He logged some AFL innings at second, learning the nuances of the position with an eye toward increasing his versatility. He's an average runner who's becoming a more aggressive baserunner. Bohn should arrive at spring training in 2015 brimming with confidence and ready for the upper minors.

Year	Club (League)	Class	AVG	G	AB	R	H	2B	3B	HR	RBI	BB	SO	SB	CS	OBP	SLG
2013	Batavia (NYP)	SS	.177	40	141	12	25	4	0	0	8	15	32	4	2	.278	.206
	Greensboro (SAL)	LoA	.250	12	48	5	12	1	0	0	2	4	12	4	0	.308	.271
2014	Greensboro (SAL)	LoA	.293	63	239	39	70	16	2	6	47	39	49	4	2	.397	.452
	Jupiter (FSL)	HiA	.296	48	199	29	59	9	3	0	12	16	45	7	3	.347	.372
Minor League Totals			.265	163	627	85	166	30	5	6	69	74	138	19	7	.348	.357

13 MATT RAMSEY, RHP

Born: Sept. 24, 1989. **B-T:** R-R. **Ht.:** 5-11. **Wt.:** 205. **Drafted:** Tennessee, 2011 (19th round). **Signed by:** Milt Hill (Rays).

The Marlins acquired Ramsey from the Rays in July 2014, sending their second, third and fourth international bonus slots—which totaled just more than $1 million—to Tampa Bay. Already in the Double-A Southern League with the Rays, he made the move from Montgomery to Jacksonville and exhibited better command with a mid-90s fastball and power curveball repertoire. After opening his season with a 1.16 WHIP while with the Biscuits, Ramsey finished the campaign with a 0.94 WHIP in Jacksonville. Talent evaluators who saw Ramsey during the Suns' SL title run—when he saved three of their six victories and struck out eight in four innings—said he was good enough to retire major league hitters. Ramsey's fastball/curve combo should get him to the big leagues at some point in 2015. Built like a bulldog, he brings those same traits to the mound. Everything about his game is power and attack. He also shows a changeup as a third offering, but rarely uses it. Added to the 40-man roster in November, Ramsey has a chance to break camp with Miami.

Year	Club (League)	Class	W	L	ERA	G	GS	CG	SV	IP	H	HR	BB	SO	K/9	WHIP	AVG
2012	Rays (GCL)	R	2	1	1.98	11	5	0	0	14	12	0	2	9	5.9	1.02	.218
2013	Bowling Green (MWL)	LoA	0	1	2.42	20	0	0	6	26	24	1	10	36	12.5	1.31	.245
	Charlotte (FSL)	HiA	1	1	3.28	12	0	0	0	25	27	0	15	22	8.0	1.70	.290
2014	Montgomery (SL)	AA	3	0	1.07	24	0	0	6	34	16	0	23	46	12.3	1.16	.148
	Jacksonville (SL)	AA	0	2	1.95	20	0	0	8	28	19	2	7	34	11.1	0.94	.190
Minor League Totals			6	5	2.08	87	5	0	20	126	98	3	57	147	10.5	1.23	.216

14 JUSTIN TWINE, SS

Born: Oct. 7, 1995. **B-T:** R-R. **Ht.:** 5-11. **Wt.:** 205. **Drafted:** HS—Falls City, Texas, 2014 (2nd round). **Signed by:** Ryan Wardinsky.

The raw but tooled-up Twine rushed for 534 yards as a sophomore for Hemphill (Texas) High, and after his family moved across state to Falls City, he scored five touchdowns on just 13 touches in his first football game. Baylor offered him a scholarship, but Twine declined in part because football might be his second-best sport. The Marlins drafted Twine as a shortstop, the position he played in the Rookie-level Gulf Coast League in 2014 after signing for $1,316,000. How his stocky frame develops and whether his throwing mechanics hold up will determine whether he stays there. Twine arrived with a tendency to throw everything to first from a low slot, giving his ball a two-seam action instead of the necessary backspin. A plus runner with plus arm strength, he also projects to have better than average power. The Marlins would like to keep him at shortstop, but his physicality makes him a candidate to move to second or third base. He didn't see a lot of quality breaking stuff in high school, so Twine tended to swing early in the count to avoid two-strike breaking stuff. His focus offensively in 2015 will be pitch recognition and strike-zone awareness. He'll need a strong spring to earn a spot at low Class A Greensboro.

Year	Club (League)	Class	AVG	G	AB	R	H	2B	3B	HR	RBI	BB	SO	SB	CS	OBP	SLG
2014	Marlins (GCL)	R	.229	44	166	19	38	8	5	1	16	6	52	5	1	.285	.355
Minor League Totals			.229	44	166	19	38	8	5	1	16	6	52	5	1	.285	.355

15 JUSTIN BOUR, 1B

Born: May 28, 1988. **B-T:** L-R. **Ht.:** 6-4. **Wt.:** 250. **Drafted:** George Mason, 2009 (25th round). **Signed by:** Billy Swoope (Cubs).

Bour rose from minor league Rule 5 draft selection in 2013 to big leaguer a year later with the Marlins, who called him up for an interleague road swing through American League parks in June to be used as a DH. He spent five seasons in the Cubs system, missing two months in 2013 with a hairline fracture in his wrist but still slugging 18 home runs at Double-A Tennessee. Nevertheless, the Marlins sought out Bour in the Triple-A phase of the 2013 Rule 5 draft and landed him for just $12,000, acquiring a slugger for their Triple-A New Orleans lineup who earned a September callup. A hulking, lumbering first baseman with bottom-of-the-scale speed, Bour has the most power in the system, with a chance to hit enough to be a regular, even at first base. He has some pre-swing movement in his swing, but when he's on time, he's short to the ball. He has the strength to drive the ball out to all fields with plus power. He has good hands at first base but below-average range. Bour's lack of athleticism and struggles with lefthanders may limit him to part-time duty. He's shown the feel for hitting and power to be a low-cost option at first base for the 2015 Marlins.

Year	Club (League)	Class	AVG	G	AB	R	H	2B	3B	HR	RBI	BB	SO	SB	CS	OBP	SLG
2012	Tennessee (SL)	AA	.283	138	506	64	143	36	0	17	110	62	115	4	1	.360	.455
2013	Tennessee (SL)	AA	.237	83	317	48	75	17	0	18	64	36	63	0	2	.313	.461
2014	New Orleans (PCL)	AAA	.306	103	385	59	118	27	0	18	72	39	57	3	1	.372	.517
	Miami (NL)	MAJ	.284	39	74	10	21	3	0	1	11	9	19	0	0	.361	.365
Major League Totals			.284	39	74	10	21	3	0	1	11	9	19	0	0	.361	.365
Minor League Totals			.279	646	2422	319	675	158	2	92	458	266	485	13	6	.351	.460

16 BRIAN SCHALES, 3B

BA GRADE

50 Risk: High

Born: Feb. 13, 1996. **B-T:** R-R. **Ht.:** 6-1. **Wt.:** 170. **Drafted:** HS— Huntington Beach, Calif., 2014 (4th round). **Signed by:** Tim McDonnell.

Schales was set to play at Long Beach State before the Marlins enticed him into pro ball with a $490,000 signing bonus as a fourth-round pick, and he may be the most accomplished of the young hitters Miami took in the 2014 draft. He has a smooth, functional swing in place and shows advanced ability to recognize pitches. He projects to have slightly above-average power and slightly below-average speed. The Marlins sent him to instructional league to work him at shortstop to get a feel for him there, though he played mostly third base after signing. Schales likely will stay at the hot corner moving forward based on his bat and an organizational logjam at shortstop. A good spring should earn him a spot at low Class A Greensboro, a step behind fellow 2014 draft pick Brian Anderson on the organizational ladder.

Year	Club (League)	Class	AVG	G	AB	R	H	2B	3B	HR	RBI	BB	SO	SB	CS	OBP	SLG
2014	Marlins (GCL)	R	.243	49	173	24	42	8	0	1	23	16	28	2	5	.318	.306
Minor League Totals			.243	49	173	24	42	8	0	1	23	16	28	2	5	.318	.306

17 J.T. RIDDLE, SS/3B

BA GRADE

45 Risk: Medium

Born: Oct. 12, 1991. **B-T:** L-R. **Ht.:** 6-3. **Wt.:** 175. **Drafted:** Kentucky, 2013 (13th round). **Signed by:** Matt Gaski

The Marlins don't anticipate having a need for a shortstop any time soon with slick-fielding Adeiny Hechavarria still in his major league infancy, but they have a nice stockpile in the minors. Riddle played mostly third and second base in the first half alongside Justin Bohn but took over as low Class A Greensboro's shortstop in the second half after Bohn's promotion, and the team didn't skip a beat. Riddle's numbers don't jump off the page, but the Marlins love his tools. Some in the organization liken him to Pirates shortstop Jordy Mercer. Riddle has all the essentials—an above-average arm, great hands and footwork—to play short at a high level. The lefthanded hitter has solid gap power, some leverage in his swing and solid-average speed. He shows good range up the middle and in the hole, and rarely does he get caught fielding a ball flat-footed. The Marlins also love Riddle's leadership ability and clubhouse presence, which along with his lefty bat profiles him well as a future utility infielder. He's headed to high Class A Jupiter with a chance to reach Double-A Jacksonville in 2015.

Year	Club (League)	Class	AVG	G	AB	R	H	2B	3B	HR	RBI	BB	SO	SB	CS	OBP	SLG
2013	Batavia (NYP)	SS	.243	59	222	38	54	10	0	2	18	10	28	6	1	.288	.315
2014	Greensboro (SAL)	LoA	.280	103	435	65	122	17	4	9	60	26	55	5	1	.323	.400
Minor League Totals			.268	162	657	103	176	27	4	11	78	36	83	11	2	.311	.371

18 ADAM CONLEY, LHP

BA GRADE

45 Risk: Medium

Born: May 24, 1990. **B-T:** L-L. **Ht.:** 6-3. **Wt.:** 210. **Drafted:** Washington State, 2011 (2nd round). **Signed by:** Gabe Sandy.

Elbow tendinitis robbed Conley of a chance to build on a stellar 2013, when he shined at Double-A Jacksonville. Limited to 12 regular season starts in 2014, mostly at Triple-A New Orleans, he was hammered in the hitter-friendly Pacific Coast League. That cost Conley an opportunity to make his major league debut in 2014, but he remains an intriguing lefty who ultimately could make a permanent move to the bullpen. He pitches off an average 88-92 mph fastball with some tailing action, with a fringe-average slider and solid-average changeup that flashes better. In spite of the elbow issue, Conley was able to repeat his delivery more consistently in 2014 than the year before. Prior to that, Conley would tend to fly open and would be late on his delivery. The Marlins are hoping that, if healthy, he will develop more of a bulldog mentality. Conley seems destined to remain in the New Orleans rotation in 2015. He's already on the 40-man roster, so he could be called upon any time he's pitching well.

Year	Club (League)	Class	W	L	ERA	G	GS	CG	SV	IP	H	HR	BB	SO	K/9	WHIP	AVG
2012	Greensboro (SAL)	LoA	7	3	2.78	14	14	0	0	74	58	4	24	84	10.2	1.10	.213
	Jupiter (FSL)	HiA	4	2	4.44	12	12	0	0	53	59	0	19	51	8.7	1.48	.282
2013	Jacksonville (SL)	AA	11	7	3.25	26	25	3	0	139	125	7	37	129	8.4	1.17	.236
2014	Jupiter (FSL)	HiA	0	1	5.06	1	1	0	0	5	9	0	2	2	3.4	2.06	.346
	New Orleans (PCL)	AAA	3	5	6.00	12	11	0	0	60	65	3	26	48	7.2	1.52	.279
Minor League Totals			25	18	3.84	67	63	3	0	333	317	14	108	316	8.5	1.28	.248

19 MICHAEL MADER, LHP

Born: Feb. 18, 1994. **B-T:** L-L. **Ht.:** 6-2. **Wt.:** 195. **Drafted:** Chipola (Fla.) JC, 2014 (3rd round supplemental). **Signed by:** Dave Dangler.

Tampa resident Chuck Hernandez, the Marlins' big league pitching coach and former assistant coach at South Florida, knew of Mader from his days Marianna (Fla.) High, which is the alma mater of Marlins backup catcher Jeff Mathis. Mader spent two years at Chipola (Fla.) JC, and the Marlins signed the 2014 supplemental third-rounder away from a Florida State scholarship for $499,500. The strong-bodied Mader impressed the Marlins with his solid delivery and three-pitch repertoire. His fastball sits 90-93 mph and he complements it with a 12-to-6 overhand curveball that flashes plus and a changeup that requires more consistency. Mader went through a transitional period in pro ball, looking tentative at times but occasionally dominating at short-season Batavia. One Marlins' front office executive said Mader improved each of the three times he saw him, and he concluded his first pro season having allowed four earned runs over his final 23 innings. He should be ready to move up to low Class A Greensboro in 2015 and has a ceiling as mid-rotation starter.

Year	Club (League)	Class	W	L	ERA	G	GS	CG	SV	IP	H	HR	BB	SO	K/9	WHIP	AVG
2014	Batavia (NYP)	SS	1	0	2.00	12	12	0	0	45	31	3	16	28	5.6	1.04	.199
Minor League Totals			1	0	2.00	12	12	0	0	45	31	3	16	28	5.6	1.04	.199

20 GABE CASTELLANOS, LHP

Born: Dec. 28, 1993. **B-T:** L-L. **Ht:** 6-1. **Wt.:** 165. **Signed:** Dominican Republic, 2010. **Signed by:** Junior Noboa.

The tall and slender Castellanos remains raw but has plenty of projectability. Through two Dominican Summer League seasons, he had trouble finding the zone, so the Marlins were prepared to keep him in the DSL a third season in 2013. However, former minor league pitching coordinator Wayne Rosenthal encouraged the club to bring Castellanos to the U.S., and the added instruction proved beneficial. While his stuff is live, he struggled with command at short-season Batavia in 2014. Nevertheless, the Marlins are excited. Castellanos has an easy delivery and good sink on the fastball, which sits 91-93 mph. Those figures should rise as he adds strength. He also throws an inconsistent slider that has flashed two-plane break at its best. Among the priorities for him in 2015 are gaining consistency with the slider and additional touch on the changeup. Castellanos will head for low Class A Greensboro in 2015.

Year	Club (League)	Class	W	L	ERA	G	GS	CG	SV	IP	H	HR	BB	SO	K/9	WHIP	AVG
2012	Marlins (DSL)	R	2	6	5.98	15	6	0	0	44	51	1	30	37	7.6	1.85	.288
2013	Marlins (GCL)	R	3	4	3.45	12	12	0	0	47	40	0	19	56	10.7	1.26	.227
2014	Batavia (NYP)	SS	2	6	4.65	13	13	0	0	62	52	1	41	54	7.8	1.50	.224
Minor League Totals			7	20	5.15	48	36	0	0	168	160	4	105	152	8.2	1.58	.250

21 ANFERNEE SEYMOUR, OF/SS

Born: June 24, 1995. **B-T:** B-R. **Ht:** 5-11. **Wt.:** 165. **Drafted:** HS—Delray Beach, Fla., 2014 (7th round). **Signed by:** Lazaro Llanes.

A product of the Bahamas who relocated to South Florida to attend high school, Seymour is the fastest player in the system after joining the Marlins as a seventh-round pick in 2014. Scouting director Stan Meek timed him at 6.14 seconds in the 60-yard dash, making him the fastest player he's ever timed. Signed for $400,000, Seymour made his debut in the Rookie-level Gulf Coast League in 2014 and stole bases on pure speed, but he also shows good technique for a player his age. He does have to work on staying low when he breaks and eliminate the tendency to make his first move standing upright. The Marlins taught Seymour to switch-hit after turning pro, and he showed an impressive feel for slashing the ball from the left side. He has shown plus range and a plus arm at shortstop, with one talent evaluator characterizing him as very good on plays he doesn't have to think about. Many of Seymour's defensive miscues came on plays where he had too much time to make his throws. He doesn't bring much power to the table, but he has the potential to be a disruptive baserunner in the Billy Hamilton mold.

Year	Club (League)	Class	AVG	G	AB	R	H	2B	3B	HR	RBI	BB	SO	SB	CS	OBP	SLG
2014	Marlins (GCL)	R	.245	26	98	24	24	0	1	0	3	12	27	11	2	.333	.265
Minor League Totals			.245	26	98	24	24	0	1	0	3	12	27	11	2	.333	.265

22 BRIAN ELLINGTON, RHP

BA GRADE

45 Risk: High

Born: Aug. 4, 1990. **B-T:** R-R. **Ht.:** 6-4. **Wt.:** 200. **Drafted:** West Florida, 2012 (16th round). **Signed by:** Brian Kraft.

Ellington took a circuitous route to pro ball. In September 2007, he had Tommy John surgery and missed his senior season at Oak Hall School in Gainesville, Fla. He had already earned a scholarship to Florida State and was ready to report as a healthy freshman. That scenario didn't materialize when Ellington and the Seminoles could not agree on a rehab plan. He went through two junior colleges in Florida before ultimately landing at Division II West Florida, which won the 2011 national championship. Fast forward to 2014 at high Class A Jupiter, where Ellington in his third pro season featured a power fastball that sat 93-97 mph and regularly touched the upper 90s, with reports of a few stray 100 mph readings. His Achilles heel was holding baserunners. After some initial struggles, his times to the plate improved from about 1.6 seconds to as fast as 1.35 seconds. Ellington throws an average slider, but his best breaking pitch is a power curve in the low 80s that flashes plus with two-plane break. He threw 13 innings in the Arizona Fall League following the 2014 season, putting him on the fast track for 2015. He'll open at Double-A Jacksonville but has a chance to take off with his power arm.

Year	Club (League)	Class	W	L	ERA	G	GS	CG	SV	IP	H	HR	BB	SO	K/9	WHIP	AVG
2012	Jamestown (NYP)	SS	2	0	2.40	18	0	0	0	30	20	2	25	33	9.9	1.50	.187
2013	Greensboro (SAL)	LoA	3	2	4.64	16	2	0	0	43	40	3	23	27	5.7	1.48	.250
	Marlins (GCL)	R	0	0	0.00	2	0	0	0	3	0	0	3	4	12.0	1.00	.000
	Batavia (NYP)	SS	1	2	3.72	6	1	0	0	19	16	0	9	21	9.8	1.29	.222
2014	Jupiter (FSL)	HiA	2	2	4.75	35	0	0	0	47	51	2	24	56	10.6	1.58	.271
Minor League Totals			8	6	3.98	77	3	0	0	142	127	7	84	141	8.9	1.48	.236

23 VIOSERGY ROSA, 1B

BA GRADE

45 Risk: High

Born: June 16, 1990. **B-T:** L-L. **Ht.:** 6-3. **Wt.:** 185. **Drafted:** Odessa (Texas) JC, 2010 (29th round). **Signed by:** Ryan Wardinsky.

Rosa attended Washington High in the Bronx, N.Y.—alma mater of Manny Ramirez—and was cut from his high school baseball team three times before sticking. He played at two junior colleges, one year at Wallace State (Ala.) CC and another at Odessa (Texas) JC before transforming himself into one of the better power prospects in the system. He followed up a 23-homer campaign at hitter-friendly low Class A Greensboro in 2013 with 13 at high Class A Jupiter in 2014, plus six more (including the postseason) during a promotion to Double-A Jacksonville. Rosa's focus in 2014 was to do more than just use the natural loft in his lefthanded swing to launch homers, and he improved at developing more of a line-drive swing. He has some feel for hitting, has added polish to his approach and isn't a strikeout machine. However, he is a below-average runner and subpar first baseman. Scouts panned Rosa's footwork at first base and think ultimately he fits best as a DH. He will return to Jacksonville to begin 2015.

Year	Club (League)	Class	AVG	G	AB	R	H	2B	3B	HR	RBI	BB	SO	SB	CS	OBP	SLG
2012	Jamestown (NYP)	SS	.279	61	197	22	55	12	0	3	25	46	45	0	0	.413	.386
2013	Greensboro (SAL)	LoA	.252	133	465	68	117	22	1	23	69	74	119	3	1	.362	.452
2014	Jupiter (FSL)	HiA	.291	116	446	52	130	25	1	13	78	42	98	0	0	.355	.439
	Jacksonville (SL)	AA	.292	20	72	15	21	4	1	2	17	14	13	0	0	.416	.458
Minor League Totals			.263	403	1412	188	371	79	4	43	219	198	355	3	2	.359	.416

24 JORGAN CAVANERIO, RHP

BA GRADE

50 Risk: Extreme

Born: Aug. 18, 1994. **B-T:** R-R. **Ht.:** 6-1. **Wt.:** 165. **Signed:** Venezuela, 2011. **Signed by:** Albert Gonzalez/Sandy Nin.

Director of international operations Albert Gonzalez just needed to see one bullpen session before signing off on Cavanerio. Though he didn't light up radar gun or exhibit any plus pitches, Cavanerio's arm action, delivery and feel for pitches all captured the Marlins' interest, as did his projectable body. Cavanerio proved hittable at short-season Batavia in 2014, but the Marlins anticipate his fastball, which sits 91-93 mph, will jump as he continues maturing physically and learns to repeat his delivery. He's not afraid to challenge hitters and throw strikes. Cavanerio also throws a plus changeup as a second offering and will continue developing a breaking pitch in 2015 when he moves up to low Class A Greensboro.

Year	Club (League)	Class	W	L	ERA	G	GS	CG	SV	IP	H	HR	BB	SO	K/9	WHIP	AVG
2012	Marlins (GCL)	R	3	2	5.13	11	9	0	0	47	61	4	13	35	6.7	1.56	.310
2013	Marlins (GCL)	R	4	1	2.74	9	8	0	0	43	43	1	10	29	6.1	1.24	.267
2014	Batavia (NYP)	SS	4	6	4.56	14	14	0	0	79	98	9	14	55	6.3	1.42	.314
Minor League Totals			11	12	4.09	46	35	0	1	198	230	17	43	148	6.7	1.38	.296

25 JAVIER LOPEZ, SS

Born: Sept. 13, 1994. **B-T:** R-R. **Ht.:** 6-3. **Wt.:** 180. **Signed:** Dominican Republic, 2011. **Signed by:** Albert Gonzalez/Alix Martinez/Sandy Nin.

BA GRADE

50 Risk: Extreme

The tooled-up Lopez was the Marlins' biggest international signee in 2011, when he received a $350,000 bonus. His minor league performances through three pro seasons are not commensurate with his top-shelf tools. After opening the 2014 season at low Class A Greensboro, he saw his development stall due in large part to a subluxed shoulder. When he got healthy, Lopez didn't hit and ultimately received a demotion to short-season Batavia. At times he struggles getting out of the batter's box or gets poor jumps on steal attempts. His shoulder issue no doubt contributed to his .223/.264/.302 batting line in 2014. Lopez has a plus arm but needs to improve his accuracy. Though Lopez has hit just two home runs in 667 professional at-bats, scouts project him to hit for average power, but it's time for him to turn his tools into production as he returns to Greensboro in 2015.

Year	Club (League)	Class	AVG	G	AB	R	H	2B	3B	HR	RBI	BB	SO	SB	CS	OBP	SLG
2012	Marlins (DSL)	R	.208	50	207	24	43	10	0	1	13	16	47	4	7	.271	.271
2013	Batavia (NYP)	SS	.174	45	155	14	27	4	3	1	13	13	47	1	2	.243	.258
2014	Greensboro (SAL)	LoA	.205	26	117	11	24	11	0	0	9	4	20	0	0	.238	.299
	Marlins (GCL)	R	.231	4	13	0	3	0	0	0	1	1	1	0	0	.286	.231
	Batavia (NYP)	SS	.234	45	175	22	41	7	3	0	8	8	38	3	1	.279	.309
Minor League Totals			.207	170	667	71	138	32	6	2	44	42	153	8	10	.261	.282

26 FELIX MUNOZ, 1B

Born: April 27, 1992. **B-T:** L-L. **Ht.:** 6-2. **Wt.:** 170. **Signed:** Dominican Republic, 2008. **Signed by:** Albert Gonzalez/Sandy Nin.

BA GRADE

45 Risk: High

In spite of what many evaluators likely rubber-stamped as a bad body, Munoz's bat and swing as an amateur were too good for the Marlins to ignore. He ranked among the top hitters in the South Atlantic League in 2014. While Greensboro's NewBridge Bank Park is a bandbox, Munoz's power is legit. He hit nearly as many homers on the road (seven) as at home (nine), and his 16 bombs led the Grasshoppers. He has strong plate discipline and strike-zone recognition to go with his pop, and he makes fairly consistent contact. He's a consistent, solid-average defender who led SAL first basemen with a .994 fielding percentage. While he's a below-average runner, Munoz could see time in left field at high Class A Jupiter.

Year	Club (League)	Class	AVG	G	AB	R	H	2B	3B	HR	RBI	BB	SO	SB	CS	OBP	SLG
2012	Jamestown (NYP)	SS	.224	35	125	13	28	5	0	2	14	4	32	0	0	.258	.312
2013	Batavia (NYP)	SS	.301	69	246	33	74	19	0	4	40	28	28	0	2	.367	.427
2014	Greensboro (SAL)	LoA	.300	126	494	81	148	31	4	16	91	57	74	1	2	.368	.476
Minor League Totals			.277	389	1485	197	411	84	6	26	219	157	208	5	6	.345	.394

27 MIGUEL DEL POZO, LHP

Born: Oct. 14, 1992. **B-T:** L-L. **Ht.:** 6-1. **Wt.:** 180. **Signed:** Dominican Republic, 2010. **Signed by:** Albert Gonzalez/Sandy Nin.

BA GRADE

45 Risk: High

Del Pozo showed an average curveball as an amateur and everything else was below-average, including his fastball, which now touches 96 mph. His curve, at times a bit slurvy, has a nice bite and finish, and the Marlins love his makeup. One talent evaluator identified Del Pozo as the safest bet to reach the majors among Marlins pitching prospects. Working exclusively in relief in the first half of 2014, he went 0-4, 6.15. He was a different pitcher after the break, lowering his ERA to 3.62 and holding opponents to a .233 average. Del Pozo also throws an average changeup with good action from a deceptive delivery, and he works with an aggressive tempo. The Marlins are debating whether to try Del Pozo, who logged 164 innings through four seasons, in a starting role at high Class A Jupiter thanks to his three-pitch mix.

Year	Club (League)	Class	W	L	ERA	G	GS	CG	SV	IP	H	HR	BB	SO	K/9	WHIP	AVG
2012	Marlins (GCL)	R	1	2	4.02	18	3	0	1	31	27	1	23	32	9.2	1.60	.225
2013	Jupiter (FSL)	HiA	0	0	0.00	2	0	0	0	2	1	0	2	0	0.0	1.50	.125
	Batavia (NYP)	SS	2	1	4.81	17	0	0	0	24	24	1	17	36	13.3	1.68	.242
2014	Greensboro (SAL)	LoA	2	6	4.91	41	0	0	4	66	59	5	19	85	11.6	1.18	.243
Minor League Totals			8	12	4.71	90	9	0	5	164	150	12	86	200	11.0	1.44	.240

28 ANDREW McKIRAHAN, LHP

BA GRADE

45 Risk: High

Born: Feb. 8, 1990. **B-T:** R-L. **Ht.:** 6-2. **Wt.:** 195. **Drafted:** Texas, 2011 (21st round). **Signed by:** Trey Forkerway (Cubs).

McKirahan pitched just 58 innings in three college seasons for Texas, then signed with the Cubs as a 21st-rounder in 2011. He had Tommy John surgery in 2012, so 2014 was his first true full season as a healthy professional. He was ready, shooting through the high Class A Florida State League to finish the year at Double-A Tennessee. He pounded the strike zone consistently with a plus fastball, sitting 92-96 mph at times with some armside run. The Cubs left him off the 40-man roster and the Marlins took him in the major league Rule 5 draft, so he has to stick on the Miami roster all year or be offered back to Chicago. McKirahan has a solid-average changeup in the mid-80s that he sells well to righthanders, and he actually had more success against them (.203 average) than same-side hitters (.301). His curveball remains inconsistent thanks to a long arm action. Mike Dunn projects to be the Marlins' lone lefty in the bullpen, so McKirahan has a fighting chance to make the roster.

Year	Club (League)	Class	W	L	ERA	G	GS	CG	SV	IP	H	HR	BB	SO	K/9	WHIP	AVG
2012	Peoria (MWL)	LoA	0	0	1.80	9	0	0	2	10	6	0	4	11	9.9	1.00	.176
2013	Cubs (AZL)	R	0	0	4.50	2	0	0	0	2	4	0	0	4	18.0	2.00	.500
	Boise (NWL)	SS	1	0	2.45	5	0	0	0	7	3	0	2	11	13.5	0.68	.120
	Kane County (MWL)	LoA	2	0	2.75	14	0	0	0	20	14	0	7	22	10.1	1.07	.200
2014	Daytona (FSL)	HiA	2	1	0.99	23	0	0	8	36	29	1	8	33	8.2	1.02	.213
	Tennessee (SL)	AA	0	3	3.45	21	0	0	2	29	28	3	6	24	7.5	1.19	.257
Minor League Totals			5	6	2.16	89	0	0	12	121	96	5	35	128	9.5	1.09	.217

29 AUSTIN BRICE, RHP

BA GRADE

50 Risk: Extreme

Born: June 19, 1992. **B-T:** R-R. **Ht.:** 6-4. **Wt.:** 205. **Drafted:** HS— Pittsboro, N.C., 2010 (9th round). **Signed by:** Joel Matthews.

Signed for $205,000, Brice has become a mainstay of the Top 30 Prospects but hasn't made it out of Class A yet. He retains one of the system's best pitches, a hard curveball that has good 12-to-6 shape and firm velocity around 80 mph when it's at its best. His fastball is a second above-average pitch, sitting 90-94 mph and bumping 95 regularly. He's shown the ability to pull the string on a changeup capably as well. Brice's issues continue to stem from his inability to repeat his delivery and find a consistent release point. While his walk rate of 3.9 per nine innings in 2014 was the best mark of his career, he still gets behind in too many counts. Brice keeps the ball in the ballpark and made progress with his control, but he may lack the command to remain a starter. He'll get a big test at Double-A Jacksonville.

Year	Club (League)	Class	W	L	ERA	G	GS	CG	SV	IP	H	HR	BB	SO	K/9	WHIP	AVG
2012	Greensboro (SAL)	LoA	8	6	4.35	25	19	0	3	110	96	13	68	122	10.0	1.50	.237
2013	Greensboro (SAL)	LoA	8	11	5.73	26	23	0	0	113	118	11	82	111	8.8	1.77	.268
2014	Jupiter (FSL)	HiA	8	9	3.60	25	24	0	0	127	114	5	55	109	7.7	1.33	.241
Minor League Totals			30	27	4.33	93	75	0	3	407	367	31	245	405	9.0	1.50	.241

30 COLBY SUGGS, RHP

BA GRADE

50 Risk: Exteme

Born: Oct. 25, 1991. **B-T:** R-R. **Ht.:** 5-11. **Wt.:** 230. **Drafted:** Arkansas, 2013 (2nd round supplemental). **Signed by:** Brian Kraft

The Marlins drafted Suggs in 2013 thinking the former Arkansas relief ace might not be long for the minors. He arrived in pro ball with a power fastball/curveball combo in place and hit some 96 mphs with his fastball in instructional league. He ended his pro debut in the high Class A Florida State League and returned to Jupiter in 2014, but he was a different pitcher. An ultra-aggressive reliever, Suggs didn't adapt well to extended outings. His ERA rose and his strikeout rate fell, and it took until August for the power on his stuff to come back. His fastball sat in the low 90s much of the season, and he couldn't locate it well thanks to the effort in his delivery. Suggs was hitting some 95s in August, and his 11-to-5 power curveball, which can reach the low 80s, remains a solid-average pitch, though he needs to land it more often. The better version of Suggs could still move quickly, with a Double-A Jacksonville test set for 2015.

Year	Club (League)	Class	W	L	ERA	G	GS	CG	SV	IP	H	HR	BB	SO	K/9	WHIP	AVG
2013	Marlins (GCL)	R	0	0	9.00	1	0	0	0	1	1	0	2	1	9.0	3.00	.250
	Batavia (NYP)	SS	1	0	1.13	7	0	0	3	8	5	0	2	11	12.4	0.88	.200
	Jupiter (FSL)	HiA	1	3	3.93	14	0	0	0	18	9	0	14	26	12.8	1.25	.141
2014	Jupiter (FSL)	HiA	1	6	5.09	46	0	0	3	58	59	3	25	47	7.3	1.44	.266
Minor League Totals			3	9	4.52	68	0	0	6	86	74	3	43	85	8.9	1.37	.235

Milwaukee Brewers

BY TOM HAUDRICOURT

Shortstop Jean Segura's poor sophomore campaign contributed to a season-ending collapse in Milwaukee in 2014

The Brewers' record stood at 73-58 on Aug. 25, and they led the National League Central by one and a half games, with a six-game margin for at least claiming a wild-card berth.

Then, the roof caved in. A nine-game losing streak morphed into a 3-16 skid, which preceded a 9-22 season-ending collapse that landed the Brewers in third place and out of the playoffs completely with an 82-80 record.

Perhaps the Brewers were just an average team that unexpectedly bolted to a 20-7 record and

went on to spend 150 days in first place. Whatever the case, the organization was left to examine how things could go so wrong.

General manager Doug Melvin and manager Ron Roenicke survived the collapse, but now must repair an offense that averaged just 2.73 runs per game in September and scored zero, one or two runs in 17 of the 31 games during the meltdown.

Three young players who appeared to form the building blocks for the club—shortstop Jean Segura, left fielder Khris Davis and second baseman Scooter Gennett—became question marks by the end of 2014.

Segura went from a brilliant all-star 2013 campaign to a season-long slump, while Davis and Gennett struggled down the stretch. The trio of young regulars combined for just 82 walks between them, epitomizing the free-swinging approach that eventually betrayed the Brewers.

Center fielder Carlos Gomez, catcher Jonathan Lucroy and veteran third baseman Aramis Ramirez all started for the NL all-star team, but none was able to duplicate his offensive exploits in the second half. Lucroy did lead the majors with 53 doubles, however, setting a major league record for a catcher.

Right fielder Ryan Braun continued to be plagued by a nerve issue in his right thumb that dramatically decreased his effectiveness, and he had a cryotherapy procedure after the season. He disappeared in September, batting .210 with one homer and five RBIs.

The good news for the Brewers was that their starters and relievers held up their end of the bargain. The former compiled a 3.69 ERA, the lowest since hitter-friendly Miller Park opened in 2001, and the latter protected late leads, led by resurgent Francisco Rodriguez's 44 saves.

The Brewers summoned top prospect right-hander Jimmy Nelson from Triple-A Nashville in the second half, but he went just 2-9, 4.93 and

TOP PROSPECTS OF THE DECADE

Year	Player, Pos.	2014 Org
2005	Rickie Weeks, 2b	Brewers
2006	Prince Fielder, 1b	Rangers
2007	Yovani Gallardo, rhp	Brewers
2008	Matt LaPorta, of	Campeche (Mexican)
2009	Alcides Escobar, ss	Royals
2010	Alcides Escobar, ss	Royals
2011	Mark Rogers, rhp	Mariners
2012	Wily Peralta, rhp	Brewers
2013	Wily Peralta, rhp	Brewers
2014	Jimmy Nelson, rhp	Brewers

moved to the bullpen in September.

With three picks in the first two rounds of the 2014 draft, the Brewers went for high school picks with high ceilings, taking lefthander Kodi Medeiros in the first round, shortstop Jacob Gatewood in the supplemental first and outfielder Monte Harrison in the second. But in a horrible turn of events, the man responsible for those picks, scouting director Bruce Seid, died unexpectedly in early September. Milwaukee hired Diamondbacks scouting director Ray Montgomery to replace Seid.

The Brewers will have two new minor league affiliates in 2015: Triple-A Colorado Springs—after long-time affiliate Nashville opted to partner with the Athletics—and Double-A Biloxi, where the Brewers will move as soon as the new park is ready and they can leave Huntsville.

General manager: Doug Melvin. **Farm director:** Reid Nichols. **Scouting director:** Ray Montgomery.

Class	Team	League	W	L	PCT	Finish	Manager
Majors	Milwaukee Brewers	National	82	80	.506	15th (30)	Ron Roenicke
Triple-A	*Nashville Sounds	Pacific Coast	77	67	.535	5th (16)	Rick Sweet
Double-A	†Huntsville Stars	Southern	77	63	.550	4th (10)	Carlos Subero
High A	Brevard County Manatees	Florida State	73	62	.541	6th (12)	Joe Ayrault
Low A	Wisconsin Timber Rattlers	Midwest	72	67	.518	t-5th (16)	Matt Erickson
Rookie	Helena Brewers	Pioneer	27	49	.355	8th (8)	Tony Diggs
Rookie	Brewers	Arizona	24	31	.436	10th (13)	Nestor Corredor
Overall Minor League Record			350	339	.508	14th (30)	

*Affiliate will be Colorado Springs (Pacific Coast) in 2015. †Franchise moves to Biloxi (Southern) in 2015.

THIS YEAR'S TOP 30

No.	Player, Pos.	Grade/Risk
1.	Tyrone Taylor, of	55/High
2.	Orlando Arcia, ss	55/High
3.	Clint Coulter, of	55/High
4.	Monte Harrison, of	55/High
5.	Gilbert Lara, 3b	55/Extreme
6.	Wei-Chung Wang, lhp	55/Extreme
7.	Taylor Williams, rhp	50/High
8.	Devin Williams, rhp	50/High
9.	Tyler Wagner, rhp	50/High
10.	Taylor Jungmann, rhp	50/High
11.	Kodi Medeiros, lhp	55/Extreme
12.	David Goforth, rhp	45/Medium
13.	Yadiel Rivera, ss/2b	50/High
14.	Michael Reed, of	50/High
15.	Jorge Lopez, rhp	50/High
16.	Miguel Diaz, rhp	50/High
17.	Jacob Gatewood, ss	50/High
18.	Victor Roache, of	50/High
19.	Kyle Wren, of	45/Medium
20.	Jed Bradley, lhp	45/Medium
21.	Johnny Hellweg, rhp	45/High
22.	Joantgel Segovia, of	50/Extreme
23.	Hobbs Johnson, lhp	45/High
24.	Tyler Cravy, rhp	45/High
25.	Brooks Hall, rhp	40/Medium
26.	Drew Gagnon, rhp	40/Medium
27.	Jason Rogers, 3b/1b	45/High
28.	Ariel Pena, rhp	45/High
29.	Mike Strong, lhp	40/Medium
30.	Damien Magnifico, rhp	45/High

LAST YEAR'S TOP 30

No.	Player, Pos.	Status
1.	Jimmy Nelson, rhp	Majors
2.	Tyrone Taylor, of	No. 1
3.	Mitch Haniger, of	(Diamondbacks)
4.	Johnny Hellweg, rhp	No. 21
5.	Victor Roache, of	No. 18
6.	Taylor Jungmann, rhp	No. 10
7.	Orlando Arcia, ss	No. 2
8.	David Goforth, rhp	No. 12
9.	Devin Williams, rhp	No. 8
10.	Hunter Morris, 1b	Dropped out
11.	Clint Coulter, c	No. 3
12.	Nick Delmonico, 3b/1b	Dropped out
13.	Yadiel Rivera, ss	No. 13
14.	Tucker Neuhaus, 3b/ss	Dropped out
15.	Ariel Pena, rhp	No. 28
16.	Tyler Wagner, rhp	No. 9
17.	Michael Blazek, rhp	Dropped out
18.	Jed Bradley, lhp	No. 20
19.	Taylor Williams, rhp	No. 7
20.	Jason Rogers, 1b/of	No. 27
21.	Kevin Shackelford, rhp	(Reds)
22.	Barrett Astin, rhp	(Reds)
23.	Damien Magnifico, rhp	No. 30
24.	Jorge Lopez, rhp	No. 15
25.	Drew Gagnon, rhp	No. 26
26.	Omar Garcia, of	Dropped out
27.	Anthony Banda, lhp	(Diamondbacks)
28.	Michael Ratterree, of	Dropped out
29.	Tyler Cravy, rhp	No. 24
30.	D'Vontrey Richardson, of	Dropped out

BEST TOOLS

Best Hitter for Average	Tyrone Taylor
Best Power Hitter	Clint Coulter
Best Strike-Zone Discipline	Jason Rogers
Fastest Baserunner	Johnny Davis
Best Athlete	Tyrone Taylor
Best Fastball	Damien Magnifico
Best Curveball	Jorge Lopez
Best Slider	Kodi Medeiros
Best Changeup	Brooks Hall
Best Control	Taylor Williams
Best Defensive Catcher	Adam Weisenburger
Best Defensive Infielder	Yadiel Rivera
Best Infield Arm	Orlando Arcia
Best Defensive Outfielder	Tyrone Taylor
Best Outfield Arm	Monte Harrison

PROJECTED 2018 LINEUP

Catcher	Jonathan Lucroy
First Base	Ryan Braun
Second Base	Scooter Gennett
Third Base	Jean Segura
Shortstop	Orlando Arcia
Left Field	Clint Coulter
Center Field	Tyrone Taylor
Right Field	Carlos Gomez
No. 1 Starter	Yovani Gallardo
No. 2 Starter	Wily Peralta
No. 3 Starter	Jimmy Nelson
No. 4 Starter	Taylor Williams
No. 5 Starter	Devin Williams
Closer	David Goforth

MILWAUKEE BREWERS

TOP 2015 ROOKIE: David Goforth, rhp. His success as a closer in the minors as well as his bulldog approach will help him find a spot in the bullpen.
BREAKOUT PROSPECT: Tyler Cravy, rhp. Be it as a starter or a reliever, he is making steady progress toward the big leagues.
SLEEPER: Brent Suter, lhp. A 31st-round pick in 2012 out of Harvard, he made steady progress in Double-A and has a chance to get to Milwaukee.

SOURCE OF TOP 30 TALENT

Homegrown	26	Acquired	4
College	11	Trades	3
Junior college	1	Rule 5 draft	1
High school	10	Independent leagues	0
Draft-and-follow	0	Free agents/waivers	0
Nondrafted free agents	0		
International	4		

LF
Victor Roache (18)
Dionis Hinojosa
Carlos Belonis
Juan Ortiz
Mitch Meyer

CF
Tyrone Taylor (1)
Monte Harrison (4)
Michael Reed (14)
Kyle Wren (19)
Joantgel Segovia (22)
D'Vontrey Richardson
Johnny Davis
Omar Garcia

RF
Clint Coulter (3)
Michael Ratterree
Jose Pena
Nicolas Pierre

3B
Gilbert Lara (5)
Nick Delmonico
Tucker Neuhaus
Michael Garza
Shea Vucinich

SS
Orlando Arcia (2)
Yadiel Rivera (13)
Jacob Gatewood (17)
Hector Gomez
Steven Halcomb
Angel Ortega

2B
Greg Hopkins
Nick Shaw
Chris McFarland
Francisco Castillo
Gregory Munoz

1B
Jason Rogers (27)
Hunter Morris
Matt Clark
Nick Ramirez
Garrett Cooper

C
Shawn Zarraga
Adam Weisenburger
Cameron Garfield
Parker Berberet
Rafael Neda
Greg McCall

LHP

LHSP	LHRP
Wei-Chung Wang (6)	Mike Strong (29)
Kodi Medeiros (11)	Brent Leach
Jed Bradley (20)	Stephen Peterson
Hobbs Johnson (23)	Tyler Alexander
Brent Suter	Trevor Seidenberger
Clint Terry	Zach Hirsch
Luis Ortega	
Tyler Linehan	

RHP

RHSP	RHRP
Taylor Williams (7)	David Goforth (12)
Devin Williams (8)	Michael Blazek
Tyler Wagner (9)	Manny Barreda
Taylor Jungmann (10)	Kaleb Earls
Jorge Lopez (15)	Greg Holle
Miguel Diaz (16)	Eric Marzec
Johnny Hellweg (21)	Casey Medlen
Tyler Cravy (24)	Tanner Poppe
Brooks Hall (25)	Tommy Toledo
Drew Gagnon (26)	Mark Williams
Ariel Pena (28)	Harvey Martin
Damien Magnifico (30)	Brandon Woodruff
Cy Sneed	
Jacob Barnes	
Andy Moye	
Austin Ross	
Chad Pierce	
Tristan Archer	
Victor Diaz	
Preston Gainey	
Chad Thompson	
J.B. Kole	

2014

BEST PURE HITTER: OF Monte Harrison (2) was more advanced after signing than the Brewers thought. His swing needs more polish and consistency, but for a three-sport prep athlete, he showed a solid approach, patience and bat speed while leading the Rookie-level Arizona League in walks.

BEST POWER HITTER: SS Jacob Gatewood (1s) entered the spring as the consensus top power hitter available, at least on the prep side. He had an iffy spring and struggled with contact issues after signing, but his 70 raw power potential remains tantalizing. He may shift to third base in 2015.

FASTEST RUNNER: The Brewers liken OF Troy Stokes (4) to Ben Revere and give him 70 grades while praising his hitting polish.

BEST DEFENSIVE PLAYER: Harrison needs reps but has a chance to be a young Torii Hunter caliber defender in center field.

BEST FASTBALL: RHP Brandon Woodruff (11) has the big arm strength that made him a fifth-rounder as a prep. His lack of command limited him to 90 innings in three seasons with Mississippi State, but he was still hitting 97 mph before and after signing. LHP Kodi Medeiros (1) has premium life and deception on his low-90s heater, which has touched 94-95.

BEST SECONDARY PITCH: Medeiros has been likened to a poor man's Madison Bumgarner for his strength, athleticism and low slot. His slider flashes present plus now and is more advanced than Bumgarner's at a similar stage of development.

BEST PRO DEBUT: Harrison hit .261/.402/.339 and led the AZL with 32 stolen bases, being caught just twice. Stokes hit .262/.363/.331 there with 19 steals. C Greg McCall (9) hit .326/.375/465 in 86 at-bats at Rookie-level Helena.

BEST ATHLETE: Harrison has burst, agility and present strength, all of which made him a Nebraska football recruit as a wide receiver. It also made him a highlight reel basketball player who excelled at finishing in transition.

MOST INTRIGUING BACKGROUND: Medeiros is the highest-drafted high school player out of Hawaii in draft history. RHP Cy Sneed (3) is the younger brother of Zeb, a righthanded reliever in the Royals system. Unsigned C J.J. Schwarz (17) is the son of Marlins minor league pitching coach Jeff Schwarz, an ex-pro.

CLOSEST TO THE MAJORS: The Brewers hope to develop the younger Sneed as a starter but were judicious with his innings after he was Dallas Baptist's ace in the spring, tossing 104 innings.

BEST LATE-ROUND PICK: Woodruff needs innings and confidence to improve his control and gain some feel for his secondary pitches. His arm strength will warrant a long look.

THE ONE WHO GOT AWAY: Schwarz headed to Florida once the Brewers quickly got their top three picks signed for more than $5.6 million. Milwaukee made more of a run at physical RHP Turner Larkins (28), now at Texas A&M.

ASSESSMENT: The Brewers gambled on upside and may have gotten the draft's top athlete (Harrison), power bat (Gatewood) and prep lefty (Medeiros), though all come with considerable risk. It was the last draft for scouting director Bruce Seid, who died in September.

2013

Milwaukee knew RHP Devin Williams (2) may take a while, so it helps that LHP Hobbs Johnson (14) got off to such a fast start. Much of the rest of the class has begun modestly.

GRADE: D

2012

OF Tyrone Taylor (2) and C/OF Clint Coulter (1) are two of the system's top prospects, with RHP Tyler Wagner (4) an intriguing arm. OF Mitch Haniger (1s) and LHP Anthony Banda (10) were dealt to Arizona for Gerardo Parra.

GRADE: B

2011

The Brewers didn't get what they hoped for our of RHP Taylor Jungmann (1) and LHP Jed Bradley (1). RHPs Jorge Lopez (2) and David Goforth (7) are prospects. What if Milwaukee had inked LHP Carlos Rodon (16)?

GRADE: B

TOP DRAFT PICKS OF THE DECADE

Year	Player, Pos.	2014 Org
2005	Ryan Braun, 3b	Brewers
2006	Jeremy Jeffress, rhp	Brewers
2007	Matt LaPorta, of	Campeche (Mexican)
2008	Brett Lawrie, c/3b	Blue Jays
2009	Eric Arnett, rhp	Out of baseball
2010	*Dylan Covey, rhp	Athletics
2011	Taylor Jungmann, rhp	Brewers
2012	Clint Coulter, c	Brewers
2013	Devin Williams, rhp (2nd round)	Brewers
2014	Kodi Medeiros, lhp	Brewers

* Did not sign

LARGEST BONUSES IN CLUB HISTORY

Rickie Weeks, 2003	$3,600,000
Taylor Jungmann, 2011	$2,525,000
Kodi Medeiros, 2014	$2,500,000
Ben Sheets, 1999	$2,450,000
Ryan Braun, 2005	$2,450,000

1 TYRONE TAYLOR, OF

Born: Jan. 22, 1994. **B-T:** R-R. **Ht.:** 6-0. **Wt.:** 185.
Drafted: HS—Torrance, Calif., 2012 (2nd round).
Signed by: Dan Huston.

The Brewers knew Taylor was a talented athlete when they selected him in the second round of the 2012 draft and signed him for $750,000. He was a standout running back in high school, and the Brewers figured he would improve when focusing on baseball only—and that's exactly what has happened. Taylor impressed in his 2012 debut in Rookie ball before a wrist injury cut short his season, and he played at low Class A Wisconsin in 2013 at age 19, where he started slow and finished strong. Taylor followed that pattern again in 2014 at high Class A Brevard County, playing better in the second half (.299 average, .350 on-base percentage) while leading the Florida State League with 45 extra-base hits. He ran out of gas in the final month (.532 OPS), but he received a promotion to Double-A Huntsville for the Southern League playoffs.

Taylor is more of a gap hitter—36 of his extra-base hits were doubles, the most in the FSL—than a bopper. He has good bat speed and is aggressive at the plate but makes contact and does not strike out much. Taylor doesn't walk much, either, and, therefore, needs to work on his plate discipline to improve his OBP. He hit lefthanders hard in 2014 (.852 OPS) and has learned how to pull inside pitches down the line for doubles. Taylor has decent speed on the bases, but he isn't a burner and has worked hard on getting jumps on the pitcher. He is a true center fielder with good range and instincts and an average, accurate arm. In 129 games in the outfield in 2014, he committed just two errors. Taylor played in a very tough park for righthanded hitters at Brevard County and should continue to be more productive.

The Brewers love Taylor's aggressiveness on the field and the way he takes to coaching. He is difficult to get off the field, and he led Brevard County by playing in 130 of 135 games. He kept going in the Arizona Fall League as well, though he hit a soft .271. Taylor will play the entire 2015 season as a 21-year-old at Double-A. The Brewers know they don't have to rush Taylor, but he continues to earn quick promotions and rapidly assumed the mantel of top prospect in the system. Taylor projects to be a top-of-the-order hitter in the majors who will be effective at the plate and in the field.

BA GRADE

55 Risk: High

SCOUTING GRADES

Batting: 60.
Power: 45.
Speed: 55.
Defense: 70.
Arm: 50.

Based on 20-80 scouting scale and future projection rather than present tools.

LGE	PA	BB%	SO%	ISO
FSL	559	7.0	10.4	.118
SL	14	7.1	35.7	.000

CLIFF WELCH

Year	Club (League)	Class	AVG	G	AB	R	H	2B	3B	HR	RBI	BB	SO	SB	CS	OBP	SLG
2012	Brewers (AZL)	R	.389	8	36	11	14	5	3	0	6	1	3	3	1	.395	.694
	Helena (PIO)	R	.385	10	39	11	15	4	0	2	5	5	8	3	2	.467	.641
2013	Wisconsin (MWL)	LoA	.274	122	485	69	133	33	2	8	57	35	63	19	8	.338	.400
2014	Brevard County (FSL)	HiA	.278	130	507	69	141	36	3	6	68	39	58	22	6	.331	.396
	Huntsville (SL)	AA	.077	5	13	0	1	0	0	0	0	1	5	1	0	.143	.077
Minor League Totals			.281	275	1080	160	304	78	8	16	136	81	137	48	17	.339	.413

2 ORLANDO ARCIA, SS/2B

Born: Aug. 4, 1994. **B-T:** R-R. **Ht.:** 6-0. **Wt.:** 170. **Signed:** Venezuela, 2010.
Signed by: Fernando Arango.

Arcia played most of the 2014 season at high Class A Brevard County at age 19, but he didn't play like a teenager. In fact, he shows uncommon maturity and a well-rounded game. He moved full-time to his natural position of shortstop at midseason when double-play partner Yadiel Rivera moved to Double-A. Arcia's older brother Oswaldo plays right field for the Twins. Arcia could probably play shortstop in the big leagues in 2015 and hold his own. He has a plus arm, great first-step quickness and above-average range. His hands are soft and his instincts are good, and he believes he can make every play. At the plate, Arcia continues to improve, with good hand-eye coordination and pitch recognition that keep his strikeouts manageable. He shows mostly gap power at present but has enough pop to stop pitchers from grooving the ball, especially for his size. With plus speed, he is a threat on the bases and an exciting, daring player to watch. Sometimes his swing gets long and his plate discipline lags, but that can improve with experience and coaching. Everyone agrees that Arcia will get to the big leagues on the basis of defense alone, but the Brewers also have high hopes for his offense. He shows leadership skills that add to the package, and it's only a matter of time before he is wearing a Brewers uniform.

BA GRADE

55 Risk: High

LGE	PA	BB%	SO%	ISO
FSL	546	7.7	11.9	.102

Year	Club (League)	Class	AVG	G	AB	R	H	2B	3B	HR	RBI	BB	SO	SB	CS	OBP	SLG
2012	Did not play—Injured																
2013	Wisconsin (MWL)	LoA	.251	120	442	67	111	14	5	4	39	35	40	20	9	.314	.333
2014	Brevard County (FSL)	HiA	.289	127	498	65	144	29	5	4	50	42	65	31	11	.346	.392
Minor League Totals			.275	311	1158	179	319	59	11	14	125	107	125	64	24	.342	.382

3 CLINT COULTER, C/OF

Born: July 30, 1993. **B-T:** R-R. **Ht.:** 6-3. **Wt.:** 215. **Drafted:** HS—Camas, Wash., 2012 (1st round). **Signed by:** Shawn Whalen.

Coulter was not ready to compete at low Class A Wisconsin in 2013 as a teenager and received a demotion to Rookie-level Helena, with injuries playing a factor in stalling his development. He made a triumphant return to the Midwest League in 2014, leading the league in home runs (22) and on-base percentage (.410). Coulter does not have a picture-perfect swing, for it involves an exaggerated load and powerful cut that makes it difficult at times to control the barrel. That combination leads to swings and misses on pitches he should hit, but when he does make contact, he does so with power (53 extra-base hits). His plate discipline improved in 2014 and he stopped getting himself out as often by swinging at pitches out of the strike zone. Coulter's defense at catcher remains a work in progress, however, particularly with his throwing mechanics and footwork. Coulter has good arm strength and is a tremendous worker, but catching is not his future.

BA GRADE

55 Risk: High

LGE	PA	BB%	SO%	ISO
MWL	529	13.8	19.5	.233

Coulter's bat will get him to the big leagues, so the Brewers sent him to instructional league and to the Arizona Fall League in 2014 to learn to play right field. They were encouraged with how quickly he improved there, though big league right fielder Ryan Braun is signed for six more years. Coulter will be tested at a challenging high Class A Brevard County ballpark in 2015.

Year	Club (League)	Class	AVG	G	AB	R	H	2B	3B	HR	RBI	BB	SO	SB	CS	OBP	SLG
2012	Brewers (AZL)	R	.302	49	169	37	51	3	3	5	33	37	40	3	5	.439	.444
2013	Wisconsin (MWL)	LoA	.207	33	116	18	24	5	1	3	13	11	31	1	0	.299	.345
	Brewers (AZL)	R	.350	17	60	12	21	5	1	3	15	5	15	1	1	.409	.617
	Helena (PIO)	R	.216	20	74	8	16	4	0	1	8	4	14	1	0	.263	.311
2014	Wisconsin (MWL)	LoA	.287	126	429	84	123	28	3	22	89	73	103	6	6	.410	.520
Minor League Totals			.277	245	848	159	235	45	8	34	158	130	203	12	12	.390	.469

4 MONTE HARRISON, OF

MIKE JANES

Born: Aug. 10, 1995. **B-T:** R-R. **Ht.:** 6-3. **Wt.:** 200. **Drafted:** HS—Lee's Summit, Mo., 2014 (2nd round). **Signed by:** Drew Anderson.

Considered by many to be the best athlete in the 2014 draft, Harrison landed with the Brewers in the second round. They forked over $1.8 million to entice him to forego a scholarship to play both baseball and football at Nebraska. Upon reporting to the Rookie-level Arizona League, Harrison put the tools on display that make him special. Harrison led the AZL with 31 walks, showcasing impressive plate discipline, and also swiped a circuit-best 32 bases while getting caught just twice. He has plus bat speed, and though his swing needs more polish and consistency, he showed an advanced approach and patience. He stood tough in the batter's box, getting hit 12 times by pitches. His speed not only makes things happen on the bases but also plays well in center field, where he just needs more experience. But he also could settle into right field, where his strong arm will play. In terms of tools and upside, Harrison might have been the most impressive player in the AZL. He showed little power, but that could come with time and isn't a necessity considering his other skills. The Brewers could challenge him by sending him to low Class A Wisconsin in 2015, but no matter where he lands, he has the makings of an exciting player to watch.

BA GRADE	
55	Risk: **High**

LGE	PA	BB%	SO%	ISO
AZL	224	13.8	21.4	.078

Year	Club (League)	Class	AVG	G	AB	R	H	2B	3B	HR	RBI	BB	SO	SB	CS	OBP	SLG
2014	Brewers (AZL)	R	.261	50	180	37	47	7	2	1	20	31	48	32	2	.402	.339
Minor League Totals			.261	50	180	37	47	7	2	1	20	31	48	32	2	.402	.339

5 GILBERT LARA, SS

MIKE JANES

Born: Oct. 30, 1997. **B-T:** R-R. **Ht.:** 6-3. **Wt.:** 205. **Signed:** Dominican Republic, 2014. **Signed by:** Eduardo Brizuela.

How badly did the Brewers want Lara? After never spending more than $800,000 for an international amateur, they committed a whopping $3.1 million to sign the 16-year-old shortstop in July 2014. The Brewers buttressed their allotted bonus pool amount of $2,611,800 by trading Cuban righthander Rodolfo Fernandez to the Athletics for slot No. 57, worth $339,000, bringing their total to $2.95 million. Thus by signing Lara, they exceeded their bonus pool by just five percent, while satisfying a goal to become more active in Latin America. Few players in Lara's signing class could match him in terms of raw power. His swing gets out of control at times, and he can be pull-happy, but those are not major issues at his age. He impressed scouts in showcases, where he drove the ball with regularity. Already big-bodied, he isn't expected to be able to stay at shortstop, which requires more dexterity. Offense is his calling card, particularly with a tremendous upside as a slugger. The Brewers are thin at third base and likely will give Lara a good look at the hot corner. That position could prove to be a challenge as well, so a move to first base or the outfield could be in his future. The Brewers might wait until 2016 before assigning Lara to Rookie ball in the U.S.

BA GRADE	
55	Risk: **Extreme**

LGE	PA	BB%	SO%	ISO
Did not play				

Year	Club (League)	Class	AVG	G	AB	R	H	2B	3B	HR	RBI	BB	SO	SB	CS	OBP	SLG
2014	Did not play—Signed 2015 contract																

6 WEI-CHUNG WANG, LHP

Born: April 25, 1992. **B-T:** L-L. **Ht.:** 6-1. **Wt.:** 180. **Signed:** Taiwan, 2011.
Signed by: Fu-Chun Chiang (Pirates).

Rule 5 draft picks don't often make prospect lists the year after their restrictions are lifted, but Wang is an exception. His initial contract with the Pirates had been voided—he required Tommy John surgery—leaving him eligible for the Rule 5 draft in 2013 when the Pirates didn't add him to the 40-man roster. Pittsburgh didn't envision any other team taking Wang to the big leagues, but the Brewers did exactly that in 2014 while pitching him 14 times. Brewers scouts who saw Wang pitch in the Rookie-level Gulf Coast League in 2013 were impressed with his command, poise and arm. The wiry lefty throws his fastball in the 91-93 mph range and touches 95 at times. He has an outstanding changeup that makes him effective against righthanders and a solid curveball as well, giving him the repertoire to be a successful starter. Those pitches, combined with his control and calm demeanor on the mound convinced the Brewers to keep the 22-year-old Wang in spring training and try to get through the season with him. When he did pitch in the majors, he wasn't sharp and often was hit hard. After Wang spent the requisite 90 days on the active roster to satisfy his Rule 5 restriction, he was shut down with a tight shoulder and later sent on a minor league rehab assignment to work as a starter. He also started and pitched well in the Arizona Fall League (23 IP, 2 BB), and likely will pitch in high Class A Brevard County's 2015 rotation.

	BA GRADE	
	55	Risk: Extreme

LGE	BF	SO%	BB%	HR/9
MWL	56	17.9	7.1	0.00
NL	92	14.1	8.7	3.12

Year	Club (League)	Class	W	L	ERA	G	GS	CG	SV	IP	H	HR	BB	SO	K/9	WHIP	AVG
2012	Did not play—Injured																
2013	Pirates (GCL)	R	1	3	3.23	12	11	0	0	47	37	2	4	42	8.0	0.87	.209
2014	Brewers (AZL)	R	0	0	0.00	2	2	0	0	4	1	0	0	3	7.4	0.27	.077
	Wisconsin (MWL)	LoA	0	2	3.29	3	3	0	0	14	13	0	4	10	6.6	1.24	.250
	Brevard County (FSL)	HiA	1	0	1.86	2	1	0	0	10	7	0	0	9	8.4	0.72	.219
	Milwaukee (NL)	MAJ	0	0	10.90	14	0	0	0	17	30	6	8	13	6.8	2.19	.361
Major League Totals			0	0	10.90	14	0	0	0	17	30	6	8	13	6.8	2.19	.361
Minor League Totals			2	5	2.91	19	17	0	0	74	58	2	8	64	7.7	0.89	.212

7 TAYLOR WILLIAMS, RHP

Born: July 21, 1991. **B-T:** B-R. **Ht.:** 5-11. **Wt.:** 180. **Drafted:** Kent State, 2013 (4th round). **Signed by:** Mike Farrell.

Williams might be smallish in stature, but he stood tall on the mound in 2014 and made a huge leap in the eyes of the organization. Working in low Class A Wisconsin's tandem starter sytem, he established himself as one of the best arms in the Midwest League, compiling a 0.94 WHIP while holding opponents to a .201 average. He struggled in five starts at high Class A Brevard County, but that did little to diminish the 2013 fourth-rounder's breakthrough season. Williams not only has a big fastball that reaches 95 mph consistently (even touching 100) and sits at 92, but he has outstanding command of his pitches. He pounds the zone with his fastball and slider, using both sides of the plate effectively. Because Williams keeps his pitches down, for the most part, he tends not to get hurt by home runs. His slider is a big out pitch against righthanders, and he keeps lefties off his hard stuff with an effective changeup. He played some middle infield as an amateur, so he's athletic and fields his position well. The Brewers like his aggressive nature on the mound, constantly pitching ahead in the count. Because of Williams' lack of size, some scouts see his future in the majors as a reliever, but the Brewers think he has the stuff to be a starter, particularly the way he commands his pitches. They plan to keep him in in the rotation at Double-A Biloxi in 2015.

	BA GRADE	
	50	Risk: High

LGE	BF	SO%	BB%	HR/9
MWL	425	26.4	5.4	0.34
FSL	108	23.1	4.6	1.42

Year	Club (League)	Class	W	L	ERA	G	GS	CG	SV	IP	H	HR	BB	SO	K/9	WHIP	AVG
2013	Helena (PIO)	R	3	1	4.25	12	6	0	0	42	42	5	17	42	8.9	1.39	.258
2014	Wisconsin (MWL)	LoA	8	1	2.36	22	12	1	4	107	78	4	23	112	9.4	0.94	.201
	Brevard County (FSL)	HiA	1	2	4.26	5	5	1	0	25	29	4	5	25	8.9	1.34	.290
Minor League Totals			12	4	3.09	39	23	2	4	175	149	13	45	179	9.2	1.11	.229

8 DEVIN WILLIAMS, RHP

Born: Sept. 21, 1994. **B-T:** R-R. **Ht.:** 6-3. **Wt.:** 175. **Drafted:** HS—Hazelwood, Mo., 2013 (2nd round). **Signed by:** Harvey Kuenn Jr.

The Brewers didn't have a first-round pick in 2013, but they considered Williams a borderline first-round talent when they took him in the second round. They signed him for $1.25 million to forego a scholarship to Missouri. Williams acquitted himself well in the Rookie-level Arizona League in 2013, holding opponents to a .215 average, but the Brewers bumped the 19-year-old only to Rookie-level Helena in 2014 because they wanted him to get his feet on the ground. Williams has a live arm, throwing his two-seam fastball in the 88-92 mph range and getting his four-seamer up to 95. When he keeps his front shoulder closed, Williams has an easy arm action and shows a feel for three pitches. His breaking ball is more of a slurve that he throws in the low 80s with good command. His changeup has good fade and sink and keeps hitters off his fastball. The Brewers were impressed with his improved maturity while pitching in the instructional league in the fall. The Brewers like Williams' athleticism and free-and-easy delivery, and at some point he might take a big leap. Until that happens, the Brewers intend to proceed cautiously, and he probably will join low Class A Wisconsin to start the 2015 season.

BA GRADE
50 Risk: High

LGE	BF	SO%	BB%	HR/9
PIO	285	23.2	7.0	0.68

Year	Club (League)	Class	W	L	ERA	G	GS	CG	SV	IP	H	HR	BB	SO	K/9	WHIP	AVG
2013	Brewers (AZL)	R	1	3	3.38	13	6	0	1	35	28	0	22	39	10.1	1.44	.215
2014	Helena (PIO)	R	4	7	4.48	15	8	0	0	66	74	5	20	66	9.0	1.42	.282
Minor League Totals			5	10	4.10	28	14	0	1	101	102	5	42	105	9.4	1.43	.260

9 TYLER WAGNER, RHP

Born: Jan. 21, 1991. **B-T:** R-R. **Ht.:** 6-4. **Wt.:** 195. **Drafted:** Utah, 2012 (4th round). **Signed by:** Jeff Scholzen.

A Las Vegas high school product, Wagner turned in one of the most impressive showings of any pitcher in the system in 2014, backing up his strong showing at low Class A Wisconsin in 2013. The closer at Utah when the Brewers drafted him in the fourth round in 2012, he has the stuff to start. He ranked among the Florida State League leaders in 2014 with a 1.86 ERA, 118 strikeouts and .221 opponent average. Wagner's bread-and-butter is a heavy sinker that has good life, and he keeps the pitch down in the zone to induce groundballs. He sits in the low to mid-90s but also reaches back for 96 mph when he needs it. For the second year in a row, he finished near the top of his league in innings (150), a tribute to his command and economy of pitches. Wagner has a sharp-breaking slider that he throws at 84-86 mph and uses to torment righthanders (.570 opponents OPS). He also has an effective changeup that keeps lefties at bay (.617 OPS). He has a high leg kick in his delivery and throws from a three-quarters arm slot with excellent command and deception. With two quality seasons under his belt, Wagner has proven he has the repertoire as well as the mentality to pitch in the rotation. He'll likely be promoted to Double-A Biloxi in 2015.

BA GRADE
50 Risk: High

LGE	BF	SO%	BB%	HR/9
FSL	595	19.8	8.1	0.60

Year	Club (League)	Class	W	L	ERA	G	GS	CG	SV	IP	H	HR	BB	SO	K/9	WHIP	AVG
2012	Helena (PIO)	R	1	4	7.77	14	13	0	0	49	63	6	22	47	8.7	1.75	.304
2013	Wisconsin (MWL)	LoA	10	8	3.21	27	25	1	0	149	129	10	56	116	7.0	1.24	.236
2014	Brevard County (FSL)	HiA	13	6	1.86	25	25	1	0	150	118	10	48	118	7.1	1.11	.221
Minor League Totals			24	18	3.26	66	63	2	0	347	310	26	126	281	7.3	1.26	.240

10 TAYLOR JUNGMANN, RHP

Born: Dec. 18, 1989. **B-T:** R-R. **Ht.:** 6-6. **Wt.:** 220. **Drafted:** Texas, 2011 (1st round). **Signed by:** Jeremy Booth.

Jungmann spun his wheels at Double-A Huntsville in 2013 and wasn't invited to big league camp in 2014. Sent back to Double-A in 2014, he made nine solid starts before earning a bump to Triple-A Nashville. The tall righty found a groove in the final weeks, posting a 1.80 ERA over his final six starts. Jungamann doesn't throw with the same velocity he did at Texas, where he often reached the high 90s, so he has to rely more on a sinker to get groundball outs. He moved to the arm side of the rubber so that his fastball caught more of the outside corner to lefthanders and his breaking stuff didn't wander too far out of the zone. Jungmann throws his fastball in the 90-92 mph range and pitches down in the zone, emphasizing contact early in the count. He throws an effective curveball at 75-78 mph that is a quality out pitch against righthanders. It took longer than expected, but Jungmann has reached Triple-A in 2014 and joined the 40-man roster after the season. He has a chance to reach a ceiling of back-end starter.

BA GRADE

50 Risk: High

LGE	BF	SO%	BB%	HR/9
SL	220	20.9	6.8	0.69
PCL	435	23.2	10.6	0.62

Year	Club (League)	Class	W	L	ERA	G	GS	CG	SV	IP	H	HR	BB	SO	K/9	WHIP	AVG
2012	Brevard County (FSL)	HiA	11	6	3.53	26	26	1	0	153	159	7	46	99	5.8	1.34	.267
2013	Huntsville (SL)	AA	10	10	4.33	26	26	0	0	139	117	11	73	82	5.3	1.36	.232
2014	Huntsville (SL)	AA	4	4	2.77	9	9	0	0	52	52	4	15	46	8.0	1.29	.264
	Nashville (PCL)	AAA	8	6	3.98	19	18	0	0	102	88	7	46	101	8.9	1.32	.235
Minor League Totals			33	26	3.79	80	79	1	0	446	416	29	180	328	6.6	1.34	.249

11 KODI MEDEIROS, LHP

BA GRADE

55 Risk: Extreme

Born: May 25, 1996. **B-T:** L-L. **Ht.:** 6-2. **Wt.:** 180. **Drafted:** HS—Hilo, Hawaii, 2014 (1st round). **Signed by:** Josh Belovsky.

The Brewers surprised many when they tabbed the prep lefty Medeiros with the 12th pick in the 2014 draft, making him the highest-drafted prep player ever out of the state of Hawaii. The Brewers scouted him extensively during his senior year and also were impressed with what he showed in a pre-draft workout in Milwaukee. In fact, they were so impressed they gave the Pepperdine recruit a $2.5 million bonus, one of the highest in club history. Medeiros throws from a low arm angle with a fastball that sits at 90-92 mph and reaches 95 at times with plus life, movement and sink. He keeps the ball down in the zone and induces groundball outs. Medeiros complements his fastball with an above-average slider that ranked as one of the best prep breaking balls in the 2014 draft class. He throws an improving changeup that has a chance to also be a plus pitch for him down the road. The Brewers believe Medeiros' athleticism and strength (in part a result of a lifelong passion for judo) will allow him to repeat his low-slot mechanics. Despite his upside, Medeiros made nine appearances in the Rookie-level Arizona League in 2014, but he logged poor results—7.13 ERA, 2.09 WHIP—so he might not be ready for full-season ball in 2015.

Year	Club (League)	Class	W	L	ERA	G	GS	CG	SV	IP	H	HR	BB	SO	K/9	WHIP	AVG
2014	Brewers (AZL)	R	0	2	7.13	9	4	0	1	18	24	2	13	26	13.2	2.09	.308
Minor League Totals			0	2	7.13	9	4	0	1	18	24	2	13	26	13.2	2.09	.308

12 DAVID GOFORTH, RHP

BA GRADE

45 Risk: Medium

Born: Oct. 11, 1988. **B-T:** R-R. **Ht.:** 6-0. **Wt.:** 187. **Drafted:** Mississippi, 2011 (7th round). **Signed by:** Joe Mason.

The Brewers have groomed Goforth as a reliever, shifting him to a closer role in 2013. He converted 27 of 33 save chances in 2014 despite a low strikeout rate. Goforth pitches off a fastball that sits in the mid-90s and has touched 100. He also started throwing more hard cutters/sliders in 2014 at 89-91 mph, pitching more to contact than trying to strike out hitters. Sometimes he overthrows the slider, but he also throws a solid curveball with good shape. He's a tremendous competitor who at least profiles as a setup reliever in the majors. Added to the 40-man roster, Goforth likely will open 2015 season at Triple-A Colorado Springs.

Year	Club (League)	Class	W	L	ERA	G	GS	CG	SV	IP	H	HR	BB	SO	K/9	WHIP	AVG
2012	Wisconsin (MWL)	LoA	10	8	4.66	28	28	0	0	151	154	16	63	93	5.6	1.44	.269
2013	Brevard County (FSL)	HiA	7	5	3.10	14	14	0	0	78	67	4	28	58	6.7	1.21	.231
	Huntsville (SL)	AA	4	3	3.28	20	4	1	5	47	32	1	18	36	6.9	1.07	.192
2014	Huntsville (SL)	AA	5	4	3.76	54	0	0	27	65	60	2	29	46	6.4	1.38	.242
Minor League Totals			26	24	3.99	135	46	1	34	381	357	28	148	275	6.5	1.33	.248

13 YADIEL RIVERA, SS/2B

BA GRADE
50 Risk: High

Born: May 1, 1992. **B-T:** R-R. **Ht.:** 6-3. **Wt.:** 180. **Drafted:** HS—Caguas, P.R., 2010 (9th round). **Signed by:** Charlie Sullivan.

The book on Rivera has not changed from past seasons. He is a quality defender who could hold his own at shortstop in the majors, but he has not proven he will hit enough to be a regular. He began the 2014 season alternating between shortstop and second base at high Class A Brevard County, then played short exclusively at Double-A Huntsville. In the field, Rivera is fun to watch. He has long, fluid strides with range to both sides and great instincts. He has soft hands and good footwork around the bag, and his plus arm makes throws from the hole look easy. Rivera remains a free swinger who draws few walks. Though his quickness plays well in the field, he has average speed on the bases and does not try many steals. He has room to mature as a hitter, and will be a 22-year-old at Double-A Biloxi in 2015. The way Rivera plays defense, he profiles as at least a dependable utility infielder.

Year	Club (League)	Class	AVG	G	AB	R	H	2B	3B	HR	RBI	BB	SO	SB	CS	OBP	SLG
2012	Wisconsin (MWL)	LoA	.247	127	465	60	115	26	5	12	49	26	119	7	3	.290	.402
2013	Brevard County (FSL)	HiA	.241	129	478	51	115	16	2	5	37	32	80	13	8	.300	.314
2014	Brevard County (FSL)	HiA	.255	66	231	35	59	8	2	3	17	16	50	5	3	.312	.346
	Huntsville (SL)	AA	.262	58	183	31	48	9	6	2	13	10	36	5	2	.304	.410
Minor League Totals			.241	535	1996	252	482	83	24	31	182	111	482	43	21	.288	.354

14 MICHAEL REED, OF

BA GRADE
50 Risk: High

Born: Nov. 18, 1992. **B-T:** R-R. **Ht.:** 6-0. **Wt.:** 200. **Drafted:** HS—Leander, Texas, 2011 (5th round). **Signed by:** Jeremy Booth.

The Brewers have had high hopes for Reed since signing him for $500,000 in 2011, but they knew that because of his youth, he would require time to fulfill his potential. The more scouts see of Reed, the more they like him, for he does many fundamental things well. Reed has the speed to handle center field, but with his strong, accurate arm he played mostly right field in 2014, in deference to Brevard teammate Tyrone Taylor. Reed has not yet shown the pop normally associated with a corner position. Though he didn't hit for a high average at Brevard, which is a tough park on righthanded hitters, he showed better discipline and took enough walks to lead the high Class A Florida State League in OBP. He must continue to work on lowering his strikeout rate and put more balls in play. Reed has had injury issues as a pro and missed about 30 games in 2014. He appears poised to move up to Double-A Biloxi in 2015.

Year	Club (League)	Class	AVG	G	AB	R	H	2B	3B	HR	RBI	BB	SO	SB	CS	OBP	SLG
2012	Huntsville (SL)	AA	.000	3	7	0	0	0	0	0	0	0	3	0	0	.000	.000
	Brevard County (FSL)	HiA	.281	11	32	5	9	0	0	0	5	8	8	3	0	.425	.281
	Helena (PIO)	R	.246	48	179	29	44	5	1	1	20	24	58	11	1	.337	.302
2013	Wisconsin (MWL)	LoA	.286	118	455	68	130	23	13	1	40	71	108	26	10	.385	.400
2014	Brevard County (FSL)	HiA	.255	110	365	50	93	20	5	5	47	78	79	33	13	.396	.378
Minor League Totals			.264	304	1094	163	289	52	21	7	117	186	273	74	24	.376	.369

15 JORGE LOPEZ, RHP

BA GRADE
50 Risk: High

Born: Feb. 10, 1993. **B-T:** R-R. **Ht.:** 6-4. **Wt.:** 185. **Drafted:** HS—Cayey, P.R., 2011 (2nd round). **Signed by:** Charlie Sullivan/Manolo Hernandez.

Selected as a raw 18-year-old in the 2011 draft, Lopez took a while to get his feet on the ground professionally. Slowed by back issues early in his career, he experienced little initial success and even moved back to the Dominican Summer League in 2012. He worked his way through continued growing pains and finally began to fulfill his potential in 2014 at high Class A Brevard County, and under the most difficult of circumstances. Lopez's infant son Mikael was seriously ill and needed constant medical care that led to considerable medical bills. But Lopez managed to keep his focus on the mound before fading in the second half. He throws his fastball in the 90-94 mph range with good movement. He has a nice, easy delivery and good sink on his two-seamer. His improved curveball has become a solid-average secondary pitch at 75-78 mph with good bite. Lopez's changeup remains a work in progress, but he is not afraid to use it. Lopez took a step forward and continues to profile as a possible back-end starter in the big leagues. He likely will be assigned to Double-A Biloxi.

Year	Club (League)	Class	W	L	ERA	G	GS	CG	SV	IP	H	HR	BB	SO	K/9	WHIP	AVG
2012	Brewers (AZL)	R	1	3	5.33	7	3	0	2	25	27	2	12	20	7.1	1.54	.270
	Brewers (DSL)	R	0	1	4.76	5	3	0	0	23	22	0	10	26	10.3	1.41	.256
2013	Wisconsin (MWL)	LoA	7	8	5.23	25	22	0	2	117	120	13	48	92	7.1	1.44	.264
2014	Brevard County (FSL)	HiA	10	10	4.58	25	25	1	0	138	144	12	46	119	7.8	1.38	.273
Minor League Totals			18	22	4.81	66	57	1	4	315	326	27	119	267	7.6	1.41	.268

16 MIGUEL DIAZ, RHP

BA GRADE:

50 Risk: High

Born: Nov. 28, 1994. **B-T:** R-R. **Ht.:** 5-11. **Wt.:** 176. **Signed:** Dominican Republic, 2011. **Signed by:** Fernando Arango.

Signed for the bargain amount of $85,000 in December 2011, Diaz quickly caught the attention of scouts while pitching in the Rookie-level Arizona League. Though small in stature, he improved his arm strength and lower-half coordination, which boosted his fastball velocity into the 94-96 mph range. He has a live, loose arm and the ball comes out of his hand well, and hitters often were late on his fastball. Diaz's slider is a quality pitch at 75-78 mph, though his command of it was spotty at times. He also throws a changeup, but it was too firm in the mid-80s and needs work. Diaz throws with a high three-quarters arm slot and sometimes had issues repeating his delivery. Regardless, his arm is electric, and if he develops his changeup, he could possibly develop into a mid-rotation starter. At the least, Diaz profiles as a power reliever. The 20-year-old probably will jump to low Class A Wisconsin in 2015.

Year	Club (League)	Class	W	L	ERA	G	GS	CG	SV	IP	H	HR	BB	SO	K/9	WHIP	AVG
2012	Brewers (DSL)	R	0	3	4.62	15	1	0	1	25	27	0	15	21	7.5	1.66	.278
2013	Brewers (DSL)	R	3	2	2.40	11	9	0	0	49	36	0	21	34	6.3	1.17	.211
2014	Brewers (AZL)	R	4	2	4.21	13	5	0	0	47	42	3	20	53	10.1	1.32	.232
Minor League Totals			7	7	3.57	39	15	0	1	121	105	3	56	108	8.0	1.33	.234

17 JACOB GATEWOOD, SS

BA GRADE

50 Risk: High

Born: Sept. 25, 1995. **B-T:** R-R. **Ht.:** 6-5. **Wt.:** 190. **Drafted:** HS—Clovis, Calif., 2014 (1st round supplemental). **Signed by:** Dan Huston.

Gatewood displayed the most raw power of any prep player in the 2014 draft, and the Brewers paid an over-slot bonus of $1.83 million to sign him. His father Henry, a catcher, was drafted in the first round of the January 1982 draft by the Dodgers, so he comes from a baseball pedigree. Gatewood won multiple home run derbies in big league stadiums in 2013. With that power comes exploitable flaws in his swing, however, and Gatewood has not proven he will hit for even a modest average. He had difficulty getting on base in his pro debut. He has good hands and impressive bat speed and leverage in his swing. A prep shortstop who stayed at that position in his first pro season, Gatewood's 6-foot-4 frame likely will push him over to third base at some point, if not to a corner-outfield spot. He has smooth actions in the field, good first-step quickness and a strong arm. His speed is average at best. Gatewood might have to repeat Rookie ball at Helena, and he has to become a better all-around hitter.

Year	Club (League)	Class	AVG	G	AB	R	H	2B	3B	HR	RBI	BB	SO	SB	CS	OBP	SLG
2014	Brewers (AZL)	R	.206	50	204	19	42	6	0	3	32	13	71	7	8	.249	.279
Minor League Totals			.206	50	204	19	42	6	0	3	32	13	71	7	8	.249	.279

18 VICTOR ROACHE, OF

BA GRADE

50 Risk: High

Born: Sept. 17, 1991. **B-T:** R-R. **Ht.:** 6-1. **Wt.:** 225. **Drafted:** Georgia Southern, 2012 (1st round). **Signed by:** Steve Smith.

The Brewers knew it would take time for Roache to get going after he missed most of his final season at Georgia Southern in 2012 with a severe wrist injury. That didn't stop them from taking him in the first round. To this point, he has been an all-or-nothing hitter because of poor plate discipline, in particular the inability to lay off breaking pitches off the plate. His raw power has been his only real tool of note, leading to 40 home runs in his first two seasons. But Roache must improve his contact rate (28 percent career strikeout rate) and on-base percentage (.310) to profile as a regular player. He is a fringe defender with an average-at-best arm, likely limiting him to left field. The Brewers like his work ethic and believe his dedication gives him a chance to make the most of his ability, but at this point he projects to be a hitter along the lines of Jonny Gomes. The Brewers probably will promote Roache to Double-A Biloxi.

Year	Club (League)	Class	AVG	G	AB	R	H	2B	3B	HR	RBI	BB	SO	SB	CS	OBP	SLG
2012	Did not play—Injured																
2013	Wisconsin (MWL)	LoA	.248	119	459	62	114	14	4	22	74	46	137	6	2	.322	.440
2014	Brevard County (FSL)	HiA	.226	122	433	46	98	17	2	18	54	37	138	11	4	.298	.400
Minor League Totals			.238	241	892	108	212	31	6	40	128	83	275	17	6	.310	.420

19 KYLE WREN, OF

BA GRADE

45 Risk: Medium

Born: April 23, 1991. **B-T:** L-L. **Ht.:** 5-10. **Wt.:** 175. **Drafted:** Georgia Tech, 2013 (8th round). **Signed by:** Brian Bridges (Braves).

The son of former Braves general manager Frank Wren, Kyle has leveraged his speed as a pro. The

Brewers acquired him in mid-November, trading righthander Zach Quintana to Atlanta after the Braves fired his father as GM. An intelligent player who plays to his strengths, Wren has an explosive first step that allows him to run down balls in the gaps and steal bases with consistency. He is aggressive on defense and gets good momentum behind his throws, which helps overcome below-average arm strength. Wren has a good feel for the strike zone and can drive the ball to the gaps despite possessing little power. An effective drag bunter, he keeps the ball on the ground to make the best use of his speed. He has great instincts on the basepaths and reads pitchers well. Wren needs to get stronger in order to hold up over a full season. He has the ceiling of a fourth outfielder and could reach Milwaukee in 2015 with a good stint at Triple-A.

Year	Club (League)	Class	AVG	G	AB	R	H	2B	3B	HR	RBI	BB	SO	SB	CS	OBP	SLG
2013	Danville (APP)	R	.409	5	22	6	9	3	1	0	4	2	3	3	0	.458	.636
	Rome (SAL)	LoA	.328	47	195	36	64	11	4	2	20	16	21	32	6	.382	.456
	Lynchburg (CAR)	HiA	.000	1	1	0	0	0	0	0	0	1	0	0	1	.500	.000
2014	Lynchburg (CAR)	HiA	.296	76	291	46	86	10	4	0	27	30	39	33	9	.359	.357
	Mississippi (SL)	AA	.283	56	205	28	58	11	4	0	16	16	40	13	5	.338	.376
Minor League Totals			.304	185	714	116	217	35	13	2	67	65	103	81	21	.362	.398

20 JED BRADLEY, LHP

Born: June 12, 1990. **B-T:** L-L. **Ht.:** 6-4. **Wt.:** 225. **Drafted:** Georgia Tech, 2011 (1st round). **Signed by:** Ryan Robinson.

Injuries and issues with maintaining a consistent delivery have sidetracked Bradley, but he took a major step forward in 2014 upon returning for a third season to high Class A Brevard County. He finally stayed healthy, threw more strikes and working ahead in the count to earn a bump to Double-A Huntsville. Bradley has not pitched with the same consistent peak velocity he showed at Georgia Tech, and he now pitches at 89-93 mph with good movement. Only one qualified minor league starter had a higher groundout/airout ratio than Bradley (2.72). Bradley has good deception and arm speed with his low-80s changeup and is not afraid to throw it when behind in the count. Bradley more closely resembles the pitcher he was in college with a delivery he repeats, and he'll give Double-A another go at Biloxi in 2015.

Year	Club (League)	Class	W	L	ERA	G	GS	CG	SV	IP	H	HR	BB	SO	K/9	WHIP	AVG
2012	Brevard County (FSL)	HiA	5	10	5.53	20	20	1	0	107	136	9	43	60	5.0	1.67	.311
2013	Brevard County (FSL)	HiA	4	4	4.14	16	16	1	0	78	81	6	39	58	6.7	1.53	.270
2014	Brevard County (FSL)	HiA	5	2	2.98	10	10	0	0	60	54	4	10	53	7.9	1.06	.240
	Huntsville (SL)	AA	5	8	4.55	17	17	0	0	87	106	8	36	71	7.3	1.63	.307
Minor League Totals			19	24	4.49	63	63	2	0	333	377	27	128	242	6.5	1.52	.288

21 JOHNNY HELLWEG, RHP

Born: Oct. 29, 1988. **B-T:** R-R. **Ht.:** 6-9. **Wt.:** 215. **Drafted:** Florida CC, 2008 (16th round). **Signed by:** Tom Kotchman (Angels).

With so many moving parts to Hellweg's 6-foot-9 frame and trouble repeating his mechanics, he seemed almost destined to blow out his elbow and require Tommy John surgery. And that's exactly what happened after just four starts at Triple-A Nashville in 2014. Hellweg always has had a big arm and seemed on the verge of big things after earning Pacific Coast League pitcher of the year honors in 2013. But he flopped badly in his big league debut in 2013, going 1-4, 6.75 in nine games. When Hellweg is at his best, he pounds the bottom half of the zone with fastballs in the 92-96 mph range with good movement and sink. He still needs to hone his secondary pitches, which consist of an average changeup and below-average, slurvy breaking ball. Still on the 40-man roster, Hellweg profiles more as a reliever.

Year	Club (League)	Class	W	L	ERA	G	GS	CG	SV	IP	H	HR	BB	SO	K/9	WHIP	AVG
2012	Arkansas (TL)	AA	5	10	3.38	21	21	1	0	120	105	8	60	88	6.6	1.38	.245
	Huntsville (SL)	AA	2	1	2.70	7	2	0	0	20	16	0	15	17	7.7	1.55	.222
2013	Wisconsin (MWL)	LoA	1	0	3.00	1	1	0	0	6	5	0	2	4	6.0	1.17	.217
	Nashville (PCL)	AAA	12	5	3.15	23	23	0	0	126	103	6	81	89	6.4	1.46	.228
	Milwaukee (NL)	MAJ	1	4	6.75	8	7	0	0	31	40	3	26	9	2.6	2.15	.325
2014	Nashville (PCL)	AAA	1	2	4.95	4	4	0	0	20	21	1	15	12	5.4	1.80	.288
Major League Totals			1	4	6.75	8	7	0	0	31	40	3	26	9	2.6	2.15	.325
Minor League Totals			32	27	3.53	162	68	1	24	477	384	20	330	446	8.4	1.50	.223

22 JOANTGEL SEGOVIA, OF

Born: Nov. 8, 1996. **B-T:** R-R. **Ht.:** 6-1. **Wt.:** 175. **Signed:** Venezuela, 2013. **Signed by:** Fernando Veracierto.

The unheralded Segovia made his pro debut in the Dominican Summer League in 2014. Playing the entire season at age 17, he led that circuit with a .384 average and was third with a .457 on-base percentage. Segovia showed a good eye at the plate and rarely struck out, though he did not flash much power. He has good knowledge of the strike zone and advanced plate coverage for a player of his age. A large majority of Segovia's hits were singles, but he showed an ability to spray the ball to all fields and occasionally to the gaps. He might not develop power but doesn't need to do so to be an offensive contributor. With above-average speed, he plays center field with ease, showing great range and good instincts. He has good work habits and excellent hand-eye coordination, hitting the ball where it is pitched. Segovia shows good poise for a teenager. The Brewers see him as a quality defender in center and leadoff hitter who puts the ball in play without chasing pitches. Look for him in the Rookie-level Arizona League in 2015.

Year	Club (League)	Class	AVG	G	AB	R	H	2B	3B	HR	RBI	BB	SO	SB	CS	OBP	SLG
2014	Brewers (DSL)	R	.384	58	224	40	86	6	4	0	21	24	19	6	8	.457	.446
Minor League Totals			.384	58	224	40	86	6	4	0	21	24	19	6	8	.457	.446

23 HOBBS JOHNSON, LHP

BA GRADE
45 Risk: High

Born: April 29, 1991. **B-T:** R-L. **Ht.:** 6-0. **Wt.:** 210. **Drafted:** North Carolina, 2013 (14th round). **Signed by:** Dan Nellum.

The Brewers really liked what they saw out of Johnson in 2014. They challenged him to work on his offspeed pitches, and he did so to become a more complete pitcher. He doesn't overpower batters, throwing his fastball in the 88-91 mph range, but he is aggressive and attacks hitters with no fear, pitching ahead in the count with consistency. Johnson's fastball has good sink and he makes a living inducing hitters to beat the ball into the ground. He throws a curve that needs more consistency, but his changeup is above-average and a prime weapon against righthanders. Because of his advanced pitchability and improved command, Johnson could move quickly. The Brewers like his bulldog approach and the way he pitches with confidence, and plan to keep him as a starter for now, but long term he is more likely a reliever. Johnson is a grinder with mental toughness and should jump to Double-A Biloxi in 2015.

Year	Club (League)	Class	W	L	ERA	G	GS	CG	SV	IP	H	HR	BB	SO	K/9	WHIP	AVG
2013	Helena (PIO)	R	0	0	1.13	4	0	0	1	8	7	0	0	9	10.1	0.88	.219
	Wisconsin (MWL)	LoA	0	0	0.69	7	0	0	1	13	13	0	4	23	15.9	1.31	.255
2014	Brevard County (FSL)	HiA	12	8	2.93	25	24	1	0	148	118	10	43	105	6.4	1.09	.221
Minor League Totals			12	8	2.67	36	24	1	2	169	138	10	47	137	7.3	1.10	.224

24 TYLER CRAVY, RHP

BA GRADE
45 Risk: High

Born: July 13, 1989. **B-T:** R-R. **Ht.:** 6-2. **Wt.:** 194. **Drafted:** Napa Valley (Calif.) CC, 2009 (17th round). **Signed by:** Justin McCray.

After a few undistinguished seasons in the bullpen, Cravy has flourished since the moving to the rotation in 2013. That was the case again in 2014 at Double-A Huntsville, where he put together a strong first half and started the Southern League all-star game. The Brewers bumped him to Triple-A Nashville, but he strained his oblique in his first start. He made up for lost time by pitching in Venezuela's winter league. Cravy works fast and pounds the zone with a 90-91 mph sinker. His slider sits at 84-86 mph with good bite, and he keeps hitters off balance with a slower curveball. Mix in a cutter and a changeup and he has a starter's repertoire and the kind of command that makes him difficult to hit. The Brewers love the way he competes and pitches with no fear, allowing weak contact and recording quick outs. Some scouts still see Cravy as a middle reliever, but the Brewers will keep him in the rotation at Triple-A Colorado Springs, where his penchant for keeping the ball down should serve him well.

Year	Club (League)	Class	W	L	ERA	G	GS	CG	SV	IP	H	HR	BB	SO	K/9	WHIP	AVG
2012	Wisconsin (MWL)	LoA	2	5	3.38	24	0	0	3	51	45	5	15	53	9.4	1.18	.231
2013	Brevard County (FSL)	HiA	4	2	2.04	25	9	0	0	79	61	1	24	59	6.7	1.07	.210
2014	Huntsville (SL)	AA	8	1	1.72	14	12	0	0	73	47	7	15	64	7.9	0.85	.184
	Nashville (PCL)	AAA	0	0	2.70	1	1	0	0	3	3	0	3	4	10.8	1.80	.250
	Brewers (AZL)	R	0	1	0.00	2	2	0	0	6	2	0	2	8	12.0	0.67	.100
Minor League Totals			28	22	3.67	122	51	0	3	412	364	27	128	402	8.8	1.19	.235

25 BROOKS HALL, RHP

BA GRADE
40 Risk: Medium

Born: June 26, 1990. **B-T:** R-R. **Ht.:** 6-5. **Wt.:** 200. **Drafted:** HS— Anderson, S.C., 2009 (4th round). **Signed by:** Ryan Robinson.

After putting Hall on the 40-man roster after the 2013 season, the Brewers expected big things from the righthander. He broke out of the gate with five strong starts, but an elbow injury stopped his season there and he never got back on the mound. To make up some of that lost time, Hall logged 19 innings in the Arizona Fall League. When healthy, he throws a 91-94 mph fastball with armside run and pitches to contact. His best secondary pitch is an above-average changeup at 79-82 mph that is effective against lefthanders. Hall mixes in a fringe-average curveball with solid rotation and isn't afraid to throw it when behind in the count. Hall projects as a back-end starter or middle reliever capable of providing multiple innings. The injury setback probably will prompt the Brewers to send him back to Double-A Biloxi.

Year	Club (League)	Class	W	L	ERA	G	GS	CG	SV	IP	H	HR	BB	SO	K/9	WHIP	AVG
2012	Brevard County (FSL)	HiA	4	3	4.33	16	13	0	1	69	72	7	35	40	5.2	1.56	.273
2013	Brevard County (FSL)	HiA	2	3	2.78	11	10	0	0	58	47	1	18	40	6.2	1.11	.217
	Huntsville (SL)	AA	2	4	4.01	17	13	0	1	61	65	8	23	39	5.8	1.45	.283
2014	Huntsville (SL)	AA	2	1	2.77	5	5	0	0	26	24	1	7	16	5.5	1.19	.264
Minor League Totals			20	20	4.00	82	66	0	2	360	372	29	124	241	6.0	1.38	.270

26 DREW GAGNON, RHP

Born: June 26, 1990. **B-T:** R-R. **Ht.:** 6-4. **Wt.:** 195. **Drafted:** Long Beach State, 2011 (3rd round). **Signed by:** Josh Belovsky.

BA GRADE
40 Risk: Medium

The Brewers were anxious to see how Gagnon would bounce back from a shaky 2013 season in which he struggled at both high Class A Brevard County and Double-A Huntsville. He had trouble controlling the ball, averaging nearly 4.0 walks per nine innings. Back at Huntsville in 2014, his control improved, with a 1.29 WHIP and .239 opponent average. The athletic Gagnon was a workhorse, ranking among the Southern League leaders in innings (155) and strikeouts (118). He uses an 88-92 mph fastball with good life and pounds the bottom of the zone. Gagnon's curveball is tough on righthanders and he did a better job of commanding it. He mixes in a fringe-average changeup with good arm action and also regularly uses a cutter to keep lefthanders off his fastball. He is prone to home runs because he pitches with little margin for error if he misses his spot in the zone. The lack of a plus pitch limits Gagnon's ceiling to back-end starter, and he faces a probable shift to the bullpen. His next stop will be Triple-A Colorado Springs in 2015.

Year	Club (League)	Class	W	L	ERA	G	GS	CG	SV	IP	H	HR	BB	SO	K/9	WHIP	AVG
2012	Wisconsin (MWL)	LoA	6	1	2.83	14	14	0	0	83	67	6	19	65	7.1	1.04	.219
	Brevard County (FSL)	HiA	1	2	2.82	11	11	1	0	67	56	3	18	49	6.6	1.10	.229
2013	Brevard County (FSL)	HiA	3	4	5.16	10	10	0	0	45	46	2	15	50	9.9	1.35	.263
	Huntsville (SL)	AA	4	9	5.57	16	16	1	0	84	94	12	42	58	6.2	1.62	.288
2014	Huntsville (SL)	AA	11	6	3.96	28	28	0	0	155	135	18	62	118	6.9	1.27	.239
Minor League Totals			25	25	4.18	87	86	2	1	453	423	42	166	367	7.3	1.30	.250

27 JASON ROGERS, 3B/1B

Born: March 13, 1988. **B-T:** R-R. **Ht.:** 6-2. **Wt.:** 245. **Drafted:** Columbus State (Ga.), 2010 (32nd round). **Signed by:** Ryan Robinson.

BA GRADE
45 Risk: High

Rogers got the Brewers' attention in 2013 with an offensive showing at Double-A that made him the organization's minor league player of the year. The Brewers sent him back to Double-A to open last season to convert from first base to third, a position of great need in the system. He fared well offensively but was a definite work in progress at third base, committing 14 errors in 66 games. Promoted to Triple-A Nashville in late June, he swung the bat even better (.947 OPS in 57 games) to earn a September callup. Rogers has good pitch recognition and discipline, which helps him limit strikeouts. He is a below-average runner with decent instincts on the bases. He'll have to tone up his stocky build if he's going to play third base regularly, but he has decent hands. His arm is borderline at third base and obviously not an issue when he plays first. He faces a probable return to Triple-A in 2015, and he could serve as insurance for both infield corners.

Year	Club (League)	Class	AVG	G	AB	R	H	2B	3B	HR	RBI	BB	SO	SB	CS	OBP	SLG
2012	Wisconsin (MWL)	LoA	.301	66	239	39	72	24	1	6	43	37	46	5	0	.394	.485
	Brevard County (FSL)	HiA	.300	67	233	33	70	11	0	5	23	42	42	7	1	.416	.412
2013	Huntsville (SL)	AA	.270	133	481	69	130	25	2	22	87	59	86	7	2	.346	.468
2014	Huntsville (SL)	AA	.282	77	287	42	81	18	2	7	43	31	56	5	1	.355	.432
	Nashville (PCL)	AAA	.316	57	206	36	65	11	4	11	39	22	38	0	0	.379	.568
	Milwaukee (NL)	MAJ	.111	8	9	0	1	1	0	0	0	1	1	0	0	.200	.222
Major League Totals			.111	8	9	0	1	1	0	0	0	1	1	0	0	.200	.222
Minor League Totals			.287	513	1873	282	537	112	12	61	307	235	353	35	8	.367	.457

28 ARIEL PENA, RHP

BA GRADE

45 Risk: High

Born: May 20, 1989. **B-T:** R-R. **Ht.:** 6-3. **Wt.:** 240. **Signed:** Dominican Republic, 2007. **Signed by:** Freddy Rodriguez (Angels).

The Brewers acquired Pena from the Angels in July 2012 as part of the Zack Greinke trade that also netted shortstop Jean Segura. Milwaukee knew Pena had a strong arm but was prone to command issues. When he throws strikes, hitters have a difficult time putting the ball in play with authority. He throws his fastball past hitters in the 92-96 mph range with good sink, and he can reach 98 with his four-seamer. He also throws a hard, late-breaking slider but still needs work on a changeup that he overthrows. He has been unable to lower a walk rate that also raises his pitch counts. Despite a revamped delivery, Pena struggles with his mechanics and release point. The Brewers have kept Pena in the rotation at Triple-A Nashville to try to help him improve his control through repetition, but that hasn't happened yet, so he faces a likely move to the bullpen. With his power arm and strikeout ability, Pena could profile as a late-inning reliever with better control. Out of minor league options, he could make the big league bullpen in 2015.

Year	Club (League)	Class	W	L	ERA	G	GS	CG	SV	IP	H	HR	BB	SO	K/9	WHIP	AVG
2012	Arkansas (TL)	AA	6	6	2.99	19	19	1	0	114	95	14	42	111	8.7	1.20	.222
	Huntsville (SL)	AA	0	2	7.24	7	7	0	0	32	40	5	23	29	8.1	1.95	.336
2013	Huntsville (SL)	AA	8	9	3.73	27	27	0	0	142	115	17	79	131	8.3	1.36	.224
2014	Nashville (PCL)	AAA	9	8	4.56	25	24	0	0	128	96	12	75	140	9.8	1.33	.208
Minor League Totals			62	46	3.73	170	161	5	0	912	791	68	450	901	8.9	1.36	.234

29 MIKE STRONG, LHP

BA GRADE

40 Risk: Medium

Born: Nov. 17, 1988. **B-T:** L-L. **Ht.:** 6-0. **Wt.:** 195. **Drafted:** Oklahoma State, 2011 (10th round). **Signed by:** Tim Collinsworth.

Strong took a big step forward in 2014 at high Class A Brevard County and the Brewers were so impressed they sent him to the Arizona Fall League, then added him to the 40-man roster in November. His fastball command was much improved, helping set up his curveball and changeup while holding his walks down considerably (2.7 per nine innings) from previous seasons. Strong throws his fastball with confidence in the 88-92 mph range with good movement. His curveball is especially tough on lefthanders, and his changeup is average and sometimes a tick above. While improving his control, Strong still recorded strikeouts (9.2 per nine). Used occasionally as a starter, he profiles as a middle reliever in the big leagues. With three serviceable pitches, he could remain a swingman capable of making starts and getting through the lineup a few times. Strong should begin 2015 at Double-A Biloxi, but the Brewers' lack of lefties—he was one of three on the 40-man roster—could earn him a quick look.

Year	Club (League)	Class	W	L	ERA	G	GS	CG	SV	IP	H	HR	BB	SO	K/9	WHIP	AVG
2012	Wisconsin (MWL)	LoA	1	1	2.76	21	0	0	3	42	30	2	26	60	12.8	1.32	.195
2013	Wisconsin (MWL)	LoA	3	4	3.31	25	8	0	1	87	79	4	45	98	10.1	1.43	.236
2014	Brevard County (FSL)	HiA	2	2	2.50	30	6	1	4	76	56	6	23	78	9.3	1.04	.207
	Huntsville (SL)	AA	0	0	0.00	1	0	0	0	4	0	0	1	6	13.5	0.25	.000
Minor League Totals			8	14	3.59	92	27	1	8	271	228	23	125	297	9.9	1.30	.225

30 DAMIEN MAGNIFICO, RHP

BA GRADE

45 Risk: High

Born: May 24, 1991. **B-T:** R-R. **Ht.:** 6-2. **Wt.:** 210. **Drafted:** Oklahoma, 2012 (5th round). **Signed by:** Tim Collinsworth.

It's one thing to be able to throw 100 mph. It's another to control it. Magnifico had trouble doing both when he was drafted out of Oklahoma in the fifth round in 2012, so he learned to dial it back a bit and trade strikeouts for better control. Magnifico, whose mechanics have been retooled considerably, still reaches the high 90s but now mostly sits around 95 mph with his fastball. His two-seamer has good sinking action when he stays on top of it, and he mixes in an improved slider. His third pitch is a changeup that needs work but is more consistent than in the past. Magnifico commanded his pitches better and found a steady routine that worked for him until he came down with arm fatigue in August. He lowered his walk rate from 4.6 per nine innings in 2013 to 3.2 in 2014. His strikeout rate also dropped to 5.7 per nine as he pitched more often to contact. Most scouts see Magnifico's future role as a late-inning reliever, and he could switch roles in 2015 at Double-A Biloxi.

Year	Club (League)	Class	W	L	ERA	G	GS	CG	SV	IP	H	HR	BB	SO	K/9	WHIP	AVG
2012	Helena (PIO)	R	0	3	5.82	9	1	0	0	22	21	2	15	25	10.4	1.66	.250
2013	Wisconsin (MWL)	LoA	5	1	3.83	11	8	0	0	54	51	4	24	46	7.7	1.39	.250
	Brevard County (FSL)	HiA	0	2	6.08	10	10	0	0	27	32	2	17	17	5.7	1.84	.311
2014	Brevard County (FSL)	HiA	8	6	3.74	22	22	2	0	120	110	11	43	76	5.7	1.27	.244
Minor League Totals			13	12	4.24	52	41	2	0	223	214	19	99	164	6.6	1.41	.254

Minnesota Twins

BY MIKE BERARDINO

A season that began with a cancer scare for general manager Terry Ryan ended with a task that was just as unpleasant and nearly as difficult: Firing his longtime friend Ron Gardenhire as Twins manager.

Four straight seasons of 92 or more losses proved too much for Gardenhire to overcome, even after leading the small-revenue club to six American League Central titles in his first nine seasons as manager, 2002-10.

The Twins ultimately hired Paul Molitor as Gardenhire's replacement, after the Hall of Famer spent the season as a baserunning and infield-defense coach for the big league team. Minnesota also interviewed high Class A Fort Myers manager Doug Mientkiewicz and Red Sox bench coach Torey Lovullo for the position.

While Molitor got the nod after spending 16 of the past 19 seasons in the organization in a variety of roles, the mere fact Lovullo made it that far spoke to the depth of the Twins' concern.

Among the most stable and loyal organizations in all of professional sports, the Twins actually were considering going outside the family for just their third manager in nearly three full decades. That period dates to the firing of Ray Miller in September 1986 and the elevation of Tom Kelly, who would lead the franchise to a pair of World Series titles in 1987 and '91.

While position prospects Danny Santana, a shortstop/center fielder, and Kennys Vargas, a first baseman, reached the majors and had success in 2014, righthander Trevor May struggled to a 7.88 ERA after getting the call in early August.

Tommy John surgery wiped out the entire season for third baseman Miguel Sano, the organization's No. 2 prospect. Top-rated center fielder Byron Buxton, meanwhile, took just 137 plate appearances thanks to a nagging left wrist injury, and his year ended in mid-August with a harrowing collision at Double-A New Britain that resulted in a concussion.

In the minors, Twins affiliates went a combined 366-327 (.528) and reached the playoffs at three levels. That included a Florida State League title for Mientkiewicz and the Miracle, a first for that franchise in 22 years as a Twins affiliate.

Despite those successes, minor league hitting coordinator Bill Springman and Fort Myers pitching coach Gary Lucas were each dismissed after 15 years in the organization. Rookie-level Gulf Coast League pitching coach Ehren Wassermann also wasn't invited back, with former journeyman

New manager Paul Molitor has spent 16 seasons in the organization as an instructor

CLIFF WELCH

TOP PROSPECTS OF THE DECADE

Year	Player, Pos.	2014 Org
2005	Joe Mauer, c	Twins
2006	Francisco Liriano, lhp	Pirates
2007	Matt Garza, rhp	Brewers
2008	Nick Blackburn, rhp	Out of baseball
2009	Aaron Hicks, of	Twins
2010	Aaron Hicks, of	Twins
2011	Kyle Gibson, rhp	Twins
2012	Miguel Sano, 3b	Twins
2013	Miguel Sano, 3b	Twins
2014	Byron Buxton, of	Twins

righthander Virgil Vasquez hired to take his place.

Second-year farm director Brad Steil made those recommendations, and Ryan honored them in hopes of expediting the Twins' turnaround.

Scouting director Deron Johnson added a third straight top-five amateur talent with the selection of Orlando prep shortstop Nick Gordon, son of former big leaguer Tom "Flash" Gordon. He joins first-rounders Buxton (2012) and Kohl Stewart (2013), a righthander, in the fold. For the second time in three years, Johnson loaded up with hard-throwing college relievers as the Twins attempt to mimic other clubs by adding pitchers who miss bats.

Internationally, the Twins added 16-year-old Dominican righthander Huascar Ynoa for $800,000 but otherwise opted for quantity over splashy signings.

General manager: Terry Ryan. **Farm director:** Brad Steil. **Scouting director:** Deron Johnson.

Class	Team	League	W	L	PCT	Finish	Manager
Majors	Minnesota Twins	American	70	92	.432	t-25th (30)	Ron Gardenhire
Triple-A	Rochester Red Wings	International	77	67	.535	5th (14)	Gene Glynn
Double-A	New Britain Rock Cats	Eastern	73	69	.514	t-4th (12)	Jeff Smith
High A	Fort Myers Miracle	Florida State	82	57	.590	1st (12)	Doug Mientkiewicz
Low A	Cedar Rapids Kernels	Midwest	73	67	.521	4th (16)	Jake Mauer
Rookie	Elizabethton Twins	Appalachian	38	30	.559	t-2nd (10)	Ray Smith
Rookie	GCL Twins	Gulf Coast	23	37	.383	t-14th (16)	Ramon Borrego
Overall Minor League Record			366	327	.528	6th (30)	

THIS YEAR'S TOP 30

No.	Player, Pos.	Grade
1.	Byron Buxton, of	75/High
2.	Miguel Sano, 3b	70/Medium
3.	Jose Berrios, rhp	55/Medium
4.	Kohl Stewart, rhp	60/High
5.	Alex Meyer, rhp	55/Medium
6.	Nick Gordon, ss	60/High
7.	Nick Burdi, rhp	50/Medium
8.	Jorge Polanco, ss/2b	50/Medium
9.	Trevor May, rhp	50/Medium
10.	Eddie Rosario, of/2b	50/High
11.	Lewis Thorpe, lhp	50/High
12.	Max Kepler, of/1b	50/High
13.	Stuart Turner, c	50/High
14.	Stephen Gonsalves, lhp	50/High
15.	Taylor Rogers, lhp	45/Medium
16.	Tyler Duffey, rhp	40/Low
17.	Adam Brett Walker, of	50/High
18.	Lewin Diaz, 1b	50/High
19.	Jake Reed, rhp	50/High
20.	J.R. Graham, rhp	50/Extreme
21.	J.T. Chargios, rhp	50/Extreme
22.	Engelb Vielma, ss	45/High
23.	Michael Cederoth, rhp	45/High
24.	Fernando Romero, rhp	50/Extreme
25.	Zack Jones, rhp	50/Extreme
26.	Amaurys Minier, of/1b	45/High
27.	Huascar Ynoa, rhp	50/Extreme
28.	Felix Jorge, rhp	45/High
29.	Niko Goodrum, 3b/ss	45/High
30.	Travis Harrison, of/3b	45/High

LAST YEAR'S TOP 30

No.	Player, Pos.	Status
1.	Byron Buxton, of	No. 1
2.	Miguel Sano, 3b	No. 2
3.	Alex Meyer, rhp	No. 5
4.	Kohl Stewart, rhp	No. 4
5.	Jose Berrios, rhp	No. 3
6.	Eddie Rosario, 2b/0f	No. 10
7.	Lewis Thorpe, lhp	No. 11
8.	Trevor May, rhp	No. 9
9.	Danny Santana, ss	Majors
10.	Jorge Polanco, 2b/ss	No. 8
11.	Max Kepler, of/1b	No. 12
12.	Fernando Romero, rhp	No. 24
13.	Stephen Gonsalves, lhp	No. 14
14.	Josmil Pinto, c	Majors
15.	Mike Tonkin, rhp	Majors
16.	Adam Brett Walker, of	No. 17
17.	Felix Jorge, rhp	No. 28
18.	Mason Melotakis, lhp	Dropped out
19.	Taylor Rogers, lhp	No. 15
20.	Kennys Vargas, 1b	Majors
21.	Lewin Diaz, of/1b	No. 18
22.	Randy Rosario, lhp	Dropped out
23.	Luke Bard, rhp	Dropped out
24.	Amaurys Minier, 3b	No. 26
25.	Travis Harrison, 3b/of	No. 30
26.	Niko Goodrum, 3b/ss	No. 29
27.	Tyler Jones, rhp	Dropped out
28.	Zack Jones, rhp	No. 25
29.	Roni Tapia, 3b	Dropped out
30.	Stuart Turner, c	No. 13

BEST TOOLS

Best Hitter for Average	Byron Buxton
Best Power Hitter	Miguel Sano
Best Strike-Zone Discipline	Jorge Polanco
Fastest Baserunner	Byron Buxton
Best Athlete	Byron Buxton
Best Fastball	Nick Burdi
Best Curveball	Alex Meyer
Best Slider	Nick Burdi
Best Changeup	Trevor May
Best Control	Jose Berrios
Best Defensive Catcher	Stuart Turner
Best Defensive Infielder	Engelb Vielma
Best Infield Arm	Niko Goodrum
Best Defensive Outfielder	Byron Buxton
Best Outfield Arm	Byron Buxton

PROJECTED 2018 LINEUP

Catcher	Stuart Turner
First Base	Joe Mauer
Second Base	Brian Dozier
Third Base	Miguel Sano
Shortstop	Nick Gordon
Left Field	Danny Santana
Center Field	Byron Buxton
Right Field	Oswaldo Arcia
Designated Hitter	Kennys Vargas
No. 1 Starter	Phil Hughes
No. 2 Starter	Jose Berrios
No. 3 Starter	Kohl Stewart
No. 4 Starter	Alex Meyer
No. 5 Starter	Kyle Gibson
Closer	Glen Perkins

MINNESOTA TWINS

TOP 2015 ROOKIE: Alex Meyer, rhp. This tower of power will be 25 on Opening Day, so it's time for him to start justifying a mountain of hype.

BREAKOUT PROSPECT: J.T. Chargois, rhp. After touching 102 mph in instructional league, this closer prospect will be nearly 19 months removed from Tommy John surgery by Opening Day.

SLEEPER: Mitch Garver, c. The hit tool is there, so now he just needs to show he can stay behind the plate.

SOURCE OF TOP 30 TALENT			
Homegrown	28	Acquired	2
College	10	Trades	2
Junior college	0	Rule 5 draft	0
High school	8	Independent leagues	0
Draft-and-follow	0	Free agents/waivers	0
Nondrafted free agents	0		
International	10		

LF	CF	RF
Eddie Rosario (10)	Byron Buxton (1)	Max Kepler (12)
Amaurys Minier (26)	Max Murphy	Adam Brett Walker (17)
Travis Harrison (30)	Jason Kanzler	Zack Larson
J.D. Williams	Zach Granite	Jeremias Pineda
	Tanner English	Roberto Gonzalez

3B	SS	2B	1B
Miguel Sano (2)	Nick Gordon (6)	Aderlin Mejia	Lewin Diaz (18)
Niko Goodrum (29)	Jorge Polanco (8)	Ryan Walker	D.J. Hicks
Roni Tapia	Engelb Vielma (22)	Levi Michael	Tyler Kuresa
Tyler Mautner	Manuel Guzman	Rafael Valera	Chad Christensen
Jonatan Hinojosa	Nelson Molina	Logan Wade	Trey Vavra
	Emmanuel Morel		

C
Stuart Turner (13)
Mitch Garver
Brian Navaretto
Jorge Fernandez
Rainis Silva

LHP		RHP	
LHSP	**LHRP**	**RHSP**	**RHRP**
Lewis Thorpe (11)	Mason Melotakis	Jose Berrios (3)	Nick Burdi (7)
Stephen Gonsalves (14)	Cameron Booser	Kohl Stewart (4)	Jake Reed (19)
Taylor Rogers (15)	Aaron Thompson	Alex Meyer (5)	J.R. Graham (20)
Jason Wheeler	Sam Clay	Trevor May (9)	J.T. Chargois (21)
Randy Rosario	Brandon Bixler	Tyler Duffey (16)	Zack Jones (25)
Brett Lee	Corey Williams	Michael Cederoth (23)	Madison Boer
Mat Batts	Brandon Easton	Fernando Romero (24)	A.J. Achter
Steven Gruver	Ryan O'Rourke	Huascar Ynoa (27)	Lester Oliveros
David Hurlbut		Felix Jorge (28)	Stephen Pryor
Jadison Jimenez		Jason Adam	C.K. Irby
Michael Theofanopoulos		Aaron Slegers	Mark Hamburger
		John Curtiss	D.J. Johnson
		Chih-Wei Hu	Brandon Peterson
		Alex Wimmers	Randy LeBlanc
		Ryan Eades	Tyler Jones
		Williams Ramirez	Brandon Poulson
		Sam Gibbons	
		Alexis Tapia	
		D.J. Baxendale	

BEST PURE HITTER: SS Nick Gordon (1) added bat speed to his quick, loose stroke that works inside the ball and hits to all fields. He projects to be an above-average hitter with strong bat-to-ball skills and projects to hit for at least average power.

BEST POWER HITTER: OF Max Murphy (9) has plus power potential and finished second in the Rookie-level Appalachian League with 10 home runs. OF Roberto Gonzalez (15) has plus raw power to his pull side from the left side of the plate.

FASTEST RUNNER: OF Tanner English (11) has at least 70-grade speed on the 20-80 scale and draws some 80 grades from scouts.

BEST DEFENSIVE PLAYER: English was one of the best defensive center fielders in college baseball at South Carolina, with first-step quickness, plus range to the gaps and a plus arm. Gonzalez had one of the best outfield arms from the prep ranks, grading as at least a 65. Gordon had one of the best prep infield arms, garnering 65 to 70 grades.

BEST FASTBALL: The Twins stocked up on power college arms and got two of the biggest fastballs from college baseball in RHPs Nick Burdi (2) and Michael Cederoth (3), who have both touched at least 100 mph. Burdi's fastball is a little bit hotter, having touched 102 and sat 96-99 with plus life. RHP Jake Reed (5) sits 93-95, touching 98 with plus arm-side run. The Twins signed RHP Brandon Poulson as a nondrafted free agent this summer after he touched 100 mph.

BEST SECONDARY PITCH: Burdi's slider is a wipeout offering that draws well above-average grades from scouts, touching as high as 93. The breaking balls for LHP Sam Clay (4; curveball), Cederoth (slider) and LHP Michael Theofanopoulos (30; curveball) all show at least plus potential.

BEST PRO DEBUT: Murphy hit .309/.403/.556 with 14 home runs across two levels. Reed had a 10.3 strikeout-walk ratio and 0.36 ERA in 25 innings at low Class A.

BEST ATHLETE: English was one of the best college athletes in this year's draft.

MOST INTRIGUING BACKGROUND: Gordon is the son of former major league all-star Tom "Flash" Gordon and the half-brother of Dodgers second baseman Dee Gordon. 1B Trey Vavra (33) is the son of longtime Twins coach Joe Vavra.

CLOSEST TO THE MAJORS: Burdi could be one of the quickest movers in the 2014 draft. Reed is in the Arizona Fall League and not far behind Burdi; it wouldn't be out of the question for either of them to reach Minnesota next season.

BEST LATE-ROUND PICK: RHP Trevor Hildenberger (22) is a strike-thrower who has been up to 92 mph from a low slot and up to 95 from over the top.

THE ONE WHO GOT AWAY: SS Dalton Guthrie (40) has big league bloodlines, advanced instincts and will likely be a very good college player at Florida.

ASSESSMENT: After getting the top up-the-middle prep player in the draft, Nick Gordon, the Twins drafted seven straight college pitchers, six of which were relievers in college.

2013

RHP Kohl Stewart (1) had an erratic first season but showed the upside of a first-round arm. C Stuart Turner (3) moved quickly so far, while LHP Stephen Gonsalves (4) looks like a potential steal.

GRADE: B

2012

While 2014 was a lost season, OF Byron Buxton (1) still excites scouts as an elite talent. RHP Jose Berrios (1s) fronts a deep pitching class including LHP Taylor Rogers (11) and RHP Tyler Duffey (5).

GRADE: A

2011

It's not over for this class, but SS Levi Michael (1) has been a bust. OF Travis Harrison (1s) is the class' top-ranked prospect, while LHP Jason Wheeler (8) has reached Triple-A.

GRADE: F

TOP DRAFT PICKS OF THE DECADE

Year	Player, Pos.	2014 Org
2005	Matt Garza, rhp	Brewers
2006	Chris Parmelee, 1b/of	Twins
2007	Ben Revere, of	Phillies
2008	Aaron Hicks, of	Twins
2009	Kyle Gibson, rhp	Twins
2010	Alex Wimmers, rhp	Twins
2011	Levi Michael, ss	Twins
2012	Byron Buxton, of	Twins
2013	Kohl Stewart, rhp	Twins
2014	Nick Gordon, ss	Twins

LARGEST BONUSES IN CLUB HISTORY

Byron Buxton, 2012	$6,000,000
Joe Mauer, 2001	$5,150,000
Kohl Stewart, 2013	$4,544,400
Nick Gordon, 2014	$3,851,000
Miguel Sano, 2009	$3,150,000

1 BYRON BUXTON, OF

Born: Dec. 18, 1993. **B-T:** R-R. **Ht.:** 6-2. **Wt.:** 190.
Drafted: HS—Baxley, Ga., 2012 (1st round).
Signed by: Jack Powell.

BA GRADE

75 Risk: High

SCOUTING GRADES

Batting: 70.
Power: 60.
Speed: 80.
Defense: 80.
Arm: 70.

Based on 20-80 scouting scale and future projection rather than present grades.

LGE	PA	BB%	SO%	ISO
FSL	134	7.5	24.6	.165

TOM DiPACE

Buxton has been named the Baseball America High School Player of the Year (2012) and its Minor League Player of the Year (2013). He jumped onto the fast track after the Twins drafted him second overall in 2012, then gave him a $6 million bonus that remains the largest in franchise history. Buxton helped Rookie-level Elizabethton win the Appalachian League title in his first professional summer and then took his game to another level in 2013, dominating the Midwest and Florida State leagues. A strained left shoulder shortened his first Arizona Fall League assignment by a couple of weeks, but that setback was nothing compared with what Buxton experienced in 2014. First, he sprained his left wrist in mid-March while attempting a diving catch on a back field. Once he made it to high Class A Fort Myers a month into the season, he re-injured the wrist five games later while sliding home. This time it took him two months to return to action. Buxton logged a .956 OPS in 15 July games before again missing time after being hit by pitch on his right (other) wrist. Sent to Double-A New Britain on Aug. 13, he struck out in his only three at-bats before suffering a harrowing outfield collision with right fielder Mike Kvasnicka. Rushed to the hospital, Buxton was fortunate to escape with only a season-ending concussion.

Widely acknowledged as the top prospect in the game by the time he played in the 2013 Futures Game, Buxton has done little to harm that reputation when healthy. Blessed with quick hands and strong wrists, he generates tremendous bat speed and keeps the bat in the zone for a long time. He has an advanced approach at the plate and shows good plate discipline, though his strikeout (24.6 percent) and walk (7.5 percent) rates diverged in his second pass through the FSL. Buxton generates easy power to all fields. Timed at 3.9 seconds from the batter's box to first base, he is an 80 runner but still must improve his reads and instincts while on base. In the field, Buxton has plus-plus arm strength and range, gliding to balls others must strain to reach. Naturally reserved and ever polite, Buxton has become more comfortable with teammates.

Sent back to the AFL for a second straight year, Buxton sustained another injury, this time a dislocated middle finger on his left hand. When he gets a fresh start in 2015, he will report to Chattanooga, the Twins' new Double-A affiliate in the Southern League, with the hope that he can resume the roll he enjoyed in 2013. Buxton turns 21 this offseason and could reach the majors by the end of 2015 with a chance to put down roots in center the following year.

Year	Club (League)	Class	AVG	G	AB	R	H	2B	3B	HR	RBI	BB	SO	SB	CS	OBP	SLG
2012	Twins (GCL)	R	.216	27	88	17	19	4	3	4	14	11	26	4	3	.324	.466
	Elizabethton (APP)	R	.286	21	77	16	22	6	1	1	6	8	15	7	0	.368	.429
2013	Cedar Rapids (MWL)	LoA	.341	68	270	68	92	15	10	8	55	44	56	32	11	.431	.559
	Fort Myers (FSL)	HiA	.326	57	218	41	71	4	8	4	22	32	49	23	8	.415	.472
2014	Fort Myers (FSL)	HiA	.240	30	121	19	29	4	2	4	16	10	33	6	2	.313	.405
	New Britain (EL)	AA	.000	1	3	0	0	0	0	0	0	0	3	0	0	.000	.000
Minor League Totals			.300	204	777	161	233	33	24	21	113	105	182	72	24	.389	.485

2 MIGUEL SANO, 3B

Born: May 11, 1993. **B-T:** R-R. **Ht.:** 6-3. **Wt.:** 232. **Signed:** Dominican Republic, 2009. **Signed by:** Fred Guerrero.

Signed out of the Dominican Republic for $3.15 million, the fifth-highest bonus in Twins history, Sano weathered a lengthy pre-signing ordeal that included an age dispute. He rocketed to the top spot on the Twins' prospect list after 2012 before stepping aside for Byron Buxton in 2013. He had Tommy John surgery in mid-March 2014, wiping out his first big league spring training as well as his entire season. Blessed with scale-busting power and an advanced understanding at the plate, Sano now is a year removed from a 35-homer season that ranked him fourth in the minors. His surgery didn't entirely come as a surprise after he missed all but two games last winter in the Dominican League with soreness in his throwing elbow. A below-average runner, he used the down time to continue shedding fat and improving his all-around athleticism. The Twins still hope to keep him at third base, though his throwing accuracy was an issue even before surgery.

BA GRADE

70 Risk: Medium

LGE	PA	BB%	SO%	ISO
Did not play

Even with incumbent third baseman Trevor Plouffe coming off surgery to repair a fractured left forearm and in line for another hefty raise via arbitration, Sano likely must wait another half-season or so before taking over the hot corner for the Twins. Adding him to the 40-man roster will finally be a necessity this November.

Year	Club (League)	Class	AVG	G	AB	R	H	2B	3B	HR	RBI	BB	SO	SB	CS	OBP	SLG
2012	Beloit (MWL)	LoA	.258	129	457	75	118	28	4	28	100	80	144	8	3	.373	.521
2013	Fort Myers (FSL)	HiA	.330	56	206	51	68	15	2	16	48	29	61	9	2	.424	.655
	New Britain (EL)	AA	.236	67	233	35	55	15	3	19	55	36	81	2	1	.344	.571
2014	Did not play—Injured																
Minor League Totals			.279	379	1375	253	384	92	17	90	291	192	423	28	13.373	.567

3 JOSE BERRIOS, RHP

Born: May 27, 1994. **B-T:** R-R. **Ht.:** 6-0. **Wt.:** 189. **Drafted:** HS—Bayamon, P.R., 2012 (1st round supplemental). **Signed by:** Hector Otero.

Selected 32nd overall out of high school in 2012, Berrios signed for $1.55 million as the highest-drafted pitcher ever from Puerto Rico. The organization's minor league pitcher of the year in 2014, he struck out Robinson Cano in the 2013 World Baseball Classic and started for the World team at the 2014 Futures Game at Target Field. Working closely with pitching coach Gary Lucas the past two seasons at low Class A Cedar Rapids and high Class A Fort Myers, Berrios has seen his confidence and mound presence blossom. An excellent athlete who fields his position and holds runners well, Berrios topped out at 98 mph, and his fastball typically sits at 92-94 and shows late life. Throwing from a three-quarters arm angle, Berrios' slurvy breaking ball comes in at 80-82 mph, but he can vary the speed and break on it. Fully committing to his changeup for the first time, Berrios used it as an out-pitch, throwing as many as 20 per game. He skipped a start in early August with shoulder stiffness, but he established a career high

BA GRADE

55 Risk: Medium

LGE	BF	SO%	BB%	HR/9
FSL	389	28.0	5.9	0.37
EL	163	17.2	7.4	0.44

with 140 innings. Bumped up to Triple-A Rochester for one start at the end of 2014, Berrios figures to return there in 2015. If he continues to progress, then he projects as a No. 3 starter with control of three average or better pitches.

Year	Club (League)	Class	W	L	ERA	G	GS	CG	SV	IP	H	HR	BB	SO	K/9	WHIP	AVG
2012	Twins (GCL)	R	1	0	1.08	8	1	0	4	17	7	0	3	27	14.6	0.60	.121
	Elizabethton (APP)	R	2	0	1.29	3	3	0	0	14	8	1	1	22	14.1	0.64	.163
2013	Cedar Rapids (MWL)	LoA	7	7	3.99	19	19	0	0	104	105	6	40	100	8.7	1.40	.262
2014	Fort Myers (FSL)	HiA	9	3	1.96	16	16	1	0	96	78	4	23	109	10.2	1.05	.218
	New Britain (EL)	AA	3	4	3.54	8	8	1	0	41	33	2	12	28	6.2	1.11	.226
	Rochester (IL)	AAA	0	1	18.00	1	1	0	0	3	7	0	3	3	9.0	3.33	.438
Minor League Totals			22	15	3.05	55	48	2	4	274	238	13	82	289	9.5	1.17	.232

4 KOHL STEWART, RHP

Born: Oct. 7, 1994. **B-T:** R-R. **Ht.:** 6-3. **Wt.:** 208. **Drafted:** HS—Houston, 2013 (1st round). **Signed by:** Greg Runser.

Passing up a chance to succeed Johnny Manziel as quarterback at Texas A&M, Stewart turned pro for $4,544,400 as the 2013 draft's fourth overall pick. A Type-1 diabetic, he has had no trouble maintaining his stamina in pro ball but has been plagued by late-season shoulder issues in both 2013 and 2014. In the latter season, Stewart topped out near 75 pitches per start and logged just five innings after July 17 after coming down with shoulder inflammation and losing velocity. Blessed with a strong, athletic frame and a clean delivery he repeats with ease, Stewart brandishes a 93-96 mph fastball that shows plus life. He also mixes in an occasional hard sinker but prefers to put hitters away with a mid-80s power slider that ranks among the best in the system. His other two pitches project to at least average but could still use some work. His curveball shows 12-to-6 action at its best, while his changeup remains inconsistent but has shown good sink and tumble.

BA GRADE

60 Risk: High

LGE	BF	SO%	BB%	HR/9
MWL	360	17.2	6.7	0.41

Perhaps because hitters could eliminate two pitches on many nights, Stewart's strikeout rate was of 6.4 per nine innings was well off the pace for top Midwest League starters. He shows competitive fire and mound swagger that can grate on opponents and umpires alike. Still just 20, Stewart should move up to high Class A Fort Myers next season, and if he can miss more bats and stay off the DL he could reach a ceiling as a No. 2 starter.

Year	Club (League)	Class	W	L	ERA	G	GS	CG	SV	IP	H	HR	BB	SO	K/9	WHIP	AVG
2013	Twins (GCL)	R	0	0	1.69	6	3	0	0	16	12	0	3	16	9.0	0.94	.188
	Elizabethton (APP)	R	0	0	0.00	1	1	0	0	4	1	0	1	8	18.0	0.50	.077
2014	Cedar Rapids (MWL)	LoA	3	5	2.59	19	19	0	0	87	75	4	24	62	6.4	1.14	.233
Minor League Totals			3	5	2.36	26	23	0	0	107	88	4	28	86	7.2	1.08	.221

5 ALEX MEYER, RHP

Born: Jan. 3, 1990. **B-T:** R-R. **Ht.:** 6-9. **Wt.:** 220. **Drafted:** Kentucky, 2011 (1st round). **Signed by:** Reed Dunn (Nationals).

Acquired from the Nationals in a straight-up trade for Denard Span, Meyer has spent the past two years marinating in the upper reaches of the system. He missed 10 weeks with a strained throwing shoulder in 2013, then remained healthy in 2014 until mild shoulder fatigue in his final start at Triple-A Rochester kept him from an expected September callup. A towering 6-foot-9 and gangly, Meyer still struggles at times to repeat his delivery. Control remains an issue, as shown by a walk rate of 4.4 per nine innings. On the plus side, Meyer led all Twins starters with 10.6 strikeouts per nine, thanks to a double-plus four-seam fastball that sits at 95-96 mph and has touched 100. He mixes in a low-90s sinker with good armside run and a power knuckle-curve that shows good depth and finish at 84-87 mph. With the help of pitching coordinator Eric Rasmussen, Meyer altered his changeup grip to more of a pitchfork style and had success turning over the

BA GRADE

55 Risk: Medium

LGE	BF	SO%	BB%	HR/9
IL	565	27.1	11.3	0.69

pitch and generating sink and fade. Meyer will be 25 when he reports to spring training, and the Twins were ready to bring him to the majors in a relief role last September until he showed signs of fatigue after throwing a career-high 130 innings. Soon enough he will join fellow 20-somethings Kyle Gibson and Trevor May in a rotation that needs all the help it can get.

Year	Club (League)	Class	W	L	ERA	G	GS	CG	SV	IP	H	HR	BB	SO	K/9	WHIP	AVG
2012	Hagerstown (SAL)	LoA	7	4	3.10	18	18	1	0	90	68	4	34	107	10.7	1.13	.210
	Potomac (CAR)	HiA	3	2	2.31	7	7	0	0	39	29	2	11	32	7.4	1.03	.213
2013	Twins (GCL)	R	0	0	1.08	3	3	0	0	8	7	0	3	16	17.3	1.20	.233
	New Britain (EL)	AA	4	3	3.21	13	13	0	0	70	60	3	29	84	10.8	1.27	.226
2014	Rochester (IL)	AAA	7	7	3.52	27	27	0	0	130	116	10	64	153	10.6	1.38	.241
Minor League Totals			21	16	3.15	68	68	1	0	338	280	19	141	392	10.4	1.25	.227

6 NICK GORDON, SS

Born: Oct. 24, 1995. **B-T:** L-R. **Ht.:** 6-1. **Wt.:** 173 . **Drafted:** HS—Orlando, 2014 (1st round). **Signed by:** Brett Dowdy.

BA GRADE

60 Risk: High

LGE	PA	BB%	SO%	ISO
APP	256	4.3	17.6	.072

Son of 21-year big league veteran Tom Gordon and younger half-brother of Dodgers second baseman Dee Gordon, Nick might be the most talented Gordon of all. Taken fifth overall in 2014 after a standout prep career at Olympia High, he signed for $3.851 million. A broken index finger on his left hand ended Gordon's season at Rookie-level Elizabethton in the first round of Appalachian League playoffs. The injury, which happened when he was jammed on a pitch, continued to slow him at his first instructional league. Some rival evaluators question whether Gordon has the quick-twitch athleticism to stay at shortstop long term, but scouting director Deron Johnson and his staff had no such doubts. He shows outstanding instincts, work ethic and makeup and quickly named Derek Jeter on draft night as his ultimate role model. With soft, sure hands and a plus arm, Gordon made just eight errors and posted the highest fielding percentage (.964) of any Appy League shortstop. At the plate, he has the ability to hit for average and power with an advanced knack for driving the ball to the opposite field. He has plenty of present bat speed, but the Twins foresee more power as he gets stronger and learns to pull the ball. His raw speed is above average but it plays down a notch out of the box due to his big swing. Gordon should open his first full pro season at low Class A Cedar Rapids, where he will get his first taste of cold weather.

Year	Club (League)	Class	AVG	G	AB	R	H	2B	3B	HR	RBI	BB	SO	SB	CS	OBP	SLG
2014	Elizabethton (APP)	R	.294	57	235	46	69	6	4	1	28	11	45	11	7	.333	.366
Minor League Totals			.294	57	235	46	69	6	4	1	28	11	45	11	7	.333	.366

7 NICK BURDI, RHP

Born: Jan. 19, 1993. **B-T:** R-R. **Ht.:** 6-4. **Wt.:** 215. **Drafted:** Louisville, 2014 (2nd round). **Signed by:** Alan Sandberg.

BA GRADE

50 Risk: Medium

LGE	BF	SO%	BB%	HR/9
MWL	54	48.1	14.8	0.00
FSL	28	42.9	7.1	0.00

After taking a 24th-round flier on Burdi out of high school in 2011, the Twins grabbed him in the second round (46th overall) after an All-America career as a closer at Louisville. Signed for $1.22 million after reaching the College World Series, Burdi made it clear he hoped to reach the majors as soon as possible, then suffered through a four-walk, no-out nightmare in his pro debut at low Class A Cedar Rapids before righting the ship. Burdi famously hit 103 mph in the Cape Cod League, owning a powerful right arm that he hones with an unconventional program of super-long toss. With an 80 fastball on the 20-80 scouting scale, Burdi's low-end velocity as a reliever is still 95-98 mph. His devastating 87-90 mph slider shows good tilt and slice. Burdi works on a changeup on the side, but so far has had no occasion to bring it into games. He stays in his max-effort delivery well, but Fort Myers pitching coach Gary Lucas had to monitor Burdi for those times when his elbow would drop or his hand would get on the side of the ball. After fanning 46 in his final 25 innings in 2014, Burdi put himself on the fast track. Considering his confident demeanor and college closing background, the Twins will let his success dictate how quickly he moves through the system. If he stays in relief, he could start at Double-A.

Year	Club (League)	Class	W	L	ERA	G	GS	CG	SV	IP	H	HR	BB	SO	K/9	WHIP	AVG
2014	Cedar Rapids (MWL)	LoA	0	0	4.15	13	0	0	4	13	8	0	8	26	18.0	1.23	.174
	Fort Myers (FSL)	HiA	2	0	0.00	7	0	0	1	7	5	0	2	12	14.7	0.95	.208
Minor League Totals			2	0	2.66	20	0	0	5	20	13	0	10	38	16.8	1.13	.186

8 JORGE POLANCO, SS/2B

Born: July 5, 1993. **B-T:** B-R. **Ht.:** 5-11. **Wt.:** 185. **Signed:** Dominican Republic, 2009. **Signed by:** Fred Guerrero.

A switch-hitter who has added 20 pounds since signing for $775,000, Polanco reached the majors briefly in 2014 and handled himself well in a five-game midseason cameo. He has shown the ability to play both middle-infield spots, and while he dominated the high Class A Florida State League, he struggled at times after making the jump to Double-A New Britain. Reminding some of a young Tony Fernandez at the plate, Polanco uses the whole field and has already learned to turn on pitches on the inner half. Polanco has at least average speed but has a long way to go with his baserunning acumen. In particular, he struggles to read pickoff moves, as shown by his career success rate of just 55 percent on stolen-base attempts. Limited mostly to second base in the low minors, Polanco made 35 errors this season at shortstop, though he has soft hands, an average arm and range that could improve to above-average as he learns to get better reads off the bat. Now 21, Polanco figures to return to Double-A in 2015. It remains to be seen whether he will stay at shortstop or move back to second. Some of that could be dictated by shortstop Danny Santana's future in Minnesota.

BA GRADE

50 Risk: Medium

LGE	PA	BB%	SO%	ISO
FSL	432	10.6	13.9	.124
EL	157	5.7	17.8	.062

Year	Club (League)	Class	AVG	G	AB	R	H	2B	3B	HR	RBI	BB	SO	SB	CS	OBP	SLG
2012	Elizabethton (APP)	R	.318	51	173	35	55	15	2	5	27	20	26	6	3	.388	.514
2013	Cedar Rapids (MWL)	LoA	.308	115	465	76	143	32	10	5	78	42	59	4	4	.362	.452
2014	Fort Myers (FSL)	HiA	.291	94	378	61	110	17	6	6	45	46	60	10	8	.364	.415
	Minnesota (AL)	MAJ	.333	5	6	2	2	1	1	0	3	2	2	0	0	.500	.833
	New Britain (EL)	AA	.281	37	146	13	41	6	0	1	16	9	28	7	3	.323	.342
Major League Totals			.333	5	6	2	2	1	1	0	3	2	2	0	0	.500	.833
Minor League Totals			.287	400	1497	223	430	85	21	19	201	150	215	36	29	.351	.410

9 TREVOR MAY, RHP

Born: Sept. 23, 1989. **B-T:** R-R. **Ht.:** 6-5. **Wt.:** 215. **Drafted:** HS—Kelso, Wash., 2008 (4th round). **Signed by:** Dave Ryles (Phillies).

Control issues led to May's inclusion along with Vance Worley in a December 2012 deal in which the Phillies acquired outfielder Ben Revere. May reached Triple-A Rochester in 2014, where he dominated to reach the majors in mid-August. A seven-walk big league debut in Oakland threatened to undercut his significant gains, but May stabilized well enough to finish out the year in the rotation. Armed with one of the best changeups in the system and the ability to miss bats, May has a strong frame and a physical presence on the mound. However, he still struggles at times with a loss of focus and fastball command. His 92-94 mph four-seamer has some run when he keeps it down in the zone, but location can be a problem. He has a 76-78 mph curveball that he still features on occasion, and his 82-85 mph slider could be sharper. High pitch counts are a common refrain for May, who falls out of attack mode too frequently and sometimes labors to finish batters. He did a much better job of working in to righthanders, producing more weak contact on the ground. May will head to spring training with a chance to extend his run in the Twins rotation. A potential No. 4 starter if he can improve his control, he would do well to continue his apprenticeship under fellow righthander Phil Hughes.

BA GRADE

50 Risk: Medium

LGE	BF	SO%	BB%	HR/9
IL	400	23.5	9.8	0.37
AL	213	20.7	10.3	1.38

Year	Club (League)	Class	W	L	ERA	G	GS	CG	SV	IP	H	HR	BB	SO	K/9	WHIP	AVG
2012	Reading (EL)	AA	10	13	4.87	28	28	0	0	150	139	22	78	151	9.1	1.45	.249
2013	New Britain (EL)	AA	9	9	4.51	27	27	2	0	152	149	14	67	159	9.4	1.42	.256
2014	Rochester (IL)	AAA	8	6	2.84	18	18	1	0	98	75	4	39	94	8.6	1.16	.209
	Minnesota (AL)	MAJ	3	6	7.88	10	9	0	0	46	59	7	22	44	8.7	1.77	.314
Major League Totals			3	6	7.88	10	9	0	0	46	59	7	22	44	8.7	1.77	.314
Minor League Totals			54	46	3.90	147	142	6	0	775	657	61	382	900	10.4	1.34	.230

10 EDDIE ROSARIO, OF/2B

Born: Sept. 26, 1991. **B-T:** L-R. **Ht.:** 6-0. **Wt.:** 180. **Drafted:** HS—Guayama, P.R., 2010 (4th round). **Signed by:** Hector Otero.

The Twins now view Rosario as the third-most prominent Puerto Rico product in the organization, behind righthander Jose Berrios and slugger Kennys Vargas. A 50-game suspension for violating baseball's recreational drug policy wiped out Rosario's first two months in 2014, and he struggled uncharacteristically once he returned. Rosario's hit tool ranks among the best in the system. He generates outstanding bat speed and plate coverage, flashing his hands through the zone and generating gap power, and he projects to hit a dozen or more home runs. Selectivity remains an issue. Defensively, his footwork and range still need work at second base, where he logged just 18 games in 2014, but in the outfield he takes good routes and shows an above-average arm. A slightly above-average runner at his best, Rosario has been successful on just 54 percent of his stolen-base attempts the past three seasons. Rosario was added to the 40-man roster this winter. With the Twins' outfield situation unsettled, Rosario's best chance to reach the majors in a hurry could be in left field to replace the traded Josh Willingham.

BA GRADE

50 Risk: High

LGE	PA	BB%	SO%	ISO
FSL	34	11.8	14.7	.000
EL	336	5.1	20.2	.158

Year	Club (League)	Class	AVG	G	AB	R	H	2B	3B	HR	RBI	BB	SO	SB	CS	OBP	SLG
2012	Twins (GCL)	R	.368	5	19	2	7	3	0	1	4	1	2	0	0	.400	.684
	Beloit (MWL)	LoA	.296	95	392	60	116	32	4	12	70	31	69	11	11	.345	.490
2013	Fort Myers (FSL)	HiA	.329	52	207	40	68	13	5	6	35	17	29	3	6	.377	.527
	New Britain (EL)	AA	.284	70	289	40	82	19	3	4	38	21	67	7	4	.330	.412
2014	Fort Myers (FSL)	HiA	.300	8	30	5	9	0	0	0	4	4	5	1	1	.382	.300
	New Britain (EL)	AA	.237	79	316	40	75	20	3	8	36	17	68	8	4	.277	.396
Minor League Totals			.294	427	1717	292	505	105	26	57	273	134	328	69	37	.343	.485

11 LEWIS THORPE, LHP

BA GRADE

50 Risk: High

Born: Nov. 23, 1995. **B-T:** R-L. **Ht.:** 6-1. **Wt.:** 208. **Signed:** Australia, 2012. **Signed by:** Howard Norsetter.

Thorpe signed for $500,000 out of Australia in 2012, then ripped through the Rookie-level Gulf Coast League in 2013. Adding 35 pounds in the first two years after signing gave Thorpe more strength to pack on his 6-foot-2 frame. His fastball sat 91-93 mph in 2014, showing sneaky late action. His changeup has good sink and fade and profiles as a potential second plus pitch. His slider will slice through the zone in the high 70s, while his curveball has good down action. Both can be average offerings at worst. Control was an issue in 2014 for Thorpe, who walked 4.5 batters per nine innings. However, the southpaw's strikeout rate jumped noticeably—73 punchouts in 54 innings—after July 1. He should begin 2015 at high Class A Fort Myers.

Year	Club (League)	Class	W	L	ERA	G	GS	CG	SV	IP	H	HR	BB	SO	K/9	WHIP	AVG
2013	Twins (GCL)	R	4	1	2.05	12	8	0	0	44	32	2	6	64	13.1	0.86	.203
2014	Cedar Rapids (MWL)	LoA	3	2	3.52	16	16	0	0	72	62	7	36	80	10.0	1.37	.232
Minor League Totals			7	3	2.96	28	24	0	0	116	94	9	42	144	11.2	1.18	.221

12 MAX KEPLER, OF/1B

BA GRADE

50 Risk: High

Born: Feb. 10, 1993. **B-T:** L-L. **Ht.:** 6-4. **Wt.:** 205. **Signed:** Germany, 2009. **Signed by:** Mike Radcliff.

Kepler still is considered the best prospect ever born and raised in Germany. Signed for $800,000 in 2009, which then was a record bonus for a European position player, he finished high school in Fort Myers, Fla. Having added nearly 20 pounds since signing, Kepler now weights in at a muscular 205. Playing first base for just a dozen games, he focused most of his effort on playing all three outfield positions at high Class A Fort Myers. His arm remains average at best, but he uses his athletic ability well to run down balls in the outfield. Kepler continues to show a balanced lefthanded swing and the ability to work counts and drive the ball to all fields. A good situational hitter, he is learning to do more damage early in counts. A tick above-average as a runner, Kepler projects more like an average hitter and fringe-average power source. Kepler will open 2015 at Double-A Chattanooga.

Year	Club (League)	Class	AVG	G	AB	R	H	2B	3B	HR	RBI	BB	SO	SB	CS	OBP	SLG
2012	Elizabethton (APP)	R	.297	59	232	40	69	16	5	10	49	27	33	7	0	.387	.539
2013	Cedar Rapids (MWL)	LoA	.237	61	236	35	56	11	3	9	40	24	43	2	0	.312	.424
2014	Fort Myers (FSL)	HiA	.264	102	364	53	96	20	6	5	59	34	62	6	2	.333	.393
Minor League Totals			.267	309	1163	172	311	64	18	25	183	121	219	22	4	.344	.418

13 STUART TURNER, C

Born: Dec. 27, 1991. **B-T:** R-R. **Ht.:** 6-2. **Wt.:** 230. **Drafted:** Mississippi, 2013 (3rd round). **Signed by:** Alan Sandberg.

BA GRADE
50 Risk: High

Signed for $550,000 as a third-round pick, Turner has displayed the leadership skills that helped make him the second college catcher drafted in 2013. Solidly built with a classic catcher's frame, he moves well behind the plate and shows a plus arm. His pitch calling improved as the season progressed, and he sets a good tone and pace with his pitchers. Offensively, he shows a short, line-drive swing and knows how to work the gaps, but he projects as a below-average hitter overall. A smart baserunner with below-average speed, Turner was perfect in seven stolen-base attempts. His catch-and-throw skills make him attractive as a potential big league backup or possibly starter if his bat develops. With Kurt Suzuki signed though 2016, Turner could push for playing time by the end of that deal.

Year	Club (League)	Class	AVG	G	AB	R	H	2B	3B	HR	RBI	BB	SO	SB	CS	OBP	SLG
2013	Elizabethton (APP)	R	.264	34	121	15	32	5	0	3	19	12	22	0	1	.340	.380
	New Britain (EL)	AA	.500	1	4	1	2	0	0	0	0	0	1	0	0	.500	.500
2014	Fort Myers (FSL)	HiA	.249	93	325	49	81	16	2	7	40	31	61	7	0	.322	.375
Minor League Totals			.256	128	450	65	115	21	2	10	59	43	84	7	1	.329	.378

14 STEPHEN GONSALVES, LHP

Born: July 8, 1994. **B-T:** L-L. **Ht.:** 6-5. **Wt.:** 195. **Drafted:** HS—San Diego, 2013 (4th round). **Signed by:** John Leavitt.

BA GRADE
50 Risk: High

As a senior at San Diego's Cathedral Catholic High, where he was a year ahead of 2014 No. 1 overall pick Brady Aiken, Gonsalves was suspended for eight games after lying to the school's dean about a roommate's drug use during a national tournament in Cary, N.C. That setback dropped the talented lefthander out of an expected draft spot in the late first round. Lanky and athletic, Gonsalves is an accomplished surfer who still has plenty of projection. His average fastball sits at 88-92 mph and will occasionally touch 94, though he needs to command the inner half better. His spike curveball and slider continue to show improvement, while his split-changeup is an average offering with the potential for more. Intelligent with a quiet competitive streak, Gonsalves should advance to high Class A Fort Myers in 2015, projecting as a No. 4 starter unless one of his pitches develops into a plus.

Year	Club (League)	Class	W	L	ERA	G	GS	CG	SV	IP	H	HR	BB	SO	K/9	WHIP	AVG
2013	Twins (GCL)	R	1	0	0.63	5	2	0	0	14	8	0	7	18	11.3	1.05	.163
	Elizabethton (APP)	R	1	1	1.29	3	3	0	0	14	10	0	4	21	13.5	1.00	.200
2014	Elizabethton (APP)	R	2	0	2.79	6	6	0	0	29	23	1	10	26	8.1	1.14	.225
	Cedar Rapids (MWL)	LoA	2	3	3.19	8	8	0	0	37	31	1	11	44	10.8	1.15	.228
Minor League Totals			6	4	2.39	22	19	0	0	94	72	2	32	109	10.4	1.11	.214

15 TAYLOR ROGERS, LHP

Born: Dec. 17, 1990. **B-T:** L-L. **Ht.:** 6-3. **Wt.:** 185. **Drafted:** Kentucky, 2012 (11th round). **Signed by:** Rick Sellers.

BA GRADE
45 Risk: Medium

An 11th-rounder who signed for $100,000 in 2012, Rogers could soon become the third or fourth ex-Kentucky Wildcat to pitch for the Twins at the big league level, depending on Alex Meyer's long-awaited arrival. Rogers touches 94 mph with his fastball, which grades as solid-average at 90-93 with late movement. He can throw his slurvy breaking ball at two different speeds, depending on the need, but he is still trying to make it sharper. Lefthanders hit just .217 and slugged .287 against Rogers, who has a solid frame and a smooth, low-effort delivery. An aggressive strike-thrower with strong command, Rogers is still working to refine his changeup, which he throws too hard at times. A good athlete with a deep competitive streak, he holds runners and fields his position. He should open 2015 at Triple-A Rochester, where he will be phone call away from continuing the Twins' Lexington pipeline.

Year	Club (League)	Class	W	L	ERA	G	GS	CG	SV	IP	H	HR	BB	SO	K/9	WHIP	AVG
2012	Elizabethton (APP)	R	2	1	1.80	6	6	0	0	30	20	2	5	39	11.7	0.83	.187
	Beloit (MWL)	LoA	2	2	2.70	9	4	0	0	33	33	5	12	35	9.5	1.35	.248
2013	Cedar Rapids (MWL)	LoA	0	1	7.20	3	3	0	0	10	14	1	4	10	9.0	1.80	.304
	Fort Myers (FSL)	HiA	11	6	2.55	22	21	3	0	131	119	5	32	83	5.7	1.16	.248
2014	New Britain (EL)	AA	11	6	3.29	24	24	1	0	145	150	4	37	110	6.8	1.29	.268
Minor League Totals			26	16	2.94	64	58	4	0	349	336	17	90	277	7.1	1.22	.254

16 TYLER DUFFEY, RHP

Born: Dec. 27, 1990. **B-T:** R-R. **Ht.:** 6-3. **Wt.:** 230. **Drafted:** Rice, 2012 (5th round). **Signed by:** Greg Runser.

BA GRADE

40 Risk: Low

Duffey evokes a young John Lackey with his durability, physical presence and competitive grit on the mound. His emotions still get the best of him at times, but he has done a better job of channeling that fire in a productive way. Making stops at each of the top three minor league levels, Duffey joined lefthander Jason Wheeler as the only Twins pitching prospects to reach 150 innings in 2014. Throwing from a three-quarters arm angle, he pitches at 90-93 mph with his fastball, touching 95 and showing late life. His slurvy breaking ball comes in at 77-80 mph and shows sweeping tilt at times. His long arm action is similar to that of Jose Berrios. His changeup can play up to average at times, but he allowed 12 homers and a .474 slugging percentage to lefthanders in 2014. Duffey's control continues to improve, and his walk rate of 1.8 batters per nine innings trailed only Aaron Slegers among Twins farmhands with at least 85 innings. He should open 2015 at Triple-A Rochester with a chance to reach the majors by midseason should a need arise.

Year	Club (League)	Class	W	L	ERA	G	GS	CG	SV	IP	H	HR	BB	SO	K/9	WHIP	AVG
2012	Elizabethton (APP)	R	2	0	1.42	12	0	0	2	19	10	1	2	27	12.8	0.63	.154
2013	Cedar Rapids (MWL)	LoA	3	2	2.78	9	9	0	0	58	49	5	6	47	7.3	0.94	.221
	Fort Myers (FSL)	HiA	4	5	4.45	15	9	0	0	63	67	3	17	44	6.3	1.34	.272
2014	Fort Myers (FSL)	HiA	3	0	2.82	4	4	0	0	22	22	0	5	13	5.2	1.21	.244
	New Britain (EL)	AA	8	3	3.80	18	18	0	0	111	104	14	19	84	6.8	1.10	.248
	Rochester (IL)	AAA	2	0	3.94	3	3	0	0	16	16	3	6	16	9.0	1.38	.258
Minor League Totals			22	10	3.51	61	43	0	2	290	268	26	55	231	7.2	1.12	.243

17 ADAM BRETT WALKER, OF

Born: Oct. 18, 1991. **B-T:** R-R. **Ht.:** 6-4. **Wt.:** 225. **Drafted:** Jacksonville, 2012 (3rd round). **Signed by:** Billy Corrigan.

BA GRADE

50 Risk: High

Blessed with outstanding raw power, Walker signed for $490,400 as a 2012 third-round pick after putting on a show during his pre-draft workout at Target Field. His strikeout rate of 28 percent in 2014 remains a concern, but he continues to do damage when he does connect. His career slugging percentage is .484, and his top exit velocity was about 1 mph lower than that of system-leader Kennys Vargas. Rival managers have voted Walker the top power prospect in the Midwest and Florida State leagues the past two years. He has gradually improved his plate discipline and pitch recognition but continues to chase breaking pitches. Walker is a tick above-average as a runner and has decent instincts on the bases. After playing mostly first base at Jacksonville, he has remained in right field for the most part. His arm strength and accuracy are merely average, but his athletic ability enables him to cover enough ground.

Year	Club (League)	Class	AVG	G	AB	R	H	2B	3B	HR	RBI	BB	SO	SB	CS	OBP	SLG
2012	Elizabethton (APP)	R	.250	58	232	44	58	7	4	14	45	19	76	4	0	.310	.496
2013	Cedar Rapids (MWL)	LoA	.278	129	508	83	141	31	7	27	109	31	115	10	0	.319	.526
2014	Fort Myers (FSL)	HiA	.246	132	505	78	124	19	1	25	94	44	156	9	5	.307	.436
Minor League Totals			.259	319	1245	205	323	57	12	66	248	94	347	23	5	.312	.484

18 LEWIN DIAZ, 1B

Born: Sept. 19, 1996. **B-T:** L-L. **Ht.:** 6-4. **Wt.:** 210. **Signed:** Dominican Republic, 2013. **Signed by:** Fred Guerrero.

BA GRADE

50 Risk: High

Signed for $1.4 million at the start of the international signing period in 2013, Diaz is more than a one-dimensional slugger. He shows the ability to hit the ball where it's pitched along with impressive raw power, reminding some in the organization of a young David Ortiz. Diaz has plus speed and an advanced feel for hitting, which enabled him to slug .451 in the Dominican Summer League in 2014 while accruing more walks than strikeouts. He also has made positive adjustments to limit pre-pitch movement that previously caused him to get jammed on occasion. Already 6-foot-4 and approaching 230 pounds, Diaz appears to have outgrown right field, playing first base exclusively in 2014. He has a plus arm but lacks the mobility needed to be a full-time outfielder, though the Twins famously value versatility in their prospects. A below-average runner, Diaz reminds some Twins officials of 2006 first-rounder Chris Parmelee, albeit with more athletic ability. The Twins like his makeup and believe in his bat, which should make its first appearance in the Rookie-level Gulf Coast League in 2015.

Year	Club (League)	Class	AVG	G	AB	R	H	2B	3B	HR	RBI	BB	SO	SB	CS	OBP	SLG
2014	Twins (DSL)	R	.257	43	144	17	37	13	0	5	27	26	24	0	0	.385	.451
Minor League Totals			.257	43	144	17	37	13	0	5	27	26	24	0	0	.385	.451

19 JAKE REED, RHP

BA GRADE
50 Risk: High

Born: Sept. 29, 1992. **B-T:** R-R. **Ht.:** 6-2. **Wt.:** 190. **Drafted:** Oregon, 2014 (5th round). **Signed by:** Trevor Brown.

Part of a run of power relievers in the Twins' 2014 draft class, Reed quickly distinguished himself at three different levels in his first pro season, reaching low Class A Cedar Rapids for 16 appearances and finishing in the Arizona Fall League. Signed for $350,000 as a fifth-rounder, Reed went nearly four and a half months and 35 2/3 innings between earned runs allowed. A starter his first two years at Oregon, he moved into the closer role as a junior and blossomed. With plus arm strength and a lean, athletic body, Reed touches 97 mph and sits at 93-95 with a fastball that shows plus life and a late, boring action that chews up righthanders. His slurvy breaking ball lags well behind his heater as a weapon but can be a strikeout pitch when he commands it. His below-average changeup gathered cobwebs after his conversion to relief, but Reed broke it out to good effect at the AFL all-star game. Reed's delivery affords him some deception, and it includes a low-three-quarters release point and an abrupt spin-off toward the first-base side. Confident and aggressive with a classic closer's mentality, he should open 2015 at high Class A Fort Myers.

Year	Club (League)	Class	W	L	ERA	G	GS	CG	SV	IP	H	HR	BB	SO	K/9	WHIP	AVG
2014	Elizabethton (APP)	R	0	0	0.00	4	0	0	3	6	1	0	0	8	12.0	0.17	.053
	Cedar Rapids (MWL)	LoA	3	0	0.36	16	0	0	5	25	10	0	3	31	11.2	0.52	.116
Minor League Totals			3	0	0.29	20	0	0	8	31	11	0	3	39	11.3	0.45	.105

20 J.R. GRAHAM, RHP

BA GRADE
50 Risk: Extreme

Born: Jan. 14, 1990. **B-T:** R-R. **Ht.:** 6-0. **Wt.:** 185. **Drafted:** Santa Clara, 2011 (4th round). **Signed by:** Tim Moore (Braves).

A Braves fourth-rounder in 2011, Graham made an immediate impact when he led the Rookie-level Appalachian League in ERA. Then a strained shoulder limited him to eight outings in 2013 and impinged on his effectiveness at Double-A Mississippi in 2014. Intrigued by arm strength Graham showed in the past, the Twins selected him in the major leauge phase of the Rule 5 draft in December. The righthander did not have surgery on his shoulder, but the ailment required an extended recovery period. The Braves moved Graham to the bullpen at Mississippi in early August. He throws a four-seam fastball in the mid-90s and a heavy two-seam fastball in the low 90s that generates lots of groundballs. Graham also mixes a tight low- to mid-80s slider that features excellent deception by mirroring his fastball. His changeup is at least average at times and keeps hitters from sitting on his heat. Though he faces serious durability concerns, he could excel as a setup man. Graham must spend 90 days on the Twins' active roster in 2015 in order to shed his Rule 5 restriction, but if he's healthy he should be able to do just that.

Year	Club (League)	Class	W	L	ERA	G	GS	CG	SV	IP	H	HR	BB	SO	K/9	WHIP	AVG
2012	Lynchburg (CAR)	HiA	9	1	2.63	17	17	1	0	103	88	6	17	68	6.0	1.02	.236
	Mississippi (SL)	AA	3	1	3.18	9	9	0	0	45	35	2	17	42	8.3	1.15	.210
2013	Mississippi (SL)	AA	1	3	4.04	8	8	0	0	36	39	0	10	28	7.1	1.37	.283
2014	Mississippi (SL)	AA	1	5	5.55	27	19	0	0	71	79	2	26	50	6.3	1.47	.289
Minor League Totals			19	12	3.37	74	61	1	0	313	293	10	83	240	6.9	1.20	.252

21 J.T. CHARGOIS, RHP

BA GRADE
50 Risk: Extreme

Born: Dec. 3, 1990. **B-T:** B-R. **Ht.:** 6-3. **Wt.:** 193. **Drafted:** Rice, 2012 (2nd round). **Signed by:** Greg Runser.

Elbow problems have essentially cost Chargois, signed for $712,600 as a second-round pick out of Rice, his first two full seasons in pro ball. After failing to progress beyond bullpen sessions in 2013, the strong-framed power reliever had Tommy John surgery that September. He failed to make it back to the mound before the regular season ended in 2014, but his fastball appeared all the way back by instructional league. At instructional league he was pitching at 96-99 and touching 102 mph. Despite the expected rust, his command was encouraging. Chargois also has a low-80s hybrid breaking ball he throws with power and depth and a much-improved changeup he may not even need as he climbs the ladder. His max-effort delivery and short arm action figure to keep him in the bullpen. With just 88 innings on the mound over his past six seasons, including three years at Rice, Chargois needs to start making up for lost time. He figures to open 2015 at low Class A Cedar Rapids.

Year	Club (League)	Class	W	L	ERA	G	GS	CG	SV	IP	H	HR	BB	SO	K/9	WHIP	AVG
2012	Elizabethton (APP)	R	0	0	1.69	12	0	0	5	16	10	0	5	22	12.4	0.94	.182
2013	Did not play—Injured																
2014	Did not play—Injured																
Minor League Totals			0	0	1.69	12	0	0	5	16	10	0	5	22	12.4	0.94	.182

22 ENGELB VIELMA, SS

BA GRADE
45 Risk: High

Born: June 22, 1994. **B-T:** B-R. **Ht.:** 5-11. **Wt.:** 152. **Signed:** Venezuela, 2011. **Signed by:** Jose Leon.

Signed out of Venezuela for $90,000 in fall 2011, the switch-hitting Vielma made gradual progress before taking a major leap forward in 2014. Even with the likes of Jorge Polanco and Nick Gordon in the system as high-end shortstops, Vielma's sure hands, range and arm all rate as plus weapons and make him the Twins' best defensive infielder by far. Showing outstanding body control, smooth actions and advanced instincts, he is a natural shortstop. He struggled in the April cold at low Class A Cedar Rapids, but his pitch selection improved as the year wore on and the temperatures climbed. Typically aggressive, he learned with the help of Kernels hitting coach Tommy Watkins to lay off breaking balls and drive fastballs he could handle into both gaps. With just average speed, Vielma still must improve his instincts as a basestealer and as a baserunner in general. He figures to open 2015 at high Class A Fort Myers.

Year	Club (League)	Class	AVG	G	AB	R	H	2B	3B	HR	RBI	BB	SO	SB	CS	OBP	SLG
2012	Twins (DSL)	R	.268	44	157	24	42	4	3	0	19	18	27	16	5	.354	.331
2013	Twins (GCL)	R	.237	42	131	20	31	3	0	0	11	15	23	7	3	.320	.260
	Elizabethton (APP)	R	.217	6	23	7	5	0	0	0	1	1	7	1	0	.308	.217
2014	Cedar Rapids (MWL)	LoA	.266	112	418	63	111	13	4	1	33	28	71	10	6	.313	.323
Minor League Totals			.259	204	729	114	189	20	7	1	64	62	128	34	14	.323	.310

23 MICHAEL CEDEROTH, RHP

BA GRADE
45 Risk: High

Born: Nov. 25, 1992. **B-T:** R-R. **Ht.:** 6-6. **Wt.:** 210. **Drafted:** San Diego State, 2014 (3rd round). **Signed by:** John Leavitt.

One of five straight college relievers the Twins drafted in 2014, Cederoth returned to the rotation at Rookie-level Elizabethton with encouraging results. Signed for $703,900 as a third-round pick, he ranked as the No. 19 prospect in the Appalachian League. A starter his first two years at San Diego State, Cederoth showed much better control his first professional summer with 3.6 walks per nine innings compared with 5.2 for the Aztecs. Tall and long-levered with a lean build and good athleticism, Cederoth hit 100 mph as a college junior but dialed it back to a peak of 96 mph, and 92-94 average, in the Appalachian League. When he stays on top of his fastball, the pitch features heavy armside run and sink from a high three-quarters arm slot. His tight curveball has the potential to be average, but command remains an issue. His changeup has flashed average but was a distant third in his narrowed summer repertoire. He still has a long arm action, but Twins pitching coaches got him to be more direct to the plate with his delivery. While Cederoth could always go back to the bullpen, the Twins intend to put him in the rotation at low Class A Cedar Rapids to open 2015.

Year	Club (League)	Class	W	L	ERA	G	GS	CG	SV	IP	H	HR	BB	SO	K/9	WHIP	AVG
2014	Elizabethton (APP)	R	4	2	3.55	11	10	0	0	46	41	1	18	42	8.3	1.29	.227
Minor League Totals			4	2	3.55	11	10	0	0	46	41	1	18	42	8.3	1.29	.227

24 FERNANDO ROMERO, RHP

BA GRADE
50 Risk: Extreme

Born: Dec. 24, 1994. **B-T:** R-R. **Ht.:** 6-0. **Wt.:** 228. **Signed:** Dominican Republic, 2011. **Signed by:** Fred Guerrero.

Signed out of the Dominican Republic for $200,000 in November 2011 at age 16, Romero vaulted all the way to No. 12 on last year's Twins prospect list. He got off to a solid start at Rookie-level Elizabethton in 2014 before elbow problems ended his year after just three outings. Despite having Tommy John surgery in June, Romero remains a solid starter prospect who should be ready for the start of the 2015 Appalachian League season in mid-June. He has allowed only one home run through 88 pro innings. Blessed with a loose, powerful arm and a projectable frame, his double-plus fastball sat at 92-94 mph before surgery and touched 97 mph. His 78-81 mph power curveball has serious down action, and his changeup has a chance to be a plus pitch as well. He easily repeats his smooth, low-effort delivery and maintains focus on the mound. Though he has experience with both starting and relieving, Romero's surgical hurdle likely means he'll spend the next couple of seasons building up his innings total in the low minors. He could reach a ceiling as a No. 3 starter if his curveball plays as a plus pitch.

Year	Club (League)	Class	W	L	ERA	G	GS	CG	SV	IP	H	HR	BB	SO	K/9	WHIP	AVG
2012	Twins (DSL)	R	1	4	4.65	14	6	0	0	31	26	0	14	28	8.1	1.29	.224
2013	Twins (GCL)	R	2	0	1.60	12	6	0	0	45	32	0	13	47	9.4	1.00	.196
2014	Cedar Rapids (MWL)	LoA	0	0	3.00	3	3	0	0	12	13	1	5	9	6.8	1.50	.289
Minor League Totals			3	4	2.86	29	15	0	0	88	71	1	32	84	8.6	1.17	.219

25 ZACK JONES, RHP

Born: Dec. 4, 1990. **B-T:** R-R. **Ht.:** 6-1. **Wt.:** 205. **Drafted:** San Jose
State, 2012 (4th round). **Signed by:** Elliott Strankman.

The hard-throwing Jones' rapid progress was slowed in 2014 by February surgery to repair an aneurysm in his upper right arm, an issue that initially began with a circulation problem that cut short his 2013 stint in the Arizona Fall League. Once he returned, he made up for lost time. Two years after signing for $356,700 as a fourth-rounder in 2012, Jones paired with fellow ex-college closer Nick Burdi to lead a shutdown bullpen at high Class A Fort Myers en route to a Florida State League title. Jones hit 100 mph several times in August and during the playoffs, and his overpowering fastball sat at 95-97 mph with late run. His 78-82 mph slider shows potential but still lags well behind the fastball. Armed with a closer mentality and a quiet confidence, he has works a lot of deep counts with career rates of 5.1 walks and 13.4 strikeouts per nine innings. His poise and mound presence are a tick better than Burdi's at this point, though the raw stuff isn't quite as good. He could open 2015 at Double-A Chattanooga with a chance to resume his progress after his health scare.

Year	Club (League)	Class	W	L	ERA	G	GS	CG	SV	IP	H	HR	BB	SO	K/9	WHIP	AVG
2012	Elizabethton (APP)	R	0	0	0.00	6	0	0	0	6	2	0	4	9	13.5	1.00	.100
	Beloit (MWL)	LoA	0	0	3.21	12	0	0	4	14	9	1	7	25	16.1	1.14	.184
2013	Fort Myers (FSL)	HiA	4	3	1.85	39	0	0	14	49	28	2	28	70	12.9	1.15	.172
2014	Twins (GCL)	R	0	0	3.38	6	1	0	0	5	3	0	4	9	15.2	1.31	.158
	Fort Myers (FSL)	HiA	0	0	0.00	5	0	0	3	5	3	0	2	5	9.0	1.00	.167
Minor League Totals			4	3	1.94	68	1	0	21	79	45	3	45	118	13.4	1.14	.167

26 AMAURYS MINIER, OF/1B

Born: Jan. 30, 1996. **B-T:** B-R. **Ht.:** 6-2. **Wt.:** 217. **Signed:** Dominican
Republic, 2012. **Signed by:** Fred Guerrero.

The burly Dominican received a $1.4 million bonus to highlight the Twins' 2012 international class. Originally signed as a shortstop, Minier spent a year at third base in 2013 before making the switch to left field and first base in 2014. Slowed early on by surgery to repair a torn labrum in his throwing shoulder and later by a hamstring injury, Minier remains a below-average defender who will only go as far as his bat takes him. He famously sent a low laser over the wall in 2013 only to be stopped at second with a ground-rule double by a disbelieving umpire. The switch-hitting Minier is a bigger threat from the left side of the plate at this point, but he has power potential from both sides, producing line drives to all fields with natural backspin. Having added nearly 20 pounds since signing, his build recalls that of Miguel Sano at a similar stage. Minier has a strong arm but must improve his accuracy and routes. His hands and footwork are below-average at first. Poor instincts and baseball awareness leave him below-average as a runner, but some of that can be remedied with more repetition.

Year	Club (League)	Class	AVG	G	AB	R	H	2B	3B	HR	RBI	BB	SO	SB	CS	OBP	SLG
2013	Twins (GCL)	R	.214	31	112	10	24	5	2	6	17	6	29	1	1	.252	.455
2014	Twins (GCL)	R	.292	53	171	25	50	11	2	8	33	29	52	2	2	.405	.520
Minor League Totals			.261	84	283	35	74	16	4	14	50	35	81	3	3	.349	.495

27 HUASCAR YNOA, RHP

Born: May 28, 1998. **B-T:** R-R. **Ht.:** 6-2. **Wt.:** 190. **Signed:** Dominican
Republic, 2014. **Signed by:** Fred Guerrero.

Six years after Dominican righthander Michael Ynoa signed with the Athletics for $4.25 million, the Twins signed his younger brother Huascar for $800,000 as their top international play in 2014. Five inches shorter than the 6-foot-7 Michael, who has struggled to stay healthy, Huascar has flashed top-of-the-rotation potential and three average to above-average pitches, but consistency has been fleeting. At his best, Ynoa throws his fastball at 88-92 mph, touching 93. Because his solid 190-pound frame lacks projection, some wonder how much velocity he'll add as he matures. His mid-70s curveball shows good depth and the potential to be an out pitch, while his low-80s changeup is a swing-and-miss pitch thrown with proper arm speed. Ynoa also shows an advanced ability to mix his pitches in any count. His delivery isn't max effort but could still use some smoothing out to keep him from throwing uphill at times. He sometimes struggles to keep the ball down in the zone. He could report to the Rookie-level Gulf Coast League in 2015.

Year	Club (League)	Class	W	L	ERA	G	GS	CG	SV	IP	H	HR	BB	SO	K/9	WHIP	AVG
2014	Did not play—Signed 2015 contract																

28 FELIX JORGE, RHP

BA GRADE

45 Risk: High

Born: Jan. 2, 1994. **B-T:** R-R. **Ht.:** 6-2. **Wt.:** 170. **Signed:** Dominican Republic, 2011. **Signed by:** Fred Guerrero.

For the second straight summer, Jorge dominated the competition in the Rookie-level Appalachian League. What didn't go as well for the wiry righthander was his first exposure to the low Class A Midwest League. Lanky and athletic with a lean lower half, Jorge signed for $400,000 and still carries significant upside. Featuring long arms and large hands and a delivery that includes some effort, he sits at 90-92 mph with his fastball, showing solid run and sink. He touches 94 mph and also features a slicing slider that shows sharp, late movement. His changeup is clearly his No. 3 pitch at this point. He holds runners and fields his position well enough. Extremely coachable, his English-speaking skills have improved greatly as well. Jorge has a quiet personality but flashes a competitive streak on the mound. He projects as a No. 4 starter if he reaches his ceiling, but he could wind up in the bullpen.

Year	Club (League)	Class	W	L	ERA	G	GS	CG	SV	IP	H	HR	BB	SO	K/9	WHIP	AVG
2012	Twins (GCL)	R	0	3	2.34	12	7	0	1	35	30	0	12	37	9.6	1.21	.221
2013	Elizabethton (APP)	R	2	2	2.95	12	12	0	0	61	56	2	18	72	10.6	1.21	.245
2014	Cedar Rapids (MWL)	LoA	2	5	9.00	12	8	0	0	39	57	9	20	23	5.3	1.97	.354
	Elizabethton (APP)	R	4	2	2.59	12	12	2	0	66	58	2	14	61	8.3	1.09	.237
Minor League Totals			10	13	3.76	57	44	2	2	228	220	13	73	219	8.7	1.29	.253

29 NIKO GOODRUM, 3B/SS

BA GRADE

45 Risk: High

Born: Feb. 28, 1992. **B-T:** B-R. **Ht.:** 6-4. **Wt.:** 190. **Drafted:** HS— Fayetteville, Ga., 2010 (2nd round). **Signed by:** Jack Powell.

Bumped off shortstop by Jorge Polanco during the first half of 2014, the strong-armed Goodrum split his time between third base and shortstop at high Class A Fort Myers after Polanco advanced to Double-A. In the Twins system, only Miguel Sano has a stronger infield arm. Signed for $514,800 as a second-round pick in 2010, Goodrum has moved slowly but steadily through the system. A home-plate collision in 2013 at low Class A Cedar Rapids cost him two weeks with a concussion, but he was durable in 2014 while slashing his strikeout rate under 20 percent for the first time. Tall and lanky with a high waist, the speedy switch-hitter has a tremendous work ethic and outgoing personality that lends itself naturally to clubhouse leadership. All three of Goodrum's homers in 2014 came from the left side, but his OPS was 87 points higher from the right side. He shows fast hands, decent gap power and an improving eye. Miracle manager Doug Mientkiewicz turned Goodrum loose on the bases, where he's both prolific and efficient. Goodrum's speed and versatility makes him a potential future utilityman.

Year	Club (League)	Class	AVG	G	AB	R	H	2B	3B	HR	RBI	BB	SO	SB	CS	OBP	SLG
2012	Elizabethton (APP)	R	.242	58	227	38	55	12	8	4	38	38	56	6	3	.349	.419
2013	Cedar Rapids (MWL)	LoA	.260	103	385	62	100	22	4	4	45	60	105	20	4	.364	.369
2014	Fort Myers (FSL)	HiA	.249	122	438	63	109	19	5	3	49	58	99	35	4	.337	.336
Minor League Totals			.247	378	1372	212	339	67	20	13	157	186	350	73	14	.339	.353

30 TRAVIS HARRISON, OF/3B

BA GRADE

45 Risk: High

Born: Oct. 17, 1992 . **B-T:** R-R. **Ht.:** 6-2. **Wt.:** 215. **Drafted:** HS—Tustin, Calif., 2011 (1st round supplemental). **Signed by:** John Leavitt.

Signed for $1.05 million as the 50th overall pick in 2011, Harrison played just 15 games at third base in 2014 as he made the transition to left field. His actions at third base were too stiff and mechanical, and he fielded just .881 at the hot corner for his career. The power-hitting Harrison struggled with his reads and routes in the outfield but relied on his plus arm and solid instincts to improve by season's end. With his improved conditioning, he projects as an average defensive left fielder in the majors. Harrison remains a below-average runner lacking in first-step quickness, but his plate discipline has greatly improved. Harrison slashed his strikeout rate from 23 percent at low Class A Cedar Rapids in 2013 to 16 percent with the Miracle. His power stroke suffered in the thick air and larger ballparks of the FSL, but his .361 on-base percentage tied for ninth in the league. He still gets too pull conscious at times and will chase breaking balls, but he has plenty of bat speed and a short swing that enables him to drive the ball to all fields. His positional value will suffer if he stays in left field, which he likely will, but he should get a chance to recapture the natural lift in his swing at Double-A Chattanooga in 2015.

Year	Club (League)	Class	AVG	G	AB	R	H	2B	3B	HR	RBI	BB	SO	SB	CS	OBP	SLG
2012	Elizabethton (APP)	R	.301	60	219	39	66	12	4	5	27	24	51	3	0	.383	.461
2013	Cedar Rapids (MWL)	LoA	.253	129	450	66	114	28	0	15	59	68	125	2	4	.366	.416
2014	Fort Myers (FSL)	HiA	.269	129	458	80	123	33	1	3	59	64	86	7	5	.361	.365
Minor League Totals			.269	318	1127	185	303	73	5	23	145	156	262	12	9	.368	.404

New York Mets

BY MATT EDDY

For the first time in a four-year tenure, general manager Sandy Alderson, his front office and field staff can glimpse light at the end of the tunnel.

While the Mets failed to crack .500 for the sixth straight season in 2014, they did manage to tie the Braves for second place in the National League East with a 79-83 record. In fact, New York finished with a positive run differential (+11) for the first time under Alderson and manager Terry Collins.

Pitching and defense have brought the Mets to the cusp of contention. While seven NL  clubs allowed fewer runs than New York in 2014, Mets pitchers allowed 3.81 runs per game, the franchise's lowest rate since 1990. They didn't rely on soft stuff and chicanery either, not with a strikeout rate of 8.0 per nine innings that ranked third in the league.

Young ace Matt Harvey spent the entire season on the shelf as he rehabbed from Tommy John surgery, so veteran import Bartolo Colon anchored a staff that featured at various points six starters who graduated from the Mets system. The list includes Zack Wheeler (32 starts), Jon Niese (30), Jake deGrom (22), Dillon Gee (22), Rafael Montero (eight) and Jenrry Mejia (seven). Righthander Noah Syndergaard and lefty Steve Matz, the system's top two prospects, figure to join the parade in 2015.

Summoned from Triple-A Las Vegas in mid-May, the 26-year-old deGrom went on to win the NL Rookie of the Year award, showcasing a strong three-pitch mix and leading all rookie starters (min. 100 innings) with a 2.69 ERA. The Mets placed a second player on the BA All-Rookie Team, though in the case of 25-year-old catcher Travis d'Arnaud, he flourished only after a midseason demotion to Las Vegas.

While the club's offensive attack once again checked in below the NL average, they inched *closer* to average in 2014. Importing free agent right fielder Curtis Granderson added power and patience to the lineup, but the emergence of first baseman Lucas Duda, who slammed 30 home runs, provided the largest jolt.

The Mets struck early in the offseason to add more offense, signing 37-year-old corner outfielder Michael Cuddyer to a two-year deal, thus sacrificing the 15th overall pick in the 2015 draft.

All seven of the Mets' domestic affiliates finished at .500 or better in 2014, giving New York a cumulative .568 winning percentage that led all organizations. Best of all, the system has begun to

Jake deGrom blossomed as a rookie in 2014, helping cover for the loss of Matt Harvey

TOP PROSPECTS OF THE DECADE

Year	Player, Pos.	2014 Org
2005	Lastings Milledge, of	Yakult (Japan)
2006	Lastings Milledge, of	Yakult (Japan)
2007	Mike Pelfrey, rhp	Twins
2008	Fernando Martinez, of	Did not play
2009	Fernando Martinez, of	Did not play
2010	Jenrry Mejia, rhp	Mets
2011	Jenrry Mejia, rhp	Mets
2012	Zack Wheeler, rhp	Mets
2013	Zack Wheeler, rhp	Mets
2014	Noah Syndergaard, rhp	Mets

shuttle position players up the ladder to pair with the quality young pitchers.

Second baseman Dilson Herrera made his big league debut in September after tearing up two minor league levels, while catcher Kevin Plawecki, shortstop Matt Reynolds and first-round outfielders Brandon Nimmo and Michael Conforto might not require much more minor league seasoning.

The signing of Cuddyer indicates that Alderson believes the rebuilding phase has ended, and that the fruits of the rebuild will end a six-year run of losing seasons.

General manager: Sandy Alderson. **Farm director:** Ian Levin. **Scouting director:** Tommy Tanous.

Class	Team	League	W	L	PCT	Finish	Manager
Majors	New York Mets	National	79	83	.488	t-16th (30)	Terry Collins
Triple-A	Las Vegas 51s	Pacific Coast	81	63	.563	t-1st (16)	Wally Backman
Double-A	Binghamton Mets	Eastern	83	59	.585	2nd (12)	Pedro Lopez
High A	St. Lucie Mets	Florida State	76	62	.551	4th (12)	Ryan Ellis
Low A	Savannah Sand Gnats	South Atlantic	85	51	.625	2nd (14)	Luis Rojas
Short season	Brooklyn Cyclones	New York-Penn	42	34	.553	t-4th (14)	Tom Gamboa
Rookie	Kingsport Mets	Appalachian	34	34	.500	6th (10)	Jose Leger
Rookie	GCL Mets	Gulf Coast	33	27	.550	7th (16)	Jose Carreno
Overall Minor League Record			434	330	.568	1st (30)	

THIS YEAR'S TOP 30

No.	Player, Pos.	Grade
1.	Noah Syndergaard, rhp	70/Medium
2.	Steve Matz, lhp	60/High
3.	Brandon Nimmo, of	55/Medium
4.	Dilson Herrera, 2b/ss	55/Medium
5.	Kevin Plawecki, c	55/Medium
6.	Amed Rosario, ss	60/High
7.	Michael Conforto, of	55/High
8.	Rafael Montero, rhp	50/Medium
9.	Marcos Molina, rhp	55/Extreme
10.	Gavin Cecchini, ss	50/High
11.	Dominic Smith, 1b	55/Extreme
12.	Matt Reynolds, ss/2b	50/Medium
13.	Michael Fulmer, rhp	50/High
14.	Jhoan Urena, 3b	55/Extreme
15.	Cory Mazzoni, rhp	50/High
16.	Gabriel Ynoa, rhp	50/High
17.	Sean Gilmartin, lhp	45/Medium
18.	Matt Bowman, rhp	50/High
19.	Akeel Morris, rhp	45/Medium
20.	Rob Whalen, rhp	50/High
21.	Casey Meisner, rhp	50/High
22.	Dario Alvarez, lhp	40/Medium
23.	Champ Stuart, of	50/Extreme
24.	Matt Koch, rhp	45/Medium
25.	Milton Ramos, ss	50/Extreme
26.	Cesar Puello, of	45/High
27.	Ali Sanchez, c	50/Extreme
28.	Eudor Garcia, 3b	45/High
29.	Brandon Brosher, c	50/Extreme
30.	Robert Gsellman, rhp	45/High

LAST YEAR'S TOP 30

No.	Player, Pos.	Status
1.	Noah Syndergaard, rhp	No. 1
2.	Travis d'Arnaud, c	Majors
3.	Rafael Montero, rhp	No. 8
4.	Dominic Smith, 1b	No. 11
5.	Kevin Plawecki, c	No. 5
6.	Wilmer Flores, 2b/3b	Majors
7.	Amed Rosario, ss	No. 6
8.	Brandon Nimmo, of	No. 3
9.	Gavin Cecchini, ss	No. 10
10.	Jake deGrom, rhp	Majors
11.	Cesar Puello, of	No. 26
12.	Steve Matz, lhp	No. 2
13.	Dilson Herrera, 2b	No. 4
14.	Michael Fulmer, rhp	No. 13
15.	Gabriel Ynoa, rhp	No. 16
16.	Cory Mazzoni, rhp	No. 15
17.	Vic Black, rhp	Majors
18.	Jeurys Familia, rhp	Majors
19.	Domingo Tapia, rhp	Dropped out
20.	Logan Verrett, rhp	Dropped out
21.	Gonzalez Germen, rhp	Majors
22.	Luis Mateo, rhp	Dropped out
23.	Jack Leathersich, lhp	Dropped out
24.	Matt Koch, rhp	No. 24
25.	Matt den Dekker, of	Majors
26.	Dustin Lawley, of/3b	Dropped out
27.	Rob Whalen, rhp	No. 20
28.	Juan Centeno, c	(Brewers)
29.	Wilfredo Tovar, ss	Dropped out
30.	Jayce Boyd, 1b	Dropped out

BEST TOOLS

Best Hitter for Average	Dilson Herrera
Best Power Hitter	Michael Conforto
Best Strike-Zone Discipline	Brandon Nimmo
Fastest Baserunner	Champ Stuart
Best Athlete	Amed Rosario
Best Fastball	Noah Syndergaard
Best Curveball	Rob Whalen
Best Slider	Michael Fulmer
Best Changeup	Akeel Morris
Best Control	Gabriel Ynoa
Best Defensive Catcher	Colton Plaia
Best Defensive Infielder	Wilfredo Tovar
Best Infield Arm	Jhoan Urena
Best Defensive Outfielder	Darrell Ceciliani
Best Outfield Arm	Cesar Puello

PROJECTED 2018 LINEUP

Catcher	Travis d'Arnaud
First Base	Lucas Duda
Second Base	Dilson Herrera
Third Base	David Wright
Shortstop	Amed Rosario
Left Field	Michael Conforto
Center Field	Juan Lagares
Right Field	Brandon Nimmo
No. 1 Starter	Matt Harvey
No. 2 Starter	Zack Wheeler
No. 3 Starter	Noah Syndergaard
No. 4 Starter	Jake deGrom
No. 5 Starter	Steve Matz
Closer	Jenrry Mejia

MINOR LEAGUE DEPTH CHART

NEW YORK METS

TOP 2015 ROOKIE: Noah Syndergaard, rhp. He spent a year wandering in Las Vegas desert, now it's time to see if plus stuff and strong control will play in the majors.

BREAKOUT PROSPECT: Brandon Brosher, c. If converted first baseman has fully recovered from broken ankle, then Mets believe he will punish pitchers with easy plus power.

SLEEPER: Corey Oswalt, rhp. He could make noise in low Class A with big league body and control of three average pitches—plus he's give up two homers in 116 pro innings.

SOURCE OF TOP 30 TALENT			
Homegrown	27	Acquired	3
College	7	Trades	2
Junior college	2	Rule 5 draft	0
High school	11	Independent leagues	0
Draft-and-follow	0	Free agents/waivers	1
Nondrafted free agents	0		
International	7		

LF
Michael Conforto (7)
Vicente Lupo

CF
Brandon Nimmo (3)
Champ Stuart (23)
Darrell Ceciliani
Kyle Johnson
Ivan Wilson
Raphael Ramirez
John Mora

RF
Cesar Puello (26)
Wuilmer Becerra
Cory Vaughn
Enmanuel Zabala

3B
Jhoan Urena (14)
Eudor Garcia (28)
Dustin Lawley
Kenny Hernandez

SS
Amed Rosario (6)
Gavin Cecchini (10)
Matt Reynolds (12)
Milton Ramos (25)
Wilfredo Tovar
Luis Guillorme
Alfredo Reyes

2B
Dilson Herrera (4)
L.J. Mazzilli
Danny Muno
T.J. Rivera

1B
Dominic Smith (11)
Jayce Boyd
Dash Winningham
Matt Oberste

C
Kevin Plawecki (5)
Ali Sanchez (27)
Brandon Brosher (29)
Colton Plaia
Dionis Rodriguez

LHP

LHSP	LHRP
Steve Matz (2)	Sean Gilmartin (17)
Blake Taylor	Dario Alvarez (22)
David Rosenboom	Jack Leathersich
Adrian Almeid	Brad Wieck
	Darin Gorski
	Paul Paez

RHP

RHSP	RHRP
Noah Syndergaard (1)	Akeel Morris (19)
Rafael Montero (8)	Matt Koch (24)
Marcos Molina (9)	Domingo Tapia
Michael Fulmer (13)	Erik Goeddel
Cory Mazzoni (15)	Jeff Walters
Gabriel Ynoa (16)	Luis Mateo
Matt Bowman (18)	Rainy Lara
Rob Whalen (20)	Miller Diaz
Casey Meisner (21)	Chase Bradford
Robert Gsellman (30)	Julian Hilario
Corey Oswalt	Beck Wheeler
John Gant	Seth Lugo
Luis Cessa	Zach Thornton
Chris Flexen	Tim Peterson
Andrew Church	Jimmy Duff
Ricky Knapp	
Josh Prevost	
Kevin McGowan	
Darwin Ramos	
Jose Celas	
Erik Manoah	

BEST PURE HITTER: The Mets like the combination of strength, polish and hitting ability of OF Michael Conforto (1) and 3B Eudor Garcia (4). Conforto's Oregon State and Team USA experience give him an edge, as he's seen better-caliber pitching.

BEST POWER HITTER: Garcia hits 'em farther and has been noted for his light-tower home runs, though some of that may stem from the thin air of the ballparks in and around El Paso CC, where he played. Conforto also has above-average power.

FASTEST RUNNER: OF Raphael Ramirez (18) is a plus runner who gives scouts occasional 70 times out of the batter's box, with his slashing approach.

BEST DEFENSIVE PLAYER: SS Milton Ramos (3) delights in playing defense even more than scouts do watching him play, and he was among the best defenders in the draft class. He plays with energy, has the arm strength and range for the play in the hole, and has the body control to make plays in front of him.

BEST FASTBALL: LHP Brad Wieck (7) can throw 92-94 mph fastballs at his best and has the biggest pure arm strength. RHP Josh Prevost (5) can hit 94 as well but generally sits 89-93, but the 6-foot-8 senior sign pitches downhill and commands his fastball better.

BEST SECONDARY PITCH: Wieck has a plus, hard breaking ball that isn't quite a true 12-to-6 curve. He throws it with power at 80-81 mph and has shown the ability to land it for strikes.

BEST PRO DEBUT: Wieck used his two-pitch mix to strike out 39 in 26 innings at short-season Brooklyn, with a 1.40 ERA and just six walks. LHP David Roseboom (17) didn't just pitch well (1.59 ERA, 30 SO in 23 IP) at Rookie-level Kingsport. His stuff played, with his fastball and breaking ball both flashing above-average.

BEST ATHLETE: Agile and nimble afoot, Ramos is an above-average runner with great first-step quickness that plays defensively. He has some wiry strength as well.

MOST INTRIGUING BACKGROUND: Ramos is originally from Colombia and is related to Braves righthander Julio Teheran. Conforto's father played football at Penn State in the 1980s and his mother Tracie Ruiz-Conforto was an Olympic gold-medalist in 1984 (and silver medallist in '88) in synchronized swimming.

CLOSEST TO THE MAJORS: Conforto has the polish to move quickly, but Wieck could beat him there as a lefty reliever.

BEST LATE-ROUND PICK: The Mets feel fortunate to have signed the speedy Ramirez. They're also encouraged by Roseboom's fast start.

THE ONE WHO GOT AWAY: Arkansas' recruiting class features two players the Mets tried hard to sign in OF Luke Bonfield (21), whom the Mets made a hard run at late in the summer, and RHP Keaton McKinney (28).

ASSESSMENT: The Mets need corner power bats, so Conforto can't arrive soon enough. An organization long on pitching got an infusion of hitters, taking bats with six of their first eight selections.

2013

Early returns weren't great for 1B Dominic Smith (1), though the Mets still believe. RHP Casey Meisner (3) and speedy OF Champ Stuart (6) lend the class some options.

GRADE: D

2012

While SS Gavin Cecchini (1) will require patience to develop physically, C Kevin Plawecki (1s), SS Matt Reynolds (2) and RHP Matt Bowman (13) have reached Triple-A.

GRADE: B

2011

OF Brandon Nimmo (1) has progressed nicely and looks like a future regular. RHPs Michael Fulmer (1s), Cory Mazzoni (2) and Logan Verrett (3), a Rule 5 loss, are in Top 30s.

GRADE: C

TOP DRAFT PICKS OF THE DECADE

Year	Player, Pos.	2014 Org
2005	Mike Pelfrey, rhp	Twins
2006	Kevin Mulvey, rhp (2nd round)	Out of baseball
2007	Eddie Kunz, rhp (1st rd. supp.)	Out of baseball
2008	Ike Davis, 1b	Pirates
2009	Steve Matz, lhp (2nd round)	Mets
2010	Matt Harvey, rhp	Mets
2011	Brandon Nimmo, of	Mets
2012	Gavin Cecchini, ss	Mets
2013	Dominic Smith, 1b	Mets
2014	Michael Conforto, of	Mets

LARGEST BONUSES IN CLUB HISTORY

Mike Pelfrey, 2005	$3,550,000
Philip Humber, 2004	$3,000,000
Michael Conforto, 2014	$2,970,800
Dominic Smith, 2013	$2,600,000
Matt Harvey, 2010	$2,525,000

1 NOAH SYNDERGAARD, RHP

Born: Aug. 29, 1992. **B-T:** L-R. **Ht.:** 6-6. **Wt.:** 240.
Drafted: HS—Mansfield, Texas, 2010 (1st round supplemental). **Signed by:** Steve Miller (Blue Jays).

BA GRADE

70 Risk: Medium

SCOUTING GRADES

Fastball: 70.
Curveball: 60.
Changeup: 55.
Control: 60.

Based on 20-80 scouting scale and future projection rather than present tools.

LGE	BF	SO%	BB%	HR/9
PCL	583	24.9	7.4	0.74

Blue Jays area scout Steve Miller correctly gauged the 17-year-old Syndergaard's upside potential as the Legacy High righthander added velocity and cruised through the Texas 4-A state playoffs in 2010. Toronto nabbed Syndergaard with the 38th pick that June and signed him for a below-slot $600,000. He rose to low Class A in the Blue Jays system before Toronto traded him, plus catcher Travis d'Arnaud, to the Mets for R.A. Dickey following the 2012 season. In the two years since the trade, Dickey has provided solid mid-rotation value for the Blue Jays, logging a 3.97 ERA and averaging 220 innings per season, while Syndergaard ranked as the top pitching prospect in the Florida State and Eastern leagues in 2013 and the Pacific Coast League in 2014. He spent all of the latter season at Las Vegas, leading the PCL with 145 strikeouts and finishing as one of just seven qualified Triple-A starters to fan at least one-quarter of opposing batters.

Syndergaard generates easy double-plus velocity from his large, 6-foot-6 frame, and unlike many young pitchers who sit in the mid-90s, he already has average control with a chance for plus big league control. He never has walked as many as three batters per nine innings in a minor league season. His delivery may not be textbook—he opens early, costing him deception—but he's strong enough to repeat his mechanics and throw strikes. Syndergaard reaches back for 98 mph when he needs it and pitches off his live, running fastball, all while the quality of his secondary pitches continues to improve. He varies the shape and speed of his curveball, often generating plus depth and low-80s velocity from a high three-quarters arm slot. At other times, the deuce arrives in the mid-70s with slurvy, lateral break. His high-80s changeup will be at least an average weapon for him after he threw it more often in 2014, when he achieved his best results yet against lefthanders. Scouts attribute Syndergaard's poor Triple-A results, including a 4.60 ERA and .293 opponent average, to a number of factors, including a tough pitcher's park at Las Vegas that accentuates both singles and home runs, spotty fastball command, a lack of deception and at times a lack of variety to his pitch sequencing. He improved in the second half, however, logging a 3.28 ERA and 3.6 SO/

BB ratio in his final 11 starts and 60 innings. Syndergaard missed two starts in 2014 while recovering from injuries to his right forearm and left shoulder.

Not only did the Mets neglect to call up Syndergaard in 2014, as they had Zack Wheeler in 2013 and Matt Harvey in 2012, they bypassed him entirely to call up Las Vegas rotation-mates Jake deGrom and Rafael Montero during the first half of the season. That won't be the case in 2015, not after Syndergaard joined the 40-man roster in November. He threw a career-high 133 innings in 2014 and could be good for 150 or more in New York this year. Syndergaard profiles as a No. 2 starter with two plus pitches, an average third and at least average control.

Year	Club (League)	Class	W	L	ERA	G	GS	CG	SV	IP	H	HR	BB	SO	K/9	WHIP	AVG
2012	Lansing (MWL)	LoA	8	5	2.60	27	19	0	1	104	81	3	31	122	10.6	1.08	.212
2013	St. Lucie (FSL)	HiA	3	3	3.11	12	12	0	0	64	61	3	16	64	9.0	1.21	.255
	Binghamton (EL)	AA	6	1	3.00	11	11	0	0	54	46	8	12	69	11.5	1.07	.228
2014	Las Vegas (PCL)	AAA	9	7	4.60	26	26	0	0	133	154	11	43	145	9.8	1.48	.293
Minor League Totals			31	19	3.25	94	84	0	1	427	399	26	124	474	10.0	1.23	.247

2 STEVE MATZ, LHP

Born: May 29, 1991. **B-T:** R-L. **Ht.:** 6-2. **Wt.:** 200. **Drafted:** HS—East Setauket, N.Y., 2009 (2nd round). **Signed by:** Larry Izzo Jr.

One of the top prep pitchers available in the 2009 draft, the Long Island-born Matz fell to the Mets with their top pick in the late second round. He missed three years after signing, however, when he had Tommy John surgery and suffered multiple setbacks. Matz finally took the mound in the second half of 2012 and subsequently breezed through three levels of the minors in 2013 and 2014, finishing the latter at Double-A Binghamton and ranking 10th in the minors with a 2.24 ERA. Matz throws with the kind of velocity (93-95 mph), looseness and direction to the plate that makes scouts drool. He can rear back for 98 mph when he needs it, earning him double-plus grades for his fastball. Matz throws a plus changeup in the mid-80s that features plus sinking action and impressive separation from his fastball. His 78-82 mph curveball functions well enough as a third pitch, and it improved in terms of power and shape under the tutelage of Binghamton pitching coach Glenn Abbott in the second half. Matz profiles as high as a No. 2 starter in a rotation because he throws two plus pitches, an average third and has average control. He could begin 2015 at Triple-A Las Vegas and supply lefty balance to the Mets rotation in the second half.

BA GRADE

60 Risk: High

LGE	BF	SO%	BB%	HR/9
FSL	289	21.5	7.3	0.00
EL	287	24.0	4.9	0.38

Year	Club (League)	Class	W	L	ERA	G	GS	CG	SV	IP	H	HR	BB	SO	K/9	WHIP	AVG
2012	Kingsport (APP)	R	2	1	1.55	6	6	0	0	29	16	1	17	34	10.6	1.14	.158
2013	Savannah (SAL)	LoA	5	6	2.62	21	21	1	0	106	86	4	38	121	10.2	1.17	.225
2014	St. Lucie (FSL)	HiA	4	4	2.21	12	12	0	0	69	66	0	21	62	8.0	1.25	.255
	Binghamton (EL)	AA	6	5	2.27	12	12	1	0	71	66	3	14	69	8.7	1.12	.248
Minor League Totals			17	16	2.32	51	51	2	0	276	234	8	90	286	9.3	1.17	.232

3 BRANDON NIMMO, OF

Born: March 27, 1993. **B-T:** L-R. **Ht.:** 6-3. **Wt.:** 205. **Drafted:** HS—Cheyenne, Wyo., 2011 (1st round). **Signed by:** Jim Reeves.

The first-ever first-rounder from Wyoming, a state that does not offer high school baseball, Nimmo hasn't let a lack of amateur experience hold him back in pro ball. He ranked third in the low Class A South Atlantic League in on-base percentage (.397) in 2013, then led the high Class A Florida State League with a .448 OBP at the time of his mid-June promotion to Double-A Binghamton in 2014, when he ranked eighth in the minors overall with 86 walks. Nimmo has added muscle since signing, steadily increasing his power output with experience. While he is more of a gap hitter now, scouts project him to develop above-average power because of his advanced hitting approach and strong lefthanded swing. He will hit for average with his all-fields approach, frequency of hard contact and willingness to attack first-pitch fastballs. An above-average runner, Nimmo has maintained his speed and fluidity even as he has bulked up, and scouts view him as a future center fielder with average range but plus instincts and reliability. He has improved his arm strength and accuracy to at least fringe-average. Few players outwork Nimmo, which combined with his average to above-average raw tools across the board should make him a quality regular. Juan Lagares has a lock on center field in New York right now, but Nimmo could begin 2015 at Triple-A Las Vegas and receive a second-half look on a corner before possibly shifting to center down the road.

BA GRADE

55 Risk: Medium

LGE	PA	BB%	SO%	ISO
FSL	279	17.9	18.3	.137
EL	279	12.9	19.4	.158

Year	Club (League)	Class	AVG	G	AB	R	H	2B	3B	HR	RBI	BB	SO	SB	CS	OBP	SLG
2012	Brooklyn (NYP)	SS	.248	69	266	41	66	20	2	6	40	46	78	1	5	.372	.406
2013	Savannah (SAL)	LoA	.273	110	395	62	108	16	6	2	40	71	131	10	7	.397	.359
2014	St. Lucie (FSL)	HiA	.322	62	227	59	73	9	5	4	25	50	51	9	3	.448	.458
	Binghamton (EL)	AA	.238	65	240	38	57	12	4	6	26	36	54	5	1	.339	.396
Minor League Totals			.268	316	1166	205	312	57	17	20	135	209	328	25	16	.387	.397

4 DILSON HERRERA, 2B/SS

Born: March 3, 1994. **B-T:** R-R. **Ht.:** 5-10. **Wt.:** 150. **Signed:** Colombia, 2010.
Signed by: Rene Gayo/Orlando Covo (Pirates).

When the Mets traded Marlon Byrd to the Pirates to acquire Herrera in August 2013, they didn't expect the low Class A second baseman to be in the big leagues a year later. That's exactly what happened in 2014, though, when Herrera hit .323/.379/.479 between stops at high Class A St. Lucie and Double-A Binghamton on his way to New York as an injury replacement for Daniel Murphy on Aug. 29. Short and compact, Herrera incorporates his hands and lower half adeptly in his swing, projecting to hit for a high average with frequent hard contact, a middle-field approach and bat speed to spare. He ranked fourth in the minors with 169 hits in 2014, thanks to a quick, repeatable swing. He hits for primarily gap power with the potential for double-digit home runs. An average runner, Herrera is no better than average defensively at second base, showing stiff actions and fringy range for some evaluators. His arm works at the keystone but is inadequate for shortstop, where he logged 27 games in 2014. The Mets love Herrera's makeup and work ethic, which factored in their decision to call him up in August, though he probably will begin 2015 at Triple-A Las Vegas while he waits for regular at-bats in New York. He can be a first-division second baseman based on his offensive ceiling.

	BA GRADE	
55	**Risk:**	
	Medium	

LGE	PA	BB%	SO%	ISO
FSL	309	5.8	14.2	.102
EL	278	10.4	18.7	.220

Year	Club (League)	Class	AVG	G	AB	R	H	2B	3B	HR	RBI	BB	SO	SB	CS	OBP	SLG
2012	Pirates (GCL)	R	.281	53	199	41	56	11	4	7	27	18	41	11	4	.341	.482
	State College (NYP)	SS	.321	7	28	7	9	1	1	1	2	1	6	1	0	.345	.536
2013	West Virginia (SAL)	LoA	.265	109	423	69	112	27	3	11	56	37	110	11	6	.330	.421
	Savannah (SAL)	LoA	.316	7	19	6	6	0	0	0	4	3	6	3	0	.417	.316
2014	St. Lucie (FSL)	HiA	.307	67	283	48	87	16	2	3	23	18	44	14	3	.355	.410
	Binghamton (EL)	AA	.340	61	241	50	82	17	3	10	48	29	52	9	4	.406	.560
	New York (NL)	MAJ	.220	18	59	6	13	0	1	3	11	7	17	0	0	.303	.407
Major League Totals			.220	18	59	6	13	0	1	3	11	7	17	0	0	.303	.407
Minor League Totals			.297	369	1407	263	418	91	18	34	187	138	299	65	25	.365	.460

5 KEVIN PLAWECKI, C

Born: Feb. 26, 1991. **B-T:** R-R. **Ht.:** 6-2. **Wt.:** 225. **Drafted:** Purdue, 2012 (1st round supplemental). **Signed by:** Scott Trcka.

An offensive-minded college catcher who signed for $1.4 million as a 2012 supplemental first-round pick, Plawecki has had no trouble adjusting to pro ball. He conquered two Class A levels in 2013, then advanced to Triple-A Las Vegas in the second half of 2014. Plawecki has hit .307/.379/.453 in full-season ball in 2013 and 2014, with strikeouts just 11 percent of the time. That sort of bat control speaks to his strong hands, all-fields approach and ability to handle varied pitch types, which will allow him to hit for average in the big leagues. While he's more of a gap hitter, he can pull the ball for power and will reach double digits for home runs. Plawecki receives the ball well behind the plate and has sure hands and solid blocking ability, but a fringe-average arm limits his defensive ceiling to average to a tick below, depending on the evaluator. His arm will play up if he can improve his footwork, transfer and arm stroke to get rid of the ball more quickly. While he doesn't offer the power-and-arm-strength profile that teams favor from catchers today, Plawecki has feel to hit, on-base ability, moderate power and the defensive chops to play every day. Mets rookie Travis d'Arnaud hit well in 2014, but his defensive struggles—he committed an National League-leading 12 passed balls—could one day create an opportunity for Plawecki to start.

	BA GRADE	
55	**Risk:**	
	Medium	

LGE	PA	BB%	SO%	ISO
EL	249	6.4	10.8	.161
PCL	170	8.2	12.4	.138

Year	Club (League)	Class	AVG	G	AB	R	H	2B	3B	HR	RBI	BB	SO	SB	CS	OBP	SLG
2012	Brooklyn (NYP)	SS	.250	61	216	26	54	8	0	7	27	25	24	0	0	.345	.384
2013	Savannah (SAL)	LoA	.314	65	245	35	77	24	1	6	43	23	32	1	0	.390	.494
	St. Lucie (FSL)	HiA	.294	60	204	25	60	14	0	2	37	19	21	0	0	.391	.392
2014	Binghamton (EL)	AA	.326	58	224	33	73	18	0	6	43	16	27	0	0	.378	.487
	Las Vegas (PCL)	AAA	.283	43	152	25	43	6	0	5	21	14	21	0	0	.345	.421
Minor League Totals			.295	287	1041	144	307	70	1	26	171	97	125	1	0	.372	.439

6 AMED ROSARIO, SS

Born: Nov. 20, 1995. **B-T:** R-R. **Ht.:** 6-2. **Wt.:** 170. **Signed:** Dominican Republic, 2012. **Signed by:** Chris Becerra/Gerardo Cabrera.

The Mets handed over $1.75 million, a franchise record for an international amateur, to sign Rosario in 2012, and he has more than justified that outlay during his first two pro seasons. He ranked as the No. 1 prospect in the Rookie-level Appalachian League in 2013 and then the top position prospect in the short-season New York-Penn League in 2014, when the 18-year-old ranked third with 77 hits despite being three years younger than the average NYP player. Rosario might have the highest ceiling among Mets position prospects because he profiles as a strong defensive shortstop who can swing the bat and run a bit. Quick, instinctual and in control, he lines the ball from gap to gap with a line drive-oriented stroke, though he might develop average power once he fills out his lean 6-foot-2 frame. He records solid-average run times but isn't a big basestealer. Rosario shines defensively, with plus range, agility and arm strength, but he can improve his efficiency by charging the ball more consistently to reduce hurried throws and errors. His quick feet make him adept at turning the double play. The Mets sent Rosario to low Class A Savannah at the end of May 2014 so that he could add game experience before joining Brooklyn in mid-June. He has the type of makeup to move quickly once he establishes himself in full-season ball, and he could grow to be an all-star shortstop.

BA GRADE

60 Risk: High

LGE	PA	BB%	SO%	ISO
NYP	290	5.9	16.2	.090
SAL	31	3.2	35.5	.167

Year	Club (League)	Class	AVG	G	AB	R	H	2B	3B	HR	RBI	BB	SO	SB	CS	OBP	SLG
2013	Kingsport (APP)	R	.241	58	212	22	51	8	4	3	23	11	43	2	6	.279	.358
2014	Savannah (SAL)	LoA	.133	7	30	2	4	0	1	1	4	1	11	0	0	.161	.300
	Brooklyn (NYP)	SS	.289	68	266	39	77	11	5	1	23	17	47	7	3	.337	.380
Minor League Totals			.260	133	508	63	132	19	10	5	50	29	101	9	9	.303	.366

7 MICHAEL CONFORTO, OF

Born: March 1, 1993. **B-T:** L-R. **Ht.:** 6-1. **Wt.:** 211. **Drafted:** Oregon State, 2014 (1st round). **Signed by:** Jim Reeves.

Conforto ranked fourth in NCAA Division I with 55 walks and a .504 on-base percentage as an Oregon State junior in 2014, when the Mets drafted him 10th overall because they were drawn to his power-and-patience approach. The first-team All-American signed for $2,970,800 and enjoyed a fine pro debut at short-season Brooklyn, showing why he ranked as the No. 1 hitter on the Mets' draft board. Conforto generates easy power in batting practice but tends to work the gaps in games with a powerful lefthanded stroke. He can hammer the ball the other way, but he still has room to unlock more power by turning on inside fastballs to pull them for home runs, and the Mets say he has the most usable power in the system. Conforto's discipline, presence and middle-field approach practically guarantee that he will hit for average, while those same attributes will help him get on base at a high clip and could help him unlock above-average power.

BA GRADE

55 Risk: High

LGE	PA	BB%	SO%	ISO
NYP	186	8.6	15.6	.117

Some scouts project his home runs potential as merely average, however. A below-average runner who already has maxed out his frame, Conforto will be limited to left field with average at best range and arm strength. By drafting Conforto, the Mets' scouting department broke a three-year run of selecting high school position players in the first round, and given his polish, he could arrive in New York at some point in 2016. The next step is high Class A St. Lucie in 2015.

Year	Club (League)	Class	AVG	G	AB	R	H	2B	3B	HR	RBI	BB	SO	SB	CS	OBP	SLG
2014	Brooklyn (NYP)	SS	.331	42	163	30	54	10	0	3	19	16	29	3	0	.403	.448
Minor League Totals			.331	42	163	30	54	10	0	3	19	16	29	3	0	.403	.448

8 RAFAEL MONTERO, RHP

Born: Oct. 17, 1990. **B-T:** R-R. **Ht.:** 6-0. **Wt.:** 185. **Signed:** Dominican Republic, 2011. **Signed by:** Rafael Perez/Ismael Cruz/Gerardo Cabrera.

Montero signed as a 20-year-old Dominican amateur in 2011 and reached the big leagues little more than three years later. He made his Mets debut one day before Jake deGrom in mid-May 2014, and while the latter went on to win the National League Rookie of the Year award, Montero showed uncharacteristically poor control and command in New York. Thus he spent most of the second half at Triple-A Las Vegas. Montero lacks a consistent plus pitch, but he has produced results in the minors with strong control and a fearless approach. He likes to pitch backwards by unleashing 92-93 mph fastballs only after setting batters up with a solid-average, mid-80s changeup and fringe-average slider. That approach didn't work so well against big league batters who recognized spin earlier out of his hand. Montero locates his fastball and changeup to both sides of the plate, though his repertoire would benefit from more angle to the plate, a sharper breaking ball or better sequencing. He missed nearly a month at midseason with an

BA GRADE

50 Risk: Medium

LGE	BF	SO%	BB%	HR/9
PCL	338	23.7	10.1	0.45
NL	194	21.6	11.9	1.62

oblique injury but otherwise has a perfect bill of health. Montero will provide major league value, most likely as a control-oriented No. 4 or 5 starter with three average to tick above pitches, though the Mets' crowded stable of power arms might ultimately force him to the bullpen.

Year	Club (League)	Class	W	L	ERA	G	GS	CG	SV	IP	H	HR	BB	SO	K/9	WHIP	AVG
2012	Savannah (SAL)	LoA	6	3	2.52	12	12	0	0	71	61	4	8	54	6.8	0.97	.223
	St. Lucie (FSL)	HiA	5	2	2.13	8	8	1	0	51	35	2	11	56	9.9	0.91	.196
2013	Binghamton (EL)	AA	7	3	2.43	11	11	0	0	67	51	2	10	72	9.7	0.92	.204
	Las Vegas (PCL)	AAA	5	4	3.05	16	16	0	0	89	85	4	25	78	7.9	1.24	.254
2014	Mets (GCL)	R	0	0	4.50	1	1	0	0	2	3	0	0	3	13.5	1.50	.333
	St. Lucie (FSL)	HiA	0	0	0.00	1	1	0	0	4	2	0	1	4	9.0	0.75	.154
	Las Vegas (PCL)	AAA	6	4	3.60	16	16	0	0	80	69	4	34	80	9.0	1.29	.231
	New York (NL)	MAJ	1	3	4.06	10	8	0	0	44	44	8	23	42	8.5	1.51	.257
Major League Totals			1	3	4.06	10	8	0	0	44	44	8	23	42	8.5	1.51	.257
Minor League Totals			34	20	2.69	82	77	1	1	434	361	20	102	413	8.6	1.07	.222

9 MARCOS MOLINA, RHP

Born: March 8, 1995. **B-T:** R-R. **Ht.:** 6-3. **Wt.:** 188. **Signed:** Dominican Republic, 2012. **Signed by:** Daurys Nin/Gerardo Cabrera.

Molina won the short-season New York-Penn League pitching triple crown in 2014 with seven wins, a 1.77 ERA and 91 strikeouts, a performance strong enough to earn him No. 1 prospect honors in the league. A year before that he was just another strong-armed, 18-year-old thrower in the Rookie-level Gulf Coast League who allowed more than a hit per inning while striking out 7.3 per nine. NYP observers remarked upon Molina's athleticism, fluidity of motion and feel for three pitches. He pitches at 93 mph and can run the ball up to 96 in crucial spots while maintaining fine control for a hard-throwing teenager. He already throws an advanced, late-breaking slider he uses to generate swings and misses, while he shows feel for a changeup that flashes plus. A lean 6-foot-3, Molina has an ideal pitcher's frame and confident mound actions, while his athleticism allows him to repeat his delivery and throw strikes. While Molina still must prove

BA GRADE

55 Risk: Extreme

LGE	BF	SO%	BB%	HR/9
NYP	296	30.7	6.1	0.24

he can maintain his stuff under a full-season workload, he outdueled the Orioles' Dylan Bundy, on a rehab assignment with Aberdeen, in a June 21 matchup by throwing seven shutout innings while allowing two hits. Though he's four levels away from the big leagues and carries significant risk, Molina has a ceiling as a No. 3 starter.

Year	Club (League)	Class	W	L	ERA	G	GS	CG	SV	IP	H	HR	BB	SO	K/9	WHIP	AVG
2012	Mets1 (DSL)	R	2	2	3.78	9	8	0	0	33	32	0	8	19	5.1	1.20	.252
	Mets2 (DSL)	R	3	0	3.27	5	5	0	0	22	16	0	6	21	8.6	1.00	.195
2013	Mets (GCL)	R	4	3	4.39	11	6	1	0	53	56	3	14	43	7.3	1.31	.271
2014	Brooklyn (NYP)	SS	7	3	1.77	12	12	0	0	76	46	2	18	91	10.7	0.84	.170
Minor League Totals			16	8	3.06	37	31	1	0	185	150	5	46	174	8.5	1.06	.219

10 GAVIN CECCHINI, SS

Born: Dec. 22, 1993. **B-T:** R-R. **Ht.:** 6-1. **Wt.:** 180. **Drafted:** HS—Lake Charles, La., 2012 (1st round). **Signed by:** Tommy Jackson.

A broken finger in 2012 and sprained ankle in 2013 undercut Cecchini's first two pro seasons, but the the 12th pick in the 2012 draft stayed completely healthy in 2014. He played at two Class A levels, batting .247/.328/.378, then made a cameo at Double-A Binghamton in time for the Eastern League playoffs. Older brother Garin made his major league debut with the Red Sox in June. Like fellow Mets first-rounder Brandon Nimmo, Cecchini has worked hard to add muscle to his frame. That work paid off in 2014 when he hit eight home runs after entering the season with only one for his career, and scouts see enough bat speed and juice to the gaps for perhaps fringe-average power. A high leg kick threw off Cecchini's timing at high Class A St. Lucie in 2014, making him late against the better fastballs in that league, though bat control and solid discipline should make him at least an average hitter. An athletic shortstop but ordinary runner, Cecchini has solid-average range and a plus arm, though his all-out, max-effort style turns off some scouts. Cecchini lacks an outstanding offensive tool but should hit enough to reach the majors in some role, perhaps as a regular shortstop or second baseman or utility infielder.

BA GRADE

50 Risk: High

LGE	PA	BB%	SO%	ISO
SAL	259	9.7	15.8	.149
FSL	271	11.8	14.8	.116

Year	Club (League)	Class	AVG	G	AB	R	H	2B	3B	HR	RBI	BB	SO	SB	CS	OBP	SLG
2012	Kingsport (APP)	R	.246	53	191	21	47	9	2	1	22	18	43	5	4	.311	.330
	Brooklyn (NYP)	SS	.000	5	5	2	0	0	0	0	0	0	1	0	0	.167	.000
2013	Brooklyn (NYP)	SS	.273	51	194	18	53	8	0	0	14	14	30	2	3	.319	.314
2014	Savannah (SAL)	LoA	.259	57	228	42	59	17	4	3	25	25	41	7	1	.333	.408
	St. Lucie (FSL)	HiA	.236	68	233	36	55	10	1	5	31	32	40	3	3	.325	.352
	Binghamton (EL)	AA	.250	1	4	1	1	0	0	0	0	0	1	0	0	.250	.250
Minor League Totals			.251	235	855	120	215	44	7	9	92	89	156	17	11	.322	.351

11 DOMINIC SMITH, 1B

BA GRADE

55 Risk: Extreme

Born: June 15, 1995. **B-T:** L-L. **Ht.:** 6-0. **Wt.:** 185. **Drafted:** HS—Gardena, Calif., 2013 (1st round). **Signed by:** Drew Toussaint.

The Mets invested $2.6 million to sign Smith, selected No. 11 overall in the 2013 draft, paying him the franchise's highest-ever bonus for a high school pick. Unlike 2011 or 2012 prep first-rounders Brandon Nimmo or Gavin Cecchini, however, Smith advanced to low Class A Savannah the year after signing, but he performed unevenly. He exceeded the South Atlantic League averages by hitting .271 with a .344 on-base percentage, but he slugged a below-average .338 and hit only one home run. Scouts laud Smith for his natural bat path, pretty lefthanded swing and strong, quick hands, projecting him to hit for a plus average. He can line the ball up the middle or to left field to keep defenses honest, but the power to right field he shows in batting practice has not transferred to games. Smith doesn't run well, but he's an agile defender at first base with strong footwork and Gold Glove potential. A lackadaisical pregame routine and low-energy approach concern scouts more than a lack of manifest power, but Smith will begin the 2015 season as a 19-year-old at high Class A St. Lucie, meaning he has nothing but time to answer his critics.

Year	Club (League)	Class	AVG	G	AB	R	H	2B	3B	HR	RBI	BB	SO	SB	CS	OBP	SLG
2013	Mets (GCL)	R	.287	48	167	23	48	9	1	3	22	24	37	2	4	.384	.407
	Kingsport (APP)	R	.667	3	6	2	4	4	0	0	4	2	0	0	0	.750	1.333
2014	Savannah (SAL)	LoA	.271	126	461	52	125	26	1	1	44	51	77	5	4	.344	.338
Minor League Totals			.279	177	634	77	177	39	2	4	70	77	114	7	8	.360	.366

12 MATT REYNOLDS, SS/2B

BA GRADE

50 Risk: Medium

Born: Dec. 3, 1990. **B-T:** R-R. **Ht.:** 6-1. **Wt.:** 198. **Drafted:** Arkansas, 2012 (2nd round). **Signed by:** Steve Gossett.

Reynolds evokes comparisons with Mark Ellis and Mark Loretta for his hard-nosed, gamer approach and his background as a college shortstop who probably fits best at second base in the majors. He challenged for the minor league batting title in 2014, ranking sixth while hitting .343/.405/.454 at Double-A Binghamton and Triple-A Las Vegas. Reynolds projects to be an average hitter, owing to his balanced, line-drive stroke and quiet hitting approach. He doesn't loft the ball for home-run power, but he can put the ball in play to the gaps for doubles, particularly to right-center field. He's a below-average runner, though quick enough to make all the routine plays at shortstop, with the sure hands and average, accurate arm to play any infield position capably. Reynolds' probable big league role ranges from utility infielder to starting second baseman, but he shouldn't require much more Triple-A time in 2015.

Year	Club (League)	Class	AVG	G	AB	R	H	2B	3B	HR	RBI	BB	SO	SB	CS	OBP	SLG
2012	Savannah (SAL)	LoA	.259	42	158	18	41	8	0	3	13	12	26	5	1	.335	.367
2013	St. Lucie (FSL)	HiA	.226	117	433	59	98	21	6	5	49	36	80	9	2	.302	.337
	Binghamton (EL)	AA	.000	1	3	0	0	0	0	0	0	0	0	0	0	.000	.000
2014	Binghamton (EL)	AA	.355	58	211	33	75	5	3	1	21	29	41	6	3	.430	.422
	Las Vegas (PCL)	AAA	.333	68	267	54	89	16	4	5	40	21	60	14	4	.385	.479
Minor League Totals			.283	286	1072	164	303	50	13	14	123	98	207	34	10	.352	.393

13 MICHAEL FULMER, RHP

BA GRADE

50 Risk: High

Born: March 15, 1993. **B-T:** R-R. **Ht.:** 6-3. **Wt.:** 200. **Drafted:** HS—Edmond, Okla., 2011 (1st round supplemental). **Signed by:** Steve Gossett.

Selected 44th overall in the 2011 draft, Fulmer spent the better part of 2013 and 2014 at high Class A St. Lucie, but few Mets pitching prospects have a superior two-pitch mix than the 6-foot-3 righthander. He threw the ball better than ever during 2014 spring training, but Fulmer's results never seemed to match his raw stuff once he took the mound in the Florida State League. He missed bats and limited walks, and the Mets indicate that many of the excess hits he allowed on balls in play resulted from a poor St. Lucie team defense that ranked last in the FSL in fielding percentage (.969). Fulmer pitches with a plus 92-94 mph fastball with good life that he locates down in the zone, backing that up with a mid-80s, power slider that consistently grades as plus. He continues to make strides with his fringe-average changeup, but it's a distinct third pitch. The organization expects that Fulmer will make rapid progress in 2015 now that he has a healthy season under his belt—knee trouble limited him to nine starts in 2013—and now that he'll have the benefit of more consistent umpires and more cohesive team defense at Double-A Binghamton.

Year	Club (League)	Class	W	L	ERA	G	GS	CG	SV	IP	H	HR	BB	SO	K/9	WHIP	AVG
2012	Savannah (SAL)	LoA	7	6	2.74	21	21	1	0	108	92	6	38	101	8.4	1.20	.227
2013	Mets (GCL)	R	1	1	3.00	2	2	0	0	12	9	0	1	13	9.8	0.83	.205
	St. Lucie (FSL)	HiA	2	2	3.44	7	7	0	0	34	24	1	18	29	7.7	1.24	.198
2014	St. Lucie (FSL)	HiA	6	10	3.97	19	19	0	0	95	112	7	31	86	8.1	1.50	.286
	Binghamton (EL)	AA	0	1	16.20	1	1	0	0	3	6	1	3	1	2.7	2.70	.375
Minor League Totals			16	21	3.62	54	53	1	0	258	252	15	95	240	8.4	1.34	.251

14 JHOAN URENA, 3B

BA GRADE

55 Risk: Extreme

Born: Sept. 1, 1994. **B-T:** B-R. **Ht.:** 6-1. **Wt.:** 200. **Signed:** Dominican Republic, 2011. **Signed by:** Rafael Perez/Sandy Rosario/Ismael Cruz/Modesto Abreu.

The Mets signed the 17-year-old Urena for $425,000 in September 2011 and have watched him make steady progress in short-season ball in three subsequent seasons. Initially drawn to Urena's physicality and power from both sides of the plate, the club has been impressed with his leaned-up physique and improved feel to hit. After not going deep in the Rookie-level Gulf Coast League in 2013, he launched five bombs at short-season Brooklyn in 2014 while hitting .300 and tying for the New York-Penn League lead with 20 doubles. Urena tends to fall into pull mode from the right side of the plate, but from the left side he shows more of an all-fields approach that could make him an above-average hitter. His power could play as plus one day with continued maturity and better pitch recognition versus breaking balls. He already has proven he can handle velocity. Urena owns the best infield arm in the system, though he's a below-average runner with heavy feet whose sure hands give him a ceiling as a fringe-average defender at third base or a solid-average fielder at first. Urena's bat will dictate his future value, but he's on track to become a run-producer at the hot corner, albeit one who is at least three years away from New York.

Year	Club (League)	Class	AVG	G	AB	R	H	2B	3B	HR	RBI	BB	SO	SB	CS	OBP	SLG
2012	Mets2 (DSL)	R	.279	64	262	37	73	15	3	4	34	20	46	12	3	.330	.405
2013	Mets (GCL)	R	.299	47	157	19	47	6	3	0	20	13	34	4	1	.351	.376
2014	Brooklyn (NYP)	SS	.300	75	283	30	85	20	1	5	47	27	58	7	9	.356	.431
Minor League Totals			.292	186	702	86	205	41	7	9	101	60	138	23	13	.345	.409

15 CORY MAZZONI, RHP

BA GRADE

50 Risk: High

Born: Oct. 19, 1989. **B-T:** R-R. **Ht.:** 6-1. **Wt.:** 200. **Drafted:** North Carolina State, 2011 (2nd round). **Signed by:** Marlin MacPhail.

The Mets like what they see from Mazzoni when he takes the mound, but that has been an increasingly rare sight the past two seasons for the 2011 second-rounder. He dealt with problems in his right knee in 2013 that ultimately resulted in surgery to repair a torn meniscus, and then he missed the first half of 2014 with a strained right lat muscle before reporting to Triple-A Las Vegas in mid-July. He made

26 starts combined during the two seasons, and he missed out on an Arizona Fall League opportunity in 2014. Mazzoni misses bats and exhibits above-average control of a power repertoire headlined by a 92-95 mph fastball he locates to both sides of the plate. His low-80s slider flashes plus and his average splitter continues to improve his effectiveness against lefthanders. A plus athlete, Mazzoni repeats his delivery consistently, but a long arm action and below-average command in the zone point to a future as a No. 4 starter or reliever. Now a member of the 40-man roster, Mazzoni will be on call at Las Vegas if the Mets need an extra arm for the back of the rotation or to serve a bullpen apprenticeship.

Year	Club (League)	Class	W	L	ERA	G	GS	CG	SV	IP	H	HR	BB	SO	K/9	WHIP	AVG
2012	St. Lucie (FSL)	HiA	5	1	3.25	12	12	0	0	64	64	3	16	48	6.8	1.26	.264
	Binghamton (EL)	AA	5	5	4.46	14	14	2	0	81	90	9	20	56	6.2	1.36	.281
2013	Binghamton (EL)	AA	5	3	4.36	13	12	0	0	66	70	4	19	74	10.1	1.35	.275
2014	Mets (GCL)	R	0	1	4.50	1	1	0	0	4	5	0	1	7	15.8	1.50	.294
	St. Lucie (FSL)	HiA	0	0	5.00	2	2	0	0	9	11	0	3	9	9.0	1.56	.297
	Binghamton (EL)	AA	2	0	4.50	2	2	0	0	12	10	0	4	10	7.5	1.17	.217
	Las Vegas (PCL)	AAA	5	1	4.67	9	9	0	0	52	54	6	12	49	8.5	1.27	.269
Minor League Totals			24	12	4.11	65	53	2	0	300	316	23	78	271	8.1	1.31	.271

16 GABRIEL YNOA, RHP

BA GRADE

50 Risk: High

Born: May 26, 1993. **B-T:** R-R. **Ht.:** 6-2. **Wt.:** 160. **Signed:** Dominican Republic, 2009. **Signed by:** Rafael Perez/Ismael Cruz/Modesto Abreu.

Ynoa's games started have outnumbered his walks issued in each of his five pro seasons, and precise control once again served as his defining characteristic in 2014 as he split the season between high Class A St. Lucie and Double-A Binghamton. He surrendered much more hard contact this time around, however, when opposing batters proved to be only too eager to see the ball consistently located in the zone. Tall, lean and in control of his emotions on the mound, Ynoa must sharpen command of his above-average, riding 92-94 mph fastball that bumps 96 to induce more weak contact and better set up his secondary pitches. He sells his plus changeup with clean mechanics and picturesque arm speed, and while his low-80s slider bumps average on occasion, he doesn't get enough velocity or depth on the pitch to serve him as a strikeout pitch. With his mound presence and precocious control, Ynoa reminds the Mets of Rafael Montero, and like him he faces a probable future as a No. 4-type starter or useful reliever.

Year	Club (League)	Class	W	L	ERA	G	GS	CG	SV	IP	H	HR	BB	SO	K/9	WHIP	AVG
2012	Brooklyn (NYP)	SS	5	2	2.23	13	13	0	0	77	61	1	10	64	7.5	0.93	.213
2013	Savannah (SAL)	LoA	15	4	2.72	22	22	1	0	136	123	9	16	106	7.0	1.02	.238
2014	St. Lucie (FSL)	HiA	8	2	3.95	14	14	0	0	82	95	7	13	64	7.0	1.32	.288
	Binghamton (EL)	AA	3	2	4.21	11	11	2	0	66	74	9	12	42	5.7	1.30	.281
Minor League Totals			38	16	3.00	86	79	4	1	489	473	32	63	338	6.2	1.10	.253

17 SEAN GILMARTIN, LHP

BA GRADE

45 Risk: Medium

Born: May 8, 1990. **B-T:** L-L. **Ht.:** 6-2. **Wt.:** 190. **Drafted:** Florida State, 2011 (1st round). **Signed by:** Hugh Buchanan (Braves).

The Mets don't typically look to the Rule 5 draft as a source of talent, but with the club casting a wide net for lefthanded relief options, they selected Gilmartin in the 2014 edition. The 28th overall pick out of Florida State in 2011, he advanced quickly to Triple-A in the Braves system, but after logging a 5.74 ERA over 17 starts in 2013, Atlanta shipped him to the Twins for Ryan Doumit. While he relies on finesse and doesn't have any one outstanding pitch, Gilmartin has three reliable offerings with which to attack batters, plus he throws an early-count, low-70s curveball to same-side batters. He pitches at 88-90 mph with his fastball and locates the ball down from a three-quarters arm slot. His low-80s slider features consistently good depth, while his high-70s, fading changeup is his best pitch for most scouts. Despite not having a wipeout breaking ball, Gilmartin dominated lefthanders as a starter at Double-A and Triple-A in 2014, holding them to a .201 average and posting a 49-to-4 strikeout-to-walk ratio. If Gilmartin makes the Opening Day roster, the Mets intend to use him in middle relief and not necessarily in a matchup role.

Year	Club (League)	Class	W	L	ERA	G	GS	CG	SV	IP	H	HR	BB	SO	K/9	WHIP	AVG
2012	Mississippi (SL)	AA	5	8	3.54	20	20	3	0	119	111	9	26	86	6.5	1.15	.248
	Gwinnett (IL)	AAA	1	2	4.78	7	7	0	0	38	41	6	13	25	6.0	1.43	.273
2013	Braves (GCL)	R	0	0	0.00	3	2	0	0	9	1	0	0	11	11.0	0.11	.034
	Rome (SAL)	LoA	1	0	1.80	1	1	0	0	5	4	0	0	5	9.0	0.80	.222
	Gwinnett (IL)	AAA	3	8	5.74	17	17	0	0	91	112	12	33	65	6.4	1.59	.304
2014	New Britain (EL)	AA	7	3	3.13	12	12	0	0	72	76	2	16	74	9.3	1.28	.275
	Rochester (IL)	AAA	2	4	4.28	14	14	0	0	74	69	7	28	59	7.2	1.32	.250
Minor League Totals			21	27	4.05	80	79	3	0	431	435	39	118	356	7.4	1.28	.263

18 MATT BOWMAN, RHP

BA GRADE

50 Risk: High

Born: May 31, 1991. **B-T:** R-R. **Ht.:** 6-0. **Wt.:** 165. **Drafted:** Princeton, 2012 (13th round). **Signed by:** Jim Thompson.

Other organizations might not be as high on Bowman as are the Mets, but the club is optimistic they have a command-oriented starter on their hands. He completed his Princeton economics degree following the 2013 season, and he naturally takes a cerebral approach with him to the mound, mixing and matching his four pitches and wearing out the strike zone. Built along the lines of Tim Lincecum, he patterns his delivery after the two-time Cy Young Award winner. He's athletic enough to do so, seeing as he played shortstop in addition to pitching in college. Bowman throws a sinker at 90-94 mph, two distinct breaking balls and a solid-average, high-70s changeup with fading action that's his go-to secondary pitch. His downer curveball and late-breaking slider feature inconsistent action and grade no better than fringe-average at present. Bowman fields his position and holds runners, but it's his plus control and natural deception that set him apart. The Mets would like to see him better establish his heavy fastball early in games before unveiling all his secondary pitches. Bowman projects as a No. 4 starter in the majors.

Year	Club (League)	Class	W	L	ERA	G	GS	CG	SV	IP	H	HR	BB	SO	K/9	WHIP	AVG
2012	Brooklyn (NYP)	SS	2	2	2.45	12	1	0	3	29	26	1	2	30	9.2	0.95	.239
2013	Savannah (SAL)	LoA	4	0	2.64	5	5	0	0	31	28	0	4	26	7.6	1.04	.237
	St. Lucie (FSL)	HiA	6	4	3.18	16	16	0	0	96	83	8	31	90	8.4	1.18	.232
2014	Binghamton (EL)	AA	7	6	3.11	17	17	0	0	98	102	7	27	92	8.4	1.31	.266
	Las Vegas (PCL)	AAA	3	2	3.47	7	6	0	0	36	38	1	9	32	7.9	1.29	.268
Minor League Totals			22	14	3.06	57	45	0	3	291	277	17	73	270	8.4	1.20	.250

19 AKEEL MORRIS, RHP

BA GRADE

45 Risk: Medium

Born: Nov. 14, 1992. **B-T:** R-R. **Ht.:** 6-1. **Wt.:** 170. **Drafted:** HS—St. Thomas, V.I., 2010 (10th round). **Signed by:** Ismael Cruz.

Morris attended high school in the U.S. Virgin Islands and turned pro as a Mets 10th-round pick in 2010 for $120,000. He struggled to throw strikes as a starter, but a full-time shift to the bullpen at low Class A Savannah in 2014 revitalized his career, for he led South Atlantic League relievers with 16 saves, a .103 opponent average and strikeout rate of 14.1 per nine innings. Thin and wiry, Morris throws from a deceptive over-the-top slot that features a slow takeaway and long arm swing. He sits at 92-94 mph with riding life on his fastball up in the zone, but his top weapon is a plus changeup that typically features up to 15 mph of separation from his heater as it dives for the bottom of the zone. He throws an occasional high-70s slider to righthanders to keep them honest, but it's a below-average pitch. Moving to the bullpen suits Morris' pitching style in which he can exert full effort on every pitch and not worry about painting corners. Expect the club to be more aggressive with him in 2015 now that he's on the 40-man roster.

Year	Club (League)	Class	W	L	ERA	G	GS	CG	SV	IP	H	HR	BB	SO	K/9	WHIP	AVG
2012	Kingsport (APP)	R	0	6	7.98	11	6	0	2	38	38	7	22	50	11.7	1.57	.253
2013	Brooklyn (NYP)	SS	4	1	1.00	14	3	0	1	45	29	1	23	60	12.0	1.16	.184
2014	Savannah (SAL)	LoA	4	1	0.63	41	0	0	16	57	19	1	22	89	14.1	0.72	.103
Minor League Totals			12	11	2.95	85	26	1	19	216	129	14	122	288	12.0	1.16	.170

20 ROB WHALEN, RHP

BA GRADE

50 Risk: High

Born: Jan. 31, 1994. **B-T:** R-R. **Ht.:** 6-2. **Wt.:** 200. **Drafted:** HS—Haines City, Fla., 2012 (12th round). **Signed by:** Mike Silvestri.

The Mets signed Whalen for an above-slot $100,000 out of the 12th round of the 2012 draft. He missed the better part of May, June and July at low Class A Savannah in 2014 after a cut on his right hand became infected and required surgery. Whalen doesn't light up radar guns, but opposing batters don't see the ball well out of his hand, which allows his average, low-90s sinking fastball and high-70s curveball to play up. His breaking ball features consistent three-quarters tilt and is the best curve in the system, projecting as plus. Whalen commands his fastball and isn't afraid to challenge hitters in the zone with good down action on his pitches. He's still fine-tuning a slider and changeup that could play as average in the future thanks to an athletic, repeatable delivery. Whalen could reach his ceiling as a mid-rotation starter with continued health and pitch refinement and should move up to high Class A St. Lucie in 2015.

Year	Club (League)	Class	W	L	ERA	G	GS	CG	SV	IP	H	HR	BB	SO	K/9	WHIP	AVG
2012	Kingsport (APP)	R	0	0	0.00	1	0	0	0	1	1	0	0	1	9.0	1.00	.333
2013	Kingsport (APP)	R	3	2	1.87	12	12	0	0	72	50	1	17	76	9.5	0.93	.187
2014	Mets (GCL)	R	0	1	1.29	3	2	0	0	7	4	0	2	10	12.9	0.86	.160
	Savannah (SAL)	LoA	9	1	2.01	11	10	0	0	63	44	2	19	53	7.6	1.01	.192
Minor League Totals			12	4	1.89	27	24	0	0	143	99	3	38	140	8.8	0.96	.189

21 CASEY MEISNER, RHP

BA GRADE

50 Risk: High

Born: May 22, 1995. **B-T:** R-R. **Ht.:** 6-7. **Wt.:** 190. **Drafted:** HS—Cypress, Texas, 2013 (3rd round). **Signed by:** Ray Corbett.

Meisner's 6-foot-7 stature helps differentiate him from the plethora of other prep righthanders in the system. His tall, lanky frame and feel for the strike zone made him a target for the Mets in the 2013 draft, despite regular velocity readings in the high 80s as a Cypress Woods High senior. They invested a third-round pick and $500,000 to sign him. Meisner throws steeply downhill with tight rotation on his pitches, pitching at 90-92 mph and topping out at 94 with his fastball in pro ball. The Mets say his high-70s curveball has become a real weapon, projecting to at least average. Only teammate Marcos Molina had more strikeouts than Meisner (67) in the short-season New York-Penn League in 2014. He throws a below-average changeup at present, and the development of that pitch probably will dictate his future role. Meisner will head to low Class A Savannah in 2015, with the chance to become a No. 4 starter, unless one of his pitches takes a giant leap forward.

Year	Club (League)	Class	W	L	ERA	G	GS	CG	SV	IP	H	HR	BB	SO	K/9	WHIP	AVG
2013	Mets (GCL)	R	1	3	3.06	10	4	0	0	35	31	0	10	28	7.1	1.16	.238
2014	Brooklyn (NYP)	SS	5	3	3.75	13	13	0	0	62	67	4	18	67	9.7	1.36	.271
Minor League Totals			6	6	3.50	23	17	0	0	98	98	4	28	95	8.8	1.29	.260

22 DARIO ALVAREZ, LHP

BA GRADE

40 Risk: Medium

Born: Jan. 17, 1989. **B-T:** L-L. **Ht.:** 6-1. **Wt.:** 170. **Signed:** Dominican Republic, 2007. **Signed by:** Sal Agostinelli/Wil Tejada (Phillies).

Released by the Phillies in August 2009 while a member of their Dominican Summer League team, Alvarez did not play affiliated ball at all from 2010 through 2012. He caught the eye of Mets international scouting director Chris Becerra in the Venezuelan League's junior-circuit Parallel League, signing in January 2013. Alvarez began 2014 as a 25-year-old at low Class A Savannah, but he dominated the league as a starter/reliever and then made nine scoreless appearances at high Class A St. Lucie and Double-A Binghamton to receive an unlikely September callup. He pitches at about 90 mph and can touch 94, but his plus 80 mph slider is a reliable out pitch now that Mets coaches have tuned down the wayward lefty's busy delivery, which once featured a full back turn to the batter. Alvarez's slider often leaves lefthanders bailing out on a pitch that begins in their batter's box and sweeps across the plate. While his ceiling is low, Alvarez can fill a specific role on a major league roster as a situational lefty, and he's ready to do so in 2015.

Year	Club (League)	Class	W	L	ERA	G	GS	CG	SV	IP	H	HR	BB	SO	K/9	WHIP	AVG
2012	Did not play																
2013	Brooklyn (NYP)	SS	2	4	3.10	12	12	0	0	58	48	1	26	57	8.8	1.28	.221
2014	Savannah (SAL)	LoA	7	1	1.32	20	6	0	1	61	43	2	14	95	13.9	0.93	.192
	St. Lucie (FSL)	HiA	2	0	0.00	4	0	0	0	6	1	0	3	10	14.2	0.63	.059
	Binghamton (EL)	AA	1	0	0.00	5	0	0	1	6	4	0	0	9	14.3	0.71	.200
	New York (NL)	MAJ	0	0	13.50	4	0	0	0	1	4	1	0	1	6.8	3.00	.500
Major League Totals			0	0	13.50	4	0	0	0	1	4	1	0	1	6.8	3.00	.500
Minor League Totals			20	14	2.66	84	44	2	4	304	242	4	116	351	10.4	1.18	.216

23 CHAMP STUART, OF

BA GRADE

50 Risk: Extreme

Born: Oct. 11, 1992. **B-T:** R-R. **Ht.:** 6-0. **Wt.:** 175. **Drafted:** Brevard (N.C.), 2013 (6th round). **Signed by:** Marlin McPhail.

A native of the Bahamas, Jervis "Champ" Stuart starred in baseball, basketball and football at high school in Asheville, N.C., before heading about 45 minutes away to NCAA Division II Brevard. A loose, long-legged athlete, Stuart is at least a double-plus runner whose speed plays on offense, in center field and on the basepaths. As with many burners, he faces questions about his batting potential. He takes a simple righthanded stroke and isn't afraid to work deep counts, though his strikeout rate at low Class A Savannah (29 percent) is much too high for a player with little home-run power. Stuart owns an average arm and plus range that will play in left or center field, and that's good because unless his bat takes a big leap forward, he probably will have the most utility to a big league club as an extra outfielder. Given that he hasn't focused solely on baseball until fairly recently, Stuart has more growth potential than most college players from his draft class. High Class A St. Lucie awaits in 2015.

Year	Club (League)	Class	AVG	G	AB	R	H	2B	3B	HR	RBI	BB	SO	SB	CS	OBP	SLG
2013	Kingsport (APP)	R	.240	43	150	26	36	8	3	1	14	34	58	11	2	.388	.353
2014	Savannah (SAL)	LoA	.256	81	285	50	73	5	5	3	28	36	97	29	4	.341	.340
Minor League Totals			.251	124	435	76	109	13	8	4	42	70	155	40	6	.359	.345

24 MATT KOCH, RHP

BA GRADE

45 Risk: Medium

Born: Nov. 2, 1990. **B-T:** L-R. **Ht.:** 6-3. **Wt.:** 185. **Drafted:** Louisville, 2012 (3rd round). **Signed by:** Jarrett England.

A closer at Louisville when the Mets made him a third-round pick in 2012, Koch moved into the low Class A Savannah rotation in 2013 before a comebacker to the head ended his season that August. He recovered to log 120 innings at high Class A St. Lucie in 2014, but his performance regressed across the board. The Mets believe Koch is around the zone too much with his 89-91 mph fastball and three average to below-average offspeed pitches. Scouts like his mid-80s slider best among his secondary weapons, followed by his fringe curveball and below-average changeup. He probably will wind up in the bullpen, and the Mets were heartened when Koch came out firing 95 mph heat and an 88 mph slider in 2014 upon entering a Double-A Binghamton playoff game in long relief. His 2015 season at Double-A will be telling.

Year	Club (League)	Class	W	L	ERA	G	GS	CG	SV	IP	H	HR	BB	SO	K/9	WHIP	AVG
2012	Brooklyn (NYP)	SS	0	2	5.01	13	2	0	0	23	25	1	7	19	7.3	1.37	.278
2013	Savannah (SAL)	LoA	6	4	4.70	18	15	1	0	82	100	7	4	68	7.4	1.26	.295
2014	St. Lucie (FSL)	HiA	10	4	4.64	22	22	0	0	120	141	7	32	63	4.7	1.44	.294
Minor League Totals			16	10	4.70	53	39	1	0	226	266	15	43	150	6.0	1.37	.293

25 MILTON RAMOS, SS

BA GRADE

50 Risk: Extreme

Born: Oct. 26, 1995. **B-T:** R-R. **Ht.:** 5-11. **Wt.:** 158. **Drafted:** HS— Plantation, Fla., 2014 (3rd round). **Signed by:** Cesar Aranguren.

Born in Colombia, Ramos moved to the U.S. at age 6. Teams viewed him as perhaps the best defensive shortstop in the 2014 draft, and he met expectations in his Rookie-level Gulf Coast League debut. After signing for $750,000 as a third-round pick, Ramos hit a light .241 and played flashy, if inconsistent, defense. He has a quick first step, sure hands and plus range to both sides, though his solid-average arm strength could limit him at shortstop. He struggled to adjust to pro pitching, though he showed gap power, fair strike-zone discipline and solid-average speed. Ramos projects to be a below-average hitter, and he turns off some evaluators with his on-field immaturity. The Mets will take it slow with Ramos, who might move up to Rookie-level Kingsport in 2015.

Year	Club (League)	Class	AVG	G	AB	R	H	2B	3B	HR	RBI	BB	SO	SB	CS	OBP	SLG
2014	Mets (GCL)	R	.241	51	166	20	40	9	5	0	29	14	34	6	6	.299	.355
Minor League Totals			.241	51	166	20	40	9	5	0	29	14	34	6	6	.299	.355

26 CESAR PUELLO, OF

BA GRADE

45 Risk: High

Born: April 1, 1991. **B-T:** R-R. **Ht.:** 6-2. **Wt.:** 220. **Signed:** Dominican Republic, 2007. **Signed by:** Ismael Cruz/Marciano Alvarez.

Puello's breakthrough performance at Double-A Binghamton in 2013 was tempered by a season-ending 50-game suspension for his involvement with the Biogenesis clinic. He flashed every tool but one—feel to hit—at Triple-A Las Vegas in 2014, and while his performance dipped compared with 2013, he finished strong by hitting .287/.401/.507 in his final 45 games. He has plus raw power and at least average in-game juice, but a wild, impatient plate approach inhibits his ability to get to it consistently. Righthanders with good breaking stuff are especially successful at retiring Puello. An average runner with the instincts to play all three outfield posts capably, he has a plus arm that will play in right field. His minor league track record suggests he could platoon against lefthanders, for he has hit .343/.419/.614 against them since 2012. Being out of minor league options can only help Puello in his quest to reach the majors in 2015.

Year	Club (League)	Class	AVG	G	AB	R	H	2B	3B	HR	RBI	BB	SO	SB	CS	OBP	SLG
2012	St. Lucie (FSL)	HiA	.260	66	227	36	59	17	4	4	21	7	58	19	2	.328	.423
2013	Binghamton (EL)	AA	.326	91	331	63	108	21	2	16	73	28	82	24	7	.403	.547
2014	Las Vegas (PCL)	AAA	.252	105	318	59	80	20	2	7	37	30	72	13	1	.355	.393
Minor League Totals			.282	577	2068	366	583	117	14	44	255	130	480	148	39	.356	.416

27 ALI SANCHEZ, C

BA GRADE

50 Risk: Extreme

Born: Jan. 20, 1997. **B-T:** R-R. **Ht.:** 6-0. **Wt.:** 175. **Signed:** Venezuela, 2013. **Signed by:** Robert Espejo/Hector Rincones.

The Mets believe they have a special talent in Sanchez, an athletic catcher they signed out of Venezuela for $690,000 in 2013. He has advanced catch-and-throw skills, and he performed in his first pro summer in the Dominican Summer League in 2014, hitting .303/.406/.394 with nearly as many walks (27) as strikeouts (31). He also ranked third among league catchers by throwing out 51 percent of basestealers.

Sanchez uses a contact-oriented, inside-out approach to hit for a high average, though with added strength and maturity he could approach average power. Sanchez is a quiet receiver with quick feet and hands, which he uses to make fluid transfers from glove to hand. Accuracy helps his average arm play up. Look for Sanchez to play catcher every day at one of the Mets' Rookie-level affiliates in 2015.

Year	Club (League)	Class	AVG	G	AB	R	H	2B	3B	HR	RBI	BB	SO	SB	CS	OBP	SLG
2014	Mets1 (DSL)	R	.303	50	175	21	53	7	0	3	24	27	31	6	6	.406	.394
Minor League Totals			.303	50	175	21	53	7	0	3	24	27	31	6	6	.406	.394

28 EUDOR GARCIA, 3B

BA GRADE

45 Risk: High

Born: May 17, 1994. **B-T:** L-R. **Ht.:** 6-1. **Wt.:** 215. **Drafted:** El Paso CC, 2014 (4th round). **Signed by:** Max Semler.

The best bat available from the state of Texas in the 2014 draft, Garcia lasted until the Mets selected him in the fourth round and signed him for an under-slot $305,000. Stocky and standing about 6 feet tall, Garcia doesn't have a classic baseball body type, but he does generate plus lefthanded power from a short, powerful swing. Assigned to Rookie-level Kingsport after signing, he hit just two home runs in 55 games, though he did show fine control of the strike zone. He has the raw ability to develop into an average hitter with at least average power. Most evaluators expect him to shift to left field or first base down the line, for his arm and range are below-average, as is his speed. The Mets project Garcia as a lefthanded power source, and one who probably will get his feet wet at low Class A Savannah at the outset of 2015.

Year	Club (League)	Class	AVG	G	AB	R	H	2B	3B	HR	RBI	BB	SO	SB	CS	OBP	SLG
2014	Kingsport (APP)	R	.262	55	202	22	53	9	1	2	28	16	32	0	0	.327	.347
Minor League Totals			.262	55	202	22	53	9	1	2	28	16	32	0	0	.327	.347

29 BRANDON BROSHER, C

BA GRADE

50 Risk: Extreme

Born: Feb. 17, 1995. **B-T:** R-R. **Ht.:** 6-3. **Wt.:** 225. **Drafted:** HS—Spring Hill, Fla., 2013 (36th round). **Signed by:** Cesar Aranguren.

Brosher is the rare right/right high school first baseman who might have a bright future in pro ball based on his double-plus raw power. A willingness to take up catcher certainly doesn't hurt, either. Selected in the 36th round of the 2013 draft, Brosher signed for $167,500 to forego an Oral Roberts commitment. He crushed four home runs in seven games at Rookie-level Kingsport in 2014 before breaking his right ankle in a freak dugout accident and missing the rest of the season. He has shown enough barrel control to profile as perhaps a fringe-average hitter. Brosher won't be the most agile defender behind the plate, but he has plus arm strength and adequate receiving potential. His arm stroke is too long and his footwork too slow at this stage to reliably retire opposing basestealers, so a return to Kingsport is possible in 2015.

Year	Club (League)	Class	AVG	G	AB	R	H	2B	3B	HR	RBI	BB	SO	SB	CS	OBP	SLG
2013	Mets (GCL)	R	.180	22	61	10	11	1	0	3	6	12	23	1	2	.324	.344
2014	Kingsport (APP)	R	.387	7	31	6	12	0	0	4	8	2	11	1	0	.424	.774
Minor League Totals			.250	29	92	16	23	1	0	7	14	14	34	2	2	.355	.489

30 ROBERT GSELLMAN, RHP

BA GRADE

45 Risk: High

Born: July 18, 1993. **B-T:** R-R. **Ht.:** 6-4. **Wt.:** 200. **Drafted:** HS—Los Angeles, 2011 (13th round). **Signed by:** Chris Beccera.

Scouts for opposing teams don't necessarily see a separating ability for Gsellman, but the Mets love his durable starter's frame, competitive fire, average control and feel for three major league average pitches. He has improved his velocity to 90-92 mph in pro ball with quality sinking life on a fastball that can bump 94 when thrown upstairs. Gsellman sells his low-80s changeup with good arm speed, and he is working to improve the spin and rotation on his curveball, but it plays as an average pitch in the low- to mid-70s at its best. His raw athleticism should allow him to reach his ceiling as a back-end starter, and he's ready for high Class A St. Lucie in 2015.

Year	Club (League)	Class	W	L	ERA	G	GS	CG	SV	IP	H	HR	BB	SO	K/9	WHIP	AVG
2012	Kingsport (APP)	R	1	3	3.92	11	5	0	0	44	42	3	18	33	6.8	1.37	.250
2013	St. Lucie (FSL)	HiA	1	0	3.00	2	2	0	0	9	5	1	5	5	5.0	1.11	.152
	Savannah (SAL)	LoA	2	3	3.72	5	5	0	0	29	35	2	6	14	4.3	1.41	.310
	Brooklyn (NYP)	SS	3	3	2.06	12	12	0	0	70	59	2	12	64	8.2	1.01	.220
2014	Savannah (SAL)	LoA	10	6	2.55	20	20	4	0	116	122	1	34	92	7.1	1.34	.275
Minor League Totals			17	15	2.85	57	45	4	1	281	278	11	77	216	6.9	1.26	.258

New York Yankees

BY JOSH NORRIS

The 2014 season represented the closing of two eras in Yankees history, one far more publicized than the other.

The first was the close of shortstop Derek Jeter's career, which featured a season-long retirement tour, a walk-off single in his final game and mountains of praise along the way. The second was the retirement of farm director Mark Newman, who had served the team for 26 seasons and had headed up minor league operations for the last 15 years. And while Jeter's successor will have a more immediate impact, the man chosen to replace Newman likely will have more significant long-term ramifications. The team's system had failed to produce capable replacements for its cavalcade of injured stars, a problem that will continue so long as aging veterans like Mark Teixeira, Carlos Beltran, Brian McCann and, yes, Alex Rodriguez remain on the roster.

The farm system did tick up this year and got good production at the major league level from righthander Shane Greene (5-4, 3.78) and Dellin Betances, who set the Yankees' record for strikeouts by a reliever with 135 in 90 innings. But there was little homegrown help for an anemic offense that ranked 20th in the majors in runs.

General manager Brian Cashman, signed to a new three-year contract in early October, used the farm system to reinforce the roster via trades, acquiring third baseman Chase Headley, versatile bat Martin Prado and righthander Brandon McCarthy, yielding mostly fringe prospects led by power-hitting catcher Peter O'Brien. McCarthy in particular played well, but the Yankees' season still ended in September, not October.

Avoiding a third straight year without a playoff spot will require better luck on the injury front, especially from Japanese import Masahiro Tanaka, who pitched like an ace in his rookie season when healthy but who is dealing with a partial ligament tear in his elbow that could require surgery. Ivan Nova will be coming back from Tommy John surgery that sidelined him after four starts, and CC Sabathia will be coming off knee surgery at age 34, two years removed from his last productive season.

Cashman is trying to make the roster younger, trading Greene to the Diamondbacks for shortstop Didi Gregorius, the only projected regular in the lineup under the age of 30. He has the unenviable task of replacing Jeter.

The Yankees did see progress in the minors, led by righthander Luis Severino, who used a powerful fastball and a well-above-average changeup to burn through both Class A levels with ease before

After two decades as the Yankees' shortstop, Derek Jeter retired at the end of 2014

TOP PROSPECTS OF THE DECADE

Year	Player, Pos.	2014 Org
2005	Eric Duncan, 3b	Out of baseball
2006	Phil Hughes, rhp	Twins
2007	Phil Hughes, rhp	Twins
2008	Joba Chamberlain	Tigers
2009	Austin Jackson, of	Mariners
2010	Jesus Montero	Mariners
2011	Jesus Montero	Mariners
2012	Jesus Montero	Mariners
2013	Mason Williams	Yankees
2014	Gary Sanchez	Yankees

ending the season at Double-A. The organization's trio of first-round picks from 2013—third baseman Eric Jagielo, lefty Ian Clarkin and outfielder Aaron Judge—each had positive seasons. Rob Refsnyder and Jose Pirela seem likely to contend for the second-base job in New York. And teenaged Dominican shortstop Jorge Mateo, the owner of the arguably best tool set in the system, dazzled in a short look before a broken left wrist ended his domestic debut season.

Most of the Yankees' top hitting prospects are at least a year away, so they'll be in the charge of new farm director Gary Denbo, who's spent years in the Yankees' system under a variety of roles. Denbo was charged with replacing the slew of other personnel—Gordon Blakeley, Pat Roessler, Trey Hillman, Butch Wynegar, Kevin Long and Mick Kelleher among them—who departed early in the offseason. More importantly, Denbo will be asked to continue the turnaround of a farm system that hasn't produced impact players capable of aiding the big league club in recent years.

General manager: Brian Cashman. **Farm director:** Gary Denbo. **Scouting director:** Damon Oppenheimer.

Class	Team	League	W	L	PCT	Finish	Manager
Majors	New York Yankees	American	84	78	.519	13th (30)	Joe Girardi
Triple-A	Scranton/W-B RailRiders	International	68	76	.472	10th (14)	Dave Miley
Double-A	Trenton Thunder	Eastern	67	75	.472	8th (12)	Tony Franklin
High A	Tampa Yankees	Florida State	71	68	.511	7th (12)	Al Pedrique
Low A	Charleston RiverDogs	South Atlantic	71	69	.507	6th (14)	Luis Dorante
Short season	Staten Island Yankees	New York-Penn	37	38	.493	t-6th (14)	Mario Garza
Rookie	Yankees1	Gulf Coast	38	22	.633	1st (16)	Travis Chapman
Rookie	Yankees2	Gulf Coast	35	25	.583	5th (16)	Pat Osborn
Overall Minor League Record			387	373	.509	12th (30)	

THIS YEAR'S TOP 30

Player, Pos.	Status
1. Luis Severino, rhp	60/High
2. Aaron Judge, of	60/High
3. Jorge Mateo, ss	60/Extreme
4. Greg Bird, 1b	50/Medium
5. Gary Sanchez, c	55/High
6. Ian Clarkin, lhp	50/High
7. Rob Refsnyder, 2b	45/Low
8. Jacob Lindgren, lhp	50/Medium
9. Luis Torrens, c	55/Extreme
10. Miguel Andujar, 3b	50/High
11. Eric Jagielo, 3b	50/High
12. Bryan Mitchell, rhp	50/High
13. Tyler Wade, ss	50/High
14. Manny Banuelos, lhp	50/High
15. Abiatal Avelino, ss	55/Extreme
16. Tyler Austin, of	45/Medium
17. Jake Cave, of	50/High
18. J.R. Murphy, c	45/Medium
19. Austin DeCarr, rhp	50/High
20. Ty Hensley, rhp	50/Extreme
21. Thairo Estrada, ss	50/Extreme
22. Angel Aguilar, ss	50/Extreme
23. Leonardo Molina, of	50/Extreme
24. Juan De Leon, of	50/Extreme
25. Dermis Garcia, 3b	50/Extreme
26. Jose Ramirez, rhp	45/Medium
27. Ramon Flores, of	45/Medium
28. Jose Pirela, 2b	45/Medium
29. Jose Campos, rhp	45/High
30. Mason Williams, of	45/High

LAST YEAR'S TOP 30

Player, Pos.	Status
1. Gary Sanchez, c	No. 5
2. Slade Heathcott, of	Free agent
3. Mason Williams, of	No. 30
4. J.R. Murphy, c	No. 18
5. Eric Jagielo, 3b	No. 11
6. Aaron Judge, of	No. 2
7. Ian Clarkin, lhp	No. 6
8. Greg Bird, 1b	No. 4
9. Luis Severino, rhp	No. 1
10. Gosuke Katoh, 2b	Dropped out
11. Manny Banuelos, lhp	No. 14
12. Abiatal Avelino, ss	No. 15
13. Jose Ramirez, rhp	No. 25
14. Jose Campos, rhp	No. 29
15. Rafael De Paula, rhp	(Padres)
16. Shane Greene, rhp	(Tigers)
17. Tyler Austin, of	No. 16
18. Miguel Andujar, 3b	No. 10
19. Luis Torrens, c	No. 9
20. Ramon Flores, of	No. 22
21. Bryan Mitchell, rhp	No. 12
22. Jake Cave, of	No. 17
23. Pete O'Brien, c/3b	(Diamondbacks)
24. Ty Hensley, rhp	No. 20
25. Angelo Gumbs, 2b	Dropped out
26. Dellin Betances, rhp	Majors
27. Brett Marshall, rhp	(Reds)
28. Thairo Estrada, ss	No. 21
29. Robert Refsnyder, 2b	No. 7
30. Vidal Nuno, lhp	(Diamondbacks)

BEST TOOLS

Best Hitter for Average	Rob Refsnyder
Best Power Hitter	Aaron Judge
Best Strike-Zone Discipline	Greg Bird
Fastest Baserunner	Jorge Mateo
Best Athlete	Jorge Mateo
Best Fastball	Luis Severino
Best Curveball	Bryan Mitchell
Best Slider	Jacob Lindgren
Best Changeup	Luis Severino
Best Control	Jaron Long
Best Defensive Catcher	Luis Torrens
Best Defensive Infielder	Cito Culver
Best Infield Arm	Cito Culver
Best Defensive Outfielder	Mason Williams
Best Outfield Arm	Aaron Judge

PROJECTED 2018 LINEUP

Catcher	Gary Sanchez
First Base	Greg Bird
Second Base	Rob Refsnyder
Third Base	Miguel Andujar
Shortstop	Didi Gregorius
Left Field	Brett Gardner
Center Field	Jacoby Ellsbury
Right Field	Aaron Judge
Designated Hitter	Brian McCann
No. 1 Starter	Masahiro Tanaka
No. 2 Starter	Luis Severino
No. 3 Starter	Ivan Nova
No. 4 Starter	Ian Clarkin
No. 5 Starter	Michael Pineda
Closer	Dellin Betances

NEW YORK YANKEES

TOP 2014 ROOKIE: Jose Pirela, 2b/of. He's not a high-ceiling talent, but Pirela can hit, second base is open, and he's coming off a strong winter campaign in his native Venezuela.

BREAKOUT PROSPECT: Eric Jagielo, 3b. He hit 18 home runs in a season shortened by injury. If he can show that power at Double-A, he'll jump way up the board.

SLEEPER: Simon de la Rosa, lhp. The 21-year-old southpaw brings a high-octane fastball to go with a high-spin curveball and changeup.

SOURCE OF TOP 30 TALENT			
Homegrown	29	Acquired	1
College	4	Trades	1
Junior college	0	Rule 5 draft	0
High school	11	Independent leagues	0
Draft-and-follow	0	Free agents/waivers	0
Nondrafted free agents	0		
International	14		

LF
Ramon Flores (27)
Ben Gamel
Michael O'Neill
Taylor Dugas

CF
Jake Cave (17)
Leonardo Molina (23)
Mason Williams (30)
Dustin Fowler
Mark Payton

RF
Aaron Judge (2)
Tyler Austin (16)
Juan De Leon (24)

3B
Miguel Andujar (10)
Eric Jagielo (11)
Dermis Garcia (25)
Dante Bichette Jr.
Rob Segedin

SS
Jorge Mateo (3)
Tyler Wade (13)
Abiatal Avelino (15)
Thairo Estrada (21)
Angel Aguilar (22)
Cito Culver

2B
Rob Refsnyder (7)
Jose Pirela (28)
Gosuke Katoh
Angelo Gumbs

1B
Greg Bird (4)
Kyle Roller
Mike Ford
Connor Spencer

C
Gary Sanchez (5)
Luis Torrens (9)
J.R. Murphy (18)

LHP

LHSP	LHRP
Ian Clarkin (6)	Jacob Lindgren (8)
Manny Banuelos (14)	James Pazos
Jordan Montgomery	Tyler Webb
Justin Kamplain	
Miguel Sulbaran	
Simon de la Rosa	

RHP

RHSP	RHRP
Luis Severino (1)	Jose Ramirez (26)
Bryan Mitchell (12)	Danny Burawa
Austin DeCarr (19)	Branden Pinder
Ty Hensley (20)	Nick Rumbelow
Jose Campos (29)	Nick Goody
Rookie Davis	Kyle Haynes
Jaron Long	Jordan Foley
Gabe Encinas	

2014

BEST PURE HITTER: OF Mark Payton (7) had a four-year track record of hitting for average and getting on base at Texas. The lefthanded hitter has a loose, quick and compact stroke that hits to all fields. His gap power will likely produce lots of doubles.

BEST POWER HITTER: 1B Chris Gittens (12) produces plus-plus raw power from the right side with a huge, physical frame. 1B Bo Thompson (13) has at least plus raw power from his 5-foot-10, 255-pound build.

FASTEST RUNNER: OF Dominic Jose (24) has at least plus speed underway, capable of running the 60-yard dash in 6.5 seconds.

BEST DEFENSIVE PLAYER: Vince Conde (9) was the starting shortstop for a College World Series-winning Vanderbilt club ahead of potential 2015 first-rounder Dansby Swanson. The surehanded Conde has the potential to remain at the position with feel for the game and defensive instincts.

BEST FASTBALL: RHP Austin DeCarr (3) has a power fastball that touches 96 mph with downhill plane from a quick arm. LHP Jacob Lindgren (2) sits 91-94, touching 95 with tremendous deception and armside run and sink. RHP Jordan Foley (5) has been up to 97. Deshorn Lake, an unsigned 12th-round out of high school who signed this summer as a nondrafted free agent, ran his fastball up to 98.

BEST SECONDARY PITCH: Lindgren has a wipe-out slider that is at least a plus offering with tilt and depth. DeCarr's downer curveball has power with at least plus potential.

BEST PRO DEBUT: Lindgren moved quickly through the minors and finished the season at Double-A Trenton, striking out an Aroldis Chapman-like 17.3 per-nine across all levels this summer. 1B Connor Spencer's (8) carrying tool is his lefthanded bat. He led the New York-Penn League in batting (.364/.489/.444) with his inside-out swing.

BEST ATHLETE: Jose has plus speed, at least an average arm with power potential from a strong, athletic build. DeCarr was recruited by colleges as a quarterback.

MOST INTRIGUING BACKGROUND: Jose is the son of former big leaguer Felix Jose.

CLOSEST TO THE MAJORS: Not only is Lindgren the closest to the majors in the system, but he also is one of the closest to the majors in the entire 2014 draft class.

BEST LATE-ROUND PICK: RHP Sean Carley (14) had the pure stuff to go in the top 10 rounds as a big-bodied strike-thrower with a fastball up to 94. RHP Matt Borens (11) has a big, projectable body at 6-foot-7 with a fastball up to 94 that he commands well.

THE ONE WHO GOT AWAY: The Yankees maxed out their signing budget and had just $70,000 left to avoid going over the 5 percent overall bonus pool threshold that would have cost them a first-round pick in 2015. Prep C Christopher Hudgins (35) has a chance to develop at Pepperdine.

ASSESSMENT: New York did not have a first-round pick for the first time since 2002 and invested heavily in pitching, selecting arms with its first five picks for the first time since 1987.

2013

While 2B Gosuke Katoh (2) took a step back last year, 3B Eric Jagielo (1), OF Aaron Judge (1) and LHP Ian Clarkin (1) and SS Tyler Wade (4) all have made strong pro debuts.

GRADE: A

2012

RHP Ty Hensley (1) hasn't been healthy yet. The Yanks traded C Peter O'Brien (2) and Corey Black (4), two of the top talents in this class. 2B/OF Rob Refsnyder (5) just keeps hitting.

GRADE: C

2011

The industry panned the $1.1 million bonus the Yankees gave 1B Greg Bird (5). He's justified the outlay as this class' top prospect, especially since the Yanks' failed to sign RHP Jon Gray (10).

GRADE: C

TOP DRAFT PICKS OF THE DECADE

Year	Player, Pos.	2014 Org
2005	C.J. Henry, ss	Out of baseball
2006	Ian Kennedy, rhp	Padres
2007	Andrew Brackman, rhp	Out of baseball
2008	*Gerrit Cole, rhp	Pirates
2009	Slade Heathcott, of	Yankees
2010	Cito Culver, ss	Yankees
2011	Dante Bichette Jr., 3b (1st round supp.)	Yankees
2012	Ty Hensley, rhp	Yankees
2013	Eric Jagielo, 3b	Yankees
2014	Jacob Lindgren, lhp (2nd round)	Yankees

*Did not sign.

LARGEST BONUSES IN CLUB HISTORY

Hideki Irabu, 1997	$8,500,000
Jose Contreras, 2002	$6,000,000
Andrew Brackman, 2007	$3,350,000
Gary Sanchez, 2009	$3,000,000
Dermis Garcia, 2014	$3,000,000

1 LUIS SEVERINO, RHP

Born: Feb. 20, 1994. **B-T:** R-R. **Ht.:** 6-0. **Wt.:** 195. **Signed:** Dominican Republic, 2011. **Signed by:** Juan Rosario.

Signed out of the Dominican Republic as a 17-year-old, Severino commanded a $225,000 signing bonus and spent a fairly anonymous debut season in the Dominican Summer League. He surrendered just 46 hits and 17 walks in 64 innings that year, and worked to a 0.98 WHIP. The strong performance continued in 2013, when he dazzled in six appearances in the Rookie-level Gulf Coast League with nearly 11 strikeouts per nine innings. The performance prompted the Yankees to jump him over short-season ball and instead send him to low Class A Charleston to close the year. Severino got hit a little harder with the RiverDogs, but positioned himself for a breakout 2014 season that arrived, as he finished in Double-A. He further enhanced his star this summer with an inning in the Futures Game that featured a strikeout of Joey Gallo, one of the minors' premier power brokers. Only a strained oblique muscle that sidelined him for three weeks slowed his progress.

Severino's build, fastball-changeup combo, Dominican heritage and dominance have earned him comparisons to Pedro Martinez. Short but not skinny, Severino utilizes a drop-and-drive delivery to bring his 94-97 fastball, which has above-average life. He touched 98 and 99 plenty of times throughout the course of the season as well. He couples the fastball with a changeup that features plenty of late fade. He's confident enough to double and triple up on the pitch at times and use it to get strikeouts against both lefthanders and righthanders. His third pitch is a mid-80s slider thrown with power, which still takes a back seat to his fastball and changeup but projects as solid-average when he's finished developing. While his size and delivery limit the amount of downward plane he can impart to his pitches, he pitches to all four quadrants of the strike zone, helping him keep the ball in the ballpark. He surrendered just three home runs on the season—one after May 25, and none at either of his stops in high Class A or Double-A. Severino presents an air of confidence in both himself and his repertoire at all times, and his demeanor helps keep him from getting flustered when breaks don't go his way behind him.

Severino clearly is on the fast track to New York.

BA GRADE

60 Risk: High

SCOUTING GRADES

Fastball: 70.
Changeup: 70.
Slider: 50.
Control: 60.

Based on 20-80 scouting scale and future projection rather than present tools.

LGE	BF	SO%	BB%	HR/9
SAL	277	25.3	5.4	0.27
EL	100	29.0	6.0	0.36

BRIAN WESTERHOLT

He's likely to start 2015 at Triple-A Scranton/Wilkes-Barre with a shot at moving into the mix of the big league staff by the end of the season if everything goes as planned.

Year	Club (League)	Class	W	L	ERA	G	GS	CG	SV	IP	H	HR	BB	SO	K/9	WHIP	AVG
2012	Yankees 1 (DSL)	R	4	2	1.68	14	14	0	0	64	46	2	17	45	6.3	0.98	.205
2013	Yankees1 (GCL)	R	3	1	1.37	6	4	0	0	26	16	0	6	32	10.9	0.84	.172
	Charleston (SAL)	LoA	1	1	4.08	4	4	0	0	18	21	1	4	21	10.7	1.42	.292
2014	Charleston (SAL)	LoA	3	2	2.79	14	14	0	0	68	62	2	15	70	9.3	1.14	.242
	Tampa (FSL)	HiA	1	1	1.31	4	4	0	0	21	11	0	6	28	12.2	0.82	.151
	Trenton (EL)	AA	2	2	2.52	6	6	0	0	25	20	1	6	29	10.4	1.04	.213
Minor League Totals			14	9	2.23	48	46	0	0	222	176	6	54	225	9.1	1.04	.217

2 AARON JUDGE, OF

Born: April 26, 1992. **B-T:** R-R. **Ht.:** 6-7. **Wt.:** 255. **Drafted:** Fresno State, 2013 (1st round). **Signed by:** Troy Afenir.

A baseball, football and basketball star in high school, Judge focused on baseball at Fresno State. His raw power didn't translate in games until his junior year, when he hit 12 home runs and slugged .655. The Yankees gave him $1.8 million with the 32nd overall pick in the draft. A torn right quad delayed his pro debut until this season. Armed with 80 raw power on the 20-80 scale, Judge takes an impressive batting practice. But unlike most players his size, Judge's in-game approach is geared to hit over power. He's just as comfortable lining pitches to the opposite power alley as he is turning on a fastball on the inner-half. His swing is shorter than most players his size. As would be expected of someone with his build, there are holes in his swing as pitchers will force him to prove he can handle pitches in. Blessed with an advanced approach, he would have led either the Sally or Florida State League in walk rate if he had enough plate appearances to qualify. He moved off of center field immediately in pro ball and is an average defender in right field with an above-average throwing arm. He's an average runner. Judge was getting extra polish in the Arizona Fall League, which should help him jump to Double-A Trenton in 2015. His tools are what scouts look for in a right fielder.

BA GRADE
60 Risk: High

LGE	PA	BB%	SO%	ISO
SAL	278	14.0	21.2	.197
FSL	285	17.5	25.3	.159

Year	Club (League)	Class	AVG	G	AB	R	H	2B	3B	HR	RBI	BB	SO	SB	CS	OBP	SLG
2013	Did not play—Injured																
2014	Charleston (SAL)	LoA	.333	65	234	36	78	15	2	9	45	39	59	1	0	.428	.530
	Tampa (FSL)	HiA	.283	66	233	44	66	9	2	8	33	50	72	0	0	.411	.442
Minor League Totals			.308	131	467	80	144	24	4	17	78	89	131	1	0	.419	.486

3 JORGE MATEO, SS

Born: June 23, 1995. **B-T:** R-R. **Ht.:** 6-0. **Wt.:** 188. **Signed:** Dominican Republic, 2010. **Signed by:** Juan Rosario.

Signed by the Yankees for $225,000 out of the Dominican Republic, Mateo has impressed when he's not sidelined in the training room, something that has slowed him in two of his three pro seasons. He missed time with a hairline fracture in his left arm in 2012. This year he missed all but 15 games after he was hit by a pitch that broke his left wrist. A top-of-the-scale 80 runner, Mateo owns a rare and enticing combination of power and speed, and has an excellent chance to stick at shortstop in the long term. His body and quick-twitch athletic abilities led one evaluator to compare him to NFL wide receiver DeSean Jackson. Before the injury, Mateo had been more than playing up to lofty expectations. He's an aggressive hitter and basestealer, and the ball jumps off his bat with pop to the gaps. He's a bit of a free swinger who needs development time to refine his plate approach and baserunning. He's got the range to stick at shortstop with a plus arm as well, and the total package evokes comparisons to Jose Reyes. Mateo has played just 93 career games, so a return to extended spring training seems likely. The Yankees then could send him to either their new Rookie-level Pulaski affiliate in the Appalachian League or short-season Staten Island.

BA GRADE
60 Risk: Extreme

LGE	PA	BB%	SO%	ISO
GCL	65	10.8	26.2	.121

Year	Club (League)	Class	AVG	G	AB	R	H	2B	3B	HR	RBI	BB	SO	SB	CS	OBP	SLG
2012	Yankees 2 (DSL)	R	.255	14	55	15	14	2	1	1	8	12	11	4	1	.382	.382
2013	Yankees 1 (DSL)	R	.287	64	258	50	74	9	6	7	26	34	52	49	10	.378	.450
2014	Yankees1 (GCL)	R	.276	15	58	14	16	5	1	0	1	7	17	11	1	.354	.397
Minor League Totals			.280	93	371	79	104	16	8	8	35	53	80	64	12	.375	.431

4 GREG BIRD, 1B

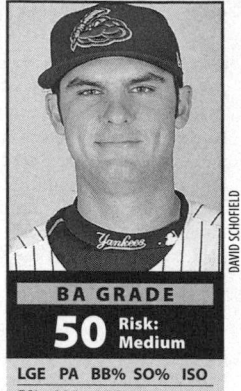

DAVID SCHOFIELD

Born: Nov. 9, 1992. **B-T:** L-R. **Ht.:** 6-3. **Wt.:** 215. **Drafted:** HS—Aurora, Colo., 2011 (5th Round). **Signed by:** Steve Kmetko.

The high school catcher for future Orioles righthander Kevin Gausman, Bird spurned an Arkansas commitment to sign with the Yankees for a $1.1 million bonus. He moved off catcher in pro ball and shifted to first base, where his recurring back spasms—which affected him in 2014 as well—would be far less likely to come into play. He has worked hard to strengthen his core but still deals with recurring back issues. Like a lot of the Yankees' better prospects, Bird is a slow-twitch player with little athleticism to speak of. What he does well is hit. He's one of the purest hitters in the system, with the ability to pepper the field from line to line and the most advanced approach in the system. He knows the strike zone and knows his own swing well. He also generates plenty of power from a short swing, and projects to hit 18-20 homers in the big leagues, a figure that could be boosted by the short porch in Yankee Stadium if he pulls the ball more often. He's average around the bag at first base and is a well below-average runner. After making up for the month or so he lost with time in the Arizona Fall League, Bird has a good shot to start 2015 in Triple-A.

BA GRADE

50 Risk: Medium

LGE	PA	BB%	SO%	ISO
FSL	325	13.8	21.5	.164
EL	116	15.5	23.3	.305

Year	Club (League)	Class	AVG	G	AB	R	H	2B	3B	HR	RBI	BB	SO	SB	CS	OBP	SLG
2012	Yankees (GCL)	R	.286	17	49	9	14	2	1	0	5	11	13	0	0	.419	.367
	Staten Island (NYP)	SS	.400	11	40	4	16	4	0	2	8	6	10	0	0	.489	.650
2013	Charleston (SAL)	LoA	.288	130	458	84	132	36	3	20	84	107	132	1	1	.428	.511
2014	Tampa (FSL)	HiA	.277	75	274	36	76	22	1	7	32	45	70	1	0	.375	.442
	Trenton (EL)	AA	.253	27	95	16	24	8	0	7	11	18	27	0	0	.379	.558
Minor League Totals			.283	264	928	149	263	72	5	36	140	188	256	2	1	.407	.488

5 GARY SANCHEZ, C

Born: Dec. 2, 1992. **B-T:** R-R. **Ht.:** 6-2. **Wt.:** 220. **Signed:** Dominican Republic, 2009. **Signed by:** Victor Mata/Raymon Sanchez.

Signed for $3 million out of the Dominican Republic in 2009, Sanchez tore through the low minors over his first four professional seasons and established himself as not only one of the best minors' best catchers, but one of the best overall prospects in the game. He's still a key member of the Yankees' farm, but middling production and repeated disciplinary issues have chipped away some of his sheen. If everything clicks, he's a frontline catcher with the potential for a .280 average and 20-25 home runs annually. His throwing arm remains an impressive tool as well, one that ranks between 70-80 on the scouting scale, and he threw out 39 percent of basestealers. But the warts are still there, too. He's still working to become more adept as a receiver and a blocker—he led the Eastern League with 17 errors and 10 passed balls—and some scouts felt he struggled to establish a proper rapport with his staff. He also was benched for five games for issues away from the field. Sanchez is ready to be tested at Triple-A and move toward the precipice of helping the big club if he can prove he's reliable.

BA GRADE

55 Risk: High

LGE	PA	BB%	SO%	ISO
EL	477	9.0	19.1	.135

Year	Club (League)	Class	AVG	G	AB	R	H	2B	3B	HR	RBI	BB	SO	SB	CS	OBP	SLG
2012	Charleston (SAL)	LoA	.297	68	263	44	78	19	0	13	56	22	65	11	4	.353	.517
	Tampa (FSL)	HiA	.279	48	172	21	48	10	1	5	29	10	41	4	0	.330	.436
2013	Tampa (FSL)	HiA	.254	94	362	38	92	21	0	13	61	28	71	3	1	.313	.420
	Trenton (EL)	AA	.250	23	92	12	23	6	0	2	10	13	16	0	0	.364	.380
2014	Trenton (EL)	AA	.270	110	429	48	116	19	0	13	65	43	91	1	1	.338	.406
Minor League Totals			.274	472	1792	245	491	104	2	71	316	166	421	23	9	.341	.453

6 IAN CLARKIN, LHP

Born: Feb. 14, 1995. **B-T:** L-L. **Ht.:** 6-2. **Wt.:** 186. **Drafted:** HS—San Diego, 2013 (1st round). **Signed by:** Dave Keith.

A star on the 2012 USA Baseball 18-and-under team that won the gold medal at the IBAF World Championship, Clarkin had a strong senior high school season, and the Yankees draft him 33rd overall in 2013. After saying he "couldn't stand" the Yankees growing up, he signed with New York for $1,650,100. His pro debut was delayed by an ankle injury that happened when he slipped on a baseball at the Yankees complex in Florida. A three-pitch lefthander, Clarkin does an excellent job of getting downhill from a high release point, generating groundball outs with his fastball, which clocks in at 90-92 mph and features modest life. Some scouts saw the need for Clarkin to add a cutter as he climbed the ladder. Under the guidance of pitching coordinator Gil Patterson, he did just that in 2014. With the new weapon in tow, he'll be able to coax even more groundballs. His best secondary pitch is a changeup, which scouts rank as plus. He also throws a big-breaking curveball in the 70-72 mph range. His delivery is clean, has some deception to it. After a cameo at high Class A Tampa, Clarkin will head back to begin 2015, with a chance at the upper levels in the second half.

BA GRADE	
50	Risk: High

LGE	BF	SO%	BB%	HR/9
SAL	284	25.0	7.7	0.77

Year	Club (League)	Class	W	L	ERA	G	GS	CG	SV	IP	H	HR	BB	SO	K/9	WHIP	AVG
2013	Yankees1 (GCL)	R	0	2	10.80	3	3	0	0	5	5	2	4	4	7.2	1.80	.263
2014	Charleston (SAL)	LoA	3	3	3.21	16	15	0	0	70	64	6	22	71	9.1	1.23	.250
	Tampa (FSL)	HiA	1	0	1.80	1	1	0	0	5	7	0	1	4	7.2	1.60	.368
Minor League Totals			4	5	3.60	20	19	0	0	80	76	8	27	79	8.9	1.29	.259

7 ROB REFSNYDER, 2B/OF

DAVID SCHOFIELD

Born: March 26, 1991. **B-T:** R-R. **Ht.:** 6-1. **Wt.:** 205. **Drafted:** Arizona, 2012 (5th round). **Signed by:** Steve Kmetko.

Refsnyder was the Most Outstanding Player in the 2012 College World Series while playing right field for Arizona. The Yankees signed him for $205,900, then moved him to second base. A short swing and excellent plate discipline help make Refsnyder a strong hitter. He's balanced at the plate, has good hand-eye coordination and has quick hands that help him catch up to good velocity. He sprays line drives all over the diamond. He's got power enough for double-digit home runs, but he's a pure hitter first before a power hitter. He's an average runner underway but a little slower out of the box. Refsnyder's bat profiles better if he can handle second base, where his lack of experience shows in his inconsistent actions, footwork and poor angles to balls. He has made strides turning double plays and reading hitters' swings, and some evaluators see him as a future fringe-average-to-average defender whose bat will help him play there. Multiple evaluators have compared Refsnyder to the Mets' Daniel Murphy, though he's a right-handed hitter. Barring a big move in free agency, he'll have a chance to win the big league second-base job out of spring training, but it's more likely he heads back to Triple-A for more seasoning.

BA GRADE	
45	Risk: Low

LGE	PA	BB%	SO%	ISO
EL	244	5.7	15.6	.206
IL	333	12.3	20.1	.157

Year	Club (League)	Class	AVG	G	AB	R	H	2B	3B	HR	RBI	BB	SO	SB	CS	OBP	SLG
2012	Charleston (SAL)	LoA	.241	46	162	22	39	8	0	4	22	16	25	11	1	.319	.364
2013	Charleston (SAL)	LoA	.370	13	54	9	20	4	1	0	6	6	12	7	0	.452	.481
	Tampa (FSL)	HiA	.283	117	413	66	117	28	2	6	51	78	70	16	6	.408	.404
2014	Trenton (EL)	AA	.342	60	228	35	78	19	5	6	30	14	38	5	5	.385	.548
	Scranton/W-B (IL)	AAA	.300	77	287	47	86	19	1	8	33	41	67	4	4	.389	.456
Minor League Totals			.297	313	1144	179	340	78	9	24	142	155	212	43	16	.389	.444

8 JACOB LINDGREN, LHP

DAVID SCHOFIELD

Born: March 12, 1993. **B-T:** L-L. **Ht.:** 5-11. **Wt.:** 180. **Drafted:** Mississippi State, 2014 (2nd round). **Signed by:** Andy Cannizaro.

A starter at Mississippi State in 2013, Lindgren converted to the bullpen in the Cape Cod League after his sophomore season and remained there in his junior year. He lost his changeup and curveball when in relief, but found less was more, leading the nation with 16.3 strikeouts per nine innings as a junior. The Yankees, who didn't pick until No. 55, popped him with their first selection and gave him $1,018,700 to turn pro and jump on the fast track. It didn't take long for Lindgren to get back in the groove. He ran through the lower minors with ease and ended his season at Double-A Trenton, his fourth level of the year. Lindgren couples a 92-94 mph fastball with deception and tremendous armside run and sink. He couples the pitch with a tight, power slider thrown in the mid-80s that already ranks as the best in the system. His control can wander a little at times, which may make the difference of whether he's a future set-up man or closer. Lindgren will have a good chance to make the Yankees' big league bullpen in 2014, perhaps after a short stint in Triple-A. He's expected to eventually pitch high-leverage innings.

BA GRADE

50 Risk: Medium

LGE	BF	SO%	BB%	HR/9
FSL	31	54.8	12.9	0.00
EL	49	36.7	18.4	0.00

Year	Club (League)	Class	W	L	ERA	G	GS	CG	SV	IP	H	HR	BB	SO	K/9	WHIP	AVG
2014	Yankees1 (GCL)	R	0	0	0.00	1	0	0	0	1	2	0	0	2	18.0	2.00	.400
	Charleston (SAL)	LoA	1	0	1.80	4	0	0	1	5	1	0	0	11	19.8	0.20	.056
	Tampa (FSL)	HiA	0	0	0.00	6	0	0	0	7	3	0	4	17	20.9	0.95	.111
	Trenton (EL)	AA	1	1	3.86	8	0	0	0	12	6	0	9	18	13.9	1.29	.154
Minor League Totals			2	1	2.16	19	0	0	1	25	12	0	13	48	17.3	1.00	.135

9 LUIS TORRENS, C

DAVID SCHOFIELD

Born: May 2, 1996. **B-T:** R-R. **Ht.:** 6-0. **Wt.:** 175. **Signed:** Venezuela, 2012. **Signed by:** Alan Atacho/Darwin Bracho/Ricardo Finol.

Torrens played in the infield in Panama's winter league on a team operated by former Yankees international scouting director Carlos Rios, who was his trainer. Torrens signed for $1.3 million and opened eyes last season with his work behind the plate and willingness to learn despite the rigors of a new position and a long season. Managers and scouts alike rave about Torrens' defensive skills, noting how advanced he is as a receiver and a blocker for someone his age and with his limited experience. He turns in 1.85-1.9-second pop times, showing a quick release and accurate throws. The Yankees aggressively moved him to low Class A Charleston to begin the year, but had to cut his time there short because a shoulder strain hindered his ability to throw. He hit better after dropping down to short-season Staten Island, where he was still young for the league. Scouts believe in his ability to hit for average in the long term, and think he'll grow into power once his body finishes developing. His swing has some loft and he's shown gap power. After a quick trip to Charleston in 2014, Torrens is likely to return there for a much longer engagement in 2015.

BA GRADE

55 Risk: Extreme

LGE	PA	BB%	SO%	ISO
NYP	202	6.9	20.3	.135
SAL	34	17.6	20.6	.115

Year	Club (League)	Class	AVG	G	AB	R	H	2B	3B	HR	RBI	BB	SO	SB	CS	OBP	SLG
2013	Yankees2 (GCL)	R	.241	48	174	17	42	7	0	1	14	27	40	2	0	.348	.299
2014	Charleston (SAL)	LoA	.154	9	26	4	4	0	0	1	3	6	7	0	0	.353	.269
	Yankees1 (GCL)	R	.250	5	16	1	4	1	0	0	1	0	2	0	0	.333	.313
	Staten Island (NYP)	SS	.270	48	185	27	50	13	3	2	18	14	41	1	2	.327	.405
Minor League Totals			.249	110	401	49	100	21	3	4	36	47	90	3	2	.338	.347

10 MIGUEL ANDUJAR, 3B

Born: March 2, 1995. **B-T:** R-R. **Ht.:** 6-0. **Wt.:** 200. **Signed:** Dominican Republic, 2011. **Signed by:** Victor Mata/Coanabo Cosme.

Andujar signed for $750,000 in 2011, but with the Yankees' third-base depth, he didn't make his full-season debut until this season. Thanks to his slow start and the fact that past top picks Dante Bichette and Eric Jagielo were a level ahead of him at high Class A Tampa, Andujar played the entire season at low Class A Charleston. After an unimpressive first half, Andujar grinded his way though and had a big second half, showing his ability to adjust. He's an aggressive hitter, especially on fastballs early in the count, and shows above-average bat speed that translates to at least average power. He showed an ability to adjust to offspeed pitches well for his age, though his inexperience showed in struggles with lefthanded pitchers (.461 OPS). Andujar's best tool is his 70 throwing arm, and he's athletic enough to throw from various angles. He needs to sharpen his reads on grounders, but he has the tools to be a tick above-average defender at third if he continues to work at improvement. If everything clicks, Andujar has a future of an everyday third baseman whose bat profiles for the position. He'll move to high Class A Tampa for 2015.

BA GRADE

50 Risk: High

LGE	PA	BB%	SO%	ISO
SAL	527	6.6	15.7	.130

Year	Club (League)	Class	AVG	G	AB	R	H	2B	3B	HR	RBI	BB	SO	SB	CS	OBP	SLG
2012	Yankees (GCL)	R	.232	50	177	21	41	9	0	1	19	13	37	1	3	.288	.299
2013	Yankees2 (GCL)	R	.323	34	133	18	43	11	0	4	25	7	21	4	1	.368	.496
2014	Charleston (SAL)	LoA	.267	127	484	75	129	25	4	10	70	35	83	5	1	.318	.397
Minor League Totals			.268	211	794	114	213	45	4	15	114	55	141	10	5	.320	.392

11 ERIC JAGIELO, 3B

Born: May 17, 1992. **B-T:** L-R. **Ht.:** 6-2. **Wt.:** 195. **Drafted:** Notre Dame, 2013 (1st round). **Signed by:** Mike Gibbons.

BA GRADE

50 Risk: High

A three-year starter at Notre Dame and a standout in the Cape Cod League, Jagielo impressed the Yankees enough to earn a $1.875 million bonus as 26th overall pick in the 2013 draft, the first of the club's three first-round selections that year. The big knock on Jagielo has been his defense at third base, where he's a slow-twitch player with limited athletic ability. He worked diligently to improve his actions and first-step quickness in 2014, and he came a long way during the course of the season. As a hitter, he produced as expected, putting forth 16 home runs at high Class A Tampa despite missing a month and change with a strained muscle near his rib cage. His power grades as at least plus, though frequent strikeouts project to make him a well below-average hitter. Slated to play in the Arizona Fall League to make up for that lost time, Jagielo was hit by a pitch during instructional league and fractured a bone in his face. After a successful stint at Tampa, Jagielo should move up to Double-A Trenton, where he will be part of a star-studded lineup with outfielder Aaron Judge. Scouts who aren't sold on his defense believe he will wind up as a first baseman in the long run.

Year	Club (League)	Class	AVG	G	AB	R	H	2B	3B	HR	RBI	BB	SO	SB	CS	OBP	SLG
2013	Yankees1 (GCL)	R	.000	1	2	1	0	0	0	0	0	0	0	0	0	.333	.000
	Yankees2 (GCL)	R	.286	3	7	2	2	2	0	0	0	1	2	0	0	.375	.571
	Staten Island (NYP)	SS	.266	51	184	19	49	14	1	6	27	26	54	0	0	.376	.451
2014	Yankees1 (GCL)	R	.217	7	23	3	5	0	0	2	4	3	1	0	0	.308	.478
	Tampa (FSL)	HiA	.259	85	309	43	80	14	0	16	54	38	93	0	0	.354	.460
Minor League Totals			.259	147	525	68	136	30	1	24	85	68	150	0	0	.360	.457

12 BRYAN MITCHELL, RHP

Born: April 19, 1991. **B-T:** R-R. **Ht.:** 6-3. **Wt.:** 205. **Drafted:** HS—Hamlet, N.C., 2009 (16th round). **Signed by:** Scott Lovekamp.

BA GRADE

50 Risk: High

After being steered away from his commitment to North Carolina, Mitchell's outlook has remained static in pro ball: The stuff is there, but the command isn't. That's still true, but on a much smaller scale in 2014. As a result, Mitchell made his big league debut, which included one start in which he allowed two runs in five innings against the Orioles in September. A righthander with a prototype power starter's body, Mitchell brings a fastball up to 97 mph, a power curveball in the high 70s to low 80s with 12-to-6 break and a developing changeup that has the potential to be average in the future. Because he's a Gil Patterson disciple, he's also added a cutter to his arsenal. Scouts both internally and externally grade the pitch, which checks in around the low 90s, as plus. Mitchell can rush his delivery at times and also gets side-to-side, which messes with his command. At worst, Mitchell could be an effective arm out of the bullpen, but the Yankees still believe he can start, and he'll likely continue to develop in that role at Triple-A Scranton Wilkes-Barre.

Year	Club (League)	Class	W	L	ERA	G	GS	CG	SV	IP	H	HR	BB	SO	K/9	WHIP	AVG
2012	Charleston (SAL)	LoA	9	11	4.58	27	26	0	0	120	107	7	72	121	9.1	1.49	.240
2013	Tampa (FSL)	HiA	4	11	5.12	24	23	1	0	127	144	5	53	104	7.4	1.56	.289
	Trenton (EL)	AA	0	0	1.93	3	3	0	0	19	14	0	5	16	7.7	1.02	.206
2014	Trenton (EL)	AA	2	5	4.84	14	13	0	0	61	64	6	29	60	8.8	1.52	.268
	Scranton/W-B (IL)	AAA	4	2	3.67	9	8	0	0	42	45	5	16	34	7.3	1.46	.281
	New York (AL)	MAJ	0	1	2.45	3	1	0	0	11	10	0	3	7	5.7	1.18	.256
Major League Totals			0	1	2.45	3	1	0	0	11	10	0	3	7	5.7	1.18	.256
Minor League Totals			22	34	4.45	102	97	1	0	476	474	30	229	433	8.2	1.48	.261

13 TYLER WADE, SS

Born: Nov. 23, 1994. **B-T:** L-R. **Ht.:** 6-1. **Wt.:** 180. **Drafted:** HS—Murrieta, Calif., 2013 (4th round). **Signed by:** David Keith.

The Yankees boast a pack of talented shortstops at the lower levels, most of them plucked from Latin America as teenagers. Wade is the exception. A prep fourth-rounder in 2013 out of the southern part of California, Wade originally was slated to split time at low Class A Charleston with Abiatal Avelino. When Avelino got hurt, however, Wade took on a bigger workload and impressed scouts along the way. A smooth, athletic defender, Wade's hands and instincts, along with just enough arm for the position, ranked him among the best glove men in the South Atlantic League. His lefthanded swing is loose and fluid, and he keeps his hands inside the ball very well, producing lots of line-drive contact. He's a tick above-average as a runner, but his 49 percent success rate shows he could stand some refinement when it comes to basestealing. Wade homered only once in 2014 but finished second on his team with 24 doubles, and scouts believe he has room to add more power to his frame. After a successful intro to full-season ball, Wade likely will spend 2014 at high Class A Tampa as a 20-year-old.

Year	Club (League)	Class	AVG	G	AB	R	H	2B	3B	HR	RBI	BB	SO	SB	CS	OBP	SLG
2013	Yankees1 (GCL)	R	.309	46	162	37	50	10	0	0	12	32	42	11	1	.429	.370
	Staten Island (NYP)	SS	.077	4	13	0	1	0	0	0	1	2	4	0	0	.200	.077
2014	Charleston (SAL)	LoA	.272	129	507	77	138	24	6	1	51	57	118	22	13	.350	.349
Minor League Totals			.277	179	682	114	189	34	6	1	64	91	164	33	14	.367	.349

14 MANNY BANUELOS, LHP

Born: March 13, 1991. **B-T:** L-L. **Ht.:** 5-10. **Wt.:** 155. **Signed:** Mexico, 2008. **Signed by:** Lee Sigman.

The bad news for Banuelos entering 2014 was simple: He'd missed nearly all of the previous two seasons, first while rehabbing his elbow in an attempt to avoid Tommy John surgery, then rehabbing from actual T.J. surgery, which took place in October 2012. The good news was, even with all the lost time, he was still just 23 years old. The returns in 2014 weren't outstanding, but they definitely provided a reason for cautious optimism. Banuelos' fastball, which had peaked at 97 mph in the past, was up to 94 by the end of the year, and was steadily in the low 90s. He didn't show the same confidence or quality with his changeup and curveball. The Yankees helped Banuelos develop a hybrid slider-cutter, which he threw in the high 80s. He showed more conviction in his stuff in instructional league, and the organization will look for more command of his offspeed stuff in 2015, which he'll begin at Triple-A Scranton/Wilkes-Barre with the chance to take a step toward fulfilling his future as a back-end starter.

Year	Club (League)	Class	W	L	ERA	G	GS	CG	SV	IP	H	HR	BB	SO	K/9	WHIP	AVG
2012	Scranton/W-B (IL)	AAA	0	2	4.50	6	6	0	0	24	29	2	10	22	8.3	1.63	.299
2013	Did not play—Injured																
2014	Tampa (FSL)	HiA	0	0	2.84	5	5	0	0	13	10	0	2	14	9.9	0.95	.213
	Trenton (EL)	AA	1	3	4.59	17	16	0	0	49	40	8	19	44	8.1	1.20	.220
	Scranton/W-B (IL)	AAA	1	0	3.60	4	4	0	0	15	14	2	10	13	7.8	1.60	.241
Minor League Totals			21	22	3.29	112	95	1	0	446	397	31	178	446	9.0	1.29	.238

15 ABIATAL AVELINO, SS

Born: Feb. 14, 1995 **B-T:** R-R. **Ht.:** 5-11. **Wt.:** 200. **Signed:** Dominican Republic, 2011. **Signed by:** Jose Sabino.

Among the Yankees' pack of talented and projectable young shortstops, Avelino stands at or near the top of the developmental chain. After impressing scouts in the Rookie-level Gulf Coast League in 2013 with his combination of offensive and defensive skills, Avelino skipped up the chain to low Class A Charleston in 2014. He split time at shortstop with Tyler Wade there, but eventually had his season severely limited by a quad injury that kept him out for two months and away from Charleston slightly longer. Avelino utilizes a stocky and strong frame to hit to all fields, albeit without much power so far in his young career (just three home runs in 671 at-bats), but he has holes in his plate coverage and ability to recognize pitches. He possesses excellent range at shortstop, but scouts question his reactions in the field at times. His arm grades as plus. He's much more instinctual on the basepaths, where he's swiped 59 bags in 70 tries (84 percent) in his young career. Avelino likely will head back to Charleston for a second try in 2015.

Year	Club (League)	Class	AVG	G	AB	R	H	2B	3B	HR	RBI	BB	SO	SB	CS	OBP	SLG
2012	Yankees 1 (DSL)	R	.302	57	222	46	67	11	1	1	25	27	34	20	2	.398	.374
2013	Yankees1 (GCL)	R	.259	17	58	14	15	2	1	0	4	7	7	9	3	.348	.328
	Yankees2 (GCL)	R	.400	17	70	21	28	5	4	0	13	9	4	17	1	.481	.586
	Staten Island (NYP)	SS	.243	17	70	10	17	2	0	0	6	4	6	2	0	.303	.271
2014	Yankees1 (GCL)	R	.355	8	31	7	11	6	0	0	3	2	4	0	0	.394	.548
	Charleston (SAL)	LoA	.232	53	220	31	51	12	1	2	12	17	44	11	5	.296	.323
Minor League Totals			.282	169	671	129	189	38	7	3	63	66	99	59	11	.361	.373

16 TYLER AUSTIN, OF/1B

BA GRADE

45 Risk: Medium

Born: Sept. 16, 1991. **B-T:** R-R. **Ht.:** 6-2. **Wt.:** 200. **Drafted:** HS—Conyers, Ga., 2010 (13th round). **Signed by:** Darryl Monroe.

The 2014 season was a tale of two halves for Austin, who spent 2013 dealing with nagging tenderness in his right wrist. He came back for Double-A Trenton's run to the Eastern League championship, but the pain cropped up again in the Arizona Fall League, and again during 2014 spring training. Over the first three months, it looked as if Austin's power was sapped. After July 1, however, he hit .302/.353/.483 with six of his nine homers and more than half of his extra-base hits. His exit velocity also crept to above-average as the year wore on. Besides getting healthy, Austin also lowered his hands at the plate, which the Yankees believe helped him as well. His defense, speed and arm in the outfield are all average, and he has dabbled at first and third base over the past few seasons. Austin's short, quick swing and power is what will get him to the big leagues, and if his power resurgence is real, then his potential as an everyday outfielder looks more realistic than it did a year ago. He likely will head to Triple-A Scranton/Wilkes-Barre in 2015, where he'll once again team up with Slade Heathcott and Ramon Flores.

Year	Club (League)	Class	AVG	G	AB	R	H	2B	3B	HR	RBI	BB	SO	SB	CS	OBP	SLG
2012	Charleston (SAL)	LoA	.320	70	266	69	85	22	5	14	54	37	68	17	2	.405	.598
	Yankees (GCL)	R	.500	2	6	1	3	0	0	1	2	1	1	0	0	.571	1.000
	Tampa (FSL)	HiA	.321	36	134	20	43	13	1	2	23	12	28	6	0	.385	.478
	Trenton (EL)	AA	.286	2	7	2	2	0	0	0	1	1	1	0	0	.375	.286
2013	Yankees2 (GCL)	R	.667	2	6	1	4	0	0	0	1	0	0	0	0	.714	.667
	Trenton (EL)	AA	.257	83	319	43	82	17	1	6	40	41	79	4	0	.344	.373
2014	Trenton (EL)	AA	.275	105	396	56	109	20	5	9	47	36	80	3	2	.336	.419
Minor League Totals			.298	349	1314	221	391	90	14	38	203	144	297	48	4	.372	.474

17 JAKE CAVE, OF

BA GRADE

50 Risk: High

Born: Dec. 7, 1992. **B-T:** L-L. **Ht.:** 6-0. **Wt.:** 179. **Drafted:** HS—Hampton, Va., 2011 (6th round). **Signed by:** Scott Lovekamp.

After a knee injury cost Cave nearly all of his first two seasons after being drafted, he put together a fine 2013 at low Class A Charleston and jumped onto the Yankees' prospect radar. Cave plays with an all-out attitude that ranks, probably for the better, just a tick below that of system-mate Slade Heathcott. Though he spent most of his time in center field, Cave can play all three outfield spots, thanks to average range and arm strength. He has no true plus tool, but everything but power is at least average. He made adjustments in 2014, including moving away from a rotational swing and learning to trust his hands more. Those adjustments paid off with a system-best 165 hits, a mark that tied him for eighth in the minors. He'll have to tap into his power more often—which plays as below-average, but the Yankees believe can produce 12-15 home runs per year—if he does wind up moving to a corner. Opposing scouts also have noted that Cave struggles with breaking pitches. After a cameo at Double-A Trenton toward the end of 2014, Cave will most likely begin 2015 back in Trenton, in the same outfield with Mason Williams and Aaron Judge.

Year	Club (League)	Class	AVG	G	AB	R	H	2B	3B	HR	RBI	BB	SO	SB	CS	OBP	SLG
2012	Did not play—Injured																
2013	Charleston (SAL)	LoA	.282	115	464	69	131	37	6	2	31	40	110	18	9	.347	.401
2014	Tampa (FSL)	HiA	.304	90	385	50	117	18	4	3	24	28	80	10	3	.354	.395
	Trenton (EL)	AA	.273	42	176	24	48	10	5	4	18	18	44	2	3	.344	.455
Minor League Totals			.288	248	1026	143	296	65	15	9	73	87	234	30	15	.349	.407

18 J.R. MURPHY, C

BA GRADE
45 Risk: Medium

Born: May 13, 1991. **B-T:** R-R. **Ht.:** 5-11. **Wt.:** 195. **Drafted:** HS—Bradenton, Fla., 2009 (2nd round). **Signed by:** Jeff Deardorff/Brian Barber.

Murphy has taken part in Mariano Rivera's final meeting at the mound in 2013 was in the dugout for Derek Jeter's final game at Yankee Stadium in 2014. Those moments would rank as nice highlights for just about any player, but Murphy reached another milestone in 2014 when he socked his first big league homer. But because he spent so much time as Brian McCann's understudy while Francisco Cervelli was on the disabled list, Murphy was rusty when he did see everyday time at Triple-A Scranton/Wilkes-Barre. Evaluators noticed it in his throws, which sometimes died as they got to second base, and in his Triple-A performance. A foul ball off the mask in August concussed Murphy, costing him about two weeks. Scouts see him as an average player in the long run, with average running and defensive abilities and a serviceable bat that could provide doubles power. With Cervelli traded to the Pirates and Gary Sanchez slated to start at Triple-A, Murphy will battle Austin Romine to be McCann's primary backup in 2015.

Year	Club (League)	Class	AVG	G	AB	R	H	2B	3B	HR	RBI	BB	SO	SB	CS	OBP	SLG
2012	Tampa (FSL)	HiA	.257	67	265	39	68	14	1	5	28	26	41	4	3	.322	.374
	Trenton (EL)	AA	.231	43	147	23	34	12	1	4	16	16	32	0	0	.306	.408
2013	Trenton (EL)	AA	.268	49	183	34	49	10	0	6	25	24	32	1	0	.352	.421
	Scranton/W-B (IL)	AAA	.270	59	230	26	62	19	0	6	21	23	41	0	1	.342	.430
	New York (AL)	MAJ	.154	16	26	3	4	1	0	0	1	1	9	0	0	.185	.192
2014	Scranton/W-B (IL)	AAA	.246	51	179	17	44	9	0	6	28	13	42	0	0	.292	.397
	New York (AL)	MAJ	.284	32	81	7	23	4	0	1	9	4	22	0	0	.318	.370
Major League Totals			.252	48	107	10	27	5	0	1	10	5	31	0	0	.286	.327
Minor League Totals			.263	451	1708	228	450	110	4	42	225	162	307	11	9	.327	.406

19 AUSTIN DeCARR, RHP

BA GRADE
50 Risk: High

Born: March 14, 1995. **B-T:** R-R. **Ht.:** 6-3. **Wt.:** 218. **Drafted:** HS—Salisbury, Conn., 2014 (3rd round) **Signed by:** Matt Hyde.

No team drafted DeCarr when he finished high school in Massachusetts in 2013, but he pulled down $1 million from the Yankees a year later after he spent a year at a prep school in Connecticut. DeCarr had a bone spur removed from his elbow as a high school junior, but his velocity has returned and he now bumps 96 mph and sits at 90-94. Besides the fastball, which he throws downhill from a high three-quarters arm slot, DeCarr also brings a hammer curveball in the low 80s that features 11-to-5 break as his clear out-pitch. He's working on further developing his mid-80s changeup, which he threw often in the Rookie-level Gulf Coast League and instructional league in 2014. DeCarr earned high marks from scouts in and out of the organization for his work ethic, mound demeanor and drive to improve. He's likely ticketed for short-season Staten Island in 2015, though he could also be bound for the new Rookie-level Pulaski affiliate.

Year	Club (League)	Class	W	L	ERA	G	GS	CG	SV	IP	H	HR	BB	SO	K/9	WHIP	AVG
2014	Yankees1 (GCL)	R	2	1	4.63	11	8	0	0	23	20	1	7	24	9.3	1.16	.222
Minor League Totals			2	1	4.63	11	8	0	0	23	20	1	7	24	9.3	1.16	.222

20 TY HENSLEY, RHP

BA GRADE
50 Risk: Extreme

Born: July 30, 1993. **B-T:** R-R. **Ht.:** 6-5. **Wt.:** 220. **Drafted:** HS—Edmond, Okla., 2012 (1st round). **Signed by:** Lloyd Simmons/Dennis Woody.

Hensley had already dealt with more than his fair share of injuries. His post-draft physical in 2012 had turned up a shoulder irregularity, and he missed all of 2013 after having surgery on both hips. He finally made it out of complex ball and under the lights in 2014 at short-season Staten Island, where the results were promising. Hensley's fastball, which touched 96-97 mph before the draft, was back up to 96 in the New York-Penn League. He pitched closer to 90-93 mph but showed he had a little extra in the tank when needed. He also found the handle on his previous out-pitch, a 12-to-6 hook in the mid-70s that reached an above-average spin rate of 2,900 revolutions per minute, according to TrackMan readings. Hensley still is working to develop his changeup and trust his stuff again after such a long layoff, but the Yankees are thrilled that he's back, healthy and pitching. He'll join low Class A Charleston in 2015.

Year	Club (League)	Class	W	L	ERA	G	GS	CG	SV	IP	H	HR	BB	SO	K/9	WHIP	AVG
2012	Yankees (GCL)	R	1	2	3.00	5	4	0	0	12	8	1	7	14	10.5	1.25	.174
2013	Did not play—Injured																
2014	Yankees1 (GCL)	R	0	0	2.37	7	6	0	0	19	16	2	9	23	10.9	1.32	.229
	Staten Island (NYP)	SS	0	0	3.86	4	4	0	0	12	11	0	2	17	13.1	1.11	.244
Minor League Totals			1	2	2.95	16	14	0	0	43	35	3	18	54	11.4	1.24	.217

21 THAIRO ESTRADA, SS

BA GRADE

50 Risk: Extreme

Born: Feb. 22, 1996. **B-T:** R-R. **Ht.:** 5-10. **Wt.:** 155. **Signed:** Venezuela, 2012. **Signed by:** Alan Atacho/Ricardo Finol.

Inked for a bonus of just less than $50,000, Estrada has proven to be a worthy investment so far for the Yankees. Though he was limited to just 21 games in 2014 with a groin injury, he still showed signs of being a player worth watching at short-season Staten Island. Despite being just 18 years old, Estrada is a heady player who reads swings well and knows how to anticipate at shortstop, which only accentuates his above-average arm and range in the field. Opposing scouts who saw him in 2014 saw a plus fielder with a bat that projects to be average in the long run. The Yankees believe he'll make contact but will also grow into below-average power in the 10-12 home run range as he grows and adds muscle to his frame. He spent time in instructional league to make up for some of the time lost to injury, and he could wind up in the New York-Penn League again in 2015 after extended spring training ends.

Year	Club (League)	Class	AVG	G	AB	R	H	2B	3B	HR	RBI	BB	SO	SB	CS	OBP	SLG
2013	Yankees2 (GCL)	R	.278	50	176	28	49	11	5	2	17	12	30	7	5	.350	.432
2014	Staten Island (NYP)	SS	.271	17	59	11	16	1	0	0	2	6	7	8	1	.348	.288
	Yankees1 (GCL)	R	.273	6	22	2	6	2	0	0	4	1	4	0	0	.304	.364
Minor League Totals			.276	73	257	41	71	14	5	2	23	19	41	15	6	.346	.393

22 ANGEL AGUILAR, SS

BA GRADE

50 Risk: Extreme

Born: June 13, 1995. **B-T:** R-R. **Ht.:** 6-0. **Wt.:** 170. **Signed:** Venezuela, 2012. **Signed by:** Cesar Suarez/Alan Atacho.

Aguilar signed out of Venezuela for $60,000 and spent his first two seasons in the Rookie-level Dominican Summer League. He wasn't in the plans to come stateside in 2014, but he forced the organization's hand. He's a heady player who shows his aptitude in the way he positions himself and reads swings on defense. Aguilar's range is solid for the position, and his hands are above-average. He's an above-average runner (6.7-second 60-yard dash times) with improving power, tying for second in the Rookie-level Gulf Coast League. Despite his lean frame, Aguilar is strong through his hands and wrists, and he uses a swing that features a leg kick as a timing mechanism and strong wrist snap at the end. He will begin 2015 in extended spring training before an assignment to one of the Yankees' three short-season clubs.

Year	Club (League)	Class	AVG	G	AB	R	H	2B	3B	HR	RBI	BB	SO	SB	CS	OBP	SLG
2012	Yankees 2 (DSL)	R	.234	49	171	19	40	3	0	0	11	8	33	1	0	.284	.251
2013	Yankees2 (DSL)	R	.262	62	229	35	60	18	3	3	37	17	44	2	1	.326	.406
2014	Yankees2 (GCL)	R	.311	39	151	34	47	11	1	7	31	14	28	8	2	.373	.536
Minor League Totals			.267	150	551	88	147	32	4	10	79	39	105	11	3	.326	.394

23 LEONARDO MOLINA, OF

BA GRADE

50 Risk: Extreme

Born: July 31, 1997. **B-T:** R-R. **Ht.:** 6-2. **Wt.:** 180. **Signed:** Dominican Republic, 2013. **Signed by:** Miguel Benitez.

The Yankees' biggest bonus baby in 2013, Molina signed for $1.4 million on Aug. 1 when he turned 16. Despite his age, he was pushed aggressively in 2014 and sent to the Rookie-level Gulf Coast League, where he was the second-youngest player in the league, older by nine days than the Phillies' Luis Encarnacion. Despite his poor performance, scouts were impressed with the quality at-bats he took and the overall package of tools. He's a 60 runner on the 20-80 scouting scale with a well above-average arm in center field. He's a larger player already at 6-foot-2 and 180 pounds, so he must watch his body going forward as he grows from what was essentially a high school sophomore into a more adult frame. As he matures, Molina should add more power, and the Yankees are excited by what they've already seen. Molina will likely spend another summer in extended spring training followed by the GCL, but an assignment to short-season Staten Island or Rookie-level Pulaski isn't out of the question.

Year	Club (League)	Class	AVG	G	AB	R	H	2B	3B	HR	RBI	BB	SO	SB	CS	OBP	SLG
2014	Yankees1 (GCL)	R	.193	53	192	18	37	10	0	1	21	19	51	6	1	.267	.260
Minor League Totals			.193	53	192	18	37	10	0	1	21	19	51	6	1	.267	.260

24 JUAN DE LEON, OF

BA GRADE

50 Risk: Extreme

Born: Sept. 13, 1997. **B-T:** R-R. **Ht.:** 6-2. **Wt.:** 185. **Signed:** Dominican Republic, 2014 **Signed by:** Esteban Castillo.

Ranked as the second-best hitter in the 2014-15 international class behind only Rays signee Adrian Rondon, De Leon signed with the Yankees on July 2 for the hefty price tag of $2 million. De Leon is big, strong and powerful, and the Yankees believe he will only grow moreso. He's cleaned up his previous all-or-nothing approach and now shows a short, quick swing with premium power generated in part by strength in his wrists and tremendous bat speed. Like most prospects his age, De Leon can get overaggressive and will fly open at times. He's a center fielder now, but scouts believe he'll eventually move to the corner, where his above-average arm will play, especially if he develops the kind of power most expect. He's an average runner at present. Like the rest of the Yankees' enormous July 2 class, he should begin 2015 in extended spring training and finish in the Rookie-level Gulf Coast League.

Year	Club (League)	Class	AVG	G	AB	R	H	2B	3B	HR	RBI	BB	SO	SB	CS	OBP	SLG
2014	Did not play—Signed 2015 contract																

25 DERMIS GARCIA, SS

Born: Jan. 7, 1998. **B-T:** R-R. **Ht.:** 6-3. **Wt.:** 200. **Signed:** Dominican Republic, 2014. **Signed by:** Miguel Benitez.

BA GRADE
50 Risk: Extreme

Trained by Moreno Tejada, whose program in the Dominican Republic helped produce the Twins' Miguel Sano and Micker Adolfo of the White Sox, Garcia signed with the Yankees for $3 million during their international spending boom in 2014. That bonus amount ties Gary Sanchez for the fifth-highest ever handed out by the franchise. Garcia already has added 15 pounds since signing, and he will most likely outgrow shortstop at some point and have to move either to third base, where his double-plus arm will play, or the outfield. He's got soft hands as well, which should help him stay in the dirt long term. Garcia also has double-plus raw power to go with the massive arm, and his overall package has drawn comparisons with Sano at the same age. The Rookie-level Gulf Coast League is his likely assignment in 2015 after extended spring training concludes.

Year	Club (League)	Class	AVG	G	AB	R	H	2B	3B	HR	RBI	BB	SO	SB	CS	OBP	SLG
2014	Did not play—Signed 2015 contract																

26 JOSE RAMIREZ, RHP

Born: Jan. 21, 1990. **B-T:** R-R. **Ht.:** 6-3. **Wt.:** 190. **Signed:** Dominican Republic, 2007. **Signed by:** Victor Mata.

BA GRADE
45 Risk: Medium

Making his fifth appearance in the Handbook, Ramirez remains a tease, with a dynamite fastball/changeup combination and developing slider. Injuries, first to his oblique in 2013 and to his lat muscles in 2014, have stunted his development and pushed him to the bullpen. Ramirez's fastball still checks in at the mid- to upper 90s with good life, and his changeup still features plenty of late fade. Those injuries may also have contributed to the control problems he's experienced after he advanced past Double-A Trenton. His long arm action, the primary culprit for his inconsistent breaking ball, also stymies his control. After a nearly-lost season, Ramirez seems destined to return to Triple-A Scranton/Wilkes-Barre.

Year	Club (League)	Class	W	L	ERA	G	GS	CG	SV	IP	H	HR	BB	SO	K/9	WHIP	AVG
2012	Tampa (FSL)	HiA	7	6	3.19	21	18	0	0	99	92	7	30	94	8.6	1.24	.239
2013	Trenton (EL)	AA	1	3	2.76	9	8	0	1	42	28	7	15	50	10.6	1.02	.192
	Scranton/W-B (IL)	AAA	1	3	4.88	8	8	0	0	31	29	3	21	28	8.0	1.60	.259
2014	New York (AL)	MAJ	0	2	5.40	8	0	0	0	10	11	2	7	10	9.0	1.80	.275
	Scranton/W-B (IL)	AAA	3	0	1.46	9	0	0	1	12	13	0	10	16	11.7	1.86	.265
Major League Totals			0	2	5.40	8	0	0	0	10	11	2	7	10	9.0	1.80	.275
Minor League Totals			29	32	3.66	114	96	0	2	506	456	39	195	486	8.6	1.29	.239

27 RAMON FLORES, OF

Born: March 26, 1992. **B-T:** L-L. **Ht.:** 5-10. **Wt.:** 150. **Signed:** Venezuela, 2008. **Signed by:** Ricardo Finol.

BA GRADE
45 Risk: Medium

As the 2013 season got underway, the Double-A Trenton outfield of Flores, Slade Heathcott and Tyler Austin was tabbed one of the most tantalizing in the sport. Two years later, only Flores, the youngest of the bunch, has reached Triple-A Scranton/Wilkes-Barre. His 2014 season was interrupted by a broken ankle at midseason, but he still put up seven home runs in 63 games, which was just four off of his career high of 11, set back in 2011 at low Class A Charleston. Flores always has had an above-average knowledge of the strike zone, as shown by his career walk rate of 11.4 percent, and feel to hit, but the development of his power will be key going forward because he doesn't have the defensive chops to play center field on an everyday basis. At 22, Flores was one of the youngest players in the International League. He'll return there in 2015 to see if he can elevate his profile past what evaluators currently peg as a useful extra outfielder.

Year	Club (League)	Class	AVG	G	AB	R	H	2B	3B	HR	RBI	BB	SO	SB	CS	OBP	SLG
2012	Tampa (FSL)	HiA	.302	131	517	83	156	29	7	6	39	54	85	24	9	.370	.420
	Trenton (EL)	AA	.400	1	5	2	2	0	0	1	2	0	0	0	0	.400	1.000
2013	Trenton (EL)	AA	.260	136	534	79	139	25	6	6	55	77	98	7	6	.353	.363
2014	Yankees2 (GCL)	R	.333	3	9	2	3	1	0	1	1	1	3	0	0	.400	.778
	Yankees1 (GCL)	R	.375	2	8	2	3	2	0	1	2	0	2	0	0	.375	1.000
	Scranton/W-B (IL)	AAA	.247	63	235	30	58	17	4	7	23	33	45	3	2	.339	.443
Minor League Totals			.271	588	2207	315	597	118	27	36	226	290	408	59	26	.358	.397

28 JOSE PIRELA, 2B

BA GRADE
45 Risk: Medium

Born: Nov. 21, 1989. **B-T:** R-R. **Ht.:** 5-11. **Wt.:** 210. **Signed:** Venezuela, 2006. **Signed by:** Cesar Suarez/Ricardo Finol.

It's taken a while for him to marinate but Pirela, signed for $300,000 as a shortstop out of Venezuela in 2006, finally made it to the major leagues toward the end of 2014. He led the Triple-A International League in hits with 163, a figure that placed him among the top 15 in the minors. Though still a question mark on defense no matter where he plays, Pirela spent time at every position except catcher and third base in 2014. He grinds out at-bats, has shown ability to go with the pitch with two strikes and in 2014 posted the highest full-season slugging percentage of his career at .441. A potential utility candidate in the mold of Yangervis Solarte, Pirela will battle with Rob Refsnyder for the Yankees' starting second base job in 2015.

Year	Club (League)	Class	AVG	G	AB	R	H	2B	3B	HR	RBI	BB	SO	SB	CS	OBP	SLG
2012	Trenton (EL)	AA	.293	82	317	55	93	19	3	8	33	26	48	9	3	.356	.448
2013	Scranton/W-B (IL)	AAA	.304	5	23	3	7	0	0	0	1	1	2	1	0	.333	.304
	Trenton (EL)	AA	.272	124	459	73	125	27	5	10	62	56	61	18	3	.359	.418
2014	Scranton/W-B (IL)	AAA	.305	130	535	87	163	21	11	10	60	37	74	15	7	.351	.441
	New York (AL)	MAJ	.333	7	24	6	8	1	2	0	3	1	4	0	0	.360	.542
Major League Totals			.333	7	24	6	8	1	2	0	3	1	4	0	0	.360	.542
Minor League Totals			.273	796	3082	464	842	137	46	45	347	281	480	110	42	.339	.391

29 JOSE CAMPOS, RHP

BA GRADE
45 Risk: High

Born: July 27, 1992. **B-T:** R-R. **Ht.:** 6-4. **Wt.:** 200. **Signed:** Venezuela, 2009. **Signed by:** Emilio Carrasquel/Patrick Guerrero (Mariners).

When pitcher after pitcher succumbed to Tommy John surgery in 2014, the Yankees were not immune. Campos, the second piece they received from the Mariners in the Michael Pineda-Jesus Montero swap, had the procedure in April. Before the operation, he featured a 91-93 mph fastball with life, a changeup at 82-84 and a downer curveball in the mid-70s. His curveball's shape varies, leading some evaluators to mistake it for a slider at times. Campos did not make it back to the mound in 2014 following surgery, and he also missed instructional league. He turns 23 during the 2015 season, but has upside potential. Now he will need to make up for lost time if he hopes to reach his ceiling of a back-end starter.

Year	Club (League)	Class	W	L	ERA	G	GS	CG	SV	IP	H	HR	BB	SO	K/9	WHIP	AVG
2012	Charleston (SAL)	LoA	3	0	4.01	5	5	0	0	25	20	2	8	26	9.5	1.14	.213
2013	Charleston (SAL)	LoA	4	2	3.41	26	19	0	2	87	82	5	16	77	8.0	1.13	.249
2014	Did not play—Injured																
Minor League Totals			21	12	3.37	71	54	1	3	283	255	14	72	270	8.6	1.16	.238

30 MASON WILLIAMS, OF

BA GRADE
45 Risk: High

Born: Aug. 21, 1991. **B-T:** L-R. **Ht.:** 6-1. **Wt.:** 180. **Drafted:** HS—Winter Garden, Fla., 2010 (4th round). **Signed by:** Jeff Deardorff.

The Yankees' No. 1 prospect entering 2013, Williams has seen his career go downhill since then, with poor performance and inconsistent effort going hand in hand. His power has vanished, with consecutive seasons of sub-.100 isolated slugging, and he was pulled on multiple occasions in 2014 for failing to run out groundballs. His jailbreak swing is largely to blame for the power outage. He still runs and defends at above-average levels when he's invested. The Yankees once were counting on Williams, but now he appears to be no more than a fourth outfielder who's likely headed for a repeat season at Double-A Trenton.

Year	Club (League)	Class	AVG	G	AB	R	H	2B	3B	HR	RBI	BB	SO	SB	CS	OBP	SLG
2012	Charleston (SAL)	LoA	.304	69	276	55	84	19	4	8	28	21	33	19	9	.359	.489
	Tampa (FSL)	HiA	.277	22	83	13	23	3	0	3	7	3	14	1	4	.302	.422
2013	Tampa (FSL)	HiA	.261	100	406	56	106	21	3	3	24	39	61	15	9	.327	.350
	Trenton (EL)	AA	.153	17	72	7	11	3	1	1	4	1	18	0	0	.164	.264
2014	Trenton (EL)	AA	.223	128	507	67	113	18	4	5	40	47	68	21	8	.290	.304
Minor League Totals			.267	409	1631	240	435	75	18	23	134	132	239	85	44	.323	.377

Oakland Athletics

BY JIM SHONERD

Take your pick of obligatory card-game metaphors. General manager Billy Beane went all in. Or maybe he said "hit me" when he already had 18 showing. The bottom line is that the Athletics raised the stakes significantly on their 2014 season, but came away with another early exit form the postseason.

The A's already had one of the best, most balanced teams in baseball through the first half when Beane upped the ante on July 4 by trading for Jeff Samardzija, one of the most sought-after arms on the market, and Jason Hammel from the Cubs.

To do so, he sacrificed the organization's two highest-ranked prospects coming into the season, shortstop Addison Russell and outfielder Billy McKinney. Russell had been Oakland's most prized prospect, its supposed future at shortstop, and the trade deprived an already middle-of-the-pack farm system of two first-round talents.

Beane made another headline-grabbing move, though it didn't affect the system, at the July 31 trade deadline when he dealt Yoenis Cespedes and a 2015 supplemental second-round pick to the Red Sox for Jon Lester and Jonny Gomes.

All the A's have to show for these and other moves is an epic second-half collapse.

The A's went just 29-38 after the all-star break, the worst second-half record of any team ever to make the playoffs. In the process, they plummeted from having the best record in baseball to barely clinching their postseason berth on the season's final day.

Oakland's relief at landing a third straight playoff trip was short lived, for the A's blew a four-run lead in the wild card game against the Royals, eventually losing 9-8 in 12 innings.

Beane stuck to his guns after the season, saying the trades were necessary or else the team wouldn't have made the playoffs at all. Say what you will about Beane, the GM is not one to sit on his hands. True to form, he immediately began overhauling the roster after the season. Beane has hit the reset button before, most recently during the 2011-12 offseason when he traded away three all-stars—Andrew Bailey, Trevor Cahill and Gio Gonzalez—for prospects. This year's A's will try to make history repeat itself, as the 2012 A's surged to an unexpected division title.

This latest round of remodeling began in November when Beane dealt all-star third baseman Josh Donaldson to the Blue Jays for Brett Lawrie and three prospects—shortstop Franklin Barreto, righthander Kendall Graveman and lefty

Billy Beane sacrificed future value in multiple trades, but Oakland still made an early exit

TOP PROSPECTS OF THE DECADE

Year	Player, Pos.	2014 Org
2005	Nick Swisher, of	Indians
2006	Daric Barton, 1b	Athletics
2007	Travis Buck, of	Padres
2008	Daric Barton, 1b	Athletics
2009	Brett Anderson, lhp	Rockies
2010	Chris Carter, 1b/of	Astros
2011	Grant Green, ss	Angels
2012	Jarrod Parker, rhp	Athletics
2013	Addison Russell, ss	Cubs
2014	Addison Russell, ss	Cubs

Sean Nolin. Samardzija and Brandon Moss were traded away during to Winter Meetings to the White Sox and Indians, respectively, to bring in more young players. As expected, Lester departed in free agency.

Aside from the new imports, the bulk of the frontline prospects Oakland has in its system played together at high Class A Stockton in 2014 and will graduate to Double-A Midland in 2015, led by shortstop Daniel Robertson and first baseman Matt Olson.

The system won't provide much help in 2015, but then it didn't in 2014 either. Sonny Gray and closer Sean Doolittle were the only players drafted and developed by Oakland to make meaningful contributions. If the A's are going to compete again in 2015, they'll once again be a team built from without.

General manager: Billy Beane. **Farm director:** Keith Lieppman. **Scouting director:** Eric Kubota.

Class	Team	League	W	L	PCT	Finish	Manager
Majors	Oakland Athletics	American	88	74	.543	t-8th (30)	Bob Melvin
Triple-A	*Sacramento River Cats	Pacific Coast	79	65	.549	4th (16)	Steve Scarsone
Double-A	Midland RockHounds	Texas	77	63	.550	2nd (8)	Aaron Nieckula
High A	Stockton Ports	California	85	55	.607	1st (10)	Ryan Christenson
Low A	Beloit Snappers	Midwest	55	84	.396	16th (16)	Rick Magnante
Short season	Vermont Lake Monsters	New York-Penn	33	43	.434	t-12th (14)	David Newhan
Rookie	AZL Athletics	Arizona	27	28	.491	7th (14)	Ruben Escalera
Overall Minor League Record			356	338	.513	11th (30)	

*Affiliate will be Nashville (Pacific Coast) in 2015.

THIS YEAR'S TOP 30

No.	Player, Pos.	Grade/Risk
1.	Daniel Robertson, ss	55/Medium
2.	Franklin Barreto, ss	60/High
3.	Matt Olson, 1b	55/High
4.	Matt Chapman, 3b	55/High
5.	Renato Nunez, 3b	55/High
6.	Chris Bassitt, rhp	50/Medium
7.	Kendall Graveman, rhp	45/Low
8.	Sean Nolin, lhp	45/Low
9.	Dillon Overton, lhp	55/High
10.	Rangel Ravelo, 1b	45/Low
11.	Raul Alcantara, rhp	50/High
12.	Chad Pinder, 2b/ss	50/High
13.	Max Muncy, 1b/3b	45/Medium
14.	Seth Streich, rhp	45/Medium
15.	Daniel Gossett, rhp	50/High
16.	Yairo Munoz, ss	50/High
17.	Joey Wendle, 2b	45/Medium
18.	Bobby Wahl, rhp	45/Medium
19.	Dylan Covey, rhp	50/High
20.	Brett Graves, rhp	50/High
21.	Boog Powell, of	45/Medium
22.	Mark Canha, 1b/of	45/Medium
23.	Ryon Healy, 3b/1b	45/Medium
24.	Billy Burns, of	45/Medium
25.	Kyle Finnegan, rhp	45/Medium
26.	Chris Jensen, rhp	45/Medium
27.	Arnold Leon, rhp	45/Medium
28.	Heath Fillmyer, rhp	50/Extreme
29.	Jordan Schwartz, rhp	50/Extreme
30.	Trace Loehr, ss	50/Extreme

LAST YEAR'S TOP 30

No.	Player, Pos.	Status
1.	Addison Russell, ss	(Cubs)
2.	Billy McKinney, of	(Cubs)
3.	Michael Choice, of	(Rangers)
4.	Raul Alcantara, rhp	No. 11
5.	Michael Ynoa, rhp	(White Sox)
6.	Renato Nunez, 3b	No. 5
7.	Max Muncy, 1b	No. 13
8.	Dylan Covey, rhp	No. 19
9.	Bobby Wahl, rhp	No. 18
10.	Daniel Robertson, ss	No. 1
11.	Nolan Sanburn, rhp	(White Sox)
12.	Matt Olson, 1b	No. 3
13.	Ryon Healy, 3b/1b	No. 23
14.	Dillon Overton, lhp	No. 9
15.	Chad Pinder, ss	No. 12
16.	Kyle Finnegan, rhp	No. 25
17.	Ronald Herrera, rhp	(Padres)
18.	Chris Bostick, 2b	(Rangers)
19.	Chris Kohler, lhp	Dropped out
20.	B.J. Boyd, of	Dropped out
21.	Arnold Leon, rhp	No. 27
22.	Miles Head, 3b	Dropped out
23.	Anthony Aliotti, 1b	Dropped out
24.	Aaron Shipman, of	Dropped out
25.	Seth Streich, rhp	No. 14
26.	Dustin Driver, rhp	Dropped out
27.	Michael Taylor, of	Free agent
28.	Bruce Maxwell, c	Dropped out
29.	Tanner Peters, rhp	Dropped out
30.	Iolana Akau, c	Dropped out

BEST TOOLS

Best Hitter for Average	Daniel Robertson
Best Power Hitter	Matt Olson
Best Strike-Zone Discipline	Rangel Ravelo
Fastest Baserunner	Billy Burns
Best Athlete	Yairo Munoz
Best Fastball	Bobby Wahl
Best Curveball	Dylan Covey
Best Slider	Daniel Gossett
Best Changeup	Dillon Overton
Best Control	Kendall Graveman
Best Defensive Catcher	Iolana Akau
Best Defensive Infielder	Matt Chapman
Best Infield Arm	Matt Chapman
Best Defensive Outfielder	Billy Burns
Best Outfield Arm	Tyler Marincov

PROJECTED 2018 LINEUP

Catcher	Derek Norris
First Base	Matt Olson
Second Base	Marcus Semien
Third Base	Matt Chapman
Shortstop	Daniel Robertson
Left Field	Brett Lawrie
Center Field	Franklin Barreto
Right Field	Josh Reddick
Designated Hitter	Renato Nunez
No. 1 Starter	Sonny Gray
No. 2 Starter	Jarrod Parker
No. 3 Starter	Chris Bassitt
No. 4 Starter	Kendall Graveman
No. 5 Starter	Sean Nolin
Closer	Sean Doolittle

OAKLAND ATHLETICS

TOP 2015 ROOKIE: Kendall Graveman, rhp. He reached the big leagues with the Blue Jays in September and now he's ready to deploy his sinker/cutter in a larger role.

BREAKOUT PROSPECT: Yairo Munoz, ss. His approach needs refinement, but Munoz's tools are as exciting as any in the system.

SLEEPER: Seth Frankoff, rhp. He could emerge as a major league bullpen candidate thanks to his command and quality secondary stuff.

SOURCE OF TOP 30 TALENT

Homegrown	20	Acquired	10
College	12	Trades	9
Junior college	2	Rule 5 draft	1
High school	3	Independent leagues	0
Draft-and-follow	0	Free agents/waivers	0
Nondrafted free agents	0		
International	3		

LF
Shane Peterson
Aaron Shipman

CF
Boog Powell (21)
Billy Burns (24)
B.J. Boyd
J.P. Sportman

RF
Jaycob Brugman
Justin Higley
Tyler Marincov
Josh Whitaker

3B
Matt Chapman (4)
Renato Nunez (5)
Ryon Healy (23)
Miles Head

SS
Daniel Robertson (1)
Yairo Munoz (16)
Trace Loehr (30)
Branden Cogswell
Edwin Diaz
Carlos Hiciano

2B
Franklin Barreto (2)
Chad Pinder (12)
Joey Wendle (17)
Jesus Lopez

1B
Matt Olson (3)
Rangel Ravelo (10)
Max Muncy (13)
Mark Canha (22)
Anthony Aliotti
Sandber Pimentel

C
Bruce Maxwell
Iolana Akau
Beau Taylor
Max Kuhn

LHP

LHSP	LHRP
Sean Nolin (8)	Jeff Urlaub
Dillon Overton (9)	Mike Fagan
Chris Kohler	
Chris Lamb	
Matt Stalcup	

RHP

RHSP	RHRP
Chris Bassitt (6)	Bobby Wahl (18)
Kendall Graveman (7)	Kris Hall
Raul Alcantara (11)	Seth Frankoff
Seth Streich (14)	Ryan Dull
Daniel Gossett (15)	Koby Gauna
Dylan Covey (19)	
Brett Graves (20)	
Kyle Finnegan (25)	
Chris Jensen (26)	
Arnold Leon (27)	
Heath Fillmyer (28)	
Jordan Schwartz (29)	
Dustin Driver	
Branden Kelliher	
Tanner Peters	
Brendan McCurry	
Drew Granier	
Deck McGuire	
Josh Bowman	

BEST PURE HITTER: 3B Matt Chapman (1) has a short, compact stroke from the right side and the ball jumps off his bat. SS Branden Cogswell (7) is an advanced college hitter with strong bat-to-ball ability from a smooth lefthanded stroke and control of the strike zone. SS Trace Loehr (6) has the skill set to become an above-average hitter, possessing feel for the zone and a quick, compact stroke from the left side.

BEST POWER HITTER: Chapman has a strong, athletic build and at least plus raw power to his pull side. He is learning to use his lower half more in his swing to allow his power and strength to play more in games.

FASTEST RUNNER: Loehr, who received a 3rd round bonus, is at least a plus runner whose speed plays even faster on the field and defensively because of his first-step quickness and baseball instincts.

BEST DEFENSIVE PLAYER: Chapman was arguably the best defensive third baseman in the draft with quick feet, soft hands and the ability to make highlight reel plays while possessing at least a 70 arm capable of touching 98 off the mound.

BEST FASTBALL: Athletic RHP Brett Graves (3) has been up to 96 mph while sitting 91-94 with a loose, quick arm. RHP Branden Kelliher (8) touches 95. Converted shortstop Heath Fillmyer (5) has been 93-95 in instructs with downhill plane.

BEST SECONDARY PITCH: The curveball for RHP Daniel Gossett (2) shows plus potential with tight 12-6 shape and downer action. His changeup has a chance to be plus as well.

BEST PRO DEBUT: Gossett had the highest strikeout-walk ratio (24.7) of any AL draftee with more than 20 pro innings. OF J.P. Sportman (27) offers positional versatility and runs well in center field, hitting .309/.365/.409 while using the whole field this summer.

BEST ATHLETE: Graves is a plus athlete for a pitcher.

MOST INTRIGUING BACKGROUND: Catcher Max Kuhn (13) was drafted by the A's out of high school as a summer follow. He has a track record of hitting in college and hit in his pro debut while transitioning behind the plate.

CLOSEST TO THE MAJORS: Chapman advanced to Double-A for the playoff run and helped Midland win the Texas League, hitting .310/.375/.586 with two home runs in the playoffs.

BEST LATE-ROUND PICK: Strike-throwing RHP Joel Seddon (11) commands his fastball that sits 88-91, touching 93 out of the pen. RHP Corey

Walter (28) has impressed since signing with a strong build and power fastball with sink that sits 90-93, touching 94.

THE ONE WHO GOT AWAY: OF Denz'l Chapman (32) is a switch-hitting burner who ran a 6.44 in the 60 at the Southern California Invitational.

ASSESSMENT: After grabbing a college position player in the first round, the A's invested in pitching. More than two-thirds of their signees were arms, and nine of their first 12 picks.

2013

The Athletics have hit on three straight first-rounders, though they traded OF Billy McKinney (1). LHP Dillon Overton (2) and SS Chad Pinder (2) are the top talents left in the system.

GRADE: B

2012

SS Addison Russell (1), traded with Billy McKinney to the Cubs for Jeff Samardzija, has superstar potential. SS Daniel Robertson (1s) and 1B Matt Olson (1s) are Oakland's top homegrown prospects.

GRADE: A

2011

Sonny Gray (1) has developed into a frontline starter. RHP Blake Treinen (7), traded in a three-team deal for John Jaso, may make the Nationals' rotation. The rest of this class hasn't delivered.

GRADE: B

TOP DRAFT PICKS OF THE DECADE

Year	Player, Pos.	2014 Org
2005	Cliff Pennington, ss	Diamondbacks
2006	Trevor Cahill, rhp (2nd round)	Diamondbacks
2007	James Simmons, rhp	Nationals
2008	Jemile Weeks, 2b	Orioles
2009	Grant Green, ss	Angels
2010	Michael Choice, of	Rangers
2011	Sonny Gray, rhp	Athletics
2012	Addison Russell, ss	Cubs
2013	Billy McKinney, of	Cubs
2014	Matt Chapman, 3b	Athletics

LARGEST BONUSES IN CLUB HISTORY

Michael Ynoa, 2008	$4,250,000
Mark Mulder, 1998	$3,200,000
Grant Green, 2009	$2,750,000
Addison Russell, 2012	$2,625,000
Renato Nunez, 2010	$2,200,000

1 DANIEL ROBERTSON, SS

Born: March 22, 1994. **B-T:** R-R. **Ht.:** 6-0. **Wt.:** 190.
Drafted: HS—Upland, Calif., 2012 (1st round supplemental). **Signed by:** Eric Martins.

Robertson always will be linked with Addison Russell, his close friend and former spring training roommate. The two shortstops, along with first baseman Matt Olson, spearheaded the Athletics' 2012 draft class in which Oakland abandoned a college-heavy acquisition strategy by taking that trio of high schoolers with its first three selections. That class casts a long shadow now that Robertson and Olson stand as the system's two best prospects, while Russell served as the key piece the A's surrendered in the blockbuster trade that brought them Jeff Samardzija from the Cubs. While losing Russell is a difficult blow to the farm system, it does speak to the faith the organization has in Robertson. Signed for $1.5 million as the 34th overall pick in 2012, he tore up the high Class A California League as a 20-year-old in 2014. The cornerstone of Stockton's prospect-laden infield, he was consistently productive, finishing third in the minors in hits (170) and leading the Cal League with 37 doubles. He also handled himself well in the Arizona Fall League, hitting .301/.398/.356 in 20 games.

Robertson has the makings of a well-rounded offensive shortstop. He has a quick swing, and he developed a much better load position in 2014, which helped him use his legs more naturally. He's a mature, professional hitter who consistently grinds out quality at-bats. He does a good job of staying inside balls, and while his approach isn't predicated on power, he has the strength to hit balls out if a pitcher makes a mistake. Robertson has gotten better about cutting his swing loose on pitches he can drive, and as he continues to mature physically he could develop into a 20-homer threat. Robertson played third base for most of his high school career, only moving to shortstop full-time as a senior. Scouts had long projected him to move back to the hot corner, especially after turning pro and teaming up with Russell. Though such a position switch still is possible, Robertson may yet have a future as a shortstop. He's a below-average runner and doesn't have flashy range, but he's almost always in the right place—a tribute both to his instincts for the game and attention to detail in his preparation. His hands are steady and he has a quick release on throws, with enough arm strength

BA GRADE	
55	**Risk:** Medium

SCOUTING GRADES

Batting: 60.
Power: 45.
Speed: 40.
Defense: 55.
Arm: 55.

Based on 20-80 scouting scale and future projection rather than present grades.

LGE	PA	BB%	SO%	ISO
CAL	642	11.2	14.6	.161

BILL MITCHELL

for either spot on the left side of the infield.

Russell's departure from the organization has changed Robertson's outlook significantly. Not only is Robertson now the organization's No. 1 prospect, but he no longer has Russell standing in his way at shortstop. Though he still faces the possibility of a position switch, Robertson's chances to stick look better today. With Jed Lowrie testing free agency, the A's will have to figure out a short-term solution at shortstop, but Robertson won't be ready to take over the job until 2016 at the earliest. First, he'll head to Double-A Midland.

Year	Club (League)	Class	AVG	G	AB	R	H	2B	3B	HR	RBI	BB	SO	SB	CS	OBP	SLG
2012	Athletics (AZL)	R	.297	29	101	25	30	10	2	4	22	16	15	2	0	.405	.554
	Vermont (NYP)	SS	.181	26	94	9	17	2	0	1	8	7	31	1	1	.238	.234
2013	Beloit (MWL)	LoA	.277	101	401	59	111	21	1	9	46	41	79	1	7	.353	.401
2014	Stockton (CAL)	HiA	.310	132	548	110	170	37	3	15	60	72	94	4	4	.402	.471
Minor League Totals			.287	288	1144	203	328	70	6	29	136	136	219	8	12	.373	.434

2 FRANKLIN BARRETO, SS

Born: Feb. 27, 1996. **B-T:** R-R. **Ht.:** 5-9. **Wt.:** 175. **Signed:** Venezuela, 2012.
Signed by: Ismael Cruz/Luis Marquez (Blue Jays).

Barreto was one of the most decorated amateurs to come out of Venezuela when he signed with the Blue Jays for $1.45 million in 2012. He had a track record of hitting against top competition during international play, and he has continued to hit after two seasons in the minors. The Athletics acquired him as the key prospect in the November trade that sent Josh Donaldson to Toronto for Brett Lawrie and pitching prospects Kendall Graveman and Sean Nolin. Barreto's top tool is his righthanded bat, and he shows tools to be become a plus hitter. He has above-average bat speed to his line-drive oriented stroke and hits the ball well to all fields. His bat speed and strength should enable at least double digit home runs and lots of doubles. He is an aggressive hitter who is still learning to lay off breaking stuff out of the zone. His athleticism, plus speed, above-average lateral range and above-average arm give him an up-the-middle profile and he will be given every opportunity to remain at shortstop, but he could move off the position at the upper levels. His .901 fielding percentage must improve, as will his ability to make accurate throws on the finishing end of the double play, the source of many of his errors. His actions are not ideal for the position, though they are improving. He could move to second base or center field. Barreto has plus speed and solid baserunning instincts. After hitting at each stop the past two summers, Barreto likely will move to low Class A Beloit in 2015 and could move quickly because of his hitting ability.

BA GRADE

60 Risk: High

LGE	PA	BB%	SO%	ISO
NWL	328	7.9	19.5	.170

Year	Club (League)	Class	AVG	G	AB	R	H	2B	3B	HR	RBI	BB	SO	SB	CS	OBP	SLG
2012	Blue Jays (DSL)	R	.292	46	171	18	50	7	1	0	9	12	23	4	3	.354	.345
2013	Blue Jays (DSL)	R	.300	64	243	56	73	14	3	0	26	31	23	19	5	.404	.383
2014	Blue Jays (GCL)	R	.288	51	170	21	49	15	0	2	16	5	14	2	3	.309	.412
Minor League Totals			.295	161	584	95	172	36	4	2	51	48	60	25	11	.364	.380

3 MATT OLSON, 1B

Born: March 29, 1994. **B-T:** L-R. **Ht.:** 6-4. **Wt.:** 236. **Drafted:** HS—Lilburn, Ga., 2012 (1st round supplemental). **Signed by:** Matt Ranson.

Olson established a fearsome reputation when he hit 30 homers over his sophomore and junior years at Parkview High, earning himself a $1,079,700 bonus as the 47th overall pick in 2012. He has kept right on mashing as a pro, swatting 37 homers at high Class A Stockton in 2014, which was good for the third-highest total in the minors. He hit 22 of those homers in the second half, during which he slugged .614 over 70 games. Olson fits the mold of a slugger, and he has legitimate plus power. Most of that pop goes to his pull side, but he does have solid plate coverage and will hit balls out the other way on occasion. Olson knows the strike zone and is very selective, which results in many deep counts and high totals for both strikeouts and walks—he led the minors in the latter with 117. He shortened his swing and moved his hands away from his body in 2014, helping him hit pitches in different parts of the zone, and he lowered his strikeout rate by nearly five percentage points. Olson can adeptly pick balls out of the dirt at first base, and he's athletic enough with a strong enough arm that the Athletics gave him a few starts in right field at the end of 2014. The A's will continue trying Olson in the outfield, envisioning him as having similar versatility as Brandon Moss. Oakland won't expect the same home run production from Olson in 2015 when he moves to Double-A Midland.

BA GRADE

55 Risk: High

LGE	PA	BB%	SO%	ISO
CAL	634	18.5	21.6	.281

Year	Club (League)	Class	AVG	G	AB	R	H	2B	3B	HR	RBI	BB	SO	SB	CS	OBP	SLG
2012	Athletics (AZL)	R	.282	46	177	29	50	16	1	8	41	16	46	0	0	.345	.520
	Vermont (NYP)	SS	.273	4	11	3	3	0	0	1	4	3	4	0	0	.438	.545
2013	Beloit (MWL)	LoA	.225	134	481	69	108	32	0	23	93	72	148	4	3	.326	.435
2014	Stockton (CAL)	HiA	.262	138	512	111	134	31	1	37	97	117	137	2	0	.404	.543
Minor League Totals			.250	322	1181	212	295	79	2	69	235	208	335	6	3	.365	.495

4 MATT CHAPMAN, 3B

BA GRADE

55 Risk: High

LGE	PA	BB%	SO%	ISO
MWL	202	3.5	22.8	.153

Born: April 28, 1993. **B-T:** R-R. **Ht.:** 6-2. **Wt.:** 205. **Drafted:** Cal State Fullerton, 2014 (1st round). **Signed by:** Eric Martins.

Chapman went undrafted out of high school yet quickly earned an everyday role with powerhouse Cal State Fullerton as a freshman. He went on to earn third-team All-America honors as a junior in 2014 when the Athletics made him the 25th overall pick in the draft and signed him for $1.75 million. Chapman might have had a future on the mound—he left scouts buzzing after making a couple pitching appearances with USA Baseball's College National Team in 2013—but he prefers hitting and the A's were adamant when they selected him that they want him for his bat. He has a physical frame and big raw power, though his in-game power plays closer to average since he hits with a line-drive, gap-to-gap style. The A's would like him to be less upright in his stance so he can create more leverage, but he stays on balls well and has a knack for driving them to right-center field. Chapman is a premium defender at the hot corner, showing good reactions, clean footwork and a cannon arm—he threw 98 mph off the mound. The A's love his polished makeup and see a future clubhouse leader as well. Chapman's profile as a third baseman suffers if he doesn't tap into more power, but he does just about everything else. He probably will begin the 2015 season at high Class A Stockton, while Renato Nunez gets reps at Midland.

Year	Club (League)	Class	AVG	G	AB	R	H	2B	3B	HR	RBI	BB	SO	SB	CS	OBP	SLG
2014	Athletics (AZL)	R	.429	3	14	1	6	1	1	0	0	1	1	0	0	.467	.643
	Beloit (MWL)	LoA	.237	50	190	22	45	8	3	5	20	7	46	2	1	.282	.389
	Midland (TL)	AA	.000	1	3	0	0	0	0	0	0	0	0	0	0	.000	.000
Minor League Totals			.246	54	207	23	51	9	4	5	20	8	47	2	1	.291	.401

5 RENATO NUNEZ, 3B

BA GRADE

55 Risk: High

LGE	PA	BB%	SO%	ISO
CAL	563	6.0	20.1	.238

Born: April 4, 1994. **B-T:** R-R. **Ht.:** 6-1. **Wt.:** 185. **Signed:** Venezuela, 2010. **Signed by:** Julio Franco.

The Athletics signed Nunez, then a touted teenager out of Venezuela, for $2.2 million in 2010, and he's beginning to prove that initial excitement was justified. He hit .301/.351/.579 with 20 homers in the second half of 2014 at high Class A Stockton and had an impressive showing at the Futures Game, hitting a single on a 98 mph fastball from Twins righthander Alex Meyer. Nunez hit behind Matt Olson in Stockton's lineup in 2014, and his raw power is in a similar class. Balls explode off his bat, and he can hit any pitch a long way when he's going well. Nunez's approach comes and goes, but at his best, he shows he can wait on breaking pitches and use the whole field. His mechanics break down when he gets pull-happy, as was the case at the end of 2014 when he started pressing to reach 30 homers. Doubts remain about Nunez's future at third base, but he showed some encouraging signs by cutting his errors to 15 after making 39 in 2013. He's a well below-average runner and has limited range, but he's working to clean up his footwork and find a consistent release point with his strong arm. Nunez may wind up shifting to first base one day, but the A's will keep him at the hot corner in 2015 as he teams up with Olson and Daniel Robertson again at Double-A Midland.

Year	Club (League)	Class	AVG	G	AB	R	H	2B	3B	HR	RBI	BB	SO	SB	CS	OBP	SLG
2012	Athletics (AZL)	R	.325	42	160	31	52	18	3	4	42	17	32	4	0	.403	.550
2013	Beloit (MWL)	LoA	.258	128	508	69	131	27	0	19	85	28	136	2	2	.301	.423
2014	Stockton (CAL)	HiA	.279	124	509	75	142	28	3	29	96	34	113	2	0	.336	.517
Minor League Totals			.275	347	1371	195	377	85	6	57	251	85	323	9	4	.327	.470

6 CHRIS BASSITT, RHP

Born: Feb. 22, 1989. **B-T:** R-R. **Ht.:** 6-5. **Wt.:** 210. **Drafted:** Akron, 2011 (16th round). **Signed by:** Phil Gulley (White Sox).

The Athletics acquired Bassitt from the White Sox in December's Jeff Samardzija trade, the third close-to-ready starting pitcher Oakland acquired in the offseason. He's somewhat similar to ex-Blue Jays Kendall Graveman and Sean Nolin in that he was an under-the-radar prospect who had seen big league time in September 2014. Bassitt is a late-bloomer who burst on the amateur scene as a fourth-year junior in 2011 and was drafted as a reliever. The White Sox put him in the rotation in 2012 and his command actually improved, and a broken right hand at Double-A Birmingham in 2014 couldn't keep him from reaching the major leagues by season's end. Bassitt pushed his fastball up as hard as 96 mph even in a starting role, and it has solid life down in the zone. While he throws consistent strikes, he doesn't command the fastball enough for him to be a frontline starter. He's focused on a slider over a curve as his breaking ball, and it gives him an average second pitch. White Sox officials believed it would play up in the bullpen to make him a potential setup reliever. His changeup remains fringe-average but has some sink as well. Bassitt impressed again in the Arizona Fall League in a relief role, but the Athletics will give him a chance to win a spot at the back of their revamped 2015 rotation.

BA GRADE: 50 Risk: Medium

Year	Club (League)	Class	W	L	ERA	G	GS	CG	SV	IP	H	HR	BB	SO	K/9	WHIP	AVG
2012	Winston-Salem (CAR)	HiA	5	4	3.66	38	10	0	4	91	74	6	54	75	7.4	1.41	.218
2013	Winston-Salem (CAR)	HiA	7	2	3.46	18	18	0	0	101	90	9	42	101	9.0	1.30	.231
	Birmingham (SL)	AA	4	2	2.27	8	8	0	0	48	35	2	17	37	7.0	1.09	.213
2014	White Sox (AZL)	R	0	0	4.15	3	2	0	0	9	9	0	3	13	13.5	1.38	.257
	Birmingham (SL)	AA	3	1	1.56	6	6	0	0	35	26	2	14	36	9.3	1.15	.206
	Chicago (AL)	MAJ	1	1	3.94	6	5	0	0	30	34	0	13	21	6.4	1.58	.286
Major League Totals			1	1	3.94	6	5	0	0	30	34	0	13	21	6.4	1.58	.286
Minor League Totals			22	10	2.97	96	44	0	5	318	263	20	138	303	8.6	1.26	.223

7 KENDALL GRAVEMAN, RHP

Born: Dec. 21, 1990. **B-T:** R-R. **Ht.:** 6-2. **Wt.:** 195. **Drafted:** Mississippi State, 2013 (8th round) **Signed by:** Brian Johnston (Blue Jays).

CLIFF WELCH

Graveman was a four-year contributor at Mississippi State and its most consistent starting pitcher as it reached its first College World Series Final in 2013. But Graveman didn't miss many bats in college (5.4 strikeouts per nine) and he signed for $5,000 as a priority senior. Barely a year later, he was in the big leagues. In November, the Jays shipped him to the Athletics in the Josh Donaldson trade. Graveman's stuff improved in his first full pro season and he became the fifth player from the 2013 draft class to reach the majors. His fastball velocity ticked up, ranging from 89-94 in the rotation while sitting 90-93 and touching 95 out of the bullpen. Graveman's sinker has above-average sink and arm-side run. With pitchability, above-average fastball life to both sides of the plate and plus control, Graveman gets outs with his heater. After throwing both a curveball and slider in college, Graveman added a cutter this season that flashed above-average and projects to be at least average. His changeup has average potential, as does his curveball, though it can be inconsistent because of his loose arm action that is long in the back. His makeup and aptitude are plusses. His groundball tendencies, home run prevention and plus control, as well as below-average strikeout rate (6.1 K/9 as a pro), make Graveman a back-end starter candidate, and he should compete for a spot in the Oakland rotation in 2015. He'll report to Triple-A Nashville if he's crowded out.

BA GRADE 45 Risk: Low

LGE	BF	SO%	BB%	HR/9
FSL	394	16.2	4.6	0.09
IL	145	15.2	3.4	0.23

Year	Club (League)	Class	W	L	ERA	G	GS	CG	SV	IP	H	HR	BB	SO	K/9	WHIP	AVG
2013	Lansing (MWL)	LoA	1	3	4.31	10	10	0	0	40	41	3	13	25	5.7	1.36	.266
2014	Lansing (MWL)	LoA	2	0	0.34	4	4	0	0	26	11	0	6	25	8.5	0.65	.126
	Dunedin (FSL)	HiA	8	4	2.23	16	16	0	0	97	89	1	18	64	6.0	1.11	.243
	New Hampshire (EL)	AA	1	0	1.50	1	1	0	0	6	8	0	2	4	6.0	1.67	.364
	Buffalo (IL)	AAA	3	2	1.88	6	6	0	0	38	34	1	5	22	5.2	1.02	.245
	Toronto (AL)	MAJ	0	0	3.86	5	0	0	0	5	4	0	0	4	7.7	0.86	.222
Major League Totals			0	0	3.86	5	0	0	0	5	4	0	0	4	7.7	0.86	.222
Minor League Totals			15	9	2.30	37	37	0	0	207	183	5	44	140	6.1	1.10	.238

8 SEAN NOLIN, LHP

Born: Dec. 26, 1989. **B-T:** L-L. **Ht.:** 6-5. **Wt.:** 235. **Drafted:** San Jacinto (Texas) JC, 2010 (6th round) Signed by: Aaron Jersild (Blue Jays).

Nolin was the second player to reach the majors from the Blue Jays' first draft of the Alex Anthopoulos era in 2010, signing for $175,000. He made a spot start for Toronto in 2013 but a groin strain slowed his development in 2014. He also joined the Athletics as part of Toronto's payment for Josh Donaldson. Nolin is a four-pitch lefthander with the potential to be a No. 4 starter with improved command of his secondary stuff and control, as his walk rate this season (3.6 per nine) was the highest of his career. Nolin's fastball sits 89-92 but can touch 95 at its best or sink in the upper 80s. His high three-quarters arm slot creates downhill plane, and his four-seam fastball has riding life through the zone when he gets extension out front. His top secondary offering is his changeup that has above-average potential, though he can slow his arm on the pitch. He has better feel for his fringy curve than his below-average slider, but he needs to land both breaking balls for strikes more often. A big-bodied lefthander with a large, durable frame, Nolin has the body to pitch in the rotation, though his physique has shown some softness in the past. Nolin is a lefthanded contrast to Kendall Graveman, the other starter Oakland acquired from Toronto, as an extreme flyball pitcher while Graveman thrives on grounders. Nolin's profile fits better in the Athletics' spacious O.Co Coliseum than it did in Toronto's Rogers Centre, and he'll compete for a rotation spot in 2015.

BA GRADE

45 Risk: Low

LGE	BF	SO%	BB%	HR/9
IL	370	20.0	9.5	0.62
AL	4	0.0	0.0	9.00

Year	Club (League)	Class	W	L	ERA	G	GS	CG	SV	IP	H	HR	BB	SO	K/9	WHIP	AVG
2012	Dunedin (FSL)	HiA	9	0	2.19	17	15	0	0	86	72	7	21	90	9.4	1.08	.226
	New Hampshire (EL)	AA	1	0	1.20	3	3	0	0	15	9	0	6	18	10.8	1.00	.170
2013	Toronto (AL)	MAJ	0	1	40.50	1	1	0	0	1	7	1	0	0	0.0	6.00	.700
	New Hampshire (EL)	AA	8	3	3.01	17	17	1	0	93	89	6	25	103	10.0	1.23	.251
	Buffalo (IL)	AAA	1	1	1.53	3	3	0	0	18	13	1	10	13	6.6	1.30	.232
2014	Blue Jays (GCL)	R	0	0	0.00	1	1	0	0	2	1	0	0	5	19.3	0.43	.125
	Dunedin (FSL)	HiA	0	1	3.68	2	2	0	0	7	4	0	4	9	11.0	1.09	.143
	Buffalo (IL)	AAA	4	6	3.50	17	17	0	0	87	74	6	35	74	7.6	1.25	.225
	Toronto (AL)	MAJ	0	0	9.00	1	0	0	0	1	1	1	0	0	0.0	1.00	.250
Major League Totals			0	1	27.00	2	1	0	0	2	8	2	1	0	0.0	3.86	.571
Minor League Totals			27	17	3.06	92	86	1	1	438	390	29	142	451	9.3	1.21	.238

9 DILLON OVERTON, LHP

Born: Aug. 17, 1991. **B-T:** L-L. **Ht.:** 6-2. **Wt.:** 172. **Drafted:** Oklahoma, 2013 (2nd round). **Signed by:** Yancy Ayres.

The Athletics signed Overton for a discounted $400,000 in the second round of the 2013 draft knowing he would need Tommy John surgery. Overton returned to the mound in late June 2014 and carved up hitters over 37 innings in short-season ball, notching 13 times as many strikeouts as walks. The 95 mph velocity Overton showed at times with Oklahoma hasn't come back yet, though the A's are hopeful that a normal offseason routine will bring about a harder fastball in the spring. He pitched at 88-91 mph in 2014, though he also dipped as low as 86 toward the end. His fastball plays up thanks to its armside sink and the fact he throws somewhat across his body, aiding his deception. Overton produced dominant results in 2014 because he has two projected plus secondary pitches in his curveball and changeup. His changeup receives the edge right now, for it looks just like a fastball out of his hand then drops off the table, but his curve has good shape and can be a chase pitch too. He brings strong control and and a fearless attitude to the mound. Prior to requiring elbow surgery, Overton was hailed as one of the elite arms in the 2013 college draft class. He will begin 2015 at one of Oakland's Class A clubs before potentially reaching Double-A Midland by season's end.

BILL MITCHELL

BA GRADE

55 Risk: High

LGE	BF	SO%	BB%	HR/9
AZL	88	35.2	3.4	0.00
NYP	58	37.9	1.7	0.00

Year	Club (League)	Class	W	L	ERA	G	GS	CG	SV	IP	H	HR	BB	SO	K/9	WHIP	AVG
2013	Did not play—Injured																
2014	Athletics (AZL)	R	0	2	1.64	7	7	0	0	22	19	0	3	31	12.7	1.00	.232
	Vermont (NYP)	SS	0	1	2.40	5	5	0	0	15	11	0	1	22	13.2	0.80	.200
Minor League Totals			0	3	1.95	12	12	0	0	37	30	0	4	53	12.9	0.92	.219

10 RANGEL RAVELO, 1B

Born: April 24, 1992. **B-T:** R-R. **Ht.:** 6-2. **Wt.:** 210. **Drafted:** HS—Hialeah, Fla., 2010 (5th round). **Signed by:** Jose Ortega (White Sox).

A relative bargain signee as a 2010 fifth-rounder for $125,000, Ravelo moved down the defensive spectrum but up the White Sox prospect list prior to being traded to the Athletics in the Jeff Samardzija deal in December. He had one of the best seasons of any organization farmhand, ranking second in the Double-A Southern League in batting (.309). Ravelo doesn't fit the typical profile of a mashing corner bat. Instead, he features an advanced approach with outstanding plate coverage. His barrel awareness allows him to square balls up, and he handles good pitching with his ability to stay inside the ball. His feel for hitting could allow him to hit for more power as he learns to keep his hips closed and pull the ball with authority. Having moved from third base to first, Ravelo defends adequately and still has solid-average arm strength. He's a below-average runner who could become a clogger if he doesn't watch his weight. If Ravelo keeps hitting, the A's will find a spot for him, possibly in a platoon role at first base or DH.

BA GRADE

45 Risk Low

LGE	PA	BB%	SO%	ISO
SL	551	10.2	14.0	.164

Year	Club (League)	Class	AVG	G	AB	R	H	2B	3B	HR	RBI	BB	SO	SB	CS	OBP	SLG
2012	Kannapolis (SAL)	LoA	.290	76	290	32	84	19	3	2	39	20	38	6	1	.343	.397
2013	Kannapolis (SAL)	LoA	.226	17	53	9	12	4	0	0	9	11	11	1	1	.364	.302
	Winston-Salem (CAR)	HiA	.312	84	301	43	94	27	2	4	53	40	46	4	1	.393	.455
2014	Birmingham (SL)	AA	.309	133	476	72	147	37	4	11	66	56	77	10	6	.386	.473
Minor League Totals			.301	421	1527	194	460	112	11	18	222	150	228	23	12	.368	.424

11 RAUL ALCANTARA, RHP

BA GRADE

50 Risk: High

Born: Dec. 4, 1992. **B-T:** R-R. **Ht.:** 6-3. **Wt.:** 225. **Signed:** Dominican Republic, 2009. **Signed by:** Manny Nanita (Red Sox).

Alcantara joined the organization in the Andrew Bailey-Josh Reddick deal with the Red Sox in 2011 and had a big 2013 at two Class A levels, prompting the Athletics to protect him on the 40-man roster. Tommy John surgery halted his momentum in 2014. When healthy, Alcantara showed a solid four-pitch mix and a smooth, repeatable delivery. His fastball and changeup highlight his repertoire, the heater sitting in the low 90s and topping out at 95 mph, while his changeup looked like a plus pitch with fading action. He had been working to improve his slider, getting more depth on it, and he also had a serviceable curveball. Alcantara's rehab has him on track to get back on the mound by July 2015. The A's won't expect much from him this year, but he has the potential to be a mid-rotation starter.

Year	Club (League)	Class	W	L	ERA	G	GS	CG	SV	IP	H	HR	BB	SO	K/9	WHIP	AVG
2012	Burlington (MWL)	LoA	6	11	5.08	27	17	0	0	103	119	12	38	57	5.0	1.53	.304
2013	Beloit (MWL)	LoA	7	1	2.44	13	13	1	0	77	84	3	7	58	6.8	1.18	.272
	Stockton (CAL)	HiA	5	5	3.76	14	14	0	0	79	73	8	17	66	7.5	1.14	.243
2014	Midland (TL)	AA	2	0	2.29	3	3	0	0	20	17	0	5	10	4.6	1.12	.250
Minor League Totals			26	24	3.45	83	73	2	0	404	402	24	87	275	6.1	1.21	.262

12 CHAD PINDER, 2B/SS

BA GRADE

50 Risk: High

Born: March 29, 1992. **B-T:** R-R. **Ht.:** 6-2. **Wt.:** 195. **Drafted:** Virginia Tech, 2013 (2nd round supplemental). **Signed by:** Neil Avent.

Pinder played primarily third base in college but not necessarily with profile power for the position. However, the Athletics felt he was underdeveloped physically for his age. Pinder worked hard in the weight room prior to 2014 and now does a better job of using his legs in his swing, lending credence to the belief he can have average power down the road. He also has an ability to backspin balls along with very quick hands. The A's hope his plate discipline improves. Transitioning to the middle of the diamond, his footwork requires cleaning up, but he can handle the routine play at second base. He still has a strong enough arm for the left side of the infield. He's a decent runner but needs to do a better job of picking his spots on the bases. He'll move with the core of the 2014 Stockton team to Double-A Midland.

Year	Club (League)	Class	AVG	G	AB	R	H	2B	3B	HR	RBI	BB	SO	SB	CS	OBP	SLG
2013	Vermont (NYP)	SS	.200	42	140	14	28	4	0	3	8	12	41	1	0	.286	.293
2014	Stockton (CAL)	HiA	.288	94	403	61	116	32	5	13	55	22	99	12	9	.336	.489
Minor League Totals			.265	136	543	75	144	36	5	16	63	34	140	13	9	.322	.438

13 MAX MUNCY, 1B/3B

BA GRADE	
45	Risk: Medium

Born: Aug. 25, 1990. **B-T:** L-R. **Ht.:** 6-0. **Wt.:** 205. **Drafted:** Baylor, 2012 (5th round). **Signed by:** Armann Brown.

Muncy hit his first real rough patch in several years in 2014. The conditions at Double-A Midland, where the wind constantly blows in, presented a stiff challenge, and his production fell. He made slight adjustments to his swing path to be able to use the whole field better and play to his strength—staying inside the ball. His swing doesn't feature much length, so he's able to cover all parts of the zone. Plate discipline is a Muncy hallmark. At the same time, his lack of power is the biggest knock on him. The A's have worked to give his swing more leverage, but Muncy still doesn't project for more than 15 homers annually. The A's tried him out at third base last season and liked what they saw. He's not tremendously athletic and has below-average speed, but he's a fundamentally-sound defender with enough arm. Muncy should continue seeing action at both corner-infield positions as he moves up to Triple-A Nashville in 2015.

Year	Club (League)	Class	AVG	G	AB	R	H	2B	3B	HR	RBI	BB	SO	SB	CS	OBP	SLG
2012	Burlington (MWL)	LoA	.275	64	229	34	63	20	2	4	23	41	37	3	1	.383	.432
2013	Stockton (CAL)	HiA	.285	93	351	67	100	13	1	21	76	64	68	1	1	.400	.507
	Midland (TL)	AA	.250	47	172	22	43	12	2	4	24	24	34	0	1	.340	.413
2014	Midland (TL)	AA	.264	122	435	59	115	23	3	7	63	87	92	7	2	.385	.379
Minor League Totals			.270	326	1187	182	321	68	8	36	186	216	231	11	5	.383	.432

14 SETH STREICH, RHP

BA GRADE	
45	Risk: Medium

Born: Feb. 19, 1991. **B-T:** L-R. **Ht.:** 6-3. **Wt.:** 210. **Drafted:** Ohio, 2012 (6th round). **Signed by:** Rich Sparks.

Streich had shown encouraging signs ever since the Athletics brought in the former Ohio two-way player in 2012, and now the results are catching up. He went to the challenging high Class A California League in 2014 and won the league ERA (3.16) title. Streich is generally more of a command pitcher, though he does show impressive stuff on his best days. His fastball sits in the low 90s but he can reach 96 mph. His heater has some natural cut at times and he can also throw two-seamers with armside sink. He doesn't have a wipeout secondary pitch in either his curveball or changeup, but both are effective and he'll use any pitch in any count. Streich's changeup has good depth, while his curve has tight top-to-bottom movement. He didn't make any real mechanical changes, but he didn't pitch as passively as in past years. He'll have to prove he's more than a back-of-the-rotation arm, with Double-A Midland his next stop.

Year	Club (League)	Class	W	L	ERA	G	GS	CG	SV	IP	H	HR	BB	SO	K/9	WHIP	AVG
2012	Athletics (AZL)	R	0	0	3.38	2	0	0	0	3	1	0	1	6	20.3	0.75	.111
	Vermont (NYP)	SS	4	1	2.60	15	4	0	0	35	26	1	17	42	10.9	1.24	.206
2013	Beloit (MWL)	LoA	10	6	3.82	21	21	1	0	111	114	2	41	82	6.7	1.40	.268
2014	Stockton (CAL)	HiA	9	6	3.16	22	22	0	0	114	110	7	22	116	9.2	1.16	.253
Minor League Totals			23	13	3.37	60	47	1	0	262	251	10	81	246	8.5	1.27	.252

15 DANIEL GOSSETT, RHP

BA GRADE	
50	Risk: High

Born: Nov. 13, 1992. **B-T:** R-R. **Ht.:** 6-2. **Wt.:** 185. **Drafted:** Clemson, 2014 (2nd round). **Signed by:** Neil Avent.

Gossett was one of the premier high school pitchers in South Carolina but chose Clemson over signing with the Red Sox as a 16th-round pick in 2011. He parlayed a 7-2, 1.93 season as a junior into a $750,000 bonus from Oakland. Gossett has a slight build but a quick arm. His lively fastball sits in the low 90s and reaches 96 mph at its best, though he has to prove he can maintain his velocity deeper into games. Scouts who saw him at Clemson preferred his curveball as his best secondary pitch, but the Athletics were impressed with his slider. His slider acted as his put-away pitch with short-season Vermont, showing depth and late break. He has a solid changeup he throws with good arm speed. Gossett's delivery looks unorthodox, but he gets in proper position eventually. He'll start his first full season at low Class A Beloit.

Year	Club (League)	Class	W	L	ERA	G	GS	CG	SV	IP	H	HR	BB	SO	K/9	WHIP	AVG
2014	Vermont (NYP)	SS	1	0	2.25	12	1	0	0	24	16	1	1	25	9.4	0.71	.188
Minor League Totals			1	0	2.25	12	1	0	0	24	16	1	1	25	9.4	0.71	.188

16 YAIRO MUNOZ, SS

BA GRADE	
50	Risk: High

Born: Jan. 23, 1995. **B-T:** R-R. **Ht.:** 6-1. **Wt.:** 165. **Signed:** Dominican Republic, 2012. **Signed by:** Amaurys Reyes.

Munoz got to showcase himself in the Under Armour All-America Game at Wrigley Field in August

2011 and went on to sign with the Athletics the following January for $280,000. Munoz is a live-bodied athlete with all kinds of tools. He has quick hands and already shows some pull-side power. His youth gets exposed at times though. He hits off his front foot and doesn't control the strike zone yet. His defense has similar issues. He has the range and plus arm to stick at shortstop, but he can be too flashy on some plays and too casual on others, evidenced by his 20 errors in 66 games at short-season Vermont. He turns in some plus running times down the line right now, though his speed will more likely end up closer to average. The Athletics won't rush Munoz, but he's earned a chance to go to low Class A Beloit in 2015.

Year	Club (League)	Class	AVG	G	AB	R	H	2B	3B	HR	RBI	BB	SO	SB	CS	OBP	SLG
2012	Athletics (DSL)	R	.229	32	105	13	24	7	3	0	22	10	23	4	3	.297	.352
2013	Athletics (AZL)	R	.194	25	67	8	13	3	0	1	5	7	11	1	0	.286	.284
2014	Vermont (NYP)	SS	.298	66	252	29	75	17	3	5	20	7	42	14	6	.319	.448
Minor League Totals			.264	123	424	50	112	27	6	6	47	24	76	19	9	.308	.399

17 JOEY WENDLE, 2B

BA GRADE
45 Risk: Medium

Born: April 26, 1990. **B-T:** L-R. **Ht.:** 5-11. **Wt.:** 190. **Drafted:** West Chester (Pa.), 2012 (6th round). **Signed by:** Brent Urcheck (Indians).

Undrafted as a junior, Wendle led Division II West Chester (Pa.)to a national title as a senior in 2012 prior to signing with the Indians for the modest sum of $10,000 as a sixth-round pick. Cleveland traded him to the Athletics for Brandon Moss in December. After a breakout year in 2013, he pulled out of an early-season slump at Double-A Akron in 2014 when a broken hamate bone in his right hand sidelined him in late June, though he did return a couple weeks before the end of the season. Wendle gets described as an old school, grinding type of player. He takes short, line-drive oriented swings from the left side with a natural feel for hitting to all fields. He hits the occasional homer, but most of his power comes in the form of doubles. Wendle's secondary tools don't stick out, but he's a reliable second baseman with good lateral mobility and a solid arm. He can play small ball too even though his speed is average at best. He will tackle the Double-A level again at Midland this time in 2015.

Year	Club (League)	Class	AVG	G	AB	R	H	2B	3B	HR	RBI	BB	SO	SB	CS	OBP	SLG
2012	Mahoning Valley (NYP)	SS	.327	61	245	32	80	15	4	4	37	15	25	4	1	.375	.469
2013	Carolina (CAR)	HiA	.295	107	413	73	122	32	5	16	64	44	79	10	2	.372	.513
2014	Indians (AZL)	R	.455	6	22	8	10	1	1	0	4	4	4	1	1	.538	.591
	Akron (EL)	AA	.253	87	336	46	85	20	5	8	50	26	56	4	2	.311	.414
Minor League Totals			.292	261	1016	159	297	68	15	28	155	89	164	19	6	.357	.471

18 BOBBY WAHL, RHP

BA GRADE
45 Risk: Medium

Born: March 21, 1992. **B-T:** R-R. **Ht.:** 6-2. **Wt.:** 210. **Drafted:** Mississippi, 2013 (5th round). **Signed by:** Kelcey Mucker.

Wahl served as the staff ace at Mississippi for two seasons, going 10-0, 2.03 as a junior in 2013, the same year the Athletics made him a fifth-round pick. However, a portent of his future came in summer 2012 when he served as the closer for USA Baseball's College National Team. After struggling as a starter early in 2013, due in part to his trying to pitch through an oblique injury, Wahl moved to the bullpen in early June and quickly settled in. His velocity diminished during his final college season but has bounced back in the shorter relief stints. Wahl has an electric fastball now, pumping mid- to upper-90s velocity. His hard curveball plays as plus when it's going well, showing tight downward break. He could probably get by with just the two pitches as a reliever, but he continues to maintain a changeup with depth as part of his arsenal. Command has been Wahl's biggest obstacle, a product of over-striding in his delivery. He has worked to shorten up and get more downward angle on his pitches. He should reach Double-A Midland in 2015, with a return to Stockton for Opening Day also a possibility.

Year	Club (League)	Class	W	L	ERA	G	GS	CG	SV	IP	H	HR	BB	SO	K/9	WHIP	AVG
2013	Athletics (AZL)	R	0	0	9.00	1	1	0	0	1	0	0	2	1	9.0	2.00	.000
	Vermont (NYP)	SS	0	0	3.92	9	4	0	2	21	20	3	6	27	11.8	1.26	.241
2014	Beloit (MWL)	LoA	0	4	5.06	20	7	0	4	43	46	5	19	43	9.1	1.52	.267
	Stockton (CAL)	HiA	0	0	4.22	9	0	0	0	11	8	2	6	19	16.0	1.31	.190
Minor League Totals			0	4	4.68	39	12	0	6	75	74	10	33	90	10.8	1.43	.247

19 DYLAN COVEY, RHP

BA GRADE
50 Risk: High

Born: Aug. 14, 1991. **B-T:** R-R. **Ht.:** 6-2. **Wt.:** 195. **Drafted:** San Diego, 2013 (4th round). **Signed by:** Eric Martins.

Covey was the 14th overall pick by the Brewers in the 2010 draft out of high school, but he decided against signing after being diagnosed with Type 1 Diabetes in an August physical. He went to the Athletics in the fourth round three years later, signing for $370,000. Splitting his 2014 season at two Class A levels, Covey struggled to find consistency. He would look unhittable at times and be incapable of getting an out at others, even within the same appearance. Covey broke out a much-improved sinking two-seamer at 88-92 mph. His four-seamer gets up to 93 mph with occasional cutting action. He can spin a plus downer curveball that's his best secondary pitch. He also features a serviceable changeup and a seldom-used slider. Covey has a starter's repertoire and a starter's frame, but he needs plenty of development. He does have some feel for pitching but his command can get erratic, and he needs to show better mound presence to limit the big innings that have been his undoing. He'll return to high Class A Stockton to open 2015.

Year	Club (League)	Class	W	L	ERA	G	GS	CG	SV	IP	H	HR	BB	SO	K/9	WHIP	AVG
2013	Vermont (NYP)	SS	0	0	0.00	4	4	0	0	12	9	0	1	15	11.3	0.83	.205
	Beloit (MWL)	LoA	1	1	4.75	10	10	0	0	47	64	4	17	31	5.9	1.71	.327
2014	Beloit (MWL)	LoA	4	9	4.81	18	17	2	0	101	99	3	26	70	6.2	1.24	.258
	Stockton (CAL)	HiA	3	5	7.15	8	8	0	0	39	49	2	15	22	5.1	1.64	.312
Minor League Totals			8	15	4.97	40	39	2	0	199	221	9	59	138	6.2	1.40	.283

20 BRETT GRAVES, RHP

BA GRADE

50 Risk: High

Born: Jan. 30, 1993. **B-T:** R-R. **Ht.:** 6-1. **Wt.:** 170. **Drafted:** Missouri, 2014 (3rd round). **Signed by:** Kevin Mello.

Graves grew up in the St. Louis area but turned down a chance to join the Cardinals organization out of high school, when he was their 26th-round pick. Also eschewing a potential college football career—he'd drawn interest as a dual-threat quarterback—he chose instead to go to Missouri on his way to landing a $510,000 bonus from the Athletics as a 2014 third-rounder. Graves has a great pitcher's body and plenty of arm strength, as he sits 94-96 mph and can reach 97. He throws strikes with his fastball and has a feel for moving it around the zone. However, his secondary stuff needs work. Both his curve and changeup will look good in flashes but are mostly below-average for now. A long arm stroke in his delivery doesn't help in this regard, though he does do a good job of repeating and gets good angle on his pitches. Graves would fit the bill as a hard-throwing reliever, but he'll remain a starter for now to see if his secondary stuff develops as he goes to low Class A Beloit in 2015.

Year	Club (League)	Class	W	L	ERA	G	GS	CG	SV	IP	H	HR	BB	SO	K/9	WHIP	AVG
2014	Athletics (AZL)	R	0	0	0.00	1	1	0	0	1	0	0	1	1	9.0	1.00	.000
	Vermont (NYP)	SS	3	2	6.86	8	2	0	0	21	24	1	6	18	7.7	1.43	.279
Minor League Totals			3	2	6.55	9	3	0	0	22	24	1	7	19	7.8	1.41	.270

21 BOOG POWELL, OF

BA GRADE

45 Risk: Medium

Born: Jan. 14, 1993. **B-T:** L-L. **Ht.:** 5-10. **Wt.:** 185. **Drafted:** Orange Coast (Calif.) CC, 2012 (20th round). **Signed by:** Rick Magnante.

Powell's nickname of Boog—his given name is Herschel—is indeed a nod to the Orioles star first baseman of the 1960s and '70s, who was one of his grandfather's favorite players. He took off with a big first half in 2014. His momentum abruptly halted on July 7 when he tested positive for an amphetamine and was hit with a 50-game suspension. Powell doesn't have any especially loud offensive tools, but he plays hard and is sound fundamentally. He has a simple swing, and while he generates little power, he hits balls hard enough to keep defenses honest. He'll drive balls to both gaps and can run into the occasional homer. He's also a highly adept bunter. Powell's plus speed plays better on defense, where he's fearless in center field, than on the bases, where poor reads and jumps hinder his basestealing capability. Down the road, Powell figures to compete with a similar player in Billy Burns for big league time, but for now he'll go back to high Class A Stockton.

Year	Club (League)	Class	AVG	G	AB	R	H	2B	3B	HR	RBI	BB	SO	SB	CS	OBP	SLG
2012	Athletics (AZL)	R	.306	35	111	20	34	1	0	0	13	15	9	5	2	.383	.315
2013	Vermont (NYP)	SS	.283	59	212	30	60	7	3	0	14	26	34	14	6	.364	.344
2014	Beloit (MWL)	LoA	.335	69	254	43	85	7	4	3	17	53	49	16	13	.452	.429
	Stockton (CAL)	HiA	.377	14	61	11	23	3	1	0	11	8	4	0	2	.449	.459
Minor League Totals			.317	177	638	104	202	18	8	3	55	102	96	35	23	.412	.384

22 MARK CANHA, 1B/ OF

BA GRADE

45 Risk: Medium

Born: Feb. 15, 1989. **B-T:** R-R. **Ht:** 6-2. **Wt.:** 195. **Drafted:** California, 2010 (7th round). **Signed by:** John Hughes (Marlins).

After five up-and-down seasons in the Marlins system, Canha joined the Athletics in December after Oakland purchased him from the Rockies, who selected him in the major league Rule 5 draft. His 2014 season at Triple-A New Orleans marked the first time he together two productive halves. He hit

.319/.394/.529 in the first half and then .271/.363/.458 after the break. One scout called him the toughest out in the Zephyrs lineup. Canha regained his power stroke in 2014, slugging 20 homers and knocking in 82 runs. His .889 OPS tied for 10th best in the PCL. Though he has below-average speed, he runs the bases well. That he doesn't excel defensively at first base, left field or third base hinders his opportunity to play every day in the majors, though he'll go as far as his bat takes him in 2015.

Year	Club (League)	Class	AVG	G	AB	R	H	2B	3B	HR	RBI	BB	SO	SB	CS	OBP	SLG
2012	Jupiter (FSL)	HiA	.293	114	406	65	119	24	3	6	68	54	75	1	3	.382	.411
2013	Jacksonville (SL)	AA	.273	128	425	63	116	32	2	13	58	54	102	6	1	.371	.449
2014	New Orleans (PCL)	AAA	.303	127	465	83	141	28	3	20	82	57	112	1	3	.384	.505
Minor League Totals			.285	496	1750	293	499	109	9	68	303	232	388	18	9	.375	.474

23 RYON HEALY, 3B/1B

BA GRADE
45 Risk: Medium

Born: Jan. 10, 1992. **B-T:** R-R. **Ht.:** 6-5. **Wt.:** 205. **Drafted:** Oregon, 2013 (3rd round). **Signed by:** Jim Coffman.

The Athletics give Healy tremendous credit for sticking with it in 2014 at high Class A Stockton, for he didn't let himself get buried by his .185 average in April and recovered to hit .326/.356/.469 in the second half. Although Healy has 20-home run potential given his size and strength, he's at his best when he stays short and focuses on driving balls up the middle. His rhythm at the plate and path to the ball improved over the course of the year, while he gets in trouble when he starts pulling off and trying too much to lift the ball. Healy mainly played first base for Oregon, but the A's are trying him out at third and found the early returns encouraging. They're hopeful he'll have the positional flexibility they so covet. His footwork at the hot corner needs cleaning up, but he can handle the routine plays and shows enough arm strength and range to handle the job, though he's a below-average runner overall. He'll continue making starts at first, third and DH as he moves up to Double-A Midland in 2015.

Year	Club (League)	Class	AVG	G	AB	R	H	2B	3B	HR	RBI	BB	SO	SB	CS	OBP	SLG
2013	Athletics (AZL)	R	.214	11	28	4	6	0	1	2	8	3	4	0	0	.273	.500
	Vermont (NYP)	SS	.233	36	146	12	34	10	0	4	21	2	24	2	1	.252	.384
2014	Stockton (CAL)	HiA	.285	136	561	73	160	28	2	16	83	28	79	0	0	.318	.428
Minor League Totals			.272	183	735	89	200	38	3	22	112	33	107	2	1	.304	.422

24 BILLY BURNS, OF

BA GRADE
45 Risk: Medium

Born: Aug. 30, 1989. **B-T:** B-R. **Ht.:** 5-9. **Wt.:** 180. **Drafted:** Mercer, 2011 (32nd round). **Signed by:** Eric Robinson (Nationals).

Burns made a splash by hitting .306 in big league spring training in 2014 but had an underwhelming season at Double-A Midland and Triple-A Sacramento. He can create havoc with his top-of-the-scale speed, but he needs to recalibrate his slap-hitting approach to maximize it. The Nationals reintroduced Burns to switch-hitting after drafting him—he hit righthanded only at Mercer after batting from both sides in high school. He still looks more comfortable and takes better swings from the right side. Burns has no over-the-fence power, but he nonetheless needs to start hitting more line drives or else upper-level pitchers and defenses can take away his strengths. He plays premium defense in center field and can steal bases at the drop of a hat. His arm rates below-average, though having a quick release helps. He'll return to Triple-A in 2015, and he'll have to show more punch if he's going to be more than an extra outfielder.

Year	Club (League)	Class	AVG	G	AB	R	H	2B	3B	HR	RBI	BB	SO	SB	CS	OBP	SLG
2012	Hagerstown (SAL)	LoA	.322	113	398	83	128	14	5	0	41	65	68	38	9	.432	.382
2013	Potomac (CAR)	HiA	.312	91	330	70	103	8	9	0	29	52	37	54	5	.422	.391
	Harrisburg (EL)	AA	.325	30	114	26	37	4	0	0	8	20	17	20	2	.434	.360
2014	Midland (TL)	AA	.250	91	364	57	91	20	3	1	23	44	65	51	5	.333	.330
	Sacramento (PCL)	AAA	.193	28	109	17	21	2	0	0	5	9	19	3	1	.254	.211
	Oakland (AL)	MAJ	.167	13	6	4	1	0	0	0	0	0	0	3	1	.167	.167
Major League Totals			.167	13	6	4	1	0	0	0	0	0	0	3	1	.167	.167
Minor League Totals			.287	385	1422	274	408	51	19	2	124	202	228	179	23	.387	.354

25 KYLE FINNEGAN, RHP

BA GRADE
45 Risk: Medium

Born: Sept. 4, 1991. **B-T:** R-R. **Ht.:** 6-2. **Wt.:** 170. **Drafted:** Texas State, 2013 (6th round). **Signed by:** Armann Brown.

While his younger brother Brandon rocketed from Texas Christian to the Royals' playoff bullpen in a span of a few months, Kyle put up a good albeit not great first full season in the Athletics system. His fastball topped out at 94 mph early in the season, but he was pitching at 87-90 by the end. The Athletics have worked with him to shorten his stride since he came into pro ball, and he started to deliver the ball out front better during instructional league, which helped him recover some velocity. Finnegan barely used his changeup in college but it has improved to the point where it has overtaken his curveball as his best secondary pitch. His changeup has nice, late sinking action and he'll use it in any count, while he struggles to maintain the consistency of his downer curve. Finnegan pitches aggressively to both sides of the plate, but his low strikeout totals are a concern. Finnegan will move up to high Class A Stockton for 2015.

Year	Club (League)	Class	W	L	ERA	G	GS	CG	SV	IP	H	HR	BB	SO	K/9	WHIP	AVG
2013	Vermont (NYP)	SS	3	3	2.70	11	11	0	0	50	43	0	12	35	6.3	1.10	.231
	Beloit (MWL)	LoA	1	1	9.82	2	2	0	0	7	12	1	6	5	6.1	2.45	.375
2014	Beloit (MWL)	LoA	7	9	3.69	23	23	1	0	120	99	12	52	55	4.1	1.26	.227
	Midland (TL)	AA	0	1	11.81	1	1	0	0	5	10	3	1	6	10.1	2.06	.455
Minor League Totals			11	14	3.90	37	37	1	0	182	164	16	71	101	5.0	1.29	.243

26 CHRIS JENSEN, RHP

BA GRADE
45 Risk: Medium

Born: Sept. 30, 1990. **B-T:** R-R. **Ht.:** 6-4. **Wt.:** 200. **Drafted:** San Diego, 2011 (6th round). **Signed by:** Jon Lukens (Rockies).

Jensen came to the Athletics along with Drew Pomeranz when Oakland sent Brett Anderson to Colorado in December 2013 and dominated in the second half at Double-A Midland, going 8-2, 2.26. Jensen pounds both sides the plate with 88-93 mph fastballs and can reach 95. Toying around with two-seam grips last offseason, he found one he was comfortable with that gave him a much-improved sinker. He gets good arm speed on his changeup and it has developed into his most useful secondary pitch. His curveball needs more work and will go a long way to determining whether he can be more than a back-of-the-rotation starter. The pitch gets slurvy at times and isn't anything more than a get-me-over breaking ball at this point, its velocity ranging from the high 60s to low 70s. Jensen also lacked extension in his delivery, though the A's believe he made improvements by the end of 2014, and he will try to keep the momentum going at Triple-A Nashville in 2015.

Year	Club (League)	Class	W	L	ERA	G	GS	CG	SV	IP	H	HR	BB	SO	K/9	WHIP	AVG
2012	Asheville (SAL)	LoA	12	3	4.28	25	25	0	0	145	148	14	50	95	5.9	1.37	.262
2013	Modesto (CAL)	HiA	5	8	4.55	28	28	0	0	152	161	15	39	136	8.0	1.31	.264
2014	Midland (TL)	AA	12	8	3.14	26	26	0	0	160	147	3	62	94	5.3	1.30	.246
Minor League Totals			31	20	3.87	87	87	0	0	495	483	33	161	353	6.4	1.30	.254

27 ARNOLD LEON, RHP

BA GRADE
45 Risk: Medium

Born: Sept. 6, 1988. **B-T:** R-R. **Ht.:** 6-1. **Wt.:** 205. **Signed:** Mexico, 2008. **Signed by:** Randy Johnson/Craig Weissmann.

Leon missed the better part of two seasons from 2010-11 after having Tommy John surgery but earned a spot on Oakland's 40-man roster after the 2012 season. He has some physicality and a low- to mid-90s fastball which he can also sink at times. His secondary pitches come and go but all are useable. He'll show a hammer 11-to-5 curveball at his best, along with a short slider and a deceptive changeup. Leon does a good job of throwing strikes, but he ran into trouble last season when he worried too much about trying to trick hitters and got away from pitching off his fastball. With only one option season remaining, Leon needs to break through to Oakland sooner than later. He could help the A's as either a starter or in the bullpen, where his stuff might play up, in 2015.

Year	Club (League)	Class	W	L	ERA	G	GS	CG	SV	IP	H	HR	BB	SO	K/9	WHIP	AVG
2012	Stockton (CAL)	HiA	0	1	5.28	12	0	0	0	15	26	1	5	25	14.7	2.02	.366
	Midland (TL)	AA	1	0	2.30	10	0	0	1	16	17	0	3	18	10.3	1.28	.288
	Sacramento (PCL)	AAA	3	0	1.77	22	0	0	0	36	26	4	15	31	7.8	1.15	.208
2013	Midland (TL)	AA	4	5	3.84	13	13	0	0	73	87	9	11	48	5.9	1.35	.295
	Sacramento (PCL)	AAA	5	3	4.42	12	11	0	0	71	81	4	13	49	6.2	1.32	.287
2014	Sacramento (PCL)	AAA	10	7	4.97	27	27	0	0	145	170	12	51	128	7.9	1.52	.295
Minor League Totals			30	21	3.92	209	63	0	5	529	560	37	170	460	7.8	1.38	.280

28 HEATH FILLMYER, RHP

BA GRADE
50 Risk: Extreme

Born: May 16, 1994. **B-T:** R-R. **Ht.:** 6-1. **Wt.:** 180. **Drafted:** Mercer County (N.J.) JC, 2014 (5th round). **Signed by:** Ron Vaughn.

The Rockies, intrigued by Fillmyer's arm strength, drafted him as a pitcher in the 28th round in 2013, even though he'd spent most of the spring playing shortstop at Mercer County (N.J.) JC, throwing just eight innings on the mound. He opted to return for a second season with MCJC to pitch full-time to see if he could raise his stock. All he did was go Fillmyer went 9-0, 0.68 to the Vikings to the Division II Junior College World Series in 2014 before landing a $305,000 bonus from the Athletics. After years of mainly being a position player, Fillmyer is still plenty raw, but he has an undeniably big arm. His fastball sits in the mid-90s with downhill angle and gets up to 97 mph. He spins a solid-average curveball that flashes plus, and while he's still learning his changeup, the pitch does show potential. Fillmyer's delivery required some extensive cleanup after the A's brought him into the fold, but he has come a long way in a short period. The team worked to get him to stay over the rubber longer and not jump at hitters, and he now throws with an easier, more repeatable motion and does a good job of throwing strikes. Fillmyer will need development time, but the A's are excited about what they have as he projects to open 2015 at low Class A Beloit.

Year	Club (League)	Class	W	L	ERA	G	GS	CG	SV	IP	H	HR	BB	SO	K/9	WHIP	AVG
2014	Athletics (AZL)	R	1	0	2.79	6	0	0	0	10	5	0	5	10	9.3	1.03	.147
Minor League Totals			1	0	2.79	6	0	0	0	10	5	0	5	10	9.3	1.03	.147

29 JORDAN SCHWARTZ, RHP

BA GRADE
50 Risk: Extreme

Born: Feb. 28, 1992. **B-T:** R-R. **Ht.:** 6-2. **Wt.:** 195. **Drafted:** Niagara, 2014 (4th round). **Signed by:** Matt Higginson.

Schwartz played outfield when he wasn't pitching for Niagara but didn't enjoy much success on the mound until his junior year. After posting ERAs north of 8.00 as a freshman and sophomore, he went 5-6, 3.12 as a junior in 2014 and led the Metro Atlantic Athletic Conference in strikeouts (109). The Athletics made Schwartz the Niagara program's highest-drafted player since 1972 when they took him in the fourth round in 2014, signing him for $175,000. He has a physical frame and fires fastballs in the mid-90s, getting up to 97 mph with some armside run. His changeup gets good depth and has a chance to be plus, putting it ahead of his slurvy breaking ball as his best secondary offering. Schwartz still has much to learn about the finer points of pitching and can struggle to repeat his delivery, leading to inconsistent command. Whether he ultimately lands in the bullpen is a question mark, but the A's will keep him in the rotation for as long as they can, beginning in 2015 at low Class A Beloit.

Year	Club (League)	Class	W	L	ERA	G	GS	CG	SV	IP	H	HR	BB	SO	K/9	WHIP	AVG
2014	Athletics (AZL)	R	0	0	4.50	1	1	0	0	2	3	0	0	4	18.0	1.50	.333
	Vermont (NYP)	SS	1	1	4.82	11	0	0	0	19	21	0	13	14	6.8	1.82	.288
Minor League Totals			1	1	4.79	12	1	0	0	21	24	0	13	18	7.8	1.79	.293

30 TRACE LOEHR, SS

BA GRADE
50 Risk: Extreme

Born: May 23, 1995. **B-T:** L-R. **Ht.:** 5-10. **Wt.:** 175. **Drafted:** HS— Milwaukie, Ore., 2014 (6th round). **Signed by:** Jim Coffman.

Loehr teamed with Pirates first-rounder Cole Tucker to form the double-play tandem for the gold-medal winning Team USA at the 2013 IBAF 18U World Cup in Taiwan. A shortstop by trade, Loehr played second base in deference to Tucker, and that versatility was one of the factors that attracted the Athletics in the draft. They spent $600,000, the third-largest bonus in their 2014 class, on the sixth-rounder to sign him away from Oregon State. He looks like a future top-of-the-order hitter. He has plus speed and takes short, quick swings. He's at his best when he focuses on line drives and keeping the ball out of the air, as he has little power, but he shows a feel for the zone and for hitting to different parts of the field. The A's see him fitting a similar mold as Cliff Pennington, their 2005 first-round pick, though Pennington was more of a pure shortstop. Scouts who watched Loehr in high school could envision him moving to second base because his arm is solid but not plus. Wherever he plays, he's a dependable defender with good instincts, and the A's like his blue-collar mentality as well. With Yairo Munoz slated to be shortstop at low Class A Beloit in 2015, Loehr may stay in extended spring training before going to short-season Vermont.

Year	Club (League)	Class	AVG	G	AB	R	H	2B	3B	HR	RBI	BB	SO	SB	CS	OBP	SLG
2014	Athletics (AZL)	R	.244	41	160	22	39	3	2	0	14	15	31	6	2	.313	.288
Minor League Totals			.244	41	160	22	39	3	2	0	14	15	31	6	2	.313	.288

Philadelphia Phillies

BY JOSH NORRIS

The writing was on the wall from the beginning for the 2014 Phillies. Their core of shortstop Jimmy Rollins, second baseman Chase Utley and first baseman Ryan Howard was back, but all a year older and looking less and less like the versions that inspired so much joy in Philadelphia from 2007-11.

The complementary pieces around that trio were not good, and certainly not good enough to back a rotation fronted by all-star lefthanders Cole Hamels and Cliff Lee. An injury-prone supporting cast in the rotation and a leaky bullpen, where only closer Jonathan Papelbon and his likely successor, dominating rookie setup man Ken Giles, pitched well consistently.

That's not to say there weren't highlights to their season. Hamels, lefty Jake Diekman, Giles and Papelbon combined to no-hit the Braves on Sept. 1. Giles debuted on June 12 and proceeded to post an ERA of 1.18 and strike out 64 over 46 innings.

The low points, however, including a no-hitter at the hands of the Dodgers' Josh Beckett, an elbow injury to Lee that killed his trade value, and Papelbon grabbing his crotch on his way off the mound after a late-season implosion, far outweighed the positives. All that added up to a second straight season with a 73-89 record, their third in a row at .500 or worse after a stretch of five straight division titles, and their first last-place finish in the National League East since the turn of the century.

General manager Ruben Amaro Jr., whose tenure began with a NL pennant in 2009 and Roy Halladay-fueled 102-win season in 2010, has overseen the slide. His predecessor, Hall of Famer Pat Gillick, took over as interim club CEO in September and proclaimed in October that "it's probably a couple of years" before the Phillies compete again.

The Phillies have slowly started to change. Scouting director Marti Wolever was fired after the season, replaced by Johnny Almaraz, previously the international scouting director with both the Rangers and Braves. Wolever oversaw a fallow period of drafts, including first-pick busts such as Anthony Hewitt (2008), Larry Greene (2011) and Shane Watson (2012), plus a level of controversy.

Baseball America revealed the Phillies had notified the NCAA that Oregon State lefthander Ben Wetzler, their unsigned fifth-round pick in 2013, had an agent acting as his advisor, a common practice that technically is against NCAA rules. As a result, Wetzler, now a Marlin and now going by the name Ben Holmes, was suspended for the first 11 games of the 2014 college season.

Rookie reliever Ken Giles ascended to the role of set-up man in what was an otherwise bleak season in Philadelphia

TOP PROSPECTS OF THE DECADE

Year	Player, Pos.	2014 Org
2005	Ryan Howard, 1b	Phillies
2006	Cole Hamels, lhp	Phillies
2007	Carlos Carrasco, rhp	Indians
2008	Carlos Carrasco, rhp	Indians
2009	Domonic Brown, of	Phillies
2010	Domonic Brown, of	Phillies
2011	Domonic Brown, of	Phillies
2012	Trevor May, rhp	Twins
2013	Jesse Biddle, lhp	Phillies
2014	Maikel Franco, 3b	Phillies

The Phillies don't have much help coming in 2015. Their best prospects—shortstop J.P. Crawford, righthander Aaron Nola and third baseman Maikel Franco—rival any organization's, but the system lacks depth, particularly in the upper levels.

It was a bad year in Philadelphia in 2014, and it looks like it will be a little while longer before Phillies fans can have high hopes once again.

General manager: Ruben Amaro Jr. **Farm director:** Joe Jordan. **Scouting director:** Johnny Almaraz.

Class	Team	League	W	L	PCT	Finish	Manager
Majors	Philadelphia Phillies	National	73	89	.451	t-22nd (30)	Ryne Sandberg
Triple-A	Lehigh Valley IronPigs	International	66	78	.458	11th (14)	Dave Brundage
Double-A	Reading Fightin Phils	Eastern	66	76	.465	t-9th (12)	Dusty Wathan
High A	Clearwater Threshers	Florida State	49	89	.355	12th (12)	Nelson Prada
Low A	Lakewood BlueClaws	South Atlantic	53	84	.387	14th (14)	Greg Legg
Short-season	Williamsport Crosscutters	New York-Penn	33	43	.434	t-12th (14)	Shawn Williams
Rookie	Phillies	Gulf Coast	36	23	.610	3rd (16)	Roly de Armas
Overall Minor League Record			**303**	**393**	**.435**	**30th (30)**	

THIS YEAR'S TOP 30

No.	Player, Pos.	Grade/Risk
1.	J.P. Crawford, ss	65/High
2.	Aaron Nola, rhp	60/Medium
3.	Maikel Franco, 3b	55/High
4.	Roman Quinn, of	50/High
5.	Carlos Tocci, of	50/High
6.	Aaron Brown, of	50/High
7.	Matt Imhof, lhp	50/High
8.	Jesmuel Valentin 2b	50/High
9.	Yoel Mecias, lhp	50/Extreme
10.	Franklyn Kilome, rhp	50/Extreme
11.	Jesse Biddle, lhp	50/Extreme
12.	Odubel Herrera, 2b/of	45/Medium
13.	Deivi Grullon, c	50/Extreme
14.	Ricardo Pinto, rhp	50/Extreme
15.	Andrew Knapp, c	45/High
16.	Dylan Cozens, of	45/High
17.	Kelly Dugan, of	45/High
18.	Zach Green, 3b	50/Extreme
19.	Severino Gonzalez, rhp	45/High
20.	Aaron Altherr, of	45/High
21.	Cord Sandberg, of	50/Extreme
22.	Cameron Perkins, of	40/Medium
23.	Victor Arano, rhp	45/High
24.	Joely Rodriguez, lhp	40/Medium
25.	Miguel Gonzalez, rhp	45/High
26.	Nefi Ogando, rhp	45/High
27.	Jose Pujols, of	50/Extreme
28.	Willians Astudillo, c/of/1b	45/High
29.	Luis Encarnacion, 1b/of	50/Extreme
30.	Elniery Garcia, lhp	50/Extreme

LAST YEAR'S TOP 30

No.	Player, Pos.	Status
1.	Maikel Franco, 3b	No. 3
2.	Jesse Biddle, lhp	No. 11
3.	J.P. Crawford, ss	No. 1
4.	Miguel Gonzalez, rhp	No. 25
5.	Carlos Tocci, of	No. 5
6.	Ethan Martin, rhp	Dropped out
7.	Cesar Hernandez, 2b/of	Majors
8.	Aaron Altherr, of	No. 20
9.	Severino Gonzalez, rhp	No. 19
10.	Roman Quinn, ss	No. 4
11.	Adam Morgan, lhp	Dropped out
12.	Cameron Perkins, of	No. 22
13.	Luis Encarnacion, 3b	No. 29
14.	Deivi Grullon, c	No. 13
15.	Zach Green, 3b	No. 18
16.	Cameron Rupp, c	Dropped out
17.	Kelly Dugan, of	No. 17
18.	Shane Watson, rhp	Dropped out
19.	Jose Pujols, of	No. 27
20.	Kenny Giles, rhp	Majors
21.	Tommy Joseph, c	Dropped out
22.	Dylan Cozens, of	No. 16
23.	Yoel Mecias, lhp	No. 9
24.	Andrew Knapp, c	No. 15
25.	Cord Sandberg, of	No. 21
26.	Jan Hernandez, 3b	Dropped out
27.	Zach Collier, of	Dropped out
28.	Malquin Canelo, ss	Dropped out
29.	Austin Wright, lhp	Dropped out
30.	Dan Child, rhp	Dropped out

BEST TOOLS

Best Hitter for Average	J.P. Crawford
Best Power Hitter	Maikel Franco
Best Strike-Zone Discipline	J.P. Crawford
Fastest Baserunner	Roman Quinn
Best Athlete	Roman Quinn
Best Fastball	Nefi Ogando
Best Curveball	Jesse Biddle
Best Slider	Ethan Stewart
Best Changeup	Aaron Nola
Best Control	Aaron Nola
Best Defensive Catcher	Deivi Grullon
Best Defensive Infielder	J.P. Crawford
Best Infield Arm	Maikel Franco
Best Defensive Outfielder	Aaron Altherr
Best Outfield Arm	Jose Pujols

PROJECTED 2018 LINEUP

Catcher	Deivi Grullon
First Base	Maikel Franco
Second Base	Jesmuel Valentin
Third Base	Cody Asche
Shortstop	J.P. Crawford
Left Field	Carlos Tocci
Center Field	Roman Quinn
Right Field	Aaron Brown
No. 1 Starter	Cole Hamels
No. 2 Starter	Aaron Nola
No. 3 Starter	Jon Pettibone
No. 4 Starter	David Buchanan
No. 5 Starter	Matt Imhof
Closer	Ken Giles

PHILADELPHIA PHILLIES

TOP 2014 ROOKIE: Maikel Franco, 3b. The powerful third baseman could earn an MLB spot out of spring training.
BREAKOUT PROSPECT: Andrew Knapp, c. A year further away from Tommy John surgery should help his bat take off.
SLEEPER: Edubray Ramos, rhp. Older Venezuelan with plus fastball is poised for full-season ball breakout.

SOURCE OF TOP 30 TALENT

Homegrown	25	Acquired	5
College	5	Trades	4
Junior college	0	Rule 5 draft	1
High school	9	Independent leagues	0
Draft-and-follow	0	Free agents/waivers	0
Nondrafted free agents	0		
International	11		

LF
Cord Sandberg (21)
Luis Encarnacion (29)
Larry Greene
Samuel Hiciano

CF
Roman Quinn (4)
Carlos Tocci (5)
Aaron Altherr (20)

RF
Aaron Brown (6)
Dylan Cozens (16)
Kelly Dugan (17)
Cameron Perkins (22)
Jose Pujols (27)

3B
Maikel Franco (3)
Zach Green (18)
Jan Hernandez
Mitch Walding
Harold Martinez

SS
J.P. Crawford (1)
Arquimedez Gamboa
Daniel Brito
Jonathan Arauz

2B
Jesmuel Valentin (8)
Odubel Herrera (12)
Andrew Pullin
Drew Stankiewicz
Angelo Mora

1B
Rhys Hoskins
Wilmer Oberto
Art Charles

C
Deivi Grullon (13)
Andrew Knapp (15)
Willians Astudillo (28)
Tommy Joseph
Cameron Rupp
Gabriel Lino
Jake Sweaney

LHP

LHSP	LHRP
Matt Imhof (7)	Joely Rodriguez (24)
Yoel Mecias (9)	Andy Oliver
Jesse Biddle (11)	Ethan Stewart
Elniery Garcia (30)	Chris O'Hare
Adam Morgan	Austin Wright

RHP

RHSP	RHRP
Aaron Nola (2)	Miguel Gonzalez (25)
Franklyn Kilome (10)	Nefi Ogando (26)
Ricardo Pinto (14)	Ethan Martin
Severino Gonzalez (19)	Colton Murray
Victor Arano (23)	Edubray Ramos
Shane Watson	Dan Child
Mitch Gueller	Colin Kleven
Tyler Viza	Mike Nesseth
Drew Anderson	
Mark Leiter Jr.	

2014

BEST PURE HITTER: 1B/OF Rhys Hoskins (5) works counts, has present strength and a good feel for hitting. He hit .326 in the Cape Cod League last summer and made good adjustments in instructional league.

BEST POWER HITTER: Hoskins has plus raw power and had a 450-foot homer in instructs. OF Aaron Brown (3) hit 13 homers in the spring for Pepperdine, best in the West Coast Conference. He has similar raw power and much more athleticism.

FASTEST RUNNER: Brown and SS Emmanuel Marrero (7) were the best of a modest class, with average speed.

BEST DEFENSIVE PLAYER: Marrero is a sure-handed, fairly smooth defender at short. If Brown ran better, he could stay in center field, which he played for the Waves, but he's a better fit in right field long-term, with a plus arm.

BEST FASTBALL: RHP Aaron Nola (1) has excellent control for an amateur and improved his fastball velocity in 2014. The Phillies saw him up to 95-96 mph. RHP Chris Oliver (4) has hit 97 in the past and sat 92-94 for most of 2014. LHP Matt Imhof (2) elicits swings and misses on an 89-93 mph fastball from a high release point.

BEST SECONDARY PITCH: Nola's changeup was the clear No. 1 in the class for the Phillies. LHP Brandon Leibrandt (6) has a fine changeup as well that earns some plus grades.

BEST PRO DEBUT: Nola reached Double-A and went 4-3, 2.93 overall with 45 strikeouts and just 10 walks in 55 innings. Imhof finished at low Class A Lakewood and struck out 40 while walking 11 in 42 innings overall.

BEST ATHLETE: Brown was a legitimate top-three-rounds talent both as a hitter and as a pitcher. His slider would rank as the best in the Phillies' draft class, as it was a true plus pitch, and he was the best player in Pepperdine's super-regional loss at Texas Christian.

MOST INTRIGUING BACKGROUND: Nola's brother Austin, whom he teamed with at Louisiana State during the 2012 season, is a shortstop in the Marlins system who played in Double-A Jacksonville this past season. Leibrandt's father Charlie won 140 games in a 14-year big league career. SS Drew Stankiewicz (11) is the son of ex-big leaguer Andy, now the head coach at Grand Canyon. Unsigned OF Tom Flacco (32) is the younger brother of quarterback Joe Flacco of the NFL's Baltimore Ravens.

CLOSEST TO THE MAJORS: If the Phillies had been in contention, Nola likely would have reached the majors with Brandon Finnegan-like speed. He'll still end up as one of the quickest movers in the 2014 draft.

BEST LATE-ROUND PICK: Physical LHP Austin Davis (12) has a durable 6-foot-5, 240-pound frame and has hit 94 mph with his fastball in the past.

THE ONE WHO GOT AWAY: The Phillies signed who they wanted to sign, but if they'd had more money they would have made a run at local SS Al Molina (29), whom they liked as a catcher. He's headed to Coastal Carolina.

ASSESSMENT: The Phillies deviated from their high-risk, prep athlete template, signing only one high school player. Marti Wolever, in charge of scouting since 2002, was let go in September.

2013

SS J.P. Crawford (1) looks like an elite prospect. C Andrew Knapp (2) and raw OF Cord Sandberg (3) are the best of the rest of the pitching-poor lot.

GRADE: B+

2012

Injuries (diabetes, shoulder surgery) to RHP Shane Watson (1s) and failing to sign RHP Alec Rash (2) thinned this pitching class. The draft's best hopes are OF Dylan Cozens (2) and OF Cam Perkins (6), who hit a wall in Triple-A.

GRADE: D

2011

OF Larry Greene (1s) looks like a bust. 3B Cody Asche (4) moved quickly, as did RHP Kenny Giles (7), and SS/OF Roman Quinn (2) has bounced back well from a torn Achilles.

GRADE: B

TOP DRAFT PICKS OF THE DECADE

Year	Player, Pos.	2014 Org
2005	Mike Costanzo, 3b (2nd round)	Reds
2006	Kyle Drabek, rhp	Blue Jays
2007	Joe Savery, lhp	Athletics
2008	Anthony Hewitt, of	Out of baseball
2009	Kelly Dugan, of (2nd round)	Phillies
2010	Jesse Biddle, lhp	Phillies
2011	Larry Greene, of (1st round supp.)	Phillies
2012	Shane Watson, rhp (1st round supp.)	Phillies
2013	J.P. Crawford, ss	Phillies
2014	Aaron Nola, rhp	Phillies

LARGEST BONUSES IN CLUB HISTORY

Gavin Floyd, 2001	$4,200,000
Aaron Nola, 2014	$3,300,900
Pat Burrell, 1998	$3,150,000
J.P. Crawford, 2013	$2,299,300
Brett Myers, 1999	$2,050,000

1 J.P. CRAWFORD, SS

Born: Jan. 11, 1995. **B-T:** L-R. **Ht.:** 6-2. **Wt.:** 189.
Drafted: HS—Lakewood, Calif., 2013 (1st round).
Signed by: Demerius Pittman.

Crawford first popped onto the Phillies' radar while they were scouting righthander Shane Watson, a high school teammate whom they eventually took as a supplemental first-round pick in 2012. They were so enamored of Crawford's overall skill set that they took him with their first-round choice in 2013 and signed him for $2,299,300, then watched as he won the batting title (.345) in the Rookie-level Gulf Coast League in his professional debut. Crawford built on that performance in 2014 with a stellar season split between low Class A Lakewood and high Class A Clearwater that cemented his status as one of the best prospects in baseball and as a shortstop who should have no problem sticking at the position longterm. He's the cousin of Dodgers outfielder Carl Crawford and the son of a former football player at Iowa State and in the Canadian Football League.

All the pieces are there for Crawford to be a potential all-star at shortstop with strong contributions on both sides of the ball. Evaluators' biggest question is how much impact he'll have at the plate. Some look at his above-average raw sock in batting practice and eight home runs in a half-season in the large parks of the Florida State League and project a player who could produce 20-25 homers annually. Others are less confident, projecting more than 10-12 homers, but the Phillies say he still has plenty of strength to gain, which of course will help his potential power output. In either case, all evaluators believe he will be an above-average hitter, especially considering the keen eye that manifested itself as a nearly 1-to-1 strikeout-to-walk ratio this summer. That was particularly impressive at Clearwater, where he played as a 19-year-old and had a stretch in July when he struck out just twice over 62 at-bats. He's capable of being a spectacular defender with strong baseball instincts and a plus arm. The Phillies worked with Crawford in instructional league on improving his comfort level on the backhanded play, for he was a bit more careless in the FSL, committing 17 of his 29 errors on the season. He shows a strong internal clock and an excellent baseball IQ, and he doesn't take his bat at-bats into the field with him. The only other area where Crawford earns below-average marks is his running, where he's below-average out of the box but uses long strides to kick it up to average underway. Multiple evaluators have noted that Crawford is a duck-footed, heel-toe style runner, which could partly contribute to his slow times to first base. He was nevertheless aggressive, if not efficient, in stealing 24 bases in 38 attempts.

Crawford is on line to head to Double-A Reading in 2015 to get his first taste of the upper levels and work toward fulfilling his role as Jimmy Rollins' heir to shortstop at Citizens Bank Park. The 36-year-old Rollins has one year left on his contract, and a strong 2015 would set up Crawford to replace him by 2016. If everything clicks, he has the potential to be an all-star for many years to come.

Year	Club (League)	Class	AVG	G	AB	R	H	2B	3B	HR	RBI	BB	SO	SB	CS	OBP	SLG
2013	Phillies (GCL)	R	.345	39	142	24	49	8	3	1	19	25	25	12	5	.443	.465
	Lakewood (SAL)	LoA	.208	14	53	10	11	1	0	0	2	7	10	2	1	.300	.226
2014	Lakewood (SAL)	LoA	.295	60	227	37	67	16	0	3	19	37	37	14	7	.398	.405
	Clearwater (FSL)	HiA	.275	63	236	32	65	7	0	8	29	28	37	10	7	.352	.407
Minor League Totals			.292	176	658	103	192	32	3	12	69	97	109	38	20	.384	.404

2 AARON NOLA, RHP

MIKE JANES

Born: June 4, 1993. **B-T:** R-R. **Ht.:** 6-1. **Wt.:** 195. **Drafted:** Louisiana State, 2014 (1st round). **Signed by:** Mike Stauffer.

Nola entered his junior year at Louisiana State with high expectations, then exceeded them in an All-America 11-1, 1.47 campaign. He ranked third in NCAA Division I in strikeouts in 2014, and the Phillies popped him seventh overall, signing him for a $3,300,900 bonus—the second-highest in team history. Nola's hallmark is his stellar command, which stems from good athletic ability and freakish flexibility. His fastball checks in at 93-95 mph and gets excellent life from a mid-three-quarters arm slot. He backs up the fastball with a slider and changeup, which each have the potential to be plus in the future. He's on a fast track for sure, but the Phillies would like to see him improve in a few areas before they consider him for the rotation. Most notably, they'd like to make sure he stays consistent with his arm slot. When it drops lower than three-quarters, his slider tends to flatten. His changeup, a plus pitch earlier in his career, has regressed. He needs to work more on controlling the running game. The Phillies' best pitching prospect by a wide margin, Nola finished his pro debut at Double-A Reading and should return there to start 2015. He should at least score a Philadelphia cameo by season's end, if he's not up sooner.

BA GRADE

60 Risk: Medium

LGE	BF	SO%	BB%	HR/9
FSL	121	24.8	4.1	1.15
EL	98	15.3	5.1	1.50

Year	Club (League)	Class	W	L	ERA	G	GS	CG	SV	IP	H	HR	BB	SO	K/9	WHIP	AVG
2014	Clearwater (FSL)	HiA	2	3	3.16	7	6	0	0	31	24	4	5	30	8.6	0.93	.214
	Reading (EL)	AA	2	0	2.63	5	5	0	0	24	25	4	5	15	5.6	1.25	.272
Minor League Totals			4	3	2.93	12	11	0	0	55	49	8	10	45	7.3	1.07	.240

3 MAIKEL FRANCO, 3B/1B

Born: Aug. 16, 1992. **B-T:** R-R. **Ht.:** 6-1. **Wt.:** 180. **Signed:** Dominican Republic, 2010. **Signed by:** Koby Perez.

Franco signed as a 17-year-old out of the Dominican Republic for $100,000. His career took off in the second half of the 2012 season at low Class A Lakewood, and he broke out in 2013, hitting 31 homers while reaching Double-A Reading. He had to rebound after a poor introduction to Triple-A Lehigh Valley in 2014, but he turned it on late in the season and earned a September callup. The biggest knock on Franco is always going to be his overaggressive approach, and his walk rate of 5.4 percent tied for fifth-worst in the International League in 2014. He's got plenty of power and makes a high rate of contact despite a swing that can get long, but he's vulnerable to velocity on his hands. Franco probably won't hit for a high average unless he tones down his approach and learns to better recognize and lay off breaking pitches out of the zone. He still draws positive reviews at third base for his quick first step—though he's a well below-average runner—and top-shelf arm strength, which allows him to unleash laser throws from all arm angles. Franco will challenge Cody Asche for the third base job with Philadelphia to open the 2015 season, but he most likely faces a return to Triple-A to work more on refining his approach.

BA GRADE

55 Risk: High

LGE	PA	BB%	SO%	ISO
IL	556	5.4	14.6	.171
NL	58	1.7	22.4	.036

Year	Club (League)	Class	AVG	G	AB	R	H	2B	3B	HR	RBI	BB	SO	SB	CS	OBP	SLG
2012	Lakewood (SAL)	LoA	.280	132	503	70	141	32	3	14	84	38	80	3	1	.336	.439
2013	Clearwater (FSL)	HiA	.299	65	264	42	79	23	1	16	52	20	39	0	0	.349	.576
	Reading (EL)	AA	.339	69	277	47	94	13	2	15	51	10	31	1	2	.363	.563
2014	Lehigh Valley (IL)	AAA	.257	133	521	64	134	33	4	16	78	30	81	3	1	.299	.428
	Philadelphia (NL)	MAJ	.179	16	56	5	10	2	0	0	5	1	13	0	0	.190	.214
Major League Totals			.179	16	56	5	10	2	0	0	5	1	13	0	0	.190	.214
Minor League Totals			.275	521	2026	271	557	131	13	66	338	140	322	7	4	.325	.450

4 ROMAN QUINN, OF/SS

DAVID SCHOFIELD

Born: May 14, 1993. **B-T:** B-R. **Ht.:** 5-10. **Wt.:** 175. **Drafted:** HS—Port St. Joe, Fla., 2011 (2nd round). **Signed by:** Aaron Jersild.

A high school quarterback at Port St. Joe (Fla.) High, Quinn passed up a scholarship to play the position at Florida State. Instead, he signed as the Phillies' second-round pick for $775,000 in 2011. He spent his first two seasons playing exclusively shortstop, but then the Phillies drafted J.P. Crawford in 2013, so Quinn moved to center field in 2014. He tore his right Achilles tendon in a workout following the 2013 season, but his top-of-the-scale speed took only a minimal hit in 2014. Quinn's calling card is blinding speed, which has allowed him to steal 94 bases in 121 tries—a 78 percent success rate—over his first three seasons. It also has been crucial to his fine play in center field, where he draws comparisons with current Phillie Ben Revere. Like Revere, Quinn's routes lack precision or polish, but his speed allows for quick corrections and minimal misplays. Given his dimensions, Quinn projects to hit for little power, but he has the skills to be an average hitter, and his fleet feet could allow him to tick up just slightly if he learns to embrace an approach more suited for his skill set. Quinn played in the Arizona Fall League in 2014 to make up for the time he missed while rehabbing from his leg injuries. He will get his first test at the upper levels in 2015 when he moves up to Double-A Reading.

BA GRADE

50 Risk: High

LGE	PA	BB%	SO%	ISO
FSL	382	9.4	20.9	.113

Year	Club (League)	Class	AVG	G	AB	R	H	2B	3B	HR	RBI	BB	SO	SB	CS	OBP	SLG
2012	Williamsport (NYP)	SS	.281	66	267	56	75	9	11	1	23	28	61	30	6	.370	.408
2013	Lakewood (SAL)	LoA	.238	67	260	37	62	7	3	5	21	27	64	32	9	.323	.346
2014	Clearwater (FSL)	HiA	.257	88	327	51	84	10	3	7	36	36	80	32	12	.343	.370
Minor League Totals			.259	221	854	144	221	26	17	13	80	91	205	94	27	.346	.375

5 CARLOS TOCCI, OF

DAVID SCHOFIELD

Born: Aug. 23, 1995. **B-T:** R-R. **Ht.:** 6-2. **Wt.:** 160. **Signed:** Venezuela, 2011. **Signed by:** Jesus Mendez.

Signed out of Venezuela for $759,000 in 2011 when he turned 16, Tocci has been pushed aggressively by the Phillies since Day One. He jumped straight to the Rookie-level Gulf Coast League as a 16-year-old and was just 17 at low Class A Lakewood in 2013, when he showcased raw skills but a severe lack of strength that showed up with a .249 slugging percentage in 421 at-bats. Tocci repeated the South Atlantic League in 2014 and grew into a touch more strength, and it showed up in his performance. He was more patient and drove the ball more frequently, hitting his first two home runs and eight triples. He still needs more strength behind his swing, which could come if he continues to mature physically. Not all scouts are convinced Tocci's body projects to add weight, but he could make it to the majors based on his defense alone. He gracefully covers tons of ground in center field with fine first-step quickness and fluid actions, and he adds an average arm for the position. He's an average runner as well. After two full seasons in Lakewood, Tocci will have to move to high Class A Clearwater in 2015. He might not be ready for the jump offensively, and at some point being young for the league won't be an excuse. If he doesn't hit more, his ceiling is that of a fourth outfielder with excellent defensive skills.

BA GRADE

50 Risk: High

LGE	PA	BB%	SO%	ISO
SAL	538	4.6	17.8	.082

Year	Club (League)	Class	AVG	G	AB	R	H	2B	3B	HR	RBI	BB	SO	SB	CS	OBP	SLG
2012	Phillies (GCL)	R	.278	38	97	13	27	2	0	0	9	6	18	9	2	.330	.299
2013	Lakewood (SAL)	LoA	.209	118	421	40	88	17	0	0	26	22	77	6	7	.261	.249
2014	Lakewood (SAL)	LoA	.242	125	487	59	118	18	8	2	30	25	96	10	11	.297	.324
Minor League Totals			.232	281	1005	112	233	37	8	2	65	53	191	25	20	.285	.291

6 AARON BROWN, OF

DAVID SCHOFIELD

Born: June 20, 1992. **B-T:** L-L. **Ht.:** 6-2. **Wt.:** 220. **Drafted:** Pepperdine, 2014 (3rd round). **Signed by:** Shane Bowers.

Drafted by the Pirates in 2011 and Indians in 2013, Brown intrigued scouts both as an outfielder and a lefthanded pitcher at Pepperdine. He throws in the low 90s off the mound and finished with the second-best ERA in the West Coast Conference in 2014, spinning seven innings in the super regional to deal Texas Christian its only loss. He signed as the Phillies' third-rounder for $750,000. The Phillies liked Brown more as an outfielder, and he could take off offensively now that pitching is in his past. He earns high marks for his work ethic, physicality, intensity and, most importantly, his well-balanced set of tools. He starts his swing with a double toe-tap of his front foot, and his stroke itself is smooth and shows the potential for above-average power due to both strength and good bat speed. Evaluators who caught Brown after he turned pro said that he must smooth out his stike-zone judgment and cover some holes, noting he was prone both to swinging through pitches in the strike zone and looking vulnerable on breaking balls off the plate. He's an above-average runner with an above-average arm and average range in right field. Brown fits the right-field profile if he reaches his ceiling, though he also can handle center in short looks. He could potentially begin 2015 at high Class A Clearwater.

	BA GRADE	
	50	Risk: High

LGE	PA	BB%	SO%	ISO
NYP	193	3.1	21.2	.100
SAL	59	1.7	32.2	.164

Year	Club (League)	Class	AVG	G	AB	R	H	2B	3B	HR	RBI	BB	SO	SB	CS	OBP	SLG
2014	Williamsport (NYP)	SS	.256	47	180	23	46	7	1	3	16	6	41	8	4	.301	.356
	Lakewood (SAL)	LoA	.309	14	55	3	17	6	0	1	5	1	19	0	1	.339	.473
Minor League Totals			.268	61	235	26	63	13	1	4	21	7	60	8	5	.310	.383

7 MATT IMHOF, LHP

DAVID SCHOFIELD

Born: Oct. 26, 1993. **B-T:** L-L. **Ht.:** 6-5. **Wt.:** 220. **Drafted:** Cal Poly, 2014 (2nd round). **Signed by:** Shane Bowers.

Looking for quicker returns in a system that had been widely panned for lack of impact at the top, the Phillies went college heavy in the 2014 draft, inking only one high schooler out of their 28-player class. Imhof, a Cal Poly lefthander who pitched on USA Baseball's College National Team in 2013 and finished seventh in NCAA Division I with 11.2 strikeouts per nine innings in 2014, was the club's second-round pick and signed for $1,187,900. Blessed with a physical pitcher's body, Imhof primarily works off his fastball, which clocks in at 86-92 mph and touched 94 in college. He couples it with a 75-80 mph curveball, which features strong overhand break out of a high three-quarters slot. He has a changeup as well, which sits in the low 80s, but he doesn't throw it often. None of his pitches grade as plus, but all are average or have the potential to be average with development. His arsenal gets a bit of a boost from the deception created when he hides the ball behind his body during delivery. A polished college arm, Imhof should begin the 2015 season at high Class A Clearwater. He projects as a back-end starter but one who could move quickly.

	BA GRADE	
	50	Risk: High

LGE	BF	SO%	BB%	HR/9
NYP	46	23.9	8.7	0.00
SAL	116	23.3	5.2	0.99

Year	Club (League)	Class	W	L	ERA	G	GS	CG	SV	IP	H	HR	BB	SO	K/9	WHIP	AVG
2014	Phillies (GCL)	R	0	0	0.00	1	1	0	0	3	2	0	1	2	6.0	1.00	.222
	Williamsport (NYP)	SS	1	0	0.75	3	3	1	0	12	6	0	4	11	8.3	0.83	.154
	Lakewood (SAL)	LoA	0	2	4.28	7	7	0	0	27	32	3	6	27	8.9	1.39	.302
Minor League Totals			1	2	2.98	11	11	1	0	42	40	3	11	40	8.5	1.20	.260

8 JESMUEL VALENTIN, 2B

Born: May 12, 1994. **B-T:** B-R. **Ht.:** 5-10. **Wt.:** 180. **Drafted:** HS—Gurabo, P.R., 2012 (1st round supplemental). **Signed by:** Robert Sidwell (Dodgers).

The Dodgers drafted Valentin, the son of longtime big league shortstop Jose Valentin, in 2012 and signed him for $984,700. He was middle-infield partners with Astros top prospect Carlos Correa at the Puerto Rico Baseball Academy. The Phillies acquired Valentin along with righthander Victor Arano in the August 2014 trade that sent veteran righty Roberto Hernandez to Los Angeles. Valentin is a second baseman with an strong set of offensive skills. He shows a quick stroke from both sides of the plate and the ability to hit line drives all over the diamond. His power is more to the gaps, but he has shown the potential for a home run every now and again. He's also got above-average speed and some aggressiveness on the bases. At second base, Valentin shows good hands and actions, albeit with a fringy arm that plays better when he's able to set his feet. He also hangs in well on double-play pivots. He's a solid runner from home to first who is faster when he gets going. After a brief stop at high Class A Clearwater following the trade, Valentin will head back there in 2015. Phillies stalwart Chase Utley, entering his age-36 season, can't last forever, so Valentin should emerge as the best in-house replacement option.

BA GRADE

50 Risk: High

LGE	PA	BB%	SO%	ISO
MWL	462	8.2	15.6	.150
FSL	49	6.1	12.2	.045

Year	Club (League)	Class	AVG	G	AB	R	H	2B	3B	HR	RBI	BB	SO	SB	CS	OBP	SLG
2012	Dodgers (AZL)	R	.211	43	152	34	32	6	2	2	18	35	24	5	2	.352	.316
2013	Great Lakes (MWL)	LoA	.212	33	99	12	21	6	1	0	5	16	28	4	3	.325	.293
	Ogden (PIO)	R	.284	62	250	53	71	10	3	4	24	33	34	11	7	.379	.396
2014	Great Lakes (MWL)	LoA	.280	108	407	73	114	22	9	7	47	38	72	24	7	.349	.430
	Clearwater (FSL)	HiA	.205	12	44	8	9	2	0	0	0	3	6	1	1	.255	.250
Minor League Totals			.259	258	952	180	247	46	15	13	94	125	164	45	20	.351	.380

9 YOEL MECIAS, LHP

DAVID SCHOFIELD

Born: Oct. 11, 1993. **B-T:** L-L. **Ht.:** 6-2. **Wt.:** 160. **Signed:** Venezuela, 2010. **Signed by:** Jesus Mendez.

Mecias has worked just 133 pro innings in four pro speasons. He spent 2011 on the restricted list, then missed half of what had been a dominant 2013 season with Tommy John surgery, which he had in June of that year. He got back on the hill in 2014 with a four-start tuneup in the Rookie-level Gulf Coast League before finishing his season with seven more starts at low Class A Lakewood. The Phillies, understandably, didn't tax Mecias terribly in 2014. He didn't throw more than five innings in any start until his last turn of the season, when he tossed six shutout innings against Hickory. At his best, he throws a fastball with armside run that sits in the low 90s and touches 93 mph. He backs it with a deceptive changeup in the low 80s and a slurvy slider that sits in the 78-80 mph range. Mecias has a deceptive delivery that features a little bit of a stab in the back. He's aggressive in the strike zone, goes after hitters without fear and when he's right can rack up strikeouts in bunches, as shown by his 11.1 punchouts per nine innings at Lakewood in 2013. With a full offseason of rest, Mecias will be pushed to high Class A Clearwater in 2015. He has to show he can stay healthy to fulfill his mid-rotation upside, and will be given that chance this year.

BA GRADE

50 Risk: Extreme

LGE	BF	SO%	BB%	HR/9
GCL	76	13.2	10.5	0.00
SAL	136	16.9	6.6	0.53

Year	Club (League)	Class	W	L	ERA	G	GS	CG	SV	IP	H	HR	BB	SO	K/9	WHIP	AVG
2012	Phillies (GCL)	R	0	2	2.16	14	4	0	2	42	32	4	11	34	7.3	1.03	.206
2013	Lakewood (SAL)	LoA	4	3	3.79	13	11	0	1	57	53	3	25	70	11.1	1.37	.244
2014	Phillies (GCL)	R	0	1	4.76	4	4	0	0	17	19	0	8	10	5.3	1.59	.279
	Lakewood (SAL)	LoA	3	3	3.21	7	7	0	0	34	29	2	9	23	6.1	1.13	.246
Minor League Totals			7	9	3.31	38	26	0	3	149	133	9	53	137	8.3	1.25	.238

10 FRANKLYN KILOME, RHP

DAVID SCHOFIELD

Born: June 25, 1995. **B-T:** R-R. **Ht.:** 6-6. **Wt.:** 198. **Signed:** Dominican Republic, 2013. **Signed by:** Koby Perez.

Signed for $40,000 in January 2013, Kilome was a project worth embarking on at 6-foot-6 and somewhere around 150 pounds. Since then, he's added plenty of bulk, which has added velocity to his arsenal. The Phillies have overhauled the long-levered righthander's delivery, incorporating his lower half more, which takes the strain off of his arm and allows him to drive the ball downhill. The result is a pitcher the Phillies consider to have as much upside as anyone in the system. More size and a better delivery have led to a spike in Kilome's velocity, including an 89-92 mph fastball that has touched 95. Evaluators inside and outside the organization praise his ability to locate the pitch to both sides of the plate. He backs his fastball with a hard curveball in the 78-80 mph range and a changeup in the low 80s. Scouts are split as to which secondary is his best. His curve needs to be tightened at this point, and his changeup needs to develop consistency. Kilome's athleticism helps him repeat his delivery, but he does get in trouble when he overthrows and leaves the ball up. Kilome has a ceiling as a strong mid-rotation starter, but he's a long way from reaching it. He should begin 2015 in extended spring training before moving to short-season Williamsport in June, and a jump to low Class A Lakewood isn't out of the question.

					BA GRADE		
					50	Risk: Extreme	

LGE	BF	SO%	BB%	HR/9
GCL	168	14.9	6.5	0.45

Year	Club (League)	Class	W	L	ERA	G	GS	CG	SV	IP	H	HR	BB	SO	K/9	WHIP	AVG
2014	Phillies (GCL)	R	3	1	3.12	11	8	0	0	40	36	2	11	25	5.6	1.17	.235
Minor League Totals			3	1	3.12	11	8	0	0	40	36	2	11	25	5.6	1.17	.235

11 JESSE BIDDLE, LHP

to Pittsburgh

BA GRADE		
50	Risk: Extreme	

Born: Oct. 22, 1991. **B-T:** L-L. **Ht.:** 6-4. **Wt.:** 225. **Drafted:** HS— Philadelphia, 2010 (1st round). **Signed by:** Eric Valent.

The Phillies popped local product Biddle with the 27th pick in the 2010 draft, and he has deep roots in the city of Philadelphia, having attended the Germantown Academy. He pushed through the low minors with relative ease, albeit with a mediocre walk rate. Biddle led the Eastern League with 154 strikeouts at Double-A Reading in 2013, but he also walked 5.3 batters per nine innings, which landed him back in the EL in 2014 for a season that turned out to be an unmitigated disaster. First he sustained a concussion in the middle of a freak springtime hailstorm in Reading, then a 10-run shellacking on June 26 earned him a demotion to high Class A Clearwater until the concussion symptoms dissipated. He ultimately returned to the Rookie-level Gulf Coast League a month later to regroup. Scouts who saw Biddle in the instructional league continue to like what they see, including his typical 91-93 mph fastball, a low-80s slider with bite and a changeup in the high 70s with good fade. He still throws his signature mid-70s curveball, but most evaluators note that he casts the pitch. He left winter ball in Puerto Rico after two starts with elbow soreness, though the Phillies protected him on the 40-man roster anyway. Biddle seems bound for Reading again in 2015, this time for a true second turn at the level. If he can get his control in order, he can make huge strides toward achieving his ceiling as a back-end starter.

Year	Club (League)	Class	W	L	ERA	G	GS	CG	SV	IP	H	HR	BB	SO	K/9	WHIP	AVG
2012	Clearwater (FSL)	HiA	10	6	3.22	26	26	1	0	143	129	10	54	151	9.5	1.28	.237
2013	Reading (EL)	AA	5	14	3.64	27	27	2	0	138	104	10	82	154	10.0	1.34	.210
2014	Phillies (GCL)	R	0	0	4.50	1	1	0	0	2	1	1	1	3	13.5	1.00	.143
	Clearwater (FSL)	HiA	2	0	0.90	2	2	0	0	10	3	0	6	9	8.1	0.90	.097
	Reading (EL)	AA	3	10	5.03	16	16	0	0	82	78	11	44	80	8.7	1.48	.250
Minor League Totals			31	39	3.55	109	108	4	0	552	459	39	273	571	9.3	1.33	.226

12 ODUBEL HERRERA, 2B/OF

BA GRADE		
45	Risk: Medium	

Born: Dec. 29, 1991. **B-T:** L-R. **Ht.:** 5-11. **Wt.:** 200. **Signed:** Venezuela, 2008. **Signed by:** Rafic Saab (Rangers).

Signed by the Rangers for $160,000 as a 16-year-old back in 2008, Herrera always has been an offensive-oriented prospect who hits for a high average—though a rough 2013 season at Double-A Frisco dropped his stock. He regrouped in 2014, winning the Texas League batting title (.321) and ranking third in on-base percentage (.373). Swimming in middle-infield prospects, the Rangers did not add Herrera to the 40-man roster, and the Phillies selected him in the major league Rule 5 draft. He has a quick, compact stroke and squares up line drives to all fields. He showed better patience at the plate in 2014 than he did the previous year, which is important because his swing doesn't have much loft and he doesn't have the power to crack double-digit homers. Despite his thick body, Herrera is a plus runner, though he needs to improve his jumps to become a more effective basestealer. Managers voted him the best defensive second baseman in the TL in 2014, a testament to the improvements he has made, along with a thin crop at the position in the league. He's still a fringy defender, but that's better than he was before, and he has an average arm. He spent some time in the outfield in the regular season, and was playing center field while leading the Venezuelan League in batting in winter ball. His versatility and bat give him a good chance to stick with the rebuilding Phillies in 2015.

Year	Club (League)	Class	AVG	G	AB	R	H	2B	3B	HR	RBI	BB	SO	SB	CS	OBP	SLG
2012	Myrtle Beach (CAR)	HiA	.284	126	500	72	142	22	6	5	46	33	99	27	7	.335	.382
2013	Frisco (TL)	AA	.257	101	389	37	100	12	7	2	30	17	67	15	5	.289	.339
	Myrtle Beach (CAR)	HiA	.295	29	95	13	28	2	1	1	5	16	19	2	2	.398	.368
2014	Myrtle Beach (CAR)	HiA	.297	29	111	26	33	3	1	0	11	23	21	9	3	.412	.342
	Frisco (TL)	AA	.321	96	368	47	118	16	4	2	48	29	70	12	7	.373	.402
Minor League Totals			.294	610	2321	347	683	98	27	13	251	197	421	128	50	.354	.377

13 DEIVI GRULLON, C

BA GRADE

50 Risk: Extreme

Born: Feb. 17, 1996. **B-T:** R-R. **Ht.:** 6-1. **Wt.:** 180. **Signed:** Dominican Republic, 2012. **Signed by:** Koby Perez.

One of best catching prospects on the international market in 2012, Grullon signed that July for $575,000, and the Phillies have reaped the benefits ever since. He spent the 2013 season in the Rookie-level Gulf Coast League before being jumped first to low Class A Lakewood, then to high Class A Clearwater for a brief cameo in 2014. Grullon draws raves mostly for his arm, which rates as a borderline double-plus tool. While his receiving and blocking have improved, he still has a ways to go in those departments, such as when he spread his legs noticeably wider in 2014 when calling for something other than a fastball. He also has been routinely praised for his leadership skills behind the plate, as well as his willingness to take initiative when it comes to improving his English and establishing a better rapport with his pitchers. While Grullon hit just .227 in 2014, scouts see both hittability and power potential in his future if he tightens his approach, but they also noted that he didn't seem to trust himself to hit the fastball at all times. Assuming the rest of the system's catchers remain healthy, Grullon should return to Lakewood in 2015 to continue to hone his skills and work toward his ceiling as a solid everyday catcher with strong defensive chops.

Year	Club (League)	Class	AVG	G	AB	R	H	2B	3B	HR	RBI	BB	SO	SB	CS	OBP	SLG
2013	Phillies (GCL)	R	.273	41	121	13	33	8	0	1	14	10	18	0	0	.333	.364
2014	Clearwater (FSL)	HiA	.200	2	10	0	2	0	0	0	1	0	1	0	0	.200	.200
	Lakewood (SAL)	LoA	.237	24	76	9	18	5	0	1	7	3	13	0	0	.275	.342
	Williamsport (NYP)	SS	.225	53	187	14	42	9	1	0	18	9	39	3	0	.268	.283
Minor League Totals			.241	120	394	36	95	22	1	2	40	22	71	3	0	.288	.317

14 RICARDO PINTO, RHP

BA GRADE

50 Risk: Extreme

Born: Jan. 21, 1994. **B-T:** R-R. **Ht.:** 6-0. **Wt.:** 185. **Signed:** Venezuela, 2011. **Signed by:** Jesus Mendez.

Signed out of Venezuela in 2011, Pinto spent two seasons putting up solid numbers in the Venezuelan Summer League before coming to the U.S. in 2014, when he pitched in extended spring training before joining short-season Williamsport in June. With the Crosscutters, Pinto kept right on performing and emerged as the staff's best arm. He sports a three-pitch mix of fastball, changeup and slider and employs a drop-and-drive delivery with crossfire action. His high-three-quarters arm slot sometimes drifts toward three-quarters. His fastball generally sits between 93-95 mph and has hit as high as 97 in the past. His changeup is his best secondary offering, sitting at 80-82 mph with excellent deception out of his hand. It projects as above-average, and the Phillies asked him to shelve it in instructional league with the hope of further developing his slider, which shows sharp but inconsistent break and could be average in the future. Pinto also throws a two-seam fastball in the low 90s and shows a willingness to attack the strike zone. He'll spend 2015 as a 21-year-old at low Class A Lakewood.

Year	Club (League)	Class	W	L	ERA	G	GS	CG	SV	IP	H	HR	BB	SO	K/9	WHIP	AVG
2012	Phillies (VSL)	R	7	3	2.74	15	10	0	1	69	70	4	20	39	5.1	1.30	.267
2013	Phillies (VSL)	R	3	5	2.86	14	14	0	0	63	55	4	12	51	7.3	1.06	.228
2014	Williamsport (NYP)	SS	1	5	2.11	9	9	0	0	47	36	4	15	48	9.2	1.09	.203
Minor League Totals			11	13	2.61	38	33	0	1	179	161	12	47	138	6.9	1.16	.237

15 ANDREW KNAPP, C

Born: Nov. 9, 1991. **B-T:** B-R. **Ht.:** 6-1. **Wt.:** 190. **Drafted:** California, 2013 (2nd round). **Signed by:** Joey Davis.

BA GRADE

45 Risk: High

Drafted in the second round in 2013 out of California, Knapp signed with the Phillies for $1,033,100. The switch-hitting catcher hit .253/.340/.401 at short-season Williamsport in his first pro campaign, but he felt his elbow pop during instructional league and needed Tommy John surgery. The procedure cost him the first month and change of 2014, and he served solely as DH until June 12. Knapp wasn't a particularly polished defender before the injury, and that remains the case. Evaluators note that he tends to stab at balls but is an adequate blocker. He understandably looked tentative on throws in 2014, and his arm, while accurate, ranged from below-average to average, throwing out just 19 percent of basestealers. He's a solid hitter who takes a good angle to the ball and keeps the barrel in the zone a long time. Knapp has pull-side power and the potential for 10-12 home runs in the big leagues. As with most catchers, he's a well below-average runner. Knapp appears destined for high Class A Clearwater in 2015 with the potential to move to Double-A Reading at midseason.

Year	Club (League)	Class	AVG	G	AB	R	H	2B	3B	HR	RBI	BB	SO	SB	CS	OBP	SLG
2013	Williamsport (NYP)	SS	.253	62	217	30	55	20	0	4	23	22	57	7	5	.340	.401
2014	Clearwater (FSL)	HiA	.157	23	83	7	13	1	0	1	7	5	26	1	0	.222	.205
	Lakewood (SAL)	LoA	.290	75	283	39	82	19	4	5	25	27	71	3	3	.354	.438
Minor League Totals			.257	160	583	76	150	40	4	10	55	54	154	11	8	.330	.391

16 DYLAN COZENS, OF

Born: May 31, 1994. **B-T:** L-L. **Ht.:** 6-6. **Wt.:** 235. **Drafted:** HS— Scottsdale, Ariz., 2012 (2nd round). **Signed by:** Brad Holland.

BA GRADE

45 Risk: High

The well-built Cozens also starred as a football defensive end in high school, but he turned pro in baseball as a 2012 second-round pick for $659,800. He possesses some of the best raw power in the organization, which manifested with 16 homers at low Class A Lakewood in 2014, but with that power came many strikeouts. Cozens fanned 147 times—or 26 percent of the time—so he needs to improve upon what is now an all-or-nothing approach that leaves him vulnerable to breaking pitches. He's a passable defender in right field with an accurate, above-average arm, but scouts worry that he may be better suited for first base or DH in the long term due to his lack of range. Despite his massive frame and lack of pure speed, Cozens' aptitude and instincts allowed him to steal 23 bases, the fourth-most in the organization, and just one fewer than top prospect J.P. Crawford. Cozens offers intriguing power potential, but without refinement to his approach, he won't hit for average, and his in-game power could decrease as he faces more experienced pitchers. He will head to high Class A Clearwater in 2015.

Year	Club (League)	Class	AVG	G	AB	R	H	2B	3B	HR	RBI	BB	SO	SB	CS	OBP	SLG
2012	Phillies (GCL)	R	.255	50	161	24	41	11	2	5	24	21	44	8	2	.341	.441
2013	Williamsport (NYP)	SS	.265	68	245	50	65	19	2	9	35	28	64	11	6	.343	.469
2014	Lakewood (SAL)	LoA	.248	132	509	69	126	25	6	16	62	40	147	23	7	.303	.415
Minor League Totals			.254	250	915	143	232	55	10	30	121	89	255	42	15	.321	.434

17 KELLY DUGAN, OF

Born: Sept. 18, 1990. **B-T:** L-R. **Ht.:** 6-3. **Wt.:** 195. **Drafted:** HS— Sherman Oaks, Calif., 2009 (2nd round). **Signed by:** Shane Bowers.

BA GRADE

45 Risk: High

After forfeiting their first-round pick to the Mariners in 2009, the Phillies used their second-round choice on Dugan, the son of Hollywood director Dennis Dugan, and signed him for $485,000 to keep him away from Pepperdine. Injuries have littered Dugan's career, including a staph infection, a stress fracture in his back, a case of turf toe and a strained oblique that cost him two months in 2014. He broke his foot toward the end of 2014 at Double-A Reading and tried to play through it briefly before landing on the disabled list. Dugan's calling card is his bat and his power, and he's showcased those skills when he's been on the field. Much like system-mate Cameron Perkins, Dugan is a bit of an awkward runner in the outfield and on the basepaths, though he grades out as an average runner and thrower and a fringe-average defender on an outfield corner. He'll need to make up for lost developmental time, and he'll try to do so at either Reading or Triple-A Lehigh Valley in 2015.

Year	Club (League)	Class	AVG	G	AB	R	H	2B	3B	HR	RBI	BB	SO	SB	CS	OBP	SLG
2012	Lakewood (SAL)	LoA	.300	117	430	83	129	33	2	12	60	48	122	5	1	.387	.470
2013	Clearwater (FSL)	HiA	.318	56	217	37	69	12	3	10	36	24	60	1	3	.401	.539
	Reading (EL)	AA	.264	56	212	25	56	12	1	10	23	5	54	0	1	.299	.472
2014	Reading (EL)	AA	.296	76	253	43	75	18	1	5	34	28	56	1	0	.383	.435
Minor League Totals			.293	425	1531	249	448	97	13	40	190	140	377	24	12	.368	.451

18 ZACH GREEN, 1B/3B

BA GRADE
50 Risk: Extreme

Born: March 7, 1994. **B-T:** R-R. **Ht.:** 6-3. **Wt.:** 210. **Drafted:** HS—Sacramento, 2012 (3rd round). **Signed by:** Joey Davis

After being selected in the third round in 2012 and mashing 13 homers in 74 games at short-season Williamsport in 2013, Green seemed primed for a breakout in 2014. Then things got weird. He started slowly at low Class A Lakewood and came down with a balky back. Upon further investigation, the Phillies found that one of Green's legs was longer than the other. Fitted with an orthotic insert to straighten things out, he returned after roughly two months away and hit .286/.325/.442 with 28 extra-base hits in 69 games the rest of the way. With his health under control, Green still has issues to correct. The Phillies played him some at first base in 2014, and scouts internally and externally believe his lack of agility and erratic arm might move him there permanently at some point. He also showed an extreme pull tendency and appeared geared toward the fastball and vulnerable to breaking pitches. Green seems destined to return to Lakewood for the first part of 2015 to make up for lost time.

Year	Club (League)	Class	AVG	G	AB	R	H	2B	3B	HR	RBI	BB	SO	SB	CS	OBP	SLG
2012	Phillies (GCL)	R	.284	47	169	20	48	13	1	3	21	8	43	2	2	.333	.426
2013	Williamsport (NYP)	SS	.252	74	270	52	68	20	1	13	41	31	91	8	5	.344	.478
2014	Lakewood (SAL)	LoA	.268	84	328	41	88	22	2	6	43	24	65	7	1	.316	.402
Minor League Totals			.266	205	767	113	204	55	4	22	105	63	199	17	8	.330	.434

19 SEVERINO GONZALEZ, RHP

BA GRADE
45 Risk: High

Born: Sept. 28, 1992. **B-T:** R-R. **Ht.:** 6-1. **Wt.:** 153. **Signed:** Panama, 2011. **Signed by:** Allen Lewis.

Gonzalez was plucked out of Panama in 2011 and spent two nondescript years in the Venezuelan Summer League before making what was supposed to be a two-start cameo at low Class A Lakewood in 2013. He was so dominant in those two starts, however, that he forced the Phillies' hand and finished the year at Double-A Reading. Gonzalez is armed with above-average command of four pitches, but the Phillies wanted to develop his changeup further in 2014. With that in mind, they took away his best pitch, a cutter thrown in the low 90s, for the first part of the season and asked him to throw more change-ups. One result was an improved change, in the mid-80s, that could be average in the future; another was a plummeting strikeout rate and the second-most home runs allowed in the Eastern League. Gonzalez throws a low-80s slider that scouts say needs to be tightened before it's considered a weapon. Gonzalez showed excellent durability for such a slight body and should move up to Triple-A Lehigh Valley in 2015. His strikethrowing ability profiles him as a back-end starter.

Year	Club (League)	Class	W	L	ERA	G	GS	CG	SV	IP	H	HR	BB	SO	K/9	WHIP	AVG
2012	Phillies (VSL)	R	7	3	1.65	14	14	2	0	93	59	4	6	86	8.4	0.70	.179
2013	Lakewood (SAL)	LoA	3	0	1.69	4	4	0	0	21	10	1	3	31	13.1	0.61	.137
	Clearwater (FSL)	HiA	3	5	2.02	20	9	0	0	76	66	4	19	82	9.8	1.12	.239
	Reading (EL)	AA	1	0	2.70	1	1	0	0	7	8	0	0	6	8.1	1.20	.308
2014	Reading (EL)	AA	9	13	4.59	27	27	0	0	159	169	23	34	115	6.5	1.28	.270
Minor League Totals			24	22	2.96	83	55	2	1	398	348	32	65	349	7.9	1.04	.234

20 AARON ALTHERR, OF

BA GRADE
45 Risk: High

Born: Jan. 14, 1991. **B-T:** R-R. **Ht.:** 6-3. **Wt.:** 190. **Drafted:** HS—Avondale, Ariz., 2009 (9th round). **Signed by:** Brad Holland

One of the finest athletes in the organization, Altherr was born in Germany, the son of a U.S. service-member mother and German soccer-playing father. Originally signed for $150,000, Altherr made his major league debut in 2014 when Tony Gwynn Jr. was placed on the bereavement list to attend the funeral of his Hall of Fame father. With his plus range and above-average throwing arm, Altherr remains the best defensive outfielder in the organization and could make the majors as a defensive-oriented extra. His offense, however, still needs more work, though he took advantage of Double-A Reading's cozy confines to set a career-high for home runs. The Phillies worked on a number of things with Altherr in 2014, including his hand positioning, being ready to hit the fastball and making more contact with two strikes. He's got long arms and will get beat inside with fastballs, and scouts noticed that his bat speed varied on fastballs and breaking pitches. He missed time early in 2014 while recovering from a broken bone in his wrist he sustained in the 2013 Arizona Fall League, and he could return to Reading in 2015.

Year	Club (League)	Class	AVG	G	AB	R	H	2B	3B	HR	RBI	BB	SO	SB	CS	OBP	SLG
2012	Lakewood (SAL)	LoA	.252	110	420	65	106	27	6	8	50	38	102	25	8	.319	.402
2013	Clearwater (FSL)	HiA	.275	123	466	57	128	36	6	12	69	45	140	23	5	.337	.455
2014	Clearwater (FSL)	HiA	.250	7	28	6	7	1	2	0	2	5	8	1	0	.364	.429

Philadelphia (NL)	MAJ	.000	2	5	0	0	0	0	0	0	0	2	0	0	.000	.000
Reading (EL)	AA	.236	120	449	54	106	27	2	14	57	26	110	12	6	.287	.399
Major League Totals		.000	2	5	0	0	0	0	0	0	0	2	0	0	.000	.000
Minor League Totals		.255	555	2072	276	528	125	22	42	260	157	509	116	30	.312	.397

21 CORD SANDBERG, OF

BA GRADE

50 Risk: Extreme

Born: Jan. 2, 1995. **B-T:** L-L. **Ht.:** 6-3. **Wt.:** 215. **Drafted:** HS—Bradenton, Fla., 2013 (3rd round). **Signed by:** Alan Marr.

Sandberg's father Chuck played in the minor leagues but also was a high school football coach. The Phillies bought Sandberg out of a Mississippi State football commitment (he was a quarterback) for $775,000 and saw progress in his first year as a full-time baseball player. Sandberg has an athletic body with some present strength and should fit an outfield corner profile if he clicks. Scouts have to project on his power future, with some seeing 20-25 homers as he learns his craft. He started to show some hitting ability, with a good stroke and a willingnss to use the whole field but remains raw thanks to his two-sport background. Sandberg needs to refine his approach and learn better pitch recognition, but the Phillies laud him for his improved two-strike approach and unquenchable work ethic. His next step will be low Class A Lakewood in 2015.

Year	Club (League)	Class	AVG	G	AB	R	H	2B	3B	HR	RBI	BB	SO	SB	CS	OBP	SLG
2013	Phillies (GCL)	R	.207	48	169	23	35	3	1	2	14	24	36	4	3	.313	.272
2014	Williamsport (NYP)	SS	.235	66	264	33	62	5	3	6	24	11	56	8	3	.267	.345
Minor League Totals			.224	114	433	56	97	8	4	8	38	35	92	12	6	.286	.316

22 CAM PERKINS, OF

BA GRADE

40 Risk: Medium

Born: Sept. 27, 1990. **B-T:** R-R. **Ht.:** 6-5. **Wt.:** 205. **Drafted:** Purdue, 2012 (6th round). **Signed by:** Nate Dion.

A third baseman at Purdue, Perkins signed for $152,900 as a sixth-rounder in 2012. He shifted to the outfield as a professional and posted a fine first full season while jumping to high Class A Clearwater, despite losing time with a broken left wrist. Perkins got off to a strong start in 2014 with Double-A Reading and was promoted to Triple-A, where he hit his first pro adversity. Looking back on it, Phillies officials concede that Perkins' move might have been too aggressive. Perkins stands upright at the plate, and scouts noticed a hitch in his hand movement and a willingness to chase breaking pitches out of the zone. He's an average runner and a passable defender on an outfield corner, but with just 13 home runs over 1,134 career at-bats, he faces legitimate questions as to whether he'll profile as an everyday right fielder. At this point, he looks like a bat off the bench, but he'll go back to Triple-A in 2015 to work on improving that outlook.

Year	Club (League)	Class	AVG	G	AB	R	H	2B	3B	HR	RBI	BB	SO	SB	CS	OBP	SLG
2012	Phillies (GCL)	R	.158	5	19	0	3	0	0	0	3	0	2	0	0	.158	.158
	Williamsport (NYP)	SS	.304	67	270	31	82	23	1	1	38	14	41	5	2	.352	.407
2013	Phillies (GCL)	R	.571	2	7	1	4	1	0	1	1	1	0	0	0	.625	1.143
	Clearwater (FSL)	HiA	.295	103	387	54	114	30	5	6	53	25	57	4	5	.346	.444
2014	Reading (EL)	AA	.342	52	196	25	67	19	1	3	34	20	30	5	3	.408	.495
	Lehigh Valley (IL)	AAA	.216	74	255	17	55	9	3	2	17	13	49	3	3	.259	.298
Minor League Totals			.287	303	1134	128	325	82	10	13	146	73	179	17	13	.338	.411

23 VICTOR ARANO, RHP

BA GRADE

45 Risk: High

Born: Feb. 7, 1995. **B-T:** R-R. **Ht.:** 6-1. **Wt.:** 208. **Signed:** Mexico, 2013. **Signed by:** Mike Brito/Pat Kelly (Dodgers).

After plucking Julio Urias and Victor Gonzalez from Mexico, the Dodgers went back to the well in 2013 and inked Arano, then watched him put together a fine season in the Rookie-level Arizona League that year. He built nicely on his debut at low Class A Great Lakes in 2014 before joining the Phillies, along with second baseman Jesmuel Valentin, in the August trade that sent righthander Roberto Hernandez to the Dodgers. The Phillies don't deny their excitement over acquiring Arano, whom they believe is loaded with upside. Evaluators who saw him in instructional league saw an 88-92 mph fastball that he could command to both sides of the plate, and he's reached 94 in shorter relief stints. He backs the fastball with a sharp 11-to-5 curveball in the 74-80 mph range and a sinking changeup in the mid-80s. He'll head to high Class A Clearwater in 2015 to work toward achieving his ceiling of a back-end starter.

Year	Club (League)	Class	W	L	ERA	G	GS	CG	SV	IP	H	HR	BB	SO	K/9	WHIP	AVG
2013	Dodgers (AZL)	R	3	2	4.20	13	8	0	0	49	52	4	13	49	8.9	1.32	.255
2014	Great Lakes (MWL)	LoA	4	7	4.08	22	15	0	3	86	88	11	20	83	8.7	1.26	.260
Minor League Totals			7	9	4.12	35	23	0	3	135	140	15	33	132	8.8	1.28	.258

24 JOELY RODRIGUEZ, LHP

BA GRADE
40 Risk: Medium

Born: Nov. 14, 1991. **B-T:** L-L. **Ht.:** 6-1. **Wt.:** 200. **Signed:** Dominican Republic, 2009. **Signed by:** Rene Gayo/Ellis Pena (Pirates).

Considered a fringe prospect in the Pirates system until having a breakout season at two Class A levels in 2013, Rodriguez joined the Phillies in December in the trade for reliever Antonio Bastardo. Rodriguez struggled at Double-A Altoona in 2014 but bounced back in the Arizona Fall League. He is intriguing despite his relative lack of success because he can throw three pitches for strikes with his 89-92 mph sinking fastball, curveball and changeup. All pitches grade as average at their best. Though he reached Double-A as a starter, Rodriguez's long-term role could be as a reliever because he tends to tire in the middle innings. The Phillies probably will keep him in the rotation at Triple-A Lehigh Valley in 2015.

Year	Club (League)	Class	W	L	ERA	G	GS	CG	SV	IP	H	HR	BB	SO	K/9	WHIP	AVG
2012	State College (NYP)	SS	3	4	4.50	14	14	0	0	64	74	2	15	32	4.5	1.39	.298
2013	West Virginia (SAL)	LoA	5	5	2.72	14	14	0	0	73	79	4	20	57	7.1	1.36	.280
	Bradenton (FSL)	HiA	4	3	2.67	12	12	0	0	67	63	4	19	44	5.9	1.22	.251
2014	Altoona (EL)	AA	6	11	4.84	30	21	2	1	134	151	10	43	73	4.9	1.45	.289
Minor League Totals			22	31	4.02	98	83	2	2	441	482	31	131	261	5.3	1.39	.281

25 MIGUEL ALFREDO GONZALEZ, RHP

BA GRADE
45 Risk: High

Born: Sept. 23, 1986. **B-T:** R-R. **Ht.:** 6-3. **Wt.:** 195. **Signed:** Cuba, 2013. **Signed by:** Sal Agostinelli.

Gonzalez emerged as the ace of the Cuban national team in 2010 after striking out 14 batters in the gold-medal game of the World University Championship, then became one of the hottest commodities on the international market when he defected in 2012. The Phillies won the bidding with a six-year, $48 million deal, but after a physical turned up shoulder issues his deal was reduced to three years and $12 million. Gonzalez made his professional debut in 2014, but had shoulder soreness in the spring, so he moved to the bullpen at high Class A Clearwater when he returned in mid-May. Gonzalez has a fastball that sits between 94-97 mph and touches higher. He backs it up with a loopy curveball that has the potential to be a tick above-average. A changeup with a chance to be average has pushed the Phillies to build him back up as a starter. Gonzalez probably will begin in the Lehigh Valley rotation in 2015.

Year	Club (League)	Class	W	L	ERA	G	GS	CG	SV	IP	H	HR	BB	SO	K/9	WHIP	AVG
2014	Clearwater (FSL)	HiA	0	2	4.70	8	3	0	0	15	20	0	9	11	6.5	1.89	.317
	Reading (EL)	AA	0	2	3.14	11	0	0	5	14	10	2	7	24	15.1	1.19	.192
	Lehigh Valley (IL)	AAA	0	1	1.62	12	0	0	2	17	10	0	10	19	10.3	1.20	.172
	Philadelphia (NL)	MAJ	0	1	6.75	6	0	0	0	5	9	1	3	5	8.4	2.25	.346
Major League Totals			0	1	6.75	6	0	0	0	5	9	1	3	5	8.4	2.25	.346
Minor League Totals			0	4	3.11	31	3	0	7	46	40	2	26	54	10.5	1.42	.231

26 NEFI OGANDO, RHP

BA GRADE
45 Risk: High

Born: June 3, 1989. **B-T:** R-R. **Ht.:** 6-2. **Wt.:** 185. **Signed:** Dominican Republic, 2010. **Signed by:** Manny Nanita (Red Sox).

The Red Sox signed Ogando and gave him a total of six starts over his first two seasons, but he has worked primarily as a reliever his entire career. The Phillies acquired him late in 2013 for shortstop John McDonald, taking a flier on Ogando's power arm, and then added him to the 40-man roster in November. Despite a fastball that touches triple-digits with regularity and a high-80s slider that occasionally shows as a wipeout pitch, Ogando was hit for a .291 average in 2014 at Double-A Reading. Scouts attribute the gory numbers to a failure to drive the fastball down in the zone, something he did with much more frequency in the Arizona Fall League. Ogando has an 70-grade fastball on the 20-80 scouting scale and a slider with the potential to be plus if he ever learns to land it for a strike. He appears ticketed for Triple-A Lehigh Valley in 2015.

Year	Club (League)	Class	W	L	ERA	G	GS	CG	SV	IP	H	HR	BB	SO	K/9	WHIP	AVG
2012	Greenville (SAL)	LoA	4	4	3.70	38	0	0	2	75	72	3	34	54	6.5	1.41	.248
2013	Salem (CAR)	HiA	2	3	4.09	33	0	0	3	55	49	5	27	44	7.2	1.38	.238
2014	Reading (EL)	AA	5	1	6.27	48	0	0	7	56	64	6	28	57	9.2	1.64	.291
Minor League Totals			15	14	4.02	145	6	0	12	278	271	17	135	224	7.3	1.46	.253

27 JOSE PUJOLS, OF

BA GRADE
50 Risk: Extreme

Born: Sept. 29, 1995. **B-T:** R-R. **Ht.:** 6-3. **Wt.:** 195. **Drafted:** Dominican Republic, 2012. **Signed by:** Koby Perez.

Inked for $540,000 in 2012, Pujols has as much raw power as any outfielder in the system. He opened 2014 in the Rookie-level Gulf Coast League at 18 years old and hit five home runs, which tied for fourth in the league, before receiving a brief taste of short-season Williamsport at season's end. As would be expected with someone his age with his power, Pujols swings and misses often and struggles with breaking pitches. Beyond the power, he's an average defender in right field. He'll need to refine his pitch recognition and an approach that right now is geared toward pulling fastballs. If Pujols can do that as he repeats Williamsport in 2015, then he could jump up the list.

Year	Club (League)	Class	AVG	G	AB	R	H	2B	3B	HR	RBI	BB	SO	SB	CS	OBP	SLG
2013	Phillies (GCL)	R	.188	45	160	27	30	7	2	6	18	19	56	1	3	.278	.369
2014	Phillies (GCL)	R	.232	41	151	21	35	8	2	5	28	12	54	1	2	.291	.411
	Williamsport (NYP)	SS	.213	16	61	3	13	5	0	0	5	0	21	0	0	.226	.295
Minor League Totals			.210	102	372	51	78	20	4	11	51	31	131	2	5	.275	.374

28 WILLIANS ASTUDILLO, 1B/C

BA GRADE

45 Risk: High

Born: Oct. 14, 1991. **B-T:** R-R. **Ht.:** 5-9. **Wt.:** 212. **Signed:** Venezuela, 2008. **Signed by:** Norman Anciani.

Astudillo has uncanny bat control, which allows him to hit fastballs and breaking balls, whether up or down, inside or outside, balls or strikes. He finds a way to put the good part of the bat on the ball and struck out just 4 percent of the time in 2014. He plays with energy, and club officials like how he calls a game when he catches. Astudillo is a bad-bodied player who doesn't profile because he doesn't draw walks, and he lacks over-the-fence power. Ideally, the Phillies would like Astudillo to commit himself to becoming a passable catcher, where his bat would profile better. He threw out just 14 percent of baserunners and had eight passed balls. He'll move up to high Class A Clearwater in 2015.

Year	Club (League)	Class	AVG	G	AB	R	H	2B	3B	HR	RBI	BB	SO	SB	CS	OBP	SLG
2012	Phillies (GCL)	R	.318	45	148	15	47	15	0	0	21	1	5	2	0	.327	.419
2013	Did not play—Injured																
2014	Lakewood (SAL)	LoA	.333	117	436	41	145	30	1	4	61	19	20	2	3	.366	.433
Minor League Totals			.319	328	1152	131	367	72	7	6	152	56	41	31	11	.364	.409

29 LUIS ENCARNACION, 1B/OF

BA GRADE

50 Risk: Extreme

Born: Aug. 9, 1997. **B-T:** R-R. **Ht.:** 6-3. **Wt.:** 215. **Drafted:** Dominican Republic, 2013. **Signed by:** Koby Perez.

The Phillies signed Encarnacion for $1 million in 2013, handing out the largest bonus in franchise history for a Latin American teen. They hoped he would transform, albeit slowly, into a third baseman with the power to hit in the middle of the order. As such, the Phillies aggressively assigned him to the Rookie-level Gulf Coast League in 2014, where at 17 years old he was one of its youngest players. And he performed like it, hitting .229/.294/.343 in 40 games with 4-to-1 strikeout-to-walk ratio. He's going to take plenty of refinement at the plate, and scouts inside and outside the organization are convinced that his lack of speed and agility will make him either a left fielder—he's got a strong arm—or a first baseman. Still, if he develops into the kind of hitter the Phillies believe he will, he'll profile at either position. He's due for a repeat of the GCL in 2015.

Year	Club (League)	Class	AVG	G	AB	R	H	2B	3B	HR	RBI	BB	SO	SB	CS	OBP	SLG
2014	Phillies (GCL)	R	.229	40	140	18	32	8	1	2	15	9	39	1	0	.294	.343
Minor League Totals			.229	40	140	18	32	8	1	2	15	9	39	1	0	.294	.343

30 ELNIERY GARCIA, LHP

BA GRADE

50 Risk: Extreme

Born: Dec. 24, 1994. **B-T:** L-L. **Ht.:** 6-0. **Wt.:** 170. **Signed:** Dominican Republic, 2011. **Signed by:** Koby Perez.

The Rookie-level Gulf Coast League is full of arms easy to dream on, and Garcia is one of the Phillies' most intriguing. He's a smooth lefthander with projection who started the year with short-season Williamsport, then missed a month with minor elbow issues before moving down to the Rookie-level Gulf Coast League. His fastball is 88-92 right now with a chance to add more velocity as he gains strength. Both of his secondary offerings are in the developmental stage, but his curveball, a true 12-6 breaker with bite in the low to mid-70s, is the better of the two. He's likely to return to extended spring and then Williamsport in 2015.

Year	Club (League)	Class	W	L	ERA	G	GS	CG	SV	IP	H	HR	BB	SO	K/9	WHIP	AVG
2012	Phillies (DSL)	R	2	1	4.18	8	3	0	0	24	23	1	8	19	7.2	1.31	.253
2013	Phillies (GCL)	R	1	3	5.15	9	9	0	0	37	43	1	14	31	7.6	1.55	.291
2014	Williamsport (NYP)	SS	0	0	5.79	4	0	0	0	5	6	1	2	5	9.6	1.71	.273
	Phillies (GCL)	R	2	2	2.08	7	4	0	0	26	26	0	4	23	8.0	1.15	.250
Minor League Totals			5	6	4.06	28	16	0	0	91	98	3	28	78	7.7	1.38	.268

Pittsburgh Pirates

BY JOHN PERROTTO

GEORGE GOJKOVICH

Rookie right fielder Gregory Polanco joined Andrew McCutchen and Starling Marte in the Pirates' rangy outfield

General manager Neal Huntington's primary goal since taking over a mess of a franchise late in the 2007 season was to turn the Pirates into perennial contenders.

Qualifying for the postseason in back-to-back years as the first National League wild card means the Pirates have certainly taken a major step toward reaching that status. However, after consecutive playoff appearances following 20 consecutive losing seasons—the longest streak in major North American professional team sports history—the Pirates are hungry for more than being a wild card.

"We need to start winning our division," said manager Clint Hurdle, whose team has finished second to the Cardinals in each of the last two seasons. "It's too risky being in the wild card game, a one-and-done situation. We need to win our division, give ourselves a little room to breathe, give ourselves a better chance of getting to the World Series."

The Pirates haven't been to the World Series since 1979 when they beat the Orioles in seven games. The 35-year Fall Classic drought is the longest in franchise history—there was a 33-year gap between 1927 and '60.

A core group of players should keep the Pirates competitive for the next few years, including a potentially star-studded outfield of center fielder Andrew McCutchen, a perennial MVP candidate, flanked by Starling Marte in left field and Gregory Polanco in right field.

Second baseman Neil Walker and first baseman Pedro Alvarez are under club control through 2016, Jordy Mercer emerged as a viable long-term answer at shortstop in 2014 and righthander Gerrit Cole, the top overall pick in the 2011 draft, has the talent, demeanor and smarts to become a No. 1 starter. And the Pirates re-signed free agent lefthander Francisco Liriano for three years.

Despite graduating a number of players to the major leagues in the last two seasons, the Pirates' farm system remains strong and includes a trio of premium pitching prospects in righthanders Tyler Glasnow, Jameson Taillon and Nick Kingham.

Switch-hitting outfielder Josh Bell had a breakout season in 2014, winning the MVP award in the high Class A Florida State League after finally being healthy for the first time since having knee surgery in 2012. He shifted to first base in instructional league because of the organization's outfield depth that includes Austin Meadows, the first of two first-round picks in 2013, who struggled with a hamstring issue for most of the 2014 season.

Reese McGuire was the other first-rounder in 2013 and he is already considered one of the best defensive catching prospects in the minors.

The Pirates will need to continue to be strong in the areas of scouting and player development. They play in one of the sport's smallest markets and have an owner in Bob Nutting who keeps a close watch on the bottom line.

TOP PROSPECTS OF THE DECADE

Year	Player, Pos.	2014 Org.
2005	Zach Duke, lhp	Brewers
2006	Neil Walker, c	Pirates
2007	Andrew McCutchen, of	Pirates
2008	Andrew McCutchen, of	Pirates
2009	Pedro Alvarez, 3b	Pirates
2010	Pedro Alvarez, 3b	Pirates
2011	Jameson Taillon, rhp	Pirates
2012	Gerrit Cole, rhp	Pirates
2013	Gerrit Cole, rhp	Pirates
2014	Gregory Polanco, of	Pirates

General manager: Neal Huntington. **Farm director:** Larry Broadway. **Scouting director:** Joe DelliCarri

Class	Team	League	W	L	PCT	Finish	Manager
Majors	Pittsburgh Pirates	National	88	74	.543	T-8th (30)	Clint Hurdle
Triple-A	Indianapolis Indians	International	73	71	.507	7th (14)	Dean Treanor
Double-A	Altoona Curve	Eastern	61	81	.430	11th (12)	Carlos Garcia
High A	Bradenton Marauders	Florida State	78	61	.561	2nd (12)	Tom Prince
Low A	West Virginia Power	South Atlantic	54	81	.400	T-12th (14)	Michael Ryan
Short season	*Jamestown Jammers	New York-Penn	35	40	.467	8th (14)	Brian Esposito
Rookie	Bristol Pirates	Appalachian	22	46	.324	10th (10)	Edgar Varela
Rookie	Pirates	Gulf Coast	20	40	.333	15th (16)	Milver Reyes
Overall Minor League Record			343	420	.450	29th (30)	

*Franchise moves to Morgantown (New York-Penn) in 2015

THIS YEAR'S TOP 30

Player, Pos.	Grade/Risk
1. Tyler Glasnow, rhp	70/High
2. Jameson Taillon, rhp	65/High
3. Austin Meadows, of	65/High
4. Josh Bell, of/1b	60/Medium
5. Reese McGuire ,c	55/Medium
6. Nick Kingham, rhp	50/Medium
7. Alen Hanson, ss/2b	50/Medium
8. Cole Tucker, ss	50/High
9. Mitch Keller, rhp	50/High
10. Harold Ramirez, of	50/High
11. Elias Diaz, c	50/High
12. Willy Garcia, of	50/High
13. JaCoby Jones, ss	50/High
14. Trey Supak, rhp	50/High
15. Adrian Sampson, rhp	45/Medium
16. John Holdzkom, rhp	45/Medium
17. Casey Sadler, rhp	45/Medium
18. Buddy Borden, rhp	50/High
19. Gage Hinsz, rhp	45/High
20. Clay Holmes, rhp	50/Extreme
21. Stetson Allie, 1b	45/High
22. Wyatt Mathisen, 3b	45/High
23. Barrett Barnes, of	50/Extreme
24. Cody Dickson, lhp	50/Extreme
25. Connor Joe, of/c	45/High
26. Luis Heredia, rhp	45/High
27. Stolmy Pimentel, rhp	40/Medium
28. Chad Kuhl, rhp	45/High
29. Tito Polo, of	45/High
30. Michael de la Cruz, of	45/Extreme

LAST YEAR'S TOP 30

Player, Pos.	Status
1. Gregory Polanco, of	Majors
2. Jameson Taillon, rhp	No. 2
3. Tyler Glasnow, rhp	No. 1
4. Austin Meadows, of	No. 3
5. Nick Kingham, rhp	No. 6
6. Alen Hanson, ss	No. 7
7. Josh Bell, of	No. 4
8. Reese McGuire, c	No. 5
9. Harold Ramirez, of	No. 10
10. Luis Heredia, rhp	No. 26
11. Brandon Cumpton, rhp	Majors
12. Wyatt Mathisen, c	No. 22
13. Barrett Barnes, of	No. 23
14. Willy Garcia, of	No. 12
15. Tony Sanchez, c	Majors
16. Stolmy Pimentel, rhp	No. 27
17. Clay Holmes, rhp	No. 20
18. Blake Taylor, lhp	(Mets)
19. JaCoby Jones, ss	No. 13
20. Cody Dickson, lhp	No. 24
21. Andrew Lambo, of	Dropped out
22. Jaff Decker, of	Dropped out
23. Stetson Allie, 1b	No. 21
24. Jin-De Jhang, c	Dropped out
25. Elvis Escobar, of	Dropped out
26. Wei-Chung Wang, lhp	(Brewers)
27. Adrian Sampson, rhp	No. 15
28. Jon Sandfort, rhp	Dropped out
29. Gift Ngoepe, ss	Dropped out
30. Joely Rodriguez, lhp	(Phillies)

BEST TOOLS

Best Hitter for Average	Josh Bell
Best Power Hitter	Stetson Allie
Best Strike-Zone Discipline	Jaff Decker
Fastest Baserunner	Alen Hanson
Best Athlete	Alen Hanson
Best Fastball	Tyler Glasnow
Best Curveball	Buddy Borden
Best Slider	Adrian Sampson
Best Changeup	Nick Kingham
Best Control	Nick Kingham
Best Defensive Catcher	Elias Diaz
Best Defensive Infielder	Gift Ngoepe
Best Infield Arm	Wyatt Mathisen
Best Defensive Outfielder	Keon Broxton
Best Outfield Arm	Willy Garcia

PROJECTED 2018 LINEUP

Catcher	Reese McGuire
First Base	Josh Bell
Second Base	Neil Walker
Third Base	Josh Harrison
Shortstop	Jordy Mercer
Left Field	Starling Marte
Center Field	Andrew McCutchen
Right Field	Gregory Polanco
No. 1 Starter	Gerrit Cole
No. 2 Starter	Tyler Glasnow
No. 3 Starter	Jameson Taillon
No. 4 Starter	Nick Kingham
No. 5 Starter	Jeff Locke
Closer	Mark Melancon

PITTSBURGH PIRATES

TOP 2015 ROOKIE: John Holdzkom, rhp. He figures to be a primary setup man after rising from the independent ranks.

BREAKOUT PROSPECT: Mel Rojas Jr., of. The son of the former big league reliver has started to turn his raw tools into production in the system's upper levels.

SLEEPER: Hector Garcia, lhp. The Dominican Republic native and his 92 mph fastball could move through the system quickly.

SOURCE OF TOP 30 TALENT

Homegrown	28	Acquired	2
College	6	Trades	1
Junior college	2	Rule 5 draft	0
High school	13	Independent leagues	1
Draft-and-follow	0	Free agents/waivers	0
Nondrafted free agents	0		
International	7		

LF
Jordan Luplow
Jonathan Schwind
Elvis Escobar

CF
Austin Meadows (3)
Harold Ramirez (10)
Barrett Barnes (23)
Michael de la Cruz (30)
Mel Rojas Jr.
Keon Broxton
Henrry Rosario

RF
Willy Garcia (12)
Connor Joe (25)
Tito Polo (29)
Jaff Decker
Andrew Lambo

3B
Wyatt Mathisen (22)
Drew Maggi
Eric Wood
Chase Simpson

SS
Cole Tucker (8)
JaCoby Jones (13)
Gift Ngoepe
Adam Frazier
Tyler Filliben

2B
Alen Hanson (7)
Dan Gamache
Erich Weiss

1B
Josh Bell (4)
Stetson Allie (21)
Jose Osuna
Edwin Espinal
Carlos Munoz

C
Reese McGuire (5)
Elias Diaz (11)
Taylor Gushue
Kevin Krause
Jin-De Jhang
Yoel Gonzalez

LHP

LHSP	LHRP
Cody Dickson (24)	Bobby LaFramboise
Hector Garcia	John Sever
Orlando Castro	Tom Harlan

RHP

RHSP	RHRP
Tyler Glasnow (1)	John Holdzkom (16)
Jameson Taillon (2)	Casey Sadler (17)
Nick Kingham (6)	Stolmy Pimentel (27)
Mitch Keller (9)	Matt Nevarez
Trey Supak (14)	Jhondaniel Medina
Adrian Sampson (15)	Yhonathan Barrios
Buddy Borden (18)	
Gage Hinsz (19)	*Traded to Brewers*
Clay Holmes (20)	
Luis Heredia (26)	
Chad Kuhl (28)	
John Kuchno	
Tyler Eppler	
Jason Creasy	
Billy Roth	
Angel Sanchez	
Frank Duncan	
Tyler DuRapau	

2014

BEST PURE HITTER: The Pirates were higher on SS Cole Tucker (1) than the industry consensus, but not by much. They believe in his command of the strike zone and feel for hitting and believe he just needs strength gains.

BEST POWER HITTER: OFs Connor Joe (1s) and Jordan Luplow (3) both have solid-average power, if not above-average, as well as the feel for hitting for their power to play. C/OF Kevin Krause (9) hit for power at Stony Brook, but the Pirates were still surprised by the sound off his bat after he signed, and he can put on a show in batting practice.

FASTEST RUNNER: Tucker is a 60 runner with long strides. His speed shows up every day he's on the diamond thanks to premium makeup and passion for the game. OF Carl Anderson (19) predicates his game on making contact and letting his 60 speed work.

BEST DEFENSIVE PLAYER: The Pirates are betting on Tucker remaining at shortstop even though at a listed 6-foot-3, he's quite tall for the position. SS Erik Forgione (25), a steady, sure-handed college defender, makes every play.

BEST FASTBALL: The Pirates spent $1 million apiece on prep RHPs Mitch Keller (2) and Trey Supak (2s), picked nine spots apart. Keller has hit 95 mph and Supak 94, and both have athleticism and loose arms. RHP Gage Hinsz (11) has a strong 6-foot-5, 210-pound body and fresh arm. The Montana native has hit 93 mph and the Pirates see more to come thanks to his strength and easy delivery.

BEST SECONDARY PITCH: Keller's changeup and curveball both flash plus. Supak's curve has similar upside but is less consistent.

BEST PRO DEBUT: Several late-round arms got off to fine starts for the Bucs, led by RHP Montana Durapau (32), who went 3-2, 2.21 with a 57-8 strikeout-walk ratio at short-season Jamestown. Former Bethune-Cookman teammate John Sever (20) dominated at Rookie-level Bristol with 63 strikeouts in 41 innings to go with a 1.33 ERA.

BEST ATHLETE: Tucker's makeup and athletic ability makes the Pirates believe he can pull off being a tall shortstop.

MOST INTRIGUING BACKGROUND: Tucker's mother Erin was a track athlete at the University of Arizona. Keller's older brother Jon pitches in the Orioles system. RHP Sam Street (16) came to the U.S. from Australia to play college baseball; he's a sidearming reliever.

CLOSEST TO THE MAJORS: The Pirates shut Joe down after he signed due to a back issue but love his makeup and bat.

BEST LATE-ROUND PICK: Hinsz stands out for his $580,000 bonus, but Sever opened eyes with his athleticism and fastball up to 93.

THE ONE WHO GOT AWAY: A late run at redshirt sophomore INF/C Paul DeJong (38), who hit 20 home runs in the Northwoods League over the summer, wasn't enough to keep him from going back to Illinois State.

ASSESSMENT: The Pirates didn't get a lot of plus present tools but believe they got a lot of good ballplayers such as Tucker and Joe. Keller, Supak and Hinsz bring upside to the mound.

2013

With an extra pick, the Pirates went young and have had good early returns from OF Austin Meadows (1) and C Reese McGuire (1), as well as SS/OF JaCoby Jones (3), LHP Cody Dickson (4) and RHPs Buddy Borden (7) and Chad Kuhl (9).

GRADE: B+

2012

Not signing RHP Mart Appel (8) hurt in the short term. RHP Adrian Sampson (5) has developed nicely, though, while OF Barrett Barnes (1s) and C/3B Wyatt Mathisen (2) still hold promise.

GRADE: C

2011

No. 1 overall pick Gerrit Cole (1) has lived up to his $8 million billing. RHP Tyler Glasnow (5) has overtaken OF/1B Josh Bell (2) as the club's top prospect. Unsigned SS Trea Turner (20) became a first-rounder three years later.

GRADE: A

TOP DRAFT PICKS OF THE DECADE

Year	Player, Pos.	2014 Org.
2005	Andrew McCutchen, of	Pirates
2006	Brad Lincoln, rhp	Phillies
2007	Daniel Moskos, lhp	Dodgers
2008	Pedro Alvarez, 3b	Pirates
2009	Tony Sanchez, c	Pirates
2010	Jameson Taillon, rhp	Pirates
2011	Gerrit Cole, rhp	Pirates
2012	*Mark Appel, rhp	Astros
2013	Austin Meadows, of	Pirates
2014	Cole Tucker, ss	Pirates

*Did not sign

LARGEST BONUSES IN CLUB HISTORY

Gerritt Cole, 2011	$8,000,000
Jameson Taillon, 2010	$6,500,000
Pedro Alvarez, 2008	$6,000,000
Josh Bell, 2011	$5,000,000
Bryan Bullington, 2001	$4,000,000

1 TYLER GLASNOW, RHP

Born: Aug. 23, 1993. **B-T:** L-R. **Ht.:** 6-7. **Wt.:** 220.
Drafted: HS—Santa Clarita, Calif., 2011 (5th round).
Signed by: Rick Allen.

Glasnow was literally a late bloomer in high school, growing 11 inches between his freshman and senior years as he grew to 6-foot-7 and separated a growth plate in his right shoulder in the process. He has grown another inch since graduating and added 25 pounds to reach 220. Lightly recruited, he committed to Portland, but the Pirates wooed the 2011 fifth-rounder to pro ball with an over-slot $600,000 bonus. Glasnow played at Hart High, which has produced such big league pitchers as James Shields and Trevor Bauer, but he did not crack the prep rotation until midway through his junior season. He comes from an athletic family. His mother Donna starred in gymnastics at Cal State Fullerton then coached at Cal State Northridge, while his father Ted and brother Ted Jr. were both decathletes at Notre Dame. The junior Ted is a member of the famed Santa Monica Track Club and aspires to make the 2016 U.S. Olympic team. Nicknamed "Baby Giraffe" and the wearer of size-15 spikes, Glasnow had a breakout season in 2013 at low Class A West Virginia when he was named the South Atlantic League pitcher of the year. He followed up by winning the same honor in the Florida State League in 2014 at high Class A Bradenton when he topped the league in ERA (1.74) and the entire minors in opponent average (.174). He was even harder to hit in 2013 with a .140 average.

Glasnow has the ability to overpower hitters with a blazing fastball that reaches the high 90s and regularly comes in at 97 mph. His heater topped out at 99 mph. Glasnow uses his long wingspan to his advantage, getting good extension on his pitches and giving batters the sense that the ball is dropping right down upon them. His 80 mph curveball has good break to it, but Glasnow must learn how to throw it for strikes more often, for too often it's a chase pitch at this point in his career. The same can be said for his changeup, though he has good velocity separation with it in the mid-80s. Glasnow does a good job of repeating his delivery, but with long levers, he is slow to the plate and can be run on. Because of his size, he is also slow getting off the mound, and opponents can take advantage of that by bunting. Glasnow is noted for his work ethic, though, and is willing to spend the time and effort necessary to address his deficiencies.

Glasnow is not a finished product, but he has had two consecutive outstanding seasons and will be tested this year when he is assigned to Double-A Altoona. Despite his credentials, Glasnow still is young for his level, and the Pirates rarely push their young players, so they will give him some necessary developmental time. With that in mind, look for him to spend the majority of the season in the Eastern League, with a late promotion to Triple-A Indianapolis possible. Glasnow likely won't see the major leagues until sometime in 2016, but he has the raw ability to eventually join Gerrit Cole at the top of the Pirates' rotation.

BA GRADE

70 Risk: High

SCOUTING GRADES

Fastball: 80.
Curveball: 60
Changeup: 50
Control: 40

Based on 20-80 scouting scale—where 50 represents major league average—and future projection rather than present tools.

LGE	BF	SO%	BB%	HR/9
FSL	493	31.8	11.6	0.22

CLIFF WELCH

Year	Club (League)	Class	W	L	ERA	G	GS	CG	SV	IP	H	HR	BB	SO	K/9	WHIP	AVG
2012	Pirates (GCL)	R	0	3	2.10	11	10	0	0	34	19	3	16	40	10.5	1.02	.156
	State College (NYP)	SS	0	0	0.00	1	1	0	0	4	4	0	1	4	9.0	1.25	.267
2013	West Virginia (SAL)	LoA	9	3	2.18	24	24	0	0	111	54	9	61	164	13.3	1.03	.142
2014	Bradenton (FSL)	HiA	12	5	1.74	23	23	0	0	124	74	3	57	157	11.4	1.05	.174
Minor League Totals			21	11	1.94	59	58	0	0	274	151	15	135	365	12.0	1.04	.160

2 JAMESON TAILLON, RHP

Born: Nov. 18, 1991. **B-T:** R-R. **Ht.:** 6-5. **Wt.:** 245. **Drafted:** HS—The Woodlands, Texas, 2010 (1st round). **Signed by:** Trevor Haley.

After a strong 2013 season that began with him pitching for Team Canada in the World Baseball Classic and finished with six strong starts at Triple-A Indianapolis, Taillon figured to make his major league debut in 2014. Instead he had to be shut down during spring training and he missed the entire season after having Tommy John surgery on April 6. It remains to be seen how surgery will affect Taillon's stuff. Before going under the knife, he routinely threw his double-plus fastball in the mid-90s while running it in on righthanders. His best pitch is a plus curveball that was of the 12-to-6 variety. However, he had started working on tightening the pitch in spring training last year in an effort to have better command of it. Taillon tends to throw his fringe-average changeup a bit too firmly, taking away its effect as offspeed pitch. Commanding his pitches has been a challenge for Taillon at times in the past. That's even more of a concern in the short term, because that is usually the last thing to come back when pitchers return from elbow surgery. Taillon likely will begin 2015 in extended spring training, then join Indianapolis in May. Before the injury, the Pirates had planned for Taillon to return to Triple-A in 2014 before calling him up during the season. That is the way the Pirates hope it plays out in 2015, though they will be cautious not to push Taillon too hard too soon.

BA GRADE

65 Risk: High

LGE	BF	SO%	BB%	HR/9
Did not play				

Year	Club (League)	Class	W	L	ERA	G	GS	CG	SV	IP	H	HR	BB	SO	K/9	WHIP	AVG
2012	Bradenton (FSL)	HiA	6	8	3.82	23	23	2	0	125	109	10	37	98	7.1	1.17	.230
	Altoona (EL)	AA	3	0	1.59	3	3	0	0	17	11	0	1	18	9.5	0.71	.183
2013	Altoona (EL)	AA	4	7	3.67	20	19	0	0	110	112	8	36	106	8.6	1.34	.257
	Indianapolis (IL)	AAA	1	3	3.89	6	6	0	0	37	31	1	16	37	9.0	1.27	.223
2014	Did not play—Injured																
Minor League Totals			16	21	3.72	75	74	2	0	382	352	28	112	356	8.4	1.21	.240

3 AUSTIN MEADOWS, OF

Born: May 3, 1995. **B-T:** L-L. **Ht.:** 6-3. **Wt.:** 200. **Drafted:** HS—Loganville, Ga., 2013 (1st round). **Signed by:** Jerry Jordan.

The ninth overall pick in the 2013 draft, Meadows suffered a strained hamstring during in a baserunning drill early in 2014 spring training while in major league camp as a non-roster invitee. His rehab had many fits and starts before he finally appeared in the Rookie-level Gulf Coast League on June 30. Meadows played well in 38 games at low Class A West Virginia to end the season and only once failed to record a hit in back-to-back games. Meadows is an excellent all-around hitter with power potential and advanced plate discipline for such a young player. He could end up as the rare player with above-average htting ability and above-average power, though the power is more projection at the moment. The Pirates project Meadows to hit in the middle of the order, but if his power doesn't blossom, he still possesses the on-base skills to bat at the top of the order. His speed will in play center field, though he's just an average defender because he has trouble with reads and routes. His below-average arm might eventually force him to left field. Meadows has played in just 93 games and logged 402 plate appearances since being drafted, so the Pirates won't rush him. He likely will split 2015 between West Virginia and high Class A Bradenton, with an eye toward reaching the majors in 2017.

BA GRADE

65 Risk: High

LGE	PA	BB%	SO%	ISO
APP	18	16.7	16.7	.000
SAL	167	8.4	18.0	.164

Year	Club (League)	Class	AVG	G	AB	R	H	2B	3B	HR	RBI	BB	SO	SB	CS	OBP	SLG
2013	Pirates (GCL)	R	.294	43	160	29	47	11	5	5	20	24	42	3	2	.399	.519
	Jamestown (NYP)	SS	.529	5	17	8	9	0	0	2	2	5	4	0	0	.636	.882
2014	Pirates (GCL)	R	1.000	2	4	1	4	2	1	0	1	2	0	0	0	1.000	2.000
	Bristol (APP)	R	.071	5	14	2	1	0	0	0	0	3	3	0	0	.235	.071
	West Virginia (SAL)	LoA	.322	38	146	18	47	13	1	3	15	14	30	2	3	.388	.486
Minor League Totals			.317	93	341	58	108	26	7	10	38	48	79	5	5	.410	.522

4 JOSH BELL, OF/1B

Born: Aug. 14, 1992. **B-T:** B-R. **Ht.:** 6-2. **Wt.:** 235. **Drafted:** HS—Dallas, 2011 (2nd round). **Signed by:** Mike Leuzinger.

Bell was hampered by a serious knee injury he suffered early in the 2012 season and needed two full years to fully recover. He started living up to his $5 million signing bonus in 2014, when he won the Florida State League MVP award at high Class A Bradenton after leading the circuit in average (.335) and slugging (.502) before a late-July promotion to Double-A Altoona. His .325 average topped the Pirates organization. Some scouts compare Bell to former Pirates slugger Bobby Bonilla because he is a large-bodied switch-hitter with power potential. Bell hasn't shown a lot of over-the-fence power so far, but it should come as his body matures because he has a natural lift to his swing. His swing is smoother from the left side, as he tends to be jumpy when batting righthanded. Bell has an extremely strong arm suited best for right field, but he does not consistently read flyballs, so the Pirates began using him at first base in instructional league and the Arizona Fall League. He has a lot of work to do there, as he's currently a well below-average fielder who has had trouble making backhanded plays. Bell does not have a quick initial burst, but he's a fringe-average runner underway. Bell will go back to Altoona to begin 2015. The Pirates would like to see him develop into a first baseman because his path is blocked in the outfield.

BA GRADE

60 Risk: Medium

LGE	PA	BB%	SO%	ISO
FSL	363	6.9	11.8	.166
EL	102	7.8	11.8	.021

Year	Club (League)	Class	AVG	G	AB	R	H	2B	3B	HR	RBI	BB	SO	SB	CS	OBP	SLG
2012	West Virginia (SAL)	LoA	.274	15	62	6	17	5	0	1	11	2	21	1	0	.288	.403
2013	West Virginia (SAL)	LoA	.279	119	459	75	128	37	2	13	76	52	90	1	2	.353	.453
2014	Bradenton (FSL)	HiA	.335	84	331	45	111	20	4	9	53	25	43	5	4	.384	.502
	Altoona (EL)	AA	.287	24	94	13	27	2	0	0	7	8	12	4	1	.343	.309
Minor League Totals			.299	242	946	139	283	64	6	23	147	87	166	11	7	.359	.452

5 REESE McGUIRE, C

Born: March 2, 1995. **B-T:** L-R. **Ht.:** 6-0. **Wt.:** 181. **Drafted:** HS—Covington, Wash., 2013 (1st round). **Signed by:** Greg Hopkins.

Selected with the second of two first-round picks in 2013, McGuire was regarded as the best defensive high school catcher available that year. He helped lead Kentwood High to the Washington Class 4A state championship as a junior in 2012, then won the USA Baseball player of the year award that summer for his play with the 18U team. McGuire's older brother Cash is a rising junior infielder at Seattle University. McGuire is noted for his defense, which is almost major league caliber in the eyes of many scouts. He works extremely well with pitchers, for he was given the responsibility of calling pitches while still in Little League. He also is an outstanding receiver with good pitch-framing skills. McGuire's arm is above-average and made even better because of his extremely quick footwork. He concentrated mainly on making contact at low Class A West Virginia in 2014, but scouts believe he will eventually hit 10-12 home runs a year because of solid bat speed and a swing that has a little length but finishes with good leverage. McGuire shows a relatively advanced understanding of his swing and uses the opposite field well. He's a fringe-average runner. McGuire's defense and off-the-chart leadership ability will get him to the major leagues, perhaps as soon as 2017. He will begin 2015 at high Class A Bradenton.

BA GRADE

55 Risk: Medium

LGE	PA	BB%	SO%	ISO
SAL	428	5.6	10.3	.072

Year	Club (League)	Class	AVG	G	AB	R	H	2B	3B	HR	RBI	BB	SO	SB	CS	OBP	SLG
2013	Pirates (GCL)	R	.330	46	176	30	58	11	0	0	21	15	18	5	1	.388	.392
	Jamestown (NYP)	SS	.250	4	16	3	4	0	0	0	0	1	1	1	0	.294	.250
2014	West Virginia (SAL)	LoA	.262	98	389	46	102	11	4	3	45	24	44	7	2	.307	.334
Minor League Totals			.282	148	581	79	164	22	4	3	66	40	63	13	3	.332	.349

6 NICK KINGHAM, RHP

Born: Nov. 8, 1991. **B-T:** R-R. **Ht.:** 6-5. **Wt.:** 220. **Drafted:** HS—Las Vegas, 2010 (4th round). **Signed by:** Larry Broadway.

Kingham grew up playing in the fertile Las Vegas area, and one of the hitters he faced consistently throughout his amateur career was Nationals star outfielder Bryce Harper. The Pirates selected Kingham in the fourth round in 2010 and signed him for $485,000, convincing him to spurn Oregon. Kingham doesn't have one clear plus pitch, but he succeeds because of his ability to mix pitches and above-average control. That comes about in part because of a clean delivery that he repeats. Kingham threw strikes on an above-average 64 percent of his pitches in 2014. He also utilizes his 6-foot-5 frame to throw all his pitches on a downhill plane. Kingham's fastball is an average offering that usually sits 92-93 mph, though he'll touch 95. His tick above-averge curveball continues to get better and is becoming a fall-off-the-table pitch. His straight changeup is an average pitch as well. It has some deception as he maintains his arm speed, but it relies on that deception as it's straight as a string. While Kingham throws strikes, he needs to improve his command within the zone. Kingham reached Triple-A Indianapolis in the second half of 2014, and the Pirates would like him to begin 2015 there. He is closing in on the major leagues and could be ready for a callup as early as June. He projects as a solid No. 4 starter.

BA GRADE

50 Risk: Medium

LGE	BF	SO%	BB%	HR/9
EL	307	17.6	8.1	0.38
IL	361	18.0	7.5	0.61

Year	Club (League)	Class	W	L	ERA	G	GS	CG	SV	IP	H	HR	BB	SO	K/9	WHIP	AVG
2012	West Virginia (SAL)	LoA	6	8	4.39	27	27	0	0	127	115	15	36	117	8.3	1.19	.243
2013	Bradenton (FSL)	HiA	6	3	3.09	13	13	0	0	70	55	6	14	75	9.6	0.99	.212
	Altoona (EL)	AA	3	3	2.70	14	12	0	0	73	70	1	30	69	8.5	1.36	.253
2014	Altoona (EL)	AA	1	7	3.04	12	12	0	0	71	71	3	25	54	6.8	1.35	.259
	Indianapolis (IL)	AAA	5	4	3.58	14	14	0	0	88	70	6	27	65	6.6	1.10	.213
Minor League Totals			27	27	3.29	97	93	0	0	503	447	36	147	429	7.7	1.18	.237

7 ALEN HANSON, SS/2B

Born: Oct. 22, 1992. **B-T:** B-R. **Ht.:** 5-11. **Wt.:** 170. **Signed:** Dominican Republic, 2009. **Signed by:** Rene Gayo/Ellis Pena.

When Hanson and Gregory Polanco arrived at low Class A West Virginia in 2012, it was Hanson who was the standout. Polanco has since sped on to the big leagues, while Hanson has seen his development slow. After reaching Double-A Altoona in 2013, he spent the entire 2014 season there again. He sat out six games at midseason for what the Pirates said was a rest but other sources said was a suspension for insubordination. Hanson is athletic with good bat and foot speed. He reached double digits in doubles (21), triples (12) and home runs (11) in 2014, an indication that he has pop despite a relatively small frame. Hanson needs to learn how to channel his aggressive play because he tends to swing at bad pitches, run into outs and try to make plays that he has no chance making. Hanson has the range to play shortstop, but his arm is well below-average and he spent his time exclusively at second base during the final month of 2014. Hanson has plenty of raw talent but has leveled off since moving up to Double-A. He will head to Triple-A Indianapolis in 2015, and if he can rein in his game and begin making more consistent contact, he could be the starting second baseman for the Pirates in 2017 when Neil Walker's contract expires. Even if he doesn't make the expected progress, he at least projects to be a utility infielder in the major leagues.

BA GRADE

50 Risk: Medium

LGE	PA	BB%	SO%	ISO
EL	527	5.9	16.7	.162

Year	Club (League)	Class	AVG	G	AB	R	H	2B	3B	HR	RBI	BB	SO	SB	CS	OBP	SLG
2012	West Virginia (SAL)	LoA	.309	124	489	99	151	33	13	16	62	55	105	35	19	.381	.528
2013	Bradenton (FSL)	HiA	.281	92	367	51	103	23	8	7	48	33	70	24	14	.339	.444
	Altoona (EL)	AA	.255	35	137	13	35	4	5	1	10	8	26	6	2	.299	.380
2014	Altoona (EL)	AA	.280	118	482	64	135	21	12	11	58	31	88	25	11	.326	.442
Minor League Totals			.289	492	1927	318	557	104	52	39	241	171	362	134	60	.351	.458

8 COLE TUCKER, SS

Born: July 3, 1996. **B-T:** B-R. **Ht.:** 6-3. **Wt.:** 185. **Drafted:** HS—Phoenix, 2014 (1st round). **Signed by:** Mike Steele.

Many other teams had pegged Tucker as a second- or third-round talent in the 2014 draft, but the Pirates were higher than the consensus on the lanky shortstop, especially after he impressed at the National High School Invitational. They signed him for $1.8 million as the 24th overall pick. Tucker's strong suit at this stage of his career is defense, for he has excellent range, a plus arm and good instincts. He is athletic enough to stay at the position despite his 6-foot-3 height. Scouts were impressed with his ability to make strong, accurate throws from a variety of arm angles. The long-armed Tucker will likely always have to prove he can handle pitches in on his hands, especially when batting from the left side. He took up switch-hitting two years ago, but he does a good job of making contact from both sides, and his lefthanded swing features good bat speed and a compact swing path. He should get stronger as he matures, but his swing is geared for line drives, which makes it hard to project more than 10 home runs a season. A long-strider who is a tick above-average runner, he shows good instincts on the basepaths. Tucker was just 17 when he made his debut in the Rookie-level Gulf Coast League, and the Pirates believe he is mature enough to handle an assignment to low Class A West Virginia in 2015.

BA GRADE

50 Risk: High

LGE	PA	BB%	SO%	ISO
GCL	217	12.0	17.5	.089

Year	Club (League)	Class	AVG	G	AB	R	H	2B	3B	HR	RBI	BB	SO	SB	CS	OBP	SLG
2014	Pirates (GCL)	R	.267	48	180	39	48	6	2	2	13	26	38	13	5	.368	.356
Minor League Totals			.267	48	180	39	48	6	2	2	13	26	38	13	5	.368	.356

9 MITCH KELLER, RHP

Born: April 4, 1996. **B-T:** R-R. **Ht.:** 6-3. **Wt.:** 195. **Drafted:** HS—Cedar Rapids, Iowa, 2014 (2nd round). **Signed by:** Matt Bimeal.

Keller seemed solid in his commitment to play college ball at North Carolina, but the Pirates were able to sign the 2014 second-rounder after offering him $1 million. His draft stock soared when his fastball jumped from the low 90s to the mid-90s as a Xavier High senior. His older brother Jon is a pitching prospect for the Orioles. Keller's plus fastball is his best pitch. He found that he was able to overpower Rookie-level Gulf Coast League hitters in 2014 nearly as easily as the high school hitters he faced in the past. Keller could well add another tick or two to his fastball because of his projectable frame. He also generates good sinking action and plenty of groundballs. His secondary pitches are not nearly as advanced and require plenty of projection. Keller needs to consistently finish his delivery on his curveball and is working to gain better feel for his changeup. He could stand to tighten his delivery in order to improve his control. The Pirates are aggressive in using defensive shifts throughout the organization, so Keller's groundball tendencies play into the philosophy very well. He will most likely begin 2015 at low Class A West Virginia. He has a lot of work to do, but the pieces are all present—including a willingness to learn—to excel as a stater.

BA GRADE

50 Risk: High

LGE	BF	SO%	BB%	HR/9
GCL	113	25.7	11.5	0.00

Year	Club (League)	Class	W	L	ERA	G	GS	CG	SV	IP	H	HR	BB	SO	K/9	WHIP	AVG
2014	Pirates (GCL)	R	0	0	1.98	9	8	0	0	27	19	0	13	29	9.5	1.17	.202
Minor League Totals			0	0	1.98	9	8	0	0	27	19	0	13	29	9.5	1.17	.202

10 HAROLD RAMIREZ, OF

Born: Sept. 6, 1994. **B-T:** R-R. **Ht.:** 5-10. **Wt.:** 210. **Signed:** Colombia, 2011. **Signed by:** Rene Gayo/Orlando Covo.

The Pirates signed Ramirez out of Colombia for $1.05 million, a hefty bonus for a player from that country, and he has looked to be worth the investment so far. He played in just 49 games at low Class A West Virginia in 2014 as he dealt with quadriceps and hamstring injuries. Ramirez, however, played winter ball in Colombia, where he sought to regain the form that made him the No. 1 prospect in the short-season New York-Penn League in 2013. Though he doesn't look the part with his stocky build, Ramirez is an athlete. His flat swing is geared more for line drives to all fields than over-the-fence power, but he projects as at least an average hitter with well below-average power. He is an above-average runner who covers a lot of ground and runs good routes in center field, though his arm is below-average, and he has problems with balls hit directly at him. Ramirez's performance in spring training will dictate which Class A roster he inhabits in 2015. In the long term, his speed and defense make him a potential everyday center fielder.

BA GRADE
50 Risk: High

LGE	PA	BB%	SO%	ISO
SAL	226	4.9	15.5	.093

Year	Club (League)	Class	AVG	G	AB	R	H	2B	3B	HR	RBI	BB	SO	SB	CS	OBP	SLG
2012	Pirates (GCL)	R	.259	39	135	18	35	5	1	1	12	6	20	9	5	.310	.333
2013	Jamestown (NYP)	SS	.285	71	274	42	78	11	4	5	40	23	52	23	11	.354	.409
2014	West Virginia (SAL)	LoA	.309	49	204	30	63	14	1	1	24	11	35	12	3	.364	.402
Minor League Totals			.287	159	613	90	176	30	6	7	76	40	107	44	19	.348	.390

11 ELIAS DIAZ, C

BA GRADE
50 Risk: High

Born: Nov. 17, 1990. **B-T:** R-R. **Ht.:** 6-1. **Wt.:** 175. **Signed:** Venezuela, 2008. **Signed by:** Rene Gayo/Rodolfo Petit.

Diaz was the breakout star in the Pirates system in 2014. The Pirates have loved his defense ever since signing him, as he's an outstanding receiver. He presents a good target, frames pitches well, possesses quick hands and feet and has an above-average arm that helped him throw out 33 percent of basestealers in 2014. After hitting .221 and .208 at low Class A West Virginia in 2011 and 2012, Diaz started to click at the plate in 2013 at high Class A Bradenton. While defense will always be his calling card, he now shows the swing that could allow him to be a .250 hitter with 5-10 home runs, which when combined with his defense will be good enough to make him a regular. Diaz will begin 2015 at Triple-A Indianapolis and could be the bridge between departed free agent Russell Martin and 2013 first-rounder Reese McGuire.

Year	Club (League)	Class	AVG	G	AB	R	H	2B	3B	HR	RBI	BB	SO	SB	CS	OBP	SLG
2012	West Virginia (SAL)	LoA	.208	92	313	32	65	14	1	3	26	22	51	2	2	.262	.288
2013	Bradenton (FSL)	HiA	.279	57	183	30	51	12	2	2	15	31	33	4	4	.382	.399
2014	Altoona (EL)	AA	.328	91	326	41	107	20	0	6	54	30	51	3	2	.378	.445
	Indianapolis (IL)	AAA	.152	10	33	4	5	1	0	0	0	3	6	0	1	.243	.182
Minor League Totals			.253	445	1555	198	394	88	9	20	196	148	285	18	16	.321	.360

12 WILLY GARCIA, OF

BA GRADE
50 Risk: High

Born: Sept. 4, 1992. **B-T:** R-R. **Ht.:** 6-3. **Wt.:** 180. **Signed:** Dominican Republic, 2010. **Signed by:** Rene Gayo/Marino Tejada.

Signed for $280,000 from the Dominican Republic in 2010, Garcia has two tools that stand out. The most notable one is a sniper rifle of an arm that enabled the right fielder to lead the Double-A Eastern League with 19 assists in 2014. The other is plus power potential. Garcia's swing is entirely geared towards driving the ball out of the park, with a big load and significant weight transfer to coil himself before taking a big cut. It leads to massive home runs when he connects, but it also makes it hard for him to make consistent contact or to go the other way with an outside pitch. He projects as a below-average hitter with frightening strikeout rates. He fanned 30 percent of the time at Double-A Altoona in 2014. Garcia also needs to shore up his route running in the outfield. He is not a burner, but he's an average runner who can get the occasional steal. The Pirates added Garcia to the 40-man roster in November, and he will begin 2015 at Triple-A Indianapolis.

Year	Club (League)	Class	AVG	G	AB	R	H	2B	3B	HR	RBI	BB	SO	SB	CS	OBP	SLG
2012	West Virginia (SAL)	LoA	.240	122	459	57	110	17	2	18	77	32	131	10	8	.286	.403
2013	Bradenton (FSL)	HiA	.256	118	449	51	115	21	6	16	60	23	154	13	6	.294	.437
2014	Altoona (EL)	AA	.271	126	439	59	119	27	5	18	63	24	145	8	4	.311	.478
Minor League Totals			.256	467	1699	221	435	85	17	58	257	104	508	46	28	.303	.428

13 JACOBY JONES, SS

BA GRADE

50 Risk: High

Born: May 10, 1992. **B-T:** R-R. **Ht.:** 6-3. **Wt.:** 200. **Drafted:** Louisiana State, 2013 (3rd round). **Signed by:** Jerome Cochran.

After Jones played all over the field at Louisiana State, the Pirates drafted him as a center fielder in 2013. However, he played exclusively at shortstop at low Class A West Virginia in 2014. Jones is a tooled-up player who is a plus runner with power, as evidenced by his 23 home runs and 17 stolen bases last season. He become enamored of hitting the ball out of the park at the expense of making contact. His all-or-nothing approach leaves him susceptible to anything but fastballs. Jones has the range to play shortstop, but most scouts don't think he'll stick there because his hands are somewhat stiff and his arm is below-average. He is a solid center fielder, where he uses his speed to his advantage. The Pirates hope Jones can stay at shortstop for the long haul, and he will play there again at high Class A Bradenton in 2015. With his tools and versatility, he could carve out a long career as a super utility player.

Year	Club (League)	Class	AVG	G	AB	R	H	2B	3B	HR	RBI	BB	SO	SB	CS	OBP	SLG
2013	Jamestown (NYP)	SS	.311	15	61	14	19	2	2	1	10	3	14	3	2	.358	.459
2014	West Virginia (SAL)	LoA	.288	117	445	72	128	21	3	23	70	33	132	17	9	.347	.503
Minor League Totals			.291	132	506	86	147	23	5	24	80	36	146	20	11	.349	.498

14 TREY SUPAK, RHP

BA GRADE

50 Risk: High

Born: May 31, 1996. **B-T:** R-R. **Ht.:** 6-5. **Wt.:** 210. **Drafted:** HS—La Grange, Texas, 2014 (2nd round supplemental). **Signed by:** Trevor Haley.

Supak became the first player in 10 years to be drafted from La Grange (Texas) High, with the last being Reds righthander Homer Bailey. The Pirates went over slot to sign him for $1 million as a supplemental second-round pick in 2014. The Pirates are intrigued by Supak's large frame and believe he can add velocity to his fastball that topped out at 94 mph in high school and usually sits 90-91, though he struggled to maintain that velocity deep in games. His heater lacks movement. His curveball flashes plus and his changeup has a chance to be at least an average pitch. Supak leverages his size very well, coming at hitters from an angle that is almost straight over the top, which makes his pitches hard to pick up. Supak lacks polish and figures to stay in extended spring training in 2015 before joining short-season Morgantown in June when the New York-Penn League season opens.

Year	Club (League)	Class	W	L	ERA	G	GS	CG	SV	IP	H	HR	BB	SO	K/9	WHIP	AVG
2014	Pirates (GCL)	R	1	3	4.88	8	6	0	0	24	27	4	11	21	7.9	1.58	.293
Minor League Totals			1	3	4.88	8	6	0	0	24	27	4	11	21	7.9	1.58	.293

15 ADRIAN SAMPSON, RHP

BA GRADE

45 Risk: Medium

Born: Oct. 7, 1991. **B-T:** R-R. **Ht.:** 6-3. **Wt.:** 200. **Drafted:** Bellevue (Wash.) CC, 2012 (5th round). **Signed by:** Greg Hopkins.

Sampson's chances of being drafted high out of high school fell apart when he needed Tommy John surgery his senior season. After that setback, Sampson decided to go to Bellevue (Wash.) CC instead of Oregon as originally planned. After not coming to terms with the Marlins as a 16th-round pick in 2011, he signed with the Pirates for $250,000 after his sophomore season in 2012. Sampson came to pro ball as a two-pitch pitcher who had a low-90s fastball and a big-breaking curve. The fastball is a tick above-average pitch because he gets some sink and tail to the offering that he can locate arm side and glove side. His curve morphed into a slurve and has now transformed into an average slider. But Sampson's development took off because of the lumps he took trying to develop his changeup in 2013. He developed feel for the pitch to the point where it played as a fringe-average offering at Double-A Altoona in 2014. It's still a little firm and he sometimes slows his arm, but he held lefties to a .703 OPS in 2014. Sampson has been somewhat under the radar to this point, but he will begin 2015 at Triple-A Indianapolis and could make it to Pittsburgh. He projects as a back-end starter or at least a useful setup man.

Year	Club (League)	Class	W	L	ERA	G	GS	CG	SV	IP	H	HR	BB	SO	K/9	WHIP	AVG
2012	State College (NYP)	SS	0	1	2.95	11	9	0	0	43	38	2	17	44	9.3	1.29	.241
2013	Bradenton (FSL)	HiA	5	8	5.14	25	24	1	0	140	177	18	22	85	5.5	1.42	.310
2014	Altoona (EL)	AA	10	5	2.55	24	24	2	0	148	125	10	30	99	6.0	1.05	.229
	Indianapolis (IL)	AAA	1	1	6.16	4	4	0	0	19	29	1	7	10	4.7	1.89	.358
Minor League Totals			16	15	3.84	64	61	3	0	350	369	31	76	238	6.1	1.27	.272

16 JOHN HOLDZKOM, RHP

Born: Oct. 19, 1987. **B-T:** R-R. **Ht.:** 6-7. **Wt.:** 225. **Drafted:** Salt Lake CC, 2006 (4th round). **Signed by:** Mike Baker (Mets).

BA GRADE

45 Risk: Medium

Though a touch old to be considered a top prospect, Holdzkom was one of the more amazing Pirates' stories in recent memory as he went from the independent American Association in June—where he caught the eye of scout Mal Fischman—to being used as a reliever in high-leverage situations during the pennant race in September. Holdzkom had battled maturity issues and frightening control problems since signing as a Mets fourth-roudner in 2006. Coming into 2014, he had walked 7.2 batters per nine innings for his career, in part because the cut he inadvertently put on the ball made it move so much that he struggled to keep it in the strike zone. A tweaked fastball grip he learned in 2014 allowed him to control his cutting action, giving him fringe-average control. That's enough for him to have success, because Holdzkom's double-plus fastball routinely hit the high 90s and has touched 100 mph. He also throws the little-seen palmball, but when he's on, he'll throw his fastball 90 percent of the time. Holdzkom will get a chance to win a setup reliever job with the Pirates in spring training and could eventually close.

Year	Club (League)	Class	W	L	ERA	G	GS	CG	SV	IP	H	HR	BB	SO	K/9	WHIP	AVG
2012	Bakersfield (CAL)	HiA	0	1	5.19	6	1	0	0	9	6	0	13	10	10.4	2.19	.194
2013	Amarillo (A-A)	IND	2	3	3.50	34	0	0	2	36	31	0	31	37	9.3	1.72	--
	Sioux City (A-A)	IND	1	1	0.00	8	0	0	0	8	5	0	5	15	17.6	1.30	--
2014	Amarillo (A-A)	IND	0	0	1.17	9	0	0	0	8	6	0	2	7	8.2	1.04	--
	San Angelo (UNI)	IND	0	0	0.00	1	0	0	0	1	1	0	0	0	18.0	1.00	--
	Altoona (EL)	AA	1	0	0.00	4	0	0	0	6	1	0	2	10	15.0	0.50	.056
	Indianapolis (IL)	AAA	2	0	2.49	18	0	0	2	22	14	1	10	27	11.2	1.11	.179
	Pittsburgh (NL)	MAJ	1	0	2.00	9	0	0	1	9	4	1	2	14	14.0	0.67	.133
Major League Totals			1	0	2.00	9	0	0	1	9	4	1	2	14	14.0	0.67	.133
Minor League Totals			11	11	4.93	85	15	0	5	162	146	6	119	190	10.5	1.63	.237

17 CASEY SADLER, RHP

Born: July 13, 1990. **B-T:** R-R. **Ht.:** 6-4. **Wt.:** 215. **Drafted:** Western Oklahoma State JC, 2010 (25th round). **Signed by:** Mike Leuzinger.

BA GRADE

45 Risk: Medium

Sadler seemed solid in his commitment to Oklahoma State coming out of junior college, but the Pirates took a shot on him in the 25th round of the 2010 draft and wound up wooing him with a $100,000 bonus. He joined the 40-man roster following the 2013 season, then made his major league debut in 2014. Sadler gets good sinking action on a fringe-average 90-91 mph fastball that will occasionally hit 94 and induce batters to hit the ball on the ground. He also mixes in a slider and changeup. Though both rate as average pitches, they work to keep hitters off his sinker. While Sadler is not overpowering, he is not afraid to attack the strike zone and rarely hurts himself with walks. He fields his position well and controls the running game, and his poise and mound presence would play well in the bullpen. Pittsburgh's rotation depth may push him to that role in 2015, which will likely include a repeat of Triple-A.

Year	Club (League)	Class	W	L	ERA	G	GS	CG	SV	IP	H	HR	BB	SO	K/9	WHIP	AVG
2012	Bradenton (FSL)	HiA	4	6	3.73	32	17	0	2	130	125	7	35	93	6.4	1.23	.255
2013	Altoona (EL)	AA	11	7	3.31	23	23	1	0	130	116	11	42	67	4.6	1.21	.242
	Indianapolis (IL)	AAA	0	0	4.50	1	1	0	0	6	7	1	1	5	7.5	1.33	.280
2014	Indianapolis (IL)	AAA	11	4	3.03	21	21	1	0	125	124	11	24	77	5.6	1.19	.263
	Pittsburgh (NL)	MAJ	0	1	7.84	6	0	0	0	10	12	0	5	7	6.1	1.65	.293
Major League Totals			0	1	7.84	6	0	0	0	10	12	0	5	7	6.1	1.65	.293
Minor League Totals			34	22	3.23	124	63	2	6	482	453	36	125	320	6.0	1.20	.251

18 BUDDY BORDEN, RHP

Born: April 29, 1992. **B-T:** R-R. **Ht.:** 6-3. **Wt.:** 210. **Drafted:** Nevada-Las Vegas, 2013 (7th round). **Signed by:** Jason Cooper.

BA GRADE

50 Risk: High

Borden went from allowing opponents to hit .392 during his freshman year at Nevada-Las Vegas to .233 in his junior season, making him one of the most improved pitchers in the nation. Borden lasted until the seventh before being picked by the Pirates. He throws a 91-93 mph fastball that reaches 96 at times, but he has improved his curveball significantly as a pro to the point where it's a plus pitch. He also throws a below-average changeup. Borden has gained better command of all of his pitches since entering the pro ranks. He will pitch at the high Class A level in 2015 and profiles as a potential back-end starter in the majors, though he has shown enough improvement to give hope more is there.

Year	Club (League)	Class	W	L	ERA	G	GS	CG	SV	IP	H	HR	BB	SO	K/9	WHIP	AVG
2013	Jamestown (NYP)	SS	0	0	1.08	6	3	0	0	17	10	0	5	23	12.4	0.90	.169
2014	West Virginia (SAL)	LoA	7	9	3.16	27	26	0	1	128	103	13	48	122	8.6	1.18	.220
Minor League Totals			7	9	2.92	33	29	0	1	145	113	13	53	145	9.0	1.15	.214

19 GAGE HINSZ, RHP

BA GRADE

45 Risk: High

Born: April 20, 1996. **B-T:** R-R. **Ht.:** 6-4. **Wt.:** 210. **Drafted:** HS— Billings, Mont., 2014 (11th round). **Signed by:** Max Kwan.

The Pirates took a shot on Hinsz in the 11th round of the 2014 draft, then took what they had left of their bonus pool money and signed the Oregon State recruit for $580,000. It's a risk because he is the kind of all-projection pitcher who often gets nabbed after three years of college development. Hinsz is intriguing because of his size and 91-93 mph fastball that looks even quicker to hitters because he throws it downhill from a three-quarters arm slot. His curveball and changeup need refinement but he is able to repeat his mechanics consistently. Hinsz is more about projection than results at this stage after logging just eight innings in the Rookie-level Gulf Coast League. The Pirates figure to take it slow with him and might even assign him to Rookie-level Bristol in 2015 following a stint in extended spring training.

Year	Club (League)	Class	W	L	ERA	G	GS	CG	SV	IP	H	HR	BB	SO	K/9	WHIP	AVG
2014	Pirates (GCL)	R	0	0	3.38	3	2	0	0	8	8	0	4	7	7.9	1.50	.267
Minor League Totals			0	0	3.38	3	2	0	0	8	8	0	4	7	7.9	1.50	.267

20 CLAY HOLMES, RHP

BA GRADE

50 Risk: Extreme

Born: March 27, 1993. **B-T:** R-R. **Ht.:** 6-5. **Wt.:** 230. **Drafted:** HS— Slocomb, Ala., 2011 (9th round). **Signed by:** Darren Mazeroski.

Holmes figured to be a tough sign out of high school in Slocomb, Ala. He was headed to Auburn after being high school valedictorian and winning the Alabama state coaches association's student-athlete of the year award. However, the Pirates won him over with a $1.2 million bonus. Holmes suffered a major setback in 2014 when he tore an elbow ligament during spring training, then missed the season after having Tommy John surgery. Many scouts viewed him as an injury waiting to happen because of his violent mechanics, and he is putting in extra work in an effort to smooth them out while he rehabs. Before being injured, Holmes had two plus pitches in a low-90s fastball he can sink and a curveball. He was also showing improvement with his changeup. Though Holmes lost a year of developmental time, he will likely be ready to pitch at either low Class A West Virginia or high Class A Bradenton by the end of April 2015.

Year	Club (League)	Class	W	L	ERA	G	GS	CG	SV	IP	H	HR	BB	SO	K/9	WHIP	AVG
2012	State College (NYP)	SS	5	3	2.28	13	13	0	0	59	35	1	29	34	5.2	1.08	.176
2013	West Virginia (SAL)	LoA	5	6	4.08	26	25	0	0	119	106	7	69	90	6.8	1.47	.240
2014	Did not play—Injured																
Minor League Totals			10	9	3.48	39	38	0	0	178	141	8	98	124	6.3	1.34	.220

21 STETSON ALLIE, 1B

BA GRADE

45 Risk: High

Born: March 13, 1991. **B-T:** R-R. **Ht.:** 6-2. **Wt.:** 238. **Drafted:** HS— Lakewood, Ohio, 2010 (2nd round). **Signed by:** Brian Tracy.

A hard-throwing pitcher in high school, Allie reached triple digits multiple times while being the winning pitcher for St. Edward High in the Ohio state championship game during his senior year in 2010. Though Allie was raw without a plus secondary pitch, many teams considered him to be a first-round talent. He suffered serious control problems early in his pro career and asked the Pirates to let him hit during extended spring training in 2012. He has turned himself back into a prospect because of his plus power and solid walk rate. Allie can be pitched to because his pull-heavy approach leaves him vulnerable to breaking balls on the outer half, but he has toned down the strikeouts—26 percent at Double-A Altoona in 2014—and will take a walk. He has worked to become an average first baseman with an arm that's wasted at the position. Allie has 20-plus home run potential, but no team has gambled a Rule 5 selection on him in either of the past two drafts. He will move to Triple-A Indianapolis in 2015.

Year	Club (League)	Class	AVG	G	AB	R	H	2B	3B	HR	RBI	BB	SO	SB	CS	OBP	SLG
2012	Pirates (GCL)	R	.213	42	150	23	32	6	2	3	19	21	50	2	0	.314	.340
2013	West Virginia (SAL)	LoA	.324	66	244	42	79	16	1	17	61	36	79	6	1	.414	.607
	Bradenton (FSL)	HiA	.229	66	236	28	54	18	0	4	25	41	82	2	3	.342	.356
2014	Altoona (EL)	AA	.246	117	407	60	100	16	0	21	62	71	127	9	6	.362	.440
Minor League Totals			.256	291	1037	153	265	56	3	45	167	169	338	19	10	.362	.446

22 WYATT MATHISEN, 3B

Born: Dec. 30, 1993. **B-T:** R-R. **Ht.:** 6-1. **Wt.:** 210. **Drafted:** HS—Corpus Christi, Texas, 2012 (2nd round). **Signed by:** Trevor Haley.

Mathisen was considered one of the best high school catchers in the 2012 draft, despite playing catcher only on the showcase circuit. He didn't wear the gear for long, for the Pirates moved him to third base at low Class A West Virginia in 2014. Defensively, Mathisen made a smooth transition. He has the potential to be an average defender with an accurate, tick above-average arm, good hands and solid range. As one would expect from a former catcher, he's a below-average runner. The bigger question is whether Mathisen can handle the offensive demands of the position. He has a strong frame, but he's shown no power as a pro with a career .336 slugging percentage. His line-drive swing features little loft; he hits for average and draws plenty of walks, but he has to learn how to drive the ball in hitter's counts. Mathisen will continue to learn the nuances of playing third base in 2015 at high Class A Bradenton.

Year	Club (League)	Class	AVG	G	AB	R	H	2B	3B	HR	RBI	BB	SO	SB	CS	OBP	SLG
2012	Pirates (GCL)	R	.295	45	139	24	41	8	0	1	15	16	19	10	8	.388	.374
2013	West Virginia (SAL)	LoA	.185	32	119	13	22	3	0	0	9	9	22	1	0	.256	.210
	Pirates (GCL)	R	.409	8	22	5	9	1	0	0	3	7	2	0	0	.552	.455
	Jamestown (NYP)	SS	.269	8	26	4	7	0	0	0	3	5	7	1	0	.394	.269
2014	West Virginia (SAL)	LoA	.280	103	375	48	105	17	2	3	42	33	54	6	2	.344	.360
Minor League Totals			.270	196	681	94	184	29	2	4	72	70	104	18	10	.348	.336

23 BARRETT BARNES, OF

BA GRADE

50 Risk: Extreme

Born: July 29, 1991. **B-T:** R-R. **Ht.:** 6-1. **Wt.:** 195. **Drafted:** Texas Tech, 2012 (1st round supplemental). **Signed by:** Mike Leuzinger.

The Pirates thought highly enough of Barnes to use the No. 45 pick on him in the 2012 draft—the highest a Texas Tech player had been selected since Matt Miller in 1996—and he has proven to be an interesting player when healthy. However, Barnes appeared in just 101 games in his first three seasons thanks to shin, back, hamstring and oblique injuries. When healthy, he has shown the ability to project as an average hitter with plus speed. He draws enough walks to be a potential top-of-the-order hitter, with the range to be at least an average center fielder with an average arm. The injuries are a bit of a puzzle because the personable Barnes is a hard worker and keeps himself in good shape. Barnes will begin 2015 at high Class A Bradenton. Under normal circumstances, he would be higher up the chain by now, so he has a lot of lost time to make up if he is going to remain on the Pirates' radar.

Year	Club (League)	Class	AVG	G	AB	R	H	2B	3B	HR	RBI	BB	SO	SB	CS	OBP	SLG
2012	State College (NYP)	SS	.288	38	125	16	36	6	0	5	24	17	21	10	6	.401	.456
2013	West Virginia (SAL)	LoA	.268	46	183	26	49	9	0	5	24	17	48	10	3	.338	.399
2014	West Virginia (SAL)	LoA	.154	4	13	1	2	0	0	0	2	2	2	2	0	.267	.154
	Pirates (GCL)	R	.313	7	16	5	5	2	0	2	5	6	3	1	0	.560	.813
	Bradenton (FSL)	HiA	.238	6	21	3	5	2	0	0	1	3	5	1	0	.333	.333
Minor League Totals			.271	101	358	51	97	19	0	12	56	45	79	24	9	.371	.425

24 CODY DICKSON, LHP

BA GRADE

50 Risk: Extreme

Born: April 27, 1992. **B-T:** L-L. **Ht.:** 6-3. **Wt.:** 180. **Drafted:** Sam Houston State, 2013 (4th round). **Signed by:** Trevor Haley.

Dickson slipped to the fourth round of the 2013 draft despite being a lefthanded starter with good stuff. Scouts dropped him because control problems forced him to move to the bullpen at Sam Houston State that spring. His wildness has followed him to pro ball, where he still has to work on the timing of his delivery. If he can throw strikes, he has the makings of a solid mid-rotation starter. Dickson throws his tick above-average fastball in the lows 90s and it will get up to 95 mph on occasion. He complements the heater with a curveball and a changeup that both flash plus, though with much inconsistency. Dickson made big strides at low Class A West Virginia in 2014. After posting a 5.58 ERA in his first 13 starts, he had a 2.45 mark in his last 14 starts. He will begin 2015 at high Class A Bradenton, but if he throws strikes consistently he could force an in-season promotion to Double-A Altoona.

Year	Club (League)	Class	W	L	ERA	G	GS	CG	SV	IP	H	HR	BB	SO	K/9	WHIP	AVG
2013	Jamestown (NYP)	SS	2	0	2.37	14	14	0	0	57	42	3	24	59	9.3	1.16	.209
2014	West Virginia (SAL)	LoA	7	9	3.90	27	27	0	0	129	138	11	58	104	7.2	1.52	.281
Minor League Totals			9	9	3.43	41	41	0	0	186	180	14	82	163	7.9	1.41	.260

25 CONNOR JOE, OF/C

Born: Aug. 16, 1992. **B-T:** R-R. **Ht.:** 6-0. **Wt.:** 205. **Drafted:** San Diego, 2014 (first round supplemental). **Signed by:** Brian Tracy.

The Pirates were criticized in some circles for selecting Joe in the supplemental first round of the 2014 draft, especially when they announced him as an outfielder rather than a catcher. Many analysts had Joe, who played first base at San Diego but caught in the Cape Cod League, going in the third round. Pittsburgh signed him for $1.25 million which was more than $200,000 under the recommended slot bonus. There are no early returns with which to judge the Pirates' decision, because Joe missed the entire short-season Jamestown slate with a back injury. His bat may be enough to handle the move to the outfield, for he projects to have potentially average power and projects as an above-average hitter. He hits the ball hard from gap to gap and has outstanding plate discipline. He is also very athletic and is an above-average runner. Joe likely will begin the 2015 season at low Class A West Virginia, and the Pirates are considering giving him some playing time behind the plate and at first base to see exactly what they have.

Year	Club (League)	Class	AVG	G	AB	R	H	2B	3B	HR	RBI	BB	SO	SB	CS	OBP	SLG
2014	Did not play—Injured																

26 LUIS HEREDIA, RHP

Born: Aug. 10, 1994. **B-T:** R-R. **Ht.:** 6-6. **Wt.:** 205. **Signed:** Mexico, 2010. **Signed by:** Rene Gayo/Chino Valdez.

The Pirates signed Heredia as an amateur free agent from Mexico for $2.6 million on his 16th birthday in 2010, though he had to give the majority of the bonus money to Veracruz, the Mexican League team that owned his rights. It remains the largest international bonus ever given by the Pirates. Heredia's father Hector pitched in the Dodgers organization and reached Triple-A before spending a number of years in the Mexican League. Though Heredia's signing came with great fanfare, he has yet to break out as a pro. He has struggled with weight issues, though he got in better shape at low Class A West Virginia in 2014, but then missed two months with shoulder tendinitis. At this point, Heredia's 92-94 mph fastball is his only plus pitch, and he actually has lost a tick of velocity since his amateur days. He also struggles to command his curveball and changeup. Heredia will move up to high Class A Bradenton in 2015 and pitch most of the season at age 20.

Year	Club (League)	Class	W	L	ERA	G	GS	CG	SV	IP	H	HR	BB	SO	K/9	WHIP	AVG
2012	State College (NYP)	SS	4	2	2.71	14	14	0	0	66	53	2	20	40	5.4	1.10	.224
2013	West Virginia (SAL)	LoA	7	3	3.05	14	13	0	0	65	52	5	37	55	7.6	1.37	.224
2014	West Virginia (SAL)	LoA	2	4	4.15	18	18	0	0	89	87	9	33	43	4.3	1.35	.258
Minor League Totals			14	11	3.55	58	56	0	0	251	220	19	109	161	5.8	1.31	.240

27 STOLMY PIMENTEL, RHP

Born: Feb. 1, 1990. **B-T:** R-R. **Ht.:** 6-3. **Wt.:** 230. **Signed:** Dominican Republic, 2006. **Signed by:** Luis Scheker (Red Sox).

Once a prospect of note for the Red Sox before struggling at the Double-A level in 2012, Pimentel joined the Pirates as part of the six-player trade following the 2012 season that sent closer Joel Hanrahan to Boston. Pimentel did well in his first season with the Pirates while splitting the season as a starter between Double-A Altoona and Triple-A Indianapolis. Ideally he would have reported back to Indianapolis in 2014, but he was out of minor league options and the Pirates kept him on the major league roster most of the season, using him in low-leverage relief situations. Pimentel has enough pitches to start with a plus, mid-90s fastball, an average split-changeup and an average curveball. He has struggled because his control is fringy. After pitching just 43 innings in 2014, Pimentel appears destined to remain in the bullpen in 2015.

Year	Club (League)	Class	W	L	ERA	G	GS	CG	SV	IP	H	HR	BB	SO	K/9	WHIP	AVG
2012	Portland (EL)	AA	6	7	4.59	22	22	1	0	116	115	9	42	86	6.7	1.36	.259
2013	Altoona (EL)	AA	4	3	3.61	13	13	1	0	77	74	8	35	61	7.1	1.41	.252
	Indianapolis (IL)	AAA	2	6	3.13	14	14	1	0	92	76	6	21	62	6.1	1.05	.224
	Pittsburgh (NL)	MAJ	0	0	1.93	5	0	0	0	9	6	0	2	9	8.7	0.86	.171
2014	Bradenton (FSL)	HiA	0	0	0.00	1	0	0	0	2	0	0	1	2	9.0	0.50	.000
	Altoona (EL)	AA	0	0	1.42	5	3	0	0	6	6	0	5	6	8.5	1.74	.261
	Indianapolis (IL)	AAA	0	0	0.00	1	0	0	1	2	0	0	0	1	4.5	0.00	.000
	Pittsburgh (NL)	MAJ	2	1	5.23	20	0	0	0	33	34	5	16	38	10.5	1.53	.264
Major League Totals			2	1	4.50	25	0	0	0	42	40	5	18	47	10.1	1.38	.244
Minor League Totals			45	50	4.10	159	150	4	1	769	746	71	253	609	7.1	1.30	.256

28 CHAD KUHL, RHP

BA GRADE

45 Risk: High

Born: Sept. 10, 1992 **B-T:** R-R. **Ht.:** 6-3. **Wt.:** 215. **Drafted:** Delaware, 2013 (9th round). **Signed by:** Brian Selman.

The high school player of the year in Delaware in 2010, Kuhl stayed home to play college ball at the University of Delaware. The youngest of five children and a history major, Kuhl is bright and absorbs instruction quickly, helping him make big strides since coming into pro ball. While his fastball usually sits at 89-91 mph, he generates good action on the pitch, and that enables him to induce a high percentage of groundballs. The sinker will need to continue to be a dominant pitch as he moves up the ladder, because his curveball and changeup project to be average at best. While he doesn't light up radar guns, Kuhl has gotten results so far in his young career, including winning 13 games at high Class A Bradenton in 2014. In addition to his intelligence, he also is noted for being an outstanding competitor. While those traits usually aren't as important having great stuff, they do give Kuhl a chance to be a decent major league starter. He will get a chance to prove himself a higher level at Double-A Altoona in 2015.

Year	Club (League)	Class	W	L	ERA	G	GS	CG	SV	IP	H	HR	BB	SO	K/9	WHIP	AVG
2013	Jamestown (NYP)	SS	3	4	2.11	13	13	0	0	55	53	0	6	33	5.4	1.07	.255
2014	Bradenton (FSL)	HiA	13	5	3.46	28	28	0	0	153	141	9	42	100	5.9	1.19	.251
Minor League Totals			16	9	3.11	41	41	0	0	209	194	9	48	133	5.7	1.16	.252

29 TITO POLO, OF

BA GRADE

45 Risk: High

Born: Aug. 23, 1994. **B-T:** R-R. **Ht.:** 5-10. **Wt.:** 150. **Signed:** Colombia, 2012. **Signed by:** Rene Gayo/Orlando Covo.

The Pirates have been one of top procurers of talent from Colombia, and Polo made a fine U.S. debut in the Rookie-level Gulf Coast League in 2014, two years after signing. He has the ability to hit for average, he runs well and is a solid defensive outfielder with the range to play center field and the above-average arm to play right. He also has decent pop for a smallish player, and that should continue to develop as he adds muscle. Polo is also a high-energy player. That did came after two fine years in the Rookie-level Dominican Summer League, so Polo is building a track record of production. Hamstring problems were a problem at times during his time in the DSL. Polo figures to be challenged in a full-season league in 2015, probably while suiting up for low Class A West Virginia.

Year	Club (League)	Class	AVG	G	AB	R	H	2B	3B	HR	RBI	BB	SO	SB	CS	OBP	SLG
2012	Pirates2 (DSL)	R	.091	7	11	1	1	0	0	0	0	0	4	0	2	.091	.091
	Pirates1 (DSL)	R	.298	48	121	26	36	7	1	2	26	16	28	17	5	.427	.421
2013	Pirates1 (DSL)	R	.275	45	160	29	44	3	3	2	16	15	41	22	5	.352	.369
2014	Pirates (GCL)	R	.291	44	158	30	46	8	6	3	25	17	34	8	4	.374	.475
Minor League Totals			.282	144	450	86	127	18	10	7	67	48	107	47	16	.375	.413

30 MICHAEL DE LA CRUZ, OF

BA GRADE

45 Risk: Extreme

Born: July 10, 1996. **B-T:** L-L. **Ht.:** 6-1. **Wt.:** 165. **Signed:** Dominican Republic, 2012. **Signed by:** Rene Gayo/Juan Mercado.

The Pirates signed de la Cruz for $700,000 from his native Dominican Republic in 2012, and he struggled mightily in his first season in the U.S. in 2014 in the Rookie-level Gulf Coast League. It was a tough year all the way around for de la Cruz, who was 17 when the GCL season began. In addition to being a homesick teenager, he also sprained his ankle and dealt with a skin condition. Despite his .165 average, Cruz did show that he is willing work the count and take a walk. He also has power potential that figures to manifest itself once he reaches adulthood and his body begins to fill out. His lone extra-base hit in 2014 was a home run. De la Cruz also has above-average speed and can steal a base, though his baserunning skills are rather rudimentary at this point. His range is plenty good enough to play center field, though he's understandably raw. If he can't stick in center, his average arm would relegate him to left field. The Pirates will likely take it slow with de la Cruz and move him up one rung to Rookie-level Bristol.

Year	Club (League)	Class	AVG	G	AB	R	H	2B	3B	HR	RBI	BB	SO	SB	CS	OBP	SLG
2013	Pirates2 (DSL)	R	.292	62	226	51	66	11	3	0	20	58	50	14	11	.436	.367
2014	Pirates (GCL)	R	.165	32	91	10	15	0	0	1	7	15	25	4	1	.287	.198
Minor League Totals			.256	94	317	61	81	11	3	1	27	73	75	18	12	.396	.319

St. Louis Cardinals

BY DERRICK GOOLD AND KARY BOOHER

Less than two weeks after their season finished in a familiar place and setting, the Cardinals had their organization and future shaken by a tragedy at the start of their offseason.

Oscar Taveras, the club's longtime elite prospect and expected everyday right fielder in 2015, was killed along with his 18-year-old girlfriend in a single-car accident in the Dominican Republic. Taveras' death at age 22 came 10 days after the Cardinals' season ended in Game Five of the National League Championship Series, and while the team mourned, it also had to reshape its future.

A team that delighted in the fact that its pursuit of what general manager John Mozeliak called "sustained success" had been defined by a strong minor league system had to dip into that depth for a short-term need.

Mozeliak denied it was a shift. "We've said all along," he insisted, "we're focused on 2015."

The Cardinals traded established starter Shelby Miller and re-established prospect Tyrell Jenkins to the Braves in a four-player deal for Jason Heyward, the new right fielder and 25-year-old pending free agent. The trade was the second in four months that the Cardinals made using young pitching—three starters and 14 years of control—to land immediate help.

The moves cleared the way for righthander Carlos Martinez or lefty Marco Gonzales to join the rotation, but it also underscored a donut hole in the farm system. The arrival of second baseman Kolten Wong, Gonzales and Martinez put the club's top prospects in the majors. The depth in pitching and impact hitters had thinned at the top levels, while the next wave of standout prospects is in the distance.

The Cardinals remain committed to youth. In manager Mike Matheny's three years, the opening lineup has seen its average age drop from 31.1 in 2012 to 29.3 in 2013 to 29.0 in 2014.

Despite leaning heavily on these homegrown players, the Cardinals have maintained their mojo. St. Louis won its second consecutive NL Central division crown and reached the NLCS for a fourth straight year in 2014. They won 90 games, but had to do so in a new fashion.

After overwhelming opponents in 2013 with a historic .330 average with runners in scoring position, the Cardinals' offense sagged, ranking last in homers, scoring a full run less per game, and for the first time since 2011 failed to lead the NL in on-base percentage. Upgrading the offense was Mozeliak's top priority, even if it cost him the

CLIFF WELCH

The death of rookie right fielder Oscar Taveras forced the Cardinals to refocus their offseason strategy

TOP PROSPECTS OF THE DECADE

Year	Player, Pos.	2014 Org
2005	Anthony Reyes, rhp	Out of baseball
2006	Anthony Reyes, rhp	Out of baseball
2007	Colby Rasmus, of	Blue Jays
2008	Colby Rasmus, of	Blue Jays
2009	Colby Rasmus, of	Blue Jays
2010	Shelby Miller, rhp	Cardinals
2011	Shelby Miller, rhp	Cardinals
2012	Shelby Miller, rhp	Cardinals
2013	Oscar Taveras, of	Cardinals
2014	Oscar Taveras, of	Cardinals

cherished pitching to do it.

While the Cardinals cultivate the next batch of talent, contending in the minors remains the rule. St. Louis affiliates had a winning record at every level except Double-A, and short-season State College won its first New York-Penn League title.

Dan Kantrovitz left for the Athletics and Chris Correa replaced him as scouting director. St. Louis likes to keep such things in house because as much as things change, the expectation to win remains the same.

General Manager: John Mozeliak. **Farm Director:** Gary LaRocque. **Scouting Director:** Chris Correa.

Class	Team	League	W	L	PCT	Finish	Manager
Majors	St. Louis Cardinals	National	90	72	.556	t-5th (30)	Mike Matheny
Triple-A	Memphis Redbirds	Pacific Coast	79	64	.552	3rd (16)	Ron Warner
Double-A	Springfield Cardinals	Texas	68	72	.486	t-5th (8)	Mike Shildt
High A	Palm Beach Cardinals	Florida State	76	63	.547	5th (12)	Dann Bilardello
Low A	Peoria Chiefs	Midwest	72	67	.518	t-5th (16)	Joe Kruzel
Short season	State College Spikes	New York-Penn	48	28	.632	t-1st (14)	Oliver Marmol
Rookie	Johnson City Cardinals	Appalachian	37	31	.544	5th (10)	Johnny Rodriguez
Rookie	GCL Cardinals	Gulf Coast	37	23	.617	2nd (16)	Steve Turco
Overall Minor League Record			**417**	**348**	**.545**	**4th (30)**	

THIS YEAR'S TOP 30

No.	Player, Pos.	Grade
1.	Marco Gonzales, lhp	55/Low
2.	Alex Reyes, rhp	60/Extreme
3.	Stephen Piscotty, of	55/Medium
4.	Randal Grichuk, of	50/Medium
5.	Rob Kaminsky, lhp	55/High
6.	Jack Flaherty, rhp	55/Extreme
7.	Tim Cooney, lhp	50/Medium
8.	Sam Tuivailala, rhp	45/Medium
9.	Charlie Tilson, of	55/High
10.	Magneuris Sierra, of	55/Extreme
11.	Aledmys Diaz, ss	55/Extreme
12.	Luke Weaver, rhp	50/High
13.	Carson Kelly, c/3b	50/High
14.	Edmundo Sosa, ss	50/Extreme
15.	Tommy Pham, of	45/Medium
16.	Ronnie Williams, rhp	50/Extreme
17.	Juan Herrera, ss	45/High
18.	Jacob Wilson, 3b/2b	45/High
19.	Xavier Scruggs, 1b	40/Low
20.	Patrick Wisdom, 3b	45/High
21.	Greg Garcia, ss/2b	40/Low
22.	Cody Stanley, c	45/High
23.	Steve Bean, c	50/Extreme
24.	Rowan Wick, of	45/High
25.	Mike Mayers, rhp	45/High
26.	Breyvic Valera, 2b	45/High
27.	Malik Collymore, 2b	50/Extreme
28.	C.J. McElroy, of	45/High
29.	Andrew Morales, rhp	45/High
30.	Mitch Harris, rhp	45/High

LAST YEAR'S TOP 30

No.	Player, Pos.	Status
1.	Oscar Taveras, of	(Deceased)
2.	Carlos Martinez, rhp	Majors
3.	Kolten Wong, 2b	Majors
4.	Stephen Piscotty, of	No. 3
5.	Marco Gonzales, lhp	No. 1
6.	Tim Cooney, lhp	No. 7
7.	Alex Reyes, rhp	No. 2
8.	James Ramsey, of	(Indians)
9.	Rob Kaminsky, lhp	No. 5
10.	Randal Grichuk, of	No. 4
11.	Carson Kelly, c/3b	No. 13
12.	Charlie Tilson, of	No. 9
13.	Patrick Wisdom, 3b	No. 20
14.	Greg Garcia, ss	No. 21
15.	Zach Petrick, rhp	Dropped out
16.	Mike O'Neill, of	Dropped out
17.	Tyrell Jenkins, rhp	(Braves)
18.	Kenny Peoples-Walls, of	Dropped out
19.	Oscar Mercado, ss	Dropped out
20.	Juan Herrera, ss	No. 17
21.	Keith Butler, rhp	Dropped out
22.	Lee Stoppelman, lhp	Dropped out
23.	Tommy Pham, of	No. 15
24.	C.J. McElroy, of	No. 28
25.	Edmundo Sosa, ss	No. 14
26.	Boone Whiting, rhp	Dropped out
27.	John Gast, lhp	Dropped out
28.	Steve Bean, c	No. 23
29.	Jacob Wilson, 2b	No. 18
30.	Xavier Scruggs, 1b	No. 19

BEST TOOLS

Best Hitter for Average	Stephen Piscotty
Best Power Hitter	Randal Grichuk
Best Strike-Zone Discipline	Mike O'Neill
Fastest Baserunner	C.J. McElroy
Best Athlete	Randal Grichuk
Best Fastball	Sam Tuivailala
Best Curveball	Rob Kaminsky
Best Slider	Dixon Llorens
Best Changeup	Marco Gonzales
Best Control	Tim Cooney
Best Defensive Catcher	Travis Tartamella
Best Defensive Infielder	Juan Herrera
Best Infield Arm	Patrick Wisdom
Best Defensive Outfielder	Tommy Pham
Best Outfield Arm	Stephen Piscotty

PROJECTED 2018 LINEUP

Catcher	Yadier Molina
First Base	Matt Adams
Second Base	Kolten Wong
Third Base	Matt Carpenter
Shortstop	Aledmys Diaz
Left Field	Stephen Piscotty
Center Field	Charlie Tilson
Right Field	Jason Heyward
No. 1 Starter	Adam Wainwright
No. 2 Starter	Lance Lynn
No. 3 Starter	Michael Wacha
No. 4 Starter	Carlos Martinez
No. 5 Starter	Marco Gonzales
Closer	Trevor Rosenthal

ST. LOUIS CARDINALS

TOP 2015 ROOKIE: Marco Gonzales, lhp. He's ready to contribute important innings, either in a starting or relief role.
BREAKOUT PROSPECT: Edmundo Sosa, ss. The Cardinals invested heavily in shortstops of late, and he may be the best one.
SLEEPER: Jorge Rodriguez, rhp. Late-blooming Dominican righthander has life on a developing low-90s fastball.

SOURCE OF TOP 30 TALENT

Homegrown	28	Acquired	2
College	12	Trades	2
Junior college	1	Rule 5 draft	0
High school	10	Independent leagues	0
Draft-and-follow	0	Free agents/waivers	0
Nondrafted free agents	0		
International	5		

LF
Nick Thompson
Mike O'Neill
Starlin Rodriguez
Vaughn Bryan

CF
Charlie Tilson (9)
Tommy Pham (15)
C.J. McElroy (28)
Blake Drake

RF
Stephen Piscotty (3)
Randal Grichuk (4)
Magneuris Sierra (10)
Rowan Wick (24)

3B
Patrick Wisdom (20)

SS
Aledmys Diaz (11)
Edmundo Sosa (14)
Juan Herrera (17)
Greg Garcia (21)
Oscar Mercado
Alex Mejia
Matt Williams

2B
Jacob Wilson (18)
Breyvic Valera (26)
Malik Collymore (27)
Ty Kelly
Daniel Seferina

1B
Xavier Scruggs (19)
Mason Katz
Bruce Caldwell

C
Carson Kelly (13)
Cody Stanley (22)
Steve Bean (23)
Ed Easley
Brian O'Keefe

LHP

LHSP	LHRP
Marco Gonazles (1)	Nick Greenwood
Rob Kaminsky (5)	Lee Stoppelman
Tim Cooney (7)	
John Gast	
Austin Gomber	
Jimmy Reed	
Ian McKinney	

RHP

RHSP	RHRP
Alex Reyes (2)	Sam Tuivailala (8)
Jack Flaherty (6)	Mitch Harris (30)
Luke Weaver (12)	Chris Perry
Ronnie Williams (16)	Dixon Llorens
Mike Mayers (25)	Landon Beck
Andrew Morales (29)	Tyler Waldron
Nick Petree	
Zack Petrick	
Boone Whiting	
Bryan Dozanski	
Kurt Heyer	

2014

BEST PURE HITTER: OF Nick Thompson (8) hit .368 in the spring for William & Mary with more walks than strikeouts, then hit .282/.396/.410 with more walks (39) than strikeouts (36) for short-season State College.

BEST POWER HITTER: Thompson controls the strike zone, has good bat speed and shows present strength in his 6-foot-1, 210-pound frame to produce above-average power.

FASTEST RUNNER: Five-foot-9 waterbug Darren Seferina (5) is a 70 runner whose speed plays on the basepaths. He stole 34 bags in the spring for Miami Dade JC, then stole 20 more for State College while being caught five times.

BEST DEFENSIVE PLAYER: OF Blake Drake (18) slipped a bit as a junior but was young for the draft class and has solid tools. His best is likely his defense, as he has above-average range and plus arm strength to go with the reads and instincts for him to fit in center field.

BEST FASTBALL: RHP Luke Weaver (1) lost some velocity in the spring but has hit 96 mph in the past and was back touching the mid-90s since signing, often with sink. RHP Daniel Poncedeleon (9), a $5,000 senior sign, has also reached 94-95 mph and has life through the strike zone as well.

BEST SECONDARY PITCH: Weaver gets plenty of groundballs with his changeup, which has excellent sink. RHP Jack Flaherty (1), a third baseman/pitcher in high school, earns lesser present grades but has the makings of a future plus changeup as he gains experience as a full-time pitcher.

BEST PRO DEBUT: Flaherty dominated the Rookie-level Gulf Coast League, posting a 28-4 strikeout-walk ratio and 1.59 ERA in 23 innings. Thompson overcame an 8-for-51 start to rank second in the New York-Penn League in OBP.

BEST ATHLETE: Flaherty was a legitimate prospect as a third baseman before emerging as a pitching prospect. His athleticism helps him repeat his delivery and pound the strike zone.

MOST INTRIGUING BACKGROUND: Poncedeleon was drafted for the fourth time this year and had a contract voided last year after agreeing to terms with the Cubs. Seferina played in the 2005 Little League World Series for Curacao, forming a double-play combination with current Rangers infielder Jurickson Profar. RHP Bryan Dobzanski (29) was a state high school wrestling champion in New Jersey in the 220-pound weight class.

CLOSEST TO THE MAJORS: RHP Andrew Morales (2s) is an accomplished strike-thrower with excellent makeup (he went 42-3 in college) and solid-average stuff.

BEST LATE-ROUND PICK: An NAIA star, Drake has shown enough offensive potential to be a fourth outfield candidate.

THE ONE WHO GOT AWAY: The Cardinals liked RHP Trevor Megill (3) but never were able to get a deal done. He returned to Loyola Marymount, while the Cardinals get a compensation pick in the third round in 2015.

ASSESSMENT: St. Louis started its draft with six straight pitchers and signed five. Jack Flaherty, Andrew Morales, Austin Gomber, Luke Weaver and Ronnie Williams provide five varied arms for the pitcher-development system.

2013

LHPs Marco Gonzales (1) and Rob Kaminsky (1) are off to by far the fastest starts in the class, with Gonzales having reached the majors already.

GRADE: B

2012

RHP Michael Wacha (1) was an almost-instant ace, though he wasn't healthy in 2014. OFs James Ramsey (1, since traded) and Stephen Piscotty (1s) are potential regulars. The class is deep with later finds such as OF Rowan Wick (9) and Jacob Wilson (10).

GRADE: A

2011

2B Kolten Wong (1) and RHP Seth Maness (11) have become key contributors in St. Louis in short order. OF Charlie Tilson (2) has moved slower but is a potential regular.

GRADE: B

TOP DRAFT PICKS OF THE DECADE

Year	Player, Pos.	2014 Org
2005	Colby Rasmus, of	Blue Jays
2006	Adam Ottavino, rhp	Rockies
2007	Pete Kozma, ss	Cardinals
2008	Brett Wallace, 3b	Blue Jays
2009	Shelby Miller, rhp	Cardinals
2010	Zack Cox, 3b	Marlins
2011	Kolten Wong, 2b	Cardinals
2012	Michael Wacha, rhp	Cardinals
2013	Marco Gonzales, lhp	Cardinals
2014	Luke Weaver, rhp	Cardinals

LARGEST BONUSES IN CLUB HISTORY

J.D. Drew, 1998	$3,000,000
Shelby Miller, 2009	$2,875,000
Rick Ankiel, 1999	$2,500,000
Chad Hutchinson, 1998	$2,300,000
Jack Flaherty, 2014	$2,000,000
Zack Cox, 2010	$2,000,000

1 MARCO GONZALES, LHP

Born: Feb. 16, 1992. **B-T:** L-L. **Ht.:** 6-0. **Wt.:** 185.
Drafted: Gonzaga, 2013 (1st round).
Signed by: Matt Swanson.

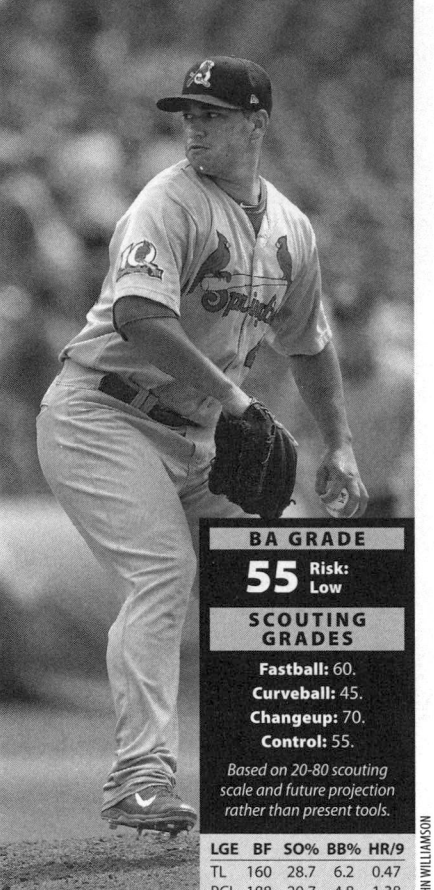

BA GRADE
55 Risk: Low

SCOUTING GRADES
Fastball: 60.
Curveball: 45.
Changeup: 70.
Control: 55.

Based on 20-80 scouting scale and future projection rather than present tools.

LGE	BF	SO%	BB%	HR/9
TL	160	28.7	6.2	0.47
PCL	188	20.7	4.8	1.38

JOHN WILLIAMSON

Following a familiar formula that led them to Michael Wacha the year before and Luke Weaver the year after, the Cardinals drafted Gonzales 19th overall in 2013 as a polished, athletic pitcher from a strong program who had a plus changeup and a history of winning. He signed quickly for $1.85 million and advanced even quicker. It took the Gonzaga product 21 starts in the minors before he made his big league debut on June 25, starting for the Cardinals at Coors Field. Gonzales grew up a Rockies fan, and thousands of friends and family made the hour drive from his hometown to see him pitch just a few blocks from where he helped his Fort Collins, Colo., high school win four consecutive state championships. His father Frank Gonzales was allowed to leave his job as pitching coach in the Rockies' minor league system to attend. It was Frank who urged his son to learn the changeup—the offspeed equalizer a mile above sea level—but the son didn't commit to pitching full time until turning pro. He led Gonzaga in hitting as a junior and gained recognition as one of the top two-way players. That kind of agility drew the Cardinals to him, and they identified him early as a lefty who could climb quickly.

Gonzales once joked that his changeup "is as much a part of me as walking." He can find the circle-change grip in the dark and never doubts his feel for what is a true swing-and-miss pitch. It has a late drop, and he adds to the deception by not varying his delivery speed or arm angle from changeup to fastball. He is willing to throw to hitters on either side of the plate, and in his debut he flummoxed Troy Tulowitzki with a series of changeups for a strikeout. His fastball hums in the 88-91 mph range and averaged 90 in the majors. The changeup runs 12 mph less, and he mixes in a sinker (89.5 mph) and an occasional curve (74.5 mph). His curve has good depth. All of that comes from an easy delivery that he is able to maintain, and that consistency aids his command, but he'll have to improve upon the control to blossom.

The Cardinals were so intrigued by Gonzales' late-season turn as a reliever that they used him in a prominent role in the postseason and intend to find some role for him in the majors in 2015. He'll come to spring training competing with Carlos Martinez for the rotation, and the Cardinals believe his future is as a starter. But an assignment to the bullpen would reduce his innings—which the team intends to do regardless of role—and let him learn while letting it loose. The giddyup they saw on Gonzales' fastball out of the bullpen means the team could fit him for a late-inning role for his first full season in the majors, just as Adam Wainwright did in 2006 before moving into the rotation.

Year	Club (League)	Class	W	L	ERA	G	GS	CG	SV	IP	H	HR	BB	SO	K/9	WHIP	AVG
2013	Cardinals (GCL)	R	0	0	5.40	4	2	0	0	7	8	0	3	10	13.5	1.65	.276
	Palm Beach (FSL)	HiA	0	0	1.62	4	4	0	0	17	10	1	5	13	7.0	0.90	.179
2014	Palm Beach (FSL)	HiA	2	2	1.43	6	6	0	0	38	34	1	8	32	7.6	1.12	.239
	Springfield, MO (TL)	AA	3	2	2.33	7	7	0	0	39	33	2	10	46	10.7	1.11	.220
	Memphis (PCL)	AAA	4	1	3.35	8	8	0	0	46	43	7	9	39	7.7	1.14	.251
	St. Louis (NL)	MAJ	4	2	4.15	10	5	0	0	35	32	4	21	31	8.0	1.53	.241
Major League Totals			4	2	4.15	10	5	0	0	35	32	4	21	31	8.0	1.53	.241
Minor League Totals			9	5	2.48	29	27	0	0	145	128	11	35	140	8.7	1.12	.234

2 ALEX REYES, RHP

Born: Aug. 29, 1994. **B-T:** R-R. **Ht.:** 6-3. **Wt.:** 185. **Signed:** Dominican Republic, 2012. **Signed by:** Rodny Jimenez/Angel Ovalles.

A high school third baseman in New Jersey who wasn't convinced he'd get attention from scouts, Reyes circumnavigated the draft by relocating to the Dominican Republic, where he lived with relatives, had a chance to focus on baseball and was, on a lark, put on the mound. He won't be leaving it. The Cardinals outmaneuvered the Astros and Royals to sign Reyes for $950,000 in 2012. He joined Carlos Martinez in that high-bonus bracket, and like Martinez, had the athleticism, untamed mechanics and power arm the Cardinals covet. Reyes has at least two plus pitches. He can locate with a 92-96 mph fastball that can reach 100. He couples that with a power curve that has sharp, 12-to-6 drop. His changeup will be an above-average pitch, and already is for the lower levels. Reyes is a strapping young man with a tight end's frame. He's already developed a reputation for durability but must maintain his conditioning. He has an easy delivery but stretches

BA GRADE

60 Risk: Extreme

LGE	BF	SO%	BB%	HR/9
MWL	465	29.5	13.1	0.49

of erratic control will have to improve. The Cardinals intend to keep the young righthander starting until they need him to relieve or want him to gain experience. Reyes has big league stuff and is primed to be the next pitcher who zooms to the upper ranks. He could reach Double-A Springfield in 2015.

Year	Club (League)	Class	W	L	ERA	G	GS	CG	SV	IP	H	HR	BB	SO	K/9	WHIP	AVG
2013	Johnson City (APP)	R	6	4	3.39	12	12	0	0	58	54	1	28	68	10.5	1.41	.249
2014	Peoria (MWL)	LoA	7	7	3.62	21	21	1	0	109	82	6	61	137	11.3	1.31	.207
Minor League Totals			13	11	3.54	33	33	1	0	168	136	7	89	205	11.0	1.34	.221

3 STEPHEN PISCOTTY, OF

Born: Jan. 14, 1991. **B-T:** R-R. **Ht.:** 6-3. **Wt.:** 210. **Drafted:** Stanford, 2012 (1st round). **Signed by:** Matt Swanson.

Piscotty has often heard questions about his power and whether it would manifest as he grew stronger and more experienced. He knows this: He's not going to force it. Piscotty has said he "knows the line-drive hitter that I am, and I'm comfortable staying with that." The Cardinals landed two compensation picks when Albert Pujols left for the Angels—one they used for Michael Wacha and the other for Piscotty. They got a level-headed and hard-hitting outfielder who may develop power but will hit for average. Piscotty has an innate feel for the strike zone (98 walks and 132 strikeouts in 303 professional games) and uses that patience to sweeten an authoritative, balanced swing built to hit .300. Piscotty keeps both hands on the bat and learned at Triple-A Memphis how to pull the ball more often instead of settling for line drives to right field. That ability to pull, coupled with more loft, is what hints at more power, though maybe in the 15-20 homer range.

BA GRADE

55 Risk: Medium

LGE	PA	BB%	SO%	ISO
PCL	556	7.7	11.0	0.118

Drafted as a third baseman, Piscotty has taken to right field where he has good instincts and where his arm is a plus asset. The Cardinals' acquisition of Jason Heyward means Piscotty is ticketed for a return to Memphis so he can continue playing every day, though he'll debut at some point in 2015 and the club has kept its roster flexibility open for him to be a regular as soon as 2016.

Year	Club (League)	Class	AVG	G	AB	R	H	2B	3B	HR	RBI	BB	SO	SB	CS	OBP	SLG
2012	Quad Cities (MWL)	LoA	.295	55	210	29	62	18	1	4	27	18	25	3	0	.376	.448
2013	Palm Beach (FSL)	HiA	.292	63	243	30	71	14	2	9	35	18	27	4	5	.348	.477
	Springfield (TL)	AA	.299	49	184	17	55	9	0	6	24	19	19	7	3	.364	.446
2014	Memphis (PCL)	AAA	.288	136	500	70	144	32	0	9	69	43	61	11	5	.355	.406
Minor League Totals			.292	303	1137	146	332	73	3	28	155	98	132	25	13	.359	.435

4 RANDAL GRICHUK, OF

Born: Aug. 13, 1991. **B-T:** R-R. **Ht.:** 6-1. **Wt.:** 195. **Drafted:** HS—Rosenburg, Texas, 2009 (1st round). **Signed by:** Kevin Ham (Angels).

Taken one spot ahead of Mike Trout by the Angels in the 2009 draft, Grichuk redefined himself as something else entirely for the Cardinals: starting right fielder. The prospect St. Louis landed from Los Angeles in a trade that featured David Freese and Peter Bourjos finished 2014 as the Cardinals' right fielder in October. Power has been Grichuk's signature tool since hitting four homers during the 2004 Little League World Series. Wrist, thumb, and knee injuries robbed Grichuk of at-bats after the draft, but in 2013 he led the Double-A Texas League in extra-base hits with 57. Grichuk earned playing time ahead of Oscar Taveras in the postseason mainly because of his defensive reliability in right field and those flickers of power. He is one of the finer athletes in the organization and his agility gives him the skills for center field. His arm is above-average for that position, catapulting from a lithe strength in the same way the ball does from his bat. Grichuk is not a hulking hitter, just one gifted with bat speed. He'll have to tame his strike-out rate to turn his starts in 2014 into a longer engagement. Though the Cardinals have a starter at all three outfield positions, Grichuk comes to spring with a chance to be a righthanded-hitting alternative in center and right.

BA GRADE

50 Risk: Medium

LGE	PA	BB%	SO%	ISO
PCL	472	5.9	22.9	.234
NL	116	4.3	26.7	.155

Year	Club (League)	Class	AVG	G	AB	R	H	2B	3B	HR	RBI	BB	SO	SB	CS	OBP	SLG
2012	Inland Empire (CAL)	HiA	.298	135	537	79	160	30	9	18	71	23	92	16	6	.335	.488
2013	Arkansas (TL)	AA	.256	128	500	85	128	27	8	22	64	28	92	9	5	.306	.474
2014	Memphis (PCL)	AAA	.259	108	436	73	113	23	2	25	71	28	108	8	5	.311	.493
	St. Louis (NL)	MAJ	.245	47	110	11	27	6	1	3	8	5	31	0	2	.278	.400
Major League Totals			.245	47	110	11	27	6	1	3	8	5	31	0	2	.278	.400
Minor League Totals			.279	541	2159	359	603	127	42	86	330	108	461	43	21	.321	.497

5 ROB KAMINSKY, LHP

Born: Sept. 2, 1994. **B-T:** R-L. **Ht.:** 5-11. **Wt.:** 191. **Drafted:** HS—Montvale, N.J., 2013 (1st round). **Signed by:** Sean Moran.

During his first visit to Busch Stadium, the New Jersey native made sure he was judged on the depth of his curve instead of the size of his jersey. "I don't think you have to be a certain height to get people out," he said. Kaminsky, a bulldog in a compact frame, passed on a commitment to North Carolina to sign for $1.785 million as a first-round pick in 2013. He had a 0.10 ERA and 126 strikeouts as a high school senior, then logged 100 innings in 2014 as one of the youngest starters in the low Class A Midwest League. Kaminsky's curveball, the pitch that created all those Ks, didn't disappoint as a pro. He raises his finger on it to give it a spike-curve look. His confidence in the deceptive pitch can make him curveball-happy at times—which is why he was asked to feature other pitches at low Class A Peoria. His fastball works around 91 mph, though he can hit 95 with it. He throws from a high three-quarters slot that adds to his offspeed pitches, especially versus righthanders. That overwhelming curve/fastball combo,

BA GRADE

55 Risk: High

LGE	BF	SO%	BB%	HR/9
MWL	407	19.4	7.6	0.18

with movement on the latter, gives some the sense he'll at least be a reliever, but a potential above-average changeup and feistiness hints the small package contains a starter. There's a spot in the high Class A Palm Beach rotation waiting for Kaminsky in 2015, and a cameo at Double-A Springfield is possible.

Year	Club (League)	Class	W	L	ERA	G	GS	CG	SV	IP	H	HR	BB	SO	K/9	WHIP	AVG
2013	Cardinals (GCL)	R	0	3	3.68	8	5	0	0	22	23	1	9	28	11.5	1.45	.261
2014	Peoria (MWL)	LoA	8	2	1.88	18	18	0	0	101	71	2	31	79	7.1	1.01	.194
Minor League Totals			8	5	2.20	26	23	0	0	123	94	3	40	107	7.9	1.09	.207

6 JACK FLAHERTY, RHP

Born: Oct. 15, 1995. **B-T:** R-R. **Ht.:** 6-4. **Wt.:** 205. **Drafted:** HS—Studio City, Calif., 2014 (1st round). **Signed by:** Mike Garciaparra.

To lure Flaherty away from North Carolina, the Cardinals signed him to the largest bonus ($2 million) of any of their 2014 draft picks and the team's fifth-largest in the past 16 years. Like most of baseball, the Cardinals first scouted Flaherty as a third baseman—one with gap power, good feel at the plate and a power arm from the corner. It became clear during his junior year, one evaluator said, that pitching was his future. He struck out 12 in his first prep start of 2014 and went to complete a 23-0, 0.63 stretch in his final two seasons in high school. Before growing into his frame and adding the strength that scouts believe will add velocity, Flaherty already has a feel for four pitches. He works from 90-92 mph with his fastball, and he has a changeup that will be a swing-and-miss pitch. His slider and curveball are clearly different from each other, not some uncommitted blend. And both pitches offer promise—with the slider being the better bet. Flaherty's fastball command is beyond his age. He has that high-angle delivery with swift arm speed that the Cardinals have sought in other tall, young righthanded pitchers. Eased into the pros in 2014, Flaherty will likely open 2015 in extended spring training with the possibility of seeing time at low Class A Peoria by summer's end.

BA GRADE

55 Risk: Extreme

LGE	BF	SO%	BB%	HR/9
GCL	94	29.8	4.3	0.40

Year	Club (League)	Class	W	L	ERA	G	GS	CG	SV	IP	H	HR	BB	SO	K/9	WHIP	AVG
2014	Cardinals (GCL)	R	1	1	1.59	8	6	0	0	23	18	1	4	28	11.1	0.97	.209
Minor League Totals			1	1	1.59	8	6	0	0	23	18	1	4	28	11.1	0.97	.209

7 TIM COONEY, LHP

Born: Dec. 19, 1990. **B-T:** L-L. **Ht.:** 6-3. **Wt.:** 195. **Drafted:** Wake Forest, 2012 (3rd round). **Signed by:** Matt Blood.

A series of injuries at the levels above him in 2013 brought Cooney to Double-A Springfield ahead of the Cardinals' plans, but the lefty hasn't shown any signs of needing to slow his advancement. He affirmed it with a complete season at Triple-A Memphis in 2014 as arguably the Redbirds' most consistent starter. Cooney was a standout in the Cape Cod League and only slipped in the draft due to a series of injuries that interrupted his junior year at Wake Forest. That year is a distant hiccup considering the relentless consistency he's brought to the pros with an average of six innings per start in 25 at Memphis. Cooney has the poise and presence expected from a college pitcher with a mature sense of his mechanics and stuff. The tall, lithe lefty brings a fastball that hums from 88-92 mph with movement, allowing him to effectively spot both sides of the plate. His changeup advanced to above-average at times in 2014, and he has a yeoman's curve that drops around 75-76 mph. He uses that spectrum of speeds to upset timing, which allows him to aggressively pitch within the strike zone. Cooney inevitably draws comparisons with Marco Gonzales because of handedness and use of the changeup, and he's right behind the touted lefty in terms of ETA. Valued for his reliability and durability, he should debut in 2015 and could receive a cameo start.

BA GRADE

50 Risk: Medium

LGE	BF	SO%	BB%	HR/9
PCL	663	17.9	7.1	1.20

Year	Club (League)	Class	W	L	ERA	G	GS	CG	SV	IP	H	HR	BB	SO	K/9	WHIP	AVG
2012	Batavia (NYP)	SS	3	3	3.40	13	11	1	0	56	56	4	8	43	7.0	1.15	.268
2013	Palm Beach (FSL)	HiA	3	3	2.75	6	6	1	0	36	38	1	4	23	5.8	1.17	.273
	Springfield (TL)	AA	7	10	3.80	20	20	0	0	118	132	8	18	125	9.5	1.27	.284
2014	Memphis (PCL)	AAA	14	6	3.47	26	25	1	0	158	158	21	47	119	6.8	1.30	.263
Minor League Totals			27	22	3.50	65	62	3	0	368	384	34	77	310	7.6	1.25	.272

8 SAM TUIVAILALA, RHP

Born: Oct. 19, 1992. **B-T:** R-R. **Ht:** 6-3. **Wt.:** 195. **Drafted:** HS—San Mateo, Calif., 2010 (3rd round). **Signed by:** Matt Swanson.

Cardinals officials had already made the decision to move Tuivailala to the mound before he hit a home run in his final game as a position player in 2012. Carried by a double-plus fastball, he sped through four levels in 2014, reaching the majors in September. With the frame of a power forward, Tuivailala is the Cardinals' latest converted power pitcher after Jason Motte and Trevor Rosenthal. He has a fastball that can touch 100 mph, and he works consistently at 98. Fine command is all he lacks with the heat. In the Arizona Fall League, Tuivailala's curve advanced. It's a 12-to-6 breaking ball that he throws hard and with a sharp drop. He also sports a changeup that he can throw when needed, giving him an offspeed entry between his two best pitches. Tuivailala once referred to pitching as his "Plan B," and in less than two years he's gone swifter and higher than his Plan A was likely to take him. If he opens the season at Triple-A Memphis as a closer, it won't be long before he's called to contribute in the majors.

BA GRADE

45 Risk: Medium

LGE	BF	SO%	BB%	HR/9
FSL	162	39.5	11.1	0.24
TL	88	34.1	10.2	0.00

Year	Club (League)	Class	W	L	ERA	G	GS	CG	SV	IP	H	HR	BB	SO	K/9	WHIP	AVG
2012	Johnson City (APP)	R	0	0	4.15	11	0	0	0	13	12	1	13	23	15.9	1.92	.235
2013	Peoria (MWL)	LoA	0	3	5.35	28	0	0	1	35	31	0	20	50	12.7	1.44	.233
2014	Palm Beach (FSL)	HiA	0	1	3.58	29	0	0	3	38	29	1	18	64	15.3	1.25	.207
	Springfield (TL)	AA	2	1	2.57	17	0	0	1	21	18	0	9	30	12.9	1.29	.234
	Memphis (PCL)	AAA	0	0	0.00	2	0	0	1	1	1	0	0	3	20.3	0.75	.200
	St. Louis (NL)	MAJ	0	0	36.00	2	0	0	0	1	5	2	2	1	9.0	7.00	.625
Major League Totals			0	0	36.00	2	0	0	0	1	5	2	2	1	9.0	7.00	.625
Minor League Totals			2	5	3.99	87	0	0	6	108	91	2	60	170	14.1	1.39	.224

9 CHARLIE TILSON, OF

MIKE JANES

Born: Dec. 2, 1992. **B-T:** L-L. **Ht.:** 5-11. **Wt.:** 175. **Drafted:** HS—Winnetka, Ill., 2011 (2nd round). **Signed by:** Kris Gross.

The reward Tilson was about to receive for a standout 2014 season was a chance to show his growth in the Arizona Fall League. An injury canceled those plans. Tilson was unable to play in the AFL because of a fracture in his foot—the most recent injury to rob him of development time. The Chicagoland speedster grabbed attention at the 2010 Area Code Games with his defense and an unexpected flash of power. The Cardinals landed him as a second-rounder in 2011 with a $1.275 million bonus, but a shoulder injury robbed him of his first pro season. The Cardinals rushed Tilson to Double-A Springfield in 2014 due to trades and injuries above him, and while his production faltered, he wasn't overmatched at the level. A high-energy outfielder, Tilson has the speed to course-correct in the field. He has a solid approach at the plate that uses the whole field. If the power doesn't come, his legs should lift his slugging percentage by finding doubles. He may have to adopt a less aggressive approach at the plate to stick at the top of a lineup. The Area Code fireworks left scouts wondering if this was his peak or a peek into his potential. Viewed by the Cardinals as a raw talent, Tilson has advanced rapidly when healthy, and his strides put him back on track for Double-A for 2015.

BA GRADE

55 Risk: High

LGE	PA	BB%	SO%	ISO
FSL	402	6.0	18.9	.105
TL	145	4.1	19.3	.086

Year	Club (League)	Class	AVG	G	AB	R	H	2B	3B	HR	RBI	BB	SO	SB	CS	OBP	SLG
2012	Did not play--Injured																
2013	Peoria (MWL)	LoA	.303	100	376	49	114	8	6	4	30	25	58	15	6	.349	.388
	Palm Beach (FSL)	HiA	.294	9	34	1	10	1	1	0	0	5	6	0	0	.385	.382
2014	Palm Beach (FSL)	HiA	.308	89	370	54	114	8	8	5	36	24	76	10	7	.357	.414
	Springfield (TL)	AA	.237	31	139	19	33	4	1	2	17	6	28	2	3	.269	.324
Minor League Totals			.296	237	946	127	280	23	16	11	88	63	172	28	16	.344	.389

10 MAGNEURIS SIERRA, OF

TONY FARLOW

Born: April 7, 1996. **B-T:** L-L. **Ht.:** 5-11. **Wt.:** 160. **Signed:** Dominican Republic, 2012. **Signed by:** Rodny Jimenez/Angel Ovalles.

As the Cardinals identified where they've best had success in Latin America, they felt that the players with mid-range bonus demands and raw tools were their ideal targets. Sierra fit that description. A left/left center fielder with a projectable frame, Sierra signed for $105,000 in 2012 and hinted at a much larger return in 2014, his first season in the U.S. He won the Rookie-level Gulf Coast League batting title (.386) and ranked third in on-base percentage (.434). He became the youngest winner of the Cardinals' minor league player of the year award. Sierra has a steady, line-drive swing with bat control that keeps the barrel in the zone. He uses all fields and figures to maintain that high-average ability as he develops an approach that could belong at the top of the order. His broad shoulders and athleticism hint at the strength he'll gain as he matures, but he doesn't have that lift for future power. He has speed on the bases and in the field, making him one

BA GRADE		
55	**Risk:**	
	Extreme	

LGE	PA	BB%	SO%	ISO
GCL	223	7.2	13.5	.119

of the finest fielders at his position in the GCL. The secret is out. A name whispered throughout the Cardinals organization is now one known beyond their academy and expectations will surge accordingly. A year at another short-season club is possible in 2015 before he slingshots to higher levels.

Year	Club (League)	Class	AVG	G	AB	R	H	2B	3B	HR	RBI	BB	SO	SB	CS	OBP	SLG
2013	Cardinals (DSL)	R	.269	63	212	44	57	6	3	1	21	29	33	15	7	.361	.340
2014	Cardinals (GCL)	R	.386	52	202	42	78	12	3	2	30	16	30	13	3	.434	.505
Minor League Totals			.326	115	414	86	135	18	6	3	51	45	63	28	10	.396	.420

11 ALEDMYS DIAZ, SS

BA GRADE		
55	**Risk:**	
	Extreme	

Born: Aug. 1, 1990. **B-T:** R-R. **Ht.:** 6-1. **Wt.:** 195. **Signed:** Cuba, 2014. **Signed by:** Matt Slater.

Major League Baseball barred Diaz, who left Cuba in 2012, from signing for a year because he misrepresented his age. The Cardinals signed him in March 2014 to a four-year, $8-million deal. Diaz hit .315/.404/.500 in his final season with Cuba's Villa Clara, and scouts saw a level swing that had some inside-out tendencies. His mannerisms reminded many scouts of Derek Jeter, and Diaz explained that's because he mimicked the Yankees great—how he ambled in the field, how he swung, his arm angle. Diaz's swing has punch that should complement the ability to hit for average with extra-base sprinkles. His bat is ahead of his fielding and some see him as a utility infielder or second baseman. The Cardinals see consistency that could stick at short. Shoulder trouble in 2014 limited Diaz to 47 games and led the Cardinals to move him to high Class A Palm Beach to be closer to the team's spring facilities. He'll start 2015 wherever there's the most playing time so the Cardinals can now see what their first foray into Cuba brought them.

Year	Club (League)	Class	AVG	G	AB	R	H	2B	3B	HR	RBI	BB	SO	SB	CS	OBP	SLG
2014	Springfield (TL)	AA	.291	34	117	15	34	8	1	3	18	2	24	6	2	.311	.453
	Palm Beach (FSL)	HiA	.227	13	44	5	10	2	0	2	6	7	10	1	0	.352	.409
Minor League Totals			.273	47	161	20	44	10	1	5	24	9	34	7	2	.324	.441

12 LUKE WEAVER, RHP

BA GRADE		
50	**Risk:**	
	High	

Born: Aug. 21, 1993. **B-T:** R-R. **Ht.:** 6-2. **Wt.:** 170. **Drafted:** Florida State, 2014 (1st round). **Signed by:** Charlie Gonzalez.

Weaver finished 2014 at high Class A Palm Beach after signing for $1.843 million as the 34th overall pick. His jump to the Florida State League did not fare well in starts, but the Cardinals are confident he can have success as he did in college at Florida State. Scouts say Weaver lost some of his looseness from 2013, when he ranked 11th in the country with 10.9 strikeouts per nine innings. That rate dipped to 7.2 in 2014, when Weaver's fastball usually sat 88-92 mph after sitting in the los 90s and touching 96 in 2013. Weaver pitches with a three-quarters arm slot, and his changeup has good deception and sinking action. However, his slider was fringy in college. Weaver might return to Palm Beach in 2015, but note that the Cardinals haven't been shy of challenging first-rounders—see: Michael Wacha or Marco Gonzales—with quick assignments to Double-A Springfield.

Year	Club (League)	Class	W	L	ERA	G	GS	CG	SV	IP	H	HR	BB	SO	K/9	WHIP	AVG
2014	Cardinals (GCL)	R	0	0	0.00	4	4	0	0	6	4	0	0	9	13.5	0.67	.190
	Palm Beach (FSL)	HiA	0	1	21.60	2	2	0	0	3	11	1	4	3	8.1	4.50	.550
Minor League Totals			0	1	7.71	6	6	0	0	9	15	1	4	12	11.6	2.04	.366

13 CARSON KELLY, C

Born: July 14, 1994. **B-T:** R-R. **Ht.:** 6-2. **Wt.:** 200. **Drafted:** HS—Portland, Ore., 2012 (2nd round). **Signed by:** Matt Swanson.

BA GRADE
50 Risk: High

The Cardinals signed Kelly for $1.6 million in 2012 after making him a second-round pick. Two years later, St. Louis moved him from third base to a full-time catching role at low Class A Peoria, and managers appreciated the way he embraced the change. Kelly's strong arm held the running game in check, and he threw out 33 percent of basestealers in 2014, though he also was charged with 13 passed balls. Kelly appeared to have lost about 15 pounds by season's end, and five of his six homers came in the season's first two months. The Cardinals believe they spotted the flaw. Kelly's eyes tended to stop tracking pitches late in the zone, creating a vulnerability on late movement. His sturdy frame has room to grow, and St. Louis is optimistic that he'll power more balls to the gaps and over the fence once he adds loft to his swing and adjusts to the rigors of catching. Kelly still drew walks and had a strong instructional league in 2014, so look for him to advance to high Class A Palm Beach in 2015.

Year	Club (League)	Class	AVG	G	AB	R	H	2B	3B	HR	RBI	BB	SO	SB	CS	OBP	SLG
2012	Johnson City (APP)	R	.225	56	213	24	48	10	0	9	25	10	33	0	0	.263	.399
2013	Peoria (MWL)	LoA	.219	43	146	18	32	6	0	2	13	13	25	0	0	.288	.301
	State College (NYP)	SS	.277	70	271	35	75	16	1	4	32	20	31	1	0	.340	.387
2014	Peoria (MWL)	LoA	.248	98	363	41	90	17	4	6	49	37	54	1	0	.326	.366
Minor League Totals			.247	267	993	118	245	49	5	21	119	80	143	2	0	.311	.370

14 EDMUNDO SOSA, SS

Born: March 6, 1996. **B-T:** R-R. **Ht.:** 5-11. **Wt.:** 170. **Signed:** Panama, 2012. **Signed by:** Arquimedes Nieto.

BA GRADE
50 Risk: Extreme

The Cardinals regarded Sosa as a top target for July 2 in 2012, when they signed the Panamanian shortstop for $425,000. He quickly rewarded the organization's confidence by performing well in the Dominican Summer League, then made a smooth transition to the U.S., playing in the Rookie-level Gulf Coast League in 2014. Sosa's baseball instincts are advanced for his age and background. He makes contact at a high clip because of his easy, level stroke and ability to control the bat head with good hand-eye coordination. He did a better job in 2014 of using the whole field and showed gap power. With his bat-to-ball skills and plus speed, he should hit for a high average and potentially be a top-of-the-order hitter if he can draw enough walks. Before signing, Sosa demonstrated above-average times in the 60-yard dash and has added strength to become a plus runner. One of the better defensive shortstops in the GCL, Sosa has good range, athleticism and quickness but also plays under control. The one knock on him is fringy arm strength, but he makes up for it with a quick release. He's primed for full-season ball in 2015.

Year	Club (League)	Class	AVG	G	AB	R	H	2B	3B	HR	RBI	BB	SO	SB	CS	OBP	SLG
2013	Cardinals (DSL)	R	.314	47	169	33	53	8	3	3	27	22	15	7	5	.396	.450
2014	Cardinals (GCL)	R	.275	52	207	37	57	8	5	1	23	18	29	8	5	.341	.377
	State College (NYP)	SS	.200	3	5	0	1	0	0	0	0	0	2	0	0	.200	.200
Minor League Totals			.291	102	381	70	111	16	8	4	50	40	46	15	10	.364	.407

15 TOMMY PHAM, OF

Born: March 8, 1988. **B-T:** R-R. **Ht.:** 6-1. **Wt.:** 185. **Drafted:** HS—Las Vegas, 2006 (16th round). **Signed by:** Manny Guerra.

BA GRADE
45 Risk: Medium

Each of Pham's prior four seasons ended prematurely because of wrist and shoulder injuries—but he finished 2014 in the majors. Pham opened 2014 as Triple-A Memphis' fourth outfielder but surged once given an everyday role. He strikes out too much, chasing pitches out of the zone, but his strength yields solid gap power once he connects. His 20 stolen bases were a career high, and he's still learning to read pitchers' tendencies. Scouts love his defense in center field, where Pham has plus range and average arm strength. His athleticism also allows for wall-scaling, home run-robbing catches. Pham fits the fourth-outfielder profile, and as a 40-man roster member will challenge for that role in St. Louis in 2015.

Year	Club (League)	Class	AVG	G	AB	R	H	2B	3B	HR	RBI	BB	SO	SB	CS	OBP	SLG
2012	Springfield (TL)	AA	.154	12	39	3	6	2	0	1	3	4	19	0	0	.233	.282
2013	Springfield (TL)	AA	.301	45	163	27	49	6	6	6	28	20	42	6	3	.388	.521
	Memphis (PCL)	AAA	.264	30	106	6	28	6	1	1	13	7	25	2	1	.310	.368
2014	Memphis (PCL)	AAA	.324	104	346	63	112	16	6	10	44	38	81	20	2	.395	.491
	St. Louis (NL)	MAJ	.000	6	2	0	0	0	0	0	0	0	2	0	0	.000	.000
Major League Totals			.000	6	2	0	0	0	0	0	0	0	2	0	0	.000	.000
Minor League Totals			.253	699	2338	360	591	113	38	58	285	271	663	113	35	.336	.408

16 RONNIE WILLIAMS, RHP

BA GRADE

50 Risk: Extreme

Born: Jan. 6, 1996 **B-T:** R-R. **Ht.:** 6-0. **Wt.:** 170. **Drafted:** HS—Hialeah, Fla., 2014 (2nd round). **Signed by:** Charlie Gonzalez.

The Cardinals usually prefer college pitchers to high school arms in the early draft rounds, but the philosophy has evolved. In 2014, Williams followed California high schooler Jack Flaherty in the second round, arriving from south Florida after signing for $833,900. Williams stands out for his athleticism. He was a two-way recruit to Florida A&M and is a plus runner. The Cardinals scouted every one of his games in the spring after seeing him in April, with two scouts struck by his athleticism and easy velocity. His fastball came on significantly as a prep senior, and his fastball touched 97 mph in 2014 after it sat 87-88 mph in the summer of 2013, when he wasn't completely healthy. Williams is better when his fastball sits in the low 90s with good armside life. He also has flashed feel for a changeup and a too-slow curveball, though he's shown some ability to spin the ball with a rudimentary slider. The Cardinals are banking on Williams' makeup, athleticism and quick arm. He appears likely to start 2015 in extended spring training with a step up to Rookie-level Johnson City in June.

Year	Club (League)	Class	W	L	ERA	G	GS	CG	SV	IP	H	HR	BB	SO	K/9	WHIP	AVG
2014	Cardinals (GCL)	R	0	5	4.71	10	8	0	1	36	39	1	9	30	7.4	1.32	.279
Minor League Totals			0	5	4.71	10	8	0	1	36	39	1	9	30	7.4	1.32	.279

17 JUAN HERRERA, SS

BA GRADE

45 Risk: High

Born: June 28, 1993. **B-T:** R-R. **Ht.:** 5-11. **Wt.:** 165. **Signed:** Dominican Republic, 2010. **Signed by:** Ramon Pena/Claudio Brito (Indians).

Herrera was acquired in a trade that sent Marc Rzepczynski to the Indians in 2013. He's an energetic type, always smiling and always with a bounce in his step. He's got a plus arm suitable for deep throws from the shortstop hole. He's not known for power, but his bat speed allows him to pepper the gaps with doubles, while his solid-average speed plays on the bases. To continue climbing the ladder, he'll need to stop giving up the outer half of the plate and also needs to moderate his hyper-aggressive approach. He reached high Class A Palm Beach in the final week of 2014 and likely will return there in 2015.

Year	Club (League)	Class	AVG	G	AB	R	H	2B	3B	HR	RBI	BB	SO	SB	CS	OBP	SLG
2012	Indians (AZL)	R	.283	39	138	28	39	11	2	0	15	26	35	8	2	.395	.391
2013	Mahoning Valley (NYP)	SS	.275	39	149	20	41	9	1	1	11	16	30	2	1	.366	.369
	State College (NYP)	SS	.067	4	15	1	1	0	0	0	0	2	1	0	0	.176	.067
	Peoria (MWL)	LoA	.271	23	85	5	23	4	0	0	3	7	22	2	0	.333	.318
2014	Peoria (MWL)	LoA	.274	101	379	50	104	22	3	2	56	24	57	27	13	.320	.364
	Palm Beach (FSL)	HiA	.194	10	31	3	6	0	0	0	0	1	5	1	0	.219	.194
Minor League Totals			.274	274	989	137	271	57	8	4	105	98	177	47	21	.347	.360

18 JACOB WILSON, 2B/3B

BA GRADE

45 Risk: High

Born: July 29, 1990. **B-T:** R-R. **Ht.:** 5-11. **Wt.:** 180. **Drafted:** Memphis, 2012 (10th round). **Signed By:** Jay Catalano.

The Conference USA player of the year as a senior in 2012, Wilson signed for just $20,000 and excited Cardinals coaches on the farm in 2014. Wilson is a high-character guy the organization desires, but he suffered a season-ending left knee injury in early June and soon required surgery. At the time, Wilson was setting the Double-A Texas League aflame in the month following a promotion from high Class A Palm Beach. His bat showed plenty of pop, as the stocky, strong righthanded hitter can turn on inside fastballs and has the strength to drive them to the gaps. Defensively, a smooth transition from third base to second base has only excited club officials more. He doesn't show great range with his fringy speed and doesn't look the part of a middle infielder, but he reads swings and has good instincts. He turns double plays well thanks to an above-average arm and fearlessness on the pivot. Wilson competed in the Arizona Fall League for a second straight season in 2014, this time to make up for lost at-bats, and should challenge for a role at Triple-A Memphis this spring.

Year	Club (League)	Class	AVG	G	AB	R	H	2B	3B	HR	RBI	BB	SO	SB	CS	OBP	SLG
2012	Batavia (NYP)	SS	.275	46	160	28	44	7	1	6	25	13	33	2	1	.341	.444
2013	Peoria (MWL)	LoA	.264	97	348	63	92	24	1	15	72	40	54	6	5	.350	.468
	Palm Beach (FSL)	HiA	.179	32	117	12	21	4	0	3	10	17	20	0	1	.294	.291
2014	Palm Beach (FSL)	HiA	.298	30	121	18	36	12	0	0	20	12	24	0	0	.358	.397
	Springfield (TL)	AA	.305	36	131	15	40	13	0	5	21	11	23	3	1	.366	.519
Minor League Totals			.266	241	877	136	233	60	2	29	148	93	154	11	8	.344	.438

19 XAVIER SCRUGGS, 1B

Born: Sept. 23, 1987. **B-T:** R-R. **Ht.:** 6-1. **Wt.:** 210. **Drafted:** Nevada-Las Vegas, 2008 (19th round). **Signed by:** Aaron Krawiec.

BA GRADE
40 Risk: Low

Scruggs has re-cast himself over the past three seasons and earned a September callup to St. Louis in 2014. Patience at the plate and enhanced conditioning keyed the turnaround. Sent to Triple-A Memphis in 2014, he trimmed his strikeout rate from 32 percent of plate appearances to 21 percent. He's consistently produced above-average power and crushes lefties (.350/.403/.686 in 2014, with OPS marks above .900 the previous two seasons), pointing to a potential platoon future. As a first baseman, Scruggs has enhanced his range and footwork in recent years and added left field duties in winter ball in the Dominican League. Scruggs is on the 40-man roster, but the signing of Mark Reynolds likely relegates him to a holding pattern back at Memphis in 2015.

Year	Club (League)	Class	AVG	G	AB	R	H	2B	3B	HR	RBI	BB	SO	SB	CS	OBP	SLG
2012	Springfield (TL)	AA	.235	130	452	64	106	26	1	22	91	58	150	8	4	.331	.442
2013	Springfield (TL)	AA	.248	133	448	67	111	18	1	29	81	82	177	11	7	.376	.487
2014	Memphis (PCL)	AAA	.286	135	472	82	135	29	3	21	87	53	114	3	5	.370	.494
	St. Louis (NL)	MAJ	.200	9	15	0	3	1	0	0	2	2	7	0	0	.333	.267
Major League Totals			.200	9	15	0	3	1	0	0	2	2	7	0	0	.333	.267
Minor League Totals			.256	771	2698	389	690	155	10	134	488	336	868	32	20	.350	.470

20 PATRICK WISDOM, 3B

Born: Aug. 27, 1991. **B-T:** R-R. **Ht.:** 6-2. **Wt.:** 210. **Drafted:** St. Mary's, 2012 (1st round supplemental). **Signed by:** Matt Swanson.

BA GRADE
45 Risk: High

The Cardinals drafted three third basemen in the first two rounds of the 2012 draft and have moved two of them, with Stephen Piscotty going to right field and Carson Kelly to catcher. Wisdom, with his double-plus throwing arm, has stayed at third and reached Double-A Springfield. It's difficult to ignore his Texas League-leading 26 errors in 2014, as the game sped up on him. He's still learning to enhance his reaction time, improve his footwork and increase his range. Offensively, Wisdom's plus raw power, especially to his pull side, at times shows through, and he led Springfield with 14 home runs. Pitchers exploited his inability to identify breaking balls, and he ranked second in the TL in strikeouts (149) and had a career-low batting average (.215). Wisdom's tools will earn him another chance at Double-A in 2015.

Year	Club (League)	Class	AVG	G	AB	R	H	2B	3B	HR	RBI	BB	SO	SB	CS	OBP	SLG
2012	Batavia (NYP)	SS	.282	65	241	40	68	16	5	6	32	31	58	2	1	.373	.465
2013	Peoria (MWL)	LoA	.231	104	372	54	86	20	4	13	62	42	114	4	1	.312	.411
	Palm Beach (FSL)	HiA	.250	25	92	8	23	4	0	2	11	9	23	1	0	.317	.359
2014	Springfield (TL)	AA	.215	128	452	49	97	19	4	14	53	39	149	5	1	.277	.367
Minor League Totals			.237	322	1157	151	274	59	13	35	158	121	344	12	3	.312	.401

21 GREG GARCIA, SS/2B

Born: Aug. 8, 1989. **B-T:** L-R. **Ht.:** 6-0. **Wt.:** 190. **Drafted:** Hawaii, 2010 (7th round). **Signed by:** Matt Swanson.

BA GRADE
40 Risk: Low

Kolten Wong's double-play partner at Hawaii and again in 2012 and 2013 at Double-A Springfield and Triple-A Memphis, Garcia received two callups to St. Louis in 2014 and remains on the 40-man roster. He's long been seen as a coach on the field, but it is probably to be expected as a third-generation player. His dad Dave was a 1978 first-round draft pick of the Yankees, and his grandfather Dave Sr. managed the Angels (1977-78) and Indians (1979-82). Garcia profiles as a big league utility man, given he plays shortstop, second base and added third base in the recent past. His feel for the game, by positioning himself well defensively and anticipating a hitter's tendencies, receives high marks. With Daniel Descalso gone via free agency to the Rockies, Garcia could make a play for the Cardinals' utility role. However, he'll need to handle the bat better, especially in dropping down bunts, and regain some of his plate discipline, which regressed last season.

Year	Club (League)	Class	AVG	G	AB	R	H	2B	3B	HR	RBI	BB	SO	SB	CS	OBP	SLG
2012	Springfield (TL)	AA	.284	124	412	81	117	20	3	10	51	80	83	10	5	.408	.420
2013	Memphis (PCL)	AAA	.271	116	354	50	96	23	4	3	35	49	70	14	2	.377	.384
2014	Springfield (TL)	AA	.333	4	15	2	5	2	0	0	1	1	4	1	0	.353	.467
	Memphis (PCL)	AAA	.272	106	382	60	104	12	3	8	40	41	95	7	5	.358	.382
	St. Louis (NL)	MAJ	.143	14	14	2	2	1	0	0	1	1	6	0	0	.333	.214
Major League Totals			.143	14	14	2	2	1	0	0	1	1	6	0	0	.333	.214
Minor League Totals			.279	513	1743	298	487	93	17	27	177	237	354	47	23	.380	.399

22 CODY STANLEY, C

BA GRADE

45 Risk: High

Born: Dec. 21, 1988 **B-T:** L-R. **Ht.:** 5-10. **Wt.:** 190. **Drafted:** UNC Wilmington, 2010 (4th round). **Signed by:** Mike Juhl.

Stanley's efforts to restore his image following a 50-game suspension for performance-enhancing drug use in 2012 materialized at Double-A Springfield in 2014. His overall game matured to the point that the Cardinals added him to the 40-man roster in November. Stanley finished fifth in the Texas League in batting (.283) and slugging (.429) in 2014, largely because he began using the whole field and exhibited more patience. Most of the lefthanded hitter's power is to his pull side, and he can drive the ball to the gaps. He remains susceptible to chase, particularly against lefthanders, who held him to a .227/.306/.309 line. For a catcher, he's fleet afoot and knows when to pick his spots. Defensively, Stanley's game-calling, handling the staff, blocking ability and control of the running game improved dramatically. He threw out a career-high 42 percent of basestealers, showing improved footwork out of the crouch. Stanley will challenge for a Triple-A Memphis role in 2015 and profiles as a solid backup catcher.

Year	Club (League)	Class	AVG	G	AB	R	H	2B	3B	HR	RBI	BB	SO	SB	CS	OBP	SLG
2012	Cardinals (GCL)	R	.300	3	10	1	3	2	0	0	0	0	4	0	0	.300	.500
	Palm Beach (FSL)	HiA	.280	45	157	11	44	8	1	3	35	6	32	1	0	.300	.401
2013	Palm Beach (FSL)	HiA	.226	23	84	7	19	1	2	1	11	2	17	0	1	.256	.321
	Springfield (TL)	AA	.250	75	272	31	68	10	0	5	34	16	54	4	0	.295	.342
2014	Springfield (TL)	AA	.283	103	385	47	109	16	2	12	43	35	68	13	2	.340	.429
Minor League Totals			.274	405	1500	186	411	73	12	38	230	107	299	30	6	.323	.415

23 STEVE BEAN, C

BA GRADE

50 Risk: Extreme

Born: Sept. 15, 1993. **B-T:** L-R. **Ht.:** 6-2. **Wt.:** 190. **Drafted:** HS— Rockwall, Texas, 2012 (1st round supplemental). **Signed by:** Aaron Looper.

The Cardinals bought Bean out of a commitment to Texas with a $700,000 bonus in 2012, when he was the 59th overall pick in the draft. Two years later, he reached low Class A Peoria but sputtered offensively. The lefty-hitting catcher split time with Carson Kelly in 2014 and saw just 34 at-bats versus lefthanders the entire season. Bean has yet to demonstrate manifest power, but scouts do seem some looseness to his swing and some pop to the gaps with a solid idea of the strike zone. The Cardinals targeted his receiving skills in instructional league after Bean threw out 27 percent of basestealers in 2014—which was down from 46 percent in 2013. He has plus arm strength, but he tended to sit back on his heels and hurry his throws. Both issues are being corrected, which will allow him to regain rhythm on his throws. Another assignment to Peoria in 2015 seems likely.

Year	Club (League)	Class	AVG	G	AB	R	H	2B	3B	HR	RBI	BB	SO	SB	CS	OBP	SLG
2012	Johnson City (APP)	R	.125	24	80	6	10	4	0	1	5	15	32	2	0	.263	.213
	Cardinals (GCL)	R	.320	15	50	8	16	4	0	0	7	8	11	0	0	.424	.400
2013	Johnson City (APP)	R	.229	32	118	15	27	4	0	2	14	11	44	0	0	.303	.314
2014	Peoria (MWL)	LoA	.235	78	260	25	61	12	0	2	30	36	67	0	0	.326	.304
Minor League Totals			.224	149	508	54	114	24	0	5	56	70	154	2	0	.320	.301

24 ROWAN WICK, OF

BA GRADE

45 Risk: High

Born: Nov. 9, 1992 **B-T:** L-R. **Ht.:** 6-3. **Wt.:** 220. **Drafted:** Cypress (Calif.) JC, 2012 (9th round). **Signed by:** Mike DiBiase.

A Canadian prep product out of the Vancouver area, Wick began his collegiate career at St. John's before transferring to Cypress (Calif.) JC. The ex-catcher intrigues because of his plus raw power and right-field profile. Scouts grade his outfield arm as double-plus, with some giving him top-of-the-scale 80 grades, and he turned in 12 outfield assists in 2014. His bat is another interesting story. Wick hit his way out of the short-season New York Penn League after 35 games, leading the league in slugging (.815) even after being penalized with the 64 hitless at-bats needed to qualify. One scout called Wick's swing "a beautiful stroke," but others consider it too grooved, in the same place at the same speed with same path, a tendency that was exploited by better pitchers at low Class A Peoria. He's a decent runner for his size. Wick's power prompted his name to come up in 2014 trade talk, and his power could push him to Double-A Springield by the end of 2015.

Year	Club (League)	Class	AVG	G	AB	R	H	2B	3B	HR	RBI	BB	SO	SB	CS	OBP	SLG
2012	Cardinals (GCL)	R	.156	23	77	9	12	4	1	1	8	5	21	1	1	.233	.273
2013	Johnson City (APP)	R	.256	56	207	28	53	11	1	10	35	30	71	2	1	.354	.464
2014	State College (NYP)	SS	.378	35	119	30	45	8	1	14	38	20	34	1	1	.475	.815
	Peoria (MWL)	LoA	.220	39	141	21	31	8	2	6	22	13	60	4	0	.299	.433
Minor League Totals			.259	153	544	88	141	31	5	31	103	68	186	8	3	.351	.506

25 MIKE MAYERS, RHP

Born: Dec. 6, 1991. **B-T:** R-R. **Ht.** 6-4. **Wt.:** 185. **Drafted:** Mississippi, 2013 (3rd round). **Signed by:** Nicholas Brannon.

An Ohio prep product, Mayers spent two years in the Mississippi rotation, then signed for $510,000 as a Cardinals third-rounder in 2013. He jumped through three levels in his first full season, finishing at Triple-A. In the Texas League, he turned in 10 quality starts out of 13 tries, working with Yadier Molina in his final Double-A start when Molina was down on an injury rehab assignment. Mayers' above-average fastball has some giddyup, topping at 97 mph, and he mixes in a sinker and slurvy slider. He didn't give up many home runs, even though he frequently missed up with his fastball. Tightening his slider, which plays fringe-average, would help improve his modest strikeout rate. Mayers learned to manage himself as a pro, showing maturity when it came to minimizing damage. He could open 2015 back at Memphis.

Year	Club (League)	Class	W	L	ERA	G	GS	CG	SV	IP	H	HR	BB	SO	K/9	WHIP	AVG
2013	Cardinals (GCL)	R	1	0	1.50	5	3	0	0	12	6	1	6	13	9.8	1.00	.146
	Peoria (MWL)	LoA	0	3	3.70	5	5	0	0	24	29	2	5	14	5.2	1.40	.302
2014	Palm Beach (FSL)	HiA	2	7	3.72	12	12	1	0	73	84	5	13	61	7.6	1.33	.294
	Springfield (TL)	AA	6	5	2.83	13	13	0	0	76	81	2	23	52	6.1	1.36	.277
	Memphis (PCL)	AAA	0	0	7.20	1	1	0	0	5	9	2	1	4	7.2	2.00	.409
Minor League Totals			9	15	3.31	36	34	1	0	190	209	12	48	144	6.8	1.35	.284

26 BREYVIC VALERA, 2B

Born: Jan. 8, 1992 **B-T:** S-R. **Ht.:** 5-11. **Wt.:** 160. **Signed:** Venezuela, 2010. **Signed by:** Jose Gregorio Gonzalez.

Valera, who joined Double-A Springfield in late June, actually made his Double-A debut two years earlier as a 19-year-old brought up from the short-season New York-Penn League in order to cover for Futures Game-bound Kolten Wong. Valera isn't flashy or overly muscular, but coaches suspect his baseball smarts will make up for both. He struck out just 6.1 percent of the time in 2014, and just two qualified minor league batters struck out less frequently. When he connects, Valera gets enough loft to lift singles over the infield—55 of his 65 Double-A Springfield hits were singles—and shows patience by drawing walks. Defensively, he mainly plays second base, where he shows nice range, soft hands, instincts and hangs in on the pivot. He can play third base and the outfield in a pinch but needs seasoning at both. Scouts see him as a big league utility infielder at best, but he'll need to enhance his bunting to stick as a National League bench player. Valera, who signed for $1,000 out of Venezuela at age 18, wasn't added to the 40-man roster and slipped through the Rule 5 draft unselected. He should return to Springfield to begin 2015.

Year	Club (League)	Class	AVG	G	AB	R	H	2B	3B	HR	RBI	BB	SO	SB	CS	OBP	SLG
2012	Springfield (TL)	AA	.200	3	5	2	1	0	0	0	1	0	0	0	0	.200	.200
	Batavia (NYP)	SS	.316	69	282	39	89	18	4	1	33	18	27	10	6	.359	.418
2013	Peoria (MWL)	LoA	.309	128	515	71	159	18	6	0	48	40	30	13	7	.358	.367
2014	Palm Beach (FSL)	HiA	.333	73	294	35	98	8	4	0	37	25	13	13	10	.385	.388
	Springfield (TL)	AA	.286	59	227	31	65	8	2	0	20	15	22	4	5	.329	.339
Minor League Totals			.313	439	1718	257	538	77	25	3	182	137	133	64	37	.365	.392

27 MALIK COLLYMORE, 2B

Born: April 29, 1995. **B-T:** R-R. **Ht.:** 5-11. **Wt.:** 190. **Drafted:** HS—Mississauga, Ont., 2013 (10th round). **Signed By:** Jason Bryans.

Collymore committed to Missouri before the Cardinals offered a $275,000 bonus after drafting the Canadian in the 10th round in 2013. He's built strong, like a running back, and could easily be mistaken for older than 19. In his first two pro seasons, Collymore's intelligence and knack for hitting the ball hard hasn't been lost on coaches. He has long demonstrated power; he hit a home run against the Astros when the Canadian junior national team was on a tour of spring training bases in Florida in his draft year. He made lots of hard contact in the Rookie-level Gulf Coast League in 2014, ranking third in the league in batting (.333) while tying for the lead with eight triples. Most of his power is to the gaps for now. He's an above-average runner who needs to polish his baserunning. He also needs to find a position. He plays second base and may give third a try, and he has the wheels to move to the outfield. He will try to earn a full-season spot in 2015 but may start the year in extended spring training.

Year	Club (League)	Class	AVG	G	AB	R	H	2B	3B	HR	RBI	BB	SO	SB	CS	OBP	SLG
2013	Cardinals (GCL)	R	.228	19	57	2	13	3	0	1	3	3	23	0	1	.267	.333
2014	Cardinals (GCL)	R	.333	54	177	34	59	7	8	1	34	18	43	9	5	.403	.480
Minor League Totals			.308	73	234	36	72	10	8	2	37	21	66	9	6	.372	.444

28 C.J. McELROY, OF

BA GRADE

45 Risk: High

Born: May 29, 1993. **B-T:** B-R. **Ht.:** 5-10. **Wt.:** 180. **Drafted:** HS—Clear Creek (Texas), 2011 (3rd round). **Signed by:** Ralph Garr Jr.

The son of former big league lefthander Chuck McElroy and nephew to all-star Cecil Cooper, C.J. McElroy surged a year after a foot injury truncated most of his 2013 season. Signed for $510,000 in 2011 as a third-round pick, he resumed working on switch-hitting upon his return to health at low Class A Peoria in 2014, incorporating batting lefthanded. It makes sense to add the feature, given his top-of-the-scale speed. While he needs polish on the bases, McElroy led the organization with 41 steals. He's not a power hitter despite his compact, muscular build. Mainly, he is a consistent singles hitter who can also draw some walks, then run his way to second and third base. McElroy's speed will come in handy in the spacious ballparks of the high Class A Florida State League in 2015.

Year	Club (League)	Class	AVG	G	AB	R	H	2B	3B	HR	RBI	BB	SO	SB	CS	OBP	SLG
2012	Johnson City (APP)	R	.271	61	247	40	67	11	2	0	22	15	42	24	5	.314	.332
2013	Cardinals (GCL)	R	.300	3	10	0	3	1	0	0	0	0	2	1	1	.364	.400
	Peoria (MWL)	LoA	.240	58	242	24	58	9	3	0	23	17	40	8	8	.288	.302
2014	Peoria (MWL)	LoA	.267	130	490	74	131	11	2	0	29	40	84	41	18	.342	.298
Minor League Totals			.259	275	1068	148	277	34	8	0	81	79	183	82	34	.321	.306

29 ANDREW MORALES, RHP

BA GRADE

45 Risk: High

Born: Jan. 16, 1993. **B-T:** R-R. **Ht.:** 6-0. **Wt.:** 185. **Drafted:** UC Irvine, 2014 (2nd round supplemental). **Signed by:** Mike DiBiase.

Morales led UC Irvine to the College World Series in 2014 and went 42-3 in his four seasons in junior college and college ball. A strike-thrower by nature despite a stiff arm action, Morales has gained strength over the course of his career and now holds his 89-91 mph fastball velocity deep into games. He'll touch 93 mph on occasion and has excellent control with a chance for major league average command. He locates his hard 79-82 mph slider as well, and he overmatched college hitters with it, leading NCAA Division I in strikeouts in 2014. He has some deception thanks to his high arm slot, and his serviceable changeup has room for improvement. He lacks projection but not heart, pitching savvy or competitiveness. Morales could be assigned back to high Class A Palm Beach in 2015 after finishing 2014 there.

Year	Club (League)	Class	W	L	ERA	G	GS	CG	SV	IP	H	HR	BB	SO	K/9	WHIP	AVG
2014	Cardinals (GCL)	R	0	1	3.60	3	2	0	0	5	2	1	3	6	10.8	1.00	.118
	Palm Beach (FSL)	HiA	1	0	1.23	2	0	0	0	7	2	0	0	6	7.4	0.27	.083
Minor League Totals			1	1	2.19	5	2	0	0	12	4	1	3	12	8.8	0.57	.098

30 MITCH HARRIS, RHP

BA GRADE

45 Risk: High

Born: Nov. 7, 1985. **B-T:** R-R. **Ht.:** 6-4. **Wt.:** 215. **Drafted:** Navy, 2008 (13th round). **Signed by:** Mike Juhl.

When the Cardinals selected Harris, a record-setting starter at Annapolis, they knew he had a commitment to his country, and they were willing to make a commitment to the Navy righthander. Harris went five years between his selection in the 2008 draft and his first inning for the Cardinals organization in 2013. He was older than his manager at short-season State College when he debuted. While he had tried to maintain his skills by throwing while on active duty for the Navy—one of his assignments was part of the drug war—the rust on his fastball was clear as it hovered in the mid-80s. A year later he saw a reassuring number: 95 mph. Aware the clock was ticking on his opportunity in pro ball, Harris has advanced swiftly as a reliever, pitching at three levels in 2014 and performing in the Arizona Fall League. He cannot be rattled on the mound, and he's developed the repertoire of other late-20s relievers who reach the majors: a cut fastball that's a legit out pitch and a split-finger fastball that the club wishes he'd throw more. Exposed in the Rule 5 draft, Harris went unselected, meaning St. Louis will bring him to spring training with a shot at the Triple-A Memphis bullpen.

Year	Club (League)	Class	W	L	ERA	G	GS	CG	SV	IP	H	HR	BB	SO	K/9	WHIP	AVG
2012	Did not play--Military List																
2013	State College (NYP)	SS	4	1	0.81	20	0	0	1	33	22	0	15	29	7.8	1.11	.193
2014	Palm Beach (FSL)	HiA	0	2	4.26	8	0	0	0	13	8	1	6	9	6.4	1.11	.178
	Springfield (TL)	AA	2	0	3.92	33	0	0	1	44	38	5	13	34	7.0	1.17	.230
	Memphis (PCL)	AAA	0	0	0.00	1	0	0	0	1	1	0	0	2	18.0	1.00	.333
Minor League Totals			6	3	2.78	62	0	0	2	91	69	6	34	74	7.3	1.14	.211

San Diego Padres

BY MATT EDDY

The Padres have averaged 87 losses per season since 2011, and they haven't qualified for the playoffs since 2006, but in recent years they lead the industry in one category: general manager hires.

A.J. Preller is the third man to hold that title in the five years since the club fired 14-year GM Kevin Towers after an 87-loss campaign in 2009. Preller follows Josh Byrnes and Jed Hoyer, the current Cubs GM whose Padres clubs followed a fluky 90-win season in 2010 with a 91-loss dud the following year.

San Diego made the GM switch during the 2014 season, firing Byrnes in mid-June and hiring Preller in early August. In between those dates, interim GM A.J. Hinch executed a number of salary-shedding, prospect-acquiring deadline deals, though he resigned his post before Preller took the reins.

Most notably, Hinch traded away veterans Chase Headley and Huston Street in mid-July, bringing back a haul of six young players that included big league third baseman Yangervis Solarte, Double-A reliever R.J. Alvarez and high Class A shortstop Jose Rondon.

Preller, most recently an assistant GM with the Rangers, managed many aspects of the two-time American League pennant winners' day-to-day operations, including the player-development and scouting departments. Prior to that, he spearheaded Texas' fruitful scouting and development program in Latin America.

Prohibited from bringing Rangers executives to San Diego to staff his front office, Preller hired Athletics international scouting coordinator Sam Geaney as farm director, promoted regional supervisor Mark Conner to scouting director and lured Logan White away from his post as Dodgers scouting director to become senior adviser and pro scouting director for the Padres. White also had interviewed for the GM job in San Diego.

The new front office has their work cut out for them. The Padres fielded the most inept lineup in the game during the first half of 2014, scoring 2.9 runs per game, but they rebounded to score 3.8 in the second half, ranking 11th in the game during that time as young veterans such as catcher Yasmani Grandal and second baseman Jedd Gyorko recovered their form.

A total of 10 teams have a lower winning percentage than the Padres in the past half-decade, but among the clubs clustered around them in the standings are the Indians, Pirates and Royals, three teams with recent playoff appearances and positive near-term outlooks. Others such as the Cubs and

Jedd Gyorko returned to form in the second half of 2014 to help revive a poor offense

TOP PROSPECTS OF THE DECADE

Year	Player, Pos.	2014 Org
2005	Josh Barfield, 2b	Out of baseball
2006	Cesar Carrillo, rhp	Laredo (American Assoc.)
2007	Cedric Hunter, of	Braves
2008	Chase Headley, 3b	Yankees
2009	Kyle Blanks, 1b	Athletics
2010	Donavan Tate, of	Padres
2011	Casey Kelly, rhp	Padres
2012	Anthony Rizzo, 1b	Cubs
2013	Casey Kelly, rhp	Padres
2014	Austin Hedges, c	Padres

Twins have elite farm systems, while the Mariners and White Sox are positioning themselves as contenders with their offseason maneuvering.

For the Padres to contend in 2015, the lineup must reprise its second-half form from 2014 and the farm system must begin feeding prospects to the big leagues.

Chief among the Padres' near-ready prospects are righthanders Matt Wisler and Joe Ross and catcher Austin Hedges. Right fielder Hunter Renfroe and shortstop Trea Turner also could move quickly after finishing 2014 with positive stints in the Arizona Fall League.

Other youngsters such as reliever Kevin Quackenbush, outfielder Rymer Liriano and second baseman Cory Spangenberg received late-season callups in 2014 and are ready for expanded roles with the Padres in 2015.

General manager: A.J. Preller. **Farm director:** Sam Geaney. **Scouting director:** Mark Conner.

Class	Team	League	W	L	PCT	Finish	Manager
Majors	San Diego Padres	National	77	85	.475	t-18th (30)	Bud Black
Triple-A	El Paso Chihuahuas	Pacific Coast	72	72	.500	10th (16)	Pat Murphy
Double-A	San Antonio Missions	Texas	68	72	.486	t-5th (8)	Rich Dauer
High A	Lake Elsinore Storm	California	75	65	.536	t-4th (10)	Jamie Quirk
Low A	Fort Wayne TinCaps	Midwest	63	76	.453	12th (16)	Michael Collins
Short-season	*Eugene Emeralds	Northwest	30	46	.395	7th (8)	Robbie Wine
Rookie	AZL Padres	Arizona	20	36	.357	13th (13)	Anthony Contreras
Overall Minor League Record			328	367	.472	23rd (30)	

*Affiliate moves to Tri-City (Northwest) in 2015

THIS YEAR'S TOP 30

No.	Player, Pos.	Grade/Risk
1.	Matt Wisler, rhp	60/Medium
2.	Trea Turner, ss	60/High
3.	Hunter Renfroe, of	60/High
4.	Joe Ross, rhp	55/High
5.	Austin Hedges, c	55/High
6.	Max Fried, lhp	60/Extreme
7.	Cory Spangenberg, 2b/of	50/Medium
8.	Rymer Liriano, of	55/High
9.	Zach Eflin, rhp	50/Medium
10.	Jace Peterson, ss/2b	50/Medium
11.	R.J. Alvarez, rhp	45/Low
12.	Fernando Perez, 2b/3b	55/High
13.	Michael Gettys, of	55/Extreme
14.	Jose Rondon, ss	50/High
15.	Jake Bauers, 1b	50/High
16.	Mallex Smith, of	50/High
17.	Casey Kelly, rhp	55/Extreme
18.	Elliot Morris, rhp	50/High
19.	Franchy Cordero, ss	55/Extreme
20.	Taylor Lindsey, 2b	45/Medium
21.	Dustin Peterson, 3b	50/High
22.	Alex Dickerson, of	45/Medium
23.	Burch Smith, rhp	45/Medium
24.	Ryan Butler, rhp	45/High
25.	Leonel Campos, rhp	45/High
26.	Zech Lemond, rhp	45/High
27.	Tayron Guerrero, rhp	45/High
28.	Keyvius Sampson, rhp	45/High
29.	Travis Jankowski, of	45/High
30.	Johnny Barbato, rhp	45/High

LAST YEAR'S TOP 30

No.	Player, Pos.	Status
1.	Austin Hedges, c	No. 5
2.	Matt Wisler, rhp	No. 1
3.	Max Fried, lhp	No. 6
4.	Hunter Renfroe, of	No. 3
5.	Casey Kelly, rhp	No. 17
6.	Rymer Liriano, of	No. 8
7.	Jace Peterson, ss	No. 10
8.	Burch Smith, rhp	No. 23
9.	Keyvius Sampson, rhp	No. 28
10.	Joe Ross, rhp	No. 4
11.	Cory Spangenberg, 2b	No. 7
12.	Franchy Cordero, ss	No. 19
13.	Joe Wieland, rhp	Dropped out
14.	Zach Eflin, rhp	No. 9
15.	Matt Andriese, rhp	(Rays)
16.	Gabriel Quintana, 3b	Dropped out
17.	Travis Jankowski, of	No. 29
18.	Juan Pablo Oramas, lhp	Dropped out
19.	Walker Weickel, rhp	Dropped out
20.	Reymond Fuentes, of	(Royals)
21.	Leonel Campos, rhp	No. 25
22.	Dustin Peterson, 3b	No. 21
23.	Tommy Medica, 1b	Majors
24.	Yeison Asencio, of	Dropped out
25.	Alex Dickerson, of/1b	No. 22
26.	Donn Roach, rhp	(Cubs)
27.	Kevin Quackenbush, rhp	Majors
28.	Adys Portillo, rhp	Dropped out
29.	Jose Urena, of	Dropped out
30.	Jonhhy Barbato, rhp	No. 30

BEST TOOLS

Best Hitter for Average	Cory Spangenberg
Best Power Hitter	Hunter Renfroe
Best Strike-Zone Discipline	Trea Turner
Fastest Baserunner	Mallex Smith
Best Athlete	Trea Turner
Best Fastball	Ryan Butler
Best Curveball	Max Fried
Best Slider	Matt Wisler
Best Changeup	Joe Ross
Best Control	Ronald Herrera
Best Defensive Catcher	Austin Hedges
Best Defensive Infielder	Trea Turner
Best Infield Arm	Carlos Belen
Best Defensive Outfielder	Hunter Renfroe
Best Outfield Arm	Michael Gettys

PROJECTED 2018 LINEUP

Catcher	Austin Hedges
First Base	Jake Bauers
Second Base	Cory Spangenberg
Third Base	Jedd Gyorko
Shortstop	Trea Turner
Left Field	Rymer Liriano
Center Field	Michael Gettys
Right Field	Hunter Renfroe
No. 1 Starter	Andrew Cashner
No. 2 Starter	Tyson Ross
No. 3 Starter	Jesse Hahn
No. 4 Starter	Matt Wisler
No. 5 Starter	Joe Ross
Closer	Kevin Quackenbush

SAN DIEGO PADRES

TOP 2015 ROOKIE: Cory Spangenberg, 2b/of. Now that he plays four positions, the speedy, lefthanded hitter could complement a righty-heavy Padres lineup.

BREAKOUT PROSPECT: Fernando Perez, 2b/3b. His impressive feel to hit and power could make him a standout in the California League.

SLEEPER: Jordan Paroubeck, of. The 2013 prep second-rounder has shown intriguing speed and feel to hit in Rookie ball.

SOURCE OF TOP 30 TALENT			
Homegrown	24	Acquired	6
College	7	Trades	6
Junior college	3	Rule 5 draft	0
High school	10	Independent leagues	0
Draft-and-follow	0	Free agents/waivers	0
Nondrafted free agents	0		
International	4		

LF
Jordan Paroubeck
Jake Goebbert
Jeremy Baltz
Nick Torres
Yale Rosen

CF
Michael Gettys (13)
Mallex Smith (16)
Travis Jankowski (29)
Auston Bousfield
Rico Noel

RF
Hunter Renfroe (3)
Rymer Liriano (8)
Franmil Reyes
Yeison Asencio
Jose Urena

3B
Fernando Perez (12)
Franchy Cordero (19)
Dustin Peterson (21)
Gabriel Quintana
Carlos Belen

SS
Trea Turner (2)
Jose Rondon (14)
Diego Goris
Stephen Carmon

2B
Cory Spangenberg (7)
Jace Peterson (10)
Taylor Lindsey (20)
Josh VanMeter
Benji Gonzalez

1B
Jake Bauers (15)
Alex Dickerson (22)
Luis Domoromo
Cody Decker

C
Austin Hedges (5)
Zach Risedorf
Griff Erickson
Dane Phillips
Ryan Miller

LHP

LHSP	LHRP
Max Fried (6)	Frank Garces
Juan Pablo Oramas	Brandon Alger
Thomas Dorminy	Kyle Bartsch
	Chris Rearick

RHP

RHSP	RHRP
Matt Wisler (1)	R.J. Alvarez (11)
Joe Ross (4)	Burch Smith (23)
Zach Eflin (9)	Ryan Butler (24)
Casey Kelly (17)	Leonel Campos (25)
Elliot Morris (18)	Zech Lemond (26)
Justin Hancock	Tayron Guerrero (27)
Joe Wieland	Keyvius Sampson (28)
Ronald Herrera	Johnny Barbato (30)
Walker Weickel	Rafael De Paula
Colin Rea	Adys Portillo
James Needy	Jerry Sullivan
Kyle Lloyd	Ben Paullus
Adrian De Horta	Nick Mutz
Walker Lockett	Mike Kelly
Mayky Perez	Erik Cabrera
	Eric Yardley
	Colby Blueberg
	Roman Madrid
	Stephen Kohlscheen

2014

BEST PURE HITTER: OF Auston Bousfield (5), one of the younger players in the college draft class, repeats his low-maintenance swing, uses the whole field and has a mature approach.

BEST POWER HITTER: College OFs Nick Torres (4) and Yale Rosen (11) have plus raw power, and Rosen wowed the Padres with a BP display in a pre-draft workout at Petco Park. But OF Michael Gettys (2) impacts the ball more than any Padres draftee, hitting four line drives at 106 mph or better since signing.

FASTEST RUNNER: The Padres would like to race top picks SS Trea Turner (1) and Gettys and grade Turner as a 70 runner. He's turned in 3.45-second times on drag bunts and knows how to use his speed on the bases.

BEST DEFENSIVE PLAYER: Scouting director Billy Gasparino projects Turner as an above-average shortstop. He has a 55 arm, sound internal clock and the body control to make all the plays. He was reliable defensively in his first pro season.

BEST FASTBALL: RHP Ryan Butler (7) has power-pitcher size at 6-foot-6, 230 pounds, and power stuff with a fastball that topped out at 97 as an amateur. He's hit 100 as a pro and throws plenty of fastball strikes as well.

BEST SECONDARY PITCH: RHP Zech Lemond (3) is the latest in a long line of Rice pitchers who gets swings and misses with a hard spike curveball. LHP Thomas Dorminy (10) pairs a fastball that reaches 92 with an average-to-plus curveball that can freeze lefthanded hitters.

BEST PRO DEBUT: Turner hit .323/.406/.448 overall in 279 at-bats, adding 23 stolen bases in 27 tries. Gettys led the Rookie-level Arizona League in hits (66) while batting .310/.353/.437 with 14 steals in 16 tries. RHP Colby Blueberg (24) shined primarily at short-season Eugene and was 3-0, 0.50 overall with a 40-8 strikeout-talk ratio in 36 innings.

BEST ATHLETE: The Padres considered Gettys one of top athletes in draft thanks to his strong 6-foot-1, 203-pound body, strength, quick acceleration and speed.

MOST INTRIGUING BACKGROUND: Unsigned RHP Cobi Johnson's (35) father Dane, an ex-big league pitcher, is Toronto's minor league pitching rover. Alex Morales, the father of SS Mitch Morales (29), scouts for the Nationals. The Padres famously drafted former Heisman Trophy-winning quarterback Johnny Manziel (28), who hasn't played baseball since high school.

CLOSEST TO THE MAJORS: Butler's move to the bullpen has him ahead of Lemond.

BEST LATE-ROUND PICK: Blueberg has some funk in his delivery and a lot of effort from a 6-foot, 185-pounder, but he pounds the zone at 92-93 mph and has an above-average slider.

THE ONE WHO GOT AWAY: The Padres liked LHP Brendan McKay (34), now at Louisville, who had a 65-inning scoreless streak over the last two years of his prep career.

ASSESSMENT: San Diego had Gettys in the mix at 13th overall and got him 51st, and was stunned to get him and Turner, Gasparino's last draft before he left for the Dodgers. Strong starts by power arms provide more positive early returns.

2013

OF Hunter Renfroe (1) has moved to Double-A quickly and has star-caliber tools. Dustin Peterson (2) moved to the outfield, and 1B Jake Bauers (7) has shown advanced hitting ability.

GRADE: B

2012

The Padres invested heavily in prep pitching, with mixed results for LHP Max Fried (1) and RHPs Zach Eflin (1s) and Walker Weickel (1s). 3B Fernando Perez (3) and OF Mallex Smith (5) have produced.

GRADE: C

2011

RHP Matt Wisler (7) has supplanted C Austin Hedges (2) as the club's top prospect, with RHP Joe Ross (1) not far behind. 2B Cory Spangenberg (1), SS Jace Peterson (1s) and RHPs Kevin Quackenbush (8), Burch Smith (14) and since-traded Matt Stites (17) have reached the majors.

GRADE: A

TOP DRAFT PICKS OF THE DECADE

Year	Player, Pos.	2014 Org
2005	Cesar Carrillo, rhp	Laredo (American Assoc.)
2006	Matt Antonelli, 3b	Out of baseball
2007	Nick Schmidt, lhp	Reds
2008	Allan Dykstra, 1b	Mets
2009	Donavan Tate, of	Padres
2010	*Karsten Whitson, rhp	Red Sox
2011	Cory Spangenberg, 2b	Padres
2012	Max Fried, lhp	Padres
2013	Hunter Renfroe, of	Padres
2014	Trea Turner, ss	Padres

*Did not sign

LARGEST BONUSES IN CLUB HISTORY

Donavan Tate, 2009		$6,250,000
Matt Bush, 2004		$3,150,000
Austin Hedges, 2011		$3,000,000
Max Fried, 2012		$3,000,000
Trea Turner, 2014		$2,900,000

1 MATT WISLER, RHP

Born: Sept. 12, 1992. **B-T:** R-R. **Ht.:** 6-3. **Wt.:** 195.
Drafted: HS—Bryan, Ohio, 2011 (7th round).
Signed by: Mark Conner.

The Padres went over slot to sign Wisler out of Bryan (Ohio) High in the 2011 draft, signing the seventh-rounder for $500,000. They would have paid much more than that had they waited for him to complete three years at Ohio State, because his performance in pro ball suggests he would have been a first-round pick in 2014. In fact, the area scout who identified Wisler's potential and signability, Mark Conner, now serves as Padres scouting director after being promoted to the position in November. He spent 2014 as Northeast regional supervisor for the club. Wisler breezed through Class A competition and dominated in 26 career starts at Double-A San Antonio in 2013 and 2014, going 9-5, 2.80 with a strikeout rate of 9.2 batters per nine innings, before meeting his first challenge in pro ball at Triple-A El Paso in 2014. Promoted to the Pacific Coast League in early May, Wisler pitched all season at age 21, and he's actually a few weeks younger than Noah Syndergaard (Mets) and Taijuan Walker (Mariners), two fellow precocious PCL right-handers with bright futures. Triple-A batters rocked Wisler for a 6.18 ERA and 11 homers in 55 innings through his first 11 starts in the hitter-friendly league, but he rebounded in the second half, going 5-1, 3.96 with 54 strikeouts and 15 walks in 61 innings over 11 starts.

Wisler tops out at 96 mph and sits 92-94 with above-average sink on his two-seamer, riding life on his four-seamer and at least average present control of his entire repertoire. His plus, low-80s slider features tight break, both lateral and vertical, and projects as a true strikeout weapon when he spots it to both sides of the plate. He must locate his breaking ball more precisely and improve his arm action on a fringe-average, fading changeup to better combat lefthanders, who hit .291 and slugged .517 against him in the PCL in 2014. He also throws a slow curveball in the low 70s for a different look. A thoughtful, analytical pitcher, Wisler can be too much of a perfectionist at times, trying to hone all his pitches in-game, rather than going with what works best that particular start. Once Wisler learns to repeat his mechanics and arm slot, scouts expect that his overall control will play as plus, and he has walked just 2.4 batters per

nine innings for his career. He logged 147 innings in 2014, even with the early struggles at Triple-A, and never has missed a start as a pro.

Wisler's plus fastball and slider combo give him an absolute ceiling of No. 2 starter—if his changeup and command come up to average. Most scouts, however, feel more comfortable projecting him as a durable No. 3 on a pennant contender. Wisler could make the Padres rotation with a strong spring, but he probably faces at least a month at Triple-A in 2015.

BA GRADE

60 Risk: Medium

SCOUTING LABEL

Fastball: 60.
Slider: 60.
Changeup: 55.
Control: 55.

Based on 20-80 scouting scale and future projection rather than present tools.

LGE	BF	SO%	BB%	HR/9
TL	120	29.2	5.0	0.60
PCL	514	19.6	7.0	1.47

JOHN WILLIAMSON

Year	Club (League)	Class	W	L	ERA	G	GS	CG	SV	IP	H	HR	BB	SO	K/9	WHIP	AVG
2012	Fort Wayne (MWL)	LoA	5	4	2.53	24	23	1	0	114	95	1	28	113	8.9	1.08	.227
2013	Lake Elsinore (CAL)	HiA	2	1	2.03	6	6	0	0	31	22	1	6	28	8.1	0.90	.196
	San Antonio (TL)	AA	8	5	3.00	20	20	0	0	105	85	7	27	103	8.8	1.07	.223
2014	San Antonio (TL)	AA	1	0	2.10	6	6	0	0	30	26	2	6	35	10.5	1.07	.234
	El Paso (PCL)	AAA	9	5	5.01	22	22	0	0	117	131	19	36	101	7.8	1.43	.279
Minor League Totals			25	15	3.40	79	77	1	0	397	361	30	105	380	8.6	1.17	.242

2 TREA TURNER, SS

Born: June 30, 1993. **B-T:** R-R. **Ht.:** 6-1. **Wt.:** 175. **Drafted:** North Carolina State, 2014 (1st round). **Signed by:** Tyler Stubblefield.

Turner's decorated college career at North Carolina State validated his decision to turn down a $500,000 bonus offer as the Pirates' 20th-round pick in 2011. He led NCAA Division I with 55 stolen bases in 2012, then helped lead the Wolfpack to the College World Series in 2013, then blasted a career-high eight homers as a junior in 2014, prompting the Padres to select the shortstop with the 13th pick in the draft and sign him for $2.9 million. Turner showed off his feel to hit and running speed during his pro debut in 2014, batting .323/.406/.448 in 279 at-bats and stealing 23 bases in 27 tries, spending most of his time at low Class A Fort Wayne. He also showcased sure-handedness by committing just four errors in 50 games. Not the rangiest shortstop around, Turner has enough lateral quickness and arm strength to grade as at least a solid-average defender. He adjusted his swing each year at N.C. State to become more direct to the ball, but even with the constant tinkering and often long swing, his bat speed and double-plus foot speed enabled him to hit .342 in college and .323 so far as a pro. He has sneaky power to his pull side, but his pro approach will center more on wearing out the gaps and reaching base via hits and walks. If he continues to hit, Turner profiles as a top-of-the-order hitter and dependable shortstop for a contending club. If he doesn't, he could bat eighth and still provide positional value and contribute with his speed. He's ready for high Class A Lake Elsinore in 2015.

BA GRADE

60 Risk: High

LGE	PA	BB%	SO%	ISO
NWL	105	10.5	18.1	.054
MWL	216	11.1	22.2	.160

Year	Club (League)	Class	AVG	G	AB	R	H	2B	3B	HR	RBI	BB	SO	SB	CS	OBP	SLG
2014	Eugene (NWL)	SS	.228	23	92	14	21	2	0	1	2	11	19	9	1	.324	.283
	Fort Wayne (MWL)	LoA	.369	46	187	31	69	14	2	4	22	24	48	14	3	.447	.529
Minor League Totals			.323	69	279	45	90	16	2	5	24	35	67	23	4	.406	.448

3 HUNTER RENFROE, OF

Born: Jan. 28, 1992. **B-T:** R-R. **Ht.:** 6-1. **Wt.:** 200. **Drafted:** Mississippi State, 2013 (1st round). **Signed by:** Andrew Salvo.

Renfroe tied for the Southeastern Conference lead with 16 home runs as a Mississippi State junior in 2013 while driving the Bulldogs to the College World Series finals. Sufficiently intrigued by Renfroe's incredible raw power, the Padres selected him 13th overall in that year's draft and signed him for $2.678 million. He led the high Class A California League with 16 home runs in the first half of 2014 before San Diego promoted him to Double-A San Antonio, where he struggled to access his power with the same frequency. Not many prospects have as much extra-base potential as Renfroe, whose uppercut swing, bat speed and double-plus power produced 21 homers and 33 doubles in 2014. Scouts expect him to continue mashing at higher levels once he learns to swing through the ball and hit straightaway, rather than trying to loft everything to his pull side. His high strikeout rate is tenable because of his correspondingly high power production and walk rate, though his big leg kick and busy swing will cap his batting-average ceiling at about .250. An average runner, Renfroe plays plus defense in right field with good closing speed and a plus, accurate arm he used to rack up 16 assists in 2014. Renfroe fits the profile for an everyday right fielder with plus power production, plus arm strength and good range. He could move quickly once he puts Double-A behind him and could be a regular in San Diego by 2016.

BA GRADE

60 Risk: High

LGE	PA	BB%	SO%	ISO
CAL	316	8.9	25.6	.270
TL	251	10.0	21.1	.121

Year	Club (League)	Class	AVG	G	AB	R	H	2B	3B	HR	RBI	BB	SO	SB	CS	OBP	SLG
2013	Eugene (NWL)	SS	.308	25	104	20	32	9	0	4	18	5	26	2	0	.333	.510
	Fort Wayne (MWL)	LoA	.212	18	66	6	14	5	0	2	7	4	23	0	0	.268	.379
2014	Lake Elsinore (CAL)	HiA	.295	69	278	46	82	21	3	16	52	28	81	9	3	.370	.565
	San Antonio (TL)	AA	.232	60	224	17	52	12	0	5	23	25	53	2	1	.307	.353
Minor League Totals			.268	172	672	89	180	47	3	27	100	62	183	13	4	.334	.467

4 JOE ROSS, RHP

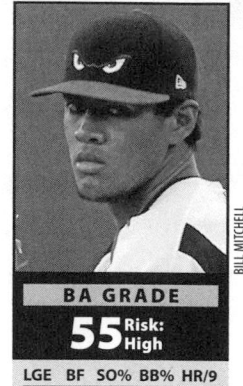

BILL MITCHELL

Born: May 21, 1993. **B-T:** R-R. **Ht.:** 6-4. **Wt.:** 205. **Drafted:** HS—Oakland, 2011 (1st round). **Signed by:** Noah Jackson.

The Padres tabbed Ross with the 25th overall pick in the 2011 draft, but not until 2014 did they know exactly what they got for their $2.75 million investment. A shoulder injury in 2012 cut his season in half, then he struck out just 5.8 batters per nine innings at low Class A Fort Wayne in 2013, a rate at odds with his pitch quality. Everything clicked into place in 2014 for Ross, the younger brother of Padres starter Tyson Ross, and he finished the season at Double-A San Antonio. Ross throws 91-93 mph fastballs from a loose, slightly crossfire delivery, and he muscles up to 96 when he needs it. He sinks the ball and runs it to his arm side well enough to record a 1.59 groundout/airout ratio in 2014 that ranked just outside the top 50 for qualified minor league starters. Ross throws two promising secondary weapons, including a plus slider in the low to mid-80s that he uses to back-foot lefties and expand the zone against righties. He throws a low-80s changeup with increasingly good arm speed and separation, and some scouts project the

BA GRADE
55 Risk: High

LGE	BF	SO%	BB%	HR/9
CAL	436	20.0	6.4	0.53
TL	84	22.6	1.2	0.90

pitch to above-average. Ross began to show a killer instinct in the second half of 2014, going after batters with his best stuff rather than pitching to contact, and the strategy paid off with the best SO/BB ratio (3.7) of his career. Ross finished the 2014 season on the disabled list with what the Padres deemed illness and fatigue, but the progress he made indicates he has a ceiling as a No. 3 starter who might be a year away from contributing. Look for him to return to the Double-A level in 2015.

Year	Club (League)	Class	W	L	ERA	G	GS	CG	SV	IP	H	HR	BB	SO	K/9	WHIP	AVG
2012	Fort Wayne (MWL)	LoA	0	2	6.26	6	6	0	0	27	33	2	11	27	8.9	1.61	.297
	Padres (AZL)	R	0	0	13.50	1	1	0	0	1	2	0	2	1	13.5	6.00	.500
	Eugene (NWL)	SS	0	2	2.03	8	8	0	0	27	16	1	9	28	9.5	0.94	.178
2013	Fort Wayne (MWL)	LoA	5	8	3.75	23	23	0	0	122	124	7	40	79	5.8	1.34	.267
2014	Lake Elsinore (CAL)	HiA	8	6	3.98	19	19	0	0	102	101	6	28	87	7.7	1.27	.256
	San Antonio (TL)	AA	2	0	3.60	4	3	0	0	20	23	2	1	19	8.6	1.20	.277
Minor League Totals			15	18	3.90	62	60	0	0	300	301	18	91	241	7.2	1.31	.261

5 AUSTIN HEDGES, C

BILL MITCHELL

Born: Aug. 18, 1992. **B-T:** R-R. **Ht.:** 6-1. **Wt.:** 190. **Drafted:** HS—San Juan Capistrano, Calif., 2011 (2nd round). **Signed by:** Josh Emmerick.

Signed for $3 million as a second-round pick out of high school in 2011, Hedges zoomed to Double-A San Antonio to finish the 2013 season, then headed back there for 2014. While his elite defensive skills distinguish him from other catchers his age, his bat needs to find another gear to allow him to contribute to a big league lineup. Hedges hit .250/.300/.400 in 220 at-bats during the first half of 2014 as a 21-year-old catcher at Double-A, and he looked for all the world like a future impact player. His production trailed off drastically in the second half, however, as he collapsed his back side and began swinging uphill, possibly as he wore down in the Texas heat under the strain of catching 106 games. When he's going well, Hedges employs a straightaway, line-drive hitting approach without an excessive number of strikeouts, and he could one day hit .260 with solid power production. Evaluators rave about Hedges' catch-and-throw skills, quick release

BA GRADE
55 Risk: High

LGE	PA	BB%	SO%	ISO
TL	457	5.0	19.5	.096

and agility behind the plate. He's a plus receiver who blocks balls in the dirt adeptly with strong hands, and his plus arm and smooth footwork helped him gun down 38 percent of basestealers in 2014. Hedges will advance to Triple-A El Paso in 2015, and if he benefits from the confidence boost that hitting in the Pacific Coast League can bestow, he could be in line for a second-half callup to San Diego.

Year	Club (League)	Class	AVG	G	AB	R	H	2B	3B	HR	RBI	BB	SO	SB	CS	OBP	SLG
2012	Fort Wayne (MWL)	LoA	.279	96	337	44	94	28	0	10	56	23	62	14	9	.334	.451
2013	Lake Elsinore (CAL)	HiA	.270	66	233	34	63	22	1	4	30	22	45	5	4	.343	.425
	San Antonio (TL)	AA	.224	20	67	4	15	3	0	0	8	6	9	3	1	.297	.269
2014	San Antonio (TL)	AA	.225	113	427	31	96	19	2	6	44	23	89	1	3	.268	.321
Minor League Totals			.251	304	1090	116	274	73	3	21	142	81	209	24	17	.311	.382

6 MAX FRIED, LHP

Born: Jan. 18, 1994. **B-T:** L-L. **Ht.:** 6-4. **Wt.:** 185. **Drafted:** HS—Studio City, Calif., 2012 (1st round). **Signed by:** Brent Mayne.

Fried and Harvard-Westlake High teammate Lucas Giolito become the seventh pair of prep teammates to be selected in the first round of the same draft in 2012. Now he and the Nationals' No. 1 prospect are linked for another reason after Fried had Tommy John surgery in late August 2014, almost exactly two years after Giolito had the same procedure. Fried came down with forearm soreness in spring training 2014 and didn't make his first appearance until July 3, when he began a rehab assignment. Five abbreviated, ineffective starts later and he was done for the year, with scouts seeing little trace of the same pitcher who showed promise at low Class A Fort Wayne in 2013. Fried has room to grow into his 6-foot-4 frame and possibly add to his 90-92 mph fastball that has topped out at 95 in pro ball. He shows uncommon feel for a power curveball with plus, 12-to-6 action and serious strikeout potential. Even when healthy in 2013, Fried had not mastered a changeup or thrown enough strikes (4.3 walks per nine innings)

BA GRADE

60 Risk: Extreme

LGE	BF	SO%	BB%	HR/9
AZL	26	30.8	11.5	0.00
MWL	24	8.3	8.3	1.59

to maximize his stuff. The Padres commend Fried for fully committing to his Tommy John rehab regimen and expect him to be ready to pitch in games late in the 2015 season. With two potential plus pitches and an average third, he has a ceiling of No. 2 starter, though his spotty pro performance record and elbow surgery enhance his risk significantly.

Year	Club (League)	Class	W	L	ERA	G	GS	CG	SV	IP	H	HR	BB	SO	K/9	WHIP	AVG
2012	Padres (AZL)	R	0	1	3.57	10	9	0	0	18	14	1	6	17	8.7	1.13	.215
2013	Fort Wayne (MWL)	LoA	6	7	3.49	23	23	0	0	119	107	7	56	100	7.6	1.37	.249
2014	Padres (AZL)	R	0	0	5.40	3	3	0	0	5	8	0	3	8	14.4	2.20	.348
	Fort Wayne (MWL)	LoA	0	1	4.76	2	2	0	0	6	7	1	2	2	3.2	1.59	.318
Minor League Totals			6	9	3.61	38	37	0	0	147	136	9	67	127	7.8	1.38	.252

7 CORY SPANGENBERG, 2B/OF

Born: March 16, 1991. **B-T:** L-R. **Ht.:** 6-0. **Wt.:** 195. **Drafted:** Indian River (Fla.) JC, 2011 (1st round). **Signed by:** Willie Bosque.

Spangenberg missed large swaths of the 2012 and 2014 seasons while suffering from concussions and their aftereffects, but he returned to Double-A San Antonio in fine form in the second half of 2014, hitting .343 in 54 games to earn a September callup to San Diego. Drafted 10th overall in 2011 on the basis of his feel to hit (.296 career minor league average) and blazing speed, he added versatility to his game by starting at four positions in 2014. Spangenberg's bat still profiles best at second base, but his rigid infield actions and fringe-average arm make him an imperfect fit. His glove has come a long way in the past two seasons, however, to the point where scouts think he's now playable at the keystone, but he also started games in center field, left field and at third base in 2014. Spangenberg hits from a wide stance, and when he keeps his hips back, he excels at lining the ball to both gaps, while occasionally dropping down a drag bunt. His double-plus speed down the line ensures that he will hit for average so long as he makes

BA GRADE

50 Risk: Medium

LGE	PA	BB%	SO%	ISO
TL	304	4.9	20.7	.139
NL	65	3.1	21.5	.161

enough contact and keeps the ball out of the air. His swing isn't geared for power, so more than a handful of home runs per year would be a surprise. Spangerberg has tools that will play in the big leagues, though he has just enough shortcomings that he might be best suited to a multi-positional role on a contender. For example, he could serve as a lefthanded-hitting complement to second baseman Jedd Gyorko in 2015.

Year	Club (League)	Class	AVG	G	AB	R	H	2B	3B	HR	RBI	BB	SO	SB	CS	OBP	SLG
2012	Lake Elsinore (CAL)	HiA	.271	98	384	53	104	12	8	1	40	26	72	27	9	.324	.352
2013	Lake Elsinore (CAL)	HiA	.296	54	226	33	67	13	6	4	31	23	51	17	3	.364	.460
	San Antonio (TL)	AA	.289	76	287	35	83	10	3	2	20	17	61	19	11	.365	.366
2014	Padres (AZL)	R	.167	2	6	3	1	0	1	0	2	2	0	0	0	.375	.500
	Eugene (NWL)	SS	.200	6	25	3	5	0	1	0	2	0	6	2	0	.200	.280
	San Antonio (TL)	AA	.331	66	281	38	93	17	8	2	22	15	63	14	9	.365	.470
	San Diego (NL)	MAJ	.290	20	62	7	18	2	1	2	9	2	14	4	2	.313	.452
Major League Totals			.290	20	62	7	18	2	1	2	9	2	14	4	2	.313	.452
Minor League Totals			.296	374	1484	220	440	69	28	12	161	128	310	104	40	.356	.405

8 RYMER LIRIANO, OF

Born: June 20, 1991. **B-T:** R-R. **Ht.:** 6-0. **Wt.:** 230. **Signed:** Dominican Republic, 2007. **Signed by:** Randy Smith/Felix Francisco.

Best power hitter. Best outfield arm. Most exciting player. Liriano has worn many crowns in the Padres system since signing for $300,000 in 2007, but until mid-August 2014 he had never played a game in the big leagues. He missed the entire 2013 season after having Tommy John surgery during spring training, but he showed no ill effects in 2014, producing his best season since Rookie ball by hitting .291/.362/.473 in 115 games, mostly at Double-A San Antonio. Built like a linebacker, Liriano has intriguing raw tools and an increasingly good idea how to put them to use, particularly his power, speed and arm strength. Between the minors and majors, he set career highs in 2014 with 15 home runs and 16 outfield assists, while stealing at least 20 bases for the fourth straight season. Liriano has the bat speed to drive any fastball out to any field, but his inability to resist offspeed pitches keeps his strikeout rate high and impedes his ability to hit for average, which should be a below-average tool for him. While not a blazer out of the batter's box, he has plus speed underway, a trait that gives him at least average range in right field. His plus arm plays up because of its accuracy. Liriano will spend most of 2015 gaining experience at Triple-A El Paso, which will give San Diego a better idea whether he profiles best as a complementary player or a run-producing corner bat.

BA GRADE
55 Risk: High

LGE	PA	BB%	SO%	ISO
TL	415	8.4	24.6	.178
NL	121	7.4	32.2	.046

Year	Club (League)	Class	AVG	G	AB	R	H	2B	3B	HR	RBI	BB	SO	SB	CS	OBP	SLG
2012	Lake Elsinore (CAL)	HiA	.298	74	282	41	84	22	2	5	41	21	69	22	7	.360	.443
	San Antonio (TL)	AA	.251	53	183	24	46	10	2	3	20	20	50	10	1	.335	.377
2013	Did not play—Injured																
2014	San Antonio (TL)	AA	.264	99	371	55	98	20	2	14	53	35	102	17	7	.335	.442
	El Paso (PCL)	AAA	.452	16	62	14	28	11	1	0	13	8	14	3	1	.521	.661
	San Diego (NL)	MAJ	.220	38	109	13	24	2	0	1	6	9	39	4	1	.289	.266
Major League Totals			.220	38	109	13	24	2	0	1	6	9	39	4	1	.289	.266
Minor League Totals			.274	607	2278	360	625	141	25	54	314	212	620	172	60	.342	.429

9 ZACH EFLIN, RHP

LARRY GOREN

Born: April 8, 1994. **B-T:** R-R. **Ht.:** 6-4. **Wt.:** 200. **Drafted:** HS—Oviedo, Fla., 2012 (1st round supplemental). **Signed by:** Willie Bosque.

Eflin pitches to his strengths like few pitchers his age. While many of his contemporaries have better raw stuff, the 2012 prep supplemental first-rounder has ranked among his league's leaders in ERA and walk rate in each of his two full seasons. After winning the low Class A Midwest League ERA title in 2013 (2.73), he ranked third in the California League in ERA (3.80) and fifth in walk rate (2.2 per nine innings) at high Class A Lake Elsinore in 2014. Eflin generates good downhill plane from a mature, 6-foot-4 frame, and he typically sits 90-92 mph with riding, sinking life to his arm side, while bumping 95 when he elevates his four-seamer. He keeps the ball on the ground by locating his pitches down in the zone, changing speeds and throwing a plus, low-80s changeup to any batter in any count. If Eflin had a reliable third pitch, he probably would have a higher strikeout rate, but his fringe-average cutter/slider hybrid doesn't typically fool batters with its minimal vertical break. Scouts see Eflin filling a big league role, with a ceiling of a durable No. 4 starter, because he commands the strike zone and works efficiently. Those same attributes make him less risky than other starters in his peer group, and he's ready for Double-A in 2015.

BA GRADE
50 Risk: Medium

LGE	BF	SO%	BB%	HR/9
CAL	536	17.4	5.8	0.63

Year	Club (League)	Class	W	L	ERA	G	GS	CG	SV	IP	H	HR	BB	SO	K/9	WHIP	AVG
2012	Padres (AZL)	R	0	1	7.71	4	3	0	0	7	9	0	3	4	5.1	1.71	.300
2013	Fort Wayne (MWL)	LoA	7	6	2.73	22	22	0	0	119	110	7	31	86	6.5	1.19	.239
2014	Lake Elsinore (CAL)	HiA	10	7	3.80	24	24	0	0	128	138	9	31	93	6.5	1.32	.281
Minor League Totals			17	14	3.41	50	49	0	0	254	257	16	65	183	6.5	1.27	.262

10 JACE PETERSON, SS/2B

Born: May 9, 1990. **B-T:** L-R. **Ht.:** 6-0. **Wt.:** 210. **Drafted:** McNeese State, 2011 (1st round supplemental). **Signed by:** Kevin Ellis.

BA GRADE
50 Risk: Medium

LGE	PA	BB%	SO%	ISO
TL	83	10.8	10.8	.081
PCL	299	14.0	16.7	.157

Until abruptly breaking the pattern in 2014, the Padres had moved Peterson methodically through the system, giving the former McNeese State shortstop/defensive back time to adjust to each new level. When San Diego needed a replacement for injured third baseman Chase Headley in April 2014, however, it called up Peterson from Double-A San Antonio, even though he had played exclusively shortstop in pro ball. While Peterson failed to hit during four stints with the Padres in 2014, going 6-for-53 (.113), he turned in a fine season at Triple-A El Paso, showing his trademark strike-zone discipline, barrel control and straightaway hitting approach. His simple, quick, lefthanded stroke and on-base ability will allow his hit tool to play near average, though his power will play only to the gaps. He sees the ball well against lefthanders and should not require a platoon partner. Peterson played plenty of second and third base at Triple-A and in the Arizona Fall League, and his average range, speed and arm strength would play better at those positions than at shortstop. Peterson has no carrying tool, but neither does he have a glaring weakness, and he profiles as a starting second baseman in the majors, possibly as soon as 2015.

Year	Club (League)	Class	AVG	G	AB	R	H	2B	3B	HR	RBI	BB	SO	SB	CS	OBP	SLG
2012	Fort Wayne (MWL)	LoA	.286	117	444	78	127	23	9	2	48	62	63	51	13	.378	.392
2013	Lake Elsinore (CAL)	HiA	.303	113	423	78	128	17	13	7	66	54	58	42	10	.382	.454
2014	San Antonio (TL)	AA	.311	18	74	10	23	3	0	1	7	9	9	4	3	.386	.392
	San Diego (NL)	MAJ	.113	27	53	3	6	0	0	0	0	2	18	2	0	.161	.113
	El Paso (PCL)	AAA	.306	68	248	44	76	21	6	2	39	42	50	12	6	.406	.464
Major League Totals			.113	27	53	3	6	0	0	0	0	2	18	2	0	.161	.113
Minor League Totals			.287	389	1465	258	421	73	33	14	187	217	233	148	42	.381	.411

11 R.J. ALVAREZ, RHP

Born: June 8, 1991. **B-T:** R-R. **Ht.:** 6-1. **Wt.:** 200. **Drafted:** Florida Atlantic, 2012 (3rd round). **Signed by:** Ralph Reyes (Angels).

BA GRADE
45 Risk: Low

An Angels third-round pick in 2012, Alvarez has had no trouble adjusting to pro ball, logging 13.4 strikeouts per nine innings, giving up two home runs and allowing a .197 opponent average through 98 minor league appearances. He didn't allow a run at Double-A Arkansas during the first half of 2014, though he also missed a month with a sore elbow. Not long after his return in late June, Alvarez joined the Padres—along with Taylor Lindsey, Elliot Morris and Jose Rondon—in the trade that sent Huston Street to the Angels. Alvarez works with two plus pitches that played against big league batters during a September callup in 2014. He averages 95 mph on his fastball and backs it with a two-plane, mid-80s slider that consistently stymies righthanders, who hit .117 against him in 2014 and .140 the year before. He throws a changeup infrequently, though like his control it grades as below-average because of a max-effort delivery that finishes with limbs flying in seemingly every direction. Alvarez profiles as a quality big league setup man, though he could close if he can lower his walk rate. He's big league ready.

Year	Club (League)	Class	W	L	ERA	G	GS	CG	SV	IP	H	HR	BB	SO	K/9	WHIP	AVG
2012	Cedar Rapids (MWL)	LoA	3	2	3.29	23	0	0	0	27	22	2	11	38	12.5	1.21	.216
2013	Inland Empire (CAL)	HiA	4	2	2.96	37	2	0	4	49	34	2	27	79	14.6	1.25	.191
2014	Arkansas (TL)	AA	0	0	0.33	21	0	0	1	27	13	0	10	38	12.7	0.85	.149
	San Antonio (TL)	AA	0	1	2.76	17	0	0	6	16	16	0	3	23	12.7	1.16	.250
	San Diego (NL)	MAJ	0	0	1.13	10	0	0	0	8	3	0	5	9	10.1	1.00	.115
Major League Totals			0	0	1.13	10	0	0	0	8	3	0	5	9	10.1	1.00	.115
Minor League Totals			7	5	2.41	98	2	0	11	119	85	4	51	178	13.4	1.14	.197

12 FERNANDO PEREZ, 2B/3B

Born: Sept. 13, 1993. **B-T:** L-R. **Ht.:** 6-0. **Wt.:** 210. **Drafted:** Central Arizona JC, 2012 (3rd round). **Signed by:** Dave Lottsfeldt.

BA GRADE
55 Risk: High

Perez injured his thumb during 2013 spring training and endured a lost year at short-season Eugene when he returned, but he's still right where he needs to be. He graduated high school a year early and attended Central Arizona JC in 2012, hitting .338 as an 18-year-old in a wood-bat conference. The Padres pounced on Perez in the third round of the 2012 draft, and two years later he's making them look smart. He tracks the ball well out of the pitcher's hand and has a knack for barreling the ball, with a picturesque lefthanded swing that delivers power to all fields. He ranked fourth in the low Class A Midwest League with 18 home runs and led the circuit with 95 RBIs in 2014. Scouts project Perez to be a plus hitter with at least average power production. He doesn't run well, and he lacks the lateral quickness to profile at second base, where he spent the most time in 2014, but his average arm will play at third base and his bat could possibly profile at first base. Look for Perez to move to high Class A Lake Elsinore in 2015.

Year	Club (League)	Class	AVG	G	AB	R	H	2B	3B	HR	RBI	BB	SO	SB	CS	OBP	SLG
2012	Padres (AZL)	R	.273	14	55	6	15	2	1	2	16	2	17	1	0	.298	.455
2013	Padres (AZL)	R	.417	4	12	3	5	1	0	1	4	1	2	0	0	.462	.750
	Eugene (NWL)	SS	.213	59	211	15	45	9	1	3	27	15	68	0	1	.270	.308
2014	Fort Wayne (MWL)	LoA	.284	116	469	69	133	24	1	18	95	25	106	3	2	.322	.454
Minor League Totals			.265	193	747	93	198	36	3	24	142	43	193	4	3	.308	.418

13 MICHAEL GETTYS, OF

BA GRADE

55 Risk: Extreme

Born: Oct. 22, 1995. **B-T:** R-R. **Ht.:** 6-1. **Wt.:** 203. **Drafted:** HS— Gainesville, Ga., 2014 (2nd round). **Signed by:** Andrew Salvo.

Gettys entered the 2014 season with first-round helium, but a poor showing at the National High School Invitational left such an impression on scouting directors that he fell to the Padres at No. 51 overall in the second round. San Diego signed him for $1.3 million, then watched the athletic center fielder lead the Rookie-level Arizona League with 66 hits and rank second with 93 total bases. Gettys tempers excitement about his hitting potential with a high strikeout rate—28 percent in 2014—but few players generate the same kind of exit velocity off the bat. Hitting for above-average power should only be a matter of adding loft and backspin to his swing, which many believe will come with maturity. Gettys records double-plus run times in the 60-yeard dash, and he has a cannon of an arm that will play at any position. His speed, first-step quickness and nose for the ball serve him well as a plus defender in center field. A power/speed threat who might be the best athlete from his draft class, Gettys has tantalizing upside, which he will unlock if he enhances his pitch recognition and contact skills at low Class A Fort Wayne in 2015.

Year	Club (League)	Class	AVG	G	AB	R	H	2B	3B	HR	RBI	BB	SO	SB	CS	OBP	SLG
2014	Padres (AZL)	R	.310	52	213	29	66	8	5	3	38	15	66	14	2	.353	.437
Minor League Totals			.310	52	213	29	66	8	5	3	38	15	66	14	2	.353	.437

14 JOSE RONDON, SS

BA GRADE

50 Risk: High

Born: March 3, 1994. **B-T:** R-R. **Ht.:** 6-1. **Wt.:** 160. **Signed:** Venezuela, 2011. **Signed by:** Lebi Ochoa/Carlos Ramirez (Angels).

The Angels jumped Rondon from the Rookie-level Pioneer League in 2013 to high Class A Inland Empire in 2014, and the 20-year-old shortstop didn't miss a beat, hitting .319/.365/.409 to rank fourth in the California League batting race. He joined the Padres—along with R.J. Alvarez, Taylor Lindsey and Elliot Morris—in a mid-July deal that sent Huston Street to the Angels. Though not flashy, Rondon has at least average range to both sides, with the sure hands and the average, accurate arm to play shortstop passably in the majors. Outside of bat control, he has no outstanding offensive skill, with well below-average power and a contact-oriented, line-drive approach that could make him an average hitter. He's also a fringe-average runner who could lose a half step. Rondon probably would be stretched as a regular shortstop on a contender, though his attributes would seem to make him a fine utility candidate if he can learn to play second and third base. Double-A San Antonio will be the next step in 2015.

Year	Club (League)	Class	AVG	G	AB	R	H	2B	3B	HR	RBI	BB	SO	SB	CS	OBP	SLG
2012	Angels (AZL)	R	.260	48	192	26	50	13	2	1	20	14	24	5	5	.314	.365
	Orem (PIO)	R	.300	6	20	4	6	1	1	0	1	2	3	1	0	.348	.450
2013	Orem (PIO)	R	.293	68	276	45	81	22	2	1	50	30	31	13	8	.359	.399
2014	Angels (AZL)	R	.125	2	8	3	1	0	0	0	0	1	0	2	1	.300	.125
	Inland Empire (CAL)	HiA	.327	72	297	40	97	17	5	0	24	17	50	8	6	.362	.418
	Lake Elsinore (CAL)	HiA	.301	37	136	18	41	9	0	1	12	13	23	3	1	.371	.390
Minor League Totals			.300	282	1094	164	328	73	12	3	128	94	147	41	25	.356	.397

15 JAKE BAUERS, 1B

BA GRADE

50 Risk: High

Born: Oct. 6, 1995. **B-T:** L-L. **Ht.:** 6-1. **Wt.:** 195. **Drafted:** HS— Huntington Beach, Calif., 2013 (7th round). **Signed by:** Josh Emmerick.

Hailing from the same Marina High program as Daric Barton, Bauers draws natural comparison with the long-time Athletics first baseman for his patient approach, lefthanded bat, fine defensive play and below-average power. A seventh-round pick in 2013, Bauers began 2014 in extended spring training before joining low Class A Fort Wayne in late April. He proceeded to hit .362 through the first half, but he regressed badly in the second. Bauers has power to his pull side, but his swing doesn't produce the loft or backspin for true power to all fields. Plus, his thick lower half and maxed-out frame leave little room to project physical gains. Bauers exercises advanced plate discipline, and he hits various pitch types with a direct-to-the-ball bat path, so he should continue to hit for average. He's also a smooth defender with an average arm. While he comes up short in some areas, Bauers possesses the all-important feel to hit, and he looks like a future second-division regular who will move up to high Class A in 2015.

Year	Club (League)	Class	AVG	G	AB	R	H	2B	3B	HR	RBI	BB	SO	SB	CS	OBP	SLG
2013	Padres (AZL)	R	.282	47	163	22	46	8	2	1	25	14	31	2	0	.341	.374
2014	Fort Wayne (MWL)	LoA	.296	112	406	59	120	18	3	8	64	51	80	5	6	.376	.414
Minor League Totals			.292	159	569	81	166	26	5	9	89	65	111	7	6	.366	.402

16 MALLEX SMITH, OF

BA GRADE

50 Risk: High

Born: May 6, 1993. **B-T:** L-R. **Ht.:** 5-9. **Wt.:** 170. **Drafted:** Santa Fe (Fla.) JC, 2012 (5th round). **Signed by:** Willie Bosque.

Another half-season at low Class A Fort Wayne was just what speedster Smith needed in 2014 to establish himself as a potential leadoff man of the future. A 5-foot-9 lefthanded hitter with at least double-plus speed, he boosted his average by 30 points year over year in the Midwest League to earn a second-half bump to high Class A Lake Elsinore in 2014. Smith put his incredible speed to good use with a minor league-leading 88 stolen bases and a focus on bunting for hits. He also led the field by being caught stealing 26 times, and his 77 percent success rate ranked middle of the road for players with at least 20 steals in 2014. With bottom-of-the-scale power, Smith must continue to make more contact, but at age 21 he already controls the strike zone fairly well, for his 69 walks ranked 11th in the minors in 2014. Most scouts see him as an average center fielder, despite his speed, and his arm plays as below-average. Smith's physique and tools earn him comparisons with the Royals' Jarrod Dyson, and that's a reasonable ceiling for him to aim for as he tastes Double-A for the first time in 2015.

Year	Club (League)	Class	AVG	G	AB	R	H	2B	3B	HR	RBI	BB	SO	SB	CS	OBP	SLG
2012	Padres (AZL)	R	.344	25	96	23	33	2	1	1	10	5	19	13	3	.379	.417
	Eugene (NWL)	SS	.188	10	32	6	6	0	0	1	5	6	8	4	1	.333	.281
2013	Fort Wayne (MWL)	LoA	.262	110	424	81	111	17	2	4	29	59	84	64	16	.367	.340
2014	Fort Wayne (MWL)	LoA	.295	65	254	56	75	13	6	0	15	38	55	48	16	.393	.394
	Lake Elsinore (CAL)	HiA	.327	55	223	43	73	16	1	5	16	31	48	40	10	.414	.475
Minor League Totals			.290	265	1029	209	298	48	10	11	75	139	214	169	46	.383	.388

17 CASEY KELLY, RHP

BA GRADE

55 Risk: Extreme

Born: Oct. 4, 1989. **B-T:** R-R. **Ht.:** 6-3. **Wt.:** 210. **Drafted:** HS—Sarasota, Fla., 2008 (1st round). **Signed by:** Anthony Turco (Red Sox).

Kelly still showed the pitch quality in 2014 that has made him a six-time Top 10 Prospect. The trouble for him is that his pitch *quantity* has been lacking since he made 27 starts at Double-A San Antonio in 2011. He rocketed to the majors in 2012, the year he first encountered elbow soreness, but then he missed all of 2013 after having Tommy John surgery in spring training. More elbow trouble limited him to just four starts in 2014, and he has totaled 87 innings in the past three seasons. However, Kelly still tantalizes scouts with three above-average pitches that all play up to plus at various times. He generates big sink and running action on a 92-93 mph fastball that batters struggle to lift, and he backs up his heater with a sharp, down-breaking curveball and a changeup that plays well off his sinker. Kelly needs only to regain the same health he showed early in his career to reach his ceiling as a No. 3 starter. The Padres aren't counting on him in 2015, but he's still talented, and he's still on the 40-man roster.

Year	Club (League)	Class	W	L	ERA	G	GS	CG	SV	IP	H	HR	BB	SO	K/9	WHIP	AVG
2012	Tucson (PCL)	AAA	0	0	2.25	2	2	0	0	12	12	0	0	14	10.5	1.00	.261
	Padres (AZL)	R	0	1	4.00	3	3	0	0	9	10	0	0	7	7.0	1.11	.250
	San Antonio (TL)	AA	0	1	3.78	3	3	0	0	17	11	1	3	18	9.7	0.84	.190
	San Diego (NL)	MAJ	2	3	6.21	6	6	0	0	29	39	5	10	26	8.1	1.69	.322
2013	Did not play—Injured																
2014	Lake Elsinore (CAL)	HiA	0	0	4.32	2	2	0	0	8	14	0	0	9	9.7	1.68	.400
	San Antonio (TL)	AA	1	0	0.75	2	2	0	0	12	11	0	1	8	6.0	1.00	.250
Major League Totals			2	3	6.21	6	6	0	0	29	39	5	10	26	8.1	1.69	.322
Minor League Totals			22	18	3.69	77	77	0	0	390	394	23	101	316	7.3	1.27	.263

18 ELLIOT MORRIS, RHP

BA GRADE

50 Risk: High

Born: April 26, 1992. **B-T:** R-R. **Ht.:** 6-4. **Wt.:** 210. **Drafted:** Pierce (Wash.) JC, 2013 (4th round). **Signed by:** Jason Ellison (Angels).

Morris lost his sophomore year at Pierce (Wash.) JC to Tommy John surgery, but he returned in strong fashion in 2013 to become the Angels' fourth-round pick that year. Los Angeles traded him to the Padres a year later in the six-player trade that sent Huston Street to the Angels. A big-bodied, 6-foot-4 right-hander with arm strength, Morris throws three average to a tick above pitches and keeps the ball off the barrel, allowing opponents to hit just .216 in 2014. He pitches with a solid-average, 91-93 mph fastball and the ability to work both sides of the plate, and he can reach 95 when he needs it. His slider and changeup could play to solid-average with continued refinement, and he generated his fair share of swings and misses with both pitches in 2014. Improved control would move Morris up the list, but as is, he's a potential No. 4 starter who will tackle Double-A competition at San Antonio in 2015.

Year	Club (League)	Class	W	L	ERA	G	GS	CG	SV	IP	H	HR	BB	SO	K/9	WHIP	AVG
2013	Orem (PIO)	R	2	2	3.95	11	2	0	0	27	29	1	11	25	8.2	1.46	.279
2014	Burlington (MWL)	LoA	2	1	2.25	8	7	0	0	40	29	2	13	44	9.9	1.05	.200
	Inland Empire (CAL)	HiA	3	3	4.17	9	9	0	0	45	37	5	28	40	7.9	1.43	.220
	Lake Elsinore (CAL)	HiA	3	3	3.56	8	8	0	0	48	40	7	11	33	6.2	1.06	.226
Minor League Totals			10	9	3.47	36	26	0	0	161	135	15	63	142	8.0	1.23	.227

19 FRANCHY CORDERO, SS

BA GRADE

55 Risk: Extreme

Born: Sept. 2, 1994. **B-T:** L-R. **Ht.:** 6-3. **Wt.:** 175. **Signed:** Dominican Republic, 2011. **Signed by:** Felix Feliz/Jose Salado/Randy Smith.

Cordero's batting potential electrified scouts in 2013, when he led the Rookie-level Arizona League in slugging (.511). Much of that goodwill evaporated in 2014 when acute throwing problems led to 51 errors in 55 games at shortstop. Cordero hit just .188 in 24 games at low Class A Fort Wayne in 2014 before being reassigned to extended spring training in late April. He regrouped at short-season Eugene in the second half, showing above-average power—his nine homers tied for third in the Northwest League—but also a long swing that contributed to a strikeout rate of 29 percent. His present strength and frequent hard contact give him a chance to hit at least .250 with solid-average power if he reaches his ceiling. He runs well for his size, but despite a strong arm, his poor footwork, hard hands and scatter arm could move him to third base or, just as likely, right field. Cordero will try the Midwest League again in 2015.

Year	Club (League)	Class	AVG	G	AB	R	H	2B	3B	HR	RBI	BB	SO	SB	CS	OBP	SLG
2012	Padres (DSL)	R	.270	61	230	39	62	9	6	1	38	37	73	14	4	.372	.374
2013	Padres (AZL)	R	.333	35	141	23	47	4	6	3	17	10	33	11	0	.381	.511
2014	Fort Wayne (MWL)	LoA	.188	22	85	5	16	2	1	0	9	4	36	3	3	.237	.235
	Eugene (NWL)	SS	.279	61	240	40	67	8	4	9	35	14	75	13	5	.329	.458
Minor League Totals			.276	179	696	107	192	23	17	13	99	65	217	41	12	.343	.414

20 TAYLOR LINDSEY, 2B

BA GRADE

45 Risk: Medium

Born: Dec. 2, 1991. **B-T:** L-R. **Ht.:** 6-0. **Wt.:** 195. **Drafted:** HS—Scottsdale, Ariz., 2010 (1st round supplemental). **Signed by:** John Gracio (Angels).

The Angels, headed by scouting director Eddie Bane, evaluated Lindsey higher than the field when they selected him with the 37th overall pick in 2010. Los Angeles' new front office didn't value Lindsey to the same degree, so they didn't hesitate to trade the organization's preseason No. 1 prospect to the Padres in the July 2014 trade that brought them Huston Street. Lindsey makes frequent contact from an upright, lefthanded stance, driving the ball only to his pull side. A below-average runner, he projects to have an average feel to hit and below-average power production. He doesn't excite scouts with his defensive potential at second base, showing only enough range for the routine play and a below-average arm. He could play every day for a second-division team, but only if he hits in his second try at Triple-A in 2015.

Year	Club (League)	Class	AVG	G	AB	R	H	2B	3B	HR	RBI	BB	SO	SB	CS	OBP	SLG
2012	Inland Empire (CAL)	HiA	.289	134	547	79	158	26	6	9	58	29	66	8	6	.328	.408
2013	Arkansas (TL)	AA	.274	134	508	68	139	22	6	17	56	48	91	4	4	.339	.441
2014	Angels (AZL)	R	.333	1	3	1	1	0	0	0	1	0	0	0	0	.500	.333
	Orem (PIO)	R	.200	1	5	0	1	1	0	0	1	0	0	0	0	.200	.400
	Salt Lake (PCL)	AAA	.247	75	295	50	73	13	4	8	30	31	44	7	2	.323	.400
	El Paso (PCL)	AAA	.219	41	146	18	32	6	1	2	17	9	15	0	2	.270	.315
Minor League Totals			.284	494	1988	306	564	108	29	45	226	143	295	37	21	.335	.435

21 DUSTIN PETERSON, 3B

Born: Sept. 10, 1994. **B-T:** R-R. **Ht.:** 6-2. **Wt.:** 180. **Drafted:** HS—
Gilbert, Ariz., 2013 (2nd round). **Signed by:** Dave Lottsfeldt.

Peterson, the younger brother of Mariners prospect D.J., led all low Class A Midwest League third basemen with 38 errors in 2014, while at the plate his production fell off a cliff after a hot start. He whips the bat through the zone with quick hands and regularly imparts backspin on the ball, which gives him above-average raw power. However, Peterson's over-aggressive approach leads to a lot of weak contact, and he hit just .199 in 61 second-half games in 2014. Scouts don't like his tentative actions or scattershot arm at third base and view him as a corner outfielder. He's a below-average runner, so Peterson's future value depends on how often he gets to his power. He would benefit from another run at low Class A in 2015.

Year	Club (League)	Class	AVG	G	AB	R	H	2B	3B	HR	RBI	BB	SO	SB	CS	OBP	SLG
2013	Padres (AZL)	R	.293	38	157	20	46	8	0	0	18	9	33	3	0	.337	.344
2014	Fort Wayne (MWL)	LoA	.233	126	527	64	123	31	3	10	79	25	137	1	3	.274	.361
Minor League Totals			.247	164	684	84	169	39	3	10	97	34	170	4	3	.288	.357

22 ALEX DICKERSON, OF/1B

Born: May 16, 1990. **B-T:** L-L. **Ht.:** 6-3. **Wt.:** 230. **Drafted:** Indiana, 2011 (3rd round). **Signed by:** Jerry Jordan (Pirates).

The Pirates traded Dickerson to the Padres following the 2013 season—for Jaff Decker and Miles Mikolas—but his Padres career got off on the wrong foot when he severely sprained his ankle during 2014 spring training, then an MRI revealed that a cyst on his left heel could jeopardize his career if left untreated. Surgery and rehab kept him out until mid-July, but Dickerson hit well enough at Double-A San Antonio when he returned to earn a spot on the 40-man roster. He stays on the ball with a balanced lefthanded swing and makes enough hard contact to project as an average hitter with fringe-average power. He's a fringe-average defender in right field with an average arm and below-average speed, making first base his best position. Dickerson has the type of bat that could be useful in a part-time role.

Year	Club (League)	Class	AVG	G	AB	R	H	2B	3B	HR	RBI	BB	SO	SB	CS	OBP	SLG
2012	Bradenton (FSL)	HiA	.295	129	488	65	144	31	3	13	90	39	93	12	7	.353	.451
2013	Altoona (EL)	AA	.288	126	451	61	130	36	3	17	68	27	89	10	7	.337	.494
2014	Eugene (NWL)	SS	.300	3	10	3	3	1	0	0	2	3	2	0	0	.462	.400
	San Antonio (TL)	AA	.321	34	137	20	44	11	2	3	24	9	28	0	1	.367	.496
Minor League Totals			.298	337	1250	177	372	96	11	36	203	94	243	22	15	.354	.478

23 BURCH SMITH, RHP

Born: April 12, 1990. **B-T:** R-R. **Ht.:** 6-4. **Wt.:** 215. **Drafted:** Oklahoma, 2011 (14th round). **Signed by:** Lane Decker.

The Padres rushed Smith to the big leagues after just six starts at Double-A San Antonio in 2013, but his development stalled in 2014 when he made two April starts, then missed the rest of the year with a forearm injury. He lacked the same zip on his pitches he had shown in 2013, when he regularly sat in the mid-90s. Smith still sits at 92 mph and can reach 95 with armside life, though now his below-average curveball looks even loopier, and he focuses more on throwing a sinker and changeup to complement his heat. Smith's physical 6-foot-4 frame and history of throwing strikes will keep him in the rotation—likely at Triple-A—for now, but his stuff probably would play up in a relief role.

Year	Club (League)	Class	W	L	ERA	G	GS	CG	SV	IP	H	HR	BB	SO	K/9	WHIP	AVG
2012	Lake Elsinore (CAL)	HiA	9	6	3.85	26	26	0	0	129	127	11	27	137	9.6	1.20	.256
2013	San Antonio (TL)	AA	1	2	1.15	6	6	0	0	31	17	1	6	37	10.6	0.73	.155
	Tucson (PCL)	AAA	5	1	3.39	12	12	0	0	61	56	4	17	65	9.6	1.20	.246
	San Diego (NL)	MAJ	1	3	6.44	10	7	0	0	36	39	9	21	46	11.4	1.65	.269
2014	El Paso (PCL)	AAA	0	2	18.56	2	2	0	0	5	13	2	5	3	5.1	3.38	.481
Major League Totals			1	3	6.44	10	7	0	0	36	39	9	21	46	11.4	1.65	.269
Minor League Totals			15	11	3.71	48	46	0	1	228	216	18	56	246	9.7	1.19	.248

24 RYAN BUTLER, RHP

Born: Feb. 23, 1992. **B-T:** R-R. **Ht.:** 6-4. **Wt.:** 225. **Drafted:** Charlotte, 2014 (7th round). **Signed by:** Tyler Stubblefield.

Butler pitched sparingly at Marshall in 2011 and not at all for Northwest Florida State JC in 2012 before having Tommy John surgery and missing 2013. He returned to make 13 starts for Charlotte in 2014, showing velocity up to 97 mph, and he signed with the Padres for $186,900 as a seventh-round pick. San Diego shifted him to the bullpen, and he breezed to low Class A Fort Wayne in July on the strength of a heavy fastball that peaked at 101 mph and sat at 97-98. Butler throws a fringe-average changeup to lefthanders, but he's working to tighten a below-average slider to keep hitters honest.

Year	Club (League)	Class	W	L	ERA	G	GS	CG	SV	IP	H	HR	BB	SO	K/9	WHIP	AVG
2014	Eugene (NWL)	SS	0	0	8.22	5	0	0	1	8	12	0	3	6	7.0	1.96	.375
	Fort Wayne (MWL)	LoA	1	1	0.83	18	0	0	10	22	17	0	6	30	12.5	1.06	.215
Minor League Totals			1	1	2.76	23	0	0	11	29	29	0	9	36	11.0	1.30	.261

25 LEONEL CAMPOS, RHP

BA GRADE
45 Risk: High

Born: July 17, 1987. **B-T:** R-R. **Ht.:** 6-3. **Wt.:** 185. **Signed:** Venezuela, 2010. **Signed by:** Yfrain Linares.

Campos signed at age 23 then had Tommy John surgery after making his first pro appearance in 2011. He returned in fine form in 2013, reaching Double-A San Antonio and striking out 106 batters in 67 relief innings. Intrigued by his athletic delivery, plus fastball and feel for two secondary pitches, the Padres tried Campos as a starter 14 times at San Antonio in 2014, though he produced a 6.61 ERA. He saws off righthanders with a riding mid-90s fastball that can touch 98 mph out of the pen, while throwing a mid-80s slider that regularly flashes plus and operates as a chase pitch. That he throws a mid-80s changeup that flashes average is a testament to his athleticism and delivery. Campos worked as a reliever at Triple-A El Paso and during a September callup, so that's the role he will reprise in 2015.

Year	Club (League)	Class	W	L	ERA	G	GS	CG	SV	IP	H	HR	BB	SO	K/9	WHIP	AVG
2012	Did not play—Injured																
2013	Fort Wayne (MWL)	LoA	2	1	2.23	28	0	0	5	36	19	2	22	63	15.6	1.13	.150
	San Antonio (TL)	AA	1	0	0.88	26	0	0	2	31	14	0	16	43	12.6	0.98	.137
2014	El Paso (PCL)	AAA	0	0	11.70	11	0	0	0	10	20	2	13	13	11.7	3.30	.408
	San Antonio (TL)	AA	2	7	5.60	31	14	0	1	72	69	6	38	95	11.8	1.48	.249
	San Diego (NL)	MAJ	0	0	5.14	6	0	0	0	7	9	0	4	9	11.6	1.86	.310
Major League Totals			0	0	5.14	6	0	0	0	7	9	0	4	9	11.6	1.86	.310
Minor League Totals			5	8	4.40	97	15	0	8	151	127	11	89	218	13.0	1.43	.224

26 ZECH LEMOND, RHP

BA GRADE
45 Risk: High

Born: Oct. 9, 1992. **B-T:** R-R. **Ht.:** 6-1. **Wt.:** 170. **Drafted:** Rice, 2014 (3rd round). **Signed by:** Kevin Ellis.

Lemond moved into the Rice rotation in time for conference play as a junior in 2014, but he made just five starts before suffering from elbow inflammation. The Padres selected him in the third round that June and signed him for $600,000, and he worked mostly as a starter during his pro debut at short-season Eugene. Lemond pitches with a plus 93-94 mph fastball he locates to both sides, and he's capable of reaching back for 96. He toned down use of his above-average spike-curveball in pro ball while working on a fringe-average changeup, though a long arm action might inhibit his feel for commanding his entire repertoire. His post-draft MRI came back clean, though, so the Padres intend to keep Lemond in the rotation as he advances to high Class A Lake Elsinore in 2015.

Year	Club (League)	Class	W	L	ERA	G	GS	CG	SV	IP	H	HR	BB	SO	K/9	WHIP	AVG
2014	Eugene (NWL)	SS	2	3	3.79	11	8	0	0	38	39	1	5	32	7.6	1.16	.262
	San Antonio (TL)	AA	0	0	0.00	1	0	0	0	4	1	0	0	2	4.5	0.25	.071
Minor League Totals			2	3	3.43	12	8	0	0	42	40	1	5	34	7.3	1.07	.245

27 TAYRON GUERRERO, RHP

BA GRADE
45 Risk: High

Born: Jan. 9, 1991. **B-T:** R-R. **Ht.:** 6-7. **Wt.:** 189. **Signed:** Colombia, 2009. **Signed by:** Robert Rowley/Felix Feliz/Marcial Del Valle.

The 6-foot-7 Guerrero had sported a walk rate of 7.3 batters per nine innings in his career until 2014, when he provided a glimpse of his future potential in the first half at low Class A Fort Wayne. He struck out 42 in 36 innings while allowing opponents to hit .169 to earn a spot in the Futures Game. Guerrero tops out near 99 mph in each outing and pitches in the mid-90s with no apparent effort, though his fastball is true and his command the very definition of imprecise. Guerrero's low-80s slider flashes plus and is tough for batters on either side of the plate to handle when it nears the plate on a fastball plane with late action. His control must improve dramatically as he repeats high Class A Lake Elsinore in 2015.

Year	Club (League)	Class	W	L	ERA	G	GS	CG	SV	IP	H	HR	BB	SO	K/9	WHIP	AVG
2012	Padres (AZL)	R	1	0	1.50	5	3	0	0	12	7	0	2	6	4.5	0.75	.175
	Eugene (NWL)	SS	0	1	3.38	4	4	0	0	13	10	0	12	11	7.4	1.65	.227
2013	Fort Wayne (MWL)	LoA	0	1	7.36	4	0	0	0	4	8	0	8	4	9.8	4.36	.471
	Eugene (NWL)	SS	1	4	4.50	15	3	0	0	32	24	1	25	35	9.8	1.53	.209
2014	Fort Wayne (MWL)	LoA	6	1	1.00	25	0	0	1	36	22	2	12	42	10.5	0.94	.169
	Lake Elsinore (CAL)	HiA	0	0	2.63	14	0	0	3	14	10	1	8	14	9.2	1.32	.200
Minor League Totals			12	13	4.17	102	20	0	5	196	169	4	140	191	8.8	1.57	.236

28 KEYVIUS SAMPSON, RHP

BA GRADE

45 Risk: High

Born: Jan. 6, 1991. **B-T:** R-R. **Ht.:** 6-0. **Wt.:** 225. **Drafted:** HS—Ocala, Fla., 2009 (4th round). **Signed by:** Rob Sidwell.

On the one hand, Sampson throws three quality pitch types and still tops out near 97 mph. On the other, his performance track record at Triple-A is dreadful, thanks to poor control. The Padres shifted him to the bullpen after he ran up a 6.71 ERA through 12 starts at El Paso in 2014. His strikeout rate spiked in relief, but he didn't shake his location problems. Scouts blame a long arm swing, wrist wrap and hard-to-repeat mechanics for Sampson's poor control, but they remain interested thanks to a 93-95 mph fastball, big-breaking 12-to-6 curveball and fading mid-80s changeup. His secondary offerings play as solid-average at times, and he might thrive in the bullpen now that he no longer has to worry about pacing.

Year	Club (League)	Class	W	L	ERA	G	GS	CG	SV	IP	H	HR	BB	SO	K/9	WHIP	AVG
2012	San Antonio (TL)	AA	8	11	5.00	26	25	0	0	122	108	11	57	122	9.0	1.35	.233
2013	San Antonio (TL)	AA	10	4	2.26	19	18	0	0	103	74	9	33	110	9.6	1.04	.199
	Tucson (PCL)	AAA	2	3	7.11	9	9	0	0	38	44	5	29	25	5.9	1.92	.306
2014	El Paso (PCL)	AAA	2	5	6.68	38	14	0	0	92	91	19	68	94	9.2	1.73	.261
Minor League Totals			37	29	4.29	130	102	0	0	524	437	56	256	560	9.6	1.32	.226

29 TRAVIS JANKOWSKI, OF

BA GRADE

45 Risk: High

Born: June 15, 1991. **B-T:** L-R. **Ht.:** 6-2. **Wt.:** 190. **Drafted:** Stony Brook, 2012 (1st round supplemental). **Signed by:** Jim Bretz.

A supplemental first-round pick in 2012, Jankowski logged just 29 games at Double-A San Antonio in 2014 when a broken wrist in late April knocked him out for nearly three months. His ticket to the big leagues will be his incredible raw speed, intelligent baserunning and plus defense in center field. He can drop down a bunt at will, doesn't strike out excessively and takes a healthy number of walks, so he's always a threat to steal when he reaches first base. He is no kind of power threat, but under the right circumstances, Jankowski would fit as a fourth or fifth outfielder on a club that values speed and defense in that role, though his below-average arm would not play in right field.

Year	Club (League)	Class	AVG	G	AB	R	H	2B	3B	HR	RBI	BB	SO	SB	CS	OBP	SLG
2012	Padres (AZL)	R	.250	2	8	1	2	0	0	0	4	0	1	0	0	.222	.250
	Fort Wayne (MWL)	LoA	.282	59	238	32	67	10	4	1	23	13	44	17	7	.318	.370
2013	Lake Elsinore (CAL)	HiA	.286	122	493	89	141	19	6	1	38	54	96	71	14	.356	.355
2014	San Antonio (TL)	AA	.240	29	100	14	24	4	1	0	10	8	14	10	2	.297	.300
Minor League Totals			.275	229	904	149	249	35	11	2	80	85	164	105	24	.338	.345

30 JOHNNY BARBATO, RHP

BA GRADE

45 Risk: High

Born: July 11, 1992. **B-T:** R-R. **Ht.:** 6-2. **Wt.:** 185. **Drafted:** HS—Miami, 2010 (6th round). **Signed by:** Rob Sidwell/Bob Filotei.

A sixth-round pick out of high school, Barbato received the highest bonus ($1.4 million) of any Padres draft pick in 2010 after first-rounder Karsten Whitson did not sign. He has worked exclusively as a reliever since he entered full-season ball in 2012, and he though he has moved slowly despite the less-demanding role. Barbato might have moved more quickly in 2014 but for an elbow injury that knocked him out of action at Double-A San Antonio in mid-June. He pitches with mid-90s velocity and verve, attacking hitters with a live fastball that sinks and runs as it nears the plate. He throws a true curveball in the high 70s that features extreme break through the zone, and he locates and mixes his two pitches well enough to boast a career strikeout rate of 9.2 per nine innings. Assuming he recovers his health, Barbato has the raw stuff to zoom to San Diego in 2015 and gradually work his way up to a setup role.

Year	Club (League)	Class	W	L	ERA	G	GS	CG	SV	IP	H	HR	BB	SO	K/9	WHIP	AVG
2012	Fort Wayne (MWL)	LoA	6	1	1.84	48	0	0	3	73	52	4	31	84	10.3	1.13	.195
2013	Lake Elsinore (CAL)	HiA	3	6	5.01	49	7	0	14	88	90	8	33	89	9.1	1.40	.269
2014	San Antonio (TL)	AA	2	2	2.87	27	0	0	16	31	26	3	10	33	9.5	1.15	.226
Minor League Totals			12	13	3.79	139	20	0	33	250	220	19	105	256	9.2	1.30	.238

San Francisco Giants

BY J.J. COOPER

At times, veterans of the industry shake their heads at the Giants.

San Francisco won its third World Series title in five years in 2014, giving them one more title this decade than the Phillies or Cubs have won in well over 100 years of trying.

Those three championships have come in dramatically different ways. The 2010 team won with a lineup of veterans on the wrong side of 30, helped by homegrown regulars Buster Posey and Pablo Sandoval and an outstanding rotation fronted by Tim Lincecum and Matt Cain (along with rookie Madison Bumgarner).

It appeared to be the kind of team that would make run and quickly fall back to the pack.

That appeared to be the case in 2011, when the Giants finished out of the playoffs. But in reality, the club managed to transition into a younger team. Homegrown draft picks Brandon Belt and Brandon Crawford worked into the lineup and reclamation project Ryan Voglesong filled a need in the rotation.

So a year later, San Francisco was ready for another run. When they needed help at the trade deadline, they landed Hunter Pence and Marco Scutaro. With Vogelsong joining Cain and Bumgarner, the pitching staff was once again good enough to win it all in 2012.

By 2014, Bumgarner has become the ace, while Posey continues to be one of the best players in the game and Sandoval and Pence drive pitchers crazy. Somehow the Giants also managed to survive the losses of Cain, Angel Pagan and Scutaro to injury. This time they added in rookies Joe Panik, Juan Perez and Andrew Susac to help Posey, Sandoval, Belt and Crawford. And once again, general manager Brian Sabean made a needed move at the deadline, this time picking up Jake Peavy.

The names on the uniforms keep changing. But the names in the front office and in the dugout have remained the same. Ask people around the game for the secret of the Giants success, and they'll point to Sabean, manager Bruce Bochy and his coaching staff, vice president of player personnel Dick Tidrow, assistant GM Bobby Evans and a long list of long-time Giants scouts, coaches and front office employees.

Stability is crucial in San Francisco. For all the Giants' titles, front office executives don't leave to take bigger jobs elsewhere. Five members of Bochy's coaching staff were with him before San Francisco won its first of these three titles.

And further down the organization chart, the Giants have many of the same area scouts, crosscheckers and instructors who have been long

San Francisco won another World Series title in 2014, this time with homegrown ace Madison Bumgarner leading the way

BILL NICHOLS

TOP PROSPECTS OF THE DECADE

Year	Player, Pos.	2014 Org
2005	Matt Cain, rhp	Giants
2006	Matt Cain, rhp	Giants
2007	Tim Lincecum, rhp	Giants
2008	Angel Villalona, 1b	Giants
2009	Madison Bumgarner, lhp	Giants
2010	Buster Posey, c	Giants
2011	Brandon Belt, 1b	Giants
2012	Gary Brown, of	Giants
2013	Kyle Crick, rhp	Giants
2014	Kyle Crick, rhp	Giants

steeped in the Giants way.

Those scouts seem to find a stream of contributors, in the draft and via pro scouting. Journeyman Travis Ishikawa hit a walkoff homer to win the National League Championship Series. Minor league free agent Gregor Blanco has become an important part of the outfield puzzle. In three years at Long Beach State, Matt Duffy slugged below .300 every season. The Giants saw something and drafted him in the 18th round. He hit .332 at Double-A Richmond, earned a callup to San Francisco, scored the tying run in one playoff game and provided a key hit in another.

It's the kind of inexplicable scouting and player-development story that leads many to shake their heads. But around the game, everyone is also tipping their caps.

General manager: Brian Sabean. **Farm director:** Shane Turner. **Scouting director:** John Barr.

Class	Team	League	W	L	PCT	Finish	Manager
Majors	San Francisco Giants	National	88	74	.543	T-8th (30)	Bruce Bochy
Triple-A	*Fresno Grizzlies	Pacific Coast	68	76	.472	13th (16)	Bob Mariano
Double-A	Richmond Flying Squirrels	Eastern	79	63	.556	3rd (12)	Russ Morman
High A	San Jose Giants	California	73	67	.521	6th (10)	Lenn Sakata
Low A	Augusta GreenJackets	South Atlantic	62	76	.449	9th (14)	Mike Goff
Short season	Salem-Keizer Volcanoes	Northwest	38	38	.500	5th (8)	Gary Davenport
Rookie	AZL Giants	Arizona	34	22	.607	2nd (13)	Nestor Rojas
Overall Minor League Record			**354**	**342**	**.509**	**13th (30)**	

*Affiliate moves to Sacramento (Pacific Coast) in 2015

THIS YEAR'S TOP 30

No.	Player, Pos.	Grade
1.	Andrew Susac, c	55/Medium
2.	Tyler Beede, rhp	60/Extreme
3.	Kyle Crick, rhp	60/Extreme
4.	Keury Mella, rhp	55/High
5.	Clayton Blackburn, rhp	50/Medium
6.	Adalberto Mejia, lhp	50/Medium
7.	Ty Blach, lhp	50/Medium
8.	Hunter Strickland, rhp	45/Low
9.	Matt Duffy, ss	45/Low
10.	Christian Arroyo, ss/2b	50/High
11.	Mac Williamson, of	55/Extreme
12.	Chris Stratton, rhp	50/High
13.	Adam Duvall, of	45/Medium
14.	Daniel Carbonell, of	55/Extreme
15.	Joan Gregorio, rhp	50/High
16.	Aramis Garcia, c	50/High
17.	Kendry Flores, rhp	50/High
18.	Michael Santos, rhp	50/Extreme
19.	Cody Hall, rhp	45/High
20.	Chase Johnson, rhp	45/High
21.	Luis Ysla, lhp	45/High
22.	Steven Okert, lhp	40/Low
23.	Derek Law, rhp	50/Extreme
24.	Ray Black, rhp	50/Extreme
25.	Chris Heston, rhp	40/Low
26.	Luis Castillo, rhp	45/High
27.	Rodolfo Martinez, rhp	50/Extreme
28.	Gary Brown, of	40/Low
29.	Logan Webb, rhp	45/High
30.	Ryder Jones, ss/3b	45/High

LAST YEAR'S TOP 30

No.	Player, Pos.	Status
1.	Kyle Crick, rhp	No. 3
2.	Edwin Escobar, lhp	(Red Sox)
3.	Chris Stratton rhp	No. 12
4.	Adalberto Mejia, lhp	No. 6
5.	Mac Williamson, of	No. 10
6.	Christian Arroyo, ss	No. 11
7.	Heath Hembree, rhp	(Red Sox)
8.	Ty Blach, lhp	No. 7
9.	Joe Panik, 2b	Majors
10.	Clayton Blackburn, rhp	No. 5
11.	Andrew Susac, c	No. 1
12.	Derek Law, rhp	No. 22
13.	Keury Mella, rhp	No. 4
14.	Kendry Flores, rhp	No. 17
15.	Ryder Jones, 3b	No. 30
16.	Angel Villalona, 1b	Dropped out
17.	Joan Gregorio, rhp	No. 15
18.	Ehire Adrianza, ss	Dropped out
19.	Gary Brown, of	No. 28
20.	Mike Kickham, lhp	Dropped out
21.	Martin Agosta, rhp	Dropped out
22.	Juan Perez, of	Majors
23.	Josh Osich, lhp	Dropped out
24.	Steven Okert, lhp	No. 26
25.	Chase Johnson, rhp	No. 20
26.	Jose DePaula, lhp	Dropped out
27.	Cody Hall, rhp	No. 19
28.	Stephen Johnson, rhp	Dropped out
29.	Roger Kieschnick, of	(Angels)
30.	Erik Cordier, rhp	Dropped out

BEST TOOLS

Best Hitter for Average	Christian Arroyo
Best Power Hitter	Adam Duvall
Best Strike-Zone Discipline	Matt Duffy
Fastest Baserunner	Daniel Carbonell
Best Athlete	Gary Brown
Best Fastball	Ray Black
Best Curveball	Derek Law
Best Slider	Kyle Crick
Best Changeup	Clayton Blackburn
Best Control	Clayton Blackburn
Best Defensive Catcher	Ty Ross
Best Defensive Infielder	Ehire Adrianza
Best Infield Arm	Chris Dominguez
Best Defensive Outfielder	Gary Brown
Best Outfield Arm	Daniel Carbonell

PROJECTED 2018 LINEUP

Catcher	Buster Posey
First Base	Brandon Belt
Second Base	Joe Panik
Third Base	Christian Arroyo
Shortstop	Brandon Crawford
Left Field	Mac Williamson
Center Field	Daniel Carbonell
Right Field	Hunter Pence
No. 1 Starter	Madison Bumgarner
No. 2 Starter	Matt Cain
No. 3 Starter	Tyler Beede
No. 4 Starter	Jake Peavy
No. 5 Starter	Kyle Crick
Closer	Hunter Strickland

SAN FRANCISCO GIANTS

TOP 2015 ROOKIE: Hunter Strickland, rhp: Yes, his postseason was awful, but also uncharacteristic. He has the stuff to be a useful setup man.

BREAKOUT PROSPECT: Ray Black, rhp: If he can handle a heavier workload, he could be in San Francisco in 2015.

SLEEPER: Christian Jones, lhp: As a lefthander with solid stuff and good feel, he could turn into a useful back-end starter.

SOURCE OF TOP 30 TALENT			
Homegrown	29	Acquired	1
College	12	Trades	0
Junior college	1	Rule 5 draft	0
High school	5	Independent leagues	0
Draft-and-follow	0	Free agents/waivers	1
Nondrafted free agents	0		
International	12		

LF
Jarrett Parker
Dylan Davis
Hunter Cole
Jean Angomas
Rafael Rodriguez

CF
Daniel Carbonell (14)
Gary Brown (28)
Mikey Edie
Seth Harrison
Gustavo Cabrera
Chris Lofton

RF
Mac Williamson (11)
Austin Slater
Chuckie Jones
Tyler Horan

3B
Ryder Jones (30)
Chris Dominguez
Nathanael Javier
Mitch Delfino

SS
Matt Duffy (9)
Ehire Adrianza
Kelvin Beltre
Manuel Geraldo

2B
Christian Arroyo (10)

1B
Adam Duvall (13)
Skyler Ewing
Brian Ragira
Angel Villalona
Miguel Gomez

C
Andrew Susac (1)
Aramis Garcia (16)
Mecky Coronado
Alilzon Rodriguez
Eric Sim

LHP

LHSP	LHRP
Adalberto Mejia (6)	Steven Okert (22)
Ty Blach (7)	Mike Kickham
Luis Ysla (21)	Josh Osich
Christian Jones	Bryce Bandilla
Matt Gage	Donald Snelten
	Carlos Diaz
	Caleb Smith

RHP

RHSP	RHRP
Tyler Beede (2)	Hunter Strickland (8)
Kyle Crick (3)	Cody Hall (19)
Keury Mella (4)	Derek Law (23)
Clayton Blackburn (5)	Ray Black (24)
Chris Stratton (12)	Luis Castillo (26)
Joan Gregorio (15)	Erik Cordier
Kendry Flores (17)	Sam Coonrod
Michael Santos (18)	Stephen Johnson
Chase Johnson (20)	Brett Bochy
Chris Heston (25)	Greg Brody
Rodolfo Martinez (27)	Pat Young
Logan Webb (29)	Dan Slania
Stetson Woods	
Martin Agosta	
Kendry Melo	

BEST PURE HITTER: C Aramis Garcia (2) nearly won the Conference USA modern triple crown in the spring, finishing second in on-base percentage after winning the batting and slugging titles. He has a balanced, strong, mature plate approach. 1B Skyler Ewing (6) has similar strength in a simple swing he repeats and controls the strike zone well.

BEST POWER HITTER: The Giants drafted the last two winners of the Cape Cod League's home run derby in Ewing (2013) and OF Dylan Davis (6, 2012), who gets Josh Willingham comparisons for his strength, bat speed and righthanded power.

FASTEST RUNNER: OF Seth Harrison (7) has posted 6.5-second times in the 60 in the past and is a plus runner.

BEST DEFENSIVE PLAYER: The Giants didn't draft a premium defender, but Garcia has the arm strength and physicality to be solid-average behind the plate.

BEST FASTBALL: RHP Tyler Beede (1) can pitch with a premium fastball at his best, sitting 92-94 mph and reaching 97. Physical RHP Sam Coonrod (5) also has hit 97 in relief.

BEST SECONDARY PITCH: Beede's changeup has evolved into his best secondary pitch, earning plus grades. His power 80-mph curve has been plus in the past but regressed this spring. Coonrod features a hard, inconsistent slider that flashes plus.

BEST PRO DEBUT: Ewing hit .291/.417/.473 with eight homers for short-season Salem-Keizer, leading the Northwest League in home runs per at-bat ratio (1 HR/22.75 ABs). OF Austin Slater (8) hit for a similar line (.347/.417/.449) in half the playing time with Salem-Keizer. RHP Greg Brody (11) struck out 27 of the 61 Rookie-level Arizona League batters he faced.

BEST ATHLETE: A former infielder, Slater (8) has speed and strength to stick on an outfield corner, while Harrison has strength and enough speed to stick in center.

MOST INTRIGUING BACKGROUND: Beede, who helped Vanderbilt win the College World Series in June, was a two-time first-rounder; he was the Blue Jays' unsigned 2011 first-rounder. Unsigned C Benito Santiago (38) is the son of the ex-big leaguer of the same name. RHPs Logan Webb (4, football quarterback) and 6-foot-8 Stetson Woods (9, basketball forward) were better known locally in Northern California for their exploits in other sports.

CLOSEST TO THE MAJORS: If he throws strikes, Beede will move to San Francisco quickly.

BEST LATE-ROUND PICK: The Giants took 3B/OF Hunter Cole (26) as a summer follow and signed him after seeing him rake (.353/.406/.565) in the Cape Cod League this summer. He's likely a better fit in the outfield than in the dirt.

THE ONE WHO GOT AWAY: The Giants went 0-for-2 against North Carolina, as RHP Benton Moss (15) returned for his senior year while hard-throwing LHP Hunter Williams (32), a two-way player at the college level, enrolled as a freshman.

ASSESSMENT: The Giants took a while to sign their players and inked just 23, but they got a balanced class with a strong group of college bats in a year that was thin on such players.

2013

The Giants bucked the industry consensus with top two picks SS/2B Christian Arroyo (1) and 3B Ryder Jones (2). So far, the industry looks right.

GRADE: D

2012

SS Matt Duffy (18) rocketed to the majors but looks more like a utility man than a regular. RHP Chris Stratton (1) and injured OF Mac WIliamson (3) stalled in 2014. LHPs Steven Okert (4) and Ty Blach (5) are solid prospects.

GRADE: C

2011

2B Joe Panik (1) was a World Series hero as a rookie. C Andrew Susac (2) supplanted RHP Kyle Crick (1s) as the club's top prospect. RHPs Ray Black (7) and Derek Law (9) throw significant gas, when healthy, while RHP Clayton Blackburn (16) has a chance to start.

GRADE: B

TOP DRAFT PICKS OF THE DECADE

Year	Player, Pos.	2014 Org
2005	Ben Copeland, of (4th round)	Out of baseball
2006	Tim Lincecum, rhp	Giants
2007	Madison Bumgarner, lhp	Giants
2008	Buster Posey, c	Giants
2009	Zack Wheeler, rhp	Mets
2010	Gary Brown, of	Giants
2011	Joe Panik, ss	Giants
2012	Chris Stratton, rhp	Giants
2013	Christian Arroyo, ss	Giants
2014	Tyler Beede, rhp	Giants

LARGEST BONUSES IN CLUB HISTORY

Buster Posey, 2008	$6,200,000
Zack Wheeler, 2009	$3,300,000
Rafael Rodriguez, 2008	$2,550,000
Angel VIllalona, 2006	$2,100,000
Tim Lincecum, 2006	$2,025,000

1 ANDREW SUSAC, C

Born: March 22, 1990. **B-T:** R-R. **Ht.:** 6-1. **Wt.:** 215.
Drafted: Oregon State, 2011 (2nd round).
Signed by: Matt Woodward.

Coming out of high school, Susac was viewed as a catch-and-throw backstop with a questionable bat. His freshman year at Oregon State in 2010 didn't change that report, as one coach described him as one of the easiest outs in the Pacific-12 Conference. But he went to the Cape Cod League that summer, gained confidence and led the Cape in slugging. That carried over into a standout sophomore year, cut short by a hamate injury. By the time he entered the 2011 draft as an eligible sophomore, scouts believed his bat was ahead of his defense. Susac again reversed the report by struggling at the plate in his 2012 pro debut while showing off an impressive arm. He gunned down Billy Hamilton five times in the California League (in 21 attempts). His bat caught up to the glove again in 2013, and after a strong start at Triple-A Fresno in 2014, he was a surprise callup to San Francisco when a concussion sidelined Hector Sanchez. He impressed enough to earn a spot on the postseason roster.

In another organization, Susac would likely be penciled in as a big league-ready everyday catcher. Because he plays for the Giants and Buster Posey isn't going anywhere, his best hope in the short term is to serve as an overqualified backup. Susac has shortened his once lengthy swing to spray more line drives. It has paid off in improved quality contact rates and hasn't really diminished his power. He projects as .250-.260 hitter with a chance to hit 15-20 home runs. He drives the ball to the opposite-field power alley with some loft and carry. His understanding of the strike zone allows him to draw plenty of walks, adding significantly to his offensive value. His plus arm regularly turns in 1.9-second pop times on throws to second base thanks to a quick release, though his arm strength seemed to taper off a little as the season wore on in 2014. Susac still is refining the rest of his work behind the plate. His pitch-calling needs to continue to improve. He's nimble enough to block pitches in the dirt and his athleticism is apparent, but he needs to quiet his hands a little more when receiving, for his pitch-framing numbers were below-average in his big league debut.

Susac's development gives the Giants the option of considering moving Posey's premium bat to first base at some point in the future. Until that happens, Susac will battle Sanchez for the backup catcher spot, with Susac likely having the edge because of his better bat. Opposing teams' scouts see Susac as an everyday catcher in his own right, making him a valuable trade chip. But if the Giants want to shift Posey to a less-demanding position, Susac gives them that option.

BA GRADE

55 Risk: Medium

SCOUTING GRADES

Batting: 50.
Power: 50
Speed: 30.
Defense: 50.
Arm: 60.

Based on 20-80 scouting scale and future projection rather than present grades.

LGE	PA	BB%	SO%	ISO
PCL	253	13.4	19.8	.183
NL	95	7.4	29.5	.193

ANDREW WOOLLEY

Year	Club (League)	Class	AVG	G	AB	R	H	2B	3B	HR	RBI	BB	SO	SB	CS	OBP	SLG
2012	San Jose (CAL)	HiA	.244	102	361	58	88	16	3	9	52	55	100	1	1	.351	.380
2013	Richmond (EL)	AA	.256	84	262	32	67	17	0	12	46	42	68	1	0	.362	.458
2014	Fresno (PCL)	AAA	.268	63	213	34	57	9	0	10	32	34	50	0	0	.379	.451
	San Francisco (NL)	MAJ	.273	35	88	13	24	8	0	3	19	7	28	0	0	.326	.466
Major League Totals			.273	35	88	13	24	8	0	3	19	7	28	0	0	.326	.466
Minor League Totals			.254	249	836	124	212	42	3	31	130	131	218	2	1	.362	.422

2 TYLER BEEDE, RHP

BILL MITCHELL

Born: May 23, 1993. **B-T:** R-R. **Ht.:** 6-4. **Wt.:** 200. **Drafted:** Vanderbilt, 2014 (1st round). **Signed by:** Andrew Jefferson.

Beede has tantalized scouts for years, but even after four years in the spotlight, he's still an intriguing blend of talent and risk. A first-round pick by the Blue Jays out of high school in 2011, he turned down $2.4 million to head to Vanderbilt. Beede was the Southeastern Conference pitcher of the year as a sophomore in 2013, sandwiching that with two erratic seasons. While Vanderbilt won the College World Series in 2014, Beede struggled in his last three postseason starts. The 14th overall pick in 2014, he signed for $2.6 million, more than he turned down out of high school. Beede has three plus pitches at his best. Blessed with an extremely quick arm, he has a well above-average fastball that sits 92-95 mph at its best and touches 97. His changeup has developed into a plus pitch as well, and he's shown a hard 80-82 mph plus curveball, though in the second half of this college season he lost the feel for it and it became much loopier. Beede is athletic, extremely competitive and has shown a feel for setting up hitters. How quickly he progresses and how far he goes depends almost entirely on him learning how to keep his delivery in sync more consistently. He's shown well below-average control everywhere he's pitched—from Vanderbilt to USA Baseball's College National Team to pro ball. The Giants are known as a team with excellent pitching instruction, and Beede has a lot of work to do, but if it all comes together, he could one day front a rotation. He'll head to either low Class A Augusta or high Class A San Jose in 2015.

BA GRADE

60 Risk: Extreme

LGE	BF	SO%	BB%	HR/9
AZL	38	28.9	10.5	0.00
NWL	30	23.3	10.0	0.00

Year	Club (League)	Class	W	L	ERA	G	GS	CG	SV	IP	H	HR	BB	SO	K/9	WHIP	AVG
2014	Giants (AZL)	R	0	1	3.12	4	4	0	0	9	8	0	4	11	11.4	1.38	.242
	Salem-Keizer (NWL)	SS	0	0	2.70	2	2	0	0	7	8	0	3	7	9.5	1.65	.308
Minor League Totals			0	1	2.93	6	6	0	0	15	16	0	7	18	10.6	1.50	.271

3 KYLE CRICK, RHP

Born: Nov. 30, 1992. **B-T:** L-R. **Ht.:** 6-4. **Wt.:** 225. **Drafted:** HS—Sherman, Texas, 2011 (1st round supplemental). **Signed by:** Todd Thomas.

Crick was better known as an infielder and defensive end at Sherman (Texas) High until his senior season. Once he got on the mound in 2011, he showed scouts where his future lay, for he dominated with a fastball that touched 97 mph. Crick has had one of the best arms in the Giants system since the day he signed as a sandwich pick, while also mixing dominant stints with ones where he can't find the strike zone. Crick still has the best pure stuff in the Giants system, and when he's on he's nearly unhittable. Crick's fastball will touch 98 mph at times, but he's generally better off when he pitches at 93-96 with better control. His control comes and goes from batter to batter and pitch to pitch. He can get 0-2 on a batter, then lose him with four straight balls. The Giants have worked on trying to get Crick to shorten his stride because his arm often is trying to catch up to his body, but so far it hasn't clicked, leaving him with well below-average control. Crick's hard 86-89 mph cutter/slider is his best secondary pitch and flashes at least average. His fringy mid-80s changeup with a late sink also has improved, and his 80-82 mph curveball is a usable below-average offering. Crick's control problems and inability to work deep in games makes it highly unlikely he'll be a big league starter, but the Giants will keep trying. San Francisco's lack of starting-pitching prospects gives them incentive to keep Crick in a starting role in 2015.

BA GRADE

60 Risk: Extreme

LGE	BF	SO%	BB%	HR/9
EL	398	27.9	15.3	0.70

Year	Club (League)	Class	W	L	ERA	G	GS	CG	SV	IP	H	HR	BB	SO	K/9	WHIP	AVG
2012	Augusta (SAL)	LoA	7	6	2.51	23	22	0	0	111	75	1	67	128	10.3	1.28	.193
2013	San Jose (CAL)	HiA	3	1	1.57	14	14	0	0	69	48	1	39	95	12.5	1.27	.201
2014	Richmond (EL)	AA	6	7	3.79	23	22	0	0	90	78	7	61	111	11.1	1.54	.234
Minor League Totals			17	14	2.79	67	58	0	0	277	210	9	175	342	11.1	1.39	.212

4 KEURY MELLA, RHP

Born: Aug. 2, 1993. **B-T:** R-R. **Ht.:** 6-2. **Wt.:** 190. **Signed:** Dominican Republic, 2011. **Signed by:** Pablo Peguero.

A product of trainer Luis Cordonado's complex that has produced Carlos Marmol and Juan Carlos Oviedo, Mella is yet another payoff from the Giants' productive scouting of older Dominican pitchers. He didn't sign until he was 18, but he still got a $275,000 thanks to his present stuff. Mella was shut down in late June 2014 with a minor rotator cuff injury. He returned to the mound six weeks later, but the Giants left him at short-season Salem-Keizer to help the team push for a playoff spot. Mella could end up with three plus pitches. He gets swings and misses with his plus 93-96 mph four-seam fastball that rides in on righthanders. Working from the extreme first-base side of the rubber, his cross-fire delivery generates some deception, and like many pitchers working from their glove side, he finds it easier to locate to both sides of the plate. His 78-80 mph curveball shows good depth and sharp 11-to-5 break at its best. It projects as another potentially above-average pitch, though it's still erratic. His changeup flashes plus as well. The Giants are impressed with Mella's tendency to remain a step ahead of hitters with an intelligent approach on the mound. Some scouts see him as a future reliever because they aren't enamored of his delivery, which has some violence and finishes with recoil, but so far he's shown the strength to repeat, and his above-average control has allowed him to regularly work six innings on limited pitch counts. Mella heads to high Class A San Jose in 2015, ready for a full workload. He has most everything scouts look for in a potential mid-rotation starter—he throws strikes with potentially above-average stuff.

BA GRADE

55 Risk: High

LGE	BF	SO%	BB%	HR/9
NWL	81	24.7	7.4	0.00
SAL	286	22.0	4.5	0.14

Year	Club (League)	Class	W	L	ERA	G	GS	CG	SV	IP	H	HR	BB	SO	K/9	WHIP	AVG
2012	Giants (DSL)	R	3	3	2.47	14	14	0	0	69	59	3	28	75	9.7	1.25	.225
2013	Giants (AZL)	R	3	2	2.25	10	9	0	0	36	34	0	11	41	10.3	1.25	.252
2014	Augusta (SAL)	LoA	3	3	3.93	12	12	1	0	66	69	1	13	63	8.5	1.24	.265
	Salem-Keizer (NWL)	SS	1	1	1.83	6	6	0	0	20	16	0	6	20	9.2	1.12	.222
Minor League Totals			10	9	2.87	42	41	1	0	191	178	4	58	199	9.4	1.23	.244

5 CLAYTON BLACKBURN, RHP

Born: Jan. 6, 1993. **B-T:** L-R. **Ht.:** 6-2. **Wt.:** 260. **Drafted:** HS—Edmond, Okla., 2011 (16th round). **Signed by:** Daniel Murray.

A high school draftee who has always pitched like a veteran, even when he was a teenager, Blackburn was a $150,000 late-round find for the Giants, as he spurned Oklahoma for pro ball. He's a 6-foot-2, thick-bodied right-hander who will have to watch his weight, and he battled pulled oblique injuries in 2014, but otherwise his weight has proven no hindrance to his clean, easy delivery. Probably the best compliment for Blackburn is that he throws every pitch with a purpose. He'll show hitters a below-average curveball pretty regularly, but it serves its purpose: misdirection. He'll flip a fringy breaking ball up early in the count for a get-me-over strike when hitters aren't looking for it, then he'll snap a plus breaking ball for strike three later in the at-bat. He also adds and subtracts off his fastball. Blackburn tosses a sinking two-seam fastball at 86 mph down in the zone in a near unhittable location, followed by a 92-94 fastball that looks harder because everything before it was softer. Blackburn is a rare minor leaguer with above-average command. His sinking fastball is an average offering, but his changeup and curveball both play as above-average and his hard cutter/slider is average. Blackburn, who got some extra work in the Arizona Fall League, projects as a No. 4 starter who could exceed that projection because of his feel and command. He's ready for Triple-A Sacramento.

BA GRADE

50 Risk: Medium

LGE	BF	SO%	BB%	HR/9
AZL	20	45.0	0.0	0.00
EL	386	22.0	5.2	0.10

Year	Club (League)	Class	W	L	ERA	G	GS	CG	SV	IP	H	HR	BB	SO	K/9	WHIP	AVG
2012	Augusta (SAL)	LoA	8	4	2.54	22	22	0	0	131	116	3	18	143	9.8	1.02	.232
2013	San Jose (CAL)	HiA	7	5	3.65	23	23	0	0	133	111	12	35	138	9.3	1.10	.224
2014	Giants (AZL)	R	0	1	3.60	2	2	0	0	5	4	0	0	9	16.2	0.80	.222
	Richmond (EL)	AA	5	6	3.29	18	18	0	0	93	94	1	20	85	8.2	1.23	.268
Minor League Totals			23	17	2.98	77	71	0	0	396	341	18	76	405	9.2	1.05	.230

6 ADALBERTO MEJIA, LHP

Born: June 20, 1993. **B-T:** L-L. **Ht.:** 6-3. **Wt.:** 205. **Signed:** Dominican Republic, 2011. **Signed by:** Pablo Peguero.

Signed for $350,000 in 2011, Mejia dominated the Dominican Summer League in his pro debut, showing excellent control and plus stuff. Since then, he's been firmly established as one of the more promising starting pitchers in the system. Mejia struggled to catch up to the speed of the Eastern League at Double-A Richmond over the first half of 2014 and didn't seem as competitive as coaches would like. But he regrouped and finished with a 2.01 ERA over his final seven starts. Mejia will miss the first 50 games of 2015 after being suspended for testing positive for Sibutramine, a stimulant used for weight loss that is banned in the U.S. As a big—if a little thick—lefthander with a plus fastball, and two other pitches that at least flash average, Mejia is a pitcher scouts can dream on since he repeats his delivery and has a tick above-average control. His 91-95 mph fastball was most effective in 2014 when he started relying on the two-seamer with

BA GRADE

50 Risk: Medium

LGE	BF	SO%	BB%	HR/9
EL	459	17.9	6.8	0.75

sink and tail more often late in the season. His average 82-84 mph slider is his best secondary pitch. His curveball might need to be shelved, as too often he gets in between and makes it a loopier slider. His changeup shows more promise. It flashes average with some late sink and fade, but it's inconsistent. Mejia has always been tough on lefties, so he should at least have a role as a lefty reliever. He can be a solid No. 4 starter if he can sharpen his secondary pitches.

Year	Club (League)	Class	W	L	ERA	G	GS	CG	SV	IP	H	HR	BB	SO	K/9	WHIP	AVG
2012	Augusta (SAL)	LoA	10	7	3.97	30	14	1	0	107	122	4	21	79	6.7	1.34	.284
2013	Fresno (PCL)	AAA	0	0	3.60	1	1	0	0	5	5	2	2	2	3.6	1.40	.250
	San Jose (CAL)	HiA	7	4	3.31	16	16	0	0	87	75	11	23	89	9.2	1.13	.228
2014	Richmond (EL)	AA	7	9	4.67	22	21	0	0	108	119	9	31	82	6.8	1.39	.283
Minor League Totals			29	22	3.50	82	65	1	0	383	379	26	85	323	7.6	1.21	.257

7 TY BLACH, LHP

Born: Oct. 20, 1990. **B-T:** R-L. **Ht.:** 6-2. **Wt.:** 210. **Drafted:** Creighton, 2012 (5th round). **Signed by:** Lou Colletti.

The Giants had a pretty good idea of what they were getting in Blach, a very durable, very successful three-year starter at Creighton. Three years later, Blach has been exactly what was expected. He's painted corners at two different levels. He doesn't dominate, but he's very consistent. He worked through the fifth inning in 22 of his 25 starts and one of the others was a game where he was pulled because of a rain delay. Blach's stuff is pretty much what it was when he signed–an 89-92 mph fastball that will touch 94 when he humps up, mixed with an 81-83 mph plus change with good late sink and a pair of fringe-average breaking balls. His slow curveball is best early in counts when hitters are looking for something to rip. His slurvy slider is a useful pitch he can use to backdoor hitters or to get them to chase out of the zone. Blach's delivery seems to have multiple parts but he repeats it, and its awkwardness adds deception. Blach's walk rate climbed last year,

BA GRADE

50 Risk: Medium

LGE	BF	SO%	BB%	HR/9
EL	596	15.3	6.5	0.51

because against more advanced hitters he found he had to nibble more often. He works fast, keeping his defense on its toes, which helps since he puts them to work. Blach's lack of swing-and-miss stuff means he'll have to be very precise when he reaches the big leagues. He is durable, throws strikes and mixes pitches, giving him a chance to be a solid back-end starter.

Year	Club (League)	Class	W	L	ERA	G	GS	CG	SV	IP	H	HR	BB	SO	K/9	WHIP	AVG
2013	San Jose (CAL)	HiA	12	4	2.90	22	20	0	0	130	124	8	18	117	8.1	1.09	.248
2014	Richmond (EL)	AA	8	8	3.13	25	25	1	0	141	142	8	39	91	5.8	1.28	.261
Minor League Totals			20	12	3.02	47	45	1	0	271	266	16	57	208	6.9	1.19	.255

8 HUNTER STRICKLAND, RHP

Born: Sept. 24, 1988. **B-T:** R-R. **Ht.:** 6-4. **Wt.:** 220. **Drafted:** HS—Zebulon, Ga., 2007 (18th round). **Signed by:** Rob English (Red Sox).

Focusing on Strickland's nightmarish 2014 postseason misses the point. He gave up a major league record six home runs in eight appearances and almost started a World Series brawl in Game Two. But the 2014 season was also Strickland's biggest triumph. Drafted by the Red Sox in the same 2007 draft as Anthony Rizzo, Strickland was traded to the Pirates in the 2009 Adam LaRoche deal, missed nearly two entire seasons with injuries and was claimed on waivers by the Giants in 2013. Strickland's stuff is unquestioned. He just needs to do a better job on pitch selection and location. In the postseason, he relied too much on four-seamers instead of pounding the bottom of the zone as he is capable of doing. Strickland has shown he can fill the zone, and he demonstrates average command in hitting his spots. His 95-100 mph fastball is a top-of-the-scale, 80-grade pitch with some armside run, and his hard 84-86 mph curveball is a plus pitch as well. He has a fringy, ineffective changeup he uses against lefties, but at his best, everything is hard. In the playoffs, his failure to locate his changeup meant he relied too much on his fastball against lefties. Strickland's durability has long been a concern. He missed time with an elbow strain in 2010, missed all of 2011 with a shoulder injury that required rotator cuff surgery and had Tommy John surgery in 2013. If he can stay healthy, Strickland has the stuff to be a setup man and possibly a closer. He will compete for a spot in the Giants bullpen in 2015.

BA GRADE
45 Risk: Low

LGE	BF	SO%	BB%	HR/9
EL	135	35.6	3.0	0.76
NL	25	36.0	0.0	0.00

Year	Club (League)	Class	W	L	ERA	G	GS	CG	SV	IP	H	HR	BB	SO	K/9	WHIP	AVG
2012	Bradenton (FSL)	HiA	2	2	2.98	10	9	0	0	45	47	5	8	25	5.0	1.21	.272
	Altoona (EL)	AA	2	2	4.46	23	0	0	2	42	50	5	15	33	7.0	1.54	.309
2013	San Jose (CAL)	HiA	1	0	0.86	20	0	0	9	21	10	1	5	23	9.9	0.71	.145
2014	San Jose (CAL)	HiA	0	0	3.00	3	0	0	0	3	2	0	0	7	21.0	0.67	.182
	Richmond (EL)	AA	1	1	2.02	38	0	0	11	36	25	3	4	48	12.1	0.81	.195
	San Francisco (NL)	MAJ	1	0	0.00	9	0	0	1	7	5	0	0	9	11.6	0.71	.200
Major League Totals			1	0	0.00	9	0	0	1	7	5	0	0	9	11.6	0.71	.200
Minor League Totals			22	21	3.65	156	55	0	23	427	442	43	86	316	6.7	1.24	.270

9 MATT DUFFY, SS

Born: Jan. 15, 1991. **B-T:** R-R. **Ht.:** 6-2. **Wt.:** 170. **Drafted:** Long Beach State, 2012 (18th round). **Signed by:** Brad Cameron.

Duffy's success has left scouts around baseball scratching their heads because the Giants seem to find successful big leaguers who had been overlooked by everyone else. In Duffy's case, it's not hard to see why other scouts missed. He didn't hit a home run or slug over .300 in three seasons at Long Beach State, but the Giants liked his glove and his ability to make frequent contact—even if he never drove the ball. With a skinny frame that could be described as scrawny, Duffy looked like a light-hitting utility infielder who would struggle to survive the higher levels. Instead, Duffy hit .332 at Double-A Richmond in 2014 to win the Eastern League batting title, while slugging .444 as he began incorporating his legs into his swing. He earned a promotion to the big leagues in 2014 and served as a utility infielder in the postseason. Duffy's average arm is a little stretched at shortstop, but he's proven to be a average defender there and a plus defender at second base. As an above-average runner, he's also useful as a pinch-runner, which he demonstrated when he scored the tying run in Game Two of the National League Division Series by scoring from second on a wild pitch by Trevor Rosenthal. Duffy looks to be a useful utility infielder for the Giants for years to come, one with some offensive value because of his speed and ability to get on base.

BA GRADE
45 Risk: Low

LGE	PA	BB%	SO%	ISO
EL	417	10.1	15.8	.112
NL	64	1.6	21.9	.033

Year	Club (League)	Class	AVG	G	AB	R	H	2B	3B	HR	RBI	BB	SO	SB	CS	OBP	SLG
2012	Salem-Keizer (NWL)	SS	.247	47	182	31	45	4	0	1	16	26	22	10	1	.361	.286
2013	Augusta (SAL)	LoA	.307	78	287	48	88	14	3	4	43	45	41	22	6	.405	.418
	San Jose (CAL)	HiA	.292	26	106	17	31	6	1	5	14	7	16	3	1	.342	.509
2014	Richmond (EL)	AA	.332	97	367	53	122	24	4	3	62	42	66	20	4	.398	.444
	San Francisco (NL)	MAJ	.267	34	60	5	16	2	0	0	8	1	14	0	1	.302	.300
Major League Totals			.267	34	60	5	16	2	0	0	8	1	14	0	1	.302	.300
Minor League Totals			.304	248	942	149	286	48	8	13	135	120	145	55	12	.387	.413

10 CHRISTIAN ARROYO, SS/2B

Born: May 30, 1995. **B-T:** R-R .**Ht.:** **6-1**. **Wt.:** 180. **Drafted:** HS—
Brooksville, Fla., 2013 (1st round). **Signed by:** Mike Metcalf.

The Giants have never had a problem bucking convention when it comes to their draft picks. In 2011, they took Joe Panik earlier than expected, and watched it pay off in the 2014 World Series. Now they hope for a similar payoff with Arroyo, a 2013 first-rounder whose future defensive home was questioned by scouts in his amateur days. He earned MVP honors for Team USA's 18U club that won the gold medal at the 2013 World Championships and was the Rookie-level Arizona League MVP in his pro debut. Sent to low Class A Augusta in 2014, Arroyo struggled and didn't turn things around until he was sent to short-season Salem-Keizer after missing time with a strained thumb. He primarily played second base with Augusta before returning to shortstop at Salem-Keizer. His limited foot speed makes him better suited for second base. He has sure hands and handles what he gets to, with an above-average arm that would also play at third base. Scouts are divided over Arroyo's future position, but few see him having a chance to stick at shortstop. At the plate, he has a balanced, simple swing with some whip that should allow him to hit for average with at least gap power, and he shows adjustments from at-bat to at-bat. He's a tick-below-average runner who will have to keep working on his agility as he matures. The Giants have shortstop Brandon Crawford and second baseman Joe Panik for the foreseeable future, so look for Arroyo to be ready to handle Augusta in 2015.

	BA GRADE	
50	Risk: High	

LGE	PA	BB%	SO%	ISO
SAL	125	3.2	17.6	.068
NWL	267	6.7	11.6	.136

Year	Club (League)	Class	AVG	G	AB	R	H	2B	3B	HR	RBI	BB	SO	SB	CS	OBP	SLG
2013	Giants (AZL)	R	.326	45	184	47	60	18	5	2	39	19	32	3	2	.388	.511
2014	Augusta (SAL)	LoA	.203	31	118	10	24	3	1	1	14	4	22	1	2	.226	.271
	Salem-Keizer (NWL)	SS	.333	58	243	39	81	14	2	5	48	18	31	6	1	.378	.469
Minor League Totals			.303	134	545	96	165	35	8	8	101	41	85	10	5	.350	.440

11 MAC WILLIAMSON, OF

	BA GRADE	
55	Risk: Extreme	

Born: July 15, 1990. **B-T:** R-R. **Ht.:** 6-4. **Wt.:** 235. **Drafted:** Wake Forest, 2012 (3rd round). **Signed by:** Jeremy Cleveland.

When Williamson was coming out of high school, he was expected to step into Wake Forest's rotation, though some scouts had also liked him as a catching prospect. A shoulder injury that required surgery meant he became the Demon Deacons best power hitter instead. He's hit for power as a pro as well, but Williamson's 2014 season never really got started. An elbow injury bothered him from day one. The Giants sent him back to high Class A San Jose so he could DH, but before long he and the club recognized he needed Tommy John surgery. He missed the rest of the year. Williamson has double-plus raw power in batting practice and has shown plus power in games thanks to excellent strength, solid bat speed and a tendency to take big cuts. He has developed a good understanding of the strike zone and draws plenty of walks to go with his home runs, though he can get pull happy and doesn't always recognize breaking balls. Despite his massive size, he's an excellent athlete whose strong, pre-injury arm was an asset in right field. He's an average runner who steals bases successfully because he gets good reads. Williamson's combination of plate discipline, immense power and surprising athleticism gives him a chance to be a productive corner outfielder. His surgery went as expected, and he was throwing in November with a chance to be ready to play right field at Double-A Richmond in 2015.

Year	Club (League)	Class	AVG	G	AB	R	H	2B	3B	HR	RBI	BB	SO	SB	CS	OBP	SLG
2012	Giants (AZL)	R	.176	4	17	4	3	0	0	2	7	2	5	0	0	.263	.529
	Salem-Keizer (NWL)	SS	.342	29	114	22	39	8	0	7	25	6	19	0	0	.392	.596
2013	San Jose (CAL)	HiA	.292	136	520	94	152	31	2	25	89	51	132	10	1	.375	.504
2014	San Jose (CAL)	HiA	.318	23	85	16	27	7	0	3	11	13	14	6	1	.420	.506
Minor League Totals			.300	192	736	136	221	46	2	37	132	72	170	16	2	.380	.519

12 CHRIS STRATTON, RHP

	BA GRADE	
50	Risk: High	

Born: Aug. 22, 1990. **B-T:** R-R. **Ht.:** 6-3. **Wt.:** 186. **Drafted:** Mississippi State, 2012 (1st round). **Signed by:** Hugh Walker.

Coming into his junior year at Mississippi State, Stratton was an enigma. He had the best stuff on the Bulldogs' staff, but he didn't capitalize it until his junior season. After a productive summer in the Cape Cod League, he became MSU's Friday starter, shutting down hitters with an excellent fastball and slider to vault into the first round of the 2012 draft. As a pro, Stratton has become an enigma again. He has rarely shown plus stuff, relying more on feel and guile. The Giants believe it's taken him a long time to fully recover from a concussion he suffered on a line drive that hit him in batting practice at short-season Salem-Keizer in 2012. After pitching at 89-92 mph in the first half of 2014, Stratton sat 90-94 again in the second half. He'll mix in two-seamers down in the zone and the occasional four-seamer up. His tight 83-85 mph slider doesn't break much, with more of a cutting action. He spots a fringe-average curveball for strikes early in the count. His fringy changeup doesn't miss bats, but it can generate weak contact. For a pitcher trying to find success by mixing pitches, he doesn't locate well enough, showing below-average control. Stratton should return to Double-A Richmond in 2015. He's shown flashes of the plus stuff required to be a mid-rotation arm, but he realistically projects as a back-end starter.

Year	Club (League)	Class	W	L	ERA	G	GS	CG	SV	IP	H	HR	BB	SO	K/9	WHIP	AVG
2012	Salem-Keizer (NWL)	SS	0	1	2.76	8	5	0	0	16	14	1	10	16	8.8	1.47	.237
2013	Augusta (SAL)	LoA	9	3	3.27	22	22	1	0	132	128	5	47	123	8.4	1.33	.258
2014	San Jose (CAL)	HiA	7	8	5.07	19	18	0	0	99	103	13	36	102	9.2	1.40	.270
	Richmond (EL)	AA	1	1	3.52	5	5	0	0	23	29	2	12	18	7.0	1.78	.315
Minor League Totals			17	13	3.92	54	50	1	0	271	274	21	105	259	8.6	1.40	.266

13 ADAM DUVALL, 3B/1B

BA GRADE

45 Risk: Medium

Born: Nov. 22, 1986. **B-T:** R-R. **Ht.:** 6-4. **Wt.:** 235. **Drafted:** Louisville, 2010 (11th round). **Signed by:** Kevin Christman.

Duvall and Chris Dominguez have been teammates both at Louisville and with the Giants. Dominguez was a higher pick (third round, 2009), but Duvall has had more success as a pro. A college shortstop and second baseman, Duvall has moved to third as a pro, but he's got below-average range there and has throwing accuracy issues that have made him unplayable in the big leagues. He stayed at first with San Francisco, where he's raw but has a chance to be a fringe-average defender. Duvall's calling card is his plus power. He has extremely strong hands that produce plenty of power, but thanks to a good understanding of the strike zone, he makes solid contact as well. His ability to backspin the ball generates plenty of carry. Duvall's power gives him a chance to stick around the big leagues, either as a backup corner bat in San Francisco or possibly for another team where he can play first base.

Year	Club (League)	Class	AVG	G	AB	R	H	2B	3B	HR	RBI	BB	SO	SB	CS	OBP	SLG
2012	San Jose (CAL)	HiA	.258	134	534	101	138	24	4	30	100	47	116	8	2	.327	.487
2013	Richmond (EL)	AA	.252	105	385	61	97	23	4	17	58	35	72	2	1	.320	.465
2014	Fresno (PCL)	AAA	.298	91	359	67	107	21	3	27	90	30	82	2	0	.360	.599
	San Francisco (NL)	MAJ	.192	28	73	8	14	2	0	3	5	3	20	0	0	.234	.342
Major League Totals			.192	28	73	8	14	2	0	3	5	3	20	0	0	.234	.342
Minor League Totals			.269	500	1901	328	512	108	16	100	353	185	413	18	10	.345	.501

14 DANIEL CARBONELL, OF

BA GRADE

55 Risk: Extreme

Born: March 29, 1991. **B-T:** R-R. **Ht.:** 6-3. **Wt.** 196. **Signed:** Cuba, 2014. **Signed by:** Joe Salermo/Pat Burrell/Mike Kendall.

In Cuba's *Serie Nacional*, Carbonell sat stuck on the Camgeury bench until Dariel Alvarez and Dayron Varona left the island to head to the U.S. Given an opportunity to play, Carbonell hit .298/.369/.449 in 2012-13 before heading to the States himself. The Giants signed him to a major league deal that included a $1 million bonus. Carbonell is athletic with a musclular build and plus-plus speed. That speed plays in center field, where he shows a above-average, if at times erratic, defense to go with an above-average arm. At the plate, scouts aren't so sure. He scrapped switch-hitting to hit righthanded only with the Giants. He has shown average raw power, but some scouts question whether he can make consistent contact with his mechanical swing. If he can become even an average hitter, the other tools will make him a big leaguer. In his first action at high Class A San Jose he mixed wild swings with impressive power displays. Carbonell could be a power/speed center fielder, but that depends on him making further strides with his bat.

Year	Club (League)	Class	AVG	G	AB	R	H	2B	3B	HR	RBI	BB	SO	SB	CS	OBP	SLG
2014	Giants (AZL)	R	.314	10	35	10	11	3	0	1	4	2	4	4	0	.368	.486
	San Jose (CAL)	HiA	.344	21	93	17	32	3	3	3	12	6	19	7	2	.390	.538
Minor League Totals			.336	31	128	27	43	6	3	4	16	8	23	11	2	.384	.523

15 JOAN GREGORIO, RHP

BA GRADE

50 Risk: High

Born: Jan. 12, 1992. **B-T:** R-R. **Ht.:** 6-7. **Wt.:** 180. **Signed:** Dominican Republic, 2010. **Signed by:** Pablo Peguero.

Gregorio announced his arrival in the U.S. by leading the Rookie-level Arizona League in ERA in 2011. The pro game since then has been more of a struggle, which continued in 2014, when he had an at times impressive but frustrating season. He had two disabled list stints at high Class A San Jose: one mostly to work on his delivery rather than any specific ailment and a second for an actual back injury. He returned to action with low Class A Augusta, pitching inconsistently and finishing strong with 10 strikeouts in his season finale. Gregorio's plus 91-95 mph fastball and 83-85 mph slider that flashes plus are enough to carve up hitters on his best nights. But his slider comes and goes, his changeup is a well-below average offering and he's just started to develop trust into throwing his secondary stuff. His control is below-average. More importantly for the Giants, they want to see Gregorio bring more competitive fire to his starts. He'll head back to San Jose for a second try in 2015. He has a likely future as a setup man, but the pieces are there to be a mid-rotation starter if he can improve his secondary offerings and control.

Year	Club (League)	Class	W	L	ERA	G	GS	CG	SV	IP	H	HR	BB	SO	K/9	WHIP	AVG
2012	Salem-Keizer (NWL)	SS	7	7	5.54	16	16	0	0	76	85	9	23	69	8.1	1.41	.272
2013	Augusta (SAL)	LoA	6	3	4.00	14	13	0	0	70	65	3	17	84	10.9	1.18	.243
2014	San Jose (CAL)	HiA	2	2	6.75	6	5	0	0	23	27	2	13	27	10.7	1.76	.303
	Augusta (SAL)	LoA	2	7	3.57	13	12	0	1	68	50	2	27	65	8.6	1.13	.204
Minor League Totals			26	22	3.94	75	72	0	1	361	335	18	113	329	8.2	1.24	.245

16 ARAMIS GARCIA, C

Born: Jan. 12, 1993. **B-T:** R-R. **Ht.:** 6-2. **Wt.:** 220. **Drafted:** Florida International, 2014 (2nd round). **Signed by:** Jose Alou.

Coming out of high school, Garcia was viewed as a solid-hitting catcher who had work to do defensively. After gaining 25 pounds of good weight at Florida International, he took a significant step forward at the plate. He has a balanced setup, present strength and a line-drive stroke that helped him lead Conference USA in batting average (.368) and slugging (.626) in 2014. The Giants didn't get to see much of that after signing him for $1.1 million, for he struggled in a short debut. Garcia has work to do behind the plate, for he is somewhat mechanical. He needs to clean up his footwork and blocking skills—he allowed six passed balls in seven games in the Rookie-level Arizona League. He turns in average pop times on throws to second base and has the tools to end up being an average defender, but it will require diligent work. Garcia has the tools to be an everyday catcher, but he's a long ways from there right now.

Year	Club (League)	Class	AVG	G	AB	R	H	2B	3B	HR	RBI	BB	SO	SB	CS	OBP	SLG
2014	Giants (AZL)	R	.219	8	32	6	7	3	0	0	3	5	6	0	0	.324	.313
	Salem-Keizer (NWL)	SS	.229	20	70	5	16	3	0	2	12	5	19	0	0	.289	.357
Minor League Totals			.225	28	102	11	23	6	0	2	15	10	25	0	0	.301	.343

17 KENDRY FLORES, RHP

Born: Nov. 24, 1991. **B-T:** R-R. **Ht.:** 6-2. **Wt.:** 175. **Signed:** Dominican Republic, 2009. **Signed by:** Pablo Peguero.

Flores has always been able to pitch, and he put together a dominant season at low Class A Augusta in 2013 that included a 15-strikeout, no-walk gem that ranked among the best starts in the minors all season, but scouts had a hard time projecting much success for a pitcher who generally threw 87-90 mph two-seamers. A year later, Flores looks much more intriguing, after he dialed his four-seamer up to 92-94 mph on a regular basis at high Class A San Jose, giving him a tick above-average fastball to go with his tick above-average changeup he can throw at any point in the count. He varies his velocity from pitch to pitch, taking some off and adding some to mess with timing. Flores also mixes in a less-consistent slider and curveball that both flash average. His delivery is clean, with little effort, and he has a pause at the start of the delivery that makes it harder to time him. Flores has the ability to be a back-end starter. He's headed for Double-A Richmond in 2015 after finishing 2014 sidelined by a shoulder injury.

Year	Club (League)	Class	W	L	ERA	G	GS	CG	SV	IP	H	HR	BB	SO	K/9	WHIP	AVG
2012	Salem-Keizer (NWL)	SS	1	3	4.46	10	8	0	0	42	44	4	11	34	7.2	1.30	.257
2013	Augusta (SAL)	LoA	10	6	2.73	22	22	1	0	142	113	11	17	137	8.7	0.92	.216
2014	San Jose (CAL)	HiA	4	6	4.09	20	20	0	0	106	101	14	32	112	9.5	1.26	.249
Minor League Totals			31	24	3.47	90	85	1	0	459	411	37	111	443	8.7	1.14	.239

18 MICHAEL SANTOS, RHP

Born: May 29, 1995. **B-T:** R-R. **Ht.:** 6-4. **Wt.:** 170. **Signed:** Dominican Republic, 2012. **Signed by:** Jesus Stephens.

The Giants signed Santos for $250,000 in January 2012, but he didn't throw his first pro pitch until late 2013 as the club worked with him to gain weight and strength. He emerged in the Rookie-level Arizona League in 2014, finishing among the league leaders in opponent average (.259) and walk rate (2.0 per nine innings). Santos appears to have plenty of projection left in his skinny but athletic frame, and his present stuff impresses with an average 90-91 mph fastball that touches 93. His slow, low-70s curveball needs more depth, but it is already a pitch he commands and throws with conviction. His promising changeup flashes average and Santos has some feel on when to mix it in. He repeats his high three-quarters delivery that shows little effort and a loose arm, though his finish has a slight recoil. He shows above-average control for his age and should be ready to handle the jump to low Class A Augusta.

Year	Club (League)	Class	W	L	ERA	G	GS	CG	SV	IP	H	HR	BB	SO	K/9	WHIP	AVG
2013	Giants (DSL)	R	1	2	2.75	4	4	0	0	20	18	0	6	18	8.2	1.22	.240
2014	Giants (AZL)	R	4	3	2.56	12	12	0	0	60	59	3	13	50	7.5	1.21	.259
Minor League Totals			5	5	2.61	16	16	0	0	79	77	3	19	68	7.7	1.21	.254

19 CODY HALL, RHP

BA GRADE

45 Risk: High

Born: Jan. 6, 1988. **B-T:** R-R. **Ht.:** 6-4. **Wt.:** 220. **Drafted:** Southern, 2011 (19th round). **Signed by:** Hugh Walker.

Hall has proven to be yet another scouting-and-development find for the Giants. whose roving pitching instructor, Lee Smith, stops in to help Southern's pitchers prior to spring training. A 19th-round pick who didn't even play high school baseball, Hall's arm strength intrigued the Giants, who figured they could work out some of the kinks in his delivery. Even after some tweaks, his delivery has plenty of effort and recoil as he finishes, but he repeats his motion and has average control. Hall's plus fastball sits at 94-97 mph, but it was at its best last year when he learned how to pitch down in the zone with it. He could then mix in the occasional elevated four-seamer for a swing and a miss. Hall has a sinking changeup that flashes average, as well as a slider that has gotten tighter but is still a fringy pitch. Hall spent most of August on the disabled list but returned healthy and dominated in winter ball, tossing 17 scoreless innings in Venezuela. That earned him a spot on the 40-man roster, and he's ready for Triple-A Sacramento.

Year	Club (League)	Class	W	L	ERA	G	GS	CG	SV	IP	H	HR	BB	SO	K/9	WHIP	AVG
2012	Augusta (SAL)	LoA	3	0	1.60	36	0	0	20	39	36	0	12	54	12.4	1.22	.247
	San Jose (CAL)	HiA	1	1	3.24	9	0	0	1	8	12	0	4	10	10.8	1.92	.333
2013	San Jose (CAL)	HiA	2	0	1.34	26	0	0	2	34	15	2	7	48	12.8	0.65	.130
	Richmond (EL)	AA	2	2	2.39	20	0	0	8	26	17	4	8	27	9.2	0.95	.181
2014	Richmond (EL)	AA	1	4	3.14	47	0	0	11	52	42	3	14	57	9.9	1.08	.225
Minor League Totals			12	8	2.31	161	0	0	46	187	143	10	64	238	11.5	1.11	.211

20 CHASE JOHNSON

BA GRADE

45 Risk: High

Born: Jan. 9, 1992. **B-T:** R-R. **Ht.:** 6-3. **Wt.:** 185. **Drafted:** Caly Poly, 2013 (3rd round). **Signed by:** Gil Kubski.

From a financial standpoint, Johnson made a great decision to go to Cal Poly. By turning down the Rangers in the 26th round out of high school, he landed a $440,000 bonus as a third-rounder in 2013. Developmentally, it cost him innings, as he worked just 107 for Cal Poly in three years. San Francisco has moved the former college closer into the rotation to get him consistent work. They also introduced a windup after he pitched exclusively from the stretch in college. Johnson is working on developing consistency. See him on the right night and he looks like a future mid-rotation power arm. On other nights, he looks overmatched. His 92-94 mph fastball will touch 96 at times. It's his one reliable pitch from start to start. In others starts, he had confidence in an average changeup. His slider is a tight pitch with some bite at its best, but it's a much slurvier offering at times. Johnson has a pitcher's body, quick arm and direct delivery, so there's lots to dream on. He'll move up to high Class A San Jose in 2015.

Year	Club (League)	Class	W	L	ERA	G	GS	CG	SV	IP	H	HR	BB	SO	K/9	WHIP	AVG
2013	Giants (AZL)	R	1	0	1.69	3	0	0	0	5	5	0	1	7	11.8	1.13	.263
	Salem-Keizer (NWL)	SS	3	2	4.17	10	10	0	0	41	36	3	12	37	8.1	1.17	.240
2014	Augusta (SAL)	LoA	4	7	4.57	23	22	0	0	110	111	5	40	94	7.7	1.37	.260
Minor League Totals			8	9	4.37	36	32	0	0	157	152	8	53	138	7.9	1.31	.255

21 LUIS YSLA, LHP

BA GRADE

45 Risk: High

Born: April 27, 1992. **B-T:** L-L. **Ht.:** 6-1. **Wt.:** 185. **Signed:** Venezuela, 2012. **Signed by:** Ciro Villalobos.

When the Giants have tried to make a big splash in Latin America, it's generally gone very poorly. But when the Giants sign older pitchers for less money, they often get a nice payoff, like what they may get from Ysla, a little-noticed, inexpensive signing from Venezuela as a 20-year-old. He dominated the Rookie-level Arizona League in his 2013 pro debut and was just as good at low Class A Augusta in 2014, leading the South Atlantic League in ERA (2.45). Ysla goes right at hitters with a high-effort, slinging delivery that leads many scouts to peg him as a future reliever. His stuff plays either as a starter or reliever.

He gets ahead of hitters by locating his 92-94 mph fastball, then his plus mid 80s mph changeup finishes them off. His 80-81 mph slider is erratic, but is average at its best. He'll help anchor the high Class A San Jose rotation in 2015.

Year	Club (League)	Class	W	L	ERA	G	GS	CG	SV	IP	H	HR	BB	SO	K/9	WHIP	AVG
2013	Giants (AZL)	R	4	0	2.65	12	12	0	0	51	38	1	13	52	9.2	1.00	.204
2014	Augusta (SAL)	LoA	6	7	2.45	24	23	0	0	121	104	8	45	115	8.5	1.23	.231
Minor League Totals			10	7	2.51	36	35	0	0	172	142	9	58	167	8.7	1.16	.223

22 STEVEN OKERT, LHP

BA GRADE

40 Risk: Low

Born: July 9, 1991. **B-T:** L-L. **Ht.:** 6-3. **Wt.:** 210. **Drafted:** Oklahoma, 2012 (4th round). **Signed by:** Dan Murray.

After being drafted twice by the Brewers and failing to sign out of junior college, Okert emerged as a weapon in the Oklahoma bullpen as a junior in 2012. Some teams thought about drafting him to start, but the Giants have kept him in the pen, and he broke through in 2014 by striking out 32.5 percent of batters faced. Okert's funky delivery begins with the lefthander lined up on the first-base side of the rubber. He then throws across his body and lands on a stiff front leg, which makes finishing pitches difficult. It's not pretty, but Okert has shown average control, and his motion helps create deception. He sits 91-95 mph with a low three-quarters arm slot that is deadly to lefthanders, especially when he mixes in his average slider. Lefties have hit .166/.259/.203 against Okert as a pro, and not one of the 245 lefthanders has ever tagged him for a home run. He's not helpless against righthanders either because he's shown he can locate to his glove side to get in on their hands. Okert shined in the Arizona Fall League. He's likely headed to Triple-A Sacramento in 2015 and may not be limited to lefty-specialist duty.

Year	Club (League)	Class	W	L	ERA	G	GS	CG	SV	IP	H	HR	BB	SO	K/9	WHIP	AVG
2012	Giants (AZL)	R	0	0	0.00	2	0	0	0	2	2	0	1	6	27.0	1.50	.250
	Salem-Keizer (NWL)	SS	2	0	2.36	15	0	0	0	27	26	0	11	22	7.4	1.39	.255
2013	Augusta (SAL)	LoA	2	2	2.97	44	0	0	2	61	55	3	24	59	8.8	1.30	.244
2014	San Jose (CAL)	HiA	1	2	1.53	33	0	0	19	35	33	2	11	54	13.8	1.25	.241
	Richmond (EL)	AA	1	0	2.73	24	0	0	5	33	24	3	11	38	10.4	1.06	.207
Minor League Totals			6	4	2.45	118	0	0	26	158	140	8	58	179	10.2	1.26	.238

23 DEREK LAW, RHP

BA GRADE

50 Risk: Extreme

Born: Sept. 14, 1990. **B-T:** R-R. **Ht.:** 6-3. **Wt.:** 210. **Drafted:** Miami Dade JC, 2011 (9th round). **Signed by:** Michael Metcalf.

If not for a midseason elbow injury in 2014 that required Tommy John surgery, Law may have pitched his way into the Giants' postseason plans. He has blazed a trail of success wherever he has gone, including a 45-to-1 strikeout-to-walk ratio at high Class A San Jose to end the 2013 season. Scouts and hitters have always been a little leery of Law because of an unconventional delivery. He uses a pronounced hip turn that turns his back to the hitter while he begins his takeaway with a pronounced stab. It makes it hard to pick up the ball, which is especially frightening when Law uncorks a plus 91-95 mph fastball that seems harder than that because of his delivery, and a plus, overhand 12-to-6 curveball that has been described as a "bowel-locker." Law also uses a below-average changeup against lefties. He'll miss at least half of the 2015 season as he rehabs from the surgery, but he has the makings of a future closer.

Year	Club (League)	Class	W	L	ERA	G	GS	CG	SV	IP	H	HR	BB	SO	K/9	WHIP	AVG
2012	Augusta (SAL)	LoA	5	2	2.91	32	0	0	2	56	45	6	23	67	10.8	1.22	.216
2013	Augusta (SAL)	LoA	0	3	2.31	19	0	0	3	35	27	1	10	48	12.3	1.06	.206
	Giants (AZL)	R	1	0	3.18	5	0	0	0	6	4	0	1	9	14.3	0.88	.200
	San Jose (CAL)	HiA	4	0	2.10	22	0	0	11	26	20	1	1	45	15.8	0.82	.208
2014	Richmond (EL)	AA	2	0	2.57	27	0	0	13	28	19	1	14	29	9.3	1.18	.198
Minor League Totals			12	5	2.57	120	0	0	33	168	131	9	51	217	11.6	1.08	.211

24 RAY BLACK, RHP

BA GRADE

50 Risk: Extreme

Born: June 26, 1990. **B-T:** R-R. **Ht.:** 6-5. **Wt.:** 225. **Drafted:** Pittsburgh, 2011 (7th round). **Signed by:** John Dicarlo.

Already a member of the 40-man roster, Black has a chance to develop into a dominant closer if he can stay healthy—but that's a big if. He had Tommy John surgery as a high school senior and redshirted his freshman year at Pittsburgh while recovering. After throwing 37 innings in two seasons in college, where knee injuries limited him, he missed his first two pro seasons because of shoulder surgery to repair his labrum. When he's healthy, Black has been the hardest-throwing pitcher in the minors. He hit 100 mph regularly in 2014 and touched 103. His fastball has boring action, even at extreme velocities. He uses it to set up a hard-breaking downer curveball that is also a plus pitch at its best. With a slinging delivery, Black likely will never have even average command, but his stuff is good enough that he just has to get it over the plate. The Giants were cautious with Black in 2014—his outings came every three days, no matter the score—and will work him into a heavier workload at Double-A Richmond in 2015.

Year	Club (League)	Class	W	L	ERA	G	GS	CG	SV	IP	H	HR	BB	SO	K/9	WHIP	AVG
2012	Did not play—Injured																
2013	Did not play—Injured																
2014	Augusta (SAL)	LoA	1	3	3.73	33	0	0	1	31	16	1	14	64	18.4	0.96	.147
	San Jose (CAL)	HiA	1	0	2.25	4	0	0	0	4	1	0	2	7	15.8	0.75	.083
Minor League Totals			2	3	3.57	37	0	0	1	35	17	1	16	71	18.1	0.93	.140

25 CHRIS HESTON, RHP

BA GRADE
40 Risk: Low

Born: April 10, 1988. **B-T:** R-R. **Ht.:** 6-3. **Wt.:** 195. **Drafted:** East Carolina, 2009 (12th round). **Signed by:** Pat Portugal.

Heston has gotten every bit out of his fringy stuff, and he earned his first big league callup in 2014 on the heels of an excellent season at Triple-A Fresno. Drafted in back-to-back seasons out of Seminole State (Fla.) JC, Heston finally signed after a solid junior year at East Carolina in 2009. Since then, he's been a crafty righthander who succeeds without any pitch that grades out as even average. Heston is direct to the plate with an 86-89 mph two-seam fastball with some armside run, a slow low-70s curveball and a fringe-average changeup. It's unlikely Heston can find big league success by letting big league hitters put pitch after pitch into play, but he will serve as a reliable emergency starter option.

Year	Club (League)	Class	W	L	ERA	G	GS	CG	SV	IP	H	HR	BB	SO	K/9	WHIP	AVG
2012	Richmond (EL)	AA	9	8	2.24	25	25	1	0	149	124	2	40	135	8.2	1.10	.230
2013	Fresno (PCL)	AAA	7	6	5.80	19	19	1	0	109	129	14	46	97	8.0	1.61	.301
2014	Fresno (PCL)	AAA	12	9	3.38	28	28	1	0	173	152	16	51	119	6.2	1.17	.233
	San Francisco (NL)	MAJ	0	0	5.06	3	1	0	0	5	6	0	3	4	6.8	1.69	.300
Major League Totals			0	0	5.06	3	1	0	0	5	6	0	3	4	6.8	1.69	.300
Minor League Totals			46	45	3.56	133	128	5	0	765	740	48	220	640	7.5	1.25	.256

26 LUIS CASTILLO, RHP

BA GRADE
45 Risk: High

Born: Dec. 12, 1992. **B-T:** R-R. **Ht.:** 6-2. **Wt.:** 170. **Signed:** Dominican Republic, 2011. **Signed by:** Jonathan Bautista.

Castillo didn't sign with the Giants until he was 19, but he's moved relatively quickly since then. He can dominate at times with a 93-96 mph fastball and a hard, low-80s curveball that flashes average. Castillo's delivery is not well-balanced. It's a high-effort delivery that finishes with him spinning toward first base, which explains why he sometimes finds the strike zone jumping around on him. He is reasonably athletic and has some present strength, so the Giants hope he can refine his delivery. He's ready to move up to high Class A San Jose as a power reliever, with a chance to eventually be a setup man.

Year	Club (League)	Class	W	L	ERA	G	GS	CG	SV	IP	H	HR	BB	SO	K/9	WHIP	AVG
2012	Giants (DSL)	R	1	3	3.31	19	0	0	2	54	47	1	22	47	7.8	1.27	.240
2013	Giants (DSL)	R	0	1	0.64	27	0	0	20	28	15	0	3	34	10.8	0.64	.150
2014	Augusta (SAL)	LoA	2	2	3.07	48	0	0	10	59	56	6	25	66	10.1	1.38	.247
Minor League Totals			3	6	2.67	94	0	0	32	141	118	7	50	147	9.4	1.19	.226

27 RODOLFO MARTINEZ, RHP

BA GRADE
50 Risk: Extreme

Born: April 4, 1994. **B-T:** R-R. **Ht.:** 6-2. **Wt.:** 180. **Signed:** Dominican Republic, 2013. **Signed by:** Jesus Stephens.

Martinez was one of the older players in the 2013 international class to land a six figure bonus. Even though he would turn 20 before he made his pro debut, he signed for $350,000 because the Giants loved his power arm. Martinez made his debut in the Rookie-level Arizona League in 2014, an aggressive assignment brought about in part because of his age, but he proved to be in over his head. It's hard to find much encouraging in his performance, but scouts saw a lot to like. Martinez showed a plus 91-97 mph fastball, a promising slider and the makings of a useable changeup. He needs to find the strike zone to let his plus stuff play, but Martinez is one of the more promising young arms in the system.

Year	Club (League)	Class	W	L	ERA	G	GS	CG	SV	IP	H	HR	BB	SO	K/9	WHIP	AVG
2014	Giants (AZL)	R	1	5	8.78	15	7	0	0	28	45	1	16	35	11.4	2.20	.375
Minor League Totals			1	5	8.78	15	7	0	0	28	45	1	16	35	11.4	2.20	.375

28 GARY BROWN, OF

BA GRADE

40 Risk: Low

Born: Sept. 28, 1988. **B-T:** R-R. **Ht.:** 6-1. **Wt.:** 190. **Drafted:** Cal State Fullerton, 2010 (1st round). **Signed by:** Brad Cameron.

Oh, what might have been. General manager Brian Sabean reportedly once turned down a trade that would have sent Brown to the Mets for Carlos Beltran. He sent Zack Wheeler instead. Brown did finally adjust to a more conventional setup at the plate as he repeated Triple-A Fresno in 2014. He used to pin his hands to his chest, which forced him to take a long path to his pre-swing load. Now his hands are further back and away from his body. The adjustment did help Brown make it to the big leagues for the first time in September. He showed he still has top-of-the-scale speed with a 3.7-seconds bunt single for his first hit. But Brown remains an inefficient basestealer. He doesn't walk enough to serve as a leadoff hitter, and he has had very little power. Brown projects as a backup outfielder who can play all three spots, though his average arm is stretched in right field.

Year	Club (League)	Class	AVG	G	AB	R	H	2B	3B	HR	RBI	BB	SO	SB	CS	OBP	SLG
2012	Richmond (EL)	AA	.279	134	538	73	150	32	2	7	42	40	87	33	18	.347	.385
2013	Fresno (PCL)	AAA	.231	137	558	79	129	29	6	13	50	33	135	17	11	.286	.375
2014	Fresno (PCL)	AAA	.271	136	536	89	145	24	6	10	53	36	119	36	20	.329	.394
	San Francisco (NL)	MAJ	.429	7	7	1	3	0	0	0	1	0	0	0	0	.429	.429
Major League Totals			.429	7	7	1	3	0	0	0	1	0	0	0	0	.429	.429
Minor League Totals			.277	550	2235	364	619	120	28	44	227	161	430	141	69	.342	.415

29 LOGAN WEBB, RHP

BA GRADE

45 Risk: High

Born: Nov. 18, 1996. **B-T:** R-R. **Ht.:** 6-2. **Wt.:** 195. **Drafted:** HS— Rocklin, Calif., 2014 (4th round). **Signed by:** Keith Snider.

A three-year starter at quarterback in high school, Webb wasn't all that well known in scouting circles heading into his senior year in 2014 because football had kept him off the showcase circuit for the most part. When he started throwing 95-96 mph off the mound as a senior, those football plans were quickly shelved. San Francisco had a built-in advantage because Rocklin, Calif., is not far from Sacramento, so they were able to run in multiple scouts to see him before signing him for $600,000 as a fourth-rounder. Webb's breaking ball has a ways to go, and the Giants will need to work with him on developing his changeup, but he's a relatively fresh, athletic arm, albeit one who was worked pretty hard during his senior season. The Giants let his arm recover in pro ball, throwing him only three times in the Rookie-level Arizona League before shutting him down until instructional league. Webb is a long way from San Francisco, but he's the kind of athletic power arm the Giants have done a great job of developing.

Year	Club (League)	Class	W	L	ERA	G	GS	CG	SV	IP	H	HR	BB	SO	K/9	WHIP	AVG
2014	Giants (AZL)	R	0	0	2.25	3	1	0	0	4	3	0	3	5	11.3	1.50	.200
Minor League Totals			0	0	2.25	3	1	0	0	4	3	0	3	5	11.3	1.50	.200

30 RYDER JONES, SS/3B

BA GRADE

45 Risk: High

Born: June 7, 1994. **B-T:** L-R. **Ht.:** 6-3. **Wt.:** 185. **Drafted:** HS—Boone, N.C., 2013 (2nd round). **Signed by:** Donnie Suttles.

When a high school player signs with Stanford, scouts often look away, believing it's usually too hard (or too expensive) to convince a player to spurn the Cardinal. But the Giants managed to talk Jones, the son of Appalachian State coach Billy Jones, into signing for the slot amount of $880,000 in the second round of the 2013 draft. Jones was considered a decent prospect as a pitcher but impressed more with his bat in high school. Few scouts projected him to stick at shortstop, but the Giants have played him there regularly. Eventually, he's expected to move to third base because of his lack of foot speed. He's already a well below-average runner, though he has a plus arm. Overmatched at shortstop, Jones must prove his hands and agility can play at third. His bat is a bigger long-term concern. His swing is geared for power with natural loft, but it's a long swing and he's struggled with velocity unless he cheats against fastballs. His long levers should bring power and strikeouts. After a tough first try at low Class A Augusta, Jones may need to return to the South Atlantic League in 2015.

Year	Club (League)	Class	AVG	G	AB	R	H	2B	3B	HR	RBI	BB	SO	SB	CS	OBP	SLG
2013	Giants (AZL)	R	.317	37	145	29	46	9	0	1	18	14	38	0	0	.394	.400
2014	Augusta (SAL)	LoA	.220	91	369	43	81	21	1	7	49	18	93	6	1	.272	.339
	Salem-Keizer (NWL)	SS	.243	27	107	17	26	5	1	3	18	7	21	1	0	.293	.393
Minor League Totals			.246	155	621	89	153	35	2	11	85	39	152	7	1	.305	.362

Seattle Mariners

BY J.J. COOPER

The Mariners experienced success in failure in 2014.

After a busy offseason in which they landed Robinson Cano, Seattle remained in the hunt for a playoff spot until the end. Needing a win and an Athletics loss on the final day of the season to force a one-game tie-breaker, the Mariners defeated the Angels 4-1 but watched Oakland shut out the Rangers to clinch the final American League wild card spot.

It was a disappointing end to the most compelling season that Seattle has seen in years. For the first time in Felix Hernandez's 10-year big league career, the Mariners played September games that mattered.

The club's battle for a playoff spot also paid off for the front office. General manager Jack Zduriencik signed a multi-year contract extension in August. He now is the club's longest-tenured GM since Woody Woodward held the job from 1988-99.

Now the Mariners face an equally compelling question: Can they keep up in the AL West, one of the most competitive divisions in baseball? For the first time in a while, the answer could be yes.

Seattle has holes to fill in the lineup in what should be a busy offseason, but those holes are at positions that are theoretically the easiest to fill. For example, getting any sort of production out of the DH spot was the Mariners' biggest problem in 2014. Corey Hart, Kendrys Morales and a host of others produced an unfathomable .190/.266/.301 batting line from the DH spot.

Center field also was a problem. Rookie James Jones swiped 27 bases in 28 tries but recorded a .278 on-base percentage. A midseason trade for the Tigers' Austin Jackson was supposed to fix the problem, but he didn't hit either. Altogether, Seattle center fielders hit .235/.271/.285.

But the Mariners also have an enviable core of both established veterans and young talent. Hernandez and Cano give the Mariners a pair of cornerstone players who are under team control for the rest of the decade. Third baseman Kyle Seager is nearly as valuable, and he's signed through 2018.

Just as importantly, Seattle has produced a wave of young pitchers to join Hernandez in the rotation. Lefthanders Roenis Elias and James Paxton both stepped into the rotation in 2014, while righthander Taijuan Walker should join them in 2015 after an impressive September stint.

Even if the pitchers aren't as effective in 2015 as they were the year before, Seattle should be competitive if they get a little more production from the lineup in home games.

Rookie southpaws James Paxton (pictured) and Roenis Elias joined Felix Hernandez and helped the Mariners lead the AL in ERA

TOP PROSPECTS OF THE DECADE

Year	Player, Pos.	2014 Org
2005	Felix Hernandez, rhp	Mariners
2006	Jeff Clement, c	Out of baseball
2007	Adam Jones, of	Orioles
2008	Jeff Clement, c	Out of baseball
2009	Greg Halman, of	Deceased
2010	Dustin Ackley, of/1b	Mariners
2011	Dustin Ackley, 2b	Mariners
2012	Taijuan Walker, rhp	Mariners
2013	Mike Zunino, c	Mariners
2014	Taijuan Walker, rhp	Mariners

After producing Elias, Paxton and Walker, the farm system is virtually exhausted of starting-pitching prospects. But part of that is by design. The Mariners have drafted position players in the first and second rounds of the past three drafts.

That position-player emphasis has provided depth for the big club. Brad Miller and Chris Taylor are expected to once again share the shortstop job in 2015, but eventually one of them could be traded.

On the horizon, 21-year-old shortstop Ketel Marte will be playing at Triple-A Tacoma, while third baseman D.J. Peterson and left fielder Patrick Kivlehan could be ready to help the lineup at some point in 2015. Plus, 2014 first-rounder Alex Jackson should be one of the fastest movers from his high school draft class.

Success in the long term can be measured only by reaching the playoffs—not merely getting close—but the outlook in Seattle is brighter today than it's been in a long time.

General manager: Jack Zduriencik. **Farm director:** Chris Gwynn. **Scouting director:** Tom McNamara.

Class	Team	League	W	L	PCT	Finish	Manager
Majors	Seattle Mariners	American	87	75	.537	11th (30)	Lloyd McClendon
Triple-A	Tacoma Rainiers	Pacific Coast	74	70	.514	T-7th (16)	Roy Howell
Double-A	Jackson Generals	Southern	63	76	.453	7th (10)	Jim Horner
High A	High Desert Mavericks	California	66	74	.471	7th (10)	Eddie Menchaca
Low A	Clinton LumberKings	Midwest	61	77	.442	T-14th (16)	Scott Steinmann
Short season	Everett AquaSox	Northwest	28	48	.368	8th (8)	Dave Valle
Rookie	Pulaski Mariners	Appalachian	36	30	.545	4th (10)	Rob Mummau
Rookie	Mariners	Arizona	31	22	.585	3rd (13)	Darrin Garner
Overall Minor League Record			359	397	.475	22nd (30)	

THIS YEAR'S TOP 30

No.	Player, Pos.	Grade
1.	Alex Jackson, of	65/High
2.	D.J. Peterson, 3b/1b	55/Medium
3.	Ketel Marte, ss/2b	50/Medium
4.	Patrick Kivlehan, 3b/1b	50/Medium
5.	Austin Wilson, of	55/Extreme
6.	Edwin Diaz, rhp	50/High
7.	Gabby Guerrero, of	50/High
8.	Luiz Gohara, lhp	55/Extreme
9.	Ryan Yarbrough, lhp	50/High
10.	Carson Smith, rhp	45/Medium
11.	Tyler O'Neill, of	50/High
12.	Gareth Morgan, of	55/Extreme
13.	John Hicks, c	45/Medium
14.	Tyler Marlette, c	50/High
15.	Jordy Lara, 1b/of	50/High
16.	Brayan Hernandez, of	55/Extreme
17.	Jack Reinheimer, ss/2b	45/Medium
18.	Joe DeCarlo, 3b	50/High
19.	Dan Altavilla, rhp	45/High
20.	Trey Cochran-Gill, rhp	45/High
21.	Erick Mejia, ss/2b	50/Extreme
22.	Rayder Ascanio, ss/2b	50/Extreme
23.	Austin Cousino, of	45/High
24.	Freddy Peralta, rhp	50/Extreme
25.	Julio Morban, of	50/Extreme
26.	Mayckol Guaipe, rhp	45/High
27.	Aaron Barbosa, of	45/High
28.	Jochi Ogando, rhp	45/High
29.	Ji-Man Choi, 1b	40/Medium
30.	Danny Hultzen, lhp	50/Extreme

LAST YEAR'S TOP 30

No.	Player, Pos.	Status
1.	Taijuan Walker, rhp	Majors
2.	D.J. Peterson, 3b	No. 2
3.	James Paxton, lhp	Majors
4.	Luiz Gohara, lhp	No. 8
5.	Edwin Diaz, rhp	No. 6
6.	Austin Wilson, of	No. 5
7.	Victor Sanchez, rhp	Dropped out
8.	Tyler Marlette, c	No. 14
9.	Chris Taylor, ss	Majors
10.	Danny Hultzen, lhp	No. 30
11.	Julio Morban, of	No. 25
12.	Patrick Kivlehan, 3b	No. 4
13.	Gabriel Guerrero, of	No. 7
14.	Carson Smith, rhp	No. 10
15.	Stefen Romero, of/2b	Majors
16.	Tyler Pike, lhp	Dropped out
17.	Abraham Almonte, of	(Padres)
18.	Tyler O'Neill, of	No. 11
19.	Jabari Blash, of	Dropped out
20.	Ketel Marte, ss/2b	No. 3
21.	Wilton Martinez, of	Dropped out
22.	Dominic Leone, rhp	Majors
23.	John Hicks, c	No. 13
24.	Timmy Lopes, 2b	Dropped out
25.	Ji-Man Choi, 1b	No. 29
26.	Jack Reinheimer, ss	No. 17
27.	James Jones, of	Majors
28.	Lars Huijer, rhp	Dropped out
29.	Guillermo Pimentel, of	Dropped out
30.	Dylan Unsworth, rhp	Dropped out

BEST TOOLS

Best Hitter for Average	Alex Jackson
Best Power Hitter	D.J. Peterson
Best Strike-Zone Discipline	Aaron Barbosa
Fastest Baserunner	Aaron Barbosa
Best Athlete	Patrick Kivlehan
Best Fastball	Edwin Diaz
Best Curveball	Matt Anderson
Best Slider	Carson Smith
Best Changeup	Ryan Yarbrough
Best Control	Daniel Missaki
Best Defensive Catcher	Steve Baron
Best Defensive Infielder	Rayder Ascanio
Best Infield Arm	Joe DeCarlo
Best Defensive Outfielder	Austin Cousino
Best Outfield Arm	Gabby Guerrero

PROJECTED 2018 LINEUP

Catcher	Mike Zunino
First Base	D.J. Peterson
Second Base	Robinson Cano
Third Base	Kyle Seager
Shortstop	Chris Taylor
Left Field	Dustin Ackley
Center Field	Ketel Marte
Right Field	Alex Jackson
Designated Hitter	Nelson Cruz
No. 1 Starter	Felix Hernandez
No. 2 Starter	James Paxton
No. 3 Starter	Taijuan Walker
No. 4 Starter	Hisashi Iwakuma
No. 5 Starter	Roenis Elias
Closer	Carson Smith

SEATTLE MARINERS

TOP 2015 ROOKIE: Carson Smith, rhp. He is ready to contribute quality innings to the big league bullpen

BREAKOUT PROSPECT: Tyler O'Neill, of. He didn't always show it in 2014, but his hitting ability could help him break out this year.

SLEEPER: Daniel Missaki, rhp. He has outstanding feel, and if he can gain a tick on his fastball, he could move quickly.

SOURCE OF TOP 30 TALENT			
Homegrown	30	Acquired	0
College	11	Trades	0
Junior college	0	Rule 5 draft	0
High school	5	Independent leagues	0
Draft-and-follow	0	Free agents/waivers	0
Nondrafted free agents	1		
International	13		

LF
Tyler O'Neill (11)
Jabari Henry
Estarlyn Morales
Dario Pizzano
Guillermo Pimentel

CF
Brayan Hernandez (16)
Austin Cousino (23)
Aaron Barbosa (27)
Luis Liberato
Leon Landry
Arby Fields

RF
Alex Jackson (1)
Austin Wilson (5)
Gabby Guerrero (7)
Gareth Morgan (12)
Julio Morban (25)
Hershin Martinez
Jabari Blash
Estarlyn Martinez
Wilton Martinez

3B
Joe DeCarlo (18)

SS
Jack Reinheimer (17)
Rayder Ascanio (22)
Tyler Smith

2B
Ketel Marte (3)
Erick Mejia (21)
Jack Marder
Timmy Lopes
Zach Shank

1B
D.J. Peterson (2)
Patrick Kivlehan (4)
Jordy Lara (15)
Ji-Man Choi (29)
Dan Paolini

C
John Hicks (13)
Tyler Marlette (14)
Steve Baron
Johan Quevedo
Marcus Littlewood
Dan Torres
Mike Dowd
Wayne Taylor

LHP

LHSP	LHRP
Luiz Gohara (8)	Spencer Hermann
Ryan Yarbrough (9)	Scott DeCecco
Danny Hultzen (30)	Nick Kiel
Tyler Pike	

RHP

RHSP	RHRP
Edwin Diaz (6)	Carson Smith (10)
Freddy Peralta (24)	Dan Altavilla (19)
Victor Sanchez	Trey Cochran-Gill (20)
Daniel Missaki	Mayckol Guaipe (26)
Zach Littell	Jochi Ogando (28)
Jordan Pries	Stephen Landazuri
Dylan Unsworth	Ronald Domiguez
Lars Huijer	Matt Brazis
	Peter Miller
	Tyler Herb
	Matt Anderson
	Logan Bawcom
	Ugueth Urbina
	Aaron Brooks
	Marvin Gorgas
	Rohn Pierce
	Emilio Pagan

2014

BEST PURE HITTER: OF Alex Jackson (1) was the top prep bat in the draft, offering plus bat speed, an advanced approach and above-average contact ability.

BEST POWER HITTER: Jackson possesses 70-grade raw power from the right side, with natural loft to his swing and the ability to drive the ball out of all parts of the ballpark. OF Gareth Morgan (2) has at least plus raw power as the ball jumps off his bat.

FASTEST RUNNER: SS Nelson Ward (12) is a plus-plus runner who puts pressure on the defense with a slashing approach from the left side. OF Austin Cousino (3) is an above-average runner with quickness who impacts games on the bases, stealing at a 94-percent clip in college.

BEST DEFENSIVE PLAYER: Cousino's speed, instincts and first-step quickness make him an above-average defender in center field with an average arm. Jackson has a plus-plus arm he is learning to use in right field.

BEST FASTBALL: LHP Ryan Yarbrough (4) saw his velocity increase in the spring and after reaching pro ball, sitting 90-93 mph, touching 95. His fastball has deception and angle. RHP Tyler Herb (29) also saw a velocity increase after working out of the pen, sitting 91-94, touching 96. RHP Dan Altavilla (5) sits 90-94 touches 96 with above-average arm-side bore.

BEST SECONDARY PITCH: Altavilla's slider flashes plus potential, as does Yarbrough's changeup. RHP Trey Cochran-Gill (17) is an athletic sinker/slider reliever with a 92-94 mph fastball and plus slider.

BEST PRO DEBUT: No pitcher with as many innings in the Northwest League (38) had a higher strikeout rate (12.3 per nine) than Yarbrough, who also had the second-lowest walk rate (0.9). Cochran-Gill allowed one earned run in 37 pro innings.

BEST ATHLETE: Morgan is a physical specimen with strong 6-foot-4, 220-pound build who moves well and has a plus arm. Cousino was a standout high school hockey player.

MOST INTRIGUING BACKGROUND: RHP Lukas Schiraldi (15), who flashes a sharp curveball, is the son of former major leaguer Calvin Schiraldi, who also pitched at Texas. Altavilla was the highest-drafted college pitcher who did not attend a Division I school.

CLOSEST TO THE MAJORS: Yarbrough can move quickly because of his ability to get out lefthanded hitters while pounding the strike zone.

BEST LATE-ROUND PICK: Herb showed a plus fastball this summer and flashed a plus breaking ball with some natural deception. Before RHP Marvin Gorgas (13) had Tommy John this summer, he showed a 91-94 mph fastball and a good breaking ball.

THE ONE WHO GOT AWAY: Prep OF DeAires Moses (31) is an 80 runner with raw physical ability. C Scott Manea (40) has defensive acumen from a strong, compact build and will head to North Carolina State.

ASSESSMENT: The Mariners invested most of their financial resources to get two of the top power hitters in the prep class and came away with arguably the top prep hitter in Alex Jackson.

2013

Seattle has gone all-in for righthanded power in recent years, with high hopes for 2013 classmates 3B/1B D.J. Peterson (1) and OFs Austin Wilson (2) and Tyler O'Neill (3).

GRADE: B

2012

C Mike Zunino (1) has shown power and defense; now if he could just hit .250. SS Chris Taylor (5) and RHP Dominic Leone (16) sped to the majors. RHP Edwin Diaz (3), 3B Pat Kivlehan (4) offer intriguing talent as well.

GRADE: B

2011

A shoulder injury has put LHP Danny Hultzen's (1) career in doubt. SS Brad Miller (2) has had his moments. RHPs Carter Capps (3s) and Carson Smith (8) have seen big league time.

GRADE: C

TOP DRAFT PICKS OF THE DECADE

Year	Player, Pos.	2014 Org
2005	Jeff Clement, c	Out of baseball
2006	Brandon Morrow, rhp	Blue Jays
2007	Phillippe Aumont, rhp	Phillies
2008	Josh Fields, rhp	Astros
2009	Dustin Ackley, of	Mariners
2010	Taijuan Walker, rhp (1st round supp.)	Mariners
2011	Danny Hultzen, lhp	Mariners
2012	Mike Zunino, c	Mariners
2013	D.J. Peterson, 3b	Mariners
2014	Alex Jackson, of	Mariners

LARGEST BONUSES IN CLUB HISTORY

Danny Hultzen, 2009	$6,350,000
Dustin Ackley, 2011	$6,000,000
Ichiro Suzuki, 2000	$5,000,000
Alex Jackson, 2014	$4,200,000
Mike Zunino, 2012	$4,000,000

1 ALEX JACKSON, OF

Born: Dec. 25, 1995. **B-T:** R-R. **Ht.:** 6-2. **Wt.:** 215.
Drafted: HS—San Diego, 2014 (1st round).
Signed by: Gary Patchett.

In scouting circles, a player who stands out in showcase after showcase is known as a famous player. Jackson is about as famous as they come. One of two two-time Under Armour All-America game participants, Jackson led all California high schoolers in home runs as a sophomore. He couldn't match that home run total as a junior or senior, but he was a three-time High School All-American and became the fifth Rancho Bernardo High product to go in the first round, joining a group that includes Cole Hamels. Jackson was in play ito go as high as No. 1 overall in the 2014 draft, but he was there for Seattle at No. 6 due in part to the pitching depth at the top of the class. Seattle signed Jackson for $4.2 million and promptly moved him from catcher to right field. He missed a month after being hit by a line drive that caused a small sinus fracture but got back on the field for the Rookie-level Arizona League's last three games.

Jackson was considered the best high school bat in the 2014 draft class, and he has the potential to be an above-average hitter with at least plus power. His swing is fluid with a picturesque finish that is usually the exclusive domain of lefthanded hitters. He combines bat speed, hand-eye coordination and a feel for controlling the barrel of the bat. He's an up-the-middle hitter with natural power to straightaway center field and the right-center gap. Because of his large number of at-bats on the showcase circuit and his participation in a highly competitive high school environment, Jackson has learned how to handle premium velocity by reducing what used to be a pronounced load at the start of his swing. He recognizes breaking balls well and should draw walks in addition to hitting for average. Jackson's plus power already plays in games, but his raw power is even more impressive. Defensively, he made a quick transition to the outfield, partly because he made a point of getting time both there and at third base during his high school career to increase his versatility. He's a below-average runner who should be at least an average right fielder long-term. His plus-plus arm recorded regular pop times of 1.8 seconds on throws to second base when he caught, and it looks to be a significant asset in the outfield, especially once he learns to take a proper outfielder's arm stroke.

Jackson has the highest ceiling among high school hitters the Mariners have drafted since they picked Alex Rodriguez No. 1 overall in 1993. By keeping Jackson away from catcher's gear, the Mariners will be able to move him up the ladder as his bat dictates instead of waiting for his defense to catch up. Jackson should be ready to head to low Class A Clinton in 2015. Long-term, if he develops as expected, he projects as a three-hole hitter who provides batting average, on-base ability and power.

BA GRADE

65 Risk High

SCOUTING GRADES

Batting: 60.
Power: 70.
Speed: 45.
Defense: 50.
Arm: 60.

Based on 20-80 scouting scale and future projection rather than present grades.

LGE	PA	BB%	SO%	ISO
AZL	94	9.6	25.5	.195

MIKE JANES

Year	Club (League)	Class	AVG	G	AB	R	H	2B	3B	HR	RBI	BB	SO	SB	CS	OBP	SLG
2014	Mariners (AZL)	R	.280	23	82	11	23	6	2	2	16	9	24	0	1	.344	.476
Minor League Totals			.280	23	82	11	23	6	2	2	16	9	24	0	1	.344	.476

2 D.J. PETERSON, 3B/1B

Born: Dec. 31, 1991. **B-T:** R-R. **Ht.:** 6-1. **Wt.:** 190. **Drafted:** New Mexico, 2013 (1st round). **Signed by:** Chris Pelekoudas.

When James Paxton failed to sign with the Blue Jays in 2009, it triggered a chain reaction that sent Peterson to New Mexico. With Paxton returning to Kentucky, the school cut its scholarship for infielder Andy Burns, so Burns transferred to Arizona. To make room for Burns, Arizona reduced its offer to Peterson, who went to UNM instead. A short-armed, stocky hitter with extremely strong arms, Peterson was hit by a pitch that broke his jaw and knocked out some teeth in 2013. He showed no ill effects in 2014. Peterson has a low trigger to his swing and is short to the ball with a pull-heavy approach. He can turn on premium velocity and shows an ability to recognize spin, but if he's going to live up to his potential to be an above-average hitter to go with his plus power, he's going to have to use the oppo-site field more. Defensively, Peterson is below-average at third base with limited range. His above-average arm is his best asset. He's a below-average runner, but he is smart on the basepaths. Peterson isn't all that far from the

BA GRADE

55 Risk: Medium

LGE	PA	BB%	SO%	ISO
CAL	299	7.7	21.7	.289
SL	248	8.9	20.6	.212

big leagues. If Seattle doesn't fill its needs at DH this offseason, he could be ready midway through 2015. Long-term, his bat should more than make up for his defensive limitations.

Year	Club (League)	Class	AVG	G	AB	R	H	2B	3B	HR	RBI	BB	SO	SB	CS	OBP	SLG
2013	Everett (NWL)	SS	.312	29	109	20	34	6	0	6	27	13	18	0	1	.382	.532
	Clinton (MWL)	LoA	.293	26	99	16	29	5	1	7	20	7	24	1	0	.346	.576
2014	High Desert (CAL)	HiA	.326	65	273	51	89	23	1	18	73	23	65	6	0	.381	.615
	Jackson (SL)	AA	.261	58	222	32	58	8	0	13	38	22	51	1	1	.335	.473
Minor League Totals			.299	178	703	119	210	42	2	44	158	65	158	8	2	.362	.552

3 KETEL MARTE, SS/2B

Born: Oct. 12, 1993. **B-T:** B-R. **Ht.:** 6-1. **Wt.:** 180. **Signed:** Dominican Republic, 2010. **Signed by:** Patrick Guerrero/Bob Engle/Franklin Taveras Jr.

Signed for $100,000 in 2010 as part of a $6 million Mariners inter-national signing class, Marte has proved to be the group's best prospect. He spent just 100 at-bats at high Class A High Desert before jumping to Double-A Jackson and made it to Triple-A Tacoma before his 21st birthday. Marte shows a compact, line-drive stroke from both sides of the plate. He is comfortable with deep counts, but he's always looking to hit. He is a difficult hitter to strike out and nearly impossible to walk. Marte has above-average speed and has developed into a solid bunter. Defensively, Marte has the easy hands and actions scouts like, but he lacks focus and his .932 fielding percentage was worst among regular Southern League shortstops. Marte's arm limits him at shortstop. He'll show above-average arm strength occasionally, but more often his throws are average at best. A number of scouts see him eventually moving to second base, where he projects as an above-average defender. Marte will be one of the youngest players in the

BA GRADE

50 Risk: Medium

LGE	PA	BB%	SO%	ISO
SL	472	4.0	13.8	.102
PCL	90	8.9	14.4	.138

Pacific Coast League in 2015. With Chris Taylor and Brad Miller at shortstop and Robinson Cano at second base in Seattle, there's no clear path to the big leagues for him right now, but time is on his side.

Year	Club (League)	Class	AVG	G	AB	R	H	2B	3B	HR	RBI	BB	SO	SB	CS	OBP	SLG
2012	Clinton (MWL)	LoA	.286	4	14	3	4	0	0	0	2	2	3	1	0	.375	.286
	Everett (NWL)	SS	.247	65	251	36	62	4	2	0	22	12	35	14	4	.281	.279
2013	Clinton (MWL)	LoA	.304	98	378	61	115	15	5	0	29	15	39	16	8	.330	.370
	High Desert (CAL)	HiA	.256	19	86	18	22	0	2	1	8	4	11	4	3	.289	.337
2014	Jackson (SL)	AA	.302	109	443	63	134	27	6	2	46	19	65	23	10	.329	.404
	Tacoma (PCL)	AAA	.313	19	80	16	25	5	0	2	9	8	13	6	0	.367	.450
Minor League Totals			.285	376	1472	241	419	56	18	7	138	86	201	80	31	.324	.361

4 PATRICK KIVLEHAN, 3B/1B

Born: Dec. 22, 1989. **B-T:** R-R. **Ht.:** 6-2. **Wt.:** 210. **Drafted:** Rutgers, 2012 (4th round). **Signed by:** Mike Moriarty.

Coming out of high school, Kivlehan had offers to play college baseball, but he opted instead to play football at Rutgers. He was a backup safety and special teams player for four years. When his football career concluded, he decided to take another crack at baseball. In his lone year of baseball at Rutgers, he finished sixth in NCAA Division I with a .693 slugging percentage. No hitting coach would teach hitting the way Kivlehan sets up for a pitch. He looks almost nervous in the box, tapping his front foot up and down, waving his bat in a circle. But his energetic setup works for him. Kivlehan is a tough out because he's a bad-ball hitter who has shown he can make in-bat adjustments. He not only punishes mistakes with average power now but he's learned to pull the ball, but he also hits line drives on pitcher's pitches. Scouts who like Kivlehan see him as having a chance to be an above-average hitter with average power. After beginning his career at third base, he now profiles best at first base or left field. He has athleticism and average running speed but lacks first-step quickness or throwing accuracy. Kivlehan's bat should make him suited for a big league role, possibly as a versatile multi-position player. He's ready for Triple-A Tacoma.

	BA GRADE	
50	Risk: Medium	

LGE	PA	BB%	SO%	ISO
CAL	157	7.6	20.4	.282
SL	431	10.2	18.1	.186

Year	Club (League)	Class	AVG	G	AB	R	H	2B	3B	HR	RBI	BB	SO	SB	CS	OBP	SLG
2012	Everett (NWL)	SS	.301	72	282	46	85	17	3	12	52	19	93	14	1	.373	.511
2013	Clinton (MWL)	LoA	.283	60	223	26	63	12	1	3	31	17	42	5	3	.344	.386
	High Desert (CAL)	HiA	.320	68	266	48	85	13	2	13	59	26	65	10	3	.384	.530
2014	High Desert (CAL)	HiA	.282	34	142	24	40	9	2	9	35	12	32	2	0	.331	.563
	Jackson (SL)	AA	.300	104	377	60	113	23	7	11	68	44	78	9	4	.374	.485
Minor League Totals			.299	338	1290	204	386	74	15	48	245	118	310	40	11	.366	.491

5 AUSTIN WILSON, OF

Born: Feb. 7, 1992. **B-T:** R-R. **Ht:** 6-4. **Wt.:** 210. **Drafted:** Stanford, 2013 (2nd round). **Signed by:** Stacey Pettis.

A possible first-round pick in 2010 coming out of high school in the Los Angeles area, Wilson's parents both held MBAs from Harvard, so teams knew that education was important to the Stanford commit and he fell to the 12th round. Three years later, Wilson fell to the second round but got first-round money ($1.7 million) to forgo his senior year. Wilson has long impressed with a physical, athletic build. Unfortunately, that physicality has not led to good health. He missed half of his junior year at Stanford with an elbow injury and missed more than a month in 2014 with a strained Achilles tendon. He then missed instructional league with minor elbow surgery. Wilson has shortened his lengthy swing as a pro, but evaluators still worry about his ability to turn on quality fastballs. He has made strides to become more fluid and athletic at the plate—he's not as upright in his stance, and he's using his legs more in his swing. He needs to take pitches on the outer half the other way more often. Defensively he's an average right fielder. Moreso than most premium college draftees, Wilson is a high-ceiling outfielder who still is a long way from that ceiling. The struggles of former Stanford outfielder Michael Taylor have led some evaluators to be more skeptical of Wilson, but if he puts it all together, he will be an impact outfielder.

	BA GRADE	
55	Risk: Extreme	

LGE	PA	BB%	SO%	ISO
MWL	299	8.7	21.7	.226

Year	Club (League)	Class	AVG	G	AB	R	H	2B	3B	HR	RBI	BB	SO	SB	CS	OBP	SLG
2013	Everett (NWL)	SS	.241	56	203	22	49	11	3	6	27	17	42	2	4	.319	.414
2014	Mariners (AZL)	R	.625	3	8	3	5	1	1	1	1	1	2	1	0	.667	1.375
	Clinton (MWL)	LoA	.291	72	261	38	76	17	3	12	54	26	65	1	1	.376	.517
Minor League Totals			.275	131	472	63	130	29	7	19	82	44	109	4	5	.356	.487

6 EDWIN DIAZ, RHP

Born: March 22, 1994. **B-T:** R-R. **Ht.:** 6-2. **Wt.:** 178. **Drafted:** HS—Caguas, P.R., 2012 (3rd round). **Signed by:** Noel Sevilla.

When the Mariners drafted Diaz, he was a raw, pencil-thin righthander with a promising arm but not enough meat on his bones. He's done a good job at adding good weight and now has the frame of a potential starter. Signed for $300,000, Diaz had only pitched for three years at that time, but he's made a quick transition to pro ball. Diaz has arguably the best arm in the system. He sits at 91-93 mph and will touch 97 on his best day. His low three-quarters arm slot is a tough look for righthanders, especially as he gets plenty of armside run. Diaz has shown average control with an ability to locate his fastball to both sides of the plate, but his delivery is long in back, with a hooking arm action and recoil as he finishes. He sometimes rushes too quickly through his delivery, though he does self-diagnose his delivery flaws as they crop up and his head remains still. Diaz's slider is an average pitch when he stays on top of it, but he too often drops his elbow and gets on the side of it. His changeup has improved to flash average. Diaz's delivery and his still-skinny frame makes some scouts project him as a reliever, but he's shown feel for setting up hitters and has the makings of three pitches. If he can survive at high Class A Bakersfield in 2015, then he'll further establish himself as the Mariners' best young arm.

BA GRADE

50 Risk: High

LGE	BF	SO%	BB%	HR/9
MWL	483	23.0	8.7	0.39

Year	Club (League)	Class	W	L	ERA	G	GS	CG	SV	IP	H	HR	BB	SO	K/9	WHIP	AVG
2012	Mariners (AZL)	R	2	1	5.21	9	1	0	0	19	12	2	17	20	9.5	1.53	.176
2013	Pulaski (APP)	R	5	2	1.43	13	13	0	0	69	45	5	18	79	10.3	0.91	.191
2014	Clinton (MWL)	LoA	6	8	3.33	24	24	1	0	116	96	5	42	111	8.6	1.19	.226
Minor League Totals			13	11	2.86	46	38	1	0	204	153	12	77	210	9.2	1.13	.210

7 GABBY GUERRERO, OF

Born: Dec. 11, 1993. **B-T:** R-R. **Ht.:** 6-3. **Wt.:** 190. **Signed:** Dominican Republic, 2011. **Signed by:** Patrick Guerrero/Bob Engle/Franklin Taveras Jr.

If your last name is Guerrero, you have a high-pocketed, limber frame and you've even worn No. 27 at times, you're going to draw comparisons with Vladimir Guerrero, especially when you're his nephew. As one opposing manager explained it, Guerrero doesn't really have an approach. He swings hard each and every time, but he is doing a better job of recognizing which pitches to lay off. Now when he swings through a breaking ball, he just might send the next one over the fence, and he will punish any pitcher who misses with a fastball. Guerrero has plus-plus raw power thanks to an extremely loose swing and strong hands. He has a chance to eventually have above-average productive power, though his free-swinging ways and long swing will limit his hitting ability. His plus-plus arm in right field keeps runners honest, though he is sometimes a little too aggressive at trying to gun down any and all. Defensively, Guerrero is still a little erratic (six errors), but he has above-average range thanks to long strides. He's a tick above-average runner underway who turns in average times out of the batter's box. Guerrero's numbers will likely take a step back as he jumps to Double-A Jackson, but he's a high-ceiling, high-risk prospect and potential everyday right fielder.

BA GRADE

50 Risk: High

LGE	PA	BB%	SO%	ISO
CAL	580	5.9	22.6	.160

Year	Club (League)	Class	AVG	G	AB	R	H	2B	3B	HR	RBI	BB	SO	SB	CS	OBP	SLG
2012	Mariners (DSL)	R	.355	50	200	38	71	9	4	11	54	21	28	4	6	.409	.605
	Mariners (AZL)	R	.333	18	75	17	25	5	0	4	18	3	13	0	0	.350	.560
2013	Clinton (MWL)	LoA	.271	125	469	60	127	23	3	4	50	21	113	12	3	.303	.358
2014	High Desert (CAL)	HiA	.307	131	538	97	165	28	2	18	96	34	131	18	6	.347	.467
Minor League Totals			.294	381	1473	236	433	74	9	38	232	93	314	38	18	.334	.434

8 LUIZ GOHARA, LHP

Born: July 31, 1996. **B-T:** L-L. **Ht.:** 6-3. **Wt.:** 210. **Signed:** Brazil, 2012. **Signed by:** Emilio Carrasquel/Hide Sueyoshi.

The word "polished" doesn't often describe a Brazilian baseball player, but Gohara fit the bill with years of baseball under his belt when he signed for $800,000 in 2012. The Mariners were impressed enough to push him right to Rookie-level Pulaski for his pro debut. Gohara's fast track through the minors hit a pothole at short-season Everett. He showed every reminder that he was one of the youngest players in the league. He struggled to repeat his delivery, didn't throw nearly enough strikes and was squared up too often when he did find the strike zone. In one start, Gohara gave up home runs to three of the first six batters he faced. In another, he walked three of the first five and hit another. The good news for Gohara is that his stuff was still apparent, and he stayed healthy after a balky shoulder limited his innings in 2013. He sits at 92-94 mph and will touch 96, and at times he showed a potentially above-average breaking ball to go with a changeup that flashes average.Gohara is farther away from the big leagues than he was when the

BA GRADE

55 Risk: **Extreme**

LGE	BF	SO%	BB%	HR/9
AZL	51	31.4	3.9	0.00
NWL	187	19.8	12.8	1.45

season began. His control and feel both took steps back, but he's still a 6-foot-3 lefty who throws in the mid-90s, so he has plenty of time to get back on track as a potential mid-rotation starter.

Year	Club (League)	Class	W	L	ERA	G	GS	CG	SV	IP	H	HR	BB	SO	K/9	WHIP	AVG
2013	Pulaski (APP)	R	1	2	4.15	6	6	0	0	22	22	1	9	27	11.2	1.43	.256
2014	Mariners (AZL)	R	1	1	2.13	2	2	0	0	13	11	0	2	16	11.4	1.03	.234
	Everett (NWL)	SS	0	6	8.20	11	11	0	0	37	46	6	24	37	8.9	1.88	.293
Minor League Totals			2	9	5.90	19	19	0	0	72	79	7	35	80	10.0	1.59	.272

9 RYAN YARBROUGH, LHP

Born: Dec. 31, 1991. **B-T:** L-L. **Ht.:** 6-5. **Wt.:** 205. **Drafted:** Old Dominion, 2014 (4th round). **Signed by:** Devitt Moore.

With the Mariners planning to go well above slot to sign second-rounder Gareth Morgan, the scouting staff knew to be on the lookout for inexpensive senior signs who could fit as top 10-rounds picks. Scout Devitt Moore hit the jackpot, for he signed fourth-rounder Yarbrough for just $40,000, then watched him make a loud debut at short-season Everett, showing better stuff than he had displayed in college. As dominant as Yarbrough's performance was in the short-season Northwest League, his stuff was equally impressive. He sat at 88-91 mph at Old Dominion, succeeding by mixing pitches and hitting spots, but with the Mariners he picked up a tick or two, sitting at 90-93 mph in shorter, three-inning stints and touching 95. Yarbrough gets excellent angle and sink on his fastball and pairs it with a changeup that is above-average at its best. His slurvy curveball has a chance to be a fringe-average pitch. All three play up because of his above-average control. Thanks to his low arm slot and deceptive delivery, Yarbrough

BA GRADE

50 Risk: **High**

LGE	BF	SO%	BB%	HR/9
APP	15	33.3	6.7	0.00
NWL	145	36.6	2.8	0.23

should be at least a useful lefty reliever. But if he can maintain his newfound velocity over longer stretches in 2015, he could climb the ladder quickly as a starter.

Year	Club (League)	Class	W	L	ERA	G	GS	CG	SV	IP	H	HR	BB	SO	K/9	WHIP	AVG
2014	Pulaski (APP)	R	0	0	0.00	2	0	0	1	4	1	0	1	5	11.3	0.50	.071
	Everett (NWL)	SS	0	1	1.40	12	10	0	0	39	25	1	4	53	12.3	0.75	.180
Minor League Totals			0	1	1.27	14	10	0	1	43	26	1	5	58	12.2	0.73	.170

10 CARSON SMITH, RHP

Born: Oct. 19, 1989. **B-T:** R-R. **Ht.:** 6-6. **Wt.:** 215. **Drafted:** Texas State, 2011 (8th round). **Signed by:** Kyle Van Hook.

The Mariners have a history of finding one useful rookie reliever per year to fit into the big league bullpen. It was Dominic Leone in 2014, Yoervis Medina in 2013, Carter Capps in 2012 and Tom Wilhelmsen in 2011. Expect Smith, a starter at Texas State who quickly moved to the pen as a Mariner, to be the next to make the jump after he impressed in a brief stint as a September callup in 2014. Pitching from the extreme glove side of the pitcher's rubber, Smith slings from an almost sidearm slot, mixing in a dive-bombing 84-86 mph slider that grades as plus. But thanks to his ability to locate to both sides of the plate and his mid-80s mph changeup, Smith is nearly as tough on lefthanders. His fastball gained a tick to sit at 92-94 mph with bumps up to 96, but it's the sink he gets when he's working down in the zone that makes his heater most effective. He has allowed just four home runs in 141 pro appearances and has racked up more than 3.5 groundouts for every airout at his last three stops. Smith isn't conventional and his delivery has plenty of effort, but he's steadily improved his control to average. He's ready to help the Mariners as a middle reliever in 2015, and he has a shot to eventually handle the eighth inning.

BA GRADE

45 Risk: Medium

	LGE	BF	SO%	BB%	HR/9
	PCL	182	24.7	7.1	0.21
	AL	29	34.5	10.3	0.00

Year	Club (League)	Class	W	L	ERA	G	GS	CG	SV	IP	H	HR	BB	SO	K/9	WHIP	AVG
2012	High Desert (CAL)	HiA	5	1	2.90	49	0	0	15	62	54	2	28	77	11.2	1.32	.234
2013	Jackson (SL)	AA	1	3	1.98	44	0	0	15	50	33	1	17	71	12.8	1.00	.183
2014	Tacoma (PCL)	AAA	1	3	2.93	39	0	0	10	43	44	1	13	45	9.4	1.33	.265
	Seattle (AL)	MAJ	1	0	0.00	9	0	0	0	8	2	0	3	10	10.8	0.60	.077
Major League Totals			1	0	0.00	9	0	0	0	8	2	0	3	10	10.8	0.60	.077
Minor League Totals			7	7	2.61	132	0	0	40	155	131	4	58	193	11.2	1.22	.227

11 TYLER O'NEILL, OF

BA GRADE

50 Risk: High

Born: June 22, 1995. **B-T:** R-R. **Ht.:** 5-11. **Wt.:** 205. **Drafted:** HS— Maple Ridge, B.C., 2013 (3rd round). **Signed by:** Wayne Norton.

Much as they did with Alex Jackson, the Mariners liked O'Neill's bat enough that they simplified his defensive responsibilities. A high school catcher, O'Neill moved to left field upon signing. Frustrated with a May 10 strikeout while with low Class A Clinton in 2014, O'Neill punched a dugout wall and broke his hand. He didn't return to action until the final day of July. In just 57 games, he led Clinton with 13 home runs. A thickly-muscled son of a body builder, O'Neill has started to reshape his body as a pro, losing some bulk in his chest while developing stronger arms, wrists and legs. He has premium bat speed and can turn on any fastball. That has partly been his downfall, because he also ends up trying to yank offspeed offerings on the outer half. He's hasn't shown the ability to adjust his approach, but he will punish a loopy breaking ball. Because of O'Neill's bat speed and a straightforward, simple swing path, a number of scouts project him to be at least an average hitter with above-average power. He's an average runner with a solid-average arm. That athleticism hasn't translated to results in left field so far, for his poor routes and reads make him a below-average defender. He will have to improve his approach at high Class A Bakersfield in 2015.

Year	Club (League)	Class	AVG	G	AB	R	H	2B	3B	HR	RBI	BB	SO	SB	CS	OBP	SLG
2013	Mariners (AZL)	R	.310	28	100	12	31	5	3	1	15	12	27	2	4	.405	.450
2014	Mariners (AZL)	R	.000	1	2	0	0	0	0	0	0	0	1	0	0	.000	.000
	Everett (NWL)	SS	.400	3	10	2	4	2	0	0	2	1	5	0	0	.455	.600
	Clinton (MWL)	LoA	.247	57	219	31	54	9	0	13	38	20	79	5	0	.322	.466
Minor League Totals			.269	89	331	45	89	16	3	14	55	33	112	7	4	.350	.462

12 GARETH MORGAN, OF

BA GRADE

55 Risk: Extreme

Born: April 12, 1996. **B-T:** R-R. **Ht.:** 6-4. **Wt.:** 220. **Drafted:** HS— Toronto, 2014 (2nd round supplemental). **Signed by:** Wayne Norton.

By taking Morgan, a Toronto prep product, in the second round of the 2014 draft, a year after selecting Tyler O'Neill, the Mariners have taken the first Canadian off the board in back-to-back years. Morgan, like O'Neill, played for Team Canada's junior national team. The Mariners signed Morgan out of the supplemental second round for $2 million. Morgan had a big league body as a high school junior, which, coupled with his mature strength, gives him plus-plus raw power. The ball flies off his bat when he connects squarely. Morgan had made significant strides over the final year of his amateur career as he started to recognize breaking balls more often. His bat suffered a relapse in his pro debut. Morgan played some center field in his debut, but he's already a below-average runner who will only slow down further. The real question is whether his strong but erratic arm will play in right. Morgan has the ceiling of an impact everyday player, but his contact issues are troubling. He probably won't be ready for low Class A Clinton in 2015.

Year	Club (League)	Class	AVG	G	AB	R	H	2B	3B	HR	RBI	BB	SO	SB	CS	OBP	SLG
2014	Mariners (AZL)	R	.148	45	155	15	23	8	1	2	12	16	73	4	1	.244	.252
Minor League Totals			.148	45	155	15	23	8	1	2	12	16	73	4	1	.244	.252

13 JOHN HICKS, C

Born: Aug. 31, 1989. **B-T:** R-R. **Ht.:** 6-2. **Wt.:** 210. **Drafted:** Virginia, 2011 (4th round). **Signed by:** Mike Moriarty.

BA GRADE
45 Risk: Medium

When area scout Mike Moriarty sat on Virginia's club, he made his time count. The Mariners drafted Cavaliers lefthander Danny Hultzen, third baseman Steven Proscia and Hicks in 2011 and followed with shortstop Chris Taylor in 2012. Hicks proved to be one of the best defenders in the organization. He lacks a standout tool, but he has an average arm and is considered an average to tick above-average receiver. Pitchers love throwing to Hicks because he calls a good game and smothers everything in the dirt. At the plate, he has made strides, but he has well below-average power to go with a tick-below average hit tool. He's gotten better at incorporating his lower half into his swing, but he still chases too many pitches and doesn't really do damage when he does connect. Hicks is an average runner, good enough that the Mariners have toyed with the idea of having him play the corner outfield. Added to the 40-man roster in November, Hicks will begin at Tacoma in 2015. He has all the tools to be a big league backup catcher.

Year	Club (League)	Class	AVG	G	AB	R	H	2B	3B	HR	RBI	BB	SO	SB	CS	OBP	SLG
2012	High Desert (CAL)	HiA	.312	121	506	87	158	32	2	15	79	28	73	22	8	.351	.472
2013	Jackson (SL)	AA	.236	80	296	40	70	14	1	4	29	22	62	13	4	.301	.331
2014	Jackson (SL)	AA	.296	53	189	29	56	10	2	3	27	20	42	6	3	.362	.418
	Tacoma (PCL)	AAA	.277	28	101	13	28	2	1	2	20	7	24	1	0	.330	.376
Minor League Totals			.288	320	1231	190	355	67	8	26	181	82	218	44	18	.337	.419

14 TYLER MARLETTE, C

Born: Jan. 23, 1993. **B-T:** R-R. **Ht.:** 5-11. **Wt.:** 195. **Drafted:** HS— Oviedo, Fla., 2011 (5th round). **Signed by:** Rob Mummau.

BA GRADE
50 Risk: High

Marlette's bat has always been ahead of his glove. He's not a smooth receiver, and he struggles to block balls in the dirt. He has yet to learn the focus to bear down pitch after pitch, and his game-calling must improve. Marlette led the California League in errors (12) and passed balls (22) at high Class A High Desert in 2014. He does show an average arm and threw out 33 percent of basestealers. At the plate, Marlette has fewer issues. He always looks to yank a fastball and do damage, and thanks to his quick hands, he can turn on inside pitches despite a significant load to start his swing. Marlette's bat gives him a chance to be an average hitter with 10-12 home runs. He's a bottom-of-the-scale runner. Marlette has a long way to go defensively, but his hitting ability will give him plenty of chances to work on his defense.

Year	Club (League)	Class	AVG	G	AB	R	H	2B	3B	HR	RBI	BB	SO	SB	CS	OBP	SLG
2012	Pulaski (APP)	R	.284	56	208	23	59	14	0	5	23	6	46	3	1	.304	.423
	Everett (NWL)	SS	.400	2	5	0	2	1	0	0	0	0	1	0	1	.400	.600
2013	Clinton (MWL)	LoA	.304	75	270	36	82	17	2	6	37	24	53	10	4	.367	.448
2014	High Desert (CAL)	HiA	.301	81	312	51	94	23	0	15	49	24	61	9	2	.351	.519
	Jackson (SL)	AA	.250	9	32	3	8	2	0	2	2	4	10	0	1	.333	.500
Minor League Totals			.289	235	872	117	252	59	2	28	113	58	184	22	9	.335	.458

15 JORDY LARA, 1B/OF

Born: **B-T:** R-R. **Ht.:** 6-3. **Wt.:** 180. **Signed:** Dominican Republic, 2008. **Signed by:** Patrick Guerrero/Luis Scheker.

BA GRADE
50 Risk: High

The frenzied hitting environment at high Class A High Desert distorts offensive production for all types of batters. Some evaluators see Lara's season as a product of that environment—he won the California League batting title (.353) and finished runner-up for on-base (.413) and slugging (.609) percentage—but others aren't so dismissive. He used the right-center field gap well and squared balls up with the approach of an above-average hitter whose solid contact from the right side leads to at least average power. Lara's well below-average running ability limits him defensively. He has a plus arm with above-average accuracy, but his range in right field is well below-average. He's an adequate first baseman. Lara doesn't get tripped up when he faces a pitcher who can spin a breaking ball, and he hits the ball where it's pitched. Lara should return to Double-A Jackson to begin 2015. As a right/right first baseman, he'll have to remain prolific to get a shot in the big leagues.

Year	Club (League)	Class	AVG	G	AB	R	H	2B	3B	HR	RBI	BB	SO	SB	CS	OBP	SLG
2012	Pulaski (APP)	R	.243	63	239	26	58	14	2	8	41	18	48	1	0	.306	.418
2013	Clinton (MWL)	LoA	.260	98	339	39	88	25	3	10	63	29	68	3	0	.317	.440
	High Desert (CAL)	HiA	.311	15	61	11	19	2	0	3	9	1	13	0	0	.333	.492
2014	High Desert (CAL)	HiA	.353	102	399	77	141	26	5	22	80	38	82	1	3	.413	.609
	Jackson (SL)	AA	.286	33	126	14	36	14	0	4	24	8	19	0	0	.326	.492
Minor League Totals			.271	473	1662	252	450	111	13	64	304	182	381	16	10	.347	.469

16 BRAYAN HERNANDEZ, OF

BA GRADE

55 Risk: Extreme

Born: Sept. 11, 1997. **B-T:** B-R. **Ht.:** 6-1. **Wt.:** 170. **Signed:** Venezuela, 2014. **Signed by:** Emilio Carrasquel/Tim Kissner.

Hernandez was considered one of the best hitters and athletes available in the 2014 international signing class, though a shoulder injury limited his throwing and kept him from switch-hitting during the leadup to the opening of the signing period on July 2. The Mariners signed him for $2 million. Hernandez showed no long-term effects from the injury and was once again swinging lefthanded during instructional league. His swing is pretty simple from both sides. He doesn't have a significant load before coming through the zone with a level swing that stays in the zone a long time. Scouts have more questions about Hernandez's power potential. He has strong wrists, but like many teenagers he'll need to fill out further to develop even average power. Hernandez is a tick above-average runner with an athletic build. He likely will start his career in center field, where his solid reads and routes should allow him to stick even if he slows down a little as he fills out.

Year	Club (League)	Class	AVG	G	AB	R	H	2B	3B	HR	RBI	BB	SO	SB	CS	OBP	SLG
2014	Did not play—Signed 2015 contract																

17 JACK REINHEIMER, SS/2B

BA GRADE

45 Risk: Medium

Born: July 19, 1992. **B-T:** R-R. **Ht.:** 6-1. **Wt.:** 175. **Drafted:** East Carolina, 2013 (5th round). **Signed by:** Devitt Moore.

Evaluators around baseball generally believe it's difficult to find a true shortstop from the four-year college ranks, where players can play the position reliably but are thought to lack the range and athleticism teams desire. The Mariners have bucked that belief and it has paid off, for they have Chris Taylor and Brad Miller, a pair of college shortstops, splitting the job in Seattle. Reinheimer could add to that trend. He has an average arm and average range, but he's an extremely steady defender with good footwork and an excellent internal clock. To avoid a utility profile, Reinheimer will have to show more pop. He needs to add upper-body strength, because he has virtually no power. He does a good job of slapping the ball to the opposite field, but he lacks the bat speed to do much more. He does have a tick above-average speed. Reinheimer most likely ends up as a steady utility player whose bat limits him from a larger role. He will move to high Class A Bakersfield in 2015.

Year	Club (League)	Class	AVG	G	AB	R	H	2B	3B	HR	RBI	BB	SO	SB	CS	OBP	SLG
2013	Everett (NWL)	SS	.269	66	249	39	67	6	1	2	30	32	51	18	5	.359	.325
2014	Clinton (MWL)	LoA	.264	110	436	69	115	17	4	2	46	39	76	34	9	.333	.335
	High Desert (CAL)	HiA	.341	20	85	15	29	5	1	1	12	4	12	5	2	.367	.459
Minor League Totals			.274	196	770	123	211	28	6	5	88	75	139	57	16	.345	.345

18 JOE DeCARLO, 3B

BA GRADE

50 Risk: High

Born: Sept. 13, 1993. **B-T:** R-R. **Ht.:** 6-0. **Wt.:** 205. **Drafted:** HS—Glen Mills, Pa., 2012 (2nd round). **Signed by:** Mike Moriarty.

A second-round pick in 2012, DeCarlo signed for $1.3 million to pass on a commitment to Georgia. He and low Class A Clinton teammates Austin Wilson and Tyler O'Neill spent too much time in Arizona rehabbing injuries in 2014 rather than anchoring the middle of the LumberKings lineup. In DeCarlo's case, he suffered a thumb injury when he was hit by a pitch on June 11. While the injury was a setback, it also served as a chance for the physical third baseman to hit the reset button after an awful start to the season. He hit .200/.311/.330 before the injury, then .349/.443/.494 after his return. DeCarlo's swing is short and direct, which should allow him to hit for at least average power with a solid-average hit tool. He's the best defensive third baseman the Mariners have in their system, with quick reactions, solid range and an above-average, accurate arm. He's a below-average runner. DeCarlo's defensive tools take some pressure off his bat, but he has modest potential at the plate as well. He'll begin 2015 at high Class A Bakersfield.

Year	Club (League)	Class	AVG	G	AB	R	H	2B	3B	HR	RBI	BB	SO	SB	CS	OBP	SLG
2012	Mariners (AZL)	R	.236	53	182	29	43	12	3	4	31	31	47	0	2	.368	.401
2013	Pulaski (APP)	R	.250	27	96	18	24	4	0	4	15	17	42	0	1	.368	.417
2014	Mariners (AZL)	R	.500	1	2	1	1	0	0	0	0	0	0	0	0	.500	.500
	Everett (NWL)	SS	.222	3	9	2	2	1	0	0	1	1	5	0	0	.364	.333
	Clinton (MWL)	LoA	.246	80	268	29	66	19	1	5	42	36	84	0	1	.351	.381
Minor League Totals			.244	164	557	79	136	36	4	13	89	85	178	0	4	.360	.393

19 DAN ALTAVILLA, RHP

BA GRADE

45 Risk: High

Born: Sept. 8, 1992. **B-T:** R-R. **Ht.:** 5-11. **Wt.:** 200. **Drafted:** Mercyhurst (Pa.), 2014 (5th round). **Signed by:** Mike Moriarty.

Scouts don't have many reasons to check out NCAA Division II schools like Mercyhurst in Erie, Pa., but every now and then, a hidden gem like Altavilla emerges. He became the highest-drafted player in Mercyhurst program history, going in the fifth round in 2014 and breaking the record previously held by Orioles outfielder David Lough, an 11th-round pick in 2007. The D-II pitcher of the year, Altavilla posted a 0.57 ERA in his senior year of high school, a 0.91 ERA as a freshman and a 1.23 ERA as a junior. So he's had long stretches of dominance against admittedly weaker competition. Altavilla's dominance comes from impressive stuff. He sits 90-94 mph and has touched 97, thanks to strong legs which he incorporates into his delivery. His fastball has boring action to the arm side. He also throws a hard 82-85 mph power slider with tilt that could give him a second plus pitch. His changeup has some late drop, but it's a little too firm. Most scouts project him as a reliever because of the effort in his delivery, though the Mariners plan to see if he can remain in the rotation.

Year	Club (League)	Class	W	L	ERA	G	GS	CG	SV	IP	H	HR	BB	SO	K/9	WHIP	AVG
2014	Everett (NWL)	SS	5	3	4.36	14	14	0	0	66	74	7	32	66	9.0	1.61	.288
Minor League Totals			5	3	4.36	14	14	0	0	66	74	7	32	66	9.0	1.61	.288

20 TREY COCHRAN-GILL, RHP

BA GRADE

45 Risk: High

Born: Dec. 10, 1992. **B-T:** R-R. **Ht.:** 5-10. **Wt.:** 190. **Drafted:** Auburn, 2014 (17th round). **Signed by:** Dustin Evans.

The Mariners' search for inexpensive college pitchers who could step in and contribute paid off with a number of intriguing arms who were better in their pro debuts than they were during their amateur careers. Lefty Ryan Yarbrough stood out the most, as his stuff jumped up a full grade, but Cochran-Gill, a three-year reliever at Auburn, also impressed with a pair of pitches that allow him to profile as a potential big league reliever. He dominated at Rookie-level Pulaski and short-season Everett with a 92-94 mph fastball that showed outstanding sink as well as a plus slider. Cochran-Gill has a compact delivery that makes it relatively easy for him to fill the zone. Unlike Yarbrough, Cochran-Gill's stuff did not improve as a pro, but his results did. He can move quickly as a two-pitch reliever with the ability to generate groundballs.

Year	Club (League)	Class	W	L	ERA	G	GS	CG	SV	IP	H	HR	BB	SO	K/9	WHIP	AVG
2014	Pulaski (APP)	R	3	0	0.35	18	0	0	8	26	14	0	3	33	11.6	0.66	.154
	Everett (NWL)	SS	2	0	0.00	7	0	0	4	11	8	0	4	11	9.3	1.13	.216
Minor League Totals			5	0	0.25	25	0	0	12	36	22	0	7	44	10.9	0.80	.172

21 ERICK MEJIA, SS/2B

BA GRADE

50 Risk: Extreme

Born: Nov. 9, 1994. **B-T:** B-R. **Ht.:** 5-11. **Wt.:** 155. **Signed:** Dominican Republic, 2012. **Signed by:** Patrick Guerrero/Franklin Taveras Jr.

If not for a separated shoulder that ended his 2013 season early, Mejia might not have had to share the middle infield in 2014 with Rayder Ascanio in the Rookie-level Arizona League. But because that injury cost him a month, he came back to the AZL where he teamed with Ascanio to form a dynamic duo. Mejia has much more present strength than his teammate, which was apparent as he finished tied for third in the AZL with six triples. An above-average runner, he shows the pop to grow into an average hitter with 5-10 home run power, and he has advanced plate discipline for his age. He's not nearly as smooth or flashy a defender as Ascanio, but he has a chance to be an average or even tick above-average second baseman who is a fringy defender at shortstop because of average actions and range. That might be selling Mejia a little short because he does have a plus arm. He may jump ahead of Ascanio to head to short-season Everett.

Year	Club (League)	Class	AVG	G	AB	R	H	2B	3B	HR	RBI	BB	SO	SB	CS	OBP	SLG
2012	Mariners (DSL)	R	.182	13	44	9	8	2	2	0	8	8	7	3	2	.308	.318
2013	Mariners (DSL)	R	.261	24	88	16	23	3	1	0	3	14	10	11	7	.365	.318
	Mariners (AZL)	R	.360	7	25	4	9	2	0	0	2	2	5	2	0	.407	.440
2014	Mariners (AZL)	R	.283	38	127	23	36	3	6	1	13	16	25	13	2	.361	.425
Minor League Totals			.268	82	284	52	76	10	9	1	26	40	47	29	11	.358	.377

22 RAYDER ASCANIO, SS/2B

BA GRADE **50** Risk: Extreme

Born: March 17, 1996. **B-T:** B-R. **Ht.:** 5-11. **Wt.:** 155. **Signed:** Venezuela, 2012. **Signed by:** Illich Salazar/Emilio Carrasquel/Tim Kissner.

Many shortstops around the minors fail to make the majors because they don't hit enough to justify giving them regular playing time, despite their excellent glovework. But every now and then, those defensive wizards add strength and turn into productive everyday shortstops. Ascanio is a long way from being a productive big leaguer, but he has a variety of the tools and skills to get there. Jack Reinheimer is the Mariners' most reliable minor league shortstop, but Ascanio grades out better in terms of raw tools, for he has plus range, outstanding hands, excellent footwork and a plus arm. Ascanio split time between second base and shortstop, but he projects as shortstop. At the plate, he has zero present power and will have to gain plenty of strength to even start stinging line-drive singles, but he does know how to draw a walk and he is a tick above-average runner. His ability to switch-hit serves him well, but he needs to improve his lefthanded swing, which produces even less thump or bat speed than his righthanded stroke.

Year	Club (League)	Class	AVG	G	AB	R	H	2B	3B	HR	RBI	BB	SO	SB	CS	OBP	SLG
2013	Mariners (VSL)	R	.266	50	143	28	38	9	3	3	18	23	33	3	3	.376	.434
2014	Mariners (VSL)	R	.133	5	15	1	2	0	0	0	0	1	3	0	0	.188	.133
	Mariners (AZL)	R	.248	51	145	28	36	9	0	0	15	25	46	5	3	.360	.310
Minor League Totals			.251	106	303	57	76	18	3	3	33	49	82	8	6	.360	.360

23 AUSTIN COUSINO, OF

BA GRADE **45** Risk: High

Born: April 17, 1993. **B-T:** L-L. **Ht.:** 5-10. **Wt.:** 178. **Drafted:** Kentucky, 2014 (3rd round). **Signed by:** Jay Catalano.

When Cousino was in high school, he injured his left shoulder playing hockey. So when baseball season rolled around, he decided to try throwing with his right arm. It didn't work—he had to sit out the season, but it illustrated his all-out approach. After turning pro for $400,000, he showed a more mature approach than he exhibited at Kentucky, vital for a player who profiles best as a top-of-the-order hitter with speed. Cousino always has been a free-swinger, but he showed a better sense of when to take a pitch in his pro debut. He has a loose swing with gap power that should provide doubles and 5-10 home runs. Cousino's calling card is his baserunning and defense. He's a tick above-average runner, and he's an above-average defender in center field thanks to excellent routes and quick, accurate reads of the ball off the bat. His average arm would be stretched in right field. He's been a successful basestealer, though his lack of pure speed likely will limit steals as he moves up. As a lefty hitter with a strong glove and an idea on the bases, Cousino can end up an extra outfielder. He should head to low Class A Clinton in 2015.

Year	Club (League)	Class	AVG	G	AB	R	H	2B	3B	HR	RBI	BB	SO	SB	CS	OBP	SLG
2014	Everett (NWL)	SS	.266	66	271	40	72	17	1	6	28	28	54	23	4	.341	.402
Minor League Totals			.266	66	271	40	72	17	1	6	28	28	54	23	4	.341	.402

24 FREDDY PERALTA, RHP

BA GRADE **50** Risk: Extreme

Born: June 4, 1996. **B-T:** R-R. **Ht.:** 5-11. **Wt.:** 175. **Signed:** Dominican Republic, 2013. **Signed by:** Eddy Toledo/Kelvin Dominguez/Tim Kissner.

Any righthander from the Dominican Republic who stands 6-foot-3 and throws 90 mph is bound for a big payday. If he stands 5-foot-11 with the same stuff, he probably will have to settle for a smaller bonus check. Peralta fits in the latter category, which explains his $137,000 bonus when he signed in April 2013. But as Johnny Cueto and Yordano Ventura have shown, teams can find bargains among Latin American righthanders with compact deliveries, quality fastballs and feel. Peralta has a relatively clean delivery, a loose arm and a quality 90-93 mph fastball. He flashes an average curveball and throws a fringy changeup that currently lacks movement or deception. With a strong extended spring he could head to short-season Everett.

Year	Club (League)	Class	W	L	ERA	G	GS	CG	SV	IP	H	HR	BB	SO	K/9	WHIP	AVG
2013	Mariners (DSL)	R	3	3	1.46	13	10	1	0	55	38	0	15	49	8.0	0.96	.198
2014	Mariners (AZL)	R	1	6	5.29	12	12	0	0	51	55	3	24	42	7.4	1.55	.275
Minor League Totals			4	9	3.30	25	22	1	0	106	93	3	39	91	7.7	1.24	.237

25 JULIO MORBAN, OF

Born: Feb. 13, 1992. **B-T:** L-L. **Ht.:** 6-1. **Wt.:** 210. **Signed:** Dominican Republic, 2008. **Signed by:** Bob Engle/Patrick Guerrero.

BA GRADE

50 Risk: Extreme

One of the higher-priced international signings the Mariners have landed in the past decade, Morban signed for $1.1 million in 2008. He's generally hit whenever healthy since then, but he's yet to play 100 games in a season. He saw his 2013 season end early when he broke his right tibia sliding into second base. He tried to return from his broken leg quickly in 2014, but he was a shell of his normal self and was shut down. He returned healthier in mid-June and once again showed hand-eye coordination and a smooth swing. Morban's swing has some length but plus bat speed allows him to handle velocity. A below-average runner, he fits best in left field, though his above-average arm works well in right. Morban has strength, but his swing is more geared for line drives than loft power. Morban is running out of time to prove he can both stay healthy and provide enough thump to be a big league corner outfielder.

Year	Club (League)	Class	AVG	G	AB	R	H	2B	3B	HR	RBI	BB	SO	SB	CS	OBP	SLG
2012	Mariners (AZL)	R	.238	6	21	2	5	0	0	0	3	0	3	0	0	.227	.238
	High Desert (CAL)	HiA	.313	76	300	56	94	16	2	17	52	21	67	5	1	.361	.550
2013	Jackson (SL)	AA	.295	86	295	46	87	20	5	7	44	28	95	7	2	.362	.468
2014	Jackson (SL)	AA	.252	30	115	14	29	5	1	1	11	9	35	0	0	.307	.339
	Tacoma (PCL)	AAA	.242	29	99	10	24	4	1	0	7	10	32	0	0	.312	.303
Minor League Totals			.277	363	1319	204	366	67	23	34	170	105	391	30	11	.334	.440

26 MAYCKOL GUAIPE, RHP

Born: Aug. 11, 1990. **B-T:** R-R. **Ht.:** 6-3. **Wt.:** 175. **Signed:** Venezuela, 2006. **Signed by:** Luis Martinez.

BA GRADE

45 Risk: High

Guaipe serves as a reminder that patience is advised when it comes to young pitchers who struggle. He signed with the Mariners out of Venezuela back in 2006 but didn't make it to the U.S. until his fifth pro season in 2011, which meant he was first eligible for the Rule 5 draft before he even advanced past Rookie-level Pulaski. But through steady development, Guaipe has smoothed out his delivery to more consistently get to his velocity, which has jumped up to 91-93 mph more consistently now, and he touches 95. Guaipe's slider flashes plus as well, though it's more erratic. After pitching well in a late-season promotion to Double-A Jackson and in the Venezuelan League following the season, the Mariners added him to the 40-man roster. Guaipe could be a useful reliever if he can maintain his fine control—he walked 1.4 batters per nine innings in 2014—and if he can sit at the upper end of his velocity range.

Year	Club (League)	Class	W	L	ERA	G	GS	CG	SV	IP	H	HR	BB	SO	K/9	WHIP	AVG
2012	Everett (NWL)	SS	2	2	4.50	2	2	0	0	12	13	1	2	6	4.5	1.25	.295
	Clinton (MWL)	LoA	5	0	3.39	11	11	0	0	58	60	4	15	34	5.2	1.29	.269
2013	High Desert (CAL)	HiA	3	4	5.64	35	3	0	5	59	59	5	29	57	8.7	1.49	.267
2014	Jackson (SL)	AA	1	3	2.89	40	0	0	12	56	45	4	9	56	9.0	0.96	.215
Minor League Totals			23	18	3.55	167	35	0	26	395	381	18	132	303	6.9	1.30	.256

27 AARON BARBOSA, OF

Born: April 14, 1992. **B-T:** L-R. **Ht.:** 5-10. **Wt.:** 160. **Signed:** Northeastern, 2013 (NDFA). **Signed by:** Brian Nichols.

BA GRADE

45 Risk: High

Barbosa has absolutely zero power. Nor does he throw as well as teams would like to see from a center fielder, and he has little pedigree. The Mariners signed him out of the Cape Cod League after he went undrafted as a Northeastern junior in 2013. But the tools Barbosa does have fit together really well. He is an 80 runner on the 20-80 scouting scale who knows how to use his speed on the basepaths, stealing 52 bases in 2014 to rank sixth in the minors. While his arm is well below-average, he covers plenty of ground in the outfield, showing plus range in center. A lefthanded hitter, Barbosa's swing is geared to flaring balls to the opposite field, and even his extra-base hit once a week is generally lined the opposite way. He's a solid bunter who can turn a grounder to third base or shortstop into an infield hit. Barbosa knows he needs to figure out any way he can to get on base. That mans that unlike many young speedsters, he looks to draw walks. He is tough to strike out and comfortable working deep counts. Slap hitters with no power like Barbosa have to excel at the little things to make the majors, but so far, he has excelled at those little things. He's ready to tackle high Class A Bakersfield in 2015.

Year	Club (League)	Class	AVG	G	AB	R	H	2B	3B	HR	RBI	BB	SO	SB	CS	OBP	SLG
2013	Pulaski (APP)	R	.356	30	101	23	36	4	1	0	6	19	14	19	3	.455	.416
2014	High Desert (CAL)	HiA	.256	34	125	26	32	1	1	0	12	28	27	10	5	.400	.280
	Clinton (MWL)	LoA	.293	81	314	53	92	8	2	0	15	43	47	42	7	.379	.331
Minor League Totals			.296	145	540	102	160	13	4	0	33	90	88	71	15	.398	.335

28 JOCHI OGANDO, RHP

BA GRADE

45 Risk: High

Born: May 27, 1993. **B-T:** R-R. **Ht.:** 6-5. **Wt.:** 210. **Signed:** Dominican Republic, 2009. **Signed by:** Bob Engle/Patrick Guerrero.

Ogando has a strong case to be considered best pure arm in the Mariners system. Now if only he could throw a strike when needed. A thick-bodied righthander with a quick arm, Ogando can carry his 92-96 mph velocity for four or five innings as a starter, and touches 99 in shorter stints. His delivery isn't smooth and it leads to issues with his well below-average control. His slider and changeup are both below-average, though his changeup will flash average on his best days. The Mariners left Ogando unprotected in the Rule 5 draft and he went unpicked. His velocity gives him a ceiling as a back-of-the-bullpen arm if he can improve his delivery and control as he heads to Double-A Jackson in 2015.

Year	Club (League)	Class	W	L	ERA	G	GS	CG	SV	IP	H	HR	BB	SO	K/9	WHIP	AVG
2012	Pulaski (APP)	R	2	3	4.17	12	12	0	0	50	49	2	23	39	7.1	1.45	.262
2013	Clinton (MWL)	LoA	1	3	3.32	33	0	0	3	60	53	1	32	56	8.4	1.42	.243
2014	Jackson (SL)	AA	0	3	5.54	4	4	0	0	13	18	0	13	14	9.7	2.38	.333
	High Desert (CAL)	HiA	4	2	7.10	22	11	0	0	58	72	6	36	52	8.0	1.85	.309
Minor League Totals			10	17	4.88	91	41	0	4	244	243	12	156	208	7.7	1.64	.262

29 JI-MAN CHOI, 1B

BA GRADE

40 Risk: Medium

Born: May 19, 1991. **B-T:** L-R. **Ht.:** 6-1. **Wt.:** 225. **Signed:** South Korea, 2009. **Signed by:** Jamey Storvick/Pat Kelly.

Choi always has been known as a hit-first player—he moved off catcher to first base in 2011—whose lack of power limits his chances of being an everyday big leaguer. So when hit with a 50-game suspension early in 2014 for using a performance-enhancing substance, he faced further skepticism. Upon his return from his suspension, Choi didn't really assuage that criticism by slugging .392. He is a pure hitter who can line the ball to all fields with a short, direct, lefthanded stroke, but he doesn't have much natural loft in his swing. His best-case scenario is as a James Loney-type offensive first baseman, but as a fringe-average defender, he lacks Loney's defensive value. The Mariners tried Choi in left field, but he's not a viable option out there. Choi will head back to Triple-A in 2015 to try to prove his doubters wrong.

Year	Club (League)	Class	AVG	G	AB	R	H	2B	3B	HR	RBI	BB	SO	SB	CS	OBP	SLG
2012	Clinton (MWL)	LoA	.298	66	242	43	72	14	1	8	43	39	55	0	2	.420	.463
2013	High Desert (CAL)	HiA	.337	48	181	34	61	24	3	7	40	27	33	0	1	.427	.619
	Jackson (SL)	AA	.268	61	198	21	53	10	3	9	39	32	28	2	2	.377	.485
	Tacoma (PCL)	AAA	.244	13	45	9	11	2	0	2	6	4	7	0	0	.333	.422
2014	Jackson (SL)	AA	.273	4	11	3	3	1	0	1	5	4	2	0	0	.467	.636
	Tacoma (PCL)	AAA	.283	70	237	41	67	7	2	5	30	36	42	2	2	.381	.392
Minor League Totals			.303	312	1092	181	331	74	12	34	193	169	206	14	8	.405	.486

30 DANNY HULTZEN, LHP

BA GRADE

50 Risk: Extreme

Born: Nov. 28, 1989. **B-T:** L-L. **Ht.:** 6-3. **Wt.** 200. **Drafted:** Virginia, 2011 (1st round). **Signed by:** Mike Moriarty.

If Hultzen's career had developed as he and the Mariners envisioned, then he would be a part of Seattle's rotation by now. Instead Hultzen has missed most of 2013-14 with a shoulder injury that eventually required rotator-cuff surgery. Pre-injury, Hultzen's fastball sat 91-94 mph and touched 96 at his best, and he also threw an above-average changeup that had deception and late fade a well as a useable slider. Nowadays, the Mariners have to hope he can simply hold up to a starter's workload. Hultzen worked off the mound late in the 2014 season, but he never saw game action before shutting it down for the winter. He did face live hitters at the organization's Arizona complex, however. His velocity wasn't back to his pre-injury form, but he did show a fastball in the high 80s and his breaking balls and changeup were both sharp at times. Hultzen always will have a crossfire delivery—it's part of what makes him tough to hit— but the Mariners have worked on ensuring he's more direct to the plate. Seattle also has been encouraged enough by his rehab to keep him on the 40-man roster, but they will have to be patient with him as he tries to work back into form after making just seven appearances in the past two seasons.

Year	Club (League)	Class	W	L	ERA	G	GS	CG	SV	IP	H	HR	BB	SO	K/9	WHIP	AVG
2012	Jackson (SL)	AA	8	3	1.19	13	13	0	0	75	38	2	32	79	9.4	0.93	.151
	Tacoma (PCL)	AAA	1	4	5.92	12	12	0	0	49	49	2	43	57	10.5	1.89	.258
2013	Mariners (AZL)	R	1	0	1.80	1	1	0	0	5	3	0	0	8	14.4	0.60	.167
	Tacoma (PCL)	AAA	4	1	2.05	6	6	0	0	31	19	1	7	34	10.0	0.85	.168
2014	Did not play—Injured																
Minor League Totals			14	8	2.82	32	32	0	0	160	109	5	82	178	10.0	1.20	.190

Tampa Bay Rays

BY BILL BALLEW

It's said that bad things happen in threes. Some believe the 2014 Rays can relate.

Considered to be the class of the American League East heading into the season, Tampa Bay got off to a terrible start, played well at midseason, and then finished as an also-ran in fourth place. Along the way the team dealt former Cy Young Award winner David Price at the trading deadline in a three-way swap with the Mariners and Tigers. The final blow came in mid-October, when vice president of baseball operations Andrew Friedman bolted for the Dodgers after nearly a decade in charge of the Rays.

All three events have implications to the Tampa Bay farm system. Having exceeded their budget in hopes of contending for a World Series title, Rays principal owner Stuart Sternberg announced at season's end that the $82 million payroll—which still ranked 25th in baseball—will be reduced for 2015. The cost-cutting should create room for another wave of young players on the major league roster, a wave bolstered in the Price deal with the acquisition of lefthander Drew Smyly, infielder Nick Franklin and minor league shortstop Willy Adames. And while Friedman's departure will be felt, there is no question that his replacement, president Matt Silverman, will remain heavily dependent on player development.

The Rays appear to be in good shape after a productive 2014 season in the farm system that included division titles for Triple-A Durham (International), short-season Hudson Valley (New York-Penn) and Princeton (Appalachian). More importantly, Tampa Bay's draft showed early promise, starting with Wichita State first baseman Casey Gillaspie in the first round followed by a plethora of young pitchers, including high school lefthander Brock Burke (third round) and righthanders Cameron Varga (second), Brent Honeywell (supplemental second), Blake Bivens (fourth) and Spencer Moran (11th).

Tampa Bay also made a bold move on the international front. After reaching the playoffs four times in six seasons despite receiving minimal contributions from their international efforts, the organization refocused its efforts in that phase, which included the signing of shortstop Adrian Rondon, deemed the top prospect on the international front, to a $2.95 million bonus. The Rays paid the 100 percent tax for exceeding their pool by more than 15 percent and won't be allowed to sign an international player for more than $300,000 during the next two signing periods, the second time the Rays have gone into the maximum penalty range for the international bonus pools. The Rays also inked fellow Dominican outfielder Jesus Sanchez for $400,000.

The Rondon signing and acquisitions of Adames and Franklin added to a core of talent up the middle that also includes Top 10 prospects such as catcher Justin O'Conner, second baseman Ryan Brett and center fielder Mikie Mahtook. The Rays have solid catching depth as well.

The system's overall depth stems from a slow-developing 2011 draft class that included 10 of the first 60 picks and a willingness to gamble on players with questionable makeup, which has caused the organization embarrassment with more than a dozen suspensions over the past three seasons. Even so, the Rays appear to have cleared many of those hurdles and look to be in solid shape to generate a flow of talent that can help the revenue-challenged club continue to compete at a high level.

CLIFF WELCH

The Rays dealt homegrown ace David Price to the Tigers in yet another build-for-the-future maneuver

TOP PROSPECTS OF THE DECADE

Year	Player, Pos.	2014 Org
2005	Delmon Young, of	Orioles
2006	Delmon Young, of	Orioles
2007	Delmon Young, of	Orioles
2008	Evan Longoria, 3b	Rays
2009	David Price, lhp	Tigers
2010	Desmond Jennings, of	Rays
2011	Matt Moore, lhp	Rays
2012	Matt Moore, lhp	Rays
2013	Wil Myers, of/3b	Rays
2014	Jake Odorizzi, rhp	Rays

General manager: Matt Silverman. **Farm director:** Mitch Lukevics. **Scouting director:** R.J. Harrison.

Class	Team	League	W	L	PCT	Finish	Manager
Majors	Tampa Bay Rays	American	77	85	.475	t-18th (30)	Joe Maddon
Triple-A	Durham Bulls	International	75	69	.521	6th (14)	Charlie Montoyo
Double-A	Montgomery Biscuits	Southern	66	74	.471	6th (10)	Brady Williams
High A	Charlotte Stone Crabs	Florida State	63	70	.474	9th (12)	Jared Sandberg
Low A	Bowling Green Hot Rods	Midwest	61	77	.442	t-14th (16)	Michael Johns
Short season	Hudson Valley Renegades	New York-Penn	46	30	.605	3rd (14)	Tim Parenton
Rookie	Princeton Rays	Appalachian	40	28	.588	1st (10)	Danny Sheaffer
Rookie	Rays	Gulf Coast	32	28	.533	8th (16)	Jim Morrison
Overall Minor League Record			383	376	.505	16 (30)	

THIS YEAR'S TOP 30

No.	Player, Pos.	Grade
1.	Willy Adames, ss	60/High
2.	Alex Colome, rhp	50/Medium
3.	Justin O'Conner, c	55/High
4.	Adrian Rondon, ss	60/Extreme
5.	Nathan Karns, rhp	50/Medium
6.	Mikie Mahtook, of	50/Medium
7.	Ryan Brett, 2b	50/Medium
8.	Brent Honeywell, rhp	60/Extreme
9.	Blake Snell, lhp	55/High
10.	Andrew Velazquez, ss/2b	50/High
11.	Casey Gillaspie, 1b	50/High
12.	Taylor Guerrieri, rhp	55/Extreme
13.	Jake Hager, ss	45/Medium
14.	Justin Williams, of	55/Extreme
15.	Nick Ciuffo, c	50/High
16.	Jose Dominguez, rhp	45/Low
17.	Tyler Goeddel, 3b	50/High
18.	Richie Shaeffer, 3b	45/Medium
19.	Tim Beckham, 2b/ss	45/Medium
20.	Enny Romero, lhp	45/Medium
21.	Hak-Ju Lee, ss	45/Medium
22.	Kean Wong, 2b	45/High
23.	Luke Maile, c	45/Medium
24.	Ryne Stanek, rhp	45/High
25.	German Marquez, rhp	45/High
26.	Patrick Leonard, 1b	45/High
27.	Johnny Field, of	45/High
28.	Andrew Toles, of	50/Extreme
29.	Yoel Araujo, of	45/High
30.	Grayson Garvin, rhp	45/High

LAST YEAR'S TOP 30

	Player, Pos.	Status
1.	Jake Odorizzi, rhp	Majors
2.	Hak-Ju Lee, ss	No. 21
3.	Taylor Guerrieri, rhp	No. 12
4.	Enny Romero, lhp	No. 20
5.	Alex Colome, rhp	No. 2
6.	Andrew Toles, of	No. 29
7.	Nick Ciuffo, c	No. 15
8.	Ryan Brett, 2b	No. 7
9.	Tim Beckham, ss/2b	No. 19
10.	Kevin Kiermaier, of	Majors
11.	Ryne Stanek, rhp	No. 24
12.	Justin O'Conner, c	No. 3
13.	Richie Shaffer, 1b/3b	No. 18
14.	Blake Snell, lhp	No. 9
15.	Jesse Hahn, rhp	(Padres)
16.	Grayson Garvin, lhp	Dropped out
17.	Felipe Rivero, lhp	(Nationals)
18.	Jake Hager, ss	No. 13
19.	Riley Unroe, ss	Dropped out
20.	Drew Vettleson, of	(Nationals)
21.	Jose Mujica, rhp	Dropped out
22.	Tyler Goeddel, 3b	No. 17
23.	C.J. Riefenhauser, lhp	Dropped out
24.	Oscar Hernandez, c	No. 27
25.	Mikie Mahtook, of	No. 6
26.	Dylan Floro, rhp	Dropped out
27.	Thomas Milone, of	Dropped out
28.	Jose Catillo, lhp	Dropped out
29.	Curt Casali, c	Dropped out
30.	Jeff Ames, rhp	Dropped out

BEST TOOLS

Best Hitter for Average	Ryan Brett
Best Power Hitter	Richie Shaffer
Best Strike Zone Discipline	Cameron Seitzer
Fastest Baserunner	Andrew Toles
Best Athlete	Mikie Mahtook
Best Fastball	Alex Colome
Best Curveball	Nathan Karns
Best Slider	Blake Snell
Best Changeup	Mike Montgomery
Best Control	Brent Honeywell
Best Defensive Catcher	Luke Maile
Best Defensive Infielder	Willy Adames
Best Infield Arm	Hak-Ju Lee
Best Defensive Outfielder	Mikie Mahtook
Best Outfield Arm	Taylor Motter

PROJECTED 2018 LINEUP

Catcher	Justin O'Conner
First Base	Casey Gillaspie
Second Base	Ryan Brett
Third Base	Evan Longoria
Shortstop	Willy Adames
Left Field	Mikie Mahtook
Center Field	Desmond Jennings
Right Field	Kevin Kiermaier
Designated Hitter	Wil Myers
No. 1 Starter	Alex Cobb
No. 2 Starter	Drew Smyly
No. 3 Starter	Matt Moore
No. 4 Starter	Chris Archer
No. 5 Starter	Alex Colome
Closer	Jose Dominguez

TAMPA BAY RAYS

TOP 2015 ROOKIE: Alex Colome, rhp. The big league rotation is deep, but the Rays feels he is ready for a full-time role after a strong September callup.
BREAKOUT PROSPECT: Justin Williams, of. He hits the ball hard consistently—career .351 average—and can unlock more power with a more refined approach.
SLEEPER: Jaime Schultz, rhp. He has a power breaking ball and a plus fastball, and he learned to command those pitches last season at Class A.

SOURCE OF TOP 30 TALENT			
Homegrown	23	Acquired	7
College	6	Trades	7
Junior college	2	Rule 5 draft	0
High school	9	Independent leagues	0
Draft-and-follow	0	Free agents/waivers	0
Nondrafted free agents	0		
International	6		

LF
Justin Williams (14)
Yoel Araujo (29)
Granden Goetzman
Hunter Lockwood
Willie Argo

CF
Mikie Mahtook (6)
Johnny Field (27)
Andrew Toles (28)
Thomas Milone
Kes Carter
Braxton Lee
Bralin Jackson

RF
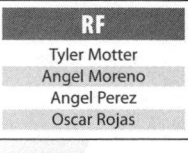
Tyler Motter
Angel Moreno
Angel Perez
Oscar Rojas

3B
Tyler Goeddel (17)
Richie Shaffer (18)

SS

Willy Adames (1)
Adrian Rondon (4)
Andrew Velasquez (10)
Jake Hager (13)
Hak-Ju Lee (21)
Riley Unroe
Brandon Martin

2B

Ryan Brett (7)
Tim Beckham (19)
Kean Wong (22)
Jace Conrad
Tommy Coyle

1B
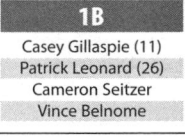
Casey Gillaspie (11)
Patrick Leonard (26)
Cameron Seitzer
Vince Belnome

C
Justin O'Conner (3)
Nick Ciuffo (15)
Luke Maile (23)
Curt Casali
Armando Araiza

LHP

LHSP	LHRP
Blake Snell (9)	Enny Romero (20)
Jose Alvarado	Grayson Garvin (30)
Mike Montgomery	C.J. Riefenhauser
Jose Castillo	

RHP

RHSP	RHRP
Alex Colome (2)	Jose Dominguez (16)
Nathan Karns (5)	Mark Sappington
Brent Honeywell (8)	Matt Lollis
Taylor Guerreri (12)	
Ryan Stanek (24)	
German Marquez (25)	
Jaime Schultz	
Greg Harris	
Henry Centeno	
Enderson Franco	
Cameron Varga	
Jose Mujica	
Dylan Floro	

2014

BEST PURE HITTER: 3B/OF Grant Kay (27) impressed with his bat in a brief Cape stint before signing and continued to impress this summer with his quick, compact stroke. 1B Casey Gillaspie (1) has plus bat speed, patience (120-63 walk-strikeout ratio in his last two college seasons) and was one of the top college bats in the class.

BEST POWER HITTER: Gillaspie has at least plus raw power from both sides of the plate with strength and leverage in his stroke, and projects to turn that into at least above-average power production. 1B Nic Wilson (24) has what one scout called "freakish raw power" and hit 10 home runs (while hitting just .207) for Rookie-level Princeton.

FASTEST RUNNER: OF Braxton Lee (12) is a 70-grade runner who runs between 3.95 and 4.00 from the left side. He is still learning to use his speed stealing bases.

BEST DEFENSIVE PLAYER: SS Alec Sole (18) is a steady, reliable defender at short with agility and a strong arm.

BEST FASTBALL: While RHP Brent Honeywell (2) has a fastball that sits 90-94, touching 96 from a quick, loose arm, his ability to command the offering and manipulate the ball is truly advanced for a 19-year-old. The competitive Honeywell pitches aggressively with his fastball and has drawn rave reviews for his intensity, pitching intelligence and preparation. RHP Kyle McKenzie (20) runs his heater up to 95.

BEST SECONDARY PITCH: Honeywell's devastating screwball is was one of the top secondary offerings in the entire draft class. Prep RHPs Cameron Varga (2) and Blake Bivens (4) both have curveballs with at least plus potential. Honeywell's changeup flashes plus as well.

BEST PRO DEBUT: Honeywell posted a 1.07 ERA and sparkling ratios of 1.6 walks and 10.7 strikeouts per nine innings for Princeton in the Appy League.

BEST ATHLETE: Lee's 70 speed plays in center field from a strong, physical 5-foot-8 frame.

MOST INTRIGUING BACKGROUND: Gillaspie is the younger brother of White Sox third baseman Conor Gillaspie, who was also a first-round pick out of Wichita State. Honeywell's father by the same name pitched for the same Princeton team in the Appy League 26 years ago as a member of the Pirates organization. Varga lived in Europe when he was younger during his father's professional basketball career.

CLOSEST TO THE MAJORS: RHP Brian Miller (15) is an experienced, battle-tested bullpen arm from a championship club at Vanderbilt who pounds the strike zone from his sidearm slot with a fastball that reaches the low 90s. Gillaspie's polish could move him quickly as well.

BEST LATE-ROUND PICK: Kay's hitting prowess and defensive versatility in the outfield corners

and at second and third differentiate him among the rest. OF Zac Law (24) impressed this summer and is very young for the class. He is a former football player with plus speed, physical strength and power potential.

THE ONE WHO GOT AWAY: OF Josh Davis (32) has some athleticism and a chance to develop at Pepperdine.

ASSESSMENT: The Rays drafted a power bat with their first pick and invested in prep pitching at the top. Brent Honeywell, the first junior college player selected, had an outstanding debut.

2013

C Nick Ciuffo (1) and raw SS Riley Unroe (2) need time, but 2B Kean Wong (4) may move quickly. Injury-plagued RHP Ryne Stanek (1) hasn't moved as fast as was hoped.

GRADE: C

2012

1B/3B Richie Shaffer (1) and C Luke Maile (8) look like potential second-division starters. Erratic OF Andrew Toles (3) took a step back in 2014.

GRADE: D

2011

With 10 of the first 60 picks, Tampa has volume, but lottery tickets RHP Taylor Guerrieri (1) and LHP Blake Snell (1s) are the only potential stars. OF Mikie Mahtook (1), SS Jake Hager (1), 3B Tyler Goeddel (1s) and LHP Grayson Garvin (1s) are intriguing potential role players.

GRADE: C

TOP DRAFT PICKS OF THE DECADE

Year	Player, Pos.	2014 Org
2005	Wade Townsend, rhp	Out of baseball
2006	Evan Longoria, 3b	Rays
2007	David Price, lhp	Tigers
2008	Tim Beckham, ss	Rays
2009	*LeVon Washington, of	Indians
2010	Josh Sale, of	Rays
2011	Taylor Guerrieri, rhp	Rays
2012	Richie Shaffer, 3b	Rays
2013	Nick Cuiffo, c	Rays
2014	Casey Gillaspie, 1b	Rays

*Did not sign

LARGEST BONUSES IN CLUB HISTORY

Matt White, 1996	$10,200,000
Rolando Arrojo, 1997	$7,000,000
Tim Beckham, 2008	$6,150,000
David Price, 2007	$5,600,000
B.J. Upton, 2002	$4,600,000

1 WILLY ADAMES, SS

Born: Sept. 2, 1995. **B-T:** R-R. **Ht.:** 6-1. **Wt.:** 180.
Signed: Dominican Republic, 2012. **Signed by:** Aldo Perez/Ramon Perez/Miguel Garcia (Tigers).

Adames was at a workout at the Tigers' Dominican complex before signing and wound up facing then-Detroit closer Jose Valverde after volunteering to jump into the batter's box. That willingness to challenge himself and ability to relish big situations helped him have a smashing first season in the U.S. Adames, Detroit's top international signing in 2012 for $420,000, ranked as the Tigers' No. 30 prospect after his Dominican Summer League debut in 2013, then jumped to the low Class A Midwest League and had a successful offensive season. After a strong first half, he became a key piece in the Rays' haul for David Price, a deal that also included big league lefthander Drew Smyly and infielder Nick Franklin. He received rave reviews in his new organization after shifting teams but staying in the same league.

Adames gives the Rays an athletic infielder who can hit. He possesses the overall package of impressive makeup and a deep set of tools. He already speaks English well and wants to improve. He also displays true passion for the game and is willing to work. Adames has good strike-zone discipline for such a young player and isn't afraid to work deep counts, which leads to walks but also some strikeouts. He generates above-average bat speed and has surprising power for his size; Tigers scouts still talk about long home runs he hit against the Cubs during the 2013 DSL playoffs. Some scouts project him to hit for above-average power, up to 20 home runs, as he matures. He ranked second in the Midwest League in triples due mostly to his power to the gaps, not his speed. He does an excellent job of driving the ball to the opposite field, and the ball tends to stay on his bat a long time. Adames' feet and hands work well on defense with solid first-step quickness despite only average running speed. His range is solid average at shortstop, although some scouts question how long he will remain at the position and see him having to move to second or third base. His arm strength rates above-average with good accuracy. Adames' body is rangy now, but some scouts are concerned he'll fill out and outgrow shortstop. He has some experience playing third base in the DSL, and that's his more likely destination if he does move.

The Rays have significant depth at shortstop, with Hak-Ju Lee and Tim Beckham at Triple-A and Jake Hager at Double-A. They will be patient with Adames, so he'll likely open the 2015 season at high Class A Charlotte. But he's already shown he is prone to accelerating timetables by putting up big numbers considering his age and the pitcher-friendly MWL in his domestic debut. If Adames can stick at short and fulfill his power potential, he could become a future all-star.

BA GRADE

60 **Risk:** High

SCOUTING GRADES

Hit: 60.
Power: 55.
Sspeed: 45.
Defense: 50.
Arm: 55.

Based on 20-80 scouting scale and future projection rather than present tools.

LGE	PA	BB%	SO%	ISO
MWL	514	10.5	24.5	.158

MIKE JANES

Year	Club (League)	Class	AVG	G	AB	R	H	2B	3B	HR	RBI	BB	SO	SB	CS	OBP	SLG
2013	Tigers (DSL)	R	.245	60	200	48	49	12	5	1	21	56	44	9	12	.419	.370
2014	West Michigan (MWL)LoA		.269	98	353	40	95	14	12	6	50	39	96	3	6	.346	.428
	Bowling Green (MWL)LoA		.278	27	97	15	27	5	2	2	11	15	30	3	0	.377	.433
Minor League Totals			.263	185	650	103	171	31	19	9	82	110	170	15	18	.375	.411

2 ALEX COLOME, RHP

Born: Dec. 31, 1988. **B-T:** R-R. **Ht.:** 6-2. **Wt.:** 210. **Signed:** Dominican Republic, 2007. **Signed by:** Eddy Toledo.

The nephew of Jesus Colome, who pitched 10 years in the big leagues, Alex has gone from a raw thrower to a promising pitcher while overcoming a handful of injuries and a 50-game suspension to open the 2014 after failing a performance-enhancing drug test. He was Tampa's only homegrown international signee on the big league roster this year. Colome is a power pitcher who works off his plus fastball that sits at 92-94 mph and reaches 97. His fastball features solid sinking action and above-average armside run. He mixes his heater with a tight power curve, a hard cutter-type slider, and a solid changeup that showed improvement in 2014. At times, Colome struggles to command his fastball because it has so much running action, but he had the best walk rate of his career in 2014 with Triple-A Durham. He's had durability issues in the past, including an elbow strain that sidelined him in 2013, but finished this season strong with a September callup. The Rays feel certain Colome, who is out of options, has nothing left to prove in the minors. His power arm would make him a good fit in the bullpen if he can't break into Tampa's crowded big league rotation. He still has the ceiling of a No. 3 starter.

BA GRADE

50 Risk: Medium

LGE	BF	SO%	BB%	HR/9
IL	369	19.8	8.1	0.21
AL	97	13.4	10.3	0.38

Year	Club (League)	Class	W	L	ERA	G	GS	CG	SV	IP	H	HR	BB	SO	K/9	WHIP	AVG
2012	Montgomery (SL)	AA	8	3	3.48	14	14	1	0	75	69	2	34	75	9.0	1.37	.252
	Durham (IL)	AAA	0	1	3.24	3	3	0	0	17	12	1	9	15	8.1	1.26	.207
2013	Durham (IL)	AAA	4	6	3.07	14	14	0	0	70	63	5	29	72	9.2	1.31	.236
	Tampa Bay (AL)	MAJ	1	1	2.25	3	3	0	0	16	14	2	9	12	6.8	1.44	.230
2014	Charlotte (FSL)	HiA	0	1	1.64	3	3	0	0	11	7	0	5	10	8.2	1.09	.179
	Durham (IL)	AAA	7	6	3.77	15	15	0	0	86	84	2	30	73	7.6	1.33	.261
	Tampa Bay (AL)	MAJ	2	0	2.66	5	3	0	0	24	19	1	10	13	4.9	1.23	.221
Major League Totals			3	1	2.50	8	6	0	0	40	33	3	19	25	5.7	1.31	.224
Minor League Totals			45	47	3.58	141	137	6	0	696	583	43	313	690	8.9	1.29	.230

3 JUSTIN O'CONNER, C

Born: March 31, 1992. **B-T:** R-R. **Ht.:** 6-2. **Wt.:** 190. **Drafted:** HS—Muncie, Ind., 2010 (1st round). **Signed by:** James Bonnici.

A high school infielder, O'Conner was the first catcher drafted by the Rays in the first round when he was the 31st overall pick in 2010. A pair of hip surgeries early in his pro career set him back a bit, but he blossomed last year in the high Class A Florida State League. O'Conner has impact tools in his arm and his bat. His arm strength earns 80 grades on the 20-80 scouting scale after he threw out 50 percent of basestealers in the FSL. His pop times have been as low as 1.7 seconds, and his throws have excellent carry and accuracy. A physical catcher with solid leadership skills, he is far from polished behind the plate with average footwork and technique. His offensive strength is his plus bat speed that produces raw power and allows him to hit top-shelf fastballs. He has an aggressive hitting approach with quick hands but tends to swing and miss at breaking balls. He has below-average speed but does not clog the base paths. The Rays believe O'Conner has matured mentally and physically, which led to major strides in his overall development. He's a high-risk, high-reward player who may never hit for high average but has the tools to impact a game. He'll return to Double-A Montgomery, where he finished the season, to start 2015.

BA GRADE

55 Risk: High

LGE	PA	BB%	SO%	ISO
FSL	340	4.4	22.9	.204
SL	84	1.2	23.8	.125

Year	Club (League)	Class	AVG	G	AB	R	H	2B	3B	HR	RBI	BB	SO	SB	CS	OBP	SLG
2012	Hudson Valley (NYP)	SS	.223	59	238	39	53	18	1	5	29	18	73	2	0	.276	.370
2013	Bowling Green (MWL)	LoA	.233	102	399	49	93	17	0	14	56	31	111	5	0	.290	.381
2014	Charlotte (FSL)	HiA	.282	80	319	40	90	31	2	10	44	15	78	0	0	.321	.486
	Montgomery (SL)	AA	.263	21	80	9	21	4	0	2	3	1	20	0	0	.298	.388
Minor League Totals			.232	358	1375	173	319	91	3	43	190	100	406	12	1	.289	.396

4 ADRIAN RONDON, SS

Born: July 7, 1998. **B-T:** R-R. **Ht.:** 6-2. **Wt.:** 180. **Signed:** Dominican Republic, 2014. **Signed by:** Danny Salazar.

CLIFF WELCH

Rondon was deemed the top international talent in 2014, and the Rays proved their interest by signing him for $2.95 million on his 16th birthday. He has consistently showed an advanced feel for the game against older competition. Rondon has a full range of tools with impressive intangibles that allow him to produce in game situations. An advanced hitter for a young international player, Rondon has good bat speed with a quick, compact stroke. His hands work well and he makes consistent contact against high velocity. He has excellent balance and does a good job of spraying line drives to all fields. He has shown above-average patience with an ability to work counts. Rondon has a live, athletic frame that should allow him to remain at short. He has soft hands and above-average arm strength, and plays under control. While he needs to improve his footwork, his range is a tick above-average and should improve with experience. Tampa Bay believes Rondon has the elite ability to become an impact player at a premium position. He has drawn comparisons to Starlin Castro and Hanley Ramirez and could move quickly once he establishes a foundation in pro ball. Rondon will make his debut next summer in the Rookie-level Dominican Summer League or Gulf Coast League.

BA GRADE

60 Risk: **Extreme**

LGE	PA	BB%	SO%	ISO
Did not play				

Year	Club (League)	Class	AVG	G	AB	R	H	2B	3B	HR	RBI	BB	SO	SB	CS	OBP	SLG
2014	Did not play—Signed 2015 contract																

5 NATHAN KARNS, RHP

Born: Nov. 25, 1987. **B-T:** R-R. **Ht.:** 6-3. **Wt.:** 230. **Drafted:** Texas Tech, 2009 (12nd round). **Signed by:** Jimmy Gonzalez (Nationals).

Karns was drafted out of high school by the Astros in 2006 and had an itinerant college career, then didn't make his pro debut with the Nationals until 2011 thanks to a torn labrum. In 2012 he led all minor leaguers with a .174 opponents average, and reached the big leagues with Washington in 2013. The Rays dealt for Karns in February, and he led the system and International League in strikeouts. A physical power pitcher who will challenge hitters, Karns mixes a 90-94 mph fastball that at times has good sinking action with a low-80s hammer curveball that's the best in the organization. He adds a low 80s-changeup that showed more consistency last year. The curveball can be a wipeout pitch when he generates good wrist snap and gets hitters to chase. His control fluctuates, particularly with his breaking ball, and his fastball lacks movement on occasion, leaving him prone to home runs. While his long arm action and stiff front leg contribute to his inconsistency in throwing strikes, the Rays believe he has made strides in commanding the strike zone since joining the organization. Karns remains in contention for a job in the big league rotation despite his advanced age and inconsistency. More control would help him realize his mid-rotation ceiling.

BA GRADE

50 Risk: **Medium**

LGE	BF	SO%	BB%	HR/9
IL	624	24.5	9.9	0.99
AL	49	26.5	8.2	2.25

Year	Club (League)	Class	W	L	ERA	G	GS	CG	SV	IP	H	HR	BB	SO	K/9	WHIP	AVG
2012	Hagerstown (SAL)	LoA	3	0	2.03	11	5	1	2	44	23	1	21	61	12.4	0.99	.148
	Potomac (CAR)	HiA	8	4	2.26	13	13	1	0	72	47	1	26	87	10.9	1.02	.190
2013	Washington (NL)	MAJ	0	1	7.50	3	3	0	0	12	17	5	6	11	8.3	1.92	.321
	Harrisburg (EL)	AA	10	6	3.26	23	23	3	0	133	109	14	48	155	10.5	1.18	.224
2014	Durham (IL)	AAA	9	9	5.08	27	27	0	0	145	142	16	62	153	9.5	1.40	.257
	Tampa Bay (AL)	MAJ	1	1	4.50	2	2	0	0	12	7	3	4	13	9.8	0.92	.163
Major League Totals			1	2	6.00	5	5	0	0	24	24	8	10	24	9.0	1.42	.250
Minor League Totals			33	21	3.45	87	81	5	2	449	350	33	190	515	10.3	1.20	.215

6 MIKIE MAHTOOK, OF

Born: Nov. 30, 1989. **B-T:** R-R. **Ht.:** 6-1. **Wt.:** 200. **Drafted:** Louisiana State, 2011 (1st round). **Signed by:** Rickey Drexler.

The Rays nabbed Mahtook with the 31st overall pick in 2011 after he earned All-America honors on two occasions and won a national championship at Louisiana State. He had two modest seasons to open his career before taking significant steps in his development last year in his first taste of Triple-A while leading the farm system in RBIs. Mahtook's impressive intangibles and strong drive allow him to get the most out of his solid-average tools. He returned to center field on a full-time basis last season after seeing most of his activity at the corners and excelled, emerging as the best defensive outfielder in the farm system. An above-average runner who takes precise routes, Mahtook has plus range and a good arm that is a tick above-average, with solid carry and accuracy. He drove the ball more consistently last year while still hitting for average. He uses the entire field and can pull the ball when needed. He is also a smart baserunner who can steal bags. Sometimes his own worst critic, Mahtook has learned to use his competitiveness to his advantage. Last season Mahtook became the player the Rays expected upon drafting him. Added experience and development could make him a starting major league outfielder. A return to Durham is likely, but he should make his big league debut at some point in 2015.

	BA GRADE	
50	**Risk:** Medium	

LGE	PA	BB%	SO%	ISO
IL	550	8.4	24.9	.166

Year	Club (League)	Class	AVG	G	AB	R	H	2B	3B	HR	RBI	BB	SO	SB	CS	OBP	SLG
2012	Charlotte (FSL)	HiA	.290	92	341	44	99	15	7	5	37	29	71	19	6	.358	.419
	Montgomery (SL)	AA	.248	39	153	17	38	10	1	4	25	11	31	4	3	.308	.405
2013	Montgomery (SL)	AA	.254	132	511	71	130	30	8	7	68	43	102	25	8	.322	.386
2014	Durham (IL)	AAA	.292	132	489	56	143	33	6	12	68	46	137	18	5	.362	.458
Minor League Totals			.274	395	1494	188	410	88	22	28	198	129	341	66	22	.342	.419

7 RYAN BRETT, 2B

Born: Oct. 9, 1991. **B-T:** R-R. **Ht.:** 5-9. **Wt.:** 180. **Drafted:** HS—Burien, Wash., 2010 (3rd round). **Signed by:** Paul Kirsch.

Brett has made a steady climb through the organization, particularly since a late 2012 suspension for testing positive for methamphetamine and an amphetamine. He spent all of 2014 at Double-A after a one-month taste of Montgomery in late 2013. Despite battling a hamstring injury for a month, Brett ranked second in the organization among full-season players in batting average and steals. A speed-oriented player with some pop, the blue-collar Brett finds a way to have success. Possessing strong, quick hands and a compact swing, he has one of the best feels for the strike zone in the organization and has strong bat-to-ball skills. He has good gap power and can drive the ball, but he also bunted for base hits for the first time in his career last year to maximize his plus speed and had excellent results. He adeptly reads pitchers, making him disruptive on the basepaths. His speed and quickness give him great range at second base. His hands are not soft but he has plenty of arm strength with good accuracy. The game continued to slow down for Brett in 2014. He is knocking on the door to the big leagues, and if the Rays try to trim payroll by dealing Ben Zobrist, Brett could get an extended look in spring training. If he opens the season in Triple-A Durham, chances are he will make his major league debut at some point during the campaign.

	BA GRADE	
50	**Risk:** Medium	

LGE	PA	BB%	SO%	ISO
SL	459	5.2	16.1	.145

Year	Club (League)	Class	AVG	G	AB	R	H	2B	3B	HR	RBI	BB	SO	SB	CS	OBP	SLG
2012	Bowling Green (MWL)	LoA	.285	100	410	77	117	20	3	6	35	37	73	48	8	.348	.393
2013	Rays (GCL)	R	.000	1	4	0	0	0	0	0	0	0	2	0	0	.000	.000
	Charlotte (FSL)	HiA	.340	51	206	38	70	11	4	4	22	15	27	22	7	.396	.490
	Montgomery (SL)	AA	.238	25	105	19	25	6	1	3	16	8	14	4	0	.289	.400
2014	Montgomery (SL)	AA	.303	107	422	64	128	25	6	8	38	24	74	27	7	.346	.448
Minor League Totals			.297	372	1476	248	439	89	21	24	144	118	231	134	28	.354	.435

8 BRENT HONEYWELL, RHP

Born: March 31, 1995. **B-T:** R-R. **Ht.:** 6-2. **Wt.:** 180. **Drafted:** Walters State (Tenn.) CC, 2014 (2nd round supplemental). **Signed by:** Brian Hickman.

Undrafted out of high school, Honeywell went to Walters (Tenn.) State JC for one year and became its highest draft pick since 1985. His status skyrocketed during pre-draft workouts last spring, and he carried that momentum into pro ball after being the 72nd overall pick and signing with the Rays for $800,000. His father, a lefty also named Brent, pitched for three seasons in the minors. Possessing a lean, athletic body with plenty of projection and tremendous intensity, Honeywell pounds the strike zone with remarkable command of five pitches and a good feel for how to attack hitters. He has a quick arm and an effortless, deceptive delivery that he repeats consistently with a short stride. He works off a plus fastball that sits at 91-94 mph and was clocked as high as 97 prior to the draft. While he mixes his two-seam and four-seam fastballs, his best pitch is a screwball that looked unhittable in the Appy League. He did not throw it often, but awareness of the pitch was enough to disrupt the mindset of opposing batters. His curveball is his least consistent offering at this point but shows tight spin and potential. Honeywell also displays a solid feel for a developing plus changeup. Honeywell exceeded expectations in his first taste of pro ball and excited the Rays with his potential. He is expected to move up to low Class A Bowling Green to open 2015.

BA GRADE

60 Risk: Extreme

LGE	BF	SO%	BB%	HR/9
APP	128	31.2	4.7	0.27

Year	Club (League)	Class	W	L	ERA	G	GS	CG	SV	IP	H	HR	BB	SO	K/9	WHIP	AVG
2014	Princeton (APP)	R	2	1	1.07	9	8	0	0	34	19	1	6	40	10.7	0.74	.161
Minor League Totals			2	1	1.07	9	8	0	0	34	19	1	6	40	10.7	0.74	.161

9 BLAKE SNELL, LHP

Born: Dec. 4, 1992. **B-T:** L-L. **Ht.:** 6-4. **Wt.:** 180. **Drafted:** HS—Shoreline, Wash., 2011 (1st round supplemental). **Signed by:** Paul Kirsch.

The Rays have limited Snell's innings since he was the 52nd overall pick in 2011 and allowed him to eclipse the century mark last year for the first time. Tampa Bay sent Snell back to low Class A Bowling Green to open the 2014 slate, giving him more time to mature physically and mentally, before promoting him to high Class A Charlotte. He finished second in the organization in ERA and third in strikeouts. The Rays love the way Snell battles on the mound, and he has developed a more advanced feel for pitching. His best pitch is an 83-84 mph slider that could be a plus offering once he adds a little more depth to it. Snell's velocity showed improvement last year. His heavy fastball resides in the low 90s, peaking at 94 mph, and has good late sinking action. He flashes an above-average changeup that has solid-average fade and depth. Pitching from the extreme third-base side of the rubber, Snell threw more strikes in 2014 but still has a walk rate too high to remain a starter. He struggles on occasion to repeat his mechanics with his stiff front leg. The organization's pitcher of the year, Snell is a potential middle-of-the-rotation pitcher in the big leagues and should make the move to Double-A this season.

BA GRADE

55 Risk: High

LGE	BF	SO%	BB%	HR/9
MWL	161	26.1	11.8	0.22
FSL	330	23.3	11.2	0.12

Year	Club (League)	Class	W	L	ERA	G	GS	CG	SV	IP	H	HR	BB	SO	K/9	WHIP	AVG
2012	Princeton (APP)	R	5	1	2.09	11	11	1	0	47	34	4	17	53	10.1	1.08	.202
2013	Bowling Green (MWL)	LoA	4	9	4.27	23	23	0	0	99	90	8	73	106	9.6	1.65	.245
2014	Bowling Green (MWL)	LoA	3	2	1.79	8	8	0	0	40	26	1	19	42	9.4	1.12	.184
	Charlotte (FSL)	HiA	5	6	3.94	16	16	1	0	75	69	1	37	77	9.2	1.41	.245
Minor League Totals			18	20	3.37	69	66	2	0	288	249	14	157	304	9.5	1.41	.235

10 ANDREW VELAZQUEZ, SS/2B

Born: July 14, 1994. **B-T:** B-R. **Ht.:** 5-8. **Wt.:** 175. **Drafted:** HS—Bronx, N.Y., 2012 (7th round). **Signed by:** Todd Donovan (Diamondbacks).

MIKE JANES

Velazquez signed for $200,000 after the Diamondbacks selected him in the seventh round of the 2012 draft. In low Class A South Bend in 2014 he made headline news with a 74-game on-base streak, then he and outfielder Justin Williams joined the Rays in a November trade involving Jeremy Hellickson. Velazquez has a good feel for hitting from both sides of the plate and good bat speed because of his strong hands, but he needs to improve his strike-zone discipline and contact rate. He showed surprising power from a small, 5-foot-8 frame. He's a plus runner with good instincts on the bases, and he led the Midwest League with 50 stolen bases after swiping just seven bags the previous year. Velazquez played entirely at shortstop in 2014 after starting his career as a second baseman and showed significant improvement with solid-average range and a strong arm. Scouts believe he best suits a utility-infield profile with his glove, speed and switch-hit bat, but some give him a chance to develop into a starting second baseman. He moves up to high Class A Charlotte in 2015.

BA GRADE

50 Risk: High

LGE	PA	BB%	SO%	ISO
MWL	623	10.0	21.8	.138

Year	Club (League)	Class	AVG	G	AB	R	H	2B	3B	HR	RBI	BB	SO	SB	CS	OBP	SLG
2012	Diamondbacks (AZL)	R	.319	29	116	33	37	8	5	1	20	18	35	20	3	.406	.500
	Missoula (PIO)	R	.220	14	50	9	11	0	2	0	4	5	12	2	0	.286	.300
2013	South Bend (MWL)	LoA	.260	65	235	23	61	10	4	0	16	21	59	7	2	.319	.336
2014	South Bend (MWL)	LoA	.290	134	544	94	158	18	15	9	56	62	136	50	15	.367	.428
Minor League Totals			.283	242	945	159	267	36	26	10	96	106	242	79	20	.356	.407

11 CASEY GILLASPIE, 1B

BA GRADE

50 Risk: High

Born: Jan. 25, 1993. **B-T:** B-R. **Ht.:** 6-4. **Wt.:** 240. **Drafted:** Wichita State, 2014 (1st round). **Signed by:** J.D. Elliby.

Gillaspie was the 20th overall pick in 2014 who signed for $2,035,500 after ranking among the national leaders in walks and on-base percentage as a junior with Wichita State. Gillaspie possesses above-average power from both sides of the plate and shows good discipline, even though he tended to chase breaking balls and changeups in his first taste of pro ball. He's more polished from the left side but shows above-average hitting instincts with the ability to make adjustments. His bat speed rates a tick above-average and tends to improve significantly when he's ahead in the count. Gillaspie has below-average athleticism that will keep him at first base. He possesses soft hands with an above-average arm and good accuracy but does not impress with either his footwork or his range. The Rays believe Gillaspie has the potential to be a middle-of-the-lineup hitter who holds down first base for an extended period of time. He will move up to the full-season ranks next year at either low Class A Bowling Green or high Class A Charlotte.

Year	Club (League)	Class	AVG	G	AB	R	H	2B	3B	HR	RBI	BB	SO	SB	CS	OBP	SLG
2014	Hudson Valley (NYP)	SS	.262	71	263	27	69	16	1	7	42	42	65	2	3	.364	.411
Minor League Totals			.262	71	263	27	69	16	1	7	42	42	65	2	3	.364	.411

12 TAYLOR GUERRIERI, RHP

BA GRADE

55 Risk: Extreme

Born: Dec. 1, 1992. **B-T:** R-R. **Ht.:** 6-3. **Wt.:** 195. **Drafted:** HS—Columbia, S.C., 2011 (1st round). **Signed by:** Brad Matthews.

The 24th overall pick in the 2011 draft, Guerrieri returned to the mound in July 2014, making five starts in the Rookie-level Gulf Coast League 11 months after having Tommy John surgery. He ranked as the No. 18 prospect in the low Class A Midwest League in 2013, the same year he was suspended 50 games for testing positive for a drug of abuse in September. Scouts love Guerrieri's lean frame and electric arm. He has the mindset of a power pitcher and works off his fastball that was clocked as high as 98 mph in high school but has resided in the low 90s and touched 95 since signing. What makes his fastball a plus offering is its hard, late sink, good armside run and his ability to throw it on both sides of the plate. Guerrieri also has a plus curveball that he struggled to command just prior to having surgery. Featuring late, hard break, the curve sits in the upper 70s and serves as an out-pitch. His changeup has been inconsistent, but he demonstrates good feel for it and could develop it into an above-average offering. Guerrieri should be at full health in 2015, when he will spend most of the season at high Class A Charlotte at age 22. Having shown added maturity and the potential to throw three pitches for strikes, he could develop into a No. 2 or 3 starter at the major league level.

Year	Club (League)	Class	W	L	ERA	G	GS	CG	SV	IP	H	HR	BB	SO	K/9	WHIP	AVG
2012	Hudson Valley (NYP)	SS	1	2	1.04	12	12	0	0	52	35	0	5	45	7.8	0.77	.186
2013	Bowling Green (MWL)	LoA	6	2	2.01	14	14	0	0	67	54	5	12	51	6.9	0.99	.225
2014	Rays (GCL)	R	0	0	0.00	5	5	0	0	9	7	0	2	10	9.6	0.96	.194
Minor League Totals			7	4	1.47	31	31	0	0	128	96	5	19	106	7.4	0.90	.207

13 JAKE HAGER, SS

BA GRADE

45 Risk: Medium

Born: March 4, 1993. **B-T:** R-R. **Ht.:** 6-1. **Wt.:** 170. **Drafted:** HS—Las Vegas, 2011 (1st round). **Signed by:** Jayson Durocher.

Hager played through nagging injuries at Double-A Montgomery, showing solid all-around skills and few weaknesses. He possesses outstanding instincts and average range, with a knack for moving in the right direction when the ball is hit and making the routine plays. He displays solid footwork and quickness on turning double plays and making relay throws. His hands are soft and he has a solid-average arm. Offensively, Hager held his own at the plate by making consistent contact with his quick hands and above-average hand-eye coordination. He still needs to add strength to improve well below-average power. He could play shortstop in the big leagues but might emerge as a utility infielder. The Rays could have a logjam of shortstops at Triple-A Durham, but Hager should make the jump, regardless, in 2015.

Year	Club (League)	Class	AVG	G	AB	R	H	2B	3B	HR	RBI	BB	SO	SB	CS	OBP	SLG
2012	Bowling Green (MWL)	LoA	.281	114	442	63	124	22	3	10	72	40	60	17	11	.345	.412
2013	Rays (GCL)	R	.500	1	4	1	2	1	0	0	1	0	0	0	0	.500	.750
	Charlotte (FSL)	HiA	.258	113	449	56	116	15	3	0	33	38	81	12	8	.318	.305
2014	Montgomery (SL)	AA	.271	114	447	42	121	27	4	4	47	30	91	4	4	.316	.376
Minor League Totals			.270	389	1535	191	415	76	11	18	170	117	258	38	30	.324	.369

14 JUSTIN WILLIAMS, OF

BA GRADE

55 Risk: Extreme

Born: Aug. 20, 1995. **B-T:** L-R. **Ht.:** 6-2. **Wt.:** 215. **Drafted:** HS—Houma, La., 2013 (2nd round). **Signed by:** Rusty Pendergrass (Diamondbacks).

Williams led the Rookie-level Pioneer League in hitting (.386), ranked third in on-base percentage (.433) and eneded his time in Missoula with a 28-game hitting streak. In November, the Diamondbacks traded him to the Rays along with shortstop Andrew Velazquez to get Jeremy Hellickson. Williams makes solid contact to all fields with his strength, hand speed and excellent hand-eye coordination. With above-average raw power, he could hit more home runs if he can generate more loft, but he needs to learn to better handle quality offspeed stuff. A shortstop in high school, he lacks experience in left field, but his defense has steadily improved, in part as a result of work done with outfield coordinator Joel Youngblood during instructional league. He continues to build arm strength and should eventually have enough to handle right field. An assignment to low Class A Bowling Green is his most likely starting point in 2015.

Year	Club (League)	Class	AVG	G	AB	R	H	2B	3B	HR	RBI	BB	SO	SB	CS	OBP	SLG
2013	Diamondbacks (AZL)	R	.345	37	148	17	51	12	0	1	32	8	35	0	1	.398	.446
	Missoula (PIO)	R	.412	11	51	12	21	6	0	0	5	1	7	0	0	.423	.529
	South Bend (MWL)	LoA	.111	3	9	3	1	0	0	0	0	2	2	0	0	.273	.111
2014	Missoula (PIO)	R	.386	46	189	31	73	6	2	2	23	17	44	1	1	.433	.471
	South Bend (MWL)	LoA	.284	28	102	16	29	6	3	2	23	7	23	0	1	.348	.461
Minor League Totals			.351	125	499	79	175	30	5	5	83	35	111	1	3	.401	.461

15 NICK CIUFFO, C

BA GRADE

50 Risk: High

Born: March 7, 1995. **B-T:** L-R. **Ht.:** 6-1. **Wt.:** 205. **Drafted:** HS—Lexington, S.C., 2013 (1st round). **Signed by:** Brian Hickman.

The second catcher selected in the 2013 draft, Ciuffo contracted a stomach virus that caused him to lose more than 15 pounds early in the season before he rebounded to put together a solid slate that included throwing out 48 percent of basestealers. Ciuffo's key strengths are his fiery approach and throwing ability, for his plus arm features a quick release and unleashes excellent throws. He also displays good athleticism behind the plate, providing a big target with the ability to block pitches in the dirt. He needs to improve his all-around technique but has the hands to do the job. Ciuffo's bat speed is fringe-average, though he does a good job of barreling pitches when he makes contact. His plate discipline and pitch recognition need work, leads to a tendency to swing and miss. Most of his power comes from pulling the ball. A bump to low Class A Bowling Green seems likely.

Year	Club (League)	Class	AVG	G	AB	R	H	2B	3B	HR	RBI	BB	SO	SB	CS	OBP	SLG
2013	Rays (GCL)	R	.258	43	159	11	41	6	1	0	25	9	40	0	0	.296	.308
2014	Princeton (APP)	R	.224	52	192	25	43	7	1	4	20	17	45	2	1	.289	.333
Minor League Totals			.239	95	351	36	84	13	2	4	45	26	85	2	1	.292	.322

16 JOSE DOMINGUEZ, RHP

BA GRADE	
45	Risk: Low

Born: Aug. 7, 1990. **B-T:** R-R. **Ht.:** 6-0. **Wt.:** 200. **Signed:** Dominican Republic, 2007. **Signed by:** Rafael Rijo (Dodgers).

Despite hitting 100 mph with regularity and striking out 11 batters per nine innings at Triple-A Albuquerque in 2013 and 2014, Dominguez logged just 14 big league appearances during two callups to the Dodgers. The Rays acquired the big-armed righthander (plus righty Greg Harris) in November when they traded Joel Peralta and Triple-A reliever Adam Liberatore to Los Angeles in a 40-man roster-shuffling deal. Dominguez, who is cousin of Rays righthander Alex Colome, doesn't rely solely on 98-100 mph velocity, but it doesn't hurt. His fastball features some downhill life that make him difficult to square up or take deep. Better command of his mid-80s slider that flirts with being a plus pitch could make him a closer, but unless that happens, Dominguez might have to settle for seventh- and eighth-inning work. Though he'll need to improve his control and stay healthy after dealing with a strained quad in 2013 and shoulder inflammation in 2014. Dominguez has weathered two drug suspensions in his career—50 games for anabolic steroid use in 2009 and 25 games for an unspecified violation in 2012—but he's ready to contribute to the big league bullpen in 2015.

Year	Club (League)	Class	W	L	ERA	G	GS	CG	SV	IP	H	HR	BB	SO	K/9	WHIP	AVG
2012	Great Lakes (MWL)	LoA	4	3	5.25	33	5	0	4	72	77	4	47	78	9.8	1.72	.268
	Chattanooga (SL)	AA	0	1	1.29	5	0	0	1	7	2	0	0	9	11.6	0.29	.095
2013	Chattanooga (SL)	AA	1	0	2.60	14	0	0	5	17	8	0	8	28	14.5	0.92	.138
	Albuquerque (PCL)	AAA	1	0	0.00	8	0	0	0	8	1	0	5	12	13.5	0.75	.040
	Los Angeles (NL)	MAJ	0	0	2.16	9	0	0	0	8	11	0	3	4	4.3	1.68	.314
2014	Los Angeles (NL)	MAJ	0	0	11.37	5	0	0	0	6	7	2	3	8	11.4	1.58	.269
	Albuquerque (PCL)	AAA	1	2	3.24	31	0	0	10	33	31	1	18	39	10.5	1.47	.244
	Ogden (PIO)	R	0	0	13.50	2	0	0	0	1	1	0	1	2	13.5	1.50	.200
Major League Totals			0	0	6.14	14	0	0	0	15	18	2	6	12	7.4	1.64	.295
Minor League Totals			18	20	4.25	141	44	0	22	318	291	16	153	353	10.0	1.40	.240

17 TYLER GOEDDEL, 3B

BA GRADE	
50	Risk: High

Born: Oct. 20, 1992. **B-T:** R-R. **Ht.:** 6-4. **Wt.:** 185. **Drafted:** HS—Mountain View, Calif., 2011 (1st round supplemental). **Signed by:** Brian Morrison.

The 41st overall pick in the 2011 draft, Goeddel struggled at the plate in May and June at high Class A Charlotte. A wiry player who possesses above-average power potential, Goeddel became more relaxed as the season progressed and learned from his mistakes. He started trusting his hands, which generate above-average bat speed, and continued to prove capable of driving the ball to all fields. Some scouts project him to a ceiling of an average hitter with average power. Goeddel is an above-average runner with good instincts on the basepaths. He also made steady improvement by learning to slow down his actions at third base, where he has good hands and a strong arm. His next stop should be Double-A Montgomery.

Year	Club (League)	Class	AVG	G	AB	R	H	2B	3B	HR	RBI	BB	SO	SB	CS	OBP	SLG
2012	Bowling Green (MWL)	LoA	.246	103	329	52	81	19	2	6	46	38	94	30	5	.335	.371
2013	Bowling Green (MWL)	LoA	.249	112	450	63	112	18	12	7	65	40	98	30	5	.313	.389
2014	Charlotte (FSL)	HiA	.269	113	424	41	114	25	8	6	61	46	98	20	9	.349	.408
Minor League Totals			.255	328	1203	156	307	62	22	19	172	124	290	80	19	.332	.391

18 RICHIE SHAFFER, 3B

BA GRADE	
45	Risk: Medium

Born: March 15, 1991. **B-T:** R-R. **Ht.:** 6-3. **Wt.:** 210. **Drafted:** Clemson, 2012 (1st round). **Signed by:** Brian Hickman.

For the first four months at Double-A Montgomery, Shaffer waved at breaking balls when behind in the count, displayed a long swing that left him late on fastballs and showed fringe-average power despite impressive batting practice displays. Shaffer tinkered with several aspects of his hitting and became quieter with his actions, which included toning down his leg kick. He finally found his groove in August, when he hit .273/.398/.591 and swatted seven of his 19 home runs. When in sync, Shaffer has a good approach but can be pull-happy. He displayed better recognition of offspeed pitches in the second half and has quick hands to hit plus fastballs. Shaffer also showed marked improvement at third base, particularly with his footwork. He has steady hands, average range and plus, accurate arm. The Rays have pushed Shaffer but may have him begin 2015 back at Montgomery. He could be a low-average, high-power third baseman.

Year	Club (League)	Class	AVG	G	AB	R	H	2B	3B	HR	RBI	BB	SO	SB	CS	OBP	SLG
2012	Hudson Valley (NYP)	SS	.308	33	117	25	36	5	2	4	26	16	31	0	0	.406	.487
2013	Charlotte (FSL)	HiA	.254	122	469	55	119	33	1	11	73	35	106	6	0	.308	.399
2014	Montgomery (SL)	AA	.222	119	427	58	95	28	4	19	64	56	119	4	0	.318	.440
Minor League Totals			.247	274	1013	138	250	66	7	34	163	107	256	10	0	.324	.426

19 TIM BECKHAM, 2B/SS

Born: Jan. 27, 1990. **B-T:** R-R. **Ht.:** 6-0. **Wt.:** 190. **Drafted:** HS—Griffin, Ga., 2008 (1st round). **Signed by:** Milt Hill.

BA GRADE
45 Risk: Medium

The first overall pick in the 2008 draft has encountered numerous hurdles over his seven seasons in the minors, ranging from a 50-game suspension he drew in 2012 after testing positive for marijuana to a torn anterior cruciate ligament in his left knee that required surgery and limited him to 95 at-bats in 2014. Beckham has impressive tools in all phases of the game with solid quick-twitch athleticism, but he has struggled to hit for average despite possessing above-average bat speed. He tends to over-swing and has not displayed good plate discipline throughout his career, resulting in high strikeouts with few walks. He generates above-average raw power but just fair in-game juice, though he can drive the ball to all fields and might hit more home runs as he matures. An average runner with decent range, Beckham has plus arm strength and consistent hands that should allow him to be a versatile infielder in the big leagues. Few see him as a starting big league shortstop, but he could see action at second and third base. Provided he opens the 2015 campaign healthy, Beckham should begin at Triple-A Durham and be a candidate to reach Tampa Bay at some point.

Year	Club (League)	Class	AVG	G	AB	R	H	2B	3B	HR	RBI	BB	SO	SB	CS	OBP	SLG
2012	Durham (IL)	AAA	.256	72	285	40	73	10	1	6	28	29	71	6	0	.325	.361
2013	Durham (IL)	AAA	.276	122	460	71	127	25	7	4	51	44	108	17	7	.342	.387
	Tampa Bay (AL)	MAJ	.429	5	7	1	3	0	0	0	1	0	0	0	0	.375	.429
2014	Rays (GCL)	R	.476	6	21	5	10	2	1	1	4	3	4	1	0	.520	.810
	Charlotte (FSL)	HiA	.167	3	12	2	2	0	0	0	0	1	4	0	0	.231	.167
	Durham (IL)	AAA	.258	15	62	8	16	2	0	0	4	2	14	0	2	.281	.290
Major League Totals			.429	5	7	1	3	0	0	0	1	0	0	0	0	.375	.429
Minor League Totals			.267	645	2503	381	669	136	22	35	291	232	600	82	39	.332	.381

20 ENNY ROMERO, LHP

Born: Jan. 24, 1991. **B-T:** L-L. **Ht.:** 6-3. **Wt.:** 170. **Signed:** Dominican Republic, 2008. **Signed by:** Eddy Toledo.

BA GRADE
45 Risk: Medium

Romero's arm strength and stuff made him one of the system's top prospects over the past several seasons, but he logged a 5.31 ERA through Aug. 1 prior to finishing strong in his last five outings, when he surrendered just four earned runs over 26 innings. Romero has a live arm that generates a fastball in the low 90s and a slurvy breaking ball in the mid-80s. He struggles with the release point of his three-quarters delivery, which led to a walk rate of 3.7 per nine innings in 2014. With a below-average changeup, Romero's two-pitch mix probably limits him to a relief future in the major leagues. His repertoire proved all too hittable against International League competition in 2014 before he made some late-season adjustments, and the Rays are hopeful that the mechanical tweaks will continue to benefit him in 2015, with a return to Durham to open the season the most realistic scenario.

Year	Club (League)	Class	W	L	ERA	G	GS	CG	SV	IP	H	HR	BB	SO	K/9	WHIP	AVG
2012	Charlotte (FSL)	HiA	5	7	3.93	25	23	1	0	126	89	5	76	107	7.6	1.31	.201
2013	Montgomery (SL)	AA	11	7	2.76	27	27	0	0	140	110	9	73	110	7.1	1.30	.215
	Durham (IL)	AAA	0	0	0.00	1	1	0	0	8	4	0	2	2	2.3	0.75	.154
	Tampa Bay (AL)	MAJ	0	0	0.00	1	1	0	0	5	1	0	4	0	0.0	1.07	.071
2014	Durham (IL)	AAA	5	11	4.50	25	25	0	0	126	128	13	52	117	8.4	1.43	.261
Major League Totals			0	0	0.00	1	1	0	0	5	1	0	4	0	0.0	1.07	.071
Minor League Totals			34	35	3.59	139	120	1	0	644	536	40	319	605	8.5	1.33	.226

21 HAK-JU LEE, SS

Born: Nov. 4, 1990. **B-T:** L-R. **Ht.:** 6-2. **Wt.:** 170. **Signed:** South Korea, 2008. **Signed by:** Steve Wilson (Cubs).

BA GRADE
45 Risk: Medium

Considered one of the system's top prospects after being acquired in January 2011 from the Cubs as part of the Matt Garza deal, Lee suffered torn ligaments in his left knee in a collision at second base in early 2013 and did not return to game action until late-April 2014. He proceeded to struggle offensively throughout the season at Triple-A Durham despite being healthy, with some scouts wondering if Lee trusted his knee after having surgery and going through a long rehabilitation. His game is based on speed and quickness. He tends to slap at pitches and use his legs to get on base, a philosophy that failed more often than not in 2014. He has 20 power on the 20-80 scouting scale, and he probably won't be better than fringe-average in terms of batting average if he doesn't recover his plate discipline. Lee has stolen 30 bases in three seasons, but he swiped just 12 in 17 attempts in 2014. His defense in 2014 remained consistent, with Lee displaying quick-twitch athleticism and above-average range at shortstop, with soft hands and plus arm strength and a quick release. He will return to Durham in 2015.

Year	Club (League)	Class	AVG	G	AB	R	H	2B	3B	HR	RBI	BB	SO	SB	CS	OBP	SLG
2012	Montgomery (SL)	AA	.261	116	475	68	124	15	10	4	37	51	102	37	9	.336	.360
2013	Durham (IL)	AAA	.422	15	45	13	19	3	1	1	7	11	9	6	2	.536	.600
2014	Durham (IL)	AAA	.203	93	315	36	64	9	1	4	23	37	86	12	5	.287	.276
Minor League Totals			.277	535	2084	356	577	80	33	17	170	232	427	145	47	.353	.371

22 KEAN WONG, 2B

BA GRADE 45 Risk: High

Born: April 17, 1995. **B-T:** L-R. **Ht.:** 5-11. **Wt.:** 190. **Drafted:** HS—Hilo Hawaii, 2013 (4th round). **Signed by:** Robbie Moen.

The brother of Cardinals second baseman Kolten Wong, the younger sibling finished second in the batting race (.306) while being tabbed the low Class A Midwest League's best batting prospect and best defensive second baseman. Wong employs a compact lefthanded swing that he uses to spray line drives to all fields. While he generates minimal power, he makes consistent contact with his advanced approach, and he hits southpaws by hanging in against breaking balls. He is a good two-strike hitter who used the bunt to his advantage last season for the first time in his career. Defensively, Wong plays a solid second base with average range that resulted in just seven errors in 2014. He has good hands but below-average arm strength caused by an unusual throwing motion. The Rays worked with him to improve crispness on his throws and produce more wrist snap to generate more velocity. His footwork is solid in turning double plays. A hard worker with a tremendous drive to succeed, Wong has the makeup to get the most out of his ability. He is in line for a promotion to high Class A Charlotte in 2015.

Year	Club (League)	Class	AVG	G	AB	R	H	2B	3B	HR	RBI	BB	SO	SB	CS	OBP	SLG
2013	Rays (GCL)	R	.328	46	177	27	58	7	2	0	22	11	22	7	1	.377	.390
2014	Bowling Green (MWL)	LoA	.306	106	422	56	129	15	3	2	24	27	73	13	7	.347	.370
Minor League Totals			.312	152	599	83	187	22	5	2	46	38	95	20	8	.356	.376

23 LUKE MAILE, C

BA GRADE 45 Risk: Medium

Born: Feb. 6, 1991. **B-T:** R-R. **Ht.:** 6-3. **Wt.:** 220. **Drafted:** Kentucky, 2012 (8th round). **Signed by:** James Bonnici.

Maile has made impressive strides in his development since being deemed an offensive-oriented receiver coming out of Kentucky in 2012. Strong hands make Maile a potential above-average receiver who frames pitches and handles a staff well, though his 11 passed balls led the Double-A Southern League. His arm also earns above-average grades with accuracy and carry on his throws; he threw out 32 percent of opposing basestealers and could improve on that with a quicker release. Maile runs enough for a catcher and has some offensive upside, with good pull power that has yet to translate consistently to games. He was a part-time catcher at Kentucky and has caught just 186 games in nearly three pro seasons, including a stint in the Arizona Fall League. Maile has to beat Justin O'Conner to the majors to be the Rays' catcher of the future. He's slated to return to Triple-A Durham in 2015 after joining the Bulls during the International League playoffs.

Year	Club (League)	Class	AVG	G	AB	R	H	2B	3B	HR	RBI	BB	SO	SB	CS	OBP	SLG
2012	Hudson Valley (NYP)	SS	.278	61	216	30	60	10	3	3	41	31	36	3	1	.377	.394
2013	Bowling Green (MWL)	LoA	.283	95	361	45	102	25	3	4	49	41	54	8	2	.351	.402
2014	Montgomery (SL)	AA	.268	97	351	43	94	19	4	5	37	35	76	1	1	.341	.387
Minor League Totals			.276	253	928	118	256	54	10	12	127	107	166	12	4	.354	.394

24 RYNE STANEK, RHP

BA GRADE 45 Risk: High

Born: July 26, 1991. **B-T:** R-R. **Ht.:** 6-4. **Wt.:** 190. **Drafted:** Arkansas, 2013 (1st round). **Signed by:** Rickey Drexler.

The 29th overall pick in 2013 after a solid college career at Arkansas, Stanek's pro career did not begin until a month into the 2014 season because a hip injury required surgical intervention. He also missed more than a month between mid-July and late August 2014 with shoulder fatigue before he returned to action and pitched well in instructional league. Possessing a quirky three-quarters delivery, Stanek is a power pitcher with a loose arm that can generate natural sink to his pitches. His fastball sits at 93-94 mph and touches 97. His slider also is a plus offering, residing in the mid-80s and topping out at 88. He shows confidence in his below-average changeup by mixing it consistently at any time in the count. Stanek is working on staying on top of the ball and improving his command after pitching up in the zone too often last season. Some teams project Stanek as a reliever, but the Rays will continue to develop him as a starter with back-end potential in the rotation. Stanek faces a likely 2015 assignment to high Class A Charlotte.

Year	Club (League)	Class	W	L	ERA	G	GS	CG	SV	IP	H	HR	BB	SO	K/9	WHIP	AVG
2014	Bowling Green (MWL)	LoA	3	4	3.63	9	9	0	0	45	47	2	13	46	9.3	1.34	.275
	Rays (GCL)	R	0	0	0.00	1	1	0	0	1	0	0	0	0	0.0	0.00	.000
	Charlotte (FSL)	HiA	1	1	5.54	3	3	0	0	13	13	0	5	4	2.8	1.38	.277
Minor League Totals			4	5	3.99	13	13	0	0	59	60	2	18	50	7.7	1.33	.271

25 GERMAN MARQUEZ, RHP

BA GRADE
45 Risk: High

Born: Feb. 22, 1995. **B-T:** R-R. **Ht.:** 6-1. **Wt.:** 185. **Signed:** Venezuela, 2011. **Signed by:** Ronnie Blanco.

Marquez signed for $225,000 in 2011 but didn't distinguish himself in his first two seasons. He struggled initially at low Class A Bowling Green in 2014, too, but he responded by not allowing more than two earned runs in any of his final last 14 starts (2.54 ERA). He has an easy arm action with clean, polished mechanics. He pounds the strike zone with above-average control and can overpower hitters with his 91-93 mph fastball that touches 96. His heater tends to jump out of his hand and possesses excellent late life. His quick arm and wrist also generate a sharp, above-average curveball, and he shows good feel for a changeup. Mature for his age, Marquez needs to fine-tune his command in the strike zone, though he does a good job of working the lower half of the zone. A potential back-end starter, Marquez should make the jump to high Class A Charlotte to open 2015.

Year	Club (League)	Class	W	L	ERA	G	GS	CG	SV	IP	H	HR	BB	SO	K/9	WHIP	AVG
2012	Rays (VSL)	R	0	2	6.82	15	6	0	0	34	43	4	20	29	7.6	1.83	.307
2013	Princeton (APP)	R	2	5	4.05	12	12	0	0	53	46	2	20	38	6.4	1.24	.232
2014	Bowling Green (MWL)	LoA	5	7	3.21	22	18	0	0	98	83	5	29	95	8.7	1.14	.228
Minor League Totals			7	14	4.12	49	36	0	0	186	172	11	69	162	7.9	1.30	.245

26 PATRICK LEONARD, 1B

BA GRADE
45 Risk: High

Born: Oct. 20, 1992. **B-T:** R-R. **Ht.:** 6-4. **Wt.:** 225. **Drafted:** HS—Houston, 2011 (5th round). **Signed by:** Brian Rhees (Royals).

Coached in high school by Craig Biggio, Leonard signed with the Royals for $600,000 as a fifth-round pick in 2011. He tied for first in the Rookie-level Appalachian League in home runs (14) and ranked third in RBIs (46) in 2012 prior to being shipped to the Rays as part of the deal that imported Wil Myers and exported James Shields. Leonard is a big-bodied, physical player with above-average power potential. Leonard has a solid approach at the plate, recognizes pitches well and rarely chases offerings outside the strike zone. He used the entire field more consistently in 2014 at high Class A Charlotte after demonstrating most of his power previously while pulling the ball. He could supply above-average power production with a strong, leveraged swing, though he probably won't hit for a high average. Regarded as the best defensive first baseman in the Florida State League in 2014, Leonard has soft hands, a good arm and moves well despite his limited range. Leonard should move to Double-A Montgomery in 2015.

Year	Club (League)	Class	AVG	G	AB	R	H	2B	3B	HR	RBI	BB	SO	SB	CS	OBP	SLG
2012	Burlington (APP)	R	.251	62	235	37	59	9	3	14	46	30	55	6	2	.340	.494
2013	Bowling Green (MWL)	LoA	.225	123	440	52	99	26	0	9	57	42	118	4	1	.303	.345
2014	Charlotte (FSL)	HiA	.284	122	455	79	129	26	5	13	58	49	107	14	0	.359	.448
Minor League Totals			.254	307	1130	168	287	61	8	36	161	121	280	24	3	.333	.418

27 JOHNNY FIELD, OF

BA GRADE
45 Risk: High

Born: Feb. 20, 1992. **B-T:** R-R. **Ht.:** 5-10. **Wt.:** 180. **Drafted:** Arizona, 2013 (5th round). **Signed by:** Jayson Durocher.

An accomplished amateur who won four state championships at Bishop Gorman High in Las Vegas, Field helped guide Arizona to College World Series title in 2012, the year he was the Pacific-12 Conference batting champion. Far from the toolsiest player in the game, Field does most things well while exhibiting a blue-collar approach and tireless work ethic. He has an excellent feel for hitting with his short stroke, and he generates fringy power. A true hustle player, he has below-average speed but shows excellent instincts in the field and on the basepaths. Field saw most of his activity in center field at low Class A Bowling Green and high Class A Charlotte in 2014 but scouts have projected a move to second base for the past two years due to his below-average arm. The Rays like versatile players and believe Field could fit the super-utility mold. Field could move up to Double-A Montgomery early in the 2015 campaign.

Year	Club (League)	Class	AVG	G	AB	R	H	2B	3B	HR	RBI	BB	SO	SB	CS	OBP	SLG
2013	Hudson Valley (NYP)	SS	.252	60	238	22	60	20	1	2	24	12	38	14	6	.299	.370
2014	Bowling Green (MWL)	LoA	.290	82	317	62	92	23	5	7	41	33	74	18	4	.367	.461
	Charlotte (FSL)	HiA	.320	40	150	33	48	13	3	5	17	13	28	5	4	.396	.547
Minor League Totals			.284	182	705	117	200	56	9	14	82	58	140	37	14	.351	.448

28 ANDREW TOLES, OF

Born: May 24, 1992. **B-T:** L-R. **Ht.:** 5-10. **Wt.:** 185. **Drafted:** Chipola (Fla.) JC, 2012 (3rd round). **Signed by:** Milt Hill.

The Rays gambled a third-round pick in 2012 on Toles, who had been dismissed from the Tennessee program in 2011, then suspended from Chipola (Fla.) JC during his draft year. He spent the first two months of 2014 at high Class A Charlotte before missing all of June, July and August (save for a week in the Rookie-level Gulf Coast League) on the inactive list for unspecified reasons. A premier athlete, Toles is a raw outfielder who grades as a plus-plus runner runner, and that speed serves him well in center field and on the basepaths. He has a quick first step and reaches top speed in a hurry, though his routes need work. Arm strength is his weakest tool, though he has above-average accuracy and does a good job of hitting cut-off men. He generates above-average bat speed to hit for a modest average but well below-average power. His pitch recognition and strike-zone judgment need work due to his over-aggressiveness at the plate. A return to Charlotte seems likely in 2015.

Year	Club (League)	Class	AVG	G	AB	R	H	2B	3B	HR	RBI	BB	SO	SB	CS	OBP	SLG
2012	Princeton (APP)	R	.281	51	199	31	56	13	3	7	33	12	36	14	5	.327	.482
2013	Bowling Green (MWL)LoA		.326	121	519	79	169	35	16	2	57	22	105	62	17	.359	.466
2014	Charlotte (FSL)	HiA	.261	46	199	28	52	10	1	1	13	12	31	18	10	.302	.337
	Rays (GCL)	R	.292	6	24	4	7	0	1	0	2	0	6	6	0	.320	.375
Minor League Totals			.302	224	941	142	284	58	21	10	105	46	178	100	32	.339	.440

29 YOEL ARAUJO, OF

Born: Dec. 3, 1993. **B-T:** R-R. **Ht.:** 6-0. **Wt.:** 190. **Signed:** Dominican Republic, 2010. **Signed by:** Eddy Toledo.

Araujo signed with the Rays in 2010 for $800,000, which represented the largest bonus in franchise history for an international amateur. After three years in Rookie ball, Araujo made his full-season debut at low Class A Bowling Green in 2014 but an arch injury and subsequent surgery sidelined him in late June. Araujo possesses plus bat speed and generates as much raw power as any player in the organization. He has a big swing that leads to high strikeout totals. Araujo gets tremendous carry on his hits due to the backspin his puts on the ball. He also has above-average athleticism and speed for his large frame. In the right field he has good arm strength but needs work on his routes. After a strong performance in instructional league, Araujo should move up to high Class A Charlotte in 2015.

Year	Club (League)	Class	AVG	G	AB	R	H	2B	3B	HR	RBI	BB	SO	SB	CS	OBP	SLG
2012	Rays (GCL)	R	.286	30	105	9	30	6	2	1	11	6	35	4	3	.339	.410
2013	Princeton (APP)	R	.223	57	206	27	46	6	0	7	26	20	66	6	3	.300	.354
2014	Bowling Green (MWL)LoA		.226	61	217	31	49	5	2	10	27	11	90	6	6	.274	.406
Minor League Totals			.233	205	718	97	167	28	6	23	87	69	267	22	14	.311	.384

30 GRAYSON GARVIN, LHP

Born: Oct. 27, 1989. **B-T:** L-L. **Ht.:** 6-6. **Wt.:** 225. **Drafted:** Vanderbilt, 2011 (1st round supplemental). **Signed by:** James Bonnici.

Garvin continued to work his way back from Tommy John surgery in 2012 and encountered stiffness and soreness in 2014 that contributed to his missing a month beginning in April. He gradually built his workload to a maximum of six innings per start by the end of the season at Double-A Montgomery. An intelligent pitcher, Garvin uses his height to his advantage by throwing downhill. He demonstrated excellent command of all his pitches in the Southern League and did a good job of keeping hitters off-balance by mixing his offerings while working off his fastball. He has smooth mechanics for a tall pitcher, which makes his 91-93 mph fastball (which touches 95) get on top of batters in a hurry. He also throws a hard cutter in the upper 80s and is making strides with an average changeup. A potential No. 5 starter or situational reliever in the big leagues, he will open 2015 at Montgomery or Triple-A Durham, based on the progress he shows in spring training.

Year	Club (League)	Class	W	L	ERA	G	GS	CG	SV	IP	H	HR	BB	SO	K/9	WHIP	AVG
2012	Charlotte (FSL)	HiA	2	4	5.05	11	10	0	0	46	45	0	19	37	7.2	1.38	.259
2013	Rays (GCL)	R	0	1	2.31	6	6	0	0	12	11	1	4	12	9.3	1.29	.244
	Charlotte (FSL)	HiA	0	1	1.08	5	5	0	0	17	8	0	4	12	6.5	0.72	.138
2014	Montgomery (SL)	AA	1	8	3.77	20	20	0	0	74	76	5	15	60	7.3	1.23	.271
Minor League Totals			3	14	3.75	42	41	0	0	149	140	6	42	121	7.3	1.22	.251

Texas Rangers

BY BEN BADLER

After the Rangers traded second baseman Ian Kinsler to the Tigers for Prince Fielder last offseason, Kinsler showed up to spring training and said he hoped the Rangers went 0-162.

He didn't get his wish, but it was otherwise as disastrous a season as possible for the Rangers, who finished with the third-worst record in baseball at 67-95. It was the franchise's worst winning percentage since 1985 and ended a run of four straight 90-win seasons.

Injuries demolished any hope the Rangers held for 2014. Starters Yu Darvish, Derek Holland, Matt Harrison and Martin Perez each missed most or all of the season with injury, as did righthander Alexi Ogando, Fielder and talented young shortstop Jurickson Profar.

With less than a month left in the season, the Rangers also lost manager Ron Washington, who resigned for undisclosed reasons. Even a strong 13-3 finish to the season hurt the organization, for it dropped the Rangers from being in position to have the No. 1 overall pick in the 2015 draft down to the fourth pick. It also cost them an estimated $750,000 in international bonus pool money for 2015. The team also lost assistant general manager A.J. Preller to the Padres, who hired him as their general manager.

As treacherous as the 2014 season was for the Rangers, few teams who finished in their neighborhood in the standings are in better position to contend in 2015, much like the Angels quickly reversed course in 2014.

The influx of talent headed to Texas will come mostly from the disabled list, but several young players are ready to take steps forward. Second baseman Rougned Odor was rushed to the big leagues in 2014 and looked over his head, but he also flashed signs of why he entered the season as the organization's top prospect.

Righthanders Jake Thompson and Alex Gonzalez both pitched at Double-A Frisco and could reach Texas in 2015, as could righthanders Luke Jackson and Alec Asher and relievers Corey Knebel and Keone Kela.

The impact position players are a little further away, but the Rangers system as a whole is on the upswing, with several high-ceiling, high-risk prospects taking steps in the right direction.

Hitters with contact issues have consistently progressed under the Rangers' watch, with third baseman Joey Gallo, catcher Jorge Alfaro and outfielders Nomar Mazara and Lewis Brinson all trimming their strikeout rates in 2014, with many

Injuries in Texas created opportunity for players like rookie Rougned Odor in 2014

TOP PROSPECTS OF THE DECADE

Year	Player, Pos.	2014 Org
2005	Thomas Diamond, rhp	Out of baseball
2006	Edinson Volquez, rhp	Pirates
2007	John Danks, lhp	White Sox
2008	Elvis Andrus, ss	Rangers
2009	Neftali Feliz, rhp	Rangers
2010	Neftali Feliz, rhp	Rangers
2011	Martin Perez, lhp	Rangers
2012	Jurickson Profar, ss	Rangers
2013	Jurickson Profar, ss	Rangers
2014	Rougned Odor, 2b	Rangers

doing it while facing better pitchers.

Gallo in particular emerged as one of the game's premium prospects. A second straight season with 40 homers made it clear his raw power is the best in the minors and among the best in the sport.

Thanks in part to one of the game's premier international programs, the Rangers have a farm system with both high-end talent at the top and a strong wave of depth behind the first wave. Most teams—such as the Cubs, Twins and Astros—need to lose at the big league level for multiple seasons in order to generate high draft picks and trade away big leaguers for prospects to build a strong farm system. But the Rangers have done it while fielding a perennial contender.

After a one-year dip, the Rangers have the pieces lined up to contend in 2015, with the young talent on the way to help keep them there.

ORGANIZATION OVERVIEW

General manager: Jon Daniels. **Farm director:** Mike Daly. **Scouting director:** Kip Fagg.

Class	Team	League	W	L	PCT	Finish	Manager
Majors	Texas Rangers	American	67	95	.414	28th (30)	R. Washington/T. Bogar
Triple-A	Round Rock Express	Pacific Coast	70	74	.486	t-11th (16)	Steve Buechele
Double-A	Frisco RoughRiders	Texas	80	59	.576	1st (8)	Jason Wood
High A	Myrtle Beach Pelicans	Carolina	82	56	.594	1st (8)	Joe Mikulik
Low A	Hickory Crawdads	South Atlantic	80	59	.576	5th (14)	Corey Ragsdale
Short season	Spokane Indians	Northwest	40	36	.526	4th (8)	Tim Hulett
Rookie	Rangers	Arizona	26	30	.464	8th (14)	Kenny Holmberg
Overall Minor League Record			**378**	**314**	**.546**	**3rd (30)**	

THIS YEAR'S TOP 30

No.	Player, Pos.	Grade
1.	Joey Gallo, 3b	70/High
2.	Jake Thompson, rhp	60/Medium
3.	Jorge Alfaro, c	60/Medium
4.	Nomar Mazara, of	60/High
5.	Nick Williams, of	60/Extreme
6.	Alex Gonzalez, rhp	55/Medium
7.	Luis Sardinas, ss	50/Low
8.	Ryan Rua, 3b/of	50/Low
9.	Luis Ortiz, rhp	55/High
10.	Josh Morgan, ss/2b	55/High
11.	Ryan Cordell, of	55/High
12.	Luke Jackson, rhp	55/High
13.	Alec Asher, rhp	50/Medium
14.	Lewis Brinson, of	55/Extreme
15.	Ti'Quan Forbes, ss/3b	55/Extreme
16.	Michael De Leon, ss	50/High
17.	Corey Knebel, rhp	45/Medium
18.	Keone Kela, rhp	45/Medium
19.	Travis Demeritte, 2b/3b	55/Extreme
20.	Andrew Faulkner, lhp	45/Medium
21.	Jose LeClerc, rhp	45/Medium
22.	Marcos Diplan, rhp	55/Extreme
23.	Jairo Beras, of	55/Extreme
24.	Delino DeShields, of	50/High
25.	Yeyson Yrizarri, ss/2b	55/Extreme
26.	Tomas Telis, c	40/Low
27.	Alexander Claudio, lhp	40/Low
28.	Ronald Guzman, 1b	50/Extreme
29.	Lisalverto Bonilla, rhp	40/Low
30.	Hanser Alberto, ss	40/Medium

LAST YEAR'S TOP 30

No.	Player, Pos.	Status
1.	Rougned Odor, 2b	Majors
2.	Jorge Alfaro, c	No. 3
3.	Nick Williams, of	No. 5
4.	Joey Gallo, 3b	No. 1
5.	Alex Gonzalez, rhp	No. 6
6.	Luis Sardinas, ss	No. 7
7.	Luke Jackson, rhp	No. 12
8.	Travis Demeritte, ss/3b	No. 19
9.	Ronald Guzman, 1b	No. 28
10.	Marcos Diplan, rhp	No. 22
11.	Akeem Bostick, rhp	Dropped out
12.	Nick Martinez, rhp	Majors
13.	Yeyson Yrizarri, ss	No. 25
14.	Alec Asher, rhp	No. 13
15.	Lewis Brinson, of	No. 14
16.	Jose Leclerc, rhp	No. 21
17.	Jairo Beras, of	No. 23
18.	Keone Kela, rhp	No. 18
19.	David Ledbetter, rhp	Dropped out
20.	Lisalverto Bonilla, rhp	No. 29
21.	Drew Robinson, 3b	Dropped out
22.	Ryan Rua, 2b/3b	No. 8
23.	Ben Rowen	Dropped out
24.	Nomar Mazara, of	No. 4
25.	Engel Beltre, of	Free agent
26.	Wilmer Font, of	Free agent
27.	Alexander Claudio, lhp	No. 27
28.	Kellin Deglan, c	Dropped out
29.	Roman Mendez, rhp	Dropped out
30.	Kelvin Vasquez, rhp	Dropped out

BEST TOOLS

Best Hitter for Average	Ryan Rua
Best Power Hitter	Joey Gallo
Best Strike-Zone Discipline	Josh Morgan
Fastest Baserunner	Chris Garia
Best Athlete	Lewis Brinson
Best Fastball	Keone Kela
Best Curveball	Corey Knebel
Best Slider	Jake Thompson
Best Changeup	Alex Claudio
Best Control	Alec Asher
Best Defensive Catcher	Pat Cantwell
Best Defensive Infielder	Hanser Alberto
Best Infield Arm	Joey Gallo
Best Defensive Outfielder	Lewis Brinson
Best Outfield Arm	Jairo Beras

PROJECTED 2018 LINEUP

Catcher	Jorge Alfaro
First Base	Prince Fielder
Second Base	Rougned Odor
Third Base	Joey Gallo
Shortstop	Elvis Andrus
Left Field	Nick Williams
Center Field	Leonys Martin
Right Field	Nomar Mazara
Designated Hitter	Shin-Soo Choo
No. 1 Starter	Yu Darvish
No. 2 Starter	Derek Holland
No. 3 Starter	Jake Thompson
No. 4 Starter	Martin Perez
No. 5 Starter	Alex Gonzalez
Closer	Keone Kela

TEXAS RANGERS

TOP 2015 ROOKIE: Ryan Rua, of/3b. Overlooked his whole life, he has mashed at every level and now gets the chance to prove he can do it again.
BREAKOUT PROSPECT: Ryan Cordell, of. His combination of size, tools and knack for the barrel could make him an 11th-round steal.
SLEEPER: Jerad Eickhoff, rhp, With a plus fastball and an average slider, he rattled off a solid Double-A campaign in 2014 and earned a spot on the 40-man roster, putting himself in the mix for 2015 if he pitches well in Triple-A.

SOURCE OF TOP 30 TALENT			
Homegrown	26	Acquired	4
College	3	Trades	3
Junior college	2	Rule 5 draft	1
High school	10	Independent leagues	0
Draft-and-follow	0	Free agents/waivers	0
Nondrafted free agents	0		
International	11		

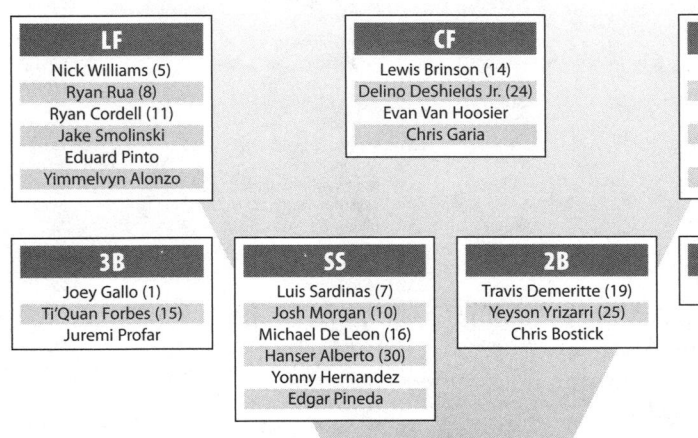

LF
Nick Williams (5)
Ryan Rua (8)
Ryan Cordell (11)
Jake Smolinski
Eduard Pinto
Yimmelvyn Alonzo

CF
Lewis Brinson (14)
Delino DeShields Jr. (24)
Evan Van Hoosier
Chris Garia

RF
Nomar Mazara (4)
Jairo Beras (23)
Luke Tendler
Drew Robinson
Jose Almonte
Preston Beck

3B
Joey Gallo (1)
Ti'Quan Forbes (15)
Juremi Profar

SS
Luis Sardinas (7)
Josh Morgan (10)
Michael De Leon (16)
Hanser Alberto (30)
Yonny Hernandez
Edgar Pineda

2B
Travis Demeritte (19)
Yeyson Yrizarri (25)
Chris Bostick

1B
Ronald Guzman (28)

C
Jorge Alfaro (3)
Tomas Telis (26)
Pat Cantwell
Jose Trevino
Kellin Deglan

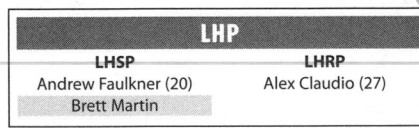

LHP

LHSP	LHRP
Andrew Faulkner (20)	Alex Claudio (27)
Brett Martin	

RHP

RHSP	RHRP
Jake Thompson (2)	Corey Knebel (17)
Alex Gonzalez (6)	Keone Kela (18)
Luis Ortiz (9)	Jose LeClerc (21)
Luke Jackson (12)	Lisalverto Bonilla (29)
Alec Asher (13)	Kyuji Fujikawa
Marcos Diplan (22)	Ben Rowen
Akeem Bostick	Roman Mendez
Sam Wolff	Abel De Los Santos
Kelvin Vasquez	Jerad Eickhoff
Richelson Pena	Phil Klein
Ariel Jurado	Jon Edwards
Jeffrey Nunez	Spencer Patton

2014

BEST PURE HITTER: SS Josh Morgan (3) has an advanced approach for a high school player. The righthanded hitter has a quick, compact stroke and level bat path conducive to producing hard line drives to all fields.

BEST POWER HITTER: OF Luke Tendler (23) has above-average raw power from the left side and tied for the Northwest League home run lead (11) and highest isolated power (.215).

FASTEST RUNNER: Morgan's body has improved since signing and his speed has also increased. He is an above-average runner who has posted some plus run times out of the box this summer. 3B Ti'Quan Forbes (2) is an average to above-average runner out of the box, but is a plus runner underway.

BEST DEFENSIVE PLAYER: Morgan is a polished, sure-handed defender who split his time between shortstop and second this summer while showing smooth actions and soft hands. He has a loose arm that is at least average. The organization is pleased with the defensive progress Jose Trevino (6) is making behind the plate after playing shortstop, third base and catcher in three years in college. He has an average arm that plays up because of a quick release.

BEST FASTBALL: RHP Luis Ortiz (1) was one of the most talented prep arms in the country with a fastball that sat 90-94 mph, touching 96 as the ball jumped out of his hand. He has an easy delivery and advanced command for a prep pitcher. LHP Brett Martin (4) has a large, projectable body, loose arm and fastball up to 95 after signing.

BEST SECONDARY PITCH: Ortiz has a wipeout slider with at least plus potential. Martin's curveball shows the makings of a plus offering. RHP John Fasola (31) is a strong-bodied reliever with a fastball up to 95 and mid-80s slider with above-average potential.

BEST PRO DEBUT: Morgan was one of the better offensive performers of any prep player drafted by an AL club, hitting .322/.436/.347 though he had just four extra-base hits.

BEST ATHLETE: Forbes was one of the top prep athletes in the class and played three sports in high school. He is a plus runner underway with at least an average arm and above-average bat speed.

MOST INTRIGUING BACKGROUND: RHP Austin Pettibone (24) is the younger brother of Phillies righthander Jonathan Pettibone. RHP Joe Watson (12), who has been up to 97, was a wide receiver in college. Trevino set a state home run record as a senior in Corpus Christi, Texas.

CLOSEST TO THE MAJORS: Ortiz and Trevino.

BEST LATE-ROUND PICK: RHP Gio Abreu (14) is an upside play as a lean, projectable prep pitcher with a loose arm.

THE ONE WHO GOT AWAY: RHP Andre Jackson (32) has a great-looking body and has a chance to turn into a good pick once he gains more strength.

ASSESSMENT: The Rangers prioritized high-upside prep players at the top of the draft with Luis Ortiz and Ti'Quan Forbes, then grabbed a collection of power arms after the 10th round.

2013

RHP Alex "Chi-Chi" Gonzalez (1) has reached Double-A with very good stuff. OF Ryan Cordell (11) looks like a steal, and there's plenty of time for raw, toolsy 2B Travis Demeritte (1) and RHP Akeem Bostick (2).

GRADE: B

2012

Seen as a boom-or-bust class at the time, 3B Joey Gallo (1s) provides plenty of boom himself. The rest of the class still has bust potential. RHPs Alec Asher (4) and Keone Kela (12) give the class intriguing arms.

GRADE: B

2011

The Rangers didn't sign 2014 first-rounders OF Derek Fisher (6), C Max Pentecost (7) and LHP Brandon Finnegan (45). The top-signed picks include since-traded RHP Kyle Hendricks (8), OF Ryan Rua (17) and RHPs Nick Martinez (18) and Phil Klein (30).

GRADE: D

TOP DRAFT PICKS OF THE DECADE

Year	Player, Pos.	2014 Org
2005	John Mayberry Jr., of	Blue Jays
2006	Kasey Kiker, lhp	Out of baseball
2007	Blake Beavan, rhp	Mariners
2008	Justin Smoak, 1b	Mariners
2009	*Matt Purke, lhp	Nationals
2010	Jake Skole, of	Rangers
2011	Kevin Matthews, lhp	Rangers
2012	Lewis Brinson, of	Rangers
2013	Alex Gonzalez, rhp	Rangers
2014	Luis Ortiz, rhp	Rangers

* Did not sign

LARGEST BONUSES IN CLUB HISTORY

Leonys Martin, 2011	$5,000,000
Nomar Mazara, 2011	$4,950,000
Mark Teixeira, 2001	$4,500,000
Jairo Beras, 2012	$4,500,000
Justin Smoak, 2008	$3,500,000

1 JOEY GALLO, 3B

Born: Nov. 19, 1993. **B-T:** L-R. **Ht.:** 6-5. **Wt.:** 205.
Drafted: HS—Las Vegas, 2012 (1st round supplemental).
Signed by: Todd Guggiana.

Tales of Gallo's prodigious power date back to his days as a youth, when he and teammate Bryce Harper were 8 and 9 years old. Gallo went on to hit 65 career home runs in high school, a Nevada state record, before signing with the Rangers for $2.25 million as the No. 39 overall pick in 2012. Gallo quickly set another home run record with 18 blasts in the Rookie-level Arizona League en route to winning the league MVP. He followed that up with a minor league-leading 40-homer season in 2013—despite missing most of July with a groin injury—then hit 42 home runs in 2014, topped in the minors only by fellow Las Vegan Kris Bryant of the Cubs, who hit 43.

Tales of Gallo's power sound like hyperbole, but scouts and coaches with 30-plus years of experience say Gallo hits balls as far as nearly anyone they have ever seen. He put on a stunning batting practice display during the Futures Game, hitting balls out of Target Field and smashing the windshield of a promotional truck set up by a sponsor on the right-field concourse. Gallo has easy, top-of-the-scale 80 raw power on the 20-80 scouting scale, which he generates with quick hands, premium bat speed and plenty of strength, leveraging the ball with majestic loft and backspin. What changed Gallo from a good young talent to one of the game's elite prospects was the improvement in his strikeout rate, which dropped from 37 percent at low Class A Hickory in 2013 to 26 percent at high Class A Myrtle Beach in 2104, though it spiked again once he reached Double-A Frisco in the second half. Gallo simplified his swing, eliminating some of the excess movement and shortening his load to be more direct to the ball. With his muscular 6-foot-5 frame, his swing always will be long and his power will come with strikeouts. But he also improved his ability to control the strike zone, which helps his hitting and boosts his on-base percentage with a high walk rate. Overall discipline still is an area he needs to hone, however, especially against high fastballs. Gallo is a below-average runner, and few players with his size play third base in the major leagues. Yet he's remarkably athletic for his size, has sound hands and a plus arm, so there's a chance he can play the hot corner. Sticking at third would boost Gallo's value, but the offensive potential is plenty for a corner outfield spot or first base, two positions he's also experimented with during instructional league.

Gallo's swing-and-miss tendencies still make him a high-risk player, but the remarkable improvement and tantalizing upside makes him a potential MVP candidate if everything clicks into place. Gallo spent the second half of 2014 at Double-A, and he probably will return to Frisco to open 2015, though he should reach Triple-A Round Rock by midseason, and possibly Texas by the end of the year.

BA GRADE
70 Risk High

SCOUTING GRADES
Batting: 50.
Power: 80.
Speed: 40.
Defense: 40.
Arm: 70.

Based on 20-80 scouting scale and future projection rather than present grades.

LGE	PA	BB%	SO%	ISO
CAR	246	20.7	26.0	.413
TL	291	12.4	39.5	.292

BILL MITCHELL

Year	Club (League)	Class	AVG	G	AB	R	H	2B	3B	HR	RBI	BB	SO	SB	CS	OBP	SLG
2012	Rangers (AZL)	R	.293	43	150	44	44	10	1	18	43	37	52	6	0	.435	.733
	Spokane (NWL)	SS	.214	16	56	9	12	2	0	4	9	11	26	0	0	.343	.464
2013	Rangers (AZL)	R	.368	5	19	4	7	4	0	2	10	2	7	1	0	.429	.895
	Hickory (SAL)	LoA	.245	106	392	82	96	19	5	38	78	48	165	14	1	.334	.610
2014	Myrtle Beach (CAR)	HiA	.323	58	189	53	61	9	3	21	50	51	64	5	3	.463	.735
	Frisco (TL)	AA	.232	68	250	44	58	10	0	21	56	36	115	2	0	.334	.524
Minor League Totals			.263	296	1056	236	278	54	9	104	246	185	429	28	4	.377	.627

2 JAKE THOMPSON, RHP

Born: Jan. 31, 1994. **B-T:** R-R. **Ht.:** 6-4. **Wt.:** 235. **Drafted:** HS—Heath, Texas, 2012 (2nd round). **Signed by:** Tim Grieve (Tigers).

The Tigers sacrificed their first-round pick in 2012 to sign Prince Fielder, so Thompson at No. 91 overall was their top selection. Detroit held him back in extended spring training the first two months of 2013, but he flew through the system after that slow start, reaching Double-A Erie as a 20-year-old in July 2014. Two starts later, the Tigers packaged him with relief prospect Corey Knebel to add reliever Joakim Soria to a thin Tigers bullpen. Thompson throws two-seam and four-seam fastballs downhill at 89-95 mph, with good sink and tail on his two-seamer. His best secondary weapon is his plus slider, a swing-and-miss pitch with two-plane break that flashes 70 on the 20-80 scale. Thompson didn't use his changeup much early in his career, but it's become an average pitch with projection to tick up. He mixes in an occasional curveball as well, and it too can be average. He's a solid strike-thrower, though he could tighten up his fastball command. The Tigers' desperation for bullpen help is the Rangers' gain. As a potential No. 2 or 3 starter, Thompson could be a steal. He's slated to return to Double-A Frisco to open 2015.

BA GRADE

60 Risk: Medium

LGE	BF	SO%	BB%	HR/9
FSL	342	23.1	7.3	0.33
TL	148	29.7	12.2	0.76

Year	Club (League)	Class	W	L	ERA	G	GS	CG	SV	IP	H	HR	BB	SO	K/9	WHIP	AVG
2012	Tigers (GCL)	R	1	2	1.91	7	7	0	0	28	14	1	10	31	9.8	0.85	.149
2013	West Michigan (MWL)	LoA	3	3	3.13	17	16	0	0	83	79	4	32	91	9.8	1.33	.244
2014	Lakeland (FSL)	HiA	6	4	3.14	16	16	0	0	83	75	3	25	79	8.6	1.20	.244
	Erie (EL)	AA	1	0	2.45	2	2	0	0	11	10	0	4	7	5.7	1.27	.238
	Frisco (TL)	AA	3	1	3.28	7	6	0	0	36	28	3	18	44	11.1	1.29	.219
Minor League Totals			14	10	2.98	49	47	0	0	241	206	11	89	252	9.4	1.22	.230

3 JORGE ALFARO, C

Born: June 11, 1993. **B-T:** R-R. **Ht.:** 6-2. **Wt.:** 185. **Signed:** Colombia, 2010. **Signed by:** Rodolfo Rosario/Don Welke.

Alfaro went from Colombia to the Dominican Republic to train, then in January 2010 signed with the Rangers for $1.3 million, a Colombian record. A broken left hand in 2013 and hamstring issues in the past have cut into his development time, but he stayed healthy and logged a career high 121 games in 2014. Alfaro has two standout tools in his power and arm strength. His bat speed, explosive hips and strength generate plus raw power, though he remains a power-over-hit prospect who's still trying to tone down his aggressive approach, improve his pitch recognition and make more contact. He could grow to be an average hitter, which is plenty good for a catcher with his power. Alfaro is athletic and is one of the fastest catchers in baseball, a legitimate average runner. His double-plus arm generates pop times of sub-1.9 seconds on throws to second base. He's never been a shutdown defender of the running game, but he threw out basestealers at a solid 28 percent clip in 2014. Alfaro has the attributes to catch, but he's

BA GRADE

60 Risk: High

LGE	PA	BB%	SO%	ISO
CAR	437	5.3	22.9	.178
TL	99	6.1	23.2	.182

still a well below-average receiver who committed 23 passed balls in 90 games in 2014. Alfaro's defensive issues are troubling, but his ceiling is as an above-average player whose power can carry him. He likely returns to Double-A Frisco to start 2015.

Year	Club (League)	Class	AVG	G	AB	R	H	2B	3B	HR	RBI	BB	SO	SB	CS	OBP	SLG
2012	Hickory (SAL)	LoA	.261	74	272	40	71	21	5	5	34	16	84	7	3	.320	.430
2013	Rangers (AZL)	R	.429	6	21	5	9	2	0	2	8	2	6	2	0	.500	.810
	Hickory (SAL)	LoA	.258	104	372	63	96	22	1	16	53	28	111	16	3	.338	.452
	Myrtle Beach (CAR)	HiA	.182	3	11	4	2	0	0	0	0	2	5	0	0	.308	.182
2014	Myrtle Beach (CAR)	HiA	.261	100	398	63	104	22	5	13	73	23	100	6	5	.318	.440
	Frisco (TL)	AA	.261	21	88	12	23	4	0	4	14	6	23	0	0	.343	.443
Minor League Totals			.262	401	1494	223	391	85	14	47	228	86	431	33	15	.326	.432

4 NOMAR MAZARA, OF

Born: April 26, 1995. **B-T:** L-L. **Ht.:** 6-4. **Wt.:** 215. **Signed:** Dominican Republic, 2011. **Signed by:** Rodolfo Rosario/Mike Daly.

Mazara set an international amateur record when he signed with the Rangers for $4.95 million on July 2, 2011. Other clubs thought the bonus was well beyond Mazara's value, and even Rangers officials worried after he struggled early. But 2014 was a breakthrough season for Mazara, who reached Double-A Frisco as a 19-year-old in August. Mazara entered pro ball with an exaggerated leg kick, which gave him timing problems once he faced better pitchers. The Rangers never told him specifically to eliminate the leg kick, but gradually he figured out that he needed to get his front foot down earlier. He now has a small toe-tap, which puts him in better position to hit, especially against good fastballs up and in. Mazara still takes a high dose of strikeouts, but he improved his contact rate, walk rate and game power in 2014. He has above-average raw power, which has always been his main draw. Defense was an adventure for Mazara early in his career, and while he's not rangy, he's become a reliable right fielder. He's also improved his throwing and now has a plus arm with good accuracy. Level-headed and mature beyond his years, Mazara has justified the Rangers' early belief in his ability. He has a chance to be an above-average everyday right fielder, and he likely returns to Double-A to open 2015.

	BA GRADE	
	60	Risk: High

LGE	PA	BB%	SO%	ISO
SAL	461	12.4	21.5	.206
TL	97	9.3	22.7	.212

Year	Club (League)	Class	AVG	G	AB	R	H	2B	3B	HR	RBI	BB	SO	SB	CS	OBP	SLG
2012	Rangers (AZL)	R	.264	54	201	40	53	13	3	6	39	37	70	5	2	.383	.448
2013	Hickory (SAL)	LoA	.236	126	453	48	107	23	2	13	62	44	131	1	2	.310	.382
2014	Hickory (SAL)	LoA	.264	106	398	68	105	21	2	19	73	57	99	4	3	.358	.470
	Frisco (TL)	AA	.306	24	85	10	26	7	1	3	16	9	22	0	0	.381	.518
Minor League Totals			.256	310	1137	166	291	64	8	41	190	147	322	10	7	.346	.434

5 NICK WILLIAMS, OF

Born: Sept. 8, 1993. **B-T:** L-L. **Ht.:** 6-3. **Wt.:** 195. **Drafted:** HS—Galveston, Texas, 2012 (2nd round). **Signed by:** Jay Heafner.

Williams had an up-and-down season as a high school senior, which is why he was available in the second round despite an explosive tool set. He crushed both Class A levels but struggled in an August 2014 bump to Double-A Frisco and during a stint in an Arizona Fall League, showcasing a tantalizing ceiling but a high-risk offensive approach. Williams has some of the fastest hands in the minors. He has a loose, free and easy swing that's quick and explosive. He has plus raw power and can go deep to any part of the park, though his stroke is more geared for line drives than loft. Scouts consistently praise Williams for his hitting actions, even though he strikes out frequently. That's because he has trouble recognizing pitches and chases too many balls out of the strike zone, which leads to excessive strikeouts and minimal walks. Williams is an above-average runner with an average arm, so he's rotated between all three outfield positions. He's still learning to become a more efficient basestealer, which will improve once he's able to time his jumps better. Scouts inclined to dream on Williams think he can become the Rangers' version of Carlos Gonzalez. If he can't shrink his strike zone, then his approach carries enough risk that the downside could be Felix Pie. He will return to a loaded Frisco team in 2015.

	BA GRADE	
	60	Risk: Extreme

LGE	PA	BB%	SO%	ISO
CAR	408	4.7	28.7	.199
TL	64	3.1	32.8	.065

Year	Club (League)	Class	AVG	G	AB	R	H	2B	3B	HR	RBI	BB	SO	SB	CS	OBP	SLG
2012	Rangers (AZL)	R	.313	48	201	34	63	9	6	2	27	16	50	15	2	.375	.448
2013	Hickory (SAL)	LoA	.293	95	376	70	110	19	12	17	60	15	110	8	5	.337	.543
2014	Rangers (AZL)	R	.308	3	13	3	4	0	1	0	2	1	2	0	0	.357	.462
	Myrtle Beach (CAR)	HiA	.292	94	377	61	110	28	4	13	68	19	117	5	7	.343	.491
	Frisco (TL)	AA	.226	15	62	4	14	2	1	0	4	2	21	1	1	.250	.290
Minor League Totals			.293	255	1029	172	301	58	24	32	161	53	300	29	15	.342	.489

6 ALEX GONZALEZ, RHP

Born: Jan. 15, 1992. **B-T:** R-R. **Ht.:** 6-2. **Wt.:** 192. **Drafted:** Oral Roberts, 2013 (1st round). **Signed by:** Jay Eddings.

Nicknamed "Chi-Chi," Gonzalez signed for $2.215 million as the No. 23 pick in the 2013 draft. He has looked the park of a polished college pitcher, moving quickly through the system to Double-A Frisco in 2014. Gonzalez commands his plus fastball to both sides of the plate, operating at 92-95 mph and touching 97. Gonzalez can cut and sink his fastball, giving it above-average movement and helping him get an abundance of grounders. He has another weapon in his plus slider, a sharp mid-80s offering that he adds and subtracts from depending on the situation. One of the focal points for Gonzalez this year was to improve his changeup, a pitch that flashes good action and sink. It has the makings of an average to a tick better offering, though he's not as consistent with the changeup yet as he is with his slider. He also started to use a solid curveball to get early-count called strikes, giving him a four-pitch mix to attack hitters. Gonzalez has all the attributes to be a mid-rotation starter. He could open 2015 at Frisco or Triple-A Round Rock, but by midseason he should be in Texas, with crisp command that should allow for a smooth transition.

BA GRADE

55 Risk: Medium

LGE	BF	SO%	BB%	HR/9
CAR	276	17.8	5.8	0.41
TL	309	20.7	8.1	0.37

Year	Club (League)	Class	W	L	ERA	G	GS	CG	SV	IP	H	HR	BB	SO	K/9	WHIP	AVG
2013	Spokane (NWL)	SS	0	4	4.56	9	9	0	0	24	30	1	7	20	7.6	1.56	.313
	Myrtle Beach (CAR)	HiA	0	0	2.84	5	5	0	0	19	15	1	9	15	7.1	1.26	.221
2014	Myrtle Beach (CAR)	HiA	5	2	2.62	11	11	0	0	65	56	3	16	49	6.8	1.10	.222
	Frisco (TL)	AA	7	4	2.70	15	14	0	0	73	67	3	25	64	7.9	1.25	.245
Minor League Totals			12	10	2.93	40	39	0	0	181	168	8	57	148	7.3	1.24	.244

7 LUIS SARDINAS, SS/2B

Born: May 16, 1993. **B-T:** B-R. **Ht.:** 6-1. **Wt.:** 170. **Signed:** Venezuela, 2009. **Signed by:** Mike Daly/Rafic Saab/Pedro Avila.

The Rangers' July 2 haul in 2009 included $1.55 million to Jurickson Profar from Curacao and $1.2 million to Sardinas out of Venezuela. Injuries slowed Sardinas his first three years, but injuries to other players in the organization helped push him up the ladder in 2014 for three separate big league stints. Sardinas isn't short, but he plays the little man's game. He has good hand-eye coordination, goes with where the ball is pitched and generally stays within the strike zone. His bat-to-ball skills are advanced, but he hits the ball on the ground frequently and has bottom-of-the-scale power, so his bat lacks impact. A double-plus runner earlier in his career, Sardinas now is a plus runner, though his stolen base total has dipped each season. He's a talented defensive shortstop with nimble feet, smooth actions, good instincts and an above-average arm. Fatigue hampered Sardinas' speed, range and even arm in 2014, so getting stronger continues to be a focal point. Sardinas is in the wrong organization, blocked by Elvis Andrus at shortstop, Rougned Odor at second and oft-injured Profar ahead of him. He should be at least a utility player, with a chance to be a defensive-oriented regular who hits at the bottom of the order.

BA GRADE

50 Risk: Low

LGE	PA	BB%	SO%	ISO
PCL	273	2.9	14.3	.084
AL	125	4.0	16.8	.052

Year	Club (League)	Class	AVG	G	AB	R	H	2B	3B	HR	RBI	BB	SO	SB	CS	OBP	SLG
2012	Hickory (SAL)	LoA	.291	96	374	65	109	14	2	2	30	29	52	32	9	.346	.356
2013	Myrtle Beach (CAR)	HiA	.298	97	383	69	114	15	3	1	31	32	54	27	8	.358	.360
	Frisco (TL)	AA	.259	29	135	12	35	4	0	1	15	4	21	5	2	.286	.311
2014	Frisco (TL)	AA	.253	21	87	12	22	5	1	0	9	3	12	1	1	.278	.333
	Round Rock (PCL)	AAA	.290	60	262	39	76	15	2	1	28	8	39	9	4	.310	.374
	Texas (AL)	MAJ	.261	43	115	12	30	6	0	0	8	5	21	5	1	.303	.313
Major League Totals			.261	43	115	12	30	6	0	0	8	5	21	5	1	.303	.313
Minor League Totals			.289	343	1396	230	404	59	9	5	128	87	203	84	27	.336	.355

8 RYAN RUA, OF/3B

Born: March 11, 1990. **B-T:** R-R. **Ht.:** 6-2. **Wt.:** 205. **Drafted:** Lake Erie (Ohio), 2011 (17th round). **Signed by:** Roger Coryell.

ROUND ROCK EXPRESS

An afterthought as a 17th-round pick out of Lake Erie College, an NCAA Division II school in Ohio, Rua got attention when he hit 32 home runs, mostly in low Class A, as a 23-year-old in 2013. He continued to rake at the upper levels in 2014, spending the last month of the season in Texas. Rua is an offensive-oriented prospect who has plus power and can take the ball out of the park to all fields. He starts his swing with a leg kick, keeps his weight back and his head still. Rua can get long to the ball, with some concerns about his ability to hit good offspeed pitches, but his swing is fluid, and he squares up the ball frequently. Rua has mostly played third base, but with Adrian Beltre stationed there in Texas, the Rangers played Rua in left field and at first base. He's surprisingly athletic for his body type, though he's a below-average runner and adequate-at-best defender wherever he goes, making the routine plays at third base with an average arm. Rua is major league ready. His easiest path to regular playing time is in left field, where he should get an opportunity to play at least semi-regularly in 2015, though the Rangers could also use him as a bat-first fill-in on the four corners.

BA GRADE

50 Risk: Low

LGE	PA	BB%	SO%	ISO
TL	288	10.4	19.1	.175
PCL	241	8.7	17.4	.192

Year	Club (League)	Class	AVG	G	AB	R	H	2B	3B	HR	RBI	BB	SO	SB	CS	OBP	SLG
2012	Spokane (NWL)	SS	.293	74	280	40	82	16	1	7	43	29	64	4	1	.368	.432
2013	Hickory (SAL)	LoA	.251	104	367	70	92	24	1	29	82	49	91	13	2	.356	.559
	Frisco (TL)	AA	.233	23	86	19	20	2	1	3	9	7	24	1	0	.305	.384
2014	Frisco (TL)	AA	.300	71	257	34	77	13	1	10	38	30	55	5	3	.375	.475
	Round Rock (PCL)	AAA	.313	58	214	31	67	13	2	8	36	21	42	1	2	.382	.505
	Texas (AL)	MAJ	.295	28	105	11	31	7	0	2	14	2	18	1	0	.321	.419
Major League Totals			.295	28	105	11	31	7	0	2	14	2	18	1	0	.321	.419
Minor League Totals			.284	382	1392	237	395	80	11	61	245	157	316	34	8	.365	.489

9 LUIS ORTIZ, RHP

Born: Sept. 22, 1995. **B-T:** R-R. **Ht.:** 6-3. **Wt.:** 230. **Drafted:** HS—Sanger, Calif., 2014 (1st round). **Signed by:** Butch Metzger.

Ortiz drew attention as a high school junior for his arm strength, but his stock soared that summer when he shed excess weight and earned MVP honors at the 18U World Championship as the closer on Team USA's gold-medal winner. Despite an inconsistent senior season, including some missed time with forearm tightness, Ortiz went 30th overall to the Rangers, then signed for $1.75 million and pitched well in his brief pro debut. Ortiz is a big-bodied pitcher and the ball comes out of his arm cleanly with sound mechanics that he repeats, which helps him command his plus fastball, a pitch that sits in the low 90s and touches 96 mph. His slider is a swing-and-miss pitch, a plus offering that he relies on to finish batters. He hasn't needed his changeup much, but it shows average potential, giving him the potential three-pitch mix to start, along with an occasional curveball. He's a consistent strike-thrower, which could help him move quickly if he remains healthy. After getting a brief trial at low Class A Hickory in 2014, Ortiz should return there to start 2015. He's still a few years away, but he has the makings of a potential mid-rotation starter.

BA GRADE

55 Risk: High

LGE	BF	SO%	BB%	HR/9
AZL	54	27.8	5.6	0.00
SAL	29	13.8	10.3	1.29

Year	Club (League)	Class	W	L	ERA	G	GS	CG	SV	IP	H	HR	BB	SO	K/9	WHIP	AVG
2014	Rangers (AZL)	R	1	1	2.03	6	5	0	0	13	12	0	3	15	10.1	1.13	.240
	Hickory (SAL)	LoA	0	0	1.29	3	1	0	1	7	4	1	3	4	5.1	1.00	.154
Minor League Totals			1	1	1.77	9	6	0	1	20	16	1	6	19	8.4	1.08	.211

10 JOSH MORGAN, SS/2B

BILL MITCHELL

Born: Nov. 16, 1995. **B-T:** R-R. **Ht.:** 5-11. **Wt.:** 185. **Drafted:** HS—Orange, Calif., 2014 (3rd round). **Signed by:** Steve Flores.

Morgan signed for $800,000 as a third-round pick, then led the Rookie-level Arizona League with a .468 on-base percentage. In a system filled with toolsy free-swingers, Morgan stands out for his plate discipline and barrel awareness. He lays off breaking balls outside the zone and uses his quick hands to unleash a fast, compact stroke to rope line drives to all fields. Morgan can put a ball in the gap, but he lacks power. A slightly above-average runner when he signed, Morgan lost around 10 pounds in pro ball and improved his speed to plus. He's a reliable defensive shortstop, with good hands, footwork and instincts that help his range play up with a solid-average arm. Some scouts in the draft questioned whether Morgan would be better suited for second base, but he played well at shortstop in his pro debut. Morgan should move on to low Class A Hickory in 2015. His potential as a high-OBP hitter in the middle of the diamond is exciting if he can develop power.

BA GRADE

55 Risk: High

LGE	PA	BB%	SO%	ISO
AZL	141	13.5	9.2	.035
NWL	102	9.8	9.8	.011

Year	Club (League)	Class	AVG	G	AB	R	H	2B	3B	HR	RBI	BB	SO	SB	CS	OBP	SLG
2014	Rangers (AZL)	R	.336	33	113	26	38	2	1	0	10	19	13	2	2	.468	.372
	Spokane (NWL)	SS	.303	23	89	11	27	1	0	0	9	10	10	1	1	.392	.315
Minor League Totals			.322	56	202	37	65	3	1	0	19	29	23	3	3	.436	.347

11 RYAN CORDELL, OF/1B

BA GRADE

55 Risk: High

Born: March 31, 1992. **B-T:** R-R. **Ht.:** 6-4. **Wt.:** 205. **Drafted:** Liberty, 2013 (11th round). **Signed by:** Jonathan George.

Cordell, who signed for $100,000 as an 11th-round pick in 2013, could be a steal. He worked to create better separation with his hands to load his swing, which helped him see the ball better and allowed him to better use his hands. Cordell's swing can get long, but he makes consistent contact, uses the whole field, shows solid strike-zone management and the power for 20 home runs. He's a good athlete for his size, a legitimate plus runner and efficient basestealer. His speed allows him to play center field, where he gets good reads off the bat, and he has a strong arm to play anywhere in the outfield. The Rangers even experimented with him in the infield before games and during instructional league at third base and shortstop, though Cordell probably will stick in the outfield. He evokes memories of Jason Bay, another physical, athletic outfielder with good tools in his early days who also was a late-round pick.

Year	Club (League)	Class	AVG	G	AB	R	H	2B	3B	HR	RBI	BB	SO	SB	CS	OBP	SLG
2013	Spokane (NWL)	SS	.241	64	232	34	56	12	0	5	23	23	53	19	4	.322	.358
2014	Hickory (SAL)	LoA	.321	73	274	53	88	18	4	8	40	27	53	18	3	.388	.504
	Myrtle Beach (CAR)	HiA	.306	16	62	12	19	2	2	5	19	7	13	3	1	.371	.645
Minor League Totals			.287	153	568	99	163	32	6	18	82	57	119	40	8	.359	.460

12 LUKE JACKSON, RHP

BA GRADE

55 Risk: High

Born: Aug. 24, 1991. **B-T:** R-R. **Ht.:** 6-2. **Wt.:** 185. **Drafted:** HS—Fort Lauderdale, 2010 (1st round supplemental). **Signed by:** Juan Alvarez.

Jackson had little trouble with Double-A hitters, but once he got to Triple-A Round Rock in late June, he got hammered in nearly every appearance. The stuff is still present for Jackson, who has a strong two-pitch mix in his fastball and slider. His four-seam fastball sits at 92-95 mph and hits 97, and he can miss bats with his plus breaking ball. The lack of a reliable third offering has hampered Jackson, who throws a below-average changeup. His long arm action also contributes to control issues, which got him into more trouble once he hit Triple-A. The Rangers plan to keep Jackson in the rotation, and he does have a chance to develop into a back-of-the-rotation type. Many others think his best fit is in the bullpen.

Year	Club (League)	Class	W	L	ERA	G	GS	CG	SV	IP	H	HR	BB	SO	K/9	WHIP	AVG
2012	Hickory (SAL)	LoA	5	5	4.92	13	13	1	0	64	63	4	33	72	10.1	1.50	.259
	Myrtle Beach (CAR)	HiA	5	2	4.39	13	13	0	0	66	67	2	32	74	10.1	1.51	.273
2013	Myrtle Beach (CAR)	HiA	9	4	2.41	19	19	0	0	101	79	6	47	104	9.3	1.25	.216
	Frisco (TL)	AA	2	0	0.67	6	4	0	0	27	13	0	12	30	10.0	0.93	.144
2014	Frisco (TL)	AA	8	2	3.02	15	14	0	1	83	58	5	24	83	9.0	0.98	.191
	Round Rock (PCL)	AAA	1	3	10.35	11	10	0	0	40	56	9	28	43	9.7	2.10	.333
Minor League Totals			35	22	4.28	96	92	1	1	456	419	35	224	484	9.6	1.41	.244

13 ALEC ASHER, RHP

Born: Oct. 4, 1991. **B-T:** R-R. **Ht.:** 6-4. **Wt.:** 225. **Drafted:** Polk County (Fla.) JC, 2012 (4th round). **Signed by:** Cliff Terracuso.

Asher signed with the Giants as a 23rd-round pick out of high school in 2010, but San Francisco voided the contract when the club found a bone chip in his elbow. Two years later, he signed with the Rangers for $150,000 as a fourth-round pick. Despite the elbow issue out of high school, Asher has been a durable innings-eater with a big-bodied frame. He repeats his delivery and commands his fastball, which parks in the low 90s and reaches 95 mph. Asher attacks hitters with downhill plane from his high arm angle, moving his fastball to all quadrants of the zone. It can flatten out at times, but his heater is his best pitch. Asher's strikeout rate has declined as he's moved up because he doesn't have a dominant secondary offering. His low-80s slider and changeup can both be average at times, with the slider occasionally a tick better, but it's a matter of refining them so they're more consistent. A potential No. 4 starter, Asher should open 2015 at Triple-A Round Rock, with a chance to make his major league debut during the season.

Year	Club (League)	Class	W	L	ERA	G	GS	CG	SV	IP	H	HR	BB	SO	K/9	WHIP	AVG
2012	Spokane (NWL)	SS	2	3	3.09	20	0	0	5	35	29	4	11	50	12.9	1.14	.221
2013	Myrtle Beach (CAR)	HiA	9	7	2.90	26	25	0	0	133	120	10	40	139	9.4	1.20	.235
2014	Frisco (TL)	AA	11	11	3.80	28	28	0	0	154	139	18	32	122	7.1	1.11	.238
Minor League Totals			22	21	3.35	74	53	0	5	322	288	32	83	311	8.7	1.15	.235

14 LEWIS BRINSON, OF

Born: May 8, 1994. **B-T:** R-R. **Ht.:** 6-3. **Wt.:** 170. **Drafted:** HS—Coral Springs, Fla., 2012 (1st round). **Signed by:** Frankie Thon.

Brinson posted a 20/20 season in his pro debut in 2013 at low Class A Hickory, but he also struck out 191 times (one behind the minor league leader) in 122 games, so he repeated the South Atlantic League in 2014. Brinson showed improvement in Hickory before a July promotion to high Class A Myrtle Beach, where he scuffled, and battled through some nagging leg injuries during the season. He already shines in center field, where he has plus speed, range and arm strength, with much-improved jumps off the bat. Brinson is a tool shed, but he's still learning the basics of hitting. His bat speed and raw power are plus, but tapping into that in games remains a struggle. He did slice his strikeout rate from 38 percent in 2013 to 25 percent in 2014, as he improved his plate coverage on the outer half and used the opposite field with more frequency, but that remains a focal point for him. So is making sure he doesn't expand the strike zone, especially against sliders. With an unorthodox swing, Brinson will always have a high swing-and-miss rate and is thus a high-risk prospect, but if he can merely be a serviceable hitter, he has the secondary skills to be a valuable player. Expect him to return to high Class A at the Rangers' new High Desert affiliate.

Year	Club (League)	Class	AVG	G	AB	R	H	2B	3B	HR	RBI	BB	SO	SB	CS	OBP	SLG
2012	Rangers (AZL)	R	.283	54	237	54	67	22	7	7	42	21	74	14	2	.345	.523
2013	Hickory (SAL)	LoA	.237	122	447	64	106	18	2	21	52	48	191	24	7	.322	.427
2014	Hickory (SAL)	LoA	.335	43	164	36	55	8	1	10	28	18	46	7	4	.405	.579
	Myrtle Beach (CAR)	HiA	.246	46	183	17	45	8	1	3	22	15	50	5	5	.307	.350
Minor League Totals			.265	265	1031	171	273	56	11	41	144	102	361	50	18	.338	.460

15 TI'QUAN FORBES, SS/3B

Born: Aug. 26, 1996. **B-T:** R-R. **Ht.:** 6-3. **Wt.:** 180. **Drafted:** HS—Columbia, Miss., 2014 (2nd round). **Signed by:** Jeff Wood.

A Mississippi prep product, Forbes signed for $1.2 million as a second-round pick in 2014, with Texas drawn to the three-sport athlete for his tools, physical projection and upside. Forbes has a sizable gap between his present ability and his future potential. He offers significant physical projection in his long, lean frame, and he already has plus bat speed despite not having a ton of strength yet. He's mostly a gap hitter, but some scouts see the potential for above-average power once he fills out. Forbes doesn't have a classic setup at the plate, starting with a hand hitch that leads to some swing-and-miss, but he has extremely quick hands and can buggy-whip the bat head through the zone. He's not a free-swinger either, so he will take his walks. Forbes is a plus runner, though he could slow down once he adds size. He has an average arm and likely fits best at third base, though he has room to improve there, with center field another option. Forbes could move on to low Class A Hickory in 2015, though given the Rangers' lower level infielders, he could open at short-season Spokane instead.

Year	Club (League)	Class	AVG	G	AB	R	H	2B	3B	HR	RBI	BB	SO	SB	CS	OBP	SLG
2014	Rangers (AZL)	R	.241	48	174	27	42	3	2	0	16	23	47	10	1	.338	.282
Minor League Totals			.241	48	174	27	42	3	2	0	16	23	47	10	1	.338	.282

16 MICHAEL DE LEON, SS

Born: Jan. 14, 1997. **B-T:** B-R. **Ht.:** 6-1. **Wt.:** 160. **Signed:** Dominican Republic, 2013. **Signed by:** Danilo Troncoso.

BA GRADE

50 Risk: High

A $550,000 signing out of the Dominican Republic on July 2, 2013, De Leon made his pro debut in Double-A on May 11 when Frisco needed a fill-in. A few days later, he went to low Class A Hickory when the Rangers were short there due to injury, and he stuck around until the end of August, when the Rangers bumped him up to high Class A Myrtle Beach to finish the season. After the season, De Leon became the youngest player in the history of the Arizona Fall League. De Leon's rapid rise was more about opportunity than him being a truly elite prospect, however. He has a simple, line-drive swing from both sides of the plate and makes frequent contact, though with minimal power, and maintains a sound approach. De Leon doesn't have flashy tools, but he's a fundamentally sound player with game awareness beyond his years. He's a smart, reliable defender at shortstop, where he has a good internal clock, smooth hands and an extremely accurate arm, though his arm strength is just average. He's a below-average runner, so he's not the rangiest shortstop, with some scouts believing he may end up at second. De Leon has a chance to be a steady, everyday middle infielder, but given his unusual career arc, where he starts 2015 is up in the air.

Year	Club (League)	Class	AVG	G	AB	R	H	2B	3B	HR	RBI	BB	SO	SB	CS	OBP	SLG
2014	Frisco (TL)	AA	.333	1	3	1	1	1	0	0	0	0	1	0	0	.333	.667
	Hickory (SAL)	LoA	.244	85	336	42	82	10	2	1	26	28	40	3	3	.302	.295
	Myrtle Beach (CAR)	HiA	.292	7	24	5	7	3	0	1	6	3	4	0	0	.370	.542
Minor League Totals			.248	93	363	48	90	14	2	2	32	31	45	3	3	.307	.314

17 COREY KNEBEL, RHP

Born: Nov. 26, 1991. **B-T:** R-R. **Ht.:** 6-3. **Wt.:** 195. **Drafted:** Texas, 2013 (1st round supplemental). **Signed by:** Tim Grieve (Tigers).

BA GRADE

45 Risk: Medium

The Tigers took Knebel with the No. 39 pick in the 2013 draft and he moved quickly, opening 2014 at Double-A Erie, reaching Triple-A Toledo in May and making his major league debut against the Rangers on May 24. In July, the Tigers traded him with righthander Jake Thompson to the Rangers to acquire reliever Joakim Soria. Knebel spent the remainder of 2014 at Triple-A Round Rock, though he came down with an elbow injury that didn't require surgery, so he spent his offseason in the Rangers' rehab program. Knebel has a lively fastball from the low 90s up to 98 mph. His low-80s curveball is a plus to double-plus pitch with tight spin and sharp, late action, giving him two swing-and-miss pitches to strike out hitters at a high clip. Knebel's delivery is full of effort and his arm action is short and funky, but he's a solid strike-thrower and the quirky mechanics give him added deception. Knebel is just about big league ready and should help the Rangers bullpen in 2015, and he offers closer potential down the line.

Year	Club (League)	Class	W	L	ERA	G	GS	CG	SV	IP	H	HR	BB	SO	K/9	WHIP	AVG
2013	West Michigan (MWL)	LoA	2	1	0.87	31	0	0	15	31	14	0	10	41	11.9	0.77	.133
2014	Erie (EL)	AA	3	0	1.20	11	0	0	1	15	8	1	8	23	13.8	1.07	.154
	Toledo (IL)	AAA	1	1	1.96	14	0	0	2	18	6	0	9	20	9.8	0.82	.109
	Detroit (AL)	MAJ	0	0	6.23	8	0	0	0	9	11	0	3	11	11.4	1.62	.306
	Round Rock (PCL)	AAA	1	0	3.75	9	0	0	0	12	9	2	5	20	15.0	1.17	.205
Major League Totals			0	0	6.23	8	0	0	0	9	11	0	3	11	11.4	1.62	.306
Minor League Totals			7	2	1.65	65	0	0	18	76	37	3	32	104	12.3	0.90	.145

18 KEONE KELA, RHP

Born: April 16, 1993. **B-T:** R-R. **Ht.:** 6-1. **Wt.:** 225. **Drafted:** Everett (Wash.) CC, 2012 (12th round). **Signed by:** Gary McGraw.

BA GRADE

45 Risk: Medium

Ar Everett (Wash.) CC, Kela's fastball went from touching the low 90s to reaching the mid-90s. The Rangers grabbed Kela for $100,000 as a 12th-round pick in 2012, and he's proved to be a late-round gem, with his velocity climbing into the triple-digits in 2013. He has one of the best fastballs in the minors, sitting in the upper 90s and reaching 100 mph with explosive late life, though there were times early in the season when his velocity dipped. Kela throws a power curveball that flashes plus with three-quarters break, a pitch he's improved but still requires more consistently. He dabbles with a changeup but is mostly a two-pitch reliever. Kela has the stuff to miss bats in the zone and generate groundballs at an above-average clip, but he needs to throw more strikes after walking 5.7 batters per nine innings in 2014, mostly at Double-A Frisco. Kela is ready for Triple-A Round Rock in 2015, but he could reach Texas quickly with a chance to pitch high-leverage innings and possibly emerge as a future closer.

Year	Club (League)	Class	W	L	ERA	G	GS	CG	SV	IP	H	HR	BB	SO	K/9	WHIP	AVG
2012	Rangers (AZL)	R	0	1	1.59	9	0	0	0	11	4	0	4	15	11.9	0.71	.105
2013	Hickory (SAL)	LoA	2	2	2.41	12	0	0	1	19	18	0	6	20	9.6	1.29	.250
	Rangers (AZL)	R	2	0	7.36	3	0	0	0	4	8	0	3	6	14.7	3.00	.421
	Spokane (NWL)	SS	1	2	3.78	12	0	0	2	17	17	1	6	26	14.0	1.38	.250
2014	Myrtle Beach (CAR)	HiA	0	1	2.61	8	0	0	5	10	9	0	4	13	11.3	1.26	.225
	Frisco (TL)	AA	2	1	1.86	36	0	0	5	39	22	1	27	55	12.8	1.27	.162
Minor League Totals			7	7	2.54	80	0	0	13	99	78	2	50	135	12.2	1.29	.209

19 TRAVIS DEMERITTE, 2B/3B

BA GRADE

55 Risk: Extreme

Born: Sept. 30, 1994. **B-T:** R-R. **Ht.:** 6-0. **Wt.:** 178. **Drafted:** HS—Winder, Ga., 2013 (1st round). **Signed by:** Derrick Tucker.

Demeritte, who signed for $1.9 million as the 30th overall pick in 2013, led all low Class A hitters with 25 home runs in 2014 at Hickory, producing power from his quick-twitch hands that generate plus bat speed. With plus power, he's a threat to go over the fence to any part of the park. Like many young Rangers prospects, Demeritte's power comes with a huge strikeout rate (37 percent) and his 171 strikeouts ranked sixth in the minors. He does draw a decent amount of walks, but he still chases too often and is working to improve his plate coverage on the outer half and use right field more frequently. An average runner, Demeritte played mostly second base in 2014. He's athletic, has a strong arm and took to the keystone quickly, with a chance to become an average defender. Demeritte's a risky player, but the upside exists to become a power-hitting second baseman. He probably follows in the footsteps of Lewis Brinson and Nomar Mazara, returning to Hickory to start 2015 with a chance to move up during the season.

Year	Club (League)	Class	AVG	G	AB	R	H	2B	3B	HR	RBI	BB	SO	SB	CS	OBP	SLG
2013	Rangers (AZL)	R	.285	39	144	31	41	5	3	4	20	29	49	5	1	.411	.444
2014	Hickory (SAL)	LoA	.211	118	398	77	84	16	2	25	66	50	171	6	2	.310	.450
Minor League Totals			.231	157	542	108	125	21	5	29	86	79	220	11	3	.338	.448

20 ANDREW FAULKNER, LHP

BA GRADE

45 Risk: Medium

Born: Sept. 12, 1992. **B-T:** R-L. **Ht.:** 6-3. **Wt.:** 200. **Drafted:** HS—South Aiken, S.C., 2011 (14th round). **Signed by:** Chris Kemp.

After signing for $125,000 in the 14th round in 2011, Faulkner then spent two nondescript seasons at low Class A Hickory. In 2014, his stock soared at high Class A Myrtle Beach when he added 20 pounds and 4 mph to his fastball with the breakout performance to match. Faulkner's best pitch is his fastball, which sits at 91-94 mph and touches 96. He throws strikes, keeps the ball down and isn't afraid to pitch inside to righthanders. After previously throwing a true splitter earlier in his career, Faulkner instead now throws a changeup with a split-like grip. It's an average pitch with good sink. He also throws a fringy slider that he needs to refine. He throws across his body and finishes with a head whack. That leads some scouts to project him as a reliever, though Faulkner has a chance to keep moving as a potential back-end starter.

Year	Club (League)	Class	W	L	ERA	G	GS	CG	SV	IP	H	HR	BB	SO	K/9	WHIP	AVG
2012	Hickory (SAL)	LoA	5	5	4.31	29	10	0	0	94	97	2	44	74	7.1	1.50	.262
2013	Hickory (SAL)	LoA	6	5	3.48	21	19	0	0	111	123	8	37	84	6.8	1.44	.280
2014	Myrtle Beach (CAR)	HiA	10	1	2.07	21	18	0	1	104	86	1	31	100	8.6	1.12	.228
	Frisco (TL)	AA	2	4	4.99	7	6	0	0	31	28	3	14	33	9.7	1.37	.237
Minor League Totals			23	17	3.33	90	60	0	1	365	351	15	130	318	7.8	1.32	.251

21 JOSE LeCLERC, RHP

BA GRADE

45 Risk: Medium

Born: Dec. 19, 1993. **B-T:** R-R. **Ht.:** 6-0. **Wt.:** 180. **Signed:** Dominican Republic, 2010. **Signed by:** Willy Espinal.

LeClerc has been a relief prospect his entire career, and it's a role that suits his power approach well. LeClerc sits at 93-95 mph and touches 97 with late life. He has one of the most unusual changeups in baseball because it has sharp cutting action instead of fade. It's a plus pitch that he can manipulate to get harder diving action at times. He adds and subtracts from his curveball, which is an average pitch that flashes better at times. LeClerc's strikeout rate has improved every year of his career, and he also induces grounders at an above-average clip. He has the stuff to pitch late-inning relief, but he needs to be more aggressive attacking hitters and throwing strikes, especially early in the count. He should move on to Double-A Frisco to begin 2015, with an outside chance of reaching Texas by the end of the season.

Year	Club (League)	Class	W	L	ERA	G	GS	CG	SV	IP	H	HR	BB	SO	K/9	WHIP	AVG
2012	Rangers (DSL)	R	3	1	1.54	19	0	0	1	47	32	1	18	41	7.9	1.07	.193
2013	Hickory (SAL)	LoA	3	4	3.36	39	0	0	5	59	53	2	21	77	11.7	1.25	.240
2014	Myrtle Beach (CAR)	HiA	4	1	3.30	42	0	0	14	57	39	8	37	78	12.2	1.33	.193
Minor League Totals			13	7	2.74	120	1	0	21	197	149	12	94	223	10.2	1.23	.209

22 MARCOS DIPLAN, RHP

BA GRADE
55 Risk: Extreme

Born: Sept. 18, 1996. **B-T:** R-R. **Ht.:** 5-10. **Wt.:** 160. **Signed:** Dominican Republic, 2013. **Signed by:** Willy Espinal/Mike Daly.

The Rangers signed Diplan on July 2, 2013 for $1.3 million, and he helped pitch the Rangers to a Dominican Summer League championship in 2014. Diplan sits at 89-93 mph and hits 95, though it can come in on a flat plane. Though he's not big, he has a quick arm, so he might have a little more velocity in the tank. Diplan flashes an above-average curveball and at times an average changeup, though both pitches are understandably inconsistent given his youth and inexperience. Diplan has the repertoire of a starter, but he needs to repeat his delivery better to throw more strikes. His herky-jerky mechanics throw him out of whack at times, which leads to bouts of wildness, though other times he just tries to toy around with hitters and doesn't attack aggressively enough, even though he's tough to hit. He's smart and athletic enough to be able to make the adjustments as he moves up. A potential mid-rotation starter, Diplan could skip the Rookie-level Arizona League and join short-season Spokane in 2015.

Year	Club (League)	Class	W	L	ERA	G	GS	CG	SV	IP	H	HR	BB	SO	K/9	WHIP	AVG
2014	Rangers (DSL)	R	7	2	1.54	13	13	0	0	64	32	2	36	57	8.0	1.06	.155
Minor League Totals			7	2	1.54	13	13	0	0	64	32	2	36	57	8.0	1.06	.155

23 JAIRO BERAS, OF

BA GRADE
55 Risk: Extreme

Born: Dec. 25, 1994. **B-T:** R-R. **Ht.:** 6-6. **Wt.:** 190. **Signed:** Dominican Republic, 2012. **Signed by:** Danilo Troncoso/Roberto Aquino/Paul Kruger/Mike Daly.

As an amateur, Beras had presented himself to major league teams as a 16-year-old eligible to sign on July 2, 2012. Shortly after the Collective Bargaining Agreement put restrictions on international signings through bonus pools set to begin on that date, Beras changed his date of birth, claiming he was in fact born one year earlier, making him 17 and eligible to sign immediately. The Rangers signed him for $4.5 million in February 2012, triggering controversy around baseball. Shortly after July 2, 2012, Major League Baseball announced that the signing would stand, but that Beras must serve a one-year suspension, which amounted to a slap on the wrist and essentially just a couple weeks of missed games. Even if Beras is a few years older, he has a promising combination of size and tools, though he remains unrefined. He has plus raw power, though he's still learning to generate more loft. He has a large strike zone to cover, can get tied up inside because of his long arms and needs to stop chasing breaking balls. He made strides at low Class A Hickory in 2014 as the season went along by keeping his weight back when he separated his hands, keeping his head locked to help him track pitches better. Beras surprises people with average speed, and that, with his plus arm, give him the ingredients to be a become a good defender in right. Beras likely follows the Nomar Mazara path, returning to Hickory in 2015 in the hopes he can have a breakout season.

Year	Club (League)	Class	AVG	G	AB	R	H	2B	3B	HR	RBI	BB	SO	SB	CS	OBP	SLG
2012	Did not play--Suspended																
2013	Rangers (AZL)	R	.250	17	64	11	16	2	2	2	15	5	19	1	0	.314	.438
2014	Hickory (SAL)	LoA	.242	110	389	38	94	18	0	7	33	33	133	5	4	.305	.342
Minor League Totals			.243	127	453	49	110	20	2	9	48	38	152	6	4	.306	.355

24 DELINO DeSHIELDS JR., OF

BA GRADE:
50 Risk: High

Born: Aug. 16, 1992. **B-T:** R-R. **Ht.:** 5-9. **Wt.:** 190. **Drafted:** HS—College Park, Ga., 2010 (1st round). **Signed by:** Lincoln Martin.

The Astros did not protect DeShields on the 40-man roster after the 2014 season, so the Rangers picked him in the Rule 5 draft. DeShields showed toughness in a quick return from being struck in the face with a fastball in April 2014, though his offensive production took a tumble. Despite a thick, stocky frame, DeShields is a 70 runner. He has average raw power, but he got homer-happy after hitting 12 in 2012 across two levels. He tries to pull the ball too often and needs to rely more on his speed to get on base. A fringy defender at second base, DeShields moved to the outfield in 2014, and with his speed, he could be above-average in left field or perhaps center, with a below-average arm. DeShields doesn't project as an everyday player, but his speed and versatility give him a chance to stick as a Rule 5 pick.

Year	Club (League)	Class	AVG	G	AB	R	H	2B	3B	HR	RBI	BB	SO	SB	CS	OBP	SLG
2012	Lexington (SAL)	LoA	.298	111	440	96	131	22	5	10	52	70	108	83	14	.401	.439
	Lancaster (CAL)	HiA	.237	24	97	17	23	2	3	2	9	13	23	18	5	.336	.381
2013	Lancaster (CAL)	HiA	.317	111	451	100	143	25	14	5	54	57	91	51	18	.405	.468
2014	Corpus Christi (TL)	AA	.236	114	411	75	97	14	2	11	57	61	112	54	14	.346	.360
Minor League Totals			.267	497	1944	375	519	86	27	37	228	259	472	241	63	.362	.396

25 YEYSON YRIZARRI, SS/2B

Born: Feb. 2, 1997. **B-T:** R-R. **Ht.:** 6-0. **Wt.:** 170. **Signed:** Dominican Republic, 2013. **Signed by:** Roberto Aquino/Gil Kim.

Yrizarri, a nephew of former big league shortstop Deivi Cruz, was born in Venezuela, but he grew up in the Dominican Republic, where he signed out of on July 2, 2013, for $1.35 million. He hit well in his first two weeks in the Dominican Summer League in 2014, then scuffled at the plate upon his promotion to the Rookie-level Arizona League. He is physically mature for his age, with strong hands and forearms that help him hit hard line drives without excessive swing-and-miss and a quick, short swing. His power is mostly to the gaps, but he projects to grow into average power. Yrizarri is an aggressive, pull-conscious hitter who will have to learn to keep his weight back and improve his pitch recognition. He split time between shortstop and second base in the AZL, looking more comfortable at second because he lacks a quick first step. His double-plus arm is his best tool. Yrizarri should have a chance to jump to low Class A Hickory in 2015, though the Rangers could hold him back to play in short-season Spokane instead.

Year	Club (League)	Class	AVG	G	AB	R	H	2B	3B	HR	RBI	BB	SO	SB	CS	OBP	SLG
2014	Rangers (DSL)	R	.302	10	43	7	13	3	1	0	6	3	4	1	1	.354	.419
	Rangers (AZL)	R	.237	50	190	23	45	13	1	1	19	9	36	5	3	.275	.332
Minor League Totals			.249	60	233	30	58	16	2	1	25	12	40	6	4	.290	.348

26 TOMAS TELIS, C

Born: June 18, 1991. **B-T:** B-R. **Ht.:** 5-8. **Wt.:** 200. **Signed:** Venezuela, 2007. **Signed by:** Edgar Suarez.

Telis hit well his first three years in the system, but his offensive performance tailed off in 2012 and 2013. He rebounded in 2014, making his big league debut in late August and sticking with the team the rest of the season. He has a knack for barreling the ball, with a flat swing path that results in more line drives and groundballs that loft, using the middle of the field with well below-average power. Telis has grown considerably as a receiver, committing just three passed balls in 82 games behind the plate in 2014, and he earns praise from other clubs for his game-calling and intangibles. Telis had Tommy John surgery in 2010, and while his arm strength is now average, controlling the running game is something he still must improve. He threw out 27 percent of basestealers in the minors in 2014, then erased just 1 of 17 in the majors. Telis could serve as the big league backup in 2015, though he might head back to Triple-A.

Year	Club (League)	Class	AVG	G	AB	R	H	2B	3B	HR	RBI	BB	SO	SB	CS	OBP	SLG
2012	Myrtle Beach (CAR)	HiA	.247	117	450	45	111	24	1	4	43	17	53	9	2	.283	.331
2013	Frisco (TL)	AA	.264	91	348	32	92	19	0	4	43	10	46	8	2	.290	.353
2014	Frisco (TL)	AA	.303	70	267	31	81	16	2	2	33	17	29	7	1	.339	.401
	Round Rock (PCL)	AAA	.345	36	139	18	48	7	2	3	17	6	12	1	1	.377	.489
	Texas (AL)	MAJ	.250	18	68	7	17	2	0	0	8	1	10	0	0	.271	.279
Major League Totals			.250	18	68	7	17	2	0	0	8	1	10	0	0	.271	.279
Minor League Totals			.291	581	2246	293	653	127	12	31	306	103	226	59	15	.325	.399

27 ALEX CLAUDIO, LHP

Born: Jan. 31, 1992. **B-T:** L-L. **Ht.:** 6-3. **Wt.:** 160. **Drafted:** HS—Juncos, P.R., 2010 (27th round). **Signed by:** Frankie Thon.

Claudio is a sidearm reliever whose fastball sits just 83-87 mph with good armside run and sink, but he still manages to strike out more than a batter per inning because of his devastating, double-plus changeup. He maintains his arm speed on his changeup, which is indistinguishable from the fastball out of his hand but travels at 66-69 mph, with late dive and tailing action that gives hitters fits. He will backdoor a slow, slurvy slider on occasion as well, but his changeup is his money maker. With long arms and legs that fly around, Claudio has deception that makes it tough for hitters to pick up the ball, and he's a consistent strike-thrower. In short stints, that works, and he should be a solid middle reliever for the Rangers in 2015.

Year	Club (League)	Class	W	L	ERA	G	GS	CG	SV	IP	H	HR	BB	SO	K/9	WHIP	AVG
2012	Rangers (AZL)	R	4	0	1.79	14	3	0	1	45	36	1	5	54	10.7	0.90	.222
2013	Hickory (SAL)	LoA	3	1	1.15	24	0	0	11	47	22	2	7	62	11.9	0.62	.139
	Frisco (TL)	AA	1	5	2.84	21	0	0	0	32	28	2	11	29	8.2	1.23	.243
2014	Myrtle Beach (CAR)	HiA	4	0	1.09	17	2	0	4	49	38	2	9	56	10.2	0.95	.216
	Frisco (TL)	AA	2	2	2.17	8	6	0	0	37	31	1	2	22	5.3	0.88	.223
	Round Rock (PCL)	AAA	0	1	3.38	2	1	0	0	5	6	0	2	6	10.1	1.50	.300
	Texas (AL)	MAJ	0	0	2.92	15	0	0	0	12	14	0	4	14	10.2	1.46	.280
Major League Totals			0	0	2.92	15	0	0	0	12	14	0	4	14	10.2	1.46	.280
Minor League Totals			19	10	2.05	114	13	0	17	259	202	10	52	273	9.5	0.98	.217

28 RONALD GUZMAN, 1B

Born: Oct. 20, 1994. **B-T:** L-L. **Ht.:** 6-6. **Wt.:** 205. **Signed:** Dominican Republic, 2011. **Signed by:** Willy Espinal/Mike Daly.

BA GRADE
50 Risk: Extreme

Several teams considered Guzman the top prospect on the international market in 2011, when he signed for $3.45 million. After a strong debut as a 17-year-old in the Rookie-level Arizona League in 2012 and a solid 2013, Guzman regressed in his return to low Class A Hickory in 2014. Then in November, Guzman was driving in the Dominican Republic when his car collided with a motorcyclist, who was killed. Guzman was released after posting bond but barred from leaving the country. At his best, he showed a mature hitting approach, making consistent contact with good pitch recognition and a hit-over-power skill set. In 2014, that approach unraveled. Guzman has average raw power, but he got caught up over-swinging. Once he started to struggle, he constantly tinkered with his stance and hand position, which made things worse. A 20 runner, Guzman has become a solid defender at first base. He gives infielders a wide margin for error on throws because he's a gigantic target with the flexibility to do splits. The 2015 season will be key for Guzman, though his legal situation clouds his status for Opening Day.

Year	Club (League)	Class	AVG	G	AB	R	H	2B	3B	HR	RBI	BB	SO	SB	CS	OBP	SLG
2012	Rangers (AZL)	R	.321	52	212	29	68	15	3	1	33	19	42	7	1	.374	.434
2013	Hickory (SAL)	LoA	.272	49	173	17	47	8	0	4	26	11	27	0	0	.325	.387
2014	Hickory (SAL)	LoA	.218	118	445	46	97	32	0	6	63	37	107	6	3	.283	.330
Minor League Totals			.255	219	830	92	212	55	3	11	122	67	176	13	4	.315	.369

29 LISALVERTO BONILLA, RHP

Born: June 18, 1990. **B-T:** R-R. **Ht.:** 6-0. **Wt.:** 175. **Signed:** Dominican Republic, 2008. **Signed by:** Sal Agostinelli (Phillies).

BA GRADE
40 Risk: Low

The Phillies signed Bonilla when he was 18 in December 2008, then almost exactly four years later traded him to the Rangers to acquire Michael Young. With experience as a starter and a reliever, Bonilla sits at 90-93 mph and touches 95, though his fastball lost a little life last year. He flashes a plus changeup at 83-86 mph that generates most of his swings and misses and a slider that vacillates between below-average to average. Bonilla's strikeout rate backed up to its lowest clip in the last three seasons in 2014, but he still recorded more than a strikeout per inning at Triple-A. He is a steady strike-thrower, though he had some trouble finding the strike zone once he got to Texas. The Rangers plan to have Bonilla compete for the No. 5 starter spot in 2015, but many scouts think he fits best in the bullpen.

Year	Club (League)	Class	W	L	ERA	G	GS	CG	SV	IP	H	HR	BB	SO	K/9	WHIP	AVG
2012	Clearwater (FSL)	HiA	1	1	1.35	10	0	0	1	13	9	0	4	18	12.2	0.98	.188
	Reading (EL)	AA	2	1	1.64	21	0	0	3	33	22	1	17	46	12.5	1.18	.193
2013	Round Rock (PCL)	AAA	5	5	7.95	26	2	0	0	43	52	8	24	56	11.7	1.77	.299
	Frisco (TL)	AA	2	0	0.30	21	0	0	6	30	16	0	9	50	14.8	0.82	.152
2014	Round Rock (PCL)	AAA	4	2	4.10	39	6	0	1	75	73	9	25	92	11.1	1.31	.253
	Texas (AL)	MAJ	3	0	3.05	5	3	0	0	21	13	2	12	17	7.4	1.21	.186
Major League Totals			3	0	3.05	5	3	0	0	21	13	2	12	17	7.4	1.21	.186
Minor League Totals			27	20	3.17	170	43	3	15	429	376	36	141	489	10.3	1.21	.232

30 HANSER ALBERTO, SS

Born: Oct. 17, 1992. **B-T:** R-R. **Ht.:** 5-11. **Wt.:** 175. **Signed:** Dominican Republic, 2009. **Signed by:** Rodolfo Rosario/Willy Espinal/Mike Daly.

BA GRADE
40 Risk: Medium

Alberto returned to Myrtle Beach for a third season to start 2014 and earned a promotion to Double-A Frisco in July. Alberto has become an above-average fielder at shortstop. He makes all the routine plays with a tick above-average, accurate arm, and he improved his range to both sides. An average runner, he has good hand-eye coordination that's evident in the field and at the plate, where he makes frequent contact. It's a line-drive stroke with well below-average power, but Alberto gets himself into trouble with his aggressive, pull-conscious approach. Alberto might never hit enough to be an everyday shortstop, but his defensive skills and contact bat could make him a nice utility player.

Year	Club (League)	Class	AVG	G	AB	R	H	2B	3B	HR	RBI	BB	SO	SB	CS	OBP	SLG
2012	Hickory (SAL)	LoA	.337	62	246	37	83	17	1	4	38	18	22	15	4	.385	.463
	Myrtle Beach (CAR)	HiA	.265	66	279	36	74	11	2	4	34	2	27	9	3	.273	.362
2013	Frisco (TL)	AA	.213	100	356	37	76	6	4	4	40	16	41	13	5	.253	.287
	Myrtle Beach (CAR)	HiA	.258	29	97	6	25	5	0	0	7	4	8	3	1	.301	.309
2014	Myrtle Beach (CAR)	HiA	.271	70	262	37	71	15	3	5	43	10	25	10	4	.301	.408
	Frisco (TL)	AA	.275	50	178	23	49	6	1	2	15	6	17	6	4	.314	.354
Minor League Totals			.276	480	1784	222	492	83	14	19	217	71	164	79	25	.309	.370

Toronto Blue Jays

BY CLINT LONGENECKER

The Blue Jays entered this season with tempered expectations after falling flat in 2013 with a roster bolstered by several big trade acquisitions and seemingly primed for a run at the American League East title.

That run came one year later, when Toronto paced the division early in the season. The Blue Jays went 21-9 in May, spent 61 days in first place and had a six-game lead in early June. But Toronto never led the division again after the Fourth of July.

So while the Jays were in playoff contention for the first time since general manager Alex Anthopoulos' inaugural year at the helm in 2010, Toronto extended its playoff drought to 21 seasons—since its back-to-back World Series championship seasons of 1992-93. With the Royals ending their streak, the Jays now own the longest empty stretch in the majors.

Toronto's offense bounced back from its league average performance in 2013, ranking fourth in runs and third in home runs. The run prevention took a step forward from last year but was roughly average at best by both traditional and advanced metrics in both the rotation and bullpen. The rotation, a liability in 2013, performed better but remained in the bottom third of major league starting staffs, while the bullpen regressed.

The trades to acquire veterans such as Mark Buehrle, R.A. Dickey and Jose Reyes two years ago shipped out numerous prospects—several of whom, such as Henderson Alvarez, Travis d'Arnaud, Adeiny Hechavarria, Justin Nicolino and Noah Syndergaard—have become useful big leaguers or top prospects with the Marlins and Mets. Still, the 2014 season started to showcase the fruits of the organization's approach in the amateur markets under Anthopoulos.

Righthander Marcus Stroman, No. 2 on this list a year ago, became one of the team's best starters as a rookie, going 11-6, 3.65, and became a rotation mainstay.

Three of the top four current prospects in the organization—lefthander Daniel Norris, righthander Aaron Sanchez and outfielder Dalton Pompey—also reached Toronto. The quartet forms the core of the next wave of Jays, with another wave coming from the lower levels and a strong 2014 draft class.

Toronto selected college players with its first two picks for the first time since 2009. Athletic righthander Jeff Hoffman (No. 9) has the potential to pitch in the front half of a rotation if he returns healthy from Tommy John surgery, which

Righthander Marcus Stroman was one of the better rookie starters in the American League in 2014

TOP PROSPECTS OF THE DECADE

Year	Player, Pos.	2014 Org
2005	Brandon League, rhp	Dodgers
2006	Dustin McGowan, rhp	Blue Jays
2007	Adam Lind, of	Blue Jays
2008	Travis Snider, of	Pirates
2009	Travis Snider, of	Pirates
2010	Zach Stewart, rhp	Braves
2011	Kyle Drabek, rhp	Blue Jays
2012	Travis d'Arnaud, c	Mets
2013	Aaron Sanchez, rhp	Blue Jays
2014	Daniel Norris, lhp	Blue Jays

he required prior to the draft. Catcher Max Pentecost (No. 11) is a premium athlete with a broad skill set and two-way ability behind the plate.

All but one who make up the Top 30 Prospects list was drafted or signed internationally by the Jays as the organization continues to invest in building homegrown internal assets.

The organization had a $137 million payroll in 2014, the largest in club history. It's unlikely the payroll will go up, so reinforcements for a 2015 will have to come internally.

Toronto boasts nearly major league-ready starters in Norris and Sanchez—though the bulk of the organization's potential impact talent is concentrated at the lower levels. Competing in the extremely difficult AL East, the Blue Jays' hope of ending the playoff drought at 21 seasons will rely very heavily on its recent influx of homegrown pitchers.

General manager: Alex Anthopoulos. **Farm director:** Tony LaCava. **Scouting director:** Brian Parker.

Class	Team	League	W	L	PCT	Finish	Manager
Majors	Toronto Blue Jays	American	83	79	.512	14th (30)	John Gibbons
Triple-A	Buffalo Bisons	International	77	66	.538	4th (14)	Gary Allenson
Double-A	New Hampshire Fisher Cats	Eastern	66	76	.465	t-9th (12)	Bobby Meacham
High A	Dunedin Blue Jays	Florida State	77	61	.558	3rd (8)	Omar Malave
Low A	Lansing Lugnuts	Midwest	62	77	.446	13th (16)	John Tamargo
Short season	Vancouver Canadians	Northwest	46	30	.605	2nd (8)	John Schneider
Rookie	Bluefield Blue Jays	Appalachian	33	35	.485	7th (10)	Dennis Holmberg
Rookie	Blue Jays	Gulf Coast	18	41	.305	16th (16)	Kenny Graham
Overall Minor League Record			379	386	.495	18th (30)	

THIS YEAR'S TOP 30

No.	Player, Pos.	Grade
1.	Daniel Norris, lhp	60/Medium
2.	Aaron Sanchez, rhp	60/High
3.	Jeff Hoffman, rhp	65/Extreme
4.	Dalton Pompey, of	55/Medium
5.	Max Pentecost, c	55/High
6.	Devon Travis, 2b/of	50/Medium
7.	Roberto Osuna, rhp	55/High
8.	Richard Urena, ss	55/High
9.	Miguel Castro, rhp	55/High
10.	Sean Reid-Foley, rhp	50/High
11.	Matt Smoral, lhp	55/Extreme
12.	Ryan Borucki, lhp	50/High
13.	Jairo Labourt, lhp	50/High
14.	Dwight Smith Jr., of	45/Medium
15.	Dawel Lugo, ss	50/High
16.	Mitch Nay, 3b	50/High
17.	Chase DeJong, rhp	50/High
18.	Anthony Alford, of	55/Extreme
19.	Lane Thomas, 3b/of	50/High
20.	Dan Jansen, c	50/High
21.	D.J. Davis, of	50/Extreme
22.	Alberto Tirado, rhp	50/Extreme
23.	A.J. Jimenez, c	45/High
24.	Andy Burns, 3b	45/High
25.	Tom Robson, rhp	50/Extreme
26.	Jesus Tinoco, rhp	50/Extreme
27.	Juan Meza, rhp	50/Extreme
28.	Nick Wells, lhp	50/Extreme
29.	Matt Boyd, lhp	45/High
30.	Rowdy Tellez, 1b	45/High

LAST YEAR'S TOP 30

No.	Player, Pos.	Status
1.	Aaron Sanchez, rhp	No. 2
2.	Marcus Stroman, of	Majors
3.	D.J. Davis, 3b	No. 21
4.	Mitch Nay, ss	No. 16
5.	Franklin Barreto, ss	(Athletics)
6.	Daniel Norris, lhp	No. 1
7.	Roberto Osuna, rhp	No. 7
8.	Alberto Tirado, rhp	No. 22
9.	Dawel Lugo, ss	No. 15
10.	Sean Nolin, lhp	(Athletics)
11.	Chase DeJong, rhp	No. 17
12.	Jairo Labourt, lhp	No. 13
13.	Matt Smoral, lhp	No. 11
14.	A.J. Jimenez, c	No. 23
15.	Clinton Hollon, rhp	Dropped out
16.	Tom Robson, rhp	No. 25
17.	Dalton Pompey, of	No. 4
18.	Rowdy Tellez, 1b	No. 30
19.	Andy Burns, 3b/2b	No. 24
20.	Kevin Pillar, of	Majors
21.	John Stilson, rhp	Dropped out
22.	Kenny Wilson, of	(Marlins)
23.	Santiago Nessy, c	(Royals)
24.	Richard Urena, ss	No. 8
25.	Matt Dean, 1b	Dropped out
26.	Miguel Castro, rhp	No. 9
27.	Dwight Smith Jr., of	No. 14
28.	Jake Brentz, lhp	Dropped out
29.	Ryan Goins, 2b/ss	Majors
30.	Yeltsin Gudino, ss	Dropped out

BEST TOOLS

Best Hitter for Average	Dwight Smith Jr.
Best Power Hitter	Rowdy Tellez
Best Strike-Zone Discipline	Dwight Smith Jr.
Fastest Baserunner	D.J. Davis
Best Athlete	Anthony Alford
Best Fastball	Aaron Sanchez
Best Curveball	Aaron Sanchez
Best Slider	Sean Reid-Foley
Best Changeup	Jeff Hoffman
Best Control	Jeremy Gabryszwski
Best Defensive Catcher	A.J. Jimenez
Best Defensive Infielder	Jonathan Berti
Best Infield Arm	Dawel Lugo
Best Defensive Outfielder	Dalton Pompey
Best Outfield Arm	Jesus Gonzalez

PROJECTED 2018 LINEUP

Catcher	Max Pentecost
First Base	Mitch Nay
Second Base	Devon Travis
Third Base	Josh Donaldson
Shortstop	Richard Urena
Left Field	Dwight Smith Jr.
Center Field	Dalton Pompey
Right Field	Jose Bautista
Designated Hitter	Edwin Encarnacion
No. 1 Starter	Marcus Stroman
No. 2 Starter	Daniel Norris
No. 3 Starter	Jeff Hoffman
No. 4 Starter	Aaron Sanchez
No. 5 Starter	Drew Hutchison
Closer	Miguel Castro

TORONTO BLUE JAYS

TOP 2015 ROOKIE: Devon Travis, 2b. He marries talent and opportunity, filling in at one of the worst positions in the AL over the last few seasons.

BREAKOUT PROSPECT: Ryan Borucki, lhp. The fastball/changeup lefthander has the potential for plus control and one of the best chances to remain a starter in the system.

SLEEPER: Connor Greene, rhp. An athletic, projectable high school righthander, Greene has shown signs of turning the corner with a fastball up to 94 mph and two average secondary offerings.

SOURCE OF TOP 30 TALENT			
Homegrown	29	Acquired	1
College	4	Trades	1
Junior college	0	Rule 5 draft	0
High school	17	Independent leagues	0
Draft-and-follow	0	Free agents/waivers	0
Nondrafted free agents	0		
International	8		

LF
Dwight Smith Jr. (14)
Freddy Rodriguez

CF
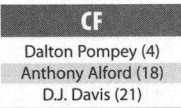
Dalton Pompey (4)
Anthony Alford (18)
D.J. Davis (21)

RF
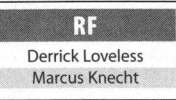
Derrick Loveless
Marcus Knecht

3B
Mitch Nay (16)
Andy Burns (24)

SS
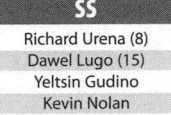
Richard Urena (8)
Dawel Lugo (15)
Yeltsin Gudino
Kevin Nolan

2B

Devon Travis (6)
Lane Thomas (19)
Jon Berti
Gunnar Heidt
Christian Lopes
Dickie Joe Thon

1B
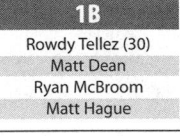
Rowdy Tellez (30)
Matt Dean
Ryan McBroom
Matt Hague

C

Max Pentecost (5)
Dan Jansen (20)
A.J. Jimenez (23)
Matt Morgan
Derrick Chung
Jack Murphy

LHP

LHSP	LHRP
Daniel Norris (1)	Colt Hynes
Matt Smoral (11)	Tyler Ybarra
Ryan Borucki (12)	Rob Rasmussen
Jairo Labourt (13)	John Anderson
Nick Wells (28)	
Matt Boyd (29)	
Jacob Brentz	
Angel Perdomo	
Daniel Lietz	
Evan Smith	
Grayson Huffman	
Shane Dawson	

RHP

RHSP	RHRP
Aaron Sanchez (2)	Ryan Tepera
Jeff Hoffman (3)	John Stilson
Roberto Osuna (7)	Jimmy Cordero
Miguel Castro (9)	Carlos Ramirez
Sean Reid-Foley (10)	Justin Shafer
Chase DeJong (17)	Brady Dragmire
Alberto Tirado (22)	Wil Browning
Tom Robson (25)	Chase Mallard
Jesus Tinoco (26)	
Juan Meza (27)	
Taylor Cole	
Connor Greene	
Clinton Hollon	
Patrick Murphy	
Adonys Cardona	

2014

BEST PURE HITTER: C Max Pentecost (1) has the tools to hit at an above-average clip and has a sustained track record of hitting, though his debut was limited because of nagging wrist injuries. The righthanded hitter has an easy, quick and short stroke conducive to line drives to all fields.

BEST POWER HITTER: Pentecost has plus raw power, though his swing path is unlikely to produce plus power production, with at least average more likely. 1B Ryan McBroom (15) has a strong, physical body and plus power potential from the left side.

FASTEST RUNNER: Both Pentecost and OF/3B Lane Thomas (5) have at least 55-grade speed that plays up because of instincts. Thomas is a plus runner underway who ran the 60 as low as 6.48 last summer.

BEST DEFENSIVE PLAYER: Pentecost's defense improved significantly over the last year, offering above-average athleticism, flexibility and better receiving to go with a plus arm that has a quick release.

BEST FASTBALL: RHP Jeff Hoffman (1) is a premier talent with an elite arm who likely would not have lasted until the ninth pick if not for his Tommy John surgery. Hoffman has a loose, easy arm action and sits 93-95 at his best, touching 98 mph.

BEST SECONDARY PITCH: Sean Reid-Foley (2) has a plus slider when he is on top of the pitch. Hoffman showed two secondary offerings with at least plus potential in his curveball and changeup. LHP Nick Wells (3) has a big, projectable body and a plus curveball that was one of the best among prep lefthanders.

BEST PRO DEBUT: Thomas, a high school draftee, was an above-average producer across two levels, finishing in the Rookie level Appalachian League while hitting .281/.369/.398. LHP Grayson Huffman (6) had an 0.95 ERA in 38 innings at two Rookie-ball stops despite 20 walks in 38 innings; he gave up just 18 hits.

BEST ATHLETE: Pentecost is a rare athlete for a catcher with a broad skill set. Hoffman was one of the most athletic pitchers in the draft and made exceptional defensive plays on the mound and highlight-reel dunks on the basketball court.

MOST INTRIGUING BACKGROUND: Shafer led his county in passing as a high school quarterback and was a two-way player at Florida.

CLOSEST TO THE MAJORS: Pentecost could move quickly as a college catcher with two-way ability. RHP Chase Mallard (14) could move quickly as a strike-thrower with pitchability and an 89-92 mph fastball and solid slider.

BEST LATE-ROUND PICK: 2B Gunnar Heidt

(13) had the tools to go in the top 10 rounds, but broke his hand in late April. He is a high-makeup grinder with some tools.

THE ONE WHO GOT AWAY: Two Illinois prep arms heading to the SEC could become good draft picks in three years, LHP Jake Latz (11; Louisiana State) and RHP Tanner Houck (12; Missouri).

ASSESSMENT: Toronto continues to covet high-ceiling power arms and athletic up-the-middle position players. Drafting Hoffman and Pentecost was a dynamic start to the overall class.

2013

Since-traded RHP Kendall Graveman (8) reached the majors quickly, but the rest of the class is leaning on LHP Matt Boyd (6) and 1B Rowdy Tellez (30) thanks to the failure to sign RHP Phil Bickford (1).

GRADE: D

2012

RHP Marcus Stroman (1) has emerged as a potential big league ace. The rest of the Jays' eggs are in the baskets of giant LHP Matt Smoral (1s) and raw OFs D.J. Davis (1) and Anthony Alford (3).

GRADE: B

2011

Top prospect LHP Daniel Norris (2) has emerged from a class that included unsigned RHP Tyler Beede (1) and big leaguers since-traded RHP Anthony DeSclafani (6) and OF Kevin Pillar (32).

GRADE: B

TOP DRAFT PICKS OF THE DECADE

Year	Player, Pos.	2014 Org
2005	Ricky Romero, lhp	Blue Jays
2006	Travis Snider, of	Pirates
2007	Kevin Ahrens, 3b	Braves
2008	David Cooper, 1b	Indians
2009	Chad Jenkins, rhp	Blue Jays
2010	Deck McGuire, rhp	Athletics
2011	*Tyler Beede, rhp	Giants
2012	D.J. Davis, of	Blue Jays
2013	*Phil Bickford, rhp	Cal State Fullerton
2014	Jeff Hoffman, rhp	Blue Jays

*Did not sign

LARGEST BONUSES IN CLUB HISTORY

Adeiny Hechavarria, 2010	$4,000,000
Jeff Hoffman, 2014	$3,080,800
Max Pentecost, 2014	$2,888,300
Adonys Cardona, 2010	$2,800,000
Ricky Romero, 2005	$2,400,000

1 DANIEL NORRIS, LHP

Born: April, 25 1993. **B-T:** L-L. **Ht.:** 6-2. **Wt.:** 180.
Drafted: HS—Johnson City, Tenn., 2011 (2nd round).
Signed by: Nate Murrie.

The Blue Jays had seven of the top 78 picks in the 2011 draft. Norris fell to the 74th overall pick with high bonus demands, which the Jays met with a $2 million bonus, the largest of their class (they failed to sign first-rounder Tyler Beede that year). Norris entered 2014 with a 4-11, 5.40 career mark and notoriety for his surfing and 1978 Volkswagen van. He turned a corner with his delivery, stuff and performance in the second half of 2013, after returning from forearm soreness. He put it all together in 2014, rocketing through four levels to reach the majors in September. The 21-year-old was the first prep lefthander and third prep pitcher overall from the 2011 class to reach the majors. He had surgery this offseason to remove loose bodies from his left elbow.

Norris has a deep repertoire, and his ability to miss bats was unparalleled in the minors this year. He had the highest strikeout rate (11.8 K/9 and 32.5 percent of plate appearances) of any qualified starter in full-season ball this year, and his strikeout rate increased at each of his three minor league stops. His fastball velocity increased this year, sitting 91-95 mph and touching 97 as a starter. Norris' loose, quick arm works easily and produces downhill plane from a high three-quarters arm slot, which is slightly raised from earlier in his career. He gets good extension out front, helping give his stuff late riding life through the zone. His top secondary offering is a sharp, tight slider with at least plus potential that flashes plus-plus at its best. He shows feel for a changeup that also has at least plus potential, though he can get around on the pitch to give it cut-like action to his glove side. A curveball that has at least average potential and 1-7 tilt is Norris' fourth offering, despite occasionally having a velocity difference of nearly 20 mph off his fastball. Norris threw more strikes (3.1 walks per nine) than he ever has in his career and projects for at least average control. Norris entered the system throwing significantly across his body; that has been reduced, although he still throws across his body some, offering natural deception. Norris is staying taller on his backside and has

reduced the rigidity to the front side of his delivery, particularly his front leg. His posture is now more upright at release after routinely being off-balance because of his cross-body direction.

Norris will likely start the year in the rotation at the upper minors, and as long as he's healthy should crack the big league rotation in the second half.

BA GRADE

60 Risk Medium

SCOUTING GRADES

Fastball: 60.
Slider: 60.
Changeup: 60.
Curveball: 50
Control: 50.

Based on 20-80 scouting scale and future projection rather than present grades.

LGE	BF	SO%	BB%	HR/9
FSL	262	29.0	6.9	0.00
EL	155	31.6	11.0	1.26

CLIFF WELCH

Year	Club (League)	Class	W	L	ERA	G	GS	CG	SV	IP	H	HR	BB	SO	K/9	WHIP	AVG
2012	Bluefield (APP)	R	2	3	7.97	11	10	0	0	35	44	4	13	38	9.8	1.63	.301
	Vancouver (NWL)	SS	0	1	10.57	2	2	0	0	8	14	0	5	5	5.9	2.48	.400
2013	Lansing (MWL)	LoA	1	7	4.20	23	22	0	0	86	84	6	44	99	10.4	1.49	.255
	Dunedin (FSL)	HiA	1	0	0.00	1	1	0	0	5	1	0	2	1	1.8	0.60	.063
2014	Dunedin (FSL)	HiA	6	0	1.22	13	13	0	0	66	50	0	18	76	10.3	1.03	.209
	New Hampshire (EL)	AA	3	1	4.54	8	8	0	0	36	32	5	17	49	12.4	1.37	.235
	Buffalo (IL)	AAA	3	1	3.18	5	4	0	0	23	14	2	8	38	15.1	0.97	.182
	Toronto (AL)	MAJ	0	0	5.40	5	1	0	0	7	5	1	5	4	5.4	1.50	.208
Major League Totals			0	0	5.40	5	1	0	0	7	5	1	5	4	5.4	1.50	.208
Minor League Totals			16	13	4.01	63	60	0	0	258	239	17	107	306	10.7	1.34	.244

2 AARON SANCHEZ, RHP

Born: July 1, 1992. **B-T:** R-R. **Ht.:** 6-4. **Wt.:** 190. **Drafted:** HS—Barstow, Calif., 2010 (1st round supplemental). **Signed by:** Blake Crosby.

One of the youngest pitchers in the 2010 draft, Sanchez has moved quickly. He threw a career-high 133 innings and finished in Toronto's bullpen. He has the stuff, body and athleticism to pitch in the front half of a rotation if he throws more strikes or profiles as a dynamic late-game reliever if he doesn't. His control took a significant step forward in the second half of 2014. Sanchez produces premium velocity with an effortless delivery and loose, quick and easy arm action as the ball explodes from his hand. His fastball sits 92-96 in the rotation, touching 98. Working out of the major league bullpen, Sanchez's fastball averaged 97 and touched 99. His two-seamer has plus-plus life with bat-breaking armside run and sink. His curveball is at least a plus offering and flashes plus-plus. Sanchez's changeup, long his third pitch, improved this season and gives him a third plus weapon. After moving across three levels in 2014, Sanchez will likely begin 2014 in the Triple-A rotation and could impact the big leagues later in the year in the rotation or out of the pen.

BA GRADE

60 Risk: High

LGE	BF	SO%	BB%	HR/9
EL	285	20.0	14.0	0.27
IL	150	18.0	11.3	1.05

Year	Club (League)	Class	W	L	ERA	G	GS	CG	SV	IP	H	HR	BB	SO	K/9	WHIP	AVG
2012	Lansing (MWL)	LoA	8	5	2.49	25	18	0	0	90	64	3	51	97	9.7	1.27	.204
2013	Dunedin (FSL)	HiA	4	5	3.34	22	20	0	0	86	63	4	40	75	7.8	1.19	.202
2014	New Hampshire (EL)	AA	3	4	3.82	14	14	0	0	66	52	2	40	57	7.8	1.39	.222
	Buffalo (IL)	AAA	0	3	4.19	8	6	0	0	34	36	4	17	27	7.1	1.54	.281
	Toronto (AL)	MAJ	2	2	1.09	24	0	0	3	33	14	1	9	27	7.4	0.70	.128
Major League Totals			2	2	1.09	24	0	0	3	33	14	1	9	27	7.4	0.70	.128
Minor League Totals			18	23	3.51	93	77	0	1	356	291	18	191	349	8.8	1.35	.226

3 JEFF HOFFMAN, RHP

Born: Jan. 1, 1993. **B-T:** R-R. **Ht.:** 6-4. **Wt.:** 192. **Drafted:** East Carolina, 2014 (1st round). **Signed by:** Chris Kline.

Hoffman was a lean, projectable righthander from upstate New York who went undrafted out of high school, but multiple teams tried to sign him in the summer before his freshman year. Hoffman's last start in college was in April when he struck out a career-high 16 in front of multiple GMs picking in the top five before undergoing Tommy John surgery in early May. Hoffman is a premium athlete with the stuff, body and athleticism to profile in the front half of a rotation. His fastball sits 93-96 mph, touching 98 with the ball jumping from his hand. Hoffman's two-seamer has at least plus life with heavy, bat-breaking sink and arm-side run to get groundballs. His drop-and-drive delivery works easy with natural fluidity and a loose arm. He offers a true downer curveball with at least plus potential that flashes plus-plus. Hoffman offers feel for a changeup that improved significantly over the last year and also has at least plus potential, flashing a full grade better.

BA GRADE

65 Risk: Extreme

LGE	BF	SO%	BB%	HR/9
Did not play				

He also mixed in a mid-80s slider with at least average potential. He fills up the zone and projects to have at least plus control. Hoffman's surgery prevented him from playing after signing but he is throwing from flat ground this fall and will likely be back in game action around midseason. Few starters in the minors can match his upside.

Year	Club (League)	Class	W	L	ERA	G	GS	CG	SV	IP	H	HR	BB	SO	K/9	WHIP	AVG
2014	Did not play—Injured																

4 DALTON POMPEY, OF

Born: Dec. 11, 1992. **B-T:** B-R. **Ht.:** 6-1. **Wt.:** 180. **Drafted:** HS—Mississauga, Ont., 2010 (16th round). **Signed by:** Jamie Lehman.

The 17-year-old Pompey was one of the youngest players in the 2010 draft and signed for $150,000. He had something of a storybook season in 2014, playing at four different levels and reaching the major leagues. A plus athlete, Pompey is a premium defender. His gap-closing defense has drawn plus-plus grades from scouts. He offers an above-average arm that could play in right field. His speed is at least plus and is capable of the occasional plus-plus time out of the box. He is a smart, efficient basestealer who can impact games on the bases. The switch-hitter could become an above-average hitter who draws walks at an above-average clip throughout his career while producing above-average contact rates. His quick-twitch athleticism translates to the batter's box with natural whip and bat speed. He will likely hit 10-15 home runs annually with lots of extra-base hits. Pompey's defensive and baserunning prowess gives him a high floor and the development of his bat could give him a well-rounded skill set capable of contributing in nearly every phase of the game.

BA GRADE

55 Risk: Medium

LGE	PA	BB%	SO%	ISO
FSL	317	11.0	17.7	.152
EL	127	11.0	14.2	.179

Year	Club (League)	Class	AVG	G	AB	R	H	2B	3B	HR	RBI	BB	SO	SB	CS	OBP	SLG
2012	Vancouver (NWL)	SS	.294	11	34	11	10	3	1	0	4	9	7	3	0	.442	.441
	Bluefield (APP)	R	.357	4	14	2	5	1	1	0	1	0	2	1	0	.357	.571
	Lansing (MWL)	LoA	.227	5	22	1	5	0	1	0	3	1	5	1	1	.261	.318
2013	Lansing (MWL)	LoA	.261	115	437	68	114	22	9	6	40	63	106	38	10	.358	.394
2014	Dunedin (FSL)	HiA	.319	70	276	49	88	12	6	6	34	35	56	29	2	.397	.471
	New Hampshire (EL)	AA	.295	31	112	20	33	5	3	3	12	14	18	8	5	.378	.473
	Buffalo (IL)	AAA	.358	12	53	15	19	5	0	0	5	3	10	6	0	.393	.453
	Toronto (AL)	MAJ	.231	17	39	5	9	1	2	1	4	4	12	1	0	.302	.436
Major League Totals			.231	17	39	5	9	1	2	1	4	4	12	1	0	.302	.436
Minor League Totals			.276	319	1221	219	337	58	23	22	121	166	272	113	20	.367	.415

5 MAX PENTECOST, C

Born: March 10, 1993. **B-T:** R-R. **Ht.:** 6-2. **Wt.:** 191. **Drafted:** Kennesaw State, 2014 (1st round). **Signed by:** Mike Tidick.

Pentecost went unsigned as a Rangers seventh-round pick out of high school partly due to a stress fracture to his right elbow. He was a top performer in college, where he won the MVP of the Cape Cod League and led Kennesaw State to its first Super Regionals appearance. Pentecost is a premium athlete for a catcher. He was a top performer in college and finished second in the NCAA in batting average this spring (.422/.482/.627). Pentecost has an easy, quick and short stroke conducive to line drives to all fields. He flashes above-average raw power to his pull side but his swing path is geared more toward line drives to the gaps. He projects to hit for 12-15 home runs annually with high doubles production. Pentecost is a plus runner at present. He has instincts on the bases and was never caught stealing in 25 tries during his college career. Pentecost has a plus arm, albeit a sometimes inaccurate one, with a quick release and his receiving improved significantly, giving him the potential to be at least an average defender. His debut was truncated because of nagging injuries, and Pentecost had surgery in October to repair a partial tear in his right labrum, but he is expected to be ready for the start of the season and will likely begin at Lansing or Dunedin.

BA GRADE

55 Risk: High

LGE	PA	BB%	SO%	ISO
GCL	22	0.0	13.6	.091
NWL	87	2.3	20.7	.096

Year	Club (League)	Class	AVG	G	AB	R	H	2B	3B	HR	RBI	BB	SO	SB	CS	OBP	SLG
2014	Blue Jays (GCL)	R	.364	6	22	2	8	2	0	0	3	0	3	0	1	.364	.455
	Vancouver (NWL)	SS	.313	19	83	15	26	2	3	0	9	2	18	2	1	.322	.410
Minor League Totals			.324	25	105	17	34	4	3	0	12	2	21	2	2	.330	.419

6 DEVON TRAVIS, 2B/OF

BILL MITCHELL

Born: Feb. 21, 1991. **B-T:** R-R. **Ht.:** 5-9. **Wt.:** 195. **Drafted:** Florida State, 2012 (13th round). **Signed by:** Jim Rough (Tigers).

Teams were wary of Travis' 5-foot-9 size, so he lasted until the 13th round in the 2012 draft, then signed with the Tigers for $200,000. That quickly looked like a bargain when he hit a combined .351/.418/.518 through two levels of Class A ball in his first full season in 2013. With Ian Kinsler blocking Travis at second base in Detroit, the Tigers traded him to the Blue Jays in November, a couple months after having core muscle surgery in September. While there's nothing flashy about Travis, he has excellent bat-to-ball skills and an extensive track record for hitting everywhere he goes. He has superb hand-eye coordination, good balance at the plate and strong bat control, which allows him to make consistent contact and use the whole field. His stance was more spread out in college, but in 2013 he adopted a more upright approach, dropped his hands and used a shorter, simpler load to be quicker to the ball and improve his plate coverage on the inner third. He

BA GRADE	
50	Risk: Medium

LGE	PA	BB%	SO%	ISO
EL	441	8.4	13.6	.162

stays within the strike zone and squares up both fastballs and offspeed pitches. Travis has the strength for 10-15 homers per year. He is an average runner who's sometimes slower going from home to first base, but he's a better runner underway and moves well going first to third. At second base, Travis is steady, making the routine play and turning double plays well with an average arm. While Travis fits the grinder mold that gets thrown on a lot of short players, he's more than just a scrappy reserve because of his bat potential. Travis has a chance to turn into a steady, average everyday second baseman for the Blue Jays, though the Tigers also had experimented with him in center field.

Year	Club (League)	Class	AVG	G	AB	R	H	2B	3B	HR	RBI	BB	SO	SB	CS	OBP	SLG
2012	Connecticut (NYP)	SS	.280	25	93	17	26	2	2	3	11	8	10	3	1	.352	.441
2013	W. Michigan (MWL)	LoA	.352	77	290	55	102	17	2	6	42	35	32	14	3	.430	.486
	Lakeland (FSL)	HiA	.350	55	214	38	75	11	2	10	34	18	32	8	1	.401	.561
2014	Erie (EL)	AA	.298	100	396	68	118	20	7	10	52	37	60	16	5	.358	.460
Minor League Totals			.323	257	993	178	321	50	13	29	139	98	134	41	10	.388	.487

7 ROBERTO OSUNA, RHP

Born: Feb. 7, 1995. **B-T:** R-R. **Ht.:** 6-2. **Wt.:** 230. **Signed:** Mexico, 2011. **Signed by:** Marco Paddy.

Osuna returned from Tommy John surgery in the second half of the season and was handled carefully upon his return, averaging less than three innings per start with the longest of his eight starts registering 4 1/3 innings. He pitched in the Arizona Fall League to get additional innings. While Osuna's fastball was not quite as firm this summer as before his injury, his heater still sat at 91-93 mph, touching 95 and could bump up a tick to its previous standards the further away from the surgery he gets. He has a loose, quick arm and throws very easily with a wrist wrap in the back. His top secondary offering is a changeup with plus potential that he has feel for. The consistency of his breaking ball will be a developmental point of emphasis, as it has flashed at least plus but consistently plays below that. Even though Osuna has routinely been one of the youngest players at each level, he has routinely missed bats, striking out 11.0 per nine in his career. His strikeout

BA GRADE	
55	Risk: High

LGE	BF	SO%	BB%	HR/9
FSL	101	29.7	8.9	1.23

rate (12.3) would have easily led the Florida State League if he had enough innings to qualify–admittedly he was roughly 90 innings short. The organization is working on getting more life to Osuna's fastball, which can play straight. Osuna will likely have a chance to move up to Double-A at some point in 2015.

Year	Club (League)	Class	W	L	ERA	G	GS	CG	SV	IP	H	HR	BB	SO	K/9	WHIP	AVG
2012	Bluefield (APP)	R	1	0	1.50	7	4	0	0	24	18	1	6	24	9.0	1.00	.209
	Vancouver (NWL)	SS	1	0	3.20	5	5	0	0	20	14	1	9	25	11.4	1.17	.192
2013	Lansing (MWL)	LoA	3	5	5.53	10	10	0	0	42	39	6	11	51	10.8	1.18	.242
2014	Blue Jays (GCL)	R	0	0	0.00	1	1	0	0	1	0	0	0	2	18.0	0.00	.000
	Dunedin (FSL)	HiA	0	2	6.55	7	7	0	0	22	28	3	9	30	12.3	1.68	.318
Minor League Totals			5	8	4.55	43	29	0	0	129	124	14	46	144	10.1	1.32	.241

8 RICHARD URENA, SS

Born: Feb. 26, 1996. **B-T:** L-R. **Ht.:** 6-1. **Wt.:** 170. **Signed:** Dominican Republic, 2012. **Signed by:** Ismael Cruz/Sandi Rosario/Luciano del Rosario.

The Blue Jays' lower minors has a talented duo of young, athletic shortstops signed from Latin America in 2011 and 2012: Dawel Lugo and Urena, who netted a $725,000 signing bonus and has the highest chance to stay at shortstop. Urena has the physical ability necessary to remain at shortstop with an arm that is at least plus and has a quick release that can throw from any angle in addition to loose, athletic actions, soft hands and above-average lateral range to both sides. He has quick-twitch athleticism but will need to cut down his defensive miscues to remain at the position after fielding .917 this summer in the Appalachian League. A natural lefthanded hitter, Urena began switch-hitting this year and impressed evaluators with his bat. He has above-average bat speed with an easy stroke, and he works inside the ball with the ability to consistently drive the ball to the gaps and opposite field. His power projects to be below-average with 6-10 home runs and lots of doubles. He is an average to above-average runner out of the box who could slow to average. Urena could be a two-way contributor and could challenge for a spot with a full-season club after being a top offensive performer in the Appy League this summer.

MIKE JANES

BA GRADE	
55	Risk: High

LGE	PA	BB%	SO%	ISO
APP	237	6.8	21.5	.115
NWL	37	8.1	13.5	.121

Year	Club (League)	Class	AVG	G	AB	R	H	2B	3B	HR	RBI	BB	SO	SB	CS	OBP	SLG
2013	Blue Jays (DSL)	R	.296	64	243	45	72	19	2	1	35	30	43	9	5	.381	.403
	Blue Jays (GCL)	R	.333	7	27	3	9	2	0	0	3	3	6	0	0	.400	.407
2014	Bluefield (APP)	R	.318	53	217	35	69	15	2	2	20	16	51	5	4	.363	.433
	Vancouver (NWL)	SS	.242	9	33	3	8	2	1	0	5	3	5	1	0	.297	.364
Minor League Totals			.304	133	520	86	158	38	5	3	63	52	105	15	9	.370	.413

9 MIGUEL CASTRO, RHP

Born: Dec. 24, 1994. **B-T:** R-R. **Ht.:** 6-5. **Wt.:** 190. **Signed:** Dominican Republic, 2011. **Signed by:** Ismael Cruz/Sandi Rosario.

In a year when the Blue Jays spent big internationally, Castro signed for $180,000 as a January signee. His 2013 stateside debut was delayed by visa issues, but he dominated the Dominican Summer League and built on that performance this year. Castro is a physical specimen with a large frame, broad shoulders, long extremities and a lean, wiry build. Castro's fastball sat in the low-90s before he signed but now sits in the mid-90s and touches 99 with a loose arm. He has a quick arm and the ball jumps from his hand with extension out front from a long-striding delivery. His low three-quarters arm slot produces plus sinking life, arm-side run and angle that projects to get groundballs at an above-average clip. Castro pitches off of his fastball and his top secondary offering is a changeup with plus potential. His slider is still in its developmental stages and is not consistently average. But his hand speed and arm slot give his sweepy slider a chance to develop. Castro's fastball velocity, life and extension make him tough on righthanded hitters. Castro will likely start the season in a Class A rotation, where the development of his breaking ball will be a focus.

BA GRADE	
55	Risk: High

LGE	BF	SO%	BB%	HR/9
NWL	201	26.4	10.0	0.36
MWL	83	24.1	8.4	0.83

Year	Club (League)	Class	W	L	ERA	G	GS	CG	SV	IP	H	HR	BB	SO	K/9	WHIP	AVG
2012	Blue Jays (DSL)	R	3	2	4.87	8	3	0	0	20	16	1	11	20	8.9	1.33	.232
2013	Blue Jays (DSL)	R	5	2	1.36	11	10	0	0	53	40	0	12	71	12.1	0.98	.208
	Blue Jays (GCL)	R	1	0	2.40	3	2	0	1	15	11	0	2	14	8.4	0.87	.212
	Bluefield (APP)	R	0	0	0.00	1	0	0	0	2	1	0	0	3	13.5	0.50	.111
2014	Vancouver (NWL)	SS	6	2	2.15	10	10	0	0	50	36	2	20	53	9.5	1.11	.202
	Lansing (MWL)	LoA	1	1	3.74	4	4	0	0	22	10	2	7	20	8.3	0.78	.133
	Dunedin (FSL)	HiA	1	0	3.12	2	1	0	0	9	4	2	3	5	5.2	0.81	.143
Minor League Totals			17	7	2.47	39	30	0	1	171	118	7	55	186	9.8	1.01	.196

10 SEAN REID-FOLEY, RHP

Born: Aug. 30, 1995. **B-T:** R-R. **Ht.:** 6-3. **Wt.:** 220. **Drafted:** HS—Jacksonville, 2014 (2nd round). **Signed by:** Matt Bishoff.

Reid-Foley was part of a standout group of prep arms in Florida in 2014. After a strong summer in 2013 on the showcase circuit, he showed consistent velocity throughout the spring—until his final outing before the draft at state's high school all-star game in Sebring, which drove down his draft stock. Reid-Foley has the stuff to profile as a mid-rotation starter and possesses a large, durable build with broad shoulders and a physical lower half. He has a quick arm that produces a fastball that sits 91-95 mph and touches 97 with downhill plane, and he has natural deception to his delivery. His top secondary offering is his slider, which has above-average potential. Reid-Foley's changeup is a point of emphasis, but it shows at least average potential. He has thrown a curveball that flashed average, but did not throw it last spring or summer. His delivery has a long stride and allows him to get extension out front, but he has a high elbow in the back that some scouts aren't fond of. Since Reid-Foley has present stuff he could vie for a rotation spot in low Class A, but the organization more commonly sends its premium high school arms to a short-season stop first.

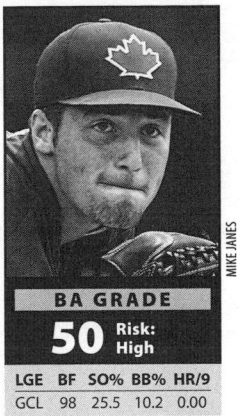

MIKE JANES

BA GRADE	
50	Risk: High

LGE	BF	SO%	BB%	HR/9
GCL	98	25.5	10.2	0.00

Year	Club (League)	Class	W	L	ERA	G	GS	CG	SV	IP	H	HR	BB	SO	K/9	WHIP	AVG
2014	Blue Jays (GCL)	R	1	2	4.76	9	6	0	0	23	21	0	10	25	9.9	1.37	.244
Minor League Totals			1	2	4.76	9	6	0	0	23	21	0	10	25	9.9	1.37	.244

11 MATT SMORAL, LHP

BA GRADE	
55	Risk: Extreme

Born: March 18, 1994. **B-T:** L-L. **Ht.:** 6-8. **Wt.:** 220. **Drafted:** HS—Solon, Ohio, 2012 (1st round supplemental). **Signed by:** Coulson Barbiche

Smoral was viewed as one of the top prep lefthanders in the 2012 draft heading into the spring, when he made only one start because of a stress fracture in his right foot. That allowed the Jays to grab him at pick No. 50 and sign him for $2 million. After not pitching in 2012 and being limited to 26 innings in 2013 because of a cracked fingernail, Smoral had his first healthy season in 2014, striking out nearly one-third of batters at Rookie-level Bluefield. His body, fastball and slider give him a foundation to be at least a mid-rotation starter, but the development of his control and changeup will dictate whether he stays in the rotation. His fastball sits at 90-93 mph, touching 95 with above-average life when down. Smoral's slider is a wipeout offering with plus potential and is a weapon against both lefthanders and righthanders. His mid-80s changeup improved in 2014 and flashed average but will need continued development. Smoral has an extra-large frame and lost weight over the 2014 season, gaining athleticism and flexibility while improving his delivery. He'll likely get his first taste of full-season ball at low Class A Lansing in 2015.

Year	Club (League)	Class	W	L	ERA	G	GS	CG	SV	IP	H	HR	BB	SO	K/9	WHIP	AVG
2012	Did not play—Injured																
2013	Blue Jays (GCL)	R	0	2	7.01	15	5	0	0	26	22	1	26	27	9.5	1.87	.237
2014	Bluefield (APP)	R	2	3	3.48	9	5	0	0	34	31	0	18	51	13.6	1.46	.230
	Vancouver (NWL)	SS	2	0	2.70	5	3	0	0	20	14	0	15	19	8.6	1.45	.219
Minor League Totals			4	5	4.42	29	13	0	0	79	67	1	59	97	11.0	1.59	.229

12 RYAN BORUCKI, LHP

BA GRADE	
50	Risk: High

Born: March 31, 1994. **B-T:** L-L. **Ht.:** 6-4. **Wt.:** 175. **Drafted:** HS—Mundelein, Ill., 2012 (15th round). **Signed by:** Mike Medici.

Borucki's father reached Triple-A as an infielder, and Ryan is making his mark on the mound. He injured his elbow as a high school senior and required Tommy John surgery after signing with the Blue Jays for $426,000 in 2012. He missed the entire 2013 season, then returned with a strong 2014 season capped by seven shutout innings in a short-season Northwest League playoff start for Vancouver. Borucki's fastball sat 90-94 mph early in the season and settled in at 88-92. He has shown pitching aptitude by reducing the effort in his delivery and reducing the height of his high elbow in the back, producing more consistent plane to his heater from his loose, quick arm action. His top secondary offering is a plus changeup. He has a feel for his changeup and for throwing strikes. Borucki currently shows a below-average to fringe-average curveball and may begin using a slider that is more conducive to his three-quarters arm slot. He will likely begin the season at low Class A Lansing and offers a lean, projectable and high-waisted build that should allow him to get stronger.

Year	Club (League)	Class	W	L	ERA	G	GS	CG	SV	IP	H	HR	BB	SO	K/9	WHIP	AVG
2012	Blue Jays (GCL)	R	1	0	3.00	4	0	0	0	6	4	1	0	10	15.0	0.67	.182
2013	Did not play—Injured																
2014	Bluefield (APP)	R	2	1	2.70	8	6	0	0	33	26	2	6	30	8.1	0.96	.211
	Vancouver (NWL)	SS	1	1	1.90	5	4	0	1	24	13	1	3	22	8.4	0.68	.159
Minor League Totals			4	2	2.43	17	10	0	1	63	43	4	9	62	8.9	0.83	.189

13 JAIRO LABOURT, LHP

BA GRADE
50 Risk: High

Born: March 7, 1994. **B-T:** L-L. **Ht.:** 6-4. **Wt.:** 204. **Signed:** Dominican Republic, 2011. **Signed by:** Marco Paddy/Hilario Soriano.

A $350,000 signing in 2011, Labourt has improved his body and his stuff significantly since then. He had a strong season in 2013 and began the 2014 campaign at low Class A Lansing, but he didn't last past April as wildness prompted a demotion to extended spring training. He returned to form at short-season Vancouver and led the Northwest League with 10.3 strikeouts per nine innings. He offers a three-pitch mix that could allow him to profile as a starter, but his below-average control will have to improve. Labourt's fastball/slider combo could make a quicker impact out of the bullpen. His fastball sits at 90-93 mph and touches 95 with two-seam sink and armside run. His slider is his top secondary offering and shows above-average potential, varying between cutter-like shape in the upper 80s and truer slider tilt in the mid-80s. While his changeup has flashed solid-average potential, it will need continued development. Labourt's delivery has improved, and he has shed bad weight and has a solid, athletic body, making him the rare physical Dominican lefthander. He likely will return to Lansing in 2015.

Year	Club (League)	Class	W	L	ERA	G	GS	CG	SV	IP	H	HR	BB	SO	K/9	WHIP	AVG
2012	Blue Jays (GCL)	R	0	3	3.79	12	12	0	0	38	38	2	23	39	9.2	1.61	.253
2013	Bluefield (APP)	R	2	2	1.92	12	8	0	0	52	39	3	14	45	7.8	1.03	.204
2014	Lansing (MWL)	LoA	0	0	6.43	6	3	0	0	14	15	1	20	11	7.1	2.50	.300
	Vancouver (NWL)	SS	5	3	1.77	15	15	0	0	71	47	0	37	82	10.3	1.18	.188
Minor League Totals			7	12	2.56	57	50	0	0	211	168	6	108	206	8.8	1.31	.217

14 DWIGHT SMITH JR., OF

BA GRADE
45 Risk: Medium

Born: Oct. 26, 1992. **B-T:** L-R. **Ht.:** 5-11. **Wt.:** 180. **Drafted:** HS— McIntosh, Ga., 2011 (1st round supplemental). **Signed by:** Eric McQueen.

The son of the former major leaguer, Smith lacks a true plus tool and will have to perform at every level. His advanced bat and secondary skills could allow him to become a regular, especially considering the lower offensive standards of this era. Smith was one of the top offensive performers in 2014 in the high Class A Florida State League, tying for the league lead in extra-base hits (48) and triples (8) while ranking second in total bases (214). His lefthanded swing features a high leg kick and high load, but he has a quick, compact and direct stroke conducive to line drives while working inside the ball well and using the opposite field. He has a strong understanding of the strike zone and feel for making adjustments. He has average pull-side power but likely will produce more doubles than home runs. Smith, who has seen most of his time in center field, has average speed and solid instincts but probably will end up on a corner, with his fringe-average arm making left field likely. He'll move up to Double-A New Hampshire for 2015.

Year	Club (League)	Class	AVG	G	AB	R	H	2B	3B	HR	RBI	BB	SO	SB	CS	OBP	SLG
2012	Bluefield (APP)	R	.226	41	159	20	36	6	0	4	21	11	22	1	1	.289	.340
	Vancouver (NWL)	SS	.175	18	63	5	11	3	1	0	8	6	11	0	0	.254	.254
2013	Lansing (MWL)	LoA	.284	109	423	57	120	17	3	7	46	52	82	25	5	.365	.388
2014	Dunedin (FSL)	HiA	.284	121	472	83	134	28	8	12	60	58	69	15	4	.363	.453
Minor League Totals			.269	289	1117	165	301	54	12	23	135	127	184	41	10	.347	.401

15 DAWEL LUGO, SS

BA GRADE
50 Risk: High

Born: Dec. 31, 1994. **B-T:** R-R. **Ht.:** 6-0. **Wt.:** 190. **Signed:** Dominican Republic, 2011. **Signed by:** Marco Paddy/Hilario Soriano.

Lugo signed for $1.3 million in 2011 but didn't reach full-season ball until last year, when he was one of the youngest position players in the low Class A Midwest League. He has a loose, handsy, line-drive stroke with above-average bat speed. He has natural feel for the barrel and has posted well above-average contact rates throughout his career. Lugo has an aggressive approach that may keep him from reaching his ceiling, however. He swings and misses against breaking pitches and has walked just 3.2 percent of the time. He flashes at least average raw power and projects to hit a dozen home runs annually with additional loft to his stroke. A below-average runner, he has smooth athletic actions, soft hands and an above-average arm, though his body and moderate range and quickness make Jhonny Peralta his best comparison defensively if he stays at short. Other scouts project a move to third base. Lugo's next stop is high Class A Dunedin.

Year	Club (League)	Class	AVG	G	AB	R	H	2B	3B	HR	RBI	BB	SO	SB	CS	OBP	SLG
2012	Blue Jays (GCL)	R	.224	47	170	20	38	2	5	2	20	7	25	5	1	.275	.329
2013	Bluefield (APP)	R	.297	51	192	28	57	11	2	6	36	5	28	1	0	.317	.469
	Vancouver (NWL)	SS	.246	16	69	6	17	4	0	1	8	1	13	0	0	.257	.348
2014	Lansing (MWL)	LoA	.259	117	474	40	123	17	2	4	53	18	72	3	3	.286	.329
Minor League Totals			.260	231	905	94	235	34	9	13	117	31	138	9	4	.288	.360

16 MITCH NAY, 3B

BA GRADE
50 Risk: High

Born: Sept. 20, 1993. **B-T:** R-R. **Ht.:** 6-3. **Wt.:** 195. **Drafted:** HS—Chandler, Ariz., 2012 (1st round supplemental). **Signed by:** Blake Crosby

Nay, the grandson of former big leaguer Lou Klimchock, signed for $1 million in 2012 and reached full-season ball in 2014. While the bat-first Nay offers plus raw power and above-average contact skills, he must continue to make offensive adjustments to reach his ceiling. He is a strong, muscular and physical presence with plus raw power to go with natural feel for the barrel and a history of high contact rates. His raw power has not translated to game action yet. His stroke can get long and leave him exposed to balls on the outer third of the plate. Nay's defense improved last year, and low Class A Midwest League managers considered him the league's best defensive third baseman. He has the above-average arm and hands for third, but fringy first-step quickness and range could move him to first base or an outfield corner. A below-average runner, Nay will return to high Class A Dunedin, where he finished the 2014 season.

Year	Club (League)	Class	AVG	G	AB	R	H	2B	3B	HR	RBI	BB	SO	SB	CS	OBP	SLG
2012	Did not play—Injured																
2013	Bluefield (APP)	R	.300	64	230	41	69	11	0	6	42	25	35	0	1	.364	.426
2014	Lansing (MWL)	LoA	.285	120	473	57	135	34	3	3	59	39	79	6	2	.342	.389
	Dunedin (FSL)	HiA	.189	11	37	2	7	1	0	0	1	3	9	0	0	.250	.216
Minor League Totals			.285	195	740	100	211	46	3	9	102	67	123	6	3	.344	.392

17 CHASE DeJONG, RHP

BA GRADE
50 Risk: High

Born: Dec. 29, 1993. **B-T:** L-R. **Ht.:** 6-4. **Wt.:** 200. **Drafted:** HS—Long Beach, 2012 (2nd round). **Signed by:** Joe Aversa.

After two Rookie-ball campaigns, DeJong made his full-season debut in 2014. While he continued to fill up the strike zone at low Class A Lansing, he didn't miss many bats and will need to sharpen his command. DeJong's fastball sat between 88-91 mph and touched 92, though his velocity could improve as he fills his athletic, angular build. His curveball is inconsistent and can range from average to plus, while his straight changeup shows average potential and flashes plus. His cross-body delivery has a short stride, causing his fastball to play below its pure velocity. He is an extremely flyball-oriented pitcher who will probably be homer-prone. The Jays have worked to try to lengthen his stride. DeJong is a good fielder who also controls the running game well. He likely will begin 2015 at high Class A Dunedin.

Year	Club (League)	Class	W	L	ERA	G	GS	CG	SV	IP	H	HR	BB	SO	K/9	WHIP	AVG
2012	Blue Jays (GCL)	R	1	0	1.50	6	0	0	0	12	7	0	1	15	11.3	0.67	.171
2013	Bluefield (APP)	R	2	3	3.05	13	10	1	0	56	58	2	10	66	10.6	1.21	.261
2014	Lansing (MWL)	LoA	1	6	4.82	23	21	0	0	97	113	12	22	73	6.8	1.39	.290
Minor League Totals			4	9	3.98	42	31	1	0	165	178	14	33	154	8.4	1.28	.273

18 ANTHONY ALFORD, OF

BA GRADE
55 Risk: Extreme

Born: July 20, 1994. **B-T:** R-R. **Ht.:** 6-1. **Wt.:** 212. **Drafted:** HS—Petal, Miss., 2012 (3rd round). **Signed by:** Brian Johnston.

Alford was one of the top athletes in the 2012 draft and was also a dual-threat high school quarterback, recognized as Mississippi's best high school football player as both a junior and senior, and best baseball player as a senior. The Blue Jays took him in the third round and signed him for an over-slot bonus of $750,000, allowing him to play football at Southern Mississippi in the fall and baseball in the summer. He left Southern Miss after his freshman year following an arrest during an on-campus fight, transferring to Mississippi, but he played just four games there before deciding to focus on baseball. Alford has barely 100 professional plate appearances, but he still intrigues because of his youth and athleticism. He has a rare power/speed combo, with the potential to remain in center field and plus-plus raw power. His hitting is understandably raw, and his uphill stroke has some length from a high load. The strong and explosive Alford might outgrow center field, and his fringe-average arm would profile in left. He's a high-ceiling, low-probability lottery ticket whom the Jays will get at-bats to make up for his lost development time.

Year	Club (League)	Class	AVG	G	AB	R	H	2B	3B	HR	RBI	BB	SO	SB	CS	OBP	SLG
2012	Blue Jays (GCL)	R	.167	5	18	1	3	0	0	1	1	2	4	4	0	.250	.333
2013	Blue Jays (GCL)	R	.227	6	22	4	5	2	1	0	2	6	6	2	0	.414	.409
2014	Bluefield (APP)	R	.207	9	29	5	6	0	0	1	2	5	13	1	0	.343	.310
	Lansing (MWL)	LoA	.320	5	25	3	8	1	0	1	3	0	8	4	0	.320	.480
Minor League Totals			.234	25	94	13	22	3	1	3	8	13	31	11	0	.339	.383

19   LANE THOMAS, 3B/OF

BA GRADE

50 Risk: High

Born: Aug. 23, 1995. **B-T:** R-R. **Ht.:** 6-1. **Wt.:** 210. **Drafted:** HS—Knoxville, 2014 (5th round). **Signed by:** Nate Murrie

Thomas, whose father is a professional drag racer, helped USA Baseball's 18-and-under team win the 2013 World Cup in Taiwan, then was a BA High School All-American who signed for $750,000 as a fifth-rounder in 2014. He has an intriguing combination of tools, athleticism and natural feel for the game with strong baseball makeup. He has natural feel for the strike zone and could become an average hitter with a quick, line-drive stroke. He flashes average raw power, though his power projects to play closer to 10-12 home runs annually. He's a plus runner who saw most of his time in high school in center field, but he split his time between center and third base in Rookie ball in 2014. He transitioned to second base during instructional league and has the hands, lateral quickness and above-average arm strength to remain in the dirt. He had a strong debut and advanced to Rookie-level Bluefield, where he could begin in 2015.

Year	Club (League)	Class	AVG	G	AB	R	H	2B	3B	HR	RBI	BB	SO	SB	CS	OBP	SLG
2014	Blue Jays (GCL)	R	.260	34	131	21	34	8	4	0	11	21	33	7	3	.362	.382
	Bluefield (APP)	R	.323	18	65	10	21	4	0	1	8	6	16	2	0	.384	.431
Minor League Totals			.281	52	196	31	55	12	4	1	19	27	49	9	3	.369	.398

20   DAN JANSEN, C

BA GRADE

50 Risk: High

Born: April 15, 1995. **B-T:** R-R. **Ht.:** 6-2. **Wt.:** 215. **Drafted:** HS—Appleton, Wis., 2013 (16th round). **Signed by:** Wes Penick

The Badger State has just four prep position players who have reached the major leagues in the last four decades, but Jansen has contributed immediately since entering pro ball and has the potential to become a two-way contributor behind the plate. He entered the 2014 season in tremendous shape and is a strong, physical and powerful presence. He offers plus bat speed from the right side along with the physical strength and leverage in his swing to hit at least 15 home runs annually. His bat-to-ball ability and knowledge of the strike zone have produced more walks than strikeouts. Jansen's stroke is geared to the pull side, and he is learning to use the opposite field. His defensive ability has improved and gives him the potential to remain behind the plate. He is working on his exchange and release, which should enable his fringe-average arm to play up. Jansen sustained a minor knee injury late in the season at Rookie-level Bluefield but is expected to be ready for spring training and could make his full-season debut in 2015.

Year	Club (League)	Class	AVG	G	AB	R	H	2B	3B	HR	RBI	BB	SO	SB	CS	OBP	SLG
2013	Blue Jays (GCL)	R	.246	36	114	19	28	4	0	0	18	21	10	0	0	.364	.281
2014	Bluefield (APP)	R	.282	38	124	22	35	10	0	5	17	16	17	2	1	.390	.484
Minor League Totals			.265	74	238	41	63	14	0	5	35	37	27	2	1	.378	.387

21   D.J. DAVIS, OF

BA GRADE

50 Risk: Extreme

Born: July 25, 1994. **B-T:** L-R. **Ht.:** 6-1. **Wt.:** 180. **Drafted:** HS—Wiggins, Miss., 2012 (1st round). **Signed by:** Brian Johnston

Davis is climbing the ladder in the same organization where his father spent his minor league career. He is a premium athlete and the ability to be an impact two-way center fielder, though feel for the game, ability to make adjustments and swing-and-miss tendencies hold him back. Davis, who has above-average bat speed, struck out nearly one-third of the time in 2014, with an aggressive approach that scouts would like to see toned down, as well as timing and pitch recognition issues. He offers surprising strength from his lean, athletic build, flashing plus raw power. He is a plus-plus runner, but his speed has not translated and he was caught (20) more times than he stole successfully (19) in 2014. He could also be a plus defender in center field if his reads improve. Davis, who has a below-average arm, will also need to cut down on his miscues after making 18 errors in 2014. He faces a likely return to Lansing in 2015.

Year	Club (League)	Class	AVG	G	AB	R	H	2B	3B	HR	RBI	BB	SO	SB	CS	OBP	SLG
2012	Blue Jays (GCL)	R	.233	43	163	30	38	7	2	4	12	18	54	18	7	.339	.374
	Bluefield (APP)	R	.340	12	47	9	16	3	1	1	6	4	10	6	2	.415	.511
	Vancouver (NWL)	SS	.167	5	18	3	3	0	0	0	0	5	6	1	1	.348	.167
2013	Bluefield (APP)	R	.240	58	225	35	54	8	7	6	25	26	76	13	8	.323	.418
2014	Lansing (MWL)	LoA	.213	121	494	56	105	13	7	8	52	36	167	19	20	.268	.316
Minor League Totals			.228	239	947	133	216	31	17	19	95	89	313	57	38	.303	.357

22 ALBERTO TIRADO, RHP

BA GRADE

50 Risk: Extreme

Born: Dec. 10, 1994. **B-T:** R-R. **Ht.:** 6-0. **Wt.:** 180. **Signed:** Dominican Republic, 2011. **Signed by:** Marco Paddy/Domingo Toribio.

Signed for $300,000, Tirado is yet another arm from the organization's big international haul in 2011. He struggled in his full-season debut last season and was demoted after two months. As a slightly built Dominican righthander with an electric arm and strike-throwing concerns, Tirado must prove that he can throw enough strikes to remain in the rotation. A plus athlete, he has a loose, quick and whippy arm and the ball explodes out of his hand with heaviness and sink. He walked 8.0 batters per nine innings in 2014, however, and his poor control stems from a long arm action, cross-body delivery and rigid lower half. Lean and athletic, Tirado has a small frame with long extremities and needs to gain strength. His fastball backed up slightly in 2014, sitting in the low 90s and touching 95 mph. His mid-80s slider shows plus potential, though he can get around on it. He was primarily a fastball/slider pitcher last season, but his changeup shows average potential and flashes better. He'll try Lansing again in 2015.

Year	Club (League)	Class	W	L	ERA	G	GS	CG	SV	IP	H	HR	BB	SO	K/9	WHIP	AVG
2012	Blue Jays (GCL)	R	1	2	2.68	11	11	0	0	37	28	0	12	34	8.3	1.08	.217
	Bluefield (APP)	R	2	0	2.45	3	3	0	0	11	4	0	5	5	4.1	0.82	.121
2013	Bluefield (APP)	R	3	0	1.68	12	8	0	0	48	41	1	20	44	8.2	1.26	.236
2014	Lansing (MWL)	LoA	1	2	6.30	13	7	0	1	40	45	3	39	40	9.0	2.10	.283
	Vancouver (NWL)	SS	1	0	3.53	17	3	0	0	36	25	1	28	36	9.1	1.49	.191
Minor League Totals			8	4	3.40	56	32	0	1	172	143	5	104	159	8.3	1.44	.228

23 A.J. JIMENEZ, C

BA GRADE

45 Risk: High

Born: May 1, 1990. **B-T:** R-R. **Ht.:** 6-0. **Wt.:** 225. **Drafted:** HS— Bayamon, P.R., 2008 (9th round). **Signed by:** Jorge Rivera.

Injuries, including Tommy John surgery in 2012, have slowed Jimenez, and he has averaged about 72 games a season in six years. He missed time last April and August with minor injuries, and the health of his arm bears monitoring. Defense is his calling card and gives him a backup catcher profile. Jimenez possesses a true plus arm and quick feet to limit running games. His caught-stealing rate of 32 percent in 2014 was the lowest of his career, and his career rate is a robust 41 percent. He is a strong receiver and blocker with athleticism, though he can have lapses of concentration. Jimenez has solid bat speed, natural feel for the barrel and uses all fields, but he projects to be a below-average to fringe-average hitter with some length to his stroke. He has a strong body and boasts at least average raw power, but his swing path and approach will likely limit him to 8-12 home runs a year. The below-average runner is on the 40-man roster and should start 2015 back at Triple-A Buffalo.

Year	Club (League)	Class	AVG	G	AB	R	H	2B	3B	HR	RBI	BB	SO	SB	CS	OBP	SLG
2012	New Hampshire (EL)	AA	.257	27	105	14	27	4	1	2	10	5	14	2	3	.295	.371
2013	Dunedin (FSL)	HiA	.429	9	28	5	12	3	0	1	9	1	3	0	0	.448	.643
	New Hampshire (EL)	AA	.276	50	203	28	56	15	0	3	29	16	37	1	2	.327	.394
	Buffalo (IL)	AAA	.233	8	30	0	7	1	0	0	0	1	2	0	1	.258	.267
2014	New Hampshire (EL)	AA	.223	25	94	11	21	8	0	1	13	6	19	1	0	.275	.340
	Buffalo (IL)	AAA	.260	58	219	21	57	13	1	2	24	13	33	1	1	.295	.356
Minor League Totals			.277	450	1654	199	458	112	4	21	228	98	317	43	17	.317	.388

24 ANDY BURNS, 3B

BA GRADE

45 Risk: High

Born: Aug. 7, 1990. **B-T:** R-R. **Ht.:** 6-2. **Wt.:** 205. **Drafted:** Arizona, 2011 (11th round). **Signed by:** Blake Crosby.

Burns sat out the 2011 season following a transfer from Kentucky to Arizona, but the Blue Jays still took him in the 11th round. Following a breakout 2013, he spent the entire 2014 season at Double-A New Hampshire, where his performance picked up in the second half. The athletic Burns has a broad skill set and spent most of his time playing third base, though he played at all four infield spots and the outfield corners. He has an aggressive, line drive-oriented stroke and works inside the ball to all fields, though his bat projects to be fringe-average because he struggles on the outer third of the plate. He flashes above-average raw power and should show average power production. Burns has the defensive ability to stick at third base with an above-average arm, natural quickness and good hands, and his athleticism makes a capable fill-in at every position but shortstop and center field. He is an average runner out of the box with above-average speed under way. Burns should head to Triple-A Buffalo in 2015.

Year	Club (League)	Class	AVG	G	AB	R	H	2B	3B	HR	RBI	BB	SO	SB	CS	OBP	SLG
2012	Lansing (MWL)	LoA	.248	78	278	57	69	25	4	9	37	38	75	15	2	.351	.464
2013	Dunedin (FSL)	HiA	.327	64	248	45	81	15	5	8	53	25	38	21	9	.383	.524
	New Hampshire (EL)	AA	.253	64	265	40	67	19	2	7	32	23	55	12	5	.309	.419
2014	New Hampshire (EL)	AA	.255	133	495	71	126	32	5	15	63	41	99	18	8	.315	.430
Minor League Totals			.266	367	1386	228	368	95	16	42	199	135	281	68	26	.333	.448

25 TOM ROBSON, RHP

BA GRADE

50 Risk: Extreme

Born: June 27, 1993. **B-T:** R-R. **Ht.:** 6-4. **Wt.:** 210. **Drafted:** HS—Ladner, B.C., 2011 (4th round). **Signed by:** Jamie Lehman

Robson had the look of a durable innings-eater until having Tommy John surgery eight starts into the 2014 season. Before the surgery, his fastball sat 89-93 mph and touched 94 with downhill plane from a high three-quarters arm slot. The addition of his two-seamer, featuring heavy, sinking life, has helped him produce above-average groundball rates. Robson offers a curveball and a mid-80s changeup with above-average potential, though the changeup can be too firm at times. His low-80s slider could be an average offering. He could return to action in the second half of 2015, likely at one of the Class A levels. If he picks up where he left off, he would project as a potential No. 3 or 4 starter.

Year	Club (League)	Class	W	L	ERA	G	GS	CG	SV	IP	H	HR	BB	SO	K/9	WHIP	AVG
2012	Bluefield (APP)	R	0	2	4.09	3	3	0	0	11	10	2	0	7	5.7	0.91	.238
2013	Bluefield (APP)	R	3	0	1.38	6	5	0	0	26	15	1	5	18	6.2	0.77	.172
	Vancouver (NWL)	SS	3	0	0.94	7	7	0	0	38	28	0	11	29	6.8	1.02	.212
2014	Lansing (MWL)	LoA	2	4	6.25	8	8	0	0	32	37	1	18	22	6.3	1.74	.303
Minor League Totals			8	6	2.94	24	23	0	0	107	90	4	34	76	6.4	1.16	.235

26 JESUS TINOCO, RHP

BA GRADE

50 Risk: Extreme

Born: April 30, 1995. **B-T:** R-R. **Ht.:** 6-4. **Wt.:** 190. **Signed:** Venezuela, 2011. **Signed by:** Marco Paddy/Rafael Moncada.

Tinoco, a Venezuelan sinkerballer with an athletic, projectable body and present strength, has drawn comparisons to a taller version of former Jays farmhand Henderson Alvarez, now with the Marlins. Tinoco looks the part on the mound. His loose, clean arm action produces heavy two-seamers at 91-94 mph that induce plenty of groundballs. He fires his four-seamer up to 95 mph. His curveball flashes plus but is inconsistent. His solid-average changeup is his most consistent secondary weapon. He made adjustments to his delivery at Rookie-level Bluefield but still spins off to first base at times, costing him control. Tinoco has the potential to be at least a No. 4 starter and could take off once he finds a more consistent delivery and throws more strikes. He'll need a strong spring to make his full-season debut in 2015.

Year	Club (League)	Class	W	L	ERA	G	GS	CG	SV	IP	H	HR	BB	SO	K/9	WHIP	AVG
2012	Blue Jays (DSL)	R	0	4	4.14	12	7	0	0	37	37	0	12	26	6.3	1.32	.266
	Blue Jays (GCL)	R	1	1	6.00	2	0	0	0	6	7	0	1	8	12.0	1.33	.280
2013	Blue Jays (GCL)	R	0	5	5.09	12	9	0	1	46	49	0	21	45	8.8	1.52	.271
2014	Bluefield (APP)	R	1	9	4.95	13	12	0	1	56	62	4	20	47	7.5	1.46	.270
Minor League Totals			2	19	4.83	39	28	0	2	145	155	4	54	126	7.8	1.44	.270

27 JUAN MEZA, RHP

BA GRADE

50 Risk: Extreme

Born: Feb. 4, 1998. **B-T:** R-R. **Ht.:** 6-2. **Wt.:** 172. **Signed:** Venezuela, 2014. **Signed by:** Ismael Cruz/Luis Marquez/Henry Sandoval.

The top international prospect from the Blue Jays' international haul in 2014, Meza signed for $1.6 million. He offers an intriguing combination of projection, present stuff and pitchability, with a lean, athletic body. His fastball velocity has crept up over the last year and has touched 93 mph while sitting 88-91 with armside run from a three-quarters arm slot. He has the foundation for a starter's delivery with a loose, quick arm and good use of his lower half. Meza also creates deception with a high glove extension. His secondary stuff projects to be at least average, though his breaking ball can get slurvy and he is still developing feel for his changeup. He has natural strike-throwing ability and feel for pitching. Meza likely will spend 2015 as a 17-year-old in the Rookie-level Gulf Coast League.

Year	Club (League)	Class	W	L	ERA	G	GS	CG	SV	IP	H	HR	BB	SO	K/9	WHIP	AVG
2014	Did not play—Signed 2015 contract																

28 NICK WELLS, LHP

BA GRADE

50 Risk: Extreme

Born: Feb. 21, 1996. **B-T:** L-L. **Ht.:** 6-5. **Wt.:** 175. **Drafted:** HS—Haymarket, Va., 2014 (3rd round). **Signed by:** Doug Witt

Long, lean and lanky, Wells has a large frame that scouts can dream on, and he took off in the spring of his senior season when his fastball sat at 87-91 mph and touched 93 with glove-side run. Signed for $661,800 as a third-round pick, Wells could see his velocity increase given his projectable, wide-shouldered build and arm speed. His top secondary offering is a big-breaking curveball that shows plus potential. He rarely needed his changeup in high school, so it is a work in progress. The Blue Jays have considered adding a slider to his repertoire. Wells is loose and athletic with natural feel for throwing strikes, projecting for at least average control. Toronto has altered Wells' delivery since signing, seeking to generate steeper plane. He'll likely open at Rookie-level Bluefield following extended spring training.

Year	Club (League)	Class	W	L	ERA	G	GS	CG	SV	IP	H	HR	BB	SO	K/9	WHIP	AVG
2014	Blue Jays (GCL)	R	1	3	5.71	11	4	0	0	35	44	1	11	18	4.7	1.59	.303
Minor League Totals			1	3	5.71	11	4	0	0	35	44	1	11	18	4.7	1.59	.303

29 MATT BOYD, LHP

BA GRADE

45 Risk: High

Born: Feb. 2, 1991. **B-T:** L-L. **Ht.:** 6-3. **Wt.:** 215. **Drafted:** Oregon State, 2013 (6th round). **Signed by:** Ryan Fox

Boyd, a distant relative of Bob Feller and former first lady Dolly Madison, did not sign with the Reds as a 13th-round pick in 2012 and returned to Oregon State for his senior season. Following a strong summer in the Cape Cod League, he was the Beavers' Friday starter, and he signed for an under-slot $75,000 in the sixth round of the 2013 draft. Boyd had raised his arm slot as a senior, boosting his velocity, and the Blue Jays raised it further to high three-quarters. It's a high-maintenance delivery that remains funky and deceptive, but he repeats it well and overcomes a long arm action with wrap in the back. The flyball-oriented Boyd is a competitor with the potential for above-average control. His fastball sits at 88-91 mph and touches 93 with average life. While none of his secondary offerings grades out as plus, all three can be at least average. His changeup shows swing-and-miss potential with late fade. The sharpness of his breaking ball has improved in pro ball. Boyd should head back to Double-A for 2015 and profiles as a back-end starter or lefty reliever.

Year	Club (League)	Class	W	L	ERA	G	GS	CG	SV	IP	H	HR	BB	SO	K/9	WHIP	AVG
2013	Lansing (MWL)	LoA	0	1	0.64	5	3	0	0	14	7	0	1	12	7.7	0.57	.140
	Dunedin (FSL)	HiA	0	2	5.40	3	2	0	0	10	7	2	3	11	9.9	1.00	.206
2014	New Hampshire (EL)	AA	1	4	6.96	10	10	0	0	43	55	5	13	44	9.3	1.59	.307
	Dunedin (FSL)	HiA	5	3	1.39	16	16	1	0	91	65	4	20	103	10.2	0.94	.196
Minor League Totals			6	10	3.09	34	31	1	0	157	134	11	37	170	9.7	1.09	.226

30 ROWDY TELLEZ, 1B

BA GRADE

45 Risk: High

Born: March 16, 1995. **B-T:** L-L. **Ht.:** 6-4. **Wt.:** 220. **Drafted:** HS—Elk Grove, Calif., 2013 (30th round). **Signed by:** Darold Brown

The Blue Jays signed Tellez for second-round money ($850,000) as a 30th-round pick in 2013, after failing to sign first-rounder Phil Bickford. Nearly all of Tellez's value will come from a bat that has the potential to make him a middle-of-the-order presence, if he hits enough to allow his plus-plus raw power to play. He took a hit-first approach in 2014, rarely swinging and missing in the strike zone. He has loose hands at the plate, with a quick lefthanded stroke that features natural extension and loft. When Tellez gets pull-happy, his swing gets long, but he has lowered his hands in his load and reduced his bat wrap, making his swing more compact. A well below-average runner with limited range and athleticism at first base, he will continue working on his fringe-average defense. His body will require continued maintenance as well. Expect Tellez to return to Lansing in 2015.

Year	Club (League)	Class	AVG	G	AB	R	H	2B	3B	HR	RBI	BB	SO	SB	CS	OBP	SLG
2013	Blue Jays (GCL)	R	.234	34	124	10	29	5	3	2	20	15	26	1	0	.319	.371
2014	Bluefield (APP)	R	.293	53	191	26	56	11	1	4	36	19	27	3	2	.358	.424
	Lansing (MWL)	LoA	.357	12	42	6	15	0	0	2	7	7	10	0	0	.449	.500
Minor League Totals			.280	99	357	42	100	16	4	8	63	41	63	4	2	.355	.415

Washington Nationals

BY AARON FITT

The Nationals rebounded from a disappointing 2013 campaign with a banner regular season, winning the National League East by 17 games and posting the best record in the NL.

Washington carried incredible momentum into the postseason, as Jordan Zimmermann threw the first no-hitter in Nats history against the Marlins on the final day of the regular season. Steven Souza recorded the final out with an incredible diving catch on the warning track in left-center field.

But Washington lost both of its home playoff games in the Division Series against the Giants,  including an 18-inning heartbreaker in Game Two, en route to a series loss in four games. The Nationals' Nos. 3 and 4 hitters, Jayson Werth and Adam LaRoche, went a combined 2-for-35 in the series, and the team's stellar pitching staff, which led the majors with a 3.03 ERA, couldn't compensate for an offense that went cold.

The Giants won the series without scoring more than three runs in any game.

Despite the bitter disappointment of Washington's postseason performance, the future remains bright for a club that boasts one of the best young cores in baseball. Righthanders Zimmermann and Stephen Strasburg are in their primes, giving the rotation an overpowering one-two punch. The emergence of righty Tanner Roark and the acquisitions of lefty Gio Gonzalez and righty Doug Fister over the last three seasons make the rotation deep.

The Nationals struck gold in 2009 and 2010 drafts with back-to-back No. 1 overall picks Strasburg and outfielder Bryce Harper, who still is just scratching the surface of his potential at age 22. They boldly landed elite talents with their first-rounders in the next two drafts when injuries caused third baseman Anthony Rendon and righty Lucas Giolito to slide.

Rendon spent one year as the team's top prospect before entrenching himself as a cornerstone piece in the majors, and he took the next step to stardom in 2014. Giolito, meanwhile, ranks atop the team's prospect list for the second straight year after making a full recovery from Tommy John surgery and dominating low Class A hitters as a 19-year-old.

The Nationals continued to be opportunistic in the draft in 2014, snatching up Nevada-Las Vegas righthander Erick Fedde, who was projected to go in the first 10 picks but slipped to No. 18 because of Tommy John surgery. They signed him for more than $2.5 million. But they were disappointed

The Nationals built a foundation for major league success thanks to hitting on their first-round picks like Stephen Strasburg

TOP PROSPECTS OF THE DECADE

Year	Player, Pos.	2014 Org
2005	Mike Hinckley, lhp	Out of baseball
2006	Ryan Zimmerman, 3b	Nationals
2007	Collin Balester, rhp	Pirates
2008	Chris Marrero, 1b	Orioles
2009	Jordan Zimmermann, rhp	Nationals
2010	Stephen Strasburg, rhp	Nationals
2011	Bryce Harper, of	Nationals
2012	Anthony Rendon, 3b	Nationals
2013	Lucas Giolito, rhp	Nationals
2014	Lucas Giolito, rhp	Nationals

that second-rounder Andrew Suarez, a lefthander for Miami, opted not to sign, thinning out the draft class.

Because several of Washington's top picks flew to the majors in a hurry, their system is top-heavy. Still, the Nationals have been rewarded for their philosophy, and they look poised to compete for championships for the foreseeable future.

Under general manager Mike Rizzo, scouting director Kris Kline and player development honcho Doug Harris, the Nats have become a model organization.

General Manager: Mike Rizzo. **Farm Director:** Mark Scialabba. **Scouting Director:** Kris Kline.

Class	Team	League	W	L	PCT	Finish	Manager
Majors	Washington Nationals	National	96	66	.593	t-2nd (30)	Matt Williams
Triple-A	Syracuse Chiefs	International	81	62	.566	1st (14)	Billy Gardner
Double-A	Harrisburg Senators	Eastern	53	89	.373	12th (12)	Brian Daubach
High A	Potomac Nationals	Carolina	78	58	.574	2nd (8)	Tripp Keister
Low A	Hagerstown Suns	South Atlantic	87	53	.621	t-3rd (14)	Patrick Anderson
Short season	Auburn Doubledays	New York-Penn	34	41	.453	9th (14)	Gary Cathcart
Rookie	Nationals	Gulf Coast	25	35	.417	t-12th (16)	Michael Barrett
Overall Minor League Record			**358**	**338**	**.514**	**10th (30)**	

THIS YEAR'S TOP 30

No.	Player, Pos.	Grade
1.	Lucas Giolito, rhp	70/High
2.	Michael Taylor, of	60/High
3.	Reynaldo Lopez, rhp	60/Extreme
4.	Erick Fedde, rhp	60/Extreme
5.	Steven Souza, of	50/Medium
6.	A.J. Cole, rhp	55/High
7.	Wilmer Difo, ss	50/High
8.	Drew Ward, 3b	50/High
9.	Brian Goodwin, of	50/High
10.	Nick Pivetta, rhp	50/High
11.	Austin Voth, rhp	50/High
12.	Tony Renda, 2b	45/Medium
13.	Pedro Severino, c	50/High
14.	Jakson Reetz, c	50/Extreme
15.	Sammy Solis, lhp	50/Extreme
16.	Taylor Hill, rhp	45/Medium
17.	Jake Johansen, rhp	50/Extreme
18.	Felipe Rivero, lhp	45/High
19.	Jefry Rodriguez, rhp	50/Extreme
20.	Rafael Bautista, of	45/High
21.	Spencer Kieboom, c	45/High
22.	Raudy Read, c	50/Extreme
23.	Matt Grace, lhp	40/Low
24.	Matt Skole, 1b	45/High
25.	Victor Robles, of	50/Extreme
26.	Drew Vettleson, of	45/High
27.	Hector Silvestre, lhp	45/High
28.	John Simms, rhp	40/High
29.	Robbie Dickey, rhp	45/Extreme
30.	Nick Lee, lhp	45/Extreme

LAST YEAR'S TOP 30

No.	Player, Pos.	Status
1.	Lucas Giolito, rhp	No. 1
2.	A.J. Cole, rhp	No. 6
3.	Brian Goodwin, of	No. 9
4.	Matt Skole, 1b/3b	No. 24
5.	Robbie Ray, lhp	(Diamondbacks)
6.	Sammy Solis, lhp	No. 15
7.	Michael Taylor, of	No. 2
8.	Jake Johansen, rhp	No. 17
9.	Nate Karns, rhp	(Rays)
10.	Steven Souza, of	No. 5
11.	Matt Purke, lhp	Dropped out
12.	Billy Burns, of	(Athletics)
13.	Tony Renda, 2b	No. 12
14.	Zach Walters, ss	Indians
15.	Austin Voth, rhp	No. 11
16.	Pedro Severino, c	No. 13
17.	Drew Ward, 3b	No. 8
18.	Aaron Barrett, rhp	Majors
19.	Jeff Kobernus, 2b/of	Dropped out
20.	Eury Perez, of	(Yankees)
21.	Jefry Rodriguez, rhp	No. 19
22.	Nick Pivetta, rhp	No. 10
23.	Blake Treinen, rhp	Majors
24.	Christian Garcia, rhp	Dropped out
25.	Brett Mooneyham, lhp	Dropped out
26.	Nick Lee, lhp	No. 30
27.	Robert Benincasa, rhp	Dropped out
28.	Rafael Bautista, of	No. 20
29.	Erik Davis, rhp	Dropped out
30.	Adrian Nieto, c	White Sox

BEST TOOLS

Best Hitter for Average	Steven Souza
Best Power Hitter	Steven Souza
Best Strike-Zone Discipline	Tony Renda
Fastest Baserunner	Rafael Bautista
Best Athlete	Michael Taylor
Best Fastball	Lucas Giolito
Best Curveball	Lucas Giolito
Best Slider	Erick Fedde
Best Changeup	Erik Davis
Best Control	Taylor Hill
Best Defensive Catcher	Pedro Severino
Best Defensive Infielder	Wilmer Difo
Best Infield Arm	Jason Martinson
Best Defensive Outfielder	Michael Taylor
Best Outfield Arm	Victor Robles

PROJECTED 2018 LINEUP

Catcher	Wilson Ramos
First Base	Ryan Zimmerman
Second Base	Tony Renda
Third Base	Anthony Rendon
Shortstop	Ian Desmond
Left Field	Steven Souza
Center Field	Michael Taylor
Right Field	Bryce Harper
No. 1 Starter	Stephen Strasburg
No. 2 Starter	Jordan Zimmermann
No. 3 Starter	Lucas Giolito
No. 4 Starter	Doug Fister
No. 5 Starter	Gio Gonzalez
Closer	Reynaldo Lopez

WASHINGTON NATIONALS

TOP 2015 ROOKIE: Steven Souza, of. After tearing up Triple-A, he has nothing more to prove in the minors, but he might be relegated to a fourth outfielder role in Washington.

BREAKOUT PROSPECT: Victor Robles, of. An electric, quick-twitch athlete with premium speed and arm strength, the 17-year-old could make a splash in his U.S. debut.

SLEEPER: Kelvin Gutierrez, 3b. He showed sure

SOURCE OF TOP 30 TALENT			
Homegrown	28	Acquired	2
College	10	Trades	2
Junior college	4	Rule 5 draft	0
High school	6	Independent leagues	0
Draft-and-follow	0	Free agents/waivers	0
Nondrafted free agents	0		
International	8		

hands and good arm strength in the Rookie-level Gulf Coast League, and his bat could come as he fills out his angular frame.

LF
Kevin Keyes
Estarlin Martinez
Oliver Ortiz

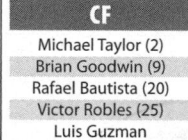

CF
Michael Taylor (2)
Brian Goodwin (9)
Rafael Bautista (20)
Victor Robles (25)
Luis Guzman

RF
Steven Souza (5)
Drew Vettleson (26)
Narciso Mesa
Brandon Miller

3B
Drew Ward (8)
Anderson Franco
Kelvin Gutierrez

SS
Wilmer Difo (7)
Jason Martinson
Stephen Perez
David Masters

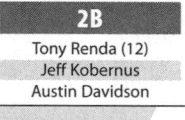

2B
Tony Renda (12)
Jeff Kobernus
Austin Davidson

1B
Matt Skole (24)
Shawn Pleffner
John Wooten
James Yezzo

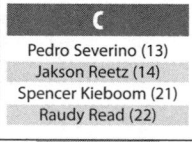

C
Pedro Severino (13)
Jakson Reetz (14)
Spencer Kieboom (21)
Raudy Read (22)

LHP

LHSP
Sammy Solis (15)
Felipe Rivero (18)
Hector Silvestre (27)
Matt Purke

LHRP
Matt Grace (23)
Nick Lee (30)
Kylin Turnbull
Brett Mooneyham

RHP

RHSP
Lucas Giolito (1)
Reynaldo Lopez (3)
Erick Fedde (4)
A.J. Cole (6)
Nick Pivetta (10)
Taylor Hill (16)
Jefry Rodriguez (19)
John Simms (28)
Robbie Dickey (29)
Wander Suero

RHRP
Jake Johansen (17)
Erik Davis
Drew Van Orden
Robert Benincasa
Derek Self
Weston Davis
Dakota Bacus
Domenick Mancini

BEST PURE HITTER: The Nationals' draft was pitcher-heavy and they didn't get a pure hitter. C Jakson Reetz (3) and OF Matt Page (10), who hit .381/.507/.700 at Oklahoma Baptist in the spring, are the best bets thanks to their professional approaches. Page missed time after signing with a hamstring injury.

BEST POWER HITTER: Unsigned 1B Austin Byler (9) was the power hitter in the class. OF Dale Carey (7), toolsier than the average senior sign, has above-average raw power and hit seven homers this spring after hitting four in his first three seasons combined, thanks to a taller setup in the box and simpler swing.

FASTEST RUNNER: Carey is an above-average runner underway, and a healthy Page is an average runner and fine baserunner. But speed was not a strength of the Nats' class.

BEST DEFENSIVE PLAYER: Reetz's glove is ahead of his bat, though both have a chance to be above-average. He has strength, soft hands and an above-average arm.

BEST FASTBALL: As usual, the Nationals emphasized velocity. RHP Erick Fedde (1) was pitching at 95-96 mph as late as the seventh inning in some starts. His combination of velocity, life and command earns 70 grades. RHP Robbie Dickey (4) can sit 94-96 and touch 97 but has to clean up his drop-and-drive delivery.

BEST SECONDARY PITCH: Fedde also pitched with a 70 slider at times this spring and flashes a plus changeup to go with it.

BEST PRO DEBUT: Reetz hit .274/.429/.368 in the Rookie-level Gulf Coast League and worked deep counts, with 26 walks and 30 strikeouts in 117 at-bats.

BEST ATHLETE: Fedde was an all-state soccer player and led Las Vegas High to a state soccer title before focusing on baseball. Carey also has above-average athleticism.

MOST INTRIGUING BACKGROUND: 1B Ryan Ripken (15) is the son of Hall of Famer Cal Ripken Jr. RHP D.J. Jauss (29) is the son of Dave Jauss, currently a coach on the Pirates' big league staff. Unsigned OF Elliott Cary (32) is the son of ex-big league pitcher Chuck Cary. RHP Kyle Simmons (24) has flashed 95 mph velocity despite pitching just $7^1/_3$ innings in four seasons at Division II Texas Lutheran.

CLOSEST TO THE MAJORS: Fedde still may move the fastest in the draft class, even after having Tommy John surgery in June.

BEST LATE-ROUND PICK: The Nats like RHPs Domenick Mancini (12), a low-slot reliever out of Miami-Dade JC, and Jim Borque (14), out of Michigan. Mancini has hit 96 mph with sink, while Borque has command issues but flashes plus pitches with his fastball and curve.

THE ONE WHO GOT AWAY: Washington thought Byler (out of Nevada) and Miami LHP Andrew Suarez (2) would sign for slot, but when they didn't, the Nats weren't able to bridge the gap. Suarez will be a redshirt junior at Miami, Byler a senior.

ASSESSMENT: The Nats have hit on injured players who fell to them (see Anthony Rendon, 2011, and Lucas Giolito, 2012), so they feel good about Fedde. Not signing Suarez and Byler hurts.

2013

Without a first-round pick, the Nats found some arms with upside in RHPs Jake Johansen (2), Nick Pivetta (4) and Austin Voth (5). 3B Drew Ward (3) is the class' best bat by a ways.

GRADE: C

2012

RHP Lucas Giolito (1) may be the minors' best pitching prospect. 2B Tony Renda (2) lacks upside but won the high Class A Carolina League batting title. C Spencer Kieboom (5) is an intriguing sleeper.

GRADE: B

2011

3B Anthony Rendon (1) has lived up to his billing as the top bat in a loaded draft class. RHP Alex Meyer (1) was traded for Denard Span. OF Brian Goodwin (1s) has an outside chance to emulate Span's career path.

GRADE: A

TOP DRAFT PICKS OF THE DECADE

Year	Player, Pos.	2014 Org
2005	Ryan Zimmerman, 3b	Nationals
2006	Chris Marrero, of	Orioles
2007	Ross Detwiler, lhp	Nationals
2008	*Aaron Crow, rhp	Royals
2009	Stephen Strasburg, rhp	Nationals
2010	Bryce Harper, of	Nationals
2011	Anthony Rendon, 3b	Nationals
2012	Lucas Giolito, rhp	Nationals
2013	Jake Johansen, rhp (2nd round)	Nationals
2014	Erick Fedde, rhp	Nationals

*Did not sign.

LARGEST BONUSES IN CLUB HISTORY

Stephen Strasburg, 2009	$7,500,000
Bryce Harper, 2010	$6,250,000
Anthony Rendon, 2011	$6,000,000
Brian Goodwin, 2011	$3,000,000
Ryan Zimmerman, 2006	$2,975,000

1 LUCAS GIOLITO, RHP

Born: July 14, 1994. **B-T:** R-R. **Ht.:** 6-6. **Wt.:** 255.
Drafted: HS—Studio City, Calif., 2012 (1st round).
Signed by: Mark Baca.

I n his full-season return from his Tommy John surgery in 2014, Giolito showed off the electrifying stuff and innate feel for pitching that had made him one of the most celebrated prep pitching prospects in recent memory heading into the spring of 2012. The son of Hollywood actors Lindsay Frost and Rick Giolito, Lucas slipped in the draft because of his elbow injury and his strong commitment to UCLA, and the Nationals took advantage by selecting him 16th overall and signing him for $2,925,000. That investment looks wise two years later, now that Giolito has established himself as one of baseball's best prospects. After pitching 37 innings in his return from surgery in 2013, he headed into 2014 healthy and confident, and he was consistent from the start of the season until the end. The Nationals had him skip a start here or there at low Class A Hagerstown and shut him down in mid-August in order to keep him around 100 innings, but they were thrilled with his developmental season.

Giolito's extra-large frame helps him generate steep downhill angle on his overpowering fastball, which ranges from 92-98 mph and sits comfortably in the mid-90s. He has touched 100 mph a handful of times over the last two years, and his fastball projects as a true 80 pitch on the 20-80 scale because of its velocity, its angle and his ability to locate it. Like any 20-year-old, Giolito has not mastered his fastball command, but he excels at throwing it for strikes, and his sound delivery and arm action suggest he should have at least average command of it, to go along with above-average control. He sometimes lands a bit stiff on his front leg, which can inhibit his ability to locate at the bottom of the zone, but his command improved as the season progressed. Giolito can throw all three of his pitches for strikes in any count, and he is learning how to set up hitters and put them away. His downer curveball can be devastating, a 12-to-6 hammer with uncommon power and sharp bite, and it should be a plus-plus pitch as he learns to repeat it more consistently. He dominated right-handers in 2014, holding them to a .175 average and .251 slugging percentage. The Nationals got Giolito to focus on developing his changeup in the second half of the 2014 season, and he gained great confidence in the pitch against lefthanded hitters.

BA GRADE

70 Risk: High

SCOUTING GRADES

Fastball: 80.
Curveball: 70.
changeup: 60.
Control: 60.

Based on 20-80 scouting scale and future projection rather than present grades.

LGE	BF	SO%	BB%	HR/9
SAL	386	28.5	7.3	0.64

ED WOLFSTEIN

It has good sinking action, and he can throw it for strikes or use it as a swing-and-miss pitch, making it another potential plus offering. Giolito also has a knack for holding baserunners and fields his position well for his size. The Nationals rave about his maturity, humility, competitiveness and diligent work habits.

With a rare combination of stuff, size, feel for pitching and makeup, Giolito has superstar potential. He'll still be just 20 years old at the start of 2015, so the Nationals won't rush him, but he should be ready to increase his workload at high Class A Potomac and could reach Double-A Harrisburg by the second half. Giolito is advanced enough to push for a big league job by 2016.

Year	Club (League)	Class	W	L	ERA	G	GS	CG	SV	IP	H	HR	BB	SO	K/9	WHIP	AVG
2012	Nationals (GCL)	R	0	0	4.50	1	1	0	0	2	2	0	0	1	4.5	1.00	.286
2013	Nationals (GCL)	R	1	1	2.78	8	8	0	0	23	19	0	10	25	9.9	1.28	.232
	Auburn (NYP)	SS	1	0	0.64	3	3	0	0	14	9	1	4	14	9.0	0.93	.191
2014	Hagerstown (SAL)	LoA	10	2	2.20	20	20	0	0	98	70	7	28	110	10.1	1.00	.197
Minor League Totals			12	3	2.17	32	32	0	0	137	100	8	42	150	9.9	1.04	.203

2 MICHAEL TAYLOR, OF

Born: March 26, 1991. **B-T:** R-R. **Ht.:** 6-3. **Wt.:** 210. **Drafted:** HS—Fort Lauderdale, 2009 (6th round). **Signed by:** Tony Arango.

Taylor has made steady progress since being drafted as a raw, athletic shortstop in 2009, first blossoming into an elite defensive center fielder and then emerging as formidable power/speed threat on offense. He posted his best offensive season in 2014, swatting 23 home runs, stealing 37 bases and ranking as the top prospect in the Double-A Eastern League before reaching the big leagues in August. The long-striding Taylor is a fluid, graceful runner with plus speed underway and plus-plus range in center field thanks to his superb instincts and quick first step. He also is a smart, efficient basestealer. Taylor's home run output spiked at Double-A Harrisburg in 2014 as he made substantial progress harnessing his plus power potential by creating more leverage in his swing. In the past, his swing often broke down on his front side, but he did a better job keeping his lower half in better position to allow him to track balls longer and keep his hands to work for him. His feel for hitting has improved, but his bat still projects as below-average and

BA GRADE

60 Risk: High

LGE	PA	BB%	SO%	ISO
EL	441	11.3	29.5	.227
IL	52	13.5	26.9	.182

strikeout-prone. Taylor can provide value even if he never hits for average, because his other tools are loud. He could become a solid everyday center fielder, and he has all-star potential if his bat takes another step forward. He figures to spend most of 2015 at Triple-A Syracuse.

Year	Club (League)	Class	AVG	G	AB	R	H	2B	3B	HR	RBI	BB	SO	SB	CS	OBP	SLG
2012	Potomac (CAR)	HiA	.242	109	384	51	93	33	2	3	37	40	113	19	9	.318	.362
2013	Potomac (CAR)	HiA	.263	133	509	79	134	41	6	10	87	55	131	51	7	.340	.426
2014	Harrisburg (EL)	AA	.313	98	384	74	120	17	2	22	61	50	130	34	8	.396	.539
	Syracuse (IL)	AAA	.227	12	44	7	10	3	1	1	3	7	14	3	1	.333	.409
	Washington (NL)	MAJ	.205	17	39	5	8	3	0	1	5	3	17	0	2	.279	.359
Major League Totals			.205	17	39	5	8	3	0	1	5	3	17	0	2	.279	.359
Minor League Totals			.261	521	1904	289	497	125	21	50	269	199	541	131	39	.335	.428

3 REYNALDO LOPEZ, RHP

Born: Jan. 4, 1994. **B-T:** R-R. **Ht.:** 6-0. **Wt.:** 185. **Signed:** Dominican Republic, 2012. **Signed by:** Virgilio De Leon.

The Nationals signed Lopez for just $17,000 in 2012, when his fastball ranged from 87-90 mph. That fall in instructional league, his velocity topped out at 94 mph, and then touched 96 the following spring. He missed nearly all of 2013 with a sore arm that was diagnosed as bone weakness. Lopez added good weight prior to the 2014 season and maintained his electric stuff into the South Atlantic League playoffs. He can overpower hitters with his top-of-the-scale fastball, which often sits at 96-99 mph early in games, and comfortably at 93-96 later in games. After struggling early in the season at low Class A Hagerstown, Lopez went down to short-season Auburn and made an adjustment to his front side, helping him create more leverage and downward angle with his fastball. It also helped his breaking ball go from a sweepy slurve to an 11-to-5 power curveball with depth. It remains a work in progress but flashes plus. His changeup and projects as an

BA GRADE

60 Risk: Extreme

LGE	BF	SO%	BB%	HR/9
NYP	138	22.5	10.9	0.00
SAL	174	22.4	6.3	0.19

average pitch as he learns to command it. Despite his 6-foot stature, Lopez's delivery and arm action have surprisingly little effort, helping him profile as a starter. Lopez has top-of-the-rotation upside if he can continue to refine his secondary stuff and stay healthy. He figures to begin 2015 at high Class A Potomac and could push for a big league job by 2016.

Year	Club (League)	Class	W	L	ERA	G	GS	CG	SV	IP	H	HR	BB	SO	K/9	WHIP	AVG
2012	Nationals (DSL)	R	1	1	3.38	5	0	0	1	11	12	1	5	9	7.6	1.59	.333
2013	Hagerstown (SAL)	LoA	0	0	6.75	1	1	0	0	4	8	1	1	4	9.0	2.25	.444
	Auburn (NYP)	SS	0	1	47.25	1	1	0	0	1	7	0	0	0	0.0	5.25	.700
2014	Auburn (NYP)	SS	3	2	0.75	7	7	0	0	36	15	0	15	31	7.8	0.83	.125
	Hagerstown (SAL)	LoA	4	1	1.33	9	9	0	0	47	27	1	11	39	7.4	0.80	.167
Minor League Totals			8	5	2.17	23	18	0	1	99	69	3	32	83	7.5	1.02	.199

4 ERICK FEDDE, RHP

BA GRADE

60 Risk: **Extreme**

LGE	BF	SO%	BB%	HR/9
Did not play				

Born: Feb. 25, 1993. **B-T:** R-R. **Ht.:** 6-4. **Wt.:** 180. **Drafted:** Nevada-Las Vegas, 2014 (1st round). **Signed by:** Mitch Sokol.

A 24th-round pick by the Padres after flashing 94 mph heat at Las Vegas High, Fedde went to Nevada-Las Vegas and spent three years in the rotation. He emerged as a likely first-rounder in 2013, but he got even better during his junior spring in 2014, when he went 8-2, 1.76 with 82 strikeouts in 77 innings before Tommy John surgery ended his season. He slipped to the Nationals at No. 18 overall and signed for $2,511,100. At his best, Fedde's fastball sat at 93-95 mph and bumped 98 in the middle innings, with angry sinking action that helped it rate as a double-plus pitch. His slider also drew some plus-plus grades at its best, when he threw it 85-88 mph with late two-plane tilt. His 83-84 mph changeup has flashed plus. His overall stuff wasn't that loud in every outing, playing down by as many as three ticks at times. Fedde has advanced command of his fastball for his age, and he is a groundball machine. He is an excellent athlete who fields his position well, though his lack of physicality raises questions about his durability. Fedde's recovery from Tommy John surgery is progressing according to schedule, and he probably will make his pro debut some time in 2015. The Nationals have nursed Stephen Strasburg, Jordan Zimmermann and Lucas Giolito through T.J. with brilliant results, so Fedde should jump on the fast track when he returns.

Year	Club (League)	Class	W	L	ERA	G	GS	CG	SV	IP	H	HR	BB	SO	K/9	WHIP	AVG
2014	Did not play—Injured																

5 STEVEN SOUZA, OF

BA GRADE

50 Risk: **Medium**

LGE	PA	BB%	SO%	ISO
L	407	12.8	18.4	.240
NL	26	11.5	26.9	.261

Born: April 24, 1989. **B-T:** R-R. **Ht.:** 6-4. **Wt.:** 225. **Drafted:** HS—Everett, Wash., 2007 (3rd round). **Signed by:** Doug McMillan.

Since the Nationals restarted Souza's career by sending him back to low Class A in 2012, he has matured, on and off the field. He followed up his 2013 breakout in Double-A by leading the Triple-A International League in hitting (.350), on-base percentage (.432) and slugging (.590), and he reached the big leagues in September. The physical, athletic Souza has multiple tools that rate better than average. His plus raw power plays in games because he excels at driving balls into the right-center field gap, and the Nationals would like to see him pull the ball with authority a bit more. Souza controls the strike zone fairly well, taking his share of walks and putting himself in good hitter's counts. He has a short swing and projects as at least a fringe-average hitter. He also has slightly above-average speed and is a smart baserunner who likes to steal bags. His speed translates to good range at either outfield corner, and his plus arm allows him to handle right field ably. Souza has nothing left to prove at Triple-A Syracuse, but he appears blocked for an everyday job in Washington, where Jayson Werth, Bryce Harper and Denard Span are entrenched in the outfield. He has a strong chance to be an everyday player given the chance.

Year	Club (League)	Class	AVG	G	AB	R	H	2B	3B	HR	RBI	BB	SO	SB	CS	OBP	SLG
2012	Hagerstown (SAL)	LoA	.290	70	262	48	76	20	2	17	72	22	49	7	7	.346	.576
	Potomac (CAR)	HiA	.319	27	91	16	29	2	1	6	13	13	25	7	1	.421	.560
2013	Nationals (GCL)	R	.200	4	10	3	2	1	0	0	2	3	4	2	0	.400	.300
	Harrisburg (EL)	AA	.300	77	273	54	82	23	1	15	44	41	76	20	6	.396	.557
2014	Hagerstown (SAL)	LoA	.500	1	2	0	1	0	0	0	1	0	1	1	0	.500	.500
	Potomac (CAR)	HiA	.111	3	9	0	1	0	0	0	1	0	4	1	0	.200	.111
	Syracuse (IL)	AAA	.350	96	346	62	121	25	2	18	75	52	75	26	7	.432	.590
	Washington (NL)	MAJ	.130	21	23	2	3	0	0	2	2	3	7	0	0	.231	.391
Major League Totals			.130	21	23	2	3	0	0	2	2	3	7	0	0	.231	.391
Minor League Totals			.260	722	2531	400	659	142	17	93	421	337	692	158	54	.354	.4406.

6 A.J. COLE, RHP

Born: Jan. 5, 1992. **B-T:** R-R. **Ht.:** 6-5. **Wt.:** 200. **Drafted:** HS—Oviedo, Fla., 2010 (4th round). **Signed by:** Paul Tinnell.

In his second season since being reacquired from the Athletics, Cole returned to Double-A Harrisburg and thrived. He spent the second half at Triple-A Syracuse and continued to hold his own, ranking as the No. 7 prospect in the International League. Cole's fastball was not quite as overpowering early in 2014 as it had been in the past, but he still pitched comfortably at 91-93 mph with decent life and bumped 96. He locates his heater well at the knees to both sides of the plate, and his sound mechanics and clean arm action give him a chance to have above-average control and solid command. Cole's second pitch remains his 83-85 mph changeup, which rates as solid-average to plus with good sinking action. Cole made progress getting more swing-throughs with his short, 81-84 mph slider in 2014, and it rates as solid-average at its best, though it can be fringy at other times. He also will occasionally steal a strike with his fringy curveball, but it is not a swing-and-miss offering. Cole figures to spend the spring in big league camp for the second straight year and open 2015 back in the rotation at Syracuse. He is a safe bet to be at least a No. 4 starter, and many scouts project him as a No. 3.

BA GRADE	
55	Risk: High

LGE	BF	SO%	BB%	HR/9
EL	308	19.8	4.9	0.13
IL	267	18.7	6.4	1.29

Year	Club (League)	Class	W	L	ERA	G	GS	CG	SV	IP	H	HR	BB	SO	K/9	WHIP	AVG
2012	Stockton (CAL)	HiA	0	7	7.82	8	8	0	0	38	60	7	10	31	7.3	1.84	.364
	Burlington (MWL)	LoA	6	3	2.07	19	19	0	0	96	78	7	19	102	9.6	1.01	.222
2013	Potomac (CAR)	HiA	6	3	4.25	18	18	0	0	97	96	12	23	102	9.4	1.22	.257
	Harrisburg (EL)	AA	4	2	2.18	7	7	0	0	45	31	3	10	49	9.7	0.90	.188
2014	Harrisburg (EL)	AA	6	3	2.92	14	14	1	0	71	79	1	15	61	7.7	1.32	.273
	Syracuse (IL)	AAA	7	0	3.43	11	11	0	0	63	69	9	17	50	7.1	1.37	.283
Minor League Totals			33	25	3.58	98	95	1	0	500	501	45	119	504	9.1	1.24	.2597.

7 WILMER DIFO, SS/2B

Born: April 2, 1992. **B-T:** B-R. **Ht.:** 6-0. **Wt.:** 175. **Signed:** Dominican Republic, 2011. **Signed by:** Modesto Ulloa.

Difo had shown flashes of potential during his first four years in pro ball, but his lack of maturity held him back. He struggled mightily to process failure, and the Nationals reset his career in 2013, sending him back to the Rookie-level Gulf Coast League to learn how to cope with the ups and downs of the game. He responded well and posted a breakout 2014 season in the low Class A South Atlantic League, winning league MVP honors. Difo has quality tools across the board. He is a plus runner who sometimes shows double-plus speed and is both aggressive and efficient as a basestealer. He has very good first-step quickness that translates to above-average range at either shortstop or second base, and his slightly above-average arm plays at either spot. A switch-hitter, Difo has a short, quick stroke and flashes average raw power from both sides, but he is stronger from the right side. He has a knack for making contact and is a good bunter, giving him a shot to be at least a solid-average hitter with fringy game power. Difo's game was ready for higher levels in 2014, but the Nationals wanted to gain confidence and earn some postseason hardware, so they left him at low Class A Hagerstown. They could push him in 2015, now that he's on the 40-man roster, with a likely assignment at high Class A Potomac and a chance to play his way to Double-A Harrisburg.

BA GRADE	
50	Risk: High

LGE	PA	BB%	SO%	ISO
SAL	610	6.1	10.7	.156

Year	Club (League)	Class	AVG	G	AB	R	H	2B	3B	HR	RBI	BB	SO	SB	CS	OBP	SLG
2012	Nationals (GCL)	R	.263	54	198	33	52	7	3	0	13	34	35	19	5	.374	.328
2013	Potomac (CAR)	HiA	.222	6	18	2	4	1	0	0	1	2	3	0	1	.300	.278
	Hagerstown (SAL)	LoA	.220	16	50	7	11	2	0	2	11	5	13	4	1	.286	.380
	Auburn (NYP)	SS	.217	33	120	15	26	3	4	1	6	10	17	3	2	.291	.333
	Nationals (GCL)	R	.211	6	19	6	4	1	0	1	3	4	3	2	0	.348	.421
2014	Hagerstown (SAL)	LoA	.315	136	559	91	176	31	7	14	90	37	65	49	9	.360	.470
Minor League Totals			.276	360	1345	213	371	55	26	19	150	145	191	120	33	.351	.398

8 DREW WARD, 3B

Born: Nov. 25, 1994. **B-T:** L-R. **Ht.:** 6-4. **Wt.:** 210. **Drafted:** HS—Leedey, Okla., 2013 (3rd round). **Signed by:** Ed Gustafson.

Ward is young for his level after he graduated high school a year early and successfully lobbied Major League Baseball to make him eligible for the 2013 draft. He held his own at low Class A Hagerstown as a 19-year-old in 2014, and the Nationals were pleased with the way he maintained a consistent approach. Ward's calling card is his lefthanded bat. He has good feel for his barrel and can spray hard line drives from the left-center field gap to the right-field line. He has a calm two-strike approach and recognizes pitches well enough that he should draw his share of walks, and he could develop into at least a solid-average hitter. Ward is learning to create more length and leverage in his swing to unlock his above-average raw power, which mostly plays to the pull side currently. He is still growing into his body, and his size-16 shoes suggest he could outgrow third base, but he made progress at the position in 2014. A well below-average runner, Ward's lateral mobility and footwork is just adequate currently, but his hands work and his solid-average arm is accurate. Ward has a chance to hit enough to become an everyday first baseman down the road, assuming he outgrows the hot corner as most evaluators expect. He'll advance to high Class A Potomac in 2015.

BA GRADE

50 Risk: High

LGE	PA	BB%	SO%	ISO
SAL	478	8.8	25.3	.144

Year	Club (League)	Class	AVG	G	AB	R	H	2B	3B	HR	RBI	BB	SO	SB	CS	OBP	SLG
2013	Nationals (GCL)	R	.292	49	168	24	49	13	0	1	28	25	44	2	4	.402	.387
2014	Hagerstown (SAL)	LoA	.269	115	431	45	116	26	3	10	73	42	121	2	2	.341	.413
Minor League Totals			.275	164	599	69	165	39	3	11	101	67	165	4	6	.359	.406

9 BRIAN GOODWIN, OF

Born: Nov. 2, 1990. **B-T:** L-R. **Ht.:** 6-0. **Wt.:** 200. **Drafted:** Miami Dade JC, 2011 (1st round supp). **Signed by:** Alex Morales.

Goodwin has yet to capitalize on the raw ability that prompted the Nationals to sign him for $3 million in 2011. They pushed him to Double-A Harrisburg by the second half of 2012, but he followed a lackluster 2013 with a horrific 2014 campaign at Triple-A Syracuse that ended on July 1 when he tore the labrum in his left shoulder sliding into second base. The Nationals believe Goodwin was just starting to make some progress before he got hurt, but scouts have been disappointed by his inability to make adjustments. He has bat speed and can turn on fastballs middle-in, but he cannot handle offspeed stuff or anything away from him. The Nationals have been trying for years to get him to stay in his legs and let his hands work for him, but he can't break the habit of pulling his lead shoulder and lunging. Goodwin has average power potential, but must become more aggressive in order to tap into it. His high walk rate is more befitting of a leadoff hitter, though. Goodwin remains a plus runner with plus defensive skills in center field and a solid-average arm. While the odds now seem remote, the Nats hope Goodwin is just a late bloomer like current center fielder Denard Span. His shoulder rehab was going well in the offseason, and the club added him to the 40-man roster in November. He faces a likely return to Syracuse in 2015, assuming he's ready to swing the bat.

BA GRADE

50 Risk: High

LGE	PA	BB%	SO%	ISO
IL	329	15.2	28.9	.109

Year	Club (League)	Class	AVG	G	AB	R	H	2B	3B	HR	RBI	BB	SO	SB	CS	OBP	SLG
2012	Hagerstown (SAL)	LoA	.324	58	216	47	70	18	1	9	38	43	39	15	4	.438	.542
	Harrisburg (EL)	AA	.223	42	166	17	37	8	1	5	14	18	50	3	3	.306	.373
2013	Harrisburg (EL)	AA	.252	122	457	82	115	19	11	10	40	66	121	19	11	.355	.407
2014	Syracuse (IL)	AAA	.219	81	274	31	60	10	4	4	32	50	95	6	4	.342	.328
Minor League Totals			.253	303	1113	177	282	55	17	28	124	177	305	43	22	.362	.409

10 NICK PIVETTA, RHP

DALE SWOPE

Born: Feb. 14, 1993. **B-T:** R-R. **Ht.:** 6-5. **Wt.:** 220. **Drafted:** New Mexico JC, 2013 (4th round). **Signed by:** Mitch Sokol.

A Canadian Junior National Team star in 2009 and 2010, Pivetta was fairly raw when he signed with the Nationals for $364,300 in 2013, but he made good progress in 2014 at low Class A Hagerstown. His velocity remained consistent all season, and he markedly improved his conditioning. Pivetta has a physical frame and a long, loose arm action that produces easy velocity. His fastball sits at 92-94 mph and bumps 96. It is effective when he repeats his delivery and pitches down in the zone with good angle, but he gets into trouble when he leaves the ball up. Likewise, the quality of his breaking ball depends upon whether he's staying over his lower half and controlling his delivery. At its best, his curveball is an above-average pitch with sharp 11-to-5 break and power, but at times he'll overthrow it. He also is developing feel for his changeup, which has good sinking action when he throws it with conviction—but he must learn to do so more consistently.

	BA GRADE	
	50	Risk: High

LGE	BF	SO%	BB%	HR/9
SAL	569	17.2	6.9	1.02

Pivetta's mechanics and command still need work, but he has upside as a potential mid-rotation starter if he can continue to progress. He figures to spend 2015 at high Class A Potomac.

Year	Club (League)	Class	W	L	ERA	G	GS	CG	SV	IP	H	HR	BB	SO	K/9	WHIP	AVG
2013	Nationals (GCL)	R	1	0	2.13	4	3	0	0	13	11	0	2	8	5.7	1.03	.234
	Auburn (NYP)	SS	0	1	3.38	5	5	0	0	21	19	1	11	17	7.2	1.41	.238
2014	Hagerstown (SAL)	LoA	13	8	4.22	26	25	0	0	132	142	15	39	98	6.7	1.37	.277
Minor League Totals			14	9	3.95	35	33	0	0	166	172	16	52	123	6.7	1.35	.269

11 AUSTIN VOTH, RHP

	BA GRADE	
	50	Risk: High

Born: June 26, 1992. **B-T:** R-R. **Ht.:** 6-1. **Wt.:** 190. **Drafted:** Washington, 2013 (5th round). **Signed by:** Fred Costello.

Voth dominated low Class A South Atlantic League hitters in the first half of 2014 to earn a promotion to high Class A Potomac, then carved up Carolina League hitters to earn a late July promotion to Double-A Harrisburg, where he struggled due in large part to fatigue. Voth stands out for his advanced command of his solid-average fastball, which sits at 88-92 mph in the early innings. He has a tendency to get stronger in the middle innings, flashing 94-95 mph heat, and his fastball has good deception and angle to both sides of the plate. His best secondary pitch is his changeup, which rates as solid-average. He has good feel for the pitch and sometimes cuts it a bit, causing it to look like a slider. His curveball remains inconsistent. He can throw it for strikes, but it is fringy and flashes solid-average. Voth lacks wipeout stuff, but his savvy and feel for pitching give him a chance to be a back-end starter. He should return to Double-A to start 2015 and could push for his first taste of the majors by the end of the season.

Year	Club (League)	Class	W	L	ERA	G	GS	CG	SV	IP	H	HR	BB	SO	K/9	WHIP	AVG
2013	Nationals (GCL)	R	0	0	0.00	2	2	0	0	5	4	0	0	4	7.2	0.80	.235
	Auburn (NYP)	SS	2	0	1.47	7	7	0	0	31	21	0	4	42	12.3	0.82	.193
	Hagerstown (SAL)	LoA	1	0	3.38	2	2	0	0	11	8	0	2	9	7.6	0.94	.195
2014	Hagerstown (SAL)	LoA	4	3	2.45	13	13	0	0	70	51	1	22	74	9.6	1.05	.206
	Potomac (CAR)	HiA	2	1	1.43	6	6	0	0	38	16	2	7	40	9.6	0.61	.126
	Harrisburg (EL)	AA	1	3	6.52	5	5	0	0	19	22	4	9	19	8.8	1.60	.286
Minor League Totals			10	7	2.50	35	35	0	0	173	122	7	44	188	9.8	0.96	.197

12 TONY RENDA, 2B

	BA GRADE	
	45	Risk: Medium

Born: Jan. 24, 1991. **B-T:** R-R. **Ht.:** 5-8. **Wt.:** 180. **Drafted:** California, 2012 (2nd round). **Signed by:** Fred Costello.

Renda's magnetic personality and dirtbag mentality make him exceptionally likable, and he has backed up his intangibles with performance. He won the high Class A Carolina League batting title at .307 in 2014 and helped lead Potomac to the league championship. The undersized Renda will never dazzle with his tools, but he does have a carrying tool in his bat, which has a chance to be above-average. He has a compact, line-drive stroke and uncommon hand-eye coordination. He excels at executing the hit-and-run and controlling the strike zone. He is tough to strike out, and he has a patient approach. Renda is strong enough to scorch liners from gap-to-gap but has well below-average home run power. He has fringe-average speed but is an instinctive, efficient basestealer. The Nationals were pleased with Renda's defensive progress, as he made strides with his footwork and his double-play pivot. He has average range at second base but is learning to take better angles. His hands work fine, and he projects as an average defender with an average arm. Renda will advance to Double-A Harrisburg in 2015, and his superb makeup and bat give him a shot to be an everyday second baseman.

Year	Club (League)	Class	AVG	G	AB	R	H	2B	3B	HR	RBI	BB	SO	SB	CS	OBP	SLG
2012	Auburn (NYP)	SS	.264	71	295	47	78	9	0	0	32	31	33	15	3	.341	.295
2013	Hagerstown (SAL)	LoA	.294	135	521	99	153	43	3	3	51	68	65	30	6	.380	.405
2014	Potomac (CAR)	HiA	.307	107	414	75	127	21	4	0	47	43	59	19	5	.381	.377
Minor League Totals			.291	313	1230	221	358	73	7	3	130	142	157	64	14	.371	.369

13 PEDRO SEVERINO, C

	BA GRADE
	50 Risk: High

Born: July 20, 1993. **B-T:** R-R. **Ht.:** 6-1. **Wt.:** 180. **Signed:** Dominican Republic, 2010. **Signed by:** Johnny DiPuglia/Moises de la Mota.

Severino struggled offensively for two and a half years, but his defensive prowess helped him move up the ladder. His bat started to come around in the second half of last season, when he .308/.379/.477 thanks to improved control of his lower half. He worked to improve his base and balance, allowing his quick hands to work and keeping his bat in the zone longer. He still hits fastballs better than breaking balls, but he has a chance to become a serviceable hitter with fringy power. Severino doesn't need to hit a ton to have value, because his defensive skills are elite. His accurate, double-plus arm sometimes produces sub-1.8-second pop times, and his transfer is smooth. A fringe-average runner, he is an excellent athlete who has lateral mobility and quickness, making him a standout blocker. He is also a good receiver with soft hands and advanced game-calling skills. Severino's defense figures to get him to the majors, and his bat will determine whether he's a quality backup or a regular. Some think he may have turned the corner at the plate, and he'll get a true test at Double-A Harrisburg in 2015.

Year	Club (League)	Class	AVG	G	AB	R	H	2B	3B	HR	RBI	BB	SO	SB	CS	OBP	SLG
2012	Nationals (GCL)	R	.220	38	109	9	24	3	1	0	8	9	9	0	0	.301	.266
2013	Hagerstown (SAL)	LoA	.241	84	282	28	68	19	2	1	45	13	54	1	0	.274	.333
2014	Potomac (CAR)	HiA	.247	94	291	41	72	15	1	9	36	21	57	2	0	.306	.399
Minor League Totals			.232	248	797	94	185	41	5	12	98	53	147	3	0	.288	.341

14 JAKSON REETZ, C

	BA GRADE
	50 Risk: Extreme

Born: Jan. 3, 1996. **B-T:** R-R. **Ht.:** 6-1. **Wt.:** 195. **Drafted:** HS—Firth, Neb., 2014 (3rd round). **Signed by:** Ed Gustafson.

A three-sport star during his prep days in Nebraska, Reetz batted .345/.459/.586 for USA Baseball's 18-and-under national team and was MVP of the Perfect Game All-American Classic in 2013. The Nationals signed him for $800,000 to lure him away from a commitment to Nebraska (where his father was a football linebacker). Reetz held his own in his pro debut, and he impressed the Nationals with his aptitude and feel for the game. He has a physical, athletic frame and soft hands behind the plate, where he quickly made adjustments with his setup, receiving and blocking. His transfer and release are sound, and his arm rates as solid-average. He needs polish, but he has the tools to become an above-average defender. Offensively, Reetz has a short righthanded stroke and a gap-to-gap approach, and he is selective for his age. He has the bat-to-ball instincts to become an average hitter, and the strength and leverage to grow into average power. He has played both outfield corners in the past, but he is a below-average runner. Reetz figures to start 2015 in extended spring training before heading to short-season Auburn.

Year	Club (League)	Class	AVG	G	AB	R	H	2B	3B	HR	RBI	BB	SO	SB	CS	OBP	SLG
2014	Nationals (GCL)	R	.274	43	117	20	32	6	1	1	15	26	30	6	3	.429	.368
Minor League Totals			.274	43	117	20	32	6	1	1	15	26	30	6	3	.429	.368

15 SAMMY SOLIS, LHP

	BA GRADE
	50 Risk: Extreme

Born: Aug. 10, 1988. **B-T:** R-L. **Ht.:** 6-5. **Wt.:** 250. **Drafted:** San Diego, 2010 (2nd round). **Signed by:** Tim Reynolds.

The Nationals continue to value Solis' ability and makeup, but he just cannot stay healthy. He battled back and leg injuries before missing all of 2012 and much of 2013 following Tommy John surgery. He had a strong showing in big league camp in 2014 and looked poised to make the Nationals' Opening Day roster, then tweaked his back at the end of spring training. After three rehab starts in mid-May, he strained his elbow and was out until late August. He was healthy heading into the offseason, and the Nationals hope a winter of rest will do him good. When healthy, Solis shows quality stuff, including an 89-93 mph fastball that bumps 95, a solid-average changeup and a slurvy breaking ball that flashes solid-average. He has No. 4 starter ability, but he needs to prove he can get through a full season, and he's now 26. Solis will be in big league spring training, but he's likely to open with an assignment to Triple-A Syracuse.

Year	Club (League)	Class	W	L	ERA	G	GS	CG	SV	IP	H	HR	BB	SO	K/9	WHIP	AVG
2012	Did not play—Injured																
2013	Nationals (GCL)	R	0	0	0.00	1	1	0	0	2	1	0	0	3	13.5	0.50	.167
	Potomac (CAR)	HiA	2	1	3.43	13	12	0	0	58	58	3	19	40	6.2	1.34	.270
2014	Hagerstown (SAL)	LoA	1	0	0.00	1	1	0	0	6	4	0	0	7	10.5	0.67	.190
	Potomac (CAR)	HiA	1	0	1.69	1	1	0	0	5	7	0	1	4	6.8	1.50	.292
	Harrisburg (EL)	AA	0	1	21.60	1	1	0	0	3	9	0	1	1	2.7	3.00	.500
	Nationals (GCL)	R	0	0	0.00	2	2	0	0	4	1	0	1	5	12.3	0.55	.083
Minor League Totals			12	5	3.32	38	37	0	0	179	182	11	45	156	7.9	1.27	.266

16 TAYLOR HILL, RHP

BA GRADE

45 Risk: Medium

Born: March 12, 1989. **B-T:** R-R. **Ht.:** 6-3. **Wt.:** 235. **Drafted:** Vanderbilt, 2011 (6th round). **Signed by:** Reed Dunn.

After spending two years in Vanderbilt's weekend rotation, Hill was drafted in 2011 as a senior and moved quickly through the Nationals system. He led the Triple-A International League in WHIP (1.12) and ranked second in ERA (2.81) in 2014 before making his major league debut in September. Hill lacks overpowering stuff, but he makes up for it with his advanced feel for pitching. He has plus control and solid-average command, and he keeps hitters off balance by throwing four pitches for strikes. His fastball sits at 90-92 mph with solid sink and occasionally bumps 94, and he pitches in with it exceptionally well. He can backdoor both of his breaking balls for called strikes. His solid-average slider is the better offering, but his curveball has become another useful pitch. He also has good feel for his average changeup. Hill is a dogged competitor who knows how to set up hitters and induce groundball outs. He fields his position and holds runners well. His upside is limited, but he has the stuff and savvy to pitch in the big leagues.

Year	Club (League)	Class	W	L	ERA	G	GS	CG	SV	IP	H	HR	BB	SO	K/9	WHIP	AVG
2012	Hagerstown (SAL)	LoA	10	6	4.92	24	20	0	0	124	144	12	31	60	4.3	1.41	.283
	Potomac (CAR)	HiA	1	1	4.80	3	3	1	0	15	17	2	3	11	6.6	1.33	.283
2013	Potomac (CAR)	HiA	6	2	2.99	15	14	2	0	84	73	6	11	54	5.8	1.00	.233
	Syracuse (IL)	AAA	1	0	4.22	2	2	0	0	11	18	0	2	9	7.6	1.88	.383
	Harrisburg (EL)	AA	2	7	2.71	11	11	0	0	70	67	7	16	41	5.3	1.19	.256
2014	Syracuse (IL)	AAA	11	7	2.81	25	24	4	1	144	136	15	25	86	5.4	1.12	.249
	Washington (NL)	MAJ	0	1	9.00	3	1	0	0	9	16	0	3	5	5.0	2.11	.410
Major League Totals			0	1	9.00	3	1	0	0	9	16	0	3	5	5.0	2.11	.410
Minor League Totals			31	25	3.49	89	79	7	1	479	487	43	91	288	5.4	1.21	.262

17 JAKE JOHANSEN, RHP

BA GRADE

50 Risk: Extreme

Born: Jan. 23, 1991. **B-T:** R-R. **Ht.:** 6-6. **Wt.:** 235. **Drafted:** Dallas Baptist, 2013 (2nd round). **Signed by:** Ed Gustafson.

Johansen followed up his dominant debut with an uneven year at low Class A Hagerstown, but he finished on a positive note after shifting to the bullpen and carried his progress over into instructional league. Big and physical, Johansen has serious arm strength. His fastball ranges from 92-99 mph in a starting role, sitting in the mid-90s with heavy life when it's down in the zone, though it is very hittable when he leaves it up. Because of the life on his heater, he often struggles to locate the pitch, and his command and control are both well below-average. His 89-91 mph cutter ranges from fringy to plus, and it generates swings and misses when he throws it right. His power curveball has good depth and rotation about once out of every four times he throws it. He has some feel for a changeup, and it showed progress late in the season, giving it a chance to be fringe-average. Most evaluators see Johansen's future in the bullpen, where he can overpower hitters in short stints without fine command. He could make a permanent transition to a relief role as soon as 2015, when he figures to advance to high Class A Potomac.

Year	Club (League)	Class	W	L	ERA	G	GS	CG	SV	IP	H	HR	BB	SO	K/9	WHIP	AVG
2013	Auburn (NYP)	SS	1	1	1.06	10	10	0	0	42	22	1	18	44	9.4	0.94	.147
	Hagerstown (SAL)	LoA	0	2	5.79	2	2	0	0	9	13	1	5	7	6.8	1.93	.317
2014	Hagerstown (SAL)	LoA	5	6	5.19	29	18	0	0	101	120	3	55	89	8.0	1.74	.302
Minor League Totals			6	9	4.08	41	30	0	0	152	155	5	78	140	8.3	1.53	.263

18 FELIPE RIVERO, LHP

BA GRADE

45 Risk: High

Born: July 5, 1991. **B-T:** L-L. **Ht.:** 6-2. **Wt.:** 195. **Signed:** Venezuela, 2008. **Signed by:** Ronnie Blanco (Rays).

Tampa Bay traded Rivero, along with Jose Lobaton and Drew Vettleson, to the Nationals for Nate Karns in February 2014. His first season in the organization was marred by injury, as he missed seven weeks in the middle of the summer with an elbow strain, but he bounced back in the Arizona Fall League, where he focused on staying closed in his delivery and improving his alignment. Rivero has a loose, quick arm, but his body awareness is still evolving, and he needs to repeat his mechanics in order to improve his command. His best pitch is a lively fastball that sits at 90-94 mph and touches 97. His breaking ball is a power slurve that is too often below-average. His remedial changeup has a tendency to get too hard, and improving it will be a point of emphasis. Rivero's command and mechanical inconsistency will likely push him to the bullpen, but his power stuff from the left side still makes him intriguing, and the Nationals aren't giving up on his chances to start. He figures to get a shot in Triple-A at some point in 2015.

Year	Club (League)	Class	W	L	ERA	G	GS	CG	SV	IP	H	HR	BB	SO	K/9	WHIP	AVG
2012	Bowling Green (MWL)	LoA	8	8	3.41	27	21	0	0	113	115	5	29	98	7.8	1.27	.266
2013	Charlotte (FSL)	HiA	9	7	3.40	25	23	2	0	127	122	7	52	91	6.4	1.37	.257
2014	Nationals (GCL)	R	0	0	0.00	3	3	0	0	6	4	0	1	6	9.0	0.83	.190
	Hagerstown (SAL)	LoA	0	0	0.00	1	1	0	0	4	3	0	0	6	13.5	0.75	.200
	Harrisburg (EL)	AA	2	7	4.12	10	10	0	0	44	45	4	18	38	7.8	1.44	.260
Minor League Totals			31	32	3.44	110	79	2	3	440	437	24	135	365	7.5	1.30	.260

19 JEFRY RODRIGUEZ, RHP

BA GRADE

50 Risk: Extreme

Born: July 26, 1993. **B-T:** R-R. **Ht.:** 6-5. **Wt.:** 185. **Signed:** Dominican Republic, 2012. **Signed by:** Johnny DiPuglia/Moises de la Mota.

A former infielder who converted to pitcher after signing with the Nationals, Rodriguez had his 2014 campaign cut short on July 1 when a comebacker hit him in his left (non-throwing) wrist, causing a hairline fracture. He returned to action in the fall and looked good in instructional league. Rodriguez is still growing into his 6-foot-5 frame, and his broad shoulders suggest he'll get stronger. He already shows premium velocity, pitching at 93-95 mph and touching 98. He'll need to learn to control his lower half better to maximize his stuff and his command. He has what the Nats call "area control," but his command has a long way to go. He flashes a bona fide plus curveball with good power, but it remains inconsistent. His changeup is in its early stages of development, but he has some feel for it. Rodriguez has tantalizing upside, and the Nats hope he is on the verge of making a leap forward, as Reynaldo Lopez did in 2014, but he comes with plenty of risk. He should return to low Class A Hagerstown in 2015.

Year	Club (League)	Class	W	L	ERA	G	GS	CG	SV	IP	H	HR	BB	SO	K/9	WHIP	AVG
2012	Nationals (DSL)	R	0	2	2.93	10	9	0	0	43	28	2	33	35	7.3	1.42	.185
2013	Nationals (GCL)	R	3	0	2.45	12	12	0	0	48	40	1	20	43	8.1	1.26	.229
2014	Hagerstown (SAL)	LoA	0	2	6.88	4	4	0	0	17	27	0	5	11	5.8	1.88	.380
	Auburn (NYP)	SS	1	0	2.76	3	3	0	0	16	16	0	4	9	5.0	1.22	.267
Minor League Totals			4	4	3.27	29	28	0	0	124	111	3	62	98	7.1	1.40	.243

20 RAFAEL BAUTISTA, OF

BA GRADE

45 Risk: High

Born: March 8, 1993. **B-T:** R-R. **Ht.:** 6-2. **Wt.:** 165. **Signed:** Dominican Republic, 2012. **Signed by:** Paul Tinnell.

Bautista led the low Class A South Atlantic League and ranked second in the minors with 69 stolen bases last season. His best tool is his well above-average speed, and he is an instinctive baserunner who gets good leads and reads. His speed also translates to center field, where he is an above-average defender with a solid-average arm. He hit at the bottom of the lineup in 2014, but he spent the second half in the leadoff spot and continued to thrive. Bautista is a slasher with good bat-to-ball instincts, and though his power is well below-average, he is wiry enough to drive the gaps for extra-base hits. He'll need to become more patient to realize his potential as a table-setter. He shows good aptitude, and he works hard to implement suggested adjustments. Bautista will advance to high Class A Potomac in 2015, and he has an outside shot to become a starting big league center fielder, though he profiles better as a speed merchant off the bench.

Year	Club (League)	Class	AVG	G	AB	R	H	2B	3B	HR	RBI	BB	SO	SB	CS	OBP	SLG
2012	Nationals (DSL)	R	.329	67	210	38	69	8	3	0	25	27	39	47	7	.419	.395
2013	Nationals (GCL)	R	.322	52	202	44	65	7	2	1	27	18	34	26	7	.400	.391
2014	Hagerstown (SAL)	LoA	.290	134	487	97	141	20	5	5	54	33	72	69	15	.341	.382
Minor League Totals			.306	253	899	179	275	35	10	6	106	78	145	142	29	.374	.387

21 SPENCER KIEBOOM, C

BA GRADE

45 Risk: High

Born: March 16, 1991. **B-T:** R-R. **Ht.:** 6-0. **Wt.:** 220. **Drafted:** Clemson, 2012 (5th round). **Signed by:** Paul Faulk.

Kieboom missed nearly all of 2013 after having Tommy John surgery, but his return to action in 2014 was a major success. A natural leader and outstanding game manager, he was Lucas Giolito's roommate for the past two years, and the Nationals say he was a positive influence on the younger righthander. Kieboom is a good receiver and blocker, with an average arm that plays up because of its accuracy. Offensively, he has an open stride and his bat stays in the zone for a long time, and he excels at driving balls to the right-center field gap. He has improved his leverage, giving him below-average to fringy power potential. Kieboom probably lacks the offensive upside to become an everyday catcher, but his defense and makeup could make him a valuable big league backup in the David Ross mold. He'll advance to Potomac in 2015.

Year	Club (League)	Class	AVG	G	AB	R	H	2B	3B	HR	RBI	BB	SO	SB	CS	OBP	SLG
2012	Auburn (NYP)	SS	.258	41	128	13	33	6	0	0	20	19	24	0	0	.362	.305
2013	Nationals (GCL)	R	.333	4	6	0	2	0	0	0	1	2	1	0	0	.500	.333
2014	Hagerstown (SAL)	LoA	.309	87	330	50	102	28	4	9	61	21	67	2	2	.352	.500
Minor League Totals			.295	132	464	63	137	34	4	9	82	42	92	2	2	.357	.444

22 RAUDY READ, C

BA GRADE

50 Risk: Extreme

Born: Oct. 29, 1993. **B-T:** R-R. **Ht.:** 6-0. **Wt.:** 170. **Signed:** Dominican Republic, 2011. **Signed by:** Moises de la Mota.

Read took a major step forward in 2014, putting together the best offensive and defensive season of his young career. He wore down a bit late in the season, causing his production to tail off, but he impressed enough to rank as the No. 13 prospect in the New York-Penn League. Read flashes above-average raw power and is learning to make use of his pop in games. He has good pitch recognition and can handle breaking balls in addition to velocity. The key to his development will be whether he takes ownership at the catcher position. He has soft hands and an above-average arm that helped him throw out 47 percent of basestealers in 2014, but he has a lot of work to do cleaning up his receiving, blocking and footwork. His pitch-calling and game management also have a long way to go. Read's bat could get him to the big leagues, but he'll need to improve behind the plate to become a regular.

Year	Club (League)	Class	AVG	G	AB	R	H	2B	3B	HR	RBI	BB	SO	SB	CS	OBP	SLG
2012	Nationals (DSL)	R	.251	62	227	33	57	16	0	9	47	18	33	3	3	.324	.441
2013	Nationals (GCL)	R	.252	40	147	9	37	5	0	2	17	6	17	2	6	.287	.327
2014	Auburn (NYP)	SS	.281	57	210	27	59	20	0	6	35	14	37	0	3	.332	.462
Minor League Totals			.242	201	724	82	175	46	1	21	121	42	107	6	13	.295	.395

23 MATT GRACE, LHP

BA GRADE

40 Risk: Low

Born: Dec. 14, 1988. **B-T:** L-L. **Ht.:** 6-3. **Wt.:** 190. **Drafted:** UCLA, 2010 (8th round). **Signed by:** Craig Kornfeld.

Grace spent most of his college career as a reliever, and after the trying him as a starter for three seasons the Nationals realized that's the role he is suited for. He dominated Double-A and Triple-A hitters last season to earn a spot on the 40-man roster. Grace's calling card is his sinker, which ranges from 88-93 mph and plays up because of its excellent life down in the zone, generating loads of groundballs. Because of his ability to locate it to either side, he could be more than just a situational reliever—though he is dominant against lefties. His No. 2 pitch is a slider that ranges from fringe-average to solid-average, and he also commands that pitch well. He also mixes in an occasional changeup against righties. Grace's ceiling is modest, but he should compete for a big league job in 2015.

Year	Club (League)	Class	W	L	ERA	G	GS	CG	SV	IP	H	HR	BB	SO	K/9	WHIP	AVG
2012	Potomac (CAR)	HiA	9	12	4.84	26	24	2	0	141	178	10	48	83	5.3	1.60	.310
2013	Potomac (CAR)	HiA	3	0	3.18	14	0	0	0	28	26	0	7	24	7.6	1.16	.245
	Harrisburg (EL)	AA	6	3	3.79	28	0	0	1	38	42	2	7	31	7.3	1.29	.284
2014	Harrisburg (EL)	AA	3	1	1.02	22	0	0	3	35	32	0	12	32	8.2	1.25	.229
	Syracuse (IL)	AAA	2	0	1.30	28	0	0	0	42	28	1	13	30	6.5	0.98	.194
Minor League Totals			36	25	4.20	154	56	2	4	444	506	22	131	303	6.1	1.44	.288

24 MATT SKOLE, 1B

BA GRADE

45 Risk: High

Born: July 30, 1989. **B-T:** L-R. **Ht.:** 6-3. **Wt.:** 225. **Drafted:** Georgia Tech, 2011 (5th round). **Signed by:** Eric Robinson.

After an injury-wracked 2013 season, Skole struggled with his swing mechanics last year. He has a lot of moving parts in his swing, and the Nationals are still trying to get him to tone down his big leg kick and exaggerated, pre-pitch bat waggle. He has a long uppercut swing, a physical frame and plus raw power to the pull side, but scouts question his ability to catch up to good fastballs, and he chases high heat too often. He takes his share of walks, but he also strikes out a lot, and he projects as a below-average hitter. A third baseman for his first two pro seasons, Skole played mostly first base in 2014, though he was a serviceable fill-in at the hot corner, where he lacks range but has a solid arm. He must unlock his power potential to have a shot at an everyday role. The Nationals could challenge Skole with an assignment to Triple-A Syracuse in 2015, which will be a crucial year for his development.

Year	Club (League)	Class	AVG	G	AB	R	H	2B	3B	HR	RBI	BB	SO	SB	CS	OBP	SLG
2012	Hagerstown (SAL)	LoA	.286	101	343	73	98	18	0	27	92	94	116	10	0	.438	.574
	Potomac (CAR)	HiA	.314	18	70	11	22	10	1	0	12	5	17	1	0	.355	.486
2013	Harrisburg (EL)	AA	.200	2	5	1	1	1	0	0	2	2	2	0	0	.429	.400
2014	Harrisburg (EL)	AA	.241	132	461	58	111	29	1	14	68	78	127	3	1	.352	.399
Minor League Totals			.270	325	1151	186	311	81	3	46	222	221	314	16	2	.387	.466

25 VICTOR ROBLES, OF

Born: May 19, 1997. **B-T:** R-R. **Ht.:** 6-0. **Wt.:** 185. **Signed:** Dominican Republic, 2013. **Signed by:** Carlos Ulloa.

The Nationals signed Robles for $225,000 in 2013, and he hit for average and showed basestealing ability in an impressive Dominican Summer League debut. A live-bodied, quick-twitch athlete with a high baseball IQ, Robles plays with energy and is learning to play under control. His raw tools are tantalizing, as he is a plus-plus runner with plus-plus arm strength and good instincts in center field. His pitch recognition and approach are advanced for his age. He has experimented with switch-hitting in the past, but for now he's a righthanded hitter with good bat speed. Robles could grow into some pop has he matures, but he has a tendency to overswing at times. Robles is very young and needs plenty of refinement, but his upside is significant. He figures to advance to the Rookie-level Gulf Coast League in 2015.

Year	Club (League)	Class	AVG	G	AB	R	H	2B	3B	HR	RBI	BB	SO	SB	CS	OBP	SLG
2014	Nationals (DSL)	R	.313	47	182	46	57	14	4	3	25	16	26	22	9	.408	.484
Minor League Totals			.313	47	182	46	57	14	4	3	25	16	26	22	9	.408	.484

26 DREW VETTLESON, OF

Born: July 19, 1991. **B-T:** L-R. **Ht.:** 6-1. **Wt.:** 185. **Drafted:** HS— Silverdale, Wash., 2010 (1st round supplemental). **Signed by:** Paul Kirsch (Rays).

Vettleson has flashed the raw ability that made him a supplemental first-round pick out of high school, where he earned publicity for being a switch-pitcher, but the Rays traded him to the Nationals along with Jose Lobaton and Felipe Rivero for Nate Karns in February 2014. After hitting home runs in both ends of an April 12 doubleheader, Vettleson was hit on the back of his left hand by a pitch, breaking a bone and sidelining him for two months. He still intrigued the Nationals for his natural feel for hitting. He can drive the ball to all fields, but he must become a more selective hitter. His body is maturing, and he could hit for average or slightly better power. He also has a well above-average arm with good accuracy and carry, giving him a chance to be a true right fielder. He has decent range but still is developing as an outfielder, where he makes his share of mistakes. Vettleson should return to Double-A Harrisburg in 2015.

Year	Club (League)	Class	AVG	G	AB	R	H	2B	3B	HR	RBI	BB	SO	SB	CS	OBP	SLG
2012	Bowling Green (MWL)	LoA	.275	132	505	80	139	24	5	15	69	51	117	20	11	.340	.432
2013	Charlotte (FSL)	HiA	.274	121	467	50	128	29	6	4	62	40	78	5	7	.331	.388
2014	Auburn (NYP)	SS	.318	8	22	3	7	1	1	0	2	3	5	1	0	.423	.455
	Harrisburg (EL)	AA	.246	75	248	24	61	14	3	8	28	11	75	3	3	.275	.423
Minor League Totals			.272	397	1476	190	401	81	19	34	201	132	328	49	27	.331	.421

27 HECTOR SILVESTRE, LHP

Born: Dec. 14, 1992. **B-T:** L-L. **Ht.:** 6-3. **Wt.:** 180. **Signed:** Dominican Republic, 2011. **Signed by:** Pablo Arias.

Lean and wiry, Silvestre is still maturing physically, but his arm action is long and loose. His low-90s fastball regularly touches 94 mph, and he isn't afraid to challenge hitters. His No. 2 pitch is a changeup with good sink that projects as an average pitch. His breaking ball remains a work in progress because he's still learning how to spin it consistently. The Nats expect the pitch to morph into a power slurve or a slider as he develops. Silvestre is a relentless strike-thrower, but he lacks a true out pitch. His arm strength and control give him a shot to become a back-end starter if he can improve his breaking ball. He'll likely return to Potomac in 2015 and could push for a promotion to Double-A Harrisburg by midseason.

Year	Club (League)	Class	W	L	ERA	G	GS	CG	SV	IP	H	HR	BB	SO	K/9	WHIP	AVG
2012	Nationals (DSL)	R	5	3	3.20	15	13	0	0	76	67	3	24	69	8.2	1.20	.241
2013	Potomac (CAR)	HiA	0	1	2.45	1	1	0	0	4	2	1	4	1	2.5	1.64	.154
	Nationals (GCL)	R	7	0	1.82	13	8	0	0	49	33	1	8	40	7.3	0.83	.190
2014	Hagerstown (SAL)	LoA	6	7	4.14	18	18	0	0	91	91	10	21	49	4.8	1.23	.259
	Potomac (CAR)	HiA	1	2	4.45	6	6	0	0	28	32	6	3	21	6.7	1.24	.283
Minor League Totals			22	14	3.18	65	53	0	0	295	257	22	83	216	6.6	1.15	.235

28 JOHN SIMMS, RHP

Born: Jan. 17, 1992. **B-T:** R-R. **Ht.:** 6-3. **Wt.:** 205. **Drafted:** Rice, 2013
(11th round). **Signed by:** Tyler Wilt.

BA GRADE
40 Risk: High

Simms split time between the rotation and the bullpen in a strong career at Rice, but his stuff went backward even as he carved up college hitters. Viewed as a potential first-round candidate after his strong freshman summer in the Cape Cod League, Simms eventually signed for $100,000 as an 11th-round pick after his junior year in 2013. He jumped to Double-A Harrisburg by the end of his first full pro season in 2014, though he tired down the stretch. Simms' best asset is his good command of his average fastball, which ranges from 88-92 mph with some sink and deception. He spots his fastball and his curveball to both sides of the plate, and the Nationals think the curve has a chance to be above-average, because it is an out pitch when he has his best feel for it. His changeup remains below-average but is improving and could wind up as a fringy pitch. Simms holds runners and fields his position well, and he is a fierce competitor. He profiles as back-end starter or a middle reliever, and his stuff has played up in the bullpen in the past. He'll likely return to Harrisburg to start 2015 but could reach Triple-A Syracuse by midseason.

Year	Club (League)	Class	W	L	ERA	G	GS	CG	SV	IP	H	HR	BB	SO	K/9	WHIP	AVG
2013	Nationals (GCL)	R	0	1	4.50	1	0	0	0	2	2	0	0	3	13.5	1.00	.250
	Auburn (NYP)	SS	0	3	5.79	11	2	0	1	28	41	0	7	31	10.0	1.71	.336
2014	Hagerstown (SAL)	LoA	0	0	0.98	5	0	0	3	18	13	0	2	20	9.8	0.82	.194
	Potomac (CAR)	HiA	2	4	4.36	10	10	0	0	54	50	2	16	49	8.2	1.23	.253
	Harrisburg (EL)	AA	2	6	5.03	11	11	1	0	59	73	6	15	42	6.4	1.49	.308
Minor League Totals			4	14	4.47	38	23	1	4	161	179	8	40	145	8.1	1.36	.283

29 ROBBIE DICKEY, RHP

Born: April 6, 1994. **B-T:** R-R. **Ht.:** 6-3. **Wt.:** 205. **Drafted:** Blinn (Texas)
JC, 2014 (4th round). **Signed by:** Tyler Wilt.

BA GRADE
45 Risk: Extreme

Dickey struck out 100 batters in 85 innings for Blinn (Texas) JC in 2014, and the Nationals signed him for $400,000 as a fourth-round pick. His stuff was live in the spring, as his fastball sat at 92 mph and often reached 94-96. But fatigue took a toll on him in his pro debut, when his fastball topped out at 92 and his breaking ball was inconsistent. At his best, Dickey flashed a plus curveball with power and depth, though it remains inconsistent. He also has feel for a changeup. He has a drop-and-drive delivery that causes his plane to flatten out a bit and his fastball to stay up in the zone, so the Nationals plan to work with him on staying taller and over the rubber. Dickey has a physical, durable frame and earns plaudits for his work ethic. He has a shot to become a back-end starter if everything comes together for him. He'll likely open 2015 at low Class A Hagerstown, where he made two starts in 2014.

Year	Club (League)	Class	W	L	ERA	G	GS	CG	SV	IP	H	HR	BB	SO	K/9	WHIP	AVG
2014	Nationals (GCL)	R	0	2	12.71	3	2	0	0	6	11	0	3	5	7.9	2.47	.407
	Auburn (NYP)	SS	0	2	2.25	5	5	0	0	20	18	0	3	13	5.9	1.05	.231
	Hagerstown (SAL)	LoA	1	0	3.00	2	2	0	0	9	10	0	5	5	5.0	1.67	.270
Minor League Totals			1	4	4.15	10	9	0	0	35	39	0	11	23	6.0	1.44	.275

30 NICK LEE, LHP

Born: Jan. 13, 1991. **B-T:** L-L. **Ht.:** 5-11. **Wt.:** 185. **Drafted:** Weatherford
(Texas) JC, 2011 (18th round). **Signed by:** Ed Gustafson.

BA GRADE
45 Risk: Extreme

Lee showed electric stuff in 2013, and continued to do so when he was healthy in 2014, but he was limited to 31 innings by an elbow strain, and his poor command got him in trouble. His inability to repeat his delivery inhibits his control, and he has averaged 4.5 walks per nine innings over the course of his pro career. He spent two years as a starter, but he spent most of 2014 in a relief role, which is where he profiles. He is strong and athletic, and his fast arm produces heat that ranges from 90-96 mph. His hammer breaking ball is a true plus pitch with power and depth at its best, and his low-80s slider has a chance to be solid-average. Lee has the ingredients to become a useful lefthanded reliever, but he has plenty of work to do. He figures to get another crack at Potomac in 2015, and if he takes to the bullpen role and stays healthy he could force his way to Double-A Harrisburg by the end of the year.

Year	Club (League)	Class	W	L	ERA	G	GS	CG	SV	IP	H	HR	BB	SO	K/9	WHIP	AVG
2012	Auburn (NYP)	SS	3	1	3.77	13	11	0	0	62	63	2	21	62	9.0	1.35	.267
2013	Hagerstown (SAL)	LoA	6	4	3.96	19	17	0	0	91	83	7	43	102	10.1	1.38	.249
2014	Potomac (CAR)	HiA	0	2	10.05	5	4	0	0	14	17	0	8	23	14.4	1.74	.283
	Nationals (GCL)	R	1	0	6.75	5	0	0	0	8	9	4	4	6	6.8	1.63	.290
	Hagerstown (SAL)	LoA	1	0	7.56	5	0	0	0	8	11	1	9	6	6.5	2.40	.314
Minor League Totals			12	7	4.61	57	32	0	0	197	199	15	100	214	9.8	1.52	.266

Baseball America national writer Ben Badler reports on international players who were free agents as the Prospect Handbook went to press but were expected to sign with major league teams for the 2015 season.

YOAN MONCADA, 2B/3B

BA GRADE

70 Risk: High

Born: May 27, 1995. **B-T:** B-R. **Ht.:** 6-0. **Wt.:** 200.

For years, teams have eagerly awaited the arrival of Moncada, the best young player to leave Cuba since Cubs outfielder Jorge Soler. Moncada first caught scouts' attention at the COPABE Pan American 16-and-under World Championship in Mexico in 2010. Moncada was 15, but he already stood out, earning tournament all-star honors at third base. Three years later in Taiwan, Moncada impressed again at the 18-and-under World Championship, and in between he dominated Cuba's youth national leagues at a level on par with what Soler and Yasiel Puig did as teenagers. Moncada is an explosive athlete with a strong track record of hitting everywhere he goes, though he hasn't been tested against much high-caliber pitching. He has premium bat speed and plus raw power, though his swing is easier and more fluid from the left side, and he's at least a plus runner. Moncada has some experience at shortstop, though scouts say he looks uncomfortable at the position. He has mostly played second and third base, which are the positions he fits best at in the majors, with good range at both spots and an arm that earns plus to plus-plus grades. He's also played occasionally in center field, where he has the speed to play. His bat projects as elite at any position, making him a potential franchise player. Once he signs, Moncada should begin his career in the minors, likely in high Class A.

HECTOR OLIVERA, 2B

BA GRADE

60 Risk: High

Born: April 5, 1985. **B-T:** R-R. **Ht.:** 6-2. **Wt.:** 195.

Olivera was a star on the Cuban national team with appearances in the 2008 Olympics, 2009 World Baseball Classic and 2010 Intercontinental Cup, where he won the MVP award. During his early-to-mid 20s from 2008-2012, Olivera was one of the best players in Cuba's Serie Nacional, but a medical condition reported in the Cuban press as thrombosis in his left biceps sidelined Olivera for the entire 2012-13 season in Cuba and kept him out of international tournaments during that time. He returned for the 2013-14 season and was still one of the top performers in Serie Nacional, then defected in September. While scouts haven't seen Olivera recently, at his peak he impressed scouts with his athleticism and well-rounded skill set. He has a loose, quick swing and a good hitting approach, consistently walking more than he struck out in Cuba. Scouts are split on his raw power, but he has a chance to hit 20 home runs. He was a plus runner in his prime with a solid arm capable of handling second or third base, though in 2013-14 he spent just 23 games of the 90-game season at second base, with the rest at DH. Given Olivera's medical history and lack of recent looks from scouts, there's a lot of uncertainty around him, but at 30 he should go straight into a major league lineup, with a chance to be an impact player if he's the same guy he was a few years ago.

ANDY IBANEZ, 2B

BA GRADE

55 Risk: High

Born: April 3, 1993. **B-T:** R-R. **Ht.:** 5-9. **Wt.:** 183.

Ibanez has been on the radar for major league scouts for several years, going back to his days representing Cuba at the 16U World Championship in Taiwan in 2009 and the 18U World Championship in Canada the following year. In 2013, Ibanez was the youngest player on Cuba's World Baseball Classic roster, though he played sparingly. He got more action that summer at the World Port Tournament in the Netherlands, where he went 9-for-15 (all singles) including a 3-for-5 showing in Cuba's victory in the title game. Ibanez was one of Cuba's top young players, though he hadn't yet had a breakout season in Serie Nacional, where he played for Isla De La Juventud. Ibanez doesn't have one electric tool or star upside, but he's a smart, fundamentally sound player who's steady across the board. He's a good hitter for his age, showing solid bat-to-ball skills with occasional power, though he's mostly a doubles threat who works the gaps. He's not a burner on the basepaths, but his athleticism and agility are evident in the field at second base, where he won Cuba's equivalent to a gold glove during his rookie season in 2011-12. He's played occasionally at third base, but his arm is a better fit at second. Once Ibanez signs, he will likely start his career at a high Class A or Double-A affiliate.

ROBERTO BALDOQUIN, SS

Born: May 14, 1994. **B-T:** R-R. **Ht.:** 5-11. **Wt.:** 186.

Baldoquin played shortstop for Cuba at the 16-and-under World Championship in Mexico in 2010, though he left Cuba before he ever had a chance to have an impact or play regularly for his Las Tunas team in Serie Nacional. Baldoquin impressed scouts with his excellent body control, sound footwork and smooth hands in the field. His body is strong and well-proportioned, but he doesn't have the prototypical lean, athletic shortstop's build. He's an average runner who should start out at shortstop with a chance to stick there, though several scouts think he would fit better at second base because of range, with lateral movement that could slow down due to his body type. His arm is average but plays up because of his quick transfer, stellar accuracy and ability to throw from a variety of angles. Reviews of Baldoquin as a hitter were mixed. His swing can get long and he's prone to collapsing his lower half and rolling over the ball. He has worked to shorten up and use the whole field, though his stroke can still get uphill. He never showed much power in Cuba, but after leaving he got stronger, increasing his bat speed and pop. He projects to be more of a doubles hitter than a home run threat, and evaluators were divided on his ability to handle premium velocity. Some scouts liked his plate discipline, while other felt he would have trouble against breaking stuff. He was reported to be close to signing as the Handbook went to press but had not officially signed. He's ready for an assignment to a Class A club.

JUNG-HO KANG, SS/2B/3B

Born: April 5, 1987. **B-T:** R-R. **Ht.:** 6-0. **Wt.:** 180.

Kang had a stellar 2014 season for the Nexen Heroes in the Korea Baseball Organization. He hit .356/.459/.739 with 40 home runs, 68 walks and 106 strikeouts in 117 games, leading the KBO in slugging and OPS, ranking second in homers and OBP, and he won the gold glove at shortstop. Those numbers are lofty, but the KBO is an extreme offensive environment, and scouts were skeptical of Kang's skill set translating into an everyday role in the majors. Kang is strong and has average raw power, with a chance for 15-20 home runs if he plays every day. While he is a solid offensive player, the consensus in the international scouting community is that he won't be an everyday payer. He doesn't have the range to play shortstop in the majors, with an average arm that would be less than ideal for the spot, and scouts also expressed concerns about his ability to make the routine plays. He's a better defensive fit at second or third base. Kang doesn't have a plus tool, but there's enough potential at the plate for him to be an offensive-oriented utility player who starts his U.S. career in the majors.

2014 DRAFT: TEAM BY TEAM SPENDING

Bonuses for the 2014 draft totaled $222,809,919, the second-largest expenditure in draft history.

It could have been the highest, surpassing the $228,009,050 spent in in 2011, had No. 1 overall pick Brady Aiken signed for the original $6.5 million deal he and the Astros agreed to in early June, or if Aiken had signed for the reported $5 million offered on deadline day and fifth-rounder Jacob Nix signed for his reported $1.5 million deal.

Teams are taxed 75 percent on every dollar spent over their bonus pool allotment, and they showed a greater willingness to spend more than their allotment. In 2012, the first year under the current collective bargaining agreement, nine teams paid a tax and 10 paid in 2013. In 2014 15 teams paid the tax, totaling $3,569,219 over their bonus pools.

No teams have been willing to incur the more significant penalty of losing draft picks, however. If teams exceed their bonus pool by more than 5 percent, they forfeit two future picks. No team in the current CBA has forfeited a pick.

Including teams that spent less than their bonus pool allotment, teams collectively spent $2.11 million more than the cumulative bonus pools. That total was $7.88 million below in 2013 and $5.62 below in 2012.

The White Sox, who finished second in total spending ($10.46 million) and bonus pool spending ($9.98), paid the most tax money at $356,175. Chicago's draft expenditure was the largest in franchise history, having signed No. 3 pick Carlos Rodon to the largest bonus in the draft at $6.58 million. Under the previous CBA from 2007-2011, the White Sox averaged $3.665 million per draft, the least of any team and only 57 percent of the average of all teams ($6.355 million).

Teams that receive revenue sharing money have greater incentive not to exceed their bonus pool. The 75 percent tax on the $3.569 million spent over the bonus pool allotment equates to $2,676,914. Teams that receive revenue sharing money and do not exceed their bonus pools receive an equal share of the tax money. Nine teams qualified and received $297,435 each.

The Marlins spent the most of any team in the draft by both total spending ($13.11 million) and bonus pool spending ($12.74 million). This marked the largest draft expenditure during the current CBA and made the Marlins the only team to spend more than $12 million in the last three drafts. The previous high water mark belonged to the 2012 Minnesota Twins ($11,938,900), who signed No. 2 pick Byron Buxton to the highest bonus in the draft class ($6,000,000) and two supplemental first-round picks (Jose Berrios and Luke Bard) for more than $1.25 million each.

Bonus pool spending ($197,972,219) accounted for 88.9 percent of the total spending, as the remaining amount was spent on draftees in rounds 11-40 who did not receive more than $100,000.

Below is a chart with total bonus spending per team. The second column is the team's total spending including money after the 10th round that did not count against the bonus pool, followed by the bonus pool spending and bonus pool allotment. The bonus pool reflects money deducted because of a player who failed to sign.

Team	Total Spending	Bonus Spending	Bonus Pool	+/- Pool	% +/- Pool	Rec'd Tax?
Marlins	$13,112,900	$12,293,400	$12,741,700	-448,300	-3.52%	Yes
White Sox	$10,460,600	$9,984,600	$9,509,700	474,900	4.99%	
Blue Jays	$9,308,700	$9,194,700	$9,458,500	-263,800	-2.79%	
Cubs	$9,783,000	$8,764,000	$8,352,200	411,800	4.93%	
Royals	$9,888,700	$8,561,700	$8,602,900	-41,200	-0.48%	Yes
Indians	$9,317,800	$8,355,300	$8,234,100	121,200	1.47%	
Rockies	$8,853,800	$8,216,300	$8,347,300	-131,000	-1.57%	Yes
Brewers	$8,102,300	$7,604,100	$7,605,600	-1,500	-0.02%	Yes
Pirates	$8,186,400	$7,412,400	$7,063,700	348,700	4.94%	
Twins	$8,067,600	$7,305,600	$7,525,600	-220,000	-2.92%	Yes
Diamondbacks	$8,357,900	$7,205,900	$7,228,300	-22,400	-0.31%	Yes
Mariners	$8,237,500	$7,085,000	$6,767,900	317,100	4.69%	
Reds	$7,929,900	$6,958,400	$6,973,400	-15,000	-0.22%	Yes
Cardinals	$7,613,800	$6,901,800	$6,582,800	319,000	4.85%	
Phillies	$7,187,800	$6,785,300	$6,896,700	-111,400	-1.62%	
Red Sox	$7,814,800	$6,559,300	$6,373,300	186,000	2.92%	
Giants	$7,275,900	$6,238,400	$5,949,800	288,600	4.85%	
Rays	$7,141,319	$6,138,319	$5,848,400	289,919	4.96%	
Padres	$6,637,600	$6,098,600	$6,098,600	0	0.00%	Yes
Angels	$6,387,500	$5,774,000	$5,774,000	0	0.00%	
Mets	$6,488,800	$5,290,800	$5,308,300	-17,500	-0.33%	
Dodgers	$5,901,100	$5,148,600	$4,947,700	200,900	4.06%	
Astros	$6,154,500	$5,090,500	$5,069,600	20,900	0.41%	
Rangers	$6,089,200	$5,047,200	$4,820,700	226,500	4.70%	
Tigers	$5,405,300	$4,782,800	$4,890,200	-107,400	-2.20%	
Athletics	$5,386,000	$4,775,000	$4,778,300	-3,300	-0.07%	Yes
Braves	$5,069,800	$4,487,800	$4,557,700	-69,900	-1.53%	
Nationals	$5,188,600	$4,349,100	$4,142,000	207,100	5.00%	
Yankees	$4,050,200	$3,290,200	$3,202,300	87,900	2.74%	
Orioles	$3,410,600	$2,273,100	$2,204,400	68,700	3.12%	
Total	**$222,809,919**	**$197,972,219**	**$195,855,700**	**2,116,519**	**1.08%**	

2014 DRAFT: TOP 50 BONUSES VS. PICK VALUES

These are the top 50 bonuses from the 2014 draft, compared with each player's overall draft position. The 2014 draft had 67 players who signed for at least $1 million, though there were 56 slots that exceeded $1 million.

The depth of the draft was in the high school class and team spending reflected that, as 60 percent of the million-dollar bonuses went to high school players. No junior college player signed for more than $1 million.

No. 3 pick Carlos Rodon (White Sox) signed for the largest bonus in the draft at $6.582 million, which was $860,500 (or 15 percent) above slot. Of the first round picks, 10 signed over-slot deals, 11 signed at slot and 12 signed for under slot.

The smallest bonus compared to slot was No. 4 pick Kyle Schwarber, who signed for $1,496,200 less than slot (32 percent). His $3,125,000 bonus accounted for the sixth-largest in the draft. The Cubs allocated those savings to sign five players to bonuses exceeding $1 million, the most of any team.

While most teams signed two players to million-dollar bonuses, three other teams signed four players: the Indians, Pirates and Royals, who were all armed with extra picks on the first day of the draft.

The Orioles, who didn't pick until the third round and whose first slot value was $594,200, were the only team to not sign a player for at least $1 million.

Rk.	Rnd.	Overall	Team. Player, Pos., School	Slot Value	Bonus	Bonus Vs. Slot
1.	1	3	White Sox. Carlos Rodon, lhp, North Carolina State	$5,721,500	$6,582,000	$860,500
2.	1	2	Marlins. Tyler Kolek, rhp, Shepherd (Texas) HS	$6,821,800	$6,000,000	($821,800)
3.	1	6	Mariners. Alex Jackson, of, HS—San Diego	$3,575,900	$4,200,000	$624,100
4.	1	5	Twins. Nick Gordon, ss, HS—Orlando	$3,851,000	$3,851,000	—
5.	1	7	Phillies. Aaron Nola, rhp, Louisiana State	$3,300,900	$3,300,900	—
6.	1	4	Cubs. Kyle Schwarber, c/of, Indiana	$4,621,200	$3,125,000	($1,496,200)
7.	1	9	Blue Jays. Jeff Hoffman, rhp, East Carolina	$3,080,800	$3,080,800	—
8.	1	10	Mets. Michael Conforto, of, Oregon State	$2,970,800	$2,970,800	—
9.	1	13	Padres. Trea Turner, ss, North Carolina State	$2,723,300	$2,900,000	$176,700
10.	1	11	Blue Jays. Max Pentecost, c, Kennesaw State	$2,888,300	$2,888,300	—
11.	1	16	D'backs. Touki Toussaint, rhp, HS—Miami	$2,338,200	$2,700,000	$361,800
12.	1	14	Giants. Tyler Beede, rhp, Vanderbilt	$2,613,200	$2,613,200	—
13.	1	15	Angels. Sean Newcomb, lhp, Hartford	$2,475,600	$2,518,400	$42,800
14.	1	18	Nationals. Erick Fedde, rhp, Nevada-Las Vegas	$2,145,600	$2,511,100	$365,500
15.	1	12	Brewers. Kodi Medeiros, lhp, HS—Hilo, Hawaii	$2,805,700	$2,500,000	($305,700)
16.	1	22	Dodgers. Grant Holmes, rhp, Conway (S.C.) HS	$1,980,500	$2,500,000	$519,500
17.	1	8	Rockies. Kyle Freeland, lhp, Evansville	$3,190,800	$2,300,000	($890,800)
18.	1	17	Royals. Brandon Finnegan, lhp, Texas Christian	$2,200,600	$2,200,600	—
19.	1	20	Rays. Casey Gillaspie, 1b, Wichita State	$2,035,500	$2,035,500	—
20.	1	23	Tigers. Derek Hill, of, Elk Grove (Calif.) HS	$1,953,100	$2,000,000	$46,900
21.	1	34	Cardinals. Jack Flaherty, rhp, HS—Studio City, Calif.	$1,650,400	$2,000,000	$349,600
22.	1.5	35	Rockies. Forrest Wall, 2b, HS—Winter Park, Fla.	$1,614,500	$2,000,000	$385,500
23.	2.5	74	Mariners. Gareth Morgan, of, HS—Toronto	$760,300	$2,000,000	$1,239,700
24.	1	19	Reds. Nick Howard, rhp, Virginia	$2,090,500	$1,990,500	($100,000)
25.	1	28	Royals. Foster Griffin, lhp, HS—Orlando	$1,815,500	$1,925,000	$109,500
26.	1	21	Indians. Bradley Zimmer, of, San Francisco	$2,008,100	$1,900,000	($108,100)
27.	1	26	Red Sox. Michael Chavis, ss/3b, HS—Marietta, Ga.	$1,870,500	$1,870,500	—
28.	1	27	Cardinals. Luke Weaver, rhp, Florida State	$1,843,000	$1,843,000	—
29.	1.5	41	Brewers. Jacob Gatewood, ss, Clovis (Calif.) HS	$1,384,900	$1,830,000	$445,100
30.	1	24	Pirates. Cole Tucker, ss, HS—Phoenix	$1,925,500	$1,800,000	($125,500)
31.	2	50	Brewers. Monte Harrison, of, HS—Lee's Summit, Mo.	$1,100,300	$1,800,000	$699,700
32.	2	56	Royals. Scott Blewett, rhp, HS—Baldwinsville, N.Y.	$1,003,200	$1,800,000	$796,800
33.	1	29	Reds. Alex Blandino, ss, Stanford	$1,788,000	$1,788,000	—
34.	1	25	Athletics. Matt Chapman, 3b, Cal State Fullerton	$1,898,000	$1,750,000	($148,000)
35.	1	30	Rangers. Luis Ortiz, rhp, Sanger (Calif.) HS	$1,760,500	$1,750,000	($10,500)
36.	1	32	Braves. Braxton Davidson, 1b, HS—Asheville, N.C.	$1,705,400	$1,705,000	($400)
37.	1	31	Indians. Justus Sheffield, lhp, Tullahoma (Tenn.) HS	$1,733,000	$1,600,000	($133,000)
38.	1.5	37	Astros. Derek Fisher, of, Virginia	$1,534,100	$1,534,100	—
39.	1	33	Red Sox. Michael Kopech, rhp, Mt. Pleasant (Texas) HS	$1,678,000	$1,500,000	($178,000)
40.	6	169	Cubs. Dylan Cease, rhp, Milton (Ga.) HS	$269,500	$1,500,000	$1,230,500
41.	1.5	40	Royals. Chase Vallot, c, HS—Lafayette, La.	$1,420,800	$1,350,000	($70,800)
42.	2	42	Astros. A.J. Reed, 1b, Kentucky	$1,350,000	$1,350,000	—
43.	2	43	Marlins. Justin Twine, ss, Falls City (Texas) HS	$1,316,000	$1,316,000	—
44.	2	51	Padres. Michael Gettys, of, Gainesville (Ga.) HS	$1,083,400	$1,300,000	$216,600
45.	2	44	White Sox. Spencer Adams, rhp, HS—Cleveland, Ga.	$1,282,700	$1,282,700	—
46.	1.5	38	Indians. Mike Papi, of, Virginia	$1,495,400	$1,250,000	($245,400)
47.	1.5	39	Pirates. Connor Joe, of, San Diego	$1,457,600	$1,250,000	($207,600)
48.	2	46	Twins. Nick Burdi, rhp, Louisville	$1,218,800	$1,218,800	—
49.	2	53	Angels. Joe Gatto, rhp, HS—Richland, N.J.	$1,050,600	$1,200,000	$149,400
50.	2	59	Rangers. Ti'quan Forbes, ss, Columbia (Miss.) HS	$957,900	$1,200,000	$242,100

SIGNING BONUSES

2013 DRAFT

Just as they did in 2012 in the first draft under the revamped rules, signing bonuses and the assigned pick values tracked each other nicely.

To give the worst teams extra spending power, the values for the selections at the top of the draft were set higher than the perceived market value. As a result, just four of the top 11 choices received their full pick value, and only three of the 33 first-rounders exceeded theirs. But all told, the top 50 bonuses added up to $110.5 million, while the first 50 pick values totaled $114.5 million. By comparison, when MLB unilaterally determined slot recommendations in the last year of the previous Collective Bargaining Agreement (2011), the total of the first 50 bonuses ($120.5 million) dwarfed that of the top 50 slots ($70 million).

Player, Pos., Team (Round/Overall Pick)	Bonus	Pick Value
1. Kris Bryant, 3b, Cubs (1st round/No. 2)	$6,708,400	$7,790,400
2. Mark Appel, rhp, Astros (1st round/No. 1)	$6,350,000	$6,708,400
3. Jonathan Gray, rhp, Rockies (1st round/No. 3)	$4,800,000	$5,626,400
4. Kohl Stewart, rhp, Twins (1st round/No. 4)	$4,544,400	$4,544,400
5. Sean Manaea, lhp, Royals (supp. 1st round/No. 34)	$3,550,000	$3,787,000
6. Colin Moran, 3b, Marlins (1st round/No. 6)	$3,516,500	$3,516,500
7. Clint Frazier, of, Indians (1st round/No. 5)	$3,500,000	$3,246,000
8. Austin Meadows, of, Pirates (1st round/No. 9)	$3,029,600	$3,137,800
9. D.J. Peterson, 3b, Mariners (1st round/No. 12)	$2,759,100	$3,029,600
10. Trey Ball, lhp, Red Sox (1st round/No. 7)	$2,750,000	$2,921,400
11. Hunter Renfroe, of, Padres (1st round/No. 13)	$2,678,000	$2,840,300
12. Dominic Smith, 1b, Mets (1st round/No. 11)	$2,600,000	$2,759,100
13. Reese McGuire, c, Pirates (1st round/No. 14)	$2,369,800	$2,678,000
14. J.P. Crawford, ss, Phillies (1st round/No. 16)	$2,299,300	$2,569,800
15. Braden Shipley, rhp, Diamondbacks (1st round/No. 15)	$2,250,000	$2,434,500
16. Alex Gonzalez, rhp, Rangers (1st round/No. 23)	$2,215,000	$2,299,300
17. Hunter Dozier, 3b, Royals (1st round/No. 8)	$2,200,000	$2,164,000
18. Tim Anderson, ss, White Sox (1st round/No. 17)	$2,164,000	$2,109,900
19. Chris Anderson, rhp, Dodgers (1st round/No. 18)	$2,109,900	$2,055,800
20. Jonathon Crawford, rhp, Tigers (1st round/No. 20)	$2,001,700	$2,001,700
21. Nick Ciuffo, c, Rays (1st round/No. 21)	$1,972,200	$1,974,700
22. Hunter Harvey, rhp, Orioles (1st round/No. 22)	$1,947,600	$1,947,600
23. Travis Demeritte, ss, Rangers (1st round/No. 30)	$1,900,000	$1,920,600
24. Christian Arroyo, ss, Giants (1st round/No. 25)	$1,866,500	$1,893,500
25. Marco Gonzales, lhp, Cardinals (1st round/No. 19)	$1,850,000	$1,866,500
26. Eric Jagielo, 3b, Yankees (1st round/No. 26)	$1,839,400	$1,839,400
27. Phillip Ervin, of, Reds (1st round/No. 27)	$1,812,400	$1,812,400
28. Billy McKinney, of, Athletics (1st round/No. 24)	$1,800,000	$1,785,300
Aaron Judge, of, Yankees (1st round/No. 32)	$1,800,000	$1,758,300
30. Rob Kaminsky, lhp, Cardinals (1st round/No. 28)	$1,785,300	$1,731,200
31. Ryne Stanek, rhp, Rays (1st round/No. 29)	$1,755,800	$1,704,200
32. Jason Hursh, rhp, Braves (1st round/No. 31)	$1,704,200	$1,677,100
33. Austin Wilson, of, Mariners (2nd round/No. 49)	$1,700,000	$1,650,100
34. Ian Clarkin, lhp, Yankees (1st round/No. 33)	$1,650,100	$1,623,000
35. Michael Lorenzen, rhp/of, Reds (supp. 1st round/No. 38)	$1,500,000	$1,587,700
Oscar Mercado, ss, Cardinals (2nd round/No. 57)	$1,500,000	$1,547,700
37. Josh Hart, of, Orioles (supp. 1st round/No. 37)	$1,450,000	$1,508,600
38. Aaron Blair, rhp, Diamondbacks (supp. 1st round/No. 36)	$1,435,000	$1,470,500
39. Corey Knebel, rhp, Tigers (supp. 1st round/No. 39)	$1,433,400	$1,433,400
40. Dustin Peterson, ss, Padres (2nd round/No. 50)	$1,400,000	$1,397,200
41. Andrew Thurman, rhp, Astros (2nd round/No. 40)	$1,397,200	$1,361,900
42. Devin Williams, rhp, Brewers (2nd round/No. 54)	$1,350,000	$1,327,600
43. Ryan McMahon, 3b, Rockies (2nd round/No. 42)	$1,327,600	$1,294,100
44. Ryan Eades, rhp, Twins (2nd round/No. 43)	$1,294,100	$1,261,400
45. Trevor Williams, rhp, Marlins (2nd round/No. 44)	$1,261,400	$1,229,600
46. Cody Reed, lhp, Royals (2nd round/No. 46)	$1,198,500	$1,198,500
47. Rob Zastryzny, lhp, Cubs (2nd round/No. 41)	$1,100,000	$1,168,200
48. Justin Williams, of, Diamondbacks (2nd round/No. 52)	$1,050,000	$1,138,800
49. Andrew Knapp, c, Phillies (2nd round/No. 53)	$1,033,100	$1,110,000
50. Tyler Danish, rhp, White Sox (2nd round/No. 55)	$1,001,800	$1,082,000
Total	**$110,511,300**	**$114,521,400**

These are the bonuses and assigned pick values for the first 100 picks of the 2012 draft. New draft rules that went into effect in 2012 establish assigned values for every pick in the first 10 rounds. The aggregate of all of a team's pick values constitute its draft signing budget. Teams are not required to adhere to the assigned value of any particular pick, but if they exceed their aggregate budget they face penalties that range from fines to lost draft picks.

FIRST ROUND

Pick Team: Player, Pos.	Pick Value	Bonus
1. Hou: Carlos Correa, ss	$7,200,000	$4,800,000
2. Min: Byron Buxton, of	$6,200,000	$6,000,000
3. Sea: Mike Zunino, c	$5,200,000	$4,000,000
4. Bal: Kevin Gausman, rhp	$4,200,000	$4,320,000
5. KC: Kyle Zimmer, rhp	$3,500,000	$3,000,000
6. ChC: Albert Almora, of	$3,250,000	$3,900,000
7. SD: Max Fried, lhp	$3,000,000	$3,000,000
8. Pit: Mark Appel, rhp	$2,900,000	Did Not Sign
9. Mia: Andrew Heaney, lhp	$2,800,000	$2,600,000
10. Col: David Dahl, of	$2,700,000	$2,600,000
11. Oak: Addison Russell, ss	$2,625,000	$2,625,000
12. NYM: Gavin Cecchini, ss	$2,550,000	$2,300,000
13. CWS: Courtney Hawkins, of	$2,475,000	$2,475,000
14. Cin: Nick Travieso, rhp	$2,375,000	$2,000,000
15. Cle: Tyler Naquin, of	$2,250,000	$1,750,000
16. Was: Lucas Giolito, rhp	$2,125,000	$2,925,000
17. Tor: D.J. Davis, of	$2,000,000	$1,750,000
18. LAD: Corey Seager, 3b	$1,950,000	$2,350,000
19. StL: Michael Wacha, rhp	$1,900,000	$1,900,000
20. SF: Chris Stratton, rhp	$1,850,000	$1,850,000
21. Atl: Lucas Sims, rhp	$1,825,000	$1,650,000
22. Tor: Marcus Stroman, rhp	$1,800,000	$1,800,000
23. StL: James Ramsey, of	$1,775,000	$1,600,000
24. Bos: Deven Marrero, ss	$1,750,000	$2,050,000
25. TB: Richie Shaffer, 3b	$1,725,000	$1,710,000
26. Ari: Stryker Trahan, c/of	$1,700,000	$1,700,000
27. Mil: Clint Coulter, c	$1,675,000	$1,675,000
28. Mil: Victor Roache, of	$1,650,000	$1,525,000
29. Tex: Lewis Brinson, of	$1,625,000	$1,625,000
30. NYY: Ty Hensley, rhp	$1,600,000	$1,200,000
31. Bos: Brian Johnson, lhp	$1,575,000	$1,575,000

SUPPLEMENTAL FIRST ROUND

Pick.Team: Player, Pos.	Pick Value	Bonus
32. Min: J.O. Berrios, rhp	$1,550,000	$1,550,000
33. SD: Zach Eflin, rhp	$1,525,000	$1,200,000
34. Oak: Daniel Robertson, 3b	$1,500,000	$1,500,000
35. NYM: Kevin Plawecki, c	$1,467,400	$1,400,000
36. StL: Stephen Piscotty, of/3b	$1,430,400	$1,430,400
37. Bos: Pat Light, rhp	$1,394,300	$1,000,000
38. Mil: Mitch Haniger, of	$1,359,100	$1,200,000
39. Tex: Joey Gallo, 3b/rhp	$1,324,800	$2,250,000
40. Phi: Shane Watson, rhp	$1,291,300	$1,291,300
41. Hou: Lance McCullers, rhp	$1,258,700	$2,500,000
42. Min: Luke Bard, rhp	$1,227,000	$1,227,000
43. ChC: Pierce Johnson, rhp	$1,196,000	$1,196,000
44. SD: Travis Jankowski, of	$1,165,800	$975,000

45. Pit: Barrett Barnes, of	$1,136,400	$1,000,000
46. Col: Eddie Butler, rhp	$1,107,700	$1,000,000
47. Oak: Matt Olson, 1b	$1,079,700	$1,079,700
48. CWS: Keon Barnum, 1b	$1,052,500	$950,000
49. Cin: Jesse Winker, of	$1,025,900	$1,000,000
50. Tor: Matt Smoral, lhp	$1,000,000	$2,000,000
51. LAD: Jesmuel Valentin, 2b	$984,700	$984,700
52. StL: Patrick Wisdom, 3b	$969,700	$678,790
53. Tex: Collin Wiles, rhp	$954,800	$975,000
54. Phi: Mitch Gueller, rhp	$940,200	$940,200
55. SD: Walker Weickel, rhp	$925,900	$2,000,000
56. ChC: Paul Blackburn, rhp	$911,700	$911,700
57. Cin: Jeff Gelalich, of	$897,800	$825,000
58. Tor: Mitch Nay, 3b	$884,100	$1,000,000
59. StL: Steve Bean, c	$870,600	$700,000
60. Tor: Tyler Gonzales, rhp	$857,200	$750,000

SECOND ROUND

Pick.Team: Player, Pos.	Pick Value	Bonus
61. Hou: Nolan Fontana, ss	$844,100	$875,000
62. Oak: Bruce Maxwell, c/1b	$831,200	$700,000
63. Min: Mason Melotakis, lhp	$818,500	$750,000
64. Sea: Joe DeCarlo, 3b	$806,000	$1,300,000
65. Bal: Branden Kline, rhp	$793,700	$793,700
66. KC: Sam Selman, lhp	$781,600	$750,000
67. ChC: Duane Underwood, rhp	$769,600	$1,050,000
68. SD: Jeremy Baltz, of	$757,900	$625,000
69. Pit: Wyatt Mathisen, c	$746,300	$746,300
70. SD: Dane Phillips, c/1b	$734,900	$450,000
71. NYM: Matt Reynolds, 3b	$723,600	$525,000
72. Min: J.T. Chargois, rhp	$712,600	$712,600
73. Col: Max White, of	$701,700	$1,000,000
74. Oak: Nolan Sanburn, rhp	$691,000	$710,000
75. NYM: Teddy Stankiewicz, rhp	$680,400	Did Not Sign
76. CWS: Chris Beck, rhp	$670,000	$600,000
77. Phi: Dylan Cozens, of	$659,800	$659,800
78. Cin: Tanner Rahier, ss	$649,700	$649,700
79. Cle: Mitch Brown, rhp	$639,700	$800,000
80. Was: Tony Renda, 2b	$630,000	$500,000
81. Tor: Chase DeJong, rhp	$620,300	$860,000
82. LAD: Paco Rodriguez, lhp	$610,800	$610,800
83. Tex: Jamie Jarmon, of	$601,500	$601,500
84. SF: Martin Agosta, rhp	$592,300	$612,500
85. Atl: Alex Wood, lhp	$583,300	$700,000
86. StL: Carson Kelly, 3b/rhp	$574,300	$1,600,000
87. Bos: Jamie Callahan, rhp	$565,600	$600,000
88. TB: Spencer Edwards, of	$556,900	$554,400
89. NYY: Austin Aune, of	$548,400	$1,000,000
90. Ari: Joe Munoz, 3b	$540,000	$520,500
91. Det: Jake Thompson, rhp	$531,800	$531,800
92. Mil: Tyrone Taylor, of	$523,600	$750,000
93. Tex: Nick Williams, of	$515,600	$500,000
94. NYY: Peter O'Brien, c	$507,800	$460,000
95. Phi: Alec Rash, rhp	$500,000	Did Not Sign

THIRD ROUND

Pick.Team: Player, Pos.	Pick Value	Bonus
96. Hou: Brady Rodgers, rhp	$495,200	$495,200
97. Min: Adam Brett Walker, 1b	$490,400	$490,400
98. Sea: Edwin Diaz, rhp	$485,700	$300,000
99. Bal: Adrian Marin, ss	$481,100	$481,100
100. KC: Colin Rodgers, lhp	$476,500	$700,000

COLLEGE TOP 100

Rank. Name, Pos., School	B-T	Ht.	Wt.	Previously Drafted
1. Brady Aiken, lhp, Uncommitted	L/L	6-4	205	Astros '14 (1)
2. Michael Matuella, rhp, Duke	R/R	6-7	220	Never
3. Kyle Funkhouser, rhp, Louisville	R/R	6-2	218	Never
4. Walker Buehler, rhp, Vanderbilt	R/R	6-1	160	Pirates '12 (14)
5. Dansby Swanson, 2b/ss, Vanderbilt	R/R	6-0	190	Rockies '12 (38)
6. Nathan Kirby, lhp, Virginia	L/L	6-2	185	Never
7. Alex Bregman, ss, Louisiana State	R/R	6-0	190	Red Sox '12 (29)
8. Riley Ferrell, rhp, Texas Christian	R/R	6-1	200	Never
9. Kyle Cody, rhp, Kentucky	R/R	6-7	245	Phillies '12 (33)
10. Carson Fulmer, rhp, Vanderbilt	R/R	5-11	195	Red Sox '12 (15)
11. Jake Lemoine, rhp, Houston	R/R	6-5	220	Rangers '12 (21)
12. Ian Happ, of, Cincinnati	S/R	6-0	205	Never
13. James Kaprielian, rhp, UCLA	R/R	6-4	200	Mariners '12 (40)
14. Phil Bickford, rhp, JC of Southern Nevada	R/R	6-4	200	Blue Jays '13 (1)
15. Kevin Newman, ss, Arizona	R/R	6-1	180	Never
16. D.J. Stewart, of, Florida State	L/R	6-0	230	Yankees '12 (28)
17. Cody Ponce, rhp, Cal Poly Pomona	R/R	6-5	235	Never
18. Gio Brusa, of, Pacific	S/R	6-3	190	Braves '12 (37)
19. Richie Martin, ss, Florida	R/R	6-0	185	Mariners '12 (38)
20. Tyler Jay, lhp, Illinois	L/L	6-1	175	Never
21. Dillon Tate, rhp, UC Santa Barbara	R/R	6-2	185	Never
22. Jon Harris, rhp, Missouri State	R/R	6-4	185	Blue Jays '12 (33)
23. Mac Marshall, lhp, Chipola (Fla.) JC	R/L	6-0	181	Astros '14 (21)
24. Marc Brakeman, rhp, Stanford	L/R	6-1	180	Never
25. Andrew Suarez, lhp, Miami	L/L	6-2	205	Nationals '14 (2)
26. Joe McCarthy, of, Virginia	L/L	6-3	215	Never
27. C.J Hinojosa, ss, Texas	R/R	5-11	179	Astros '12 (26)
28. Tyler Ferguson, rhp, Vanderbilt	R/R	6-3	225	Giants '12 (40)
29. Alex Young, lhp, Texas Christian	L/L	6-2	205	Rangers '12 (32)
30. Blake Trahan, ss Louisiana-Lafayette	R/R	5-9	180	Never
31. Brett Lilek, lhp, Arizona State	L/L	6-4	194	Mariners '12 (37)
32. Christin Stewart, of Tennessee	L/R	6-0	205	Never
33. Steven Duggar, of, Clemson	L/R	6-2	190	Never
34. Mark Mathias, 2b/3b, Cal Poly	R/R	6-0	185	Never
35. Chris Shaw, 1b, Boston College	L/R	6-3	248	Mets '12 (26)
36. Justin Garza, rhp Cal State Fullerton	R/R	5-11	160	Indians '12 (26)
37. Kyle Twomey, lhp, Southern California	L/L	6-3	175	Athletics '12 (3)
38. Thomas Eshelman, rhp Cal State Fullerton	R/R	6-3	190	Never
39. Brandon Waddell, lhp, Virginia	L/L	6-3	180	Never
40. Tyler Alexander, lhp, Texas Christian	L/L	6-3	180	Tigers '13 (23)
41. Mikey White, ss, Alabama	R/R	6-1	195	Mets '12 (34)
42. Garrett Cleavinger, lhp, Oregon	L/L	6-0	220	Never
43. Daniel Pinero, ss, Virginia	R/R	6-5	210	Astros '13 (20)
44. Ryan Burr, rhp, Arizona State	R/R	6-4	224	Rangers '12 (33)
45. Alex Robinson, lhp, Maryland	L/L	6-3	225	Never
46. A.J. Minter, lhp, Texas A&M	L/L	6-0	210	Tigers '12 (38)
47. Eric Hanhold, rhp, Florida	R/R	6-5	195	Phillies '12 (40)
48. Josh Sborz, rhp, Virginia	R/R	6-3	225	Never
49. Kyle Holder, ss, San Diego	L/R	6-1	185	Never
50. Andrew Sopko, rhp, Gonzaga	R/R	6-2	200	Padres '12 (14)

Rank. Name, Pos., School	B-T	Ht.	Wt.	Previously Drafted
51. Kevin Duchene, lhp, Illinois	L/L	6-2	210	Never
52. Zack Erwin, lhp, Clemson	L/L	6-5	195	Never
53. Isiah Gilliam, of, Chipola (Fla.) JC	S/R	6-2	215	Cubs '14 (23)
54. Kal Simmons, ss, Kennesaw State	S/R	6-1	195	Never
55. Jon Duplantier, rhp, Rice	L/R	6-4	210	Never
56. Kyri Washington, of, Longwood	R/R	6-1	215	Never
57. Justin Jacome, lhp, UC Santa Barbara	L/L	6-6	215	Never
58. Kolton Mahoney, rhp, Brigham Young	R/R	6-0	195	Brewers '14 (23)
59. Ryan Perez, lhp/rhp, Judson (Ill.)	S/S	6-2	190	Never
60. David Thompson, 1b/3b, Miami	R/R	6-2	207	Yankees' 12 (38)
61. Braden Bishop, of, Washington	R/R	6-1	188	Braves '12 (36)
62. Logan Taylor, ss, Texas A&M	R/R	6-1	195	Never
63. John La Prise, 3b/2b, Virginia	L/R	6-3	180	Never
64. Ryan Kellogg, lhp, Arizona State	R/L	6-5	225	Blue Jays '12 (12)
65. Trey Killian, rhp, Arkansas	R/R	6-3	200	Never
66. Chandler Eden, rhp, JC of Southern Nevada	R/R	6-2	165	Marlins '13 (36)
67. Blake Hickman, rhp, Iowa	R/R	6-5	210	Cubs '12 (20)
68. Edwin Rios, 2b/3b/1b, Florida International	L/R	6-3	202	Never
69. Grayson Long, rhp, Texas A&M	R/R	6-5	215	Mariners '12 (39)
70. Skye Bolt, of, North Carolina	S/R	6-2	175	Nationals '12 (26)
71. Tate Matheny, of, Missouri State	R/R	6-0	185	Cardinals '12 (23)
72. John Kilichowski, lhp, Vanderbilt	L/L	6-5	210	Never
73. Austin Byler, 1b, Nevada	L/R	6-3	225	Nationals '14 (9)
74. Dylan Nelson, rhp, Radford	R/R	6-2	165	Never
75. Reilly Hovis, rhp, North Carolina	R/R	6-3	190	Never
76. Cody Poteet, rhp, UCLA	R/R	6-1	188	Nationals '12 (27)
77. Scott Kingery, 2b/of, Arizona	R/R	5-10	175	Never
78. Rhett Wiseman, of, Vanderbilt	L/R	6-1	205	Cubs '12 (25)
79. Matt Rose, rhp/3b, Georgia State	R/R	6-4	195	Blue Jays '12 (24)
80. Jacob Drossner, lhp, Maryland	R/L	6-3	205	Cubs '12 (23)
81. Taylor Ward, c Fresno State	R/R	6-2	190	Rays '12 (31)
82. Mitchell Traver, rhp, Texas Christian	R/R	6-7	255	Astros '12 (39)
83. Josh Staumont, rhp, Azusa Pacific (Calif.)	R/R	6-2	205	Never
84. Trent Thornton, rhp, North Carolina	R/R	6-0	170	Never
85. Travis Bergen, lhp, Kennesaw State	L/L	6-0	195	Never
86. Jaylin Davis, of, Appalachian State	R/R	6-1	195	Never
87. Andrew Stevenson, of, Louisiana State	L/L	6-0	188	Never
88. David Graybill, rhp/of, Arizona State	R/R	6-5	244	Yankees '14 (32)
89. Cam Gibson, of, Michigan State	L/R	6-1	190	Diamondbacks '12 (38)
90. Cole Irvin, lhp, Oregon	L/L	6-3	182	Blue Jays '12 (29)
91. Conor Costello, rhp, Oklahoma State	R/R	6-3	204	Reds '11 (16)
92. Tyler Stubblefield, lhp, Texas A&M	L/L	6-4	210	Braves '13 (36)
93. Trevor Megill, rhp, Loyola Marymount	L/R	6-8	245	Cardinals '14 (3)
94. Harrison Bader, of, Florida	R/R	5-11	180	Never
95. Mark Laird, of, Louisiana State	L/L	6-1	172	Never
96. David Fletcher, ss, Loyola Marymount	R/R	5-10	175	Never
97. Andrew Benintendi, of, Arkansas	L/L	5-10	180	Reds '13 (31)
98. Jacob Cronenworth, rhp, Michigan	L/R	6-1	167	Never
99. Ian Gibaut, rhp, Tulane	R/R	6-3	220	Never
100. Seth McGarry, rhp, Florida Atlantic	R/R	6-1	180	Never

HIGH SCHOOL TOP 100

Rank.	Player	Position	B/T	Ht.	Wt.	High School	Commitment
1.	Brendan Rodgers	SS	R/R	6-0	190	Lake Mary (Fla.) HS	Florida State
2.	Kolby Allard	LHP	L/L	6-1	175	San Clemente (Calif.) HS	UCLA
3.	Justin Hooper	LHP	L/R	6-7	230	De La Salle HS, Concord, Calif.	UCLA
4.	Trenton Clark	OF	L/L	6-0	200	Richland HS, North Richland Hills, Texas	Texas Tech
5.	Daz Cameron	OF	R/R	6-0	186	Eagle's Landing Academy, McDonough, Ga.	Florida State
6.	Nick Plummer	OF	L/L	5-11	199	Brother Rice HS, Bloomfield Hills, Mich.	Kentucky
7.	Chris Betts	C	L/R	6-2	200	Woodrow Wilson HS, Long Beach, Calif.	Tennessee
8.	Ashe Russell	RHP	R/R	6-4	201	Cathedral HS, Indianapolis	Texas A&M
9.	Mike Nikorak	RHP	R/R	6-04	197	Stroudsburg (Pa.) HS	Alabama
10.	Garrett Whitley	OF	R/R	6-2	200	Niskayuna (N.Y.) HS	Wake Forest
11.	Demi Orimoleye	OF	R/R	6-3	225	St. Matthew HS, Ottawa, Ont.	Oregon
12.	Beau Burrows	RHP	R/R	6-2	200	Weatherford (Texas) HS	Texas A&M
13.	Kyle Tucker	OF	L/R	6-03	184	Plant HS, Tampa	Florida
14.	Austin Smith	RHP	R/R	6-4	215	Park Vista HS, Boynton Beach, Fla.	Florida Atlantic
15.	Cornelius Randolph	INF	L/R	6-1	190	Griffin (Ga.) HS	Clemson
16.	Juan Hillman	LHP	L/L	6-2	183	Olympia HS, Orlando, Fla.	Central Florida
17.	Donnie Everett	RHP	R/R	6-1	231	Clarksville (Tenn.) HS	Vanderbilt
18.	Triston McKenzie	RHP	R/R	6-5	160	Royal Palm Beach (Fla.) HS	Vanderbilt
19.	Chandler Day	RHP	R/R	6-4	165	Watkins Memorial HS, Pataskala, Ohio	Vanderbilt
20.	Cole McKay	RHP	B/R	6-5	230	Smithson Valley HS, Spring Branch, Texas	Louisiana State
21.	Alonzo Jones	2B/OF	B/R	5-9	190	Columbus (Ga.) HS	Vanderbilt
22.	Kyler Murray	MIF/OF	R/R	5-10	175	Allen (Texas) HS	Texas A&M
23.	Kyle Molnar	RHP	R/R	6-3	205	Aliso Niguel HS, Aliso Viejo, Calif.	UCLA
24.	Dakota Chalmers	RHP	R/R	6-3	175	Lakeview Academy, Gainesville, Ga.	Georgia
25.	Luken Baker	1B/RHP	R/R	6-4	240	Oak Ridge HS, Conroe, Texas	Texas Christian
26.	Bryce Denton	OF	R/R	6-1	195	Ravenwood HS, Brentwood, Tenn.	Vanderbilt
27.	Jake Woodford	RHP	R/R	6-4	215	Plant HS, Tampa	Florida
28.	Bryan Hoeing	RHP	R/R	6-5	185	Batesville (Ind.) HS	Louisville
29.	Eric Jenkins	OF	L/R	6-2	165	West Columbus HS, Cerro Gordo, N.C.	UNC Wilmington
30.	Cadyn Greiner	SS	R/R	5-10	180	Bishop Gorman HS, Las Vegas	Oregon State
31.	Jalen Miller	SS	R/R	6-1	185	Riverwood Charter HS, Sandy Springs, Ga.	Clemson
32.	Ke'Bryan Hayes	3B	R/R	6-1	207	Concordia Lutheran HS, Tomball, Texas	Tennessee
33.	Nick Madrigal	SS	R/R	5-5	155	Elk Grove (Calif.) HS	Oregon State
34.	Kep Brown	OF	R/R	6-5	195	Wando HS, Mt Pleasant, S.C.	Miami
35.	Cole Sands	RHP	R/R	6-2	200	North Florida Christian HS, Tallahassee, Fla.	Florida State
36.	Mitchell Hansen	OF	L/L	6-3	197	Plano Senior (Texas) HS	Stanford
37.	Reggie Pruitt	OF	R/R	6-1	168	Kennesaw (Ga) Mountain HS	Vanderbilt
38.	Tristan English	RHP	R/R	6-2	180	Pike County HS, Zebulon, Ga.	Georgia Tech
39.	Joe DeMers	RHP	R/R	6-2	215	College Park HS, Pleasant Hill, Calif.	Washington
40.	Nick Neidert	RHP	R/R	6-0	185	Peachtree Ridge HS, Suwanee, Ga.	South Carolina
41.	Ryan Johnson	OF	L/R	6-3	205	College Station (Texas) HS	Texas Christian
42.	Nick Shumpert	SS	R/R	6-0	180	Highlands Ranch (Colo.) HS	Kentucky
43.	Gray Fenter	RHP	R/R	5-11	190	West Memphis (Ark.) HS	Mississippi State
44.	Riley Thompson	RHP	L/R	6-4	185	Christian Academy, Louisville	Louisville
45.	Blake Perkins	OF	R/R	6-0	180	Verrado HS, Buckeye, Ariz.	Arizona State
46.	Hogan Harris	LHP	R/L	6-2	195	St Thomas More HS, Lafayette, La.	Louisiana-Lafayette
47.	Jahmai Jones	OF	R/R	6-0	210	Wesleyan HS, Norcross, Ga.	North Carolina
48.	Austin Riley	RHP	R/R	6-3	240	DeSoto Central HS, Southaven, Miss.	Mississippi State
49.	Desmond Lindsay	OF/1B	R/R	6-0	200	Out-Of-Door Academy, Sarasota, Fla.	North Carolina
50.	Ryan McKenna	OF	R/R	5-10	180	St Thomas Aquinas, Dover, N.H.	Liberty

Rank. Player	Position	B/T	Ht.	Wt.	High School	Commitment
51. John Aiello	3B	S/R	6-2	200	Germantown Academy, Ft Washington, Pa.	Wake Forest
52. Josh Naylor	1B	L/L	6-0	230	St. Joan of Arc Catholic SS, Mississauga, Ont.	Texas Tech
53. Tyler Williams	OF	R/R	6-3	210	Raymond S Kellis HS, Glendale, Ariz.	Arizona State
54. D.J. Wilson	OF	L/R	5-8	170	Canton (Ohio) South HS	Vanderbilt
55. Brendan Davis	3B/SS	R/R	6-4	170	Lakewood (Calif.) HS	Cal State Fullerton
56. Cody Morris	RHP	R/R	6-4	200	Reservoir HS, Fulton, Md.	South Carolina
57. Brendon Little	LHP	L/L	6-2	195	Conestoga HS, Berwyn, Pa.	North Carolina
58. Lucas Herbert	C	R/R	6-1	195	San Clemente (Calif.) HS	UCLA
59. Peter Lambert	RHP	R/R	6-1	185	San Dimas (Calif.) HS	UCLA
60. Garrett Wolforth	C	S/R	6-3	190	Concordia Lutheran HS, Tomball, Texas	Dallas Baptist
61. Thomas Szapucki	LHP	L/R	6-2	190	Dwyer HS, Palm Beach Garden, Fla.	Florida
62. Brady Singer	RHP	R/R	6-5	180	Tavares (Fla.) HS	Florida
63. Lucius Fox Jr.	2B/SS	B/R	6-0	160	American Heritage HS, Plantation, Fla.	N.C. State
64. Antonio Santillan	RHP	R/R	6-3	195	Seguin HS, Arlington, Texas	Texas Tech
65. Ryan Mountcastle	OF/1B	R/R	6-4	190	Hagerty HS, Oveido, Fla.	Central Florida
66. Daniel Reyes	OF	R/R	6-1	200	Mater Academy Charter HS, Hialeah Gardens, Fla.	Florida
67. Parker Ford	RHP	R/R	6-2	210	Lufkin (Texas) HS	Mississippi State
68. Luke Wakamatsu	SS	B/R	6-3	185	Keller (Texas) HS	Rice
69. Doak Dozier	OF	L/R	6-3	180	Arlington Heights HS, Fort Worth	Virginia
70. Greg Pickett	1B	L/R	6-4	205	Legend HS, Parker, Colo.	Mississippi State
71. Chad Smith	OF	L/L	6-2	200	South Gwinnett HS, Snellville, Ga.	Georgia
72. Hunter Bowling	LHP	R/L	6-6	220	American Heritage HS, Plantation, Fla.	Florida
73. Nick Lee	RHP	R/R	6-4	190	South Beauregard HS, Longville, La.	Lousiana-Lafayette
74. Wyatt Cross	C	L/R	6-3	197	Legacy HS, Broomfield, Colo.	North Carolina
75. Isaiah White	OF	R/R	6-0	175	Greenfield HS, Wilson, N.C.	East Carolina
76. Cody Deason	RHP	R/R	6-3	210	Nordhoff HS, Ojai, Calif.	Oregon
77. Jonathan India	2B/3B	R/R	6-0	190	American Heritage School, Plantation, Fla.	Florida
78. Xavier LeGrant	2B	R/R	6-0	180	Berry Academy, Charlotte	North Carolina State
79. AJ Graffanino	SS	B/R	6-2	165	Northwest Christian HS, Phoenix	Washington
80. Elih Marrero	C	B/R	5-9	190	Coral Gables (Fla.) HS	Mississippi State
81. Matt McGarry	RHP	R/R	6-3	185	Menlo HS, Atherton, Calif.	Vanderbilt
82. Michael Benson	C	R/R	6-0	190	Rancho Buena Vista HS, Vista, Calif.	UCLA
83. Nolan Kingham	RHP	R/R	6-3	185	Sierra Vista HS, Las Vegas	Texas
84. Devin Davis	1B	R/R	6-2	220	Valencia (Calif.) HS	Loyola Marymount
85. Dayton Dugas	OF	R/R	6-3	225	Sam Houston HS, Lake Charles, La.	Wichita State
86. Joe Davis	C/1B	R/R	6-0	220	Bowie (Texas) HS	Houston
87. Patrick Sandoval	LHP	L/L	6-2	190	Mission Viejo (Calif.) HS	Vanderbilt
88. Logan Gillaspie	RHP/C	B/R	6-2	195	Frontier HS, Bakersfield, Calif.	Seattle
89. Drew Finley	RHP	R/R	6-3	200	Rancho Bernardo HS, San Diego	Southern California
90. Chris Chatfield	OF	L/L	6-3	190	Spoto HS, Tampa	South Florida
91. Kyle Dean	OF	R/R	6-1	195	Rancho Bernardo HS, San Diego	Uncommitted
92. Corey Zangari	RHP	R/R	6-5	230	Carl Albert HS, Midwest City, Okla.	Oklahoma State
93. Nic Enright	RHP	R/R	6-3	230	Steward School, Richmond, Va.	Virginia Tech
94. Noah Burkholder	RHP	R/R	6-6	210	Crown Point (Ind.) HS	Louisville
95. Hunter Parsons	RHP	R/R	6-2	195	Parkside HS, Salisbury, Md.	Maryland
96. Michael Zimmerman	LHP	L/L	6-3	180	Gulf Coast HS, Naples, Fla.	Florida
97. Julian Infante	3B	R/R	6-3	205	Westminster Christian HS, Miami	Vanderbilt
98. Austin Rubick	RHP	R/R	6-4	205	Buena HS, Ventura, Calif.	Arizona
99. Tyler Stephenson	C/OF	R/R	6-4	210	Kennesaw Mountain HS, Kennesaw, Ga.	Georgia Tech
100. Ethan Paul	2B/SS	L/R	5-9	175	Newport HS, Bellevue, Wash.	Vanderbilt

FROM EVERY MINOR LEAGUE

As a complement to the organization prospect rankings, Baseball America also ranks prospects in all the minor leagues at the end of their seasons. Like the organization lists, they place more weight on potential than performance and should not be regarded as all-star teams. Unlike the organization lists, which are from more of a scouting perspective, the minor league lists reflect the views of minor league managers, who give more weight to what a player does on the field now. We think both perspectives are useful, so we give you both, even though they don't always match up. For a player to qualify for a league prospect list, he must have spent at least one-third of the season in a league. Also unlike the organization lists, players can make the league lists even if they exhausted their rookie eligibility during the 2014 season. Players are listed with the minor league teams and organizations they were with during the 2014 season.

TRIPLE-A

INTERNATIONAL LEAGUE
1. Gregory Polanco, of, Indianapolis (Pirates)
2. Mookie Betts, 2b/of, Pawtucket (Red Sox)
3. Francisco Lindor, ss, Columbus (Indians)
4. Maikel Franco, 3b/1b, Lehigh Valley (Phillies)
5. Steven Souza, of, Syracuse (Nationals)
6. Anthony Ranaudo, rhp, Pawtucket (Red Sox)
7. AJ .Cole, rhp, Syracuse (Nationals)
8. Alex Meyer, rhp, Rochester (Twins)
9. Robbie Ray, lhp, Toledo (Tigers)
10. Christian Bethancourt, c, Gwinnett (Braves)
11. Casey Sadler, rhp, Indianapolis (Pirates)
12. Giovanny Urshela, 3b, Columbus (Indians)
13. Rob Refsnyder, 2b/of, Scranton/WB (Yankees)
14. Micah Johnson, 2b, Charlotte (White Sox)
15. Alex Colome, rhp, Durham (Rays)
16. Christian Vazquez, c, Pawtucket (Red Sox)
17. Trevor May, rhp, Rochester (Twins)
18. Hernan Perez, ss/2b, Toledo (Tigers)
19. Allen Webster, rhp, Pawtucket (Red Sox)
20. Nick Kingham, rhp, Indianapolis (Pirates)

PACIFIC COAST LEAGUE
1. Kris Bryant, 3b, Iowa (Cubs)
2. Joc Pederson, of, Albuquerque (Dodgers)
3. Javier Baez, 2b, Iowa (Cubs)
4. Noah Syndergaard, rhp, Las Vegas (Mets)
5. Andrew Heaney, lhp, New Orleans (Marlins)
6. Oscar Taveras, of, Memphis (Cardinals)
7. Jon Singleton, 1b, Oklahoma City (Astros)
8. Jimmy Nelson, rhp, Nashville (Brewers)
9. Taijuan Walker, rhp, Tacoma (Mariners)
10. Arismendy Alcantara, ss/2b/of, Iowa (Cubs)
11. Rafael Montero, rhp, Las Vegas (Mets)
12. Andrew Susac, c, Fresno (Giants)
13. Tim Cooney, lhp, Memphis (Cardinals)
14. Stephen Piscotty, of, Memphis (Cardinals)
15. Kyle Hendricks, rhp, Iowa (Cubs)

16. Kevin Plawecki, c, Las Vegas (Mets)
17. Matt Wisler, rhp, El Paso (Padres)
18. Nick Ahmed, ss, Reno (Diamondbacks)
19. Mike Foltynewicz, rhp, Oklahoma City (Astros)
20. Luis Sardinas, ss, Round Rock (Rangers)

DOUBLE-A

EASTERN LEAGUE
1. Michael Taylor, of, Harrisburg (Nationals)
2. Mookie Betts, 2b/of, Portland (Red Sox)
3. Francisco Lindor, ss, Akron (Indians)
4. Steve Matz, lhp, Binghamton (Mets)
5. Aaron Sanchez, rhp, New Hampshire (Blue Jays)
6. Henry Owens, lhp, Portland (Red Sox)
7. Eduardo Rodriguez, lhp, Bowie/Portland, (Orioles/Red Sox)
8. Blake Swihart, c, Portland (Red Sox)
9. Brian Johnson, lhp, Portland (Red Sox)
10. Elias Diaz, c, Altoona (Pirates)
11. Gary Sanchez, c, Trenton (Yankees)
12. Dilson Herrera, 2b/ss, Binghamton (Mets)
13. Rob Refsnyder, 2b, Trenton (Yankees)
14. Kevin Plawecki, c, Binghamton (Mets)
15. A.J. Cole, rhp, Harrisburg (Nationals)
16. Kennys Vargas, 1b, New Britain (Twins)
17. Willy Garcia, of, Altoona (Pirates)
18. Steven Moya, of, Erie (Tigers)
19. Deven Marrero, ss, Portland (Red Sox)
20. Nick Kingham, rhp, Altoona (Pirates)

SOUTHERN LEAGUE
1. Kris Bryant, 3b, Tennessee (Cubs)
2. Addison Russell, ss, Tennessee (Cubs)
3. Corey Seager, ss, Chattanooga (Dodgers)
4. Robert Stephenson, rhp, Pensacola (Reds)
5. C.J. Edwards, rhp, Tennessee (Cubs)
6. Jose Peraza, 2b, Mississippi (Braves)
7. J.T. Realmuto, c, Jacksonville (Marlins)
8. D.J. Peterson, 1b/3b, Jackson (Mariners)
9. Jake Lamb, 3b, Mobile (Diamondbacks)
10. Archie Bradley, rhp, Mobile (Diamondbacks)
11. Aaron Blair, rhp, Mobile (Diamondbacks)
12. Michael Lorenzen, rhp, Pensacola (Reds)
13. Andrew Heaney, lhp, Jacksonville (Marlins)
14. Chris Reed, lhp, Chattanooga (Dodgers)
15. Ketel Marte, ss/2b, Jackson (Mariners)
16. Micah Johnson, 2b, Birmingham (White Sox)
17. Scott Schebler, of, Chattanooga (Dodgers)s
18. Albert Almora, of, Tennessee (Cubs)
19. Justin Nicolino, lhp, Jacksonville (Marlins)
20. Ben Lively, rhp, Pensacola (Reds)

TEXAS LEAGUE
1. Joey Gallo, 3b, Frisco (Rangers)
2. Jon Gray, rhp, Tulsa (Rockies)
3. Eddie Butler, rhp, Tulsa (Rockies)
4. Austin Hedges, c, San Antonio (Padres)
5. Alex Gonzalez, rhp, Frisco (Rangers)
6. Hunter Dozier, 3b, Northwest Arkansas (Royals)
7. Luke Jackson, rhp, Frisco (Rangers)
8. Rymer Liriano, of, San Antonio (Padres)
9. Ryan Rua, 3b, Frisco (Rangers)
10. Jorge Bonifacio, of, Northwest Arkansas (Royals)
11. Tyler Anderson, lhp, Tulsa (Rockies)

12. Alec Asher, rhp, Frisco (Rangers)
13. James Ramsey, of, Springfield (Cardinals)
14. Alex Yarbrough, 2b, Arkansas (Angels)
15. Tony Kemp, 2b, Corpus Christi (Astros)
16. Dan Winkler, rhp, Tulsa (Rockies)
17. Cam Bedrosian, rhp, Arkansas (Angels)
18. Jason Adam, rhp, Northwest Arkansas (Royals)
19. R.J. Alvarez, rhp, Arkansas/San Antonio (Angels/Padres)
20. Delino DeShields, of, Corpus Christi (Astros)

HIGH CLASS A

CALIFORNIA LEAGUE
1. Carlos Correa, ss, Lancaster (Astros)
2. Corey Seager, ss, Rancho Cucamonga (Dodgers)
3. Julio Urias, lhp, Rancho Cucamonga (Dodgers)
4. Braden Shipley, rhp, Visalia (Diamondbacks)
5. Aaron Blair, rhp, Visalia (Diamondbacks)
6. Joe Ross, rhp, Lake Elsinore (Padres)
7. Daniel Robertson, ss/2b, Stockton (Athletics)
8. Vince Velasquez, rhp, Lancaster (Astros)
9. Hunter Renfroe, of, Lake Elsinore (Padres)
10. D.J. Peterson, 1b/3b, High Desert (Mariners)
11. Chris Anderson, rhp, Rancho Cucamonga (Dodgers)
12. Jesse Winker, of, Bakersfield (Reds)
13. Matt Olson, 1b, Stockton (Athletics)
14. Gabby Guerrero, of, High Desert (Mariners)
15. Renato Nunez, 3b, Stockton (Athletics)
16. Ben Lively, rhp, Bakersfield (Reds)
17. Billy McKinney, of, Stockton (Athletics)
18. Brandon Drury, 3b, Visalia (Diamondbacks)
19. Teoscar Hernandez, of, Lancaster (Astros)
20. Lance McCullers Jr., rhp, Lancaster (Astros)

CAROLINA LEAGUE
1. Joey Gallo, 3b, Myrtle Beach (Rangers)
2. Jorge Alfaro, c, Myrtle Beach (Rangers)
3. Jose Peraza, 2b, Lynchburg (Braves)
4. Raul A. Mondesi, ss, Wilmington (Royals)
5. Sean Manaea, lhp, Wilmington (Royals)
6. Hunter Dozier, 3b, Wilmington (Royals)
7. Lucas Sims, rhp, Lynchburg (Braves)
8. Tim Anderson, ss, Winston-Salem (White Sox)
9. Courtney Hawkins, of, Winston-Salem (White Sox)
10. Alex Gonzalez, rhp, Myrtle Beach (Rangers)
11. Nick Williams, of, Myrtle Beach (Rangers)
12. Tyler Danish, rhp, Winston-Salem (White Sox)
13. Christian Binford, rhp, Wilmington (Royals)
14. Francellis Montas, rhp, Winston-Salem (White Sox)
15. Lewis Brinson, of, Myrtle Beach (Rangers)
16. Miguel Almonte, rhp, Wilmington (Royals)
17. Andrew Faulkner, lhp, Myrtle Beach (Rangers)
18. Pedro Severino, c, Potomac (Nationals)
19. Jose Leclerc, rhp, Myrtle Beach (Rangers)
20. Alex Claudio, lhp, Myrtle Beach (Rangers)

FLORIDA STATE LEAGUE
1. Tyler Glasnow, rhp, Bradenton (Pirates)
2. J. P. Crawford, ss, Clearwater (Phillies)
3. Daniel Norris, lhp, Dunedin (Blue Jays)
4. Kyle Schwarber, c/of, Daytona (Cubs)
5. Dalton Pompey, of, Dunedin (Blue Jays)
6. Jose Berrios, rhp, Fort Myers (Twins)
7. Steve Matz, lhp, St. Lucie (Mets)
8. Josh Bell, of, Bradenton (Pirates)
9. Orlando Arcia, ss/2b, Brevard County (Brewers)

10. Justin O'Conner, c, Charlotte (Rays)
11. Albert Almora, of, Daytona (Cubs)
12. Dilson Herrera, 2b/ss, St. Lucie (Mets)
13. Jake Thompson, rhp, Lakeland (Tigers)
14. Jorge Polanco, 2b/ss, Fort Myers (Twins)
15. Aaron Judge, of, Tampa (Yankees)
16. Tyrone Taylor, of, Brevard County (Brewers)
17. Brandon Nimmo, of, St. Lucie (Mets)
18. Billy McKinney, of, Daytona (Cubs)
19. Dwight Smith Jr., of, Dunedin (Blue Jays)
20. Colin Moran, 3b, Jupiter (Marlins)

LOW CLASS A

MIDWEST LEAGUE
1. Alex Reyes, rhp, Peoria (Cardinals)
2. Trea Turner, ss, Fort Wayne (Padres)
3. Braden Shipley, rhp, South Bend (Diamondbacks)
4. Michael Feliz, rhp, Quad Cities (Astros)
5. Willy Adames, ss, West Michigan/Bowling Green (Tigers/Rays)
6. Kohl Stewart, rhp, Cedar Rapids (Twins)
7. Clint Coulter, c, Wisconsin (Brewers)
8. Brett Phillips, of, Quad Cities (Astros)
9. Clint Frazier, of, Lake County (Indians)
10. Buck Farmer, rhp, West Michigan (Tigers)
11. Amir Garrett, lhp, Dayton (Reds)
12. Jesmuel Valentin, 2b, Great Lakes (Dodgers)
13. Carson Kelly, c, Peoria (Cardinals)
14. Austin Kubitza, rhp, West Michigan (Tigers)
15. Zach Bird, rhp, Great Lakes (Dodgers)
16. Andrew Velazquez, ss/2b, South Bend (Diamondbacks)
17. Kyle Farmer, c, Great Lakes (Dodgers)
18. Duane Underwood, rhp, Kane County (Cubs)
19. Mitch Brown, rhp, Lake County (Indians)
20. Jake Bauers, 1b, Fort Wayne (Padres)

SOUTH ATLANTIC LEAGUE
1. Lucas Giolito, rhp, Hagerstown (Nationals)
2. J.P. Crawford, ss, Lakewood (Phillies)
3. Reynaldo Lopez, rhp, Hagerstown (Nationals)
4. Luis Severino, rhp, Charleston (Yankees)
5. Reese McGuire, c, West Virginia (Pirates)
6. Austin Meadows, of, West Virginia (Pirates)
7. David Dahl, of, Asheville (Rockies)
8. Aaron Judge, of, Charleston (Yankees)
9. Manuel Margot, of, Greenville (Red Sox)
10. Hunter Harvey, rhp, Delmarva (Orioles)
11. Ryan McMahon, 3b, Asheville (Rockies)
12. Raimel Tapia, of, Asheville (Rockies)
13. Nomar Mazara, of, Asheville (Rangers)
14. Wilmer Difo, 2b/ss/ Hagerstown (Nationals)
15. Ian Clarkin, lhp, Charleston (Yankees)
16. Domingo German, rhp, Greensboro (Marlins)
17. Wendell Rijo, 2b, Greenville (Red Sox)
18. Chance Sisco, c, Delmarva (Orioles)
19. Mike Yastrzemski, of, Delmarva (Orioles)
20. Lewis Brinson, of, Asheville (Rangers)

SHORT-SEASON

NEW YORK-PENN LEAGUE
1. Marcos Molina, rhp, Brooklyn (Mets)
2. Reynaldo Lopez, rhp, Auburn (Nationals)
3. Amed Rosario, ss, Brooklyn (Mets)
4. Luis Torrens, c, Staten Island (Yankees)

5. Bradley Zimmer, of, Mahoning Valley (Indians)
6. Yairo Munez, ss, Vermont (Athletics)
7. Michael Conforto, of, Brooklyn (Mets)
8. Derek Fisher, of, Tri-City (Astros)
9. Francisco Mejia, c, Mahoning Valley (Indians)
10. Jhoan Urena, 3b, Brooklyn (Mets)
11. A.J. Reed, 1b, Tri-City (Astros)
12. Casey Gillaspie, 1b, Hudson Valley (Rays)
13. Raudy Read, c, Auburn (Nationals)
14. Enderson Franco, rhp, Hudson Valley (Rays)
15. Sam Travis, 1b, Lowell (Red Sox)
16. Joe Musgrove, rhp, Tri-City (Astros)
17. Rowan Wick, of, State College (Cardinals)
18. Aaron Brown, of, Williamsport (Phillies)
19. Joe Jimenez, rhp, Connecticut (Tigers)
20. Kevin McAvoy, rhp, Lowell (Red Sox)

NORTHWEST LEAGUE

1. Franklin Barreto, ss, Vancouver (Blue Jays)
2. Christian Arroyo, ss, Salem-Keizer (Giants)
3. Jairo Labourt, lhp, Vancouver (Blue Jays)
4. Miguel Castro, rhp, Vancouver (Blue Jays)
5. Trea Turner, ss, Eugene (Padres)
6. Jeffrey Baez, of, Boise (Cubs)
7. Franchy Cordero, ss, Eugene (Padres)
8. Max Pentecost, c, Vancouver (Blue Jays)
9. Mark Zagunis, c/of, Boise (Cubs)
10. Josh Morgan, 2b/ss/ Spokane (Rangers)
11. Ryan Castellani, rhp, Tri-City (Rockies)
12. Ryan Yarbrough, lhp, Everett (Mariners)
13. Richelson Pena, rhp, Spokane (Rangers)
14. Erick Leal, rhp, Boise (Cubs)
15. Jose Trevino, c/3b/2b, Spokane (Rangers)
16. Austin Cousino, of, Everett (Mariners)
17. Helmis Rodriguez, lhp, Tri-City (Rockies)
18. Rashad Crawford, of, Boise (Cubs)
19. Zac Curtis, lhp, Hillsboro (Diamondbacks)
20. Roemon Fields, of, Vancouver (Blue Jays)

ROOKIE

APPALACHIAN LEAGUE

1. Ozhaino Albies, ss, Danville (Braves)
2. Nick Gordon, ss, Elizabethton (Twins)
3. Richard Urena, ss, Bluefield (Blue Jays)
4. Foster Griffin, lhp, Burlington (Royals)
5. Brent Honeywell, rhp, Princeton (Rays)
6. Scott Blewett, rhp, Burlington (Royals)
7. Matt Smoral, rhp, Bluefield (Blue Jays)
8. Alec Grosser, rhp, Danville (Braves)
9. Nick Ciuffo, ss, Princeton (Rays)
10. Angel Moreno, of, Princeton (Rays)
11. Chase Vallot, c, Burlington (Royals)
12. Ryan Borucki, lhp, Bluefield (Blue Jays)
13. Riley Unroe, 2b/ss, Princeton (Rays)
14. Marten Gasparini, ss, Burlington (Royals)
15. Tanner Murphy, c, Danville (Braves)
16. Dan Jansen, c, Bluefield (Blue Jays)
17. Oscar Mercado, ss, Johnson City (Cardinals)
18. Wuilmer Becerra, of, Kingsport (Mets)
19. Michael Cederoth, rhp, Elizabethton (Twins)
20. Niklas Stephenson, rhp, Burlington (Royals)

ARIZONA LEAGUE

1. Alex Jackson, of Mariners
2. Grant Holmes, rhp, Dodgers
3. Bobby Bradley, 1b, Indians
4. Justus Sheffield, lhp, Indians
5. Spencer Adams, rhp, White Sox
6. Alex Verdugo, of, Dodgers
7. Monte Harrison, of, Brewers
8. Michael Gettys, of, Padres
9. Carson Sands, lhp, Cubs
10. Michael Santos, rhp, Giants
11. Cody Reed, lhp, Diamondbacks
12. Yu-Cheng Chang, ss/3b, Indians
13. Eloy Jimenez, of, Cubs
14. Gleyber Torres, ss, Cubs
15. Jose Herrera, c, Diamondbacks
16. Ricardo Sanchez, lhp, Angels
17. Dillon Overton, lhp, Athletics
18. Miguel Diaz, rhp, Brewers
19. Josh Morgan, ss/2b, Rangers
20. Yeyson Yrizarri, ss, Rangers

GULF COAST LEAGUE

1. Rafael Devers, 3b, Red Sox
2. Tyler Kolek, rhp, Marlins
3. Ozhaino Albies, ss, Braves
4. Jorge Mateo, ss, Yankees
5. Jack Flaherty, rhp, Cardinals
6. Derek Hill, of, Tigers
7. Javier Guerra, ss, Red Sox
8. Sean Reid-Foley, rhp, Blue Jays
9. Michael Chavis, ss/3b, Red Sox
10. Edmundo Sosa, ss, Cardinals
11. Cole Tucker, ss, Pirates
12. Braxton Davidson, of, Braves
13. Mitch Keller, rhp, Pirates
14. Jakson Reetz, c, Nationals
15. Angel Aguilar, ss, Yankees
16. Magneuris Sierra, of, Cardinals
17. Jose Alvarado, lhp, Rays
18. Jomar Reyes, 3b, Orioles
19. Francis Martes, rhp, Marlins/Astros
20. Isael Soto, of, Marlins

PIONEER LEAGUE

1. Aristides Aquino, of, Billings (Reds)
2. Forrest Wall, 2b, Grand Junction (Rockies)
3. Jose De Leon, rhp, Ogden (Dodgers)
4. Alex Blandino, ss, Billings (Reds)
5. Ryan O'Hearn, 1b, Idaho Falls (Royals)
6. Julian Leon, c, Ogden (Dodgers)
7. Justin Williams, of, Missoula (Diamondbacks)
8. Wyatt Strahan, rhp, Billings (Reds)
9. Sergio Alcantara, ss, Diamondbacks
10. Cody Bellinger, 1b, Ogden (Dodgers)
11. Kevin Padlo, 3b, Grand Junction (Rockies)
12. Taylor Sparks, 3b, Billings (Reds)
13. Jeff Brigham, rhp, Ogden (Dodgers)
14. Dom Nunez, c, Grand Junction (Rockies)
15. Tyler Mahle, rhp, Billings (Reds)
16. Devin Williams, rhp, Helena (Brewers)
17. Samir Duenez, 1b, Idaho Falls (Royals)
18. Wes Rogers, of, Grand Junction (Rockies)
19. Natanael Delgado, of, Orem (Angels)
20. Luis Jean, ss/2b, Grand Junction (Rockies)

INDEX

De Leon, Michael (Rangers)	457	Frazier, Clint (Indians)	131	Guerrieri, Taylor (Rays)	439
Dean, Austin (Marlins)	247	Freeland, Kyle (Rockies)	147	Gunkel, Joe (Red Sox)	76
DeCarlo, Joe (Mariners)	425	Frias, Carlos (Dodgers)	236	Gustave, Jandel (Royals)	205
DeCarr, Austin (Yankees)	314	Fried, Max (Padres)	389	Guzman, Ronald (Rangers)	461
DeJong, Chase (Blue Jays)	473	Fry, Jace (White Sox)	104		
Del Pozo, Miguel (Marlins)	252	Fuentes, Steven (Tigers)	168		
Delgado, Natanael (Angels)	220	Fulenchek, Garrett (Braves)	38	**H**	
Demeritte, Travis (Rangers)	458	Fulmer, Michael (Mets)	296	Hader, Josh (Astros)	183
DeSclafani, Anthony (Reds)	117			Hager, Jake (Rays)	440
DeShields Jr., Delino (Rangers)	459			Haley, Justin (Red Sox)	77
Devers, Rafael (Red Sox)	69	**G**		Hall, Brooks (Brewers)	268
Diaz, Aledmys (Cardinals)	375	Gagnon, Drew (Brewers)	268	Hall, Cody (Giants)	410
Diaz, Edwin (Mariners)	421	Gallagher, Cam (Royals)	205	Haniger, Mitch (Diamondbacks)	27
Diaz, Elias (Pirates)	359	Gallo, Joey (Rangers)	450	Hannemann, Jacob (Cubs)	89
Diaz, Isan (Diamondbacks)	28	Garcia, Aramis (Giants)	409	Hanson, Alen (Pirates)	357
Diaz, Jairo (Rockies)	152	Garcia, Dermis (Yankees)	316	Harris, Mitch (Cardinals)	381
Diaz, Lewin (Twins)	281	Garcia, Elniery (Phillies)	349	Harrison, Monte (Brewers)	260
Diaz, Miguel (Brewers)	265	Garcia, Eudor (Mets)	301	Harrison, Travis (Twins)	285
Dickerson, Alex (Padres)	395	Garcia, Greg (Cardinals)	378	Hart, Josh (Orioles)	60
Dickey, Robbie (Nationals)	493	Garcia, Jarlin (Marlins)	247	Harvey, Hunter (Orioles)	51
Dickson, Cody (Pirates)	363	Garcia, Jason (Orioles)	57	Hawkins, Courtney (White Sox)	102
Difo, Wilmer (Nationals)	485	Garcia, Julio (Angels)	215	Healy, Ryon (Athletics)	331
Diplan, Marcos (Rangers)	459	Garcia, Onelki (White Sox)	108	Heaney, Andrew (Angels)	210
Dominguez, Jose (Rays)	441	Garcia, Willy (Pirates)	359	Hedges, Austin (Padres)	388
Dosch, Drew (Orioles)	56	Garcia, Yimi (Dodgers)	231	Heim, Jonah (Orioles)	61
Downes, Brandon (Royals)	204	Garrett, Amir (Reds)	117	Hellweg, Johnny (Brewers)	266
Dozier, Hunter (Royals)	196	Garvin, Grayson (Rays)	445	Hensley, Ty (Yankees)	314
Drury, Brandon (Diamondbacks)	21	Gasparini, Marten (Royals)	203	Heredia, Luis (Pirates)	364
Dubon, Mauricio (Red Sox)	75	Gatewood, Jacob (Brewers)	265	Hernandez, Brayan (Mariners)	425
Duffey, Tyler (Twins)	281	Gatto, Joe (Angels)	213	Hernandez, Elier (Royals)	203
Duffy, Matt (Giants)	406	Gerber, Mike (Tigers)	170	Hernandez, Teoscar (Astros)	182
Dugan, Kelly (Phillies)	345	German, Domingo (Marlins)	245	Herrera, Dilson (Mets)	292
Duvall, Adam (Giants)	408	Gettys, Michael (Padres)	392	Herrera, Jose (Diamondbacks)	24
Dykstra, James (White Sox)	108	Gillaspie, Casey (Rays)	439	Herrera, Juan (Cardinals)	377
		Gilmartin, Sean (Mets)	297	Herrera, Odubel (Phillies)	343
E		Giolito, Lucas (Nationals)	482	Herrera, Rosell (Rockies)	150
Eaves, Kody (Angels)	216	Givens, Mychal (Orioles)	60	Hess, David (Orioles)	58
Edwards, C.J. (Cubs)	84	Glasnow, Tyler (Pirates)	354	Heston, Chris (Giants)	412
Eflin, Zach (Padres)	390	Goeddel, Tyler (Rays)	441	Hicks, John (Mariners)	424
Elizalde, Sebastian (Reds)	124	Goforth, David (Brewers)	263	Hill, Derek (Tigers)	163
Ellington, Brian (Marlins)	251	Gohara, Luiz (Mariners)	422	Hill, Taylor (Nationals)	489
Ellis, Chris (Angels)	212	Gonsalves, Stephen (Twins)	280	Hinshaw, Chad (Angels)	221
Emanuel, Kent (Astros)	188	Gonzales, Marco (Cardinals)	370	Hinsz, Gage (Pirates)	362
Encarnacion, Luis (Phillies)	349	Gonzalez, Alex (Rangers)	453	Hockin, Grant (Indians)	141
Engel, Adam (White Sox)	107	Gonzalez, Brian (Orioles)	59	Hoffman, Jeff (Blue Jays)	467
Ervin, Phillip (Reds)	120	Gonzalez, Erik (Indians)	134	Holdzkom, John (Pirates)	361
Escobar, Edwin (Red Sox)	73	Gonzalez, Miguel Alfredo (Phillies)	348	Holmberg, David (Reds)	122
Estevez, Carlos (Rockies)	156	Gonzalez, Rayan (Rockies)	154	Holmes, Clay (Pirates)	362
Estrada, Thairo (Yankees)	315	Gonzalez, Severino (Phillies)	346	Holmes, Grant (Dodgers)	228
		Goodrum, Niko (Twins)	285	Honeywell, Brent (Rays)	438
F		Goodwin, Brian (Nationals)	486	Houser, Adrian (Astros)	186
Farmer, Buck (Tigers)	163	Gordon, Nick (Twins)	277	Howard, Nick (Reds)	116
Farmer, Kyle (Dodgers)	237	Gossett, Daniel (Athletics)	328	Howard, Sam (Rockies)	155
Faulkner, Andrew (Rangers)	458	Gott, Trevor (Angels)	216	Hultzen, Danny (Mariners)	429
Featherston, Taylor (Angels)	215	Grace, Matt (Nationals)	491	Hursh, Jason (Braves)	36
Fedde, Erick (Nationals)	484	Graham, J.R. (Twins)	282		
Feliz, Michael (Astros)	180	Graveman, Kendall (Athletics)	325	**I**	
Fernandez, Pedro (Royals)	202	Graves, Brett (Athletics)	330	Ibanez, Andy (Appendix)	494
Field, Johnny (Rays)	444	Gray, Jon (Rockies)	147	Iglesias, Raisel (Reds)	115
Fields, Daniel (Tigers)	172	Green, Chad (Tigers)	173	Imhof, Matt (Phillies)	341
Fillmyer, Heath (Athletics)	332	Green, Hunter (Angels)	217		
Finnegan, Brandon (Royals)	195	Green, Zach (Phillies)	346	**J**	
Finnegan, Kyle (Athletics)	331	Gregorio, Joan (Giants)	408	Jackson, Alex (Mariners)	418
Fisher, Derek (Astros)	184	Greiner, Grayson (Tigers)	171	Jackson, Luke (Rangers)	455
Flaherty, Jack (Cardinals)	373	Grichuk, Randal (Cardinals)	372	Jagielo, Eric (Yankees)	311
Flores, Kendry (Giants)	409	Griffin, Foster (Royals)	197	Jaime, Juan (Braves)	42
Flores, Ramon (Yankees)	316	Grosser, Alec (Braves)	41	Jankowski, Travis (Padres)	397
Flynn, Brian (Royals)	199	Grullon, Deivi (Phillies)	344	Jansen, Danny (Blue Jays)	474
Foltynewicz, Mike (Astros)	179	Gsellman, Robert (Mets)	301	Jenkins, Tyrell (Braves)	37
Forbes, Ti'Quan (Rangers)	456	Guaipe, Mayckol (Mariners)	428	Jensen, Chris (Athletics)	332
Franco, Maikel (Phillies)	339	Guerra, Javier (Red Sox)	72	Jewell, Jake (Angels)	218
Franco, Wander (Royals)	204	Guerrero, Alexander (Dodgers)	234	Jimenez, A.J. (Blue Jays)	475
		Guerrero, Gabby (Mariners)	421		
		Guerrero, Tayron (Padres)	396		

Name	Page		Name	Page		Name	Page
Jimenez, Eloy (Cubs)	90		Lopez, Eduar (Angels)	219		Moncrief, Carlos (Indians)	137
Jimenez, Emerson (Rockies)	152		Lopez, Javier (Marlins)	252		Mondesi, Raul A. (Royals)	194
Jimenez, Joe (Tigers)	168		Lopez, Jorge (Brewers)	264		Montas, Francellis (White Sox)	100
Jiminian, Johendi (Rockies)	157		Lopez, Reynaldo (Nationals)	483		Montero, Rafael (Mets)	294
Joe, Connor (Pirates)	364		Lorenzen, Michael (Reds)	116		Morales, Andrew (Cardinals)	381
Johansen, Jake (Nationals)	489		Lowry, Thaddius (White Sox)	105		Moran, Colin (Astros)	181
Johnson, Brian (Red Sox)	68		Lugo, Dawel (Blue Jays)	472		Morban, Julio (Mariners)	428
Johnson, Chase (Giants)	410		Lugo, Luis (Indians)	138		Morgan, Gareth (Mariners)	423
Johnson, Hobbs (Brewers)	267		Lutz, Donald (Reds)	125		Morgan, Josh (Rangers)	455
Johnson, Micah (White Sox)	100					Morris, Akeel (Mets)	298
Johnson, Pierce (Cubs)	86		**M**			Morris, Elliot (Padres)	394
Jokisch, Eric (Cubs)	91		Machado, Dixon (Tigers)	167		Moscot, Jon (Reds)	122
Jones, Brent (Diamondbacks)	28		Mader, Michael (Marlins)	250		Moya, Steven (Tigers)	162
Jones, JaCoby (Pirates)	360		Magnifico, Damien (Brewers)	269		Muncy, Max (Athletics)	328
Jones, Ryder (Giants)	413		Mahle, Greg (Angels)	220		Munoz, Felix (Marlins)	252
Jones, Zack (Twins)	284		Mahle, Tyler (Reds)	124		Munoz, Yairo (Athletics)	328
Jorge, Felix (Twins)	285		Mahtook, Mikie (Rays)	437		Murphy, J.R. (Yankees)	314
Judge, Aaron (Yankees)	307		Maile, Luke (Rays)	443		Murphy, Tanner (Braves)	41
Jungmann, Taylor (Brewers)	263		Manaea, Sean (Royals)	195		Murphy, Tom (Rockies)	149
			Mancini, Trey (Orioles)	61		Musgrove, Joe (Astros)	186
K			Mantiply, Joe (Tigers)	172			
Kaminsky, Rob (Cardinals)	372		Margot, Manuel (Red Sox)	69		**N**	
Kang, Jung-Ho (Appendix)	495		Marin, Adrian (Orioles)	58		Naquin, Tyler (Indians)	133
Karns, Nathan (Rays)	436		Marlette, Tyler (Mariners)	424		Nay, Mitch (Blue Jays)	473
Kela, Keone (Rangers)	457		Marquez, German (Rays)	444		Nesbitt, Angel (Tigers)	170
Keller, Jon (Orioles)	56		Marrero, Deven (Red Sox)	70		Newcomb, Sean (Angels)	211
Keller, Mitch (Pirates)	358		Marte, Ketel (Mariners)	419		Nicolino, Justin (Marlins)	243
Kelly, Carson (Cardinals)	376		Martes, Francis (Astros)	185		Nimmo, Brandon (Mets)	291
Kelly, Casey (Padres)	393		Martin, Cody (Braves)	42		Nola, Aaron (Phillies)	339
Kemp, Tony (Astros)	185		Martinez, Jose (Diamondbacks)	24		Nolin, Sean (Athletics)	326
Kepler, Max (Twins)	279		Martinez, Luis (White Sox)	106		Norris, Daniel (Blue Jays)	466
Kieboom, Spencer (Nationals)	490		Martinez, Rodolfo (Giants)	412		Northcraft, Aaron (Braves)	45
Kilome, Franklyn (Phillies)	343		Mateo, Jorge (Yankees)	307		Norwood, James (Cubs)	93
Kime, Dace (Indians)	138		Mathisen, Wyatt (Pirates)	363		Nunez, Dom (Rockies)	153
Kingham, Nick (Pirates)	357		Matz, Steve (Mets)	291		Nunez, Renato (Athletics)	324
Kivel, Jeremy (Reds)	125		May, Jacob (White Sox)	103			
Kivlehan, Patrick (Mariners)	420		May, Trevor (Twins)	278		**O**	
Kline, Branden (Orioles)	60		Mayers, Mike (Cardinals)	380		O'Brien, Chris (Dodgers)	236
Knapp, Andrew (Phillies)	345		Mazara, Nomar (Rangers)	452		O'Brien, Pete (Diamondbacks)	22
Knebel, Corey (Rangers)	457		Mazzoni, Cory (Mets)	296		O'Conner, Justin (Rays)	435
Koch, Matt (Mets)	300		McCann, James (Tigers)	165		O'Hearn, Ryan (Royals)	204
Kolek, Tyler (Marlins)	242		McCullers Jr., Lance (Astros)	183		O'Neill, Tyler (Mariners)	423
Kopech, Michael (Red Sox)	72		McElroy, C.J. (Cardinals)	381		Oberg, Scott (Rockies)	155
Kubitza, Austin (Tigers)	166		McGowin, Kyle (Angels)	215		Ogando, Jochi (Mariners)	429
Kubitza, Kyle (Braves)	39		McGuire, Reese (Pirates)	356		Ogando, Nefi (Phillies)	348
Kuhl, Chad (Pirates)	365		McKinney, Billy (Cubs)	85		Ohlman, Mike (Orioles)	58
			McKirahan, Andrew (Marlins)	253		Okert, Steven (Giants)	411
L			McMahon, Ryan (Rockies)	148		Olivera, Hector (Appendix)	494
Labourt, Jairo (Blue Jays)	472		Meadows, Austin (Pirates)	355		Olson, Matt (Athletics)	323
Lamb, Jake (Diamondbacks)	21		Mecias, Yoel (Phillies)	342		Orlando, Paulo (Royals)	205
Lara, Gilbert (Brewers)	260		Medeiros, Kodi (Brewers)	263		Ortiz, Luis (Rangers)	454
Lara, Jordy (Mariners)	424		Meisner, Casey (Mets)	299		Osuna, Roberto (Blue Jays)	469
LaValley, Gavin (Reds)	121		Mejia, Adalberto (Giants)	405		Overton, Dillon (Athletics)	326
Law, Derek (Giants)	411		Mejia, Erick (Mariners)	426		Owens, Henry (Red Sox)	67
LeClerc, Jose (Rangers)	458		Mejia, Francisco (Indians)	133			
Lee, Hak-Ju (Rays)	442		Mejia, Jefferson (Diamondbacks)	27		**P**	
Lee, Nick (Nationals)	493		Mejias-Brean, Seth (Reds)	123		Padlo, Kevin (Rockies)	152
Lee, Zach (Dodgers)	232		Mella, Keury (Giants)	404		Palka, Daniel (Diamondbacks)	29
Lemond, Zech (Padres)	396		Mercedes, Melvin (Tigers)	172		Pankake, Joey (Tigers)	173
Leon, Arnold (Athletics)	332		Merejo, Luis (Braves)	45		Papi, Mike (Indians)	132
Leon, Julian (Dodgers)	231		Merritt, Ryan (Indians)	140		Parker, Kyle (Rockies)	154
Leonard, Patrick (Rays)	444		Meyer, Alex (Twins)	276		Parsons, Wes (Braves)	41
Leyba, Domingo (Diamondbacks)	22		Meza, Juan (Blue Jays)	476		Patterson, Jordan (Rockies)	156
Light, Pat (Red Sox)	77		Michalczewski, Trey (White Sox)	102		Paulino, Dorssys (Indians)	140
Lindgren, Jacob (Yankees)	310		Middleton, Keynan (Angels)	221		Pederson, Joc (Dodgers)	227
Lindor, Francisco (Indians)	130		Minier, Amaurys (Twins)	284		Pena, Ariel (Brewers)	269
Lindsey, Taylor (Padres)	394		Mitchell, Bryan (Yankees)	311		Pena, Francisco (Royals)	204
Liriano, Rymer (Padres)	390		Mitchell, Jared (White Sox)	109		Pena, Roberto (Astros)	187
Lively, Ben (Reds)	119		Mitchell, Kevonte (Cubs)	92		Pentecost, Max (Blue Jays)	468
Lobstein, Kyle (Tigers)	168		Molina, Leonardo (Yankees)	315		Peralta, Freddy (Mariners)	427
Loehr, Trace (Athletics)	333		Molina, Marcos (Mets)	294		Peralta, Ofelky (Orioles)	61
Longhi, Nick (Red Sox)	76		Moll, Sam (Rockies)	154			
			Moncada, Yoan (Appendix)	494			

Peraza, Jose (Braves) 34
Perez, Arvincent (Tigers) 167
Perez, Carlos (Angels) 220
Perez, Fernando (Padres) 391
Perez, Hernan (Tigers) 164
Perez, Roberto (Indians) 136
Perez, Williams (Braves) 42
Perkins, Cam (Phillies) 347
Peter, Jake (White Sox) 107
Peterson, D.J. (Mariners) 419
Peterson, Dustin (Padres) 395
Peterson, Jace (Padres) 391
Pham, Tommy (Cardinals) 376
Phillips, Brett (Astros) 181
Pimentel, Stolmy (Pirates) 364
Pinder, Chad (Athletics) 327
Pinto, Ricardo (Phillies) 344
Pirela, Jose (Yankees) 317
Piscotty, Stephen (Cardinals) 371
Pivetta, Nick (Nationals) 487
Plawecki, Kevin (Mets) 292
Plutko, Adam (Indians) 139
Polanco, Jorge (Twins) 278
Polo, Tito (Pirates) 365
Pompey, Dalton (Blue Jays) 468
Povse, Max (Braves) 42
Powell, Boog (Athletics) 330
Prime, Correlle (Rockies) 155
Puello, Cesar (Mets) 300
Pujols, Jose (Phillies) 348

Q

Quinn, Roman (Phillies) 340

R

Rademacher, Bijan (Cubs) 90
Railey, Matt (Diamondbacks) 29
Ramirez, Harold (Pirates) 359
Ramirez, Jose (Yankees) 316
Ramos, Henry (Red Sox) 77
Ramos, Milton (Mets) 300
Ramsey, James (Indians) 135
Ramsey, Matt (Indians) 248
Ranaudo, Anthony (Red Sox) 73
Ravelo, Rangel (Athletics) 327
Ray, Robbie (Diamondbacks) 23
Read, Raudy (Nationals) 491
Realmuto, J.T. (Marlins) 243
Reed, A.J. (Astros) 185
Reed, Chris (Dodgers) 231
Reed, Cody (Diamondbacks) 24
Reed, Jake (Twins) 282
Reed, Michael (Brewers) 264
Reetz, Jakson (Nationals) 488
Refsnyder, Rob (Yankees) 309
Reid-Foley, Sean (Blue Jays) 471
Reinheimer, Jack (Mariners) 425
Renda, Tony (Nationals) 487
Renfroe, Hunter (Padres) 387
Reyes, Alex (Cardinals) 371
Reyes, Elmer (Braves) 45
Reyes, Jomar (Orioles) 55
Reyes, Victor (Braves) 43
Reynolds, Danny (Angels) 217
Reynolds, Matt (Mets) 295
Rhame, Jacob (Dodgers) 235
Richy, John (Dodgers) 235
Riddle, J.T. (Marlins) 249
Rijo, Wendell (Red Sox) 75
Rivera, Yadiel (Brewers) 264
Rivero, Felipe (Nationals) 489
Roache, Victor (Brewers) 265

Robertson, Daniel (Athletics) 322
Robles, Victor (Nationals) 492
Robson, Tom (Blue Jays) 476
Rodgers, Brady (Astros) 187
Rodon, Carlos (White Sox) 98
Rodriguez, Eduardo (Red Sox) 68
Rodriguez, Helmis (Rockies) 157
Rodriguez, Jefry (Nationals) 490
Rodriguez, Joely (Phillies) 348
Rodriguez, Nellie (Indians) 138
Rodriguez, Ronny (Indians) 141
Rodriguez, Yorman (Reds) 119
Rogers, Jason (Brewers) 268
Rogers, Taylor (Twins) 280
Rogers, Wes (Rockies) 157
Romano, Sal (Reds) 120
Romero, Avery (Marlins) 244
Romero, Enny (Rays) 442
Romero, Fernando (Twins) 283
Rondon, Adrian (Rays) 436
Rondon, Bruce (Tigers) 166
Rondon, Cleuluis (White Sox) 105
Rondon, Jose (Padres) 392
Rosa, Viosergy (Marlins) 251
Rosario, Amed (Mets) 293
Rosario, Eddie (Twins) 279
Ross, Joe (Padres) 388
Rua, Ryan (Rangers) 454
Rucinski, Drew (Angels) 217
Ruiz, Rio (Astros) 182
Russell, Addison (Cubs) 83

S

Sadler, Casey (Pirates) 361
Saladino, Tyler (White Sox) 106
Salazar, Carlos (Braves) 44
Sampson, Adrian (Pirates) 360
Sampson, Keyvius (Padres) 397
Sanchez, Aaron (Blue Jays) 467
Sanchez, Ali (Mets) 300
Sanchez, Carlos (White Sox) 103
Sanchez, Gary (Yankees) 308
Sanchez, Ricardo (Angels) 211
Sandberg, Cord (Phillies) 347
Sands, Carson (Cubs) 92
Sano, Miguel (Twins) 275
Santana, Domingo (Astros) 183
Santos, Michael (Giants) 409
Sardinas, Luis (Rangers) 453
Schales, Brian (Marlins) 249
Schebler, Scott (Dodgers) 230
Schwarber, Kyle (Cubs) 84
Schwartz, Jordan (Athletics) 333
Scruggs, Xavier (Cardinals) 378
Seager, Corey (Dodgers) 226
Segovia, Joantgel (Brewers) 267
Senzatela, Antonio (Rockies) 150
Severino, Luis (Yankees) 306
Severino, Pedro (Nationals) 488
Seymour, Anfernee (Marlins) 250
Shaffer, Richie (Rays) 441
Shane, Casey (Indians) 140
Shaw, Travis (Red Sox) 74
Sheffield, Justus (Indians) 132
Shepherd, Zac (Tigers) 167
Sherfy, Jimmie (Diamondbacks) 25
Shipley, Braden (Diamondbacks) 19
Shreve, Chasen (Braves) 39
Sierra, Magneuris (Cardinals) 375
Silvestre, Hector (Nationals) 492
Simmons, Shae (Braves) 40
Simms, John (Nationals) 493
Sims, Lucas (Braves) 35

Sisco, Chance (Orioles) 52
Skoglund, Eric (Royals) 200
Skole, Matt (Nationals) 491
Smith Jr., Dwight (Blue Jays) 472
Smith, Burch (Padres) 395
Smith, Carson (Mariners) 423
Smith, Dominic (Mets) 295
Smith, Kevan (White Sox) 104
Smith, Mallex (Padres) 393
Smith, Nate (Angels) 216
Smoral, Matt (Blue Jays) 471
Snell, Blake (Rays) 438
Sobotka, Chad (Braves) 43
Soler, Jorge (Cubs) 83
Solis, Sammy (Nationals) 488
Sosa, Edmundo (Cardinals) 376
Soto, Isael (Marlins) 245
Souza, Steven (Nationals) 484
Spangenberg, Cory (Padres) 389
Sparkman, Glenn (Royals) 201
Sparks, Taylor (Reds) 121
Stamets, Eric (Angels) 219
Stanek, Ryne (Rays) 443
Stankiewicz, Teddy (Red Sox) 74
Stanley, Cody (Cardinals) 379
Starling, Bubba (Royals) 202
Stassi, Max (Astros) 186
Steele, Justin (Cubs) 90
Stephenson, Niklas (Royals) 203
Stephenson, Robert (Reds) 114
Stewart, Brock (Dodgers) 237
Stewart, Kohl (Twins) 276
Stinnett, Jake (Cubs) 87
Story, Trevor (Rockies) 151
Strahan, Wyatt (Reds) 123
Stratton, Chris (Giants) 407
Streich, Seth (Athletics) 328
Strickland, Hunter (Giants) 406
Stripling, Ross (Dodgers) 233
Strong, Mike (Brewers) 269
Stuart, Champ (Mets) 299
Suarez, Jose (Angels) 218
Suggs, Colby (Marlins) 253
Supak, Trey (Pirates) 360
Susac, Andrew (Giants) 402
Sweeney, Darnell (Dodgers) 233
Swihart, Blake (Red Sox) 66
Syndergaard, Noah (Mets) 290

T

Taillon, Jameson (Pirates) 355
Tapia, Raimel (Rockies) 151
Tarpley, Stephen (Orioles) 57
Taylor, Michael (Nationals) 483
Taylor, Tyrone (Brewers) 258
Telis, Tomas (Rangers) 460
Tellez, Rowdy (Blue Jays) 477
Thomas, Lane (Blue Jays) 474
Thompson, Jake (Rangers) 451
Thompson, Trayce (White Sox) 105
Thorpe, Lewis (Twins) 279
Thurman, Andrew (Astros) 189
Tilson, Charlie (Cardinals) 374
Tinoco, Jesus (Blue Jays) 476
Tirado, Alberto (Blue Jays) 475
Tocci, Carlos (Phillies) 340
Toles, Andrew (Rays) 445
Tomas, Yasmany (Diamondbacks) 20
Torrens, Luis (Yankees) 310
Torres, Gleyber (Cubs) 86
Torreyes, Ronald (Astros) 187
Torrez, Daury (Cubs) 93
Toussaint, Touki (Diamondbacks) 20

Towey, Cal (Angels)	221
Trahan, Stryker (Diamondbacks)	26
Travieso, Nick (Reds)	118
Travis, Devon (Blue Jays)	469
Travis, Sam (Red Sox)	71
Trexler, David (White Sox)	107
Tropeano, Nick (Angels)	214
Tseng, Jen-Ho (Cubs)	87
Tucker, Cole (Pirates)	358
Tucker, Preston (Astros)	184
Tuivailala, Sam (Cardinals)	374
Turnbull, Spencer (Tigers)	169
Turner, Stuart (Twins)	280
Turner, Trea (Padres)	387
Twine, Justin (Marlins)	248

U

Underwood, Duane (Cubs)	87
Urena, Jhoan (Mets)	296
Urena, Jose (Marlins)	244
Urena, Richard (Blue Jays)	470
Urias, Julio (Dodgers)	227
Urrutia, Henry (Orioles)	56
Urshela, Giovanny (Indians)	135

V

Valdez, Jose (Tigers)	169
Valentin, Jesmuel (Phillies)	342
Valera, Breyvic (Cardinals)	380
Vallot, Chase (Royals)	199
Vanegas, A.J. (Dodgers)	237
Vasquez, Danry (Astros)	189
Velasquez, Vince (Astros)	180
Velazquez, Andrew (Rays)	439

Verdugo, Alex (Dodgers)	228
VerHagen, Drew (Tigers)	169
Verrett, Logan (Orioles)	59
Vettleson, Drew (Nationals)	492
Vielma, Engelb (Twins)	283
Vizcaino, Arodys (Braves)	39
Vogelbach, Dan (Cubs)	92
Voth, Austin (Nationals)	487

W

Wade, Tyler (Yankees)	312
Wagner, Tyler (Brewers)	262
Wahl, Bobby (Athletics)	329
Waldrop, Kyle (Reds)	120
Walker, Adam Brett (Twins)	281
Walker, Christian (Orioles)	51
Wall, Forrest (Rockies)	149
Wallach, Chad (Reds)	124
Wang, Wei-Chung (Brewers)	261
Ward, Drew (Nationals)	486
Weaver, Luke (Cardinals)	375
Webb, Logan (Giants)	413
Wells, Nick (Blue Jays)	477
Wendle, Joey (Athletics)	329
Whalen, Rob (Mets)	298
Wick, Rowan (Cardinals)	379
Wilkins, Andy (White Sox)	109
Williams, Devin (Brewers)	262
Williams, Justin (Rays)	440
Williams, Mason (Yankees)	317
Williams, Nick (Rangers)	452
Williams, Ronnie (Cardinals)	377
Williams, Taylor (Brewers)	261
Williams, Trevor (Marlins)	246
Williamson, Mac (Giants)	407

Wilson, Austin (Mariners)	420
Wilson, Jacob (Cardinals)	377
Wilson, Marcus (Diamondbacks)	27
Wilson, Tyler (Orioles)	55
Windle, Tom (Dodgers)	230
Winker, Jesse (Reds)	115
Winkler, Dan (Braves)	44
Wisdom, Patrick (Cardinals)	378
Wisler, Matt (Padres)	386
Wojciechowski, Asher (Astros)	189
Wolters, Tony (Indians)	141
Wong, Kean (Rays)	443
Wren, Kyle (Brewers)	266
Wright, Mike (Orioles)	54
Wright, Steven (Red Sox)	75

Y

Yarbrough, Alex (Angels)	214
Yarbrough, Ryan (Mariners)	422
Yastrzemski, Mike (Orioles)	54
Ynoa, Gabriel (Mets)	297
Ynoa, Huascar (Twins)	284
Ynoa, Michael (White Sox)	108
Yrizarri, Yeyson (Rangers)	460
Ysla, Luis (Giants)	410

Z

Zagunis, Mark (Cubs)	88
Zastryzny, Rob (Cubs)	88
Zimmer, Bradley (Indians)	131
Zimmer, Kyle (Royals)	196
Ziomek, Kevin (Tigers)	164